THE ST. JAMES WOMEN FILMMAKERS ENCYCLOPEDIA

also from visible ink press

The St. James Film Directors Encyclopedia Edited by Andrew Sarris, noted film critic and American father of the auteur theory, this is a masterful guide to the fascinating history of film direction. *The St. James Film Directors Encyclopedia* is an essential and reasonably-priced source for everyone who appreciates the art of filmmaking. It is international in scope and covers 208 up-and-coming and "classic" directors.

ISBN 1-57859-028-0 • 7¼″ x 9¼″ • 692 pages • 204 photographs

The St. James Fashion Encyclopedia: A Survey of Style from 1945 to the Present Edited by Richard Martin, Curator of the Costume Institute of the Metropolitan Museum of Art, this is the most thorough survey of the contemporary world of fashion to date. It covers more than 200 famous and fledgling artists and houses from all over the world, including clothing designers, milliners, footwear designers and textile houses.

ISBN 0-7876-1036-4 • 7¼″ x 9¼″ • 438 pages • 100 photographs

The St. James Opera Encyclopedia: A Guide to People and Works The history of opera, in all its drama and pageantry, is thoroughly explored in this lavishly illustrated book. Covering the art from its beginnings to the present day, *The St. James Opera Encyclopedia* presents 500 in-depth entries on operas, composers and performers.

ISBN 0-7876-1035-6 • 7¼″ x 9¼″ • 958 pages • 94 photographs

THE ST. JAMES WOMEN FILMMAKERS ENCYCLOPEDIA

Women on the Other Side of the Camera

Edited by Amy L. Unterburger
Foreword by Gwendolyn Audrey Foster

VISIBLE INK PRESS

DETROIT • SAN FRANCISCO • LONDON • BOSTON • WOODBRIDGE, CT

The St. James Women Filmmakers Encyclopedia

Visible Ink Press is a division of the Gale Group
27500 Drake Road
Farmington Hills, MI 48331-3535

Most Visible Ink Press® books are available at special quantity discounts when purchased in bulk by corporations, organizations, or groups. Customized printings, special imprints, messages, and excerpts can be produced to meet your needs. For more information, contact Special Markets Manager, The Gale Group, 27500 Drake Road, Farmington Hills, MI 48331-3535. Or call 1-800-776-6265.

Cover Photo: Jodie Foster on the set of *Little Man Tate,* 1991.

Cover Design: Pamela A. E. Galbreath

Library of Congress Cataloging-in-Publication Data

The St. James women filmmakers encyclopedia : women on the other side of the camera.
p. cm.
ISBN 1-57859-092-2 (softcover)
1. Women motion picture producers and directors—Biography—Dictionaries. 2. Motion pictures—Biography—Dictionaries. 3. Women in the motion picture industry. I. St. James Press. II. Title: Saint James women filmmakers encyclopedia. III. Title: Women filmmakers encyclopedia.
PN1998.2.S683 1999
791.43'082—dc21
[B] 99-23149
CIP

ISBN 1-57859-092-2
Printed in the United States of America

10 9 8 7 6 5 4 3 2 1

about the foreword writer

Gwendolyn Audrey Foster has been actively working in the study and archiving of the works of women directors since 1985, when she began to write and direct her documentary on early women film directors of the silent era. With the production of this documentary, *The Women Who Made the Movies* (1992), Foster began her career in film studies and her academic work specializing in women's film and literature and cultural studies in general. Foster published one of the first encyclopedias of women directors, entitled *Women Film Directors: An International Bio-Critical Dictionary*, in 1995. Next, Foster began to focus on women filmmakers of the African, African American, and Indian diasporas for her second book, published in 1997, *Women Filmmakers of the African and Asian Diaspora: Decolonizing the Gaze, Locating Subjectivity*. This is the first book-length study of women filmmakers of color, including chapters on Ngozi Onwurah, Pratibha Parmar, Zeinabu irene Davis, Julie Dash, and Mira Nair. Foster has also edited an anthology on the films of Chantal Akerman, forthcoming in 1999.

contents

WOMEN FILMMAKERS

Introduction xi

Foreword xiii

Chronology of Women Filmmakers xix

Picture Acknowledgments xxv

a . . . . . . Gilda de Abreu. . . **1** Marianne Ahrne. . . **2** Chantal Akerman. . . **4** Zoë Akins. . . **5** Maryse Alberti. . . **7** Dede Allen. . . **9** Jay Presson Allen. . . **12** Suzana Amaral. . . **13** Allison Anders. . . **15** Maya Angelou. . . **17** Annette Apon. . . **19** Gillian Armstrong. . . **21** Dorothy Arzner. . . **25** Jacqueline Audry. . . **27**

b . . . . . . Beth B. . . **30** Rakhshan Bani-Etemad. . . **32** Joy Batchelor. . . **34** Anne Bauchens. . . **36** María Luisa Bemberg. . . **38** Kathryn Bigelow. . . **40** Antonia Bird. . . **42** Margaret Booth. . . **44** Lizzie Borden. . . **46** Betty E. Box. . . **48** Muriel Box. . . **50** Leigh Brackett. . . **52** Anja Breien. . . **53** Jutta Brückner. . . **56** Mary Ellen Bute. . . **58**

c . . . . Jane Campion. . . **61** Corinne Cantrill. . . **64** Ana Carolina. . . **67** Liliana Cavani. . . **69** Suso Cecchi d'Amico. . . **71** Ayoka Chenzira. . . **74** Abigail Child. . . **76** Joyce Chopra. . . **78** Christine Choy. . . **80** Vera Chytilová. . . **83** Michelle Citron. . . **86** Shirley Clarke. . . **87** Lenore J. Coffee. . . **90** Janis Cole and Holly Dale. . . **92** Colette. . . **94** Betty Comden. . . **96** Martha Coolidge. . . **99** Jill Craigie. . . **101** *d* ...... Julie Dash... 105 Zeinabu irene Davis... 107 Storm De Hirsch... 109 Donna Deitch... 112 Claire Denis... 114 Maya Deren... 116 Carmen Dillon... 118 Doris Dörrie... 120 Germaine Dulac... 122 Marguerite Duras... 124

e .... Judit Elek... 127 Nora Ephron... 129 Marie Epstein... 132 Valie Export... 133

f .... Safi Faye... 137 Marcela Fernández Violante... 139 Verna Fields... 140 Jodie Foster... 142 Su Friedrich... 144

g ...... Lillian Gish... 147 Elinor Glyn... 150 Jill Godmilow... 152 Sara Gómez... 154 Frances Goodrich... 155 Bette Gordon... 157 Marleen Gorris... 159 Helen Grayson... 161 Maggie Greenwald... 163 Agnès Guillemot... 165 Alice Guy... 167

h .... Randa Haines... 171 Barbara Hammer... 173 Marion Hänsel... 175 Leslie Harris... 178 Joan Harrison... 180 Edith Head... 181 Amy Heckerling... 189 Birgit Hein... 191 Astrid Henning-Jensen... 193 Agnieszka Holland... 195 Faith Elliott Hubley... 197 Ann Hui... 199 Danièle Huillet... 201

i-j .... Irene... 203 Wanda Jakubowska... 206 Dorothy Jeakins... 208 Ruth Prawer Jhabvala... 209

k .... Nelly Kaplan... 212 Diane Keaton... 214 Beeban Kidron... 217 Barbara Kopple... 220 Ester Krumbachová... 223 Diane Kurys... 225

l .... Matilde Soto Landeta... 229 Alile Sharon Larkin... 231 Clara Law... 232 Caroline Leaf... 234 Isobel Lennart... 236 Sonya Levien... 237 Carol Littleton... 239 Lynne Littman... 240 Jennie Livingston... 242 Anita Loos... 244 Ida Lupino... 247 Lottie Lyell... 250

m ..... Alison Maclean... 253 Jeanie Macpherson... 255 Cleo Madison... 258 Sarah Maldoror... 260 Marilú Mallet... 262 Frances Marion... 264 Penny Marshall... 267 June Mathis... 269 Elaine May... 271 Melanie Mayron... 275 McDonagh sisters (Isobel, Phyllis, Paulette)... 278 Jeanine Meerapfel... 280 Deepa Mehta... 282 Marie Menken... 284 Bess Meredyth... 286 Márta

Mészáros. . . 287 Pilar Miró. . . 290 Kira Muratova. . . 293 Jane Murfin. . . 296 Brianne Murphy. . . 297 Musidora. . . 299

n . . . . . . Mira Nair. . . 302 Gunvor Nelson. . . 304 Elvira Notari. . . 306 María Novaro. . . 309

o . . . . Alanis Obomsawin. . . 312 Yoko Ono. . . 315 Ulrike Ottinger. . . 318

p . . . . . . Euzhan Palcy. . . 321 Claire Parker. . . 324 Pratibha Parmar. . . 326 Christine Pascal. . . 328 Peng Xiaolian. . . 330 Eleanor Perry. . . 332 Mary Pickford. . . 333 Anne-Claire Poirier. . . 336 Léa Pool. . . 338 Sally Potter. . . 340 Olga Preobrazhenskaya. . . 342

r . . . . Yvonne Rainer. . . 345 Lotte Reiniger. . . 346 Alma Reville. . . 349 Leni Riefenstahl. . . 351 Helen Rose. . . 355 Shirley Russell. . . 357

s . . . . Leontine Sagan. . . 359 Helke Sander. . . 361 Helma Sanders-Brahms. . . 363 Valeria Sarmiento. . . 365 Nancy Savoca. . . 367 Greta Schiller. . . 370 Carolee Schneemann. . . 372 Thelma Schoonmaker. . . 375 Susan Seidelman. . . 379 Coline Serreau. . . 382 Irene Sharaff. . . 384 Larissa Shepitko. . . 386 Nell Shipman. . . 387 Esther Shub. . . 390 Joan Micklin Silver. . . 391 Vera Šimková-Plívová. . . 394 Yulia Solntseva. . . 395 Dorothy Spencer. . . 397 Penelope Spheeris. . . 399 Dawn Steel. . . 401 Barbra Streisand. . . 405

t . . . . Kinuyo Tanaka. . . 409 Betty Thomas. . . 411 Wendy Toye. . . 414 Monika Treut. . . 416 Trinh T. Minh-Ha. . . 417 Nadine Trintignant. . . 419

u-v . . Liv Ullmann. . . 423 Christine Vachon. . . 426 Helen van Dongen. . . 429 Theadora Van Runkle. . . 431 Virginia Van Upp. . . 432 Agnès Varda. . . 435 Patrizia von Brandenstein. . . 437 Thea von Harbou. . . 439 Margarethe von Trotta. . . 441

w . . . . . Lois Weber. . . 444 Claudia Weill. . . 446 Lina Wertmüller. . . 449 Mae West. . . 452 Joyce Wieland. . . 455 Oprah Winfrey. . . 456

contents

y-z . . . Tizuka Yamasaki. . . **460** Mai Zetterling. . . **462** Zhang Nuanxin. . . **464**

Notes on Contributors 467

Nationality Index 473

Index 475

introduction

The more than 200 filmmakers within *The St. James Women Filmmakers Encyclopedia* encompass not only directors but also women in many important behind-the-camera vocations, including producers, animators, art directors, editors, writers, and costume designers. Each of these entries consists of a brief biography, a complete filmography, and an expository essay by a specialist in the field.

The selections within this book are intended to represent the wide range of interests within North American and European film scholarship and criticism. The entries selected were deemed to be both interesting and of lasting importance. The eclecticism in both the list of entries and the critical stances of the different writers emphasizes the multifarious notions of the cinema.

Non-English-language film titles are ordinarily given in the original language or a transliteration of it. Alternate release titles in the original language(s) are found in italics within parentheses, followed by release titles in English (American, then British, if there is a difference) and translations. The date of a film is understood to refer to its year of release in its country of origin unless stated otherwise.

In the list of films in each entry, a name in parentheses following a film title is that of the director(s). Information within the parentheses following the director's name modifies, if necessary, then adds to the subject's principal function(s).

The most common abbreviations used in *The St. James Women Filmmakers Encyclopedia* are:

anim	animator or animation
assoc	associate
asst	assistant

d	director
des	designer
ed	editor
exec pr	executive producer
mus	music
ph	cinematographer or director of photography
pr	producer
ro	role
sc	scenarist or scriptwriter
st	story

"Co-" preceding a function indicates collaboration with one or more persons. Other abbreviations that may be used to clarify the nature of an individual film are "doc"—documentary, and "ep"—episode.

foreword

The history of women filmmakers is a rich and fertile body of knowledge that has been largely ignored, until recently, by mainstream film historians. Nevertheless, women were very much involved in the creation of the visual art form known as motion pictures from its beginnings until the present. In fact, women were at one time far more prominent in film production circles than they are now. In the early days of film, women such as Alice Guy, Gene Gauntier, Hanna Henning, Ida May Park, Olga Preobrazhenskaya, Nell Shipman, Ruth Stonehouse, Lucille McVey Drew, Elvira Notari, Lois Weber, Dorothy Arzner, Germaine Dulac, Marie Epstein, Grace Cunard, and many others were involved in creating the new visual format. Unfortunately, when the first surveys of film history were written, and when the first pantheons of directors and major players were drawn up, most of the accomplishments of women directors, producers, and scenarists were overlooked. Even feminists tended to believe that there simply were no women involved in the production end of early films; women were viewed as objects of a voyeuristic "male gaze," in films that were supposedly all directed and created by men.

Women were written out of history as active participants in the production and creation of film, film movements, special effects, the star system, the studio system, independent and experimental forms, and genres. It seems as if historians were primarily interested in women in front of the camera as actors and sex objects. Creative women, however, were very much participants in the history of filmmaking. For example, Alice Guy, a French woman director, is generally credited as having directed the first "narrative" film. Her film, *La Fée aux choux,* is in many ways a film like that of her male contemporaries; it tells the story of a fairy tale in which a woman who cannot bear children creates them in a cabbage patch. Guy was instrumental in the development of such early pioneering techniques as special effects (masking, superimposition, and other in-camera effects). She was also very much a pioneer of the very first genre vehicles, yet Alice Guy is rarely cited as the originator of these genres. The hundreds of films she directed include everything from melodramas to gangster films, horror films, fairy tales, and even short music films featuring famous opera singers—forerunners to today's music videos.

It is hard to overestimate the talented contributions of this pioneering woman director who worked in early primitive color techniques such as hand-painting and stamping and also created some of the first examples of sound films, recorded on wax cylinders. And Alice Guy was not by any means the only woman producer/writer/director to contribute to the development of the film form. Internationally, many other women, most of whom are barely remembered today, were also prominent in silent-film production. For example, in Australia, the McDonagh sisters (Paulette, Phyllis, and Isobel) taught themselves filmmaking from the vantage point of actresses. Their early films were only recently "rediscovered" and written back into Australian film history. Hanna Henning, a German director who made many silent films, awaits rediscovery, as does Ida May Park, an American director who made scores of films in the silent-film period. The years have been a bit kinder to Lois Weber, Cleo Madison, Dorothy Davenport Reid, and Dorothy Arzner, all of whom have had their films survive and who have been rediscovered and celebrated in film festivals and archival retrospectives such as those at the Museum of Modern Art in New York and the American Museum of the Moving Picture in Astoria.

Women directors thrived during a short period in the beginning of filmmaking production, especially in the teens and early 1920s. In this period, before film directing was seen as primarily a "masculine" occupation, women directors were numerous and busy. This period is well covered by Anthony Slide in his book, *Early Women Directors*. So many women were active in film production: Julia Crawford Ivers, Nell Shipman, Ruth Stonehouse, Lottie Lyell, Musidora, Margery Wilson, and many others. Many women were employed at the Universal Studios, where Carl Laemmle was not averse to hiring women as directors. Women were also highly active in this period as screenwriters.

Many women directors of color worked outside the studio system as independent producer/directors. African American women directors such as Eloice Gist and Zora Neale Hurston developed and introduced the independent personal film. Gist was a preacher who wrote, produced, directed, and self-distributed her own films; she lectured with them as she went from town to town, speaking with films such as her *Hellbound Train,* which depicted the narratives of figures bound for hell because of various moral trespasses. Zora Neale Hurston, as many now know, pioneered the ethnographic film that featured the insider informant. Hurston's films were ahead of their time in that she understood the value of herself as an insider informant in the stories she told about the African American community.

Beyond the United States, women were instrumental in pioneering schools of film. Women such as French filmmakers Germaine Dulac and Marie Epstein were groundbreakers in the experimentation with film. Dulac is now finally hailed as one of the champions of the experimental French film. She was loosely associated with the Surrealists, the Impressionists, and the poetic realists. Her films are currently championed and lionized as part of a canon of important experimental films that challenged the borders of poetic filmic expression. Epstein is also being reconfigured into the landscape of film history. Her pioneering and mastery of poetic realism, combined with her narrative techniques, are finally being included in film history. Agnès Varda, the Belgian woman director who helped pioneer the New Wave, is also finally being credited for her contribution to the development of the new school of filmmaking previously only attributed to directors such as François Truffaut, Jean-Luc Godard, and other male directors. In Italy, as Giuliana Bruno uncovered, the early silent filmmaker Elvira Notari was already beginning to embrace the artistic precepts behind Neorealism, a school of film that arose in Italy many years after her death.

By the 1930s there were fewer and fewer women directors. Film was beginning to be viewed as an art form and as a powerful medium in the marketplace. Many women directors left the field when it was clear that society no longer approved of women working in such a high-profile job that clearly indicated power in the public sphere. Among the exceptions were German director Leni Riefenstahl, who is universally credited with pioneering the documentary form and the technique of propaganda. Dorothy Arzner, a lesbian filmmaker, was one of the few prominent women directors in the 1930s. Mary Field is credited with pioneering the British nature film at about this time. Mary Ellen Bute was one of the pioneers of the experimental film in the United States. Her use of oscillated light to form patterns choreographed to music was far ahead of its time.

The 1940s were a fertile time for experimental women filmmakers. In this era, Maya Deren and Marie Menken introduced many of the ideas and forms of experimental avant-garde cinema. In Britain, Joy Batchelor created animated films. In France, Jacqueline Audry directed glossy studio-produced films. In the Soviet Union, Wanda Jakubowska pioneered many of the Soviet ideals of the social document film. In Mexico, Matilde Landeta fought to direct her own productions after having served as an assistant director for many, many years. She managed to direct a few of her own projects despite the sexism of the industry.

In the 1950s, Ida Lupino claimed that she did her work simply because there was no one else available, but the passion of her efforts belies such modesty. She tackled controversial subject matter and invented many of the techniques and themes associated with film noir. In the 1960s many women directed personal experimental films. Mai Zetterling, for example, began as an actress, but soon tired of working within the confines of a male-dominated system, and created her own visions of the world. Sara Aldrege was another important innovator in experimental film. One of the greatest of the experimental directors of the 1960s, Carolee Schneemann deals with issues of sexuality, power, and gender, as does Barbara Hammer, who began working as a director in the early 1970s. The multiplicity of visions among women directors is startling; it forces us to look at ourselves as women, and as members of society, in a series of entirely new and enlightening ways.

foreword

In the 1970s, 1980s, and the 1990s, there has been an international rise in the number of women filmmakers, both independent and studio directors. Women have been prominent as filmmakers in both developed and developing countries. Despite the rise in the number of women filmmakers, the auteur film director continues to be thought of as male. Despite women's contributions to the development of the art form and many of its pivotal movements (from Surrealism to New Wave to documentary and the personal film), women filmmakers continue to be marginalized in dominant discourse. Women filmmakers, through their exclusion from history books, have been denied a sisterhood. Each generation of women filmmakers stands apart from its earlier predecessors. Remedying the paucity of scholarship on women directors is compounded by an unavailability of many of the films made by women in the early days of cinema, many of which have been lost, neglected, or destroyed. Film scholars have produced a remarkably persuasive body of film criticism that begins the belated recognition process of women film directors and their achievements.

Despite a clear lineage, women filmmakers have managed to be influenced by one another, even if they have been marginalized or excluded from film scholarship. Barbara Hammer and several women directors credit, for example, the work of Maya Deren, whose experimental films were profoundly personal and expressed a female camera-eye. Diana Barrie claims she was most influenced by Deren's *Meshes of the Afternoon*. Alice Guy was a mentor and influence on Lois Weber, who followed in her footsteps to produce, write, and direct her own material. Weber, in turn, had a profound effect upon the career of Dorothy Arzner, who had a successful directorial career within the confines of the studio system of Hollywood in the 1930s.

Dorothy Arzner, however, admitted she stifled her criticism of other filmmaker's studio projects. As the only woman director in the studio system, she felt she "ought not complain," and yet she carefully maintained that no obstacles were put in her way by men in the business. Elinor Glyn, the famous author and early filmmaker, seemingly did not recognize the clearly sexist critical lambasting she received for her adroit and sharply observed comedy, *Knowing Men*. Ida May Park, another woman among many who directed in the 1920s, refused her first job directing, thinking it an unfeminine job. Even contemporary women directors find the notion of a feminist approach to filmmaking incompatible with their need for acceptance in the industry. The recently deceased Shirley Clarke refused invitations to women's film festivals, even if she agreed that women directors should be recognized. French filmmaker Diane Kurys finds the idea of women's cinema "negative, dangerous, and reductive," at the same time claiming, "I am a feminist because I am a woman, I can't help it."

Other women directors make absolutely no excuses for their feminism. Carolee Schneemann, Yvonne Rainer, and Barbara Hammer, for example, make films that deal directly and uncompromisingly with issues of sexuality, power, and gender. Donna Deitch was primarily motivated to make *Desert Hearts* because she saw a lack of films—especially commercial films—that center around a lesbian relationship. Hammer was drawn to experimental formalist filmmaking precisely because it did not seem to be (yet) the exclusive domain of men.

Some women directors wish to make films that employ newly defined heroines or that reverse gender expectations. Sally Potter's *The Gold Diggers* is a case in point. Michelle Citron's *Daughter Rite* consists of a narrative about two sisters and their mother and ignores the trappings of heroism. Doris Dörrie's film *Men. . .* is an attempt to see men as comic gender reversals of the mythic Marilyn Monroe type. Social concerns are also prevalent in the films and voices of women directors. Barbara Kopple's *American Dream* covers union battles. Marguerite Duras, a French critic and writer, and Trinh T. Minh-ha, a Vietnamese deconstructionist critic and documentarian, are centrally concerned with deprivileging the screen from its power to distort social reality. Trinh T. Minh-ha questions the ability of the image itself as a historicist account of truth. Clearly then, women directors are often compelled to redefine the boundaries of cinema.

Women directors face a lack of support not only as a result of their gender, but also because they have a remarkable tendency to choose "controversial" or "difficult" subject matter. Shirley Clarke had enormous difficulties funding *The Cool World,* an early 1960s experimental film (shot in 35mm) about racism and drug dependency. British feature director Muriel Box faced similar difficulties proving herself in a male-dominated industry. Jodie Foster and Penny Marshall stand as proof that some women manage to find funding and support from Hollywood executives, but both have had to use their acting as leverage in the decision-making process.

Racism in Hollywood is a problem only compounded by sexism against women of color. The new African American "wave" of feature filmmaking is predominated by men such as Spike Lee and John Singleton. African American women directors such as Julie Dash, Kathleen Collins, Alile Sharon Larkin, and Barbara McCullough have so far not been offered lucrative package deals by industry executives. Similarly, Asian American women directors have had major difficulties finding funding and distribution. Christine Choy faced enormous interference and lack of support in the production of her film *Who Killed Vincent Chin?,* a film about violence and racism directed against Asian Americans. Kathleen Collins spent more than a year trying to fund her film *Women, Sisters, and Friends*.

Julie Dash continues to have to search aggressively for funding, even after the critical success of her Afrocentric *Daughters of the Dust.* Claire Denis was forced to face humiliation and scorn when attempting to finance her independent feature *Chocolat,* a film that directly attacks African colonization. Similarly, Ann Hui's *Boat People,* a critically successful film that documents the harsh realities of Vietnamese refugees, clearly deserves wider distribution. Distribution and finance remain as formidable barriers that independent filmmakers find themselves up against. An unbelievable amount of hardship seems to have been suffered by women directors, yet an unrivaled degree of perseverance seems to be a common factor in many of their experiences. Early pioneering film director Dorothy Davenport Reid faced the resentment of her male colleagues as she struggled to create her own cinematic visions of the woman's plight in American society. Yet Reid went on to make a series of intensely personal films that argued against drug addiction, prostitution, and sexism. Yvonne Rainer recently managed to fund a film about menopause, *Privilege,* despite its supposedly taboo subject matter, because of an incredibly loyal following and an intense determination to make the film. For all of these women, the need to make films is a fierce desire they must simply obey, no matter the cost.

Whether working in the industry or making films with the aid of grants and personal financial subsidies, women filmmakers have helped to shape the world of film as it is today. Some women film practitioners see themselves as harbingers of change, instructional forces, barometers of social reintegration; other women see themselves as workers within a tradition that they attempt to subvert from within. The immense contribution made by these women is a legacy that is rich in personal insight, hard work, careful study, and often sacrifice to achieve the aims they held for their creative endeavors.

Gwendolyn Audrey Foster

chronology of film history

Note: Also featured in this chronology are seminal film history events of a general nature, which are included for the sake of context.

1893

Thomas Alva Edison (1847-1931) shoots *Fred Ott's Sneeze,* which in 1894 becomes the first whole film on record at the Library of Congress. Edison's early films are shot using the Kinetograph, his motion-picture camera, and are viewed through the Kinetoscope, his peephole viewer.

1895

The Lumière brothers of France—Louis (1864-1948) and Auguste (1862-1954)—shoot their first film, *La Sortie des Usines Lumière* (*Workers Leaving the Lumière Factory*), which then becomes the first film to be projected in a theater. Their early films utilize their Cinématographe, a combination camera-projector.

The first movie theater opens in Paris on 28 December.

1896

French producer-director Alice Guy (1873-1968), the world's first woman filmmaker, exhibits her film *La Fée aux choux* (*The Cabbage Fairy*) at the International Exhibition in Paris. Some historians contend this was the first fictional film.

1906

Elvira Notari (1875-1946), Italy's first—and most prolific—female filmmaker, begins directing, co-producing, and writing films. By 1930, she will have worked on about 60 feature films and more than 100 documentaries and shorts.

1913

Olga Wohlbrück becomes the first German woman filmmaker with the release of *Ein Mädchen zu Verschenken* (*A Girl for Giving Away*), the only film she directs.

1915

American director Julia Crawford Ivers becomes the first woman general manager of a Hollywood studio, Bosworth, Inc.

American Viola Lawrence (d. 1973), considered the first female film editor, begins her career. She will later work with such noted Hollywood directors as John Ford, Howard Hawks, and Orson Welles.

Lois Weber (1882-1939), the first consistently successful American woman filmmaker, is hired by Universal Studios at the then-astounding salary of $5,000 per week. She is the highest-paid director at Universal and the highest-paid woman director of the silent era.

1916

American screenwriter Anita Loos (1888-1981) writes subtitles for D. W. Griffith's *Intolerance.* Loos is considered the first to use only "talking titles" (titles that convey dialogue) in silent films.

Canadian-born actress Mary Pickford (1893-1979) creates the Mary Pickford Film Corporation in Hollywood, becoming the first movie star to form and own a film company.

Russian filmmaker Olga Preobrazhenskaya (1881-1971), considered Russia's first female director, is co-director of *Baryshnia krestianka* (*The Lady Peasant*), her directorial debut.

American filmmaker Lois Weber (1882-1939) directs two important films: *Where Are My Children?,* a groundbreaking movie about birth control, which costs $12,000 to make and reportedly earns $500,000; and the major historical drama *The Dumb Girl of Portici,* which introduces the Russian ballerina Anna Pavlova to the screen.

1917

The Technicolor Corporation is founded in the United States and begins experimenting with color film.

American actress Marion E. Wong is the first president of the Mandarin Film Company of Oakland, California. This organization, the first film production company to be staffed entirely by Chinese Americans, had its own studio and starred Wong and her sister in its first movie, *The Curse of Quon Qwan,* released in 1917.

1918

French director-actress-writer Musidora (1889-1957) forms her own production company, La Société des Films Musidora.

1919

American film editor Anne Bauchens (1882-1967) becomes the first film editor to be written into a director's contract, that of Cecil B. DeMille. She edits all of DeMille's films from this year forward.

Australian director-actress Lottie Lyell (1890-1925) is the screenwriter, art director, editor, and production assistant (and uncredited co-director or director) of her masterpiece, *The Sentimental Bloke,* in which she also stars. The film brings in more money than any previous Australian film and earns enormous praise.

Mary Pickford co-founds United Artists with D. W. Griffith, Charlie Chaplin, and Douglas Fairbanks, Sr.

1920

American actress Lillian Gish (1896-1993) makes her only foray into directing with *Remodeling Her Husband.* In an "all-woman" production, Gish co-writes the screenplay with her sister Dorothy, who also stars, and recruits the American writer Dorothy Parker to write the intertitles.

1922

American writer Jane Murfin (1893-1955) is the first person to write a film script starring a dog. Starting in 1922, five pictures were made for First National that were written by Murfin and starred Strongheart, a German shepherd who had formerly served in a Red Cross unit in the army.

1926

Working as a production team, the McDonagh sisters—Isobel (1899-1982), Paulette (1901-78), and Phyllis (1900-78)—are the first women in Australia to produce a feature film, with their debut, *Those Who Love.*

German-born British filmmaker Lotte Reiniger (1899-1981) creates the first full-length animated film *Die Geschichte des Prinzen Achmed* (*The Adventures of Prince Achmed*), working in Germany and using silhouette figures made out of cardboard, tin, and paper.

1927

The Academy of Motion Picture Arts and Sciences is founded on 4 May.

The sound era begins when *The Jazz Singer* opens on 6 October featuring a synchronized soundtrack on its musical numbers.

British writer Bryher (1894-1983) founds *Close-Up,* the first serious film journal, in Vevey, Switzerland.

French filmmaker Germaine Dulac (1882-1942) is the first person to make a surrealist film, *La Coquille et le clergyman* (*The Seashell and the Clergyman*).

Soviet Ukrainian filmmaker Esther Shub (1894-1959), a pioneer of the Soviet compilation film, creates two of her best-known works, *Padenye dinastii romanovykh* (*The Fall of the Romanov Dynasty*) and *Veliky put'* (*The Great Road*), both compiled for the tenth anniversary of the Russian Revolution.

German writer Thea von Harbou (1888-1954) writes the screenplay for *Metropolis,* which is directed by her then-husband, Fritz Lang.

1928

The first all-talking film, *The Lights of New York,* is released.

1929

American director Dorothy Arzner (1900-79) is the first woman to direct a sound film, with *The Wild Party.* In the process, she creates the first overhead microphone by attaching a mike to a fishing pole.

The first Academy Awards are presented on 16 May.

1931

American writer-director Frances Marion (1890-1973), who earned the moniker "Dean of Hollywood Screenwriters" in the 1920s and 1930s, wins an Academy Award for *The Big House* (1930). She wins again in 1932 for *The Champ*.

Austrian filmmaker Leontine Sagan (1899-1974) directs *Mädchen in Uniform,* notable for its all-woman cast, its antifascist stance, and its groundbreaking treatment of lesbian themes. Made in Germany, it is the first German film directed by a woman and the first German film whose profits are shared cooperatively. The film is later banned by German Minister for Propaganda Joseph Goebbels.

American film animator Claire Parker (1906-81) co-invents (with Russian filmmaker Alexander Alexeieff) the "pinboard" animation technique, a process analogous to using halftones in black-and-white photography. Parker and Alexeieff first use this technique in *Une Nuit sur le Mont Chauve* (*Night on Bald Mountain*), released in 1933.

1935

German documentary filmmaker Leni Riefenstahl (1902—) directs *Triumph des Willens* (*Triumph of the Will*).

1937

Walt Disney (1901-66) produces *Snow White and the Seven Dwarfs,* the first feature-length animated cartoon in color.

1938

American costume designer Edith Head (1897-1981) becomes the first woman to head a studio design department, when she attains the post of chief designer at Paramount Studio. Over the course of her long career, Head is nominated for 35 Academy Awards, and wins the award eight times, garnering her more Oscars than any other designer in history.

Olympia, Leni Riefenstahl's documentary about the 1936 Olympic Games in Berlin, makes its premiere on Adolf Hitler's birthday.

1939

The first Cannes International Film Festival is held in the resort town of Cannes, France, with opening night on 1 September.

American film editor Margaret Booth (1898—), having edited a number of noted MGM films, including *The Barretts of Wimpole Street, Romeo and Juliet,* and *Camille,* is appointed head of editing at MGM and will supervise the editing of MGM films for the next three decades. She is awarded an honorary Academy Award in 1977 "for 62 years of exceptionally distinguished service to the motion picture industry as a film editor."

American film editor Dorothy Spencer (1909—) is nominated for an Academy Award for her work on *Stagecoach*. Over a 50-year career, she is nominated for three more Oscars—never winning—and edits numerous noted films, including *To Be or Not to Be* (1942), *My Darling Clementine* (1946), *Decision before Dawn* (1952), *Cleopatra* (1963), and *Earthquake* (1974).

1940

British animator Joy Batchelor (1914-91) co-founds Halas & Batchelor Cartoon Films in England with her husband, the Hungarian animator John Halas. Over the next five decades, this company, an innovator in the production of animated film, produces and directs hundreds of cartoons for cinema, television, and commercials as well as for promotional, scientific, and instructional films.

American Anne Bauchens (1882-1967)—the editor of every one of Cecil B. DeMille's films from *We Can't Have Everything* in 1918 to his last in 1956—becomes the first woman to receive an Academy Award for film editing for her work on *Northwest Mounted Police*.

1942

American costume designer Irene (1901-62) becomes chief designer at MGM, a position she will hold through 1950, during which time she will design costumes for dozens of films.

1945

American writer and producer Virginia Van Upp (1902-70) is made executive producer for Columbia Pictures, second-in-command to studio boss Harry Cohn.

1946

British writer-director Muriel Box (1905-91) shares an Academy Award for original screenplay with her husband Sydney for *The Seventh Veil*.

Russian-born American Maya Deren (1917-61), the first woman to succeed as an independent filmmaker, is awarded a Guggenheim Fellowship for work in creative film. Deren, whose seminal work is the 1943 film *Meshes of the Afternoon,* is the first person to receive an award from the John Simon Guggenheim Memorial Foundation.

Danish filmmaker Astrid Henning-Jensen (1914—) serves as assistant director to husband Bjarne on their breakthrough film, *Ditte Menneskebarn* (*Ditte: Child of Man*).

1947

Polish filmmaker Wanda Jakubowska (1907—), co-founder in 1930 of the radical Society of the

Devotees of the Artistic Film (START), directs *Ostatni etap* (*The Last Stop*), one of the first films about the Nazi concentration camps, basing it on her own experiences.

1949
French filmmaker Jacqueline Audry (1908-77) directs *Gigi,* the first of several films she will make based on the writings of Colette.

1951
The first Berlin International Film Festival is held.

Irene Sharaff (1910-93), American costume designer, handles the costume design for *An American in Paris,* for which she is awarded an Academy Award, her first of five Oscars.

1953
First film produced in CinemaScope, *The Robe,* is released.

American director-actress Ida Lupino (1918-95) directs and co-writes *The Hitch-Hiker,* her most successful film, both critically and commercially.

Japanese director-actress Kinuyo Tanaka (1910-77) directs *Koibumi* (*Love Letters*), becoming the first Japanese female director.

1954
Agnès Varda (1928—), the Belgian filmmaker known as the "grandmother of the New Wave" of French filmmaking, writes, produces, and directs what some consider the first film of the French New Wave, *La Pointe courte,* which juxtaposes twin story lines, one fictional, one real.

1959
French director-writer Marguerite Duras (1914-96) writes the screenplay for the acclaimed *Hiroshima mon amour.*

1961
Agnès Varda writes and directs *Cléo de cinq à sept* (*Cleo from 5 to 7*), noteworthy for its groundbreaking use of physical time, with events happening at the same tempo as they would in real life.

1962
Vera Chytilová (1929—), perhaps the most important woman director of the Czech cinema, makes her directorial debut with *Strop* (*The Ceiling*), for which she also wrote the screenplay.

American filmmaker Shirley Clarke (1925-97) cofounds, with Jonas Mekas, the New York Filmmakers Cooperative, a nonprofit distribution company for independent films.

French film editor Agnès Guillemot (1931—), who edited all of Jean-Luc Godard's films from 1961 to 1969, edits Godard's *Vivre sa vie* (*My Life to Live*).

1963
Shirley Clarke (1919-97), an American filmmaker, directs *The Cool World,* the first commercial film to be shot on location in Harlem.

American writer Ruth Prawer Jhabvala (1927—) is the screenwriter for *The Householder,* the first of her numerous collaborations with Merchant Ivory Productions.

1967
In recognition of her skill and creativity in editing *Bonnie and Clyde,* American film editor Dede Allen (1925—) is the first person in her field to receive a solo credit among the screen titles. For the same film, Theadora Van Runkle (c. 1940—) made her debut as a costume designer, garnering an Academy Award nomination in the process.

American filmmaker Carolee Schneemann (1939—) directs *Fuses,* generally considered her best film and a key film of the 1960s avant-garde film movement.

1971
Actress Barbara Loden (1934-80) becomes the first American feminist film director with her direction of *Wanda,* winner of the International Critics Prize, Venice.

1972
The First International Festival of Women's Film is held in New York City.

French filmmaker Sarah Maldoror (1929—), of Guadeloupian descent, directs *Sambizanga,* a film about a female revolutionary in Angola and a prizewinner at several international film festivals.

1973
Pamela Douglas becomes the first black woman producer at a major motion-picture studio, namely Universal Pictures.

British/American cinematographer-director Brianne Murphy (1937—) becomes the first woman member of the American Society of Cinematographers.

1974
Julia Miller Phillips (1944—) is the first woman to win an Academy Award as a producer, for *The Sting,* which wins the Oscar for best picture.

1975

Belgian filmmaker Chantal Akerman (1950—), who was the first to work with an all-female staff of technicians, directs the acclaimed *Jeanne Dielman, 23 Quai du Commerce, 1080 Bruxelles.*

American director Dorothy Arzner is honored for her career by the Directors Guild of America, becoming the first woman member of the Directors Guild.

Award-winning Mexican director-writer Marcela Fernández Violante (1941—) becomes the first woman to join the Mexican film director's union.

American Verna Fields (1918-82) is the editor on the blockbuster *Jaws,* for which she is awarded an Academy Award. The following year, Universal Pictures promotes her to vice president of feature productions, a post she holds for the remainder of her life.

1976

American documentary filmmaker Barbara Kopple (1946—) directs and produces *Harlan County, U.S.A.,* the first feature-length documentary about a labor dispute. Among several other honors, the film is awarded the Academy Award for best feature documentary.

Italian director Lina Wertmüller (1928—) is nominated for an Academy Award for *Pasqualino settebellezze* (*Seven Beauties*), becoming the first woman ever nominated in the category of best director.

1979

The first International Women's Film Festival is held in Sceaux, France, with a total audience of 3,000 moviegoers. In later years, this showcase for women filmmakers the world over is held in Créteil, France, and by the 1990s attendance surpasses 35,000.

Australian filmmaker Gillian Armstrong (1950—) directs her first feature film, the acclaimed *My Brilliant Career.* The film is reportedly the first commercial feature film directed by an Australian woman in 46 years.

1980

American film editor Thelma Schoonmaker (1940—) edits Martin Scorsese's *Raging Bull,* for which she receives an Academy Award. She will edit all of Scorsese's films from this date forward.

1982

Spanish director Pilar Miró (1940-97), an award-winning and commercially successful filmmaker, is appointed Culture Ministry director general of cinematography for the Spanish government, a post she will hold until 1985. While in office, the "Miró Law" is passed, which provides generous subsidies to Spanish filmmakers, including such notables as Pedro Almodóvar and Fernando Trueba.

Filmmaker Susan Seidelman (1952—) is the first American to direct an independent film (*Smithereens*) shown in competition at the Cannes International Film Festival in France. Three years later, she directs the surprise box-office hit *Desperately Seeking Susan.*

1983

Euzhan Palcy (1957—), French West Indian director-writer-producer, writes and directs the internationally acclaimed *La Rue cases nègres* (*Sugar Cane Alley*), her feature-film debut.

Barbra Streisand (1942—) is the first woman to produce, direct, co-write, star in, and sing in a major motion picture, performing multiple roles in her film *Yentl.*

1985

The first Sundance Film Festival is held in Sundance, Utah, bringing attention to the world of independent filmmakers.

Polish filmmaker Agnieszka Holland (1948—) gains major international acclaim with her direction of *Bittere ernte* (*Angry Harvest*), which is nominated for best foreign-language film.

1986

American filmmaker Donna Deitch (1945—) directs *Desert Hearts,* the first lesbian love story to obtain mainstream distribution.

1987

American movie executive Dawn Steel (1946-97) is named presdent of Columbia Pictures, a post she holds until 1991.

1988

Christine Choy (1952—) co-directs the Academy Award-nominated *Who Killed Vincent Chin?* Choy, an American filmmaker born in China to a Korean father and a Chinese mother, is the first Asian-American woman to achieve a successful career in documentary filmmaking.

American filmmaker Penny Marshall (1942—) directs the box-office smash *Big.*

Mira Nair (1957—), Indian filmmaker, directs her breakthrough film, *Salaam Bombay!,* about street children of Bombay. The film is nominated for an Academy Award for best foreign-language film, is awarded several prizes at international film festivals, and enjoys considerable box-office success in India and the West.

1989

Russian/Ukrainian director Kira Muratova (1934—), whose pre-glasnost films were consistently banned, creates her most highly regarded film, *Astenicheskii Sindrom* (*The Asthenic Syndrome*). Despite glasnost, this film too is banned, but only for a brief time.

With the release of her *A Dry White Season,* French West Indian director-writer-producer Euzhan Palcy (1957—) is the first black woman to direct a feature-length Hollywood film.

1990

Dutch filmmaker Annette Apon (1949—) directs her best-known film, the quirky comedy *Krokodillen in Amsterdam* (*Crocodiles in Amsterdam*).

1992

Leslie Harris (1959—) writes, produces, and directs *Just Another Girl on the I.R.T.,* making her the first African American woman to release her own feature film.

1993

New Zealand director Jane Campion's (1954—) film *The Piano* wins the Palme d'Or at the Cannes International Film Festival.

Canada-based Native American documentary filmmaker Alanis Obomsawin (1932—) directs *Kanehsatake: 270 Years of Resistance,* winner of 18 awards and international acclaim for its coverage of the 1990 standoff between Mohawks and the government in Quebec.

1995

Dutch director-writer Marleen Gorris's (1948—) *Antonia* (*Antonia's Line*) earns international renown, and garners the best foreign-language film Academy Award.

1996

Australian-based Chinese filmmaker Clara Law (1957—) directs the first Australian feature film that is not mostly in English, *Floating Life,* which wins the Silver Leopard at the Locarno International Film Festival.

1997

El perro del hortelano (*The Dog in the Manger*), directed by Spaniard Pilar Miró in 1995, wins seven prizes at the 1997 Goya Awards, including best director.

1998

American filmmaker Lisa Cholodenko makes her feature debut as director and screenwriter with *High Art,* an official selection at the 1998 Cannes Film Festival. She is awarded the Waldo Salt Screenwriting Award at the 1998 Sundance Film Festival.

Donna Dewey and Carol Pasternak, American filmmakers, are awarded the Academy Award for best short subject documentary, for *A Story of Healing*.

For the first time, two female-directed films—Mimi Leder's *Deep Impact* and Betty Thomas's *Dr. Doolittle*—surpass the $100 million mark at the U.S. box office during a single year. In fact, both films gross more than $150 million domestically during 1998.

1999

American filmmaker Elaine May (1932—) receives her second Academy Award nomination for screenplay adaptation for her work on *Primary Colors*.

picture acknowledgments

Photographs in *The St. James Women Filmmakers Encyclopedia* have been used with the permission of the following organizations and individuals:

AP/Wide World Photos: Randa Haines; Diane Keaton; Lynne Littman; Betty Thomas; Oprah Winfrey.

Archive Photos, Inc.: Dawn Steel.

Columbia Pictures (courtesy Kobal Collection): Claudia Weill.

Di Novi/Columbia (courtesy Kobal Collection): Gillian Armstrong.

Films de la Pleiade (courtesy Kobal Collection): *Vivre sa vie*.

Filmworld International (courtesy Kobal Collection): Maggie Greenwald.

Flach-TFI-Soprofilm/Sam Goldwyn (courtesy Kobal Collection): *Trois hommes et un couffin*.

Handmade Films (courtesy Kobal Collection): Mai Zetterling.

IRS Media (courtesy Kobal Collection): Penelope Spheeris.

The Kobal Collection: Allison Anders; Dorothy Arzner; Lizzie Borden; Betty Box; Muriel Box; Jane Campion; Liliana Cavani; Vera Chytilová; Shirley Clarke; Betty Comden; Martha Coolidge; Donna Deitch; *Deutschland bleiche Mutter;* Marguerite Duras; Nora Ephron; Lillian Gish; Elinor Glyn; *Harlan County, U.S.A.;* Edith Head; Irene; Ruth Prawer Jhabvala; Diane Kurys; Anita Loos; Ida Lupino; Jeanie Macpherson; *Männer. . .*; Frances Marion; Penny Marshall; June Mathis; Márta Mészáros; Mary Pickford; *Qingchunji;* Lotte Reiniger; Alma Reville; Leni Riefenstahl; Shirley Russell; Helke Sander; Irene Sharaff; Wendy Toye; Nadine Trintignant; Virginia Van Upp; Margarethe von Trotta; Lina Wertmuller; Mae West.

MGM (courtesy Kobal Collection): Euzhan Palcy.

MGM/UA Entertainment (courtesy Kobal Collection): Barbra Streisand.

New Line Cinema (courtesy Kobal Collection): Nancy Savoca.

Norsk Film A/S (courtesy Kobal Collection): Anja Breien.

Orion Pictures Corp. (courtesy Kobal Collection): Jodie Foster; Susan Seidelman.

Outlook (courtesy Kobal Collection): Jill Craigie.

Paramount Pictures (courtesy Kobal Collection): Elaine May.

The Rank Organisation plc (courtesy Kobal Collection): Carmen Dillon.

20th Century Fox (courtesy Kobal Collection): Amy Heckerling.

United Artists (courtesy Kobal Collection): *Raging Bull.*

Universal/Amblin (courtesy Kobal Collection): Beeban Kidron.

Universal-Jewel (courtesy Kobal Collection): Lois Weber.

Vestron (courtesy Kobal Collection): Kathryn Bigelow.

Walker Art Center (courtesy of the filmmakers): Jill Godmilow; Barbara Hammer (photograph by Glenn Halverson).

Warner Bros. (courtesy Kobal Collection): *Girlfriends;* Liv Ullmann.

The following photos are courtesy of the filmmakers: Maryse Alberti (photograph by Richard Foreman); Corinne Cantrill; Ayoka Chenzira (photograph by André Harris); Janis Cole and Holly Dale (photograph by John Walker); Claire Denis; Safi Faye; Su Friedrich (photograph by James Hamilton); *Fuses* (Carolee Schneemann); Ann Hui; Nelly Kaplan; Mira Nair (photograph by Prabhuddo Dasgupta); Joan Micklin Silver (photograph by Joyce Ravid); Christine Vachon.

Abreu, Gilda de

Brazilian director, writer, and actress

Born *1905.* ***Family*** *Married Vicente Celestino.* ***Career*** *With her husband, staged light operas with their own production company; she also performed as a singer and actress in theater, radio, and the cinema; 1946—directed her first film,* The Drunkard, *which became a box-office success; 1951—formed film production company, Pro-Arte.* ***Died*** *June 1979.*

Films as Director: 1946: *O Ébrio* (*The Drunkard*) (+ sc, pr). **1949:** *Pinguinho de Gente* (*Tiny Tot*) (+ sc). **1951:** *Coração Materno* (*A Mother's Heart*) (+ ro, sc, pr). **1977:** *Cançao de Amor* (*Song of Love*) (short).

Films as Writer: 1955: *Chico Viola Não Morreu* (*Chico Viola Didn't Die*) (Vinoly Barreto). **1974:** *Mestiça, a Escrava Indomavel* (Perroy).

A standard introduction to Brazilian cinema cannot begin without mentioning the important role that women have played in the industry, not only as actresses, but as writers, directors, and producers. Gilda de Abreu's contributions include producing, writing, directing, screenwriting, acting, songwriting, and singing.

A multitalented performer, Abreu acted and sang in radio, theater, and film. She wrote novels, plays, and songs in addition to adapting other authors' novels and plays for the stage and screen. With her husband Vicente Celestino, Abreu staged light operas in Rio de Janeiro through the couple's production company.

Abreu's directorial film debut, *O Ébrio* seemed to position her for instant stardom within the industry. An adaptation of a play by Celestino, *O Ébrio,* a musical melodrama and biopic, was wildly popular in Brazil and a record five hundred prints were struck in order to meet theatrical exhibition demand for the film.

The 1940s, however, were a difficult time to be a woman producing and directing films in Brazil. The famed Brazilian "machismo" made it difficult for Abreu to gain the respect of her crew, largely male, who had a hard time taking orders from a woman. Abreu wore pants on the set of *O Ébrio,* reportedly to minimize her female appearance in an effort to gain her crew's confidence. Despite the success of *O Ébrio,* Abreu was hindered by this gender divide and found it nearly impossible to round up a crew and financing for her second feature. This film, *Pinguinho de Gente,* was not nearly as well-received as her first. Consequently, Abreu's problems as a woman in the film industry continued.

Abreu took matters into her own hands by producing herself a third feature, *A Mother's Heart*. In addition to producing, writing, and directing the film, Abreu acted in it, proving once again her versatility.

A combination of factors, including *machista* attitudes and Brazil's economic situation, caused Abreu to quit filmmaking after *A Mother's Heart*. She was persuaded in 1955 to write the script for *Chico Viola Didn't Die* and later, in 1973, Lenita Perroy talked her into adapting one of her own stage plays for the screen.

The incredible box-office success of *O Ébrio* and the relative success of her third feature and her screenwriting efforts leave the aficionado of Brazilian cinema wondering how much more she might have contributed to the evolution of a national art form had she not been thwarted because of her sex. As late as 1979, just before her death, Abreu continued writing novels and plays, proving that her diverse talents remained vital even though she was out of the public eye.—ILENE S. GOLDMAN

Ahrne, Marianne

Swedish director

Born *Lund, Sweden, 1940.* ***Education*** *Attended University of Lund, foreign languages, B.A. 1966; entered the Stockholm Film School, 1967.* ***Career*** *Late 1960s—actress at the Student Theater at the University of Lund, in France at Théâtre des Carmes (Avignon), and in Denmark at the experimental theater Odinteatret; early 1970s—launched directing career making documentaries for Swedish and Italian TV, producing a number of documentaries in France; 1976—directed first full-length feature film,* Near and Far Away; *1991—directed TV series* Rosenholm, *parts 1-17.* ***Awards*** *Swedish Gold Bug for Best Director, Swedish Film Institute, for* Near and Far Away, *1976.*

Films as Director: **1970:** *Balladen om Therese* (*The Ballad of Therese*); *Illusionernas Natt* (*Palace of Illusions*); *Ferai.* **1971:** *Få mig att skratta* (*Make Me Laugh*); *Abortproblem i Frankrike* (*Abortion Problems in France*) (doc); *Skilsmässoproblem i italien* (*Divorce Problems in Italy*) (doc). **1972:** *Den sista riddarvampyren* (*The Last Knight Vampire*) (short); *Storstadsvampyrer* (*Big-City Vampires*); *Camargue, det forlorade landet* (*Camargue—The Lost Country*). **1973:** *Fem dagar i Falköping* (*Five Days in Falköping*) (+ co-sc, ed) (released in 1975 as half of *Två kvinnor* [*Two Women*], a double feature packaged as one film). **1974:** *Drakar, drümmar och en flicka från verkligheten* (*Dragons, Dreams—and a Girl from Reality*); *Promenad i de gamlas land* (*Promenade in the Land of the Aged*) (doc for TV). **1975:** *Pamend I de gamlas land* (for TV). **1976:** *Långt borta och nära* (*Near and Far Away*) (+ co-sc, ed). **1978:** *Frihetens murar* (*Roots of Grief*; *The Walls of Freedom*) (+ co-sc, ed). **1981:** *Svenska färger* (for TV). **1986:** *På liv och död* (*A Matter of Life and Death*) (+ co-sc, ed). **1989:** *Maskrosbarn* (*Dandelion Child*) (for TV) (+ sc). **1991:** *Rosenholm* (for TV). **1995:** *Gott om pojkar—ont om män?* (*Plenty of Boys, Shortage of Men?*) (+ ro, sc, ed). **1997:** *Flickor, kvinnor och en och annan drake* (*Girls, Women—and Once in a While a Dragon*).

Other Films: 1968: *Fanny Hill* (*The Swedish Fanny Hill*) (Ahlberg) (ro). **1990:** *Jag skall bli Sveriges Rembrandt eller dö!* (Grunér) (ro as Madame Dupuis).

Swedish filmmaker Marianne Ahrne—who is also an accomplished novelist and journalist—began her film career as an actress at the Student Theater at the University of Lund, following that with stints at the Théâtre des Carmes in Avignon, France, and the experimental theater Odinteatret in Denmark. She entered the Stockholm Film School in 1967 to study acting, but by 1970 she had begun directing, initially making documentaries for Swedish and Italian television. Although Ahrne dislikes being considered a "woman filmmaker" with its limiting connotations, her films have often focused on "women's" or feminist issues, as evidenced by her early documentaries *Abortion Problems in France* and *Divorce Problems in Italy,* as well as by 1974's *Promenade in the Land of the Aged,* her collaboration with Simon de Beauvoir, and a film considered one of her most important. The latter was one of many early documentaries that she made in France.

Several of Ahrne's initial forays into fictional film were fantasies: *The Last Knight Vampire* and *Big-City Vampires* from 1972 and *Dragons, Dreams—and a Girl from Reality* from 1974 (she would return to this genre in 1997 with *Girls, Women—and Once in a While a Dragon*). In 1973 Ahrne directed *Five Days in Falköping,* which depicts a 29-year-old film actress's five-day-long return to the town where she grew up. This 45-minute-long film was released—at least in the United States—in an odd 1975 double-feature package as the second part of *Two Women* (the first part being Stig Bjorkman's *The White Wall*).

In 1976, Ahrne made her first full-length feature film, *Near and Far Away,* for which she won a Gold Bug award for best director from the Swedish Film Institute. In it, a female student (Mania, played by Finland's Lilga Kovanko) helping at a mental institution befriends a mute young man on her ward, eventually encouraging him to speak (he is played by Britain's Robert Farrant). In addition to depicting the developing relationship between these two misfits, the film also functions as a very effective attack on psychiatrists—his muteness is not a result of illness but rather a matter of choice. Reviewed rather harshly in the United States, *Near and Far Away* was received much more warmly in Europe.

In Ahrne's next feature, 1978's *Roots of Grief,* she tells the story of a young Argentinean immigrant (Sergio, played by Italian Renzo Casali, who also co-wrote the screenplay with Ahrne), who—having fled from political oppression—finds his new home of Stockholm to be rather cold in more ways than one. Sergio does befriend his elderly translator-landlady, a younger switchboard operator cum jazz singer, and the singer's nine-year-old daughter, but each of the female characters becomes jealous of the attention Sergio pays to the others, and eventually he decides to leave Sweden for warmer climes closer to his Argentinean roots. Although critical of the film's clichés, a *Variety* reviewer said, "[Ahrne's] people and her action comes alive in both a humorous and truly affecting way by the leading actresses and by rotund Renzo Casali."

Ahrne has increasingly spent time writing novels and other books in the 1980s and 1990s, but has continued to make motion pictures as well (in addition to her work for television). In 1986 she directed the semiautobiographical *A Matter of Life and Death,* which details a woman's long relationship with a married man. Both this film and *Roots of Grief* are particularly evocative of Ahrne's disdain for "women's films," since she treats her male characters with particular sensitivity. For *A Matter of Life and Death,* she has said that a main theme of the film is the difficulty that many men have in "speaking about their private emotions"—that, unlike relationship-centered women, men often believe that "if they had this emotional quality . . . it would be considered a weakness."

Given her string of varied cinematic achievements—not to mention her ability to effectively handle both male and female characters—one can only hope that Ahrne's fascinatingly diverse oeuvre will eventually receive the attention that it deserves in the United States.—DAVID E. SALAMIE

Akerman, Chantal

Belgian director

Born *Brussels, 6 June 1950.* ***Education*** *Attended INSAS film school, Brussels, 1967-68; studied at Université Internationale du Théâtre, Paris, 1968-69.* ***Career*** *1971—*Blow up My Town *entered in Oberhausen festival; 1972—lived in New York; 1973—returned to France; 1997—instructor at Harvard University.* ***Address*** *c/o National Tourist Office, 61 Rue de Marche Aux Herbes, Brussels, B1000, Belgium.*

Films as Director: 1968: *Saute ma ville* (*Blow up My Town*) (short) (+ ro). **1971:** *L'Enfant aimé* (*The Beloved Child*) (short). **1972:** *Hotel Monterey* (short); *La Chambre 1*; *La Chambre 2*. **1973:** *Le 15/8* (co-d); *Hanging out—Yonkers* (unfinished). **1974:** *Je, tu, il, elle* (+ sc, ro as Julie). **1975:** *Jeanne Dielman, 23 Quai du Commerce, 1080 Bruxelles* (+ sc, ro as voice of neighbor). **1977:** *News from Home* (+ sc, ro as voice). **1978:** *Les Rendez-vous d'Anna* (+ sc). **1980:** *Dis-moi* (*Tell Me*) (for TV). **1982:** *Toute une nuit* (*All Night Long*) (+ sc). **1983:** *Les Années 80* (*The Eighties*) (co-sc); *Un Jour Pina m'a demandé* (*One Day Pina Asked Me*) (for TV). **1984:** *L'Homme à la valise* (*The Man with the Suitcase*) (for TV); "J'ai faim, j'ai froid" ("I'm Hungry, I'm Cold") ep. of *Paris vu par. . . 20 ans après*; *Family Business* (short—for TV); *New York, New York Bis* (short); *Lettre d'un cineaste* (*Letter from a Filmmaker*) (short—for TV). **1986:** *Le Marteau* (*The Hammer*) (short); *La Paresse* (*Sloth*) (short); *Window Shopping* (*The Golden Eighties*). **1987:** *Seven Women, Seven Sins* (co-d). **1989:** *Les Trois dernières sonatas de Franz Shubert* (*Franz Schubert's Last Three Sonatas*) (short); *Trois strophes sur le nom de Sacher* (*Three Stanzas on the Name Sacher*) (short); *Histoires d'Amérique: Food, Family and Philosophy* (*American Stories*). **1991:** *Nuit et jour* (*Night and Day*) (+ co-sc); *Contre l'oubli* (*Against Oblivion*) (co). **1993:** *D'est* (+ sc); *Moving In* (*Le Déménagement*) (for TV). **1994:** *Portrait d'une jeune fille de la fin des années 60 à Bruxelles* (*Portrait of a Young Girl at the End of the 1960s in Brussels*) (+ sc). **1996:** *Un Divan à New York* (*A Couch in New York*) (+ co-sc).

Other Film: 1985: *Elle à passe tant d'heures sous les sunlights* (Garrel) (ro).

At the age of 15 Chantal Akerman saw Godard's *Pierrot le fou* and realized that filmmaking could be experimental and personal. She dropped in and out of film school and has since created short and feature films for viewers who appreciate the opportunity her works provide to think about sounds and images. Her films are often shot in real time, and in space that is part of the characters' identity.

During a self-administered apprenticeship in New York (1972-73) shooting short films on very low budgets, Akerman notes that she learned much from the work of innovators Michael Snow and Stan Brakhage. She was encouraged to explore organic techniques for her personal subject matter. In her deliberately paced films there are long takes, scenes shot with stationary camera, and a play of light in relation to subjects and their space. (In *Jeanne Dielman, 23 Quai du Commerce, 1080 Bruxelles,* as Jeanne rides up or down in the elevator, diagonals of light from each floor cut across her face in a regular rhythm.) Her films feature vistas down long corridors, acting with characters' backs to the camera, and scenes concluded with several seconds of darkness. In Akerman films there are hotels and journeys, little conversation. Windows are opened and sounds let in, doors opened and closed; we hear a doorbell, a radio, voices on the telephone answering machine, footsteps, city noises. Each frame is carefully composed, each gesture the precise result of Akerman's directions. A frequent collaborator is her sensitive cameraperson, Babette Mangolte, who has worked with Akerman on such works as *Jeanne Dielman, News from Home,* and *Toute une nuit.* Mangolte has also worked with avant-gardists Yvonne Rainer, Marcel Hanoun, and Michael Snow.

Plotting is minimal or nonexistent in Akerman films. Old welfare clients come and go amid the impressive architecture of a once-splendid hotel on New York's Upper West Side in *Hotel Monterey.* New York City plays its busy, noisy self for the camera as Akerman's voice on the soundtrack reads concerned letters from her mother in Belgium in *News from Home.* A young filmmaker travels to Germany to appear at a screening of her latest film, meets people who distress her, and her mother who delights her, and returns home in *Les Rendez-vous d'Anna.* Jeanne Dielman, super-efficient housewife, earns money as a prostitute to support herself and her son. Her routine breaks down by chance, and she murders one of her customers.

The films (some of which are semiautobiographical) are not dramatic in the conventional sense, nor are they glamorized or eroticized; the excitement is inside the characters. In a film which Akerman has called a love letter to her mother, Jeanne Dielman is seen facing the steady camera as members of a cooking class might see her, and she prepares a meat loaf—in real time. Later she gives herself a thorough scrubbing in the bathtub; only her head and the motion of her arms are visible. Her straightening and arranging and smoothing are seen as a child would see and remember them.

In *Toute une nuit* Akerman displays her precision and control as she stages the separate, audience-involving adventures of a huge cast of all ages that wanders out into Brussels byways on a hot, stormy night. In this film, reminiscent of Wim Wenders and his wanderers and Marguerite Duras's inventive soundtracks, choreography, and sense of place, Akerman continues to explore her medium using no conventional plot, few spoken words, many sounds, people who leave the frame to a lingering camera, and appealing images. A little girl asks a man to dance with her, and he does. The filmmaker's feeling for the child and the child's independence cannot be mistaken.

Akerman's *Moving In,* meanwhile, centers on a monologue delivered by a man who has just moved into a modern apartment. A film of "memory and loss," according to *Film Comment,* he has left behind "a melancholy space of relations, relations dominated by his former neighbors, a trio of female 'social science students.'"—LILLIAN SCHIFF

Akins, Zoë

American writer

Born *Humansville, Missouri, 30 October 1886.* ***Family*** *Married Hugo Rumbold, 1932 (died 1932).* ***Career*** *Playwright: plays produced from 1915, with much critical attention after success of* Déclassée, *1919; 1930—first solo screenplay,* Sarah and Son; *1930-31—*

contract as writer with Paramount, and with MGM, 1934-38. ***Awards*** *Pulitzer Prize (for drama) for* The Old Maid, *1936.* ***Died*** *In Los Angeles, California, 20 October 1958.*

Films as Writer (often in collaboration): 1925: *Eve's Secret* (Badger); *Déclassée* (*The Social Exile*) (Vignola) (play). **1929:** *Her Private Life* (A. Korda) (play). **1930:** *Anybody's Woman* (Arzner); *The Right to Love* (Wallace); *Sarah and Son* (Arzner); *Ladies Love Brutes* (R. V. Lee) (st); *The Furies* (st). **1931:** *Women Love Once* (Goodman); *Once a Lady* (McClintic); *Working Girls* (Arzner); *Girls about Town* (Cukor) (st). **1932:** *The Greeks Had a Word for Them* (*Three Broadway Girls*) (L. Sherman) (play). **1933:** *Christopher Strong* (Arzner); *Morning Glory* (L. Sherman) (play). **1934:** *Outcast Lady* (Leonard). **1936:** *Accused* (Freeland); *Lady of Secrets* (Gering). **1937:** *Camille* (Cukor). **1938:** *The Toy Wife* (Thorpe); *Zaza* (Cukor). **1939:** *The Old Maid* (E. Goulding). **1947:** *Desire Me* (Cukor and LeRoy). **1953:** *How to Marry a Millionaire* (Negulesco) (co-play). **1958:** *Stage Struck* (Lumet) (play).

Zoë Akins is best known as the winner of the Pulitzer Prize for drama for *The Old Maid* and as a playwright of light comedies and social dramas. Unfortunately she has not been recognized as a screenwriter excelling in adapting plays and novels—her own and several from French and Hungarian sources—to film form. Her woman-centered scripts portrayed feminine consciousness in American and Continental settings with shocking candor and worldly wit. She deftly chronicled her characters' conflicts with shifting social standards within the complete spectrum of comedy, from slapstick farce to sentimental romance to urbane satire. Many of her stage plays, among them *Déclassée, Her Private Life,* and *The Furies,* were adapted to the screen by others. Two of her plays, relatively unsuccessful in the United States, were produced abroad: *Papa* (1919) in Germany and *The Human Element* (1939) in Hungary. Akins's ability for dramatic adaptation was the key to her success as a screenwriter.

Her first plays, *Papa* and *The Magical City,* were produced by the Washington Square Players in 1919. Akins's first hit play, *Déclassée,* portrayed marital infidelity and the consequences of divorce for the wife. It was one of Ethel Barrymore's most popular vehicles, "the richest and most interesting play that has fallen to her in all her years upon the stage" (*The New York Times*). The screen version was titled *Her Private Life.*

Throughout Akins's twin careers, her works consistently received mixed reviews, with the exceptions of her hit plays, *Déclassée, The Greeks Had a Word for Them, The Old Maid* and its film version, and the film *Camille.* George Jean Nathan attributed to her plays "grace and humor and droll insight."

Subsequent to her Broadway productions of the 1920s—*Moonflower, Daddy's Gone A-Hunting, First Love, The Furies,* and *The Love Duel*—Akins earned her first screenwriting credit, with G. Morris and Doris Anderson, for *Anybody's Woman.* Next she captured the antics and anxieties of three young models searching for wealthy husbands in *The Greeks Had a Word for Them.* This very funny and popular comedy also pleased audiences of the film version, which was adapted by Sidney Howard. (The 1953 film *How to Marry a Millionaire* was based both on the Akins play and *Loco,* by Dale Eunson and Katharine Albert.) Akins then wrote the screenplay for *Women Love Once,* based on her play *Daddy's Gone A-Hunting,* which was a moderate success. Her next assignment was the adaptation of Gilbert Frankau's novel *Christopher Strong*. It starred Katharine Hepburn as an aviatrix facing a career/marriage choice. Critics at the time disliked it, and the film failed. *Variety* stated: "The story is a weak vehicle for a new star . . . so overloaded with playwright device that it is just that and nothing more. . . . The people are merely glamorous puppets."

When Akins's most successful play, *The Old Maid,* based on the Edith Wharton novel chronicling the woes of an unmarried mother and her daughter, won the Pulitzer Prize, many protests were voiced. Enraged New York drama critics formed their own group, the Drama Critics Circle, to give their own awards. Judith Anderson and Helen Menken starred in the play; Bette Davis and Miriam Hopkins in the film that Akins scripted. Critics rated the film pictorially perfect, the acting superb, and the production nearly flawless.

Writing with Frances Marion and James Hilton, Akins scripted the critically and commercially successful *Camille,* starring Greta Garbo and Robert Taylor. According to *Time* the film kept "intact the story's inherent emotional vitality." *The Toy Wife* and *Zaza* were rated mediocre successes. Critics faulted *Desire Me,* written with Marguerite Roberts, for a labored story line that was a variant of the Enoch Arden tale, and for miscast actors.

Akins differed from her Pulitzer Prize-winning dramatist peers Zona Gale and Susan Glaspell in two ways. Unlike them, she was essentially a comedic writer; and she wrote for stage and screen simultaneously for two decades. She was considered the best-known woman playwright of her time, achieving the record of 16 plays on Broadway in 16 years. Her reputation rests primarily upon her prolific and lengthy career as a playwright and secondarily upon her success as a screenwriter skilled in adapting literary works to film.—LOUISE HECK-RABI

Alberti, Maryse

American cinematographer

Born *Langon, France, 10 March 1954.* ***Family*** *Son, Marley.* ***Career*** *Entered the industry as assistant to cinematographer Steven Fierberg on* Vortex, *1982.* ***Awards*** *Best cinematography award at Sundance for* H2 Worker, *1989, and for* Crumb, *1995.*

Films as Cinematographer: 1989: *H2 Worker.* **1990:** *The Golden Boat.* **1991:** *Poison*; *Paris Is Burning.* **1992:** *Zebrahead*; *Incident at Oglala.* **1993:** *Confessions of a Suburban Girl*; *Dottie Gets Spanked* (for TV); *Deadfall.* **1994:** *Crumb*; *Dutch Master*; *Moving the Mountain*; *She Lives to Ride.* **1996:** *When We Were Kings*; *I Love You, I Love You Not.* **1997:** *Inspirations*; *Dear Diary*; *Stag.* **1998:** *Velvet Goldmine*; *Happiness.*

Maryse Alberti. Photograph by Richard Foreman.

Maryse Alberti is a rarity in today's flourishing, and increasingly ego-centered, independent film market. Though still one of the few women cinematographers in the United States, she is content to bring her vast technical expertise to a project and allow it to be tempered both by her intuition and the director's own vision. What results is a body of work that is both impressive in it's unconventional variety, and seductive in it's distinctive, if sometimes almost invisible, Alberti stamp.

Alberti was raised on her grandmother's farm in France, and first came to the United States at the age of 19. She had long dreamt of seeing Jimi Hendrix in concert (she's still an avid rock fan), but soon discovered he was already dead. She worked as an au pair for a time, hitchhiked across the United States, and then started edging her way into the business as a still photographer for the *New York Rocker* and on porn films. "I was broke," she told Linda Lee in the *New York Times* (24 January 1999), "and I said, 'Why not?' I loved being on the movie set." (Next year she hopes to mount a tableau exhibition in New York of some of the porn, rock, and travel photographs she's shot over the years).

This ease with which Alberti inhabits a set, coupled with a working expertise in the use of lights, gels, lenses, mirrors, and cameras themselves, has become an instilling trademark. In *Paris Is Burning,* a groundbreaking documentary of African-American male "divas" in Harlem dressing in drag and staging an extravagant, all-night pageant, Alberti and her team (which included co-cinematographer Paul Gibson) are ever in the midst of the two-snaps-up action, swirling around like so much fluttering silk. And as director Todd Haynes, with whom Alberti did *Poison* and *Velvet Goldmine,* has noted, "she creates an atmosphere on the set among her crew and particularly among actors that's extremely trusting. They feel a kind of security with her that they might not feel in an all-male, macho kind of environment." (*American Cinematographer,* November, 1998).

Not that Alberti can't be stubborn too, according to some of her colleagues, but she's never been afraid to push and learn, and listen to input from all sides. On making her first film, *Vortex,* a low-budget, punk film-noir shot cheaply on 16-millimeter, Alberti recalled to Lee that "Steven Fierberg (the cinematographer) believed I knew what I was doing until the first day of shooting. But he was real nice, and I learned a lot."

Alberti says her preparation for any project, big or small, now involves working like an architect, discussing the vision, imagining, drawing, and then matching the more ethereal concepts to the "big machine" of cameras, tools and crew. Alberti's two recent small-budget successes—*Happiness* and *Velvet Goldmine*—are as different as Des Moines and Times Square, but each attests to a clarity-of, adherence-to, and a fighting-for the director's vision before any filming actually begins.

In *Velvet,* for example, a glittery "rock *Citizen Kane*" focusing on the rise (and fall) of glam-rock stars, director Haynes was adamant about employing the dated camera vernacular of the 1970s—lots of zooming, panning, and swishing through space in an effort to isolate and caress certain scenes. "This was the first movie I've done where I used so many colored gels," Alberti told *American Cinematographer.* But when asked why she chose certain shades, pale greens and blues with edges of lavender to symbolize the end of an era, she readily admits there's little method to the madness. "They just felt right," she says. "(You) learn your technique, but don't let it be the driving force. Instead, trust your intuition and instincts." *Happiness* was an opposing experience, using a more subdued camera—and Alberti's keen instincts—to tell a moving story about pedophilia. When shooting a scene where the father is confronted by his son about his sexual abuse, for example, Alberti and director Todd Solondz noticed that the child actor began to cry off-camera. They decided to immediately re-shoot the son's scene, and what results is some raw emotion that is brilliantly captured.

Despite her success with dramas, Alberti claims the documentary is still her first love. "I like to go back and forth actually," she told this writer, "but the documentary is important for my soul." *Inspirations,* a feature-length documentary look at the creative process she filmed for director Michael Apted (with whom she also did *Incident at Oglala* and *Moving the Mountain*) and showcasing celebrity artists like Roy Lichtenstein and Alberti-favorite David Bowie, received rave reviews for her top-notch camerawork. "There is a lot of pressure on feature films because there's so much money involved," she told Lee. "A documentary, at this point in my life, I just go in with just two people, my little camera on my shoulder, and I just enter the world [she uses her own Aaton 16-millimeter]. There is no take two."—JEROME SZYMCZAK

Allen, Dede

American editor

Born *Dorothea Carothers Allen in Cincinnati, Ohio, 1925.* ***Family*** *Married the director Stephen Fleischman, one son and one daughter.* ***Career*** *1943—worked as messenger, then in sound laboratory and as assistant editor for Columbia; editor on commercial and industrial films before becoming feature-film editor; 1981—received Academy Award* *nomination for editing of* Reds. ***Awards*** *British Academy of Film and Television Arts Award, for* Dog Day Afternoon, *1975.* ***Address*** *c/o United Talent, 9560 Wilshire Boulevard, Suite 500, Beverly Hills, CA 90212, U.S.A.*

Films as Editor: **1948:** *Story of Life* (*Because of Eve*) (Bretherton). **1957:** *Endowing Your Future* (Engel—short). **1958:** *Terror from the Year 5000* (*Cage of Doom*) (Gurney). **1959:** *Odds against Tomorrow* (Wise). **1961:** *The Hustler* (Rossen). **1964:** *America, America* (*The Anatolian Smile*) (Kazan). **1965:** *It's Always Now* (Wilmot—short). **1967:** *Bonnie and Clyde* (A. Penn). **1968:** *Rachel, Rachel* (P. Newman). **1970:** *Alice's Restaurant* (A. Penn); *Little Big Man* (A. Penn). **1972:** *Slaughterhouse-Five* (G. R. Hill). **1973:** *Serpico* (Lumet) (co); *Visions of Eight* (A. Penn) (co). **1975:** *Night Moves* (A. Penn); *Dog Day Afternoon* (Lumet). **1976:** *The Missouri Breaks* (A. Penn) (co). **1977:** *Slap Shot* (G. R. Hill). **1978:** *The Wiz* (Lumet). **1981:** *Reds* (Beatty) (co, + co-exec pr). **1984:** *Harry & Son* (P. Newman); *Mike's Murder* (Bridges) (co). **1985:** *The Breakfast Club* (Hughes). **1986:** *Off Beat* (Dinner) (co). **1988:** *The Milagro Beanfield War* (Redford) (co). **1989:** *Let It Ride* (Pytka) (co). **1990:** *Henry and June* (Kaufman) (co). **1991:** *The Addams Family* (Sonnenfeld) (co).

Film as Production Assistant: **1969:** *Storia di una donna* (*Story of a Woman*) (Bercovici).

Between 1961 and 1981, Dede Allen reigned as American cinema's most celebrated editor. This period championed the auteur director and Allen emerged as an auteur editor, working with many of Hollywood's best auteurs (Arthur Penn, Sidney Lumet, Robert Wise, Robert Rossen, Elia Kazan, and George Roy Hill) and developing her own editorial signature.

Her first important feature film (after 16 years in the industry) was *Odds against Tomorrow.* Urged by Robert Wise to experiment, Allen developed one of her major techniques: the audio shift. Instead of stopping both a shot and its accompanying audio at the same time (the common practice), she would overlap sound from the beginning of the next shot into the end of the previous shot (or vice versa). The overall effect increased the pace of the film—something always happened, visually or aurally, in a staccato-like tempo.

When she started work on her next feature, *The Hustler,* the French Nouvelle Vague and the British "angry young men" films hit America. The realism of the British school and the radical editing of the French school made strong impressions on Allen. She credits Tony Gibbs's editing on *Look Back in Anger* (1959) as very influential. *The Hustler* employs a similar style: lengthy two-shots, unexpected shot/reverse-shot patterns, and strategically placed "jump cuts." "Jump cutting" helped launch the Nouvelle Vague, and before Allen began editing, Robert Rossen asked her to watch Jean-Luc Godard's *A bout de souffle,* one of the seminal films of the French movement. Although she felt the jump cuts were only partially successful, she incorporated the basic principle into *The Hustler* by using a straight cut instead of a dissolve or an invisible continuity edit. The combination of these two schools and the focus on character over a seamless narrative flow gives *The Hustler* its unique quality of realism and modernism.

With *Bonnie and Clyde* (the first of six films with Arthur Penn), Allen further developed the principle of the jump cut by marrying it to classical Hollywood editing and television commercial editing. Instead of using the jump cut as a modernist reflexive device or a stylistic flourish, Allen combined its spatial and temporal discontinuity with a clear narrative and strong character identification (from Hollywood) and nontraditional shot combinations and short duration shots (from television commercials). Allen's synthesis of the Nouvelle Vague, the angry young men, Hollywood, and television defined her other major editing technique, what Andrew Sarris called "shock cutting . . . wild contrasts from one shot to the next, which give the film a jagged, menacing quality and create a sort of syncopated rhythm." Bonnie's sexual frustration and ennui at the start of *Bonnie and Clyde* find perfect expression in a series of jump/shock cuts.

The chaos of the gun fights and the immeasurably influential ending (which also shows Allen's debt to Eisenstein's montage) pushed screen violence to a new, visually stunning level.

In short, Allen must be credited with bringing modernist editing to Hollywood. Whether labeled American New Wave or Postclassical Hollywood, *The Hustler* and *Bonnie and Clyde* stand as benchmark films in the history of editing. And like *A bout de souffle, The Hustler* and *Bonnie and Clyde* deviated enough from the norm to be originally perceived as "badly edited," a perception fully inverted today.

Allen's "shock cutting" in *Bonnie and Clyde* produced two long-lasting effects: 1) the American public began to recognize and openly discuss editing as an art form; and 2) the standard was set for rapid editing in every subsequent action film. From Sam Peckinpah to John Woo, editorial pacing continually moved toward shorter and flashier sequences. Her influence also manifests itself in other visual media; television commercials, music videos, animation, and children's television compress many images into very short sequences. Almost every music video owes its rapid, nontraditional editing constructs to Dede Allen. In retrospect, Allen expresses concern about her contribution to increased editing tempo—"I wonder if we're raising enough people in a generation who are able to sit and look at a scene play out without getting bored if it doesn't change every two seconds. We talk an awful lot about cutting; we talk very little about not lousing something up by cutting just to make it move faster. I'm afraid that's the very thing I helped promulgate. . . . It may come to haunt us, because attention spans are short."

Allen continued to refine her editorial signature (audio shifts, shock cutting, and montage) through her subsequent films, especially the temporal and spatial jumps of *Slaughterhouse-Five* and *Dog Day Afternoon* (her first Academy Award nomination). In *Dog Day Afternoon,* after a slow, tension-building opening, the protagonist's discovery of the SWAT team unleashes a brief moment of chaos which Allen augments into ten breathless seconds of screen time by overlapping audio, intercutting multiple interior and exterior locations, and employing jarring shot combinations and temporal ellipses. Since Sidney Lumet used a double camera setup on Al Pacino and Chris Sarandon during their phone conversations, Allen used various takes of each, which produced jump cuts and violated screen direction, but intensified their performances. In *Reds,* Allen combined documentary editing and her signature narrative techniques to weave a historical and biographical tapestry of refined complexity. This documentary/narrative blend won her an Academy Award.

Since *Reds,* Allen's work remains consistently professional, especially in the usually overlooked dialogue scenes, but fails to convey the innovation of the 1960s and 1970s. This is not her fault. In the 1980s, not only did Hollywood become more an industry and less a developer of film artists, but Allen's techniques became fully integrated into everyday film and television editing. What once appeared radical became commonplace. When asked to edit *The Addams Family,* Allen needed to balance special effects, a greater emphasis on spectacle and set design, the demands of stars, shorter viewer attention span, a more cost-conscious Hollywood, and a script based on a 1960s television show. These constraints resulted in a polished film, but one with little of her signature, except for the loony glee of the vault slide and the intercutting of Gomez's train sequence. When working on independent projects, more of her creativity emerges. The curious jumble of edgy character interaction in *The Breakfast Club* and *Let It Ride* depends on the pacing her editing provides. In *Henry and June,* she experimented with fades and partial fades to blur time and point of view.

Allen has co-edited most of her films since *Reds* with younger editors, providing invaluable training for them. Her mentoring of others has produced a new generation of top-rank editors. After nearly 40 years in Hollywood, Allen's style, technical skill, groundbreaking films, and teaching secure her status as a legend of American editing.—GREG S. FALLER

Allen, Jay Presson

American writer

Born *Jacqueline Presson in San Angelo, Texas, 3 March 1922.* ***Family*** *Married the producer Lewis Maitland Allen (second marriage), 1955, one daughter: Brooke.* ***Career*** *Author—first novel published in 1948; 1963—film version of her play* Wives and Lovers *produced by Paramount; 1964—first film script,* Marnie; *1969—play adaptation of the novel* The Prime of Miss Jean Brodie *published; also wrote screen version; 1976-80—creator and script consultant, TV series* Family; *1980—produced first film,* Just Tell Me What You Want, *first of several films with Sidney Lumet; 1995—appeared on camera and provided commentary in the documentary* The Celluloid Closet. ***Agent*** *ICM Agency, 40 West 57th Street, New York, NY 10019, U.S.A.*

Films as Writer: 1964: *Marnie* (Hitchcock). **1969:** *The Prime of Miss Jean Brodie* (Neame). **1972:** *Cabaret* (Fosse); *Travels with My Aunt* (Cukor) (co). **1973:** *The Borrowers* (Miller). **1975:** *Funny Lady* (Ross) (co). **1980:** *Just Tell Me What You Want* (Lumet) (+ co-pr). **1981:** *Prince of the City* (Lumet) (co, + pr). **1982:** *Deathtrap* (Lumet) (+ exec pr). **1986:** *The Morning After* (Lumet) (co). **1990:** *Lord of the Flies* (Hook); *Year of the Gun* (Frankenheimer) (co). **1995:** *Copycat* (Amiel) (co).

Other Films: 1980: *It's My Turn* (Weill) (pr). **1988:** *Hothouse* (*The Center*) (Gyllenhaal) (pr). **1995:** *The Celluloid Closet* (Epstein and Friedman—doc) (interviewee).

Jay Presson Allen is a curiously overlooked screenwriter whose work has never received the attention it deserves. This may be in part because of a debut film which seemed inauspicious at the time, but which has grown in critical estimation: her screenplay for Alfred Hitchcock's *Marnie.* Although criticized at the time for what was regarded as facile psychoanalyzing, the screenplay is actually a finely constructed work, presenting with great subtlety, voyeurism, and yet sympathy, an emotionally disturbed woman who can hold her own with those female creations of Bergman and Antonioni of the same period, but who, perhaps typical of her American context, is able to overcome her problems. Providing Hitchcock with the screenplay for this, one of his two or three greatest films, is certainly a notable achievement, even more apparent if one is familiar with the original novel by Winston Graham and knows how well (and radically) Allen adapted the material. Her power to adapt brilliantly is present also in her screenplay for *The Prime of Miss Jean Brodie,* based on the novel by Muriel Spark, which once again presented sympathetically a three-dimensional, deeply disturbed woman.

Allen's greatest critical acclaim came for her adaptation for Bob Fosse of *Cabaret,* which not only threw out most of the sentimental trappings of the Broadway musical, but also had the courage to go back to the original Christopher Isherwood stories and to make explicit in the film itself the central homosexuality of the character generally patterned on Isherwood. By providing Fosse with a screenplay which allowed him to express his characteristic cynicism in great displays of technical razzle-dazzle, Allen made an inestimable contribution to the institution of the American musical; in its portrait of Nazism and German society, *Cabaret* claimed definitively for the musical a kind of laudable pretension and seriousness, as well as providing for Liza Minnelli one of the American cinema's great roles—yet another of Allen's portraits of neurotic women.

Allen's most underrated screenplay is the surprising *Just Tell Me What You Want,* directed by Sidney Lumet, which offered an excellent Hollywood story and provided Ali McGraw the chance to turn in her most accomplished performance. Allen expanded the scope of her career somewhat by writing the screenplay for Sidney Lumet's *Prince of the City,* with its largely masculine milieu and adapting (again for Lumet) the thriller *Deathtrap,* perhaps her least interesting or successful project. Like many of her screenwriting colleagues, Allen became a sometime hyphenate, taking increased control of her work by functioning as her own producer as well. She also expanded into television and theater work.

Tru, a one-man show based on the life of Truman Capote which she wrote and directed, had great success on Broadway. Allen's theatrical follow-up was *The Big Love,* adapted from a novella by Florence Aadland. Co-written with Allen's daughter, Brooke Allen, the play was produced by Allen's husband, Lewis Allen, and Home Box Office, and later appeared on the cable network. In 1994 Allen returned to film, discussing her work on *Cabaret* in *The Celluloid Closet,* a documentary on gay representations in Hollywood films. Allen also co-wrote the script for *Copycat,* a thriller featuring Sigourney Weaver as an agoraphobic psychologist. The apologetic mother (Tracey Ullman) in *The Big Love* and *Copycat*'s distraught detective (Holly Hunter) and paranoid psychologist are further examples of Allen's effective portraits of neurosis.—CHARLES DERRY and MARK JOHNSON

Amaral, Suzana

Brazilian director

Born *São Paolo, Brazil, 1933.* ***Education*** *Attended film schools at the University of São Paolo and New York University; attended acting and directing classes at New York's Actors Studio.* ***Family*** *Married to a physician and divorced, nine children.* ***Career*** *Decided she wanted to pursue a career after 12 years of marriage and motherhood; early 1970s—worked as a public television station news reporter; mid-1970s—began working on television documentaries, eventually making 50 one-hour films examining various social issues; 1980s—worked in television after living in New York for three years; 1985—directed her first feature,* The Hour of the Star. ***Awards*** *Best Film, Havana Film Festival, Best Film, Brasilia Film Festival, Best Director, International Woman's Film Festival, for* The Hour of the Star, *1985.* ***Address*** *Concine/National Cinema Council, Rua Mayrink Velga 28, Rio de Janeiro, Brazil.*

Films as Director: **1971:** *Semana de 22* (*The Week of 1922*). **1972:** *Coleçao de marfil* (*Ivory Collection*). **1980:** *Projeto pensamiento e linguajen* (*A Project for Thought and Speech*) (short). **1981:** *São Paolo de todos nos* (*Our São Paolo*). **1985:** *A Hora da Estrêla* (*The Hour of the Star*) (+ co-sc).

Other Film: **1996:** *O Regresso do Homem Que Não Gostava de Sair de Casa* (Costa e Silva) (ro).

The cliché "better late than never" perfectly describes the career of Suzana Amaral. She had been married to a physician for 12 years and had eight of her nine children when she decided that she also wanted an education, and a vocation. She enrolled at the University of São

Paolo along with her eldest son; the pair even shared some of the same classes. Eventually, she worked as a public-television news reporter, and made 50 hour-long documentaries. By the time Amaral directed *The Hour of the Star,* she was 50-plus, and a divorcee with seven grandchildren.

The Hour of the Star not only is Amaral's first feature, but it is her lone feature to date. Notwithstanding, it is one of the top Brazilian films of the 1980s: a neorealist slice-of-life, set in São Paolo, which records the plight and fate of Macabea, a thoroughly ordinary, virginal 19 year old. Macabea is employed as a typist, even though she barely can type and is oblivious to her inadequacies. She is an orphan who is all alone in the world and new to the city; she is a *baiano,* a northeastern Brazilian who migrates south.

Macabea is plain-looking and slow-witted, unhygienic and uncouth. She always is apologizing, even when there is nothing for which to be sorry. At one point, she declares, "I'm not much of a person." Her favorite off-hours activity is riding the São Paolo subway, which she describes as "nice." In her own way, she is as disconnected from the world around her as Travis Bickle, Martin Scorsese's *Taxi Driver.*

Macabea may have romantic fantasies (which involve her staring longingly at a wedding dress-garbed mannequin in a store window and dreaming of becoming a movie star) and sexual longings (which she fulfills via masturbation), but she is socially and sexually inept. She only can envy a bitchy, voluptuous co-worker, who brags about all her boyfriends and abortions. At one point, Macabea thinks two men are admiring her. The first is a transit cop, who tells her that she is standing beyond a subway station safety line. The second reveals himself to be blind.

For a good portion of *The Hour of the Star,* Macabea dates the pretentious and self-involved Olimpico, who sports his own delusions of grandeur. It remains a mystery why he agrees to see her beyond their first meeting, and their relationship (which is devoid of romance or sex) consists of her asking him the meanings of words and spouting factoids she has heard on the radio. When he finally breaks off with her, he does so by pronouncing, "You're a hair in my soup." At the finale, a fortune-teller reports to Macabea that her life will change. Her now ex-boyfriend will want to marry her. Her boss will not fire her. A wealthy foreigner, a "gringo," will give her lots of money, as well as love her and marry her. The scenario segues into fantasy as Macabea purchases a sunny blue-and-white polka-dot dress. But the "gringo" hits her with his car, leaving her a bloody corpse. He gets out of the car, and runs toward her. Then, magically, she comes alive, and runs toward him. . . .

Amaral paints a fully developed portrait of Macabea, whose thickheadedness ordinarily might make her easy to dismiss. Yet as her hopes and fantasies are visualized, Macabea becomes a three-dimensional character whose shallowness makes her sympathetic. *The Hour of the Star* works as a chronicle of the manner in which lack of money and knowledge may cause a person to feel (and, in many ways, be) less-than-human, and a reminder that even those who are unattractive and none-too-bright are individuals, with their very own feelings and longings. And in more political terms, it is a vivid depiction of disenfranchisement of the poor in a modern industrial society.

The Hour of the Star was an impressive first film for Amaral. Unfortunately, it apparently will be her lone directorial credit. Given her age, and the time that has passed since its release, it is highly unlikely that she will be adding additional credits to her filmography.—ROB EDELMAN

Anders, Allison

American director

Born *Ashland, Kentucky, 16 November 1954; daughter of the actress Luana Anders.* ***Education*** *Attended junior college and was graduated from the University of Southern California at Los Angeles, School of Theater, Film and Television.* ***Family*** *Two daughters.* ***Career*** *Early 1980s—became acquainted with Wim Wenders; 1983—kept a journal while on the set of Wenders's* Paris, Texas; *1988—co-directed first feature,* Border Radio; *1992—earned international acclaim for second feature,* Gas Food Lodging. ***Awards*** *Nicholl Fellowship, Academy of Motion Picture Arts and Sciences; Samuel Goldwyn Award, for screenplay* Lost Highway; *Best New Director, New York Film Critics Circle, for* Gas Food Lodging, *1992.* ***Address*** *Cineville, Inc., Skywalker Studios, 1861 South Bundy Drive, Los Angeles, CA 90025, U.S.A.*

Films as Director and Writer: 1988: *Border Radio* (co-d with Lent, co-sc). **1992:** *Gas Food Lodging.* **1993:** *Mi Vida Loca* (*My Crazy Life*). **1995:** "The Missing Ingredient" ep. of *Four Rooms.* **1996:** *Grace of My Heart.*

Allison Anders's most consequential film to date is *Gas Food Lodging,* a sharply observed character study which is most effective as a refreshingly realistic look at the travails of motherhood without fatherhood. Set within a family whose members are all women, it is a story of motherly love and concern, daughterly yearnings for freedom and independence, the realities of romantic love, and the characters' vulnerabilities and cravings for compassion and understanding.

Allison Anders directing *Grace of My Heart.*

Anders tells the story of Nora Evans (Brooke Adams), a truck-stop waitress in the dusty town of Laramie, New Mexico. Nora is attempting to rear her two teenaged daughters, whose father "walked off" when they were very young. The eldest, 17-year-old Trudi (Ione Skye), is as rebellious and promiscuous as she is pretty. She has accumulated one too many unexcused absences from school; among her peers, she has earned a reputation for being "easy." Nora and Trudi constantly squabble, most particularly over Trudi's arrival home at ungodly hours after hot-and-heavy dates with men who promise her the love and affection she covets. Nora is distressed because she does not want Trudi to be victimized by suitors who will promise commitments they have no intention of keeping.

Trudi's kid sister, Shade (Fairuza Balk), is a sweetly innocent romantic who has not yet discovered the pitfalls of sexuality. Her concept of love has been gained from watching corny Spanish-language movies at the local theater. Shade longs for the traditional nuclear family, and is intent upon instigating a relationship between her mom and a man—just about any male who might make an appropriate mate for Nora and stepdad for her and Trudi. Will such a situation ever be possible? Or will there always be roadblocks that will prevent Shade's dream from becoming real (or, more to the point, from reflecting the outcomes of the movies to which she is addicted)?

The latter is certain to be the case, because Anders's characters exist within a world that is more reflective of reality. Unlike more traditional celluloid portraits of women on their own, none of the characters ends up being saved by a man. There are no handsome hunks on white horses to whisk them away from the drudgery of their lives. *Gas Food Lodging* is the polar opposite of a Hollywood assembly-line product such as *Pretty Woman,* a Cinderella story whose spunky, squeaky-clean heroine just so happens to be a Hollywood Boulevard whore. She may love old movies just as passionately as Shade, do dental floss rather than crack, and be played by Julia Roberts; her savior may be a profiteer, but he is cute, doesn't drink, says no to drugs, and is transformed by love into a constructive citizen. *Pretty Woman* is a sugary entertainment package which, in its own perverse way, serves as a recruiting poster for a career as a hooker. It is also the type of film which, one safely assumes, would disgust Allison Anders.

Furthermore, in *Gas Food Lodging* Anders depicts characters you rarely see in Hollywood films: blue-collar workers who live ordinary lives and struggle for survival in unglamorous environments. Nora's plight as a single mother may be common in today's society, but it is one that rarely is acknowledged with any thought or depth in mainstream movies. Yet the lives of such characters are rich in dramatic possibility. At the core of *Gas Food Lodging* is an intelligent, nonsensationalistic story featuring women's points-of-view regarding men, sex, love, and dreams. Additionally, the film is highly autobiographical. While trying to jump-start her career, Anders herself worked as a waitress—and she is the single mother of two daughters (born in 1974 and 1977). The filmmaker has claimed, however, that she modeled the character of Nora Evans after her own mother.

The films Anders made before and after *Gas Food Lodging* have been much less spectacular. *Border Radio,* set amid the Los Angeles punk scene, was barely noticed. *Mi Vida Loca (My Crazy Life)* is a well-intentioned chronicle of the plights of Latina gang members in East Los Angeles. Unlike most "teen-gang" movies, which focus on the personalities of males—with their female counterparts appearing as either decorations or prizes to be won in rumbles—*Mi Vida Loca* offers portraits of adolescent girls. Their evocative nicknames—Sad Girl, Mousie, Whisper—tell you all you need to know about them. And here, too, Anders is mostly interested in the manner in which the characters share camaraderie and form identities apart from the men. Unfortunately, the result is dramatically vague, a series of pasted-together episodes that do not add up to a cohesive whole.

Anders's attempt at a full-bodied portrayal of Latino girls in *Mi Vida Loca* may be linked to a secondary plot line in *Gas Food Lodging*. At one point, Trudi callously dismisses a young Mexican-American busboy as a wetback; later on, a friend of Shade whispers that the same character is a *cholo*, a gangster and dope dealer who robs pizza deliverymen and steals car radios to support his illegitimate children. The lad, of course, proves to be something else altogether, an entirely sympathetic character.

Anders's segment in *Four Rooms,* a four-part feature co-directed with Alexandre Rockwell, Robert Rodríguez, and Quentin Tarantino, is equally run-of-the-mill. Titled "The Missing Ingredient" it is the senseless story of a coven of witches who go about trying to raise their goddess from the dead.

Anders's career is at a crossroads. Will she be able to come up with a commendable follow-up to *Gas Food Lodging,* or will history prove her a one-shot artist, a footnote among women filmmakers?—ROB EDELMAN

Angelou, Maya

American writer and producer

Born *Marguerite Annie Johnson in St. Louis, Missouri, 4 April 1928.* ***Education*** *Attended George Washington High School, San Francisco; studied dance with Pearl Primus, New York City; studied acting with Frank Silvera; numerous honorary degrees.* ***Family*** *Married 1) Tosh Angelos (divorced); 2) Vusumzi Make (divorced 1963); 3) Paul DuFeu, 1973; son: Guy Johnson.* ***Career*** *Taught modern dance; 1960s—northern co-ordinator Southern Christian Leadership Conference; 1963-65—writer for the Ghanaian Broadcasting Corporation; 1969—published first novel, the critically acclaimed best-seller* I Know Why the Caged Bird Sings; *1970—writer-in-residence University of Kansas-Lawrence; 1972—wrote the script and score for* Georgia, Georgia; *1977—appeared in TV miniseries* Roots; *since 1981—Reynolds Professor of American Studies at Wake Forest University; 1993—delivered her poem "On the Pulse of Morning" at Presidential inauguration; 1998—directed first feature film,* Down in the Delta. ***Agent*** *Dave La Camera, Lordly & Dame, Inc., 51 Church Street, Boston, MA 02116-5493, U.S.A.* ***Address*** *Reynolds Professor, Wake Forest University, Box 7314, Winston-Salem, NC 27109.*

Films as Writer: 1972: *Georgia, Georgia* (Bjorkman) (+ score). **1979:** *I Know Why the Caged Bird Sings* (Cook—for TV) (co-sc). **1982:** *Sister, Sister* (Berry—for TV, produced 1980) (+ co-pr). **1996:** *America's Dream* (Barclay, Duke, and Sullivan) (sc based on story "The Reunion").

Other Films: 1957: *Calypso Heat Wave* (Sears) (ro as herself). **1993:** *Poetic Justice* (Singleton) (poetry, + ro as Aunt June); *There Are No Children Here* (Addison) (ro as grandmother). **1995:** *How to Make an American Quilt* (Moorhouse) (ro as Anna). **1998:** *Down in the Delta* (d).

Truly a renaissance woman, Maya Angelou has had an enchantingly colorful career. Nicknamed "Maya" by her beloved older brother Bailey, she has worked as a dancer, composer, poet, historian, author, actress, playwright, civil-rights activist, in addition to film producer, screenwriter, and director. She was even the first black and female streetcar fare collector in San Francisco. In the realm of motion pictures, she has been nothing less than a pioneer for women of color; and, like most pioneers, she faced enormous challenges in her early efforts to bring more varied, realistic, and nuanced portrayals of African Americans to film and television screens.

Angelou was the first African-American woman to write the script and musical score for a feature film, *Georgia, Georgia.* Adapted from one of her stories, it is about a beautiful, sharp-tongued black woman, played by Diana Sands, from an impoverished Southern background who has gained international fame as a pop singer. On tour in Sweden, she responds flippantly when reporters ask her about a number of "Black issues," and later, supposedly caught in the throes of the so-called "white fever," she has a relationship with a handsome, white photographer. But the heroine's attraction to white culture creates a conflict with her black companion, a grandmotherly woman who hates whites as much as Georgia loves them. Angelou was thoroughly dissatisfied with the completed film because she disagreed with the approach of the director, Stig Bjorkman. She considered that as a Swedish man, Bjorkman had no understanding of African Americans and had failed to bring the essence of her work, especially its romance, to the screen. While in Sweden, Angelou assiduously studied the craft of cinematography, as she explained, learning everything from "breaking down a script and putting it on a 'day chart' to breaking down a camera." Consequently, she was prompted to pursue work as a director in order to attempt to more effectively convey the multifaceted "rhythms" of African-American life on-screen. Subsequently, producer David Wolper cast her in the monumental television miniseries *Roots,* with the understanding that she would later be a given a project of her own to direct; however, her chance was lost when Wolper sold his production company.

In 1972 Angelou optioned her autobiography, *I Know Why the Caged Bird Sings,* with a film producer who agreed to let her direct her own project, but he later reneged. So, she bought her script back and proclaimed that she would write and direct any film she made in the future. Nevertheless, in 1978, she reluctantly signed a contract with CBS Television that limited her involvement in the production of *I Know Why the Caged Bird Sings* to co-writing the script. She later confessed to a *New York Times* interviewer that she made the deal with CBS because she felt compelled to abandon her long-held conviction that black films should be produced by black filmmakers, though she maintained that it behooved white filmmakers to actively endeavor to learn about and to respect black sensibilities. The resulting film was acclaimed for offering a poignant account of Angelou's childhood during the Great Depression in the segregated South, especially her close relationships with her brother Bailey and with her grandparents who raised the two after their parents divorced, as well as of the rape that rendered her mute for several years after her rapist was killed by outraged friends. Critics likewise boasted that the film represented one of television's infrequent efforts to examine racism and the African-American family in more contemporary terms, outside the context of slavery. Although Angelou herself was pleased with the results, she lamented that, in general, there were considerable strains for an author working in television where, as she put it, "everyone and his dog has a chance to pick at a writer's work."

Seeking a more advantageous relationship with Hollywood, Angelou signed a writer-producer contract with 20th Century-Fox in 1978 that made her the first African-American woman to sign such a deal with a major production company. As a result, she made a television movie for NBC entitled *Sister, Sister,* which she wrote and co-produced with a one-and-a-half million dollar budget. Dubbed Angelou's "black-Americanization of Chekhov" by an NBC executive, the network was notably reticent about releasing it: it was four years before the film was screened. In addition, Angelou was informed that in order to procure the director the executive producer wanted, she would have to agree to share her co-producer credit. She agreed, but the producer later insisted that he wanted sole producer credit or he would file a complaint with the Writers Guild in order to acquire half of the writing credit.

Angelou has had several stage and screen acting parts over the years and she has made hundreds of guest appearances on television. Furthermore, she has directed plays for public television, and has written, directed, and produced television documentaries, including *Black! Blues! Black!* for the National Education Television network. In the 1970s Angelou had vehemently objected to Hollywood's depictions of blacks and singled out the "blaxploitation" film genre, in particular, for what she claimed were their demeaning, distorted, and stereotypical conceptions. Further, she advocated the notion of black investment in black film projects in order to counter prevailing stereotypes. But, she questioned whether the ideal situation was for black filmmakers to make films about black people, or to produce films that have nothing to do with being black. Notably, since that time, and with Angelou's considerable assistance, her dream has become a reality on both counts as increasing numbers of black directors, screenwriters, and producers have recently made many successful feature films, thus inspiring some critics to declare the 1990s a period of "black renaissance" in Hollywood.—CYNTHIA FELANDO

Apon, Annette

Dutch director

Born *The Netherlands, 1949.* ***Education*** *Graduated from the Netherlands Film Academy, Amsterdam, 1972.* ***Career*** *1973—made first film,* Eigen Haard is Goud Waard; *1973 to about 1980—made documentaries with the Amsterdam City Newsreel collective; 1982—gained recognition for her first full-length feature film,* Golven; *1990—released best-known film,* Krokodillen in Amsterdam. ***Address*** *c/o* Skrien*: Vondepark 3, 1071 AA, Amsterdam, Netherlands.*

Films as Director: 1973: *Eigen Haard is Goud Waard* (short). **1974:** *Overloop is Sloop* (short). **1975:** *Van Brood Alleen Kan een Mens Niet Leven* (short). **1976:** *Een Schijntje Vrijheid* (short). **1978:** *Het Bosplan* (short). **1979:** *Politiewerk* (short). **1980:** *Kakafonische Notities* (short). **1982:** *Golven* (*The Waves*) (+ sc). **1983:** *Giovanni* (+ sc). **1984:** *Projekties.* **1985:** *Ornithopter.* **1988:** *Reis Zonder Einde.* **1990:** *Krokodillen in Amsterdam* (*Crocodiles in Amsterdam*) (+ co-sc). **1993:** *Naarden Vesting.* **1994:** *Een Winter in Zuiderwoude* (*A Winter in Zuiderwoude*) (doc, short) (+ sc, ed); *Wakers en Dromers* (*Wakers and Dreamers*) (doc) (+ sc, ed). **1996:** *Het is de Schraapzucht, Gentlemen* (for TV) (+ sc).

Other Film: 1995: *Laagland* (Entius—for TV) (scenario adviser).

Filmmaker Annette Apon is well known in the Netherlands, though her work is generally unknown in the United States. She has directed several low-budget, long and short films—both fiction and documentary, but is known primarily for her documentary work. In addition, she has written extensively on the subject of film and is a co-founder of the serious film journal *Skrien,* as well as a co-founder of the Amsterdam City Newsreel collective. In general, her films feature clever styles and structures that refuse familiar narrative conventions in favor of more personal, experimental approaches that combine realism and antirealism.

After spending seven years making documentaries with the Amsterdam City Newsreel collective, Apon garnered critical praise for her first full-length feature film, *Golven,* in which she returned to the experimental forms of her earlier short films. Adapted from Virginia Woolf's novel *The Waves,* it was praised by critics who predicted that it heralded a promising career for Apon. Set in the 1920s, *Golven* is a decidedly low-key, yet fascinating, exploration of the thoughts and feelings of six people, on the verge of adulthood, as they prepare for and attend a farewell dinner party for the mysterious Percival, an important figure in each of their lives. Their varied personalities, lost hopes, insecurities, mixed emotions, and ambitions are conveyed via their thoughts, which are related in offscreen and on-screen monologues set in the present. The film's performances are especially interesting, inasmuch as the acting is mostly confined to facial expression.

The central element of Apon's absorbing second full-length feature film, *Giovanni* (funded in part by the Netherlands's Film Fund), is a Rome hotel room, in which a fashion photographer is staying for work and to look for a man she once knew—Giovanni. The film's clever conceit is that the camera remains trained on the hotel room even when the photographer is gone, thus revealing a motley assortment of events—from the room's changing light and sounds, to the maid and valet who go through her things, and a trysting couple who briefly spend time there. Eventually, even Giovanni visits, but the photographer is destined to miss the note he leaves, as a man with a gun wound climbs into and out of her room, thus making the police suspicious about her and her untidy room. The film ends compellingly anticlimactically, with the photographer's departure after less than 48 hours as the maid prepares the room for the next guests.

In the United States, *Crocodiles in Amsterdam* is Apon's best-known feature film, in which she wittily crafts a distinctly fantastic world where it seems that crocodiles could indeed roam through Amsterdam. Critics were generally enthusiastic, appreciating in particular its wacky sense of fun and humor, as well as its crafty reworking of the conventions of the buddy movie so as to feature lesbians. One critic characterized the film as a "whimsical allegory of lesbian desire." It is indeed a quirky comedy, which follows an unlikely couple on a series of wild adventures. Politically committed Nina wants to attack a bomb factory but her plans are thwarted by Gino's impetuous ideas. Consequently, their shaky relationship seems on the verge of an explosive dissolution.

Another noteworthy Apon film is *A Winter in Zuiderwoude,* a short black-and-white documentary that has been characterized as a study of the Dutch winter in variations of white, black, and gray. Entirely without interviews, voice-over narration, or dialogue, the film provides a fascinating portrait of a Dutch landscape throughout several cold winter months. Filmed with a static camera that shows a changing exterior of snow and freezing weather, as well as a collection of cows in their snug sheds waiting impatiently for spring.

Wakers and Dreamers is another documentary that focuses on the Dutch landscape, in this case, to explore the way that the Netherlands's many dikes shape the landscape and enrich the Dutch language. The function of dikes to control water by keeping it in or keeping it out, serves as a metaphor for society's unrelenting urge to likewise channel and regulate. Thus, people craft a set of fish stairs to accommodate fish that are unable to swim upstream, but they erect barriers against the "flood" of foreign immigrants into the Netherlands. Indeed, as Apon's film suggests, both protest and contradiction are essential parts of the urge to create.

Although her films are not as well-known as those of her contemporary, Marleen Gorris, Apon's films have been screened internationally on the film festival circuit, including Berlin; Films de Femmes in Créteil, France; Montreal Women's Film Festival; and New York and San Francisco's International Lesbian and Gay film festivals.—CYNTHIA FELANDO

Armstrong, Gillian

Australian director

Born *Melbourne, 18 December 1950.* ***Education*** *Attended Swinburne College, studied filmmaking in Melbourne and at Australian Film and Television School, Sydney.* ***Family*** *Married the editor John Pfeffer, two daughters.* ***Career*** *Worked as production assistant, editor, art director, and assistant designer, and directed several short films; 1979—directed first feature,* My Brilliant Career; *1984—directed first American film,* Mrs. Soffel; *1987—returned to Australia to direct* High Tide; *has since made films both in Australia and the United States; also director of documentaries and commercials.* ***Awards*** *Best Short Fiction Film, Sydney Festival, for* The Singer and the Dancer, *1976; British Critics' Award, and Best Film and Best Director, Australian Film Institute Awards, for* My Brilliant Career, *1979.* ***Agent*** *Judy Scott-Fox, William Morris Agency, 151 El Camino Drive, Beverly Hills, CA 90212, U.S.A.*

Films as Director: **1970:** *Old Man and Dog* (short). **1971:** *Roof Needs Mowing* (short). **1973:** *Gretel*; *Satdee Night*; *One Hundred a Day* (short). **1975:** *Smokes and Lollies* (doc). **1976:** *The Singer and the Dancer* (+ pr, sc). **1979:** *My Brilliant Career.* **1980:** *Fourteen's Good, Eighteen's Better* (doc) (+ pr); *Touch Wood* (doc). **1982:** *Starstruck.* **1983:** *Having a Go* (doc); *Not Just a Pretty Face.* **1984:** *Mrs. Soffel.* **1986:** *Hard to Handle: Bob Dylan with Tom Petty and the Heartbreakers.* **1987:** *High Tide.* **1988:** *Bingo, Bridesmaids and Braces* (doc) (+ pr). **1991:** *Fires Within.* **1992:** *The Last Days of Chez Nous.* **1994:** *Little Women.* **1996:** *Not Fourteen Again* (doc) (+ sc, co-pr). **1997:** *Oscar & Lucinda.*

While women directors in film industries around the world are still seen as anomalous (if mainstream) or marginalized as avant-garde, the Antipodes have been home to an impressive cadre of female filmmakers who negotiate and transcend such notions.

Before the promising debuts of Ann Turner (*Celia*) and Jane Campion (*Sweetie*), Gillian Armstrong blazed a trail with *My Brilliant Career,* launching a brilliant career of her own as an international director. Like Turner and Campion, Armstrong makes films that resist easy categorization as either "women's films" or Australian ones. Her films mix and intermingle genres in ways which undermine and illuminate afresh, if not openly subvert, filmic conventions—as much as the films of her male compatriots, such as Peter Weir, Bruce Beresford, or Paul Cox. Formally, however, the pleasures of her films are traditional ones, such as sensitive and delicate cinematography (often by Russell Boyd), fluid editing, an evocative feel for setting and costume, and most importantly, a commitment to solid character development and acting. All in all, her work reminds one of the best of classical Hollywood cinema, and the question of whether her aim is parody or homage is often left pleasingly ambiguous.

Although Armstrong has often spoken in interviews about her discomfort at being confined to the category of woman filmmaker of women's films, and has articulated her desire to reach an audience of both genders and all nationalities, her work continually addresses sexual politics and family tensions. Escape from and struggle with traditional sex roles and the pitfalls

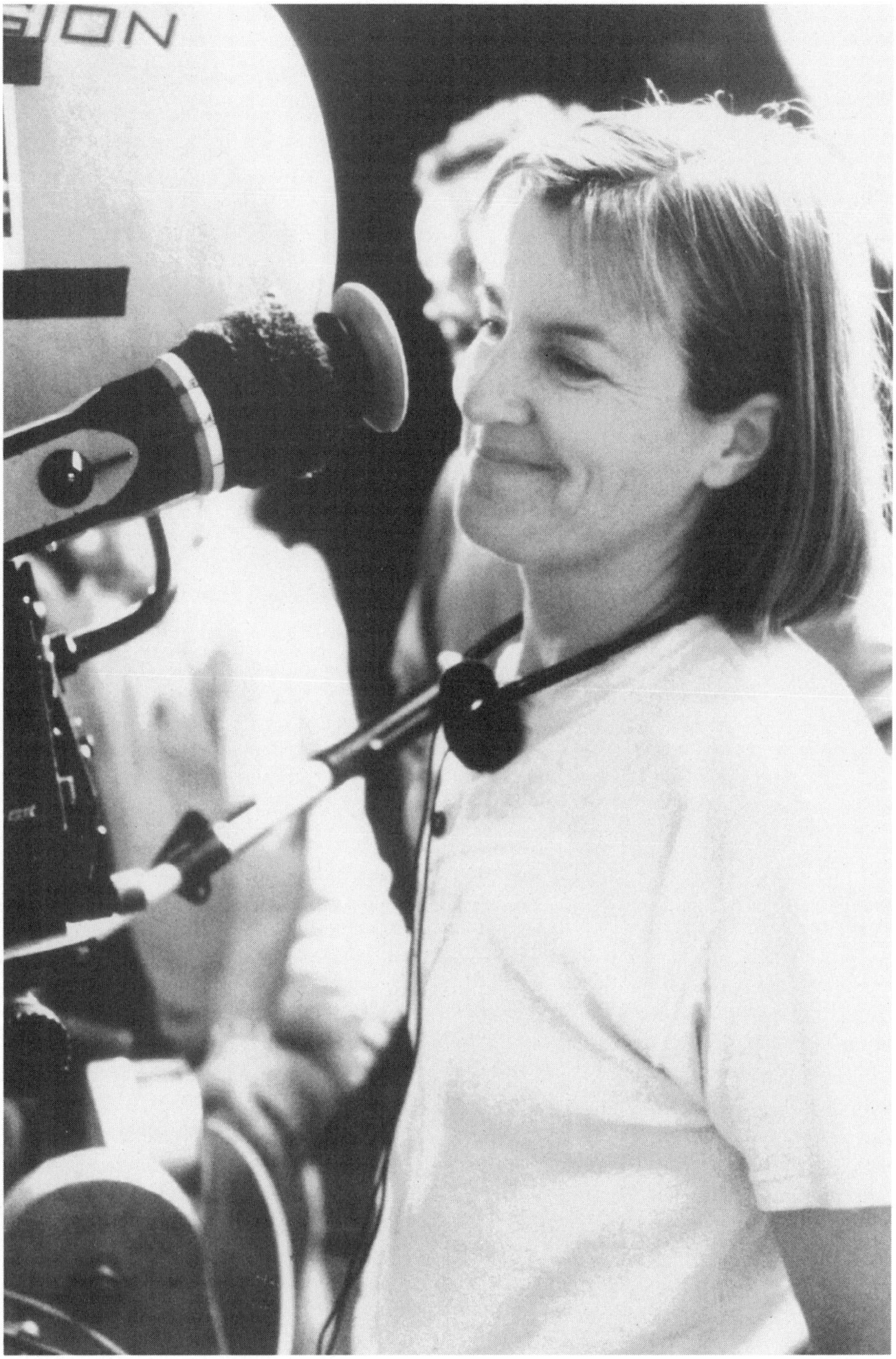

Gillian Armstrong on the set of *Little Women.*

and triumphs therein are themes frequently addressed in her films—from *One Hundred a Day,* her final-year project at the Australian Film and Television School, through *My Brilliant Career,* her first and best-known feature, to *High Tide.* Even one of her earliest films at Swinburne College, the short *Roof Needs Mowing,* obliquely tackled this theme, using a typical student filmmaker's pastiche of advertising and surrealism. Like most maturing filmmakers with an eye on wider distribution, Armstrong dropped the "sur" from surrealism in her later work, so that by *One Hundred a Day*—an adaptation of an Alan Marshall story about a shoe-factory employee getting a back-street abortion in the 1930s—she developed a more naturalistic handling of material, while her use of soundtrack and fast editing remained highly stylized and effective.

Made on a tiny budget and heavily subsidized by the Australian Film Commission, the award-winning *The Singer and the Dancer* was a precocious study of the toll men take on women's lives that marked the onset of Armstrong's mature style. On the strength of this and *One Hundred a Day,* producer Margaret Fink offered Armstrong the direction of *My Brilliant Career.* Daunted at first by the scale of the project and a lack of confidence in her own abilities, she accepted because she "thought it could be bungled by a lot of men."

While *The Singer and the Dancer* had been chastised by feminist critics for its downbeat ending, in which the heroine returns to her philandering lover after a halfhearted escape attempt, *My Brilliant Career* was widely celebrated for its feminist fairy-tale story as well as its employment of women crew members. Adapted from Miles Franklin's semiautobiographical novel, *My Brilliant Career,* with its turn-of-the-century setting in the Australian outback, works like *Jane Eyre* in reverse (she does not marry him), while retaining the romantic allure of such a story and all the glossy production values of a period setting that Australian cinema had been known for up until then. Distinguished by an astonishing central performance by the then-unknown Judy Davis (fresh from playing Juliet to Mel Gibson's Romeo on the drama-school stage), the film managed to present a positive model of feminine independence without belying the time in which it was set. Like Armstrong's later *Mrs. Soffel, My Brilliant Career* potently evokes smothered sensuality and conveys sexual tension by small, telling details, as in the boating scene.

Sadly, few of Armstrong's later films have been awarded commensurate critical praise or been as widely successful, possibly because of her refusal to conform to expectations and churn out more upbeat costume dramas. Her next feature, *Starstruck,* although it too features a spunky, ambitious heroine, was a rock musical set in the present and displaying a veritable rattle bag of influences—including Judy Garland-Mickey Rooney "let's-put-on-a-show" films, Richard Lester editing techniques, new-wave pop videos, and even Sternberg's *Blond Venus,* when the heroine sheds her kangaroo suit to sing her "torch song" à la Marlene Dietrich. Despite a witty script and fine bit characters, the music is somewhat monotonous, and the film was only mildly successful.

Armstrong's first film to be financed and filmed in America was *Mrs. Soffel.* Based on a true story and set at the turn of the century, it delineated the tragic story of a prison warden's wife who falls in love with a convict, helps him escape, and finally runs off with him. The bleak, monochrome cinematography is powerfully atmospheric but was not to all reviewers' tastes, especially in America. For Armstrong, the restricted palette was quite deliberate, so that the penultimate images of blood on snow would be all the more striking and effective. A sadly underrated film, it features some unexpectedly fine performances from Diane Keaton in the title role, Mel Gibson as her paramour (a fair impersonation of young Henry Fonda), and the young

Matthew Modine as his kid brother. At its best, it recalls, if not *McCabe and Mrs. Miller,* then at least *Bonnie and Clyde.*

High Tide returns to Australia for its setting in a coastal caravan park, and comes up trumps as an unabashedly sentimental weepie, and none the worse for it. It features three generations of women: Lilli (Judy Davis again), backup singer to an Elvis impersonator and drifter; Ally (Claudia Karvan), the pubescent daughter she left behind; and mother-in-law Bet (Jan Adele), who vies with Lilli for Ally's affections. In terms of camera work, it is Armstrong's most restless film, utilizing nervous zip pans, fast tracking, and boomshots, and then resting for quiet, intense close-ups on surfboards, legs being shaved, and shower nozzles, all highly motivated by the characters' perspectives. Like *Mrs. Soffel, High Tide* uses colors symbolically to contrast the gentle tones of the seaside's natural landscape with the garish buildings of the town called Eden.

Armstrong wears her feminist credentials lightly, never on her sleeve. Nevertheless, her fiction films—like her documentaries, which have followed three women from the ages of 14 to 25—can be seen as charting over the years the trajectory of the women's movement: *My Brilliant Career* in the 1970s celebrated women's independence, as Sybylla rejects the roles of wife and mother; *Mrs. Soffel* in the mid-1980s reopens negotiations with men (with tragic results); and finally *High Tide* returns to the rejected motherhood role, with all its attendant joys and anxieties.

Fires Within is a well-meaning but insipid tale of a Cuban political prisoner and his encounter with his family in Miami. A fiasco, Armstrong lost control of the project during post-production. The filmmaker bounced back strongly, however, with two impressive films centering on the relationships between female siblings.

The Last Days of Chez Nous, which Armstrong directed back in Australia, is a thoughtful, well-acted drama focusing on the emotional plight of a pair of sisters. One (Lisa Harrow) is a bossy, fortysomething writer, and the other (Kerry Fox) has just emerged from an unhappy love affair. The scenario centers on events that take place after the latter becomes romantically involved with the former's husband (Bruno Ganz). The film's major strength is the depth and richness of its female characters. Its theme, consistent with Armstrong's best previous work, is the utter necessity of women's self-sufficiency.

Little Women, based on Louisa May Alcott's venerable 1868 novel of four devoted sisters coming of age in Concord, Massachusetts, during the Civil War, was Armstrong's first successful American-made film. It may be linked to *My Brilliant Career* as a story of feminine independence set in a previous era. Alcott's book had been filmed a number of times before: a silent version, made in 1918; most enjoyably by George Cukor, with Katharine Hepburn, in 1933; far less successfully, with a young Elizabeth Taylor (among others), in 1949; and in a made-for-television movie in 1978. Armstrong's version is every bit as fine as the Cukor-Hepburn classic. Her cast is just about perfect, with Winona Ryder deservedly earning an Academy Award nomination as the headstrong Jo March. Ryder is ably supported by Trini Alvarado, Claire Danes, Samantha Mathis, and Kirsten Dunst, and Susan Sarandon offers her usual solid performance as Marmee, the March girls' mother. If the film has one fault, it is the contemporary-sounding feminist rhetoric that Marmee spouts: the dialogue is completely out of sync with the spirit and reality of the times. But this is just a quibble. This new *Little Women* is a fine film, at once literate and extremely enjoyable.—LESLIE FELPERIN and ROB EDELMAN

Arzner, Dorothy

American director

Born *San Francisco, 3 January 1900.* ***Education*** *Studied medicine at University of Southern California.* ***Military Service*** *Ambulance driver in World War I, 1917-18.* ***Career*** *1919—typist for William C. de Mille, at Famous Players-Lasky (Paramount); 1922—editor for "Realart," a subsidiary of Paramount; 1926—wrote and edited* Old Ironsides; *1929—directed Paramount's first sound film,* The Wild Party; *1943—retired from directing.* ***Awards*** *Honored at First International Festival of Women's Films, New York, 1972, and by Director's Guild of America, 1975.* ***Died*** *In La Quinta, California, 1 October 1979.*

Films as Director: **1927:** *Fashions for Women*; *Get Your Man*; *10 Modern Commandments*. **1928:** *Manhattan Cocktail*. **1929:** *The Wild Party* (+ ro). **1930:** "The Gallows Song—Nichavo" sequence in *Paramount on Parade*; *Anybody's Woman*; *Sarah and Son*; *Behind the Makeup* (co-d); *Charming Sinners* (co-d, uncredited). **1931:** *Honor among Lovers*; *Working Girls*. **1932:** *Merrily We Go to Hell*. **1933:** *Christopher Strong*. **1934:** *Nana* (*Lady of the Boulevards*). **1936:** *Craig's Wife*. **1937:** *The Bride Wore Red*; *The Last of Mrs. Cheyney* (co-d, uncredited). **1940:** *Dance, Girl, Dance*. **1943:** *First Comes Courage*.

Other Films: **1922:** *Blood and Sand* (Niblo) (ed). **1923:** *The Covered Wagon* (Cruze) (ed). **1924:** *Inez from Hollywood* (A. E. Green) (ed, sc); *The Bread of the Border* (sc); *The No-Gun Man* (sc). **1925:** *Red Kimono* (W. Lang) (sc); *When Husbands Flirt* (Wellman) (sc). **1926:** *Old Ironsides* (Cruze) (ed, sc). **1936:** *Theodora Goes Wild* (Boleslawski) (pr).

Dorothy Arzner's career as a commercial Hollywood director covered little more than a decade, but she had prepared for it by extensive editing and script-writing work. Ill health forced her to abandon a career that might eventually have led to the recognition she deserved from her contemporaries. One of only a handful of women operating within the structure of Hollywood's post-silent boom, Arzner has been the subject of feminist critical attention, with film retrospectives of her work both in the United States and United Kingdom in the 1970s, when her work was "rediscovered."

Most feminists would recognize that the mere reinsertion of women into a dominant version of film history is a dubious activity, even while asserting that women's contributions to cinema have been excluded from most historical accounts. Recognition of the work of a "popular" director such as Arzner and an evaluation of her contribution to Hollywood cinema must be set against an awareness of her place in the dominant patriarchal ideology of classic Hollywood cinema. Arzner's work is particularly interesting in that it was produced *within* the Hollywood system with all its inherent constraints (time, budget, traditional content requirements of particular genres, etc.).

While Arzner directed "women's pictures"—classic Hollywood fare—she differed from other directors of the genre in that, in place of a narrative seen simply from a female point of view, she actually succeeded in challenging the orthodoxy of Hollywood from within, offering perspectives that questioned the dominant order.

The films often depict women seeking independence through career—a burlesque queen and an aspiring ballerina (*Dance, Girl, Dance*), a world-champion aviatrix (*Christopher Strong*). Alternatively, the escape route can be through exit from accepted female positions in the

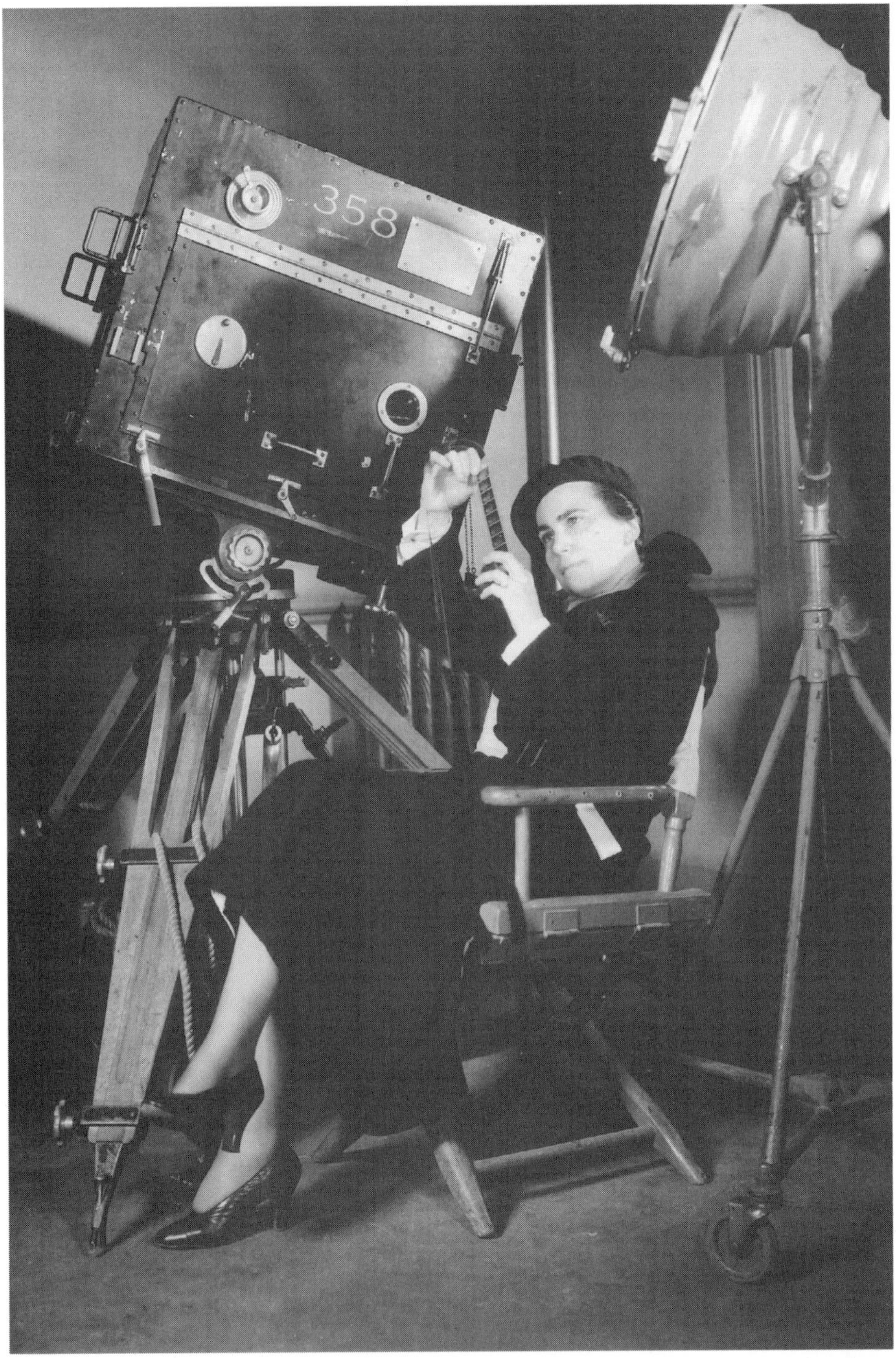

Dorothy Arzner

hierarchy—a rich daughter "escaping" into marriage with a poverty-stricken drunk (*Merrily We Go to Hell*). Even excess can be a way of asserting independence, as with the obsessive housekeeper rejecting family relationships in favor of a passion for domesticity and the home (*Craig's Wife*).

The films frequently play with notions of female stereotyping (most notably in *Dance, Girl, Dance,* with its two central female types of Nice Girl and Vamp). Arzner's "nice girls" are likely to have desires that conflict with male desires, while narrative requirements will demand that they still please the male. While these tensions are not always resolved, Arzner's strategies in underlining these opposing desires are almost gleeful at times.

In addition, Arzner's films offer contradictions that disturb the spectator's accepted relationship with what is on screen—most notably in *Dance, Girl, Dance,* when dancer Judy O'Brien turns on her burlesque (male) audience and berates them for their voyeurism. This scene has been the focus for much debate about the role of the spectator in relation to the woman as spectacle (notably in the work of Laura Mulvey).

Although the conventions of plot and development are present in Arzner's films, Claire Johnston sees these elements as subverted by a "women's discourse": the films may offer us the kinds of narrative closure we expect from the classic Hollywood text—the "happy" or the "tragic" ending—but Arzner's insistence on this female discourse gives the films an exciting and unsettling quality. In Arzner's work, Johnston argues, it is the male universe which invites scrutiny and which is "rendered strange."

Dorothy Arzner's position inside the studio system has made her a unique subject for debate. As the women's movement set about reassessing the role of women in history, so feminist film theorists began not only to reexamine the role of women as a creative force in cinema, but also to consider the implications behind the notion of women as spectacle. The work of Dorothy Arzner has proved a rich area for investigation into both these questions.—LILIE FERRARI

Audry, Jacqueline

French director

Born *Orange, France, 25 September 1908.* ***Family*** *Married the writer Pierre Laroche.* ***Career*** *1933—entered the French film industry as a script girl; 1930s—became an assistant director, working with G. W. Pabst, Max Ophüls, Jean Delannoy, and others; 1943—directed her first short,* Les Chevaux du Vercors; *1945—directed her first feature,* Les Malheurs du Sophie. ***Died*** *Poissy, France, 1977.*

Films as Director: **1943:** *Les Chevaux du Vercors* (short). **1945:** *Les Malheurs du Sophie.* **1948:** *Sombre dimanche.* **1949:** *Gigi.* **1950:** *Minne, l'Ingénue libertine* (*Minne, the Innocent Libertine*). **1951:** *Olivia* (*Pit of Loneliness*). **1953:** *La Caraque blonde* (*The Blonde Gypsy*). **1954:** *Huis clos* (*No Exit*). **1956:** *Mitsou.* **1957:** *La Garçonne*; *C'est la faute d'Adam.* **1958:** *L'École des cocottes* (*School for Coquettes*). **1960:** *Le Secret du Chevalier d'Éon.* **1961:** *Les Petits matins*; *Cadavres en Vacances.* **1966:** *Fruits amers* (*Bitter Fruit*; *Soledad*) (+ co-sc). **1971:** *Le Lis de mer.* **1972:** *Un grand amour de Balzac.*

Jacqueline Audry's career is significant not only because she was one of the rare female directors working in a motion-picture industry dominated by men, but because she created a body of work that consistently featured strong-willed and independent-minded female characters. Audry often depicted her heroines in psychological terms, with more than a few of her films touching on open sexuality or lesbianism. Yet while behaving in ways that were anything but conventional, her characters never were viewed as oddities or aberrations who needed to be roped in and tamed by good, strong males—unlike the propaganda found in countless postwar Hollywood films featuring self-reliant female characters who by the finale had to be taught that true happiness only came with subservience to men.

Audry's heroines generally are perceptively and sensitively realized, with their alternative lifestyles becoming models of liberation. While she directed with a sure hand, however, her films on occasion are visually unimaginative; they lack the originality and flair that was to characterize the French New Wave that practically all of her films predated.

Most of Audry's films are literary adaptations based on the work of both male and female writers, and were scripted by her husband, Pierre Laroche. Three of the more notable—each starring Danièle Delorme—are from the writings of Colette (who worked closely with Audry and Laroche in developing the scripts). The first, *Gigi,* the story of a girl who is trained by her aunt to be a high-class courtesan but who rebelliously opts for love and marriage, was released nine years before the Academy Award-winning Hollywood musical version. While the title character chooses a traditional lifestyle, the point is that it is her option; she is active rather than passive as she goes against the teachings of her aunt and, in the process, reforms the playboy whom she weds. *Minne, l'Ingenue libertine* tells of a disaffected married woman who distances herself sexually from her husband and drifts into a pair of extramarital relationships as she searches for love. Because of its theme, and the depiction of its heroine, *Minne, l'Ingenue libertine* became the initial film to earn an "X" certificate in Great Britain. In a *New York Times* review, it was noted that the film "has been somewhat abridged, for reasons of moral discretion, from its original length." Finally, *Mitsou* chronicles the predicament of a young, uncultivated chorus girl who seeks the help of an older and more experienced paramour in order to improve herself. Here, too, the female character does not remain submissive but chooses to take action to alter her life.

Easily Audry's most notorious—and, arguably, best-known—film is *Olivia,* a landmark of lesbian cinema if only because it was produced during an era in which even hints of same-sex relationships were practically absent from the screen. *Olivia* (which was retitled *Pit of Loneliness* for its American release) is set in the late 19th century, and is based on an autobiographical novel by Lytton Strachey's sister, Dorothy Bussy (which originally was published under a pseudonym). It is thematically reminiscent of *Mädchen in Uniform* in that it depicts the stirrings of a romantic relationship that develops between the title character, a new student at an all-girls' boarding school, and one of her headmistresses. Not surprisingly, the film was heavily censored; 11 minutes were snipped from it prior to its release in England. Another important Audry credit is her version of *No Exit,* based on Jean-Paul Sartre's existential play about three individuals who have died, and who find themselves trapped in a hotel room where they are fated to remain together for eternity.

Additional Audry heroines include a blond gypsy who has become a celebrated dancer (in *La Caraque blonde*); a young woman who exerts her independence upon discovering her fiancé is cheating on her (*La Garçonne*); a flirt who becomes celebrated throughout Paris after having an affair with a pianist (*L'École des cocottes*); and a young hitchhiker who attracts many men while traveling from Belgium to the Riviera (*Les Petits matins*). The characters in each are placed in romantic or sexual situations. They may evolve in a Pygmalion-like manner, fall in love and are cheated on, have many sexual liaisons, or choose to forgo sex altogether until they find love. But again, their ultimate courses of action are theirs. And in her latter films Audry expanded her gallery of women, depicting them as revolutionaries (*Fruits amers*) and as being forced to pose as boys to win inheritances (*Le Secret du Chevalier d'Éon*).

As with so many other proficient but lesser-known film makers of both sexes, little has been written about Audry in the standard film references. Most certainly, her career is ripe for a further, deeper analysis.—ROB EDELMAN

B, Beth

American director

Born *New York, 14 April 1955.* ***Education*** *Attended San Diego State University and the University of California, Irvine; graduated from the School of Visual Arts.* ***Family*** *Married the filmmaker Scott B (divorced).* ***Career*** *Late 1970s-early 1980s—with her then-husband, Scott B, emerged as a prominent figure in the New York independent/underground/No-Wave film scene; 1980—co-directed (with Scott B) her first feature,* The Offenders; *1984-86—directed the music videos* Dominatrix, Joan Jett: I Need Someone, *and* Taka Boom; *1987—directed her first feature on her own,* Salvation!; *1980s-90s—created multimedia environments, art exhibits/installations and photographic series, which have been exhibited around the world; 1995—a retrospective of her work presented at New York's Anthology Film Archive.* ***Awards*** *New York Film Festival Award, for* Vortex, *1983.* ***Address*** *B Movies Inc., 45 Crosby Street, New York, NY 10012, U.S.A.*

Films as Director: 1978: *G-Man* (co-d with Scott B—short); *Black Box* (co-d with Scott B—short). **1979:** *Letters to Dad* (co-d with Scott B—short). **1980:** *The Offenders* (co-d with Scott B, + co-sc, co-ph, co-music). **1981:** *The Trap Door* (co-d with Scott B, + co-sc, co-pr, co-ph, co-music). **1983:** *Vortex* (co-d with Scott B, + co-sc, co-ed, co-music). **1987:** *Salvation!* (*Salvation! Have You Said Your Prayers Today?*; *Benefactors*) (+ co-sc, co-pr, music). **1989:** *Belladonna* (co-d with Applebroog—short) (+ ro). **1991:** *Thanatopsis* (short); *Stigmata* (short); *Shut Up and Suffer* (short). **1992:** *Amnesia* (short). **1993:** *Two Small Bodies* (+ sc, co-pr); *Under Lock and Key* (short). **1994:** *High Heel Nights* (short). **1995:** *Out of Sight/Out of Mind* (short). **1996:** *Visiting Desire* (doc) (+ ph, pr, sound).

During the late 1970s-early 1980s, Beth and Scott B were among the most significant proponents of the No-Wave, no-budget style of underground punk filmmaking. Working out of New York's East Village in conjunction with performance artists and musicians and in the Super-8mm format, they created a series of noisy, scruffy, deeply personal short films in which they combine violent themes and darkly sinister images to explore the manner in which the individual is constrained by society.

These films are at once contemplative and confrontational, penetrating and politically loaded. In *G-Man,* Beth and Scott B attack society's power structures as they depict a cop who feels compelled to employ a dominatrix. In *Letters to Dad,* various people read letters to the camera (and the viewer, who takes on the role of "dad"). At the finale, it is disclosed that the letters were written by followers of notorious cult leader Jim Jones immediately prior to their mass suicide. The result is that the viewer has unknowingly assumed the part of Jones. *Black Box* is the name of a torture contraption that was devised in the United States and utilized in foreign nations. In the film, a man is imprisoned in one such box, where he is tortured—and the viewer endures his suffering.

The brief length of these films allows them to effectively assault the viewer in a hit-and-run, belt-in-the-gut manner. But when Beth and Scott B ventured into the realm of feature-length filmmaking, they were unable to attain a similar effect. *The Offenders,* also shot in Super-8mm, is a poorly photographed, acted, and directed punk melodrama about a kidnapping; it originally was presented as a serial that was screened at New York's Max's Kansas City. *The Trap Door,* their final Super-8mm production, is the muddled account of the plight of an unemployed and directionless man. *Vortex,* shot in 16mm, is a monotonous, film noirish drama featuring frequent Beth B collaborator Lydia Lunch as a detective who becomes immersed in corporate chicanery and the exploitation of politicians by companies soliciting defense contracts.

After *Vortex,* Beth and Scott B ended their partnership. The feature films Beth B has since made on her own are ambitious in content. Her most consistent themes, which are extensions of her earlier work, are sexual repression and violence, the boundaries of sexual desire, and the manner in which authority figures act out their own neuroses while trying to control others. Unfortunately, these films have too often fallen short in execution. *Salvation!* is her first major solo credit, a black comedy about a hypocritical television evangelist who preaches hellfire-and-brimstone sermons while becoming involved in a sex scandal. Despite some genuinely funny moments, this potentially explosive material mostly is squandered. The film has the look of a music video, which disrupts the narrative flow, and the characters are cliched and underdeveloped. *Visiting Desire* is a structural throwback to her earliest work. Its premise is intriguing: Strangers come together to act out their sexual fantasies in the presence of each other, and the camera. The encounters are titled Aggression, Innocence, Trust, Loss of Innocence, Control, Vulnerability. . . . Unfortunately, the result is boring and pretentious.

Two Small Bodies may be linked to *Visiting Desire* as an exploration of eroticism and fantasy. And it is Beth B's most effective feature to date, a bizarre but compelling two-character psychodrama in which a distrustful cop investigates the disappearance of the two children of a divorcee who works as a cocktail waitress in a strip joint, and who appears to be curiously unmoved by her predicament. The cop is at once attracted to and disturbed by the woman's unconventional behavior. Meanwhile, she psychologically toys with him, resulting in a sexual power struggle which is fascinating yet depressing, given that both characters are thoroughly wretched individuals.

Easily Beth B's best later works are her short films. *Thanatopsis,* performed and written by Lydia Lunch, is a pointed meditation on the absurdity and inevitability of war in a male-dominated society. *Stigmata* poignantly charts the disturbing stories of six drug addicts. Especially noteworthy is *Belladonna,* co-directed by Beth B and her mother, installation artist/painter Ida Applebroog, which was screened as part of one of Applebroog's exhibitions. It consists of rapidly intercut close-ups of talking heads reading statements from a Sigmund Freud case history; affidavits attesting to the atrocities of Dr. Josef Mengele, the Nazi war criminal; and journals from the trial of New Yorker Joel Steinberg, accused of killing his adopted daughter. "What emerges here," wrote Eleanor Heartney, reviewing the film in *Art in America,* "is a picture of a chain of abuse in which victims become victimizers and disturbed individuals hold together their fragile egos by compartmentalizing their darker urges even as they act upon them. . . . This film offers a degree of understanding, but no comfort. Violence breeds violence, the child who suffers becomes the adult who inflicts suffering. Human cruelty here is a closed circuit which feeds off its own energy."

Early in her career, Beth B's films were purposefully noncommercial. They were meant to be screened in lofts, clubs, and alternative spaces, rather than cinemas. Indeed, they might be described as anti-cinema and, like the punk rock movement which they parallel, they are nihilistic. Ironically, her more recent features, while maintaining their individual edges, are more commercially structured. "No matter how modest the distribution deal, a theatrical release is why I continue to make films," she wrote in a "filmmaker diary" at the 1996 Independent Feature Film Market, which she attended to pitch a new project, titled *The Naked Bride.*—ROB EDELMAN

Bani-Etemad, Rakhshan

Iranian director

Born *Tehran, 1954.* ***Education*** *Attended Tehran's College of Dramatic Arts, 1975-79, graduating with a degree in film directing.* ***Family*** *Married (second) to the film producer Jahan gir Kousari, 1983; son: Tandis Ghahremani, and daughter: Baran.* ***Career*** *1979-83—"script girl" and reporter for National Iranian Radio and Television (NIRT); 1980—assistant director on Mehdi Sabaghzadeh's* Aftab Nechinha; *1983-87—directed four documentaries for NIRT; 1988—directed her first feature,* Off the Limits, *a comedy that became a box-office hit.* ***Awards*** *Crystal Simorgh for Best Director, Fajr International Film Festival, Tehran, and Best Film of the Year, Iranian Film Critics, for* Nargess, *1992; Crystal Simorgh for Best Script, Fajr International Film Festival, Tehran, Bronze Leopard, Locarno International Film Festival, and Silver Award, Iranian Society of Filmmakers, for* The Blue-Veiled, *1995.* ***Agent*** *Farabi Cinema Foundation, 55 Sie-Tir Avenue, IR Tehran 11358, Iran.*

Films as Director: 1984: *Farahang-e-Massraffi* (*Consumer Culture*) (doc—for TV). **1985:** *Mohojereen Roustai* (*Employment of the Rural Migrants in Town*) (doc—for TV). **1986:** *Ta'dabir Eghtessadi-y-Janghi* (*Economic Measures at the Time of War*) (doc—for TV). **1987:** *Tamarkoze* (*Centralization*) (doc—for TV). **1988:** *Kharejaz Mahdoudeh* (*Off the Limits*). **1989:** *Zard-e Ghanari* (*Canary Yellow*) (+ co-sc). **1990:** *Poul-e Khareji* (*Foreign Currency*). **1992:** *Nargess* (+ co-sc). **1992-94:** *Report of 1993* (doc, video); *Spring to Spring* (doc, video); *To Whom Are You Showing These Films?* (doc, video). **1995:** *Rusariye Abi* (*The Blue-Veiled*) (+ sc). **1996:** *The Last Visit to Ms. Iran Daftari* (doc, video). **1997:** *Under the Skin of the City* (doc, video). **1998:** *The May Lady.*

Other Films: 1980: *Aftab Nechinha* (Sabaghzadeh) (asst d). **1983:** *Golhayeh Davoodi* (Sadr Ameli) (planning manager). **1984:** *Tanoureh Deev* (Ayari) (planning manager). **1985:** *Tohfehha* (Vahidzadeh) (planning manager).

One of the nine women currently working as feature-film directors in Iran, Rakhshan Bani-Etemad has imposed herself both at home and abroad by a rigorous filmic *écriture* and a powerful mise en scène. Having started her career as a documentarist for television, she combines an acute, sometimes ironical, sense of observation with a compassionate gaze and the construction of characters firmly rooted in reality. Even after she started directing features, she never stopped getting involved with documentary issues, and, in the early 1990s, she used video to continue exploring the topics she was interested in while waiting for the green light for her next feature.

Her early documentaries, dealing with peasant migration to the cities, war efforts, or postrevolutionary consumerism, were controversial, but her first feature, *Off the Limits,* a satire of bureaucratic mix-ups, struck an immediate chord with local Iranian audiences. It was followed by two pungent comedies, one, *Canary Yellow,* plunging into darker waters in which economic survival and personal integrity overlap, while *Foreign Currency* takes an affectionate poke at the mores and foibles of the Iranian bourgeoisie. With *Nargess,* her first international success, Bani-Etemad staged two powerful figures of women from the most disenfranchised classes. Before writing the script, she interviewed women jailed for theft and prostitution: "I do not do research to find a story," she says, "but to get closer to people." While bringing her father to the hospital, Nargess, a poor, but sweet and delicate young woman, meets the attractive Adel, unaware that he is in fact hiding from the police after a botched burglary. For Adel, Nargess represents an impossible dream of salvation, and he persuades his "mother," Afagh, to propose marriage. Once abandoned in the streets, Adel was raised as a thief by Afagh who later became his lover. Afagh, a complex, tormented character, accepts the arrangement, and the marriage takes place. Love and ignorance blind Nargess to the abjection her new husband is struggling to escape, till reality catches up. As Adel gradually becomes a pitiful character, Bani-Etemad depicts the relationship between the two women with master strokes. Afagh shows surprising resilience in her passion for Adel, and even the "innocent" Nargess proves a tiger ready to fight for what she believes.

In *The Blue-Veiled,* Bani-Etemad switches the action from the lower depths of Tehran to the countryside. Rashul, a good-natured widower and the wealthy owner of a large tomato plantation, adored by his married daughters, seems content with his lot. Yet, a newly hired young peasant, Nobar, slowly tears apart the shroud of his fake happiness. After resisting their mutual feelings of attraction, Nobar and Rashul eventually start living together "on the sly," until societal pressure, in the guise of Rashul's "well-meaning" but class-conscious daughters, brings trouble in paradise. "In *Nargess* and *The Blue-Veiled,* I show women who don't have childhood, don't have youth, who become older too soon; they don't have anybody to support them, and because they have to stand on their own feet, they bear a lot of hardship," says Bani-Etemad. "I would like for people to pay attention to them, but I also want to show their hidden roles, their hidden loves, and their hidden goals."

Bani-Etemad, who refuses to be considered a "female director," but a director who happens to be a woman, nevertheless takes pride in her portrayal of strong, believable, complex female characters. Her latest film, *The May Lady,* just released in Iran, shows the plight of a professional woman through a combination of documentary and fiction. As the director herself is the first to admit, under the chador a woman can virtually go anywhere in Iran, even in places where men can not, and bring to the silver screen stories and characters that their male colleagues might have passed by.—BÉRÉNICE REYNAUD

Batchelor, Joy

British animator

Born *Watford, Hertfordshire, England, 12 May 1914.* ***Family*** *Married the Hungarian animator John Halas in late 1930s, two children.* ***Career*** *1935—began working in films as artist; 1937—hired as designer and animator to work on* The Music Man; *1940—with John Halas, co-founder of Halas & Batchelor Cartoon Films; 1940-45—made numerous information and propaganda films for British government; 1951-54—produced only feature-length British cartoon,* Animal Farm, *based on George Orwell novel; 1968—Halas & Batchelor bought by Trident Television; Batchelor and Halas concentrated on individual projects working through their other company, Educational Film Centre; from 1968-72—not responsible for films produced by Halas & Batchelor production company; 1974—Halas & Batchelor sold back to Halas after losing money for corporation; 1973—Batchelor retired but continued to act as adviser to animation students at International Film School, London.* ***Died*** *In London, 14 May 1991.*

Films as Co-Director with John Halas: 1940: *Train Trouble* (+ co-pr, anim); *Carnival in the Clothes Cupboard* (+ co-pr, co-des, co-anim). **1941:** *Filling the Gap* (+ co-pr, co-sc, co-anim); *Dustbin Parade* (+ co-pr, co-sc, co-des, co-anim); *The Pocket Cartoon* (+ co-sc, co-anim) (may not have been released); *The Brave Tin Soldier* (+ co-sc, co-anim) (may not have been released). **1942:** *Digging for Victory* (+ co-pr, co-sc, co-anim, des). **1943:** *Jungle Warfare* (+ co-pr, co-des, co-anim). **1944:** *Cold Comfort* (+ co-pr, co-sc, co-anim); *From Rags to Stitches* (+ co-pr, co-sc, co-anim); *Blitz on Bugs* (+ co-pr, co-sc, co-anim); *Mrs. Sew and Sew* (+ co-pr, co-sc, co-anim); *Christmas Wishes* (+ co-pr, co-sc, co-anim). **1945:** *Tommy's Double Trouble* (+ co-pr, co-anim); *Six Little Jungle Boys* (+ co-anim). **1946:** *Modern Guide to Health* (+ co-pr, co-des; sc); *Old Wives' Tales* (+ co-pr, co-des; sc); *Road Safety* (+ co-pr, co-anim); *Britain Must Export* (+ co-pr, co-anim); *Export or Die* (+ co-pr, co-anim); *Export! Export! Export!* (+ co-pr, co-anim); *The Keys of Heaven* (+ co-pr, co-anim); *Good King Wenceslas* (+ co-pr, co-anim). **1947:** *First Line of Defence* (+ co-pr, co-sc); *This Is the Air Force* (+ co-pr, co-sc); *What's Cooking?* (+ co-pr, co-des, sc); *Dolly Put the Kettle On* (+ co-pr, co-des, sc). **1948:** *Oxo Parade* (+ co-pr, co-des, sc); *Heave Away My Johnny* (+ co-pr, co-sc). **1949:** *The Shoemaker and the Hatter* (+ co-pr, co-sc, co-des); *Submarine Control* (co-d with Privett and Crick); *Fly about the House* (+ co-pr, co-des, sc); *A Well Kept Machine* (+ co-pr); *A Little Forethought* (+ co-pr); *A Better Spirit* (+ co-pr); *Start with What Is under Your Nose* (+ co-pr). **1950:** *The British Army at Your Service* (+ co-pr). **1951:** *The Flu-ing Squad* (+ co-pr). **1952:** *Linear Accelerator.* **1953:** *The Figurehead.* **1954:** *Animal Farm* (feature, begun 1951) (+ co-pr, co-sc, co-des). **1956:** *The Candlemaker* (+ co-sc). **1958:** *Dam the Delta* (+ sc). **1959:** *All Lit Up* (+ co-pr, sc); *Piping Hot* (+ co-pr, sc); *For Better for Worse* (+ co-pr, sc). **1973:** *Contact* (+ co-sc).

***Abu* Series: 1943-44:** *Abu's Dungeon*; *Abu's Poisoned Well*; *Abu's Harvest*; *Abu Builds a Dam* (+ co-pr, co-anim).

***Charley* Series: 1946-49:** *Charley in the New Towns*; *Charley in the New Schools*; *Charley in "Your Very Good Health"*; *Charley in the New Mines*; *Charley Junior's Schooldays*; *Charley's March of Time* (+ co-pr, co-sc, co-des); *Robinson Charley* (+ co-pr, co-des); *Farmer Charley* (+ co-pr, co-sc); *Charley's Black Magic* (+ co-pr, co-sc).

Other Films: 1938: *The Music Man* (Halas) (co-anim). **1944-45:** *Handling Ships* (Halas and Privett—feature) (co-pr). **1948:** *Magic Canvas* (Halas) (co-pr); *Water for Firefighting* (feature) (Halas and Crick) (co-pr). **1950:** *As Old as the Hills* (Privett) (co-pr); *Fowl Play* (Dyer and Kirley) (co-pr). **1951:** *Moving Spirit* (co-d: Halas) (co-sc). **1952:** *We've Come a Long Way* (co-sc); *Service: Garage Handling* (Crick and Privett) (co-pr, co-sc); *The Owl and the Pussycat* (Halas and Borthwick) (co-pr). **1953:** *Power to Fly* (co-sc); *The Figurehead* (Crick) (co-pr); *Coastal Navigation and Pilotage* (Dahl) (co-pr). **1954:** *Down a Long Way* (Privett) (co-sc). **1955:** *Animal Vegetable Mineral* (co-sc); *The World That Nature Forgot* (co-pr); *Basic Fleetwork* (co-pr); *Refinery at Work* (co-pr). **1956:** *To Your Health* (co-sc); *The World of Little*

Ig (Halas) (sc, co-pr); *Think of the Future* (co-pr); *Invisible Exchange* (co-pr). **1957:** *Midsummer Nightmare* (Halas) (co-pr, co-sc); *Queen of Hearts* (co-anim); *History of the Cinema* (Halas) (co-pr). **1958:** *Speed the Plough* (Privett) (co-sc); *The First Ninety-Nine* (d, co-pr, co-sc); *The Christmas Visitor* (co-pr, co-sc); *Best Seller* (Potterton) (co-pr, co-sc). **1959:** *How to Be a Hostess* (live action) (sc); *Energy Picture* (sc, co-pr). **1960:** *The Wonder of Wool* (Halas) (co-pr). **1961:** *The Monster of Highgate Pond* (sc); *Hamilton the Musical Elephant* (Halas) (co-pr); *Hamilton in the Musical Festival* (Halas) (co-pr). **1962:** *Barnaby—Father Dear Father* (Halas) (co-pr); *Barnaby—Overdue Dues Blues* (Halas) (co-pr). **1963:** *Automania 2000* (Halas) (co-pr, co-sc); *Pulmonary Function* (Halas) (co-pr). **1964:** *Paying Bay* (co-sc, co-pr); *Follow that Car* (co-sc, co-pr); *Ruddigore* (feature) (d, co-pr, sc). **1966:** *Dying for a Smoke* (Halas) (co-sc). **1967:** *The Colombo Plan* (d, co-pr, sc); *The Commonwealth* (d, co-pr, sc). **1968:** *Bolly* (d, co-pr, sc). **1970:** *Short Tall Story* (Halas) (co-pr); *The Five* (d, co-pr, sc); *Wot Dot* (d, co-pr, sc); *Flurina* (Halas) (co-pr); *Sputum* (Borthwick) (pr); *This Love Thing* (Dunbar) (co-pr). **1971:** *Children and Cars* (Halas) (co-pr, co-sc). **1973:** *Children Making Cartoons* (P. Halas) (co-pr, co-sc). **1974:** *The Ass and the Stick* (d, co-sc); *Christmas Feast* (Halas) (co-sc); *Carry on Milkmaids* (d, sc). **1977:** *How the Motor Car Works: The Carburettor* (Seager) (co-anim). **1979:** "No. 10" ep. of *Ten for Survival* (*Together for Children: Principle 10*) (Halas) (sc).

***Poet and Painter* Series: 1951:** Programme 1: *Twa Corbies*; *Spring and Winter*; Programme 2: *Winter Garden*; *Sailor's Consolation*; *Check to Song*; Programme 3: *In Time of Pestilence*; *The Pythoness*; Programme 4: *John Gilpin* (Halas) (co-pr).

***Foo-Foo* Series: 1960:** *The Scapegoat*; *The Gardener*; *The Birthday Treat*; *A Denture Adventure*; *A Misguided Tour*; *The Caddies*; *Burglar Catcher*; *The Art Lovers*; *The Three Mountaineers*; *Foo-Foo's New Hat*; *The Big Race*; *The Treasure Hunt*; *The Magician*; *The Spy Train*; *Insured for Life*; *Automation Blues*; *The Beggar's Uproar*; *Sleeping Beauty*; *The Reward*; *The Dinner Date*; *Beauty Treatment*; *The Ski Resort*; *Lucky Street*; *The Stowaway*; *A Hunting We Will Go*; *The Pearl Divers*; *Foo-Foo's Sleepless Night*; *The Salesman*; *Art for Art's Sake*; *The Dog Pound*; *The Hypnotist*; *Low Finance* (co-pr).

***Snip and Snap* Series: 1960:** *Bagpipes*; *Treasure of Ice Cake Island*; *Spring Song*; *Snakes and Ladders*; *In the Jungle*; *Lone World Sail*; *Thin Ice*; *Magic Book*; *Circus Star*; *Moonstruck*; *Snap and the Beanstalk*; *Goodwill to All Dogs*; *In the Cellar*; *The Grand Concert*; *The Beggar's Uproar*; *The Birthday Cake*; *Snap Goes East*; *The Hungry Dog*; *Tog Dogs* (co-d: Halas) (co-pr).

***Classic Fairy Tales* Series: 1966:** 6 films (d, sc, co-pr).

Joy Batchelor is one of the rare pioneer female animators, working in a discipline historically dominated by men. She began her career as a commercial artist and, in the late 1930s, met Hungarian-born animator John Halas, whom she was to join in a full professional partnership. Batchelor and Halas, who later were married, maintained control of their work by establishing, in 1940, their own production company, Halas & Batchelor Cartoon Films. Over the next five decades it was to become one of the most active animation houses in Europe, with Batchelor and Halas producing an extraordinary array of films: informational and propaganda pieces for the British government; scientific, educational, industrial, and promotional films; television entertainment programs and commercials; animated short subjects on more artistic topics; and, most significantly, a version of George Orwell's *Animal Farm*, the first-ever British feature-length animated film. Their studio even became a haven in which other animators from Europe and America could work and thrive.

The first film Batchelor and Halas made at their studio was *Train Trouble*, a celluloid commercial for Kellogg's Cornflakes. During World War II, they produced more than 70 original and cleverly animated government films: how-to instructionals, which were meant to educate the public on ways to help contribute to victory against the Axis, and more technical-oriented training films. One of the latter, *Handling Ships*, an instructional film financed by the British Admiralty, was the first-ever British cartoon in Technicolor.

After the war, Batchelor and Halas turned to more aesthetic subjects. Working in collaboration with Henry Moore, Ronald Searle, and others, they created a *Poet and Painter* series of animated shorts. They worked experimentally with stereoscopy, the prototypical three-projection form of Cinerama, and sophisticated forms of film puppetry. They created the initial animated version of a Gilbert and Sullivan operetta, *Ruddigore,* and won an Academy Award nomination for *Automania 2000,* an animated vision of a future dominated by cars. Among their more commercial projects were the *Foo-Foo* and *Snip and Snap* cartoon series, produced for television, with the latter introducing paper-sculpture animals.

Batchelor and Halas's best-known work is *Animal Farm,* released in 1954 after three years in production. The film is of further note for its portrayal of animated animal characters who are seriously dramatic, rather than the sweet and lovable inhabitants of escapist children's fantasies. In Batchelor's *Variety* obituary, it was noted that *Animal Farm* was the film that "put Britain on the world animation map."

The scenario follows what happens when a group of animals assume operation of a farm upon successfully revolting against their brutal overseer. It is a sobering and distinctly political allegory, with a point of view that those who lead democratic uprisings against oppressors may become just as despotic once they gain power. Batchelor and Halas chose to caricature the heavies of the story—most especially the pigs who lead the revolt—while realistically representing the other animals.

In a bow to commercial considerations, Batchelor and Halas altered and brightened the story's original ending, going against Orwell's pessimistic view regarding the future of democratic movements. Nonetheless, their *Animal Farm* does put forth a jarringly unsentimental world view, one that differs markedly not just from other animated features but from most other 1950s' cinematic fare. This is most fully illustrated by the fate of Boxer, a courageous horse who ends up not emerging triumphant but being carted off to the glue factory.

In no way was Joy Batchelor the passive partner in her relationship with John Halas. She is most deserving of her place, alongside her husband and the likes of J. Stuart Blackton, Winsor McCay, Emile Cohl, Chuck Jones, Ub Iwerks, Dave and Max Fleischer, Walt Disney, and all the rest, as an innovative and influential animator.—ROB EDELMAN

Bauchens, Anne

American editor

Born *St. Louis, Missouri, 2 February 1882 (some sources say 1881).* ***Education*** *Studied drama with actor-director Hugh Ford; later studied dancing and gymnastics.* ***Career*** *Worked as a telephone operator at the* St. Louis Post-Dispatch; *moved to New York City with the intention of becoming a Broadway actress; worked as a secretary in a real-estate company; 1912—hired as a secretary to William C. de Mille; 1915—accompanied de Mille to Hollywood; 1918—worked as an assistant and script supervisor to Cecil B. DeMille and began editing DeMille-directed films; 1934—first of four Academy Award nominations for best film editing, for* Cleopatra; *worked for DeMille until his death, at which point she retired in 1959.* ***Awards*** *Academy Award, Best Film Editing, for* Northwest Mounted

Police, *1940; ACE (Achievement Award of the American Cinema Editors), for* The Greatest Show on Earth, *1952.* ***Died*** *In Woodland Hills, California, 7 May 1967.*

Films as Editor: 1918: *We Can't Have Everything* (C. B. DeMille) (co-d); *Till I Come Back to You* (C. B. DeMille); *The Squaw Man* (C. B. DeMille). **1919:** *Male and Female* (C. B. DeMille); *For Better, for Worse* (C. B. DeMille); *Don't Change Your Husband* (C. B. DeMille). **1920:** *Why Change Your Wife?* (C. B. DeMille); *Something to Think About* (C. B. DeMille). **1921:** *Forbidden Fruit* (C. B. DeMille); *Fool's Paradise* (C. B. DeMille); *The Affairs of Anatol* (C. B. DeMille). **1922:** *Saturday Night* (C. B. DeMille); *Manslaughter* (C. B. DeMille). **1923:** *The Ten Commandments* (C. B. DeMille); *Adam's Rib* (C. B. DeMille). **1924:** *Triumph* (C. B. DeMille); *Feet of Clay* (C. B. DeMille). **1925:** *The Road to Yesterday* (C. B. DeMille); *The Golden Bed* (C. B. DeMille). **1926:** *The Volga Boatman* (C. B. DeMille). **1927:** *The King of Kings* (C. B. DeMille) (co); *Chicago* (Urson). **1928:** *Ned McCobb's Daughter* (Cowan); *Craig's Wife* (W. C. de Mille). **1929:** *Noisy Neighbors* (Reisner); *The Godless Girl* (C. B. DeMille); *Dynamite* (C. B. DeMille). **1930:** *Lord Byron of Broadway* (Nigh and Beaumont); *This Mad World* (W. C. de Mille) (co); *Madam Satan* (*Madame Satan*) (C. B. DeMille). **1931:** *The Squaw Man* (*The White Man*) (C. B. DeMille); *Guilty Hands* (Van Dyke); *The Great Meadow* (Brabin) (co). **1932:** *The Sign of the Cross* (C. B. DeMille); *The Beast of the City* (*City Sentinel*) (Brabin); *The Wet Parade* (Fleming). **1933:** *Tonight Is Ours* (Walker); *Cradle Song* (Leisen); *This Day and Age* (C. B. DeMille). **1934:** *Four Frightened People* (C. B. DeMille); *Cleopatra* (C. B. DeMille); *Menace* (Murphy); *Mrs. Wiggs of the Cabbage Patch* (Taurog); *One Hour Late* (Murphy). **1935:** *The Crusades* (C. B. DeMille). **1936:** *The Plainsman* (C. B. DeMille). **1937:** *This Way Please* (Florey). **1938:** *Bulldog Drummond in Africa* (L. King); *Hunted Men* (*Crime Gives Orders*) (L. King); *Sons of the Legion* (Hogan); *The Buccaneer* (C. B. DeMille). **1939:** *Television Spy* (Dmytryk); *Union Pacific* (C. B. DeMille). **1940:** *Women without Names* (Florey); *Northwest Mounted Police* (C. B. DeMille). **1941:** *Land of Liberty.* **1942:** *Reap the Wild Wind* (C. B. DeMille); *Mrs. Wiggs of the Cabbage Patch* (Murphy). **1943:** *The Commandos Strike at Dawn* (Farrow). **1944:** *The Story of Dr. Wassell* (C. B. DeMille); *Tomorrow the World* (Fenton). **1945:** *Love Letters* (Dieterle). **1947:** *Unconquered* (C. B. DeMille). **1949:** *Samson and Delilah* (C. B. DeMille). **1952:** *The Greatest Show on Earth* (C. B. DeMille). **1956:** *The Ten Commandments* (C. B. DeMille).

"Some hundreds of millions of people, at least, have seen Anne Bauchens' name on the screen as film editor," wrote Cecil B. DeMille in his autobiography. "It has meant nothing to them—except to the few who know that gracious white-haired lady or who know, as we in the business know, how much a film's success or failure is due to the way it is edited."

While it was fitting for DeMille to cite Bauchens and praise her profession in his book (which was published posthumously in 1959), the fact remains that the status of film editors was considered lowly for decades. It was deemed not so much a profession as a craft—and this was one reason why women were allowed to become editors. The insignificance of editors is reflected by the listings in the section headed "Personnel of Studios—U.S. & Canada," published in the 1928 *Film Daily Year Book.* Cited under the heading Pathé-DeMille Studio are employees from President (Cecil B. DeMille) down through Technical Director (Ted Dickson, Julia Heron), Chief of Props (William House), Chief Electrician (William Whistler), Still Cameraman (Fred Archer) and Paymaster (I. F. Dawson). There is no listing for Editor, and no mention of Bauchens.

Nevertheless, Bauchens (whom DeMille called "Annie B.") is as much a movie industry pioneer as the man who steadily employed her for just under four decades. She had worked as secretary to DeMille's brother William C. de Mille, a director-playwright-screenwriter, before becoming C.B.'s assistant, script supervisor, and finally editor (or cutter, as they were called when she earned her first screen credit). DeMille's decision to train Bauchens resulted in her becoming one of the industry's first script supervisors and female editors. (Many sources credit Bauchens as the very first female editor; however, Viola Lawrence [also known as Viola Mallory], for one, predated her by two years.) She developed into a solid and strong-willed craftswoman, and a pivotal member of DeMille's moviemaking team. Her various Academy Award nominations, and her Oscar for editing *Northwest Mounted Police,* attest to her editing acumen.

On occasion, Bauchens worked on the films of other directors (including William Dieterle, John Farrow, Victor Fleming, and Mitchell Leisen). But she was almost exclusively employed by DeMille, editing every one of his films from *We Can't Have Everything* in 1918 all the way to his last, 1956's *The Ten Commandments,* made when she was in her mid-seventies. On *The Ten Commandments,* Bauchens was entrusted to retain the story's thrust and dramatic power while editing down to 12,000 feet the 100,000-plus feet of film shot by DeMille.

When a film was in its editing stage, Bauchens was known to work 16-plus hour days. And she was no shrinking violet who would acquiesce without comment to DeMille's demands; she would offer creative input, and even argue with her boss if she felt strongly about her point of view.

Later in his career, whenever DeMille signed a contract to direct a film, he claimed to have insisted on the inclusion of a clause stipulating that Bauchens would be hired as editor. "This is not sentiment, or at least not only sentiment," DeMille explained in his autobiography. "She is still the best film editor I know."—ROB EDELMAN and AUDREY E. KUPFERBERG

Bemberg, María Luisa

Argentinean director and writer

Born *Buenos Aires, 14 April 1922.* ***Family*** *Divorced, four children.* ***Career*** *Established Argentina's Teatro del Globo theater company, 1950s; wrote her first screenplay,* Chronicle of a Woman, *1971; moved to New York and attended the Strasberg Institute, late 1970s; returned to Argentina and directed her first feature,* Momentos, *1981.* ***Died*** *7 May 1995.*

Films as Director and Writer: 1981: *Momentos* (*Moments*). **1982:** *Señora de Nadie* (*Nobody's Woman*). **1984:** *Camila.* **1987:** *Miss Mary.* **1990:** *Yo, la peor de todas* (*I, the Worst of Them All*). **1993:** *De eso no se habla* (*I Don't Want to Talk about It*) (co-sc).

Films as Writer Only: 1971: *Cronica de una Señora* (*Chronicle of a Woman*) (de la Torre). **1972:** *El Mundo de la Mujer* (short). **1975:** *Triangulo de Cuatro* (Ayala). **1978:** *Juguetes* (short).

María Luisa Bemberg entered the filmmaking world only after leading an "asphyxiating and uneventful" life (her own words). Born into one of the wealthiest families in Buenos Aires, she entered the film industry at age 46, after her children had grown and she had obtained a divorce. Despite her belated entry into the profession, Bemberg was one of the most subversive and popular Argentinean directors. In addition, she was acclaimed in Europe and the States.

Bemberg's first (semiautobiographical) screenplay, *Chronicle of a Woman,* gained acclaim as a contemporary domestic drama, focusing on a regressive political system as it affected the female protagonist. Wishing to exert more control over her screenplays, but with no formal training, she spent three months as an actress at the Lee Strasberg Institute in New York and returned to Argentina to direct. In 1982 she caused a stir with *Nobody's Woman,* which featured a friendship between a gay man and a separated woman, challenging in one swoop the sacred notions of marriage, family, and the Church. Released on the day that Argentina invaded the Malvinas (Falklands), the film's impact was overshadowed somewhat by political events, but the crumbling state of the military regime (which had exerted so much censorship and control over the country's film industry that by the late 1970s only 12 films were being produced per year) ultimately helped the film succeed. Hugely popular with female audiences, it made a powerful and overtly feminist intervention into a culture crippled by its own repression and machismo.

After the overthrow of the military regime, and the humiliation of defeat in the Falklands War, Bemberg still saw much to come to terms with and much to struggle against in her national identity. She felt that her role as a filmmaker, and as a woman in a fiercely patriarchal society, was to explore political oppression as a backdrop and context for intense personal conflict. Her films dwell anxiously on Argentina's troubled past, and suggest that only by coming to terms with it can the nation—and the individual—put it to rest.

In 1984 Bemberg directed *Camila,* the first Argentinean film ever to break into the American market. Recipient of an Oscar nomination for best foreign-language film, it is all the more remarkable in that many other directors who wanted to film this true story of illicit love between a priest and a young woman in 1847 had previously been prevented from doing so by the government. By casting the priest as a beautiful object of desire and Camila (historically portrayed as the innocent victim) as the temptress, Bemberg created a passionate melodrama in which she consciously moved away from her earlier, hard-bitten domestic dramas into a more emotional, lyrical sphere. The historical basis of *Camila* offers a mythical arena in which to explore her very real contemporary political concerns.

Miss Mary continues to focus on these concerns, exploring English influence over the Argentinean upper class in the years before World War II through the crucial figure of the nanny. Politics and history are expressed through family structures, sexuality, and human behavior. Female characters, even the repressed and unsympathetic nanny (played by Julie Christie), are portrayed with understanding—although Miss Mary is a reactionary agent of oppression, the film works to explore *why* she is so—in an attempt to study the forces that could create her and the sick family for which she works.

Bemberg's strong sense of the melancholy is an integral part of her work, causing an uneasy tension in all her films: while all her works indict the reactionary political system, they are also impregnated with a tragic sensibility that presents events as somehow out of the protagonists' control. The bleak endings (in which transgressors are punished and traditional structures remain apparently intact) of Bemberg's films might seem pessimistic. But the very expression of transgression in the films—along with the tentative exploration of the disruptions that inevitably threaten an apparently monolithic system—by an individual who could so easily be a victim of that system (female, bourgeois, divorced), is not merely laudable, but remarkable.

Camila and *Miss Mary* remain exceptional films, the former a passionate and profound examination of a doomed romance and the latter a sumptuous, evocative account of a repressed woman. If both films are not overtly autobiographical, they do deal in very personal ways with Bemberg's own identity as a woman existing in a male-dominated society. A third, most impressive, feature from Bemberg is *I, the Worst of Them All,* set in Mexico during the 17th century. Her heroine is a nun possessed of a deep thirst for knowledge who becomes a writer. She also is destined to become the antagonist of her country's misogynist archbishop. Bemberg followed that up with *I Don't Want to Talk about It,* a fitfully interesting drama about two women—one a dwarf and the other her physically appealing but obnoxiously controlling mother—who become involved with an aging but still-suave bachelor (impeccably played by Marcello Mastroianni).

The unfortunate aspect of Bemberg's career is that it began so late in her life, thus robbing her of time to write and direct other films. Still, she was able to transcend the repressive political forces at work in her country and the constraints placed upon her because of her sex. Moreover, her films show her ability to discerningly philosophize about these aspects of existence in her country.—SAMANTHA COOK and ROB EDELMAN

Bigelow, Kathryn

American director and writer

Born *San Francisco, 1953.* ***Education*** *After high school, studied art at the San Francisco Art Institute, graduated in 1972; won scholarship to the Whitney Museum in New York, in 1972, where she switched to film studies; moved to Columbia Graduate Film School, studied under Milos Forman, graduated in 1979.* ***Family*** *Married the director James Cameron, 1989 (divorced 1991).* ***Career*** *Worked with radical NY British art collective, Art and Language; photographed by Robert Mapplethorpe; 1978—directed short graduation film,* The Set-Up; *1982—co-directed debut feature,* The Loveless; *1983—lectured in film at California Institute of the Arts; 1993—co-directed TV miniseries,* Wild Palms. ***Agent*** *Creative Artists Agency, 9830 Wilshire Boulevard, Beverly Hills, CA 90212, U.S.A.*

Kathryn Bigelow on the set of *Blue Steel.*

Films as Director: **1978:** *The Set-Up* (short). **1982:** *The Loveless* (*Breakdown*) (co-d with M. Montgomery, + co-sc). **1987:** *Near Dark* (+ co-sc). **1990:** *Blue Steel* (+ co-sc). **1991:** *Point Break*. **1995:** *Strange Days*. **1997:** *Ohio*.

Other Films: **1980:** *Union City* (Reichert) (script supervisor). **1983:** *Born in Flames* (Borden) (ro as newspaper editor). **1995:** *Undertow* (Red) (sc).

If nothing else, Kathryn Bigelow has lastingly scotched the assumption that the terms "woman director" and "action movie" are somehow incompatible. She herself has grown understandably weary of questioning along these lines, responding tersely that she does not see directing as "a gender-related job." But it is undeniable that no other female director has shown herself so adept at handling the intricate, kinetic ballets of stylized violence indispensable to the current Hollywood action genre. At the same time, Bigelow has never been content simply to adopt the language of the genre to produce routine, competent roller-coaster exercises; instead, she transforms it, through her own preoccupations and distinctive vision, into something wholly individual.

Not content with simply colonizing genre material, Bigelow bends and blends it into fertile new mutations. Her co-directed first feature, *The Loveless,* put a dreamy Sirkian spin on the standard biker movie. *Near Dark* is a vampire Western, *Blue Steel* laces a cop drama with horror film conventions, and *Point Break* crosses a surfing movie with a heist thriller. For *Strange Days* Bigelow mixed an even richer cocktail: science fiction plus love story plus political satire plus murder mystery. All, though vigorously paced and tinged with ironic humor, are shot through with Bigelow's dark romanticism; and all of them, by delving deeper into formal, psychological, and thematic patterns than mainstream Hollywood generally cares to, lift their material some way towards the condition of art-house fare.

The complexity of Bigelow's moral and aesthetic concerns has meant that, though her films are avowedly aimed at a wide audience ("I see film as an extraordinary social tool that could reach tremendous numbers of people"), as a filmmaker she remains a slightly marginal figure. It is a stance reflected in her choice of protagonists: for her, as two decades earlier for Arthur Penn, "a society has its mirror in its outcasts." The black-leather bikers of *The Loveless,* the nomadic vampire clan of *Near Dark,* the surfing bank robbers of *Point Break* are all seemingly defined by their opposition to conventional mores, yet they represent an alternative dark-side structure, respectable society's hidden needs and appetites made manifest. A local citizen, gazing fascinated at the bikers' remote otherness, fantasizes about being "them for a day or two"; while Bodhi, leader of the surfboard criminals, even claims their heist exploits are aimed at inspiring the downtrodden masses. "We show them that the human spirit is still alive!" he exults.

Bigelow's artistic training—prior to becoming a filmmaker, she worked, in her own words, as "a conceptual artist and poststructuralist theoretician"—shows in the stylized and highly textured look of her films. Her images are tactile, often sensual to the point of fetishism: in the opening shot of *Blue Steel,* light caresses the curves of a handgun in extreme close-up, transforming it into an abstract study of curves and shadows. This close-grained visual intensity becomes another means of subverting and reappropriating generic material, turning it to her own ends—just as her dark, at times nihilistic plots serve as prelude to soft-edged, sentimental denouements in which love conquers all. Not least of the contradictions that fuel her work is that, while not shying away from graphic incidents of violence against women—the rape scene in *Strange Days* sparked widespread outrage—her films generally feature women as the strongest, most focused characters, acting as mentors and protectors to the self-doubting males.

In her first three solo films Bigelow played these various tensions off against each other, deftly maintaining a balance between mainstream and "serious" audience appeal. With *Strange Days* the strategy came unstuck. Bigelow herself describes the film as "the ultimate Rorschach," an artifact lending itself to as many interpretations as it has viewers. Drawing its inspiration from an eclectic multiplicity of sources—Hawks, Hitchcock, and Ridley Scott; cyberpunk fiction; and Michael Powell's *Peeping Tom*—the film torments and probes us, forcing us to question not only what we are seeing but our own motives in wanting to watch it. In creating such an intricate, demanding collage, inviting simultaneous engagement on any number of levels, Bigelow may have outpaced her public. *Strange Days,* though raved over by many if not all reviewers, stalled badly at the box office and dented its director's career, setting back her long-cherished Joan of Arc project, *Company of Angels.* Only temporarily, it is to be hoped. Few current directors are better placed than Bigelow to give us a fresh take on the woman who most famously trespassed on sacrosanct male territory.—PHILIP KEMP

Bird, Antonia

British director

Born *1959.* ***Career*** *1974-76—ran away from home at age 16 to pursue a career as an actress, and worked for two years in a repertory theater; 1970s-80s—switched to directing, helming mostly new plays by Hanif Kureishi, Jim Cartwright, and Trevor Griffiths, and became Resident Director of the Royal Court Theatre in London, a post she held for six years; began directing television dramas, series, and miniseries, with her credits including* Submariners, *1983,* TECX, *1990,* The Men's Room, *1990,* Inspector Morse, *1991, and* A Masculine Ending, *1992; 1993—directed her first television feature,* Safe; *1994—directed her first theatrical feature,* Priest. ***Awards*** *Named best TV film, British Academy of Film and Television Arts, Charles Chaplin Prize for Best First Feature, Edinburgh International Film Festival, and Special Jury Prize (Silver Hitchcock), Dinard Film Festival, for* Safe, *1993; People's Choice Award, Toronto International Film Festival, and Michael Powell Award, Best British Feature, Edinburgh International Film Festival, FIPRESCI International Critics Prize, Berlin International Film Festival, Alexander Korda Award, Best British Feature Film, for* Priest, *1994.*

Films as Director: 1987: *Inspector Morse* (for TV). **1988:** *Thin Air* (for TV). **1990:** *TEXC* (for TV). **1991:** *The Men's Room* (for TV). **1992:** *A Masculine Ending* (for TV). **1993:** *Safe* (for TV). **1994:** *Priest.* **1995:** *Mad Love.* **1997:** *Face.* **1998:** *Without Apparent Motive.*

If women filmmakers are supposed to be preoccupied with making the kinds of movies that it is assumed women only want to see—touchy-feely dramas, for example, or romantic soapers, female bonding stories and explorations of budding female sexuality—then Antonia Bird is one woman filmmaker who has little interest in making "women's films." She is fully capable of directing action scenes, and one can see her helming a special effects-laden, mega-budget epic. Only that film would not focus solely on explosions and glitz. Amid the mayhem would be complex characters whose deep conflicts are explored within the framework of the scenario, and an unyielding point-of-view regarding human relations and the manner in which society attempts to control its unruly outsiders and nonconformists.

To date, Bird's best films have been jarring, hit-'em-in-the gut dramas featuring characters who are deeply troubled, or on-the-edge. After establishing herself as a director of British television action/detective dramas and miniseries, she won acclaim for *Safe,* a based-on-fact feature made for the BBC. *Safe* is an uncompromisingly (but necessarily) grim portrait of homelessness and hopelessness in contemporary London, centering on 48 hours in the lives of two young street people. Next came her debut theatrical release, the thoughtful—and controversial—*Priest.* The media hype surrounding the film was that it chronicled the predicament of a pastor who just so happens to be gay. In this regard, *Priest* is a powder keg of a movie. But the film is about so much more than a cleric who is a sexually active homosexual. It is a riveting drama that opens up for discussion a wealth of moral, ethical, and religious issues.

The scenario centers around the conflict of a young Catholic priest, Father Greg Pilkington (Linus Roache), who is assigned to a working-class parish in urban England. At first, Father Greg is presented as a holier-than-thou prig who preaches conventionally meaningless rhetoric at his parishioners without having any understanding of the realities of their lives. He declares that it is up to each person to make moral choices not to sin, as if the daily pressures one experiences have no bearing on individual thought or action. This generic "just say no" approach is frowned upon by Father Greg's outspoken fellow priest, Father Matthew. In turn, Father Greg chastises the liberal Father Matthew for sermonizing about social responsibility, not to mention breaking his vow of chastity by having a relationship with a woman. "We're not bloody social workers," Father Greg exclaims. He is convinced that a priest's sole responsibility begins and ends with offering his parishioners "moral guidance."

What qualifies a priest to offer moral guidance? What if that priest is himself in dire need of instruction and direction regarding his own conduct? These are but a few of the questions posed in *Priest.*

Furthermore, in the course of the story, a 14-year-old girl tells Father Greg at the confessional that she is being sexually abused by her father. The terrified child refuses to inform her mother, or any other adult. If he intercedes on her behalf, Father Greg will be breaking the confidentiality of the confessional. If he does not, the child's suffering will continue unabated.

While all this is transpiring, Father Greg himself is harboring a secret. One evening, he removes his collar, shows up in a gay bar and promptly hooks up with another man for a night of sex. He does not want to quit the priesthood, because he firmly believes that "God wanted me to be a priest." Here, another question arises, How can Father Greg reconcile his own actions with the content of his sermons, let alone the teachings of the church that homosexuality is a sin and a priest's celibacy is "a gift from God?"

The point of the film is that men of the cloth are human beings, with human needs. But Bird and her scriptwriter, Jimmy McGovern, stretch this view to the furthest degree. They put forth the premise that it is unnatural to sublimate those needs even if they entail a physical attraction to a person of the same sex. Herein lies the controversy surrounding the film.

Priest is an intricate film that astutely examines what it means to be truly religious, and how one goes about practicing that religion. Other concerns are the priestly relationship with Christ, and clergy who care more about the trappings of power than the teachings of Christ. *Priest* may be a film about ideas and issues, but it never, ever becomes pedantic or boring. Beyond the points it tackles, it works as a highly entertaining drama sprinkled with clever touches of dark humor.

The same may be said of *Face,* which deals with an entirely different set of characters. At its core, *Face* is a combination taut crime drama/allegory about political idealism gone awry in post-Thatcherite London. It tells the story of Ray (Robert Carlyle), a streetwise, working class antihero who once was a political activist but has since channeled his outside-the-system rage into a career as an armed robber.

On one level, *Face* is a conventional genre film as Ray and his mates plot out and pull off a major heist. Only their take is less than expected, and the scenario goes on to chart their subsequent violent falling-out. Nevertheless, unlike action dramas that spotlight in-your-face theatrics at the expense of relationships and emotion, Bird adds deep humanity to all the characters. Ray is the primary one, and he is a classic antihero: a lawbreaker who is sympathetically presented. He is a kindhearted soul who exists in a world in which all that counts is the size of the wad of cash in a man's pocket. Good and evil have become irrelevant, as are cops and robbers, politics, friendship, and even sex. Ray has come to believe that the world never will be changed by political activism. So he lives aimlessly, steals for a living and at one point tellingly declares, "I'm just chasin' money like everybody else."

By abandoning his ideals and becoming a thief, Ray has lost his soul. His most meaningful human connections are destroyed by greed, and the violence that results from an "I want it all" world view. He is a casualty of the British class system, just as Father Greg is a casualty of religious dogma.

Bird's direction of *Face* is seamless. The film is visually dazzling, with its loud and busy soundtrack paralleling the camera movement and editing. On strictly genre terms, *Face* is a first-rate thriller. Like *Priest,* however, it is radical in theme. Its intention is to make you think as well as entertain you. This becomes clear when Bird intersperses scenes of a gun battle between the thieves and the cops with shots of the police violently breaking up a political demonstration.

In between *Priest* and *Face,* Bird slumped with her American debut, *Mad Love,* a superficial teen-lovers-against-the-world road movie but with a twist: the heroine is "clinically depressed," and a typical Bird character in that she is an outsider who is misunderstood by her strict, controlling father. Despite this misstep, one can look toward to Bird's future film projects with anticipation—just so long as she remains on her home turf, and is not further lured by Hollywood. If they are anything like her best earlier work, they will be made with intelligence and compassion.—ROB EDELMAN

Booth, Margaret

American editor

Born *Los Angeles, 1898; sister of the actor Elmer Booth.* ***Career*** *Entered films as "joiner" for D. W. Griffith; then worked in Paramount Laboratories; 1921—assistant editor for Mayer (later MGM); 1939-68—supervising film editor, MGM.* ***Awards*** *Special Academy Award, 1977.*

Films as Editor: 1924: *Why Men Leave Home* (Stahl) (co); *Husbands and Lovers* (Stahl) (co). **1925:** *Fine Clothes* (Stahl) (co). **1926:** *Memory Lane* (Stahl); *The Gay Deceiver* (Stahl). **1927:** *The Enemy* (Niblo); *Bringing Up Father* (Conway); *Lovers?* (Stahl); *In Old Kentucky* (Stahl) (co). **1928:** *Telling the World* (Wood) (co); *The Mysterious Lady* (Niblo); *A Lady of Chance* (Leonard). **1929:** *The Bridge of San Luis Rey* (Brabin); *Wise Girls (Kempy)* (E. M. Hopper). **1930:** *The Rogue Song* (L. Barrymore);

Redemption (Niblo); *Strictly Unconventional* (Burton); *The Lady of Scandal* (*The High Road*) (Franklin); *A Lady's Morals* (*The Soul Kiss*; *Jenny Lind*) (Franklin). **1931:** *New Moon* (Conway); *The Southerner* (*The Prodigal*) (Pollard); *It's a Wise Child* (Leonard); *The Cuban Love Song* (Van Dyke); *Five and Ten* (*Daughter of Luxury*) (Leonard); *Susan Lenox, Her Fall and Rise* (*The Rise of Helga*) (Leonard). **1932:** *Lovers Courageous* (Leonard); *Smilin' Through* (Franklin); *Strange Interlude* (*Strange Interval*) (Leonard); *The Son-Daughter* (C. Brown). **1933:** *White Sister* (Fleming); *Peg o' My Heart* (Leonard); *Storm at Daybreak* (Boleslavsky); *Bombshell* (Fleming); *Dancing Lady* (Leonard). **1934:** *Riptide* (E. Goulding); *The Barretts of Wimpole Street* (Franklin). **1935:** *Reckless* (Fleming); *Mutiny on the Bounty* (Lloyd). **1936:** *Romeo and Juliet* (Cukor). **1937:** *Camille* (Cukor).

Films as Editorial Supervisor: **1937:** *A Yank at Oxford* (Conway). **1970:** *The Owl and the Pussycat* (Ross). **1972:** *Fat City* (J. Huston). **1973:** *The Way We Were* (Pollack). **1975:** *The Sunshine Boys* (Ross); *The Black Bird* (Giler) (uncredited); *Funny Lady* (Ross). **1976:** *Murder by Death* (Moore). **1977:** *The Goodbye Girl* (Ross). **1978:** *California Suite* (Ross). **1979:** *Chapter Two* (Moore) (+ assoc pr). **1980:** *Seems Like Old Times* (J. Sandrich) (+ assoc pr). **1982:** *Annie* (J. Huston).

Other Films: **1963:** *The V.I.P.s* (Asquith) (prod adviser). **1978:** *The Cheap Detective* (Moore) (assoc pr). **1982:** *The Toy* (R. Donner) (assoc pr). **1985:** *The Slugger's Wife* (Ashby) (exec pr).

Margaret Booth was one of the great film editors in Hollywood history. She started out as a patcher (film joiner) for D. W. Griffith and ended her career some 60 years later as one of the true insiders at MGM. The classic Hollywood film is surely defined by its characteristics of editing. Booth was one of the innovators who shepherded the classic Hollywood editing style through the coming of sound, color, and wide-screen.

Like many of her contemporaries, Booth joined the American film industry without any formal training. She took her first job with D. W. Griffith's company right out of high school. She then moved to Famous Players and the Mayer studios. By the early 1930s she ranked as one of the top editors at MGM. In 1939 she was appointed MGM's supervising film editor, a position she held until the studio collapsed in 1968.

Booth was, if anything, a survivor. Once she left MGM, she began to work as a freelance editor on such 1970s blockbusters as *The Way We Were, The Sunshine Boys,* and *Murder by Death.* She was one of those rare individuals whose career encompassed the history of Hollywood from its beginnings through the studio years into the age of television.

There have been few opportunities for women behind the camera in Hollywood. "Film editing," noted the *New York Times* in 1936, "is one of the few important functions in a studio in which women play a substantial part." And at MGM Booth was able to advance in the ranks so that she held a position of substantial creative power in the 1930s and 1940s. Her patron was Louis B. Mayer himself, for Booth had worked as a secretary with the old Mayer studio before it ever merged into MGM.

Booth's career neatly divides into two parts. During the first, up through her appointment as head of editing at MGM, she cut many a noted film. These include a number of MGM classics: *The Barretts of Wimpole Street, Romeo and Juliet,* and *Camille.* Somewhat surprisingly for one with so much industry power and influence, Booth received only one Academy Award nomination for film editing. This was for the 1935 version of *Mutiny on the Bounty.* She did not win the award. Nevertheless, it should be noted that Booth did get an honorary Oscar in 1977 to denote "62 years of exceptionally distinguished service to the motion picture industry as film editor."

In the second half of her career Margaret Booth worked strictly as an editing supervisor. According to her, she did no actual editing for 30 years. But she assigned those who did, and approved their work and performance. As such she held immense power and continued the tradition of a style of classic editing for which Hollywood films of the studio years have now become famous. All filmmakers from the late 1930s through the late 1960s who worked at MGM had, in the end, to go through Booth to have the final editing of sound and image approved. Thus for three decades she represented one of the truly important but relatively unknown powers in the history of Hollywood filmmaking.—DOUGLAS GOMERY

Borden, Lizzie

American director

Born *Linda Elizabeth Borden in Detroit, Michigan, 3 February 1950.* ***Education*** *Studied painting at Wellesley College, Massachusetts, received degree in fine arts.* ***Career*** *1976—made first film* Regrouping; *formed production company, Alternate Current; 1983—directed widely discussed feature film* Born in Flames; *1986—second feature film* Working Girls; *from 1992—director of Hollywood feature films and TV anthologies.*

Films as Director: 1976: *Regrouping.* **1983:** *Born in Flames* (+ sc, ph). **1986:** *Working Girls* (+ pr, sc, ed). **1988:** *Monsters* (for TV). **1992:** *Inside Out* (for TV); *Love Crimes* (+ co-pr). **1994:** "Let's Talk about Sex" ep. of *Erotique* (for TV) (+ co-sc). **1995:** "Juarez" ep. of *Red Shoe Diaries* (for TV).

Lizzie Borden emerged on the film scene as part of the new generation of American independent women filmmakers in the 1970s and early 1980s, when she earned a reputation for making feminist films that offer unflinching examinations of a range of women's issues.

After writing art criticism for *Artforum* which she did after graduation from university, Borden decided she wanted to pursue a career as a filmmaker. She determined to teach herself filmmaking and editing. In 1976 she made a film titled *Regrouping,* and then founded her own production company, Alternate Current. Subsequently, she started planning her first feature film, the radical science-fiction masterpiece *Born in Flames,* which exploded on the feminist film scene in 1983. Widely praised by critics, it garnered Borden considerable publicity despite a low budget—about $30,000. The film was much discussed in feminist circles and was much appreciated given the increasing political conservatism of the early Reagan era.

Set in a postapocalyptic near-future in a place much like lower Manhattan, *Born in Flames* is a radical feminist allegory about sexism, racism, classism, and the media's complicity in maintaining them. Likewise, it disputes the utopian notion that a single sweeping social revolution will entirely eliminate oppression. It portrays the process by which a seemingly successful cultural revolution only ten years old begins to unravel and return to the old patterns of male dominance and the marginalization of women and their issues. In response, several apparently disparate groups of women who refuse to "grin and bear" it—including blacks, Latinas, lesbians, intellectuals, activists, and punks, among others—build a coalition by acknowledging rather than ignoring the differences, in order to battle the forces that aim to keep them divided. The film has a distinctively feminist perspective, but Borden does not conceive of her audience as homogeneous, so *Born in Flames* provides a range of possible identifications. In part, the film reflects upon the invisibility of black women and lesbians in films produced by white women, and in feminism in general. Borden developed the script in close collaboration with the performers who played the main characters, so the script ultimately combined her original plan with the actors' ideas. The film has a challenging, unconventional form that is characterized by a fragmented narrative, quick editing, a documentary look with a science-fiction sensibility, a fast-paced music track, and an incoherence between soundtrack and screen. Borden also refused to visually objectify women, thus asking her viewers to question the more familiar cinematic representations of women. Her purported aim was to question the characteristics of narrative in general, as well as those of race and class. Since its release, *Born in Flames* has become a part of the feminist independent film canon; however, some feminists have objected to its utopian suggestion that women can work together despite disparate racial and class positions.

Lizzie Borden

Borden's next independent feature film, *Working Girls,* attracted even more attention for its distinctly feminist perspective, and because its simpler narrative treated a more familiar subject—prostitution. It offers a fascinating and occasionally amusing account of a day in the lives of ten prostitutes who work in a nondescript, middle-class Manhattan brothel that serves a procession of male clients. Borden's best-known film, it offers a trenchant portrayal of the prostitutes' motivations for working, the details of their workaday routine, as well as telling glimpses of the johns. Along with its striking look at a much-mythologized world—especially by Hollywood—it refreshingly demystifies prostitution and denies the male fantasy of mutual ecstasy. Inspired by her association with COYOTE, the coalition of feminist prostitutes working to legalize prostitution, Borden depicts prostitution as a viable economic alternative for women who are marginalized in the labor market. Prior to making *Working Girls,* Borden eschewed traditional narrative filmmaking. Yet, although this film has a more conventional organization, it retains her commitment to feminism and a willingness to treat controversial women's issues.

Throughout her film career, sparse though it has been, Borden has retained a commitment to making films that are entertaining, even if the larger purpose seems to be audience edification or the confrontation of passive viewers, as in her early career. Yet feminist critics who praised her choice to avoid objectifying women's bodies in her first two features, chastised her for featuring them in *Love Crimes,* and accused her of losing her personal vision to work in mainstream Hollywood. An erotic thriller, it tells the story of a female district attorney who is enticed into sadomasochistic sex games with a photographer-murderer who "enlightens" her about her sexual desires. The film's abrupt ending is due to the studio's refusal to use Borden's original ending, and their substitution of a new one. Since then, she has been directing episodes of soft-core series for cable television.—CYNTHIA FELANDO

Box, Betty E.

British producer

Born *Beckenham, Kent, 25 September 1920; sister of the writer/producer Sydney Box.* ***Family*** *Married second husband, producer Peter Rogers, 1949.* ***Career*** *Trained as a commercial artist; began as tea girl at Gainsborough Studios, worked at Verity Films, and moved back to Gainsborough as successful producer.* ***Awards*** *British Women in Films Achievement Award, 1992. Commander, Order of the British Empire, 1958.* ***Died*** *15 January 1999.*

Films as Producer: 1945: *The Seventh Veil* (Bennett) (assoc). **1946:** *The Years Between* (Bennett) (assoc). **1947:** *Dear Murderer* (Crabtree); *When the Bough Breaks* (Huntington). **1948:** *Miranda* (Annakin); *The Blind Goddess* (French); *Vote for Huggett* (Annakin); *Here Come the Huggetts* (Annakin). **1949:** *Don't Ever Leave Me* (Crabtree); *The Huggetts Abroad* (Annakin); *Marry Me!* (Fisher); *It's Not Cricket* (Roome and Rich). **1950:** *So Long at the Fair* (Fisher and Darnborough); *The Clouded Yellow* (Thomas). **1951:** *Appointment with Venus* (*Island Rescue*) (Thomas). **1952:** *The Venetian Bird* (*The Assassin*) (Thomas). **1953:** *A Day to Remember* (Thomas). **1954:** *Doctor in the House* (Thomas); *Mad about Men* (Thomas). **1955:** *Doctor at Sea* (Thomas). **1956:** *Checkpoint* (Thomas); *Iron Petticoat* (Thomas). **1957:** *Doctor at Large* (Thomas). **1958:** *Campbell's Kingdom* (Thomas); *A Tale of Two Cities* (Thomas); *The Wind Cannot Read* (Thomas). **1959:** *The 39 Steps* (Thomas); *Upstairs and Downstairs* (Thomas). **1960:** *Conspiracy of Hearts* (Thomas); *Doctor in Love* (Thomas). **1961:** *No Love for Johnnie* (Thomas); *No, My Darling Daughter* (Thomas); *A Pair of Briefs* (Thomas). **1962:** *The Wild and the Willing* (*Young and Willing*) (Thomas). **1963:** *Doctor in Distress* (Thomas). **1964:** *Hot Enough for June* (*Agent 8¾*) (Thomas). **1965:** *The High Bright Sun* (*McGuire, Go Home!*) (Thomas). **1966:** *Deadlier than the Male* (Thomas); *Doctor in Clover* (*Carnaby, M.D.*) (Thomas). **1968:** *Nobody Runs Forever* (*The High Commissioner*) (Thomas). **1969:** *Some Girls Do* (Thomas). **1970:** *Doctor in Trouble* (Thomas); *Percy* (Thomas). **1972:** *The Love Ban* (*It's a 2′ 6″ above the Ground World*) (Thomas). **1974:** *It's Not the Size that Counts* (*Percy's Progress*) (Thomas).

Betty Box and her work are at the center of a dynastic structure in British postwar cinema that is as complex as anything in the Hollywood system. Sister of Sydney Box, and sister-in-law of Muriel Box, she gained her first experience of film production working for Sydney's companies in the 1940s; she then embarked on a collaboration with director Ralph Thomas which lasted more than 20 years, while her husband, Peter Rogers, formed an equally prolific producer/director association with Ralph's brother, Gerald. In contrast to the relentless homogeneity of the Rogers/Thomas output (some low-budget action films, and then the *Carry On* series), the work of Box/Thomas is striking in its generic variety, moving easily between comedy, thriller, and melodrama. The films are, however, consistent in the level of their aim—the middlebrow popular domestic audience—and in the correspondingly unadventurous cinematic strategies they adopt.

Box and Thomas operated as a production team within the Rank Organisation, and their films, more than anyone else's, typify the style of Rank's product from the early 1950s onward. At the end of World War II, Rank had expanded boldly, confident of finding a place in the American market for high-quality British films, but the industry's postwar financial crisis forced a change in policy. Ambitious independents such as Powell and Pressburger, David Lean, and Launder and Gilliat went to work elsewhere, and more pragmatic operators such as Box and Thomas moved in. Their first big success was *Doctor in the House* in 1954, a comedy about medical trainees which led to several sequels and established a pattern of casting which served them well in other films too: its stars, Dirk Bogarde and Kenneth More, were supported by a multitude of British character actors each doing their economical, predictable bit. Bogarde and More belonged to the last generation of actors to get the old-fashioned star buildup in the British market, and Box and Thomas assiduously built many films around them and contemporaries such as Michael Craig: More starred in their lightweight remake of *The 39 Steps,* and Bogarde alternated the *Doctor* sequels with roles as adventurer (*Campbell's Kingdom*) and romantic hero (*The Wind Cannot Read*).

Betty E. Box

In their prolific 1950s output, Box and Thomas played the domestic market with energy and expertise; when that market changed in the 1960s they adapted by putting more sex in the comedies and more violence in the adventure films, and also attempting some New Wave subjects such as politics (*No Love for Johnnie*) and youth (*The Wild and the Willing*), but the days of their kind of British cinema, based on a modest continuity of production, were clearly numbered. They did, however, have a late one-off commercial success with *Percy,* the story of a penis transplant.

Throughout the long and evidently harmonious partnership with Ralph Thomas, Betty Box received at least equal attention in the press—Miss Box-Office was a label that stuck. This was partly due to the novelty value of a high-profile woman filmmaker operating in a male-dominated industry, but it also reflected her creative role as producer. It would be hard to do much with an auteurist study of Ralph Thomas, in terms of directorial signature, nor (one feels) would he have been interested in such an approach. These are producer's films, packages created by careful planning, casting, budgeting, scheduling, and marketing. Box brought to her work for Rank the knowledge of all sides of the business, and the rigorous financial discipline that she had learned in working for her brother Sydney, latterly at Gainsborough; such productions as *The Seventh Veil* (1945) had also enhanced her understanding of how to reach the female audience. Her Rank films, typically of the decade, were lacking in strong female stars (though she was proud of introducing a youthful Bardot in *Doctor at Sea*) but they appealed consistently to women through their artful presentation of heroes in need of motherly attention: Dirk Bogarde's romantic image and box-office status were built up largely through these films. Along with Michael Balcon at Ealing, Betty Box can be called the dominant British feature producer of the early postwar years.—CHARLES BARR

Box, Muriel

British writer and director

Born *Violette Muriel Baker in Tolworth, Surrey, 22 September 1905.* ***Family*** *Married 1) the writer/producer Sydney Box, 1935 (divorced 1969); 2) Lord Gardiner, 1970.* ***Career*** *1920s-30s—typist, continuity girl, and script editor at British Instructional Films, and at Elstree with Michael Powell, and at Gaumont; directed shorts and documentaries for*

Muriel Box with Thomas Mitchell

Sydney Box's production company, Verity Films; 1946—became head of Script Department at Gainsborough Studios, collaborated with Sydney Box writing and directing numerous films; 1952—directed first solo feature, The Happy Family; *mid-1960s—retired from filmmaking and set up publishing house, Femina Books, with the novelist Vera Brittain.* ***Awards*** *Academy Award, for* The Seventh Veil, *1945.* ***Died*** *In London, 18 May 1991.*

Films as Writer with Sydney Box: **1935:** *Alibi Inn* (Tennyson). **1945:** *The Seventh Veil* (Bennett); *29 Acacia Avenue* (*Facts of Love*) (Cass). **1946:** *The Years Between* (Bennett); *The Girl in a Million* (Searle). **1947:** *The Brothers* (Macdonald); *Daybreak* (Bennett); *Dear Murderer* (Crabtree) (+ pr); *Holiday Camp* (Annakin); *The Man Within* (*The Smugglers*) (Knowles) (+ pr); *When the Bough Breaks* (Huntington). **1948:** *The Blind Goddess* (French); *Easy Money* (Knowles); *Portrait from Life* (*The Girl in the Painting*) (Fisher); *Here Come the Huggetts* (Annakin). **1949:** *Christopher Columbus* (D. Macdonald). **1950:** *So Long at the Fair* (Fisher and Darnborough); *The Astonished Heart* (Fisher and Darnborough) (sole writer); *Good Time Girl* (D. Macdonald).

Films as Writer and Director: **1949:** *The Lost People* (*Cockpit*) (Knowles) (additional scenes only). **1952:** *The Happy Family* (*Mr. Lord Says No!*). **1953:** *Street Corner* (*Both Sides of the Law*; *The Gentle Arm*; *The Policewoman*). **1957:** *The Passionate Stranger* (*A Novel Affair*). **1958:** *The Truth about Women* (+ pr).

Films as Director: **1953:** *A Prince for Cynthia.* **1955:** *The Beachcomber.* **1956:** *To Dorothy a Son* (*Cash on Delivery*); *Simon and Laura*; *Eyewitness.* **1959:** *This Other Eden* (+ co-pr); *Subway in the Sky.* **1960:** *Too Young to Love*; *The Piper's Tune.* **1964:** *Rattle of a Simple Man.*

Muriel Box was a true craftswoman of the cinema, as director as well as screenwriter. Her prolific output in both roles spanned more than 30 years: the three decades that saw the rise and fall of British cinema production through the documentary movement of the 1930s, the boom years of war and its aftermath, the precarious continuity of the 1950s, then decline in the 1960s.

Box's apprenticeship as a writer was served as a playwright. Always a popular storyteller rather than an "artist," she aimed her plays mainly at repertory groups and amateur dramatic societies. She became a sought-after writer of plays for all-women casts—many are still performed today—which strikingly anticipated her future work (in partnership with her first husband, Sydney Box) for Gainsborough Studios, with its dominant roles for women stars and its strong appeal to female audiences.

Although she had worked in the film industry for many years, it was the outbreak of war in 1939 which offered Muriel (like many other women) the chance to progress. It was for Verity Films—the production company Sydney had formed—that Muriel had her first solo credits both as a writer (the road safety film *A Ride with Uncle Joe,* commissioned by the Ministry of Information), and as a director (the short documentary on *The English Inn,* commissioned by the British Council).

In the boom conditions of postwar cinema the Box partnership moved into independent feature production and almost immediately had a huge popular and critical success with *The Seventh Veil,* for which they won a joint screenwriting Oscar. Gainsborough Studios signed them up, Sydney as head of production and Muriel as script editor.

Gainsborough had become a household name during World War II for their vigorous melodramas, especially popular with women, who could identify with their romantic often transgressive heroines, motivated by romantic and sexual desire. Muriel supervised, and often herself wrote, a series of woman-centered postwar melodramas both historical/costume (such as *Jassy*) and contemporary (for example, *Good Time Girl*), films which contrast starkly with the more tasteful middle-class products of, for example, Ealing Studios under Michael Balcon.

Significantly, it was Balcon who had turned her down as a director, declaring that a woman "didn't have the strength" to handle a film unit. During the 1950s and early 1960s she was to prove him spectacularly wrong, directing 14 features across a wide range of mainstream genres. Many of these she also wrote herself (including the typically unpretentious but carefully crafted drama *Street Corner* about female police officers) or adapted from short stories and plays; one example of the latter, *Simon and Laura,* a comedy about live television production, has a wit and sharpness not since rivaled by films on similar themes.

It was another adaptation, *Rattle of a Simple Man,* which effectively ended Box's career as a director in 1964. Perceived at the time as a "sex comedy" and poorly received, this story of an encounter between prostitute and client can be seen today as a rather audacious film, ahead of its time in its treatment of the ideology of the male group and its crude sexism. Indeed the same kind of rereading can be applied to many of Box's films, as a new generation of feminist critics has enthusiastically discovered.

Along with many other filmmakers of her generation, Muriel Box's career in cinema ended in the 1960s. Her activities as a writer and a feminist, however, continued undiminished. She began to write novels; the first to be published was *The Big Switch,* which had a strong feminist theme. In 1966 she co-founded Britain's first feminist press, Femina Books, and edited the first book to be published under its imprint—*The Trial of Marie Stopes.*—CAROLINE MERZ

Brackett, Leigh

American writer

Born *Leigh Douglass Brackett in Los Angeles, 7 December 1915.* ***Family*** *Married the writer Edmond Hamilton, 1946 (died 1977).* ***Career*** *Freelance writer; first novel published,* No Good from a Corpse, *1944; 1945—first film as writer,* The Vampire's Ghost; *1946—first of several films for Howard Hawks,* The Big Sleep; *also worked for TV series* Checkmate, Suspense, *and* Alfred Hitchcock Presents. ***Died*** *In Lancaster, California, 18 March 1978.*

Films as Writer: 1945: *The Vampire's Ghost* (Selander). **1946:** *The Big Sleep* (Hawks) (co); *Crime Doctor's Man Hunt* (Castle). **1959:** *Rio Bravo* (Hawks). **1961:** *Gold of the Seven Saints* (G. Douglas). **1962:** *Hatari!* (Hawks); *13 West Street* (*The Tiger among Us*) (Leacock) (st only). **1967:** *El Dorado* (Hawks). **1970:** *Rio Lobo* (Hawks). **1973:** *The Long Goodbye* (Altman). **1980:** *The Empire Strikes Back* (Kershner) (co).

Upon being asked about Leigh Brackett's work on *El Dorado* in the book *Hawks on Hawks,* director Howard Hawks replied: "She wrote that like a man. She writes good." Therein lies not only Hawks's opinion of Brackett but also his screen heroes' reaction to a person who comes through in a tight spot. "You were good back there" (*The Big Sleep*), "You were good in there tonight" (*Rio Bravo*), were the best compliments that a Hawks character could pay. And Brackett did come through for Hawks, writing screenplays for five of his films, beginning with *The Big Sleep.*

By the time that Brackett began working with Hawks, the director already had a definite style. The "Hawksian woman" as she is now known—a strong-willed character who gambles, drinks, can use a gun, and still remains feminine—had made appearances in previous films. Hawks normally shaped his action around two or more men and their reaction to pressure and to the Hawksian woman. Brackett's contribution as one of Hawks's screenwriters was to hone the male-female relationships, and to connect scenes and action that Hawks gave her. Hawks preferred his writers to be present on the set, and there was constant rewriting as dialogue was changed and then changed again. During their period together, Brackett and Hawks produced ensemble films in which the hero is helped by a group of oddball characters who surround him and aid him in a life or death situation. In four of the five films they did together (*Rio Bravo, Hatari!, El Dorado, Rio Lobo*), John Wayne was that hero.

Brackett believed, as Hawks did, that the usual Hollywood leading ladies were not very strong or interesting, and the Hawksian woman was a necessary character in their films. The screenwriter and the director also agreed that you had to depend on yourself because others can fail you in any situation—especially love. And while the characters of their films reject help in a tight situation, they receive it from unexpected places. On the subject of love, the characters usually have an unlucky past record with someone who left them, and they are wary of new relationships. Both the hero and the heroine tentatively approach a possible relationship by sarcastic bantering back and forth, testing the waters, aware that it might not last. Even the first kiss is a test: "I'm glad we tried it a second time. It's better when two people do it," Feathers tells Chance in *Rio Bravo*. But once started, the relationship is strong.

Without Hawks, Brackett wrote the script for *The Long Goodbye,* directed by Robert Altman and, like *The Big Sleep,* based on a Raymond Chandler story. This script, however, was more brutal than anything that Brackett wrote for Hawks, and it portrayed a modern-day Marlowe who, like the 1940s detective, has definite values of honor and trust and plays down danger with a flippant attitude. This Marlowe reacts to events with "O.K. with me," but, unlike his 1940s counterpart, he is truly alone. He is betrayed by everyone, including his cat, and in the end he shoots a friend, Terry, who has deceived him. Brackett admitted that she changed the ending of the Chandler story because she felt Marlowe could not walk away from such a betrayal. Later, in *Take One,* she explained, in typically graphic terms, "It seemed that the only satisfactory ending was for the cruelly diddled Marlowe to blow Terry's guts out . . . something the old Marlowe would never have done."

Shortly before she died Brackett wrote a draft for *The Empire Strikes Back.* Concerned for the most part with Luke Skywalker's battle against evil (in others and in himself), the film has Brackett touches—most obviously the strong sarcastic Leia, the daring Han Solo, and their relationship. When Solo attempts to kiss her, Leia says, "Being held by you isn't quite enough to get me excited." But the attraction was there, and like Vivian and Marlowe, and Feathers and Chance, it is only a matter of time.—ALEXA L. FOREMAN

Breien, Anja

Norwegian director

Born *Oslo, 12 July 1940.* ***Education*** *Studied filmmaking in Paris at the IDHEC film school.* ***Career*** *1966—worked as a script girl and assistant to Henning Carlsen; 1967—*

Anja Breien

began making short films and documentaries; 1971—directed her first feature, Rape—The Anders Case; *1972—directed the Norwegian television documentaries* Herbergisterne, *about alcoholism, and* Mine soskend Goddad, *1973, about artist Arne Bendik Sjur; 1975—won international success with* Hustruer; *has also directed for the Norwegian stage.* ***Awards*** *Best Short Film, Oberhausen Film Festival, for* 17 May, a Film about Rituals, *1969; Special Mention, Cannes Film Festival, for* Next of Kin, *1979; Special Mention, Venice Film Festival, for* The Witch Hunt, *1981; Amanda (Norwegian Academy Award), Best Film, for* Wives: 10 Years After, *1985.* ***Address*** *Mellbydalen 8, 0287 Oslo, Norway.*

Films as Director: 1967: *Jostedalsrypa* (short). **1969:** *Anskiter* (*Faces*) (short); *17, maj—en film om ritualer* (*17 May, a Film about Rituals*) (short). **1971:** *Voldtekt-Tilfellet Anders* (*Rape—The Anders Case*). **1975:** *Hustruer* (*Wives*) (+ sc). **1977:** *Den Allvarsamma leken* (*The Serious Game*; *Games of Love and Loneliness*) (+ co-sc). **1979:** *Arven* (*Next of Kin*; *L'Heritage*) (+ co-sc). **1981:** *Forfølgelsen* (*The Witch Hunt*) (+ sc). **1985:** *Papirfuglen* (*Pappersdraken*; *Paper Bird*) (+ sc); *Hustruer—10 år etter* (*Wives: 10 Years After*) (+ co-sc). **1990:** *Smykketyven* (*Twice upon a Time*) (+ co-sc). **1996:** *Hustruer III* (*Wives III*) (+ co-sc).

Other Films: 1966: *Sult* (*Hunger*; *Svält*) (Carlsen) (continuity girl). **1994:** *Trollsyn* (*Second Sight*) (Solum) (sc).

In England over the course of three decades, Michael Apted produced a series of sociological documentaries, titled *7 Up, 14 Up, 21 Up, 28 Up,* and *35 Up,* in which he filmed a group of individuals, from all British classes, beginning in 1963 and starting at age seven. Then he reappeared every seven years to find out how they had matured, and if their youthful aspirations had been met as they reached adulthood.

In Norway, Anja Breien created an equally unique and absorbing series with her fictional *Wives* trilogy: three films, the first directed in 1975 with each follow-up coming a decade later, which chronicle the lives of a trio of women played by the same actresses: Anne Marie Ottersen (cast as Mie); Katja Medboe (playing Kaja); and Froydis Armand (in the role of Heidrun). While Breien is credited as the screenwriter or co-screenwriter of each film, she worked in conjunction with the actresses to create characterizations and dialogue. The result is a revealing look at the evolution of contemporary middle-class women and their enduring friendship.

The first installment is titled, simply, *Wives.* Its scenario is inspired by *Husbands,* the 1970 John Cassavetes feature which charts the response of three middle-aged suburbanites to the sudden death of their best friend; *Wives* also predates John Sayles's *The Return of the Secaucus Seven,* Lawrence Kasdan's *The Big Chill* and Anne-Claire Poirier's *Over Forty* as a generational reunion movie. The women once were close friends, but had not seen each other in years. Now, all are married, with two already mothers and the third pregnant. They come together after a school reunion and spend three days in each other's company where they recollect old times and, as they are picked up by a pair of men, explore the choice of marital fidelity versus infidelity.

More to the point, the women collectively rekindle a girlish spirit and sense of freedom they had not experienced in ages. They do express some desperation over and disappointment with the course of their present lives; still, *Wives* primarily is a vigorous, clever, and quick-witted story of female friendship, and the bond that exists across the years among friends both male and female, if that friendship is predicated on emotional honesty.

In *Wives: 10 Years After,* the same three characters first meet on Christmas Eve, and then spend several days sharing their company and updating each other (and the audience) on the progress of their lives—especially the children they are raising, and the men to whom they are married (contrasted to those they really want to be with). In this installment, the characters must deal with the reality that time is passing. They are becoming even further separated from their girlish pasts as they are fast approaching 40—and middle age.

In *Wives III,* the women reunite for Kaja's surprise birthday party, an event that symbolizes the further passage of time. Here, the characters are well-ensconced in middle age, but their fantasies and dreams are just as distinctly portrayed. Their lives may be disparate, but the feelings, thoughts, tears, and smiles they share attest to the substance of their lifelong bond. Indeed, the camaraderie between Mie, Kaja and Heidrun is extra-special, and transcends their individual relationships with their husbands.

In countless movies, an earlier photograph of an actor may be placed on a wall or desk to add authenticity to a setting. But because of the unique structure of the *Wives* trilogy, and the fact that the same actresses are cast in each film, Breien is able to include flashbacks, made up of footage from the previous films. Thus, the audience sees the characters literally age before their eyes—the same feature which makes Apted's documentaries so riveting.

Beyond the *Wives* trilogy, Breien has worked successfully in a variety of genres. Her debut feature, *Rape—The Anders Case,* is a jarring black-and-white chronicle of a rape case told from the point of view of the accused. *The Serious Game,* a project Breien took over when its original director, Per Blom, became ill, is the story of a newspaperman whose rigidity prevents him from marrying his true love. *Next of Kin* is a comedy about the manner in which various family members react upon inheriting immense wealth. *The Witch Hunt,* set in the 17th century, chronicles the plight of a woman whose independent spirit and open sexuality results in her being prosecuted (and eventually beheaded) as a witch. *Paper Bird* may be a thriller about a woman who attempts to solve the mystery surrounding the death of her father, but it primarily explores the personality of the protagonist. *Twice upon a Time* is the story of a middle-aged Casanova who has lost his touch with women; its point of view is that relations between the sexes must be predicated on emotional commitment, rather than sexual conquest.

The films of Anja Breien are collectively ambitious and provocative, as well as intensely personal—particularly when they spotlight the intimate connections between individuals, and the absolute need for (as well as benefits of) integrity in interpersonal relationships.—ROB EDELMAN

Brückner, Jutta

German director

Born *Düsseldorf, Germany, 25 June 1941.* ***Education*** *Studied political science, philosophy, and history in Berlin, Paris, and Munich, granted a Ph.D. in 1973.* ***Career*** *1976—wrote film scripts,* Coup de grâce, *with Margarethe von Trotta, directed by Volker Schlöndorff, and* A Woman with Responsibility *for TV, directed by Ula Stöckl, 1977; has also written essays in film theory, film reviews, and radio plays; has been a professor at the* Hochschule der Künste, *in Berlin.* ***Address*** *Brückner Filmproduktion, Goltzstrasse 13A, 10781 Berlin, Germany.*

Films as Director: 1975: *Tue recht und scheue niemand* (*Do Right and Fear No-one*). **1977:** *Ein ganz und gar verwahrlostes Mädchen* (*A Thoroughly Demoralized Girl: A Day in the Life of Rita Rischak*).

1979: *Hungerjahre* (*Years of Hunger*). **1980:** *Laufen lernen* (*Learning to Run*). **1982:** "Luftwurzeln" ep. of *Die Erbtöchter* (*The Daughter's Inheritance* (six-part omnibus co-d with Stöckl and Sanders-Brahms). **1984:** *Kolossale Liebe* (*Colossal Love*). **1986:** *Ein Blick—und die Liebe bricht aus* (*One Glance, and Love Breaks Out*).

Films as Writer: 1976: *Der Fangschuss* (*Coup de grâce*) (Schlöndorff) (co). **1977:** *Eine Frau mit Verantwortung* (*A Woman with Responsibility*) (Stöckl—for TV).

Jutta Brückner's career as a filmmaker coincided with the strongest historical moments of feminism in West Germany. Feminism flourished in West Germany starting in the mid-1970s, provoked by a variety of historical factors—the failure of the student movement to enact change, the rise of terrorism, and the general collapse of collectivity and consensus among the German left. These factors—coupled with the rise of international feminism—stimulated women to strike out on their own; they were bound by their rejection of violent solutions to political problems, as well as their disapproval of dogmatic, hard-line Marxism. The other major crucible for Brückner was her adolescence in postwar Germany, as part of a generation of *trümmerkinden,* raised amidst the ruins left by Allied bombings. Brückner witnessed a Germany rebuilt according to the status quo. A galvanic force for women growing up in the postwar period was the immediate reinstatement of the ruinous authoritarian patriarchal order, and the unquestioning submission of their mothers to the restoration of this destructive state of affairs.

Unlike other women filmmakers of her generation, Brückner has a strong academic background (a doctorate in political science and philosophy), and did not study at a film school, nor undergo a variety of apprenticeships before making her first film. She wrote several screenplays for other directors (Volker Schlöndorff and Ula Stöckl) before sending a synopsis of a script to a section of West German television (DGZ) that encouraged experimental work—*das kleine Fernschspiel* [The little television play]—and was a boon to emerging women filmmakers. Much to her surprise, they agreed to produce the film.

Brückner's first film, *Do Right and Fear No-One,* was prompted by a series of mysterious illnesses, which the director felt were connected to repressed material from her childhood, and which she needed to express through her filmmaking. *Do Right,* like most of Brückner's films, is highly autobiographical; it is a portrait of her mother. The director assembled a montage of still photos from family albums and history books, intermingled with photographs by August Sander. Brückner was interested in exploring not only the life of her mother, but the impact of class and history on the individual. Her mother, not given to self-reflection, at first refused to participate in the project, but finally became intensely involved, ultimately supplying the voice-over ruminations that mark the film's narrative. When the film was shown, Brückner's mother forced her dying husband to watch the film when it was televised, saying, "in it are all the things you don't know about me."

Brückner is greatly concerned with the investigation of private life, using her personal experience as a springboard to larger issues, and the recognition of what she calls "collective gestures," among women. She claims, in her theoretical writings, that women's perception of time and space is different from men's, that the oppression of women by the patriarchy has resulted not only in a distortion of their sexuality, but also of their very physical being and perceptual abilities. She believes that film empowers women to display this psychic and physical disintegration, a capacity that literature does not have. Brückner sees film as nothing less than a recovery for women of the ability to look, to perceive.

The director's next work was also commissioned for German television, and is called *A Thoroughly Demoralized Girl: A Day in the Life of Rita Rischak.* The film is a melange of docudrama-style scenes accompanied by the voice-over of the protagonist's interior thoughts, mixed with Rita being interviewed. It is the story of an office worker, longing for different forms of fulfillment, but with only the most chaotic ideas of how to achieve her desires. The film details her problematic relations with her parents, child, lovers, and work. Again, Rita's personal problems and self-destructive tendencies are tied to the social structure in which she is mired.

The film for which Brückner is justifiably most well known, *Hunger Years,* followed, and was screened at the Berlin Film Festival. The film was universally well-received, except in France, where the director's audacious shot of a bloody sanitary napkin was considered tasteless. *Hunger Years* takes place between 1953 and 1956, the years of the West German "economic miracle." It details the upsurge of material prosperity, the increasing grip of cold war politics and the rehabilitation of numerous Nazis. The repression, denial, and soullessness of the sociopolitical milieu is mirrored by the adolescent Ursula's family life, particularly in the disavowal by the girl's mother of her daughter's developing body and sexuality. The mother's disgust with her own body—she says at one point, "We should be able to tear out our ovaries"—is communicated all too clearly to Ursula, who comes to despise who and what she is. Psychologically and physically, Ursula desperately attempts to obliterate her feelings of self-alienation, and fill her emptiness with secret eating binges, which not only exacerbate her negative self-image, but also further isolate her from the social world. The young girl sinks further into self-mutilation, silence, and finally, a suicide attempt.

Brückner says, "this film is an attempt at a psychoanalytic cinematic form." The film's interest lies not only in the complexity with which she treats the subject matter, but also in formal play with narrative voice, documentary footage intercut with the fiction, inner monologues, poems, nursery rhymes, and fantasies that serve to reveal the inner life of the protagonist. The bloody sanitary napkin is an emblem of all those things in women's lives that cannot be shown. As Brückner says, "Film can integrate and release women's collective neuroses and maimings . . . , because film creates a public space for experience."

The director's remaining films, *Learning to Run,* about a woman whose breast cancer scare causes her to rethink her life, *The Daughter's Inheritance,* an omnibus film made with other women directors, and *One Glance, and Love Breaks Out,* a series of performance pieces revolving around sadomasochistic fantasies have received little critical attention. Jutta Brückner appears to have stopped making films, and taken a position in academia.—CAROLE ZUCKER

Bute, Mary Ellen

American abstract filmmaker and animator

Born *Houston, Texas, 1904.* ***Education*** *Attended Yale School of Drama, graduated 1925.* ***Family*** *Married the cinematographer Ted Nemeth, 1940, two sons: Theodore Jr. and James.* ***Career*** *1925—drama director for "floating university," on a cruise around the world; worked with Thomas Wilford designing Clavilux light organ; joined studio of Leon Theremin; directed visual department of Gerard Warburg Studio, headed by Joseph Schillinger; 1932—provided abstract drawings for* Synchronization, *an unfinished work by Schillinger and filmmaker, later film historian, Lewis Jacobs; 1934-59—worked with*

Ted Nemeth and others on short abstract animated films, first in black and white then in color after Parabola, *1937, set to musical works in the mainstream classical repertory; 1936—began self-distribution of films to Radio City Music Hall and similar venues; 1950—began working with Dr. Ralph Potter of Bell Telephone Laboratories to develop circuit to use oscilloscope as controlled source of light for drawing, first used for* Abstronic, *1952; 1956—produced live-action short film,* The Boy Who Saw Through, *directed by George Stoney; 1965—directed live-action feature film based on James Joyce novel,* Finnegans Wake. *The Mary Ellen Bute papers are stored at Yale University.* ***Awards*** *Best Short Film, Brussels International Experimental Film Festival, for* Mood Contrasts, *1953.* ***Died*** *In New York, 17 October 1983.*

Abstract Films (in collaboration with Ted Nemeth, 1934-59): 1932: *Synchromy No. 1 (Synchronization)* (unfinished; collaborators: Joseph Schillinger and Lewis Jacobs). **1934:** *Rhythm in Light* (collaborators: Melville Webber and Ted Nemeth). **1935:** *Synchromy No. 2.* **1936:** *Dada (Universal Clip)*; *Anitra's Dance.* **1937:** *Parabola* (collaborators: Rutherford Boyd, Ted Nemeth, and Bill Nemeth); *Escape (Synchromy No. 4)* (collaborators: Ted Nemeth and Bill Nemeth); *Evening Star.* **1939:** *Spook Sport* (collaborators: Norman McLaren and Ted Nemeth). **1940:** *Tarantella (Synchromy No. 9)*; *Toccata and Fugue.* **1947:** *Polka Graph (Fun with Music)*; *Mood Lyric.* **1948:** *Color Rhapsodie.* **1950:** *Pastorale* (collaborators: Ted Nemeth and Hillary Harris). **1952:** *Abstronic.* **1953:** *Mood Contrasts.* **1958:** *Imaginations.* **1959:** *RCA: New Sensations in Sound.* **1964:** *The Skin of Our Teeth.*

Live-Action Films: 1956: *The Boy Who Saw Through* (Stoney) (pr). **1965:** *Finnegans Wake (Passages from James Joyce's Finnegans Wake)* (d, pr).

Mary Ellen Bute grew up in Texas, painting pictures of cows and horses à la Rosa Bonheur. Her interest in the depiction of motion took her to the Pennsylvania Academy of Fine Arts, where she studied with Henry McCarter. There, like contemporary European artists such as Hans Richter and Viking Eggeling, she rapidly became disenchanted with the limitations of painting and switched her artistic concerns to multimedia creations. This led her to study stage lighting and design at the Yale School of Drama, from which she was graduated in 1925.

Bute was fascinated by the possibilities of various technologies for the creation of works which could express movement and controlled rhythms, to achieve as she put it, "a time element in abstract forms." Since music generated the strongest creative impulses in her, she began to explore the new light organs developed by such scientists as Thomas Wilford and Leon Theremin. In 1932 she delivered a collaborative paper on the synchronization of light and sound before the New York Musicological Society, while Theremin provided an electronic demonstration.

Through her association with Theremin she was introduced to Joseph Schillinger, a composer and mathematician with whom she went to work at the Gerard Warburg Studio. It was there that she learned a valuable lesson. Bute explained:

> Visual composition is a counterpart of the sound composition, and . . . I began to seek for a medium for combining these two and found it in films. I was determined to express this feeling for movement in visual terms, which I had not been able to achieve in painting, and I was determined to paint in film, and that is why I actually started.

After working with Schillinger and filmmaker Lewis Jacobs on an unfinished animation project, Bute set out on her own to make films. In 1934 she used a personal bank loan to pay for a five-minute black-and-white film called *Rhythm in Light,* accompanied by music from Edvard

Grieg's *Peer Gynt Suite*. She recruited cinematographer Ted Nemeth for this project, which led to a close collaboration over the next two decades. Bute married Nemeth in 1940; all of her films through *Pastorale* in 1950 were produced by Ted Nemeth Studios. In the 1950s, at least a decade before Nam June Paik, she began using an oscilloscope, her "pencil of light," to generate images that could move without the need for animation techniques.

Bute's films were designed to accompany mostly familiar classical music selections by composers such as Bach, Wagner, Grieg, Saint-Saëns, Liszt, Rimsky-Korsakov, and Shostakovich. This, combined with her aggressive theatrical promotion of her films, made them more popularly available than other similar works. As early as 1935 her *Rhythm in Light* was run as an accompaniment to a feature film in New York's Radio City Music Hall. Her films played there and at other commercial movie theaters around the country well into the 1950s.

Because her unusual marketing of her films set her at odds with the prevailing anticommercial stance of the avant-garde and modernist art communities, Bute eventually fell into an undeserved obscurity. Her work and reputation began to be revived in the 1980s, as part of the feminist project of reclamation of marginalized work by women in film and other arts. Bute is now recognized, along with Oskar Fischinger, as one of the most important avant-garde filmmakers to work in the United States before World War II.—STEPHEN BROPHY

Campion, Jane

New Zealander director

Born *Wellington, New Zealand, 30 April 1954; daughter of the opera/theater director Richard Campion and the actress/writer Edith Campion; sister of the director Anna Campion.* ***Education*** *Attended Victoria University, Wellington, B.A. in structural arts; Chelsea School of Arts, London, diploma in fine arts (completed at Sydney College of the Arts); Australian Film and Television School, diploma in direction.* ***Family*** *Married the television producer/director Colin Englert.* ***Career*** *Late 1970s—became interested in filmmaking and began making short films; 1981—short film,* Tissues, *led to acceptance into the Australian Film and Television School; 1984—took job with Australia's Women's Film Unit; 1986—directed an episode of the television drama* Dancing Daze; *1989-90—short films* Peel, *Passionless Moments, and* Girl's Own Story *released theatrically in the United States.* ***Awards*** *Palme d'Or, Best Short Film, Cannes Film Festival, for* Peel, *1982; Best Experimental Film, Australian Film Institute Awards, for* Passionless Moments, *1984; Best Direction and Screenplay, Australian Film Institute Awards, for* Girl's Own Story, *1984; Best Director and Best TV Film, Australian Film Institute Awards, for* 2 Friends, *1985; Academy Award, Best Original Screenplay, and Best Director and Screenplay, Australian Film Institute Awards, for* The Piano, *1993.* ***Address*** *Big Shell Films Pty Ltd, P.O. Box 266, Vaucluse, NSW 2030, Australia.*

Films as Director: 1981: *Tissues* (short). **1982:** *Peel* (short) (+ sc). **1984:** *Mishaps of Seduction and Conquest* (video short) (+ sc); *Passionless Moments* (short) (co-d, + co-sc); *Girl's Own Story* (short) (+ sc); *After Hours* (short) (+ sc). **1985:** *2 Friends* (for TV). **1989:** *Sweetie* (+ co-sc). **1990:** *An Angel at My Table* (for TV; edited version released theatrically). **1993:** *The Piano* (+ sc). **1996:** *The Portrait of a Lady.* **1999:** *Holy Smoke.*

Whatever their quality, all of Jane Campion's feature films have remained consistent in theme. They depict the lives of girls and women who are in one way or another separate from the mainstream, because of physical appearance (if not outright physical disability) or personality

Jane Campion directing *The Portrait of a Lady.*

quirk, and she spotlights the manner in which they relate to and function within their respective societies.

Campion began directing features after making several highly acclaimed, award-winning short films which were extensively screened on the international film festival circuit. Her first two features are alike in that they focus on the relationships between two young women, and how they are affected by the adults who control their world. Her debut, *2 Friends,* was made for Australian television in 1985 and did not have its American theatrical premiere until 1996. It is a depiction of the connection between a pair of adolescents, focusing on the changes in their friendship and how they are influenced by adult authority figures. The narrative is told in reverse time: at the outset, the girls are a bit older, and their developing personalities have separated them; as the film continues, they become younger and closer.

Sweetie, Campion's initial theatrical feature, is a pitch-black comedy about a young woman who is overweight, overemotional, and even downright crazy, with the scenario charting the manner in which she relates to her parents and her skinny, shy, easily manipulated sister. The film was controversial in that critics and viewers either raved about it or were turned off by its quirky nature. While not without inspired moments, both *Sweetie* and *2 Friends* lack the assurance of Campion's later work.

The filmmaker's unequivocal breakthrough as a world-class talent came in 1990 with *An Angel at My Table.* The theatrical version of the film is 158 minutes long and is taken from a three-part miniseries made for New Zealand television. *An Angel at My Table* did not benefit from the media hype surrounding *The Piano,* Campion's 1993 international art-house hit, but it is as equally fine a work. It is an uncommonly literate portrait of Janet Frame, a plump, repressed child who was destined to become one of New Zealand's most renowned writers. Prior to her fame, however, she was falsely diagnosed as a schizophrenic, passed eight years in a mental hospital, and received more than 200 electric shock treatments.

Campion evocatively depicts the different stages of Frame's life; the filmmaker elicits a dynamic performance from Kerry Fox as the adult Janet and, in visual terms, she perfectly captures the essence of the writer's inner being. At the same time, Campion bitingly satirizes the manner in which society patronizes those who sincerely dedicate their lives to the creation of art. She depicts pseudo-artists who would not know a poem from a Harlequin Romance, and publishers who think that for Frame to truly be a success she must have a best-seller and ride around in a Rolls-Royce.

If *An Angel at My Table* spotlights the evolution of a woman as an intellectual being, Campion's next work, *The Piano,* depicts a woman's development on a sexual and erotic level. *The Piano,* like *The Crying Game* before it and *Pulp Fiction* later on, became the cinematic cause celebre of its year. It is a deceptively simple story, beautifully told, of Ada (Holly Hunter, in an Academy Award-winning performance), a mute Scottish woman who arrives with her nine-year-old daughter (Anna Paquin, who also won an Oscar) in remote New Zealand during the 1850s. Ada is to be the bride in an arranged marriage with a stern, hesitant farmer (Sam Neill). But she becomes sexually and romantically involved with Baines (Harvey Keitel), her illiterate, vulnerable neighbor to whom she gives piano lessons: an arrangement described by Campion as an "erotic pact."

Campion succeeds in creating a story about the development of love, from the initial eroticism between the two characters to something deeper and more romantic. Ada has a symbolic relationship with the piano, which is both her refuge and mode of self-expression. *The Piano* is an intensely haunting tale of exploding passion and deep, raw emotion, and it put its maker at the forefront of contemporary, world-class cinema. Campion's most recent project is *The Portrait of a Lady,* based on the Henry James novel.—ROB EDELMAN

Cantrill, Corinne

Australian director

Born *Corinne Mozelle Joseph, in Sydney, 6 November 1928.* ***Education*** *Studied botany at Sydney University; studied music in Paris with Nadia Boulanger.* ***Family*** *Married the filmmaker and her collaborator, Arthur Cantrill, 1960, two children.* ***Career*** *1960-63—made documentaries, experimental shorts, and a series of children's art and craft films for*

Corinne Cantrill in her film *In This Life's Body.*

the Australian Broadcasting Service; 1969-70—spent a highly productive period of personal/experimental filmmaking, which was enabled by Arthur's Fellowship in the Creative Arts at the Australian National University in Canberra; 1971—began editing and publishing the independent film journal, Cantrill's Filmnotes; *1974—made her film,* At Eltham; *1982-84—made her masterpiece,* In This Life's Body. ***Awards*** *Silver Award, Australian Film Institute, for* Earth Message, *1970; Second Prize, St. Kilda Film Festival, for* In This Life's Body, *1984.* ***Address*** *Box 1295 L, GPO, Melbourne, Victoria 3001, Australia.*

Films as Co-Director with Arthur Cantrill (unless otherwise noted): 1963: *Mud*; *Galaxy*; *Nebulae*; *Kinegraffiti.* **1964-65:** *Robert Klippel Sculpture Studies* (5 films). **1965:** *Robert Klippel Drawings, 1947-1963.* **1966:** *The Incised Image*; *Dream*; *Adventure Playground.* **1968:** *Henri Gaudier-Brzeska*; *Red Stone Dancer.* **1969:** *Rehearsal at the Arts Laboratory*; *Imprints*; *Fud 69*; *Home Movie—A Day in the Bush*; *Eikon*; *White-Orange-Green.* **1970:** *Bouddi*; *4000 Frames, an Eye-Opener Film*; *Earth Message*; *Harry Hooton.* **1971:** *New Movements Generate New Thoughts*; *The Boiling Electric Jug Film*; *Blast*; *Meditations*; *Nine Image Film*; *Milky Way Special*; *Zap*; *Video Self-Portrait*; *Gold Fugue*; *Pink Metronome*; *Room*; *The City*; *Fragments*; *Island Fuse.* **1973:** *Skin of Your Eye.* **1974:** *At Eltham*; *Reflections on Three Images by Baldwin Spencer, 1901*; *Negative/Positive on Three Images by Baldwin Spencer, 1901.* **1975:** *Studies in Image (De)Generation* (Nos. 1, 2, and 3). **1976:** *Three Colour Separation Studies—Landscapes*; *Three Colour Separation Studies—Still Lifes*; *Simple Observations of a Solar Eclipse.* **1977:** *Touching the Earth Series: Ocean at Point Lookout, near Coober Pedy, at Uluru, Katatjuta.* **1978:** *Moving Picture Postcards*; *Heat Shimmer*; *Hillside at Chauritchi*; *Near Wilmington*; *Meteor Crater, Gosse Bluff*; *Ocean*; *Interior/Exterior.* **1979:** *Angophora and Sandstone*; *Coast at Pearl Beach*; *Notes on the Passage of Time.* **1980:** *Grain of the Voice Series: Rock Wallaby and Blackbird*; *Two Women*; *Seven Sisters*; *Unthurqua*; *Warrah*; *Experiments in Three-Colour Separation*; *Two-Colour Separation Studies*; *Pan/Colour Separations.* **1981:** *The Second Journey (To Uluru)*; *Wilpena*; *Time/Colour Separations*; *Floterian—Hand Printings from a Film History.* **1983:** *Corporeal*; *Passage.* **1984:** *At Black Range*; *Waterfall*; *In This Life's Body.* **1986:** *Notes on Berlin, the Divided City.* **1987:** *Walking Track*; *The Berlin Apartment.* **1988:** *Projected Light.* **1989:** *Myself When Fourteen* (with Ivor Cantrill). **1990:** *Bali Film.* **1990-97:** *The Bemused Tourist.* **1991:** *Agung Gives Ivor a Haircut.* **1992:** *View from the Balcony of the Marco Polo Hotel* (revised 1993); *Rendra's Place, Depok.* **1993:** *Walking to Yeh Pelu*; *The Pause between Frames*; *In the Shadow of Gunung Batur*; *Ming-Wei to Singaraja.* **1994:** *Ivor's Tiger Xmas Card.* **1995:** *Ivor's Exhibition*; *Ramayana/Legong*; *Jalan Raya, Ubud*; *Early Morning at Borobudur*; *Ivor Paints.*

Corinne Cantrill is one of Australia's preeminent experimental filmmakers, whose long-term collaboration with her husband Arthur has proved to be both prolific and influential. Before embarking on her film career, Corinne spent time in Europe where she studied music in Paris, sang in a choir in Denmark, and taught English in Italy. After she married Arthur Cantrill, she began making films with him in 1960. Since then, the Cantrills have made more than 150 films, including seven feature-length films.

In the early years of their film career, the Cantrills made a series of documentaries about children and art, and the occasional experimental short. Moreover, they used the money they made selling their films to the Australian Broadcasting Service to purchase a camera and other equipment. Consequently, throughout their productive careers, they have worked at home using their own equipment, without resorting to the more typical film industry mode of hiring facilities and crews.

In 1965 the Cantrills moved to London to seek treatment for their autistic son, and while in Europe they attended an experimental film festival that inspired their full-time commitment to avant-garde cinema. In 1969 they returned to Australia where Arthur accepted a university fellowship, which was instrumental in terms of enabling them to be enormously productive as filmmakers. Since then, they have worked exclusively in the field of personal and experimental film. Over the years, their work has explored numerous aspects of film, including multi-screen projections and film performance, single-frame structuring of film, landscape films that relate film forms to land forms, and works that have addressed the history of film and film technologies. On all of the films, they have worked closely together as equals, though some, such as *At Eltham* and *In This Life's Body* were mainly Corinne's projects. She has explained that she is drawn to experimental filmmaking strategies in particular for the ability they provide to "open up new areas of the film experience."

The Cantrills' extensive body of work ranges from the two-minute *Zap* to the 148-minute *In This Life's Body*. A significant part of their work displays their intense fascination with the landscape, an interest that began with their 1962 film series, *The Native Trees of Stradbroke Island*. Subsequent landscape films include *Bouddi*—filmed on the coast, *Earth Message*—with views of Canberra and its flora, and *Island Fuse*—also made at Stradbroke Island. The films convey a sense of awe for the landscape, and a respect for nature that is almost religious. In addition, the Cantrills have pursued their interest in the materiality and formal properties of film and image analysis, as in *Island Fuse,* in which they reworked existing film footage by refilming it and coloring it with filters frame by frame. Indeed, their formalist films have employed a variety of means to refer to and acknowledge the elements and basic properties of filmmaking, such as how the camera registers and records images, the mutability of celluloid, and projection properties, as well as the larger issues of how a film can structure space, time, and perception. Thus, the Cantrills have explored the properties of film stock, speed, and three-color separation (i.e., by using black-and-white film with red, green, and blue filters), as in their *Three Colour Separation Studies—Landscapes, Still Lifes,* and *Waterfall*. In the latter film, the Cantrills both create and discover many chance happenings and transformations in the natural setting. Also, they have interrogated the history of film form; thus, they have discovered in the anthropological films of Walter Baldwin Spencer a notable intersection between early silent cinema and the materialist concerns of later avant-garde filmmakers. Furthermore, they have explored personal experience and history, as in *In This Life's Body* in which Corinne used a collection of photographs to construct her autobiography. Similarly, Corinne has noted that their affinity for returning to the sites of earlier films is a theme that runs through their body of work, as in 1983's *Corporeal,* which was filmed at the site of their 1979 film, *Angophora and Sandstone* and 1980's *Warrah*.

Corinne's film *At Eltham* continued her fascination with the Australian landscape and it developed her ideas about "playing" the camera's functions like a musical instrument. It depicts the quintessential Australian landscape of eucalyptus-covered hills and the Yarra river seen through the trees. The soundtrack consists of a recording of the natural sounds at Eltham's birds and the river. In one of her essays, Corinne subtitled the film "A Metaphor on Death," thus referring to the Cantrills' despair, at the time, about their future as filmmakers in Australia and their decision to leave the country temporarily to pursue their dreams.

In This Life's Body is undoubtedly Corinne's career masterpiece. A personal and deeply contemplative documentary-autobiography, it provides a simple account of her life and work. She was prompted to make the film after a bout of illness when she became committed to preparing for the "inevitability of death," and had resolved to review and search for meaning in her life. Constructed almost totally with a collection of hundreds of still photographs—

snapshots, studio portraits, and self portraits of Corinne alone and with her family and friends—along with bits of her movies, the film has a remarkable additive effect. Specifically, sequences of photographs are accompanied by Corinne's spoken narration, which at one point explains that she is using the photographs to re-create "her own history, her own story." The film's title refers to Corinne's "undogmatic" belief in reincarnation and to the possibility of changing one's life and of creating different stories about one's life. Critics consider it among the most powerful of such personal films.

The Cantrills' work has been screened internationally at film festivals, film museums, and art galleries. Together they have been instrumental in lecturing and writing about Australia's avant-garde film scene and history. And, since 1971, they have published and edited the film journal *Cantrill's Filmnotes,* a bi-annual review of innovative independent film and video that emphasizes experimental film, animation, video art, digital media and works of performance, sound and installation art from Australia and around the world, and that has made a significant contribution to the field of experimental film in Australia.—CYNTHIA FELANDO

Carolina, Ana

Brazilian director and writer

Pseudonym *Full name, Ana Carolina Teixeira Soares.* ***Born*** *São Paulo, Brazil, 1943.* ***Education*** *Studied journalism and photography at the Universidade da São Paulo.* ***Career*** *1967-74—made short and medium length films; 1974—first feature film, the documentary* Getúlio Vargas.

Films as Director: 1968: *A Feira* (short); *Lavrador* (short) (co-d). **1969:** *Indústria* (short); *Articulações* (short). **1970:** *Tres Desenhos* (short); *Monteiro Lobato* (short) (co-d with Sarno); *As Fiandeiras* (short). **1972:** *Guerra do Paraguai* (*War of Paraguay*) (doc, short). **1973:** *Pantanal* (doc, short); *O Sonho Acabou* (short). **1974:** *Getúlio Vargas* (doc). **1977:** *Mar de Rosas* (*Sea of Roses*) (+ sc). **1979:** *Nelson Pereira Dos Santos* (doc); *Anatomía do Espectador* (short—16mm). **1982:** *Das Tripas Coração* (*Hearts and Guts*) (+ sc). **1987:** *Sonho de Valsa* (*The Lady in Shining Armor*) (+ sc).

Brazilian Ana Carolina arrived at filmmaking after first pursuing a career in medicine and then in journalism and photography. Her ultimate career choice did not reflect a childhood of moviegoing, in fact her family rarely went to the movies. A medical student in the turbulent sixties, Carolina found herself more attracted to the university's cultural activities and academics than to her medical courses. She fell in love with a film student and began to make films with him. He wanted to make documentaries and that led Carolina first to the production of documentary films. As Carolina commented to Luis Trelles Plazaola in a 1989 interview, "I had no ideology, neither as a cinephile nor in any way." From this rather odd beginning, Carolina quickly progressed to writing, producing, and directing her own films.

In the late 1960s, Brazilian life was ruled by a repressive dictatorship. Brazilian filmmakers concentrated on politicized projects, striving to use film to engage the audience and to incite change. Carolina entered the scene making social, cultural, poetic, and political documentaries, films for which she was imprisoned twice. Made in 1974, her first feature film, *Getúlio Vargas,* documented the political life of Vargas, who ruled Brazil as president from 1930 to 1945 and again from 1951 to 1954, his rule ending with his suicide. With this film, Carolina learned about the commercial aspects of filmmaking, working with producers, restructuring her approach to cinematic time to suit the rhythm of a feature-length film, and anticipating a more commercial audience.

In a 1985 interview, Carolina commented that it was the experience of making *Getúlio Vargas* that made her see the possibility of making feature films. Not only were documentaries not commercially viable, but it was very difficult to express political views in such a "real" way given Brazil's repressed political culture. So, she went inside herself and followed *Getúlio Vargas* with a trilogy of films centered around female protagonists confronting and sometimes subverting their roles within a patriarchal society. It is difficult to classify neatly *Sea of Roses, Hearts and Guts,* or *The Lady in Shining Armor* as any one genre. Here we defer to Carolina who describes the films as "dramatic comedy," lacking any more well-defined category for them.

In *Sea of Roses,* Carolina's best-known film, two generations are contrasted: The mother is pushed around by the macho husband and, even though she attempts to flee with her daughter, she ultimately has no way out. Her daughter, however, might escape the controlling patriarchal family structure. With its nonsensical, even hysterical dialogue, the film might at first seem absurd. Yet, the tension between man and woman and between generations is very real and quite poignant. Called "modern and inventive" by one critic, "at once iconoclastic and malicious" by another, and "schizophrenic" by a third, *Sea of Roses* offers characters informed by Carolina's own experiences, as both the daughter in a patriarchally ordered family and a daughter of Brazil.

Tereza, the protagonist of *The Lady in Shining Armor,* is a single 30-something woman who lives with and seems to have strangely close relationships with her father and brother. The film examines her near-hysterical search for a man, literally a "Prince Charming" who will love her unconditionally for the rest of her life, and her continual disappointment. This plot summary, however, is misleading because it omits the central elements of the film—Tereza's fantasies or nightmares, filled with religious imagery that are at once both humorous and scandalous. Another child of Brazil's recent repressive regime, Tereza's quest for love belies her search for herself—as she says herself early in the film, she has no identity.

Set in a girls' boarding school, *Hearts and Guts* explores the hypocrisy and educational atmosphere that control the students' behavior. The 16- and 17-year-old girls are rebellious and curious. Confused about their identities, especially their sexual identities, these girls go on hysterical (both pathologically and humoristically) romps through the school, obsessing about each other and their teachers.

It is fitting that Carolina's first feature examined Vargas's life, as her subsequent films are peopled by the generation most affected by his rule, and the generation perhaps most responsible for the pushing Brazil toward a representative democracy in the 1960s. Carolina speaks often of "power" and believes that her generation never had any sense of their own power, as individuals or as a group, because of Vargas's paternalistic, repressive regime. Her characters struggle with this, and amuse their audiences with their attempts at rebellion.—ILENE S. GOLDMAN

Cavani, Liliana

Italian director and writer

Born *Emilia, Italy, 12 January 1937.* ***Education*** *Attended University of Bologna, B.A. in classic literature; graduated from Rome's film school, Centro Sperimentale di Cinematografia.* ***Career*** *Early 1960s—directed documentaries and dramas for RAI (Italian television); 1966—made her first feature film,* Francesco d'Assisi; *1974—made her most famous feature film,* The Night Porter. ***Awards*** *Ciak d'Oro, Migliore Allievo al Centro Sperimentale di Cinematografia.* ***Address*** *via Filangeri 4, Rome, Italy.*

Films as Director: 1961: *Incontro notturno.* **1962:** *L'evento.* **1962-63:** *Storia del terzo Reich* (*Story of the Third Reich*) (doc for TV). **1963:** *L'eta' di Stalin* (*The Age of Stalin*) (doc for TV). **1964:** *La Casa in Italia* (*The House in Italy*) (doc for TV). **1965:** *Philippe Pétain: Processo a Vichy* (*Philippe Petain: Trial at Vichy*) (doc for TV); *La Donna Nella Resistenza* (*Women of the Resistance*) (doc for TV); *Gesu' mio Fratello* (*Jesus, My Brother*) (doc for TV); *Il Giorno Della Pace* (*The Day of Peace*) (doc for TV). **1966:** *Francesco d'Assisi* (+ co-sc). **1968:** *Galileo* (+ co-sc, co-st). **1969:** *I Cannibali* (*The Cannibals*) (+ co-sc, st). **1971:** *L'Ospite* (*The Hospital; The Guest*) (+ co-sc, st). **1973:** *Milarepa* (+ co-sc, st). **1974:** *Il Portiere di notte* (*The Night Porter*) (+ co-sc, st). **1977:** *Al di là del bene e del male* (*Beyond Good and Evil; Oltre il Bene e il Male*) (+ co-sc, st). **1981:** *La Pelle* (*The Skin*) (+ co-sc). **1983:** *Beyond the Door* (*Oltre la Porta*) (+ co-sc, co-st). **1986:** *Interno Berlinese* (*The Berlin Affair, Affair in Berlin*) (+ co-sc). **1988:** *Francesco* (*St. Francis of Assisi*) (+ co-sc, st). **1993:** *Dove siete? Io sono qui* (*Where Are You? I'm Here*) (for TV) (+ co-sc, co-st). **1999:** *Dissociated States.*

Since the 1960s, Italian director Liliana Cavani has been a prolific filmmaker. Her film career began when she directed a series of documentary histories and dramas for RAI—Italian

Liliana Cavani

television. RAI eventually produced her first feature film, and since then Cavani has focused on making commercial fiction films.

In general, Cavani's films are known for their emphasis on the pleasure and danger of power and politics. Her early work provided compelling new perspectives on historical and mythological figures, including *Francesco d'Assisi, Galileo, The Cannibals,* and *Milarepa.* Her first fiction feature, for example, was *The Cannibals,* which revisits the myth of Antigone in relation to contemporary political revolts against state repression in Italy. In addition, Cavani has been drawn to German culture themes, as in *Beyond Good and Evil,* about Nietzsche and Lou Andreas Salomé; *The Night Porter,* which looks at Nazism from the perspective of sexual politics; and *The Berlin Affair,* about a Japanese-German lesbian couple—from a Japanese novel that she set in Germany. Cavani's films may be characterized as critiques of political hierarchies, though, interestingly, it is the male characters who embody the critique and speak for change. Her primary interest in male characters and performers is revealed in her strange claim that "each of my [male] actors looks a bit like me." Although most of her films have central male characters, *The Berlin Affair* is about a lesbian relationship; similarly, *Women of the Resistance* is about the struggle of women who fought against fascism. Like her contemporary, Lina Wertmüller, to whom she is often compared, Cavani's films do not typically focus on female protagonists; it is male characters who occupy the privileged positions, in terms of both image and story. Additional exceptions are the female figures of Antigone in *The Cannibals,* and the psychoanalyst Lou Andreas Salomé in *Beyond Good and Evil.*

In the United States, Cavani's best-known work is *The Night Porter,* a difficult and challenging film that tells the dark, melancholy story of a sadomasochistic love affair between an ex-Nazi officer and the concentration camp inmate (Lucia) he raped 15 years earlier. The man, Max, is part of a group of Nazis who have avoided conviction for their crimes when key evidence is destroyed and crucial witnesses are murdered. As a result, Max and Lucia meet again accidentally, in 1957, when he is working as the night porter at a Vienna hotel; soon they resume their relationship. As depicted by Cavani, their "love affair" is a twisted psychological game that allegorically alludes to the unequal yet mutually dependent relationship between oppressor countries and the weaker countries over which they exert their wicked dominance. Critics in the United States panned the film, especially for its "kinky" fascist imagery, but it proved to be financially successful and garnered considerable attention for Cavani.

Cavani has consistently rejected the notion that she brings a different, gender-based perspective to her work; nevertheless, feminist film critics have found ways to read feminist empowerment into her films, inasmuch as they offer unconventional representations of sexuality and they question knowledge and its relation to power. Similarly, her films usually focus on social and political issues; in addition to treating themes of violence and sex. Feminist film scholar Kaja Silverman has argued that Cavani should be considered a true auteur because, in addition to featuring a coherence of themes, her work is unique in relation to both mainstream and experimental cinemas. In addition, she contends that Cavani's films are "neither classically 'feminine' nor overtly feminist." Silverman readily notes the difficulties that feminist viewers have had with her work, since not one of her many features explicitly treats the subject of sexual oppression or depicts active feminist resistance to it. Certainly, Cavani's work is not about women specifically, as are the films of Laura Mulvey, Michelle Citron, and Lizzie Borden, for example; so, her female characters seem to have little to offer feminist analyses. But, Silverman contends that Cavani's films hold the possibility of feminist readings because they demonstrate the "fatal lure of masochism" for their male characters, and they work to elide the boundaries between male and female identity (as when *The Night Porter*'s Max and Lucia trade roles in their sadomasochistic scenarios). Indeed, Silverman suggests that Antigone's male cohort in *The Cannibals*, *The Night Porter*'s Max, and Paul in *Beyond Good and Evil* all occupy "feminine" positions that demand passivity, suffering, and sacrifice. Likewise, in her earlier film, *Francesco d'Assisi*, Francesco continually gives away his material possessions—clothing, money, and furniture—thus implying his increasing cultural alienation. That is, his acts are a means by which to refuse power and privilege and to thereby assert the equality between himself and the people around him. Interestingly, Cavani revisited this character in 1988 with *Francesco*, which likewise traces the spiritual awakening of the decadent son of a rich merchant, who experiences a religious call and subsequently abandons his past to help the poor and needy in his community.

In recent years, Cavani has been spending more time directing stage productions and seems to have moved away from film.—CYNTHIA FELANDO

Cecchi d'Amico, Suso

Italian writer

Born *Giovanna Cecchi in Rome, 21 July 1914; daughter of the writer Emilio Cecchi.* ***Education*** *Studied in Rome and Cambridge.* ***Family*** *Married the music critic Fedele D'Amico.* ***Career*** *Journalist; translator of English-language plays; 1946—first film as writer,* Mio figlio professore; *1977—co-writer for TV miniseries* Gesù di Nazareth (Jesus of Nazareth*); writer for TV,* Una moglie, *1987,* Quattro storie di donne, *1990.* ***Awards*** *Best script award, Sindicato Nazionale Giornalisti Cinematografici Italiani, for* Let's Hope It's a Girl, *1986.* ***Address*** *via Paisiello 27, 00198 Rome, Italy.*

Films as Writer: 1946: *Mio figlio professore* (*Professor My Son*) (Castellani); *Vivere in pace* (*To Live in Peace*) (Zampa); *Roma città libera* (Pagliero). **1947:** *Il delitto di Giovanni Episcopo* (*Flesh Will Surrender*) (Lattuada); *L'onorevole Angelina* (*Angelina*) (Zampa). **1948:** *Fabiola* (Blasetti); *Ladri di biciclette* (*The Bicycle Thief*) (De Sica) (co); *Patto col diavolo* (Chiarini); *Cielo sulla palude* (*Heaven over the Marshes*) (Genina). **1949:** *Le mura di Malapaga* (*The Walls of Malapaga*) (Clément) (co-sc Italian version); *Prohibito rubare* (*Guaglio*) (Comencini). **1950:** *Miracolo a Milano* (*Miracle in Milan*) (De Sica) (co); *E primavera* (*It's Forever Springtime*) (Castellani); *E più facile che un cammello* (Zampa); *Romazo d'amore* (*Toselli*) (Coletti). **1951:** *Due mogli sono troppe* (*Honeymoon Deferred*) (Camerini); *Bellissima* (Visconti). **1952:** "Primo amore" ep. of *Altri tempi* (*Times Gone By*) (Blasetti); *Processo alla città* (*A Town on Trial*) (Zampa); *Buon Giorno, elefante!* (*Hello, Elephant!*; *Pardon My Trunk*) (Franciolini); *I vinti* (*I nostri figli*) (Antonioni); *Il mondo le condanna* (*His Last Twelve Hours*) (Franciolini). **1953:** *Siamo donne* (*We the Women*) (Visconti); "Il pupo" ep. of *Tempi nostri* (*Anatomy of Love*) (Blassetti); *Febbre di vivere* (Gora); *La signora senza camelie* (*Camille without Camellias*; *The Lady without Camellias*) (Antonioni); *Cento anni d'amore* (de Felice). **1954:** *Graziella* (Bianchi); *Senso* (*The Wanton Contessa*) (Visconti); *L'allegro squadrone* (Moffa); *Peccato che sia una canaglia* (*Too Bad She's Bad*) (Blasetti); *Proibito* (Monicelli). **1955:** *Le amiche* (*The Girlfriends*) (Antonioni). **1956:** *La fortuna di essere donna* (*Lucky to Be a Woman*) (Blasetti); *La finestra sul Luna Park* (Comencini); *Kean* (Gassman); *Difendo il mio amore* (Sherman) (co). **1957:** *Le notti bianche* (*White Nights*) (Visconti); *Mariti in città* (Comencini). **1958:** *Nella città l'inferno* (*And the Wild, Wild Women*) (Castellani); *La sfida* (*The Challenge*) (Rosi); *I soliti ignoti* (*Big Deal on Madonna Street*) (Monicelli). **1959:** *Estate violenta* (*Violent Summer*) (Zurlini); *I magliari* (Rosi). **1960:** *La contessa azzurra* (Gora); *Rocco e i suoi fratelli* (*Rocco and His Brothers*) (Visconti) (co); *Risate di gioia* (*The Passionate Thief*) (Monicelli); *It Started in Naples* (Shavelson). **1961:** *Salvatore Giuliano* (Rosi); *Il relitto* (*The Wastrel*) (Cacoyannis); *I due nemici* (*The Best of Enemies*) (Hamilton). **1962:** "Il lavoro" ("The Job") and "Renzo e Luciana"

("Renzo and Luciana") eps. of *Boccaccio '70* (Visconti and Monicelli); "Le Lièvre et la tortue" ("The Tortoise and the Hare") ep. of *Les Quatre Vérités* (*Three Fables of Love*) (Blasetti). **1963:** *Il gattopardo* (*The Leopard*) (Visconti) (co); *Gli indifferenti* (*Time of Indifference*) (Maselli). **1965:** *Casanova '70* (Monicelli); *Vaghe stelle dell'orsa* (*Sandra*) (Visconti). **1966:** *Io, io, io . . . e gli altri* (Blasetti); "Queen Armenia" ep. of *Le fate* (*The Queens*) (Monicelli); *Spara forte, più forte . . . non capisco* (*Shout Loud, Louder . . . I Don't Understand*) (De Filippo); *The Taming of the Shrew* (Zeffirelli). **1967:** *Lo straniero* (*The Stranger*) (Visconti); *L'uomo, l'orgoglio, la vendetta* (*Man, Pride and Vengeance*) (Bazzoni). **1969:** *Metello* (Bolognini); *Infanzia, vocazione, e prime esperienze di Giacomo Casanova, Veneziano* (Comencini); *Senza sapere nulla di lei* (Comencini). **1971:** *La mortadella* (*Lady Liberty*) (Monicelli). **1972:** *Pinocchio* (Comencini—for TV); *Fratello sole, sorella luna* (*Brother Sun, Sister Moon*) (Zeffirelli); *Il diavolo nel cervello* (Sollima); *I figli chiedono perche* (Zanchin). **1973:** *Ludwig* (Visconti); *Amore e ginnastica* (L. F. d'Amico). **1974:** *Gruppo di famiglia in un interno* (*Conversation Piece*; *Violence et Passion*) (Visconti); *Prete, fai un miracolo* (Chiari); *Amore amaro* (Vancini) (co). **1976:** *L'innocente* (*The Innocent*) (Visconti); *Caro Michele* (Monicelli); *Dimmi che fai tutto per mei* (Festa Campanile). **1980:** *La velia* (Ferrero). **1983:** *Lighea* (Tuzii) (co); *Les Mots pour le dire* (Pinheiro) (co). **1984:** *Cuore* (Comencini—for TV); *Uno scandale per bene* (Festa Campanile); *Bertoldo, Bertoldino e Cacasenno* (Monicelli) (co). **1985:** *Le due vite di Mattia Pascal* (*The Two Lives of Mattia Pascal*) (Monicelli) (co). **1986:** *I soliti ignoti vent'anni dopo* (*Big Deal on Madonna Street. . . 20 Years Later*) (Todini) (co); *Speriamo che sia femmina* (*Let's Hope It's a Girl*) (Monicelli) (co); *La storia* (*History*) (Comencini) (co). **1987:** *L'inchiesta* (Damiani) (co); *Oci ciornie* (*Dark Eyes*) (Mikhalkov) (co); *I picari* (Monicelli). **1988:** *Ti presento un'amica* (Massaro). **1989:** *Stradivari* (Battiato) (co). **1990:** *Il male oscuro* (Monicelli); *Rossini, Rossini* (Monicelli). **1992:** *Parenti serpenti* (Monicelli) (co). **1993:** *La fine e nota* (Cristina Comencini); *Cari fottutissimi amici* (Monicelli) (co). **1995:** *Facciamo paradiso* (Monicelli). **1996:** *Bruno aspetta in macchna* (Camerina) (co-st only). **1998:** *La Stanza dello scirocco*; *Der Letzte Sommer-Wenn Du nicht Willst.* **1999:** *Panni sporchi*; *Il Dolce cinema* (for TV).

Suso Cecchi d'Amico is undoubtedly best known as Visconti's regular scriptwriter, however her work, either alone or in collaboration, with a large number of other directors is at the core of a long list of films which embodies the development of postwar Italian cinema from Blasetti to De Sica, from Rosi to Zeffirelli and Antonioni. It is undoubtedly a tribute to her work that her scripts achieve a certain "transparency," becoming all-but-inextricable from the finished film itself.

She has all too modestly described her work as akin to that of the artisan. This emphasizes her professionalism, the literate well-craftedness of her scripts, and her endless adaptability to the contrasting needs of filmmakers working within competing stylistic conventions. It glosses over the acuteness of her appraisal of particular projects and particular directors. Luigi Comencini may be no great stylist, as she has remarked, his films stand or fall by their overall effect. *Cuore* is a tender and ironic melodrama but anchored cogently to moments in Italian history. Zampa may be a minor talent but with *To Live in Peace* Cecchi d'Amico wrote to the project's integrity and antiheroic pacifism. Her script gives Genina's strange melodrama about a peasant girl's rape and subsequent sanctification, *Heaven over the Marshes,* a much-needed steely quality.

Writing for De Sica made other demands. Cecchi d'Amico has spoken of his need "to borrow from and reproduce" reality, a need that predated any theorization of neorealism. The moral catch-22 behind *The Bicycle Thief* lends De Sica's slice-of-life a bitter edge. Her collaboration with Francesco Rosi has been equally rewarding. A trial transcript provided the source for Salvatore Giuliano's script, the framework for a film of epic dimension honed from events both sordid and sadly routine. But where she worked with a director whose own drive was towards honing away excesses and revealing a structure, the results were less happy. Where Antonioni saw his films as the bare rendition of reality, Cecchi d'Amico saw contemporary fables.

It was the opportunity posed by working for Visconti with his concern for the firm location of characters within a specific time, place, and history that drew from her her best work. She has said that his clarity of vision and sureness made him an easy person to work for, and there is an obvious complementarity between her spareness and Visconti's rhetorical visual style. Initial efforts for him required copious pruning to adapt them to his particular "cinematic rhythm." So completely did Visconti make his projects his own that they escape the category of "literary adaptation," and are rewritten and reformed to his own vision. Where a subject interested him but a suitable text could not be found, Cecchi d'Amico has spoken of the preparation of a script only after a considerable amount of research had been done. Even a contemporary subject might have a literary analogue. Thus Dostoyevsky was a touchstone for *Rocco and His Brothers.*

Rocco, an original story, knits its moral conundrum into a precisely located mise-en-scène, as it follows the attempts of a Southern peasant family to adjust to a new life in the North, and in doing so charts the stresses attendant upon Italy's own path to industrialization.

The script's major coup is the withholding of an explicit statement of the immigrant's code of morality until the final section, where it acquires an especially revelatory force, marking a passage from the certainties of an agrarian society, to notions of compromise embodied in a trade-off between rights and duties. The concern for issues of morality, betrayal, and personal and national history that are present here also underlie many of her other projects for Visconti, including *The Innocent, Senso, Ludwig,* and *Conversation Piece.*

The same concerns give her extraordinary gallery of female characters a memorable distinctiveness. Often transgressive they are always true to their time and place and never airbrushed into stereotype. Another consistent thread has been her collaborations with Monicelli, a director known for his humorously ironic tales of bourgeois life. The 1990 *Il male oscuro* was scripted with Tonino Guerra from a prize-winning 1960s novel (translated as *Incubus* in the United States) by Giuseppe Berto. It studies the relationships between a mediocre writer undergoing analysis, his younger wife, and his obsessive, ambivalent relationship with his father. The family theme is continued with *Parenti serpenti,* an examination of the tensions that arise as three generations of an extended family attempt Christmas together. Humor and irony also underlie her contributions to the script for Mikhalkov's *Dark Eyes.*

Her experience of writing a supposedly "Ben Hecht" script for Wyler's *Roman Holiday* (she took the job out of admiration for the director), which involved stringing together a series of banal generic elements, merely confirmed her observations of the wholly pernicious effect of Hollywood's postwar incursion into Italian filmmaking. (The Italian industry was, in her opinion, to be destroyed and the country opened up as a market for U.S. product.) Occasionally there were other international co-productions, including the Taylor-Burton *The Taming of the Shrew* for which her early experience as a translator of English literature into Italian might in part have prepared her, and on which she worked with Paul Dehn. But her preoccupations lay elsewhere. Cecchi d'Amico has always believed in the necessity of developing a national cinema that would "tell its own stories." It has been an unstinting dedication to this principle which underlies her work.—VERINA GLAESSNER

Chenzira, Ayoka

American producer, director, animator, and writer

Born *Philadelphia, 1956.* ***Education*** *Attended New York University, B.F.A. 1975; Columbia University/Teachers College, M.A.* ***Family*** *Married the choreographer Thomas Osha Pinnock, daughter: Haj.* ***Career*** *1981-84—program director of the Black Filmmakers Foundation; 1984—one of seven writer/directors selected for the Sundance Institute; mid-1980s—formed Red Carnelian, a production and distribution company in New York; founding board member, Production Partners, New York; professor and chair, department of communications, film, and video, City College of New York; 1993—producer/director of a series of animated shorts for the Children's Television Workshop; 1996—consultant to M-Net Television, South Africa.* ***Awards*** *Brooklyn Cultural Crossroads*

Ayoka Chenzira. Photograph by André Harris.

Achievement Award, 1981; Paul Robeson Award, 1984; First Place/Cultural Affairs, National Black Programming Consortium, 1984; Mayor's Award—New York, Outstanding Contributions to the Field, 1987; Mayor's Award—Detroit, Contributions to the Field, 1987; First Place for Animation, Black Filmmakers Hall of Fame, for Zajota and the Boogie Spirit, *1990; Best Producer, National Black Programming Consortium, 1990; Silver Apple, National Educational Film and Video Festival, 1990; First Place, Sony Innovator Award in Media, 1991; First Place, John Hanks Award, 1991; First Place, Dance Screen, 1992; Best Overall, Best Drama, and Community Choice Award, Black Filmmakers Hall of Fame, for* MOTV, *1993.* **Address** *Red Carnelian, 1380 Dean Street, Brooklyn, NY 11216, U.S.A.*

Films as Director: 1979: *Syvilla: They Dance to Her Drum* (doc, short) (+ pr, sc). **1982:** *Flamboyant Ladies Speak Out* (short). **1984:** *Hair Piece: A Film for Nappyheaded People* (animated short) (+ pr, sc, co-ed, art work, animation). **1985:** *Secret Sounds Screaming* (doc, short) (+ pr, mus). **1986:** *Five Out of Five* (mus video) (+ ed). **1988:** *Boa Morte* (doc, short) (+ co-pr). **1989:** *The Lure and the Lore* (short) (+ pr, ed). **1990:** *Zajota and the Boogie Spirit* (short) (+ pr, sc, ed, animation). **1992:** *Pull Your Head to the Moon* (short—for TV); *Williamswood* (short—for TV) (+ ed). **1993:** *Love Potion* (short) (+ pr); *Alma's Rainbow* (+ co-pr, sc); *MOTV (My Own TV)* (+ pr). **1994:** *Snowfire* (short) (+ pr, sc, mus, ph). **1995:** *Sentry at the Gate: The Comedy of Jane Galvin-Lewis* (+ co-pr, ph). **1997:** *In the Rivers of Mercy Angst* (short) (+ pr, sc, ph).

Other Film: 1986: *On Becoming a Woman* (Chisolm) (animation).

Ayoka Chenzira, considered one of the first African-American women animators, is an independent film and video artist who has received international renown in the areas of dramatic narrative, experimental, documentary, animation, and cross-genre productions. She brings to her work a diverse background in the arts, including photography, theater, music, and dance. Like many other African-American media artists, Chenzira can also be considered a media activist because her work challenges the exclusionary practices of mainstream media and frees African Americans from the confines of one-dimensional stereotypes. But she can also be considered a media activist in a stricter sense because of her efforts as an educator and her efforts on behalf of other film and video artists. Chenzira's most well-known works are *Hair Piece: A Film for Nappyheaded People* (1984), *Secret Sounds Screaming* (1985), and *Alma's Rainbow* (1993), three very different films, with differing subjects and styles—demonstrating Chenzira's varied talents as a film and video artist.

Hair Piece is a satirical animated short film about the cultural politics of African-American hairstyles. Chenzira uses humor to comment on a very serious and rarely discussed subject—the internalization of European standards of beauty by African Americans and its negative effects. Like "colorism," the preference for lighter-skin tones over darker, the delineation of "good hair" from "bad hair" has had severe consequences for the African-American community, affecting familial relationships, employment, education, and self-esteem. By affirming the natural beauty of natural hair styles over processed, *Hair Piece,* as Gloria Gibson-Hudson states, "dramatizes that exploration and affirmation of self can bring a keener sense of one's personal and cultural identity."

Chenzira was one of the first media producers to address the widespread problem of sexual child abuse with her documentary *Secret Sounds Screaming*. Rather than approaching the subject as one consisting of isolated cases, Chenzira places the abuse of children within a social and cultural context. It is a unique documentary, as it allows individuals from different aspects of the problem to directly address the audience: survivors of sexual child abuse, parents of abused children, and social-service professionals.

Alma's Rainbow, Chenzira's first feature-length film, is a contemporary drama set in Brooklyn, New York. As a coming-of-age film it is uncommon, because it is centered on the experiences of an African-American girl and her relationship with two other female characters: her aunt and her mother.

In addition to her work as a media artist, Chenzira is also a professor of communications, film, and video at City College of New York. Chenzira has been an important force in the lives of the students, department, and institution. In addition to her contributions in the classroom, her tenure at the college has included service as the director of the B.F.A. program in production, development of special workshops and seminars, and facilitating the participation of media professionals such as director Julie Dash, cinematographer Robert Shepard, and editor Lillian Benson, the first African-American woman accepted into the American Cinema Editors union.

In the mid-1980s Chenzira formed Red Carnelian, a New York-based production and distribution company that focuses on media production depicting the life and culture of African Americans. In addition to its successful distribution division, Black Indie Classics, Red Carnelian also provides instruction in film and video making. By providing such a service at a minimal cost to participants, Chenzira is helping to make the field of media production more inclusive, providing access to communities and individuals normally without access and without voice.

She also works as an arts administrator and lobbyist for independent cinema, distributing and exhibiting hundreds of films by African-American artists internationally. As a founding board member of Production Partners, a New York-based nonprofit organization developed for the purpose of increasing the visibility of African-American and Latino films, she was instrumental in providing support for such films as Charles Lane's award-winning feature *Sidewalk Stories*. Chenzira has also served as a media panelist for the Jerome Foundation, the National Endowment for the Arts, and the New York State Council on the Arts. As a panelist for the Minority Task Force on Public Television, her work, along with 14 other panelists, resulted in the establishment of the first Multi-cultural Public Television Fund.—FRANCES K. GATEWARD

Child, Abigail

American director

***Born** 1948. **Career** Lecturer, filmmaker; mid-1970s—began working in cinema in San Francisco on documentary films before shifting to experimental film; 1980—moved to New York.*

Films as Director: **1970:** *Except the People.* **1972:** *Game.* **1975:** *Tar People.* **1977:** *Some Exterior Presence, Peripeteia I.* **1978:** *Daylight Test Section, Peripeteia II.* **1979:** *Pacific Far East Line, Ornamentals.* **1996:** *B/Side.*

***Is This What You Were Born For?* collection:** **1981:** *Prefaces* (Part 1). **1983:** *Mutiny* (Part 3). **1984:** *Covert Action* (Part 4). **1986:** *Perils* (Part 5). **1987:** *Mayhem* (Part 6). **1988:** *Both* (Part 2). **1989:** *Mercy* (Part 7).

New York-based filmmaker Abigail Child is primarily known for a seven-part series of films entitled *Is This What You Were Born For?* This intellectually challenging group of films explores genre, issues of representation, sexual identity, and body politics. The films are also significant explorations into film form, including the aesthetic possibilities of sound in cinema. As Lotz claims "Child's short, dense, and highly poetic films work to de-stabilize familiar images, sequences, and tableaux, insistently exploring the artifices which structure narrative, and probing them for moments of rupture and excess." Child's films use radical editing patterns, repetitions, image and sound fragments, and found footage to create their highly stylized, rigorous forms. Her films explicitly reference narrative genres such as film noir and melodrama in their interrogation of narrative codes and theories of representation. Child is representative of those avant-garde filmmakers in the late 1970s and early 1980s who combined the severe structuralist preoccupations of the early 1970s with more explicit ideological explorations. Child's films differ from other theory films of the period in that their ideological inquiry does not overwhelm the formal experimentation and visual poetry in the films. Her work is also intensely musical, and has as much connection to certain kinds of language poetry and experimental music of the 1980s as to other avant-garde films. *Perils,* one of the films from this series, features music by John Zorn on the soundtrack.

Child's most significant and best-known film is the 1987 *Mayhem,* which is specifically concerned with sexual politics and how narrative codes position the viewer ideologically. A difficult work that ends with a sequence from a Japanese pornographic film from the 1920s, *Mayhem* is infused with references to the rhetoric of film noir and melodrama, and creates an elaborate structure to explore the cinematic representation of male and female bodies. Child has stated that this film is her attempt "to create a film in which sound is the character, and to do so focusing on sexuality and the erotic" (Child, "Program Notes," 1990). *Mayhem* includes many shots that employ single-source lighting common to film noir of the 1940s to create highly expressionist images. Characters are dressed in 1940s attire and are frequently framed in ritualized poses. The images constantly intercut between characters looking and being looked at, and individuals engaged in continuous pursuit. Child takes the rhetoric of the 1940s detective genre, a genre associated with danger, desire, violence, narrative entanglement, and obsessive behavior, and omits the narrative context for this rhetoric. *Mayhem* has no story because a story would be irrelevant to the film's project. The film is more interested in examining the language of film and how we position ourselves as viewers.

The most radical aspects of *Mayhem* are its montage, which constantly cuts off shots and scenes before we can make sense of them, and the film's sound construction, which also relies on fragmentation and repetition for its effectiveness. The formal severity of image and sound strategies make it an extremely abstract work despite its reliance on representational imagery. The film undoubtedly invokes the Russian Formalist precept of "laying bare" the workings of art by making the viewer aware of its construction. The rhetoric of discontinuity is paramount in *Mayhem* just as continuity is the primary mode in Hollywood classical cinema. Child's feminist project in *Mayhem* also includes portraying the film's male figures as sex objects. The film's nonlinear, fragmentary style and use of negative imagery creates a kind of dream logic to the proceedings. *Mayhem* ends with a now notorious sequence of two Japanese women engaged in a sex act being observed by a male thief, who is then captured by the women and forced to engage in sex with them. The sound that has been added to this sequence is a jaunty musical tune overlaid with voices of women. In fact, the human voice is a key articulating device throughout the film.

The notion of musicality also enters into *Mercy,* a film that functions altogether differently than *Mayhem*. It includes much found footage and is constructed in a collage style with many images referencing the organic and the body. The human figure is presented in a variety of contexts and in radically different film forms. Child includes footage from Hollywood movies, nonfiction films, and her own footage as well. The film also intermingles black-and-white stock with color footage. *Mercy* is a vibrant exploration of the rhythmical principle in cinema, and is much less concerned with sexual politics and feminist ideology than *Mayhem*. It is reminiscent of the films of Bruce Conner and Arthur Lipsett, filmmakers known for their collage stylistics, image and sound interaction, and use of found footage. Once again, sound plays a key role in *Mercy* as it does in most of Child's other work.

Abigail Child is one of the most intriguing filmmakers to emerge in the last 15 years, and her films explore the more complex possibilities of formal experimentation in both image and sound. Her work is aesthetically groundbreaking and deserves thoughtful in-depth analysis, something it has rarely received since much of the critical comment around her films has tended to place her within the narrow context of sexual politics and lesbian filmmaking. Her artwork is much more than that.—MARIO FALSETTO

Chopra, Joyce

American director

Born *1938.* ***Education*** *Studied comparative literature at Brandeis University, graduated; studied acting at the Neighborhood Playhouse in New York City.* ***Family*** *Married the screenwriter Tom Cole, one daughter.* ***Career*** *1960s—started Club 47, a coffeehouse for folksingers; 1972—co-directed renowned feminist short for PBS,* Joyce at 34; *1985—directed critically well-received first feature film* Smooth Talk; *1990s—works as television movie director.* ***Awards*** *Bronze Award, Venice International Film Festival, for* A Happy Mother's Day, *1963; Grand Jury Prize, Sundance Film Festival, for* Smooth Talk, *1985.* ***Agent*** *Paul Allan Smith, Broder Kurland Webb Uffner, 9242 Beverly Boulevard, Los Angeles, CA 90210, U.S.A.*

Films as Director: 1963: *A Happy Mother's Day* (doc—co-d with Leacock). **1972:** *Joyce at 34* (co-d with Weill—doc short). **1975:** *Girls at 12* (doc); *David Wheeler: Theater Company of Boston* (doc). **1976:** *Clorae & Albie.* **1978:** *That Our Children Will Not Die* (doc). **1980:** *Martha Clarke Light and Dark: A Dancer's Journal* (co-d, + ed, pr). **1985:** *Smooth Talk.* **1989:** *The Lemon Sisters.* **1992:** *Baby Snatcher* (for TV); *The Danger of Love* (for TV); *Murder in New Hampshire: The Pamela Wojas Smart Story* (for TV). **1993:** *The Disappearance of Nora* (for TV); *Angel Falls* (for TV). **1994:** *The Corpse Had a Familiar Face* (for TV). **1995:** *Deadline for Murder: From the Files of Edna Buchanan* (for TV). **1997:** *L.A. Johns* (*Confessions*) (for TV); *Convictions* (for TV). **1999:** *Murder in a Small Town* (for TV).

Joyce Chopra gained renown in the early 1970s, especially among feminists, as the co-director and star of *Joyce at 34,* a feminist independent documentary short. She continued to make documentaries until 1986, when she garnered attention for her well-regarded first fiction feature *Smooth Talk.*

Joyce at 34 was one of the earliest and most respected feminist documentaries, like Kate Millett's *Three Lives* and Donna Deitch's *Woman to Woman,* which used simple formats to depict the ordinary details of real women's lives, along with the constraints and successes attached to their endeavors to move into traditionally male realms of work and power. In the case of *Joyce,* the real woman is Chopra herself; she speaks directly to an intended female audience about her life, in particular about the possibilities that marriage, family, and career can be harmoniously combined, and also about the conflicts between her pregnancy and filmmaking aspirations. The film scholar E. Ann Kaplan, however, criticized the film for assuming a position of absolute knowledge, so that viewers are forced into the position of passive consumers. Nevertheless, it has long held a firm position in the feminist film canon.

Chopra was considered by many critics to be a "new" director in 1985 when she made *Smooth Talk,* despite more than ten years of filmmaking experience; yet, the film marked a breakthrough in her career. It focuses on the emergent sexuality of an adolescent young woman who radiates a palpable sensuality, but seems unaware of its power.

Originally intended as a one-hour film for PBS's *American Playhouse,* it developed into a feature film at the script-writing stage. The producer obtained additional funding with the stipulation that the film would screen on PBS 18 months after the theatrical release. The extremely low-budget feature was shot in 32 days entirely on location, and cast and crew all worked for scale. Adapted by her screenwriter-husband Tom Coles from the well-known Joyce Carol Oates short story "Where Are You Going, Where Have You Been?," it minimized the metaphysical elements of Oates's story to focus instead upon the realistic intimations of a young woman's sexual coming-of-age. Notably, it depicts the complexities of both youth and femininity, rather than the mall, fast food, and often insipid, masculine milieu of Hollywood's more typical teenpics. Laura Dern convincingly plays the young heroine who clashes with her family, while finding a giddy camaraderie with her teenage girlfriends, until she is seduced and then raped by a menacing man. As a result, according to some feminist critics, the film seemed to fly in the face of traditional feminism.

That is, mainstream critics praised the film, but many feminist critics disparaged it, especially the formidable B. Ruby Rich who chastised Chopra for depicting a regressive puritanical sexual double standard that seems to punish its young heroine for her sexuality. Rich complained that Chopra's message was intended to stifle youthful feminine sexuality because to express it would ensure that "a grownup bogeyman Arnold Friend will come and get you." She further determined that Chopra was motivated by the fact that she herself had been the mother of a teenage daughter when she made the film. But the film can be interpreted rather differently, in terms of its depiction of the pleasure as well as the dangers of feminine sexual initiation. Further, while the rape of the young heroine is problematic, it nevertheless adheres to Oates's story. Indeed, other feminist critics praised Chopra for the film's refreshing balance between the characters of the mother and the daughter. Chopra manages to convey the engagingly exuberant yet disturbingly naive sexuality of the daughter as well as her indifference to the adults around her. On the other hand, the mother's poignantly conveyed love, anger, and worry for her daughter, and her regret that they are no longer close is equally important to the film. Certainly, Chopra goes far beyond the usual teenpics with their absent or unjustifiably shrill mothers to give this teen heroine's mother a voice.

Chopra claimed that her primary goal in *Smooth Talk* was to portray the teenagers as "full humans" who speak with individual voices in order to counter the stereotypical teenage voices that predominated in other films. Accordingly, she cited her documentary about 12-year-old girls in Waltham, Massachusetts, as a source for much of *Smooth Talk,* including a moving scene she re-created in which Dern's character sits alone stringing beads in her bedroom. In addition,

Chopra's 14-year-old daughter reportedly provided snippets of conversations she had heard at school to add subtlety to the characterizations. Thus, Chopra succeeded in offering a nuanced, realistic depiction of a young woman, who is played with a poignant charm by Dern, during her ambivalent coming-of-age—which is highlighted by her wary sexual attraction to the macho stranger, played with a sinister appeal by Treat Williams.

Following the release of *Smooth Talk,* Chopra was deluged with scripts to direct more typical teenpics. She eventually agreed to direct the film adaptation of Jay McInerney's best-seller, *Bright Lights, Big City,* but three weeks into the production she was replaced by James Bridges (known for directing *The China Syndrome, Urban Cowboy,* and *Perfect*), apparently because the studio considered her feminist perspective problematic. Her second feature film, *The Lemon Sisters,* was produced by Diane Keaton who also starred with Carol Kane. It tells the touching story of an enduring friendship between three girlfriends, from childhood to middle age, who as youngsters growing up in a more-innocent Atlantic City jauntily dubbed themselves the "Lemon Sisters." Despite their relationships with men, both alive and dead, the characters' most important relationships are with each other. The story was loosely inspired by the real-life friendship of the three lead actresses and their shared nostalgia for Atlantic City. A more recent directorial assignment for Chopra was the well-realized television movie, *Murder in New Hampshire,* about the notorious young high-school teacher, Pamela Smart, who was convicted of murder for persuading her teenage lover to kill her husband.

In general, Chopra's work treats the themes of sexuality and sensuality of women; further, her films often focus on the transitional periods in women's lives—puberty in *Smooth Talk,* pregnancy in *Joyce at 34,* as well as the new boyfriends, new lifestyles, and new business ventures that are depicted in *The Lemon Sisters.* In addition, she typically employs fairly conventional filmmaking strategies, including the cinema verité of *Joyce* and the traditional narrative of *Smooth Talk, The Lemon Sisters,* and *Murder in New Hampshire.* Currently, Chopra works as a director of television series and movies.—CYNTHIA FELANDO

Choy, Christine

American director and cinematographer

Born *Chai Ming Huei, in the People's Republic of China, 1952, to a Chinese mother and Korean father.* **Education** *Studied architecture at New York's Manhattanville College of the Sacred Heart; Columbia University, master's degree in urban planning.* ***Career*** *1960s—became interested in film while living in Korea; 1966—came to the United States by herself; 1971—became involved with Newsreel; 1971—began working in documentary film as an editor and animator; 1972—directed her first documentary,* Teach Our Children; *mid-1970s—became executive director of Third World Newsreel; became associate professor at (and, later, chairperson of) the graduate film/TV department of New York University's Tisch School of the Arts; 1988—received Academy Award nomination for Best Documentary as co-director of* Who Killed Vincent Chin?; *1991—"Christine Choy: A Retrospective" presented at the Queens (New York) Museum of Art.* ***Awards*** *First Prize, International Black Film Festival, for* Teach Our Children, *1972; Best Subject Matter, Ann Arbor Film Festival, for* To Love, Honor, and Obey, *1980; Alfred DuPont Columbia University Award, George Foster Peabody Award, Outstanding Film, London Internation-*

al Film Festival, Best Documentary, Hawaii International Film Festival, and Award Winner at U.S. Film Festival, for Who Killed Vincent Chin?, *1988; Ace Award for Best Documentary Special, and First Place, Mannheim International Film Festival, for* Best Hotel on Skid Row, *1989; Juror's Citation, Black Maria Film Festival, for* Yellow Tale Blues, *1991; Golden Gate Award, San Francisco Film Festival,* Homes Apart: Korea, *1991; Achievement Award, Hong Kong International Film Festival, for* Mississippi Triangle, *1992; Cinematography Award, Sundance Film Festival, for* My America, *1996.* ***Address*** *Graduate Film Department, Tisch School of the Arts, New York University, 721 Broadway, New York, NY 10003, U.S.A.*

Films as Director: **1972:** *Teach Our Children* (co-d, + ph, ed). **1975:** *Fresh Seeds in a Big Apple* (co-d, + ed, sound); *Generation of the Railroad Builder* (+ ed). **1976:** *From Spikes to Spindles* (+ pr). **1977:** *History of the Chinese Patriot Movement in the U.S.* (+ ed); *North Country Tour* (+ sound rec). **1978:** *Inside Women Inside* (co-d, + exec pr, ph); *Loose Pages Bound* (+ pr). **1980:** *To Love, Honor, and Obey* (co-d, + ph). **1981:** *Bittersweet Survival* (co-d, + pr, 2nd camera); *White Flower Passing.* **1982:** *Go Between* (+ pr). **1983:** *Mississippi Triangle* (*Mississippi Mah Jong Blues*) (co-d with Long and Siegel, + pr, ph, researcher); *Fei Tien, Goddess in Flight.* **1984:** *Namibia, Independence Now* (co-d). **1985:** *Monkey King Looks West* (+ ph). **1986:** *Permanent Wave* (co-d). **1988:** *Shanghai Lil's* (+ pr); *Who Killed Vincent Chin?* (co-d with Tajima, + ph). **1989:** *China Today* (+ pr); *Best Hotel on Skid Row* (co-d, + co-pr, ph); *Fortune Cookies: The Myth of the Model Minority* (+ pr). **1991:** *Yellow Tale Blues: Two American Families* (co-d with Tajima); *Homes Apart: Korea* (*Homes Apart: The Two Koreas*) (co-d, + pr, ph, interviewer). **1993:** *SA-I-GU* (co-d with Kim-Gibson, + pr, ph). **1995:** *In the Name of the Emperor* (co-d with Tong, + ph); *Not a Simple Story*; *Out in Silence.* **1997:** *The Shot Heard 'Round the World* (co-d with Lampros, + pr).

Other Films: **1971:** *The Dead Earth* (ed, anim). **1973:** *Nigeria, Nigeria One* (ed). **1975:** *In the Event That Anyone Disappears* (ed). **1978:** *A Dream Is What You Wake Up From* (exec pr). **1979:** *People's Firehouse Number 1* (exec pr); *Percussion, Impression & Reality* (exec pr). **1981:** *The American Writer's Congress* (unit d); *Boy and Tarzan Appear in a Clearing* (unit d, camera). **1984:** *Chronicle of Hope: Nicaragua* (pr). **1987:** *Audre Lord Story* (pr, ph); *Haitian Corner* (pr); *Making of the Sun City* (unit d). **1995:** *Litany for Survival: The Life and Work of Audre Lord* (co-ph). **1996:** *My America . . . or Honk if You Love Buddha* (ph).

Christine Choy uses film as a political/humanist tool. Most specifically, she is concerned with injustice as it is perpetrated on individuals or entire peoples. Her films work as oral and visual histories and records of events, with one of her major concerns being the manner in which people of color are represented on screen.

Choy is most involved with issues relating to Asia and Asian Americans, and this is a direct reflection of her own heritage. By exploring the life of an individual or the sides of an issue, Choy wishes to educate and enlighten—and help sustain political and social change. Those of her films that focus on contemporary problems effectively bring these problems to the forefront. Those that spotlight incidents out of history serve as indispensable documents of that history, and become visual records that help ensure that the events chronicled will not be lost in the pages of time. The best-case scenario is that these incidents now will be well remembered and, if they involve injustice, that injustice will not be repeated in the future.

In the early 1970s Choy worked as a film cleaner/cataloguer/sometime editor at Newsreel (later known as Third World Newsreel), an alternative media arts organization that describes itself as being "committed to the creation and appreciation of independent and social issue media by and about people of color, and the peoples of developing countries around the world." Choy recalls: "When the inmates of Attica prison rebelled in 1971, I submitted a proposal to Newsreel. I argued that it was fine for white, upper-middle-class males to document the struggles of the Third World communities, but it was about time that the Third World people have an opportunity to express themselves. I raised some funds and with two other black women I produced my first documentary on Attica, called *Teach Your Children*"—thus beginning a prolific and multi-award-winning directorial career.

A number of Choy's films are portraits of Asian-American individuals, families, and communities. Here, she emphasizes the manner in which individuals live within communities, co-exist with their neighbors, and respond to the world around them. *Mississippi Triangle,* co-directed with Worth Long and Allan Siegel, is a portrait of life on the Mississippi Delta, where Chinese, African Americans, and whites coexist. The history of the area's various communities is placed within the framework of daily life and culture, class and gender, racial friction, and the civil rights movement. *SA-I-GU,* co-directed with Daisil Kim-Gibson, is a look at the citizens of Los Angeles's Koreatown after the Rodney King verdict, with a focus on the effect of the subsequent riots on Korean-American women. Perhaps her most personal film is *Yellow Tale Blues: Two American Families,* co-directed with Renee Tajima, a portrait of the filmmakers' contrasting families—Choy's is immigrant and working class while Tajima's is fourth generation and middle class—and the manner in which their members have assimilated into the American melting pot. The emphasis in *Monkey King Looks West* is the maintenance of cultural tradition. Here, Choy charts the attempts by classically trained Chinese opera performers to pass on their heritage and their art form to young Chinese Americans as they struggle to survive economically in New York's Chinatown. And *Not a Simple Story* and *Out in Silence* are portraits of two Asian Americans living under the specter of AIDS, and who have become AIDS activists: Vince, a gay man, and Robin, a widow who contracted the disease from her husband.

A number of Choy's films deal directly with racism and violence. *Who Killed Vincent Chin?,* also co-directed with Tajima, is arguably Choy's best-known film. She and Tajima investigate the economic and political factors that led to the death of Chin, a 27-year-old Chinese American celebrating his upcoming marriage, in a Detroit bar in 1982. He got into an argument with Ron Ebens, an unemployed auto worker, and Ebens—who thought Chin was Japanese—eventually beat Chin to death with a baseball bat. Similarly, *The Shot Heard 'Round the World,* co-directed with Spiro Lampros, explores the events surrounding the killing of Yoshi Hattori, a Japanese high-school exchange student, who was shot to death in a Baton Rouge suburb in 1992 while attempting to ask directions to a party. These films emphasize the manner in which the fear of individuals who look or speak differently may result not only in miscommunication and racism but violence, and the negligence of the American judicial system with regard to the issue of equal justice for all.

Additionally, Choy is concerned with events out of the past as they relate to her mother continent. *In the Name of the Emperor,* co-directed with Nancy Tong, documents what has come to be known as the "Rape of Nanjing": the massacre of more than 300,000 Chinese civilians by the Japanese during a six-week-long period in 1937, all "in the name of Emperor Hirohito." The film works as a clear-minded record of an event that is little known in the West, that Japan would much rather ignore, and that is in danger of being forgotten forever. Its point, soberingly made, is that the Nazi extermination of the Jews was not the lone Holocaust of the 1930s-40s.

When examining the films of Christine Choy, a question arises: Is it important to evaluate the impact of her work in fostering racial, political, and social enlightenment? After all, Vincent Chin was killed in 1982. Ten years later, Yoshi Hattori lost his life in an act of violence that was just as random and racist. In a perfect world, every hatemonger would view *Who Killed Vincent Chin?* and *The Shot Heard 'Round the World* and come away with an aroused conscience while summarily counting him or herself an ex-racist.

Ultimately, the point is not how effective her films have been in perpetuating social change, but that they have been made and seen in the first place—and the result is the potential to impact positively on even one viewer, and compel even one individual to reevaluate his or her world view. It remains essential that dedicated and fair-minded political filmmakers such as Choy—whose concerns are not altered by what is currently in fashion—persist in producing films that are politically savvy, and that seek to expose the bitter truths of their subject matter.

Finally and happily, in her position as an educator at New York University's Tisch School of the Arts, Choy is in the position to positively influence the upcoming generation of documentary filmmakers.—ROB EDELMAN

Chytilová, Věra

Czech director

***Born** Ostrava, 2 February 1929. **Education** Studied architecture at Charles University; Film Academy (FAMU), Prague, 1957-62. **Family** Married the cinematographer Jaroslav Kučera. **Career** 1956—assistant director on* 3 Men Missing; *1962—directed first film,* The Ceiling; *1969-76—forbidden to direct or work for foreign producers. **Address** c/o Barrandov Studios, Prague, Czech Republic.*

Films as Director: 1962: *Strop* (*The Ceiling*) (+ sc); *Pytel blech* (*A Bag of Fleas*) (+ sc). **1963:** *O něčem jiném* (*Something Different*; *Something Else*; *Another Way of Life*) (+ sc). **1965:** "Automat Svět" ("The World Cafe") ep. of *Perličky na dně* (*Pearls of the Deep*) (+ co-sc). **1966:** *Sedmikrásky* (*Daisies*) (+ co-sc). **1969:** *Ovoce stromů rajských jíme* (*The Fruit of Paradise*; *We Eat the Fruit of the Trees of Paradise*) (+ co-sc). **1977:** *Hra o jablko* (*The Apple Game*) (+ sc). **1978:** *Cas je neúprosný* (*Inexorable Time*) (short). **1979:** *Panelstory* (*Prefab Story*) (+ co-sc). **1980:** *Kalamita* (*Calamity*) (+ co-sc). **1981:** *Chytilová versus Forman*. **1983:** *Faunovo prilis pozdni odpoledne* (*The Very Late Afternoon of a Faun*) (+ co-sc). **1985:** *Praha, neklidne srace Europy* (*Prague, the Restless Heart of Europe*) (short). **1986:** *Vlci bouda* (*Wolf's Hole*) (+ co-sc). **1987:** *Sasek a kralovna* (*The Jester and the Queen*); *Kopytem Sem, Kopytem Tam* (*Tainted Horseplay*) (+ sc). **1990:** *T.G.M.—Osvoboditel* (*Tomas G. Masaryk—The Liberator*) (+ sc). **1991:** *Mi Prazane me Rozùmeji* (*My Praguers Understand Me*). **1992:** *Dědictví aneb Kurvahošigutntag* (*The Legacy*; *The Inheritance or Fuckoffguysgoodbye*). **1993:** *Kam Parenky* (+ sc). **1998:** *Pasti, Pasti, pasticky* (*Trap, Trap, Little Trap*).

Other Films: 1956: *Ztracenci* (*3 Men Missing*) (asst d). **1958:** *Konec jasnovidce* (*End of a Clairvoyant*) (ro as girl in bikini). **1991:** *Face of Hope* (sc).

So far the only important woman director of the Czech cinema is Věra Chytilová, its most innovative and probably most controversial personality. She is the only contemporary Czech filmmaker to work in the Eisensteinian tradition. She combines didacticism with often daring experimentation, based in essence on montage. Disregarding chronology and illustrative realism, she stresses the symbolic nature of images as well as visual and conceptual shock. Influenced to some extent also by cinema verité, particularly by its female representatives, and militantly feminist in her attitudes, she nevertheless made excellent use of the art of her husband, the cameraman Jaroslav Kučera, in her boldest venture to date, *Daisies*. This film, Chytilová's best known, is a dazzling display of montage, tinting, visual deformation, film trickery, color

Věra Chytilová

processing, etc.—a multifaceted tour de force which, among other things, is also a tribute to the classics of the cinema, from the Lumière brothers to Chaplin and Abel Gance. It contains shots, scenes, and sequences that utilize the most characteristic techniques and motives of the masters. *Daisies* is Chytilová at her most formalist. In her later films, there is a noticeable shift towards realism. All the principles mentioned above, however, still dominate the more narrative approach, and a combination of unusual camera angles, shots, etc., together with a bitterly sarcastic vision, lead to hardly less provocative shock effects.

The didactical content of these highly sophisticated and subtly formalist works of filmic art, as in Eisenstein, is naive and crude: young women should prefer "useful" vocations to "useless" ones (*The Ceiling*); extremes of being active and being inactive both result in frustration (*Something Different*); irresponsibility and recklessness lead to a bad end (*Daisies*); a sexual relationship is something serious, not just irresponsible amusement (*The Apple Game*); people should help each other (*Prefab Story, Calamity*). Given the fact that Chytilová has worked mostly under the conditions of an enforced and harshly repressive establishment, a natural explanation of this seeming incongruity offers itself: the "moral messages" of her films are simply libations that enable her, and her friends among the critics, to defend the unashamedly formalist films and the harshly satirical presentation of social reality they contain. This is corroborated by Chytilová's many clashes with the political authorities in Czechoslovakia: from an interpellation in the Parliament calling for a ban of *Daisies* because so much food—"the fruit of the work of our toiling farmers"—is destroyed in the film, to her being fired from the Barrandov studios after the Soviet invasion in 1968, and on to her open letter to President Husák printed in Western newspapers. In each instance she won her case by a combination of publicly stated kosher ideological arguments, stressing the alleged "messages" of her works, and of backstage manipulation, not excluding the use of her considerable feminine charm. Consequently, she is the only one of the new wave of directors from the 1960s who, for a long time, had been able to continue making films in Czechoslovakia without compromising her aesthetic creed and her vision of society, as so many others had to do in order to remain in business (including Jaromil Jireš, Hynek Bočan, Jaroslav Papoušek, and to some extent Jiří Menzel).

Prefab Story and *Calamity* earned her hateful attacks from establishment critics and intrigues from her second-rate colleagues, who thrived on the absence of competition from such exiled or banned directors as Miloš Forman, Ivan Passer, Jan Němec, Evald Schorm, and Vojtěch Jasný. The two films were practically withdrawn from circulation and can be occasionally seen only in suburban theaters. In 1982 *Film a doba,* Czechoslovakia's only critical film periodical, published a series of three articles which, in veiled terms and using what playwright Václav Havel calls "dialectical metaphysics" ("on the one hand it is bad, but on the other hand it is also good"), defended the director and her right to remain herself. In her integrity, artistic boldness, and originality, and in her ability to survive the most destructive social and political catastrophes, Chytilová was a unique phenomenon in post-invasion Czech cinema. Unfortunately, during the last years of Communist rule in Czechoslovakia, she seems to have lost something of her touch, and her latest films—such as *The Very Late Afternoon of a Faun* or *The Jester and the Queen*—are clearly not on the level of *Daisies* or *Prefab Story*.

However, since the "velvet revolution" she has maintained her independence as idiosyncratically as ever. Refusing to take up any comfortably accommodating position, she has been accused of nostalgia for the Communist years. This would be to misrepresent her position. A fierce campaigner for a state subsidy for the Czech film industry, she cannot but lament the extent to which the implementation of the ideology of the "free market" has been allowed to accomplish what the Soviet regime never quite could—the extinguishing of Czech film culture.

She has made a number of documentary films for television as well as a 1992 comedy about the deleterious effects of sudden wealth, which was publicly well-received but met with critical opprobrium. She has so far failed to find funding for a long-cherished project, *Face of Hope,* about the 19th-century humanist writer Bozena Nemcova. The continuing relevance of *Daisies,* and its depiction of philistinism in several registers, is surely the strongest argument in support of Chytilová's position. It is a film which shines with the sheer craftsmanship Czech cinema achieved in those years.—JOSEF SKVORECKÝ and VERINA GLAESSNER

Citron, Michelle

American director

Born *1948.* ***Education*** *Studied psychology and film production at University of Wisconsin—Madison; earned Ph.D. in cognitive psychology.* ***Career*** *1974—taught film and television at Temple University; 1975-78—taught film at William James College in Grand Rapids, Michigan; 1978—first feature film,* Daughter Rite; *1979 to present—professor of film production at Northwestern University.* ***Address*** *Radio, TV, Video and Film Department, 1905 Sheridan Road, Northwestern University, Evanston, IL 60208, U.S.A.*

Films as Director: 1973: *Self-Defense*; *April 3, 1973.* **1974:** *Integration.* **1975:** *Parthenogenesis.* **1978:** *Daughter Rite.* **1983:** *What You Take for Granted* (+ sc, pr, ed); *Mother Right.*

Michelle Citron is well-known as a feminist independent filmmaker. Her best-known films are *Daughter Rite* and *What You Take for Granted,* both of which explore the concepts of realism, modernism, and manipulation of film form. She started as an avant-garde filmmaker and over the years she has gradually moved towards narrative filmmaking.

Unlike many filmmakers who have backgrounds in some area of the arts, Citron was inspired to become a filmmaker during the course of her doctoral studies in cognitive psychology, when she began taking film courses to enhance her dissertation project. In part, she was lured to film as a result of her commitment to political activism—she wanted to make films with which the scores of women involved in feminist "consciousness raising" could identify. In addition, she wanted to make films that challenged passive viewing habits and addressed feminist issues to advantage by using purely formal cinematic methods. Accordingly she experimented with blending documentary filmmaking's more familiar conventions with those of melodrama. In this way, she believed, women would be engaged by their recognition of certain genre characteristics and would perhaps be moved to question the "reality" of cinematic representations of women.

Citron's distinctive and overtly feminist films come from real experiences. For example, *Parthenogenesis* is a study of her sister's concert violin studies with a female instructor. In addition, the stories for *Daughter Rite* and *What You Take for Granted* were developed from her many interviews with women, which she conducted on the model of the feminist consciousness-raising group. From the interviews, Citron identified certain common experiences as the themes of the films. As she puts it, "There needs to be a synthesis between the world and my imagination." Thus her characters are composites of the many women she interviewed.

The experimental film *Daughter Rite* combined fictional, documentary, and experimental elements and proved to be a touchstone in the emerging realm of feminist independent filmmaking. Inspired, in part, by male avant-garde filmmaking, it bridges the gap between narrative and documentary films and uses a mock cinema-verité style to tell the story of two fictional sisters exploring their childhood together—as sisters and as daughters. American cinema verité purported to present objective looks at "reality," without imposing a viewpoint on that which was filmed. *Daughter Rite*'s "documentary" scenes, in which the sisters discuss their mother, employ the visual conventions of cinema-verité (e.g., shots of long duration, zooms in for closer shots, awkward unsteady camera, and on-screen focusing) and are quite convincing and easily confused with "reality." In one compelling scene, the sisters riffle through and comment upon their dead mother's personal belongings for clues about her personality and the details of her life. Further, the documentary-style scenes are intercut with home movies of two little girls with their mother that are slowed to a crawl and looped to run repeatedly; they are accompanied by a woman's voice-over reading journal entries in a thoughtful, flat tone. And, unlike traditional documentaries that use the "voice of god"-style of narration to lend a tone of authority, in *Daughter Rite* the voice-over is ambivalent and fails to provide easy answers or precise meanings; indeed, the voice-over occasionally does not seem to relate to the accompanying images at all. Based on her preliminary interviews, Citron discovered that there were some women who tried to carefully analyze their relationships with their mothers, while others told stories that displayed little self-awareness. The two types are represented in the film: one by the narrator and the other by the two sisters in the "documentary." Interestingly, Citron was surprised that audiences are so attuned to documentary film conventions that they typically believe the pseudo-documentary sequences are real. Indeed, that the film is mostly fictional becomes clear only as the end credits start to roll.

Citron's next film, *What You Take for Granted,* is about both professional and working-class women who work in a variety of jobs traditionally held by men. It suggests that the social and political realities of women doing "men's work" resonate in their personal lives, and that such work comes with heavy challenges, including the hostility of men and isolation. Also a pseudo-documentary, she developed six fictional women based on her preliminary interviews who describe their jobs and how and why they are doing them. Notably, the characters are identified in the film not by name, but by occupation—doctor, sculptor, philosophy professor, carpenter, cable-splicer, and truck driver—in order to generalize their commentary to the larger community of working women. Further, their "interviews" are edited so as to illuminate the similarities and differences of their varied experiences. These sequences alternate with narrative sequences that depict a friendship developing between the doctor and truck driver.

Daughter Rite and *What You Take for Granted* can be understood in the context of the 1970's call for a feminist cinematic language that would effectively "deconstruct" patriarchal film conventions and representations of women, but without providing easy answers. Both films, therefore, suggest that although documentaries pose as more truthful than fiction films, they cannot provide a privileged view of reality and actually may be more deceptive.

Citron is currently working on a feature film entitled *Heartland,* and finishing a book entitled *Home Movies, Autobiography, and Other Necessary Fictions,* about autobiographical film. She is also a professor of film production in the Radio, Television, Video, and Film Department at Northwestern University.—CYNTHIA FELANDO

Clarke, Shirley

American director

Born *Shirley Brimberg in New York City, 2 October 1919.* ***Education*** *Attended Stephens College, Johns Hopkins University, Bennington College, and University of North Carolina.* ***Family*** *Married the lithographer Bert Clarke, 1943; one daughter, Wendy.* ***Career*** *1946-53—dancer with Martha Graham and Doris Humphrey, also chairwoman, National Dance Foundation; 1954—made first film,* A Dance in the Sun; *1962—co-founder, with Jonas Mekas, Film-Makers Cooperative; late 1960s—worked with Public Broadcast*

Lab (fired 1969); 1975-85—professor of film and video at University of California, Los Angeles. ***Awards*** *Maya Deren Award, American Film Institute, 1989.* ***Died*** *In Boston, 23 September 1997.*

Films as Director: 1954: *A Dance in the Sun* (+ pr, ph, ed, co-choreo); *In Paris Parks* (+ pr, ph, ed, co-choreo). **1955:** *Bullfight* (+ pr, co-ph, ed, co-choreo). **1957:** *A Moment in Love* (+ pr, co-ph, ed, co-choreo). **1958:** *The Skyscraper* (co-d, pr); *Brussels "Loops"* (12 film loops made for Brussels Exposition, destroyed) (+ pr, co-ph, ed). **1959:** *Bridges-Go-Round* (+ pr, co-ph, ed). **1960:** *A Scary Time* (+ co-sc, ph). **1961:** *The Connection* (+ co-pr, ed). **1963:** *The Cool World* (+ co-sc, ed); *Robert Frost: A Lover's Quarrel with the World* (co-d). **1967:** *Portrait of Jason* (+ pr, ed, voice); *Man in Polar Regions* (11-screen film for Expo '67). **1978:** *Trans*; *One Two Three*; *Mysterium*; *Initiation* (all video). **1981:** *Savage/Love* (video). **1982:** *Tongues* (video/theater collaboration with Sam Shepard). **1985:** *Ornette, Made in America.*

Other Films: 1959: *Opening in Moscow* (Pennebaker) (co-ed). **1969:** *Lions Love* (Varda) (ro as herself). **1977:** *March on Paris 1914—Of General Obrest Alexander von Kluck—and His Memory of Jessie Holladay* (Gutman) (co-ed).

Shirley Clarke was a leader and major filmmaker in the New York film community in the 1950s and 1960s. Her films, which exemplify the artistic directions of the independent movement, are classic examples of the best work of American independent filmmaking. Clarke began her professional career as a dancer. She participated in the late 1940s in the avant-garde dance community centered around New York City's Young Men's-Young Women's Hebrew Association's (YM-YWHA) performance stage and Hanya Holm's classes for young choreographers. In 1953 Clarke adapted dancer-choreographer Daniel Nagrin's *Dance in the Sun* to film. In her first dance film, Clarke relied on editing concepts to choreograph a new cinematic space and rhythm. She then applied her cinematic choreography to a nondance subject in *In Paris Parks,* and further explored the cinematic possibilities for formal choreography in her dance films, *Bullfight* and *A Moment in Love.*

During this period, Clarke studied filmmaking with Hans Richter at the City College of New York and participated in informal filmmaking classes with director and cinematographer Peter Glushanok. In 1955 she became an active member of the Independent Filmmakers of America (IFA), a short-lived New York organization that tried to improve promotion and distribution for independent films. Through the IFA, Clarke became part of the Greenwich Village artistic circle that included avant-garde filmmakers Maya Deren, Stan Brakhage, and Jonas Mekas. It also introduced her to the importance of an economic structure for the growth of avant-garde film, a cause she championed throughout the 1960s.

Clarke worked with filmmakers Willard Van Dyke, Donn Alan Pennebaker, Ricky Leacock, and Wheaton Galentine on a series of film loops on American life for the U.S. Pavilion at the 1958 World's Fair in Brussels. With the leftover footage of New York City bridges, she then made her experimental film masterpiece, *Bridges-Go-Round,* utilizing editing strategies, camera choreography, and color tints to turn naturalistic objects into a poem of dancing abstract elements. It is one of the best and most widely seen examples of cinematic abstract expressionism in the 1950s.

Clarke made the documentary film *The Skyscraper* in 1958 with Van Dyke, Pennebaker, Leacock, and Galentine, followed by *A Scary Time* (1960), a film commissioned by the United Nations International Children's Emergency Fund (UNICEF). Clarke also began work on a public television film on Robert Frost, *A Lover's Quarrel with the World,* but due to artistic disagree-

Shirley Clarke

ments and other commitments she left the project before the film's completion while retaining a credit as co-director.

Influenced by the developing cinema-verité style in the documentary films of Leacock and Pennebaker, Clarke adapted cinema verité to two feature-length dramatic films, *The Connection* and *The Cool World*. *The Connection* was a landmark for the emergence of a New York independent feature-film movement. It heralded a new style that employed greater cinematic realism and addressed relevant social issues in black-and-white low-budget films. It was also important because Clarke made the film the first test case in a successful fight to abolish New York State's censorship rules. Her next feature film, *The Cool World,* was the first movie to dramatize a story on black street gangs without relying upon Hollywood-style moralizing, and it was the first commercial film to be shot on location in Harlem. In 1967 Clarke directed a 90-minute cinema-verité interview with a black homosexual. *Portrait of Jason* is an insightful exploration of one person's character while it simultaneously addresses the range and limitations of cinema-verité style. Although Clarke's features had only moderate commercial runs and nominal success in the United States, they have won film festival awards and critical praise in Europe, making Clarke one of the most highly regarded American independent filmmakers among European film audiences.

In the 1960s Clarke also worked for the advancement of the New York independent film movement. She was one of the 24 filmmakers and producers who wrote and signed the 1961 manifesto, "Statement for a New American Cinema," which called for an economic, artistic, and political alternative to Hollywood moviemaking. With Jonas Mekas in 1962, she co-founded Film-Makers Cooperative, a nonprofit distribution company for independent films. Later, Clarke, Mekas, and filmmaker Louis Brigante co-founded Film-Makers Distribution Center, a company for distributing independent features to commercial movie theaters. Throughout the 1960s, Clarke lectured on independent film in universities and museums in the United States and Europe, and in 1969 she turned to video as her major medium in which to work.—LAUREN RABINOVITZ

Coffee, Lenore J.

American writer

Born *San Francisco, California, c. 1896.* ***Education*** *Attended Dominican College, San Rafael, California.* ***Family*** *Married the director William J. Cowen, one son and one daugher.* ***Career*** *1919—first film as writer,* The Better Wife; *then writer for Metro, First National, Paramount, MGM in the 1930s, and Warner Bros.; retired to England, but then returned to the Motion Picture Home in California.* ***Died*** *In Woodland Hills, California, 2 July 1984.*

Films as Writer: 1919: *The Better Wife.* **1920:** *The Forbidden Woman* (Garson); *For the Soul of Rafael* (Garson) (uncredited); *The Fighting Shepherdess* (*Vindication*) (Jose) (uncredited). **1921:** *Ladyfingers* (*Alias Ladyfingers*) (Veiller); *Hush* (Garson) (uncredited). **1922:** *The Face Between* (Veiller); *The Light That Failed* (Veiller); *Sherlock Brown* (Veiller); *The Dangerous Age* (Stahl) (uncredited). **1923:** *Temptation* (Le Saint); *Wandering Daughters* (J. Young); *The Age of Desire* (Borzage); *Daytime Wives* (Chautard); *Thundering Dawn* (Garson); *Strangers of the Night* (Niblo) (uncredited); *The Six Fifty* (N. Ross). **1924:** *Fool's Highway* (Cummings); *Bread* (Schertzinger); *The Rose of Paris* (Cummings); *The Great Divide* (Barker) (uncredited). **1925:** *Hell's Highroad* (Julian); *East Lynne* (Flynn); *The Swan* (Buchowetzki) (uncredited); *Graustark* (Buchowetzki) (uncredited). **1926:** *The Volga Boatman* (C. B. DeMille); *For Alimony Only* (W. de Mille); *The Winning of Barbara Worth* (H. King) (uncredited). **1927:** *The Night of Love* (Fitzmaurice); *Lonesome Ladies* (Henabery); *Chicago* (Urson); *The Angel of Broadway* (L. Weber); *The Love of Sunya* (Albert Parker) (uncredited). **1928:** *Ned McCobb's Daughter* (Cowan) (uncredited). **1929:** *Desert Nights* (Nigh). **1930:** *Street of Chance* (Cromwell); *The Bishop Murder Case* (Grinde and Burton); *Mother's Cry* (Henley). **1931:** *Possessed* (C. Brown); *The Squaw Man* (*The White Man*) (C. B. DeMille); *The Honor of the Family* (L. Bacon). **1932:** *Arsène Lupin* (Conway); *Night Court* (*Justice for Sale*) (Van Dyke); *Downstairs* (Bell); *Rasputin and the Empress* (Boleslawski) (uncredited). **1933:** *Torch Singer* (Hall and Somnes). **1934:** *Evelyn Prentice* (W. K. Howard); *Four Frightened People* (C. B. DeMille); *Such Women Are Dangerous* (Flood); *All Men Are Enemies* (Fitzmaurice). **1935:** *Age of Indiscretion* (Ludwig); *Vanessa: Her Love Story* (W. K. Howard); *David Copperfield* (Cukor) (uncredited). **1936:** *Suzy* (Fitzmaurice). **1937:** *Parnell* (Shahl) (uncredited). **1938:** *Four Daughters* (Curtiz) (co); *White Banners* (E. Goulding). **1939:** *Good Girls Go to Paris* (Hall). **1940:** *My Son, My Son!* (C. Vidor); *The Way of All Flesh* (L. King). **1941:** *The Great Lie* (E. Goulding). **1942:** *The Gay Sisters* (Rapper); *We Were Dancing* (Leonard) (uncredited). **1943:** *Old Acquaintance* (V. Sherman). **1944:** *Till We Meet Again* (Borzage); *Marriage Is a Private Affair* (Leonard). **1946:** *Tomorrow Is Forever* (Pichel). **1947:** *The Guilt of Janet Ames* (Levin); *Escape Me Never* (Godfrey) (uncredited). **1949:** *Beyond the Forest* (K. Vidor). **1951:** *Lightning Strikes Twice* (K. Vidor). **1952:** *Sudden Fear* (D. Miller). **1955:** *Young at Heart* (G. Douglas); *The End of the Affair* (Dmytryk); *Footsteps in the Fog* (Lubin). **1958:** *Another Time, Another Place* (L. Allen) (st only). **1960:** *Cash McCall* (Pevney).

Lenore J. Coffee's own success story is almost as incredible as one of her most romantic screenplays. Born in San Francisco at the turn of the century, Coffee was an avid moviegoer, often unimpressed by the caliber of screenplays she saw. When she read in *The Motion Picture Exhibitor's Herald* that the silent star Clara Kimball Young was looking for a good story, she wrote one. Coffee sent "The Better Wife" to the Garson Studio, they bought it for $100, and less than six months later the aspiring writer was on her way to Hollywood with a one-year contract.

Beginning with that first original story in 1919, Lenore Coffee wrote steadily for motion pictures for 35 years, earning her last credit in 1960. Throughout the 1920s she wrote scenarios as well as title cards for silent films. She worked at various studios—Metro, First National, and DeMille Pictures—writing mostly romances and melodramas.

Her first important picture was *The Volga Boatman,* directed by Cecil B. DeMille. By the end of the decade, Coffee was writing for Hollywood's biggest stars. *The Night of Love* teamed one of the silent screen's most popular couples, Ronald Colman and Vilma Banky. And *Desert Nights* was especially tailored for John Gilbert. To protect the actor as long as possible from the feared transition to sound, Coffee's script had accompanying music and effects, but no dialogue.

During the 1930s Coffee settled in at MGM and continued to specialize in romantic dramas—so-called women's pictures—and mystery-thrillers, establishing her competence in two distinctly different Hollywood genres. While such films as *The Bishop Murder Case, Street of Chance,* and *Arsène Lupin* required fast pacing, intricate plotting, and rapid dialogue, her women's pictures, *Evelyn Prentice, Torch Singer,* and *Vanessa: Her Love Story,* focused on relationships and feelings rather than action. Coffee's script for *Possessed,* starring Joan Crawford and Clark Gable, stands out as one of the most inventive of Crawford's many Cinderella stories at MGM.

In 1938 Coffee left Metro, co-wrote *Four Daughters* with Julius Epstein for Warner Bros., and was nominated for an Academy Award. The story capitalized on her abilities to sensitively portray family conflict and established her, along with Casey Robinson, as the studio's resident women's film expert.

Over the next few years, she wrote some of the romantic genre's best pictures—particularly *The Great Lie, The Gay Sisters,* and *Old Acquaintance.* Coffee brought plausibility, freshness, and even, on occasion, depth of character to these overworked stories. She was able to temper the often maudlin characteristics of the pieces with humor, but never lost sight of the fact that the genre's fundamental appeal lay in the suffering and sacrifice of the leading ladies.

Her later women's films were less successful. *Tomorrow Is Forever,* a reworking of *Ethan Frome*'s plot, was formulaic and tired, and *Beyond the Forest,* despite its eventual cult popularity, was a critical and box-office failure when it was released. In director King Vidor's hands, it became a cynical perversion of the women's film and marked the end of Bette Davis's long career at Warner Bros. Coffee's suspense melodramas of the late 1940s and early 1950s met with mixed reception. The best known are the Joan Crawford vehicle, *Sudden Fear,* and the adaptation of Graham Greene's novel, *The End of the Affair.* Surprisingly, her last screen credit was a comedy, *Cash McCall,* based on a Cameron Hawley novel.—JOANNE L. YECK

Cole, Janis and Holly Dale

Canadian directors, producers, writers, and editors

COLE. Born *Canada, 1954.* ***Education*** *Attended Sheridan College, Toronto.* ***Awards*** *Best Short Film, Toronto Festival of Festivals, for* Shaggie, *1990; Top Ten Award, Writers Guild of Canada, and Bronze Plaque, Columbus Festival, for* Dangerous Offender, *1996.*

DALE. Born *Toronto, 1953.* ***Education*** *Attended Sheridan College, Toronto; the Centre for Advanced Film Studies, 1988.* ***Career*** *1996—directed episode of TV series* Traders, *and TV commercials.* ***Awards*** *Bessie Award, for commercial directing.*

In 1976—completed first film together, as students, Cream Soda; *1977—completed critically acclaimed and best-known film,* The Thin Line; *1990s—co-operators of Spectrum Films.* ***Awards*** *Best Theatrical Documentary, Genie Award, Red Ribbon, American Film Festival, and Grand Prize-Best Human Condition Category and Best Cinematography, York Film & Video Festival, for* P4W, *1982; Gold Medal, Chicago Film Festival, for* Hookers on Davie, *1984; Theatrical Producers Achievement Award, Canadian Film and Television Association, 1988; Lillian Gish Award, Los Angeles Women in Film Festival, for* Calling the Shots, *1988; Toronto Arts Award in Media, 1994.* ***Address*** *Canadian Filmmakers Distribution Centre, 37 Hanna Avenue, Suite 220, Toronto, Ontario M6K 1W8, Canada.*

Films as Co-Directors: 1976: *Cream Soda* (+ pr, ed); *Minimum Charge No Cover* (+ pr, ed). **1977:** *Nowhere to Run* (+ pr, ed); *The Thin Line* (*The Thin Blue Line*) (+ pr, ed). **1982:** *P4W* (*Prison for*

Janis Cole (right) and Holly Dale. Photograph by John Walker.

Women) (+ pr, ed). **1984:** *Hookers on Davie* (+ pr, ed). **1985:** *Quiet on the Set: Filming Agnes of God* (*The Making of Agnes of God*) (+ pr, ed). **1988:** *Calling the Shots* (+ pr, ed).

Other Films: **1977:** *Starship Invasions* (*Alien Encounter*) (E. Hunt) (Dale: asst pr). **1990:** *Shaggie* (Cole: d). **1995:** *Blood & Donuts* (Dale: d). **1996:** *Dangerous Offender* (for TV) (Dale: d; Cole: sc).

"We want to make films so that people can see what they normally are not exposed to and have some kind of understanding." Such are the noble intentions of Janis Cole and Holly Dale, the highly esteemed independent documentary filmmakers from Canada, whose fruitful collaborations have involved sharing the duties of director, producer, and editor. Their films have been widely screened at film festivals around the world, including Berlin, Sydney, Paris, London, Créteil, Los Angeles, and Lyon. Associated with Canada's film boom of the 1970s, their work has been praised for tackling marginal, daring, offbeat subjects, including prostitutes, cross-dressers, criminally insane men, and female prisoners, albeit with unusual sensitivity and commitment. Early in their career, they earned a reputation for focusing on those members of society who endure class, gender, and other institutional oppressions—including women film directors. Thus, one critic commented upon their remarkable courage and determination, "Like the best young filmmakers, they don't know that it's impossible to make films, so they go ahead and make them."

Cole and Dale started collaborating as college students when they were 20 years old. Their student film *Cream Soda* provides an unflinching cinema-verité look at massage parlors in downtown Toronto, including footage of the women workers as they chat in their dressing room, and of the customers as they furtively come and go. *Minimum Charge No Cover* is about prostitution, homosexuals, transsexuals, and female impersonators. Interestingly, the film begins without revealing the identity of its subjects, because Cole and Dale wanted to encourage the audience to identify with them as "ordinary people." Critics often have been intrigued about the team's success in getting willing participants to reveal themselves to their cameras; but, as Dale casually explained to an interviewer, "Well, they're all friends of ours." Indeed, at the age of 20, Dale had worked as an assistant manager at the French Connection, a Toronto massage parlor.

The Thin Line was their first widely seen film, and like their previous work, it explores a usually hidden aspect of society: the therapeutic treatment of criminally insane inmates at a maximum-security prison in Ontario. Cole and Dale use interviews and therapy sessions with patients to reveal the deep capacity for understanding among the men who have committed some of society's most horrible crimes—including rape, assault, and murder—and thereby to humanize them.

Cole and Dale's feature-length films are *P4W* and *Hookers on Davie,* both of which performed well at the box office. *P4W* provides a compelling look at the love and isolation among women in prison—the result of a four-year struggle to gain access to the facility. They collected interviews, monologues, and cinema-verité sequences that poignantly demonstrate the will to survive among a tightly knit community of female prisoners. *Hookers on Davie* provides an excursion into the realm of Vancouver sex workers. Its setting is the Davie strip, Canada's capital of prostitution and its only significant pimp-free zone, where the prostitutes are in charge of their own business. The film is surprising, amusing, and sad; moreover, like all of Cole and Dale's work, it belies expectations about the world of prostitution by refusing conventional morality and presenting the perspectives of the prostitutes themselves. In addition, it celebrates the strength, solidarity, and defiance of the prostitutes who formed the Alliance for the Safety of Prostitutes and distributed "bad trick sheets" to warn colleagues about dangerous customers.

Cole and Dale turned their attention to the world of filmmaking with *Quiet on the Set: Filming Agnes of God,* a behind-the-scenes account of the production of Norman Jewison's 1985 film. Then, a few years later, in *Calling the Shots,* they illuminated the vast contribution of women filmmakers to the world of cinema, as well as the remarkable diversity of their personalities and films. It features interviews with a variety of well- and lesser-known women film workers from around the world about the constraints and successes of their careers in the 1970s and 1980s, including producers, scriptwriters, studio executives, and directors, such as Agnès Varda, Amy Heckerling, Joan Micklin Silver, Martha Coolidge, Lizzie Borden, Susan Seidelman, Ann Hui, Penelope Spheeris, Lee Grant, Joyce Chopra, and Jeanne Moreau. The women tell horror stories as well as amusing and dramatic anecdotes about what drew them to filmmaking and about the subject matter of their work. Notably, the film includes brief segments of women on-the-job: at production meetings and directing scenes. Interestingly, the filmmakers excluded in *Calling the Shots* are Cole and Dale themselves.

Recently, Cole and Dale have each pursued individual projects; perhaps not surprisingly, they chose to tackle subjects and themes that live on the margins of society. In 1990 Cole directed the film short *Shaggie,* about Marlene Moore, who was sent to a juvenile detention center when she was 13 and was incarcerated for the next 20 years, until 1988, when she committed suicide in Kingston's Prison for Women. In 1995 Dale made the revealingly titled film, *Blood & Donuts*.—CYNTHIA FELANDO

Colette

French writer and actress

Born *Sidonie-Gabrielle Colette in Saint-Sauveur en Puisaye (Yvonne), France, 28 January 1873.* ***Education*** *Received Primary Education Certificate.* ***Family*** *Married 1) Henry Gauthier-Villars (known as Willy), 15 years her senior, 1893 (divorced 1907); 2) the newspaper editor Henry de Jouvenel, 1912 (divorced 1925), daughter, Colette ("Bel-Gazou"); 3) Maurice Goudeket, 17 years her younger, 1935.* ***Career*** *1900-05—forced by husband Willy, a publisher, to spend four hours a day writing stories about her youth which he then published under his name (the "Claudine" novels); 1906-10—performed as a mime and dancer in music halls; 1911—began journalism career as drama critic; 1914—first film criticism; 1916—first film scenario based on her own novel,* La Vagabonde; *1919—directed a play,* En Camarades, *in which she also performed; 1920—success of* Chéri *established her reputation as a novelist; 1924—began use of "Colette" only; 1932—opened a beauty salon selling her own line of products; 1942—suffered severe arthritis and oversaw the publication of the 15 volumes of her* Oeuvres complètes, *containing none of her film scripts and very little of her writing on cinema; assisted with film adaptations of her novels.* ***Awards*** *Elected member, Belgian Royal Academy, 1936; elected member, Goncourt Academy, 1945; Grand Officer of the Legion of Honor, 1953.* ***Died*** *In Paris, 3 August 1954.*

Films as Writer: **1918:** *La Vagabonde* (*The Vagabond*) (Perego). **1920:** *La Flamme cachée* (*The Hidden Flame*) (Musidora and Lion, produced in 1918). **1932:** *La Vagabonde* (Bussi) (remake with additional scenes by Colette). **1935:** *Divine* (Max Ophüls) (+ dialogue based on her *L'Envers du Music Hall*).

Films as Dialogue Writer: **1934:** *Lac-aux-Dames* (M. Allégret) (based on a 1932 novel by Vicki Baum). **1949:** *Gigi* (Audry). **1950:** *Chéri* (Billon).

Other Films Adapted from Her Novels (uncredited): **1916:** *Minne* (Musidora) (adaption by Jacques de Baroncelli of *L'Ingénue libertine*, unreleased). **1937:** *Claudine à l'école* (*Claudine at School*) (de Poligny). **1950:** *Julie de Carneilhan* (Manuel); *Minne, l'Ingénue libertine* (*Minne, the Innocent Libertine*) (Audry). **1952:** "L'Envie" ("Envy") ep. of *Les Sept péchés capitaux* (*The Seven Deadly Sins*) (Rossellini) (based on *La Chatte*). **1953:** *Le Blé en herbe* (*The Game of Love*) (Autant-Lara). **1956:** *Mitsou* (Audry). **1958:** *Gigi* (Minnelli). **1980:** *La Naissance du jour* (for TV). **1990:** *La Seconde* (for TV); *Duo* (for TV); *Le Blé en herbe* (for TV).

During her lifetime, she was considered the greatest French female writer ever and was the first French female writer not of the aristocracy. Because Colette herself considered her role in cinema subservient to that of the novelist or playwright, it was largely overlooked by film histories until Alain and Odette Virmaux collected both her criticism and scripts into a single volume in 1975. Though participating actively in the later film adaptations of her novels, her influence on the new art was strongest in the era of silent films. Acting as film critic during the war years, she pointed out America's creative contribution to a cinematic language where European productions slavishly imitated theater. Whereas the rest of France saw only a pro-Japanese issue in Cecil B. DeMille's *The Cheat,* Colette underscored the significance of Sessue Hayakawa's internalized style of acting, more appropriate for cinema with its close-ups and the antithesis of exaggerated theatrical expression. She lauded filming in natural rather than studio settings and movies that dealt with ordinary daily life rather than dramatic and heroic plots.

When Philippe de Rothschild wanted a part in the cinematic enterprise as producer of *Lac-aux-Dames,* to be shot on location, he turned to his old acquaintance Colette for the dialogue. Though based on someone else's novel, she made it her own and much that is in her novels can be found in it: the combination of purity and provocation, the male as object. *Divine* was based on her own novel, *L'Envers du Music Hall,* and directed by the then newcomer Max Ophüls. The star, an already famous French actress and producer, Simone Berriau, was a friend of Colette's and would play the music hall girl.

Colette's first-known newspaper article, written in 1914, praised the documentary character of *The Scott Expedition* and is worth quoting for its foresight as it reads like a commentary of television in the 1990s: "When Scott and his companions, before perishing at the South Pole, capture for the inhabited world living images, animated portraits of an unknown land, . . . [the spectacle] honors—should we say rehabilitates?—the cinema . . . [which] ceases in short to be merely a tool of vaudeville and grotesque imbroglios." Her "Short Manual for the Aspiring Scenario Writer" is still a valid satire of the artifice of many Hollywood studio films.

The qualities of her best novels—such as *Chéri* (1920) or *Le Blé en herbe* (1923)—are found in her films as well as her criticism. Like her novels, her films are primarily stories of love, both sought and feared by the principal characters, women. The female, however, like her mother Sido, is seen as subject, not object, in the relationship. The subject matter, as in all truly modern art since Impressionism, was not the most significant aspect of her work. From her mother she had learned to delight continually in plants and animals. This sense of renewed discovery and wonder within the everyday world is her hallmark. Her fresh approach often shocked by its naturalness, its lack of moral intent or attempt to instruct. Colette did not see people or things as black and white; she did not judge. Her world is firmly grounded in the five physical senses. Her dialogues express sensitivity through the use of peasant idioms or the often crude language of actresses, the demimonde. To affirm her liberation from her first husband Willy, she wrote her novels in the first person. As Claude Pichois succinctly observes, her stories tend to be collections of brief scenes, a succession of pleasures that, having no hierarchy, become prose poems, rendering plot subservient to the joy of self-expression. All physical pleasures delight and interest her—and they are in motion. The moving image was, therefore, already inherent in her novelistic orientation as were a succession of scenes; the adaptation of her novels to film was inevitable.—EMILY ZANTS

Comden, Betty

American writer and lyricist

Born *Betty Cohen in Brooklyn, New York, 3 May 1917.* ***Education*** *Attended New York University, B.S. in drama, 1937.* ***Family*** *Married Steven Kyle, 1942 (died 1979), children: Susanna and Alan.* ***Career*** *1940-44—with partner Adolph Green performed with Judy Holliday, John Frank, and Alvin Hammer in cabaret group The Revuers; 1944—wrote first Broadway musical,* On the Town *(later musicals include* Billion Dollar Baby, *1945,* Bonanza Beyond, *1947,* Two on the Aisle, *1951,* Wonderful Town, *1953,* Bells Are Ringing, *1956,* Say Darling, *1958,* Do Re Mi, *1960,* Subways Are for Sleeping, *1961,* Fade Out—Fade In, *1964,* Hallelujah, Baby, *1967,* Applause, *1970,* Lorelei, or Gentlemen Still Prefer Blondes, *1974,* By Bernstein, *1975,* On the Twentieth Century, *1978,* A Doll's Life, *1981, and* Will Rogers Follies, *1991); 1947—first film as writers,* Good News; *1953—first Academy Award nomination for Best Original Screenplay, for* The Band Wagon; *1955—second Academy Award nomination for Best Original Screenplay, for* It's Always Fair Weather. ***Awards*** *Six Tony Awards, for* Wonderful Town, *1953,* Hallelujah, Baby, *1967,* Applause, *1970,* On the Twentieth Century *(two), 1978,* Will Rogers Follies, *1991; Writers Guild Awards, for* On the Town, *1949,* Singin' in the Rain, *1952, and* Bells Are Ringing, *1960.* ***Agent*** *ICM Agency, 40 West 57th Street, New York, NY 10019, U.S.A.*

Films as Co-Writer and Co-Lyricist with Adolph Green: 1947: *Good News* (Walters). **1948:** *Take Me Out to the Ball Game* (*Everybody's Cheering*) (Berkeley) (lyricists only); *The Barkleys of Broadway* (Walters) (sc only). **1949:** *On the Town* (Donen and Kelly). **1952:** *Singin' in the Rain* (Donen and Kelly) (one song, "Moses Supposes"). **1953:** *The Band Wagon* (Minnelli) (sc only). **1955:** *It's Always Fair Weather* (Donen and Kelly). **1958:** *Auntie Mame* (da Costa) (sc only). **1960:** *Bells Are Ringing* (Minnelli). **1964:** *What a Way to Go!* (J. L. Thompson).

Films as Actress: 1944: *Greenwich Village* (W. Lang). **1984:** *Garbo Talks* (Lumet). **1989:** *Slaves of New York* (Ivory) (as Mrs. Wheeler).

With her longtime creative partner, Adolph Green, Betty Comden has co-written the scenarios and lyrics for two of the most beloved and entertaining of the classic MGM musicals, *Singin' in the Rain* and *The Band Wagon*. And her other credits are anything but chopped liver! Nevertheless, even with a string of musical film credits that reads like a Hollywood honor role, Comden has not transcended her identity as the other half of Adolph Green's enormous talent. (One cannot even call her Green's better half, since that role has been held by Phyllis Newman

Betty Comden and Adolph Green

for close to 40 years.) Moviegoers have a sense that they know Adolph Green because they have seen him appear on-screen in various frenetic, sometimes self-parodying roles in *My Favorite Year* and *Lily in Love*; Green is so effusive that he practically jumps off the screen and into the viewer's lap. On the other hand, rare Comden screen performances have not been telling or expressive. In some ways, Comden is like Greta Garbo—whom she plays in the final scene of *Garbo Talks*—in that her film-going admirers have not had the opportunity to get to know her very well.

Hidden or perhaps guarded as she remains, the key to Comden actually is apparent to all who have seen the films she and Green wrote. Look closely at the original screen musicals *The Barkleys of Broadway, Singin' in the Rain,* and *The Band Wagon,* and you will recognize Comden in the vivacious, puckish, and well-developed female characters.

In *Barkleys* she is Dinah Barkley, an attractive, charming, and independent woman who is very close to what the French refer to as *d'un certain âge*. Dinah has lots of talent and a quick temper, which flares frequently as she vents frustration in being one half of a well-established creative partnership (even if the other half *is* Fred Astaire), rather than as a star in her own right with her name solely filling a marquee. A good deal of the scenario features Dinah complaining and plotting and finally striking out on her own as a serious dramatic actress—a metaphor, perhaps, for a fantasy of Comden's breaking loose from her Siamese coupling with Green in order to prove that her talents stand firm on their own.

As Kathy Selden in *Singin' in the Rain,* we may be seeing the early Comden, with a youthful positivism and collaborative spirit, trying to break into show business—as she did as one quarter of the cabaret act The Revuers. When Kathy has to sacrifice her own chance to be a movie star in order to save the motion picture, that is Comden as a happy team player, in love with show business and her fellow artists and primarily concerned with the success of the project. Whether it is the unique spirit of Debbie Reynolds in the role or the quality of the character as developed on the written page, Kathy has a freshness, vigor, drive, and camaraderie that are unusual to female characters of the post-World War II silver screen.

In *The Band Wagon,* Comden's alter-ego is Lily Marton, who with her husband Lester is writing a Broadway musical for a Hollywood star-pal. The Martons are as consolidated as Tweedledee and Tweedledum: a spunky, wisecracking couple who ache with separation pangs any time they do not share the frame. Lester is the homely, eccentric image of Green, and Lily is the pretty, sweet-natured, nurturing partner. This is the public image of Comden and Green—and, if you will, it is their legend. The showbiz-savvy, bubbly creations of Lily and Lester Marton, as concocted by Comden and Green, make for self-reflexive cinema that is uncommon in MGM musicals. This is the Comden imagined by most movie enthusiasts. She is a willing partner and good sport who complements the more famous, more capricious personality of Adolph Green.

Even with the publication of her memoir *Off Stage* in 1995, Betty Comden probably always will be remembered as one half of the successful creative team of Comden and Green. Perhaps this is destined by Comden. For after all, under her creative will, even tempestuous Dinah Barkley goes back to being one of the two *Barkleys of Broadway*.—AUDREY E. KUPFERBERG

Coolidge, Martha

American director

Born *New Haven, Connecticut, 1946.* ***Education*** *Studied animation at Rhode Island School of Design; attended New York University to study filmmaking; took film classes at the School of Visual Arts, and Columbia Graduate School.* ***Career*** *1968—directed children's program for Canadian TV; 1972-75—made a series of radical feminist documentaries that were screened at film festivals; 1975—made the much-admired feminist feature,* Not a Pretty Picture; *1978—hired by Francis Ford Coppola's Zoetrope Studio to develop the never-produced film* Photoplay; *1982—directed first fiction feature* City Girl *(released in 1984); 1983—directed first commercially successful film,* Valley Girl; *1991—directed the critically acclaimed independent feature,* Rambling Rose. ***Agent*** *Ken Stovitz, Creative Artists Agency, 9830 Wilshire Boulevard, Beverly Hills, CA 90212, U.S.A.*

Films as Director: **1972:** *David: Off and On* (+ pr, sc, ed). **1973:** *More Than a School* (+ sc, ed). **1974:** *Old-Fashioned Woman* (+ pr, sc, ed). **1975:** *Not a Pretty Picture* (+ pr, sc, co-ed). **1978:** *Bimbo* (+ pr, ed). **1979:** *The Troubleshooters.* **1980:** *Strawberries and Gold* (for TV). **1983:** *Valley Girl.* **1984:** *City Girl* (produced in 1982) (+ pr); *Joy of Sex.* **1985:** *Real Genius*; "Night of the Meek" ep. of *The Twilight Zone* (for TV). **1986:** *Hammered: The Best of Sledge* (for TV); "Quarantine" ep. of *The Twilight Zone* (for TV). **1987:** "Shelter Skelter" ep. of *The Twilight Zone* (for TV). **1988:** *Plain Clothes*; *Roughhouse.* **1989:** *Trenchcoat in Paradise* (for TV). **1990:** *The Friendly*; *Rope Dancing.* **1991:** *Bare Essentials* (for TV); *Rambling Rose.* **1992:** *Crazy in Love* (for TV). **1993:** *Lost in Yonkers.* **1994:** *Angie.* **1995:** *Three Wishes.* **1997:** *Out to Sea.* **1999:** *Dorothy Dandridge* (for TV).

Other Films: **1971:** *Passing Quietly Through* (pr, ed). **1990:** *That's Adequate* (H. Hurwitz) (ro). **1994:** *Beverly Hills Cop III* (Landis) (ro as security woman).

Martha Coolidge

Martha Coolidge has proved to be one of Hollywood's most successful commercial directors, male or female. Early in her career, however, she garnered critical success as an independent documentary filmmaker. While still a film student at New York University, an instructor hired her to direct an hour-long documentary about a Long Island "free school," which was eventually screened on public television. Thereafter, she made several documentaries that were shown on the film festival circuit, one of which, *Not a Pretty Picture,* was widely respected. A semiautobiographical feature about a woman filmmaker directing a re-creation of a rape attack, *Not a Pretty Picture* now occupies an honored place in the feminist film canon. During this period, Coolidge was a vociferous champion of independent film and she wrote numerous articles about the obstacles to finding financial support and distribution deals.

Impressed by *Not a Pretty Picture,* Francis Ford Coppola invited Coolidge to develop a rock 'n' roll love story entitled *Photoplay* for his Zoetrope Studio. But, after working on it for two-and-a-half years, the financially strapped studio abandoned the project. Frustrated, Coolidge returned to Canada where she soon found work directing a television miniseries for the Canadian Broadcasting Corporation. While there, she was finally invited to direct her first fiction feature film, *City Girl,* a film she is proud to call a "woman's film." But, before *City Girl* found a distributor in 1984, Coolidge directed her breakthrough hit, the low-budget teenpic, *Valley Girl.*

Subsequently, Coolidge was offered numerous teen sex movies to direct. She finally agreed to make *Joy of Sex* (1984) for Paramount, a typical but unsuccessful teen comedy. To its predictably thin plot, she managed to provide some feminist perspective about the subjects of contraception, menstruation, and pregnancy. But, at the time, she implied in interviews that she really wanted to make other kinds of films. She ultimately left the project during postproduction and then tried to distance herself from the final product.

Next she directed a big-budget feature, the teen science-fiction comedy, *Real Genius.* With a nearly all-male cast, Coolidge's goal was to depict the young men as more vulnerable than she thought a male director would have, and to present the challenges of scientific conquest as fun, and more importantly, as respectable. *Real Genius* also marked the entry of females into the cherished multimillion dollar special effects' turf of male directors. Following *Real Genius,* however, she worked steadily in television and continued to pursue feature-film projects that would provide greater opportunities for artistic expression.

In 1991 she scored a critical hit with *Rambling Rose,* a coming-of-age story adapted by Calder Willingham from his novel. Upon discovering the script in a "dead script" file after it had been rejected by a series of Hollywood producers, Coolidge struggled for five years to get it made. It was Renny Harlin, known for directing action films, who finally agreed to produce the independent feature. With an impressive cast and quiet, thoughtful performances, the film treats the subject of feminine sexuality in the sexually constrained 1930s. It tells the story of Rose, a guilelessly promiscuous young woman hired to work as a housemaid for a Southern family who wants to prevent her from becoming a prostitute. Coolidge masterfully portrays Rose as a girl-woman who longs for affection, but confuses it with sex. *Rambling Rose* remains Coolidge's masterpiece, and it proved to be her ticket off the teenpic track.

The big-budget film *Angie,* a vehicle for the big-budget movie-star Geena Davis, restored Coolidge's reputation as a major studio director. It tells the story of a single, working-class Brooklynite who becomes unexpectedly pregnant. Coolidge's feminist touch permeates the movie, importantly, in her depiction of Angie as an engaging but, refreshingly, not always sympathetic heroine. The director also cleverly reworks the conventions of the melodrama by respecting rather than condemning Angie's pregnancy, by playing with the notion of the single girl who gets "in trouble," by implicating the fathers who fail to stick around, and by celebrating the community of women. Indeed, the film's most important relationship is between Angie and her best girlfriend.

Coolidge's 1997 feature film, *Out to Sea,* reunited Jack Lemmon and Walter Matthau in a shipboard sex farce that critics have praised as funny and smart about love and mortality. In addition to proving once again that Coolidge is a bankable, big-budget director, it is noteworthy for depicting one of Hollywood's most enduring taboos—against portraying older women as sexually desiring or desirable. Now a firmly established director, Coolidge's champions often note that she continues to bring fresh perspectives to her often predictable scripts; likewise, her body of work demonstrates a special talent for enabling inspired performances and for working with ensemble casts. Thus, as she explained in the early 1990s, her biggest lesson as a director was learning that she could express herself creatively, even under the most constrained filmmaking conditions.—CYNTHIA FELANDO

Craigie, Jill

British director and writer

Born *7 March 1914.* ***Education*** *Attended various boarding schools.* ***Family*** *Married 1) the screenwriter, director, and novelist Jeffrey Dell; 3) member of Parliament Michael Foot, 1949.* ***Career*** *1932—journalist on teenage magazine, then for London branch of Hearst Newspapers; 1940-42—scriptwriter on documentaries for the British Council; 1944—signed up by producer Filippo del Giudice for Two Cities Film, directed first film,* Out of Chaos; *1948—formed production company, Outlook; 1949—directed first feature film,* Blue Scar; *after 1951—gave up directing, but continued to write journalism, scripts for the BBC, and occasional film scripts.* ***Addresses*** *c/o Michael Foot, The Labour Party, 150 Walworth Road, London SE17, England; and 308 Gray's Inn Road, London WC1X 8DY, England.*

Films as Director: 1944: *Out of Chaos* (doc, short) (+ sc). **1946:** *The Way We Live* (doc) (+ sc, pr). **1948:** *Children of the Ruins* (doc, short). **1949:** *Blue Scar* (+ sc). **1951:** *To Be a Woman* (doc, short) (+ sc, pr). **1994:** *Two Hours from London* (doc for TV, produced 1992) (+ sc).

Other Films: 1937: *Make-Up* (Zeisler) (ro as Tania). **1943:** *The Flemish Farm* (Dell) (co-sc). **1953:** *The Million Pound Note* (*Man with a Million*) (Neame) (sc). **1957:** *Windom's Way* (Neame) (sc).

Jill Craigie was not, as is sometimes claimed, the first British woman film director. That distinction should probably go to Dinah Shurey, director of patriotic features in the 1920s, followed by Mary Field, who made documentaries, children's films, and the occasional short feature in the 1930s. But Craigie was the first British woman to direct features that gained widespread distribution and publicity: *The Way We Live* is said to have had as many column inches devoted to it at the time of its release as Olivier's near-contemporary *Henry V.* And she was certainly the first British director—of either sex—to bring a consistently feminist and socialist viewpoint to her work.

Jill Craigie

Having worked as a journalist and—briefly—as an actress, Craigie spent the war years writing scripts for British Council documentaries. This, and the experience of working with her then-husband, the novelist and director Jeffrey Dell, on the script of *The Flemish Farm,* convinced her that she too could direct. "I developed a great urge to make a documentary for myself," she later recalled. "I did decide quite deliberately, why shouldn't a woman make a film? It was a male-dominated industry from top to bottom." She cut her teeth on a short subject not far different from those she had been scripting for the British Council. *Out of Chaos,* featuring interviews with such artists as Henry Moore and Graham Sutherland, was a pioneering attempt to use cinema to introduce people to modern art.

With the British documentary movement at its wartime-boosted height, Craigie ambitiously embarked on a feature-length documentary intended for general distribution. She got backing from the open-minded impresario Filippo del Giudice, whose company Two Cities Films had released *Out of Chaos,* through the Rank Organisation. *The Way We Live* was something quite new: it set out to show how planning, that panacea of the postwar Labour government, affected the lives of "ordinary people"—and how they, in their turn, could influence the planning process. She chose to focus on the port city of Plymouth, shattered by wartime bombing, where enlightened town planners were proposing a radically redesigned housing system.

Focusing chiefly on one bombed-out family and working with an almost entirely amateur cast, Craigie set out "to show that Town Planning must be integrated with everyday life. . . I went to people and asked them what they really wanted. . . not what I wanted. The whole content of the film came from the people, from the architects, from the Town Councillors, and I was just the interpreter." The film climaxes in a procession of several thousand people to the Town Hall to demand that the new plan be put into effect, carrying banners with slogans derived from the vox populi comments Craigie had gleaned. The film exhilarates with its mood of buoyant postwar optimism, the sense that given the energy and will, anything is possible. But more, it was an exceptional—and in Britain, virtually unheard-of—example of filmmaking as activism, the creative and political processes intertwining and advancing each other in a way that even the Soviet filmmakers of the 1920s had only rarely achieved.

After directing a documentary short, *Children of the Ruins,* on UNESCO's work to rehabilitate war-traumatized children, Craigie formed her own production company, Outlook, with the producer William McQuitty, to make a fiction feature, *Blue Scar.* A drama set—and largely filmed—in the mining valleys of South Wales, it mixed professional actors with local amateurs to tell the story of a young woman, a miner's daughter, enticed away from the valleys and her colliery sweetheart by the lure of a shallow social life in London. With the British film industry in crisis and Del Giudice ousted by hostile forces, financing proved elusive. Craigie and McQuitty raised the whole budget themselves with the help of friends, and converting a disused Welsh cinema into a studio, made the film with no distribution guarantee.

The film is uneven, often awkward—Craigie herself now dismisses it as "amateurish"—and betrays her inexperience in handling fictional drama. But, as Andy Medhurst observes, "what is so startling, and fascinating, about *Blue Scar*. . . is that it is a British feature film that is consciously political, avowedly socialist." It was certainly the politics, not the awkwardness, that led the major circuits to deny *Blue Scar* a booking, and the film was only shown after a skillful press campaign had roused public opinion in its favor.

But Craigie was increasingly disheartened by the dual struggle of being a female and independent director in an industry where the opinions were narrowing. After making a last documentary short for Outlook, *To Be a Woman,* a heartfelt plea for equal pay for women, she moved into screenwriting, scripting two comedies for Rank. In 1958 she suggested to Michael Balcon, head of Ealing, that she should make films for him featuring fully realized female characters—a rarity, she argued, in British films. Ealing, though, was nearing its last gasp, and nothing came of the idea. Craigie's filmmaking career seemed to be over.

Nevertheless, she unexpectedly returned to directing in 1992 with *Two Hours from London,* a documentary made for television. With her husband, the MP and former Labour leader Michael Foot, as on-screen presenter, it was a scathing and unashamedly partisan indictment of the passivity of the Western powers in the face of Serbian aggression in former Yugoslavia. The film had to wait 18 months before being transmitted by the BBC, and then only in a truncated form, but it proved that in her long absence from filmmaking Craigie had lost none of the deep-felt political and humanist passions. Too bad that her most cherished project, a fictionalized drama about the suffragette movement, never came to fruition; few directors could have been more ideally suited to the subject.—PHILIP KEMP

Dash, Julie

American director and writer

***Born** New York City, 1952. **Education** Attended City College of New York, studying film production, B.A. 1974; American Film Institute, 1975; University of California, Los Angeles, M.F.A. 1986. **Career** 1973-91—made a series of short films, including the critically well-received* Illusions; *1978-80—worked for the Motion Picture Association of America's Classifications and Rating Administration, assigning ratings to films awaiting theatrical distribution in the United States; 1989—started production on her first feature film,* Daughters of the Dust; *1992—*Daughters of the Dust *finally released; 1990s—directed music videos, including* Lost in the Night *(for Peabo Bryson), 1992,* Give Me One Reason *(for Tracy Chapman), and* More Than One Way Home, *1996,* Thinking of You *(for Tony, Toni, Tone), 1997; and anthology television; 1996—directed an episode of the HBO series* Subway Stories. ***Awards** Fulbright Fellowship, 1991; Dorothy Arzner Award, Women in Film, 1992; Best Film, Black Filmmaker's Hall of Fame, for* Daughters of the Dust, *1992; Maya Deren Award, American Film Institute, 1993; John Simon Guggenheim Memorial Foundation Fellowship. **Address** Geechee Girls Productions, Inc., 137 North Larchmont Boulevard, Box 244, Los Angeles, CA 90004, U.S.A.*

Films as Director: 1973: *Working Models of Success* (doc). **1975:** *Four Women* (short). **1977:** *Diary of an African Nun* (short). **1983:** *Illusions* (short). **1988:** *Breaking the Silence.* **1989:** *Preventing Cancer, Phillis Wheatley* (doc, short). **1990:** *Relatives* (short, for TV). **1992:** *Praise House* (short, for TV); *Daughters of the Dust* (+ pr). **1994:** *Breaths* (short, for TV). **1997:** *Grip Till It Hurts* (for TV); *Subway Stories: Tales from the Underground.* **1998:** *Black South: The Life and Lifework of Zora Neale Hurston* (doc). **1999:** *Funny Valentine* (for TV).

Independent filmmaker Julie Dash was the first African-American woman to produce a full-length, theatrically released film, 1992's *Daughters of the Dust*. Born and raised in New York City, it was her uncle who first gave her a camera, after which she studied film production in an after-school program in Harlem, and in college at the City College of New York, the American

Film Institute, and the University of California, Los Angeles. Subsequently, she made short films for several years before she made her first feature, the critically acclaimed *Daughters of the Dust*. Dash's avowed intentions are to correct the white distortions that have predominated in Hollywood films, to reflect the realities of black life and history, and to craft positive black images that will counter those of the mainstream cinema. She specifically cites the novelists Alice Walker, Toni Cade Bambara, and Zora Neale Hurston for providing important inspiration.

Dash's early short films include *Diary of an African Nun,* an adaptation of an Alice Walker short story, and *Four Women,* an experimental dance poem based on a Nina Simone song. Her best-known short film is *Illusions*. Like all of her work, it reveals an acute sense of racial and sexual oppression and is concerned with the images and identities of black women. *Illusions* has been the subject of considerable critical attention and adulation, among feminists in particular, for its unique examination of the issue of black female identity in the realm of Hollywood's mythmaking. Set during World War II, it tells the story of Mignon Dupree, a light-skinned black woman who "passes" as white and thereby works her way to the executive suites of a movie studio; and Ester Jester, a black woman who is hired to dub the voice of a white Hollywood movie star. It is only when she befriends Ester that Mignon realizes the irony of her position, in terms of her participation in constructing Hollywood's illusions and in maintaining the invisibility of black women and their stories. Ultimately, she decides to stay to fight the system from within. The film's compelling narrative confirms the means by which the film industry has perpetuated racism and sexism by depicting one-dimensional stereotypes that ignore the diversity of African Americans and women. Accordingly, Dash's work suggests the power of the medium of film to enlighten audiences about the realities and intersections of black history and women's history. Notably, after she made *Illusions,* critics championed Dash, along with filmmaker Alile Sharon Larkin, as the forerunners of an emerging African-American cinema.

Dash's first feature film and reigning masterpiece is *Daughters of the Dust,* a hauntingly poetic work that celebrates African culture, the oral tradition, and the Gullah people. Focusing on a matriarchal clan of a Gullah family (or Geechee—from the descendants of the freed slaves who settled on the islands off the coast of South Carolina and Georgia), it tells the story of a turn-of-the-century gathering that marks the occasion of some of the Peazant family's departure to the mainland. Dash shot the film on the Sea Islands, a location of enormous significance due to its isolation, which has meant the retention of its West African cultural traditions. *Daughters* employs a uniquely drawn combination of narrative and nonnarrative elements to illuminate issues of family, migration and exile, sex, race, and nationality, and does so from personal, political, and historical perspectives. Visually the film is highly stylized, using painterly colors, natural lighting, and slowed action, to achieve a poetic sensuality. Dash has explained that she used slow motion, in particular, to give viewers a sense of memory or déjà vu. Interestingly, she first conceived of the film in 1975; then, after she made *Illusions* she undertook extensive research for *Daughters*—collecting stories from her relatives, and studying at the National Archives in Washington, D.C., the Library of Congress, the Smithsonian Institution, Harlem's Schomburg Center for Research in Black Culture, and at the Penn Center on St. Helena Island. In addition, she struggled for several years to raise the production money. Consequently, the film is a remarkable achievement and evidence of her deep commitment to capturing and celebrating the realistic and subtle details of African-American cultures, especially the rituals and relationships of women. Thus, as Dash put it, *Daughters* is "about abandoning your home, but not your culture."

Dash notes that her films are about women facing pivotal moments in their lives; for example, those who are juggling complex psyches and those who communicate with fractured sentences and familiar gestures. That is, the kinds of women who surrounded her as a child. In addition, her work reflects her belief that our identities are shaped by the intersections of histories and personal influences. Accordingly, Dash proudly acknowledges the importance to her work of the "old souls" who preceded her; in particular, she cites the influence of largely forgotten filmmakers such as Oscar Micheaux and Spencer Williams Jr. For example, the baptism scene in *Daughters of the Dust* was inspired by a scene in Williams's *The Blood of Jesus*. Likewise, the enchanting tree scene in which Trula's legs hang into the frame was inspired by a similar scene in Bill Gunn's *Ganja and Hess*.

In recent years, Dash has directed a number of music videos, including "Give Me One Reason" for Tracy Chapman, and "Lost in the Night" for Peabo Bryson. She is currently writing for Dutton Signet books, developing multimedia projects for her company, Geechee Girls Productions, Inc., and planning a futuristic film (set in 2050), to be called *Bone, Ash and Rose*.—CYNTHIA FELANDO

Davis, Zeinabu irene

American director and producer

Born *Irene Davis in Philadelphia, 13 April 1961.* ***Education*** *Attended Brown University, B.A., 1983; University of California, Los Angeles, M.A. in African Studies, 1985, M.F.A. in Motion Picture and Television Production, 1989.* ***Family*** *Married the screenwriter Marc Arthur Chéry.* ***Career*** *1987—selected as Most Promising Filmmaker by the National Black Filmmakers Hall of Fame; 1996—awarded tenure at Northwestern University.* ***Awards*** *Best Drama, National Black Programming Consortium, Best of category (Experimental), Black Filmmakers Hall of Fame, for* Cycles, *1989; Best Narrative, Lawrence Kasdan Award, 30th Ann Arbor Film Festival, Best Experimental Narrative, ETA Creative Arts Foundation (Chicago), for* A Powerful Thang, *1991; Best Film and Video, Children's Jury, 12th Annual Chicago International Children's Fest, Best Short Feature, 6th New England Children's Film Festival, Best of Category, Chris Award, 34th Columbus International Film Festival, Silver Hugo, Chicago International Film and Video Festival, for* Mother of the River, *1995.* ***Address*** *Department of Radio-TV-Film, Northwestern University, 1905 Sheridan Road, Evanston, IL 60208, U.S.A.*

Films as Director: **1982:** *Filmstatement* (+ pr, sc). **1983:** *Recreating Black Women's Media Image* (doc). **1986:** *Sweet Bird of Youth* (doc) (+ pr); *Crocodile Conspiracy.* **1987:** *Canta for Our Sisters* (+ pr). **1989:** *Cycles* (short) (+ pr, ed); *Trumpetistically, Clora Bryant* (doc) (+ pr). **1990:** *Kneegrays in Russia* (doc) (+ pr). **1991:** *A Period Piece* (+ pr); *A Powerful Thang* (+ pr, sc, ed). **1995:** *Mother of the River* (+ pr). **1997:** *Compensation* (+ pr).

Equally talented in the mediums of film and video, Zeinabu irene Davis is an internationally renowned African-American producer and director who, rather than following conventional film form and narrative styles, works to create what she describes as "a visual language that is representative of the African American female experiences." A recipient of grants from such prestigious organizations as the Illinois Arts Council, the Rockefeller Foundation, the Paul Robeson Fund for Independent Media, the National Endowment for the Arts, the American Film

Institute, and the National Black Programming Consortium, her work includes documentaries, short narratives, experimental pieces, and music videos. Though diverse in subject and style, Davis's productions are consistent in that they construct African-American female subjectivity through the everyday experience and draw upon the culture of the African diaspora through the use of music and symbols of Pan African spirituality.

As an undergraduate student of law at Brown University, Davis was introduced to media production while serving as an intern at WSBE, the Public Broadcasting Station in Providence, Rhode Island. Working closely with African-American Gini Booth—host and producer of the minority affairs program *Shades*—Davis became increasingly aware of the power media wields in the arenas of ideology and culture. Her interest in media was furthered in 1981, while studying in Kenya. During her year abroad, Davis worked with Kenyan playwright Ngugi wa Thiong'o on a multimedia staging of one of his works, and also observed European film crews shooting ethnographic films of "exotic" Africa. Determined to become a film director, Davis enrolled in UCLA's graduate program in African Studies, earning a Master's of Arts degree in 1985, and a Master of Fine Arts degree in Motion Picture and Television Production four years later.

The name of her production company, Wimmin with a Mission, reflects Davis's approach to film and video production. Her work differs significantly from the Hollywood tradition of movies and television not only in terms of form, but also because it focuses on the lives of women of color, particularly African-American women—presenting characters far from the characteristic misrepresentations and one-dimensional stereotypes common in the media. One can look to her most noted works, *Cycles, A Powerful Thang,* and *Mother of the River* to view representations of African-American women rarely seen, constructed in a style that Gwendolyn Foster characterizes as "poetic (re)constructions of time, the body, and an exploration of spatial configurations."

Cycles, a provocative and innovative black-and-white experimental short, explores an important aspect of women's lives—the act of waiting. The film combines live action, still photography, animation, and pixilation to reflect the mood and feelings of the protagonist Rasheeda Allen as she awaits the start of menstruation. A complex and dense film, *Cycles* gives voice to women's experiences through its multilayered soundtrack of dialogue spoken by several women. Through the use of music by such artists as South African Miriam Makeba, Haitian Martha Jean-Claude, and American trumpeter Clora Bryant and the images of a Haitian Veve, ground paintings drawn during Vodun ceremonies, Davis links the culture of African Americans to the larger diaspora.

Like *Cycles,* the first feature-length film directed by Davis, *A Powerful Thang,* also embraces Pan African culture. The performance of Afro-Haitian dance, the use of *djembe* drums and jazz in the soundtrack, and the braided hair of the lead female character Yasmine, illustrate the diversity and richness of culture in this film, which focuses on friendship and intimacy in the lives of an African-American couple.

A Powerful Thang is also illustrative of Davis's dedication as an educator. The film was produced while Davis worked as an assistant professor at Antioch College, where she was the first African-American woman to teach. Working with her on the film were several professionals in the field: cinematographer S. Toriano Berry, art director Claudia Springer, and editor Casi Pacilio. But the crew also included several production students from the college's Institute of

Communications and Media Arts. This inclusion was instrumental in demystifying the filmmaking process for the students, and provided an opportunity for them to gain production experience.

Like other filmmakers of color, Davis is concerned with the issue of invisibility. Given age, race, and gender, the group rendered in film most rarely are African-American girls. Davis and African-American women media artists such as Debra J. Robinson, Ayoka Chenzira, and Alile Sharon Larkin are filling the gap with productions that depict the lives and unique perspectives of African-American girls. In 1995 Davis directed a script written by her husband Marc Arthur Chéry. *Mother of the River,* produced for ITVS, the Independent Television Service, is a 30-minute narrative based on an African coming-of-age folktale. It takes place on a plantation in the Southern United States, and concerns the relationship between an enslaved girl and a magical older woman, the Mother of the River. An innovative film, it is one of the first to present slavery from a girl's perspective.

Davis was once quoted as saying that film is an articulation of voice and vision. Her work in the media arts, while giving voice to persons and issues not usually discussed in film and video, itself presents a distinct voice and unique vision. Her legacy as a filmmaker will be a great one, adding diverse perspectives, creative stylings, and serving as an inspiration to countless generations of filmmakers to come.—FRANCES K. GATEWARD

De Hirsch, Storm

American director

Born *Lillian Malkin in New Jersey, 9 December 1912.* ***Family*** *Following a stormy relationship with her parents, she left home at an early age for an artistic life as a painter and poet in New York City, where she married an artist named De Hirsch, a union that lasted some 20 years; married 2) Louis Brigante one of the early editors of* Film Culture *magazine, during the latter part of their 25-year relationship which ended only with his death in 1975.* ***Career*** *1963—first film,* Goodbye in the Mirror, *feature-length narrative shot in Rome and later blown up to 35mm for possible showings in movie theaters, with disappointing results (Brigante assisted her on this and subsequent films); 1963-73—made a dozen or so short abstract animation and live-action films, using many experimental techniques including cameraless etching and painting directly onto film, multiple images, dual-screen projection, and in-camera masking; 1968—only woman winner of American Film Institute's first round of $10,000 grants to independent filmmakers; 1973—retrospective film showing at Whitney Museum of American Art; 1973-74—made ten or more very short, silent Super-8mm films and became a pioneer advocate of this low-cost, easily accessible medium of artistic expression. Throughout her film career, lectured and taught at major institutions throughout the United States, including a course in visionary film at New York's School of Visual Arts; forced to give up her studio after Brigante's death in 1975, she made no more films and suffered a gradual decline in health that has turned into a long and tragically debilitating case of Alzheimer's disease.*

Films as Director: **1963:** *Journey around a Zero.* **1964:** *Goodbye in the Mirror* (produced 1963). **c. 1965:** *Newsreel: Jonas in The Brig.* **1966:** *Sing Lotus* (music of Manipur, Kashmir, and Nepal). **1968:**

Trap Dance; Third Eye Butterfly (dual screen projection). **1969:** *The Tattooed Man.* **1971:** *An Experiment in Meditation.* **1975:** *Geometrics of the Kabballah* (16mm, silent).

***"The Color of Ritual, The Color of Thought"* Series: 1964-67:** *Divinations; Shaman: A Tapestry for Sorcerers; Peyote Queen.*

***"Hudson River Diary"* Series: 1967:** *Cayuga Run.* **1973:** *Wintergarden; River-Ghost.*

***"Cine-Sonnets"* Series (Silent Super-8mm): 1973-74:** *Lace of Summer; September Express; Charlotte Moorman's Avant-Garde Festival #9; Malevitch at the Guggenheim; Ives House: Woodstock; Deep in the Mirror Embedded; Silently, Bearing Totem of a Bird; A Reticule of Love; Aristotle; The Recurring Dream.*

Storm De Hirsch made her first motion picture in 1963, two years after the untimely death of Maya Deren, the woman who had virtually masterminded the avant-garde film movement in the United States. Although De Hirsch was born five years earlier than Deren, she was a mature artist—over 40 years old—when she began her filmmaking career. Deren was only 25 when she made her first film—the classic *Meshes of the Afternoon*—and at the age of 44, she died.

Though they may never have known each other, they had quite a bit in common. Both women had created new names and personas for themselves; Deren's were earthy and radical, De Hirsch's more imposing and regal. Both had backgrounds in poetry and other arts; they were also deeply involved with primitive cultures and the occult. In making their first films, both were supported by their husbands. In Maya Deren's case, it was an inspired artistic collaboration with Alexander Hammid in a short-lived marriage; Storm De Hirsch's first professional collaboration with Louis Brigante was disappointing, but the personal relationship endured. Both women made lasting contributions to the American avant-garde film scene, within the limits of their times and talents.

The 1960s offered Storm De Hirsch many more options than the 1940s had offered Deren, allowing her to start big, with an ambitious feature-length story about three young women, living in Rome, loosely based on a poem she had written and on her own experiences. Brigante was associate director. Called *Goodbye in the Mirror,* part scripted, part improvised, it was shot on 16mm and later blown up to 35mm, at a total cost of some $20,000. *Variety*'s reviewer found it too uneven for a feature, and thought it might have been a sharp, incisive short. Even before its release, De Hirsch already had begun making short films that were much more suited to her painterly and poetic roots.

Independent, cheaply made underground films, she later said, were not merely a futile rebellion against Hollywood's slickness, but were spontaneous efforts to create the equivalent of off-Broadway theater in the medium of film. De Hirsch's first short film, *Journey around a Zero,* was made without a camera, simply because she did not have one. Using old black-and-white film stock and some rolls of 16mm sound tape, she painted and etched images of her imagination with a variety of discarded surgical instruments and the sharp edge of a screwdriver. Compared to the $20,000 cost of *Goodbye in the Mirror, Journey*'s cost was cheap indeed—practically zero. The visuals were pure abstract animation, which De Hirsch described as "a phallic invocation." In her writing and especially in making her animation abstractions De Hirsch felt she became both man and woman, or either one—not for lack of sexual identification but with an awareness of a cosmic sexuality.

De Hirsch's trilogy entitled *The Color of Ritual, The Color of Thought,* explored relationships of abstract animated imagery (this time in color) with live photography and what she called "voyages into buried continents of the self." The very titles indicated her penchant for magic, myth, and ritual: *Divinations, Shaman: A Tapestry for Sorcerers, Peyote Queen*. In 1968 Storm De Hirsch was awarded $10,000 in the American Film Institute's first round of grants to independent filmmakers—the only woman among the winners. With the money she made a mini-feature called *The Tattooed Man,* based on her poem of the same name; it was more episodic than her first film had been, like a "happening" more than a dramatic film, and more representative of her times. For her tenth film, *Third Eye Butterfly,* De Hirsch used dual screens, side-by-side, creating a 70mm effect. One critic wrote that this encouraged the viewer's mind to give the two horizontal images a third meaning, as Eisenstein's montage of two images on a strip of film gave them an implied third meaning.

In 1973, for her Hudson River Diary series, De Hirsch used a handheld 16mm camera to create cinematic landscapes and waterscapes shot from a moving train (*Cayuga Run*) or walking along the frozen water's edge (*Wintergarden*). These films began to look more like visual poems than movies based on poems or films for which she had written poetic descriptions. Sometimes for convenience or safety's sake, she shot on Super-8 which later was blown up to 16mm. When she was given a cartridge loading Super-8 camera to take to the Venice Film Festival, she began her Cine-Sonnets series. Filmed in England's Heathrow Airport, on the train from Rome to Venice, or in her Venice hotel room, each was three or four minutes long, short and edited in the camera. No random shots of this and that—as her first European film had been—each carefully selected shot was framed by her eye and mind and hand, beautifully lighted by nature or perhaps by God Himself. As the films outwardly became shorter and simpler, inwardly they grew richer and more revealing.

With Louis Brigante's death in 1975, Storm De Hirsch lost not only her much-loved companion of some 25 years, but also the studio where they had worked, much of her creative energy, and ultimately her health. As she succumbed slowly to Alzheimer's disease, eventually she lost all memory of her achievements in film—the retrospectives at New York's Whitney Museum and the Museum of Modern Art; her classes in visionary filmmaking at the School of Visual Art; lectures and screenings in Pennsylvania and Ohio, Vancouver, and Brussels, and at many film festivals and women's programs. At the time of this writing, Storm De Hirsch continues to survive in a Manhattan nursing home with this long and devastating illness. Her fascinating role in independent cinema has yet to be well documented and assessed.

Comparison with Maya Deren deserves these further comments. Deren was something of a genius, far ahead of her times in virtually everything she did. Storm De Hirsch was an extremely talented filmmaker of her time, exploring many aspects of film as an artist's medium. The very title of her film, *Peyote Queen,* shows her to be an outspoken product of those times—the rebellious sixties, the Beat Generation, the hallucinatory decade. It is a sad footnote to those times that although P. Adams Sitney played a major role in one of her major films (*The Tattooed Man,* 1968), Sitney's seminal book on American avant-garde cinema (*Visionary Films,* 1974) does not even mention her name.—CECILE STARR

Deitch, Donna

American director

Born *8 June 1945.* ***Education*** *Studied painting and photography as an undergraduate; studied film production as a University of California, Los Angeles, graduate student.* ***Career*** *1970s—made a series of documentary films; 1975—gained recognition from feminists for the documentary,* Woman to Woman; *1986—directed first feature film,* Desert Hearts; *1989—directed TV miniseries* The Women of Brewster Place; *1990s—worked as a television director on series including:* Murder One, NYPD Blue, *and* ER. ***Awards*** *Honorable Mention, Sundance Film Festival, for* Desert Hearts, *1986.* ***Agent*** *William Morris Agency, 151 El Camino Drive, Beverly Hills, CA 90212, U.S.A.* ***Address*** *c/o Desert Heart Productions, 685 Venice Boulevard, Venice, CA 90291, U.S.A.*

Films as Director: 1968: *Berkeley 12 to 1.* **1969:** *Memorabilia P P 1.* **1970:** *She Was a Visitor.* **1972:** *Portrait.* **1975:** *"For George, Love Donna"* (short); *Woman to Woman* (doc). **1978:** *The Great Wall of Los Angeles* (doc). **1986:** *Desert Hearts* (+ pr, ro as Hungarian gambler). **1989:** *The Women of Brewster Place* (for TV). **1991:** "Esperanza" ep. of *Prison Stories: Women on the Inside* (for TV). **1992:** *Sexual Advances* (for TV). **1993:** "Dead Man Talking" ep. of *NYPD Blue* (for TV). **1994:** *Criminal Passion*; *A Change of Place* (for TV). **1995:** "Full Moon, Saturday Night" ep. of *E.R.* (for TV); "Home" ep. of *E.R.* (for TV). **1997:** *Angel on My Shoulder*; *Murder One: Diary of a Serial Killer* (for TV); "The Devil's Rainbow" ep. of *The Visitor* (for TV).

Feminist filmmaker Donna Deitch is known for making films that feature strong, cleverly nuanced female characters who find particular strength in the community of women. Her first feature was the independently produced *Desert Hearts,* which earned the praise of feminist critics for its unusual depiction of a lesbian love affair. Early in her career, Deitch worked as a still photographer, camerawoman, and editor, in addition to directing several documentaries, film shorts, and commercials. But, like many feminist filmmakers who started working in the 1970s, Deitch eventually moved from making documentary films to fiction features.

As a film student at UCLA, Deitch displayed a cheeky irreverence with her short film, *"For George, Love Donna,"* which consisted of a close shot of an erect penis that was meant to call attention to and challenge the sexism of her male student colleagues. Her interest in operating outside the conventions of male Hollywood directors is evident in her early documentaries as well, which include *Woman to Woman* about women's social roles, or, as Deitch put it, about "hookers, housewives, and other mothers"; and *The Great Wall of Los Angeles* about a mile-long mural in the Tujunga Wash of Los Angeles.

Her best-known film, *Desert Hearts,* was the product of more than two years of intensive fund-raising on Deitch's part to acquire $1.5 million in financing. She found most of her investors among women who sympathized with her desire to avoid the studio system and to retain control of her vision for the film. Indeed, Deitch was determined to deal with her subject frankly and realistically, in order to resist the depictions of lesbian relationships more typically found in American films. *Desert Hearts* tells the story of Columbia English professor Vivian Bell, a 30-something blond sophisticate who arrives in Reno in 1959 to get a divorce. In order to meet the state's residency requirements for divorce, she settles temporarily at a dude ranch run by a salty older woman. Though Vivian intends to spend her time studying, the openly lesbian and younger Cay Rivers, a lithe, bold, yet casual Westerner, attracts her attention. Vivian is not, however, initially comfortable with Cay's sexuality—or with her own. The emotions unleashed by their developing intimacy, and Vivian's ambivalence and insecurity about her feelings towards Cay, are played out against a rocky Western landscape usually associated with masculinity. Importantly, it is the female gaze that moves the film, as in a scene in which the two women eye each other while Cay dances with a man, but does not look at him. Also, more so than in the novel, Deitch effectively conveys Vivian's intrapersonal conflict, between the world of respectable heterosexuality and the challenges and rewards of a lesbian relationship.

Donna Deitch

Desert Hearts has been favorably compared to two other features from the 1980s about lesbian relationships: John Sayles's 1983 *Lianna* and Robert Towne's 1982 *Personal Best,* both of which feature less-than-happy endings for their lesbian heroines. Deitch explained that she wanted to make *Desert Hearts* because American films had failed to show a relationship between women that did not end with some "suicides, murders, or convoluted bisexual triangles." Adapted from Jane Rule's novel *Desert of the Heart,* Deitch's film is a sincere lesbian love story. Interestingly, before she agreed to sell them to Deitch, the novelist turned down a studio's offer to buy the rights to her novel, because she expected that they would alter her story beyond recognition. With its 1950s Reno setting, Deitch was drawn especially to Rule's tender love story and its key metaphor—gambling. That is, while people gamble with their money in the casinos, *Desert Hearts*'s two heroines gamble with their sexuality and social identities by pursuing a "taboo" but true love.

Critics praised *Desert Hearts*'s love scene for being highly erotic without resorting to the voyeurism or objectification of women's bodies that are typical of lesbian love scenes crafted for the "male gaze," such as *Personal Best,* whose exploitative sex scenes serve as a prelude for the heterosexual love scene; or, like *Lianna,* which means well but fails to convey any level of eroticism. Accordingly, B. Ruby Rich approvingly called *Desert Hearts* a "lesbian heart-throb movie." Indeed, as Deitch explained, "I wanted to make just a love story, like any other love story between a man and a woman, handled in a frank and real way." Thus, her film is not heavy-handed about its sexuality or sexual politics; that is, it presents the women's relationship as fully romantic, healthy, and true without forcing the characters to take on the world's homophobia on any large scale.

Deitch's next film was for Oprah Winfrey, who recruited her to direct her pet project *Women of Brewster Place,* a four-hour television miniseries adapted from Gloria Naylor's award-winning novel. It tells the story of a strong community of seven black women, including a church woman, a welfare mother, and a yuppie lesbian couple. Their collective strength is tested by the city's attempt to thwart their neighborhood's newly thriving community by erecting a brick wall to separate it from the rest of the neighborhood.

More recently, Deitch directed *Criminal Passion,* a fairly conventional story about a detective who falls in love with her prime murder suspect, thus impossibly blurring the lines between passion and police work. In the 1990s, Deitch has found success as a television director, for both movies and episodic dramas, such as *Murder One* and *ER.* In addition, she directed one of the three episodes of the cable-television anthology *Prison Stories: Women on the Inside,* which aimed to bring attention to the problems prison mothers endure. Certainly, however, the independent films from the 1990s that have achieved success featuring lesbian relationships owe a debt of gratitude to Deitch's groundbreaking *Desert Hearts* and its affirmations of lesbian love.—CYNTHIA FELANDO

Denis, Claire

French director and writer

Born *Paris, France, 21 April 1948.* ***Education*** *Attended Institut des Hautes Cinématographiques in Paris, graduated in 1972.* ***Career*** *Mid-1970s to mid-1980s—worked on short films and was an assistant director for Costa-Gavras, Wim Wenders, and Jim Jarmusch; 1988—completed her first feature, the widely seen* Chocolat; *1996—completed award-winning film,* Nénette et Boni. ***Awards*** *Golden Leopard, Locarno International Film Festival, for* Nénette et Boni, *1996.* ***Address*** *c/o: Flach Pyramide International, 5 Rue Richepanse, 75008 Paris, France.*

Films as Director: 1973-74: *Chroniques de France.* **1988:** *Chocolat* (*Chocolate*) (+ co-sc). **1989:** *Man No Run* (+ co-sc); *Jacques Rivette, Le Veilleur* (for TV). **1990:** *S'en fout la mort* (*No Fear, No Die*) (+ co-sc). **1991:** *Contre l'oubli* (*Against Oblivion*) (co, + co-sc); *Keep It for Yourself* (*Moyen Montrage*); *Ni Une, Ni Deux* (for TV). **1992:** *La Robe à Cerceaux* (*The Hoop Skirt*) (for TV). **1993:** *J'ai pas sommeil* (*I Can't Sleep*) (+ co-sc). **1994:** *Boom, Boom; U.S. Go Home* (+ co-sc) (for TV). **1995:** *Nice, Very Nice* (for TV). **1996:** *Nénette et Boni* (*Nénette and Boni*) (+ co-sc).

Claire Denis (right)

Other Films: **1978:** *Mais où et donc Ornicar* (van Effenterre) (ro, asst d). **1984:** *Paris, Texas* (Wenders) (asst d). **1986:** *Down by Law* (Jarmusch) (asst d). **1987:** *Der Himmel über Berlin* (*Wings of Desire*) (Wenders) (asst d). **1995:** *En avoir (ou pas)* (*To Have [or Not]*) (Masson) (ro as Alice's mother).

Over the course of the last ten years, Claire Denis has created an impressive body of work that ranges from narrative features and music documentaries to films for television. Known worldwide as an inspired director with a vivacious, trenchant perspective, she has been called "one of the great directors of our time," and enjoys a reputation as an extraordinarily inventive and influential independent filmmaker.

When she was two months old, Denis's parents moved to Africa, where, while her father worked in the French civil service, they lived in a series of countries until she was 14 years old. When she finished college, Denis took a position as a trainee at a company that made short educational films, whereupon she decided to attend film school in Paris. After she was graduated from film school in Paris, she worked her way from production assistant to assistant director for several highly esteemed filmmakers, such as Jacques Rivette, Constantin Costa-Gavras, Wim Wenders, and Jim Jarmusch. In a few years she was writing scripts; four years later she made her first feature film, the sublimely beautiful, much-praised, *Chocolat*. In general, her films are rich, complex combinations of intimate drama and acute sociological and political awareness.

It was while working as an assistant director on Wim Wenders's *Paris, Texas* in 1984 that she had the idea for her first feature film. The southwestern landscape prompted her memories of Africa, and the result was *Chocolat,* a fictional rendering of her own experience as a privileged, white female in colonial West Africa and of the emotional conflicts generated by colonialism. It is an altogether subtle, sophisticated film that features the aptly named character, "France," a French woman who returns as an adult to her childhood home in postcolonial Cameroon, where her father had been a district officer in the late 1950s, during the last years of French colonialism. France's story and growing racial consciousness are revealed via a long flashback to her life as an eight-year-old girl. Denis has explained that the film was fictional rather than a documentary account of her own experiences, since "when you make fiction you talk about yourself."

After *Chocolat* Denis switched gears and made *Man No Run,* a documentary about the Cameroon band Les Têtes Brûlées on their first French tour. Her next feature was *No Fear, No Die,* which offered a brutal depiction of the strange and metaphorical realm of cockfighting. *I Can't Sleep,* based on a true story, is about the infamous "granny killer" of Paris. It features the beautiful Daiga, who has emigrated from Lithuania to Paris and is looking for work; Theo, a struggling musician; and Theo's brother Camille, a transvestite dancer. It is one of the three who might be linked to the serial killer who has been terrorizing Paris, but strangely, no one notices them. The film's loose narrative evokes the work of director Eric Rohmer, but is distinctively Denis's, inasmuch as characters are revealed via their brief intersections and subtle gestures.

U.S. Go Home was part of the series *Tous les garçons et les filles* [All the boys and girls in their time], a collection of ten coming-of-age movies by esteemed French directors. Denis's highly energetic contribution is set in 1965 France and considers the pervasive influence of American culture, especially upon 14-year-old heroine Marlene who attends a party with a single-minded goal—to lose her virginity. She fails at the party, but while hitchhiking home, she meets an American serviceman. Denis brilliantly conveys Marlene's likable charm, as well as her ambivalence—both fascination and fear—of sex.

Denis routinely collaborates with Jean-Pôl Fargeau on the screenplays for her films. Her films share a commitment to examining racism and colonialism (as in *No Fear, No Die* and *Chocolat*). Further, several of her films feature characters who are siblings, including *U.S. Go Home, I Can't Sleep,* and *Nénette et Boni,* because she is drawn to the complexities, and, as she puts it, the weirdness of sibling relationships. Critics laud her moviemaking strategies, especially her knack for "committing the texture of life to film." Likewise, she has a canny sense of people and place, a compelling approach to film time and space, and she is known for her effective use of non-actors, such as the female leads in *U.S. Go Home,* and the male lead in *I Can't Sleep.*

Denis's most recent film is the award-winning *Nénette et Boni,* an impressionistic and hauntingly heartfelt, yet unsentimental look at sibling ties and immature teenage emotions. Notably, the film's characterizations and story are built in layers of metaphor and scene fragments. In the southern port city of Marseilles, Boni is a 19-year-old pizzeria worker with an active sex-fantasy life, and Nénette is his 15-year-old sister who discovers that she is pregnant and runs away from boarding school. When she unexpectedly arrives on Boni's doorstep, the two eye each other suspiciously. Both sister and brother are tough and uncompromising, as they are used to years of tribulations and coping with the legacy of their father, whom they hate. Slowly Nénette's pregnancy brings the two together, though Nénette is apparently indifferent to the baby, and it means perhaps too much to Boni.

Like Denis's other work, *Nénette et Boni* is deeply sensual. Indeed, all of her deeply evocative and unpredictable films avoid the slick production values of commercial cinema in favor of a sense of intimacy and sincerity. Nevertheless, they are remarkably varied, both visually and thematically. As a result, her many-layered films are always memorable—and occasionally haunting.—CYNTHIA FELANDO

Deren, Maya

American director

Born *Kiev, 1917, became U.S. citizen.* ***Education*** *Attended the League of Nations School, Geneva, Switzerland; studied journalism at University of Syracuse, New York; New York University, B.A.; Smith College, M.A.* ***Family*** *Married (second time) the Czech filmmaker Alexander Hackenschmied (Hammid), 1942 (divorced); later married Teijo Ito.* ***Career*** *1922—family emigrated to America; 1943—made first film* Meshes of the Afternoon; *1946—traveled to Haiti; 1960—secretary for Creative Film Foundation.* ***Awards*** *Guggenheim Fellowship for work in creative film, 1946.* ***Died*** *Of a cerebral hemorrhage in Queens, New York, 13 October 1961.*

Films as Director: 1943: *Meshes of the Afternoon* (with Alexander Hammid) (+ ro); *The Witches' Cradle* (unfinished). **1944:** *At Land* (+ ro). **1945:** *A Study in Choreography for Camera*; *The Private Life of a Cat* (home movie, with Hammid). **1946:** *Ritual in Transfigured Time* (+ ro). **1948:** *Meditation on Violence.* **1949:** *Medusa.* **1951:** *Divine Horsemen*; *Ensemble for Somnambulists.* **1959:** *The Very Eye of Night.* **1960:** *Haiku* film project.

Film as Writer: 1961: *Maeva* (*Wahine*) (Bonsignori).

Maya Deren was the best-known independent, experimental filmmaker in the United States during and after World War II. She developed two types of short, subjective films: the psychodrama and the ciné-dance film. She initiated a national nontheatrical network to show her six independently made works, which have been referred to as visual lyric poems, or dreamlike trance films. She also lectured and wrote extensively on film as an art form. Her films remain as provocative as ever, her contributions to cinematic art indisputable.

Intending to write a book on dance, Deren toured with Katherine Dunham's dance group as a secretary. Dunham introduced Deren to Alexander Hammid, and the following year the couple made *Meshes of the Afternoon*. Considered a milestone in the chronology of independent film in the United States, it is famous for its four-stride sequence (from beach to grass to mud to pavement to rug). Deren acted the role of a girl driven to suicide. Continuous action is maintained while time-space unities are severed, establishing a trancelike mood by the use of slow motion, swish-pan camera movements, and well executed point-of-view shots.

In her next film, *At Land,* a woman (Deren) runs along a beach and becomes involved in a chess game. P. Adams Sitney refers to this work as a "pure American trance film." The telescoping of time occurs as each scene blends with the next in unbroken sequence, a result of planned editing. *At Land* is also studded with camera shots of astounding virtuosity.

Other films include Deren's first ciné-dance film, the three-minute *A Study in Choreography for Camera*. Filmed in slow motion, a male ballet dancer, partnered by the camera, moves through a variety of locales. Continuity of camera movement is maintained as the dancer's foot changes location. Space is compressed while time is expanded. According to Sitney, the film's importance resides in two fresh observations: space and time in film are *created* space and time, and the camera's optimal use is as a dancer itself. *Ritual in Transfigured Time,* another dance-on-film, portrays psycho-dramatic ritual by use of freeze frames, repeated shots, shifting character identities, body movements, and locales. *Meditation on Violence* explores Woo (or Wu) Tang boxing with the camera as sparring partner, panning and zooming to simulate human response. *The Very Eye of Night* employed Metropolitan Ballet School members to create a celestial ciné-ballet of night. Shown in its negative state, Deren's handheld camera captured white figures on a total black background. Over the course of her four dance-films Deren evolved a viable form of ciné-choreography that was adapted and adjusted to later commercial feature films. In cases such as *West Side Story,* this was done with great skill and merit.

Deren traced the evolution of her six films in "A Letter to James Card," dated April 19, 1955. *Meshes* was her "point of departure" and "almost expressionist"; *At Land* depicted dormant energies in mutable nature; and *Choreography* distilled the essence of this natural changing. In *Ritual* she defined the processes of changing, while *Meditation* extends the study of metamorphosis. In *The Very Eye* she expressed her love of life and its living. "Each film was built as a chamber and became a corridor, like a chain reaction."

In 1946 Deren published *An Anagram of Ideas on Art, Form, and the Film,* a monograph declaring two major statements: the rejection of symbolism in film, and strong support for independent film after an analysis of industrial and independent filmmaking activities in the United States.

Although *Meshes* remains the most widely seen film of its type, with several of its effects unsurpassed by filmmakers, Deren had been forgotten until recently. Her reputation now enjoys a well-deserved renaissance, for as Rudolf Arnheim eulogized, Deren was one of film's "most delicate magicians."—LOUISE HECK-RABI

Dillon, Carmen

British art director

Born *Cricklewood, London, 1908.* ***Education*** *Attended New Hall Convent, Chelmsford, Essex; qualified as architect.* ***Career*** *Actress and designer for amateur dramatics; 1934—assistant to Ralph Brinton, Wembley Studios; then long association with Two Cities and Rank.* ***Awards*** *Academy Award, for* Hamlet, *1948; Venice Festival prize, for* The Importance of Being Earnest, *1952.*

Films as Art Director: **1937:** *The Five Pound Man* (Albert Parker). **1938:** *Who Goes Next?* (Elvey). **1939:** *French without Tears* (Asquith) (asst); *The Mikado* (Schertzinger) (asst). **1940:** *Freedom Radio* (*The Voice in the Night*) (Asquith). **1941:** *Quiet Wedding* (Asquith). **1942:** *Unpublished Story* (French); *The First of the Few* (*Spitfire*) (L. Howard); *Secret Mission* (French). **1943:** *The Gentle Sex* (L. Howard); *The Demi-Paradise* (*Adventure for Two*) (Asquith). **1945:** *Henry V* (Olivier); *The Way to the Stars* (*Johnny in the Clouds*) (Asquith). **1946:** *Carnival* (Haynes); *School for Secrets* (Ustinov). **1947:** *White Cradle Inn* (*High Fury*) (French). **1948:** *Vice Versa* (Ustinov); *Woman Hater* (T. Young); *Hamlet* (Olivier). **1949:** *Cardboard Cavalier* (Forde). **1950:** *The Reluctant Widow* (Knowles); *The Woman in Question* (*Five Angles on Murder*) (Asquith); *The Rocking-Horse Winner* (Pelissier). **1951:** *The Browning Version* (Asquith). **1952:** *The Story of Robin Hood and His Merrie Men* (*The Story of Robin Hood*) (Annakin); *The Importance of Being Earnest* (Asquith); *Meet Me Tonight* (Pelissier). **1953:** *The Sword and the Rose* (Annakin); *Rob Roy, the Highland Rogue* (French). **1954:** *Doctor in the House* (Thomas); *One Good Turn* (Carstairs). **1955:** *Richard III* (Olivier); *Doctor at Sea* (Thomas). **1956:** *Simon and Laura* (M. Box); *The Iron Petticoat* (Thomas); *Checkpoint* (Thomas). **1957:** *The Prince and the Showgirl* (Olivier); *Miracle in Soho* (Amyes). **1958:** *A Tale of Two Cities* (Thomas). **1959:** *Sapphire* (Dearden). **1960:** *No Kidding* (*Beware of Children*) (Thomas); *Watch Your Stern* (Thomas); *Carry on Constable* (Thomas); *Please Turn Over* (Thomas); *Kidnapped* (Stevenson); *Make Mine Mink* (Asher). **1961:** *The Naked Edge* (M. Anderson); *Raising the Wind* (*Roommates*) (Thomas). **1962:** *Carry on Cruising* (Thomas); *Twice 'round the Daffodils* (Thomas). **1963:** *The Iron Maiden* (*The Swingin' Maiden*) (Thomas). **1964:** *The Chalk Garden* (Neame). **1965:** *The Battle of the Villa Fiorita* (Daves); *The Intelligence Men* (*Spylarks*) (Asher). **1966:** *Sky, West, and Crooked* (*Gypsy Girl*) (Mills). **1967:** *Accident* (Losey). **1968:** *A Dandy in Aspic* (A. Mann and Harvey); *Otley* (Clement). **1969:** *Sinful Davey* (J. Huston). **1970:** *The Rise and Rise of Michael Rimmer* (Billington). **1971:** *Catch Me a Spy* (Clement); *The Go-Between* (Losey). **1973:** *Lady Caroline Lamb* (Bolt); *A Bequest to the Nation* (*The Nelson Affair*) (J. C. Jones). **1974:** *Butley* (Pinter). **1975:** *In This House of Brede* (Schaefer—for TV); *Love among the Ruins* (Cukor—for TV). **1976:** *The Omen* (R. Donner). **1977:** *Julia* (Zinnemann). **1978:** *The Sailor's Return* (Gold). **1979:** *The Corn Is Green* (Cukor—for TV).

Carmen Dillon was born in 1908 in London. As did so many art directors, she originally studied architecture. Dillon worked as a set dresser and art director on many pictures for Two Cities and Rank, and for nearly a quarter of a century she was the only woman art director working in English films.

Early in her career Dillon collaborated with the great British art directors Paul Sheriff and Roger Furse. She assisted Sheriff on Olivier's *Henry V,* and the sets of Olivier's *Hamlet* were by Dillon with design by Furse. These two pictures were very significant in the history of film design. *Henry V* changed style from a "realistic" look at an historic (Elizabethan) time, to an historic theatrical setting, and finally to a re-creation of the style, color, and spatial sense of medieval illuminated manuscripts. It was a daring and successful undertaking. As a contrast to the highly colored spectacle of *Henry V,* Olivier filmed the tragedy of *Hamlet* in black and white. The impression was that of an etching. The design emphasized spaces, with ominous repeating arches and geometric platforms, giving a sense of modern minimal theater as well as that of a dark and drafty castle.

Dillon did several historical reconstruction films. *The Importance of Being Earnest* and *The Go-Between* amply illustrate her skills as a researcher. In 1977 Dillon worked with Gene Callahan and Willy Holt on *Julia*. This film had great potential as a costumer. Art Deco was enjoying a revival and there were enough scenes of the wealthy, the bohemians, and the decadents for some standard streamlining and a bit of neon here and there. But the picture had none of that. Except for a calendar on the wall and the political events taking place it could have represented any time. This is critical. It gives the film a timeless meaning that speaks beyond a particular era and style. This story does not only tell specifically about Julia fighting Nazi atrocities but also how a brave human can stand up against injustice and evil. It is not just about the author Lillian Hellman and her deep relationship with a childhood companion, but of the strength of loving friendships. Furthermore, this film concerns nonmaterialistic characters who care more about feelings and ideas than decor. Dillon must convey that tone.

Carmen Dillon

Julia uses clean simple lines. Dillon emphasizes few objects, and only then with the precision of a still life. Objects, when shown, have specific relationships to the story. They are never there just for local color. Again, the sets are painted with the sparsity of a modern minimalist stage set. Often, particularly in the scenes of Hellman and Dashiell Hammett, darkness forms a cover. At times it serves as a protective blanket, at others as a threat of the unknown. Sometimes it serves for dramatic composition. Light also plays many roles—exposing, attacking, enlightening. Scene after scene features silhouettes and outlines, lamps and lighting fixtures. Ceilings are shown, giving a feeling of claustrophobia.

Dillon characterizes Julia's childhood in strongly lit reflective surfaces broadcasting to the viewer the opulent wealth of her family. There are few objects—the highly polished silver, the crystal chandeliers, the red velvet chairs. The rest of the house is almost bare, even the few hanging paintings blend into the blankness of the walls. The tall arches throughout oppress and intimidate. The staircase at the end of the film serves a similar function. Julia's room, in contrast, feels cozy, an all-white interior which symbolizes purity rather than coldness.

In *Julia* Dillon's free use of space and lighting as key elements in design goes back to her earlier work on *Hamlet*. These elements project inner feelings and serve a purpose other than that of decorative surface trappings. Dillon's versatility allows her to use detail or to eliminate it, in her pursuit of achieving an appropriate narrative effect.—EDITH C. LEE

Dörrie, Doris

German director and writer

Born *Hanover, West Germany, 26 May 1955.* ***Education*** *Studied theater at the University of the Pacific in Stockton, California; philosophy, psychology, and semantics at the New School for Social Research in New York; and film and television at the Hochschule für Film und Fernsehen in Munich, where she received a diploma in directing.* ***Career*** *1976-86—wrote film criticism for* Süddeutsche Zeitung; *1979-86—directed documentaries for German television; 1983—directed her first feature,* Straight through the Heart; *1986—won international acclaim for directing* Men. . . . ***Agent*** *ICM, 40 West 57th Street, New York, NY 10019, U.S.A.* ***Address*** *Tengstrasse 16, 8000 Munich 40, Germany.*

Doris Dörrie: *Männer*. . .

Films as Director and Writer/Co-Writer: 1976: *Ob's stürmt oder schneit* (*Come Rain or Shine*) (co-d). **1977:** *Ene, mene, mink* (short). **1978:** *Der Erste Walzer* (*The First Waltz*) (short); *Hättest was Gescheites gelernt* (for TV); *Alt werden in der Fremde.* **1979:** *Paula aus Portugal.* **1980:** *Von Romantik keine Spur* (*No Trace of Romanticism*) (for TV); *Katharina Eiselt.* **1981:** *Dazwischen* (*In Between*) (co-d with Reichel—for TV); *Unter Schafen* (*Among Noisy Sheep*). **1983:** *Mitten ins Herz* (*Straight through the Heart*) (for TV). **1985:** *Im Innern des Wals* (*In the Belly of the Whale*). **1986:** *Männer. . .* (*Men. . .*); *Paradies* (*Paradise*). **1987:** *Ich und Er* (*Me and Him*). **1989:** *Geld* (*Money*); *Love in Germany.* **1991:** *Happy Birthday Türke!* (*Happy Birthday!*). **1993:** *What Can It Be.* **1994:** *Keiner Liebt Mich* (*Nobody Loves Me*).

Other Films: 1977: *Der Hauptdarsteller* (Hauff) (ro). **1984:** *King Kongs Faust* (Stadler) (ro). **1987:** *Wann—Wenn Nicht Jetzt?* (Juncker) (sc).

Doris Dörrie's most consistent cinematic themes are sexual politics and the chasms existing between men and women. In her films, it is almost as if the opposite sexes have evolved from different species. Women are looking for emotional honesty and sexual pleasure in relationships, and attempt to connect with men in what are fated to be hapless, luckless searches for everlasting love. Men, on the other hand, are emotionally unavailable. They are obsessed with the power of their sex organs, yet become sexually unresponsive once they are married (or, for that matter, regularly sharing the same bed with the woman they have so ardently pursued). Dörrie's heroines may be unable to break through to the men in their midst, but they are not perfect either. They might be flaky or self-absorbed, and this adds resonance to her work. Furthermore, Dörrie's films are consistently offbeat. Her characters in the best of them, while existing in real worlds and facing genuine emotional dilemmas, respond to situations in altogether humorous, original, and unusual ways.

Men. . ., Dörrie's biggest hit to date, is a razor-sharp feminist satire. It is a farcical portrait of the manner in which a pompous middle-class married man responds upon learning that he is being cheated on by his sexually ignored wife. By having this affair, she has struck a blow for independence after years of devotion to a womanizing husband. An outlandish scenario unfolds, involving the cuckold befriending his wife's lover and transforming him into a clone of himself, knowing full well that his wife will become bored. *Men. . .* is an astute portrayal of the casual attitudes many men have toward women and the manner in which men view each other, all filtered through the sensibilities of a woman writer/director.

Unfortunately, Dörrie has been unable to repeat the international box-office success and win the critical raves achieved by *Men. . . . Me and Him,* her follow-up to *Men. . .*, was a major let-down: a stupefyingly unfunny parody—based, no less, on a novel by Alberto Moravia—about an architect whose penis begins offering him guidance on how to live his life. In *In the Belly of the Whale* and *Paradise,* Dörrie repeats the plot structure of *Men. . .*: a third party comes to play a key role in a less-than-sound two-person, opposite-sex familial relationship. The cornerstone of *In the Belly of the Whale* is the sadomasochistic connection between a 15-year-old girl and her policeman father. The girl runs away, in search of her mother (who also was physically abused by her father), and becomes involved with a young man who previously had conflicted with the father. *Paradise* is the story of a married couple who are more concerned with their hobbies and professions than with each other; furthermore, the husband is disinterested in satisfying the wife sexually. The third party here is the wife's former schoolmate.

Men. . ., however, is far from Dörrie's lone artistic success. *Straight through the Heart,* her debut feature (after working for German television and making shorts and documentaries), is a sharply observed exploration of the relationship between a pair of lonely neurotics: a 20-year-old woman seeking her identity and a reclusive middle-aged dentist. While the latter is willing to pay the former to move in with him, he offers her no companionship; he is interested solely in a lively female presence in his life. She becomes psychologically connected to him, but is unsuccessful in her attempt to make him love her.

In *Happy Birthday, Türke!,* an entertaining noirish detective film (as well as Dörrie's one major thematic departure), the filmmaker touches on the issue of ethnic identity. It is the story of a Turkish-born private eye who was raised by German parents and speaks only German; as a result, he is mistrusted by the Turkish community and subjected to ethnic slurs by Germans. He is hired by a Turkish woman to locate her missing husband, and becomes immersed in a scenario involving murder, prostitution, and police corruption.

Nobody Loves Me is a quirky chronicle of the trials of a lonely, death-obsessed airport security officer who is about to turn 30 and senses that life is passing her by. She declares she does not need a man, but still is desperate to find one. Her gay next-door neighbor (who is a psychic, as well as her kindred spirit) declares that she momentarily will meet her perfect love match. Could he be the new manager of their apartment building, whose primary interests are seducing attractive blonds and collecting the compensation to be gained by redoing the building into an extravagant living space?

In the end, Dörrie's heroine is left only with the companionship of her neighbor. One of the points of *Nobody Loves Me* is that, within the framework of heterosexual relations, it nearly is impossible for a man and a woman to be friends. In fact, the only male who can express compassion and remain loyal to a woman is a gay male; the emotional honesty that exists between the heroine and her neighbor is able to flourish because of the absence of sexual expectation.

Over the years, the heterosexual men in Dörrie's films have not changed. But the women have. The heroines in *Straight through the Heart* and *Nobody Loves Me* may be unsuccessful in their quests for love. In the former, the result is tragedy, while in the latter (which was made a decade later), the heroine undergoes a transformation, becoming less self-indulgent and more independent. This is her triumph, and it is one that reflects the evolution of Dörrie's view of the plight and fate of women.—ROB EDELMAN

Dulac, Germaine

French director

Born *Charlotte Elisabeth Germaine Saisset-Schneider in Amiens, France, 17 November 1882.* ***Family*** *Married Marie-Louis Albert Dulac, 1905 (divorced 1920).* ***Career*** *1909-13—writer and editor for feminist journal* La Française; *1914—offered position as camerawoman on* Caligula *by actress friend Stacia de Napierkowska; formed production company with husband and scenarist Irène Hillel-Erlanger; 1915—directed first film,* Les Soeurs enemies; *1921—traveled to United States to observe production techniques; from 1922—general secretary of Ciné-Club de France; 1930s—directed newsreels for Gaumont; formed production company, Delia Film.* ***Died*** *In Paris, July 1942.*

Films as Director: 1915: *Les Soeurs enemies.* **1916:** *Géo le mystérieux; Vénus Victrix; Dans l'ouragan de la vie.* **1917:** *Ames de fous* (+ sc). **1918:** *Le Bonheur des autres.* **1919:** *La Fête espagnole; La Cigarette*

(+ co-sc). **1920:** *Malencontre; La Belle dame sans merci.* **1921:** *La Mort du soleil.* **1922:** *Werther* (incomplete). **1923:** *La Souriante Madame Beudet* (*The Smiling Madame Beudet*); *Gossette.* **1924:** *Le Diable dans la ville.* **1925:** *Ame d'artiste* (+ co-sc); *La Folie des vaillants.* **1926:** *Antoinette Sabrier.* **1927:** *La Coquille et le clergyman* (*The Seashell and the Clergyman*); *L'Invitation au voyage; Le Cinéma au service de l'histoire.* **1928:** *La Princesse Mandane; Disque 927; Thèmes et variations; Germination d'un haricot.* **1929:** *Etude cinégraphique sur une arabesque.*

Other Films: 1928: *Mon Paris* (Guyot) (supervision). **1932:** *Le Picador* (Jacquelux) (supervision).

Before becoming a film director, Germaine Dulac had studied music, was interested in photography, and had written for two feminist journals—all of which played a role in her development as a filmmaker. There were three phases to her filmmaking career: in commercial production, in the avant-garde, and in newsreels. In addition, filmmaking was only one phase of her film career; she also was prominent as a theorist and promoter of the avant-garde film, and as an organizer of the French film unions and the ciné-club movement. The French historian Charles Ford wrote in *Femmes Cinéastes* that Dulac was the "heart" of the avant-garde in France, that without her there would have been no avant-garde. Her role in French film history has been compared to that of Maya Deren in the United States three decades later.

Dulac learned the rudiments of filmmaking by assisting a friend who was making a film in 1914. The following year she made her first film, *Les Soeurs enemies,* which was distributed by Pathé. It was the ideal time for a woman to enter commercial production, since many men had been called into the army. After directing several other conventional story films, Dulac became more and more drawn to the avant-garde cinema, which she defined in 1927 as "lines, surfaces, volumes, evolving directly without contrivance, in the logic of their forms, stripped of representational meaning, the better to aspire to abstraction and give more space to feelings and dreams—INTEGRAL CINEMA."

It is generally reported that Dulac was introduced to the French film avant-garde movement through her friendship with Louis Delluc; but Ester Carla de Miro claims that it was in fact through Dulac that he became involved in film. Delluc wrote that Dulac's first film was worth "more than a dozen of each of her colleagues. . . . But the cinema is full of people . . . who cannot forgive her for being an educated woman . . . or for being a woman at all."

Dulac's best-known and most impressive film (of the few that have been seen outside France) is *The Smiling Madame Beudet,* based on a play by André Obey. It depicts the life and dreams of a small-town housewife married to a coarse, if not repulsive, businessman. The film created a sensation in its day. Dulac succeeded with what was, at the time, signal originality in expressing by pictorial means the atmosphere and implications of this study of domestic conflict.

Showings of *The Seashell and the Clergyman,* based on an original screenplay by Antonin Artaud, have generally been accompanied by program notes indicating Artaud's outrage at Dulac's "feminized" direction. Yet as P. Adams Sitney points out in his introduction to *The Avant-Garde Film,* Artaud praised the actors and thanked Dulac for her interest in his script in an essay entitled "Cinema et l'abstraction." (Wendy Dozoretz has pointed out that the protest aimed against Dulac at the film's Paris opening in 1928 was based on a misunderstanding; at least one protester, Georges Sadoul, later said he had thought he was protesting against Artaud.)

At the other end of the cinema spectrum, Dulac began to use time-lapse cinematography to reveal the magical effects of tiny plants emerging from the soil with leaf after leaf unfolding and stretching to the sun. "Here comes Germaine Dulac and her lima bean," became a popular joke among film-club devotees, a joke that did not exclude admiration.

The last decade of Dulac's life was spent directing newsreels for Gaumont. She died in 1942, during the German occupation. Charles Ford, who has collected her articles, indicates that she expressed ideas in "clear and accessible language" which others often set forth "in hermetic formulas." One American writer, Stuart Liebman, sums up the opposing view: "Despite their undeniable importance for the film culture of the 1920s, the backward-looking character of Dulac's film theory, constituted by her nostalgia for the aesthetic discourse of the past, both defines and delimits our interest in her theoretical contributions today." The final assessment of Germaine Dulac's life and work as filmmaker and theorist may depend on the arrival of a well-documented biography, and greater access to all her writings (some short pieces are now available in English translations) and all her existing films.—CECILE STARR

Duras, Marguerite

French director and writer

Born *Marguerite Donnadieu in Giadinh, French Indo-China, 2 April 1914.* ***Education*** *Educated in mathematics, law, and political science at the Sorbonne, Paris.* ***Career*** *1943—published first novel,* Les Impudents; *subsequently novelist, journalist and playwright; 1966—directed first film,* La Musica. ***Awards*** *Prix Goncourt for novel* L'Amant, *1984, Ritz Paris Hemingway, Paris, 1986.* ***Died*** *In Paris, 3 March 1996.*

Films as Director: 1966: *La Musica* (co-d with Seban, sc). **1969:** *Détruire, dit-elle* (*Destroy, She Said*) (+ sc). **1971:** *Jaune le soleil* (+ pr, co-ed, sc, from her novel *Abahn, Sabana, David*). **1972:** *Nathalie Granger* (+ sc, music). **1974:** *La Femme du Ganges* (*Woman of the Ganges*) (+ sc). **1975:** *India Song* (+ sc, voice). **1976:** *Des journées entières dans les arbres* (*Days in the Trees*) (+ sc); *Son nom de Venises dans Calcutta désert* (+ sc). **1977:** *Baxter, Vera Baxter* (+ sc); *Le Camion* (*The Truck*) (+ sc, ro). **1978:** *Le Navire Night* (+ sc). **1978/79:** *Aurélia Steiner* (4-film series): *Cesarée* (1978) (+ sc); *Les Mains négatives* (1978) (+ sc); *Aurélia Steiner—Melbourne* (1979) (+ sc); *Aurélia Steiner—Vancouver* (1979) (+ sc). **1981:** *Agatha et les lectures limitées* (*Agatha*) (+ sc). **1983:** *Il Dialogo di Roma* (doc) (+ sc). **1985:** *Les Enfants* (*The Children*).

Other Films: 1958: *La Diga sul Pacifico* (*This Angry Age*; *The Sea Wall*) (Clémént) (st only). **1959:** *Hiroshima mon amour* (Resnais) (sc). **1960:** *Moderato Cantabile* (P. Brook) (sc, co-adapt from her novel). **1961:** *Une Aussi longue absence* (*The Long Absence*) (Colpi) (co-sc from her novel). **1964:** *Nuit noire, Calcutta* (Karmitz) (short) (sc). **1965:** "Les rideaux blancs" (Franju) episode of *Der Augenblick des Friedens* (*Un Instant de la paix*) (for W. German TV) (sc); *Mademoiselle* (Richardson). **1966:** *10:30 P.M. Summer* (*Dix heures et demie du soir en été*) (Dassin) (co-sc uncredited, from her novel); *La Voleuse* (Chapot) (sc, dialogue). **1967:** *The Sailor from Gibraltar* (Richardson) (st only). **1992:** *The Lover* (Annaud) (st only).

As a writer, Marguerite Duras's work is identified, along with that of such authors as Alain Robbe-Grillet and Jean Cayrol, with the tradition of the New Novel. Duras began working in film as a screenwriter, with an original script for Alain Resnais's first feature, *Hiroshima mon amour*. She subsequently wrote a number of film adaptations from her novels. She directed her first film, *La Musica,* in 1966. If *Hiroshima mon amour* remains her best-known work in cinema, her later films have won widespread praise for the profound challenge they offer to conventional dramatic narrative.

Marguerite Duras

The nature of narrative and the potential contained in a single text are major concerns of Duras's films. Many of her works have appeared in several forms, as novels, plays, and films. This not only involves adaptations of a particular work, but also extends to cross-referential networks that run through her texts. The film *Woman of the Ganges* combines elements from three novels—*The Ravishing of Lol V. Stein, The Vice-Consul,* and *L'Amour*. *India Song* was initially written as a play, taking characters from *The Vice-Consul* and elaborating on the structure of external voices developed in *Woman of the Ganges*. *India Song* was made as a film in 1975, and its verbal track was used to generate a second film, *Son nom de Venises dans Calcutta désert*.

This process of transformation suggests that all works are "in progress," inherently subject to being reconstructed. This is partly because Duras's works are more concerned with the quality or intensity of experience than with events per se. The films present narrative rather than a linear, unambiguous sequence of events. In *Le Camion,* two characters, played by Gérard Depardieu and Duras, sit in a room as the woman describes a movie about a woman who hitches a ride with a truck driver and talks with him for an hour and 20 minutes. This conversation is intercut with scenes of a truck driving around Paris, and stopping for a female hitchhiker (with Depardieu as the driver, and Duras as the hitchhiker). Thus, the verbal description of a potential film is juxtaposed by images of what that film might be.

An emphasis on the soundtrack is also a crucial aspect of Duras's films; her verbal texts are lyrical and are as important as the images. In *India Song,* sound and image function contrapuntally, and the audience must actively assess the relation between them, reading across the body of the film, noting continuities and disjunctions. The verbal text often refers in past tense to events and characters on screen, as the viewer is challenged to figure out the chronology of events described and depicted—which name on the soundtrack corresponds to which actor, whether the voices belong to on- or off-screen characters, and so forth. In this way the audience participates in the search for a story, constructing possible narratives.

As minimal as they are, Duras's narratives are partially derived from melodrama, focusing on relations between men and women, the nature or structure of desire, and colonialism and imperialism in both literal and metaphoric terms. In pursuing these issues through nonconventional narrative forms, and shifting the burden of discovering meaning to the audience, Duras's films provide an alternative to conventional ways of watching movies. Her work is seen as exemplifying a feminine writing practice that challenges the patriarchal domination of classical narrative cinema. In an interview, Duras said, "I think the future belongs to women. Men have been completely dethroned. Their rhetoric is stale, used up. We must move on to the rhetoric of women, one that is anchored in the organism, in the body." It is this new rhetoric, a new way of communicating, that Duras strived for in her films.—M. B. WHITE

Elek, Judit

Hungarian director

Born *Budapest, 10 November 1937.* ***Education*** *Graduated from Hungary's Academy of Theater and Film Arts.* ***Career*** *Early 1960s—became a member of the Béla Balázs Studio of young Hungarian filmmakers, a workshop for experimental film; 1963—directed her first documentary,* Encounter; *1968—directed her first fiction feature,* Island on the Continent. ***Awards*** *Chevalier de l'Ordre des Arts et des Lettres, 1987; Ecumenical Prize, Montreal World Film Festival, for* Memoirs of a River, *1988; main prize, Salerno Film Festival, for* Awakening, *1994.*

Films as Director: **1963:** *Találkozás* (*Encounter*) (short). **1966:** *Kastélyok lakói* (*Occupants of Manor Houses*; *Tenants of Castles*; *Inhabitants of Castles*) (short) (+ sc). **1967:** *Meddig él az ember?* (*How Long Does Man Matter?*). **1968:** *Sziget a szárazföldön* (*Island on the Continent*; *The Lady from Constantinople*). **1971:** *Találkozunk 1972-ben* (*We'll Meet in 1972*) (short). **1974:** *Istenmezején 1972-73* (*A Hungarian Village*). **1975:** *Egyszerű történet* (*A Simple Story*; *A Commonplace Story*) (+ sc). **1980:** *Majd holnap* (*Maybe Tomorrow*); *Martinovics* (for TV). **1983:** *Mária-nap* (*Maria's Day*). **1988:** *Tutajosok* (*Memoirs of a River*; *The Raftsmen*) (+ sc). **1994:** *Ébredés* (*Awakening*) (+ sc, ed). **1996:** *Mondani a mondhatatlant: Elie Wiesel üzenete* (*To Speak the Unspeakable: The Message of Elie Wiesel*) (+ sc, ed).

Other Film: **1976:** *Árvácska* (G. Mészáros and Ranódy) (sc).

The films of Judit Elek serve as textbook examples of art as a reflection of personal experience and political/humanist commitment. The works of many of our foremost contemporary filmmakers are autobiographical: In his films, Woody Allen consistently focuses on the neuroses of middle-class Jewish New Yorkers whose childhood insecurities and Brooklyn roots forever affect their actions as adults; the films of Martin Scorsese often spotlight the Italian-American tough guys and tough-guy wannabes of the director's youth. Yet Elek goes Allen and Scorsese one better as she combines autobiography with a sensitivity towards human suffering that is a direct outgrowth of her own youthful experience.

As a child, World War II raged around her. Elek's father, a bookstore owner, was exiled to a Nazi labor camp, and she and her family were confined to the Budapest ghetto until the Allied liberation in 1945. While they all survived, Elek did witness the obliteration of her own community, not to mention the entire Eastern European Jewish culture.

And so her films are both humanist and activist in content. They serve as testimonials to the brutalization of the human spirit, as historical records and heartfelt contemplations of anti-Semitism, and as warnings of the folly of sitting idly by in the face of genocidal racial and ethnic hatred.

From the outset, Elek has been a trailblazer. She was the lone woman in her class at her country's Academy of Theater and Film Arts. In the early 1960s she and her fellow young Hungarian filmmakers, including István Szabó, Pál Gabór, Imre Gyongyossy, and Zsolt Kedzi-Kovács, were lauded as Hungary's "first generation" of filmmakers. This "generation of 1956" trained at the Béla Balázs Studio, a workshop that served as an experimental and bureaucracy-free learning center for young directors. Summarily, Elek was acknowledged as one of the notable members of Hungary's "direct cinema" movement, whose constituents went about portraying history in realistic and factual (rather than idealized, Hollywoodized) terms as they directly confronted the grisly realities of fascism and violence in their homeland's recent and distant past.

Throughout her career, Elek has directed both documentaries and fiction features. Thematically speaking, they spotlight individuals who most often are young, and who suffer through troubled childhoods and summarily must struggle to overcome childhood constraints. They are girls coming of age in a man's world, or girls and boys confronting the bleak realities of life in wartime or under totalitarianism. By exploring the plight of abandoned or abused children and charting the harsh realities of the Holocaust, it is as if Elek is affirming her own survival and exorcising her own ghosts.

Occasionally, Elek's films explore the intricacies of familial relationships. *Maybe Tomorrow* is a portrait of a family devastated by resentment, brutality, and adultery. *Maria's Day* is a Chekhovian account of the familial and political tensions that arise during the summer reunion of an aristocratic family. Here, a recurring theme is the place and role of women within the patriarchal family structure. Similarly, the docudramas *A Hungarian Village* and *A Simple Story* chart the plights of young women aspiring to dodge the limitations placed upon them because of their gender in a Hungarian village. Elek's approach to filmmaking is never casual. While making *A Hungarian Village* and *A Simple Story,* she relocated herself and spent four years in the village researching her subject.

The pressures on Elek's main characters also may result from events that transcend familial conflict. *Awakening* is the story of Kati, a young teenager coming of age in Stalinist Budapest during the 1950s. Upon the exile of her father and the death of her mother, she is forced to her own devices and ends up residing in a communal apartment. In order to get on with her life, she must face up to her growing loneliness and psychological isolation and come to terms with her mother's death.

Arguably Elek's most acclaimed film is *Memoirs of a River,* a commanding and haunting examination of anti-Semitism. Its fact-based story—one she had wanted to tell for two decades—is set in Austria-Hungary in 1882, with the core of its scenario involving the apprehension and persecution of a group of Jewish and non-Jewish loggers who are falsely accused of the ritualistic murder of a 14-year-old Christian girl. In *Memoirs of a River,* Elek contrasts pastoral countryside images with sudden and quick bursts of violence. She effectively re-creates a shtetl world—a world of her own ancestors, if you will—which is devastated by anti-Semitism.

Elek had wanted to make *Memoirs of a River* for two decades. Significantly, when the film opened in Hungary, she was harassed by anonymous threats and hate mail, and her car was vandalized.

Her most recent film, *To Speak the Unspeakable: The Message of Elie Wiesel,* is a poignant documentary that charts the journey of Nobel Peace Prize-winner/Holocaust survivor Elie Wiesel back to his hometown in the Carpathian mountains. Wiesel recalls the destruction of his village by the Nazis, and the tragic plight of him and his family as they are deported to Auschwitz-Birkenau and Buchenwald. Wiesel in fact tours what remains of the concentration camps, and his recollections are gut-wrenchingly painful as he recounts his final memories of his sister and mother and how his father died. Yet Wiesel—as well as Elek—emerges as a survivor, a storyteller and a recorder of history, and this is their triumph.

Elek has noted that *To Speak the Unspeakable* is "dedicated to our children." She has also observed: "Although I haven't lost as much as Elie Wiesel, I have the feeling [that] despite all, we are like sister and brother. And I wish to share our common fate, our common responsibility, with the people who will see the film. We are both convinced our mission is to keep the memory alive and pass on to our children this history we've inherited from those who lost their life [sic]. It is the only way to protect the living and do the dead justice."—ROB EDELMAN

Ephron, Nora

American writer, director, and producer

Born *New York City, 19 May 1941; daughter of screenwriters and playwrights Phoebe and Henry Ephron; sister of the novelist Amy Ephron; sister of the journalist-novelist and her frequent screenwriting collaborator Delia Ephron.* ***Education*** *Graduated from Beverly Hills High School, California, 1958, and Wellesley College, Massachusetts, 1962.* ***Family*** *Married 1) Dan Greenburg, 1967 (divorced); 2) Carl Bernstein, 1976 (divorced 1979), two sons: Jacob and Max Bernstein; 3) Nicholas Pileggi.* ***Career*** *1963-68—worked as a newspaper journalist at the New York Post; 1968-78—wrote personally inflected social criticism for popular American magazines, including monthly columns as a contributing editor at* Esquire *(1972-73 and 1975-78) and* New York *(1973-74); published three books collecting these essays in the 1970s; 1978—wrote Lauren Bacall's telefilm debut,* Perfect Gentlemen; *1983—published* Heartburn, *a best-selling novel drawn from her marriage to Watergate muckraker Bernstein, and also co-wrote with Alice Arlen the screenplay of* Silkwood, *directed by Mike Nichols; 1986—wrote the screenplay for Nichols's film version of* Heartburn; *1989—wrote and associate produced* When Harry Met Sally . . . , *directed by Rob Reiner, also made a cameo appearance in Woody Allen's* Crimes and Misdemeanors; *1992—co-wrote with her sister Delia her own directorial debut,* This Is My Life, *did another Allen cameo in* Husbands and Wives; *1993—co-wrote and directed* Sleepless in Seattle. ***Agent*** *Sam Cohn, International Creative Management, 40 West 57th Street, New York, NY 10019, U.S.A.*

Films as Director and Co-Writer: **1992:** *This Is My Life.* **1993:** *Sleepless in Seattle.* **1994:** *Mixed Nuts.* **1996:** *Michael* (+ pr). **1998:** *You've Got Mail.*

Films as Writer: **1978:** *Perfect Gentlemen* (Jackie Cooper—for TV). **1983:** *Silkwood* (M. Nichols) (co-sc). **1986:** *Heartburn* (M. Nichols). **1989:** *Cookie* (S. Seidelman) (co-sc, + exec pr); *When Harry Met Sally . . .* (R. Reiner) (+ assoc pr). **1990:** *My Blue Heaven* (H. Ross) (+ exec pr). **1999:** *Hanging Up* (+ pr).

Films as Actress: **1989:** *Crimes and Misdemeanors* (W. Allen) (as wedding guest). **1992:** *Husbands and Wives* (W. Allen) (as dinner party guest).

During the 1980s, Nora Ephron wrote or co-wrote five Hollywood features. So far in the 1990s she has directed four films. She is one of the most prolific and commercially successful female filmmakers in Hollywood history.

In a 1972 essay called "Fantasies," Ephron wrote that the women's movement helped her see the need for new types of stories which would free women from sexual submissiveness (and men from constant dominance), but she felt hampered in her (culture's) ability to think of any. Ephron's films give center stage to daughters of the feminist revolution in that her heroines enjoy sex and happily pursue careers which often grant them power and wealth. Nevertheless, her women propel themselves fundamentally not toward self-sufficiency or toward the affection of women friends but toward male approval.

Though Ephron's genre of choice is the romantic comedy, her heroines suffer. They generally suggest, in Ephron's rapid-fire dialogue, that their tragedy is the inability of men and women to overcome gender differences—differences that the stories nonetheless posit as essential to their own structures and thus to the viability of the characters' love. A viewer who believes that a woman need not look solely and unilaterally to men to secure her identity might feel that the tinge of sadness to Ephron's movies comes from the heroines' constant efforts to employ a means of self-definition which they know does not work.

Ephron's first script is anomalous in her oeuvre for its genre but not its plot construction. *Silkwood,* directed by Mike Nichols and co-written with Alice Arlen, builds from the true story of a nuclear power plant worker (Meryl Streep) who died under suspicious circumstances while attempting to expose her bosses' abuses. The film expresses its passion for Silkwood's causes by training a sharp eye on the characters from a respectful distance. Still, the script shapes Silkwood's story into a thwarted quest for family, for one good man. Silkwood's work as a union leader (so threatening that someone at her plant deliberately contaminates her and her house with plutonium) functions in the film, however abstrusely, as a painful interruption to her romance with her boyfriend.

The subtlety (and resultant poignancy and realism) with which *Silkwood* approaches Ephron's central theme is abandoned in her later projects, which are consumed with Woman's search for Man to complete her. After Academy Award nominations all around for *Silkwood,* Ephron, Nichols, and Streep reprised their respective jobs in *Heartburn.* The film ends with its heroine finally leaving her husband, long after she discovers his ongoing affair during her second pregnancy. The story makes it hard to understand why she wants to be married to him from the start.

Heartburn was not a hit, but Ephron received a second Academy Award nomination for writing the popular *When Harry Met Sally . . .* (directed by Rob Reiner). Famously, Sally (Meg Ryan) demonstrates to pal Harry (Billy Crystal)—who denies, with the film, that he can be "just" her pal—that women fake orgasm. The puncturing of a male ego is equaled by what may be taken as a celebration of female self-denial. Earlier in the film, Sally has humiliated herself in a similar diner setting by speaking too loudly about sex, while Harry never humiliates himself at all.

Nora Ephron

A second of Ephron's screenplays produced in 1989, *Cookie* (directed by Susan Seidelman), also finds humor in its heroine's humiliation. The title character is an adolescent girl (Emily Lloyd) who wins the respect of her long-lost father (Peter Falk), a gangster, by engineering his escape from his enemies and his legal wife of convenience, so that he can run off with her mother. Mother and daughter only bond via the daughter's facilitation of the mother's still-healthy lust for the father, and this androcentrism is rigidly enforced. Early on, her father slaps Cookie for defending her mother, and it is played for laughs as she falls backward over a rack of Santa suits to a jolly tune.

This Is My Life (1992), Ephron's directorial debut, allows for patriarchal failure within the familial framework it shares with *Cookie*. Its young heroines' absentee father turns out to be less than inspiring, and they return to their mother who—in a slant unaffected by feminists' then 20-year-old arguments that motherhood and working need not be mutually exclusive—has disappointed them by leaving their sides to become a stand-up comedy star. By the end, both the older daughter and the mother have paramours, and even the prepubescent younger girl has a present from the man on whom she has a crush. Even without the father, the (formerly) all-female family unit is undergirded by each member's relationship with a man.

Ephron's second directorial effort, *Sleepless in Seattle,* did wonderfully at the box office and won her a third Oscar nomination for writing. A love story about lovers who do not meet until the final scene, *Sleepless* represents its protagonists' passion as substanceless, formalizing a certain lack of conviction about its fantasy of ironclad romantic destiny. Some critics have suggested that Ephron's doubts about the old forms of storytelling which she favors make her films popular in an age where viewers want to have their fun and scoff at it too. Maybe it is to be expected that blockbusters about women's desire, still rare enough, should ask us to mock as well as identify with them. On the flip side, it may be not the active femininity of the characters but their exaggerated dependence on men which makes the ambivalence appear, and sell.

After *Sleepless,* Ephron directed two little-seen films. The most recent, *Michael,* uses its archangel fallen to Earth as a cupid, his other divine powers only spicing up the love story. *Mixed Nuts* is the second of Ephron's projects to star Steve Martin—she wrote *My Blue Heaven* in 1990—and both Martin films vary from Ephron's usual pattern. Her only films with male protagonists, both side with oddballs and underdogs, both create a community rather than just one couple, and both feature a midpoint dance between two men. Ephron's work studiously avoids homoerotic tension between women, but the men's dances infuse these films with energy—though all homoeroticism transmutes into hetero-romance. As one of Hollywood's biggest female hit-makers, Ephron seems in the position of an ultimate inside outsider. It would be interesting to see her expand the comparative mess and liveliness of her Martin films to bring more of the outside in.—SUSAN KNOBLOCH

Epstein, Marie

French director, writer, and editor

Born *Marie-Antonine Epstein, 1899; sister of the director Jean Epstein.* ***Career*** *1923—assistant director and actress in Jean Epstein's avant-garde film* Coeur fidèle; *1925-27—wrote screenplays and co-directed films for Jean Epstein; 1927—began collaboration with Jean Benoît-Lévy with film* Âmes d'enfants, *which she co-wrote, co-edited, and co-directed; 1933—co-scripted, co-edited, and co-directed best-known film* La Maternelle; *1940-77—worked in film reconstruction and restoration as director of technical services at Cinémathèque Française, until she retired; 1953—sole director of* La Grande espérance. ***Awards*** *Grand Prix du Film Français at French Exposition, for* La Mort du cygne, *1937.* ***Died*** *1995.*

Film as Director and Writer: 1953: *La Grande espérance.*

Films as Writer and Co-Director and Co-Editor with Benoît-Lévy: 1927: *Âmes d'enfants* (*Children's Souls*) (co-sc). **1928:** *Peau de pêche.* **1929:** *Maternité.* **1930:** *Jimmy Bruiteur.* **1931:** *Le Coeur de Paris.* **1933:** *La Maternelle* (*Children of Montmartre*; *The Nursery School*). **1934:** *Itto.* **1936:** *Hélène.* **1937:** *La Mort du cygne* (*The Dying Swan*). **1938:** *Altitude 3200* (*Youth in Revolt*). **1939:** *La Feu de paille* (*Fire in the Straw*; *The Straw Fire*).

Other Films: 1923: *L'Auberge rouge* (Jean Epstein) (ro); *Coeur fidèle* (Jean Epstein) (ro as Mlle. Marice). **1925:** *L'Affiche* (Jean Epstein) (sc); *Mauprat* (Jean Epstein) (ro). **1927:** *Six et demi-onze* (*6½ x 11*) (co-d with Jean Epstein, sc).

Recently, film historians have rediscovered Marie Epstein's contributions to French cinema as one of the few French women filmmakers of the 1920s and 1930s. Although she worked as a screenwriter, director, and editor, she was typically unacknowledged in film histories in favor of her two collaborators, brother Jean Epstein and Jean Benoît-Lévy.

Marie Epstein began her film career as an actress, most notably as the crippled neighbor of the heroine in Jean's 1923 film *Coeur fidèle.* Her work as a screenwriter began when she won first prize in a scenario-writing competition with *Les Mains qui meurent,* which was never produced. Subsequently, she wrote two scripts for her brother, *L'Affiche* and *6½ x 11.* The compelling *L'Affiche* includes many of the themes that would characterize her subsequent films. It begins classically, with a woman's seduction and abandonment by a man; when the baby she conceives is born, she enters its photograph in a contest for the most beautiful baby in Paris, to be used in an extensive advertising campaign. Soon after winning, the baby dies and as the grieving woman wanders through Paris, she is besieged by images of her baby. The scenario was inspired by an actual soap advertisement, which illustrates Epstein's assertion that the best scenarios are discovered in "all the little details of life." It also demonstrates her interest in the still image, a theme taken up again in *6½ x 11,* whose title refers to the dimensions of a Kodak print.

Epstein's major work was produced in collaboration with Jean Benoît-Lévy, with whom she scripted, co-directed, and edited 11 films, although they are usually attributed to Benoît-Lévy alone. Their egalitarian professional relationship was one of the earliest and most productive in France. In addition, their films feature themes rarely depicted on screen, such as the desires of mothers for children and children for mothers. In *Maternité* a woman who regrets her decision not to have children discovers that there are equally rewarding opportunities to nurture the children of friends as well as the poor children in orphanages. Likewise, in *La Maternelle* an orphaned girl longs for a mother and ultimately finds one in a tenderhearted cleaning woman. And, *The Dying Swan* features a maternal relationship between a 12-year-old ballerina and the object of her adoration, the star dancer of a stage troupe.

Along with Epstein's interest in offering realistic depictions of motherhood, childhood, domesticity, and the friendship among females, the Epstein-Benoît-Lévy films also emphasize Benoît-Lévy's commitment to using film in the service of moral education. Consequently, *Children's Souls* extols the virtues of good parenting and sanitary healthy housing by contrasting two children of poor families—one neglected and the other carefully supervised. The Epstein-Benoît-Lévy films likewise address the issue of personal responsibility and moral choices, especially the weighty ethical dilemmas that accompany various social conditions. Thus, *Hélène* tells the story of a single woman who endeavors to raise her child on her own after the father commits suicide, though she must overcome a variety of obstacles. Nevertheless, despite their shared themes, the Epstein-Benoît-Lévy films looked different from one another, revealing Epstein's remarkable visual vocabulary and versatility. Indeed, she was especially interested in using poetic imagery and sophisticated, often avant-garde, cinematic techniques to convey the subjectivity of her characters.

Epstein and Benoît-Lévy's masterpiece and most successful work was *La Maternelle*. An early sound film loosely based on Léon Frapié's populist novel, its heartbreaking story takes place in the nursery school of a Paris slum. It looks like a documentary, much as the later Italian Neorealist and French "poetic realist" films did, and offers authentic observations of its largely nonprofessional cast—a group of actual slum children. A tender and haunting film, it tells the story of an newly orphaned little girl, Marie, who immediately develops an intense attachment to the new cleaning woman at her nursery school. Although the woman is lovingly attentive to her, Marie sees the school director propose to the woman and Marie becomes distraught anticipating a second abandonment. She tries to kill herself by flinging herself into a river, but she eventually reunites with her substitute *maternelle* and the film ends happily.

After World War II, Epstein and Benoît-Lévy made a short series of television documentaries about the ballet (*Ballets de France*). During the Cold War Epstein made a documentary about atomic power, *La Grande espérance*. Thereafter, she worked as a film archivist at the Cinémathèque Française, where she restored and reconstructed silent films, including some of her own, until she retired at age 76 in 1977.—CYNTHIA FELANDO

Export, Valie

Austrian director

Born *Waltraut Lehner in Linz, Austria, 1940.* ***Education*** *Attended the Vienna College for Textile Art and Industry, B.A. 1964.* ***Family*** *1 daughter: Perdita.* ***Career*** *Since 1967—*

created "expanded cinema" performances, often in collaboration with Peter Weibel; 1968—performed well-known "touch cinema" piece, Tapp und Tastkino, *co-founded the Austrian Filmmakers Cooperative; 1970—began creating "video-actions" with* Split Reality; *1975—was an associate founding member of the Graz Writers' Conference and a founding member of Film Women International (UNESCO); 1976—completed first feature-length film,* Invisible Adversaries; *1989—professor of film and video, School of Fine Arts, University of Wisconsin, Milwaukee.* **Awards** *Prize for most political film, Third Maraisiade, for* Ping Pong, *1968; Special Jury Prize, Mostra Internationale de Film d'Autore, for* Invisible Adversaries, *1976; Special Jury's Prize, 27th Bilbao International Film Festival, for* Syntagma, *1983; Festival Prize, Daniel Wadsworth Memorial Video Festival, for* A Perfect Pair, or, Indecency Sheds Its Skin, *1986.*

Films as Director: 1967: *Menstruationsfilm* (*Menstruation Film*). **1967-68:** *Ars Lucis*; *Abstract Film No. 1*; *Cutting*. **1968:** *Ohne Titel Nr. 2* (*Without Title No. 2*) (co-d with Weibel); *Ohne Titel xn* (*Without Title xn*) (co-d with Weibel); *Der Kuss* (*The Kiss*) (co-d with Weibel); *Ein Familienfilm von Waltraut Lehner* (*A Family Film by Waltraud Lehner*); *Instant Film* (co-d with Weibel); *Valie Export* (co-d with Weibel); *Wor(l)d Cinema: Ein Sprachfest* (*Wor[l]d Cinema: A Festival of Languages*) (co-d with Weibel); *Gesichtsgrimassen* (*Facial Grimaces*); *Ansprache Aussprache* (*Speak to, Speak Out*); *Splitscreen-Solipsismus*; *Tapp und Tastkino* (*Touch Cinema*); *333*; *Ping Pong*; *Sie Suesse Nummer: Ein Konsumerlebnis*; *Sehtext: Fingergedicht*; *Auf+Zu+Ab+An* (*Up+Down+On+Off*); *Vorspann: Ein Lesefilm* (*Cast and Credits: A Film to Be Read*). **1969:** *Proselyt* (*Proselyte*); *Eine Reise ist eine Reise Wert* (*A Journey Is Worth the Trip*) (co-d with Weibel); *Das Magische Auge* (*The Magical Eye*) (co-d with Weibel); *Tonfilm* (*Sound Film*); *Genitalpanik* (*Genital Panic*). **1970:** *Split Reality*. **1971:** *Facing a Family*; *Eros/ion*. **1971-72:** *Interrupted Line*; *Stille Sprache* (*Silent Language*). **1973:** *Hyperbulie* (*Hyperbulia*); *Adjungierte Dislokationen* (*Adjoined Dislocations*); *Asemie* (*Asemia*); *Mann & Frau & Animal* (*Man, Woman and Animal*); *. . . Remote . . . Remote . . .*; *Sehtext: Fingergedicht* (*Sight Poem: Finger Poem*); *Die Süsse Nummer: Ein Konsumerlebnis* (*The Sweet One: A Consumer Experience*); *Hauchtext: Liebesgedicht (1970)* (*Love Poem*); *Touching (1970)*. **1974:** *Body Politics*; *Raumsehen und Raumhören* (*Seeing Space and Hearing Space*) (+ co-sound). **1976:** *Unsichtbare Gegner* (*Invisible Adversaries*) (+ co-sc, pr); *Homometer II*; *Wann ist der Mensch eine Frau?* (*When Is a Human Being a Woman?*); *Schnitte* (*Cuts*). **1977:** *Delta: Ein Stück* (*Delta: A Piece*). **1978:** *I [(Beat) It]*. **1979:** *Restringierter Code* (*Restricted Code*); *Menschenfrauen* (+ co-sc, pr). **1982:** *Das Bewaffnete Auge* (*The Armed Eye*) (doc) (+ sc). **1983:** *Syntagma* (+ sc, pr). **1984:** *Die Praxis der Liebe* (*The Practice of Love*) (+ sc, pr). **1985:** *Tischbemerkungen-November 1985* (*Table Quotes-November 1985*) (doc). **1986:** *Die Zweiheit der Natur* (*The Duality of Nature*) (+ pr); *Ein Perfektes Paar oder die Unzucht wechselt ihre Haut* (*A Perfect Pair, or, Indecency Sheds Its Skin*) (+ sc, pr); *Yukon Quest* (co-d with I. Wiener, O. Weiner, and E. Forster). **1987:** *Maschinenkörper-Körperraum-Körpermaschinen* (*Machine-Bodies/Body-Space/Body-Machines*); *Mental Images, Oder der Zugang der Welt* (*Mental Images, or, the Gateway to the World*) (co-d). **1988:** *Dokumente zum Internationalen Aktionismus*; *Unica*. **1989:** *Die Meta-Morphose* (*The Meta-Morphosis*) (+ co-sc).

As Annie, a character in Valie Export's first feature film, *Invisible Adversaries*, explains, "images penetrate me like psychic meteors, they frighten me—but they mirror the reality that surrounds me as a paranoid." Throughout her long career as an artist, Export has emphasized the amazing power of images to shape psychic and external realities, especially when the images depict women's bodies. With an international reputation as a challenging and prolific avant-garde artist, Export has noted that her body of work includes "films, expanded movies, video, body actions (body-material-interactions), photography, drawings." In general, her work explores psychoanalytic themes regarding femininity, sexuality, and desire, and critics have complimented her imaginative use of film to counter the conventions of mainstream narrative films and their depictions of the female body.

In the 1960s Export earned recognition for her avant-garde performance pieces, films, videos, and installation work. She has explained that her work is linked to and inspired by the avant-garde movements of the first half of the 20th century and their developments after World War II. In addition, her artistic development is productively understood in relation to contemporary art trends in Vienna, especially to the work of progressive artists who sought to connect with prewar trends and deployed a variety of media in their work to question the relationship between and meanings of language, culture, and reality.

Export is the author of several brave and challenging works that suggest an acute interest in contemporary feminist film theoretical and critical attention to the function of the female body, along with a remarkable willingness to put her body on the line—literally. One of her most acclaimed "expanded films," *Tapp und Tastkino,* considered the kind of cinematic male voyeurism and fetishism of the female body that film scholar Laura Mulvey gained renown for writing about much later, in her 1975 article, "Visual Pleasure and Narrative Cinema." Export titled the piece "touch cinema" because it consisted of inviting a "spectator" to take pleasure in a real woman's body: Export's own. Specifically, she donned a "movie theater"—a box with curtains that contained her bare chest, while Peter Weibel encouraged passersby to participate by touching her breasts.

Indeed, much of Export's work uses the female body as a primary material element of film in order to suggest the interrelationships between the body and its social and cultural environments. *. . . Remote . . . Remote . . .* and *Man, Woman, and Animal* are short 16mm films that depict the body as the site of psychological and sociological examination, via both pain and pleasure. *Man, Woman, and Animal* investigates women's pleasure by depicting a woman's genitals as she masturbates in the bath. *. . . Remote . . . Remote . . .* shows a woman who methodically undertakes the bloody mutilation of her hands by cutting away her cuticles with an Exacto blade. At intervals, she washes the blood in a bowl of milk that sits in her lap. Significantly, she is linked symbolically to a poster-size black-and-white photograph of two infants who were abused by their parents and are apparently being exploited by their rescuers—the legal authorities who have permitted the children's pain to be recorded by a news photographer. The film foregrounds Export's interest in making internal states visible; as she puts it, she is preoccupied with "the pictorial representation of psychic conditions, with the responses of the body when its loses its identity."

The defining characteristics of Export's work are her emphasis on materials and objects, spontaneity and randomness, transgressions of the lines between art media and between life and art. Moreover, her aim is to alter the conventions that govern typical depictions of the female body and to intervene in the audience's passive consumption of more typical representations. Her expanded cinema pieces from the 1960s and 1970s experimented with new considerations of the film medium, and include a number of works that documented the multimedia events or "happenings" she created, occasionally with her collaborator Peter Weibel. Among her best-known expanded films are *Cutting,* and *Genital Panic,* in which she walked through a row of spectators with the front of her pants cut out. Likewise, her expanded films *Instant Film* and *The Magical Eye* elide the gap between production and consumption so as to force spectators out of their typically passive viewing modes into a more active engagement with the film experience. Thus, *Instant Film,* which Export also called an "object film," consists of a sheet of transparent plastic that viewers were encouraged to look through to create their own "films."

Export's first feature, *Invisible Adversaries,* enjoyed critical acclaim for its meditations on feminine identity and representation and for the refusal to provide unambiguous meanings. The film echoes *Invasion of the Body Snatchers* to the extent that it features a photographer, Anna, who is convinced that unknown forces are controlling the minds of the people around her. Specifically, she believes that Earth has been colonized by a foreign enemy, the Hyksos—an ancient Egyptian tribe known for sudden appearances and disappearances. Unlike the earlier film, however, the mind control to which Export's film refers is related to patriarchal attitudes about and representations of the female body. Accordingly, Anna, like Export, uses the tools of her trade to observe hidden "truths" that reveal how the female body has been "constructed" by male artists and medical discourses. For example, the men in the film either are uninterested in taking up Anna's system of understanding or they think she is crazy. Thus, when she confides her concerns about the "invisible adversaries," her doctor recommends drugs to control her "hallucinations."

Export's second feature, *Menschenfrauen,* works like a "consciousness-raising" film in its focus on the "true" life stories of four women. Her third feature film, *The Practice of Love* is about a professional journalist, Judith, who discovers during a criminal investigation that she is surrounded by corruption when she learns that one of her two lovers is an illegal arms dealer. Part of the film's task is to consider the integration of the public and private realms, a salient theme in much of Export's work.

In addition to her work as an artist, Export has written several published pieces on the subjects of contemporary art and feminist theory. Like her films and performances, her writing offers poetically jarring, direct challenges to the function of patriarchal language to deindividuate women and it exhorts viewers to challenge dehumanizing "realities." Accordingly, she has advised that "if sentences devoid of general meaning are spoken . . . then it is no longer a question of testing a theory of existence but of saving individuation, naked existence in a reality of senseless destruction."—CYNTHIA FELANDO

Faye, Safi

Senegalese director and writer

Born *Dakar, Senegal, 22 November 1943.* ***Education*** *Received teaching certificate from Rufisque Normal School, 1963; studied ethnology at the École Pratique des hautes Études and filmmaking at the Louis Lumière Film School during the 1970s; University of Paris, Ph.D. in Ethnology, 1979; degree in ethnology from the Sorbonne, 1988.* ***Family*** *Daughter, Zeiba.* ***Career*** *Ethnologist, filmmaker; 1963-69—teacher, Dakar school system; 1972—began filmmaking; 1979-80—guest lecturer, Free University of Berlin.* ***Awards*** *Georges Sadoul Prize, Festival International du Film de l'Ensemble Francophone (Geneva), and International Film Critics Award, Berlin Film Festival, for* Kaddu Beykat, *1975; Award, Carthage Film Festival, for* Fad'jal, *1979; Special Prize, Leipzig Festival (Germany), for* Selbé One among Others, *1982.* ***Address*** *12 Rue Morère, 75014 Paris, France; B P 1352, Dakar, Senegal.*

Films as Director: 1972: *La Passante* (*The Passerby*) (short) (+ sc, ro). **1973:** *Revanche* (*Revenge*) (short). **1975:** *Kaddu Beykat* (*Lettre paysanne, Peasant Letter, Letter from the Village*). **1979:** *Fad'jal* (*Come and Work, Grand-père raconte*) (+ sc); *Goob na nu* (*La Récolte est finie, The Harvest Is In*) (short). **1980:** *Man Sa Yay* (*I, Your Mother, Moi, ta mère*). **1981:** *Les Âmes au soleil* (*Souls in the Sun*) (short). **1982:** *Selbé et tant d'autres* (*Selbé One among Others*) (doc). **1983:** *3 ans 5 mois* (*3 Years Five Months*) (short). **1984:** *Ambassades Nourricières* (*Culinary Embassies*) (doc). **1985:** *Racines noires* (*Black Roots*) (short); *Elsie Haas* (*Elsie Haas: Femme peintre et cinéaste d'Haiti*). **1989:** *Tesito* (short). **1990:** *Tournage Mossane* (short). **1996:** *Mossane* (*Beauty*) (+ sc).

Film as Actress: 1972: *Petit à petit ou Les Lettres persanes 1968* (*Little by Little, 1968 Persian Letters*) (Rouch).

Considered the first woman filmmaker of sub-Saharan Africa, Safi Faye remains one of the few active black African women directors. Born in Dakar, Faye's family belongs to the Serer ethnic group, and comes from Fad'jal, the village upon which she would base her fourth film.

Safi Faye

Trained as an educator, Faye was introduced to filmmaking by Jean Rouch, the ethnographic filmmaker credited with the term cinema verité and known for films that Fatimah Tobing Rony, in her book *The Third Eye,* describes as "increasingly self-reflexive and collaborative cinema" that "gets beyond scientific voyeurism." Rouch and Faye met in 1966, while Faye was working as an official hostess for the 1966 Dakar Festival of Negro Arts. Her first entry into the cinema was not as a filmmaker, but as an actress. She appeared in Rouch's film *Little by Little*. The filmmaker encouraged Faye to pursue her interest in ethnographic film, and she did so in 1972, traveling to Paris to study both filmmaking and ethnology.

Her first film, *The Passerby,* in which she stars, was made while Faye was still a film student. The film is a critique of the neocolonialist introduction of agricultural monoculture—shifting farming from varied crops of use to the community to a single crop for export. As Sheila Petty states, this film, as well as *Fad'jal* "attempts to bring a feminist consciousness to African film by revealing rather than glossing over, certain structures or uses of structures that continue to deny women equality."

Using money earned from her first film, Faye shot her first feature-length docudrama with a budget of only $20,000, *Kaddu Beykat*. The film was completed three years later, and garnered international attention and awards. As Françoise Pfaff states, the film was "literally meant to give a voice to Senegalese peasants," and like *Fad'jal,* to "condemn the precariousness of [a] base on the whims of peanut monoculture." But rather than focus solely on the role of foreign markets in the oppression of African people, the film also critiques the role of the Senegalese government. As Faye noted in the *Guardian,* "It is all too easy and convenient to place the blame for Africa's present ills uniquely on the past or on outside forces."

One of her best-known films is the documentary *Selbé One among Others* produced in 1982. This film was part of a unique and innovative program funded by UNICEF. Several filmmakers were chosen to direct films documenting the everyday experiences of women in different countries. Faye focused on her native Senegal, and Selbé Diout, a 39-year-old woman struggling in a village for the survival of herself and her children. Selbé, whose husband has left the community for a job in the city, is only one of many women who are the sole providers for their families. With no jobs and no viable incomes, the women work endlessly making and selling goods, foraging for food, and tending small subsistence plots of land.

Faye's international reputation is defined not only by her vision, but also by her style, for she brought to African ethnographic film the perspective not of the "outsider" observing the exotic, but that of a member of the culture. Her method is participatory and as she herself states: "I do not work singlehandedly, but rather through and with people. I go to talk to farmers in their village, we discuss their problems and I take notes. Even though I may write a script for my films, I basically leave the peasants free to express themselves in front of a camera and I listen. My films are collective works in which everybody takes an active part."—FRANCES K. GATEWARD

Fernández Violante, Marcela

Mexican director and writer

Born *Mexico City, 9 June 1941.* ***Education*** *Centro Universitario de Estudios Cinematográficos (CUEC), Universidad Nacional Autonoma de México (UNAM).* ***Family*** *Divorced; sons: Roberto and Jaime.* ***Career*** *1971 to present—professor at CUEC; 1974-75—feature film debut,* Whatever You Do, You Lose; *1975—first woman to join Mexican film director's union; 1978-82—technical secretary, CUEC; 1988-91—director of CUEC; director, Sección de Autores del Sindicato de Trabajadores de la Industria Cinematográfica (Authors' Section, Film Industry Workers Union).* ***Awards*** *Diosa de la Plata, critics'award for best experimental short, for* Blue, *1966; Ariel, Best Documentary Short, Mexican Academy of Motion Picture Arts and Science, and Diosa de la Plata for best documentary short, for* Frida Kahlo, *1971; Ariel, Best Feature Film, Mexican Academy of Motion Picture Arts and Science, for* Whatever You Do, You Lose, *1975; Ariel, Best Feature Film, and Best Director, Mexican Academy of Motion Picture Arts and Science, and Jury's Special Award, Mystery International Film Festival, for* Mystery, *1979.* ***Address*** *c/o Mexican Film Institute (IMCINE), Ateletas 2 Country Club, Coyoacán, DF 14220, Mexico.*

Films as Director: 1966: *Azul* (*Blue*) (experimental short). **1968:** *Gayosso de descuentos* (unfinished short). **1971:** *Frida Kahlo* (doc, short) (+ sc). **1975:** *De todos modos Juan te llamas* (*In Any Case, Your Name Is Juan*; *Whatever You Do, You Lose*; *The General's Daughter*) (+ sc). **1977:** *Cananea.* **1979:** *Misterio* (*Mystery*) (+ sc). **1980:** *En el país de los pies ligeros* (*El niño Raramuri*; *The Raramuri Boy*; *In the Country of Fast Runners*) (+ co-sc). **1986:** *Nocturno amor que te vas* (*Nocturnal Love That Leaves*). **1991:** *Golpe de suerte* (*Stroke of Luck*; *Lucky Break*). **1998:** "Música, risa y llanto" ep. of *Enredando Sombras.*

Other Film: 1990: *My Filmmaking, My Life: Matilde Landeta* (P. Diaz and J. Ryder—doc) (appearance).

In each of its important moments, Mexican cinema has been able to boast at least one prominent woman producer, director, or screenwriter. In the 1970s, the woman of note was Marcela Fernández Violante, who wrote and directed award-winning short films and feature films. She studied at the film school at the Universidad Nacional Autonoma de México in the late 1960s, where she learned her trade from film professionals. In 1971 she was invited back to the university to be trained as a professor and to teach in the film program. Since then, Fernández Violante has taught film, eventually being promoted to the leadership of the department in 1988.

From the beginning, Fernández Violante caught Mexico's and the international film community's attention. She won the 1966 Diosa de la Plata's critics' award for her first directorial effort, an experimental short entitled *Blue*. Her 1971 documentary about Frida Kahlo preceded the deification of Kahlo as perhaps the greatest and most misunderstood of Mexico's women painters. Winning both an Ariel (Mexico's equivalent of the Academy Award) and a Diosa de la Plata for best documentary, *Frida Kahlo* arguably primed the public for Paul Leduc's magnificent biopic, *Frida* (1982).

Fernández Violante has directed five feature films, each one critically acclaimed. In 1975, after the release of *Whatever You Do, You Lose,* she became the first woman to join the Mexican director's union. Her first feature analyzes the role of the military in Mexico through its treatment of the Cristero War of 1926, a conflict that revolved around religious questions. According to Fernández Violante, the film looks at "how the revolution was betrayed and the different aspects of loyalty to one's convictions and how one betrays them." Written and produced during a tense moment in Mexico's contemporary history, *Whatever You Do, You Lose* allowed her to explore how Mexico's military has traditionally dealt with opposition while avoiding the sensitive contemporary issues of Marxism and the tumultuous era of student uprisings of the late 1960s. She believes that the film, which was funded by UNAM, was only possible because it was made during a period of political rapprochement under President Luis Echevarría. Although she was criticized for not dealing specifically with the betrayal of peasants, Fernández Violante made a strong and lasting impression on Mexican critics and audiences with this sensitive portrayal of Mexican army officers and their families.

Fernández Violante's subsequent feature films have won vast critical acclaim, but have not succeeded at Mexico's box offices. Her second feature film, *Cananea,* is based on the real experiences of William C. Greene, a U.S. entrepreneur whose copper mine, Cananea, suffered a workers' strike in 1906 which finally had to be settled by the Texas Rangers. In this film, Fernández Violante partnered with Mexico's premier cinematographer, Gabriel Figueroa, whose cinematography defined the Mexican Cinema's Golden Age from the mid-1930s to the 1950s.

In 1979 Fernández Violante turned toward contemporary Mexico as the setting for her next feature film *Mystery*. Adapted by Vicente Leñero from his own novel *Studio Q, Mystery* is a self-reflexive tale about a soap-opera actor whose life begins to mirror that of his screen character. *Mystery* is a complex, twisted story in which the perennial question "does life imitate art or does art imitate life?" resounds loudly. This third feature won eight Ariels, including best director and best feature film.

Despite financing problems and shifting governmental support of the Mexican film industry, Mexican filmmakers in the 1980s and early 1990s affected a slow but steady renaissance of Mexican cinema. Fernández Violante was instrumental in this rebirth, both as a filmmaker and as a professor of cinema and, from 1988 to 1991, the director of UNAM's film school. Her 1991 film, *Stroke of Luck,* achieved not only critical acclaim, but perhaps more important, successful commercial exhibition in Mexico. This triumph, coupled with the domestic success of *Like Water for Chocolate* (directed by Alonso Arau, 1992) and *Danzón* (directed by María Novaro, 1990), truly demonstrates that Mexicans are returning to their own films, reveling in the opportunity to see themselves on screen. Fernández Violante's perseverance has certainly contributed to the audience's newly reborn respect and enthusiasm for Mexican film.—ILENE S. GOLDMAN

Fields, Verna

American editor

Born *1918.* ***Family*** *Married the film editor Sam Fields (died 1954), two sons.* ***Career*** *1940s—assistant editor on Hollywood films; 1950s-early 1960s—assistant editor on TV series* The Whistler, *1954-55,* The Lone Ranger, *1954-57,* Death Valley Days, *1955-58,* Sky

King, *1955-58,* Wanted: Dead or Alive, *1959-60, and* The Tom Ewell Show, *1960-61; taught film editing, University of Southern California, Los Angeles; from 1960—film editor; 1976-82—vice-president of Feature Productions, Universal.* ***Awards*** *Academy Award, for* Jaws, *1975.* ***Died*** *30 November 1982.*

Films as Editor: 1944: *Belle of the Yukon* (Seiter) (asst); *Casanova Brown* (Wood) (asst); *The Woman in the Window* (F. Lang) (asst). **1945:** *Along Came Jones* (Heisler) (asst). **1960:** *The Savage Eye* (Maddow, Meyers, and Strick); *Studs Lonigan* (Lerner); *The Sword and the Dragon* (English-language version of *Ilya Mourometz*) (Ptushko). **1963:** *An Affair of the Skin* (Maddow); *Cry of Battle* (Lerner) (supervisor). **1964:** *The Bus* (Wexler) (co). **1966:** *Country Boy* (Kane); *Deathwatch* (Morrow). **1967:** *The Legend of the Boy and the Eagle* (Couffer) (co); *Search for the Evil One* (Kane); *Track of Thunder* (Kane). **1968:** *The Wild Racers* (Haller) (co). **1969:** *Medium Cool* (Wexler). **1971:** *Point of Terror* (Nicol) (supervisor). **1972:** *What's Up, Doc?* (Bogdanovich). **1973:** *American Graffiti* (Lucas) (co); *Paper Moon* (Bogdanovich). **1974:** *Daisy Miller* (Bogdanovich); *The Sugarland Express* (Spielberg) (co); *Memories of Us* (Dyal) (co). **1975:** *Jaws* (Spielberg).

Other Films: 1956: *While the City Sleeps* (F. Lang) (sound ed). **1958:** *Snowfire* (D. & S. McGowan) (sound ed). **1961:** *El Cid* (A. Mann) (sound ed). **1963:** *The Balcony* (Strick) (sound ed); *A Face in the Rain* (Kershner) (sound ed). **1967:** *Targets* (Bogdanovich) (sound ed). **1968:** *Journey to the Pacific* (d). **1969:** *It's a Good Day* (d).

Verna Fields became one of the American film industry's most famous editors during the 1970s, and in the process was able to accumulate considerable power. Since she had helped with so many blockbusters of the decade, including *Jaws* and *American Graffiti,* Fields was promoted by a grateful Universal Pictures into the executive suite as vice president of feature films. She held that post until her death in 1982.

Unfortunately all this fame and power at the end of her long career only served to remind close observers of the American film industry that like in other multibillion dollar institutions, few women ever accumulated a measure of true power. Since the beginnings of the film industry, however, film editing had been one of the few arenas open to women. Fields, like Margaret Booth before her (at MGM), used this opening to become a force at a major Hollywood studio.

Indeed during the heyday of the "Movie Brats" of the 1970s, many looked to Fields as a symbolic breakthrough. Here was a person who had worked on many a low-budget independent film being elevated into a real position of power. She was so "in" that in 1974 *Newsweek* featured an article on her—one of the few in a popular magazine about a film editor.

Verna Fields's father helped her move into the film industry. Through him she met her husband Sam Fields, who was a film editor, in the 1940s. Sam died in 1954, leaving two sons to support. Verna returned to work that year and learned her craft on television fare such as *The Lone Ranger, Wanted: Dead or Alive, Death Valley Days,* and *Sky King*. She made her big splash in Hollywood as the sound editor for *El Cid*.

But her greatest impact came when she began to teach film editing to a generation of students at the University of Southern California. She then operated on the fringes of the film business, for a time making documentaries for the Office of Economic Opportunity. The end of that federal agency pushed her back into mainstream Hollywood, then being overrun by her former students.

Cutting *What's Up, Doc?* for Peter Bogdanovich represented her return, but her real influence began when she helped a former USC student, George Lucas, persuade Universal to distribute *American Graffiti*. A grateful Lucas, the story goes, presented her with a brand new BMW automobile in return. *Jaws* for Steven Spielberg "made" Fields's career.

She was quoted in the 1970s, at the height of her influence, saying that she believed editing should be invisible. She sought to play down her own influence, preferring to let the director dictate the terms. Thus she worked in a variety of projects equally well—from melodrama to comedy to classic genre films. Certainly that is precisely what the new young Hollywood generation liked about her. She was a great technician who was sympathetic to their projects and visions. She wanted to help them—unlike the rest of the Hollywood establishment of the day which fought their very entry into the system. It is for this support that Verna Fields will long be remembered.—DOUGLAS GOMERY

Foster, Jodie

American director and actress

Born *Alicia Christian Foster in Los Angeles, 19 November 1962.* ***Education*** *Attended Lycée Français, Los Angeles; Yale University, B.A., 1985.* ***Career*** *Acted in TV commercials from the age of three; 1969—acting debut on TV in* Mayberry R.F.D.; *1972—feature film acting debut in* Napoleon and Samantha; *1991—directorial film debut with* Little Man Tate. ***Awards*** *U.S. National Film Critics Award, and Los Angeles Film Critics Award, for* Taxi Driver, *1976; BAFTA Awards for Best Supporting Actress and Most Promising Newcomer, for* Taxi Driver *and* Bugsy Malone, *1976; Academy Awards for Best Actress, for* The Accused, *1988, and for* The Silence of the Lambs, *1991; Chevalier dans l'Orde des*

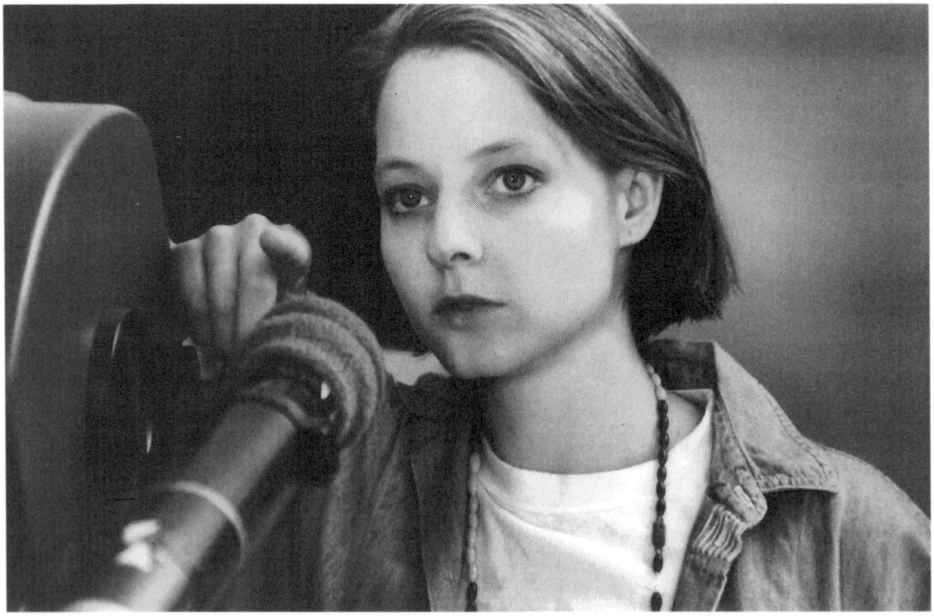

Jodie Foster directing *Little Man Tate.*

Arts et de Lettres, 1995; Governors Award, American Society of Cinematographers, 1996. **Agent** *ICM, 8942 Beverly Boulevard, Beverly Hills, CA 90211, U.S.A.*

Films as Director: 1991: *Little Man Tate* (+ ro as Dede Tate). **1995:** *Home for the Holidays* (+ co-pr).

Films as Actress: 1970: *Menace on the Mountain* (McEveety—for TV) (as Suellen McIver). **1972:** *Napoleon and Samantha* (McEveety) (as Samantha); *Kansas City Bomber* (Freedman) (as Rita). **1973:** *Tom Sawyer* (Taylor) (as Becky Thatcher); *One Little Indian* (McEveety) (as Martha); *Rookie of the Year* (Elikann—for TV). **1974:** *Alice Doesn't Live Here Anymore* (Scorsese) (as Audrey); *Smile Jenny, You're Dead* (Thorpe—for TV) (as Liberty). **1976:** *Echoes of a Summer* (*The Last Castle*) (Taylor) (as Deirdre Striden); *Freaky Friday* (Nelson) (as Annabel Andrews); *Bugsy Malone* (Alan Parker) (as Tallulah); *Taxi Driver* (Scorsese) (as Iris Steensman). **1977:** *The Little Girl Who Lives down the Lane* (Gessner) (as Rynn Jacobs); *Candleshoe* (Tokar) (as Casey Brown); *Il Casotto* (*The Beach House*) (Citti) (as Teresina). **1978:** *Moi, Fleur Bleue* (*Stop Calling Me Baby!*) (as Fleur Bleue). **1980:** *Foxes* (Lyne) (as Jeanie); *Carny* (Kaylor) (as Donna). **1983:** *O'Hara's Wife* (Bartman) (as Barbara O'Hara); *Le Sang des autres* (*The Blood of Others*) (Chabrol) (as Hélène); *Svengali* (Harvey—for TV) (as Zoe Alexander). **1984:** *The Hotel New Hampshire* (Richardson) (as Franny Berry). **1986:** *Mesmerized* (*Shocked*) (Laughlin) (as Victoria, + co-pr). **1987:** *Siesta* (Lambert) (as Nancy). **1988:** *Five Corners* (Bill) (as Linda); *The Accused* (Kaplan) (as Sarah Tobias); *Stealing Home* (Kampmann) (as Katie Chandler). **1989:** *Backtrack* (*Catchfire*) (D. Hopper—released in U.S. in 1991) (as Anne Benton). **1991:** *The Silence of the Lambs* (J. Demme) (as Clarice Starling). **1992:** *Shadows and Fog* (W. Allen) (as prostitute). **1993:** *Sommersby* (Amiel) (as Laurel); *It Was a Wonderful Life* (Ohayon—doc) (as narrator). **1994:** *Nell* (Apted) (title role, + co-pr); *Maverick* (R. Donner) (as Annabelle Bransford). **1997:** *Contact* (Zemeckis) (as Dr. Eleanor Arroway).

A wunderkind stage-managed by a pushy mother who enrolled her in a French-speaking school for gifted children and succeeded in bringing her to the notice of fledgling director Martin Scorsese, Jodie Foster has in many ways lived up to her early promise, winning Academy Awards for her performances in *The Accused* and *The Silence of the Lambs* and graduating with honors from Yale. After notable appearances as a child actress in *Alice Doesn't Live Here Anymore* and *Taxi Driver* (the only performance to inspire a would-be presidential assassin?), Foster suffered through the reactionary and overly conventional 1980s with few real opportunities to display her acting talents. Both *The Accused* and *Silence of the Lambs,* however, afforded her the opportunity once again to make an impression on mainstream cinema with finely crafted portraits of morally ambiguous women who, though victimized, maintain their integrity and self-respect.

Though urged by talent and inclination toward the director's chair, Foster has directed only two films. Perhaps too much was expected of her maiden effort (Foster appeared on the cover of *Time* immediately upon the release of *Little Man Tate,* which the magazine enthusiastically reviewed). Critics and audiences alike, however, generally did not like the film. Foster was undoubtedly attracted to the project to some extent by the subject matter, which has strong resonances with her own life and experiences. Fred Tate is also a wunderkind, whose only problem is that he needs more stimulation than his loving, though terribly low-brow, mother (played by Foster) is able to provide. Enter Jane Grierson, head of a school for gifted children, who wants to take charge of Fred's education. Dede Tate reluctantly agrees, and the remainder of the film treats the struggle between these two mothers, with their different parenting styles, for control of Fred.

Never a fan of mainstream cinema's glitz and fascination with (particularly) violent spectacle, Foster seems to have found in this story by Scott Frank the material for a dramatically effective small film. And yet Foster's handling (not discounting the problems in Frank's screenplay) does not do the material justice. Because Fred has no conflicts, except for finding a proper environment, he is rightly displaced from the story's center. And yet the conflict between the two women is not adroitly handled. Dede's decision to let Jane have Fred is not clearly dramatized; in fact, a number of scenes that begin with some promise of illuminating the similarities and differences of the two women end confusingly. Lacking the essential Aristotelian elements of a linear movement toward a conclusion and clearly drawn characters, the film becomes tedious and pointless; it is not rescued by an improbable conclusion and out-of-place melodramatic touches along the way. If Foster's point is to make some point about a mother's need to combine career aspirations for her child with unconditional elemental love and respect, the film only confusingly endorses such a position.

Foster waited four years before directing her follow-up effort, *Home for the Holidays,* in 1995. Continuing with the theme of parent-child relationships, the film stars Holly Hunter as the estranged daughter of a dysfunctional family who returns home to attempt to make peace. *Home for the Holidays* received mixed reviews, with some critics praising its dark humor and on-target picture of family life, while others claimed that the repeated clashes between parents and siblings made it difficult to watch. At any rate, the release of the film demonstrated that the multitalented Foster does intend to continue her pursuit of a directorial career.—R. BARTON PALMER

Friedrich, Su

American director

Born *New Haven, Connecticut, 1954.* ***Education*** *Attended the University of Chicago, 1971-72; Oberlin College, art and art history, B.A., 1975.* ***Career*** *1976—moved to New York; 1978—made her first film,* Hot Water; *part-time teacher of film production at the Millennium Film Workshop, New School for Social Research, and New York University; films have been the subject of retrospectives at numerous venues, including the Whitney Museum of American Art, National Film Theater (London), Stadtkino (Vienna), American Cinematheque (Los Angeles), and Anthology Film Archives (New York); active in many film-related and feminist endeavors.* ***Awards*** *Special Merit Award, Athens Film Festival, for* Cool Hands, Warm Heart, *1979; Best Experimental Film Award, Athens Film Festival, and Best Experimental Narrative Award, Atlanta Film Festival, for* Damned if You Don't, *1987; Guggenheim Foundation Fellowship, 1989; Golden Gate Award, San Francisco Film Festival, Gold Juror's Choice Award, Charlotte Film and Video Festival, and Grand Prix, Melbourne Film Festival, for* Sink or Swim, *1990; Rockefeller Foundation Fellowship, 1990; National Endowment for the Arts grant, 1994; Best Narrative Film Award, Athens International Film Festival, and Outstanding Documentary Feature, Outfest '97, for* Hide and Seek, *1996; Alpert Award, 1996.* ***Address*** *222 East 5th Street, #6, New York, NY 10003, U.S.A.*

Films as Director: **1978:** *Hot Water* (short) (+ sc, ph, ed). **1979:** *Cool Hands, Warm Heart* (short) (+ sc, ph, ed); *Scar Tissue* (short) (+ sc, ph, ed). **1980:** *I Suggest Mine* (short) (+ sc, ph, ed). **1981:** *Gently down the Stream* (short) (+ sc, ph, ed). **1982:** *But No One* (short) (+ sc, ph, ed). **1984:** *The Ties That Bind* (+ sc, ph, ed). **1987:** *Damned if You Don't* (+ sc, ph, ed). **1990:** *Sink or Swim* (+ sc, ph, ed). **1991:** *First Comes Love* (short) (+ sc, ph, ed). **1993:** *Rules of the Road* (+ sc, ph, ed); *The Lesbian Avengers Eat Fire Too* (video) (co-d with Baus, + co-ed). **1996:** *Hide and Seek* (+ co-sc, ed).

Su Friedrich is a New York-based independent filmmaker whose work is intensely personal and often centers around issues of feminism, gender, identity, family, body politics, and sexuality. Her work comes out of several key traditions within the American avant-garde such as structural, poetic, and autobiographical film. Friedrich's earliest short films in the late 1970s often revolved around specific female rituals such as shaving, or were primarily formal explorations concerned with the materiality of film. Friedrich achieved a certain maturity as a filmmaker with *Gently down the Stream* (1981), a film that combines formal experimentation and sophisticated film techniques with provocative subject matter. The film includes hand-scratched material (poetic text that was taken from a dream journal kept by the filmmaker over a period of several years), and photographed imagery that makes extensive use of the optical printer and rephotographed images. The film is primarily concerned with the emotional conflict between the filmmaker's Roman Catholic upbringing and her lesbian desires.

Su Friedrich. Photograph by James Hamilton.

The hand-scratched poetic text and the lack of a soundtrack make watching *Gently down the Stream* a highly individuated experience since reading each word of scratched text as it is projected is an essential part of the viewing experience. The film is related in some ways to earlier structural films of the late 1960s and early 1970s by filmmakers such as Hollis Frampton and Owen Land (George Landow) whose films also contained rigorous structures and often involved the active participation of the viewer in similar forms of direct address. Friedrich's film has the added appeal of working with very emotional and intense subject matter. *Gently down the Stream* breaks new ground in its formal experimentation and the way it encourages a kind of cinematic stream of consciousness. This creates a particularly subjective film experience that also links Friedrich to Maya Deren and Stan Brakhage, who pioneered the experimental poetic form and also explored dream states in their films.

Friedrich's autobiographical explorations can be seen most clearly in *The Ties That Bind* (1984), one of her most well-known, longer-form films. This film is an evocative examination of the filmmaker's relationship to her mother. The film's structure revolves around Friedrich's mother answering the filmmaker's questions about her life in Germany in the 1930s and 1940s. The questions are once again scratched onto the celluloid. The photographed imagery not only includes footage of the filmmaker's mother at the present moment but images made while the filmmaker traveled in Germany, as well as footage from an antinuclear demonstration at a U.S. army base, archival war footage, home movies of Friedrich's parents together, footage from an early silent film, and other kinds of visual material. The sheer variety of photographed images in the film is astounding and is skillfully edited into a complex shape with the addition of the voice of the filmmaker's mother and scratched text. The complexities of the film extend to include an analysis of the filmmaker's views about war and the nature of human conflict, the positioning of women in society, and an examination of the filmmaker's German identity. The film is also significant within Friedrich's oeuvre in that the material is fairly accessible to an audience not necessarily familiar with or particularly interested in avant-garde cinema. But as Friedrich has stated, she herself enjoys "films that are both sensual and entertaining, that engage me emotionally as well as intellectually. I'm so bored by most films that are made in response to current film theory, and I've never felt obliged to use that sort of language in my own work."

Damned if You Don't, another key film from the 1980s, once again examines the filmmaker's Catholic upbringing and lesbian sexuality but in a more analytical way than the earlier films. It incorporates images from Pressburger and Powell's *Black Narcissus* (1947), one of the most sumptuous films made in the 1940s that, to some extent, depends on its extraordinary color photography for its aesthetic effect. Friedrich chooses to deliberately cut in black-and-white images from the film that have been transmitted on a television screen, thus neutralizing the aesthetic power of the Pressburger/Powell film almost entirely. The effect of this strategy is to allow Friedrich to explore the world of nuns in a more critical way and create her own discourse revolving around lesbian desire, the church, repression, and sexual politics. It is also a film that has a fair degree of humor in it, something absent from Friedrich's earlier work. The film offers the unstartling observation that some nuns suffer from sexual frustration and are attracted to other women. Whatever one may feel about the politics of the film and its critique, there is no denying that Friedrich created one of the most controversial and complex avant-garde films of the 1980s. Friedrich returned to specifically autobiographical investigations in one of her most recent long-form films, *Sink or Swim,* which is concerned with her relationship to her father. Once again Friedrich works with highly structured, rigorous forms, but as with all her work, the emotional, highly charged material makes watching the film a more engaging experience than earlier structuralist films.

Su Friedrich has undoubtedly created one of the most impressive bodies of work in recent years. Her explorations into cinematic form include exploring the film frame and screen surface, layering of the image and soundtrack, complex editing patterns, and the rhythmical possibilities of cinema. What sets her work apart, however, is that she never sacrifices emotional content in creating these complex forms. She is a filmmaker of great integrity and skill who continues to experiment with the film medium in ways that continually surprise and astonish audiences.—MARIO FALSETTO

Gish, Lillian

American director and actress

Born *Lillian Diana Gish in Springfield, Ohio, 14 October 1896 (some sources say 1893); sister of the actress Dorothy Gish.* ***Education*** *Briefly attended Ursuline Academy, East St. Louis, Illinois.* ***Career*** *About 1902—stage debut in Rising Sun, Ohio, in* The Little Red Schoolhouse; *1903-04—with mother and sister Dorothy, toured in* Her First False Step; *1905—danced with Sarah Bernhardt production in New York City; 1908-11—lived with aunt in Massillon, Ohio, and with mother in East St. Louis, and briefly with father in Oklahoma; 1912—film debut as featured player, with sister, in* An Unseen Enemy *for D. W. Griffith; 1913—in Belasco production of* A Good Little Devil *starring Mary Pickford; collapsed during run of play with pernicious anemia; 1920—directed sister Dorothy Gish in* Remodeling Her Husband *for D. W. Griffith; 1921—last film under Griffith's direction,* Orphans of the Storm; *joined Inspiration Films; 1924—$800,000 contract with MGM; 1930—first talkie,* One Romantic Night; *resumed stage career in* Uncle Vanya; *1930s—began working in radio; 1948—TV debut in Philco Playhouse production* The Late Christopher Bean; *1969—began giving film lecture "Lillian Gish and the Movies: The Art of Film, 1900-1928"; 1987—starred in her last film, with Bette Davis, in* The Whales of August. ***Awards*** *Honorary Academy Award, "for superlative artistry and for distinguished contribution to the progress of motion pictures," 1970; Life Achievement Award, American Film Institute, 1984; D. W. Griffith Award, for "an outstanding career in motion pictures," 1987.* ***Died*** *In New York City, 27 February 1993.*

Film as Director: 1920: *Remodeling Her Husband* (+ co-sc).

Films as Actress: 1912: *An Unseen Enemy* (D. W. Griffith); *Two Daughters of Eve* (D. W. Griffith); *In the Aisles of the Wild* (D. W. Griffith); *The One She Loved* (D. W. Griffith); *The Musketeers of Pig Alley* (D. W. Griffith); *My Baby* (F. Powell); *Gold and Glitter* (F. Powell); *The New York Hat* (D. W. Griffith); *The Burglar's Dilemma* (D. W. Griffith); *A Cry for Help* (D. W. Griffith). **1913:** *Oil and Water* (D. W. Griffith); *The Unwelcome Guest* (D. W. Griffith); *The Stolen Bride* (O'Sullivan); *A Misunderstood Boy*

(D. W. Griffith); *The Left-Handed Man* (D. W. Griffith); *The Lady and the Mouse* (D. W. Griffith); *The House of Darkness* (D. W. Griffith); *Just Gold* (D. W. Griffith); *A Timely Interception* (D. W. Griffith); *Just Kids* (Henderson); *The Mothering Heart* (D. W. Griffith); *During the Round Up* (D. W. Griffith); *An Indian's Loyalty* (F. Powell); *A Woman in the Ultimate* (D. W. Griffith); *A Modest Hero* (D. W. Griffith); *So Runs the Way* (D. W. Griffith); *The Madonna of the Storm* (D. W. Griffith); *The Blue or the Gray* (Cabanne); *The Conscience of Hassan Bey* (Cabanne); *The Battle at Elderbush Gulch* (D. W. Griffith). **1914:** *The Green-Eyed Devil* (Kirkwood); *The Battle of the Sexes* (D. W. Griffith); *The Hunchback* (Cabanne); *The Quicksands* (Cabanne); *Home, Sweet Home* (D. W. Griffith); *Judith of Bethulia* (D. W. Griffith) (as the young mother); *Silent Sandy* (Kirkwood); *The Escape* (D. W. Griffith); *The Rebellion of Kitty Belle* (Cabanne); *Lord Chumley* (Kirkwood); *Man's Enemy* (F. Powell); *The Angel of Contention* (O'Brien); *The Wife*; *The Tear that Burned* (O'Brien); *The Folly of Anne* (O'Brien); *The Sisters* (Cabanne); *His Lesson* (Crisp) (as extra). **1915:** *The Birth of a Nation* (D. W. Griffith) (as Elsie Stoneman); *The Lost House* (Cabanne); *Enoch Arden* (*As Fate Ordained*) (Cabanne); *Captain Macklin* (O'Brien); *Souls Triumphant* (O'Brien); *The Lily and the Rose* (P. Powell). **1916:** *Daphne and the Pirate* (Cabanne) (as Daphne); *Sold for Marriage* (Cabanne); *An Innocent Magdalene* (Dwan); *Intolerance* (D. W. Griffith); *Diane of the Follies* (Cabanne) (title role); *Pathways of Life*; *Flirting with Fate* (Cabanne); *The Children Pay* (Ingraham). **1917:** *The House Built upon Sand* (Morrissey). **1918:** *Hearts of the World* (D. W. Griffith) (as the Girl, Marie Stephenson); *The Great Love* (D. W. Griffith); Liberty Bond short (D. W. Griffith); *The Greatest Thing in Life* (D. W. Griffith); *The Romance of Happy Valley* (D. W. Griffith). **1919:** *Broken Blossoms* (D. W. Griffith) (as Lucy Burrows); *True Heart Susie* (D. W. Griffith) (title role); *The Greatest Question* (D. W. Griffith). **1920:** *Way Down East* (D. W. Griffith) (as Anna Moore). **1921:** *Orphans of the Storm* (D. W. Griffith) (as Henriette Girard). **1923:** *The White Sister* (H. King) (as Angela Chiaromonte). **1924:** *Romola* (H. King) (title role). **1926:** *La Bohème* (K. Vidor) (as Mimi); *The Scarlet Letter* (Seastrom) (as Hester Prynne). **1927:** *Annie Laurie* (Robertson) (title role); *The Enemy* (Niblo). **1928:** *The Wind* (Seastrom) (as Letty Mason). **1930:** *One Romantic Night* (Stein) (as Alexandra). **1933:** *His Double Life* (Hopkins and W. B. deMille) (as Mrs. Alice Hunter). **1942:** *The Commandos Strike at Dawn* (Farrow) (as Mrs. Bergesen). **1943:** *Top Man* (*Man of the Family*) (Lamont) (as Beth Warren). **1946:** *Miss Susie Slagle's* (Berry) (title role); *Duel in the Sun* (K. Vidor) (as Mrs. Laura Belle McCanles). **1948:** *Portrait of Jennie* (*Jennie*) (Dieterle) (as Mother Mary of Mercy). **1955:** *The Cobweb* (Minnelli) (as Victoria Inch); *The Night of the Hunter* (Laughton) (as Rachel); *Salute to the Theatres* (supervisor: Loud—short) (appearance). **1958:** *Orders to Kill* (Asquith) (as Mrs. Summers). **1960:** *The Unforgiven* (J. Huston) (as Mattilda Zachary). **1963:** *The Great Chase* (Killiam—doc). **1966:** *Follow Me, Boys!* (Tokar) (as Hetty Seiber). **1967:** *Warning Shot* (Kulik) (as Alice Willows); *The Comedians* (Glenville) (as Mrs. Smith); *The Comedians in Africa* (short) (appearance). **1970:** *Henri Langlois* (Hershon and Guerra) (as guest). **1976:** *Twin Detectives* (Day—for TV). **1978:** *A Wedding* (Altman) (as Nettie Sloan). **1981:** *Thin Ice* (Aaron—for TV). **1983:** *Hobson's Choice* (Cates—for TV). **1984:** *Hambone and Hillie* (Watts) (as Hillie). **1986:** *Sweet Liberty* (Alda) (as Cecelia Burgess); *The Adventures of Huckleberry Finn* (Hunt). **1987:** *The Whales of August* (L. Anderson) (as Sarah Webber).

In 1919 Lillian Gish was one of Hollywood's most respected performers and D. W. Griffith's favorite actress. That year, confident that her knowledge of the movies was equal to his own, Griffith asked her to direct a movie starring her sister Dorothy for Paramount. Convinced that women had already proven to be proficient directors, Gish happily accepted the offer. Griffith gave her a $50,000 budget and total liberty in the production. He also asked, however, that she supervise the conversion of a recently acquired Long Island estate into a studio, which was far from properly equipped for film production. It proved to be an enormous task, but she completed both it and the film successfully.

Believing that Dorothy's considerable charm and comedic skills had never been fully captured on film by her directors, Lillian was committed to doing a better job. In addition, she wanted the production to be an "all-woman picture," so she recruited Dorothy Parker to bring her immense wit to the task of writing the intertitles, a first for Parker. The Gish sisters worked together to develop a comedy scenario that was inspired by a "little piece of business" that Dorothy had discovered in a magazine. The result was *Remodeling Her Husband,* which provides a clever take on the notions of male prerogative and feminine "charms," with a heroine who was quite different from the fragile, demure, and often-victimized heroines Lillian usually played. Specifically, a husband complains that his wife is so dowdy that she never attracts the admiring gazes of men. Furious, the wife determines to teach him a lesson by insisting that he follow her as she walks down the street. Each time she passes a man she makes amusing or seductive faces at him, which her husband cannot see. Consequently, each man turns to stare intently at her and she successfully convinces her surprised husband that he is wrong about her lack of sex appeal. The film gently mocks masculine expectations about femininity as its heroine cleverly avoids making herself over to satisfy her husband—a common theme in films at the time. Instead, she uses her natural charms to entice the looks of men, and more importantly, to "remodel" her husband's opinion of her.

Lillian Gish

In addition to preparing Griffith's studio for film production in general, Gish recalled her overwhelming responsibilities during the production of *Remodeling Her Husband,* including designing and furnishing all of the sets, coordinating the costumes, negotiating the hazards of filming in winter, and calming the frazzled nerves of the cinematographer—a shell-shocked war veteran. One of Gish's favorite anecdotes about the production involved learning the day before shooting one of the film's most complicated scenes that a police permit was required. Set in downtown Manhattan—where a bus on which Dorothy was riding would pass a taxicab that held her husband and another woman—the scene was crucial to the narrative. So, because it would take several days to acquire one, and because she was without the budget to pay her crew in the meantime, Gish decided to film the scene as scheduled. Risking jail, the film company agreed to the plan. Their gamble paid off, with the help of a sympathetic policeman—a fan of Lillian's—who allowed the cast and crew to continue shooting after he discovered them breaking the law. In the end, she was able to complete the film for $58,000 and it netted more than $460,000. Interestingly, the film erroneously credited Gish with being the first woman director; that is, it included an introductory title card that suggested that because the modern woman was becoming active in all of the arts, it was time for her to undertake motion picture directing.

When *Remodeling Her Husband* was completed, Griffith praised Lillian's work but the critics were less kind, suggesting that Dorothy's performance was its only strength. In any event, the film marked the beginning and the end of Lillian Gish's career as a director. She subsequently told an interviewer that she thought directing was "no career for a lady," mostly because she was not enamored of the myriad administrative details it requires. By the time she left Griffith's employ, Gish had acquired considerable filmmaking expertise, and her subsequent studio contracts gave her unusual power in the production of her films; at both the smaller Inspiration Pictures studio and later for MGM, she had script control and her choice of directors. Thus, in the mid-1920s, she made two of her most memorable films, which were directed by two virtuoso directors: *La Bohème* directed by King Vidor, and *The Scarlet Letter* directed by Victor Seastrom. In addition, she diligently scouted locations and sought to bring authenticity to her films and performances.—CYNTHIA FELANDO

Glyn, Elinor

British director and writer

Born *Elinor Sutherland in Jersey, England, 17 October 1864; sister of the fashion designer Lady Lucy Duff Gordon.* ***Education*** *Taught at home by a series of governesses until age 14.* ***Family*** *Married Clayton Glyn, 1892 (died 1915), daughters: Margot and Juliet.* ***Career*** *1900—published first novel,* The Visits of Elizabeth; *1907—gained fame as a novelist with* Three Weeks; *1920—wrote first screenplay,* The Great Moment; *1921—gained fame in Hollywood for second screenplay,* Beyond the Rocks; *1928—helped adapt her 1926 novel,* It, *for the screen; 1930—directed two films in England, both were failures that precipitated her retirement from the movies; 1936—published her autobiography,* Romantic Adventure. ***Died*** *In London, 23 September 1943.*

Films as Director: 1930: *Knowing Men* (+ pr, co-sc); *The Price of Things* (+ pr, sc).

Films as Writer: 1920: *The Great Moment* (Woods). **1921:** *Beyond the Rocks* (Woods). **1923:** *Six Hours* (Rabin); *Three Weeks* (*The Romance of a Queen*) (Crosland). **1924:** *His Hour* (K. Vidor). **1925:** *Man and Maid* (Schertsinger); *Love's Blindness* (Dillon). **1926:** *The Only Thing* (Conway). **1927:** *Ritzy* (Rosson). **1928:** *It* (Badger) (+ ro as herself, co-pr); *Red Hair* (Badger).

Film as Actress: 1921: *The Affairs of Anatol* (C. B. DeMille) (as bridge player).

Elinor Glyn was one of Hollywood's most famous screenwriters in the 1920s, when she was known for her bold and sexy scenarios. She began her writing career as a romantic novelist, and in 1908 when her immensely popular novel *Three Weeks* was published, she earned a salacious notoriety in the United States. The novel scandalized conservatives at the time for featuring a married woman's passionate and illicit love affair—conducted atop a tiger skin rug. During the 1910s and 1920s, Glyn enjoyed continued fame for her daring novels and expert advice on the subjects of love, femininity, and most importantly, "sex appeal."

Based on her immense popularity as a novelist, in 1920, at the age of 56, Glyn was invited to Hollywood by Jesse Lasky of Famous Players-Lasky to write and supervise the production of a scenario. She was part of the wave of well-known authors, including F. Scott Fitzgerald and Somerset Maugham, who were recruited to the film capital to write original scenarios or to adapt their existing works for the movies so as to lend Hollywood a tone of sophistication. Although she had no practical knowledge about filmmaking, Glyn proved to be one of the most adaptable and successful at the venture.

Credited with putting "sex appeal" on screen, Glyn's early screenplays were tremendous hits, including *The Great Moment* written especially for Gloria Swanson, *Beyond the Rocks* (adapted from her novel) with Swanson and Rudolph Valentino, and the screen adaptation of *Three Weeks*. *The Great Moment* featured the adventures of an English socialite who falls in love with a macho Westerner who saves her from a rattlesnake bite and discovers the wild gypsy streak she inherited from her mother. Although she returns home with her father and finds a millionaire to marry, she is miserable until her reunion with her rugged hero, who has in the meantime become wealthy. Like *The Great Moment,* Glyn's early screenplays were all lush, extravagantly costumed, and overwrought romances set in mythical pasts, which shared her favorite themes—of love, passion, sex, and danger. But the formula eventually lost its appeal, and after the failure of *Man and Maid* and *The Only Thing* she attempted to modernize her screenplays. The result was *Ritzy,* an absurd farce about a young woman hunting a duke in Paris, who is duped by another duke who loves her but masquerades as poor to teach her a lesson. It was a box-office failure.

Elinor Glyn

But, in 1926, Glyn's popular reputation was restored when her serialized novella *It* was published. Although nearly everyone knew that "It" translated as sex appeal, Glyn took credit for discovering it, thus prompting widespread discussions about what "It" was, who had "It," and how to cultivate "It." She then reached the height of her Hollywood career in 1928 after Famous Players-Lasky purchased the movie rights to *It* and she was linked with Clara Bow's quickly rising star. Intended as a comedy vehicle for Bow specifically, the film has almost nothing in common with the novel other than a seductive title, but it includes Glyn's campy "grande dame" cameo appearance in which she explains the meaning of "It." The movie's credits list Glyn as "author and adaptor" [sic], and the writing team of Hope Loring and Louis D. Lighton received the "scenario" credit. Jesse Lasky confirmed in his memoirs that it was Loring and Lighton, the studio's top writing team, who were responsible for the screenplay. In any event, the film was a popular phenomenon of huge proportions, and since then it has been fixed in popular memory as the quintessential "Jazz Age"—and Elinor Glyn—movie. In addition, *It* was both a smash hit and a distinctive example of Hollywood's "flapper movies." Its extraordinary success was due, in large part, to Bow's compelling performance as a sexy, free-spirited shop-girl who is smitten by and ultimately wins her boss, a department-store heir. Glyn's last Hollywood film, *Red Hair,* was another comedy vehicle for Bow with a slim story meant to demonstrate the passion of red-haired people.

In addition to her screenwriting success, Glyn was famous for cultivating an aristocratic star persona, which Hollywood's elite obliged by dubbing her "Madame Glyn." But, in literary circles she was decidedly less celebrated and critics disparaged her novels and scenarios as simple, melodramatic potboilers. Nevertheless, Glyn audaciously lamented that her literary skills were less valued in Hollywood than her famous name. After *Red Hair,* Glyn left Hollywood to return to England, where she financed and directed the film *Knowing Men*. About an heiress who pretends to be her aunt's penniless companion in order to ascertain the character of her beaux, the film was an abysmal, amateurish failure, against which the screenwriter Edward Knoblock brought legal action to prevent its release. Nevertheless, she made one more film, the never-released *The Price of Things*. Both films were old-fashioned and slow-paced affairs that exhausted her finances and hastened Glyn's return to writing novels and articles for magazines and newspapers.—CYNTHIA FELANDO

Godmilow, Jill

American director

Born *Philadelphia, 1943.* ***Education*** *Attended the University of Wisconsin, B.A., 1965.* ***Career*** *Late 1960s—worked as a freelance editor on commercials and industrial films, and for San Francisco's KQED; 1973—co-directed her first documentary feature,* Antonia: A Portrait of the Woman, *which received an Academy Award nomination; 1970s-80s—directed videos and documentaries for television; 1992—associate professor, then full professor, Communication & Theatre, at the University of Notre Dame, teaching film and video production.* ***Awards*** *Best Documentary, Independent New York Film Critics Awards, and Emily Award, American Film Festival, for* Antonia: A Portrait of the Woman, *1973; Red Ribbon, American Film Festival, for* Nevelson in Process, *1976; Grand Jury Prize, Sundance Film Festival, for* Waiting for the Moon, *1987.* ***Address*** *Department of Communication and Theatre, University of Notre Dame, 320 O'Shaughnessy Hall, Notre Dame, IN 46556, U.S.A.*

Films as Director: 1967: *La Nueva Vida* (co-d—doc, incomplete). **1969:** *Tales* (co-d—doc short). **1973:** *Antonia: A Portrait of the Woman* (co-d with J. Collins). **1974:** *Where Have All the Mentally Ill Gone?* (doc short). **1976:** *Nevelson in Process* (co-d) (doc short). **1977:** *The Popovich Brothers of South Chicago* (doc). **1979:** *With Grotowski at Nienadowka* (short). **1980:** *The Vigil* (short); *The Odyssey Tapes* (*Odyssey*) (short). **1981:** *Far from Poland.* **1984:** *The Theory of Ideas* (co-d—short). **1987:** *Waiting for the Moon* (+ sc). **1995:** *Roy Cohn/Jack Smith.* **1996:** *What's Underground about Marshmallows.* **1997:** *What Farocki Taught* (short).

Other Film: 1976: *Pleasantville* (Locker) (ed).

Jill Godmilow won her initial acclaim for co-directing (with folksinger Judy Collins) *Antonia: A Portrait of the Woman,* a documentary look at the life of pioneer orchestra conductor Antonia Brico. The film is a compelling portrayal of Brico, who was 73 when the film was released, and how her desire to conduct a major symphony orchestra was continually thwarted because of sexism and discrimination. Brico poignantly describes how a musician who is not part of an orchestra at least may practice on her own to hone her skills, but a conductor—whose instrument is her orchestra—is not allowed the same luxury. At the time of its release, just as the women's movement was beginning to make headway among the masses of American baby boomers, *Antonia: A Portrait of the Woman* served as a valuable feminist testament of how sexism thwarts personal ambition.

Godmilow's most challenging undertaking was *Far from Poland,* the title of which alludes to *Far from Vietnam,* a French-made antiwar film consisting of individual meditations on the war in Southeast Asia. *Far from Poland* started out as a documentary on the then-burgeoning Solidarity movement. When martial law was declared in Poland, however, Godmilow was denied access to the country. Rather than abandon the project, she resolved to make a film about her experience. The result unfolds in three acts and an epilogue, with each consisting of a dramatic re-creation of the contents of published interviews, given during Solidarity's ascendance—by a shipyard laborer, a coal miner, and a government censor. Also included are a mix of fake documentary footage and real interviews and newsreel footage, and a conjured up ending in which Solidarity triumphs over its enemies. The result not only interprets a time and place in history but explores the same question posed in *Far from Vietnam*: What can a filmmaker do to aid a peoples' struggle against tyranny?

Jill Godmilow

On a more theoretical/cinematic level, this question segues into the issue of documentary objectivity: Does a recorder of events need to be impartial about those events as she selects the material that will appear on screen, along with the order in which it will be presented? Indeed, is it possible for a filmmaker to remain impartial while researching and recording controversial events? What is the effect of her imprint on the material? What happens when it is altered, or reinterpreted? Finally, what is the effect of the filmmaker's decision to appear on screen—as Godmilow does in *Far from Poland*?

Godmilow entered the realm of feature-length narrative filmmaking with *Waiting for the Moon,* an account of the lasting friendship and complex relationship between Gertrude Stein and her secretary-companion, Alice B. Toklas. *Waiting for the Moon* was a disappointment: a slow, lifeless semi-biography. The film also caused a minor controversy in that it is clear that Stein and Toklas are a couple, yet their romantic/sexual relationship is not depicted on screen. Godmilow's other major feature is *Roy Cohn/Jack Smith,* which may be linked to *Far from Poland* as an interpretation of real-life experience via performance. *Roy Cohn/Jack Smith* is a record of actor/performance artist Ron Vawter's theatrical exploration of the lives of two very dissimilar individuals who are linked in that both were gay, and died of AIDS (as did the actor who plays them). The first is Roy Cohn, the right-wing lawyer and Joseph McCarthy underling who refused to acknowledge his sexual preference while publicly condemning gay lifestyles; in the film, the hypocritical Cohn offers a lecture at a banquet for an organization called the American Society for the Protection of the Family. The second is Jack Smith, the legendary (as well as unabashedly out-of-the-closet) underground filmmaker, who appears in drag in a campy Arabian Nights setting. *Roy Cohn/Jack Smith* is worth seeing for the contrasts and ironies of its subjects. But the film is dramatically and visually static, with Godmilow unable to overcome the obstacle of transforming a stage performance into visually arresting cinema.

Prior to *Antonia: A Portrait of the Woman,* Godmilow started (but did not complete) her first film, *La Nueva Vida,* a documentary about New York's Spanish Harlem. Beyond *Antonia* and the ambitious and provocative *Far from Poland,* her best work has been her documentaries in which she explores diverse subject matter. Her topics have ranged from perspectives on sexuality (*Tales*) to the mental health establishment (*Where Have All the Mentally Ill Gone?*), fine artists and their creativity (*Nevelson in Process,* a portrait of artist Louise Nevelson) to musical traditions (*The Popovich Brothers of South Chicago,* a chronicle of Serbian dance music over a 50-year period).—ROB EDELMAN

Gómez, Sara

Cuban director

Born *Havana, 1943.* ***Education*** *Attended the Conservatory of Music, Havana.* ***Career*** *Since 1961—assistant director at Instituto Cubano del Arte e Industria Cinematograficos (ICAIC), under Tomás Gutiérrez Alea, Jorge Fraga, and Agnès Varda; 1964—directed first film,* Iré a Santiago; *1974—shot and edited first feature,* De cierta manera; *1974-76—original negative, damaged in processing, restored under supervision of Gutiérrez Alea and Rigoberto López.* ***Died*** *Of acute asthma, 2 June 1974.*

Films as Director: **1964:** *Iré a Santiago* (*I Shall Go to Santiago*). **1965:** *Excursion a Vueltabajo* (*Outing to Vueltabajo*). **1967:** *Y tenemos sabor* (*And We've Got "Sabor"*). **1968:** *En la otra isla* (*On the Other Island*). **1969:** *Isla del tesero* (*Treasure Island*). **1970:** *Poder local, poder popular* (*Local Power, People's Power*). **1971:** *Un documental a proposito del transito* (*A Documentary about Mass Transit*). **1972:** *Atencion prenatal* (*Prenatal Care in the First Year*); *Año uno.* **1973:** *Sobre horas extras y trabajo voluntario* (*About Overtime and Voluntary Labor*). **1977:** *De cierta manera* (*One Way or Another*).

We shall never know all that Sara Gómez might have given to us. We have her one feature film, the marvelous *De cierta manera,* and a few short documentaries to indicate what might have been had she lived beyond the age of 31. But we will never really know all that this prodigiously talented woman was capable of.

Sara Gómez could be seen as prototypical of the new Cuban directors. Entering the Cuban Film Institute (ICAIC) at an early age, she worked as assistant director for various cineastes, including Tomás Gutiérrez Alea, whose influence marked her work as it has so many young directors. During a ten-year period (1964-74) she fulfilled the usual apprenticeship among Cuban cineastes by directing documentary films. Documentaries are seen as an important training ground for Cuban directors because they force them to focus on the material reality of Cuba and thus emphasize the use of cinema as an expression of national culture. As Gutiérrez Alea noted, "the kind of cinema which adapts itself to our interests, fortunately, is a kind of light, agile cinema, one that is very directly founded upon our own reality." This is precisely the kind of cinema Sara Gómez went on to produce, beginning work on *De cierta manera* in 1974 and finishing the editing of the film shortly before her death of acute asthma.

Gómez's early training in documentaries and the influence of Gutiérrez Alea is evident in *De cierta manera.* The film combines the documentary and fiction forms so inextricably that they are impossible to disentangle. Through this technique, she emphasized the material reality that is at the base of all creative endeavor and the necessity of bringing a critical perspective to all forms of film.

In choosing this style, which I call "dialectical resonance," Gómez appeared to follow Gutiérrez Alea's example in the superb *Memories of Underdevelopment.* But there is a crucial difference between the two films—a difference that might be said to distinguish the generation of directors who came of age before the triumph of the revolution (e.g., Gutiérrez Alea) from those who have grown up within the revolution. In spite of its ultimate commitment to the revolutionary process, *Memories* remains in some ways the perspective of an "outsider" and might be characterized as "critical bourgeois realism." Nevertheless, *De cierta manera* is a vision wholly from within the revolution, despite the fact that every position in the film is subjected to criticism—including that of the institutionalized revolution, which is presented in the form of an annoyingly pompous omniscient narration. Thus, the perspective of Gómez might be contrasted to that of *Memories* by calling it "critical socialist realism." The emphasis on dialectical criticism, struggle, and commitment is equally great in both films, but the experience of having grown up within the revolution created a somewhat different perspective.

Despite its deceptively simple appearance—a result of being shot in 16mm on a very low budget—*De cierta manera* is the work of an extremely sophisticated filmmaker. Merely one example among many of Gómez's sophistication is the way in which she combined a broad range of modern distanciation techniques with the uniquely Cuban tropical beat to produce a film that is at once rigorously analytic and powerfully sensuous—as well as perhaps the finest instance to date of a truly dialectical film. Although we are all a little richer for the existence of this work, we remain poorer for the fact that she will make no more films.—JOHN MRAZ

Goodrich, Frances

American writer

Born *Belleville, New Jersey, 1890.* ***Education*** *Attended Passaic Collegiate High School, graduated 1908; Vassar College, Poughkeepsie, New York, graduated 1912; New York School of Social Work, 1912-13.* ***Family*** *Married 1) the actor Robert Ames, 1917 (divorced 1923); 2) the writer Henrik Willem Van Loon, 1927 (divorced 1930); 3) Albert Hackett, 1931.* ***Career*** *1913—stage debut in Massachusetts; 1916—Broadway debut in* Come Out of the Kitchen; *1927—actress in a Denver stock company, in which Albert Hackett was also a member; 1930—first writing collaboration with Hackett, on the play* Up Pops the Devil; *1933-39—writer, with Hackett, for MGM, and for Paramount, 1943-46, and MGM again after 1948.* ***Awards*** *Writers Guild Award, for* Easter Parade, *1948,* Father's Little Dividend, *1951,* Seven Brides for Seven Brothers, *1954, and* The Diary of Anne Frank, *1959; Pulitzer Prize (for drama), for* The Diary of Anne Frank, *1956.* ***Died*** *Of cancer, in New York City, 29 January 1984.*

Films as Co-Writer with Albert Hackett: **1933:** *The Secret of Madame Blanche* (Brabin); *Penthouse* (*Crooks in Clover*) (Van Dyke). **1934:** *Fugitive Lovers* (Boleslawsky) (co); *The Thin Man* (Van Dyke); *Hide-Out* (Van Dyke). **1935:** *Naughty Marietta* (Van Dyke) (co); *Ah, Wilderness!* (C. Brown). **1936:** *Rose Marie* (Van Dyke) (co); *Small Town Girl* (Wellman) (co); *After the Thin Man* (Van Dyke). **1937:** *The Firefly* (Leonard). **1939:** *Another Thin Man* (Van Dyke); *Society Lawyer* (Ludwig) (co). **1943:** *Doctors at War* (Shumlin—short). **1944:** *Lady in the Dark* (Leisen); *The Hitler Gang* (Farrow). **1946:** *The Virginian* (Gilmore); *It's a Wonderful Life* (Capra) (co). **1948:** *The Pirate* (Minnelli); *Summer Holiday* (Mamoulian); *Easter Parade* (Walters) (co). **1949:** *In the Good Old Summertime* (Leonard) (co). **1950:** *Father of the Bride* (Minnelli). **1951:** *Father's Little Dividend* (Minnelli); *Too Young to Kiss* (Leonard). **1954:** *Give a Girl a Break* (Donen); *Seven Brides for Seven Brothers* (Donen) (co); *The Long, Long Trailer* (Minnelli). **1956:** *Gaby* (Bernhardt) (co). **1958:** *A Certain Smile* (Negulesco). **1959:** *The Diary of Anne Frank* (Stevens). **1962:** *Five Finger Exercise* (Daniel Mann). **1980:** *The Diary of Anne Frank* (Sagal).

Although the screenwriting team of Frances Goodrich and Albert Hackett received critical and popular acclaim for the 1959 adaptation of their Pulitzer Prize-winning stage play, *The Diary of Anne Frank,* most of their creative efforts were not "serious" works. Schooled in the sophisticated stage comedies of the late 1920s and early 1930s, Goodrich and Hackett adapted *The Thin Man* in 1934, and it is a work that now as then is considered to be the best of the cinema's detective comedies. They followed this exceptional adaptation with an excellent *After the Thin Man* and an effective *Another Thin Man,* in both of which they succeeded in translating the work of Dashiell Hammett to the screen while managing to maintain the quality of his stories.

While it might appear that these screenplays owed much of their wit to the novelist, Goodrich and Hackett contributed the dramatic sense and skills they developed from almost two decades of working as actors and writers on the theatrical stage. The co-adapters could translate from one verbal medium to another, developing the story through dramatic dialogue. It was a special talent that both executed in unison so that it was difficult to trace which one contributed the most to a specific scene. One of their early collaborations on an original story was a sophisticated comedy stage play, *Up Pops the Devil* (1930) which was converted to a screenplay in 1931 and revised in a successful remake as a Bob Hope vehicle, *Thanks for the Memory* (1938).

From their sophisticated comedy background on the stage and screen, Goodrich and Hackett moved to the adaptation of the so-called light opera of the past. They were not happy with this assignment, but it was part of their MGM contract. In the mid 1930s they adapted two vehicles for Jeanette MacDonald and Nelson Eddy, *Naughty Marietta* and *Rose Marie,* reworking some of the stilted dialogue and simplifying the plots from the stage versions so that the works were more contemporary and more fluid. The pair also produced two splendid screen musicals—the flashy, colorful *The Pirate* in the late 1940s and the innovative *Seven Brides for Seven Brothers* in the mid-1950s. Less inventive musicals were their *Easter Parade* (1948) and *In the Good Old Summertime* (1949).

In the 1940s the couple's credits for director Frank Capra's *It's a Wonderful Life* seemed to be unusual for their background. The work's warmth and humanity seemed more likely to have been the work of Robert Riskin, Capra's frequent collaborator, than that of Goodrich and Hackett. Critics now regard *It's a Wonderful Life* as an outstanding achievement—for its screenplay as well as its execution. It was certainly a major film in Capra's career (coming ironically just when his fortunes were on the wane with the Hollywood establishment), and it is certainly one of the couple's significant contributions to the movies.

A switch in handling another comedy genre emerged in the early 1950s when the screenwriters integrated social commentary into the humorous works *Father of the Bride* and *Father's Little Dividend.* The originally released *Father* focused on a rite of passage, marriage, while the sequel rite stressed the event of becoming a grandfather. The two films provided a boost to the career of Spencer Tracy in the lead role.

Only two movie adaptations seemed to be beyond the scope of the writers. These works were a Western, *The Virginian* (1946) starring Joel McCrea and a slapstick farce, *The Long, Long Trailer* (1954), featuring Lucille Ball and Desi Arnaz. The genre most effectively executed by the screenwriters proved to be variations of comedy: the sophisticated, witty comedy; the musical; and the genteel, humorous drama. There were a few exceptions, namely *The Diary of Anne Frank,* a drama that they wrote for the stage in 1958 and adapted to cinema in 1959.

An evaluator today probably could discern the specific contribution of Frances Goodrich by examining the strong female portraits, such as Nora Charles in the 1936 *The Thin Man* and Anne Frank. Goodrich's best work gives her a place as one of the leading writers for the screen. *Wonderful Life, Anne Frank,* and *The Thin Man* are works that meet high standards of dramatic writing with excellent dialogue and characters. The fresh handling of plot and character in the designed-for-the-screen musicals, *The Pirate* and *Seven Brides,* also serves to suggest that Goodrich and Hackett still remain the most eclectic screenwriters that Hollywood has produced. Their scope has not yet been matched by any other team.—DONALD W. McCAFFREY

Gordon, Bette

American director

Born *1950.* ***Education*** *Attended the University of Wisconsin, Madison, B.A. in French, 1972, M.A. in radio, television, and film, 1975, and M.F.A. in film, 1976.* ***Family*** *Married the filmmaker James Benning (divorced), one daughter, Lili.* ***Career*** *1970s—began making experimental films with James Benning while a graduate student, and also on her own; 1976-79—assistant professor at the School of Fine Arts, University of Wisconsin, Milwaukee; 1979—moved to New York City; 1979-94—adjunct professor and assistant professor, Hofstra University; from 1980—edits television films and documentaries, directs plays and stage readings, and directs music videos and films for television, including episodes in Laurel Entertainment's* Monsters *series, Playboy Channel's "Director's Showcase," and short films for HBO and Showtime; 1990s—contributing editor of* BOMB *magazine; from 1991—adjunct professor and associate professor in Columbia University Graduate Film Division; 1993-95—instructor at the School of Visual Arts; 1996—*Variety *and* Empty Suitcases *presented as part of the Whitney Museum's "New York/No Wave" retrospective; 1997—began principal photography on feature film* History of Luminous Motion. ***Awards*** *Director's Choice Award, Sinking Creek Film Celebration, for* Still Life, *1975.* ***Address*** *School of Arts, Columbia University, 512 Dodge Hall, MC 1805, 2960 Broadway, New York, NY 10027, U.S.A.*

Films as Director: 1973: *Michigan Avenue* (co-d—short). **1974:** *1-94* (co-d—short). **1975:** *Still Life* (short); *United States of America* (co-d—short). **1976:** *Noyes* (short). **1977:** *An Algorithm* (short). **1979:** *Exchanges* (short). **1980:** *Empty Suitcases* (+ sc, ed, pr, sound recording, voice, ro). **1983:** *What Is It, Zach* (short—for TV). **1984:** *Variety* (+ original st, additional ph). **1987:** "Greed" ep. of *Seven Women, Seven Sins* (for TV) (co-sc).

Other Film: 1985: *The Boy Next Door* (Schidor) (asst d).

Bette Gordon is a feminist filmmaker/theorist whose special concerns are sexual subjugation and the sexual politics that sully male-female relations. To date, her best-known film is *Variety,* a low-budget, independently produced allegory about female empowerment linked to the manner in which men watch women on celluloid, and a chronicle of the manner in which pornographic images affect both sexes.

Variety is the story of Christine, unemployed and desperate to find a job, who is hired as a cashier in a New York City porn movie theater: a venue where men come to be voyeurs, to stare in silence at a screen and watch pornographic images of women. Two questions immediately become apparent. How will these men view Christine, as they purchase their $2 tickets? How will her duties, and her surroundings, influence Christine?

On her first day at work, Christine takes a break in the theater lobby. As she paces back and forth and smokes, she cannot help but overhear a woman oohing and aahing on screen, and a male voice declaring, "You're a whore, aren't you." She then peeks in on the film, which upsets her so that she promptly spills a soda she has purchased.

Because of Christine's sex, she is supposed to be passive. As she sits in the ticket booth, men may fantasize about her: What sort of woman would take such a job? One even attempts to grab her hand as he purchases his ticket. At one point Christine observes that the patrons see her as "some sort of attraction." At another, she receives an obscene phone call on her answering machine.

Christine turns the tables and takes control upon being approached by Louis, one of the customers, a well-dressed man who rides around in a chauffeured car. Louis is mysterious and patronizing as he not so much asks as orders her to join him for an evening at Yankee Stadium, and wants her to admit that she enjoys watching the porn movies. Christine eventually begins following him around, spying on him and his activities. In so doing, the woman becomes the aggressor, the voyeur, while the man becomes the passive visual object, who is spied on by prying eyes.

By the very nature of her employment, Christine already has become a voyeur. "I sit in a glass booth between the lobby and the street," is how she describes her job. In so doing, she has become a watcher of men as she handles their admission fees. But her presence in the booth still is demeaning. Her pay is low; she must receive permission to take a break; and she is scrutinized by the men who enter the theater. Only when Christine takes charge, and begins following Louis, does she become in any way empowered.

Variety is a story of sexual politics, and the silent, invisible walls existing between men and women. Just about all of the men in the story view Christine as an object. Even her co-worker at the theater, who initially is a sympathetic character, eventually hits on Christine. When she tells her boyfriend about her new job, he hardly reacts, and then leaves. The only genuine communication is between women: Christine and her bartender friend, and the various women who hang out in the latter's saloon.

At the same time, *Variety* depicts the impact of pornography on a woman's soul. Christine's job and surroundings affect her psyche. She becomes obsessed/disturbed by the sounds and images of pornography. She begins frequenting porn parlors, blurting out erotic stories, dressing as a seductress/whore. At one point, she even imagines herself and Louis in a porn movie.

While an individual may receive instant gratification from pornography, that gratification is not the result of real sexual/human contact. And so, as her attraction to pornographic images becomes imbedded within her, Christine is disconnected from her life. What will be her plight, and her fate? Gordon chooses to leave this up in the air, as the film concludes on an ambiguous note.

Despite all these subtexts, the ultimate theme of *Variety* is voyeurism. This is apparent at the film's outset, as Christine and her bartender friend chat in a locker room while the latter removes her clothes. So even here, as the camera records these images, the viewer becomes a voyeur.

Gordon's other directorial credits range from early experimental short films made on her own and in conjunction with former husband James Benning; to her subsequent work for television; to her direction of the "Greed" episode in *Seven Women, Seven Sins,* produced for German television, in which seven women filmmakers examine the seven deadly sins. Especially outstanding are the two films she made upon coming to New York in 1979, both of which are thematically linked to *Variety* in that they explore and deconstruct female images. *Exchanges* depicts various women switching clothes, resulting in a demystification of the image of women undressing; the 50-odd-minute-long, semiautobiographical *Empty Suitcases* explores the view of women as seductive objects as it presents a single woman who is at once a mistress, terrorist, struggling artist, and professor.

After *Variety,* Bette Gordon spent several years working on an adaptation of Catherine Texier's novel, *Love Me Tender,* a project which was not realized. It was not until 13 years after the release of *Variety* that she began principal photography on her next feature, *History of Luminous Motion.* This enormous time gap is a pity, if only because of the combination of intelligence and potential she demonstrated in *Variety.*—ROB EDELMAN

Gorris, Marleen

Dutch director and writer

Born *Holland, 1948.* ***Education*** *Studied English and theater in Holland; attended the University of Birmingham, England, master's in drama.* ***Career*** *1981—directed acclaimed groundbreaking debut feature* A Question of Silence; *1995—earned international renown with* Antonia's Line. ***Awards*** *Best Feature, Dutch Film Days, and Women's Festival Prize, Sceaux, France, for* A Question of Silence, *1981; Best Foreign Language Film, Academy Award, Best Picture, Toronto International Film Festival, Best Screenplay, Chicago International Film Festival, and Best Director, Hampton's International Film Festival, for* Antonia's Line, *1995.* ***Address*** *c/o First Look Pictures, 8800 Sunset Boulevard, Los Angeles, CA 90069, U.S.A.*

Films as Director: 1981: *De Stilte Rond Christine M* (*A Question of Silence*) (+ sc). **1984:** *Gebroken Spiegels* (*Broken Mirrors*) (+ sc). **1991:** *The Last Island* (+ sc). **1993:** *Tales from a Street* (for TV). **1995:** *Antonia* (*Antonia's Line*) (+ sc). **1997:** *Mrs. Dalloway.* **1998:** *Come West with Me.*

Dutch director and screenwriter Marleen Gorris has several respected and commercially successful feature-film credits to her name—all of which express her abiding interest in women-centered stories and feminist issues. Her work treats themes of female identity, strength, and solidarity in the face of male oppression and exploitation, though she leavens them with sharp doses of wry, self-reflective humor. Interestingly, Gorris freely acknowledges her feminist perspective, "both by temperament and intellect," and that her films inevitably are influenced by that perspective, but she denies that she emphasizes "political or moral lessons." Yet more than a few, usually male, critics insist that her films are "anti-male."

Without any previous film experience, Gorris took her screenplay for *A Question of Silence* to the Dutch government and was given the funding to finance the project. As her directorial debut, it was her best-known work until 1995's *Antonia's Line. A Question of Silence* was commercially successful and enjoys a well-deserved reputation as a feminist classic. Its conventional, easily accessible narrative structure belies its status as a notoriously subversive film that expresses anger about a capitalist system that functions to demean and oppress women. The story concerns three women who spontaneously come together to viciously murder a man, though they are all strangers at the time. At first, the women seem a rather disparate group: a zaftig, jolly middle-aged divorcée working as a waitress; a dowdy housewife with a stiff, silent demeanor; and an attractive and smart executive secretary. It is while engaging in a typically feminine pursuit, shopping in a dress boutique, that the women join forces: when the housewife boldly lifts an item and the smug male shopkeeper attempts to retrieve it from her bag, she resists and the other two women boldly begin shoplifting too until, together, they beat him to death. Thereafter, they, and four strangely calm women who have silently witnessed their deed, each leave the shop. After their arrest, the three women, each of whom refuses to deny her deed or to reveal her motives, come under the purview of a female, court-appointed psychiatrist who is expected to evaluate their sanity. Soon, however, the psychiatrist loses her professional "objectivity" and develops a deep identification with the women. Her conclusion: that the women are all sane but wearied by the constraints and abuses of male domination.

The title of *A Question of Silence* works on several levels. First, it suggests the patriarchal refusal to hear women's voices: at business meetings, the secretary's insights are ignored; the waitress routinely endures her male customers' sexist remarks; and the housewife bears a poignant isolation and melancholy. The title also alludes to the women's shared silence, suggesting that it can function as a tool of solidarity and empowerment. Indeed, in the film's courtroom scene, Gorris cleverly underscores the myriad connections between the three women with a series of exchanged looks, with each other and with the four unidentified women who witnessed the killing. When the prosecutor makes the absurd declaration that it would make no difference if it had been three men who had killed one woman, rather than vice versa, it provokes peels of laughter among the women, including the psychiatrist. Nevertheless, the men involved in the case (cops, lawyers, judges) simply fail to understand the women's motivations. Although the women's shared act of violence can be read metaphorically, as symbolic of the potential power of women to fight sexism, not a few film critics (including some feminists) were shocked by the violence and rejected it as "extreme," especially the murder scene, which includes an offscreen genital mutilation. Not surprisingly, male critics were generally angered or confused by the film and produced vitriolic reviews.

Gorris's second feature was *Broken Mirrors,* a much darker film about seven prostitutes and a psychopath who beats and imprisons them until they die of hunger. It was not as well-received critically or commercially as *A Question of Silence*. Her third film, *The Last Island,* is about a group of plane-crash survivors who find themselves stranded on a desert island; they eventually come to the conclusion that they might be the last people on Earth. The men in the group thereby begin pressuring the only potential child-bearing woman in the group to breed so as to ensure the survival of the human race. Soon, however, she becomes frustrated as she watches the men argue and endeavor to destroy each other.

Antonia's Line brought Gorris international fame as a gifted, award-winning filmmaker. It is indeed a visually rich, beautiful film. On the last day of her life, 90-year-old Antonia lies quietly and recalls her return, shortly after World War II, to the village of her birth. Gorris traces the subsequent 50 years in Antonia's eventful life, including its dark secrets, violence, humor, and intense emotions—along with the array of eccentric female descendants who constitute her "line." The film differs from Gorris's earlier works in that the female characters are strong and happy, and the tone is generally warmer and lighter. The extraordinary success of *Antonia's Line* gave Gorris the cachet to direct the adaptation of Virginia Woolf's novel, *Mrs. Dalloway*. At a party she is hosting in her elegant home, Mrs. Dalloway is surprised by a former suitor whom she rejected over 30 years earlier. His sudden appearance prompts her to consider what might have been had she accepted rather than feared his passionate love, and chosen him instead of the dull, reliable, and respectable Mr. Dalloway. Both *Antonia's Line* and *Mrs. Dalloway* treat the subject of memory and the complex human emotions that characterize women's lives, and both films indicate Gorris's ability to direct women-centered films that speak to larger audiences. Accordingly, her next film suggests the confidence the major studios have in her continued success; she is currently at work on Twentieth Century-Fox's romance/drama, *Come West with Me,* from Beth Henley's play *Abundance*.—CYNTHIA FELANDO

Grayson, Helen

American director

Born *Helen Steel Grayson, 1902.* ***Education*** *Privately tutored in France in her early years; graduated from Bryn Mawr College, 1926.* ***Career*** *Late 1920s-early 1930s—studied acting with Maria Ouspenskaya at New York's American Laboratory Theatre; became a dress and costume designer for New York avant-garde artists; later in the depression years, an adviser to the Federal Theatre Costume Workshop, an unemployment relief project; film career began during World War II at the Office of War Information in New York, as an assistant on the production* Salute to France, *and on the filming of a tour of the United States by a group of French journalists that included the young Jean-Paul Sartre; 1945—first directing assignment, the OWI's* The Cummington Story; *1953—directed the U.S. State Department's most widely shown films, a trio of documentaries on American history and culture; late 1950s-early 1960s—spent her last half-dozen years as an unofficial U.S. representative at film festivals in Europe and Canada, writing articles, and attempting unsuccessfully to find sponsors for two films she was eager to direct: one on Balanchine's young New York City Ballet and one on Benjamin Franklin in France.* ***Died*** *Of cancer, in New York City, 5 May 1962.*

Films as Director: 1945: *The Cummington Story.* **1947:** *Starting Line.* **1948:** *Bryn Mawr College.* **1949:** *Wings to Hawaii.* **1951:** *The House in Sea Cliff.* **1953:** *The New World; To Freedom; A Nation Sets Its Course.*

Other Films: 1943: *Salute to France* (asst to producers). **1944:** Newsreel sequence on American tour of visiting French journalists (asst d).

Although virtually unknown today, Helen Grayson was prominent among the first generation of American women who directed documentary films. As was typical of the 1940s and 1950s, most of Grayson's films were shot on 35mm film by all-male crews, with little or no sync sound—with real people reenacting scripted versions of realistic situations in real locations. Her friend and colleague, Ricky Leacock, called it "the dark ages of documentary." Within these and other limitations, in their day Grayson's films ranged form average (*Bryn Mawr College*) to outstanding (*The Cummington Story*).

Most of the men she worked with in her ten-year career described her in glowing terms. Guy Glover, who produced and scripted the premature babies film, *Starting Line,* called her "a Beautiful Person—intelligent, kind, civilized and knowledgeable about film—a rare combination." Glover spent the rest of his life as a leading producer at the National Film Board of Canada. George Justin, who shot the same film, remembered Grayson as a "sensitive, artistic director. . . brilliantly organized [with] a fine sense of drama. . . camera. . . and all the technical things that go into making a film." Justin eventually became an executive production manager at Orion Pictures and later senior vice president at MGM. Ricky Leacock, who photographed the American history series Grayson directed, called her "a joy to work with. . . imaginative. . . and responsive to the ideas of those she worked with." Leacock later became an international icon for his role in helping develop the new documentary technique called cinema verité, and a longtime film teacher and guru at the Massachusetts Institute of Technology.

Anyone who was not close to the New York documentary-film scene in those early years might well wonder why the career of this capable woman came to a sudden halt. For one reason there were virtually no female mentors, models, or allies Grayson could turn to for a hand-up. Most of the women filmmakers who had preceded her (Osa Johnson, Frances Flaherty, Margaret Mead) worked only, or mainly, with their husbands. Lee Burgess Dick, who set up her own company to produce and direct documentary films in the late 1930s, soon abandoned it to work as an editor and occasional director for a commercial production company in New York. Virginia Bell, who became a highly successful filmmaker in the 1950s—in a company she had founded with her husband Robert—adopted the androgenous name of Tracy Ward to disguise her female identity. Shirley Clarke, who briefly joined Leacock, Donn Pennebaker, and Willard Van Dyke in a loose affiliation called Filmmakers, Inc., soon found herself on her own while the others moved on to more rewarding opportunities.

For another reason, Grayson was more than 50 years old when she directed her last film in an era when women that age were rarely considered employable: Dorothy Arzner was only 43 when she directed her last Hollywood feature. Yet in the mid-1950s, Grayson set out to find sponsorship for two films that would have capitalized on her early ties to Europe. One was on George Balanchine's new, exciting New York City Ballet, and the other (which she hoped to co-produce with the French filmmaker William Novik) on the charismatic Benjamin Franklin's years in Paris. Despite her endeavors, funding was not forthcoming.

Instead, Grayson spent those last years as unofficial goodwill ambassador, selecting and promoting America's outstanding documentaries for European film festivals—and vice versa. During her frequent stays in Paris, she often attended Jean-Paul Sartre's weekly literary circle—and was said to be the only American he ever invited. In New York she remained an active member of the Screen Directors Guild, as she had been for more than a dozen years. Helen Grayson died of cancer in New York City in 1962, after several years' illness. The Prix Helen Grayson was established that year at the Annecy (France) Animation Festival, and her good friend Jay Leyda dedicated to her his book, *Films Beget Films.*

Some years later, research on pioneer American women filmmakers revealed some of the obstacles Grayson had faced in her film career. "We were cruel to her," Larry Madison admitted to one researcher, recalling how he and some of the technical crew had tried to undermine her authority when she was directing *The Cummington Story*. He had already asked for and in some publications received co-credit as the film's director. To set the record straight, Grayson had published in the *Bryn Mawr Alumnae Bulletin* a lengthy account of her work as director and his as director of photography. (Later, Frances Flaherty published a full-page report on Grayson's *Bryn Mawr* film in that same publication, and later still Grayson's close friend Claire Parker wrote of her work in pinboard animation with Alexander Alexeieff. Lee Burgess, another pioneer filmmaker, also attended Bryn Mawr, an all-women's college, which specialized in the arts.)

Although he was the producer of many films Grayson had directed, Willard Van Dyke stated after her death that Grayson's sole significance was that she had directed "one quite good documentary." Unfortunately for her, that film and others she directed have rarely been shown in the United States. Perhaps it is for this reason that Helen Grayson's name is rarely found in any film books, even those devoted only to women filmmakers.—CECILE STARR

Greenwald, Maggie

American director and writer

Born *23 June 1955.* ***Career*** *Began her career as an actor then a dancer; in her early twenties spent a year at film school, subsequently made several short films and moved into the postproduction phase of the film industry; she was a picture editor for several years and then shifted to sound editing; 1987—made her first feature,* Home Remedy; *1989—made* The Kill-Off, *from the novel by Jim Thompson; 1993—made the highly acclaimed* The Ballad of Little Jo; *mid-1990s—adjunct associate professor, Columbia University School of the Arts.* ***Awards*** *Best Director Award, Turin Film Festival, for* The Kill-Off, *1989; Special Jury Award, Rome-Florence Film Festival, for* The Ballad of Little Jo, *1994.* ***Address*** *c/o Sloss Law Offices, 170 Fifth Avenue, 8th Floor, New York, NY 10010, U.S.A.*

Films as Director and Writer: 1987: *Home Remedy.* **1989:** *The Kill-Off.* **1993:** *The Ballad of Little Jo.*

Best known for the cross-dressing, revisionist Western *The Ballad of Little Jo* (1993), Maggie Greenwald began her artistic career as a dancer and actor before embarking on a career in the film industry. Greenwald made several short films before gaining experience as a picture editor and sound editor. Her first feature as a director was the 1987 *Home Remedy,* followed by *The Kill-Off* (1989). According to Greenwald, it took five years to get the $200,000 needed to finance *Home Remedy*. Her first two films had short commercial lives with neither film making much of an impression on commercial critics. *The Kill-Off* is interesting because it represents Greenwald's first foray into a traditionally male genre, the film noir. Based on a Jim Thompson novel, Greenwald claims to have been attracted to the material by Thompson's use of language, his exploration of "low-lifes," and the opportunity to work on characters from an internal perspective. As she states, "You are reading stories about people who are doing incredibly vicious things, you are inside of them and experiencing the world from their point of view of being vulnerable and fragile. And I consider that perspective to be very feminine."

Greenwald is also one of the few women film directors to work in the traditionally male Western genre. Modleski claims *Little Jo* is the "first Western written and directed by a woman since the silent era." The strengths of this revisionist, feminist Western lie in Suzy Amis's compelling portrait of a 19th-century Eastern society woman who is ostracized from her community after the illegitimate birth of a child. The character ends up in the Far West where she encounters poverty and attempted rape and finally decides the only way to survive is to pass as a

Maggie Greenwald

man. Eventually Jo becomes a miner then a sheepherder and falls in love with a Chinese man, Tinman (David Chung). Although they privately live as man and woman, the rest of the world believes Jo to be a man until her secret is discovered after her death. The central conceit of cross-dressing might have come across as a gimmick in less capable directorial hands, but added to the persuasive, sensitive performance by Amis, the film is genuinely moving and convincing. The film also features a surprisingly strong performance from Bo Hopkins, best known for his work in Peckinpah's *The Wild Bunch*. It also features, not surprisingly, a wonderfully detailed performance by Ian McKellen as Percy, a character who struggles with his own sexuality and displays a strong hatred for women.

The inspiration for this tale was a real individual although Greenwald claims that the only things she knew for certain about Josephine Monaghan are what was published in newspaper articles at the time of her death. Greenwald has taken the basic facts of the character's beginnings and the end of her life and imagined much of the rest. But that seems fair and honest within the context of a fiction film. *Little Jo* harkens back to earlier films like the Jack Nicholson/Monte Hellman "existential" Westerns of the mid-1960s, *Ride in the Whirlwind* and *The Shooting* in its level of realism. There is good attention to period detail in the film as well as an accuracy in the dialogue, which nicely captures the flavor and speech idioms common to the period. The re-creation of Ruby City is particularly well done and there is a real sense of life lived in the town scenes. One feels that people could very well have lived like this at the time and the viewer actually learns something about the Old West. Greenwald claims that most of the research for the film was based on looking at photographs—unlike the Nicholson Westerns, which were inspired by real cowboy diaries.

Little Jo is strong in its visual style and montage, and nicely captures the sense of expanse and lyricism of the landscape. Viewer involvement is also enhanced by a lovely, emotional music score. Another strength of the film is the sudden shifts in tone and mood that occur within a scene. One particularly fine example occurs when the character played by Ian McKellen goes mad and attacks a deaf, mute whore. The sense that death or physical harm could explode at any instant in this world is well communicated by this scene. The sequence also communicates the character's self-loathing as well as his misogynistic streak. The film's pacing is leisurely but maintains interest throughout.

To say that the film is flawless, however, would be inaccurate. There are occasionally awkward moments, and the film's ideological project is at times too pat and obvious. One major flaw in the film is Jo's lack of an interior life. The film might have gained in complexity if it had tried to illustrate what this intriguing character felt or thought about her life, but that never happens. Greenwald's interest in the subjectivity of the noir genre might well have been transposed to this film. Nonetheless, *The Battle of Little Jo* is a serious contribution to the contemporary Western genre and offers a genuinely fresh spin on some well-worn territory. The film may not be as subversive as some have claimed, but it is a genuine accomplishment. Greenwald has a sure command of the medium and is clearly a director who merits attention.—MARIO FALSETTO

Guillemot, Agnès

French editor

Born *Agnès Perche in Roubaix, 1931.* ***Education*** *Attended IDHEC, Paris, 1956-57.* ***Family*** *Married the director Claude Guillemot.* ***Career*** *1956-57—editor for Télévision Canadienne (Télé-France); 1957-59—assistant editor at IDHEC; 1960—worked on TV news series, and then on series* L'Education sentimentale, *1971,* L'Amour du métier, *1972,* La Clé des champs, *1973, and* Les Secrets de la Mer Rouge, *1974; since 1980—teacher of film editing at IDHEC.*

Films as Editor: 1953: *La Faute des autres* (Guez—short). **1955:** *Walk into Paradise* (*L'Odyssée du Capitaine Steve*) (Robinson and Pagliero) (asst). **1958:** *Vous n'avez rien contre la jeunesse* (Logereau—short); *Voyage en Boscavie* (Herman—short). **1959:** *Voiles à Val* (Perol—short). **1960:** *Le Gaz de Lacq* (Lanoe—short); *Thaumetopoea* (Enrico—short); *Un Steak trop cuit* (Moullet—short). **1961:** *La Quille* (Herman—short); *Une Femme est une femme* (*A Woman Is a Woman*) (Godard). **1962:** *Une Grosse Tête* (De Givray); *Vivre sa vie* (*My Life to Live*) (Godard); "Il Nuovo mondo" ep. of *Rogopag* (Godard). **1963:** *Le Petit Soldat* (*The Little Soldier*) (Godard—produced 1960) (co); *Les Hommes de la Wahgi* (Villeminot—short); *Les Carabiniers* (Godard); *Le Mépris* (*Contempt*) (Godard); "Le Grand Escroc" ep. of *Les Plus Belles Escroqueries du monde* (*The Beautiful Swindlers*) (Godard); *Jérôme Bosch* (Weyergans—short); *Une Semaine en France* (C. Guillemot and Chambon—short). **1964:** *Bande à part* (*Band of Outsiders*) (Godard); *Une Fille à la dérive* (Delsol); *Rues de Hong Kong* (C. Guillemot—short); *La Jonque* (C. Guillemot—short); *Les Tourbiers* (Weyergans—short); *De l'amour* (Aurel); *Une Femme mariée* (*The Married Woman*) (Godard) (co). **1965:** *Alphaville* (*Une étrange aventure de Lemmy Caution*; *Alphaville: A Strange Adventure of Lemmy Caution*; *Tarzan versus I.B.M.*) (Godard). **1966:** *Masculin-féminin* (*Masculine-Feminine*) (Godard); *Dialectique* (C. Guillemot—short); *Le Chien fou* (Matalon); *Nature morte* (C. Guillemot—short); *Made in U.S.A.* (Godard). **1967:** "Anticipation" ep. of *Le Plus Vieux Métier du monde* (*The Oldest Profession*) (Godard); *La Chinoise* (Godard); *Weekend* (Godard). **1968:** *Les Gauloises bleues* (Cournot); *Baises volés* (*Stolen Kisses*) (Truffaut); *One Plus One* (*Sympathy for the Devil*) (Godard); *La Trêve* (C. Guillemot). **1969:** "L'amore" ep. of *Amore e rabbia* (*Vangelo '70*) (Godard); *La Sirène du Mississippi* (*Mississippi Mermaid*) (Truffaut); *L'Enfant sauvage* (*The Wild Child*) (Truffaut). **1970:** *Domicile conjugal* (*Bed and Board*) (Truffaut). **1974:** *L'Age tendre* (Laumet). **1975:** *Le Grand Matin* (C. Guillemot—short); *Cousin cousine* (Tacchella). **1976:** *Un Type comme moi ne devrait jamais mourir* (Vianey); *Le Pays bleu* (*The Blue Country*) (Tacchella). **1977:** *Monsieur Badin* (Ceccaldi); *Jean de la lune* (Villiers); *Les Violons parfois* (Ronet). **1978:** *Folies douces* (Ronet); *Le Concierge revient de suite* (Wyn). **1979:** *Il y a longtemps que je t'aime* (Tacchella). **1982:** *Invitation au voyage* (Del Monte). **1983:** *La Diagonale du fou* (*Dangerous Moves*) (Dembo). **1985:** *Escalier C* (Tacchella). **1987:** *La Brute* (C. Guillemot); *Fuegos* (C. Guillemot). **1988:** *La Lumière du lac* (Comencini). **1990:** *Un Week-End sur deux* (*Every Other Weekend*) (N. García); *Sale comme un ange* (*Dirty Like an Angel*) (Breillat). **1995:** *N'oublie pas que tu vas mourir* (*Don't Forget You're Going to Die*) (Beauvois); *Memoires d'un jeune con* (Aurignac). **1996:** *Parfait amour.*

Agnès Guillemot's 45-year career places her as one of France's most important, respected, and influential editors. She teaches editing at IDHEC in Paris, edits television series, documenta-

Agnès Guillemot: *Vivre sa vie* production still.

ries, and narrative features, and through the 1960s, established the basic editing style of modernist filmmaking, contemporary television commercials, and music videos. She began cutting film during the Nouvelle Vague and remains strongly associated with that era.

As Jean-Luc Godard's favorite editor, Guillemot edited all of his films from 1961 to 1969, with the exceptions of *Pierrot le fou, Deux ou trois choses que je sais d'elle* (both edited by one of her former assistants, Françoise Collin), and *Le Gai savoir.* Collaborating with Godard on 13 features and four episodes of compilation films, and having an assistant edit two others, she must share responsibility for the deconstructive narrative techniques and reflexive visual style usually credited to Godard. Although the similarity of the editing strategies in *Deux ou trois choses* and *Pierrot le fou* to all Godard's other films suggests the director's overriding influence, and Guillemot herself admits that an editor must embrace the personal rhythm of each director and not impose her own, Guillemot's reification of Godard's theories cannot be underestimated. By introducing a sense of musical rhythm and a disregard for spatial and temporal continuity, her work with Godard avoided the realist dictates of linear narrative and provided a locus for ideological analysis. This radicalizing of conventional editing eventually emerged as her most important legacy.

Within any one film, Guillemot's editing appears contradictory, or perhaps dialogic; in any case, her work seems, at first glance, an impossible melange of styles. She combines or juxtaposes the formal symmetry of long takes, the precise rigor of classical match-action editing and shot/reverse shot, the playfulness of reflexivity, and the spontaneity of jump cuts. These characteristics exactly demonstrate the musical and open narrative signature of the Nouvelle Vague. Guillemot cites her strongest work as *A Woman Is a Woman,* with its interplay of words and music as in an opera, and *Les Carabiniers* for the crescendo of the postcard sequence. In *Alphaville,* she reinforces Godard's parody of American science fiction by employing standard editing techniques only to abandon them at moments of highest narrative expectation. In *Contempt,* she uses jump cuts sparingly as a metaphor for Camille's confused mind, ironically embedding them in a fluid pattern of graceful tracking shots. In *Masculine-Feminine,* she plays off the symmetrical tension of the title to visually explore the energy of romance; initially, fast-paced jump cutting represents a new love, slowing to long takes as the romance dissolves. In *Weekend,* she summarizes her collaboration with Godard by fully exhibiting her varied and "contradictory" style of editing, a style perfectly suited for encapsulating Godard's "end of cinema."

Guillemot's late career allowed her to adapt radical Nouvelle Vague modernism for more mainstream cinema; as New Wave stylistics became accepted and standardized, she expanded the confining logic and limitations of classic linear narrative. She edited films for François Truffaut (including two of the Antoine Doinel series), Jean-Charles Tacchella (including the Oscar-nominated *Cousin cousine*), and Richard Dembo (the Academy Award-winning *Dangerous Moves*). By comparing these films to her Godard period, one can easily see Guillemot's influence on contemporary film editing. Eschewing only the reflexivity of her Godard period, she employs the other techniques (especially visual and aural jump cuts) to stress spatial and temporal ellipses. Contained within classical match action and shot/reverse shot sequences and countered with long takes, these ellipses open up a narrative, regardless of how confining (*Dangerous Moves*'s chess match) or how limited (*Cousin cousine*'s conventional love story) and offer the potential for social critique. Her editing on *La Lumière du lac* and *Every Other Weekend* accomplishes exactly this—expanding the parameters of linear narrative with humorous spontaneity, rhythmic pacing, and critical observations of modern society. She has also edited ten shorts and features by her husband Claude Guillemot, alternating between traditional documentary style and her Nouvelle Vague techniques.

Agnès Guillemot's New Wave cutting also influenced most contemporary film and television editing. Even though the link between her editing during the 1960s and today's television commercials and music videos loses its political edge, the continuation of her style in these formats seems incontrovertible (the 1989 Lee Jeans ads, particularly, acting as a direct homage). The formal symmetry of shot/reverse shot placed within long takes, invisible match-action editing alternating with jump cuts, a playful reflexivity, and loosely structured "nonnarratives" are now accepted as standard practice (almost every music video is edited this way). Like most historical avant-garde artists, her work seems much less radical today because of its wide appropriation. Nevertheless, Guillemot must be credited with modernizing editing during the 1960s, an accomplishment which continues to influence visual media today.—GREG S. FALLER

Guy, Alice

French director and writer

Pseudonym *Also known as Alice Guy-Blaché and Alice Blaché.* ***Born*** *Saint-Mandé, 1 July 1873.* ***Education*** *Attended the Convent du Sacré-Coeur, Viry, France 1879-85; religious school at Ferney, and brief term in Paris; studied stenography.* ***Family*** *Married Herbert Blaché-Bolton, 1907 (divorced 1922), two children.* ***Career*** *1895—secretary to Léon Gaumont; 1896 (some sources give 1900)—directed first film,* La Fée aux choux; *1897-1907—director of Gaumont film production; 1900—using Gaumont "chronophone," made first sound films; 1907—moved to United States with husband, who was to supervise Gaumont subsidiary, Solax; 1917—ceased independent production, lectured on filmmaking at Columbia University; 1919-20—assistant director to husband; 1922—returned to France; 1964—moved to United States.* ***Awards*** *Legion of Honor, 1953.* ***Died*** *In Mahwah, New Jersey, 24 March 1968.*

Films as Director and Writer: 1896: *La Fée aux choux* (*The Cabbage Fairy*). **1897:** *Le Pêcheur dans le torrent*; *Leçon de danse*; *Baignade dans le torrent*; *Une nuit agitée*; *Coucher d'Yvette*; *Danse fleur de lotus*; *Ballet Libella*; *Le Planton du colonel*; *Idylle*; *L'Aveugle*. **1897/98:** *L'Arroseur arrosé*; *Au réfectoire*; *En classe*; *Les Cambrioleurs*; *Le Cocher de fiacre endormi*; *Idylle interrompue*; *Chez le magnétiseur*; *Les Farces de Jocko*; *Scène d'escamotage*; *Déménagement à la cloche de bois*; *Je vous y prrrends!*. **1898/99:** *Leçons de boxe*. **1899/1900:** *Le Tondeur de chiens*; *Le Déjeuner des enfants*; *Au cabaret*; *La Mauvaise*

Soupe; *Un Lunch*; *Erreur judiciaire*; *L'Aveugle*; *La Bonne Absinthe*; *Danse serpentine par Mme Bob Walter*; *Mésaventure d'un charbonnier*; *Monnaie de lapin*; *Les Dangers de l'acoolisme*; *Le Tonnelier*; *Transformations*; *Le Chiffonier*; *Retour des champs*; *Chez le Maréchal-Ferrant*; *Marché à la volaille*; *Courte échelle*; *L'Angélus*; *Bataille d'oreillers*; *Bataille de boules de neige*; *Le marchand de coco.* **1900:** *Avenue de l'Opéra*; *La petite magicienne*; *Leçon de danse*; *Chez le photographe*; *Sidney's Joujoux* series (nine titles); *Dans les coulisses*; *Au Bal de Flore* series (three titles); *Ballet Japonais* series (three titles); *Danse serpentine*; *Danse du pas des foulards par des almées*; *Danse de l'ivresse*; *Coucher d'une Parisienne*; *Les Fredaines de Pierrette* series (four titles); *Vénus et Adonis* series (five titles); *La Tarantelle*; *Danse des Saisons* series (four titles); *La Source*; *Danse du papillon*; *La Concierge*; *Danses* series (three titles); *Chirurgie fin de siècle*; *Une Rage de dents*; *Saut humidifié de M. Plick.* **1900/01:** *La Danse du ventre*; *Lavatory moderne*; *Lecture quotidienne.* **1900/07:** (Gaumont "Phonoscènes," i.e., films with synchronized sound recorded on a wax cylinder): *Carmen* (twelve scenes); *Mireille* (five scenes); *Les Dragons de Villars* (nine scenes); *Mignon* (seven scenes); *Faust* (twenty-two scenes); *Polin* series (thirteen titles); *Mayol* series (thirteen titles); *Dranem* series of comic songs (twelve titles); Series recorded in Spain (eleven titles); *La Prière* by Gounod. **1901:** *Folies Masquées* series (three titles); *Frivolité*; *Les Vagues*; *Danse basque*; *Hussards et grisettes*; *Charmant FrouFrou*; *Tel est pris qui croyait prendre.* **1902:** *La fiole enchantée*; *L'Equilibriste*; *En faction*; *La Première Gamelle*; *La Dent récalcitrante*; *Le Marchand de ballons*; *Les Chiens savants*; *Miss Lina Esbrard Danseuse Cosmopolite et Serpentine* series (four titles); *Les Clowns*; *Sage-femme de première classe*; *Quadrille réaliste*; *Une Scène en cabinet particulier vue à travers le trou de la serrure*; *Farces de cuisinière*; *Danse mauresque*; *Le Lion savant*; *Le Pommier*; *La Cour des miracles*; *La Gavotte*; *Trompé mais content*; *Fruits de saison*; *Pour secourer la salade.* **1903:** *Potage indigeste*; *Illusioniste renversant*; *Le Fiancé ensorcelé*; *Les Apaches pas veinards*; *Les Aventures d'un voyageur trop pressé*; *Ne bougeons plus*; *Comment monsieur prend son bain*; *La Main du professeur Hamilton ou Le Roi des dollars*; *Service précipité*; *La Poule fantaisiste*; *Modelage express*; *Faust et Méphistophélès*; *Lutteurs américains*; *La Valise enchantée*; *Compagnons de voyage encombrants*; *Cake-Walk de la pendule*; *Répétition dans un cirque*; *Jocko musicien*; *Les Braconniers*; *La Liqueur du couvent*; *Le Voleur sacrilège*; *Enlèvement en automobile et mariage précipite.* **1903/04:** *Secours aux naufragés*; *La Mouche*; *La Chasse au cambrioleur*; *Nos Bon Etudiants*; *Les Surprises de l'affichage*; *Comme on fait son lit on se couche*; *Le Pompon malencontreux 1*; *Comment on disperse les foules*; *Les Enfants du miracle*; *Pierrot assassin*; *Les Deux Rivaux.*

1904: *L'Assassinat du Courrier de Lyon*; *Vieilles Estampes* series (four titles); *Mauvais coeur puni*; *Magie noire*; *Rafle de chiens*; *Cambrioleur et agent*; *Scènes Directoire* series (three titles); *Duel tragique*; *L'Attaque d'un diligence*; *Culture intensive ou Le Vieux Mari*; *Cible humaine*; *Transformations*; *Le Jour du terme*; *Robert Macaire et Bertrand*; *Electrocutée*; *La Rêve du chasseur*; *Le Monolutteur*; *Les Petits Coupeurs de bois vert*; *Clown en sac*; *Triste fin d'un vieux savant*; *Le Testament de Pierrot*; *Les Secrets de la prestidigitation dévoilés*; *La Faim . . . L' occasion . . . L'herbe tendre*; *Militaire et nourrice*; *La Première Cigarette* (*The First Cigarette*); *Départ pour les vacances*; *Tentative d'assassinat en chemin de fer*; *Paris la nuit ou Exploits d' apaches à Montmartre*; *Concours de bébés*; *Erreur de poivrot*; *Volée par les bohémiens* (*Rapt d'enfant par les romanichels*); *Les Bienfaits du cinématographe*; *Pâtissier et ramoneur*; *Gage d'amour*; *L'Assassinat de la rue du Temple* (*Le Crime de la rue du Temple*); *Le Réveil du jardinier*; *Les Cambrioleurs de Paris.* **1905:** *Réhabilitation*; *Douaniers et contrebandiers* (*La Guérité*); *Le Bébé embarrassant*; *Comment on dort á Paris!*; *Le Lorgnon accusateur*; *La Charité du prestidigitateur*; *Une Noce au lac Saint-Fargeau*; *Le Képi*; *Le Pantalon coupé*; *Le Plateau*; *Roméo pris au piége*; *Chien jouant á la balle*; *La Fantassin Guignard*; *La Statue*; *Villa dévalisée*; *Mort de Robert Macaire et Bertrand*; *Le Pavé*; *Les Maçons*; *La Esmeralda*; *Peintre et ivrogne*; *On est poivrot, mais on a du cœur*; *Au Poulailler!.* **1906:** *La Fée au printemps*; *La Vie du marin*; *La Chaussette*; *La Messe de minuit*; *Pauvre pompier*; *Le Régiment moderne*; *Les Druides*; *Voyage en Espagne* series (15 titles); *La Vie du Christ* (25 tableaux); *Conscience de prêtre*; *L'Honneur du Corse*; *J'ai un hanneton dans mon pantalon*; *Le Fils du garde-chasse*; *Course de taureaux à Nîmes*; *La Pègre de Paris*; *Lèvres closes* (*Sealed Lips*); *La Crinoline*; *La Voiture cellulaire*; *La Marâtre*; *Le Matelas alcoolique*; *A la recherche d'un appartement.* **1907:** *La vérité sur l'homme-singe* (*Ballet de Singe*); *Déménagement à la cloche de bois*; *Les Gendarmes*; *Sur la barricade* (*L'enfant de la barricade*). **1910:** *A Child's Sacrifice* (*The Doll*). **1911:** *Rose of the Circus*; *Across the Mexican Line*; *Eclipse*; *A Daughter of the Navajos*; *The Silent Signal*; *The Girl and the Bronco Buster*; *The Mascot of Troop "C"*; *An Enlisted Man's Honor*; *The Stampede*; *The Hold-Up*; *The Altered Message*; *His Sister's Sweetheart*; *His Better Self*; *A Revolutionary Romance*; *The Violin Maker of*

Nuremberg. **1912:** *Mignon or The Child of Fate; A Terrible Lesson; His Lordship's White Feather; Falling Leaves; The Sewer; In the Year 2000; A Terrible Night; Mickey's Pal; Fra Diavolo; Hotel Honeymoon; The Equine Spy; Two Little Rangers; The Bloodstain; At the Phone; Flesh and Blood; The Paralytic; The Face at the Window; A Detective's Dog; Canned Harmony; The Girl in the Armchair; The Making of an American Citizen; The Call of the Rose; Winsome but Wise.* **1913:** *The Beasts of the Jungle; Dick Whittington and His Cat; Kelly from the Emerald Isle; The Pit and the Pendulum; Western Love; Rogues of Paris; Blood and Water; Ben Bolt; The Shadows of the Moulin Rouge; The Eyes that Could Not Close; The Star of India; The Fortune Hunters; A House Divided; Matrimony's Speed Limit.* **1914:** *Beneath the Czar; The Monster and the Girl; The Million Dollar Robbery; The Prisoner of the Harem; The Dream Woman; Hook and Hand; The Woman of Mystery; The Yellow Traffic; The Lure; Michael Strogoff or The Courier to the Czar; The Tigress; The Cricket on the Hearth.* **1915:** *The Heart of a Painted Woman; Greater Love Hath No Man; The Vampire; My Madonna; Barbara Frietchie* (co-d). **1916:** *What Will People Say?; The Girl with the Green Eyes; The Ocean Waif; House of Cards.* **1917:** *The Empress; The Adventurer; A Man and the Woman; When You and I Were Young; Behind the Mask.* **1918:** *The Great Adventure; A Soul Adrift.* **1920:** *Tarnished Reputations.*

Other Films: 1919: *The Divorcee* (asst d); *The Brat* (asst d). **1920:** *Stronger than Death* (asst d).

Alice Guy was the first person, or among the first, to make a fictional film. The story-film was quite possibly "invented" by her in 1896 when she made *The Cabbage Fairy.* Certain historians claim that films of Louis Lumière and Georges Méliès preceded Guy's first film. The question remains debatable; Guy claimed precedence, devoting much effort in her lifetime to correcting recorded errors attributing her films to her male colleagues, and trying to secure her earned niche in film history. There is no debate regarding Guy's position as the world's first woman filmmaker.

Between 1896 and 1901 Guy made films averaging just 75 feet in length; from 1902 to 1907 she made numerous films of all types and lengths using acrobats, clowns, and opera singers as well as large casts in ambitious productions based on fairy and folk tales, Biblical themes, paintings, and myths. The "tricks" she used—running film in reverse and the use of double exposure—were learned through trial-and-error. In this period she also produced "talking pictures," in which Gaumont's Chronophone synchronized a projector with sound recorded on a wax cylinder.

One of these sound films, *Mireille,* was made by Guy in 1906. Herbert Blaché-Bolton joined the film crew of *Mireille* to learn directing. Alice Guy and Herbert were married in early 1907. The couple moved to the United States, where they eventually set up a studio in Flushing, New York. The Blachés then established the Solax Company, with a Manhattan office. In its four years of existence, Solax released 325 films, including westerns, military movies, thrillers, and historical romances. Mme. Blaché's first picture in the United States was *A Child's Sacrifice* (in 1910), which centers on a girl's attempts to earn money for her family. In her *Hotel Honeymoon* of 1912, the moon comes alive to smile at human lovers, while in *The Violin Maker of Nuremberg,* two apprentices contend for the affections of their instructor's daughter.

The Blachés built their own studio at Fort Lee, New Jersey, a facility with a daily printing capacity of 16,000 feet of positive film. For its inauguration in February of 1912, Mme. Blaché presented an evening of Solax films at Weber's Theatre on Broadway. In that year she filmed two movies based on operas: *Fra Diavolo* and *Mignon,* each of which were three-reelers that included orchestral accompaniment. Her boldest enterprises were films using animals and autos.

Cataclysmic changes in the film industry finally forced the Blachés out of business. They rented, and later sold, their studio, then directed films for others. In 1922 the Blachés divorced.

Herbert directed films until 1930, but Alice could not find film work and never made another film. She returned to France, but without prints of her films she had no evidence of her accomplishments and could not find work in the French film industry either. She returned to the United States in 1927 to search the Library of Congress and other film depositories for her films, but her efforts were in vain: only a half-dozen of her one-reelers survive. In 1953 she returned to Paris, where, at age 80, she was honored as the first woman filmmaker in the world. Her films, characterized by innovation and novelty, explored all genres and successfully appealed to both French and American audiences. Today she is finally being recognized as a unique pioneer of the film industry.—LOUISE HECK-RABI

Haines, Randa

American writer and director

Born *Los Angeles, California, 20 February 1945.* ***Education*** *School of Visual Arts, New York; studied acting with Lee Strasberg; accepted into American Film Institute's Directing Workshop for Women, 1975.* ***Career*** *Directed and co-wrote short film* August/September *while with AFI, which led to work as writer for TV series,* Family. *Also Directed episodes of the TV series* Knots Landing, Hill Street Blues, Tucker's Witch, *and* Tales From the Crypt. ***Awards*** *Emmy nomination for TV movie* Something about Amelia, *1984; first woman to be nominated for Director's Guild of America Award for* Children of a Lesser God, *1986.*

Films as Director: 1979: *Under This Sky* (for TV). **1980:** *The Jilting of Granny Weatherall* (for TV). **1982:** *Just Pals.* **1984:** *Something About Amelia* (for TV). **1985:** *Alfred Hitchcock Presents* (co-d) (for TV). **1986:** *Children of a Lesser God.* **1991:** *The Doctor.* **1993:** *Wrestling Ernest Hemingway.* **1998:** *Dance With Me.*

Born in Los Angeles, but raised in New York City, Randa Haines' first love was the theater. She even briefly studied acting before landing a job as a script supervisor for a New York production company in the mid-1960s. The task of "bird-dogging" the set to prevent visual inconsistencies from one take to the next "was better than film school," she told *Time* magazine in 1991. "You learn how directors see a film, why they make certain decisions."

It wasn't long before Haines was taking her experience behind the camera. Following a workshop with the AFI in 1975, she began directing in television—*Family, Knot's Landing, Hill Street Blues*—and earned critical acclaim with the groundbreaking *Something About Amelia* in 1984, which dealt unflinchingly with incest. Her first feature film project, *Children of a Lesser God,* was thought to be a story (from the award-winning Broadway play) impossible to translate to the screen. Haines perservered and successfully unveiled not only the hidden world of deaf culture, but told a touching story of love between a new teacher (William Hurt) and an angry deaf janitor (Marlee Matlin, who won the Oscar for Best Actress).

Randa Haines

"I'm always attracted to stories that reflect how very much alone we are in life and the never-ending need to connect," Haines says. With this in mind, she resisted the temptation to jump right into another project following the success of *Children* and instead searched for just the right script. In 1991, she found it in *The Doctor,* another collaboration with Hurt that told the story of a carve-more-and-care-less cardiac surgeon who suddenly finds himself on the other end of the scalpel. The film was both lauded for its visceral realism and criticized for its descent into soap-opera pathos. In 1993, a project written by 21-year-old author Steve Conrad grabbed Haines. *Wrestling Ernest Hemingway* became something of a sleeper hit that examined the loneliness of old age and the uneasy comfort of companionship among even the most disparate of characters (Robert Duvall, Richard Harris, Shirley MacLaine, Piper Laurie).

Haines' 1998 film, *Dance With Me,* has been called her most personal, portraying as it does the concomittant primal sense of pride, family and culture she herself discovered while dancing at Los Angeles' salsa clubs. Despite (again) being criticized as melodramatic and predictable,

Haines (again) scored a popular hit in her portrayal of people fighting to find each other across a chasm of loneliness and divergent cultures, this time accomplished with a vibrant, Latin-beat sensuality. In Haines' capable directorial hands—variously described as both sensitive and black-comedic—it seems safe to say we can look forward to more well-chosen, if infrequent, projects with the same timeless theme.—JEROME SZYMCZAK

Hammer, Barbara

American director and writer

Born *1939.* ***Education*** *Attended University of California, Los Angeles, B.A. in psychology, 1961; San Francisco State University, M.A. in English literature, 1963, M.A. in film, 1975.* ***Family*** *Married once (divorced c. 1968); domestic partner, Florrie Burke, 1988.* ***Career*** *After undergraduate study, taught at Marin County Juvenile Hall; after graduate study in film, began career as avant-garde, feminist filmmaker whose body of work has become known for its exploration and articulation of lesbian concerns. Has taught at State University of New York at Binghamton; Columbia College, Chicago; San Francisco State University; San Francisco Art Institute; California College of Arts and Crafts; University of Iowa, Iowa City; Art Institue of Chicago; New School for Social Research; School for Visual Arts, New York; and School of the Museum of Fine Arts, Boston.* ***Awards*** *First Prize, Ann Arbor Film Festival, for* Optic Nerve, *1985; First Prize, Black Maria Film Festival, and First Prize, Bucks County Film Festival, for* Endangered, *1988; Atlanta Film/Video Festival, Women in Film Award, for* Still Point, *1989; Jurors' Award, Black Maria Film Festival, and Best Experimental Film, Utah Film Festival, for* Vital Signs, *1991; Polar Bear Award for Lifetime Contribution to Lesbian/Gay Cinema, Berlin International Film Festival, 1993; Isabel Liddell Art Award, Ann Arbor Film Festival, and Director's Choice, Charlotte Film Festival, for* Tender Fictions, *1995.* ***Address*** *55 Bethune Street, #114G, New York, NY 10014, U.S.A.*

Films and Videotapes as Director and Writer: **1968:** *Schizy.* **1969:** *Barbara Ward Will Never Die.* **1970:** *Traveling: Marie and Me.* **1972:** *The Song of the Clinking Cup.* **1973:** *I Was/I Am.* **1974:** *Sisters!*; *A Gay Day*; *Dyketactics*; *X*; *Women's Rites or Truth Is the Daughter of Time*; *Menses.* **1975:** *Jane Brakhage*; *Superdyke*; *Psychosynthesis*; *Superdyke Meets Madame X* (co-d with Almy). **1976:** *Moon Goddess* (co-d with Churchman); *Eggs*; *Multiple Orgasm*; *Women I Love*; *Stress Scars and Pleasure Wrinkles.* **1977:** *The Great Goddess.* **1978:** *Double Strength*; *Home*; *Haircut*; *Available Space*; *Sappho.* **1979:** *Dream Age.* **1980:** *See What You Hear What You See.* **1981:** *Our Trip*; *Arequipa*; *The Lesbos Film*; *Machu Picchu*; *Pictures for Barbara*; *Pools* (co-d with Klutinis); *Sync Touch.* **1982:** *Pond and Waterfall*; *Audience.* **1983:** *Bent Time*; *New York Loft*; *Stone Circles.* **1984:** *Doll House*; *Pearl Diver*; *Bamboo Xerox.* **1985:** *Optic Nerve*; *Tourist*; *Parisian Blinds*; *Would You Like to Meet Your Neighbor?*; *Hot Flash.* **1986:** *Bedtime Stories.* **1987:** *Place Mattes*; *No No Nooky TV.* **1988:** *Endangered*; *The History of the World According to a Lesbian*; *Two Bad Daughters* (co-d with Levine). **1989:** *Hot Flash*; *Snow Job: The Media Hysteria of Aids*; *Still Point*; *T.V. Tart.* **1990:** *Sanctus.* **1991:** *Vital Signs*; *Dr. Watson's X-Rays.* **1993:** *Nitrate Kisses.* **1994:** *Out in South Africa.* **1995:** *Tender Fictions.* **1997:** *The Female Closet.*

The impressive body of work created by Barbara Hammer during the last three decades exists at the intersection of developments in contemporary American avant-garde film/video practice, and the proactive lesbian feminist community that emerged in the 1970s. Consistently engaged in exploring alternative means of expression, Hammer has moved from experimental

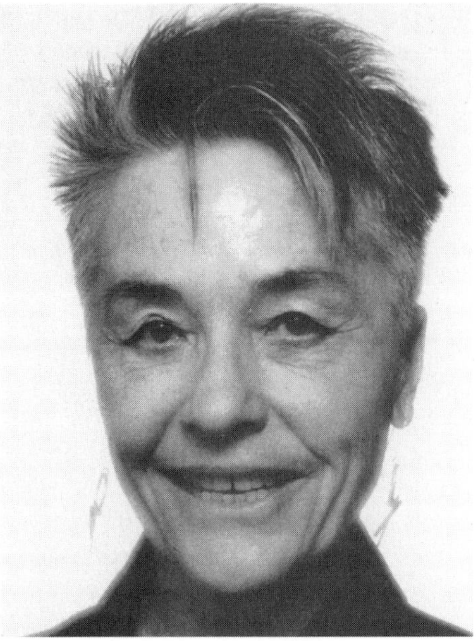

Barbara Hammer. Photograph by Glenn Halverson.

film to performance art to feature-length projects to designing sites in cyberspace. Pursuing a path consciously at odds with commercial cinema and structures endemic to patriarchal society, Hammer has worked to generate audience participation, and to that end has employed a collection of strategies—from post-screening discussions, to projection arrangements that create not just moving but mobile images, to website construction that invites visitors to contribute to cyberspace archives. Throughout her career, Hammer's writings, interviews, and screening performances have not only allowed her to provide a context for her creative work, they have also underscored the autobiographical character of her projects, and further, the role her creative work has played in the development of her identity as someone who, as she explained to Holly Willis in 1993, has dedicated her life to advancing film and lesbian studies.

After getting a bachelor's degree in psychology in 1961, and a master's in English literature in the mid-1960s, Hammer took stock of her life, caught the culture's wave of discontent and experimentation, and left her husband and the United States in 1968 to set off on a global tour with her lesbian lover. She returned to San Francisco in 1972, enrolled in graduate school—this time in cinema—and in the next few years, became one of the central figures of lesbian feminist cinema. Hammer's early trilogy, composed of *I Was/I Am* (1973), *X* (1974), and *Psychosynthesis* (1975) recounts, as Jacqueline Zita aptly explains, a transition from "anger directed outward [to] a synthesis of selves collaged in the symbol of Jungian archetypes." In making that transition, these (and other Hammer) films embrace central features of lesbian feminist art of the 1970s, for they are marked by—autobiographical and participatory, as opposed to voyeuristic—representations of lesbian sexuality; a focus on the lesbian body as beautiful, as opposed to abhorrent; an exploration of women's lives and women's bodies as being in touch with nature and spirituality, as opposed to being sites of artifice and deviance.

Hammer's body-centered films of the 1970s include a series of landmark films. *Dyketactics* (1974), a four-minute film in which each image focuses our attention on the sense of touch, is recognized as the first representation of lesbian sexuality by a lesbian. *Multiple Orgasm* (1977), with its celebration of the female genitalia, confirmed lesbian feminists' emphasis on sexuality—rather than procreativity—as the core of women's identity. *Women I Love* (1976), which emerged from Hammer's personal experience, explored and thus gave credence to women's sexuality as well as women's domain (cooking, craft work, gardening). *Double Strength* (1978), which recalled Hammer's relationship with trapeze artist Terry Sendgraff, not only created and valorized images of female power, like parallel strategies in other Hammer films, its use of sepia tones and muted colors helped to define an alternative aesthetic. Perhaps what is most remarkable is that Hammer's work during this time (as in later periods) ranged from the humor of such films as *Superdyke* (1975), to the spirituality of films such as *Moon Goddess* (1976).

As Hammer explains in her essay, "Politics of Abstraction," a 1979 Film Forum program in Los Angeles was the first time her work was screened "outside the supportive lesbian feminist community." That moment also serves as marker for a shift in her creative work, for in contrast to the 1970s, throughout the 1980s Hammer's more abstract films emphasize the role of the filmmaker in creating meaning. In this collection of work, films such as *Parisian Blinds* (1985), *Tourist* (1985), *Optic Nerve* (1985), *Place Mattes* (1987), and *Endangered* (1988) represent some of Hammer's best and well-known work.

In 1993 Hammer created her 50th film, *Nitrate Kisses*. Her first feature-length piece, *Nitrate Kisses* is, as Holly Willis points out, a "critique of the marginalization of gays and lesbians from 'common history,'" and an account of lesbian and gay culture that "attempts to show the processes of history-making." The film creates complex levels of meaning by intercutting, among other things, quotes from the texts that helped shape her conception of the film; archival footage from *Lot in Sodom* (1930), perhaps the first gay film made in America; and footage she shot in Super 8 of places that held the dramatic stories of ordinary lesbians—from long-closed, off-limit bars to sites of former concentration camps. After completing *Nitrate Kisses,* Hammer has continued to produce lengthier pieces. In 1994 she documented the first gay and lesbian film festival in Africa in her work, *Out of South Africa,* and in 1995 she completed an autobiographical work entitled *Tender Fictions*.

Most recently, Hammer has been engaged in creating a website which she describes as a "Lesbian Community in Cyberspace." The site's interactive character and its role in making lesbian experience visible emerge from concerns that have informed Hammer's work from the beginning. In very practical terms, the site makes possible projects she has been working towards for some time. As early as 1982 Hammer sought to make an international compilation film consisting of women expressing what for them was erotic. Today, one component of the website's continuously developing archive is a collection of diverse expressions of women who have visited the website (www.echonyc.com/~lesbians).

Barbara Hammer is not the first American filmmaker to explore women's sexuality—Hammer has acknowledged the influence of American avant-garde filmmaker Maya Deren—nor is she the only filmmaker whose work helps to write the history of lesbian experience. She is, however, a pioneer, a force to be reckoned with, for, as she has explained to Jacqueline Zita, "to live a lesbian life, to make it real, to validate it in film, is a revolutionary act." As Zita convincingly suggests, we should see Barbara Hammer as "a woman artist struggling to redefine the medium in a form and content commensurate with the requirements of a new lesbian aesthetic."—CYNTHIA BARON

Hänsel, Marion

French/Belgian director and writer

Born *Marseille, France, 12 February 1949; moved to Antwerp, Belgium, as a child.* ***Education*** *Studied acting and mime; attended the French Circus School; studied at the Lee Strasberg Actor's Studio, New York.* ***Career*** *1970s—worked as an actress, and worked*

briefly with the Fratellini circus act in Paris; 1977—established her own company, Man's Films, and directed her first short film, Equilibres; *1979—directed three documentaries,* Gongola, Hydraulip, *and* Bakti; *1982—directed her first feature,* The Bed; *1987—named Belgium's Woman of the Year; 1988—elected president of the Belgium Film Selection Board.* ***Awards*** *Silver Lion, Venice International Film Festival, for* Dust, *1985.* ***Address*** *Man's Films, 65 avenue Mostinck, 1150 Brussels, Belgium.*

Films as Director: 1977: *Equilibres* (short). **1979:** *Sannu batture* (*Welcome, Foreigner*) (short); *Gongola*; *Hydraulip*; *Bakti.* **1982:** *Le Lit* (*The Bed*) (+ sc, pr). **1985:** *Dust* (+ sc, co-pr). **1987:** *Les Noces barbares* (*Cruel Embrace*) (+ co-sc, pr). **1989:** *Il Maestro* (*The Maestro*; *Musical May*) (+ co-sc). **1993:** *Sur la terre comme au ciel* (*Between Heaven and Earth*; *In Heaven as on Earth*; *Entre el cielo y la tierre*) (+ co-sc, co-pr). **1995:** *Between the Devil and the Deep Blue Sea* (*Li*) (+ co-sc, co-pr). **1998:** *The Quarry.*

Other Films: 1976: *De guerre lasse* (Grospierre) (ro); *Berthe* (Ledoux). **1977:** *L'Une chante l'autre pas* (*One Sings, the Other Doesn't*) (Varda) (ro); *Ressac* (L. Buñuel) (ro); *La belle affaire* (Arago) (ro). **1987:** *Love Is a Dog from Hell* (Deruddere) (co-assoc pr). **1988:** *Baptême* (Feret) (assoc pr). **1989:** *Blueberry Hill* (De Hert) (assoc pr).

Marion Hänsel makes intricately detailed and deeply personal films that most often explore adult-child relationships. She primarily is concerned with the manner in which adults relate to (and learn from) children and, on the downside, the emotional dependence of a child—even one who has grown to adulthood—on even the most cruelly insensitive parent. Her films often are punctuated by lengthy shots and long silences, with cameras lingering on scenes and recording their details or slowly tracking across landscapes.

Hänsel's most characteristic films fit into two groupings: those that explore positive, hopeful adult-child connections (*Between Heaven and Earth* and *Between the Devil and the Deep Blue Sea*); and those that explore tumultuous relationships between parent and offspring (*Dust* and *Cruel Embrace*). *Between Heaven and Earth* is the story of Maria, a high-powered and unmarried television journalist who has devoted herself to her career and ignored the ticking of her biological time clock. After an erotic encounter in a stalled elevator, Maria finds herself pregnant. She feels she can effortlessly juggle motherhood and career, and so she decides to have the child. Notwithstanding, as her pregnancy progresses Maria begins to question her decision to bring a human being into the world. While completing some job-related research, she watches a videotape of emaciated children. She covers a bomb blast at a university and is jarred by the sight of terrorized young people and how this place of learning—where her child just might be in 20 years—can be rocked by violence and death. She also comes in touch with the more general issue of how mankind is mistreating the environment, and is no longer in harmony with nature.

The most telling relationship in *Between Heaven and Earth* is between Maria and Jeremy, a little boy whose parents recently moved into her apartment building. They are never around (and are not seen on camera), and Maria observes Jeremy's resentment over his situation. Maria and Jeremy bond and, despite his youth, he takes on the role of her teacher. She feels that she can leave her baby at a nursery; he points out that maybe the baby would not want to be abandoned in such a way.

Then Maria comes to believe that her fetus is communicating with her, and telling her that it does not want to be born into a world that is so hostile to children. After refusing an induced labor and endangering the life of the baby, Maria realizes that, despite the world's ills, giving birth is an affirmation, an act of faith. At the finale she has her baby, with whom she shares the kind of harmony she could not have conceived scant months earlier.

Between Heaven and Earth is a profoundly intellectual film. Hänsel points out that, on one hand, science has allowed mankind to produce test-tube babies. Yet in a society in which adults are increasingly career-oriented and self-involved, there is no longer room for children: witness Jeremy, who is all by himself and has neither a place to play nor children with whom to be friends.

The closeness and understanding that develops between Maria and Jeremy mirrors the primary relationship in *Between the Devil and the Deep Blue Sea,* which chronicles the passing friendship between Nikos, a rootless, opium-addicted sailor whose ship docks in Hong Kong, and Li, a bright ten-year-old who earns her living by cleaning the ships in the harbor. Li is an involuntary participant in a sampan subculture in which she is little more than an indentured servant. Yet despite her plight, her optimism has allowed her to preserve her innocence. Here, too, the adult learns from the child. When Nikos asks Li why she takes on responsibility, she responds, "That's what life is all about."

Between Heaven and Earth and *Between the Devil and the Deep Blue Sea* make stark contrasts to *Dust* and *Cruel Embrace. Dust* (which, tellingly, Hänsel dedicates "to my father") is a psychological portrait of Magda, a woman who lives with her father (who is nameless) in a remote region of South Africa, where they tend a small sheep farm. Magda's life is not so much one of isolation as frustration and regret. At the outset, she expresses her thoughts about how, over the years, she and her father have faced each other in silence. She craves his love and attention, yet her connection to him is strictly servile. In their first scene together he barks out her name. She promptly enters the room, offers him a drink, and removes his boots.

"I should have been a man," Magda declares. "I would have spent my days in the sun, doing whatever it is that men do." Rather than leaving her father and going off to make her own life, Magda is living a self-imposed prison sentence with her father as her jailor: a situation that results in her growing psychological breakdown, and her eventually murdering him after watching him seduce the shy wife of their farm's foreman. Magda cannot bear that her father is giving this young woman the attention—sexual and otherwise—that she covets.

Cruel Embrace also depicts a less-than-idyllic parent-child relationship. It is the story of a boy named Ludovic, who is despised by Nicole, his emotionally tormented and alcoholic mother, because he was conceived while she was brutally raped. Ludovic first is locked in an attic, and then is committed to an insane asylum. Yet like Magda, his need for, and love of, his parent transcends the manner in which he is so heartlessly treated.

In *Between Heaven and Earth* and *Dust,* Hänsel explores the interior lives and complex emotional states of women. In this regard, they are linked to *The Bed,* her debut feature, the story of a desperately ill man and the two women, his first and present wives, who are at his bedside as he approaches death.

In most of her films, however, Hänsel's primary concern is a fascination with children and their world views, and the manner in which they cope within their often hostile environments. "Childhood. . . clear of mind, unprejudiced and uncompromising," she has declared, "children with their courage (which we adults lack) have the power to change us. . . the world. To watch them, to listen and to stay close to them, reassures, guides and helps me to make my films."—ROB EDELMAN

Harris, Leslie

American director

Born *Cleveland, Ohio, 1959.* ***Education*** *Attended Denison University, M.F.A. in painting.* ***Career*** *1980s—moved to New York and worked for an advertising agency; directed television commercials.* ***Awards*** *Special Jury Prize for a First Feature, Sundance Film Festival, for* Just Another Girl on the I.R.T., *1993; Open Palm, Independent Feature Project Gotham Award, 1993.*

Film as Director, Writer, and Producer: 1992: *Just Another Girl on the I.R.T.*

At the end of *Just Another Girl on the I.R.T.*—independently produced and shot in 17 days—the audience is informed that they have just sat through "A Film Hollywood Dared Not Do." This is true insofar as Hollywood has denied access to African-American women filmmakers, and *Just Another Girl on the I.R.T.* was directed, produced, and scripted by an African-American woman, Leslie Harris. Prior to its release, among the tens of thousands of films made in Hollywood across the decades, Euzhan Palcy's *A Dry White Season* was the *lone* one directed by a black woman. This fact speaks volumes about racism and sexism in Hollywood and American history.

Nevertheless, any film made by any filmmaker whether inside or outside the cinema mainstream must be held to artistic and technical standards. A film should not automatically be financed and released, critically acclaimed and showered with prizes solely because its maker is a woman or a person of color, and its content is politically correct.

In the case of *Just Another Girl on the I.R.T.*, it would fair to surmise that the movie industry powers-that-be passed on it not because of a conspiracy to silence the voices of African-American women filmmakers. Instead, maybe they nixed it because its script was appallingly simplistic, and annoyingly manipulative.

Just Another Girl on the I.R.T., which to date is Harris's only feature, is significant insomuch as it tells the story of a black adolescent female who is more than on-screen window dressing in a male-dominated scenario. She is Chantel (Ariyan Johnson, whose likable performance is the film's sole saving grace), a spirited 17-year-old African American and child of inner-city hip-hop culture who desires to flee her stifling Brooklyn housing project by heading off to college, and then to medical school. But her plans are altered when she discovers she is pregnant.

Cinematically, *Just Another Girl on the I.R.T.* is astonishingly amateurish. The climactic scene, in which Chantel gives birth, is especially embarrassing as it is so poorly staged. And what of Harris's script? It is shrill and one-note, as well as racially loaded. For one thing, Harris hypocritically depicts her only two white characters in broad, mean-spirited terms. One is a snooty lady, a customer in the store in which Chantel works after school. This character acts as if she is the mistress of an antebellum plantation. The other is a narrow-minded Jewish history instructor who only wants to teach his all-black class about the Holocaust. He does not cite instances in which blacks have been discriminated against over the centuries. He responds to Chantel's complaints with a shrug, as he notes that he only is teaching what is in his curriculum.

In the production notes of *Just Another Girl on the I.R.T.,* Harris is quoted as follows: "It's time that we start seeing characters on the screen that are real." Yet the manner in which she depicts the customer and history teacher is broadly cliched, and serves as evidence that an African-American filmmaker can be as thoughtless, insensitive, and racist as a white one.

Chantel may be 17, with her bravado masking a child-woman who is scared and confused, but it is hard to feel anything for her but contempt. This is because, ultimately, she is a fraud. This shining beacon of feminism spouts rhetoric about a woman's right to self-determination. Yet she dumps her boyfriend, Gerard, who is as poor as she is and only can take her out on dates on the subway. What is her attraction to her new boyfriend, Tyrone? He has money. He drives a jeep. And, conveniently, the actor who plays him is attractive and charming, while the actor cast as Gerard is comically goofy.

After impregnating Chantel, Tyrone gives her $500 for an abortion. What does Chantel do with the money? She irresponsibly squanders it in one afternoon, on a shopping spree with a girlfriend.

Just Another Girl on the I.R.T. may be compared to *Girls Town,* another film which depicts the experience of inner city adolescent females. *Girls Town,* directed by Jim McKay, is a vivid slice-of-life about an interracial quartet of working-class teens who are completing their senior year in high school. At the outset, one of the group—a bright and attractive African American—inexplicably commits suicide. There is much soul-searching and sharing of feelings among the survivors; on one level, watching *Girls Town* is like taking a peek at a group therapy session involving these characters.

Girls Town is a story of female bonding, and female friendship. The few adults in the film have had little impact on the characters' lives. Furthermore, their involvement with males mostly is contentious. Boys either do not understand them, or regard them merely as receptacles for physical and verbal abuse and sex. *Girls Town* is extremely effective as a feminist tract about how girls can be as tough and self-sufficient as boys. They must not allow themselves to be victimized by boys. In fact, they must demand nothing less than respect from the opposite sex. Unlike *Just Another Girl on the I.R.T., Girls Town* is emotionally honest. It portrays the confusion of youth without making excuses for its characters' lack of judgment or life experience.

In the 1990s, a list of films, directed by African-Americans, which offer illuminating, multilayered scenarios and characterizations just begins with *Boyz N the Hood, Menace II Society, Dead Presidents, Daughters of the Dust, To Sleep with Anger, Clockers, Malcolm X, Get on the Bus.* While these films vary in quality and subject matter, all have what *Just Another Girl on the I.R.T.* sorely lacks: maturity and integrity. As film critic Gene Seymour, in his *Newsday* review of the film, observed, "The best you could say about *I.R.T.* is that it gives you a view of life you don't often see in the movies. But as the African-American film movement continues to grow in ambition and achievement, just getting these stories on screen won't be enough. Thinking them through and making them sturdy will."—ROB EDELMAN

Harrison, Joan

British writer and producer

***Born** Guildford, Surrey, England, 20 June 1909.* ***Education** Attended the Sorbonne, Paris; Oxford University, B.A.* ***Family** Married the writer Eric Ambler, 1958.* ***Career** Secretary; 1935—began working as Alfred Hitchcock's secretary; 1937—first film as writer for Hitchcock,* Young and Innocent; *accompanied Hitchcock to the United States; 1944—first film as producer,* Phantom Lady; *1953-64—producer of the TV series* Alfred Hitchcock Presents; *1964—co-founder, Tarantula Productions.* ***Died** 14 August 1994.*

Films as Writer: 1937: *Young and Innocent* (*The Girl Was Young*) (Hitchcock). **1939:** *Jamaica Inn* (Hitchcock). **1940:** *Rebecca* (Hitchcock); *Foreign Correspondent* (Hitchcock). **1941:** *Suspicion* (Hitchcock). **1942:** *Saboteur* (Hitchcock). **1943:** *Shadow of a Doubt* (Hitchcock). **1944:** *Dark Waters* (de Toth).

Films as Producer: 1944: *Phantom Lady* (Siodmak) (+ co-sc). **1945:** *Uncle Harry* (*The Strange Affair of Uncle Harry*) (Siodmak). **1946:** *Nocturne* (Marin) (+ co-sc). **1947:** *They Won't Believe Me* (Pichel); *Ride the Pink Horse* (Montgomery) (+ co-sc, uncredited). **1949:** *Once More, My Darling* (Montgomery). **1950:** *Your Witness* (*Eye Witness*) (Montgomery) (+ co-sc); *Circle of Danger* (J. Tourneur).

Those who think that there were no women producers in the old Hollywood studio system have perhaps never heard of the remarkable Joan Harrison. A wise woman who always made the most of her opportunities, the young Harrison took a job as secretary to Alfred Hitchcock, with a reduction in salary and status from her former position in an advertising department of a London newspaper. ("I am probably the worst secretary Hitch ever had," she once told *Modern Screen* magazine.) Working for Hitchcock in the British film industry, she was able to invade every department and learn all aspects of the business, so when her opportunity to become a Hollywood producer came along, she was more than prepared. In her eight years with Hitchcock, she collaborated with him on several of his best screenplays: *Rebecca, Foreign Correspondent, Suspicion,* and *Saboteur* among them. Ultimately she returned to work with him as the producer of his acclaimed television series, *Alfred Hitchcock Presents.*

Harrison's mark was made in various types of crime films, particularly those which featured a woman in jeopardy. She had always been interested in criminal cases, and had followed many of England's more colorful examples through the courts of London. (She married the famous spy genre author Eric Ambler.) Her first film away from Hitchcock in Hollywood, as writer and associate producer, was *Dark Waters,* directed by Andre de Toth. It established the Harrison style in that it was a story about a young woman (Merle Oberon) caught in a *Gaslight* situation, being driven mad by a group of false relatives. Harrison's first feature as full producer was the much respected low-budget film noir *Phantom Lady,* directed by Robert Siodmak, starring Ella Raines as a fearless secretary bent on proving her boss did not actually murder his wife. These two excellent small pictures illustrate what would always be true of Harrison's work—she was a totally competent producer capable of making stylish mystery films from the woman's angle. They also illustrate a handicap she was never able to overcome in terms of critical acceptance: she seemed forever destined to remain in Hitchcock's shadow. In addition, her solo productions are almost all directed by men such as de Toth and Siodmak, who, like Hitchcock, are well known for a personal vision. Thus, it was not only difficult to identify what might be her touch, but no one seemed willing to try to do so. Perhaps the outstanding thing that can be said for Harrison is that the films she produced were often complimented for "being in the

Hitchcock tradition." This meant that she had learned her lessons well from the master, and that she *was* capable of putting that stamp on her movies. All of Harrison's films have these qualities in common: excellent women characters, who are frequently intrepid in their response to danger and death; a low-key, subtle suggestion of violence rather than overt blood and gore; and elegant production values, with handsome sets and modish costumes.

A thoughtful woman who always utilized what she had learned in her experience with Hitchcock, Harrison commented on what made an effective suspense thriller by saying:

> There is a difference between violence and action. The two are not synonymous. This is a very important point to consider. Displayed violence, blow-by-blow account violence is irresponsible, unnecessary, and unworthy of creativity. Action, on the other hand, cannot be totally implied or merely suggested. For whodunits, no action is pretty bloody dull. Many persons equate in their minds action and violence. They speak of one when they mean the other. Each is an individual property, and suggested violence is much more interesting. I see no point in plunging a dagger in someone's chest and the viewer watching this unfold. One should see the dagger in the hand of the manipulator and then shift—the horror that results! This way is suspenseful and the audience gets involved.

Although her list of films is small, it displays subtle, tasteful suspense work in well-photographed, stylish films. It is also unique because few women achieved her status. Commenting on her unusual role as Hollywood's top female producer in the 1940s, Harrison remarked, "We women have to work twice as hard to be recognized in our own fields. But today there is more recognition of women's talents than ever before. Those women who want a career can certainly have one." The most obvious thing to say about Harrison's career is that what is remarkable about it is that it exists at all. Her work, however, is of a level of taste and intelligence that qualifies her as something more than an oddity or a footnote, and certainly has earned her the right to be seen separately from, if not equal to, Alfred Hitchcock.—JEANINE BASINGER

Head, Edith

American costume designer

Born *Edith Claire Posener in San Bernardino, California, 28 October 1897.* ***Education*** *Attended elementary school in Redding, California to 1911; schools in Los Angeles; University of California, Berkeley; Stanford University; also attended classes at Otis Art Institute and Chouinard Art School, both in Los Angeles.* ***Family*** *Married 1) Charles Head (divorced 1938); 2) the designer Wiard Ihnen, 1940 (died 1979).* ***Career*** *1923—French, Spanish, and art teacher at Bishop School for Girls, La Jolla, California, and at Hollywood School for Girls; 1924-27—sketch artist; 1927-38—assistant to Travis Banton; 1938-66—head of design, Paramount; then chief designer at Universal until her death; also designed for other studios, for stage shows, and for commercial companies; 1945-52—regular appearances on the radio show* Art Linkletter's House Party *(and on TV, 1952-69); 1949-51—lecturer, University of Southern California, Los Angeles (also in 1973); 1978—designed for the TV miniseries* Little Women. ***Awards*** *Academy Awards, for* The Heiress, *1949,* Samson and Delilah, *1949,* All about Eve, *1950,* A Place in the Sun, *1951,* Roman

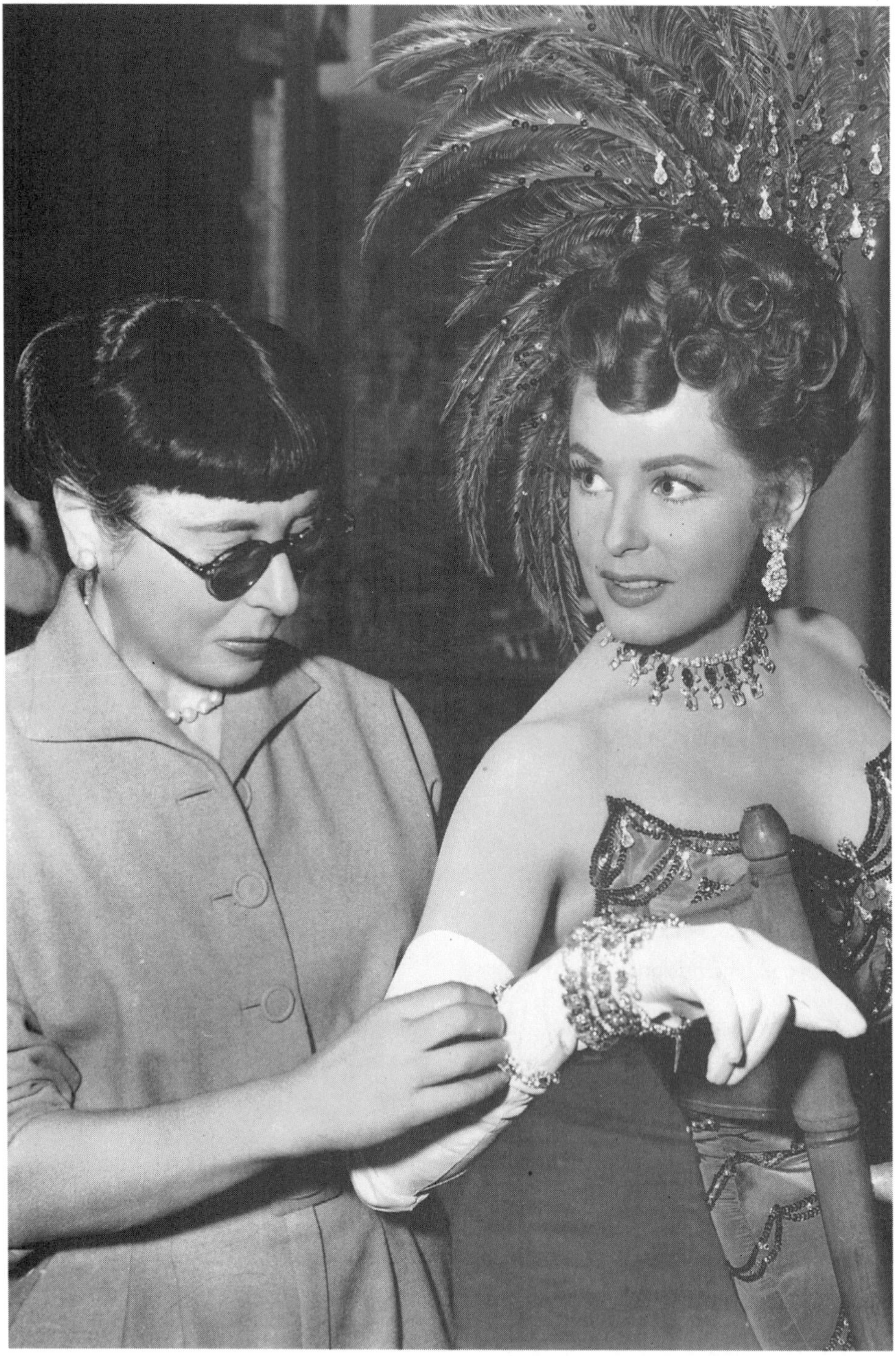

Edith Head (left) with Arlene Dahl

Holiday, *1953,* Sabrina, *1954,* The Facts of Life, *1960, and* The Sting, *1973.* ***Died*** *In Los Angeles, 24 October 1981.*

Films as Costume Designer: 1924: *Peter Pan* (Brenon) (co). **1925:** *The Golden Bed* (C. B. DeMille) (co); *The Wanderer* (Walsh) (co). **1926:** *Mantrap* (Fleming). **1927:** *Wings* (Wellman). **1929:** *The Saturday Night Kid* (Sutherland) (co); *The Virginian* (Fleming); *The Wolf Song* (Fleming). **1930:** *Along Came Youth* (Corrigan and McLeod); *Follow the Leader* (Taurog); *Only the Brave* (Tuttle); *The Santa Fe Trail* (Brower and Knopf). **1932:** *The Big Broadcast of 1932* (Tuttle); *A Farewell to Arms* (Borzage) (co); *He Learned about Women* (Corrigan); *Hot Saturday* (Seiter); *Love Me Tonight* (Mamoulian); *The Sign of the Cross* (Banton) (co); *Two Kinds of Women* (W. de Mille); *Undercover Man* (Flood); *Wayward* (Sloman). **1933:** *A Cradle Song* (Leisen) (co); *Crime of the Century* (Beaudine) (co); *Duck Soup* (McCarey); *Gambling Ship* (Gasnier and Marcin); *Hello, Everybody* (Seiter); *I'm No Angel* (Ruggles) (co); *She Done Him Wrong* (L. Sherman); *Sitting Pretty* (H. Brown); *Strictly Personal* (Murphy); *White Woman* (Walker) (co). **1934:** *Ladies Should Listen* (Tuttle); *Little Miss Marker* (Hall); *Many Happy Returns* (McLeod); *The Notorious Sophie Lang* (Murphy) (co); *The Pursuit of Happiness* (Hall); *The Witching Hour* (Hathaway); *You Belong to Me* (Werker). **1935:** *The Big Broadcast of 1936* (Taurog); *Car 99* (Barton); *The Crusades* (C. B. DeMille) (co); *Father Brown, Detective* (Sedgwick); *Four Hours to Kill* (Leisen); *The Glass Key* (Tuttle); *Here Comes Cookie* (McLeod); *Hold 'em, Yale* (Lanfield); *The Last Outpost* (Barton and Gasnier); *The Lives of a Bengal Lancer* (Hathaway) (co); *Man on the Flying Trapeze* (Bruckman); *Men without Names* (Murphy); *Mississippi* (Sutherland); *People Will Talk* (Santell); *Peter Ibbetson* (Hathaway); *Ruggles of Red Gap* (McCarey) (co); *Stolen Harmony* (Werker); *Two for Tonight* (Tuttle); *Wings in the Dark* (Flood). **1936:** *The Accusing Finger* (Hogan); *The Big Broadcast of 1937* (Leisen); *Border Flight* (Lovering); *College Holiday* (Tuttle); *Collegiate* (Murphy); *Hollywood Boulevard* (Florey); *The Jungle Princess* (Thiele); *Lady Be Careful* (Reed); *The Milky Way* (McCarey); *Murder with Pictures* (Barton); *Poppy* (Sutherland); *The Return of Sophie Lang* (Archainbaud); *Rhythm on the Range* (Taurog); *Rose Bowl* (Barton); *The Texas Rangers* (K. Vidor); *Thirteen Hours by Air* (Leisen); *Three Cheers for Love* (McCarey); *Till We Meet Again* (Florey); *Too Many Parents* (McGowan); *Wedding Present* (Wallace); *Wives Never Know* (Nugent) (co); *Woman Trap* (H. Young). **1937:** *Arizona Mahoney* (Hogan); *Artists and Models* (Walsh) (co); *The Barrier* (Selander); *Blonde Trouble* (Archainbaud); *Blossoms on Broadway* (Wallace); *Borderland* (Watt); *Born to the West* (Barton); *Bulldog Drummond Comes Back* (L. King); *Bulldog Drummond Escapes* (Hogan); *Bulldog Drummond's Revenge* (L. King); *Clarence* (Archainbaud); *The Crime Nobody Saw* (Barton); *Daughter of Shanghai* (Florey); *A Doctor's Diary* (C. Vidor) (co); *Double or Nothing* (Reed); *Easy Living* (Leisen) (co); *Ebb Tide* (Hogan); *Exclusive* (Hall); *Forlorn River* (Barton); *Girl from Scotland Yard* (Vignola); *The Great Gambini* (C. Vidor); *Her Husband Lies* (Ludwig) (co); *Hideaway Girl* (Archainbaud); *Hills of Old Wyoming* (Watt); *Hold 'em, Navy* (Neumann); *Hopalong Rides Again* (Selander); *Hotel Haywire* (Archainbaud); *Interns Can't Take Money* (Santell); *John Meade's Woman* (Wallace) (co); *King of Gamblers* (Florey); *The Last Train from Madrid* (Hogan); *Let's Make a Million* (McCarey); *Love on Toast* (Dupont); *Make Way for Tomorrow* (McCarey); *Midnight Madonna* (Flood); *Mind Your Own Business* (McLeod); *Mountain Music* (Florey); *Murder Goes to College* (Riesner); *Night Club Scandal* (Murphy); *A Night of Mystery* (Dupont); *North of the Rio Grande* (Watt); *On Such a Night* (Dupont); *Outcast* (Florey); *Partners in Crime* (Murphy); *Partners of the Plains* (Selander); *Rustler's Valley* (Watt); *She Asked for It* (Kenton); *She's No Lady* (C. Vidor); *Sophie Lang Goes West* (Riesner) (co); *Souls at Sea* (Hathaway); *Texas Trail* (Selman); *This Way, Please* (Florey); *Thrill of a Lifetime* (Archainbaud); *Thunder Trail* (Barton); *True Confession* (Ruggles) (co); *Turn Off the Moon* (Seiler); *Waikiki Wedding* (Tuttle); *Wells Fargo* (Lloyd); *Wild Money* (L. King). **1938:** *The Arkansas Traveler* (Santell); *Bar 20 Justice* (Selander); *Artists and Models Abroad* (Leisen) (co); *The Big Broadcast of 1938* (Leisen); *Booloo* (Elliott); *The Buccaneer* (C. B. DeMille); *Bulldog Drummond in Africa* (L. King); *Campus Confessions* (Archainbaud); *Bulldog Drummond's Peril* (Hogan); *Cassidy of Bar 20* (Selander); *Coconut Grove* (Santell); *College Swing* (Walsh); *Dangerous to Know* (Florey); *Doctor Rhythm* (Tuttle) (co); *The Frontiersman* (Selander); *Give Me a Sailor* (Nugent); *Heart of Arizona* (Selander); *Her Jungle Love* (Archainbaud); *Hunted Men* (L. King); *Illegal Traffic* (L. King); *In Old Mexico* (Venturini); *King of Alcatraz* (Florey); *Little Orphan Annie* (Holmes); *Men with Wings* (Wellman); *The Mysterious Rider* (Selander); *Pride of the West* (Selander); *Prison Farm* (L. King); *Professor Beware* (Nugent); *Ride a Crooked Mile* (A. E. Green); *Say It in French* (A. L. Stone); *Scandal Sheet* (Hogan); *Sing, You Sinners* (Ruggles); *Sons of the Legion* (Hogan); *Spawn of the North* (Hathaway); *Stolen Heaven* (A. L. Stone); *The Texans* (Hogan); *Thanks for* *the Memory* (Archainbaud); *Tip-Off Girls* (L. King); *Tom Sawyer, Detective* (L. King); *Touchdown Army* (Neumann); *Tropic Holiday* (Reed); *You and Me* (F. Lang). **1939:** *All Women Have Secrets* (Neumann); *Arrest Bulldog Drummond* (Hogan); *Back Door to Heaven* (W. K. Howard); *The Beachcomber* (Pommer); *Beau Geste* (Wellman); *Boy Trouble* (Archainbaud); *Bulldog Drummond's Bride* (Hogan); *Café Society* (E. Griffith); *Bulldog Drummond's Secret Police* (Hogan); *The Cat and the Canary* (Nugent); *Death of a Champion* (Florey); *Disbarred* (Florey); *Disputed Passage* (Borzage); *Geronimo* (Sloane); *The Gracie Allen Murder Case* (A. E. Green); *Grand Jury Secrets* (Hogan); *The Great Victor Herbert* (A. L. Stone); *Heritage of the Desert* (Selander); *Honeymoon in Bali* (E. Griffith); *Hotel Imperial* (Florey); *Invitation to Happiness* (Ruggles); *Island of Lost Men* (Neumann); *I'm from Missouri* (Reed); *King of Chinatown* (Grinde); *The Lady's from Kentucky* (Hall); *Law of the Pampas* (Watt); *The Llano Kid* (Venturini); *The Magnificent Fraud* (Florey); *Man about Town* (M. Sandrich); *Man of Conquest* (Nicholls) (co); *Midnight* (Leisen) (co); *Million Dollar Legs* (Grinde); *Never Say Die* (Nugent); *The Night of Nights* (Milestone); *Night Work* (Archainbaud); *$1,000 a Touchdown* (Hogan); *Our Leading Citizen* (Santell); *Our Neighbors, the Carters* (Murphy); *Paris Honeymoon* (Tuttle); *Persons in Hiding* (L. King); *Range War* (Selander); *The Renegade Trail* (Selander); *Rulers of the Sea* (Lloyd); *Silver on the Sage* (Selander); *Some Like It Hot* (Archainbaud); *The Star Maker* (Del Ruth); *St. Louis Blues* (Walsh); *Sudden Money* (Grinde); *The Sunset Trail* (Selander); *Television Spy* (Dmytryk); *This Man Is News* (McDonald); *Undercover Doctor* (L. King); *Union Pacific* (C. B. DeMille); *Unmarried* (Neumann); *What a Life* (Reed); *Zaza* (Cukor).

1940: *Adventure in Diamonds* (Fitzmaurice); *Arise, My Love* (Leisen) (co); *The Biscuit Eater* (Heisler); *Buck Benny Rides Again* (M. Sandrich); *The Cherokee Strip* (Selander); *Christmas in July* (P. Sturges); *Comin' round the Mountain* (Archainbaud); *Dancing on a Dime* (Santley); *Doctor Cyclops* (Schoedsack); *Emergency Squad* (Dmytryk); *The Farmer's Daughter* (Hogan); *French without Tears* (Asquith) (co); *Golden Gloves* (Dmytryk); *The Ghost Breakers* (George Marshall); *The Great McGinty* (P. Sturges); *Hidden Gold* (Selander); *I Want a Divorce* (Murphy); *Knights of the Range* (Selander); *Light of Western Stars* (Selander); *The Light That Failed* (Wellman); *Love Thy Neighbor* (M. Sandrich); *Moon over Burma* (L. King); *Mystery Sea Raider* (Dmytryk); *A Night at Earl Carroll's* (Neumann); *Northwest Mounted Police* (C. B. DeMille) (co); *Opened by Mistake* (Archainbaud); *A Parole Fixer* (Florey); *The Quarterback* (Humberstone); *Queen of the Mob* (Hogan); *Rangers of Fortune* (Wood); *Remember the Night* (Leisen); *Rhythm on the River* (Schertzinger); *Road to Singapore* (Schertzinger); *Safari* (E. Griffith); *Santa Fe Marshal* (Selander); *Seventeen* (L. King); *The Showdown* (Bretherton); *Stagecoach War* (Selander); *Texas Rangers Ride Again* (Hogan); *Those Were the Days* (Reed); *Three Men from Texas* (Selander); *Typhoon* (L. King); *Untamed* (Archainbaud); *Victory* (Cromwell); *The Way of All Flesh* (L. King); *Women without Names* (Florey); *World in Flames* (Richard). **1941:** *Aloma of the South Seas* (Santell); *Among the Living* (Heisler); *Bahama Passage* (E. Griffith); *Ball of Fire* (Hawks); *Birth of the Blues* (Schertzinger); *Border Vigilantes* (Abrahams); *Buy Me That Town* (Forde); *Caught in the Draft* (D. Butler); *Doomed Caravan* (Selander); *Flying Blind* (McDonald); *Forced Landing* (Wiles); *Glamour Boy* (Tetzlaff); *Henry Aldrich for President* (Bennett); *Here Comes Mr. Jordan* (Hall); *Hold back the Dawn* (Leisen); *I Wanted Wings* (Leisen); *In Old Colorado* (Bretherton); *Kiss the Boys Goodbye* (Schertzinger); *The Lady Eve* (P. Sturges); *Las Vegas Nights* (Murphy); *Life with Henry* (Reed); *The Mad Doctor* (Whelan); *The Monster and the Girl* (Heisler); *New York Town* (C. Vidor); *The Night of January 16th* (Clemens); *Nothing But the Truth* (Nugent); *One Night in Lisbon* (E. Griffith); *The Parson of Panamint* (McGann); *Pirates on Horseback* (Selander); *Power Dive* (Hogan); *Reaching for the Sun* (Wellman); *Road to Zanzibar* (Schertzinger); *Roundup* (Selander); *Secret of the Wastelands* (Abrahams); *Shepherd of the Hills* (Hathaway); *Skylark* (M. Sandrich) (co); *Sullivan's Travels* (P. Sturges); *Virginia* (E. Griffith); *There's a Magic in the Music* (Stone); *West Point Widow* (Siodmak); *Wide-Open Town* (Selander); *World Premiere* (Tetzlaff); *You Belong to Me* (Ruggles); *You're the One* (Murphy). **1942:** *Are Husbands Necessary?* (Taurog); *Beyond the Blue Horizon* (Santell); *The Fleet's In* (Schertzinger); *The Gay Sisters* (Rapper) (co); *The Glass Key* (Heisler); *The Great Man's Lady* (Wellman); *Henry Aldrich, Editor* (Bennett); *Holiday Inn* (M. Sandrich); *I Married a Witch* (Clair); *The Lady Has Plans* (Lanfield); *Lucky Jordan* (Tuttle); *The Major and the Minor* (Wilder); *Mrs. Wiggs of the Cabbage Patch* (Murphy); *My Favorite Blonde* (Lanfield); *My Heart Belongs to Daddy* (Siodmak); *The Palm Beach Story* (P. Sturges) (co); *The Remarkable Andrew* (Heisler); *Road to Morocco* (D. Butler); *Star-Spangled Rhythm* (George Marshall); *This Gun for Hire* (Tuttle); *Wake Island* (Farrow); *Young and Willing* (E. Griffith). **1943:** *China* (Farrow); *The Crystal Bell* (Nugent); *Five Graves to Cairo* (Wilder); *Flesh and Fantasy* (Duvivier) (co); *For Whom the Bell Tolls* (Wood); *The Good Fellows* (Graham); *Happy Go Lucky* (Bernhardt); *Henry Aldrich Gets Glamour* (Bennett); *Hostages* (Tuttle); *Henry Aldrich Haunts a House* (Bennett); *Lady Bodyguard* (Clemens); *Lady of Burlesque* (Wellman) (co); *Let's Face It* (Lanfield); *Night Plane from Chungking* (Murphy); *No Time for Love* (Leisen) (co); *Riding High* (George Marshall); *Salute for Three* (Murphy); *Tender Comrade* (Dmytryk) (co); *They Got Me Covered* (D. Butler) (co); *True to Life* (George Marshall). **1944:** *And Now Tomorrow* (Pichel); *And the Angels Sing* (George Marshall); *Double Indemnity* (Wilder); *Going My Way* (McCarey); *The Great Moment* (P. Sturges); *Hail the Conquering Hero* (P. Sturges); *Henry Aldrich's Little Secret* (Bennett); *The Hitler Gang* (Farrow); *Here Come the Waves* (M. Sandrich); *The Hour before the Dawn* (Tuttle); *I Love a Soldier* (M. Sandrich); *I'll Be Seeing You* (Dieterle); *Lady in the Dark* (Leisen) (co); *The Man in Half Moon Street* (Murphy); *Ministry of Fear* (F. Lang); *The Miracle of Morgan's Creek* (P. Sturges); *National Barn Dance* (Bennett); *Rainbow Island* (Murphy); *Our Hearts Were Young and Gay* (L. Allen); *The Uninvited* (L. Allen); *Standing Room Only* (Lanfield); *Till We Meet Again* (Borzage); *You Can't Ration Love* (Fuller). **1945:** *The Affairs of Susan* (Seiter); *The Bells of St. Mary's* (McCarey); *Bring on the Girls* (Lanfield); *Christmas in Connecticut* (Godfrey) (co); *Duffy's Tavern* (Walker) (co); *Hold That Blonde* (George Marshall); *Incendiary Blonde* (George Marshall); *The Lost Weekend* (Wilder); *Love Letters* (Dieterle); *Masquerade in Mexico* (Leisen); *A Medal for Benny* (Pichel); *Miss Susie Slagle's* (Berry) (co); *Murder, He Says* (George Marshall); *Out of this World* (Walker); *Road to Utopia* (Walker); *Salty O'Rourke* (Walsh); *The Stork Club* (Walker); *You Came Along* (Farrow). **1946:** *The Blue Dahlia* (George Marshall); *Blue Skies* (Heisler) (co); *The Bride Wore Boots* (Pichel); *Monsieur Beaucaire* (George Marshall); *My Reputation* (Bernhardt) (co); *Notorious* (Hitchcock); *Our Hearts Were Growing Up* (Russell); *The Perfect Marriage* (L. Allen); *The Strange Love of Martha Ivers* (Milestone); *To Each His Own* (Leisen); *The Virginian* (Gilmore); *The Well-Groomed Bride* (Lanfield). **1947:** *Blaze of Noon* (Farrow); *Calcutta* (Farrow); *California* (Farrow) (co); *Cross My Heart* (Berry); *Cry Wolf* (Godfrey) (co); *Dear Ruth* (Russell); *Desert Fury* (L. Allen); *Easy Come, Easy Go* (Farrow); *I Walk Alone* (Haskin); *The Imperfect Lady* (L. Allen) (co); *My Favorite Brunette* (Nugent); *The Other Love* (de Toth) (co); *The Perils of Pauline* (George Marshall); *Ramrod* (de Toth); *Road to Rio* (McLeod); *The Trouble with Women* (Lanfield); *The Two Mrs. Carrolls* (Godfrey) (co); *Variety Girl* (George Marshall) (co); *Welcome Stranger* (Nugent); *Where There's Life* (Lanfield); *Wild Harvest* (Garnett). **1948:** *The Accused* (Dieterle); *Arch of Triumph* (Milestone) (co); *Beyond Glory* (Farrow); *The Big Clock* (Farrow); *Dream Girl* (Leisen); *The Emperor Waltz* (Wilder) (co); *Enchantment* (Reis) (co); *A Foreign Affair* (Wilder); *Isn't It Romantic?* (McLeod); *June Bride* (Windust) (co); *Miss Tatlock's Millions* (Haydn); *My Own True Love* (Bennett); *The Night Has a Thousand Eyes* (Farrow); *Saigon* (Fenton); *Rachel and the Stranger* (Foster); *The Sainted Sisters* (Russell); *The Sealed Verdict* (L. Allen); *So Evil My Love* (L. Allen) (co); *Sorry, Wrong Number* (Litvak); *Whispering Smith* (Fenton) (co). **1949:** *The Great Gatsby* (Nugent); *Beyond the Forest* (K. Vidor); *The Great Lover* (Hall); *The Heiress* (Wyler) (co); *Malaya* (Thorpe) (co); *Manhandled* (Foster); *My Foolish Heart* (Robson) (co); *My Friend Irma* (George Marshall); *Red, Hot, and Blue* (Farrow); *Rope of Sand* (Dieterle); *Samson and Delilah* (C. B. DeMille) (co); *Song of Surrender* (Leisen).

1950: *All about Eve* (J. Mankiewicz) (co); *Copper Canyon* (Farrow) (co); *The Dark City* (Dieterle); *Fancy Pants* (George Marshall); *The File on Thelma Jordan* (Siodmak); *The Furies* (A. Mann); *Let's Dance* (McLeod); *Mr. Music* (Haydn); *My Friend Irma Goes West* (Walker); *Paid in Full* (Dieterle); *No Man of Her Own* (Leisen); *Riding High* (Capra); *September Affair* (Dieterle); *Sunset Boulevard* (Wilder). **1951:** *The Big Carnival* (Wilder); *Branded* (Maté); *Crosswinds* (Foster); *Darling, How Could You?* (Leisen); *Dear Brat* (Seiter); *Detective Story* (Wyler); *Here Comes the Groom* (Capra); *Hong Kong* (Foster); *The Last Outpost* (Foster); *The Lemon Drop Kid* (Lanfield); *My Favorite Spy* (McLeod); *Payment on Demand* (Bernhardt) (co); *Peking Express* (Dieterle); *A Place in the Sun* (Stevens); *Rhubarb* (Lubin); *Silver City* (Haskin); *The Stooge* (Taurog); *Submarine Command* (Farrow); *That's My Boy* (Walker); *When Worlds Collide* (Maté). **1952:** *Aaron Slick from Punkin Crick* (Binyon); *Caribbean* (Ludwig); *Anything Can Happen* (Seaton); *Carrie* (Wyler); *Come Back, Little Sheba* (Daniel Mann); *Denver and Rio Grande* (Haskin); *The Greatest Show on Earth* (C. B. DeMille) (co); *Hurricane Smith* (J. Hopper); *Jumping Jacks* (Taurog); *Just for You* (Nugent) (co); *My Son John* (McCarey); *Red Mountain* (Dieterle); *Road to Bali* (Walker); *Ruby Gentry* (K. Vidor); *Sailor Beware* (Walker); *The Savage* (George Marshall); *Somebody Loves Me* (Brecher); *Something to Live For* (Stevens); *Son of Paleface* (Tashlin); *This Is Dynamite* (Dieterle); *The Turning Point* (Dieterle). **1953:** *Arrowhead* (Warren); *The Caddy* (Taurog); *Forever Female* (Rapper); *Here Come the Girls* (Binyon); *Houdini* (George Marshall); *Jamaica Run*

(Foster); *Little Boy Lost* (Seaton); *Off Limits* (George Marshall); *Pleasure Island* (Hugh); *Pony Express* (J. Hopper); *Roman Holiday* (Wyler); *Sangaree* (Ludwig); *Scared Stiff* (George Marshall); *Shane* (Stevens); *Stalag 17* (Wilder); *The Stars Are Singing* (Taurog); *Those Redheads from Seattle* (L. R. Foster); *Thunder in the East* (C. Vidor); *Tropic Zone* (Foster); *The Vanquished* (Ludwig); *War of the Worlds* (Haskin). **1954:** *About Mrs. Leslie* (Daniel Mann); *Alaska Seas* (J. Hopper); *The Bridges at Toko-ri* (Robson); *The Country Girl* (Seaton); *Elephant Walk* (Dieterle); *Jivaro* (Ludwig); *Knock on Wood* (Panama and Frank); *Living It Up* (Taurog); *Money from Home* (George Marshall); *Mr. Casanova* (McLeod); *The Naked Jungle* (Haskin); *Rear Window* (Hitchcock); *Red Garters* (George Marshall) (co); *Sabrina* (Wilder); *Secret of the Incas* (J. Hopper); *Three-Ring Circus* (Pevney); *White Christmas* (Curtiz). **1955:** *Artists and Models* (Tashlin); *Conquest of Space* (Haskin); *The Desperate Hours* (Wyler); *The Far Horizon* (Maté); *The Girl Rush* (Pirosh); *Hell's Island* (Karlson); *Lucy Gallant* (Parrish); *The Rose Tattoo* (Daniel Mann); *Run for Cover* (N. Ray); *The Seven Little Foys* (Shavelson); *Strategic Air Command* (A. Mann); *To Catch a Thief* (Hitchcock); *The Trouble with Harry* (Hitchcock); *You're Never Too Young* (Taurog). **1956:** *Anything Goes* (R. Lewis); *The Birds and the Bees* (Taurog); *The Come-On* (Birdwell); *The Court Jester* (Panama and Frank) (co); *Hollywood or Bust* (Tashlin); *The Leather Saint* (Ganzer); *The Man Who Knew Too Much* (Hitchcock); *The Mountain* (Dmytryk); *Pardners* (Taurog); *The Proud and the Profane* (Seaton); *The Rainmaker* (Anthony); *The Scarlet Hour* (Curtiz); *The Search for Bridey Murphy* (Langley); *The Ten Commandments* (C. B. DeMille) (co); *That Certain Feeling* (Panama and Frank); *Three Violent People* (Maté). **1957:** *Beau James* (Shavelson); *The Buster Keaton Story* (Sheldon); *The Delicate Delinquent* (McGuire); *The Devil's Hairpin* (Wilde); *Fear Strikes Out* (Mulligan); *Funny Face* (Donen) (co); *Gunfight at the O.K. Corral* (J. Sturges); *Hear Me Good* (McGuire); *The Joker Is Wild* (C. Vidor); *The Lonely Man* (Levin); *Loving You* (Kanter); *The Sad Sack* (George Marshall); *Short Cut to Hell* (Cagney); *The Tin Star* (A. Mann); *Wild Is the Wind* (Cukor); *Witness for the Prosecution* (Wilder). **1958:** *As Young as You Are* (Gerard); *The Buccaneer* (Quinn) (co); *The Geisha Boy* (Tashlin); *Hot Spell* (Daniel Mann); *Houseboat* (Shavelson); *Maracaibo* (Wilde); *I Married a Monster from Outer Space* (Fowler); *King Creole* (Curtiz); *The Matchmaker* (Anthony); *Me and the Colonel* (Glenville); *The Party Crashers* (Girard); *Rock-a-Bye Baby* (Tashlin); *Separate Tables* (Delbert Mann) (co); *St. Louis Blues* (Reisner); *Teacher's Pet* (Seton); *Vertigo* (Hitchcock). **1959:** *Alias Jesse James* (McLeod); *The Black Orchid* (Ritt); *But Not for Me* (W. Lang); *Career* (Anthony); *The Hangman* (Curtiz); *Don't Give Up the Ship* (Taurog); *The Five Pennies* (Shavelson); *A Hole in the Head* (Capra); *The Jayhawkers* (Frank); *Last Train from Gun Hill* (J. Sturges); *That Kind of Woman* (Lumet); *Too Young for Love* (Girard); *The Trap* (Panama); *The Young Captives* (Kershner).

1960: *The Bellboy* (J. Lewis); *A Breath of Scandal* (Curtiz); *Cinderfella* (Tashlin); *The Facts of Life* (Frank) (co); *G.I. Blues* (Taurog); *Heller in Pink Tights* (Cukor); *It Started in Naples* (Shavelson); *Pepe* (Sidney); *The Rat Race* (Mulligan); *A Touch of Larceny* (Hamilton); *Visit to a Small Planet* (Taurog). **1961:** *All in a Night's Work* (Anthony); *Blue Hawaii* (Taurog); *Breakfast at Tiffany's* (Edwards) (co); *The Errand Boy* (J. Lewis); *The Ladies' Man* (J. Lewis); *Love in a Goldfish Bowl* (Sher); *Mantrap* (O'Brien); *On the Double* (Shavelson); *The Pleasure of His Company* (Seaton); *Pocketful of Miracles* (Capra); *Summer and Smoke* (Glenville). **1962:** *The Counterfeit Traitor* (Seaton); *Escape from Zahrain* (Neame); *A Girl Named Tamiko* (J. Sturges); *Girls! Girls! Girls!* (Taurog); *Hatari!* (Hawks); *It's Only Money* (Tashlin); *The Man Who Shot Liberty Valance* (Ford); *My Geisha* (Cardiff); *The Pigeon That Took Rome* (Shavelson); *Too Late Blues* (Cassavetes); *Who's Got the Action?* (Daniel Mann). **1963:** *The Birds* (Hitchcock); *Come Blow Your Horn* (Yorkin); *Critic's Choice* (Weis); *Donovan's Reef* (Ford); *Fun in Acapulco* (Thorpe); *Hud* (Ritt); *I Could Go On Singing* (Neame); *My Six Loves* (Champion); *Love with the Proper Stranger* (Mulligan); *A New Kind of Love* (Shavelson) (co); *The Nutty Professor* (J. Lewis); *Papa's Delicate Condition* (George Marshall); *Who's Been Sleeping in My Bed?* (Daniel Mann); *Who's Minding the Store?* (Tashlin); *Wives and Lovers* (Rich). **1964:** *The Carpetbaggers* (Dmytryk); *The Disorderly Orderly* (Tashlin); *A House Is Not a Home* (Rouse); *Lady in a Cage* (Grauman); *Men's Favorite Sport?* (Hawks); *Marnie* (Hitchcock); *The Patsy* (J. Lewis); *Roustabout* (Rich); *Sex and the Single Girl* (Quine) (co); *Thirty-Six Hours* (Seaton); *What a Way to Go* (J. L. Thompson) (co); *Where Love Has Gone* (Dmytryk). **1965:** *Boeing, Boeing* (Rich); *The Family Jewels* (J. Lewis); *The Great Race* (Edwards) (co); *The Hallelujah Trail* (J. Sturges); *Harlow* (G. Douglas) (co); *Inside Daisy Clover* (Mulligan) (co); *John Goldfarb, Please Come Home* (J. L. Thompson) (co); *Love Has Many Faces* (Singer); *Red Line 7000* (Hawks); *The Slender Thread* (Pollack); *The Sons of Katie Elder* (Hathaway); *Sylvia* (G. Douglas); *Who Has Seen the Wind?* (Sidney); *The Yellow Rolls-Royce* (Asquith) (co). **1966:**

Assault on a Queen (Donohue); *The Last of the Secret Agents* (Abbott); *Nevada Smith* (Hathaway); *Not with My Wife, You Don't!* (Panama); *The Oscar* (Rouse); *Paradise, Hawaiian Style* (Moore); *Penelope* (Hiller); *The Swinger* (Sidney); *This Property Is Condemned* (Pollack); *Torn Curtain* (Hitchcock); *Waco* (Springsteen). **1967:** *Barefoot in the Park* (Saks); *The Caper of the Golden Bulls* (Rouse); *Chuka* (G. Douglas); *Easy Come, Easy Go* (Rich); *Hotel* (Quine) (co); *Warning Shot* (Kulik). **1968:** *In Enemy Country* (Keller); *Madigan* (Siegel); *The Pink Jungle* (Delbert Mann); *The Secret War of Harry Frigg* (Smight); *What's So Bad about Feeling Good?* (Seaton). **1969:** *Butch Cassidy and the Sundance Kid* (G. R. Hill); *Downhill Racer* (Ritchie); *Eye of the Cat* (Rich); *The Hellfighters* (McLaglen); *House of Cards* (Guillermin); *The Lost Man* (Arthur); *Sweet Charity* (Fosse); *Tell Them Willie Boy Is Here* (Polonsky); *Topaz* (Hitchcock); *Winning* (Goldstone).

1970: *Airport* (Seaton); *Colossus: The Forbin Project* (Sargent); *Myra Breckinridge* (Sarne) (co); *Skullduggery* (G. Douglas and Wilson); *Story of a Woman* (Bercovici). **1971:** *Red Sky at Morning* (Goldstone); *Sometimes a Great Notion* (P. Newman). **1972:** *Hammersmith Is Out* (Ustinov); *Pete 'n' Tillie* (Ritt); *The Screaming Woman* (Smight); *The Life and Times of Judge Roy Bean* (J. Huston) (co). **1973:** *Ash Wednesday* (Peerce); *A Doll's House* (Losey) (co); *Divorce His, Divorce Hers* (Hussein); *The Sting* (G. R. Hill); *The Don Is Dead* (Fleischer); *The Showdown* (Seaton). **1974:** *Airport 75* (Smight). **1975:** *The Great Waldo Pepper* (G. R. Hill); *Rooster Cogburn* (Miller); *The Man Who Would Be King* (J. Huston). **1976:** *The Bluebird* (Cukor); *Family Plot* (Hitchcock); *Gable and Lombard* (Furie); *W. C. Fields and Me* (Hiller); *The Disappearance of Aimee* (Harvey). **1977:** *Airport 77* (Hiller); *Sex and the Married Woman* (Arnold); *Sunshine Christmas* (G. Jordan). **1978:** *The Big Fix* (Kagen); *Olly Olly Oxen Free* (Colla); *Sextette* (Hughes). **1979:** *The Last Married Couple in America* (Cates). **1982:** *Dead Men Don't Wear Plaid* (C. Reiner).

For many people, Edith Head and film costume design are synonymous. Other designers may have been more flamboyantly creative, or more consistently original, but no one did more to earn this art form popular recognition. Her guiding principle was that costume should support, rather than compete with, story and character development. Better than most, perhaps, she understood that clothing is not merely a matter of adornment, but a potent method of communication working in tandem with a film's sound and other visual elements. Her longevity, her productivity, her frequent touches of genius, and her talent for self-promotion secured her a celebrity status rare among Hollywood's legions of production artists. Moviegoers have long remained oblivious to the identities of those who work in the shadow of the stars, but they seem to have found a place in their consciousness for this tiny, austere-looking woman who wove illusions out of beads and cloth.

Unlike most of her peers, Head entered film costuming without relevant training or experience. When Howard Greer, Paramount's chief designer, hired her as a sketch artist in 1923, she was a high school teacher of French and art looking for a way to supplement her income. She learned quickly, however, honing her skills by observing the masters at work. From Greer she learned the value of attention to detail. From Travis Banton, another outstanding member of Paramount's design team, she learned how to fabricate the highest standards of glamour and elegance.

In her early years at the studio, Head mainly dressed minor characters and animals, or generated wardrobes for the countless B pictures then in production. Gradually she progressed to creating costumes for stars with whom the senior designers lacked the time or inclination to work. Among her first major assignments were Clara Bow, Lupe Velez, and Mae West. Head became Paramount's chief designer in 1938, when Banton, who replaced Greer as head designer in 1927, left to start a couture business. She remained at the studio for another three decades, working with most of Hollywood's major actresses and some of its best-known actors. When

Paramount was sold in 1967, she became chief designer at Universal, where she worked until her death.

During her career, which spanned nearly six decades, Head's productivity achieved legendary proportions. In 1940 alone, she supervised costumes for 47 films. She is estimated to have contributed to more than 1,000 movies during her lifetime. In terms of formal recognition, her record is equally staggering. She received 34 Academy Award nominations, of which eight resulted in an Oscar. Costume design did not become an Academy Award category until 1948. For the first 19 years in which this honor was given, Head was nominated at least once every year. Had the award been introduced earlier, she would surely have earned additional nominations for such distinctive creations as Dorothy Lamour's sarongs in *The Jungle Princess* or Barbara Stanwyck's Latin-inspired garments for *The Lady Eve.*

Much of her best work was executed in the 1950s, when glamour and high-fashion were the keynotes of costume design. Among the enduring images her designs helped promote were Grace Kelly's refined allure in *Rear Window* and *To Catch a Thief,* Elizabeth Taylor's incandescent sensuality in *A Place in the Sun,* Audrey Hepburn's chic individuality in *Sabrina,* Bette Davis's mature sophistication in *All about Eve,* and Gloria Swanson's anachronistic glamour in *Sunset Boulevard.* This was also an era in which Head's public visibility reached its zenith. Already a fashion magazine editor, columnist, and regular contributor to Art Linkletter's radio show *House Party,* Head now made frequent television appearances, acted as consultant for the Academy Awards show, and published her first book. The diversity of her activities helped to extend her influence well beyond the realm of motion pictures.

Perhaps her greatest asset was her adaptability. Entering the business when limitless spending permitted designers broad artistic license, she later had to adjust to the restrictions imposed by wartime shortages of luxury textiles and the government's L-85 ruling on the amount of materials which could be used in clothing manufacture. Following the return to glamour and clothing-as-special-effects during the 1950s, Head made yet another successful transition when the 1960s ushered in a new emphasis on realism.

Head was also able to adjust to widely varying ideas about her role among the directors with whom she worked. Attitudes ranged from Alfred Hitchcock and George Roy Hill's close involvement in design, to the laissez-faire approach of Joseph Mankiewicz. Describing herself on one occasion as "a better politician than costume designer," Head was expert at handling star temperament, preferring to yield ground on a neckline or dress length than engage in a battle of wills. The conservative, neutral-colored suits she perennially wore symbolized her willingness to suppress her individuality in the interests of her craft. With the exception of a dispute over whether she or Givenchy deserved the credit for Audrey Hepburn's famous bow-tied neckline in *Sabrina,* her career was unruffled by controversy.

Although she created a number of outstanding designs for period movies, most notably *The Heiress* and *Samson and Delilah,* she preferred to dress films with a contemporary theme, believing that they afforded more scope for originality. She also preferred to dress men rather than women, on the grounds that they were easier to deal with. One of her most effective wardrobes was the clothing worn by Robert Redford and Paul Newman in *The Sting,* in which her subtle use of accessories, especially hats, was brilliantly executed. Her designs, on occasion, set fashion trends, but she did not deliberately set out to influence what the public wore. She placed far more importance on enabling stars to assume their characters' identities. She also believed it essential to create designs that would not cause a movie to date prematurely. This preference for a middle-of-the-road approach dates from 1947, when Dior's "New Look" exploded onto the fashion scene, making Head's streamlined designs seem instantly outmoded.

Head's excellence as a designer was augmented by her keen understanding of the technical constraints within which she operated. She was acutely aware of the different requirements created by variations in lighting, sound, and color. She also believed in close collaboration with her fellow production artists. Although she worked in an industry in which honors and public recognition are focused on individual achievement, Head truly was a team player. She may have enjoyed the celebrity status earned by her television appearances and writing, but when it came to practicing her craft, aligning her skills with the needs of directors, cinematographers, art directors, and others is what mattered most. It was her capacity for partnership that helped her become one of Hollywood's preeminent production artists.—FIONA VALENTINE

Heckerling, Amy

American director

Born *The Bronx, New York, 7 May 1954.* ***Education*** *Attended Art and Design High School, New York; studied film at New York University Film School; earned a master's degree from the American Film Institute.* ***Family*** *Married the writer/director Neal Israel.* ***Career*** *1982—directed first feature film, the hit* Fast Times at Ridgemont High; *1986—producer for TV series* Fast Times; *1989—revived her feature film career with the commercially successful* Look Who's Talking; *1995—directed the critically and commercially successful* Clueless; *1996—executive producer for TV series* Clueless. ***Agent*** *Richard Lovett, Creative Artists Agency, 9830 Wilshire Boulevard, Beverly Hills, CA 90212, U.S.A.*

Films as Director: 1977: *Getting It Over With.* **1982:** *Fast Times at Ridgemont High.* **1984:** *Johnny Dangerously.* **1985:** *National Lampoon's European Vacation.* **1989:** *Look Who's Talking* (+ sc). **1990:** *Look Who's Talking Too* (+ co-sc). **1995:** *Clueless* (+ sc).

Other Films: 1985: *Into the Night* (Landis) (ro as ship's waitress). **1988:** *Life on the Flipside* (for TV) (pr). **1997:** *Frank Capra's American Dream* (Bowser—doc for TV) (ro as herself). **1998:** *A Night at the Roxbury* (Fortenberry and Markle) (co-sc, co-pr).

Amy Heckerling is an enormously successful commercial Hollywood director whose forte is comedy filmmaking. After film school, she worked as a television editor where she learned to create effective comic rhythms. Subsequently, her first feature, the smash hit *Fast Times at Ridgemont High* was a career-making effort. The film was based on Cameron Crowe's novel about his return to high school to examine what contemporary teenagers were doing. A hilarious parody of high school teenpics, it was enthusiastically endorsed by several critics. It is also noteworthy as the film that introduced Sean Penn and Jennifer Jason Leigh to mainstream audiences.

Heckerling's second feature, however, *Johnny Dangerously,* performed poorly at the box office, though it is a clever comic spoof of the 1930s gangster movies, in which an honest man turns to crime to fund his mother's surgeries. Likewise, *National Lampoon's European Vacation,* a fluffy comedy with an anemic screenplay that seems to gently mock the all-American family, was not a box-office success. Nevertheless, Heckerling has demonstrated a tenacious will to

Amy Heckerling (center) on the set of *Look Who's Talking Too* with John Travolta and Kirstie Alley.

succeed in Hollywood. For example, when her screenplay *My Kind of Guy* unsuccessfully made the rounds of the studios, from Warner Bros., to Universal, to MGM, she responded by working on another screenplay—for *Look Who's Talking,* which was inspired by her own pregnancy. It ultimately proved to be a smash hit and marked her career "comeback." In addition, it prompted two sequels, the first of which she also directed, *Look Who's Talking Too.* In *Look Who's Talking,* an unmarried woman played by Kirstie Alley pursues her quest to find the perfect father for her baby. She finds him, unexpectedly, in an unconventional candidate—a taxi driver (played by John Travolta). The film's hook is baby Mikey's amusing impressions of his experiences between the time of his conception and his first birthday.

Heckerling had another huge commercial and critical hit with *Clueless,* a charming contemporary adaptation of Jane Austen's *Emma.* Arguably, it represents a career summation film, one that evokes prevalent issues and themes from her earlier movies. Yet, it is utterly original. Her most feminist film, it features a heroine who is a spoiled yet engaging Beverly Hills incorrigible who indefatigably endeavors to arrange and manipulate the romances of her high school cohorts, while she puts her own love life in neutral. Much of its considerable appeal is due to its clever take on the fads, slang, and other preoccupations of teenagers, especially girls. Like *Fast Times at Ridgemont High,* and unlike most teenpics, it attracted both teen and adult audiences. But, whereas the earlier film had a more realistic look and tone, in addition to more explicit depictions of youthful sexuality, *Clueless* revels in bright colors, quick, witty repartee, and camp sensibilities—especially in terms of the slightly-over-the-top performances Heckerling elicited from the film's leads, including Alicia Silverstone in her career-making role.

Heckerling has spoken of the pressure she felt in Hollywood whereby male directors can make a string of bad films before they finally succeed and are considered "hot directors"—a path she had never seen a female director tread. Therefore, she felt compelled to work without stopping so that she would not be forgotten in Hollywood. Her critics, therefore, often charge that her eye is focused entirely upon the box office. But, as she herself explained, it would be great if a woman director could make "tons of money" since the "best and the worst thing about this industry is that that's the bottom line." Furthermore, her critics complain that her films look as though they were directed by men—sometimes leering men. They point to her first film, *Fast Times at Ridgemont High,* in which it is only the males who are fully developed characters, while the girls are obsessed with their looks and with boys, and whose bodies are featured in various states of undress.

Despite such criticisms, Heckerling's comic scripts boast fast-paced dialogue and clever humor that occasionally point to the sexism and superficialities of American consumer culture, as they mock and celebrate the insipid yet well-intentioned values of suburbia, even in upscale Beverly Hills. Likewise, they include subversive feminine humor despite their big studio backing. Thus, in *Look Who's Talking,* the babies voice the absurdities of their adult companions, and in *Clueless,* the teenage heroine expresses a clever awareness of the superficialities of consumer obsessions and of sexism. Accordingly, astute critics have compared her films to those of Jerry Lewis and Frank Tashlin. They are well-produced, technically proficient, and engaging works that employ the narrative conventions and formulae that predominate in commercial Hollywood movies. In addition, they are testimony to Heckerling's considerable skill in evoking humorously engaging performances from her actors.

Heckerling's résumé includes directorial assignments for television, including several episodes of the series *Fast Times.* Recently, she has worked as a producer on the feature film, *A Night at the Roxbury.*—CYNTHIA FELANDO

Hein, Birgit

German director

Born *West Germany, 1942.* ***Education*** *Studied art history.* ***Family*** *Married the filmmaker Wilhelm Hein.* ***Career*** *Late 1960s to late 1970s—produced several abstract formalist films with Wilhelm Hein, in addition to collaborating on multimedia events, and performances; 1978—the Heins started to incorporate certain representative images into their nonrepresentative works; since 1970s—written and published extensively on the subjects of art history and avant-garde film.*

Films as Co-Director with Wilhelm Hein: 1967: *S&W*; *Ole*; *Und Sie?.* **1968:** *Grün*; *Werbefilm Nr. 1: Bamberg*; *Rohfilm*; *Reproductions.* **1969:** *625*; *Square Dance*; *Work in Progress Teil A* (*Work in Progress Part A*); *Sichtbarmachung der Wirkungsweise optischer Gesetze am einfachen Beispiel.* **1970:** *Work in Progress Teil B* (*Work in Progress Part B*); *Porträts I*; *Auszüge aus einer Biographie*; *Madison/Wis*; *Replay*; *Foto-Film*; *Filmraum: Reproduktionsimmanente Ästhetik.* **1971:** *Porträts. 4. Nina I-III*; *Autobahn. 2 Teile*; *Work in Progress Teil C* (*Work in Progress Part C*); *Work in Progress Teil D* (*Work in Progress Part D*); *Doppelprojektion I*; *I Want You to Be Rich*; *Altes Material*; *Zoom—lange Fassung*; *Zoom—kurze Fassung*; *Videotape I*; *Liebesgrüsse*; *Yes to Europe.* **1972:** *Porträts. Kurt Schwitters I, II, III*; *Porträts*; *Doppelprojektion II-IV*; *Aufblenden (Abblenden)*; *Dokumentation*; *Fussball.* **1973:** *Ausdatiertes Material*; *God Bless America*; *Stills*; *London*; *Zu Lucifer Rising von Kenneth Anger.* **1974:** *Strukturelle Studien*; *Jack Smith*; *Künstlerfilme I*; *Künstlerfilme II.* **1975:** *Porträts II.* **1976:** *Materialfilme I*; *Materialfilme II.* **1977:** *Porträts III.* **1978:** *Kurt Kren. Porträt eines experimentellen Fulmmachers.* **1978-79:** *Verdammt in alle Ewigkeit (From Here to Eternity).* **1980:** *Superman und Superwoman.* **1981:** *Die Medien und das Bild. Andy Warhol's Kunst.* **1982:** *Love Stinks—Bilder des taeglichen Wahnsinns*; *American Graffiti.* **1984-85:** *Verbotene Bilder.* **1986:** *Fusswaschung* (in *Jesusfilm*). **1987-88:** *Die Kali-filme* (*The Kali Films*). **1992:** *Die Unheimlichen Frauen* (*The Frightening Women*) (+ ed, ph, sc, pr). **1995:** *Baby, I Will Make You Sweat* (+ ed, ph, sc).

Since the late 1960s, the internationally renowned German avant-garde artist Birgit Hein has collaborated with her husband Wilhelm Hein on experimental films, multimedia projects, and performances. Known for their difficult "structural-materialist" films, the Heins have created an impressive body of work with determinedly political intentions. Though Birgit declared in 1978 that "art cannot change society," she conceded that it did, however, have a significant part to play in the struggle for progressive goals by conveying ideas that cannot be conveyed via other means. In addition to her avant-garde motion-picture collaborations with Wilhelm, Birgit is also a well-known and often-published art historian and avant-garde film critic.

Like other experimental filmmakers in the 1960s, the Heins's early films used the medium to explore the language of cinema and to challenge viewers' perceptions, and they employed abstract formalist techniques to challenge the strategies of mainstream cinema. Such techniques included using scratched film, visible sprocket holes, and experimenting with purely formal notions. *625,* for example, consisted of several sequences produced by photographing a television screen at different speeds to reveal the television's bar line. The aptly titled *Strukturelle Studien* was a compilation of 33 shorts made over the course of many years, each of which demonstrates either a factor related to film's ability to produce the illusion of movement, such as persistence of vision, or to investigate the camera's fundamental functions, such as focus and zoom.

In 1978 Birgit wrote that the Heins's perspective on the social function of art was characterized by two extremes: a leftist political agenda and a formal, nonnarrative film aesthetic. But she noted that formal nonrepresentational art was being rejected on both sides of the political spectrum. Interested only in critics on the left, who charged that abstract work was a manifestation of reactionary bourgeois politics and, therefore, was socially irrelevant, Birgit countered that purely formal works cannot be characterized as either reactionary or progressive simply for being nonrepresentational. Instead, she insisted that it is solely how art is used that can be judged as progressive or reactionary. She acknowledged, however, that in order to appreciate abstract art it was necessary to learn how to "decode" the information it presented, and that she was often advised to combine film formalism with narrative to make their work more accessible. So, by 1980, the Heins announced that their recent works marked a move away from strict abstract formalism and included representational images. Their decision followed serious meditation about whether or not their formal film exercises had simply become self-perpetuating. Consequently, the Heins started incorporating into their works a variety of popular generic elements, which they called "emotion, sentiment, triviality." The films included attention to their personal lives and relationship, and offered weighty reflections about female sexuality. In addition, the Heins explored some of the more taboo areas of female sexuality such as those that countered passive femininity, such as aggressive feminine sexuality. For example, *The Kali Films* depict women using weapons to attack men, along with clips from horror movies and women-in-prison films. Their work suggests that female sexuality can exist outside the realm of masculine voyeurism, and can be explored productively by women and men together.

One of the Heins's most famous films, *Love Stinks,* was shot during a year the filmmakers spent in New York, and it cleverly conveys the experience of life in a foreign land. Subtitled "Pictures of Everyday Madness," it includes footage of marital sex and shots of their surroundings, from the Bowery to the downtown art scene to the Lower East Side, where they found the graffiti that inspired the film's subtitle. One of the film's tasks is to locate signs of Germany in the States, such as graffiti swastikas, decimated tenements, and a television broadcast of *Inside the Third Reich*. But at least one critic commended the Heins for providing a comically witty investigation of New York's subway graffiti, especially their study of a series of vandalized movie posters for *Mommie Dearest* and *Rocky III.*

From Here to Eternity is a multimedia piece whose title was inspired by the 1953 Hollywood film and which consists of the earlier film's dubbed German trailer, in addition to popular music, live performances by the Heins, and multiscreen projections of both representational and nonrepresentational films. One of the work's themes concerns the notion of role-playing as an act of masquerade or ritual. Accordingly, the Heins performed as Frankenstein, in matching black suits and masks, by first dancing together slowly and mechanically on stage, and then by jumping offstage to dance crazily to rock and roll. To add further complications, the work's soundtrack presents a disjunction between the voice and the body, includes film images of a Marilyn Monroe impersonator, long home-movie sequences, and segments of scratched celluloid. Critics have suggested, however, that the work's combination of disparate elements failed to illuminate any new understandings regarding the processes of film and seeing.—CYNTHIA FELANDO

Henning-Jensen, Astrid

Danish director

Born *Astrid Smahl in Frederiksberg, Denmark, 10 December 1914.* ***Family*** *Married the director Bjarne Henning-Jensen, 6 October 1938, son: Lars.* ***Career*** *1931-38—actress at "Riddersalen," Copenhagen; 1941—assistant director, then director, 1943, at Nordisk Films Kompagni; 1950-52—Norsk Film A/S, Oslo; since early 1950s—Astrid and Bjarne both worked as freelance writers and directors for film, theater, radio, and television.* ***Awards*** *Director Prize, Venice Film Festival, for* Denmark Grows Up, *1947; Cannes Film Festival Prize, for* Palle Alone in the World, *1949; Catholic Film Office Award, Cannes Festival, and Technik Prize, for* Paw, *1960; Best Director, Berlin Festival, for* Winter Children, *1979.* ***Address*** *Frederiksberg Allé 76, DK-1820 Copenhagen V, Denmark.*

Films as Director: 1945: *Dansk politi i Sverige* (*The Danish Brigade in Sweden*). **1947:** *Denmark Grows Up* (co-d). **1949:** *Palle alene i Verden* (*Palle Alone in the World*). **1951:** *Kranes Konditori*

(*Krane's Bakery Shop*). **1952:** *Ukjent mann* (*Unknown Man*). **1954:** *Ballettens børn* (*Ballet Girl*). **1955:** *Kaerlighed pa kredit* (*Love on Credit*) (+ sc). **1959:** *Hest på sommerferie* (*Horse on Holiday*); *Paw* (*Boy of Two Worlds*; *The Lure of the Jungle*) (+ co-sc). **1961:** *Een blandt mange* (*One among Many*). **1965:** *De blå undulater.* **1966:** *Utro* (*Unfaithful*). **1967:** *Min bedstefar er en stok.* **1968:** *Nille.* **1969:** *Mej och dej* (*Me and You*; *Mig og dig*) (+ sc). **1978:** *Vinterbørn* (*Winter Children*; *Winterborn*) (+ sc, ed). **1980:** *Øjeblikket* (*The Moment*) (+ sc). **1985:** *Hodja fra Pjort.* **1986:** *Barndommens gade* (*Street of My Childhood*; *Early Spring*) (+ sc).

Films as Co-Director with Bjarne Henning-Jensen: **1943:** *S.O.S. Kindtand* (*S.O.S. Molars*). **1945:** *Flyktingar finner en hamn* (*Fugitives Find Shelter*); *Folketingsvalg 1945.* **1947:** *Stemning i April* (*Impressions of April*); *De pokkers unger* (*Those Blasted Kids*). **1948:** *Kristinus Bergman.* **1950:** *Vesterhavs drenge* (*Boys from the West Coast*). **1953:** *Solstik* (+ st). **1954:** *Tivoligarden spiller* (*Tivoli Garden Games*). **1991:** *In Spite Of.* **1995:** *Bella, My Bella.*

Other Films: **1937:** *Cocktail* (ro). **1943:** *Naar man kun er ung* (*While Still Young*) (B. Henning-Jensen) (asst d). **1946:** *Ditte Menneskebarn* (*Ditte: Child of Man*) (B. Henning-Jensen) (asst d). **1962:** *Kort år sommaren* (*Short Is the Summer*) (B. Henning-Jensen) (co-sc). **1982:** *Napló gyermekeimnek* (*Diary for My Children*) (Mészáros) (co-production supervisor). **1984:** *Forbrydelsens Element* (*The Element of Crime*) (von Trier) (ro as Osborne's housekeeper). **1996:** *Danske piger viser alt* (Blair and others) (as herself).

Astrid Henning-Jensen's film career is closely linked with that of her husband, the director Bjarne Henning-Jensen, but includes significant solo projects as well. Both started as stage actors, but shortly after they married in 1938 they began working in films. Bjarne Henning-Jensen directed several government documentaries beginning in 1940 and he was joined by Astrid in 1943. At that time the Danish documentary film, strongly influenced by the British documentary of the 1930s, was blooming, and the Henning-Jensens played an important part in this. In 1943 they made their first feature film, Astrid serving as assistant director. *Naar man kun er ung* was a light, everyday comedy, striving for a relaxed and charming style, but it was too cute, and it was politely received. Their next film, *Ditte Menneskebarn*—again with Astrid as assistant director—was their breakthrough, and the two were instantly considered as the most promising directors in the postwar Danish cinema. The film was an adaptation of a neoclassical novel by Martin Andersen-Nexø. It was a realistic story of a young country girl and her tragic destiny as a victim of social conditions. The novel, published between 1917 and 1921, was in five volumes, but the Henning-Jensens used only parts of the novel. The sentimentality of the book was, happily, subdued in the film, and it is a sensitive study of a young girl in her milieu. The film was the first example of a more realistic and serious Danish film and it paralleled similar trends in contemporary European cinema, even if one would refrain from calling the film neorealistic. It was a tremendous success in Denmark and it also won a certain international recognition.

Astrid and Bjarne Henning-Jensen's film was a sincere attempt to introduce reality and authentic people to the Danish film. They continued this effort in their subsequent films, but a certain facile approach, a weakness for cute effects, and a sensibility on the verge of sentimentality made their films less and less interesting. In the 1950s Bjarne Henning-Jensen returned to documentaries, while Astrid Henning-Jensen—who had made her debut as a solo director in 1945—continued making films on her own. She made two carefully directed and attractive films in Norway, and in the 1960s she tried to keep up with the changing times in a couple of films. But it was not until the late 1970s that she regained her old position. In 1978's *Vinterbørn,* about women and their problems in a maternity ward, and in 1980's *Øjeblikket,* treating the problems of a young couple when it is discovered that the woman is dying of cancer, she worked competently within an old established genre in Danish films, the problem-oriented popular drama—in both cases writing the screenplay as well as directing.—IB MONTY

Holland, Agnieszka

Polish director and writer

Born *Warsaw, Poland, 28 November 1948.* ***Education*** *Graduated from the Filmova Akademie Muzickych Umeni (FAMU) film school in Prague, 1971, where she studied directing.* ***Career*** *1970—maintained her studies in Prague even after the Soviet invasion; was jailed by the authorities after months of harassment by police; 1972—returned to Poland and became member of film collective "X," headed by Andrzej Wajda; 1973—began career as a production assistant to director Krzysztof Zanussi on* Illumination; *1970s—worked in Polish theater and television; 1979—began writing scripts for films directed by Wajda, directed first feature,* Provincial Actors; *1981—moved to Paris after the declaration of martial law in Poland, and began making documentaries for French television; 1985—earned first major international acclaim for* Angry Harvest; *member of board of directors of Zespoly Filmowne; member of board of directors of Polish Filmmakers Association.* ***Awards*** *Golden Globe Award, Best Foreign Language Film, and National Board of Review, Best Foreign Language Film, 1990,* for Europa, Europa. ***Agent*** *William Morris Agency, 151 El Camino Drive, Beverly Hills, CA 90212, U.S.A.*

Films as Director and Writer: 1974: *Wieczór u Abdona* (*Evening at Abdon's*; *An Evening at Abdon*) (for TV). **1976:** *Niedzielne Dzieci* (*Sunday Children*) (for TV). **1977:** *Zdjecia probne* (*Screen Tests*) (ep. in sketch film); *Cós za cós* (*Something for Something*) (for TV—co-d with Wajda). **1979:** *Aktorzy prowincjonalni* (*Provincial Actors*). **1981:** *Gorączka* (*Fever*; *The Fever: The Story of the Bomb*). **1982:** *Kobieta samotna* (*A Woman Alone*; *A Lonely Woman*) (co-d). **1985:** *Bittere ernte* (*Angry Harvest*). **1988:** *To Kill a Priest* (*Le complot*) (co-sc). **1990:** *Europa, Europa.* **1991:** *Olivier, Olivier.*

Films as Director: 1990: *Largo Desolato* (co-d with Zizka—for TV). **1993:** *The Secret Garden.* **1995:** *Total Eclipse.* **1997:** *Washington Square.*

Other Films: 1978: *Dead Case* (sc); *Bez znieczulenia* (*Without Anesthesia*; *Rough Treatment*) (Wajda) (sc). **1981:** *Człowiek z Żelaza* (*Man of Iron*) (Wajda) (sc). **1982:** *Przesluchanie* (*The Interrogation*) (Bugajski—released 1990) (ro as Witowska). **1983:** *Danton* (Wajda) (co-sc). **1984:** *Ein Liebe en Deutschland* (*A Love in Germany*) (Wajda) (co-sc). **1987:** *Anna* (Bogayevicz) (sc); *Les Possedes* (sc). **1988:** *La Amiga* (*Die Freundin*) (Meerapfel) (co-sc). **1990:** *Korczak* (Wajda) (sc). **1993:** *Trois Coleurs: Bleu* (*Three Colors: Blue*) (Kieslowski) (additional dialogue). **1994:** *Trois Coleurs: Blanc* (*Three Colors: White*) (Kieslowski) (co-sc).

The death camps were liberated decades ago. Auschwitz and Birkenau, Chelmno and Dachau—the ABCDs of the Final Solution—have long been silent memorials to the mass murder of millions. Despite this passage of time—and despite the media-induced impression that Steven Spielberg's *Schindler's List* is the only movie ever made which confronts the mass extermination of a people during World War II—the Holocaust has long been a topic for filmmakers. One such filmmaker is director Agnieszka Holland.

Holland is a Polish Jew who was born scant years after the end of World War II. The legacy of that era has influenced her life, and her work. She is not so much interested in the politics of the war, in how and why the German people allowed Hitler to come to power. Rather, a common theme in her films is the manner in which individuals responded to Hitler and the Nazi scourge. This is most perfectly exemplified in what is perhaps her most distinguished film to date: *Europa, Europa*, a German-made feature based on the memoirs of Salamon Perel, who as a teenaged German Jew survived World War II by passing for Aryan in a Hitler Youth academy.

This thoughtful, tremendously moving film was the source of controversy on two accounts: it depicts a Jew who compromises himself in order to ensure his survival; and it was not named as Germany's official Best Foreign Language Film entrant, making it ineligible in that category for an Academy Award. Nevertheless, it did earn Holland a nomination for Best Screenplay (based on material from another medium).

Even though Holland only wrote the screenplay for *Korczak*—the film was directed by her mentor, Andrzej Wajda—it too is one of her most impassioned works. Her simple, poignant script chronicles the real-life story of a truly gentle, remarkable man: Janusz Korczak (Wojtek Pszoniak), a respected doctor, writer, and children's rights advocate who operated a home for Jewish orphans in Warsaw during the 1930s. Korczak's concerns are people and not politics. "I love children," he states, simply and matter-of-factly. "I fight for years for the dignity of children." In his school, he offers his charges a humanist education. And then the Nazis invade his homeland. Given his station in life, Korczak easily could arrange his escape to freedom. But he chooses to remain with his children and do whatever he must to keep his orphanage running and his children alive, even after they all have been imprisoned in the Warsaw Ghetto.

After directing several theatrical and made-for-television features in Poland, Holland came to international attention in 1985 with *Angry Harvest*, a superb drama about a wealthy farmer who offers to shelter a Jewish woman in his cellar in World War II Poland. His repressed sexuality transforms this act of kindness into one of hypocrisy, as he attempts to abuse his guest. Films such as *Angry Harvest*, *Korczak*, and *Europa, Europa* serve a necessary, essential purpose: they are tools that can be used to educate young people, Jew and non-Jew alike, about the exploitation and extermination of a race. They are monuments—as much to the memory of generations past as to the survival of generations to come.

Not all of Holland's films have dealt directly with the Holocaust. Another of her themes—which also may be linked to the Holocaust by its very nature—is the loss of innocence among children that occurs not by the natural progression of growing into adulthood, but by odd, jarring circumstances. *Olivier, Olivier*, like *Europa, Europa* and *Korczak*, also is a narrative based on fact. It is the intricate account of a country couple whose youngest offspring, Olivier, mysteriously disappears. Six years later he "reappears," but is no longer the special child who was a joy to his family. Rather, he is a Parisian street hustler who claims to have forgotten his childhood. One also can understand Holland's attraction to *The Secret Garden*, an adaptation of the Frances Hodgson Burnett children's story about a ten-year-old orphan who revitalizes a neglected garden in her uncle's Victorian mansion.

Most of Holland's films have been artistically successful. Two exceptions have been *To Kill a Priest*, an ambitious but ultimately clumsy drama about an ill-fated activist priest in Poland; and *Total Eclipse*, about the relationship between French poets Arthur Rimbaud and Paul Verlaine (and based on a play by Christopher Hampton), which was a fiasco—one of the more eagerly anticipated yet disappointing films of 1995. Thankfully, however, these failures comprise the minority of Holland's filmic output.—ROB EDELMAN

Hubley, Faith Elliott

American animator, producer, and director

Born *Faith Chestman in New York City, 16 September 1924.* ***Education*** *Attended Art Students League, New York City.* ***Family*** *Married (second) the animator John K. Hubley, 1955 (died 1977), four children: Mark, Ray, Emily, Georgia.* ***Career*** *1943-55—film editor, script supervisor, music editor; 1955-president, The Hubley Studio; 1972—senior critic, Yale University School of Art.* ***Awards*** *Academy Award (with John Hubley), Best Short Subjects, Cartoons, for* The Hole, *1962; Academy Award (with John Hubley), Best Short Subjects, Cartoons, for* Herb Alpert and the Tijuana Brass Double Feature, *1966; honorary doctorate, Columbia College, Chicago, 1990; honorary doctorate, Hofstra University, 1995; 14 CINE Golden Eagle awards.* ***Address*** *Hubley Studio Inc., 2575 Palisade Avenue, Apartment 12L, Riverdale, NY 10463-6127, U.S.A.*

Films as Co-Producer and Co-Director with John Hubley: **1956:** *Adventures of an **. **1957:** *Harlem Wednesday.* **1958:** *The Tender Game.* **1959:** *Moonbird.* **1960:** *Children of the Sun.* **1961:** *Of Stars and Men* (+ ed). **1962:** *The Hole.* **1964:** *The Hat.* **1966:** *Herb Alpert and the Tijuana Brass Double Feature*; *Urbanissimo.* **1968:** *Windy Day.* **1969:** *Of Men and Demons.* **1970:** *Eggs.* **1972:** *Dig: A Journey into the Earth.* **1973:** *Cockaboody.* **1974:** *Voyage to Next.* **1975:** *People People People.* **1976:** *Everybody Rides the Carousel.* **1977:** *The Doonesbury Special* (for TV) (+ co-sc).

Films as Producer and Director: **1975:** *W.O.W.* (*Women of the World*). **1976:** *Second Chance: Sea.* **1977:** *Whither Weather.* **1978:** *Step by Step.* **1980:** *Sky Dance.* **1981:** *The Big Bang and Other Creation Myths*; *Enter Life.* **1983:** *Starlore.* **1984:** *Hello.* **1985:** *The Cosmic Eye* (+ sc). **1987:** *Time of the Angels.* **1988:** *Yes We Can.* **1989:** *Who Am I.* **1990:** *Amazonia.* **1991:** *Upside Down.* **1992:** *Tall Time Tales.* **1993:** *Cloudland.* **1994:** *Seers & Clowns.* **1995:** *Rainbows of Hawai'i.* **1996:** *My Universe Inside Out.* **1997:** *Beyond the Shadow Place.*

Other Films: **1957:** *Twelve Angry Men* (Lumet) (script supervisor). **1966:** *The Year of the Horse* (Sunasky) (co-sc).

When Faith Elliott married John Hubley in 1955, they agreed that they would make one independently financed short film a year, and that they would always eat dinner at the table with their children. They upheld their agreement for 22 years, co-directing and co-producing films and animated shorts. After John's death in 1977, Faith Hubley, in spite of a lengthy battle with breast cancer, continued to produce and direct on her own. By then her own children had grown up, and several were working with her, while she continued to raise new generations of "children": her students at Yale.

In Hell's Kitchen as a young woman, Faith Chestman's parents had wanted her to become a dentist, and conflicts became heated when they realized that she had other plans. She showed ability as a visual artist, but she drifted toward theater work instead: already a dedicated radical, Chestman worked in People's Theatre in New York while studying with the New Theatre League. After a brief, failed marriage that left her with little more than the new surname of Elliott, she moved to Los Angeles, where she went to work in a factory. By that time, the Soviet Union had entered World War II against Nazi Germany, so she had become an enthusiastic proponent of the war, and she was fired for being overly zealous in organizing the workers to make war against fascism.

Faith Elliott got a job as a messenger for a film studio, where the war had opened up more film jobs for women. Over the next decade, she progressed through a variety of jobs at Columbia,

Goldwyn, and Republic, gaining experience by working with The Three Stooges. She met John Hubley, a Disney animator who had worked on such classics as *Dumbo* and *Bambi*. John helped form United Productions of America, where Faith first worked with him on an educational film about menstruation—hardly typical subject matter in the 1940s.

John Hubley had left Disney after a 1941 strike, and as he and Faith became collaborators in life and work, Disney's negative influence would become a significant motivating factor for both of them. The animated films the Hubleys made, from the 1950s on, would mark a dramatic departure from the glossy style of Disney. Instead of bright, sharp colors, they used muted tones influenced not only by cubist art, but by ancient cave paintings and children's drawings. Those three influences—modernism, primitivism, and a celebration of the child—would become the pillars of the couple's joint projects and later of Faith Hubley's solo work.

Given John's work as an animator and Faith's earlier explorations in visual art, animated shorts made a natural basis for the Hubley Studio, formed in 1955, the year of their marriage. These were usually outlandish films such as *The Hole* (featuring their friend Dizzy Gillespie), in which two construction workers in a manhole discuss the future of the world. *The Hole* was decades ahead of its time, prefiguring the style of 1990s television shows such as *Seinfeld* with their concentration on quirky dialogue over plot, and it won an Academy Award.

But the Hubleys also showed a talent for innovation in their more commercial work, projects they did chiefly to pay the bills and finance their experimental and avant-garde projects. One of the most famous "films" to come out of the Hubley Studio, in fact, was the "Markie Maypo" cereal commercial in 1959. Hubley later described it as a "non-commercial," and like *The Hole,* it belonged more to the 1990s than the 1950s. Using the voice of their own son, the Hubleys created the character of "Markie Maypo," who despises Maypo cereal and dismisses it with a "Yuck!" This form of anti-selling proved enormously popular with the public, yet it did not gain common usage until the 1990s, with "anti" campaigns employed by Sprite, McDonald's (for the Arch Deluxe burger), and others.

In spite of such successes, or the acclaim given to other commercial works such as a 1966 documentary about Herb Alpert's Tijuana Brass or a 1977 television special based on the *Doonesbury* cartoon, the Hubleys' first love was their cutting-age, sardonic, and highly innovative animation work. Just as they visually contrasted with Disney cartoons, the Hubleys' cartoons were markedly different in their political and "progressive" undertones. A number of films emphasized feminist themes, including *Windy Day* (1968), which used their daughters' voice-overs; and 1975's *W.O.W.* Faith Hubley's later work, such as *Amazonia* (1990) and *Rainbows of Hawai'i* (1995), explores environmental issues.

Ironies abound in Faith Hubley's lengthy career. A feminist married to a man who shared her views, she saw their joint efforts routinely categorized as "Films by John Hubley" or "John Hubley *with* Faith Hubley." A communist sympathizer in the Stalin era and a "progressive" in the years since, she has routinely eschewed public grants for her films, financing them through her own efforts. (She has also described herself as "not [a] very populist person.") Finally, there is the irony of her films' distributorship. In the 1990s, a number of the animated shorts from earlier decades became available on video from Pyramid Films, but before that, their chief distributor had been the Hubleys' arch-nemesis: Disney.—JUDSON KNIGHT

Hui, Ann

Chinese/Hong Kong director

Pseudonyms *Xu Anhua, Hsu An-hua, Ann Huio On-Wah.* ***Born*** *Anshan, Liaoning province, Manchuria, China, 23 May 1947; moved to Hong Kong in 1952.* ***Education*** *Attended Hong Kong University, graduated with a degree in English and comparative literature; attended the London Film School for two years.* ***Career*** *1975-77—worked as assistant to Hong Kong director King Hu and directed drama series and short documentaries for the TVB television station; 1977—produced and directed six one-hour films for Hong Kong's Independent Commission against Corruption; 1978—directed three episodes for the RTHK series* Below the Lion Rock; *1979—directed first feature,* The Secret; *1997—Fellow, Academy for Performing Arts.* ***Awards*** *Best Picture and Best Director, Hong Kong Film Awards, for* Boat People, *1982; Best Film, Asian Pacific Festival, and Best Film, Rimini Festival, for* Song of the Exile, *1990; Best Picture and Best Director, Hong Kong Film Awards, Best Picture and Best Director, Golden Bauhinia Awards, Best Picture, Hong Kong Film Critics Society, Golden Horse Award, Taipei Golden Horse Film Festival, and Best Film, Creteil International Festival of Women's Films, all for* Summer Snow, *1994; awarded MBE (Member of British Empire), 1997.* ***Address*** *1-7 Shell Street, 7B, Hong Kong.*

Films as Director: 1979: *Feng Jie* (*The Secret*). **1980:** *Zhuang Dao Zheng* (*The Spooky Bunch*; *Xiaojie Zhuang Dao Gui*). **1981:** *Hu Yueh Te Ku Shih* (*The Story of Woo Viet*; *Huyue de gushi*). **1982:** *T'ou-Pen Nu-Hai* (*Boat People*; *Tou Bun No Hoi*). **1984:** *Qing Cheng Zhi Lian* (*Love in a Fallen City*). **1987:** *Xiang Xiang Gong Zhu* (*Princess Fragrance*) (+ sc); *Shu Jian En Chou Lu* (*The Romance of Book & Sword*) (+ co-sc). **1988:** *Jinye Xingguang Canlan* (*Starry Is the Night*). **1990:** *Ketu Qiuhen* (*Song of the Exile*); *Xiao Ao Jiang Hu* (*Swordsman*; *Siu Ngo Gong Woo*) (co-d). **1991:** *Jidao Zhuizhong* (*Zodiac Killer*). **1992:** *Shanghai Jiaqi* (*My American Grandson*) (+ sc). **1994:** *Xiatian de Xue* (*Nuren sishi*; *Summer Snow*) (+ co-pr). **1996:** *Ah Kam* (*A Jin de gu shi*; *The Stunt Woman*; *Stuntwoman Ajin*). **1997:** *Personal Memoir of Hong Kong: As Time Goes By* (+ co-pr, sc); *Sixteen Springs*.

Other Films: 1993: *Fong Sai-Yuk* (*The Legend of Fong Sai-Yuk*) (Yuen Kwai) (production). **1994:** *Tianguo Niezi* (*The Day the Sun Turned Cold*) (Yim Ho) (co-pr). **1996:** *He Liu* (*The River*) (Tsai Ming-liang). **1997:** *Yi Sheng Yitai Xi* (*A Little Life-Opera*) (Fong) (exec pr).

Ann Hui is one of the most distinguished directors in the first new wave of Hong Kong film making, which emerged on the international cinema scene during the 1980s. While many of the period's films are Eastern variations on the popular gangster and action-adventure genres of Hollywood, Hui's best work is more personal in nature. Her films reflect on cultural displacement, and the effect on individuals who are uprooted from one country and culture and planted in another, either by personal choice or political or economic necessity. Hui is especially concerned with how her characters respond to their new surroundings, and how they are affected when they return—also by choice or necessity—to their homelands.

Hui also has directed films that are more generic in nature. *The Secret,* her first feature, is a based-on-fact suspense drama about a double murder. *The Spooky Bunch,* her follow-up, is a satiric ghost story. Her major cinematic concerns emerged in *The Story of Woo Viet,* a drama about a South Vietnamese refugee in Manila, and *Boat People,* her most lauded early film, a semidocumentary account of the plight of downtrodden Vietnamese after the 1975 Liberation, whose only hope for survival lies in their becoming boat people.

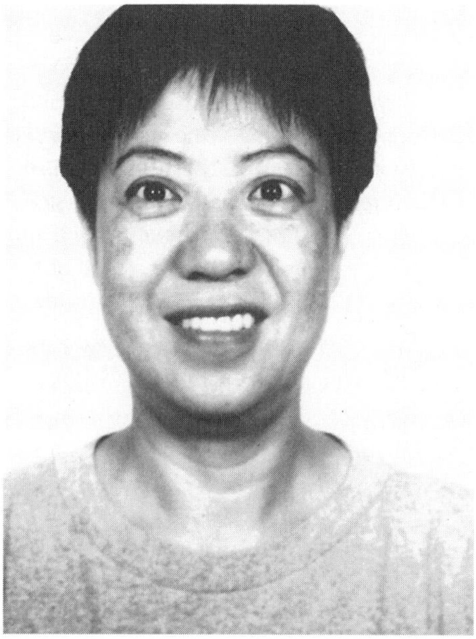

Ann Hui

Familial conflict is a key theme in Hui's work. In the two-part historic epic *Princess Fragrance* and *The Romance of Book & Sword,* she focused on the dissension between two brothers, one a Manchurian emperor and the other the head of the secret anti-Manchu Red Flower Society. *My American Grandson* is the story of an elderly Chinese man looking after his 12-year-old American grandson. Here, Hui acutely examines the cultural differences between East and West, the manner in which American-reared Chinese have lost touch with their native culture, and the importance of understanding that culture. By far her best recent film is *Summer Snow,* a family comedy-drama about May Sun, a working woman with a husband and teenage son, who has never gotten along with her father-in-law but must take him in upon the death of his wife. The scenario follows May Sun's struggle to deal with the situation, which is exacerbated when the father-in-law is afflicted with Alzheimer's disease.

To date, *Song of the Exile* is Hui's most intensely intimate work, if only because it so obviously is semiautobiographical. This slice-of-life, set in 1973, tells the story of Hueyin, a 25-year-old woman who (like Hui) was raised in Hong Kong and, at the scenario's outset, completes a film school education in London. Hueyin returns to Hong Kong to attend her younger sister's wedding, where she recalls the supportive grandparents with whom she spent much of her childhood and clashes with her manipulative mother who attempts to stifle her dreams and her individuality.

For Hueyin, the cultural revolution in China and the war in Vietnam are little more than news items reported on television. As such, she pays them no mind. Yet in the wake of such events, families are separated and individuals are forced to flee their homes and become refugees. If she ever is to attain self-understanding, Hueyin must realize that the wars and revolutions of the recent past, coupled with economic realities, have separated, and affected, the various members of her family.

On the surface, *Song of the Exile* chronicles the clashing personalities and value-systems of a mother and daughter. But more to the point, it is the story of a displaced family and the cultural and nationalistic barriers that isolate its members. Hueyin's mother was born in Japan, lived most of her adult life in Hong Kong, and in the film's final section returns to Japan. Hueyin's grandparents reside in Canton, and resent her mother because she is Japanese. Hueyin spent her youth in Canton as well as Hong Kong, studied in London, returns to Hong Kong, travels with her mother to Japan, and visits her grandparents in Canton. Upon her marriage, Hueyin's sister and her husband emigrate to Canada.

When an individual moves to a foreign country out of choice, as Hueyin did when she went off to study in London, it can be an enlightening experience. But when you are forced to move, the result is altogether different as the individual sadly and tragically feels displaced and loses touch with native culture and familial roots. Hueyin comes in touch with this differentiation as she spends time with her mother, and journeys with her back to Japan. At the outset of *Song of the Exile,* Hueyin merrily romps through the London streets with her classmates. She is an idealistic schoolgirl, with the promise of a happy life before her. But in the course of the story, she changes as she becomes more worldly and realizes there is much more between herself and her mother than superficial generational conflict. She comes to understand the source of her mother's unhappiness and frustration. Indeed, in the last shot of the film, Hueyin is crying.

During the 1990s, Ann Hui has gravitated to directing commercial genre films, and working in behind-the-scenes capacities for other filmmakers. One of her latest works, *The Stunt Woman,* tells the story of Ah Kam, a movie stuntwoman. But even here, the theme of displacement is present: Ah Kam is born in China but comes to Hong Kong to pursue her career; she is separated from her family, and struggles to acclimate herself to her new environment. In the mid-1990s, Hui unsuccessfully attempted to raise money for an ambitious, potentially controversial project: a film about the people of Hong Kong at the time of the Tiananmen Square massacre.—ROB EDELMAN

Huillet, Danièle

French director

Born *France, 1 May 1936.* ***Education*** *Studied film at universities in Nancy and Strasbourg.* ***Family*** *Married the director Jean-Marie Straub, 1959.* ***Career*** *1954—began collaboration with Jean-Marie Straub; 1959—Straub and Huillet moved to Munich; 1963—collaborated on their first film,* Machorka-Muff; *1969—moved to Italy.* ***Address*** *c/o French Film Office, 745 5th Avenue, New York, NY 10151, U.S.A.*

Films as Co-Director with Jean-Marie Straub: 1963: *Machorka-Muff* (+ sc, co-ed, co-sound). **1965:** *Nicht versöhnt oder Es hilft nur Gewalt, wo Gewalt herrscht* (*Es hilft nicht, wo Gewalt herrscht*; *Not Reconciled*) (+ sc, co-ed, co-ph). **1968:** *Chronik der Anna Magdalena Bach* (*Chronicle of Anna Magdalena Bach*) (+ sc); *Der Bräutigam, die Komödiantin und der Zuhälter* (*The Bridegroom, the Comedienne and the Pimp*) (+ sc, co-ed). **1969:** *Othon* (*Les Yeux ne veulent pas en tout temps se fermer ou Peut-être qu'un jour Rome se permettra de choisir à son tour*; *Die Augen wollen sich nicht zu jeder Zeit schliessen oder Vielleicht eines Tages wird Rom sich erlauben, seinerseits zu wählen*; *Eyes Do Not Want to Close at All Times or Perhaps One Day Rome Will Permit Herself to Choose in Her Turn, Othon*) (+ sc, co-ed); *Einleitung zu Arnold Schoenberg Begleit Musik zu einer Lichtspielscene* (*Introduction to Arnold Schoenberg's Accompaniment for a Cinematographic Scene*) (for TV) (+ sc, co-pr, co-ed). **1972:** *Geschichtsunterricht* (*History Lessons*) (+ sc, co-pr, co-ed). **1975:** *Moses und Aron* (*Moses and Aaron*) (+ sc, co-ed). **1976:** *Fortini/Cani* (*I cani del Sinai*; *The Dogs of Sinai*) (+ sc, co-ed). **1977:** *Toute révolution est un coup de dés* (*Every Revolution Is a Throw of the Dice*) (+ sc, ed). **1979:** *Della nube alla resistenza* (*From the Cloud to the Resistance*) (+ sc, ed). **1982:** *En Rachachant.* **1983:** *Trop tot, trop tard* (*Zu früh, zu spät*; *Too Early, Too Late*). **1985:** *Klassenverhältnisse* (*Class Relations*) (+ co-sc, ed). **1986:** *Der Tod des Empedokles* (*The Death of Empedocles*) (+ ed, costumes). **1989:** *Schwarze Sunde* (*Black Sins*) (+ ed); *Cézanne.* **1992:** *Antigone.* **1994:** *Lothringen!* (+ ed).

In Ephraim Katz's *Film Encyclopedia,* Jean-Marie Straub is given his own entry, in which he is described as "a leading voice in the New German Cinema." Meanwhile, the entry for his wife and co-creator, Danièle Huillet, is cross-referenced to Straub. She is not mentioned until the final sentence, which reads, "His wife, Danièle Huillet, collaborates on his films as producer and writer."

In *Cinema: A Critical Dictionary,* an anthology edited by Richard Roud, Straub is cited on 13 pages. Huillet is mentioned only on one, in Roud's essay on Straub, and it is an ever-so casual citation.

Is this lack of attention the result of an assumption that the male automatically is the more important contributor in a male-female collaboration? Or is it an offshoot of the auteurist theory that Straub, as the officially credited director, is the foremost contributor to a film while Huillet, as collaborator/producer/writer, is rendered merely an asterisk?

In these post-feminist times, the latter would seem to be the case, if only because contemporary women directors (rather than their male scriptwriters, producers, or "collaborators") are the ones who take center stage at film festivals and are the focus of press interviews and critical analysis. And after all, the direction of Straub and Huillet's earliest films *was* credited only to Straub. For example, *Nicht versöhnt oder Es hilft nur Gewalt, wo Gewalt herrscht,* based on a novel by Heinrich Böll, is listed as a Straub-Huillet production, directed by Straub and scripted by Straub and Huillet.

Still, there is more-than-ample evidence pointing to Huillet's omission as a case of wholesale sexism. This is because, from the early 1970s on, Huillet has shared directorial credit with Straub. They are listed as co-directors of *Geschichtsunterricht,* based on Bertolt Brecht's *The Affairs of Mr. Julius Caesar.* Yet in the body of the *Variety* review, only Straub is cited. Huillet may be mentioned in the *Variety* critique of *Moses und Aron,* an adaptation of Arnold Schoenberg's biblical opera, but she is immediately referred to as "Mrs. Straub," while Straub alone is the focus of the critical commentary. This dismissal directly segues into the space (or lack of) devoted to Huillet by Katz and Roud.

As with many intimate, long-lasting two-person collaborations, the boundaries of who does what over the course of many years and many films often becomes fuzzy. So the point really is not who directed what, who scripted what, who photographed what—and who was credited with what. Straub and Huillet are equal partners. When one discusses one, one certainly must cite the other.

Beyond giving acknowledgment where acknowledgment is due, it is reasonable to assume that Straub and Huillet never will be as celebrated as fellow New German filmmakers Rainer Werner Fassbinder, Volker Schlöndorff, Werner Herzog, or Wim Wenders. Nevertheless, their unconventionally structured, gloriously uncommercial experimental minimalist films, which more often than not spotlight German literature and music, are sharply visual and mind-massagingly cerebral. They abandon naturalism and conventional narrative and combine images, sounds, and words to create impressions and emotions, with the use of music taking on a special emphasis as a tool of communication.

Most significantly, Straub and Huillet place demands on their audiences to interact with and respond to their work. Some critics and film goers have written off their efforts as static, uncinematic, even downright boring. But as Dave Kehr so succinctly put it in a review of *Moses und Aron,* "Straub and Huillet's investigation of the medium is an important experience for anyone interested in the way film represents reality—or fails to."—ROB EDELMAN

Irene

American costume designer

Born *Irene Lentz in Montana, 1901.* ***Family*** *Married the screenwriter Elliot Gibbons.* ***Career*** *1932—first costume designs for film* The Animal Kingdom; *1942-50—chief designer for MGM; 1950—formed own design manufacturing company, with some freelance film work in early 1960s.* ***Died*** *(Suicide) in Hollywood, 15 November 1962.*

Films as Costume Designer: **1932:** *The Animal Kingdom* (E. H. Griffith) (co). **1933:** *Goldie Gets Along* (St. Clair); *Flying Down to Rio* (Freeland) (co). **1936:** *The Unguarded Hour* (Wood). **1937:** *Vogues of 1938* (Cummings) (co); *Shall We Dance* (M. Sandrich); *Topper* (McLeod) (co). **1938:** *Algiers* (Cromwell); *Merrily We Live* (McLeod) (co); *There Goes My Heart* (McLeod); *Trade Winds* (Garnett) (co); *Vivacious Lady* (Stevens) (co); *You Can't Take It with You* (Capra) (co); *Blockade* (Dieterle); *Service De Luxe* (R. V. Lee). **1939:** *Bachelor Mother* (Kanin); *Eternally Yours* (Garnett); *Intermezzo* (Ratoff); *Topper Takes a Trip* (McLeod); *Midnight* (Leisen) (co); *The Housekeeper's Daughter* (Roach); *In Name Only* (Cromwell) (co). **1940:** *Arise My Love* (Leisen) (co); *Lucky Partners* (Milestone) (co); *Seven Sinners* (Garnett) (co); *The House Across the Bay* (Mayo); *He Stayed for Breakfast* (Hall) (co); *Too Many Husbands* (Ruggles). **1941:** *That Uncertain Feeling* (Lubitsch); *Skylark* (M. Sandrich) (co); *Sundown* (Hathaway) (co); *Escape to Glory* (*Submarine Zone*) (Brahm); *Bedtime Story* (Hall); *This Thing Called Love* (Hall); *Mr. and Mrs. Smith* (Hitchcock). **1942:** *The Lady Is Willing* (Leisen); *The Palm Beach Story* (P. Sturges); *The Talk of the Town* (Stevens); *They All Kissed the Bride* (Hall); *To Be or Not to Be* (Lubitsch) (co); *Twin Beds* (Whelan) (co); *Take a Letter, Darling* (*The Green Eyed Woman*) (Leisen) (co); *Reunion in France* (*Mademoiselle France*) (Dassin); *You Were Never Lovelier* (Seiter); *Tales of Manhattan* (Duvivier) (co); *The Wife Takes a Flyer* (*A Yank in Dutch*) (Wallace). **1943:** *Three Hearts for Julia* (Thorpe); *Song of Russia* (Ratoff); *The Heavenly Body* (Hall); *Cry Havoc* (Thorpe); *Lost Angel* (Rowland); *The Youngest Profession* (Buzzell); *Above Suspicion* (Thorpe); *Thousands Cheer* (Sidney); *Slightly Dangerous* (Ruggles); *The Human Comedy* (C. Brown); *The Man from Down Under* (Leonard); *Dr. Gillespie's Criminal Case* (Goldbeck); *Whistling in Brooklyn* (Simon); *Cabin in the Sky* (Minnelli) (co); *Assignment in Britanny* (Conway) (co); *Du Barry Was a Lady* (Del Ruth) (co); *Swing Shift Maisie* (*The Girl in Overalls*) (McLeod); *Best Foot Forward* (Buzzell) (co); *No Time for Love* (Leisen) (co); *Broadway Rhythm* (Del Ruth) (co). **1944:** *Between Two Women* (Goldbeck); *The Seventh Cross* (Zinnemann); *Two Girls and a Sailor* (Thorpe); *An American Romance* (K. Vidor); *Nothing but Trouble* (Taylor); *Andy Hardy's Blonde Trouble* (Seitz); *A Guy Named Joe* (Fleming); *See Here, Private Hargrove* (Ruggles); *Maisie Goes to Reno* (Beaumont); *Kismet* (Dieterle); *Mrs. Parkington* (Garnett) (co); *The*

Irene

White Cliffs of Dover (C. Brown) (co); *Meet the People* (Riesner) (co); *Two Girls and a Sailor* (Thorpe) (co); *Bathing Beauty* (Sidney) (co); *Gaslight* (*Murder in Thornton Square*) (Cukor) (co); *Three Men in White* (Goldbeck); *The Thin Man Goes Home* (Thorpe) (co); *Marriage Is a Private Affair* (Leonard) (co); *Blonde Fever* (Whorf); *Thirty Seconds over Tokyo* (LeRoy) (co); *Music for Millions* (Koster) (co); *Dragon Seed* (Conway and Bucquet) (co); *National Velvet* (C. Brown) (co). **1945:** *The Picture of Dorian Gray* (Lewin) (co); *Adventure* (Fleming); *The Sailor Takes a Wife* (Whorf) (co); *Weekend at the Waldorf* (Leonard) (co); *This Man's Navy* (Wellman) (co); *Keep Your Powder Dry* (Buzzell) (co); *Anchors Aweigh* (Sidney) (co); *The Clock* (*Under the Clock*) (Minnelli) (co); *Without Love* (Bucquet) (co); *Son of Lassie* (Simon); *Valley of Decision* (Garnett) (co); *Thrill of a Romance* (Thorpe) (co); *Twice Blessed* (Beaumont) (co); *The Hidden Eye* (Whorf) (co); *Our Vines Have Tender Grapes* (Rowland) (co); *Abbott and Costello in Hollywood* (Simon) (co); *Dangerous Partners* (Cahn) (co); *She Went to the Races* (Goldbeck); *What Next Corporal Hargrove?* (Thorpe). **1946:** *Up Goes Maisie* (*Up She Goes*) (Beaumont); *Bad Bascomb* (Simon); *Easy to Wed* (Buzzell) (co); *Holiday in Mexico* (Sidney) (co); *Undercurrent* (Minnelli); *Two Smart People* (Dassin) (co); *Courage of Lassie* (Wilcox); *Boys' Ranch* (Rowland); *Lady in the Lake* (Montgomery); *Love Laughs at Andy Hardy* (Goldbeck); *The Secret Heart* (Leonard); *No Leave No Love* (Martin); *The Green Years* (Saville) (co); *Faithful in My Fashion* (Salkow) (co); *The Postman Always Rings Twice* (Garnett) (co); *Little Mister Jim* (Zinnemann) (co); *Three Wise Fools* (Buzzell) (co); *Undercurrent* (Minnelli); *My Brother Talks to Horses* (Zinneman) (co); *The Mighty McGurk* (Waters) (co); *Till the Clouds Roll By* (Whorf); (co); *The Yearling* (C. Brown) (co); *The Harvey Girls* (Sidney); *The Hoodlum Saint* (Taurog) (co); *Ziegfeld Follies* (Minnelli) (co). **1947:** *Fiesta* (Thorpe) (co); *This Time for Keeps* (Thorpe) (co); *The Arnelo Affair* (Obeler); *The Beginning of the End* (Taurog); *Undercover Maisie* (Beaumont); *Dark Delusion* (Goldbeck); *High Barbaree* (Conway); *Desire Me* (Cukor and others—uncredited); *The Hucksters* (Conway); *Cynthia* (*The Full Rich Life*) (Leonard); *Merton of the Movies* (Alton) (co); *Living in a Big Way* (La Cava) (co); *Song of Love* (Franklin and Marion) (co); *The Romance of Rosy Ridge* (Rowland) (co); *Song of the Thin Man* (Buzzell) (co); *The Unfinished Dance* (Koster) (co); *Green Dolphin Street* (Saville) (co); *10th Avenue Angel* (Rowland); *If Winter Comes* (Saville); *Cass Timberlane* (Sidney). **1948:** *Summer Holiday* (Mamoulian); *Three Daring Daughters* (Wilcox); *State of the Union* (Capra); *Easter Parade* (Walters) (co); *Julia Misbehaves* (Conway); *On an Island with You* (Thorpe); *B.F.'s Daughter* (Leonard). **1949:** *The Bribe* (Leonard); *The Great Sinner* (Siodmak) (co); *Neptune's Daughter* (Buzzell); *Malaya* (Thorpe) (co); *The Barkleys of Broadway* (Walters); *In the Good Old Summertime* (Leonard) (co); *The Sun Comes Up* (Thorpe); *The Shadow on the Wall* (Jackson); *The Scene of the Crime* (Rowland). **1950:** *Please Believe Me* (Taurog); *Key to the City* (Sidney). **1960:** *Midnight Lace* (Miller). **1961:** *Lover Come Back* (Delbert Mann). **1963:** *A Gathering of Eagles* (Delbert Mann) (co).

Film as Actress: 1922: *A Tailor Made Man* (De Grasse).

Irene's first work in Hollywood was as a movie extra, but after studying at the Wolfe School of Design, she opened a dress shop at the University of California, Los Angeles, which attracted the likes of Lupe Velez and Dolores Del Rio. The actresses loved Irene's elegant evening gowns and gladly recommended her to their celebrity friends. Following a trip to Europe, where she studied the couturier collections in search of inspiration, Irene opened an even larger boutique, catering to scores of Hollywood starlets. Her reputation soon landed her a position as head of Bullock's Wilshire Custom Salon, and while there she often received commissions to dress such clients as Ginger Rogers, Myrna Loy, Rosalind Russell, Irene Dunne, and Claudette Colbert for their film roles. Her designs lent the actresses the level of taste and sophistication they sought to exude, both privately and on screen, and, in turn, the starlets were willing to champion Irene's work in film. By 1942 Irene had signed a seven-year contract with MGM to be Adrian's successor as executive designer

Irene's film specialty was an extension of her boutique work—the fabulous evening gown. Her soufflé gowns were soft and classic, draped elegantly, and would cling in such a way as to accentuate the flowing lines of the women she dressed. Those women were often likened to moving sculptures, and are best represented by Claudette Colbert in *The Palm Beach Story* and Rita Hayworth in *You Were Never Lovelier.* Irene was not limited to one style, though. Among her most famous works was Lana Turner's midriff blouse/turban/hot pants ensemble from *The Postman Always Rings Twice.*

Irene was one of the most prolific designers in the screwball comedy genre. She dressed the actresses in confident-yet-feminine outfits that the strong female characters in these films begged for, such as with Carole Lombard in *Mr. and Mrs. Smith* and Claudette Colbert in *Midnight.* In addition, Irene perfected the sensible career gal look, which she favored for herself. Her suits were worn with flair by Rosalind Russell in *Take a Letter, Darling* and Joan Crawford in *They All Kissed the Bride.*

Unfortunately, Irene's costumes had a reputation for being quite costly. A custom tailored Irene gown sold for double what a Paris original of equal quality did, and her film designs were often just as extravagant. One failed outlandish outfit for *Kismet* had Marlene Dietrich wearing pants made entirely of hundreds of tiny gold chains, a creation that fell apart once Dietrich began performing in them. The mistake raised the ire of Irene's boss, Louis B. Mayer, who felt his executive designer wasted too much money. Irene's penchant for costly designs is very apparent in her period dresses. Because she was not comfortable with historical costumes, her designs were as indicative of the times Irene lived as of the times they were meant to depict. *The Great Sinner,* which took place in Germany in the 1800s, featured elegant gowns in the soft fabrics popular in the 1940s, not the stiff silk used in the era. Period pictures dressed by Irene (such as the Oscar nominated *Mrs. Parkington*) were noted for their asymmetrical rayon crepe gowns draped with layered chiffon and other couture fabrics, resembling creations out of her own boutiques. But what Irene lacked in authenticity, she more than made up for in beauty, with her sharp inventiveness in costuming.

Obviously suited for more personal and singular design work, and convinced her stint with MGM had been a mistake, Irene left the field of costume design almost completely in 1949, preferring to devote her full attentions to her boutiques, which she had launched in 1947. She was lured back on a few occasions, most notably to dress Doris Day in a couple of films in the early 1960s. In *Midnight Lace,* Irene created a very popular and memorable black-lace negligee for Day to wear, earning the designer an Academy Award nomination. In *Lover Come Back,* Irene furthered Day's cheerleader chic image with more white hats, dresses, and gloves, as well as favorable use of furs. Her last film *A Gathering of Eagles* was completed shortly before her suicide in 1962. By the time Irene leapt from the Knickerbocker Hotel, the era of glamour which she had helped clothe so immaculately was long gone.—JOHN E. MITCHELL

Jakubowska, Wanda

Polish director

Born *Warsaw, 10 October 1907.* ***Education*** *Studied architecture and arts.* ***Career*** *1930—co-founder of Society of Devotees of the Artistic Film (START); 1930s—made short documentary films; 1937—co-founder of the Cooperative of Film Authors (SAF); 1939—directed first feature film,* On the Neman River*—which has been lost; 1942—arrested by German Nazis and imprisoned in concentration camps Oświęcim (Auschwitz) and Ravensbrück; 1947—first feature film after the war,* The Last Stop; *1949-74—lecturer at Łódź Film School; 1955-68—artistic director of START film unit.*

Films as Director: 1932: "Impresje jesienne" ("Autumn Impressions") ep. of *Reportaż nr 1* (*Reportage no. 1*) (co-d with Cękalski and Zarzycki—doc, short); *Morze* (*The Sea*) (co-d with Cękalski and Wohl—doc, short). **1934:** *Budujemy* (*We Are Building*) (co-d with Cękalski, Emmer, and Maliniak—doc, short). **1937:** *Ulica Edisona* (*Edison Street*) (doc, short). **1939:** *Nad Niemnem* (*On the Neman River*) (co-d with Szołowski—unreleased). **1946:** *Budujemy nowe wsi* (*We Are Building New Villages*) (doc, short). **1947:** *Ostatni etap* (*The Last Stop*; *The Last Stage*) (+ co-sc). **1953:** *Żołnierz zwycięstwa* (*The Soldier of Victory*) (+ sc). **1954:** *Opowieść Atlantycka* (*The Atlantic Story*). **1956:** *Pożegnanie z diabłem* (*Farewell to the Devil*) (+ co-sc). **1957:** *Król Maciuś I* (*King Matthias I*; *King Matthew I*). **1960:** *Spotkania w mroku* (*Begegnung im Zwielicht*; *Encounters in the Dark*) (+ co-sc); *Historia współczesna* (*Modern Story*). **1963:** *Koniec naszego świata* (*The End of Our World*) (+ sc). **1965:** *Gorąca linia* (*The Hot Line*). **1971:** *150 na godzinę* (*150 km per Hour*). **1978:** *Biały mazur* (*The White Mazurka*; *Dance in Chains*) (+ sc). **1986:** *Zaproszenie* (*The Invitation*) (+ sc). **1988:** *Kolory kochania* (*The Colors of Love*) (+ co-sc).

Other Film: 1962: *Wielka Wielksza Najwielksza* (*The Great Big World and Little Children*) (Sokolowska) (production supervisor).

Wanda Jakubowska decided to become a film director at a time when this occupation was rather unusual for a woman. It was even more unusual in a country such as Poland where the economical and technical conditions for film development were lacking. In spite of that fact, towards the end of the silent film era many people appeared who were enchanted by the medium of film and at the same time realized its social and artistic power. Those enthusiasts, Jakubowska among them, founded an avant-garde group, START (Society of Devotees of the Artistic Film), which began to bring to life—from the theoretical to the practical—their ideas of how to elevate the film. They found their models in the Soviet documentary film, especially those of Dziga Vertov, and later within the British documentary school.

Under the influence of those trends, Jakubowska shot her first short films and her first feature film, *On the Neman River*. The latter never reached an audience. The premiere should have taken place in September 1939, the very month that World War II began with the attack on Poland. In the apocalypse that followed, the film was entirely lost. Jakubowska was soon arrested and imprisoned in Auschwitz and Ravensbrück.

Shortly after the war she directed her most famous film, *The Last Stop,* which was based on the horror of the concentration camps. It was one of the first films about the fascist "death factories." Jakubowska had started to work on the film in 1946, at a time when there were still rows of prison houses, when an Auschwitz commander waited for his verdict, and when the new and more horrible crimes of fascism were still being revealed at the Nuremberg Tribunal. Although the recent past was alive, Jakubowska was able to keep her recollections in check and collect facts using a strict selection. She consciously refused to shock spectators with drastic scenes and decided to convey the testimony of modest and nonpathetic heroes who even under the pressure of suffering and fear managed to keep their human dignity and sensitivity. On the other hand she did not conceal the truth about those who had been broken by a cruel system. A few trite, unbelievable motives and too pathetic an end disturb a bit the integrity of the film.

But for all that, *The Last Stop* is a significant piece of art born out of real suffering, from love of people and the desire to fight to stay alive. Thanks to this desire Jakubowska survived: "I might owe my life to my desire to shoot this film. This desire saved me from going through my experience in Auschwitz too subjectively, it allowed me to perceive everything around me as a special kind of documentation" (*Historia filmu polskiego III,* 1966-85).

Jakubowska devoted all her active life to film. For decades she was active in various organizations, involved with education, and continued in film production. At the same time she stayed faithful to the main principles of START, which aimed to create socially useful and committed films. Following *The Last Stop,* she unfortunately was not able to realize these principles with a sufficient artistic might.

The gigantic two-part epopee about General Świerczewski (*The Soldier of Victory*) was schematic and false, tributary to the aesthetics of socialistic realism. Her effort to express up-to-date contemporary problems was converted to a direct political proclamation (*Modern Story*). Even the films where she evoked her experience from the war lacked an artistic persuasiveness and impressiveness. Perhaps only *King Matthias I* is worth mentioning for its design.

Only *The Last Stop* guarantees a place for Jakubowska in film history—this is more significant than it might seem. With this film, Jakubowska opened the way for Polish film to reach the world. Only in its wake came the "Polish film school" of the 1950s and 1960s.—BLAŽENA URGOŠÍKOVÁ

Jeakins, Dorothy

American costume designer

Born *San Diego, California, 11 January 1914.* ***Education*** *Attended Otis Art Institute, 1931-34; Guggenheim fellowship, to Japan, 1961.* ***Family*** *Married Raymond Eugene Dane, 1940 (divorced 1946), sons: Peter Dane and Stephen Dane.* ***Career*** *Stage and TV designer; 1948—first film as costume designer,* Joan of Arc; *1967-70—curator of textiles, Los Angeles County Museum of Art.* ***Awards*** *Academy Awards, for* Joan of Arc, *1948,* Samson and Delilah, *1950, and* The Night of the Iguana, *1964.* ***Died*** *In Santa Barbara, California, 21 November 1995.*

Films as Costume Designer: **1948:** *Joan of Arc* (Fleming) (co). **1949:** *Samson and Delilah* (C. B. DeMille) (co). **1952:** *Belles on Their Toes* (Levin); *The Big Sky* (Hawks); *The Greatest Show on Earth* (C. B. DeMille) (co); *Les Misérables* (Milestone); *Lure of the Wilderness* (Negulesco); *My Cousin Rachel* (Koster); *The Outcasts of Poker Flat* (J. Newman); *Stars and Stripes Forever* (Koster); *Treasure of the Golden Condor* (Daves). **1953:** *Beneath the Twelve Mile Reef* (Webb); *City of Bad Men* (H. Jones); *Inferno* (R. W. Baker); *The Kid from Left Field* (H. Jones); *Niagara* (Hathaway); *Titanic* (Negulesco); *White Witch Doctor* (Hathaway). **1954:** *Three Coins in the Fountain* (Negulesco). **1956:** *Friendly Persuasion* (Wyler). **1957:** *The Ten Commandments* (C. B. DeMille) (co). **1958:** *South Pacific* (Logan). **1959:** *Green Mansions* (M. Ferrer). **1960:** *Elmer Gantry* (R. Brooks); *Let's Make Love* (Cukor); *The Unforgiven* (J. Huston). **1961:** *The Children's Hour* (Wyler). **1962:** *All Fall Down* (Frankenheimer); *The Music Man* (da Costa). **1964:** *The Best Man* (Schaffner); *Ensign Pulver* (Logan); *The Night of the Iguana* (J. Huston). **1965:** *The Fool Killer* (*Violent Journey*) (Gonzalez); *The Sound of Music* (Wise). **1966:** *Any Wednesday* (R. E. Miller); *Hawaii* (G. R. Hill) (+ ro as Hepzibah Hale). **1967:** *The Flim-Flam Man* (Kershner); *Reflections in a Golden Eye* (J. Huston). **1968:** *Finian's Rainbow* (F. F. Coppola); *The Fixer* (Frankenheimer); *The Stalking Moon* (Mulligan). **1969:** *True Grit* (Hathaway). **1970:** *Little Big Man* (A. Penn); *The Molly Maguires* (Ritt). **1972:** *Fat City* (J. Huston); *Fuzz* (Colla). **1973:** *The Iceman Cometh* (Frankenheimer); *The Way We Were* (Pollack) (co). **1974:** *Young Frankenstein* (M. Brooks). **1975:** *The Hindenburg* (Wise); *The Yakuza* (Pollack). **1977:** *Audrey Rose* (Wise). **1978:** *The Betsy* (Petrie). **1979:** *North Dalls Forty* (Kotcheff); *Love and Bullets* (Rosenberg). **1981:** *The Postman Always Rings Twice* (Rafelson); *On Golden Pond* (Rydell). **1987:** *The Dead* (*The Dubliners*) (J. Huston).

Dorothy Jeakins was abandoned by her natural parents for unknown reasons, and had an unhappy childhood. She lived with a foster mother who frequently whipped her and threatened to send her to reform school. Often left alone, as a young child she would roam the streets of Los Angeles and ask people for free food and clothes. She called it a "Dickensian existence." She has described herself as "pathologically shy and neurotically modest," but very secure in her sense of taste and style, with the "sensitive soul of an artist." Perhaps as a result of her shyness, virtually nothing has been written about Jeakins or her impressive film credits.

At Fairfax High School she found plays to be a "sweet escape into fantasy." Encouraged into drama by sympathetic teachers, she discovered her vocation when she visited a costume house and found a means of interpreting the plays she loved through costume. She attended Otis Art Institute on a scholarship and continued to frequent the public library to read and illustrate the characters of plays.

She worked for the WPA at the age of 19 during the Great Depression, and then moved on to Disney studios as an illustrator for $16 a week until a strike left her unemployed. She next became an illustrator of fashion layouts for I. Magnin's advertising department. Eventually a studio art director saw her sketches and hired her as an assistant designer for *Joan of Arc*—her first major film for which she won her first Oscar. (She had also been an assistant to the designer Ernst Dryden for *Dr. Rhythm,* 1938.)

Jeakins had an impressive number of credits, almost equally divided between the theater and motion pictures, and some plays she designed for Broadway she later designed as films, such as *South Pacific* and *The Sound of Music.*

Jeakins's noted specialty was for ethnic and period costumes, and also for her use of color. With each film Jeakins considered how she could use costume in a new way, and when searching for inspiration for the color scheme would consider such natural elements as "wet stones or peonies or pullet-eggs beige and white or Chinese-coolie blues." The designer Edith Head once commented that Jeakins had a particularly good eye for color. On a separate occasion, Jeakins said candidly of Edith Head that "her work is extremely mediocre . . . but Edith deserves a lot of credit for hanging in there." Jeakins was also budget-conscious when she worked on films and could make elegant costumes with inexpensive muslin. As a designer, she said of herself, "I'm dependable, experienced, organized, aesthetic, creative."—SUSAN PEREZ PRICHARD

Jhabvala, Ruth Prawer

American writer

Born *Cologne, Germany, of Polish parents, 7 May 1927; emigrated to England as a refugee, 1939; naturalized, 1948; became U.S. citizen, 1986.* ***Education*** *Attended Hendon County School, London; Queen Mary College, University of London, M.A. in English literature, 1951.* ***Family*** *Married Cyrus Jhabvala, 1951, three daughters.* ***Career*** *1951-75—lived in India; 1955—first novel published; 1963—began association with producer Ismail Merchant and director James Ivory: first collaborative film,* The Householder; *1975—moved to New York.* ***Awards*** *Booker Prize, 1975; British Academy Award,* *for* Heat and Dust, *1983; Academy Awards, for* A Room with a View, *1986, and* Howards End, *1992.* ***Address*** *400 East 52nd Street, New York, NY, 10022, U.S.A.*

Films as Writer for Director James Ivory: 1963: *The Householder.* **1965:** *Shakespeare Wallah.* **1968:** *The Guru.* **1970:** *Bombay Talkie.* **1975:** *Autobiography of a Princess* (co). **1977:** *Roseland.* **1978:** *Hullabaloo over Georgie and Bonnie's Pictures.* **1979:** *The Europeans.* **1980:** *Jane Austen in Manhattan.* **1981:** *Quartet.* **1983:** *Heat and Dust.* **1984:** *The Bostonians.* **1986:** *A Room with a View.* **1990:** *Mr. and Mrs. Bridge.* **1992:** *Howards End.* **1993:** *The Remains of the Day.* **1995:** *Jefferson in Paris.* **1996:** *Surviving Picasso.* **1998:** *A Soldier's Daughter Never Cries* (co).

Other Films as Writer: 1982: *The Courtesans of Bombay* (Merchant—doc). **1988:** *Madame Sousatska* (Schlesinger) (co).

Since the 1960s, Ruth Prawer Jhabvala has enjoyed a unique position among screenwriters as one of the principal collaborators in Merchant Ivory Productions, the independent film company headed by the Indian producer Ismail Merchant and the American director James Ivory. Jhabvala has supplied the scripts for a majority of the company's productions, in a happy blend of narrative styles and thematic concerns that has proven so seamless it is often difficult to tell where the writer's influence ends and the filmmaker's begins.

Jhabvala was born in Germany and emigrated with her parents to England in 1939. She later married the architect Cyrus Jhabvala and moved with him to India, where she lived for 24 years. (She eventually was to divide her time between India and New York City.) Her life in India became the source of many of her richest early works, and fostered within her a fascination with the country which she shares with Ivory. Beginning with *The Householder*, an adaptation of one of her own novels, Jhabvala wrote a series of films for Merchant Ivory Productions which helped establish both the company itself and James Ivory's reputation as a director. All of these films are set in India and deal with cultural clashes of one kind or another, a theme that would become a hallmark of the company's output. The best known of the group, *Shakespeare Wallah*, follows the fortunes of a British touring theatrical company, sadly out of place in modern India yet determined to hang on to their traditional way of life. Conflicts between East and West, tradition and change, or simply different strata of the same society recur throughout the Jhabvala-Ivory collaborations, with the stories' characters trying—and often failing—to reconcile themselves to their differences in culture and class.

Ruth Prawer Jhabvala

Ivory's films are exquisite, leisurely portraits of minutely observed people and places, and Jhabvala's screenplays lend themselves admirably to the director's style. Subtle nuances of dialogue reveal shifts in a character's thoughts or emotions, while the story is allowed to unfold through delicately sketched character interaction rather than dynamic physical activity. The themes that mark the team's earliest films were applied on a more diverse scale in their collaborations between the mid-1970s and mid-1980s, with *The Europeans*, adapted from Henry James's novel, exploring the conflicts between British and American culture; *The Bostonians*, again adapted from James, examining the problematic interplay between men and women; and *Roseland* depicting the gulf between reality and imagination in its stories of the people who frequent an outmoded New York ballroom. *Autobiography of a Princess* and *Heat and Dust* find Jhabvala and Ivory returning again to the Anglo-Indian cultural conflict, with a particular emphasis on the differences between present-day India and the India of the British Raj.

Merchant-Ivory's 1986 adaptation of E. M. Forster's *A Room with a View* introduced new audiences to the style of filmmaking that had won them a hitherto select—but devoted—following. Its story of a young Englishwoman's emotional and sexual awakening in the face of the beauty and passion of Florence was ideally suited to Ivory's and Jhabvala's long-standing concerns, and the latter's witty, literate script is alive with carefully shaded characterizations. The same can be said for *Howards End*, also based on Forster, which explores class distinctions in 1910 England (and is considered the penultimate Merchant-Ivory-Jhabvala collaboration); and *The Remains of the Day*, adapted from Kazuo Ishiguro's novel, about an efficient, mindlessly selfless professional servant, in which most of the narrative occurs between the World Wars. Less successful (but no less ambitious) were *Mr. and Mrs. Bridge* (about the manner in which the passage of time affects a Midwestern couple) and *Jefferson in Paris* (chronicling Thomas Jefferson's experiences while serving as the U.S. ambassador to France).

In the 1990s, the ever-thinning line between Hollywood and the world of independent cinema may be best symbolized by Merchant-Ivory's inking a three-film pact with the Walt Disney Company. Nonetheless, Merchant-Ivory—and Ruth Prawer Jhabvala—have sustained the conviction that the tradition of the intelligent, thoughtful film, brimming with observations on the complexities of human nature, a conviction which seems so out of place in contemporary Hollywood, remains safe and alive in their hands.—JANET LORENZ and ROB EDELMAN

Kaplan, Nelly

Argentinean/French director and writer

Born *Buenos Aires, Argentina, 1936.* ***Education*** *Studied economics at the University of Buenos Aires.* ***Career*** *1954—met and became assistant of the French director Abel Gance; 1961—directed a series of prize-winning short documentaries about artists; 1967—directed feature* Le Regard Picasso *for a retrospective on Picasso's 85th birthday;*

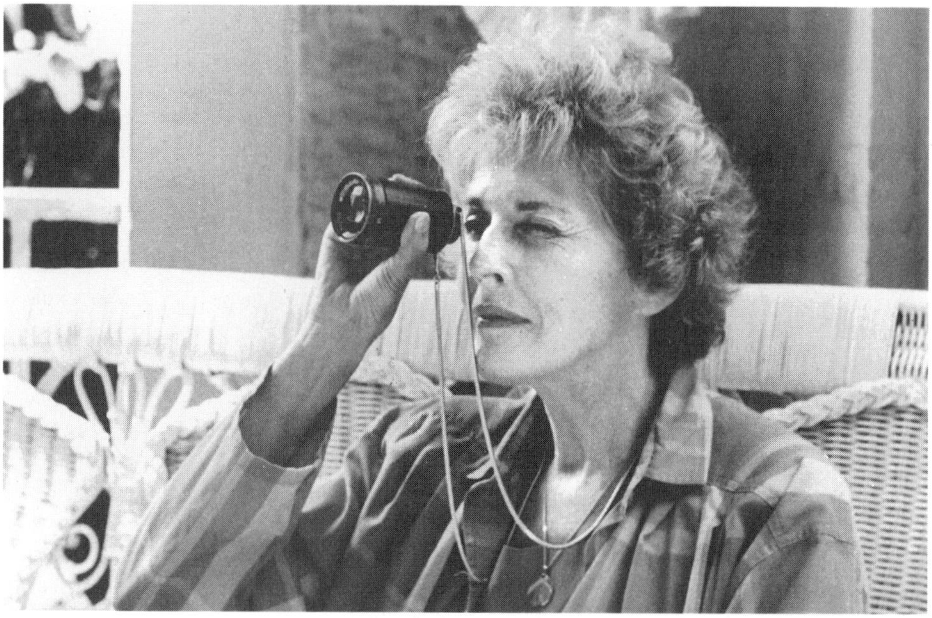

Nelly Kaplan

1969—directed first full-length fiction feature, La Fiancée du pirate. ***Awards*** *Golden Lion Award, Venice International Film Festival, for* Le Regard Picasso, *1967; Chevalier dans l'Ordre National de la Légion d'Honneur, 1996.* ***Address*** *Cythere Films, 34 Champs Elysees, 75008 Paris, France.*

Films as Director: 1961: *Gustave Moreau* (doc short) (+ sc, ed); *Rodolphe Bresdin 1825-1885* (doc short) (+ sc, ed). **1963:** *Abel Gance, hier et demain* (doc short) (+ sc, ed). **1965:** *À la source, la femme aimée* (doc short) (+ sc, ed). **1966:** *Les Années 25* (+ sc, ed); *La Nouvelle orangerie* (+ sc, ed); *Dessins et merveilles* (doc short) (+ sc, ed). **1967:** *Le Regard Picasso* (+ sc, ed). **1969:** *La Fiancée du pirate* (*A Very Curious Girl*; *Dirty Mary*) (+ co-sc, co-ed). **1971:** *Papa les petits bateaux* (+ co-sc, ro as Belen). **1976:** *Néa* (*A Young Emmanuelle*) (+ co-sc, ro as librarian). **1979:** *Charles et Lucie* (+ ro as Belen). **1983:** *Abel Gance et son Napoléon* (+ sc, pr). **1986:** *Pattes de Velours.* **1994:** *Plaisir d'amour.*

Other Films: 1954: *La Tour de Nèsle* (Gance) (ro). **1960:** *Austerlitz/Napoleone ad Austerlitz* (*The Battle of Austerlitz*) (Gance) (asst d, ro). **1963:** *Cyrano et d'Artagnan* (Gance) (co-d). **1964:** *La prima donna* (Lifchitz) (ro). **1974:** *Au Verre de l'amitié* (Makovski) (co-sc). **1975:** *Il faut vivre dangereusement* (Makovski) (co-sc). **1980:** *Livingstone* (Chapot—for TV) (co-sc). **1981:** *La Tentation d'Antoine* (Chapot—for TV) (co-sc); *Un Fait d'hiver* (Chapot—for TV) (co-sc). **1982:** *Ce fut un bel été* (Chapot—for TV) (co-sc, ro). **1984:** *Regard dans le miroir* (Chapot—for TV) (co-sc). **1992:** *Honorin et la Lorelei* (Chapot—for TV) (co-sc); *Polly West est de retour* (Chapot—for TV) (co-sc). **1993:** *Honorin et l'Enfant prodigue* (Chapot—for TV) (co-sc). **1994:** *Les Mouettes* (Chapot) (co-sc).

The controversial French feminist filmmaker Nelly Kaplan is known for her fantastic films that utilize her unique combination of gentleness, grotesquerie, vulgarity, boldness, and contradiction. Kaplan came to filmmaking by way of her work as an archivist for the Argentine cinematheque. After traveling to Paris to represent her native Argentina at an International Congress of film archivists, she decided to remain to work as a correspondent for Argentinean film journals. In 1954 she met the legendary French director Abel Gance and became his assistant. He taught her film production—though they had different ideological perspectives—and they worked together on four films. In the early 1960s, Kaplan directed her first short films, including the short documentaries about artists: *Gustave Moreau, Rodolphe Bresdin, Dessins et merveilles, Abel Gance, hier et demain,* and *À la source, la femme aimée.* Subsequently she gained renown as a successful feminist feature-film director. Kaplan's renderings of feminine sexuality celebrate female fantasies of desire and do so with lovely and slightly surreal images that suggest the power of feminine pleasure and the possibility that fantasy may be a liberating urge. But her films have provoked considerable controversy among feminists, with some charging that her films are nothing more than commercial pornography.

Kaplan's first feature film, *La Fiancée du pirate* tells the story of a young Gypsy girl who returns to her small village to exact a sometimes hilarious revenge upon the people who sexually enslaved her. She becomes the village whore and makes herself up with makeup, scents, sexy attire, and an amusing collection of cheesy consumer items in order to showcase her sexuality and to conquer and destroy her enemies, while making them pay for it, pitting them against each other, and destroying the community's economy. The film was distributed as soft-core pornography, but Kaplan has said that her aim was to make an allegorical fantasy of the avenging archetypal witch/prostitute woman. As she explained, "I wanted to tell a story in which witches burn the others." Her second feature likewise depicted a woman in revolt. *Papa les petits bateaux* is a satirical, indirect tribute to Tex Avery and Betty Boop that has a relentlessly improbable cartoonish fantasy of a luscious heiress, Cookie, who is kidnapped by a gang of ugly bumblers who hold her in a suburban house. Despite their imagined macho, Cookie manages with her single-minded determination and rapier wit rather than violence to eliminate them one by one, and thus to emerge victorious. Further, she succeeds in getting her father's ransom for herself and then decides to "kidnap Daddy" himself. Kaplan's first two features both have strong fantastic elements because Kaplan preferred to avoid neorealist strategies in order to employ myths, and because she believed it is possible to focus on realistic subjects in fantastic ways.

Néa reveals the feminist politics that characterizes all of Kaplan's work. One feminist critic described it as a feminist "erotic art" movie in which its adolescent heroine unabashedly seeks sexual experiences. Accordingly, it is vastly different from the pornography made for male spectators that depicts women as the passive objects of male sexual desires. Nevertheless, in England *Néa* received an "adults only" rating, was retitled *A Young Emmanuelle,* and was screened in soft-core pornography theaters. Its heroine Sybille is the daughter of wealthy straight-arrow parents from Geneva who finds personal liberation by writing an erotic novel. Constrained by her prejudiced father and a hypocritical family existence, she becomes determined to publish the novel anonymously, to urge her lesbian mother to leave her father for her lover, and to take her own lover in order to attain the experiences she lacks. During the course of her writing, Sybille sees and experiences a panoply of sexual activities, and she is presented as having supernatural powers that she deploys to get precisely what she desires. In the whimsical *Charles et Lucie,* a romantic comedy, an elderly working-class couple tries to secure a fortune and happiness by gambling, though they are swindled to the point of pennilessness. They are hunted by the law through the south of France so that they must use their wits to survive. Ultimately, their unhappiness with each other is replaced by a rekindling of their love. Although the film is sentimental, Kaplan brings her usual ironic sense of humor and a surreal absurdity to her offbeat story.

Some critics allege that Kaplan is a technically proficient filmmaker, but that her work fails to challenge conventional filmmaking. Her early films were influenced by surrealism and by Freud. An admitted feminist, Kaplan also has confessed to a weakness for animated cartoons, humor, audacity, nonsense, and the absurd, in order to counter the more familiar stereotypical ideas about women depicted on-screen. She explained that to combat 40 centuries of "slavery," any extreme was permitted. Further, her films are not only radical but generous, clever, and engaging. In her recent work, Kaplan has moved toward less radical themes though her stories are still generally female dominated. For example, her film, *Plaisir d'amour* concerns three generations of women. In addition, although she has not gained wide recognition in the United States, Kaplan continues to enjoy success in the arena of feminist commercial filmmaking in France.—CYNTHIA FELANDO

Keaton, Diane

American actress and director

***Born** Diane Hall in Los Angeles, California, 5 January 1946.* ***Education** Studied drama at Santa Ana College and with Sanford Meisner at New York's Neighborhood Playhouse.* ***Family** Never married; adopted a baby girl in 1996.* ***Career** Late 1960s—appeared in summer stock and on various television series, including* The FBI, Night Gallery, Mannix *and* Love, American Style; *1968—appeared on Broadway in the rock musical* Hair; *1969—appeared on Broadway in Woody Allen's* Play It Again, Sam; *1970—made her screen debut in* Lovers and Other Strangers; *1971—was directed by, and appeared with,*

Woody Allen in the 25-minute television film Men in Crisis: The Harvey Wallinger Story; *1972—appeared opposite Woody Allen for the first time on screen in* Play It Again, Sam; *1973—was directed for the first time on screen by Woody Allen in* Sleeper; *1980—published* Reservations, *a book of photographs; 1987—directed her first feature film, the documentary* Heaven; *1988—directed the television series* China Beach; *1990—directed the television series* Twin Peaks; *1995—directed her first major theatrical feature,* Unstrung Heroes; *1999—co-produced the television mini-series* Oh What a Time It Was *with Linda Ellerbee and Whoopi Goldberg.* ***Awards*** *1977—Best Actress Academy Award, National Society of Films Critics Award, New York Film Critics Circle Award, British Academy Award, Golden Globe Award as Best Motion Picture Actress-Comedy, and National Board of Review Best Supporting Actress Award, all for* Annie Hall; *1991—Woman of the Year, Harvard University's Hasty Pudding Theatricals.* ***Address*** *William Morris Agency, 151 El Camino Drive, Beverly Hills, CA 90212.*

Films as Director: 1982: *What Does Dorrie Want* (short doc). **1987:** *Heaven* (doc). **1990:** *The Girl With the Crazy Brother* (short) (for TV). **1991:** *Wildflower* (for TV). **1995:** *Unstrung Heroes.* **1999:** *Mother's Helper*; *Hanging Up* (+ role).

Films as Actress: 1970: *Lovers and Other Strangers* (Howard) (as Joan Vecchio). **1971:** *Men in Crisis: The Harvey Wallinger Story* (Allen) (short, for TV). **1972:** *The Godfather* (Coppola) (as Kay Adams); *Play It Again, Sam* (Ross) (as Linda). **1973:** *Sleeper* (Allen) (as Luna Schlosser). **1974:** *The Godfather, Part II* (Coppola) (as Kay Corleone). **1975:** *Love and Death* (Allen) (as Sonja). **1976:** *Harry and Walter Go to New York* (Rydell) (as Lissa Chestnut); *I Will, I Will . . . For Now* (Panama) (as Katie Bingham). **1977:** *Looking for Mr. Goodbar* (Brooks) (as Theresa Dunn); *Annie Hall* (Allen) (as Annie Hall). **1978:** *Interiors* (Allen) (as Renata). **1979:** *Manhattan* (Allen) (as Mary Wilke). **1981:** *The Wizard of Malta* (Davis) (narrator); *Reds* (Beatty) (as Louise Bryant). **1982:** *Shoot the Moon* (Parker) (as Faith Dunlap). **1984:** *Mrs. Soffel* (Armstrong) (as Kate Soffel); *The Little Drummer Girl* (Hill) (as Charlie). **1986:** *Crimes of the Heart* (Beresford) (as Lenny Magrath). **1987:** *Baby Boom* (Shyer) (as J.C. Wiatt); *Radio Days* (Allen) (as New Year's Singer). **1988:** *The Good Mother* (Nimoy) (as Anna Dunlap). **1990:** *The Lemon Sisters* (Chopra) (as Eloise Hamer) (+ co-pr); *The Godfather, Part III* (Coppola) (as Kay Adams). **1991:** *Father of the Bride* (Shyer) (as Nina Banks). **1992:** *The Godfather Trilogy: 1901-1980* (Coppola) (as Kay Adams); *Running Mates* (Lindsay-Hogg) (as Aggie Snow) (for TV). **1993:** *Manhattan Murder Mystery* (Allen) (as Carol Lipton); *Look Who's Talking Now* (Ropelewski) (as the voice of Daphne). **1994:** *Amelia Earhart: The Final Flight* (Simoneau) (as Amelia Earhart) (for TV). **1995:** *Father of the Bride, Part II* (Shyer) (as Nina Banks). **1996:** *The First Wives Club* (Wilson) (as Annie MacDuggan Paradis); *Marvin's Room* (Zaks) (as Bessie). **1997:** *The Only Thrill* (Masterson) (as Carol Fitzsimmons); *Northern Lights* (Yellen) (as Roberta) (for TV) (+ co-exec pr). **1999:** *The Other Sister* (Marshall) (as Elizabeth Tate); *Town and Country* (Chelsom).

Diane Keaton is best-known as the la-de-dah actress of *Annie Hall*, who since the 1970s has amassed a substantial inventory of screen credits. She created the role of Kay, girlfriend and wife of Michael Corleone, in the *Godfather* films. She gave fine dramatic performances as an ill-fated schoolteacher in *Looking for Mr. Goodbar*, the bohemian journalist Louise Bryant in *Reds*, and a middle-aged woman who has taken on the role of caregiver to her invalid father and ditsy aunt in *Marvin's Room.* Most memorably, she starred opposite Woody Allen in some of his best comedies, playing the female Anglo counterpart to Allen's prototypical Jewish urban nebbish-neurotic who passes his adult life flitting from relationship to relationship. Keaton's star-making, career-defining role was *Annie Hall*, for which she earned a Best Actress Academy Award.

While remaining among the upper echelon of respected middle-aged actresses who still command high-profile screen roles, Keaton has also begun a directorial career. In 1987, she made her first feature, *Heaven*: an extremely personal documentary examination of the way in

Diane Keaton

which individuals of varying backgrounds view death and the afterlife. Keaton loaded the film with interviews, plus sequences from films and television shows that visualize heavenly existence. Her old friend Woody Allen might have suggested she pose one of the film's more intriguing questions: Does sex exist in heaven?

Keaton honed her directorial skills shooting music videos and various television series episodes. Her most personal small-screen work has been *Wildflower*, a made-for-TV movie, and *The Girl With the Crazy Brother*, a 44-minute-long film shot for the anthology series *Wonderworks*. Both are humanistic, character-driven explorations of the manner in which adolescent girls relate to those who have deeply suffered, and who might be dismissed by society-at-large because they do not fit neatly into the mainstream. *Wildflower* is the story of two rustic teens who befriend a deaf epileptic who has been severely mistreated by her father, while *The Girl With the Crazy Brother* is a drama about a girl who struggles to accept her schizophrenic sibling.

In 1995, Keaton directed her first theatrical feature, *Unstrung Heroes*: an affecting film about a boy who is unable to relate to his parents because they are immersed in their own problems, and who finds unlikely role models in other more unconventional grown-ups. *Unstrung Heroes*, based on a childhood memoir by Franz Lidz, offers commentary on the pop culture view of what constituted an American family during the 1950s-early 1960s. Its scenario contradicts the notion, perpetuated by the era's fashionable family-oriented television sitcoms, that all children are blessed with healthy, well-adjusted, ever-helpful moms and dads. The youngsters on *The Adventures of Ozzie & Harriet*, *Leave It to Beaver*, *Father Knows Best* and *The Donna Reed Show* all had two parents: a mother, who stayed at home and baked cookies all day; and a father, who was never too busy to offer sage advice to his offspring. Of course, back when everybody liked Ike, there also were single-parent (or impending single-parent) households, which is the theme Keaton explores in *Unstrung Heroes*.

The primary character is 12-year-old Steven Lidz. As the story opens, both of Steven's parents are alive. He and his kid sister are an integral part of a happy, likably nutty family. Sid, Steven's father, is genuinely sweet, while Selma, his mother, is aptly described as an "American beauty." Then Selma becomes terminally ill. She is hospitalized for long stretches, and consequently then passes most of her time in her bedroom. Sid becomes preoccupied with his wife's condition, and is so consumed by his anger over her plight that he becomes insensitive to Steven's needs. So the boy looks to his two eccentric uncles—the "unstrung heroes" of the title—for companionship. Both exist on society's edge. One is a rotund, none-too-bright oddball. The other is a paranoid who has been psychologically affected by the era's McCarthyist hysteria to the point where he enters rooms through windows and sees political conspiracies lurking everywhere. Both characters play against the essentially sad situation at the core of the scenario. In so doing, they prove to be Steven's salvation.

In *Unstrung Heroes*, Keaton beautifully captures a time and a place, and her film features richly developed characterizations. Like many performers-turned-filmmakers, she is especially sympathetic to the needs of her actors. "Diane is good at knowing what's good for a scene, and then letting the actor find his own way," Andie MacDowell (who plays Selma) noted at the 1995 Toronto Film Festival, where *Unstrung Heroes* was screened. Regarding the manner in which she approached the film's direction, Keaton explained, "I think you do have instincts, and you follow them."

Keaton won kudos for her work on *Unstrung Heroes.* "She knows how to touch on an emotion without squeezing every last tear out of it," wrote critic Richard Schickel, adding, "she knows how to get a laugh without bringing down the whole fragile edifice of her film." Roger Ebert observed that *Unstrung Heroes* was directed "with an unusual combination of sentiment and quirky eccentricity. There are moments so touching that the heart almost stops. . . ." David Ansen declared that "the guiding spirit is clearly Keaton's, whose touch is both delicate and assured. You can detect her sensibility in every detail." Barbara Shulgasser noted, "Keaton possesses such crucial directorial gifts as good taste, intelligence, and subtlety. . . . The one thing I feel sure of after seeing this movie is that Diane Keaton knows how to direct."

Unstrung Heroes deserves to be the starting point of an important career behind the camera for Diane Keaton.—ROB EDELMAN

Kidron, Beeban

British director

Born *London, 1961.* ***Education*** *Studied film at Britain's National Film and Television School.* ***Career*** *1970s—worked as an assistant to photographer Eve Arnold; 1981—made a short film,* With or Without (Sugar*), as part of a three-day film course at the South Bank Poly, London; 1983—co-directed (with Amanda Richardson) the documentary* Carry Greenham Home *while a student at the National Film and Television School; 1986—directed a second documentary,* Global Gamble, *for the BBC; 1988—directed* Vroom, *her first feature; 1991—her success with* Antonia & Jane *led to her coming to Hollywood to make* Used People, *1992.* ***Awards*** *Hugo Award, Chicago Film Festival, for* Carry Greenham Home, *1983; Audience Award for Best Feature, San Francisco International Lesbian and Gay Film Festival, and Cable ACE Award, for* Oranges Are Not the Only Fruit, *1989.* ***Agent*** *United Talent Agency, 9560 Wilshire Boulevard, 5th Floor, Beverly Hills, CA 90212, U.S.A.*

Films as Director: 1981: *With or Without (Sugar)* (short). **1983:** *Carry Greenham Home* (co-d with A. Richardson—doc). **1985:** *Alex* (unfinished). **1986:** *Global Gamble* (doc). **1988:** *Vroom.* **1989:** *Itch*; *Oranges Are Not the Only Fruit.* **1991:** *Antonia & Jane.* **1992:** *Used People.* **1993:** *Hookers, Hustlers, Pimps and Their Johns* (doc); *Great Moments in Aviation (Shades of Fear).* **1995:** *To Wong Foo, Thanks for Everything! Julie Newmar.* **1997:** *Swept from the Sea* (+ co-pr).

Beeban Kidron

Throughout her career, Beeban Kidron has made films that explore the need for individuals to be who they are, and take and maintain control of their lives. They might be young heterosexual women (*Antonia & Jane*) or older heterosexual women (*Used People*), gay women (*Oranges Are Not the Only Fruit*) or gay men (*To Wong Foo, Thanks for Everything! Julie Newmar*).

To date, two of Kidron's best films—as well as those that established her international reputation—are among her first: *Oranges Are Not the Only Fruit* and *Antonia & Jane,* low-budget, character-oriented dramas made for British television. Both depict complex, tug-of-war relationships between two distinctly different women. In *Oranges Are Not the Only Fruit,* they are a stridently religious mother and her adopted daughter, who grows up to be a lesbian; in *Antonia & Jane,* they are two contemporaries who form an unlikely friendship despite their polar-opposite personalities.

Oranges Are Not the Only Fruit, adapted by lesbian writer Jeanette Winterson from her semiautobiographical first novel, is the story of Jess, who is depicted in the scenario at ages seven and 16. Jess is brought up by a strict, fanatically religious foster mother who spends her life at revival meetings and constantly spouts on about how she "met the lord" and gave "my heart to Jesus." The mother refuses to allow the daughter any friends her own age, and maintains that school is little more than a "den of vice." She wants Jess to grow up to be a missionary. "The world is full of sin," she declares. "You can change the world."

As an impressionable seven year old, Jess is little more than a receptacle for her mother's fanaticism. But by the time she is 16, she has developed into a headstrong young woman who knows her own mind, exudes a zest for life, and verbalizes her feelings about the narrow-mindedness in her midst. Additionally, Jess is in the process of realizing that she is physically attracted to her own sex. To date, her sole friend in the world is 82-year-old Elsie, the lone member of her mother's religious group who attempts to understand her and give her space in which to grow. Then Jess meets Melanie, who becomes her first friend her own age—as well as her first lover. Their relationship is discovered and exposed, leading to bitter conflict with her mother, and her church.

According to the church, Jess's love for Melanie is an "illness," and "the devil inside her." But Jess has become acutely aware that the love is natural, joyous, and of her own free will. So as Jess comes to separate herself from her mother and church—at the film's finale she is accepted at Oxford, where she will "read a lot more books than the Bible" and her life truly will begin—*Oranges Are Not the Only Fruit* becomes a story of sexual and spiritual liberation triumphing over sexual and spiritual repression.

Antonia & Jane chronicles the relationship between two friends, Antonia McGill and Jane Hartman, who are a study in contrast and irony. Jane, who is unmarried, is plain, obsessive, unassertive. "At parties, I always get stuck with the resident loser," she tells her therapist (whom she unknowingly shares with Antonia). Whenever she is treated rudely, Jane is incapable of complaining, and only can smile meekly. It is no understatement when she admits, "I've always had difficulty expressing my feelings."

Jane is envious of Antonia, who is pretty and outwardly successful. Antonia is married to Howard, Jane's first-ever boyfriend; Antonia and Howard had an affair when he and Jane were supposed to be "ecstatically in love." Jane even went to the wedding, and watered Antonia's plants while she and Howard were on their honeymoon.

Nonetheless, Antonia's life really is not so perfect. Her marriage and publishing industry job are less ideal than she lets on to Jane, and she is jealous of the latter's freedom. "Jane always makes me feel middle-aged," Antonia observes. "Every time we meet, she's into something new . . . I'm in a rut, and she keeps moving." Unlike Jane, Antonia may be able to say what she feels. But then she acts in a manner that is diametrically opposed to what she says, and how she feels.

Antonia & Jane is a carefully realized examination of the manner in which these two characters perceive each other, and the boundaries and subtleties of female friendship. But primarily (and like *Oranges Are Not the Only Fruit*), it is about the need for women (or, actually, anyone) to take and maintain control of their lives. It also mirrors the manner in which people perceive each other. You might expect a plain Jane to be jealous of an attractive Antonia, yet the latter also might think she has a legitimate reason to envy the former.

Kidron's success with *Oranges Are Not the Only Fruit* and *Antonia & Jane* led to her coming to Hollywood. The two American films she has made to date, *Used People* and *To Wong Foo, Thanks for Everything! Julie Newmar,* are, thematically speaking, way outside the movie industry mainstream. They are similar to her earlier work in that they focus on human relationships and unlikely personal connections. *Used People* chronicles the courtship of a middle-aged, just-widowed Jewish woman, who is surrounded by neurotic relatives, by an Italian gentleman who for decades has loved her from afar. *To Wong Foo. . .* is the story of three drag queens driving cross-country and their positive impact on the inhabitants of a small town. Neither film is particularly successful. *Used People* is dramatically heavy-handed, and none-too convincing. *To Wong Foo. . .*, a poor relation of *The Adventures of Priscilla, Queen of the Desert,* is simplistic and infuriatingly uneven (not to mention highly improbable). Both films are Hollywood "product," lacking the natural flow and believability of *Oranges Are Not the Only Fruit* and *Antonia & Jane.*

To her credit, Kidron has not abandoned her cinematic roots. Since heading for Hollywood, she has returned to England to direct *Great Moments in Aviation,* scripted by Jeanette Winterson and set in the 1950s, whose main character is a young woman bent on becoming a flyer; and *Hookers, Hustlers, Pimps and Their Johns,* a documentary (made for Britain's Channel 4) about New York City's multibillion-dollar prostitution industry, in which Kidron offers a nonjudgmental portrait of her subject. Her most recent project is *Swept from the Sea,* inspired by the Joseph Conrad novella *Amy Foster.*—ROB EDELMAN

Kopple, Barbara

American director

***Born** New York City, 30 July 1946. **Education** Graduated from Northeastern University with degree in psychology. **Career** Assisted documentary filmmakers as an editor, sound recordist, and camerawoman; 1973-76—spent four years in coal fields of Harlan County, Kentucky, recording struggles of unionized miners for documentary* Harlan County, U.S.A; *1996—directed episode of TV series* Homicide: Life on the Streets. ***Awards** Academy Award, Best Feature Documentary, and designation by Congress as American Film Classic in National Film Registry, for* Harlan County, U.S.A., *1976; National Endowment for the Arts Fellowships, 1970s and 1980s; Academy Award, Best Feature Documentary, and Best Feature Documentary, Directors Guild of America, for* American Dream, *1991; John Simon Guggenheim Memorial Foundation Fellowship, 1992; Dorothy Arzner Directing Award, Women in Film, 1993; Outstanding Directorial Achievement,*

Barbara Kopple: *Harlan County, U.S.A.*

Directors Guild of America, for Fallen Champ, *1993; Maya Deren Award, American Film Institute, 1994.* **Address** *58 East 11th Street, New York, NY 10003, U.S.A.* **Agent** *William Morris Agency, 151 El Camino Drive, Beverly Hills, CA 90212, U.S.A.*

Films as Director: 1972: *Winter Soldier* (co-d). **1976:** *Harlan County, U.S.A.* (+ sound, pr). **1981:** *No Nukes* (co-d with Wexler). **1983:** *Keeping On* (+ exec pr). **1989:** *Civil Rights: The Struggle Continues* (+ pr). **1990:** *Out of Darkness* (co-d). **1991:** *American Dream* (+ sound, co-pr). **1992:** *Beyond JFK: The Question of Conspiracy* (co-d); *Locked Out: Ravenswood.* **1993:** *Fallen Champ: The Untold Story of Mike Tyson* (for TV) (+ pr). **1994:** *Century of Women* (segment d). **1995:** *Prisoners of Hope* (co-d). **1997:** *With Liberty and Justice for All.* **1998:** *Wild Man Blues; Woodstock '94.*

Other Films: 1974: *Richard III* (pr, sound, ed). **1986:** *Hurricane Irene* (pr). **1995:** *Nails* (segment pr).

Barbara Kopple got her start in film working for Albert and David Maysles. In order to make films, she decided it was necessary to learn all aspects of their production. At the Maysles' studio, she became familiar with the craft—from getting coffee to reconstituting trims, no job was trivialized. She became an assistant editor for the Maysles and began working as editor and sound recordist for other producers.

After gaining enough experience and confidence, Kopple decided it was time to direct her own films. Her crews consisted of a camera operator and sound recordist, of which she was the sound recordist. As with most documentaries, such a small crew was an economic necessity, but it also enhanced the filmmaker's intimacy with the subject. According to Kopple, recording sound brought her "deeper into what was happening"; she was "hearing" and participating in the filmic process on multiple levels. As a technician, interviewer, and director, she is both observer and participant. In supervising post-production she becomes the storyteller.

Most of Kopple's independent films require her constant attention to fund-raising. Winning the Academy Award for Best Feature-length Documentary for *Harlan County, U.S.A.* did not ensure funds for another project. While shooting *American Dream,* rather than process film, she bought freezers to store the exposed rolls until money could be raised for lab expenses. Kopple thinks "small crews are great, but sometimes it's better to have money and hire a sound recordist."

Kopple was influenced by the Maysles brothers and D. A. Pennebaker, exponents of Direct Cinema. Her method of filmmaking, though owing much to her predecessors, is very much a result of form following content. Though her style may differ slightly from film to film because of the organic strategy she employs for each story, there is an overriding consistency to her work. She gives those not normally heard a voice—the audience of most films are her subjects. Her documentaries have become emblematic of social change films.

Most of Kopple's films have no simple beginning—we enter a story that has already begun. The audience may know the outcome, yet we are engaged in the suspense of how we arrived at that point. Her films examine the antecedents of power relationships, how people are affected, respond, and make sense of their own actions and those of others. Though the chronology of a film may shift through history, intercutting past events with the contemporary, we experience the action in the present tense. Her endings are never clean, sometimes with story updates occurring under the end credits. Kopple's films create a discourse that cuts through historical time in an attempt to understand where we are today.

Kopple's films create such intimacy of identity that we feel sure she lived the experience. Nevertheless, *Harlan County, U.S.A.* took only 13 months to make. After reading about the death of Joseph Yablonski, his wife, and daughter, and the formation of Miners for Democracy, she decided to make the film and secured a $10,000 loan from Tom Brandon. The film develops small stories to contextualize a larger narrative.

The Consolidation Coal Mannington Mine Disaster of 1968, the Yablonski family murder in 1970, and the union election places the Harlan strike in a national relationship. History is seen as a growing organism and montage moves the discourse through time. John L. Lewis is cut against Carl Horn, president of Duke Power, as though they were engaged in debate. Yet the film is faithful to and references the chronology of the Harlan strike.

Kopple uses music to remind the audience of our folk storytelling tradition. In geographically isolated regions such as Harlan, music has been a way of sharing experience, creating a unifying identity. In the film, music functions to evoke cultural memory and meaning. Though we may be thousands of miles from Harlan, we share a common heritage of labor struggle. The voice of the film is the voice of many. There is no one hero, but a common chorus of purpose uniting gender and race.

"Which Side Are You On" functions as *Harlan County, U.S.A.*'s theme song. The film is about choice. Kopple is asked by Duke Power's thugs to identify herself; there is no question of her allegiance. Kopple thinks that being a woman may have contributed to the local police letting her film in jail. They did not consider her a threat. There is no question that the film threatened Duke Power; the camera is beaten. And the film is very much about violence: everyday life seems harsh, and the strike heightens the brutality. The audience must look at the conflict's viscera—pieces of lung and brains in the dirt—and ultimately the death of striker Lawrence Jones. The strike may be won, but it is a momentary victory. The struggle continues without end through the credits.

Kopple continues themes developed in *Harlan County, U.S.A.* in *American Dream,* but the story and issues have become more complicated. Again she films a strike, a labor crisis, and documents the crisis of labor. At issue is whether the union movement will be destroyed by Reaganism, or whether it will transform and once again play an active role in the American drama. The film follows Local P-9 of the United Food and Commercial Workers International Union as the rank and file struggles with the International leadership and dissidents among its own membership, as well as labor's traditional antagonist, in this case Hormel and Company.

Again a strike is the motivating force for communality. But because labor is divided—brother pitted against brother—*American Dream* evokes the heartbreak of the Civil War. The labor movement has lost its innocence, yet Local P-9 seems naive. They lack a historical perspective to labor negotiations. When the strike is going well they are enthusiastic, but they succumb to moral self-righteousness when frustrated. Recognizing stasis in the International, they hire an outside labor consultant, Ray Rogers of "Corporate Campaign," whose strategy is to effect economic distress on Hormel, build solidarity with other locals, and make the strike "newsworthy." He packages the strike for television, but we are not sure which side of the camera he prefers to be on since he seems to be playing a role from *Norma Rae* (Rogers was the organizer at J. P. Stevens). Authenticity becomes problematic.

As in *Harlan County, U.S.A.,* there is no doubt that Kopple's camera is on the side of labor. In *American Dream,* however, the camera repositions itself to show the conflicting points of view within the labor movement. The camera is with Local P-9 leader Jim Guyette, then with Lewie Anderson, director of the International Union's Meatpacking Division. It is in a car with dissidents as they defy the Local and go back to work. But the camera does not cross the picket line with them; it watches the dissidents go through the gate from the vantage point of the strikers.

In *American Dream,* Kopple utilizes various documentary styles. Direct Cinema techniques are combined with conventional sit-down interviews and narration. The voice of the film is that of labor, but unlike *Harlan County, U.S.A., American Dream* employs narration. Guyette and Anderson provide commentary for their own stories. And Kopple personally announces voice-over information necessary to move the story forward. As the film proceeds to its end, we are aware of a distance and dislocation of voice and character not experienced in *Harlan County, U.S.A.* The grand narrative of American labor is fractured, and we wonder if the Dream can ever be reconstructed. The film ends with an *American Graffiti*-style montage of character updates. But it is the 1980s, and although there may be personal change, one story remains the same: company profits continue to grow while workers are paid less.

Kopple thinks of herself as a filmmaker of traditional dramas, examining how people behave in moments of crisis and change. Her films question the construct of the "American Dream" and the price we pay in its attainment; how this "Dream" influences and informs our collective and individual identity and what we value; and how we are equipped to deal with and interpret issues of justice and change.—JUDY HOFFMAN

Krumbachová, Ester

Czech costume designer, writer, and director

Born *Brno, Czechoslovakia, 12 November 1923.* ***Education*** *Studied at the University of the Arts, finishing in 1948.* ***Family*** *Married the director Jan Němec, 1965 (divorced 1968).* ***Career*** *From 1954—worked at Czech theaters; from 1961—began work in the cinema; 1970—first and last feature film as director,* Murder of Mr. Devil; *also worked in television.* ***Died*** *13 January 1996.*

Films as Costume Designer: 1961: *Ztracená revue* (*The Lost Revue*) (Podskalský—for TV). **1962:** *Život bez kytary* (*Life without a Guitar*) (Hanibal). **1967:** *Muž, který stoupl v ceně* (*A Man Who Rose in Price*) (Moravec); *Ta naše písnička česká* (*Love with a Song*) (Podskalský). **1969:** *Ezop* (*Aesop*) (Valczanov). **1970:** *Archa bláznů aneb Vyprávění z konce života* (*Ark of Fools*) (Balada); *Vražda ing. Čerta* (*Murder of Mr. Devil*) (+ d, co-sc). **1971:** *Psi a lidé* (*Dogs and People*) (Schorm); *Slaměný klobouk* (*Straw Hat*) (Lipský); *Tajemství velikého vypravěče* (*The Secret of the Great Story-Teller*) (Kachyňa). **1989:** *Království za kytaru* (*The Kingdom for a Guitar*) (Králová). **1990:** *Poslední motýl* (*The Last Butterfly*) (Kachyňa). **1996:** *Marian* (Václav) (+ set designer).

Films as Artistic Collaborator: 1961: *Muž z prvního století* (*The Man from the First Century*) (Lipský); *Medvěd* (*A Bear*) (Frič—for TV). **1962:** *Král Králu* (*The King of Kings*) (Frič); *Transport z ráje* (*A Convoy Leaving Paradise*) (Brynych); *Slzy, které svět nevidí* (*The Tears That the World Doesn't See*) (Frič—for TV). **1963:** *Ikarie XB 1* (*Icarus XB 1*) (Polák); *Uspořená libra* (*A Saving Pound*) (Svitáček and Roháč—for TV). **1964:** *Démanty noci* (*Diamonds of the Night*) (Němec); *Kdyby tisíc klarinetu* (*If a Thousand Clarinets . . .*) (Roháč and Svitáček); *. . . a pátý jezdec je Strach* (*The Fifth Horseman Is Fear, . . . and the Fifth Rider Is Fear*) (Brynych) (+ co-sc). **1965:** *At žije republika* (*Long Live the Republic!*) (Kachyňa); *Nikdo se nebude smát* (*Nobody Gets the Laugh*) (Bočan). **1966:** *Hotel pro cizince* (*Hotel for Strangers*) (Máša); *Kočár do Vídně* (*A Carriage Going to Vienna*) (Kachyňa); *Mučedníci lásky* (*Martyrs of Love*) (Němec) (+ co-sc); *O slavnosti a hostech* (*The Party and the Guests*) (Němec) (+ co-sc); *Romance pro křídlovku* (*Romance for Cornet*) (Vávra); *Sedmikrásky* (*Daisies*) (Chytilová) (+ co-sc). **1967:** *Pension pro svobodné pány* (*Boarding House for Single Gentlemen*) (Krejčík); *Mother and Son*

(Němec—short) (+ co-sc). **1968:** *Všichni dobří rodáci* (*All Good Countrymen . . .*) (Jasný); *Náhrdelník melancholie* (*Necklace of Melancholy*) (Němec—for TV). **1969:** *Kladivo na čarodějnice* (*The Witch Hunt*) (Vávra) (+ co-sc); *Ovoce stromů rajských jíme* (*The Fruit of Paradise*; *We Eat the Fruit of the Trees of Paradise*) (Chytilová). **1970:** *Ucho* (*The Ear*) (Kachyňa); *Už zase skáču přes kaluže* (*I Can Jump over Puddles Again*) (Kachyňa); *Valerie a týden divů* (*Valerie and a Week of Wonders*) (Jireš) (+ co-sc). **1973:** *Dny zrady* (*The Days of Betrayal*) (Vávra). **1975:** *O neposedném knoflíčku* (*A Fidgety Little Bouton*) (Seko—animated short). **1976:** *Malá mořská víla* (*Little Mermaid*) (Kachyňa). **1981:** *O Honzovi, Jakubovi Kostečkovi a papírovém okénku* (*Honza, Jakub Kosteczka and a Little Paper Window*) (Bočik—animated short) (+ co-sc). **1983:** *Faunovo prilis pozdni odpoledne* (*The Very Late Afternoon of a Faun*) (Chytilová) (+ co-sc); *O statečném kováři* (*Brave Blacksmith*) (Švéda). **1984:** *Shoe show aneb Botky mají pré* (*Shoe Show*) (Seko—animated short). **1987:** *O živej vode* (*Live Water*) (Balada). **1988-89:** *Pravdivý příběh Josta Buergiho* (*The True Story of Jost Buergi*) (Havas—doc for TV). **1996:** *Co dělat?* (*Cesta z Prahy do Českého Krumlova aneb Jak jsem sestavoval novou vládu*; *What to Do?*) (Vachek).

Other Films: **1968:** *Třináctá komnata* (*The Thirteenth Chamber*) (Vávra) (words of songs). **1985:** *Leoš Janáček* (Havas—doc) (co-sc). **1986:** *Figure behind the Glass* (Stevens) (co-sc). **1995:** *Genus: Život Jitky a Květy Válových* (*Genus: The Life of Jitka and Květa Válovy*) (d, sc—doc, short, for TV); *Genus: Život divadelníka Oty Ornesta* (*Genus: The Live of Theater Maker Ota Ornest*) (d, sc—doc, short, for TV); *Winner Takes All* (d of musical clip).

Czechoslovakian filmmaking became considerably well known abroad in connection with the so-called Czech New Wave in the 1960s. In that time—actually a span of just a few years—many films were shot in Czechoslovakian film studios, and they have been shown at cinemas and various retrospective programs into the present day. Not just men, but women too found success in this new trend. Probably the best known is the director, Věra Chytilová, but another remarkable Czech woman filmmaker was Ester Krumbachová, whose influence upon the Czech New Wave is undoubted. Her former colleagues said that she was imbued with a versatile talent; they compare her to a renaissance type of an artist, and she was in fact a costume designer, scriptwriter, and director.

Krumbachová was most active in the artistic area of filmmaking, which was natural because she had studied at the University of the Arts, in the art and graphics branch. After finishing her studies, she worked as a set designer and a costume designer in a few Czech theaters. Then in 1961 she began her film career, also in art and costume design, helping to give a new and modern face to Czech film. She participated in the films of the most significant directors and worked in different genres—contemporary, historical, science-fiction settings. Her participation was always welcomed because for each film Krumbachová approached the problem of design from a global view. Her costumes together with the idea of the work shaped the necessary atmosphere, enforced the story, and defined each character. She had an extraordinarily developed sense of material and color thanks to inspiration from painting. She also managed to work with a wide scale of shades in black-and-white films. For example, in Jaromil Jireš's *Valerie and a Week of Wonders,* Krumbachová effectively brought black-and-white sequences into harmony with colored ones; in the process, an imaginative story clearly came out of the contours of narrative levels.

Another chapter in Krumbachová's career is her work as a scriptwriter, which directly influenced the essence of the Czech New Wave. She co-wrote such significant films as *Martyrs of Love, The Party and the Guests,* and *Daisies.*

The versatility of her talent—the separate elements of which complemented each other—led her to work as an independent director. In 1970 she finished the comedy *Murder of Mr. Devil,* the first and last film she would direct for the cinema. Krumbachová not only directed the film, but also wrote the script and served as the art designer and the costume designer. The film was truly her own. *Murder of Mr. Devil* is a rather peculiar story with morbid elements about a woman who is gatecrashed by the Devil under the pretext of marrying her. But the Devil is more interested in good food and drinks and the woman must get rid of him later.

If we look back at Krumbachová's lifetime of work we find that the high point came in the 1960s. During that time she absorbed the atmosphere of permissive politics and the ideas of the Prague Spring of 1968; in turn, her work influenced the politics of the day. Her opinions on life, the status of man in society, and freedom had their own moral dimension. Krumbachová did not change them, either after the Soviet occupation or during the ominous years that followed. Therefore she could not devote herself entirely to her work and develop her talent to its full extent. Unfortunately, her modest contributions to film during the 1990s stopped entirely and suddenly with her death in early 1996.—BLAŽENA URGOŠÍKOVÁ

Kurys, Diane

French director and writer

Born *Lyon, 3 December 1948, to Russian-Jewish immigrants.* ***Education*** *Attended Lycée Jules Ferry, Paris.* ***Family*** *Married to the director-producer Alexandre Arcady.* ***Career*** *1970—joined Jean-Louis Barrault's theater group; 1977—directed first feature film,* Peppermint Soda, *the year's largest-grossing film in France; 1983—international success of* Entre nous. ***Awards*** *Prix Louis Delluc, Best Picture, for* Peppermint Soda, *1977.* ***Agent*** *William Morris Agency, 151 El Camino Drive, Beverly Hills, CA 90212, U.S.A.*

Films as Director and Writer: 1977: *Diabolo menthe* (*Peppermint Soda*). **1980:** *Cocktail Molotov* (*Molotov Cocktail*). **1983:** *Coup de foudre* (*Entre nous*; *Between Us*; *At First Sight*). **1987:** *A Man in Love* (*Un Homme amoureux*) (co-sc, + pr). **1990:** *La Baule-les-Pins* (*C'est la vie*) (+ pr). **1992:** *Après l'amour* (*Love after Love*) (co-sc). **1994:** *À la folie* (*Alice et Elsa*; *Six Days, Six Nights*; *To the Limit*). **1999:** *Les Enfants du siècle.*

Other Films: 1972: *Poil de carotte* (*Carrot Top*) (Graziani) (ro as Agathe); *Elle court, elle court la banlieue* (Pirès) (ro). **1976:** *Casanova* (*Il Casanova di Federico Fellini*) (Fellini) (ro). **1992:** *Pour Sacha* (*For Sasha*) (Arcady) (co-pr).

It is not unusual for young independent filmmakers to create an autobiographical first or second feature: perhaps a tale of struggling adolescence on the model of Truffaut's *The Four Hundred Blows*. But *Peppermint Soda,* Diane Kurys's first film, a resounding critical and box-office success in France, was highly unusual in 1977 for having a female perspective on teenage rites of passage. It also initiated a remarkable group of films—one that does not follow the same characters through a series of sequels, à la Truffaut's Antoine Doinel cycle, but focuses upon essentially the same family (with slightly different names and played by different actors), rather the way some novelists and playwrights have circled around the same traumatic event, catching it from different angles, different characters' viewpoints, in work after work. Though Kurys has created some other striking films—concerned chiefly with self-defeating sexual games—her most enduring works to date may be those about a divorce in a French-Jewish family and the children who witness the breakup.

Diane Kurys

The title of that first film refers to the "grown-up" drink young Anne Weber orders in a café—until Frédèrique, her older sister and sometime confederate, humiliatingly sends her home. This and many other painful moments of budding youth are presented—sometimes with heartfelt intensity, sometimes with a cool comic edge—in vignettes that take us into the sisters' Paris lycée (schoolyard secrets, wretched teachers) and their lives outside it (mother-daughter conflicts, reluctant encounters with the divorced father, and most disturbingly, Frédèrique's near-seduction by a school-friend's father). Politics intersect with private life (the year is 1963, marked by Kennedy's assassination): a girl tells of witnessing a police riot, and Frédèrique's antifascist student group is disparaged by her principal as well as attacked by neo-Nazi thugs. Quiet observations of character, sudden explosions of emotion, unexpected turns of plot, touches of ironic humor—such hallmarks of Kurys's later work are already evident in this first feature.

Molotov Cocktail, at least a peripheral chapter in the family saga, is marked as a sequel by the title's ironic echo of the first film's less potent concoction, and by the name of the young protagonist. We are now in May 1968, though ironically Anne is off on an excursion with two male friends, exploring sexuality and independence from her mother, while missing the political events back in Paris. Nevertheless, Kurys's third film, *Entre nous,* is more directly a prequel, centering upon the girls' mother and her intense friendship with another woman, with the subsequent breakups of both their marriages. The film became Kurys's greatest international success to date and certainly her most controversial film.

Entre nous has been admired by some as a superbly powerful and subtle drama, gorgeously realized, while others have dismissed it as too vague in its sexual politics, too chic, too conservative in its filmmaking style. Much of the debate over the film centered upon the question of whether it should be categorized as a "lesbian film." The original title ("Stroke of Lightning," an idiom for love at first sight) may suggest as much, and several scenes between Lena and Madeleine certainly have an erotic charge, though the women are never shown to make love. Lena's husband accuses her of leaving him for a "dyke," but his outrage is colored by Madeleine's earlier rejection of his sexual advances.

A sympathetic reading of the film—or more, an argument that it is a major achievement in French cinema of recent years—might stress its refusal to reduce love relationships to the binary "sexual/nonsexual," or to make characters simply likable or dislikable. Lena's husband is heroic in rescuing her from probable death in a concentration camp, tender with his daughters, and quite vicious with Madeleine. The women, memorably played by Isabelle Huppert and Miou-Miou, are seen as both admirable in their quest for independence and selfish—or curiously absentminded—in their consideration of others; sometimes the viewer's sympathies seem intended to shift not just from scene to scene but from shot to shot. (Consider the episode of Lena losing little Sophie on the bus, or her encounter with the soldiers on the train and later confession to Madeleine.) The dramatic canvas is broad, with its wartime prologue, crosscutting between Michel's rescue of Lena (which has its comic moments) and the violent death of Madeleine's first husband; the women's first meeting in the 1950s and ultimate decision to move to Paris; and the startling shift to an autobiographical mode (Sophie's point of view) in the film's last moments. Kurys's consistently brilliant use of wide-screen Panavision, whether in the epic views of a Pyrenees prison camp or the languid reclinings of the two women, is essential to the film's overall effect, as is the attention to period detail, particularly fashions and music, as a way of dramatizing the 1950s context (the war years seemingly long past, the possibilities for women's independence largely in the future) and underlining the women's interest in fashion as a career. Perhaps most striking, though difficult to pinpoint, is the film's ability to present scenes with a full sense of immediacy and yet as if we were watching a reenactment of family legends from a distance.

The story is once again told in *C'est la vie,* named after the seaside resort where the entire film takes place. The daughters are once again the central characters, while Madeleine has metamorphosed into Lena's stepsister (though the same actor, the one carryover, plays her husband), and Lena is having an affair with another man. The film records the usual lazy amusements of a long summer at the beach, but also the girls' growing anxiety over their parents' impending separation. Lena is cruelly distant (literally and figuratively) at times, warmly affectionate at others. The eruption of violence in this film, when Michel attacks his wife, is truly shocking in its suddenness and brutality (i.e., in the staging of the scene, the editing, the performances); yet the placidities of beach life continue for the children, for some weeks/scenes to come, as they might indeed in life.

A Man in Love, made in between *Entre nous* and *C'est la vie,* is equally interested in passion at first sight, adultery, and flares of temper, and has a similar eye for wide-screen compositions, but this international co-production has quite a different setting: the glamour world of international filmmaking, where an American movie star, hired to play Cesare Pavese in an Italian biopic, has a steamy affair with his co-star, who abandons her French lover though the American will not give up his wife. The film has a great many fine moments which, however, do not add up to a coherent whole, and the actor remains uninterestingly egocentric, thanks to some combination of the screenwriting and Peter Coyote's wooden performance. A more successful, though certainly peculiar, tale of people involved in ludicrously neurotic love relationships is *Love after Love,* in which a cluster of affluent Parisians make themselves miserable by oscillating between their old and new lovers. One can only assume the tone is one of detached amusement, as one assumes too of *Six Days, Six Nights,* in which a house guest disrupts a pair of lovers. Whether Kurys can find a new theme which can bring out the full range of talent displayed in *Entre nous* is yet uncertain.—JOSEPH MILICIA

Landeta, Matilde Soto

Mexican director and writer

Born *Mexico City, 20 September 1910.* ***Education*** *Attended Colegio de las Damas del Sagrado Corazón in San Luis Potosí (Mexico); boarding schools in St. Louis, Missouri, and Mexico City.* ***Family*** *Married Martín Toscano, a colonel in the Mexican army, 1933 (divorced 1942).* ***Career*** *1933-45—continuity person for several Mexican producers, including Films Mundiales; 1945-48—assistant to various directors, including Emilio Fernández, Mauricio Magdaleno, Julio Bracho, and Alfredo Crevena; 1948—directed first film,* Lola Casanova; *1953—directed 110 half-hour children's television programs; 1950s-70s—taught screenwriting, wrote scripts, worked in television, ran a movie theater, worked as government liaison on foreign films shot in Mexico; 1975—"rediscovered" when her* The Black Angustias *was screened during "The Woman Filmmaker" series, part of the International Woman's Year celebrations; 1991—returned to feature filmmaking with* Nocturne for Rosario. ***Awards*** *Ariel, for best screenplay, Mexican Academy of Motion Picture Arts and Science, for* Los Caminos de la vida, *1956; lifetime achievement award, Mexican film institute (IMCINE), 1992.*

Films as Director: 1948: *Lola Casanova* (+ pr, co-sc). **1949:** *La Negra Angustias* (*The Black Angustias*) (+ pr, co-sc). **1951:** *Trotacalles* (*Streetwalker*) (+ pr, co-sc). **1990:** *Islas Revillagigedo* (*Revillagigedo Islands*). **1991:** *Nocturno a Rosario* (*Nocturne for Rosario*) (+ sc).

Films as Writer: 1956: *Los Caminos de la vida* (Corona Blake). **1957:** *Siempre estaré contigo* (co).

The only woman to have broken into the male-dominated Mexican film industry during its "golden age" (1930-50s), Landeta directed three successful fictional features but was forced to give up her career by male bias. Estranged from filmmaking for 40 years, she was rediscovered as a pioneer woman filmmaker in the 1970s and 1980s and finally received national tributes and many international acknowledgments (at festivals in such locations as Havana, London, Tokyo, Barcelona, Créteil, Buenos Aires, and San Francisco).

Born into a distinguished family the same year that the Mexican revolution broke out, Landeta was orphaned early and she and her brother Eduardo were raised in the family's grand ancestral home in San Luis Potosí by their maternal grandmother. Eventually but separately, both were sent to the United States to study, but Landeta and her brother reunited in Mexico City in the 1930s, a time of great postrevolutionary ferment in the arts and culture. Eduardo became a film actor and Landeta, although still a schoolgirl, decided that she also wanted a career in the movies. Despite her family's protests, she became a "script girl" (continuity person) and went on to work with some of the Mexican cinema's greatest directors and stars. After working on more than 75 feature films, she fought her way through the professional hierarchy of the Mexican film-workers union to become an assistant director, working on 14 films. She eventually succeeded in becoming the first recognized woman director in the Mexican film industry—and the first female in Latin America to direct within a studio-based production system—though she had to attend a union meeting dressed as a man in order to get the promotion.

Working in a highly competitive industrial system, Landeta co-scripted, produced, and directed three feature films before hostile producers and distributors blocked her from the industry. All of her three films adopt a clear women-centered perspective and simultaneously work within and against the predominant genres of the Mexican industry at the time. Each film invokes a distinct moment in Mexican history—the Spanish colony in *Lola Casanova,* the Mexican revolution in *The Black Angustias,* and modern urbanization in *Streetwalker*—with narratives centered upon a conflicted heroine who assumes a contestatory social position. In *Lola Casanova,* for example, a tale of Creole gentry captured by Indians, the captured heroine (Meche Barba, successfully cast against type) does not attempt to either civilize the Indians or escape and chooses instead to remain with them and adapt to their ways. In the revolutionary melodrama *The Black Angustias,* the mulatta Angustias (María Elena Marquez), an outcast in her own village, redefines the role of women in the Mexican revolution not as a *soldadera* (camp follower), but as a powerful leader of men in battle. The film addresses not only questions of gender, but also explores the tensions produced by racial and class differences. *Streetwalker* works within the *fichera* or prostitute melodrama subgenre. The narrative focuses on the parallel stories of two sisters, María (Edna Peralta), a prostitute who is exploited and abused by Rodolfo, her pimp, and Elena (Miroslava), the pampered wife of a rich older businessman who begins an affair with Rodolfo unaware of his relationship to her sister. In a clear reversal of the prevailing bourgeois morals, Landeta positions the married woman as the real prostitute, both within and outside her marriage.

In the 1950s Landeta had a fourth film in the works, a script that she had long nurtured entitled *Tribunal de menores*; a duplicitous producer, however, tricked her into ceding him the rights to the script and it was filmed by Alfonso Corona Blake as *Los Caminos de la vida*. Landeta had to sue to get her name included in the credits, and the Ariel prize (the Mexican equivalent of the Oscar) she won for the script was a most bittersweet triumph. As a result of her confrontations with the director of the National Cinema Bank, she was effectively barred from the industry.

Although eagerly awaited, her 1990s comeback film, *Nocturne for Rosario,* was not well received by critics. Its evocation of end-of-the-century romanticism through the failed love affair between a poet and a powerful and seductive older woman failed to impress even Landeta's most ardent supporters. Landeta is currently working on her memoirs.—ANA M. LÓPEZ

Larkin, Alile Sharon

American director

Born *Chicago, 6 May 1953.* ***Education*** *Attended the University of Southern California, B.A. Humanities (creative writing); University of California, Los Angeles, M.F.A., film and television production.* ***Career*** *1979—began filmmaking career with* Your Children Come Back to You; *co-founder of Black Filmmakers Collective; educator-writer-activist and advocate of children's educational television; 1982—directed* A Different Image; *1989—formed NAP productions.* ***Awards*** *First prize, Black American Cinema Society, for* A Different Image, *1982.*

Films as Director: 1979: *Your Children Come Back to You.* **1982:** *A Different Image.* **1984:** *My Dream Is to Marry an African Prince* (for TV). **1986:** *What Color Is God?* (doc—for TV). **1987:** *Miss Fluci Moses* (doc—for TV). **1991:** *Dreadlocks and the Three Bears.*

African-American independent filmmaker Alile Sharon Larkin burst onto the fresh and electrifying world of the black cinema movement in 1979 when she completed her production of *Your Children Come Back to You* while still a film student. After studying creative writing and earning a bachelor's at the University of Southern California, Larkin entered the M.F.A. program in film and television production at the University of California, Los Angeles. Along with classmates Barbara McCullough and Carroll Blue, together they helped form the second wave of black "womanist" filmmakers.

Her 1979 film explores issues concerned with the "blind" assimilation of Western culture. Larkin is perhaps best known, however, for her award-winning 1982 production of the film, *A Different Image*. Simple in construction but powerful in message, *A Different Image* explores the exploitation of women's bodies and the sexism and racism of Western culture—all against a backdrop of "Pan-African consciousness."

It is the story of Alana, a young, free-spirited African-American woman, and her best friend Vincent. Though their relationship has always been platonic, Vincent allows himself to become influenced by an older male friend, who teases him about not having "gotten over" on Alana. Vincent's world is the real world: billboards adorned with erotic images of scantily clad women dot the highway; men's magazines exploit the sacredness of the female body. Larkin intersperses this imagery of sexism and exploitation with a montage of other images; that of photographs of black American and African women of all shapes, sizes, hues, dress, and ethnicity—including women of cultures where various states of undress are the norm and not a means of exploitation and for the selling of products.

In a moment of supreme weakness, Vincent attempts to molest a tired and sleeping Alana who accuses him of rape. He has violated the sanctity of their friendship. Noting his stack of Penthouse magazines, she cries at him in desperation: "We see you! Why can't you see us?"

A Different Image received a great deal of well-deserved accolades and a good measure of recognition, including a first place award from the Black American Cinema Society. Though largely well-received, Larkin's work has also endured some criticism. As she has noted in various interviews, she was sometimes maligned by "radical feminists," who would have preferred that her work contain more of a general condemnation of black men. Some felt that she should align herself with white women against patriarchy. Larkin is very clear in her position on these and other issues in her essay on black women filmmakers that appears in a book edited by E. Deidre Pribram, "White feminists' insistence that black women condemn Black men is seen by many of us as a tactic . . . to divide and conquer us as a people." Further, she states, "many Black women see feminism as a 'white women's movement,' not at all separate from the rest of white society."

Like her contemporaries, Larkin concerns herself with much more than simply "women's stories," but seeks to explore themes rarely dealt with realistically by the mainstream film industry. Issues of assimilation, Western beauty standards, sexism, stereotyping, and the history of the African-American experience are appropriate fodder for her work, just as they are for many black women filmmakers. Black women filmmakers, too, share the same difficulties, most notably the challenge of procuring funding for their work.

In addition to her work in film, Larkin is a videographer and has produced or co-produced material for television. Larkin is a co-founder of the Black Filmmakers Collective. This group of independent filmmakers, with a grant from the California Foundation for Community Service Cable Television, produced the 1984 cable program *My Dream Is to Marry an African Prince.* It focused on the effects that racial stereotyping has on the psyche of young black children. "I believe it is important for Black people to control their own image," she states, "Black people working in the established 'Western' film industry do not have the power that we [independent filmmakers] have." In 1985 she began an examination of racism and sexism in contemporary Christianity in the production of *What Color Is God?*

In 1987, through a commission from the Woman's Building, she produced *Miss Fluci Moses,* a documentary of the life of African-American poet and educator Louise Jane Moses. This presentation was screened on cable television. Larkin, a stanch advocate of children's education television in 1989 formed NAP productions for the purpose of producing quality education children's television and video.—PAMALA S. DEANE

Law, Clara

Chinese director

Born *Clara Law Chuck-Yiu, in Macao, China, 29 May 1957.* ***Education*** *Studied English literature at the University of Hong Kong, graduated; attended National Film and Television School in England, 1982-85.* ***Family*** *Married the screenwriter Eddie Ling-Ching Fong.* ***Career*** *1978—production assistant with Radio Television Hong Kong (RTHK); 1978-81—directed 12 single-episode television dramas; 1985—directed first feature, the student film,* They Say the Moon Is Fuller Here; *returned to Hong Kong to continue working for RTHK directing fiction and docudramas; 1988—directs first professional feature,* The Other Half and the Other Half; *1990—migrated to Australia.* ***Awards*** *Golden Leopard, Locarno International Film Festival, for* Autumn Moon, *1992; Silver Leopard, Locarno International Film Festival, for* Floating Life, *1996.* ***Address*** *c/o Southern Star Film Sales, Level 10, 8 West Street, North Sydney, NSW 2060, Australia.*

Films as Director: 1985: *They Say the Moon Is Fuller Here.* **1988:** *Wo ai tai kung ten* (*The Other Half and the Other Half*). **1989:** *Pan jin lian zhi qian shii jin sheng* (*The Reincarnation of Golden Lotus*). **1990:** *Ai zai biexiang de jijie* (*Farewell China*); *Yes! Yi zu* (*Fruit Bowl*; *Fruit Punch*). **1991:** *It's Now or Never.* **1992:** *Qiuyue* (*Autumn Moon*) (+ co-pr). **1993:** *You seng* (*Temptation of a Monk*). **1994:** "Wonton Soup" ep. of *Erotique* (for TV). **1996:** *Floating Life* (+ co-sc).

Internationally acclaimed director Clara Law was born in Macao, China, raised in Hong Kong, and emigrated to Australia as an adult. As a filmmaker, she is an esteemed part of Hong Kong's thriving and enormously creative film industry. She has been directing films since the mid-1980s, and has proven to be an important, provocative, and inventive director who is praised for her intimate modern dramas. Starting with her student feature film, her work has been screened throughout the world on the film-festival circuit. In addition, she has been characterized as a representative of the so-called "diasporic multicultural cinema." Indeed, themes of anxiety about emigration are present in *Floating Life* and *Autumn Moon*. Moreover, her first professional film, *The Other Half and the Other Half,* explored the problems of married couples who live apart due to emigration. In general, Law's films have complex, metaphorically charged narratives, and although, on occasion, mainstream U.S. critics have expressed dissatisfaction with her pacing and characterizations, her films have been the subject of enthusiastic praise at film festivals.

The Reincarnation of Golden Lotus, Law's most successful film in Hong Kong, is about China's ancient myth of the notorious fallen woman, which is integrated with a contemporary love story. The mythical fallen woman is reincarnated as Lotus, though she, like her forebear, is fated for tragedy due to her innocent desires. In the political turbulence of 1966 Shanghai, Lotus is unfairly labeled a counterrevolutionary and thus her tragic story begins again. When the 20th-century Lotus reads the old myth, the two stories join for a romantic yet tragic ending. Much of Law's focus in the film is the connectedness of the political and personal.

Farewell China is Law's fourth feature, whose themes concern cultural dislocation and individual disconnection. Filmed on location in New York, it stars the beautiful and hugely popular Hong Kong star Maggie Cheung. It tells the compelling story of Li, who, after many failed attempts to get a visa to the United States, finally succeeds and makes the trip. Although she expects that her husband and child will eventually join her, within a year she writes home for a divorce. But her husband illegally immigrates to search for her. With a Chinese-American teenager as his guide, he discovers the people and places Li has known, and it is not until he finally begins to get on with his life that the two meet again. But Li has changed, with ultimately tragic results.

Law's first costume drama, *Temptation of a Monk,* demonstrates her skillful blending of two genres—art film and action film. It is a historical allegory set in early Tang dynasty China (A.D. 626), which is based on a story by popular Hong Kong writer Lilian Lee. It is a richly textured accomplishment, despite a relatively small budget, in which Law employs and intensifies the imagery of sword films and conveys a tasteful and even-handed eroticism. In addition, it deftly juxtaposes disparate elements—quiet contemplation and chaotic violence, the spiritual and worldly. According to Law, she wanted the film to be theatrical, with masklike makeup and stiff body movements, and a stagelike delivery of dialogue in order to expose the thoughts rather than faces of the characters. It tells the story of two imperial princes who are fighting for the old emperor's throne as he is dying. The hero is General Shi, who serves one of the brothers but believes his master is incompetent to rule the empire and inevitably will destroy it. Therefore, Shi betrays the prince and subsequently his former master is brutally murdered. Shi's guilt about his treason prompts him to leave the princess he loves and escape to his ancestral home. But he is pursued by his nemesis, General Huo, and much bloody battling ensues—whose slow motion sequences evoke Peckinpah's scenes of cine-violence. Eventually Shi seeks refuge in an isolated Buddhist monastery where he develops a deep self-awareness and decides to become a monk, but his evil past and pursuers continue to haunt him. As Law explained: "With the present world, where chaos reigns, values are confused, and countries are deep in turmoil . . . only a return to the origin can lend us clarity."

Law gained international acclaim with *Autumn Moon,* a study of alienation in modern Hong Kong. Along with its beautiful cinematography, Law carefully combines humor and nostalgia. The film traces two parallel love affairs, but Law's focus is really on Hong Kong's erasure of its past and the alienation of its modern conveniences and pastimes, as well as the encroachment of foreign, especially Western, influences, which is underscored by the presence of three languages. *Autumn Moon* expresses Law's concern for modern Chinese children: "As our culture fades away, what will they remember? Will they be nomadic modernists that wander, with no attachments, no memories, no dreams?"

Floating Life is Law's most recent film and her first Australian project, which has personal resonances given her emigration to Australia from Hong Kong with her husband in the early 1990s. The film is also noteworthy as the first Australian feature film that was not mostly in English. With her husband, she wrote the screenplay, which draws from their own experiences. Set in the context of the Chinese takeover of Hong Kong, the film examines what it means to live as an exile from a home country as well as the meaning of "home" itself. It tells the story of the Chan family—father, mother, and two sons—who emigrate to their second daughter's home in Australia out of anxiety about Beijing's leaders. In Australia, their domineering daughter tries to run their lives and to frighten them with tales of the country's dangers, including dogs and criminals. Law treats the cultural gaps and stresses between the emigrants and their new country in depth. Visually she underscores the disparities by contrasting the daughter's brightly lit, sterile, and mechanized home with the warm overcrowding of Hong Kong.

The themes Law explores in her work include migration, exile, loyalty, love and sensual pleasures, and family. Despite their shared themes, each of Law's films is quite different. Indeed, her work has been praised for its assured use of a broad range of visual styles, genres, and narrative rhythms.—CYNTHIA FELANDO

Leaf, Caroline

American/Canadian animator and director

Born *Seattle, 12 August 1946.* ***Education*** *Studied art at Radcliffe College, 1964-68.* ***Career*** *1968—while at college, invented the technique of creating animated movement with sand on glass; 1972—moved to Montreal, and started work in the animation department of the National Film Board of Canada, serving as a staff animator and director from 1979 until she left in 1991; 1977—received Academy Award nomination for* The Street; *1990s—focused on painting in oils and mixed media; has done several 30-second animation commercials; 1997—visiting lecturer, Harvard University.* ***Awards*** *Wendy Michener Award, Canadian Film Awards, 1976; Grand Prix, Ottawa International Animation Festival, for* The Street, *1976; Grand Prix, Melbourne Film Festival, for* Interview, *1979; Grand Prix, and Best Story Award, Ottawa International Animation Festival, for* Two Sisters, *1990; Norman McLaren Award, Ottawa, 1994; Life Achievement*

Award, Zagreb, 1996. **Agent** *Acme Filmworks, 6525 Sunset Boulevard, Garden Suite 10, Hollywood, CA 90028, U.S.A.*

Films as Animator/Director (shorts and commercials): 1969: *Sand or Peter and the Wolf.* **1972:** *Orfeo; How Beaver Stole Fire.* **1974:** *Le Mariage du Hibou* (*The Owl Who Married a Goose*). **1976:** *The Street.* **1977:** *The Metamorphosis of Mr. Samsa.* **1979:** *Interview* (co-animator, co-d with V. Soul). **1983:** *War Series* title. **1988:** *Paradise Found.* **1990:** *Entre Deux Soeurs* (*Two Sisters*) (+ sc). **1991:** *I Met a Man.* **1993:** *Bell Partout.* **1994:** *Fleay's Fauna Centre.* **1995:** *Brain Battle; Radio Rock Detente.*

Other Films: 1981: *The Right to Refuse?* (co-sc, co-pr); *Kate and Anna McGarrigle* (doc, short) (d, co-ed). **1982:** *An Equal Opportunity* (short) (d, co-sc). **1983:** *Pies* (Cohen—animation) (pr). **1985:** *The Owl and the Pussycat* (d, designer, pr). **1986:** *The Fox and the Tiger* (d, designer); *A Dog's Tale: A Mexican Parable* (short) (d).

Serendipity is the hallmark of this animated life, ironically because Caroline Leaf plans so well. Her professional serendipity and planning began at Harvard when as a Radcliffe College senior she ambled into the Harvard classroom of Derek Lamb. Having previously taken no film courses, unskilled at drawing, surely unaware that her teacher would become the head of the English animation division of the National Film Board of Canada (NFBC), unsure whether this course was preferable to the documentary course she also considered, Leaf responded just as casually to an early homework assignment, "Bring an object to class tomorrow, something we can animate." Her classmates brought the expected: things that easily fit in one's pocket. Leaf brought sand, which she photographed on an opaque glass lit from below. Six months later she had completed her first film, *Sand,* in tribute to the unusual medium. To praise it as a first film is insufficient since its virtuosity well exceeds this definition. Already she understood the need to personalize her material, to control her medium, to invent as a complement to planning, and to grasp instinctively animated motion's secret ingredient, timing.

After a year of drawing in Italy, a Harvard postdoc (*Orfeo*), and St. Louis freelancing (*How Beaver Stole Fire*), she began work at the NFBC in the Arctic, where for a year and a half she worked with an Eskimo legend and twice daily collaborated with an Eskimo artist (*The Owl Who Married a Goose*).

The Street required a comparably arduous 18 months that she spent finger-painting tempera watercolors and oil on glass. Her dabbing and erasing create stunningly mobile transitions that whirl the viewer through a complex overlay of emotionally moving characters and richly colored moods. The soundtrack interacts gracefully with the ever-changing visuals, anticipating and reading what we feel we see. Across decades buildings, cars, families, porches, stairs, and furniture all speak to us with tradition-rich insistence. In animation people are somehow more human for losing the fixity of time and space that binds literal bodies. Here both the visual and aural tracks continually re-create reality with force and power that challenge our minds and hearts. Ten minutes on Mordecai Richler's St. Urbain Street becomes timeless. Of all her highly honored films, this one has earned the most awards, and the ambiguous benefice of an Academy Award nomination.

Although Franz Kafka persuaded his publisher not to illustrate his short story about a man turned into an insect, the problem of literal representation has never existed for Leaf. In *The Metamorphosis of Mr. Samsa* external shape poses no barrier to our emotional identification with the soul of this allegorical fantasy. Caroline Leaf herself now undergoes metamorphosis, pursuing for ten years a series of cinematic projects and experiments that derive from her earlier work with animation and prepare her for new directions.

A strong sense of individuality and difference drive her and other women animators, often of her generation. They usually avoid the studio worlds of Hollywood and New York, rejecting Disneyfication and the soul-shackling prescriptions of its assembly-line laws. Rather than devising cartoon ideas, she and they begin with a feeling and create personal connections between altogether elective forms and content. This freedom arises from a college milieu rather than from a cartoon studio.

Defining employment as a means to new, creative directions Leaf has continued to experiment plastically, with new definitions of documentary, interactions between it and animation, between theater and animation, between theater, film, and music. In the 1990s she has created the emotionally and dramatically compelling *Two Sisters* by scratching her color images directly on 70mm film. A staunch promoter of independent animation, she has traveled the world doing screenings and animation workshops.—ARTHUR G. ROBSON

Lennart, Isobel

American writer

Born *Brooklyn, New York, 18 May 1915.* ***Family*** *Married the actor John Harding, one son and one daughter.* ***Career*** *1939-45—twice member of the Communist Party (testified before the House committee, 1952); 1943—first film as writer,* A Stranger in Town; *1964—wrote successful Broadway play* Funny Girl. ***Awards*** *Writers Guild Award for* Love Me or Leave Me, *1955;* Funny Girl, *1968.* ***Died*** *In an automobile accident in California, 25 January 1971.*

Films as Writer: 1943: *A Stranger in Town* (Rowland); *The Affairs of Martha* (*Once upon a Thursday*) (Dassin); *Lost Angel* (Rowland). **1945:** *Anchors Aweigh* (Sidney). **1946:** *Holiday in Mexico* (Sidney). **1947:** *It Happened in Brooklyn* (Whorf). **1948:** *The Kissing Bandit* (Benedek). **1949:** *Holiday Affair* (Hartman). **1950:** *East Side, West Side* (LeRoy); *A Life of Her Own* (Cukor). **1951:** "Rosika, the Rose" ep. of *It's a Big Country* (C. Vidor). **1952:** *Skirts Ahoy!* (Lanfield); *My Wife's Best Friend* (Sale). **1953:** *The Girl Next Door* (Sale); *Latin Lovers* (LeRoy). **1955:** *Love Me or Leave Me* (C. Vidor). **1956:** *Meet Me in Las Vegas* (Rowland). **1957:** *This Could Be the Night* (Wise). **1958:** *Merry Andrew* (Kidd); *The Inn of the Sixth Happiness* (Robson). **1960:** *The Sundowners* (Zinnemann); *Please Don't Eat the Daisies* (Hill). **1962:** *Period of Adjustment* (G. R. Hill); *Two for the Seesaw* (Wise). **1967:** *Fitzwilly* (Delbert Mann). **1968:** *Funny Girl* (Wyler).

Isobel Lennart began writing Hollywood screenplays in the 1940s and specialized in frothy entertainments such as *Anchors Aweigh, Holiday in Mexico, It Happened in Brooklyn,* and *The Kissing Bandit* and an occasional melodrama such as *East Side, West Side*. Finally, in 1955, with Daniel Fuchs, she fashioned the gritty and often bitter screenplay *Love Me or Leave Me,* based on the life of Ruth Etting, the popular singer of the 1920s and 1930s. This sadomasochistic love story between Etting (Doris Day) and her crippled, racketeer husband (James Cagney) was a far cry from the whitewashed musical biographies so familiar to moviegoers. With Charles Vidor directing, and a score of such excellent musical standards as "Ten Cents a Dance," "You Made Me Love You," "Mean to Me," and the title song, the film is a hard-hitting and true-to-life look at show business. Lennart and Fuchs received Academy Award nominations for best screenplay, and Fuchs won an Oscar for best original story.

Lennart seemed to hit her stride with screen biographies, and her next good script was for *The Inn of the Sixth Happiness,* based on the life of Gladys Aylward, the English servant girl who becomes a missionary in China. Unlike *Love Me or Leave Me,* this script *was* a romanticized biopic, but was saved by the excellent acting of Ingrid Bergman and Robert Donat. Two years later Lennart adapted for the screen the Jon Cleary novel *The Sundowners*. This rambling story of an Irish sheepdrover and his itinerant family in Australia was beautifully directed by Fred Zinnemann, expertly acted by Deborah Kerr and Robert Mitchum (probably his best screen performance), and earned Lennart a second Academy Award nomination.

Following *Fitzwilly,* Lennart created her greatest work, *Funny Girl,* the Barbra Streisand tour de force. Drawing upon the style used in *Love Me or Leave Me,* Lennart wrote the original Broadway play version of this life of the great comic Fanny Brice, focusing on her tempestuous love affair with the gangster Nicky Arnstein. The Broadway version made Streisand a star, and the film version, for which Lennart wrote the screenplay and which William Wyler directed, made Fanny Brice's story a permanent part of Hollywood musical history.—RONALD BOWERS

Levien, Sonya

American writer

Born *Near Moscow, Russia, 25 December 1888; emigrated to the United States with her parents when she was a child.* ***Education*** *Attended New York University, law degree.* ***Family*** *Married the writer Carl Hovey, 1917 (died 1956), children: Tamara and Serge.* ***Career*** *Practiced law briefly; 1916-20—staff member,* Woman's Journal *and* Metropolitan *magazines; 1919—first film writing credit,* Who Will Marry Me?; *1929-41—writer for 20th Century-Fox, and for MGM, 1941-56; 1956—joined George Sidney Productions.* ***Award*** *Screen Writers Guild, Laurel for Achievement Award, 1953; Academy Award, for* Interrupted Melody, *1955.* ***Died*** *Of cancer, in Hollywood, 19 March 1960.*

Films as Writer: **1919:** *Who Will Marry Me?* (Powell). **1921:** *Cheated Love* (Baggot); *First Love* (Campbell). **1922:** *The Top of New York* (Taylor); *Pink Gods* (Stanlaws). **1923:** *The Snow Bride* (Kolker); *The Exciters* (Campbell). **1925:** *Salome of the Tenements* (Olcott). **1926:** *The Love Toy* (Kenton); *Christine of the Big Top* (Mayo). **1927:** *The Princess from Hoboken* (Dale); *The Heart Thief* (Chrisander); *A Harp in Hock* (R. Hoffman). **1928:** *A Ship Comes In* (*His Country*) (W. K. Howard); *The Power of the Press* (Capra); *Behind that Curtain* (Cummings); *The Younger Generation* (Capra); *Trial Marriage* (Kenton); *Lucky Star* (Borzage); *They Had to See Paris* (Borzage); *South Sea Rose* (Dwan); *Frozen Justice* (Dwan). **1930:** *Song o' My Heart* (Borzage); *So This Is London* (Blystone). **1931:** *Delicious* (D. Butler). **1932:** *She Wanted a Millionaire* (Blystone); *After Tomorrow* (Borzage). **1933:** *State Fair* (H. King); *Warrior's Husband* (W. Lang); *Berkeley Square* (Lloyd); *Mr. Skitch* (Cruze). **1934:** *Change of Heart* (Blystone); *The White Parade* (Cummings). **1935:** *Here's to Romance* (A. E. Green); *Navy Wife* (Dwan); *Paddy O'Day* (Seiler) (st only). **1936:** *The Country Doctor* (H. King); *Reunion* (Taurog). **1938:** *In Old Chicago* (H. King); *Kidnapped* (Werker); *Four Men and a Prayer* (Ford). **1939:** *Drums along the Mohawk* (Ford); *The Hunchback of Notre Dame* (Dieterle). **1941:** *Ziegfeld Girl* (Leonard). **1943:** *The Amazing Mrs. Holliday* (Manning); *Rhapsody in Blue* (Rapper); *State Fair* (W. Lang). **1946:** *The Green Years* (Saville); *The Valley of Decision* (Garnett); *Ziegfeld Follies* (Minnelli). **1947:** *Cass Timberlane* (Sidney). **1948:** *Three Daring Daughters* (Wilcox). **1951:** *The Great Caruso* (Thorpe). **1952:** *The Merry Widow* (Bernhardt). **1954:** *The Student Prince* (Thorpe). **1955:** *Hit the Deck* (Rowland); *Interrupted Melody* (Bernhardt); *Oklahoma!* (Zinnemann); *Bhowani Junction* (Cukor). **1957:** *Jeanne Eagels* (Sidney). **1960:** *Pepe* (Sidney).

Films as Co-writer with S. N. Behrman: **1930:** *Lightnin'* (H. King); *Liliom* (Borzage); *The Brat* (Ford); *Surrender* (W. K. Howard). **1931:** *Daddy Long Legs* (Santell). **1932:** *Rebecca of Sunnybrook Farm* (Santell); *Tess of the Storm Country* (Santell). **1933:** *Cavalcade* (Lloyd). **1934:** *As Husbands Go*

(MacFadden). **1935:** *Anna Karenina* (C. Brown). **1938:** *The Cowboy and the Lady* (H. C. Potter). **1951:** *Quo Vadis* (LeRoy).

Throughout the golden era of the Hollywood studio system, Sonya Levien wrote enough screenplays (sometimes as many as five per year) to qualify her as a guaranteed professional name, but on most of her films she shared the writing credit, so that identifying her personal trademarks becomes difficult. Nevertheless, despite a minimum of biographical knowledge and no opportunity to examine the evolution of any single screenplay she worked on, it is still possible to assume three primary characteristics to her career: a strong tendency toward co-authorship, a talent for adaptation, and a flair for creating women characters who are intelligent, noble, and independent, but who are also searching to define their particular roles in life.

When Levien was paired with an established male author, it seems possible to assume she was hired to represent the feminine point of view, and to enhance the female characters. For instance, she was paired more than once with such different writers as S. N. Behrman, Lamar Trotti, and William Ludwig. As might be expected, the Behrman films are sophisticated comedies, the Trotti are prestige productions of an epic scale, and the Ludwig are musical adaptations. Since in all three cases she is working with an established writer with a personal style, her contribution is an enrichment of the leading female roles. The best example is probably the Trotti-Levien adaptation of *Drums along the Mohawk,* in which the central role of Lana, played by Claudette Colbert, is a classic example of the pioneer wife, feminine and attractive but strong enough to survive the dangers and hardships presented in the story line.

Levien's association with what were termed "quality" projects led her to work on many adaptations of novels, plays, and musicals. One of her most successful solo efforts was her adaptation of Sinclair Lewis's *Cass Timberlane,* in which the plot was restructured to reflect the postwar era in which it was released by including a character who sold faulty war materials for profit. Her skill at updating projects is also reflected in the three versions of *State Fair* she worked on, as well as in her refurbishing of such older musicals as *The Merry Widow* and *The Student Prince.* In all cases, she maintains the essential characters and overall ambience of the original, while removing outdated attitudes, particularly toward women and sex.

Given the number of collaborations Levien was involved in, it is difficult to identify exactly what she might have contributed to a specific characterization. Nevertheless, it is obvious that the assignments she was given—and took—are frequently stories about women. It must have been assumed that her name and her talent enhanced a project that would feature a leading actress. Thus, her work for Greer Garson in *The Valley of Decision,* and Eleanor Parker in *Interrupted Melody,* created strong roles for which both actresses were nominated for Oscars. In addition, such sex symbols as Lana Turner, Ava Gardner, and Kim Novak found parts that stretched their reputations and abilities in *Cass Timberlane* and *Ziegfeld Girl, Bhowani Junction,* and *Jeanne Eagels,* respectively. The difficulty of untangling "who is responsible for what" in Sonya Levien's prolific and successful career points to the problems of historical research, and illustrates how much is yet to be learned about many of Hollywood's most influential writers.—JEANINE BASINGER

Littleton, Carol

American editor

Born *Oklahoma, c. 1948.* ***Education*** *Attended University of Oklahoma; received Fulbright Fellowship, Paris, France.* ***Family*** *Married the cinematographer John Bailey.* ***Career*** *1972-77—owned company which made commercial ad spots; 1977—began as editor with director Karen Arthur on* Legacy, *followed by Arthur's* The Mafu Cage *in 1978 before her first major commercial release with 1979's* French Postcards; *1982—Academy Award nomination for editing Steven Spielberg's* E.T.—The Extraterrestrial; *1987—elected president of Editors Guild Local 776 (West Coast); member, Board of Governors, Academy of Motion Picture Arts & Sciences.* ***Agent*** *c/o United Talent, 9560 Wilshire Boulevard, Suite 500, Beverly Hills, CA 90212, U.S.A.*

Films as Editor: **1977:** *Legacy* (Arthur). **1978:** *The Mafu Cage* (*My Sister, My Love*) (Arthur). **1979:** *French Postcards* (Huyck). **1980:** *Roadie* (Rudolph). **1981:** *Body Heat* (Kasdan). **1982:** *E.T.—The Extraterrestrial* (Spielberg). **1983:** *The Big Chill* (Kasdan). **1984:** *Places in the Heart* (Benton). **1985:** *Silverado* (Kasdan). **1986:** *Brighton Beach Memoirs* (Saks). **1987:** *Swimming to Cambodia* (J. Demme). **1988:** *Vibes* (Kwapis); *The Accidental Tourist* (Kasdan). **1990:** *White Palace* (Mandoki). **1991:** *The Search for Signs of Intelligent Life in the Universe* (Bailey); *Grand Canyon* (Kasdan). **1993:** *Benny & Joon* (Chechik). **1994:** *China Moon* (Bailey) (co); *Wyatt Earp* (Kasdan). **1996:** *Diabolique* (Chechik). **1998:** *Beloved* (Demme); *Twilight* (Benton).

Editor Carol Littleton's music training is evident in the lyrical images that open *Places in the Heart.* Pictures of people populating a dust-bowl town during the Great Depression may epitomize her work, a gentle evocation of humanity undergoing some emotionally trying struggle of common rather than Herculean tests.

Her greatest achievements in structuring film images seem to fall into quiet, understated imagery. Even with the fantastical elements of *E.T.,* for which she received an Academy Award nomination for her editing, Littleton emphasized the simple magic of the friendship between the boy, Elliott, and his alien visitor in a manner suitable to François Truffaut. While it may have been an unlikely approach to science-fiction fantasy, it surely had much to do with why audiences responded to the fable. Even hardened audiences warmed to this sentimental and charming story.

With frequent collaborator Lawrence Kasdan, Littleton has helped bring warmth to *The Accidental Tourist* and the entertaining *The Big Chill,* two of his successes. The stylish *Body Heat,* revisiting Hollywood's film noir, brought imitation after imitation, perhaps including Littleton's own collaboration with her husband, cinematographer John Bailey, in his foray as director with *China Moon.* Kasdan and Littleton also worked together on two Westerns, *Silverado* and *Wyatt Earp,* the former a superficial homage to childhood oaters and the latter windy, dry, and far too long.

Littleton has said that simplicity is the key and that, while many editors have great technical knowledge, those that "can make a film purely emotional at the same time" are rarer. And in fact Littleton's best work seems simple on the surface but has an underlying emotional core that strikes a real note for audiences. Friendship could be said to be at the heart of *E.T., Places in the Heart,* and most of her work with director Kasdan—and this is some of her most successful work artistically.

Even in the less-pleasing films Littleton has edited, such as *Vibes, Brighton Beach Memoirs,* and the recent remake of *Diabolique,* critics take note of the assistance that she has given the work. The film may not be good but Littleton as editor has helped make it a little better.

The editor's role is unspecific and anonymous, according to Littleton; it is much like that of a symphony conductor who pulls diverse elements together in an attempt to make a cohesive whole. Her best work seems to emphasize affection and humanity that is clearly heart-felt.—ALLEN GRANT RICHARDS

Littman, Lynne

American director and producer

Born *New York City, 26 June 1941.* ***Education*** *Bachelor of Arts, Sarah Lawrence College, B.A. 1962; student at The Sorbonne, Paris, 1960-61.* ***Family*** *One son; one stepson, Rio Hackford.* ***Career*** *Researcher/associate producer for National Educational Television; 1963-67—researcher for Jay McMullen, CBS Reports; 1965—Assistant to Agnes Varda on* Lions Love *(theatrical feature); 1968—Associate Producer, David Wolper Films, Los Angeles; 1969—Director, NIMH series on drugs at UCLA Media Center (first time director), short documentaries; 1969—producer and director for documentary films, news, and public-affairs series for KCET Community TV, Southern California; 1971-77—directed feature documentary for WNET's Non-Fiction Lab,* Once A Daughter; *1978—executive producer, Movies for TV, ABC; 1993—director of* Oscar Tribute to Women, *which premiered at the 65th Annual Academy Awards; 1996—director* Cagney & Lacey: True Convictions, *series finale; 1997—director* Marie Taquet, *for Showtime cable network.* ***Awards*** *Winner of four Los Angeles Emmy awards, 1972, 1973, 1974, 1977; Academy award for best short documentary,* Number Our Days; *1977—Winner, 4 Cine Golden Eagle awards.*

Films as Director and Producer: 1974: *In The Matter of Kenneth* (short doc); *Wanted: Operadadoras* (short doc). **1975:** *Women in Waiting* (short doc); *Till Death Do Us Part* (short doc). **1976:** *Number Our Days* (+ro) (short doc). **1978:** *It's All Right Now* (doc). **1979:** *Once a Daughter* (doc). **1982:** *Running My Way* (short). **1983:** *Testament* (co-p). **1985:** *In Her Own Time* (doc). **1998:** *Freak City* (for TV). **1999:** *Having Our Say: The Delany Sisters first 100 Years* (doc) (for TV).

Other Films: 1987: *Legacy of the Hollywood Blacklist* (creative consultant) (for TV).

Lynne Littman is a prolific producer and director whose documentary shorts and features invariably aim for the heart of our collective human social consciousness. From her first National Institute of Mental Health documentaries on drugs for UCLA's media center (1970), to her feature-length drama on the aftermath of a nuclear attack (*Testament,* 1983), Littman has distinguished herself as a film-journalist with a decidedly female sensibility for getting to the core of concerns shared by all of us. "It's funny and sad to me when a woman says, 'I'm not a woman. I'm a director.' Baloney!," Littman said to author Sharon Smith.

What is perhaps most impressive about Littman's numerous and varied projects is that she received all her training in the field. Not enamored with the academic route for filmmaking, she started as a secretary in the publicity department for WNET (New York) and, after a series of freelance jobs, came to work for National Educational Television's Mort Silverstein in the early

1970s. It was Silverstein's dedication to Edward R. Murrow-style reporting that formed her lifelong commitment to hard hitting news and issues. With Silverstein, she made *What Harvest for the Reaper*, a ten-year follow-up to Murrow's celebrated *Harvest of Shame*, which portrayed the plight of migrant laborers on Long Island. Later, she joined KCET-TV as an associate producer-reporter in its current affairs department where, in 1974 alone, she won Los Angeles Emmys for *In The Matter of Kenneth* and *Wanted: Operadoras,* as well as a Golden Mike Award for investigative reporting and a Los Angeles Press Club Award for Best TV Documentary. Other signature short films of this period include a film based on the fieldwork of anthropologist Barbara Myerhoff called *Number Our Days* (a 1977 Academy award winner for best short documentary); *Once a Daughter* (1979); and *Running My Way* (a 1982 Cine Golden Eagle award winner).

Lynne Littman

Lynne Littman made her feature film directing debut in 1984 with *Testament,* which earned Jane Alexander an Academy award nomination for Best Actress. An original member of the AFI's Women's Directing Program, she also developed years of projects for Rastar, Warner Brothers, Paramount, and most successfully for Disney, with *Beaches.* She is an enthusiastic board member of the International Documentary Association and chaired the 1996 International Documentary Congress sponsored by the IDA and the Motion Picture Academy.

If it can be said there is a thread running through all of Littman's films, it is an underlying belief in—and what might be termed a solemn enthusiasm for—the power of human faith. In *In Her Own Time,* for instance, Littman looks at the last days of Barbara Myerhoff who, dying of cancer, comes to terms with her own Jewish roots. Littman interprets Myerhoff's final religious acts among Orthodox Jews and religious Soviet Jewish immigrants in the Fairfax district of Los Angeles—purification rituals, re-establishment of her soul through an orthodox divorce, taking a new and sanctified name—as reflecting a need we all feel for some synthesis of spirit and intellect. Myerhoff discovers that while she is deeply drawn to the security enjoyed by orthodox women, her own scientific and feminist mind rejects their unquestioning conformity and faith. "I look (at them)," she says in the film, "across a vast and acceptable distance."

Littman recently completed the feature *Freak City,* starring Natalie Cole, Marlee Matlin, Samantha Mathis, Estelle Parsons, Jonathan Silverman and Peter Sarsgaard. She also recently completed *Having Our Say,* a Kraft premiere movie for CBS based on the best-selling book and Broadway play about the extraordinary centenarian Delany sisters. The film stars Ruby Dee, Diahann Carroll, Amy Madigan, Richard Roundtree, Lonette McKee, Audra Macdonald, Mykelti Williams and Lisa Arrindel-Anderson. Both productions are scheduled to premiere on television in 1999 on the same day, at the same time.

The irony of this half-full/half-empty situation is not lost on Ms. Littman who, for almost ten years, put her directing career on hold in order to function as a single mother. The day her sons' applications for college went into the mail, Littman returned to filmmaking. "Returning to work was a more difficult battle than making the initial breakthrough as a woman director," she told this author in March of 1999. However, armed with the strength gained as a mother, she has completed two films in less than one year—"making up for lost time," as she says—and is keen to tap the sense of humor and humility she feels only time and experience has taught her. "I was thrilled to re-discover—that I do indeed love making films. That's a tremendous relief!"—JEROME SZYMCZAK

Livingston, Jennie

American director

Born *Los Angeles, 1960.* ***Education*** *Graduated from Yale University, with a major in art, 1983; took summer school filmmaking class at New York University.* ***Career*** *1985—moved to New York City; 1986—began working on, and raising funds to complete, what was to be the documentary feature,* Paris Is Burning; *early 1990s—wrote* Not for Profit, *her first screenplay, which was not produced; mid-1990s—at work on two film projects,* Prenzlauerberg *and* Who's the Top? ***Awards*** *Grand Jury Prize, Best Documentary, Sundance Film Festival, Best Documentary, New York Film Critics Circle, Best Documentary, Los Angeles Film Critics, Best Documentary, National Society of Film Critics, Open Palm, Independent Feature Project Gotham Award, and Teddy Award for Best Documentary, all for* Paris Is Burning, *1990; Vito Russo Film Award, GLAAD Media Awards, 1992.* ***Agent*** *William Morris Agency, 151 El Camino Drive, Beverly Hills, CA 90212, U.S.A.*

Films as Director: 1990: *Paris Is Burning* (doc) (+ co-pr, still ph, co-sound recording). **1993:** *Hotheads* (short).

To date, Jennie Livingston is a one-film filmmaker. But what a film it is! *Paris Is Burning* is an exemplary documentary, a vivid and ultimately bittersweet portrait of an authentic American/New York City subculture and one of the most acclaimed early examples of 1990s New Queer Cinema.

The Blacks and Latinos in *Paris Is Burning* are outside the mainstream because they are minorities, and they are poor—and they are outcasts from their families because they are transsexuals and drag queens. So they exist within their own subculture in which they establish extended families and join different "houses" which serve to forge their identities. They not only fit in and find acceptance here but attend competitive, dress-up drag balls. Going to one, and vogueing at one (or dancing and striking poses in imitation of high-fashion images), is the closest they ever will come to experiencing "the way rich people live." As they walk at a ball, they live out the "fantasy of being a superstar." And by winning a trophy, they attain a certain kind of fame within the subculture.

These balls have their own history. Decades ago, drag queens attended them garbed as Las Vegas showgirls. In the 1970s, participants attempted to imitate movie stars like Marilyn Monroe and Elizabeth Taylor. In the 1980s, they were copying supermodels, like Christie Brinkley and Iman.

Participants also dress up to resemble (and take on the superficial personalities of) character types they never could be in the real world: preppie college students and smartly dressed business executives, wealthy ladies of leisure and immaculately uniformed military personnel. The point is to create a sense of "realness," to capture "the great white way of living or looking or dressing or speaking," to look so authentic as to be able to blend in on Wall Street or a military base or a college campus without revealing sexual preference. As one of the participants pointedly observes: "The fact that you are not an executive is merely because of the social standing of life. . . . Black people have a hard time getting anywhere. Those that do are usually straight. In a ballroom you can be anything you want. . . . You're showing the straight world that I can be an executive. If I had the opportunity, I could be one . . . and that is like a fulfillment."

Nevertheless, there is a melancholy edge to *Paris Is Burning,* in that many of those depicted feel cheated because of their "sad backgrounds," their coming from "broken homes, or no homes at all." After a ball is over, they do not retire to limousines and Park Avenue duplexes. Unlike wealthy New York gays, they do not own West Village brownstones or summer in chic beach communities. Rather, they often are homeless, and come to balls starving. The fantasies they create for themselves are affectations, which exist only for a short time; within them remains a yearning for permanency which never can be fulfilled. Person after person, they talk about making it in the "real world" as models or dancers or actors, and attaining the affluence they see as being an intrinsic part of straight, white America. Yet their view of affluence is distorted. It comes not from real life experience but from watching television shows such as *Dynasty* and perusing ads in slickly designed high-fashion magazines.

The one true realist in the group is Dorian Corey, an aging drag queen who is well aware that her dreams of mainstream stardom can never be achieved. It is "a small fame," she declares, of her status within the subculture: "But you accept it. And you like it." Later on, she adds, "As you get older, you aim a little lower." Age has taught her that "you've left a mark on the world if you just get through it, and a few people remember your name."

The most tragic of *Paris Is Burning*'s subjects is Venus Xtravaganza, a petite blond boy-girl who declares: "I would like to be a spoiled rich white girl. They get what they want, whenever they want. They really don't have to struggle with finances." Venus wants a sex change operation, which will make her "complete." She admits that, to make money, she has turned tricks. Near the finale, she adds, "I want a car. I want to be with the man I love. I want a nice home, away from New York City, up the Peekskills [sic] or maybe in Florida, somewhere far away where no one knows me . . . I want to get married in church, in white. . . I want to be a complete woman." It then is revealed that Venus was murdered in a sleazy hotel room. She was strangled, and her body went undiscovered for four days. The violent death of Venus is of course unplanned, and lamentable. But it adds an unexpected resonance—and an uncompromising dose of reality—to *Paris Is Burning*.

The film was not without controversy. An organization called the Christian Film and Television Commission announced that "all moral Americans" should boycott *Paris Is Burning,* indicting it as a "homosexual propaganda film." Nonetheless, it is anything but a gay indoctrination tract. The lives depicted on screen are not glorified, but rather are tinged with sadness, and the film is as much about cultural and economic disenfranchisement as sexual preference.

Unfortunately, the success of *Paris Is Burning* has not translated into a prolific directorial career for Jennie Livingston. In 1993 she made *Hotheads,* a three-minute video on the subject of violence against women. She wrote *Not for Profit,* her first screenplay, which she described to filmmaker Sarah Jacobson as being about "a rapist of indeterminate gender who attacks famous straight white guys. . . . There's this fundraising PR agency where this Jewish girl works, and they get approached by this coven of witches who want to better the image of pagans in the eyes of the public. The Jewish girl falls in love with the witch who is head of the coven." Livingston was unable to raise the funds to have *Not for Profit* produced. By the mid-1990s she had two projects in the works: *Prenzlauerberg,* "an ensemble piece, like a *Nashville* or *Short Cuts*. It takes place among artists and writers in Berlin—some of whom are informants for the secret police—and among artists and writers in New York during the kind of art boom of the 1980s, just before the stockmarket crashed"; and *Who's the Top?,* a lesbian sex comedy which is "kind of like *She's Gotta Have It* meets *Belle du Jour* meets *8½*. The theme is how do you live in a world where maybe you have one partner, you have one girlfriend, and you know your fantasies and possibilities are endless. What decisions do you make and how do you deal with that when those fantasies comes to call?"—ROB EDELMAN

Loos, Anita

American writer and producer

Born *Corinne Anita Loos in Sissons (now Mount Shasta), California, 26 April 1888.* ***Education*** *Attended schools in San Francisco and San Diego.* ***Family*** *Married 1) Frank Pallma Jr., 1915 (divorced 1915); 2) the director and writer John Emerson, 1920 (died 1956), one adopted daughter.* ***Career*** *Child actress briefly; 1912—first film as writer,* The New York Hat, *followed by a large number of films for D. W. Griffith; 1916—collaborator with Emerson, and co-producer with Emerson from 1919; 1925—published the novel* Gentlemen Prefer Blondes *(play version, 1926, film version, 1928); other plays include* The Whole Town's Talking, The Fall of Eve, The Social Register, Happy Birthday, Gigi, The Amazing Adèle, Chéri, Gogo Love You; *1963—one-woman show,* An Evening of Theatrical Reminiscences. ***Died*** *In New York City, 18 August 1981.*

Films as Writer: 1912: *The New York Hat* (D. W. Griffith); *My Baby* (F. Powell); *The Musketeers of Pig Alley* (D. W. Griffith). **1913:** *The Power of the Camera*; *The Telephone Girl and the Lady* (D. W. Griffith—short); *A Horse on Bill* (Powell); *The Hicksville Epicure* (Henderson); *Highbrow Love* (O'Sullivan); *Pa Says* (Henderson); *The Widow's Kids* (Powell); *The Lady in Black*; *His Hoodoo* (Powell); *A Fallen Hero* (Powell); *A Cure for Suffragettes* (Kirkwood); *The Suicide Pact* (Powell); *Bink's Vacation* (*Bink Runs Away*); *How the Day Was Saved* (Powell); *The Wedding Gown* (Powell); *Gentleman or Thief*; *For Her Father's Sins* (O'Brien); *A Narrow Escape*; *The Mother*; *The Lady and the Mouse* (D. W. Griffith) (short); *The Mistake* (D. W. Griffith) (short). **1914:** *Hickville's Finest*; *His Awful Vengeance*; *The Saving Grace* (Cabanne); *A Bunch of Flowers*; *When a Woman Guides*; *The Road to Plaindale*; *The Saving Presence*; *The Meal Ticket*; *The Suffering of Susan*; *Nearly a Burglar's Bride*; *Some Bull's Daughter*; *The Fatal Dress Suit*; *The Girl in the Shack*; *The Stolen Masterpiece* (Pollard); *A Corner in Hats*; *The Million Dollar Bride*; *A Flurry in Art*; *Billy's Rival* (*Izzy and His Rival*) (Taylor—short); *The Last Drink of Whiskey* (Dillon); *Nell's Eugenic Wedding*; *The White Slave Catchers*; *The Deceiver* (Dillon); *How to Keep a Husband*; *The Gangsters of New York* (Cabanne and Kirkwood) (short); *The Hunchback* (Cabanne); *A Lesson in Mechanics*. **1915:** *The Deacon's Whiskers* (Dillon); *The Tear on the Page*; *Pennington's Choice* (Lund); *Sympathy Sal*; *Mixed Values* (Dillon); *The Fatal Finger Prints* (Dillon); *Lord Chumley* (Kirkwood); *The Sisters* (Cabanne) (short); *A Ten-Cent Adventure* (short); *When the Road Parts* (short); *Double Trouble* (Cabanne); *The Lost House* (Cabanne). **1916:** *The Little Liar* (Ingraham); *A Corner in Cotton* (Balshofer); *Intolerance* (D. W. Griffith); *Macbeth* (Emerson); *Stranded* (Ingraham); *Wild Girl of the Sierras* (Powell); *A Calico Vampire*; *Laundry Liz*; *The French*

Anita Loos (right) with Jean Harlow

Milliner, *The Wharf Rat* (Withey); *The Half-Breed* (Dwan); *American Aristocracy* (Ingraham); *A Daughter of the Poor* (Dillon). **1917:** *Wild and Woolly* (Emerson); *Down to Earth* (Emerson); *The Deadly Glass of Beer*. **1927:** *Stranded* (Rosen); *Publicity Madness* (A. Ray). **1932:** *Red-Headed Woman* (Conway); *Blondie of the Follies* (E. Goulding). **1933:** *The Barbarian* (Wood); *Hold Your Man* (Wood); *Midnight Mary* (Wellman). **1934:** *Biography of a Bachelor Girl* (E. Griffith); *The Merry Widow* (Lubitsch) (uncredited). **1935:** *Riffraff* (Ruben). **1936:** *San Francisco* (Van Dyke). **1937:** *Mama Steps Out* (Seitz); *Saratoga* (Conway). **1939:** *The Women* (Cukor). **1940:** *Susan and God* (*The Gay Mrs. Trexel*) (Cukor). **1941:** *They Met in Bombay* (C. Brown); *Blossoms in the Dust* (LeRoy); *When Ladies Meet* (Leonard). **1942:** *I Married an Angel* (Van Dyke).

Films as Co-writer with John Emerson: **1916:** *His Picture in the Papers* (Emerson); *Manhattan Madness* (Powell); *The Matrimaniac* (P. Powell); *The Social Secretary* (Emerson). **1917:** *In Again, Out Again* (Emerson); *Reaching for the Moon* (Emerson); *The Americano* (Emerson). **1918:** *Let's Get a Divorce* (Giblyn); *Hit-the-Trail Holliday* (Neilan); *Come on In* (Emerson) (+ co-pr); *Good-bye-Bill* (Emerson) (+ co-pr). **1919:** *Oh, You Women!* (Emerson); *The Isle of Conquest* (Jose); *Under the Top* (Crisp); *Getting Mary Married* (Dwan) (+ co-pr); *A Temperamental Wife* (Emerson) (+ co-pr); *A*

Virtuous Vamp (Kirkland) (+ co-pr). **1920:** *In Search of a Sinner* (Kirkland) (+ co-pr); *The Perfect Woman* (Kirkland); *The Love Expert* (Kirkland) (+ co-pr); *Two Weeks* (Franklin); *The Branded Woman* (Albert Parker). **1921:** *Dangerous Business* (Neill); *Mama's Affair* (Fleming); *A Woman's Place* (Fleming). **1922:** *Polly of the Follies* (Emerson); *Red Hot Romance* (Fleming) (+ co-pr). **1923:** *Dulcy* (Franklin). **1924:** *Three Miles Out* (Willat). **1925:** *Learning to Love* (Franklin). **1928:** *Gentlemen Prefer Blondes* (St. Clair). **1929:** *The Fall of Eve* (Strayer). **1931:** *The Struggle* (D. W. Griffith). **1934:** *The Girl from Missouri* (*One Hundred Percent Pure*) (Conway).

Films Based on Loos's Writings: 1926: *The Whole Town's Talking* (Edward Laemmle). **1931:** *Ex-Bad Boy* (Moore). **1934:** *The Social Register* (Neilan). **1953:** *Gentlemen Prefer Blondes* (Hawks). **1955:** *Gentlemen Marry Brunettes* (Sale).

At the early age of 16, Anita Loos began her career in films by scripting more than 100 scenarios for D. W. Griffith's Biograph Company. She is credited with writing the subtitles for *Intolerance* (1916), and is regarded as one of the first screenwriters to employ intertitles to silent films. Although she wrote serious plots for silent films (*Wild Girl of the Sierras* and *Stranded*), her early success came as a satirist of everyday events. Indeed, her original use of intertitles provided her with the opportunity to let loose with her wisecracks that teased the picture. She was also proficient in slapstick comedy and wrote a number of half-reels featuring the Keystone Kops.

It was Loos, with her husband, the director John Emerson (who assumed much of the credit for her creative endeavors) who first realized that Douglas Fairbanks's acrobatics were an extension of his effervescent personality. Loos, Emerson, and Fairbanks worked as a unit in Griffith's company and parlayed Fairbanks's natural athletic ability into swashbuckling adventure roles. Never missing a chance for satire, Loos (the "O'Henrietta of the Screen") parodied not only the nouveau riche American industrialist but also Fairbanks's own star persona in *American Aristocracy*. The scenario for the film is typical of Loos's humor: Fairbanks foils a buccaneer who is sending powder to Mexico in the guise of malted milk and as the result of his adventurous exploits wins the heart of a hat-pin king's daughter. In pursuit of the villain, Fairbanks vaults a dozen walls and fences. He readies himself to leap at a window ten feet above the ground when he suddenly decides to take the easy way out and opens a basement window, climbing in the building like an ordinary mortal. Loos wrote other humorous films that firmly established Fairbanks as a major leading man of the American screen. Americans' love of publicity was ridiculed in *His Picture in the Papers* and pacifism was satirized in *In Again, Out Again*.

Loos left the Griffith studio in 1925 and moved east with her husband. During her brief "retirement" from the film colony she wrote the durable story of Lorelei Lee, *Gentlemen Prefer Blondes*. The story was quite successful as a novel, Broadway musical, and film. Loos and Herman J. Mankiewicz co-wrote the intertitles for the original silent film version directed by Mal St. Clair in 1928. Howard Hawks's *Gentlemen Prefer Blondes* (1953) was an adaptation of the stage play and featured Marilyn Monroe as Lorelei and Jane Russell as her dark-haired girlfriend. Through the perils of Lorelei, the amoral and dim-witted young blond from Little Rock, Loos poked fun at male-female relationships. The blond's flirtations and the gullible millionaires who surrounded her provided Loos with rich material to gleefully expose the merchandising of sexuality.

Loos returned to Hollywood and worked for MGM during the Irving Thalberg reign. She took over the writing duties from F. Scott Fitzgerald on the Harlow vehicle *Red-Headed Woman*. She also wrote *Hold Your Man* starring Harlow and Clark Gable. Gable, Jeanette MacDonald, and Spencer Tracy were featured in the Loos script for *San Francisco*. This large-scale Hollywood soap opera evolved around San Francisco at the time of the great earthquake. Loos and the veteran MGM scriptwriter Jane Murfin adapted Clare Boothe Luce's venomous comedy *The Women* to the screen; it featured an all-woman cast including Norma Shearer, Rosalind Russell, Paulette Goddard, and Joan Crawford.—DOREEN BARTONI

Lupino, Ida

American director and actress

Born *London, 4 February 1918; daughter of the actor Stanley Lupino and the actress Connie Emerald; became U.S. citizen in 1948.* ***Education*** *Attended Clarence House School, Hove, Sussex; Royal Academy of Dramatic Art, London.* ***Family*** *Married 1) the actor Louis Hayward, 1938 (divorced 1945); 2) the writer Collier Young, 1948 (divorced 1951); 3) the actor Howard Duff, 1951 (divorced 1972), daughter: Bridget.* ***Career*** *Stage debut at Tom Thumb Theatre, London, at age 12; late 1920s—extra in films for British International Studios; 1932—first lead role in* Her First Affaire; *1933-37—contract with Paramount; 1939—success in* The Light that Failed; *contract with Warner Brothers; 1949—co-founder, with Anson Bond, Emerald Productions: producer, co-director, and co-scriptwriter of* Not Wanted; *1950—director of the film* Never Fear; *1950-80—co-owner, with Collier Young, Film-makers Company; 1952—co-founder, with Dick Powell, Charles Boyer, and David Niven, Four Star Productions for television; 1956—director for TV series* On Trial; *1957-58—in TV series* Mr. Adams and Eve; *1957-66—worked exclusively in television.* ***Awards*** *Best Actress, New York Film Critics, for* The Hard Way, *1943.* ***Died*** *Of cancer, in Burbank, California, 3 August 1995.*

Films as Director: 1949: *Not Wanted* (co-d with Clifton, + pr, co-sc). **1950:** *Never Fear* (*The Young Lovers*) (+ pr, co-sc); *Outrage* (+ co-pr, co-sc). **1951:** *Hard, Fast, and Beautiful* (+ co-pr). **1953:** *The Hitch-Hiker* (+ co-pr, co-sc); *The Bigamist* (+ co-pr, ro as Phyllis Martin). **1966:** *The Trouble with Angels* (+ co-pr).

Films as Actress: 1932: *Her First Affaire* (Dwan) (as Anne). **1933:** *Money for Speed* (Vorhaus) (as Jane); *High Finance* (G. King) (as Jill); *The Ghost Camera* (Vorhaus) (as Mary Elton); *I Lived with You* (Elvey) (as Ada Wallis); *Prince of Arcadia* (Schwartz) (as Princess). **1934:** *Search for Beauty* (Kenton) (as Barbara Hilton); *Come on, Marines!* (Hathaway) (as Esther Cabot); *Ready for Love* (Gering) (as Marigold Tate). **1935:** *Paris in Spring* (Milestone) (as Mignon De Charelle); *Smart Girl* (Scotto) (as Pat Reynolds); *Peter Ibbetson* (Hathaway) (as Agnes). **1936:** *Anything Goes* (*Tops Is the Limit*) (Milestone) (as Hope Harcourt); *One Rainy Afternoon* (*Matinee Scandal*) (R. V. Lee) (as Monique Pelerin); *Yours for the Asking* (Hall) (as Gert Malloy); *The Gay Desperado* (Mamoulian) (as Jane). **1937:** *Sea Devils* (Stoloff) (as Doris Malone); *Let's Get Married* (A. E. Green) (as Paula Quinn); *Artists and Models* (Walsh) (as Paula Sewell); *Fight for Your Lady* (Stoloff) (as Marietta). **1939:** *The Lone Wolf Spy Hunt* (Godfrey) (as Val Carson); *The Lady and the Mob* (Stoloff) (as Lila Thorne); *The Adventures of Sherlock Holmes* (Werker) (as Ann Brandon); *The Light that Failed* (Wellman) (as Bessie Broke). **1940:** *They Drive by Night* (Walsh) (as Lana Carlsen). **1941:** *High Sierra* (Walsh) (as Marie Garson); *The Sea Wolf* (Curtiz) (as Ruth Webster); *Out of the Fog* (Litvak) (as Stella Goodwin); *Ladies in Retirement* (C. Vidor) (as Ellen Creed). **1942:** *Moontide* (Mayo) (as Ada); *The Hard Way* (V. Sherman) (as Helen Chernen); *Life Begins at 8:30* (*The Light of Heart*) (Pichel) (as Kathi Thomas). **1943:** *Forever and a Day* (Clair and others) (as Jenny); *Thank Your Lucky Stars* (D. Butler) (appearance). **1944:** *In Our Time* (V. Sherman) (as Jennifer Whittredge); *Hollywood Canteen* (Daves) (appearance). **1945:** *Pillow to Post* (V. Sherman) (as Jean Howard). **1946:** *Devotion* (Bernhardt) (as Emily Brontë); *The Man I Love* (Walsh) (as Petey Brown). **1947:** *Deep Valley* (Negulesco) (as Libby); *Escape Me Never* (Godfrey) (as Gemma Smith). **1948:** *Road House* (Negulesco) (as Lily Stevens). **1949:** *Lust for Gold* (Simon) (as Julia Thomas); *Woman in Hiding* (Gordon) (as Deborah Chandler Clark). **1951:** *On Dangerous Ground* (N. Ray) (as Mary Malden).

1952: *Beware, My Lovely* (Horner) (as Mrs. Helen Gordon). **1953:** *Jennifer* (Newton) (as Agnes). **1954:** *Private Hell 36* (Siegel) (as Lilli Marlowe, + co-sc). **1955:** *Women's Prison* (Seiler) (as Amelia Van Zant); *The Big Knife* (Aldrich) (as Marion Castle). **1956:** *While the City Sleeps* (F. Lang) (as Mildred); *Strange Intruder* (Rapper) (as Alice). **1969:** *Backtrack* (Bellamy) (as Mama Delores). **1972:** *Junior Bonner* (Peckinpah) (as Elvira Bonner); *Deadhead Miles* (Zimmerman) (as herself); *Women in Chains* (Kowalski—for TV) (as Tyson); *The Strangers in 7A* (Wendkos—for TV) (as Iris Sawyer). **1973:** *Female Artillery* (Chomsky—for TV) (as Martha Lindstrom); *I Love a Mystery* (L. Stevens—for TV) (as Randolph Cheyne); "Dear Karen" ep. of *The Letters* (Krasny—for TV) (as Mrs. Forrester). **1975:** *The Devil's Rain* (Fuest) (as Mrs. Preston). **1976:** *Food of the Gods* (B. I. Gordon) (as Mrs. Skinner). **1978:** *My Boys Are Good Boys* (Buckalew).

One of the few female directors to enjoy success in Hollywood in the 1950s, Ida Lupino was perhaps destined to work in the realm of entertainment, as she was descended from ancestors who had worked as performers during the Renaissance. After studying at London's Royal Academy of Dramatic Art, she went to Hollywood in 1934 and enjoyed a successful career as a film actress before she embarked upon a career as a film director. Specifically, during a period of suspension from Warner Bros. and because of general frustration as an actress after she was unable to work for 18 months in the mid-1940s, Lupino was inspired to direct movies rather than to star in them, as she put it to "fill the time." With her second husband, Collier Young, she founded her own film company, Film-makers, for which she controlled the production, direction, and screenplays of its films. Between 1949 and 1954, she made six feature films. She took over the directorial duties on her first film, *Not Wanted,* when director Elmer Clifton had a heart attack. She was uncredited, however. Subsequently, she and Collier co-wrote and co-produced, and she directed, each of their films.

As a film director Lupino can be characterized as a social realist because she relished tackling daring topics that were usually overlooked in Hollywood at the time. Critics have praised her as an *auteur* (i.e., as the author of her films) because her work reveals a consistency of themes and motifs. Certainly she often selected controversial social issues as the subjects of her films, such as rape, promiscuity, single motherhood, and bigamy, though she provided no easy answers and the films themselves often end ambiguously. Typically, her characters are from the working class, and often her male characters are the dangerous or questionable figures who are usually portrayed in film noir by women. In addition, her films explore the themes of feminine sexuality, independence, and dependence, and her female characters are as likely to be villains, or at least morally questionable, as they are to be heroines. Likewise, her films convey the tensions of disillusioned characters who are trapped by their surroundings. For example, *Never Fear* concerns the travails of a female dancer who is stricken by polio; *Not Wanted* is about unwed mothers, and tells the story of a promiscuous teenage girl who takes up with men she meets in bars, thus becoming pregnant in the process. *Hard, Fast, and Beautiful* is about a bored mother filled with dreams for her tennis-champion daughter, though the film denounces her for what it suggests are her unhealthy ambitions and the daughter ultimately chooses marriage over her tennis career. *Outrage* treats the subject of rape by focusing on the trauma endured by a rape victim who finds comfort in the arms of a paternal man. And, in *The Bigamist* the central character is a man who is driven by his wife's professional ambitions to an affair and it earned the praise of critics for its empathetic account of the ambiguous origins of a couple's double affair. Critics have pointed out that for Lupino's characters, the problem is not about the difficulties of being reintegrated into the mainstream of society, but rather about the superficiality of that mainstream.

Critics generally agree that *The Hitch-Hiker* is Lupino's best directorial accomplishment; it was her biggest critical and commercial success. Made the same year as her impressive melodrama *The Bigamist,* this film is nonetheless entirely different. It is an unrelentingly tense story of two businessmen on a fishing holiday who pick up a hitchhiker—a murdering psychopath—and are held as his captives. They are forced at gunpoint to drive him through the southwest and into Mexico until he no longer needs them. Lupino demonstrated a deft hand at crafting a dismal noir atmosphere, in coaxing riveting performances, and avoiding suspense-film clichés. She also effectively revealed the changes of the victimized men's relationship as they argue about what to do, and she suggests that their survival depends on their union more than anything else.

Ida Lupino

Lupino's technically proficient films boasted small budgets, usually less than $200,000, and no stars; they were usually shot in about 13 days. Not surprisingly, given her extensive acting experience, actors especially appreciated her directorial skills. Nonetheless, Lupino proclaimed distinctly antifeminist aims and ultrafeminine means, to the chagrin of many feminist film scholars. She freely admitted to using a soft touch as a director; i.e., she cooed instructions to her cast and crew, and encouraged them to call her "mother" because she wanted her productions to operate like a big, happy family. Nevertheless, she approached her duties with determination and extensive preparation. And, though she was apparently rhetorically unconcerned with feminist issues, in her own life she worked prolifically, and critics have astutely noted that her rhetoric about feminism was belied by the way she conducted her own life. In her later years, however, Lupino softened her rhetoric and lamented that there were not more women working as directors and producers in Hollywood.

Lupino and Collier's mistake was going into distribution, a move to which she objected because she considered herself a creative worker rather than a businessperson. But, when their film company folded in 1954, Lupino went to work in television. Initially reluctant, she was persuaded to work as an actress for two years. She loved it. Eventually, she moved into television directing and ultimately, she directed at least a hundred episodes for series television, though she claimed to have directed hundreds. She was praised for her use of a mobile camera during a time when camera work tended to be static. Among the series she directed were *Gunsmoke, Have Gun Will Travel, Sunset Strip, The Untouchables,* and *Alfred Hitchcock Presents.* Interestingly, as a television director, Lupino became pigeonholed as a director who was best at Westerns and action shows, though she longed to do a love story. Eventually, she directed Anne Baxter and Ronald Reagan in a teleplay for *General Electric Theater.* After a lengthy period directing for television, Lupino returned to feature film work with *The Trouble with Angels,* a frothy movie about an all-girls religious academy whose educational goals are compromised by the high jinks of a pair of wild, boy-crazy girls. It was her last Hollywood feature film.—CYNTHIA FELANDO

Lyell, Lottie

Australian director and actress

Born *Lottie Edith Cox in Sydney, 23 February 1890.* ***Family*** *Married the director Raymond Longford, 1925.* ***Career*** *1907—professional stage debut as the female lead in* An Englishman's Home; *1911—appeared on-screen for the first time, in a supporting role with Raymond Longford in* Captain Midnight, the Bush King; *made her first film with Longford,* The Fatal Wedding; *1919—her masterpiece,* The Sentimental Bloke *was released; 1922—Longford and Lyell formed the Longford-Lyell Australian Picture Productions Limited in order to fight Australia's ongoing problems of exhibition and distribution; 1924—Longford and Lyell re-formed their production company as Longford-Lyell Productions.* ***Died*** *Of tuberculosis, in Australia, 21 December 1925.*

Films as Actress: 1911: *Captain Midnight, the Bush King* (Rolfe) (as Thelma); *Captain Starlight*; *The Life of Rufus Dawes.*

Films as Actress (all films directed by Longford): 1911: *The Fatal Wedding*; *The Romantic Story of Margaret Catchpole* (title role). **1912:** *The Tide of Death*; *The Midnight Wedding.* **1913:** *Australia Calls*; *Pommy Arrives in Australia*; *'Neath Austral Skies.* **1914:** *The Swagman's Story*; *Trooper Campbell*; *Taking His Chance*; *The Silence of Dean Maitland.* **1915:** *We'll Take Her Children in Amongst Our Own*; *Ma Hoggan's New Boarder.* **1916:** *A Maori Maid's Love* (+ sc); *The Mutiny of the Bounty* (as Nessie Heywood, + sc, ed). **1917:** *The Church and the Woman.* **1918:** *The Woman Suffers* (as Marjorie Manton). **1919:** *The Sentimental Bloke* (as Doreen, + sc, art d, ed, production asst). **1920:** *Ginger Mick* (+ sc). **1921:** *Rudd's New Selection* (as Nell). **1923:** *The Dinkum Bloke* (+ co-d, sc, pr).

Other Films: 1921: *The Blue Mountains Mystery* (co-d with Longford, sc, ed). **1923:** *Australia Calls* (sc); *An Australian by Marriage* (sc, + possibly ro). **1924:** *Fisher's Ghost* (sc, pr). **1925:** *The Bushwackers* (sc, pr). **1926:** *Peter Vernon's Silence* (sc, pr); *The Pioneers* (Longford) (sc).

Lottie Lyell is credited with being the first Australian movie star, but she is also noteworthy as a director, producer, writer, art director, and editor. For more than a decade, during the 1910s and early 1920s, she enjoyed a productive personal and professional partnership with filmmaker Raymond Longford. Nevertheless, her long career was overlooked by Australian film historians, despite her status as a cinema pioneer. Indeed, as film historian Andrée Wright contends, Lyell is "the outstanding Australian personality of early film."

Lyell's acting career began in the theater in 1907, and by 1909 she was performing on stage with Longford. Then, in 1911 she and Longford made a momentous decision—to make movies. Together, they made 28 films and Lyell starred in 21 of them, although only a few survive. Film historians have bemoaned the fact that primary evidence about Lyell's early career is so sparse, but she is presumed to have combined her role as an actress with that of director for many years. Reportedly, Lyell co-directed all of her films, though such accomplishments went uncredited. Indeed, many of her production colleagues steadfastly maintained that she was the primary director of the Lyell-Longford productions. Her contributions were so great, that one of her acting colleagues alleged that she, rather than Raymond, had the skills to direct a film alone, and further credited her with using her power with "reserve and discretion."

During a period when screen roles for women were fairly narrow, Lyell enacted an important depiction of Australian femininity that was both demure and defiant, quiet and daring—the "girl of the bush," in films such as *The Tide of Death* and *'Neath Austral Skies*. In the latter film she rides to the rescue of a trooper who has been bound and tossed into a river by cattle thieves. While her man takes care of the gang, Lyell, with knife clenched between her teeth, dives to the rescue. Critics at the time enthusiastically characterized Lyell as like the "all-Australian heroine" she often played, especially for her skills as a horsewoman. Notably, more recent film critics have observed the tendency for Lyell's heroines to blur the distinction between good and evil. In other words, in the Longford-Lyell films it was the men who caused women to go "wrong." Thus, in the most-cited example, *The Woman Suffers,* two women are seduced and abandoned after they become pregnant. The first woman commits suicide in desperation, while the second (played by Lyell) attempts a self-induced abortion without success. But rather than ensuring a hopeless future, her act leads her lover to acknowledge his wrong and to marry her, which seems to guarantee a happy future.

Despite considerable opposition from critics and investors, Lyell and Longford determined to adapt C. J. Dennis's popular 1915 book *The Songs of a Sentimental Bloke* for the screen. *The Sentimental Bloke,* a romantic comedy about the working class, proved to be their masterpiece, and moreover, it achieved legendary status as the earliest Australian feature to be considered a classic. It successfully blends love story, social comedy, and a working-class setting—though without featuring the extreme class conflict as did other films of the time that featured the poor. Like Dennis's volume, nearly all of the film's titles consist of dialected verse from the Bloke's point of view, which lent considerably to its Australian humor and spirit. The film is largely unknown outside Australia, though local historians consider it one of the world's best films made before 1920. Among its other noteworthy attributes, it is considered innovative for its realistic ambience and an unusually respectful depiction of the working poor, unlike other films that associated the city with vice and the country with virtue. Lyell played the Bloke's true love, the sweet factory-girl Doreen for whom he goes straight. Most of the movie's narrative concerns their courtship, which is broken when they argue about a rival for Doreen's affection. After they reconcile and marry, the Bloke goes astray from his vow to give up drinking and gambling with his pub mates. Eventually Doreen's uncle arrives and presents the couple with an enticing opportunity—to take over his country orchard, where they find happiness in hard work. When their baby boy is born, their future seems assuredly idyllic.

When it was released, *The Sentimental Bloke* made more money than any previous Australian film and it earned enormous praise. Indeed, in Australia it was considered a landmark of quality until the end of the silent era. Its performances are especially noteworthy, in large part, due to Lyell's restrained, sympathetic, and realistic style of acting. She has been credited with being one of the first Australian performers to adapt her performance style to the film medium, by avoiding the exaggerated gestures that were necessary on stage but not on-screen. In addition, reportedly, Longford encouraged the actors to spend time in a working-class Sydney suburb to prepare for their roles. After *The Sentimental Bloke,* Longford and Lyell made two sequels, *Ginger Mick* and *The Dinkum Bloke,* which no longer survive, though historians have presumed they followed the formula established in *The Sentimental Bloke.*

Lyell's first screen credit for directing did not come until 1921's *The Blue Mountains Mystery,* for which she also adapted the script from Harrison Owen's novel, *The Mount Maranga Mystery.* The film features an innocent young heroine who is contrasted with the mean and mysterious sophisticate, Belle Vere. The sophisticate, however, was not entirely irredeemable, as she eventually confesses her role in falsely convicting the innocent woman of manslaughter, and then kills herself.

In the early 1920s, Lyell started to experience diminishing health due to tuberculosis; then, after living together for 13 years, Longford secured a divorce and married her only weeks before her death at the age of 35. One obituary appropriately described her passing as "a distinct blow to the motion picture industry of this country and the loss of one who has left the mark of her genius on Australia's screen progress." After her death, Longford directed *The Pioneers* from a script Lyell had written, though without her other skills, his career declined rapidly thereafter.—CYNTHIA FELANDO

Maclean, Alison

Canadian/New Zealander director

Born *Ottawa, Ontario, Canada, 31 July 1958; moved to New Zealand in 1972.* ***Education*** *Attended Auckland University, BFA, majored in sculpture.* ***Career*** *1982—directed first short film,* Taunt, *the year she was graduated from Auckland University; 1989—moved to Sydney, Australia; 1992—directed her first feature,* Crush; *1992—directed "Greed," an episode of the Australian TV series* The Seven Deadly Sins; *moved to New York City; 1990s—contributing editor of* BOMB *magazine; 1995—directed* The Adventures of Pete & Pete *for Nickelodeon; 1996—directed "Subway Kick," an episode of the HBO series* Subway Stories; *mid-1990s—in development on several projects, including a remake of* Bedlam, *originally produced by Val Lewton and starring Boris Karloff;* Iris, *produced by Good Machine; and an untitled "Chrome Dragon" project, an action film set in Bangkok; 1997—directed episode of TV series* Homicide: Life on the Streets. ***Awards*** *Best Short Film, New Zealand Film and Television Awards, for* Talkback, *1987; Best Short Film, New Zealand Film Awards, for* Kitchen Sink, *1989.* ***Agent*** *William Morris Agency, 151 El Camino Drive, Beverly Hills, CA 90212, U.S.A.*

Films as Director: **1982:** *Taunt* (short) (+ sc). **1985:** *Rud's Wife* (short) (+ co-sc). **1987:** *Talkback* (short) (+ co-sc). **1989:** *Kitchen Sink* (short) (+ sc). **1992:** *Crush* (+ co-sc). **1993:** *Positive* (short).

Alison Maclean is one of a group of Australasian women filmmakers—the list only begins with Jane Campion, Gillian Armstrong, and Jocelyn Morehouse—who have brought distinctly female perspectives to a male-dominated movie industry. In her films, Maclean has exhibited a special concern for gender roles and empowerment; words and their meanings; and the manner in which women communicate (as well as lack of communication and its ramification).

All of these issues are articulated in *Talkback,* one of Maclean's earlier short films, the story of a female talkback radio producer who replaces a male host. The producer must acclimate herself to her new role, and her new power to communicate, as she converses with her callers.

Maclean's follow-up, *Kitchen Sink,* is a small masterpiece: a riveting—and wordless—12-minute-long surreal horror film about a woman and the man-monster/paramour who emerges from the hair in her sink. *Kitchen Sink* works as an exploration of an evolving male-female relationship and a textbook example of the often overlooked power of the short film. It is tightly directed, and exudes a nonstop energy that would be impossible to maintain in a feature-length film.

Maclean's debut feature is *Crush,* an oddly compelling psychological thriller. *Crush* is the story of New Zealander Christina, a literary critic who has set up an interview with Colin, a reclusive writer. Her American womanfriend Lane is at the wheel as the pair drive to meet Colin. Seemingly inexplicably, Lane begins speeding. The car crashes. Christina is nearly killed; she ends up hospitalized, comatose, and with massive head injuries. Lane leaves the accident scene without summoning help. She shows up at the home of Colin, where she encounters his unpolished 15-year-old daughter, Angela. Both Angela and Colin are attracted to Lane, who begins seducing her way into their lives.

This triangle is dissolved upon the reappearance of Christina. Angela, who is confused by her conflicting feelings and her father's developing relationship with Lane, switches her attention to Christina. The adolescent visits the invalid in the hospital, assists in her therapy, and contaminates her mind against Lane. Christina's physical condition improves to the point where she can spend a weekend with Colin, Angela, and Lane; however, she is bound to a wheelchair, and her speech is slurred.

The film concludes with the characters spending a day by a waterfall, with Lane aspiring to clear the air with both Angela and Christina (who is still in her wheelchair). When the others are not around, Christina rises from the chair and shoves Lane to her death over the waterfall cliff.

During the course of the film, many questions emerge. Exactly what is the nature of Lane and Christina's relationship? Are they merely friends, or have they been lovers? What spurred on Lane's actions in the car? Had she and Christina had some kind of spat just before the film opens? Has Lane abandoned Christina out of selfishness or thoughtlessness, or has she been psychologically jarred (if not physically damaged) by the accident? Why does Lane relate to Colin and Angela in the manner in which she does? And what is the true extent of Christina's injuries? Can she think clearly, and is unable to communicate because of her physical limitations, or has the accident shattered her mind and memory? (More clear are Angela's motivations for her connecting with Lane and Christina. She is no manipulative devil, but rather a lonely, attention-seeking innocent who seeks female camaraderie with Lane and at the same time is dazzled by her and attracted to her because of her fear of heterosexual sex. When Angela sees Lane linking romantically with her father, and thus becoming a rival for his affection, she switches her attention to Christina. As Christina has been rendered mute and physically helpless, Angela can exercise power in her presence.)

At the outset, Lane's actions make her appear to be the rogue, while helpless Christina suffers dearly because of Lane. As the scenario develops, however, these roles become more ambiguous. At the end, it is purposefully unclear which character truly is the villain and which is the victim—or, indeed, if either one can be labeled or judged as "good" or "evil."

These questions—and their lack of answers—are what gives *Crush* its appeal. Maclean does not in any way transform Lane or Christina into feminist heroines. She does not define their motivations; the viewer has to figure them out. The result is a tale of deep and complex emotions, which is at its most compelling when exploring the intricate connection between Lane, Christina, and Angela. Meanwhile, a masculine point of view is practically missing from the film, as the role of Colin is more of a catalyst for the actions of the other characters.

Crush is a highly unconventional film, and Alison Maclean is a gifted cinematic voice. As of mid-1997 she was living in New York, where she was "in development" on several projects (one of which is a remake of the 1946 Val Lewton-produced chiller, *Bedlam*). One hopes that her promising feature film career will not end with *Crush*.—ROB EDELMAN

Macpherson, Jeanie

American writer, director, and actress

Born *Boston, 18 May 1884.* ***Education*** *Attended Mademoiselle DeJacque's School, Paris.* ***Career*** *1907-14—stage and film actress: member of the chorus, Chicago Opera House, film debut in* Mr. Jones at the Ball, *1908, and in road companies of* Cleopatra *and* Strongheart *and on Broadway in* Havana; *1912—directed and appeared in new version of lost film,* The Tarantula; *1915—began long association with Cecil B. DeMille.* ***Died*** *Of cancer, in Hollywood, 26 August 1946.*

Films as Writer for Director Cecil B. DeMille: **1915:** *The Unafraid*; *The Captive* (+ ro); *Chimmie Fadden Out West*; *The Golden Chance.* **1916:** *Maria Rosa*; *Temptation*; *The Trail of the Lonesome Pine*; *The Heart of Nora Flynn*; *The Dream Girl.* **1917:** *Joan the Woman*; *A Romance of the Redwoods*; *The Little American*; *The Woman God Forgot*; *The Devil Stone.* **1918:** *The Whispering Chorus*; *Old Wives for New*; *Till I Come Back to You.* **1919:** *Don't Change Your Husband*; *For Better, for Worse*; *Male and Female.* **1920:** *Something to Think About.* **1921:** *Forbidden Fruit*; *The Affairs of Anatol.* **1922:** *Saturday Night*; *Manslaughter.* **1923:** *Adam's Rib*; *The Ten Commandments.* **1924:** *Triumph.* **1925:** *The Golden Bed*; *The Road to Yesterday.* **1927:** *The King of Kings.* **1929:** *The Godless Girl*; *Dynamite.* **1930:** *Madam Satan.* **1935:** *The Crusades.* **1936:** *The Plainsman.* **1938:** *The Buccaneer.* **1939:** *Land of Liberty* (doc); *Union Pacific.* **1940:** *Northwest Mounted Police.* **1942:** *Reap the Wild Wind* (uncredited). **1944:** *The Story of Dr. Wassell.*

Other Films as Writer: **1912:** *The Tarantula* (+ d, ro). **1913:** *The Sea Urchin* (E. August) (+ ro as lover); *Red Margaret, Moonshiner* (Dwan). **1914:** *The Ghost Breaker* (+ d); *The Lie* (Dwan). **1916:** *The Love Mask* (Reicher) (co). **1926:** *Red Dice* (W. K. Howard); *Young April* (Crisp); *Her Man o' War* (Reicher). **1933:** *Fra Diavolo* (*The Devil's Brother*) (Roach and Rogers).

Jeanie Macpherson with Cecil B. De Mille

Films as Actress for Director D. W. Griffith: 1908: *Mr. Jones at the Ball*; *The Fatal Hour*; *The Vaquero's Vow*; *Father Gets in the Game*; *The Devil*; *Concealing a Burglar*; *The Curtain Pole*; *The Clubman and the Tramp*; *Mrs. Jones Entertains*; *The Test of Friendship*; *A Wreath in Time*; *Tragic Love*. **1909:** *Mr. Jones Has a Card Party*; *Trying to Get Arrested*; *The Medicine Bottle*; *Lady Helen's Escapade*; *A Rude Hostess*; *Confidence*; *The Peach Basket Hat*; *The Faded Lilies*; *The Message*; *The Seventh Day*; *With Her Card*; *Lines of White on the Sullen Sea*; *A Midnight Adventure*; *The Death Disc*; *A Corner in Wheat*; *The Call*. **1910:** *The Newlyweds*; *The Way of the World*; *A Victim of Jealousy*; *An Affair of Hearts*; *The Impalement*; *A Flash of Light*; *In Life's Cycle*; *The Iconoclast*; *Winning Back His Love*; *A Wreath of Orange Blossoms*; *Heart Beats of Long Ago*. **1911:** *Fisher Folks*; *The Spanish Gypsy*; *Enoch Arden*; *The Blind Princess and the Poet*; *The Last Drop of Water*; *Out from the Shadow*. **1914:** *The Desert's Sting* (d unknown).

Other Films as Actress: 1914: *Rose of the Rancho* (C. B. DeMille); *The Ghost Breaker* (C. B. DeMille and Apfel); *The Merchant of Venice* (Weber and Smalley) (as Merrissa). **1915:** *The Girl of the Golden West* (C. B. DeMille); *Carmen* (C. B. DeMille). **1923:** *Hollywood* (Cruze) (as herself).

Jeanie Macpherson was not a screenwriter when she was introduced to Cecil B. DeMille. She had been a director at Universal at one time, but when she met DeMille she was concentrating on acting. Due to her dark features, however, she was being typecast as either a gypsy or a Spaniard. Macpherson was cast by DeMille to act in a few of his features (*Rose of the Rancho, The Girl of the Golden West, Carmen,* and *The Captive*—the last of which she also wrote) before she decided to turn exclusively to screenwriting. There was mutual attraction between Macpherson and DeMille from the start: she loved the challenge of working with a hard-driving perfectionist; he was drawn to her spirit and courage. It was a partnership that would last more than 25 years.

Macpherson and DeMille held a common belief that would be the basis for every screenplay on which they collaborated: they despised weakness in men and women. In Macpherson's scripts, weak men were taken advantage of and degraded, and weak women were shallow, gold-digging, and destructive creatures who went from one rich man to the next. The screenwriter believed that men and women could learn from experience, however, and change weak or evil ways, and she demonstrated this in her early social dramas. Both Macpherson and DeMille celebrated the hero and the heroine—biblical, historical, or fictional—and praised their courage and perseverance.

Macpherson's strength was writing historical dramas. When she began her work for DeMille, she assisted the director in writing features for Geraldine Farrar, the operatic star, including *Maria Rosa, Temptation,* and *Joan the Woman*. This last was based on the life of Joan of Arc. While DeMille created the huge frame around the French girl's life with his grandiose settings and hundreds of extras, Macpherson fashioned a human drama with which the audience could identify. Thus, while Joan was part of a spectacular event, upon a closer look she was seen as a frightened young girl driven by her spiritual beliefs. The title, Macpherson's idea, emphasized the view of Joan as a human being rather than an indestructible saint. This same viewpoint was used in the DeMille epic *The King of Kings*. Based on the life of Jesus Christ, the film portrayed Mary Magdalene as a woman who was not evil but misguided, and Jesus as a virile and strong man.

The end of World War I ushered in the era of the Roaring Twenties and by then Macpherson had begun writing contemporary drama rather than historical projects. The liberal moral climate gave rise to the flapper, the sexually aware young woman who rejected conventional mores. Some of the best films DeMille and Macpherson created were responses to America's change in mood and fashion: *Old Wives for New, Don't Change Your Husband, Male and Female, The Affairs of Anatol, Manslaughter,* and *Adam's Rib*. *Male and Female,* an update of the play *The Admirable Crichton,* introduced a new element into Macpherson's screenplays: the blending together of past and present stories. Macpherson interwove episodes from history and the Bible into modern dramas to demonstrate moral lessons. These lessons warned audiences of the excesses of the 1920s and what the future would hold if the warnings were not heeded. Flashbacks were used as lessons, such as the prologue to *The Ten Commandments* which concerned Moses and the story of the commandments (this version of *Ten Commandments* had a modern-day plot). *Male and Female* contained a flashback to Babylon, *Manslaughter* to ancient Rome, *Adam's Rib* to prehistoric times, *Triumph* to Romeo and Juliet, and *The Road to Yesterday* to 17th-century England. These screenplays offered audiences not only an admonishment for their money, but also the attraction of seeing stars in the period costumes that each flashback required.

In 1933, while DeMille was busy with other projects, Macpherson wrote the screenplay for *Fra Diavolo* for Laurel and Hardy, before rejoining the director for several films celebrating heroes: King Richard the Lionhearted in *The Crusades,* Wild Bill Hickok in *The Plainsman,* Jean Lafitte in *The Buccaneer,* the men who started the transcontinental railroad in *Union Pacific,* Canadian Mounties in *Northwest Mounted Police,* and Dr. Corydon E. Wassell in *The Story of Dr. Wassell.* In 1939 she co-wrote and narrated the DeMille film *Land of Liberty,* a historical look at America for the New York World's Fair. These last research and writing projects were done mostly without credit. Before she could finish her research work on *Unconquered* for DeMille, Macpherson died of cancer in 1946. Her screenplays had gone full circle from the early escapist and historical films to realistic and social dramas and back to escapist and historical pictures again.—ALEXA L. FOREMAN

Madison, Cleo

American director and actress

Born *Bloomington, Indiana, 1883.* ***Career*** *1900s—worked as an actress on the legitimate stage and in vaudeville; 1910s—moved to California and acted with the Santa Barbara Stock Company; 1913—made her screen debut as an actress; 1914—won stardom for her performance in* The Trey O'Hearts; *1915—began directing and co-directing Universal shorts and features; 1924—retired from movies.* ***Died*** *Burbank, California, 11 March 1964.*

Films as Actress and/or Director: 1913: *The Trap* (August—short); *The Heart of a Cracksman* (Reid and Robards—short); *Cross Purposes* (short); *The Buccaneers* (short); *Captain Kidd* (short); *Shadows of Life* (Weber—short); *His Pal's Request* (+ d, uncredited—short); *Under the Black Flag* (short). **1914:** *The Trey O' Hearts* (W. Lucas—serial) (as Ruth/Judith); *Samson* (J. F. Macdonald) (as Jasmine, the Philistine); *Damon and Pythias* (Turner) (as Hermion); *The Master Key* (serial); *Dead Man Who Killed* (*Eye for an Eye*; *The Dead Man That Kills*) (short); *The Feud* (short); *The Last of Their Race* (short); *The Law of Their Kind* (short); *The Love Victorious* (short); *The Man Between* (short); *The Mexican's Last Raid* (short); *The Mystery of Wickham Hall* (short); *Sealed Orders* (short); *The Severed Hand* (short); *The Strenuous Life* (short); *Unjustly Accused* (short). **1915:** *The Pine's Revenge* (DeGrasse—short); *A Mother's Atonement* (DeGrasse—short) (as Alice/Jen); *The Fascination of the Fleur de Lis* (DeGrasse—short) (as Lisette); *Alas and Alack* (DeGrasse—short) (as Wife); *Agnes Kempler's Sacrifice* (short); *Liquid Dynamite* (+ d—short); *The Ring of Destiny* (+ d—short); *The Power of Fascination* (+ d—short); *The Dancer* (Park—short); *Extravagance* (Giblyn—short); *Faith of Her Fathers* (Giblyn—short); *A Fiery Introduction* (Giblyn—short); *The Flight of a Nightbird* (Giblyn—short); *The People of the Pit* (Giblyn—short); *A Wild Irish Rose* (Giblyn—short); *Haunted Hearts* (short); *The Mother's Instinct* (short); *Their Hour* (short); *The Ways of a Man* (short); *A Woman's Debt* (short). **1916:** *A Soul Enslaved* (as Jane, + d); *The Chalice of Sorrow* (Ingram) (as Lorelei); *Her Bitter Cup* (as Rethna, + d, sc); *Her Defiance* (+ co-d with J. King—short); *Alias Jane Jones* (+ co-d—short); *Along the Malibu* (+ co-d with Mong—short); *His Return* (+ d—short); *Eleanor's Catch* (+ d—short); *Virginia* (+ d—short); *When the Wolf Howls* (+ co-d—short); *The Crimson Yoke* (+ co-d with Mong—short); *Priscilla's Prisoner* (+ d—short); *The Girl in Lower 9* (+ co-d—short); *The Guilty One* (+ co-d—short); *The Triumph of Truth* (+ d—short); *To Another Woman* (+ co-d with Mong—short); *Cross Purposes* (short); *The Heart's Crucible* (+ co-d with Kerrigan—short); *The Mystery Woman* (short); *Tillie, the Little Swede* (+ co-d with Mong—short). **1917:** *Black Orchids* (Ingram) (as Marie De Severac/Zoraida); *The Girl Who Lost* (Cochrane—short); *The Web* (Cochrane—short); *The Woman Who Would Not Pay* (Baldwin—short); *The Sorceress* (short). **1918:** *The Romance of Tarzan* (Meredyth and W. Lucas) (as La Belle Odine); *The Flame of the West* (short). **1919:** *The Girl from Nowhere* (W. Lucas) (as "Gal"). **1919-20:** *The Great Radium Mystery* (R. F. Hill and Broadwell—serial). **1920:** *The Price of Redemption* (Fitzgerald) (as Anne

Steel). **1921:** *Ladies Must Live* (Tucker) (as Mrs. Lincourt); *The Lure of Youth* (Rosen) (as Florentine Fair). **1922:** *The Dangerous Age* (Stahl) (as Mary Emerson); *A Woman's Woman* (Giblyn) (as Iris Starr). **1923:** *Gold Madness* (Thornby) (as Olga McGee); *Souls in Bondage* (Clifford) (as The Chameleon). **1924:** *Discontented Husbands* (Le Saint) (as Jane Frazer); *The Lullaby* (Bennett) (as Mrs. Marvin); *The Roughneck* (Conway) (as Anne Delaney); *True as Steel* (Hughes) (as Mrs. Parry); *Unseen Hands* (Jaccard) (as Mataoka).

Cleo Madison found a steady job acting and writing for Carl Laemmle at Universal studios in 1913. She appeared in a steady flow of short films, serials, and occasionally a feature length drama, working with a stream of skilled technicians, including pioneer women directors Lois Weber and Ida May Park who would become mentors to Madison. Particularly in the 1914 serial *The Trey O' Hearts,* Madison won the hearts of fans starring in the dual role of an innocent but resilient heroine Ruth, and her evil identical twin Judith. As such, she remarkably survived through 15 episodes of apparently relentless action, including a car crash, forest fire, shooting, and death-threatening curse. As Madison became established as an on-screen personality, she became self-confident that she could do equally well working behind the camera. According to a fan magazine story of the mid-teens, she asked the company bosses to allow her to direct, and when they refused she became so difficult to work with—a prima donna à la Sarah Bernhardt—that they finally relented and gave her her own small production company.

As a combination film star and director, Madison was living in the limelight, bringing a number of feminist cinema pieces to the screen, and receiving a steady paycheck. Yet life at Universal was a mixed blessing. As silent-film historian Richard Koszarski has pointed out, Universal was one of the low-paying Hollywood studios. Perhaps that is why they hired so many women for directorial jobs that the other studios offered only to men. If you could bring a picture in on time and under budget and make it a crowd-pleaser to boot, then "Uncle Carl" Laemmle was happy to have you on the director's payroll. By 1915 there was an outstanding group of capable women directing at Universal, including Weber and Park, Nell Shipman, Ruth Ann Baldwin, Grace Cunard and others. Most of these women did their most prolific and effective work before and during the World War I years when men were in uniform. And while it cannot be said that women obtained director jobs before the war because men were not available, an argument can be made that some of these women lost their jobs when the war ended and a population of males sought to replace military duty with private-sector jobs.

Between 1915 and the end of 1916, Madison directed, or co-directed, and also starred in close to 20 films at Universal. Most were two-reeler shorts. Of these, very few survive due to the fact that Universal, in a classic example of corporate shortsightedness, burned its silent film material (shot on flammable and chemically unstable nitrate film stock) because they foresaw no further financial gain to be had from silent product. The surviving evidence of her film work shows that Madison was concerned with telling stories of social significance that center on the plight of working-class women.

A Soul Enslaved, a feature starring and directed by Madison, is about Jane, a poor girl working in a factory, who has a brief affair with the rich factory owner. As a result, years after her marriage to another man, she is castigated by her husband for being "damaged goods." *Her Bitter Cup,* a feature in which Madison starred as well as directed and wrote, relates the story of yet another factory laborer, Rethna, who organizes her fellow workers against a merciless factory owner. While a romance between Rethna and the factory owner's son provides the audience with entertainment, there also is a strong message that women working in factories must band together to fight for improved working conditions. One of the few films directed by Madison that does survive is a 23-minute short entitled *Her Defiance.* In this photoplay, a young woman (Madison) becomes pregnant by a lover who appears to abandon her. She chooses to bear the bastard child and then finds work as a cleaning woman to support herself and baby, rather than follow her brother's instructions to marry a wealthy old man. Film historian and archivist Eileen Bowser comments on this film in the Museum of Modern Art Circulating Film Library Catalog, "[it is] noteworthy for its own defiance of thematic taboos and its avoidance of a stereotypical portrayal of women." From these examples, it is clear that Madison, as Lois Weber did before her, was creating a body of work devoted to a social and moralistic view of lower- and middle-class women's lifestyles, paying detailed attention to the individual rights of women and society's power to control women's destinies.

After 1916 Madison either quit or was asked to leave the Universal lot. One can imagine an argument over a much deserved raise or perhaps a desire to work on more carefully structured features, rather than an assembly line of shorts, as reason for her termination. Or perhaps she, or the physically disabled sister for whom she took responsibility, became ill. In any case, there are no director credits for her in 1917. After that, she appears to have taken work wherever it could be found. She appeared in a single feature for a variety of studios and independent producers. She even returned to work as a lead in a Universal serial in 1919—quite a challenge for a 36-year-old veteran.

Age actually may have been Madison's worst enemy. And the Hollywood system has never had much patience with women aging. By 1924 she was playing the part of an Indian woman in a rather undistinguished scenario. Then she disappeared from the Hollywood scene. As happened with so many of the men and women pioneers of the silent screen, her skills lay dormant as sound films took over, and new, younger talents were imported to Hollywood. Only with the recent rise of interest in feminist cinema has Cleo Madison's name been resurrected. One only hopes that archivists will recover any privately held prints of the films she created—examples of an early feminist cinema—one that predates the Jazz Age, before women got the vote. Only then will her body of work be viewed with authority, and only then will her creativity and message truly be recognized.—AUDREY E. KUPFERBERG

Maldoror, Sarah

French director

Born *Sarah Ducados, in Condom, Gers, France.* ***Education*** *Attended École Dramatique de la rue Blanche, Paris, 1958-60; studied with Mark Donskoï at University Lomonosov, All-Union State Institute of Cinematography (VGIK), Moscow, 1961-62.* ***Family*** *Companion to the president/founder of the Popular Movement for Angolan Liberation (MPLA) Mario de Andrade (died 1990), two daughters: Anna Ginga and Heinda Lucia.* ***Career*** *1960-62—founded the black theater company Les Griots in which she also worked as director and actor; 1965—assistant to Gillo de Pontercorvo on* The Battle of Algiers; *1969—directed her first short in Algeria,* Monangambée; *1970—directed her first feature in Guinea-Bissau,* Guns for Banta. ***Awards*** *First Prize, Dinard Film Festival, and Best Director Award, Carthage Film Festival, for* Monangambée, *1969; Golden Tanis, Carthage Film Festival, and International Catholic Film Office award, Ouagadougou Film Festival, Upper Volta, for* Sambizanga, *1972; Label de la Qualité, for* Vlady-Peintre, *1988;*

First Prize, Milan Film Festival, and Jury Prize and Critics Prize, Cairo Film Festival, for Léon G. Damas, *1996.* **Address** *14, Avenue Jean Moulin, Bat B1, Appt. 22, 93200 Saint Denis, France.*

Films as Director: 1969: *Monangambée* (short). **1970:** *Des Fusils pour Banta* (*Guns for Banta*). **1971:** *Carnaval en Guinée-Bissau* (*Carnival in Guinea-Bissau*) (short); *Saint-Denis sur Avenir* (*The Future of Saint Denis*) (featurette). **1972:** *Sambizanga.* **1977:** *Un carnaval dans le Sahel* (*Carnival in Sahel*) (short); *Fogo, Ile de Feu* (short); *Et les Chiens se taisaient* (*And the Dogs Kept Silent*) (short); *Un Homme, une Terre* (*A Man, a Country*) (featurette). **1980:** *La Basilique de Saint Denis* (short); *Un dessert pour Constance* (*A Dessert for Constance*) (featurette—for TV). **1981:** *Le Cimetière du Père Lachaise* (short); *Miró* (short); *Alberto Carliski, Sculpteur* (short). **1982:** *Robert Lapoujade, Peintre* (short); *Toto Bissainte, Chanteuse* (short); *René Depestre, Poète* (short); *L'hôpital de Leningrad* (*Leningrad Hospital*) (featurette—for TV). **1983:** *La littérature tunisienne de la Bibliothèque Nationale* (*Tunisian Literature at the National Library*) (for TV); *Un Sénégalais en Normandie* (*A Senegalese in Normandy*) (for TV); *Robert Doisneau, Photographe* (for TV); *Le racisme au quotidien* (*Daily-Life Racism*) (for TV). **1985:** *Le passager du Tassili* (*The Tassili Passenger*) (for TV). **1986:** *Aimé Césaire, le masque des mots* (*Aimé Césaire, Words as Masks*) (short). **1988:** *Emmanuel Ungaro, Couturier* (short); *Louis Aragon—Un Masque à Paris* (short); *Vlady, Peintre* (short). **1996:** *Léon G. Damas* (short). **1997:** *L'enfant-cinéma* (*Cinema-Child*) (short). **1998:** *La tribu du bois de l'é* (*The Tribe of the "E" Wood*).

There are unsolved questions, gaps, mysteries, and misunderstandings (willful or not) in Sarah Maldoror's career and biography that are best summarized by the origin of her name: Maldoror is the title of one of the "venomous" flowers of French culture, *The Songs of Maldoror,* a book-length descent into hell written by 19th-century-poet Lautréamont. By choosing this name as an alias, Maldoror posited herself within French culture—claiming some of its most sophisticated, albeit slightly elitist aspects—while simultaneously embracing its iconoclastic tradition (Lautréamont is hailed as an ancestor to Rimbaud and the Surrealists). In one word, she paid homage to the dilemma of the French-speaking black intellectual: in love with and a part of French culture, yet deeply aware that he/she will never belong to the "mainstream." Another tantalizing question: where does Maldoror come from? Even though she made some of her better-known movies in Africa, she was born in France, and is discreet about the nature of her West Indian (Guadeloupean) descent. The point is, like many children of mixed parentage, Maldoror proudly claims her black heritage, and identifies with it. The most puzzling question: why wasn't Maldoror given the opportunity to direct more feature films after *Sambizanga*? As it stands now, her filmography is particularly impressive, as she has turned her camera, her incisive and generous gaze, her sense of rhythm and poetry, to a number of subjects, from the history of the Saint Denis Cathedral to African immigration in Paris, from the work of poets, fashion designers, sculptors, and singers (including the legendary Haitian Toto Bissainte, one of the four members of the theater group "Les Griots" she founded in the early 1960s), to adaptation of literary works (such as *L'hôpital de Leningrad,* from a short story by Victor Serge, or *Le passager du Tassili,* from a novel by Akli Tadjer). Yet, after *Monangambée, Guns for Banta,* and mostly *Sambizanga,* our appetite was whetted, and we were expecting more African revolutionary movies from Sarah Maldoror. Not only because there are still so few women working as directors in the African continent, but because *Sambizanga,* combining a superb mastery of cinematic language with a unique sensibility, both Pan-African and feminine, expressed a new, powerful voice in world cinema: African women had never been shown with such compassion, understanding, and love, with such a keen attention to detail, body language, and modes of communication. When Maria's husband is brutally kidnapped by the police, she is immediately surrounded by a group of village women of all ages who cry and mourn with her, comfort her, eventually pacify her. After a long and exhausting journey in her search for her jailed husband, she arrives at the home of friends, where she is welcomed by a community of women; one of them takes Maria's baby in her arms and suckles him. bell hooks wrote: "[in *Sambizanga*] there are black women imaged, constructed there so differently from what i had seen before. i remember the cries of these black women in their sister bonding . . . their cries haunt me these mourning black women, their grief unmediated, different."

Yet Maldoror's life also articulates the essential *displacement* which defines women in the African diaspora; her own situation is made more complex by her involvement with Mario de Andrade, a complex, charismatic figure who was a writer, artist, and poet as well as a political leader who contributed to the Revolution in Angola. In the early 1960s, they received scholarships to go to Moscow (where she studied with Mark Donskoï and met Ousmane Sembene, the "father" of African cinema), as the Soviet Union sought to play a role in the emerging African countries and train its new elites. At that time, the left-wing intelligentsias in Europe, Latin America, and Africa believed that only the "Third World" could foster world revolution. This was a time of struggle and utopia. For some African essentialists, though, Maldoror is still considered a "foreigner," only redeemed by "her long service to the black and African causes and her marriage [sic] to a prominent African nationalist." Significantly, the same writer adds that "[*Sambizanga*'s] deliberate feminist slant . . . dilutes the impact of the film's concern with armed guerrilla struggle," forgetting to mention that *Sambizanga* is one of Angela Davis's personal favorites.

When Maldoror came back to live in France and started working for television in the late 1970s, she was faced with another aspect of this cultural dilemma (characterized by the French as *métissage*): as she claims at once French, West Indian, and African cultures, she is considered from neither place (not African enough for some, too black for others), and, as a woman, she has to fight across-the-border prejudices at a professional level. Moreover, French television is not known for the cultural diversity of its programs, as it postulates an average white *téléspectateur*. It is, therefore, a testimony to Maldoror's stamina, strength, and determination that, as funding for another feature film keeps eluding her, she has managed to work within a variety of formats (shorts, TV films, featurettes), and, among a series of more or less commissioned works, insert the object of her real desire, the telling, uncovering, and celebration of the stories, myths, traditions, memories of a multifaceted African diaspora. In Martinique, she shot *Aimé Césaire, Words as Masks,* a multi-voiced, sensual, impressionist portrait of the French-speaking poet/playwright/politician who developed the concept of *négritude*. In Guyana, another documentary, *Léon G. Damas* was filmed. In Réunion Maldoror made *The Tribe of the "E" Wood*. And she is still trying to raise money for *Colonel Delgrès,* a feature about a colonel from the West Indies, who loved classical music, fought in Napoleon's armies, came to believe in the ideas of liberty, equality, fraternity, but found, upon returning to his native island of Guadeloupe, that slavery has been reestablished. A man who, like Maldoror, knew the price of treading the narrow line between races and cultures.—BÉRÉNICE REYNAUD

Mallet, Marilú

Chilean director and writer

Born *Santiago, Chile, 1945.* ***Education*** *Attended Université de Montréal, received M.A., working on Ph.D., in literature and cinema.* ***Family*** *Married, one son.* ***Career*** *1973—*

fled Chile for Montreal; made films with the support of the National Film Board of Canada; two collections of short stories published in French; 1980—co-founder with Dominique Pinel, Les Films de l'Atalante; assistant professor of cinema, University of Montreal, Concordia University. ***Awards*** *Festival awards, Locarno Film Festival and Strasbourg Film Festival, for* There Is No Forgetting, *1975; Filmmaking Award, John Simon Guggenheim Fellowship; Meilleur Documentaire d'Essai à Création, FIPA, for* Dear America, *1989.* ***Address*** *Department of Cinema, Concordia University, Sir George Williams Campus, 1455 De Maisonneuve Boulevard West, Suite VA 035-1, Montreal, PQ H3G 1M8, Canada.*

Films as Director: 1971: *Amuhuelai-Mi* (doc). **1972:** *A.E.I.* (doc). **1973:** *Donde voy a encontrar otra Violeta* (*Where Am I Going to Find Another Violeta*) (unfinished). **1974:** *Lentement* (*Slowly*). **1975:** *Il n'y à pas d'oubli* (*There Is No Forgetting*) (doc) (co-d with Fajardo and R. González). **1978:** *Los Borges* (doc). **1979:** *L'évangile à Solentiname*; *Musique d'Amérique latine* (doc). **1986:** *Journal inachevé* (*Unfinished Diary*) (doc). **1988:** *Mémoires d'un enfant des Andes* (*Child of the Andes*) (doc). **1989:** *Chère Amérique* (*Dear America*) (doc). **1995:** *2, Rue de la Memoire.*

Chilean-born Marilú Mallet began her filmmaking career during the Popular Unity government led by Salvador Allende (1970-73). Like many of her compatriots, Mallet fled Chile in the wake of the 1973 military coup that installed the repressive regime of General Pinochet. She settled in Montreal, Quebec, and embarked on a dual career of filmmaking and writing. In addition to making documentary films and working for television, Mallet has published two collections of short stories.

Mallet's oeuvre is marked by a continual exploration of the condition and experience of the immigrant-exile and the process of adjusting to a new country and trying to make it one's own. She blends fiction with documentary discourse, allowing her characters to react to situations from the depth of their own experiences. In the process of unraveling her own painful isolation, Mallet has created a personal, poetic film language which uses everyday behavior as a lens through which to examine gender, language, immigration, and exile. One sees how the subjective, personal experiences blends with and/or abuts collective experience. Mallet's innovative filmmaking carries on a pan-American dialogue with other feminist filmmakers and with Latin American political documentary. As one of a handful of prominent Chilean women making films in exile, Mallet also contributes to an international Chilean cinema that, especially in its early years (1973-79), concerned itself with identity issues and with the hope of returning to a Chile where economic and social disparities might be eradicated.

Mallet's most well-known film, *Unfinished Diary* exemplifies her aesthetic and political approach to film. Made as part of the filmmaker's own struggle with alienation and language, *Unfinished Diary* reveals Mallet's relationship with her English-speaking husband, himself a prominent filmmaker, and with their young Quebec-born son who speaks only French. Verbal language separates and unites this family, creating gender boundaries when Mallet reverts to her native Spanish. Moreover, her husband's objective approach to filmmaking clashes with Mallet's more personal, subjective style. When he criticizes her use of film language, we understand the profundity of linguistic and emotional isolation Mallet feels. Interviews with the writer Isabel Allende and other Chilean exiles uncover the universality of these language and gender problems within the female exile community.

Ultimately *Unfinished Diary* is both an analysis of and a product of exile culture. The film reveals the process of exile—a journey that begins with separating from one's home for political or ideological reasons and that can lead to a permanent struggle to balance one's identity with one's new surroundings. It is about negotiating the slippages of identity, gender, language, and exile, about ambivalence and resistance, and about getting through.

Many of Mallet's films focus on the exile or the immigrant condition in Quebec. In *Les Borges* she documents the small Portuguese community in Montreal, centering particularly on the family of Manuel Borges who arrived in Montreal in 1967. The Borges family's personal experiences serve as a meditation on how immigrants learn to live in a country that they wish to make their own. Ten years later Mallet continues to struggle with questions of how an individual consciously alters his or her life's course—in her 1989 *Dear America* two women from Montreal talk about their lives and the choices they have made. The younger, Quebec native Catherine, has the very contemporary dream of having children without neglecting her musical career. Céleste, a Portuguese woman, considers how she sacrificed her children's love by leaving them in Portugal while she sought her fortune in America. Ultimately, like most of Mallet's documentary subjects and protagonists, Catherine and Céleste struggle for happiness.—ILENE S. GOLDMAN

Marion, Frances

American writer

Born *Frances Marion Owens in San Francisco, 18 November 1890.* ***Education*** *Attended Hamilton Grammar School; St. Margaret's Hall; University of California, Berkeley.* ***Family*** *Married 1) Wesley De Lappé, 1907 (divorced 1909); 2) Robert Pike, 1910 (divorced); 3) Fred Thomson (died 1928), sons: Fred Jr. and Richard; 4) the director George William Hill, 1930 (divorced 1931).* ***Career*** *1909—reporter, San Francisco* Examiner; *then commercial artist, advertising designer, model, and poster painter for Oliver Morosco's Theatre; 1914—assistant to Lois Weber; 1915-17—writer for World Company Films (association with Mary Pickford), and Paramount; 1918-19—war correspondent in France; after 1920—wrote for Hearst's Cosmopolitan Studios, MGM, and Columbia; 1925—first novel published; 1940—retired from screenwriting; taught scriptwriting at the University of Southern California, Los Angeles.* ***Awards*** *Academy Awards, for* The Big House, *1929-30, and* The Champ, *1931-32.* ***Died*** *In Los Angeles, 12 May 1973.*

Films as Writer: 1915: *Camille* (Capellani); *'Twas Ever Thus* (Janis) (+ ro); *Nearly a Lady* (Janis) (+ ro); *Fanchon, the Cricket* (Kirkwood). **1916:** *The Foundling* (O'Brien); *The Yellow Passport* (E. August); *Then I'll Come Back to You* (Irving); *The Social Highwayman* (E. August); *The Feast of Life* (Capellani); *Tangled Fates* (Vale); *La Vie de Bohème* (Capellani); *The Crucial Test* (J. Ince and Thornby); *A Woman's Way* (O'Neil); *The Summer Girl* (August); *Friday, the 13th* (Chautard); *The Revolt* (O'Neil); *The Hidden Scar* (O'Neil); *The Gilded Cage* (Knoles); *Bought and Paid For* (Knoles); *All Man* (Chautard); *The Rise of Susan* (S. E. Taylor); *On Dangerous Ground* (Thornby); *The Heart of a Hero* (Chautard). **1917:** *A Woman Alone* (Davenport); *Tillie Wakes Up* (Davenport); *The Hungry Heart* (Chautard); *A Square Deal* (Knoles); *A Girl's Folly* (M. Tourneur); *The Web of Desire* (Chautard); *The Poor Little Rich Girl* (M. Tourneur); *As Man Made Her* (Archainbaud); *The Social Leper* (Knoles); *Forget-Me-Not* (Chautard); *Darkest Russia* (Vale); *The Crimson Dove* (Fielding); *The Stolen Paradise* (Knoles); *The Divorce Game* (Vale); *The Beloved Adventuress* (Brady and Cowl); *The Amazons* (Kaufman); *Rebecca of Sunnybrook Farm* (Neilan); *A Little Princess* (Neilan); *The Pride of the Clan* (M. Tourneur). **1918:** *Stella Maris* (Neilan); *Amarilly of Clothes-Line Alley* (Neilan); *M'Liss* (Neilan); *How Could You, Jean?* (W. Taylor); *The City of Dim Faces* (Melford); *Johanna Enlists* (W. Taylor); *He Comes Up Smiling* (Dwan); *The Temple of Dusk* (J. Young); *The Goat* (Crisp). **1919:** *Captain Kidd, Jr.* (W. Taylor); *The Misleading*

Frances Marion

Widow (Robertson); *Anne of Green Gables* (W. Taylor); *A Regular Girl* (J. Young); *The Dark Star* (Dwan). **1920:** *The Cinema Murder* (G. D. Baker); *Pollyanna* (P. Powell); *Humoresque* (Borzage); *The Flapper* (Crosland); *The Restless Sex* (Leonard and d'Usseau); *The World and His Wife* (Vignola). **1921:** *Just around the Corner* (+ d); *The Love Light* (+ d); *Straight Is the Way* (Vignola). **1922:** *Back Pay* (Borzage); *The Primitive Lover* (Franklin); *Sonny* (H. King); *East Is West* (Franklin); *Minnie* (Nielan and Urson); *The Eternal Flame* (Lloyd). **1923:** *The Voice from the Minaret* (Lloyd); *The Famous Mrs. Fair* (Niblo); *The Nth Commandment* (Borzage) (+ artistic supervisor); *Within the Law* (Lloyd); *The Love Piker* (E. M. Hopper); *Potash and Perlmutter* (Badger); *The French Doll* (Leonard). **1924:** *The Song of Love* (+ co-d with Franklin, co-ed); *Through the Dark* (G. Hill); *Abraham Lincoln* (Rosen); *Secrets* (Borzage); *Cytherea* (Fitzmaurice); *Tarnish* (Fitzmaurice); *In Hollywood with Potash and Perlmutter* (*So This Is Hollywood*) (Green); *Sundown* (Trimble and Hoyt). **1925:** *A Thief in Paradise* (Fitzmaurice); *The Lady* (Borzage); *The Flaming Forties* (Forman); *His Supreme Moment* (Fitzmaurice); *Zander the Great* (G. Hill); *Lightnin'* (Ford); *Graustark* (Buchowetzki); *The Dark Angel* (Fitzmaurice); *Lazy Bones* (Borzage); *Thank You* (Ford); *Simon the Jester* (Melford) (+ pr); *Stella Dallas* (H. King). **1926:** *The First Year* (Borzage); *Partners Again* (H. King); *Paris at Midnight* (E. M. Hopper) (+ pr); *The Son of the Sheik* (Fitzmaurice); *The Scarlet Letter* (Sjöström); *The Winning of Barbara Worth* (H. King). **1927:** *The Red*

Mill (Goodrich); *The Callahans and the Murphys* (G. Hill); *Madame Pompadour* (Wilcox); *Love* (E. Goulding). **1928:** *Bringing Up Father* (Conway); *The Cossacks* (G. Hill); *Excess Baggage* (Cruze); *The Wind* (Sjöström); *The Awakening* (Fleming); *The Masks of the Devil* (Sjöström). **1929:** *Their Own Desire* (E. M. Hopper and Forbes). **1930:** *Anna Christie* (C. Brown); *The Rogue Song* (L. Barrymore); *The Big House* (G. Hill); *Let Us Be Gay* (Leonard); *Good News* (Grinde and MacGregor); *Min and Bill* (G. Hill); *Wu Li Chang* (Grinde). **1931:** *The Secret Six* (G. Hill); *The Champ* (K. Vidor). **1932:** *Emma* (C. Brown); *Blondie of the Follies* (E. Goulding); *Cynara* (K. Vidor). **1933:** *Secrets* (Borzage); *Peg o' My Heart* (Leonard); *Dinner at Eight* (Cukor); *The Prizefighter and the Lady* (Van Dyke); *Going Hollywood* (Walsh). **1935:** *Riffraff* (Ruben). **1937:** *Camille* (Cukor); *Love from a Stranger* (R. V. Lee); *Knight without Armour* (Feyder); *The Good Earth* (Franklin) (uncredited). **1940:** *Green Hell* (Whale).

Films as Writer, Actress, and Editor/Assistant Editor: 1914: *False Colors*; *Hypocrites*; *It's No Laughing Matter*; *Like Most Wives*; *Traitor*. **1915:** *Sunshine Molly*.

Films as Actress: 1915: *Caprices of Kitty* (Janis); *Betty in Search of a Thrill* (Janis); *A Girl of Yesterday* (Dwan) (as Rosanna Danford); *City Vamp*; *The Wild Girl from the Hills*; *Captain Courtesy* (stunt double).

Generally ranked with the leading screenwriters of all time, Frances Marion had more than 130 screen credits during her 25-year career, spanning the years 1915 to 1940, from the rise of the star-laden silent features to the height of the Golden Age of talkies. Her work encompasses such diversities as the 1915 *Camille* starring Clara Kimball Young and the 1937 Garbo version; *The Poor Little Rich Girl* with Mary Pickford in 1917 and *Riffraff* with Jean Harlow in 1935; but she was best known for her "four-handkerchief" pictures (*Stella Dallas, The Champ*) and high dramas (*The Big House, Dinner at Eight*).

Frances Marion arrived in Los Angeles from San Francisco in 1913 at age 23, twice married and divorced, talented and ambitious, having already worked as a journalist, artist's and photographer's model, commercial artist/illustrator, and writer of published stories and verse. She got into film work under a system that today would be called "networking," when her close friend Adela Rogers St. Johns introduced her to director-producer-writer Lois Weber, who took Marion into Bosworth studios as her protégée, doing a little bit of everything—acting, writing, cutting, publicity. There Marion met actor Owen Moore who introduced her to his wife, Mary Pickford; Marion and Pickford became and remained the best of friends, and frequent colleagues, for life.

If that sounds like the start of a heartwarming movie script, one could add other similar episodes. Friendship was one of Frances Marion's special talents, so when Lois Weber died penniless and forgotten after a significant career, it was Marion who, at the peak of her own fame and fortune, arranged and paid for Weber's funeral. When Marie Dressler, another old friend, could not get work on stage or screen, Marion revitalized her career with lively hand-tailored scripts—and helped get her cast as Marthy in *Anna Christie* which Marion had also scripted. After that, there was no stopping Dressler, who consulted Frances Marion at every turn. Among other close friends for whom Marion wrote scripts were Alice Brady, Elsie Janis, Billie Burke, and Marion Davies. She also wrote vehicles for Ronald Colman, Rudolph Valentino, John Gilbert, and Wallace Beery, and helped discover Gary Cooper and Clark Gable.

Although by tradition Hollywood writers usually travel in their own circles, Frances Marion also had many good friends among producers: William A. Brady, who gave her a writing contract at $200 a week in 1917; William Randolph Hearst, who let her direct her first film, *Just around the Corner*, in 1921; Joe Kennedy, who encouraged her third husband, the ex-chaplain and college athlete Fred Thomson, to star in Westerns; Samuel Goldwyn, her favorite producer, who called her his favorite scriptwriter; Irving Thalberg, who over several years sought her advice on production problems and on other writers' scripts.

What distinguished Marion's scripts, according to DeWitt Bodeen (who researched and interviewed Frances Marion in her later life), were her original characters with their dramatic but genuinely human conflicts, and her eye-minded stories, written always with the camera in mind. Her screenplays *moved,* and could be *acted,* Bodeen wrote. As one of the few scriptwriters who made a successful transition from silent films to talkies, Marion often wrote sequences without any dialogue, relying on pantomime (and the especially expressive faces of Garbo, Beery, and Dressler) to reach audiences more effectively than words could.

Soon after Marion started a long-term $3,500-a-week contract at MGM, as one of Hollywood's highest paid scriptwriters, tragedy came into her life: her husband died suddenly of tetanus, leaving their two young sons for her to raise alone. A later short-lived marriage to George W. Hill, a director-friend, was followed by his suicide a few years after their divorce. Already feeling vulnerable, as screenwriting was being handled more and more on an assembly-line basis, Marion decided that she would have to be a writer-director or writer-producer to maintain the integrity of her scripts.

She had already tried directing and it seemed to go nowhere. Following her first effort for Hearst in 1921, Marion had directed Mary Pickford in *The Love Light.* A few years later, when the film's director was too ill to work, Marion had finished directing her own script for *The Song of Love,* a Norma Talmadge production. But her efforts to produce her own scripts in the late 1930s and 1940s never got off the ground. She turned instead to magazine stories and serials. Her book *How to Write and Sell Film Stories* emphasizes visual over verbal communication, stresses simplicity and detail, colorful personalities, and everyday emotions. Her later book of reminiscences, *Off with Their Heads!,* tells more about her friends than about herself. She mentions merely in passing that she directed three films but writes nothing about her experiences or why she stopped.—CECILE STARR

Marshall, Penny

American director and actress

Born *New York City, 15 October 1942 (some sources say 1943).* ***Education*** *Attended the University of New Mexico, majored in math and psychology.* ***Family*** *Married 1) Michael Henry (divorced), one daughter, Tracy; 2) the actor/director Rob Reiner, 1971 (divorced 1979).* ***Career*** *1960s—began acting, appearing in stock productions; 1967-68—network acting debut on* The Danny Thomas Hour; *1970—auditioned unsuccessfully for the role of Gloria on the television sitcom* All in the Family; *1971-75—initially attracted notice for recurring role as Jack Klugman's secretary on TV's* The Odd Couple; *1970s—acted on television series, including* The Mary Tyler Moore Show, Taxi, Mork and Mindy, *and* Happy Days; *1976—became a television star on* Laverne & Shirley; *late 1970s-1980s—directed commercials, several episodes of* Laverne & Shirley, *two episodes of* The Tracey Ullman Show, *and TV pilot* Working Stiffs; *1985—made stage debut in off-Broadway play* Eden Court; *1986—directed first feature,* Jumpin' Jack Flash; *1990—signed a three-*

Penny Marshall on the set of *Big*.

picture deal with Columbia Pictures. **Agent** *c/o Todd Smith, Creative Artists Agency, 9830 Wilshire Boulevard, Beverly Hills, CA 90212, U.S.A.*

Films as Director: **1986:** *Jumpin' Jack Flash.* **1988:** *Big.* **1990:** *Awakenings* (+ co-exec pr). **1992:** *A League of Their Own* (+ exec pr). **1994:** *Renaissance Man* (+ co-exec pr). **1996:** *The Preacher's Wife.* **2000:** *Time Tunnel: The Movie.*

Films as Actress: **1968:** *The Savage Seven* (Rush) (as Tina); *How Sweet It Is!* (Paris) (as tour girl). **1970:** *The Grasshopper* (Paris) (as Plaster Caster). **1971:** *The Feminist and the Fuzz* (Paris—for TV). **1972:** *Evil Roy Slade* (Paris—for TV) (as bankteller); *The Crooked Hearts* (J. Sandrich—for TV); *The Couple Takes a Wife* (Paris—for TV). **1975:** *How Come Nobody's on Our Side?* (Michaels) (as Theresa); *Let's Switch* (Rafkin—for TV). **1978:** *More than Friends* (Burrows—for TV). **1979:** *1941* (Spielberg) (as Miss Fitzroy). **1984:** *Love Thy Neighbor* (Bill—for TV) (as Linda). **1985:** *Movers & Shakers* (Asher) (as Reva); *Challenge of a Lifetime* (Mayberry—for TV). **1991:** *The Hard Way* (Badham) (as Angie). **1993:** *Hocus Pocus* (Ortega). **1995:** *Get Shorty* (Sonnenfeld) (as herself).

Other Films: **1993:** *Calendar Girl* (Whitesell) (exec pr). **1996:** *Getting Away with Murder* (H. Miller) (co-pr). **1998:** *Saving Grace* (pr); *With Friends Like These. . . (Mom's on the Roof)* (co-pr). **1999:** *Live From Baghdad* (pr).

Had Penny Marshall not had show business connections—she is the younger sister of director-producer-writer Garry Marshall—she might not have been allowed the opportunities she received first as an actress, then as a director. But this can be said for any second- or third-generation Hollywood name, from Bridges to Fonda, Carradine to Sheen. Besides, had Marshall lacked the requisite abilities, her career might not have flourished as it has in both venues. Marshall has become one of a generation of actors—Ron Howard and Rob Reiner, her former husband, are others who come to mind—who first earned popularity as stars of television situation comedies, and then went on to forge major careers behind the cameras.

Marshall cut her teeth as an actress, appearing first in a handful of features and made-for-television movies, then in a quartet of television situation comedies: *The Odd Couple* (as Myrna Turner, 1971-75, co-produced by brother Garry); *The Bob Newhart Show* (as Miss Larson, 1972-73); *Paul Sand in Friends and Lovers* (as Janice Dreyfuss, 1974-75); and, most notably, *Laverne & Shirley* (as Laverne De Fazio, 1976-83, co-created and produced by brother Garry), a spin-off of *Happy Days*. The success of the latter made Marshall a household name. In 1978 she co-starred with Reiner in *More than Friends,* a made-for-television romantic comedy based on their courtship.

Marshall initially began directing episodes of *Laverne & Shirley*. Her feature-film directorial debut, *Jumpin' Jack Flash,* was inauspicious: one of Whoopi Goldberg's pitifully unfunny post-*Color Purple* fiascos. More recently, Marshall made *Renaissance Man,* an overlong (at 129 minutes), generic comedy about an advertising man (Danny DeVito) who finds himself suddenly unemployed, and accepts a job tutoring a bunch of none-too-bright Army recruits. In between, however, Marshall made a trio of popular features that firmly established her as a leading Hollywood director. Each is a commercially viable film that combines solid entertainment value with a humanistic, life-affirming story line.

Big is by far the best in a string of late 1980s fantasy-comedies (including *Like Father, Like Son*; *Vice Versa*; and *18 Again!*) which are variations on the same theme: the souls of young people are transferred into the bodies of their elders (and vice versa). *Big* is the story of a preteen boy who, like many kids, wishes he were older. Miraculously, this request is granted—and the boy, now trapped in the body of a man almost three times his age, is thrust into the adult world. The adult is played by Tom Hanks, giving a performance which earned him his first Academy Award nomination and solidified his status as an A-list movie star. The based-on-fact *Awakenings* features superlative performances by Robin Williams (as Oliver Sacks, a reticent research doctor working in a hospital ward which houses the chronically ill) and Robert De Niro (as a patient who awakens from a 30-year coma). *A League of Their Own* mixes fiction with fact as it tells the story of the trailblazing women athletes who played professional baseball in the All-American Girls Professional Baseball League during the 1940s and 1950s.

Along with fellow television refugees Reiner and Howard, Marshall has been able to entertain audiences while making them think and feel: an impressive accomplishment in an era dominated by crass, in-your-face, assembly-line Hollywood product.—ROB EDELMAN

Mathis, June

American writer

Born *Leadville, Colorado, 1892.* ***Family*** *Married the director Silvanio Balboni, 1924.* ***Career*** *1910-16—stage and vaudeville actress; 1918—hired at Metro as writer; 1919—appointed head of script department; associated with the performers Nazimova, Valentino, and Colleen Moore, and the director Rex Ingram during the next few years; 1923—edited von Stroheim's* Greed *down from 18 to 10 reels.* ***Died*** *In New York City, 26 July 1927.*

Films as Writer: **1917:** *Red, White and Blue Blood* (Brabin); *Blue Jeans* (Collins); *Aladdin's Other Lamp* (Collins). **1918:** *To Hell with the Kaiser* (Irving); *An Eye for an Eye* (Capellani); *Social Quicksands* (Brabin). **1919:** *Out of the Fog* (Capellani); *The Red Lantern* (Capellani); *The Brat* (Blaché); *Satan Junior* (Blaché and Collins); *The Microbe* (Otto); *The Man Who Stayed at Home* (Blaché); *The Island of Intrigue* (Otto); *The Divorcee* (Blaché). **1920:** *Old Lady 31* (J. Ince); *Hearts Are Trumps*; *Polly with a*

Past (De Cordova); *The Saphead* (Blaché); *The Right of Way* (Dillon); *Parlor, Bedroom and Bath* (Dillon). **1921:** *The Four Horsemen of the Apocalypse* (Ingram); *The Conquering Power* (Ingram); *A Trip to Paradise* (Karger); *Camille* (Smallwood); *The Idle Rich* (Karger). **1922:** *Turn to the Right* (Ingram); *Kisses* (Karger); *Hate* (Karger); *Blood and Sand* (Niblo); *The Young Rajah* (Rosen). **1923:** *Three Wise Fools* (K. Vidor); *The Spanish Dancer* (Brenon); *In the Palace of the King* (Flynn); *Greed* (von Stroheim) (re-write, re-edit). **1924:** *Three Weeks* (Crosland) (+ ed). **1925:** *Sally* (A. E. Green); *The Desert Flower* (Cummings); *Classified* (Santell); *We Moderns* (Dillon). **1926:** *Ben-Hur* (Niblo); *Irene* (A. E. Green); *The Greater Glory* (Rehfeld); *The Masked Woman* (Balboni); *The Magic Flame* (H. King).

Film as Actress: 1923: *Souls for Sale* (R. Hughes) (as celebrity).

June Mathis in her short but brilliant career (she died in her mid-thirties) was one of the most influential women in Hollywood production during the silent film era, becoming chief of Metro's script department in 1919 when she was only 27. Her family had a background in the theater, and she had already begun to write for the theater when she secured a job with Metro as scenario-writer in 1918, and was immediately responsible for scripting a range of films with titles such as *To Hell with the Kaiser, An Eye for an Eye, Hearts Are Trumps,* and *Polly with a Past*. This initial work culminated in her notable adaptation of the famous war novel by Vicente Blasco Ibánez, *The Four Horsemen of the Apocalypse*. By this stage she was influential enough to succeed in her insistence with Metro on the appointment of her young friend Rex Ingram (aged 29) as the film's director, though his postwar reputation rested only on the direction of a few minor features, and on the casting of Rudolph Valentino (then only a bit-player) as the star, so establishing his meteoric career (like hers, to be only too short) as the embodiment of the erotic imaginings of the mass international female film-going public. Mathis went on to script and supervise a range of Valentino's subjects, including *Camille, Blood and Sand,* and *The Young Rajah*.

Mathis, it would appear, had by now extended her status in the studios to that of an associate producer, and she was to assume a similar responsibility of scripting and cutting (then often a producer's prerogative) over a considerable range of films. According to Lewis Jacobs, in his authoritative book *The Rise of the American Film,* she was the "most esteemed scenarist in Hollywood." Her strength lay in careful preparation of the shooting script along with the director, cutting out waste in production while at the same time sharpening narrative continuity. She became in effect head, or one of the heads, of the Metro and Samuel Goldwyn units, and joined with other youthful women writers (such as Anita Loos and Bess Meredyth) in establishing the importance of the basic screenplay-scenario in silent American film. It was she who was in good measure responsible for persuading Metro-Goldwyn to agree to sponsor Erich von Stroheim's celebrated film *Greed,* and so became notorious among film devotees, who

June Mathis

see the company she represented as "betraying" one of the greatest artists of silent cinema, and all but destroying one of its potentially greatest films. *Greed* as initially shot and assembled by Stroheim ran to 42 reels (ten hours), following every detail of Frank Norris's novel *McTeague*; Stroheim himself reduced this to 24 reels (six hours), hoping the film could then be screened with intermissions in two successive evenings. But Metro-Goldwyn-Mayer (as the company had now become) demanded more drastic cutting. At Stroheim's request, his close friend Rex Ingram reduced it to 18 reels (4½ hours). But Mathis was instructed to reduce the film on her own initiative (without consultation with Stroheim) to ten reels (2½ hours), which she undertook with the aid of a routine cutter, Joseph W. Farnham, "on whose mind was nothing but a hat," as Stroheim put it. The exact nature of this drastic cutting of an overlong masterpiece of realistic, psychological cinema is detailed by Joel W. Finler in his edition of Stroheim's full-scale original script *Greed*.

Mathis went on to script and supervise the adaptation of the "epic" *Ben-Hur* for Goldwyn, finally after much trouble directed by Fred Niblo and starring Francis X. Bushman and Ramon Novarro. Mathis, however, was withdrawn from the film by MGM while on location in Italy, but in any case she disowned what had initially been shot by the film's first director, Charles Brabin, whom she had chosen. Her final films included *Irene* for Colleen Moore and *The Magic Flame* with Ronald Colman and Vilma Banky. Mathis died suddenly in 1927.—ROGER MANVELL

May, Elaine

American writer, director, and actress

Born *Elaine Berlin in Philadelphia, 21 April 1932; moved to Los Angeles, California, 1942; daughter of the theater director Jack Berlin and the actress Jeannie Berlin.* ***Education*** *Attended University of Chicago and Playwrights Theatre in Chicago, 1950.* ***Family*** *Married 1) Marvin May, 1949, daughter: Jeannie Berlin; 2) the lyricist Sheldon Harnick, 1962 (divorced 1963).* ***Career*** *1947—studied acting under Maria Ouspenskaya; 1953-57—member of the improvisational theater group, the Compass Players, where began partnership with Mike Nichols; 1957—performed in New York clubs with Nichols, made several TV appearances; 1960—Broadway debut in the revue* An Evening with Mike Nichols and Elaine May; *1960s—wrote, directed, and acted in the theater, also wrote and performed for radio; recorded comedy albums; 1971—directed her first feature film,* A New Leaf. ***Address*** *c/o Julian Schlossberg, Castle Hill Productions, 1414 Avenue of the Americas, New York, NY 10019, U.S.A.*

Films as Writer: 1971: *Such Good Friends* (Preminger) (under pseudonym Esther Dale). **1978:** *Heaven Can Wait* (Beatty and Henry) (co). **1982:** *Tootsie* (Pollack) (co—uncredited). **1995:** *Dangerous Minds* (J. Smith) (co—uncredited). **1996:** *The Birdcage* (M. Nichols). **1998:** *Primary Colors* (M. Nichols).

Films as Writer and Director: 1971: *A New Leaf* (+ ro as Henrietta Lowell). **1976:** *Mikey and Nicky.* **1987:** *Ishtar.*

Film as Director: 1972: *The Heartbreak Kid.*

Films as Actress: 1966: *Enter Laughing* (C. Reiner) (as Angela). **1967:** *Luv* (C. Donner) (as Ellen Manville); *Bach to Bach* (Leaf—short). **1978:** *California Suite* (Ross) (as Millie Michaels). **1990:** *In the Spirit* (Seacat) (as Marianne Flan).

Elaine May on the set of *A New Leaf.*

Elaine May's historical importance as a female writer/director pioneer in the 1970s has not been diminished by her inability to live up to her reputation as a groundbreaking filmmaker such as Ida Lupino or Dorothy Arzner. Because May carved a niche for herself out of a traditionally male workplace, contemporary Hollywood hyphenates such as Penny Marshall and Barbra Streisand owe her a debt of gratitude. Despite her unassailable originality, however, May's post-*Heartbreak Kid* assignments (*Mikey and Nicky,* 1976, and *Ishtar,* 1987) have been exercises in character-driven chaos that yielded mixed results. Scattering her talent through the fields of screenwriting, directing, playwriting, and performing, this comic iconoclast has not been able to channel her energies safely and commercially like her more successful, less inspiring, former partner Mike Nichols.

Having been a child actress with the Yiddish Theater run by her father, Jack Berlin, May attended the University of Chicago and joined the Compass Players, a precursor of the Second City Troupe. May's formative years in sketch comedy inform all her subsequent work. Paired with the equally deadpan Mike Nichols, May shot to stardom as half of a droll duo, whose improvisation-derived material remains more sophisticated than today's stand-up acts. After conquering cabaret, television, and Broadway, Nichols and May amicably parted company. Hailed for his directorial achievements in New York, in 1966 Nichols became Hollywood's fair-haired boy with *Who's Afraid of Virginia Woolf?* (Nichols and May later starred in a stage version of the play at the Long Wharf Theatre in 1980.)

Throughout the 1960s, May honed her playwriting skills, most notably with the one-act *Adaptation*. As a screen comedienne, she offered two bewitchingly offbeat interpretations of urban insecurity in *Enter Laughing* and *Luv*. Considering May's estimable behind-the-scenes accomplishments, a preference for her performing talent may seem like heresy. In her directorial debut, *A New Leaf* (1971), she also stars, with virtuoso skill, as a wallflower heiress victimized by her lawyer, her servants, and her gaslighting husband, but protected from harm by cosmic clumsiness. This endearingly wacky directorial bow plays like a riff on the Charlie Chaplin/Martha Raye rowboat scene in *Monsieur Verdoux*. In 1990 May replanted herself in front of the cameras in the slapdash female buddy comedy, *In the Spirit,* which she did not direct. As Marianne Flan, a shopaholic stripped of consumer power, May wings it with a jubilantly hilarious turn. Her study of fraying equanimity is a classic comic tour de force.

It is her love for actors, and her insistence on allowing them breathing space that is the one constant of May's filmmaking style. Her penchant for thespic improvisation, and her directorial curiosity in permitting characters to reach the end of their rope, is an essential element of May's moviemaking modus operandi. Unfortunately, such freewheeling methods fly in the face of Hollywood convention. Right off the bat, May resisted Hollywood logic. Having crafted a zany update on 1930s screwball comedy with *A New Leaf,* May handed in a 180-minute black comedy that the studio cut and sweetened into a 102-minute weird romance. May had the last laugh with her next film, *The Heartbreak Kid,* an exhilarating soufflé whipped up from potentially sour ingredients. In a dazzling tightrope walk, with pathos and slapstick on either side, May maintained perfect comic balance. Although screenwriter Neil Simon had been knocked for his formulaic style, May dived headfirst into the wisecracking neurosis that made him a household name and emerged with a literally painfully funny exposé of romantic self-absorption. In essence, *The Heartbreak Kid* was a series of sharply written sketches cemented by Simon's professionalism and May's risk-taking. She created an off-kilter comic momentum as the film's self-deluded characters talked themselves into corners marked "Be Careful What You Wish For."

Despite the cruel treatment of the heroines in these films, May's sympathies lie with the passive martyrs of *A New Leaf* and *The Heartbreak Kid*; the more her male protagonists wrangle and prevaricate, the deeper a hole they dig for their own happiness.

The assurance of May's first two films has never been recaptured. Based on her unproduced play, *Mikey and Nicky* emerged as a John Cassavetes film without that maverick director's edge. This bleak fable about a small-time gangster marked for sacrifice attracted a cult following, but May's collaboration with her actors rambled on without a focus. For May, exercising a variety of choices became a liability. You can feel her confidence wane as *Mikey and Nicky* unravels before your eyes.

Pilloried in the press as an example of fiscal mismanagement and ego-fueled disorder, the floundering *Ishtar* struck critics as less defensible than the equally undisciplined *Mikey and Nicky*. Heralded as a May-Day version of a Hope-Crosby "Road" picture, *Ishtar* offered further proof of May's fussiness as a director and her deteriorating knack for following through on ideas as a writer. Although the movie's early scenes sparkled with show biz savvy, May proved to be incompatible with the adventure-flick elements of her own screenplay about Middle East intrigue. *Ishtar* revisited a dead genre known for vaudevillian energy and re-killed it with feeble directorial pacing and two over-intellectualized leading performances that lacked personality-powered oomph.

As a writer-for-hire, May remains highly regarded. Having won an Oscar nomination for updating *Here Comes Mr. Jordan* as *Heaven Can Wait* and having won industry plaudits for doctoring the script of *Tootsie,* May contributed greatly to her reunion with Mike Nichols on *The Birdcage*. Astutely relocating the classic French farce *La Cage aux Folles* to South Beach, Florida, May incorporated contemporary broadsides that made *The Birdcage* politically correct if sexually backward in its treatment of gay stereotypes. In director Nichols's hands, May's screenplay was a polished laugh-getter, although their remake is neither as liberatingly amusing nor as moving as the original. They re-teamed on *Primary Colors* in 1997, for which May received a Best Screenplay Academy Award nomination.

Whatever May's filmmaking shortcomings were, they never stemmed from commercial compromise. When her skewered world-view sustained itself in *A New Leaf* and *The Heartbreak Kid,* the audience became willing participants in comic hijackings that May transformed into joyrides. Even when her failures of nerve produced the spotty *Ishtar* and the protracted *Mikey and Nicky,* May's bracing originality always flickered. Bolstered by the acclaim of *The Birdcage,* May starred on Broadway in 1998 in one acts co-written by Alan Arkin and herself. Perhaps, she will rekindle her film directing desire with a screenplay written by a sympathetic co-conspirator, a script that May could translate into her own wacky vernacular.

Wonderfully expressive as a wordsmith, and provisionally gifted as a moviemaker, May is irreplaceable as a comic voice and as a comedienne. In front of or behind the cameras, she is a modern screwball born in a trunk and raised on an analyst's couch.

Unlike some of her directorial successors (e.g., Jane Campion, Claudia Weill), filmmaker May was never obsessed with feminist causes. Her distinctively hapless heroines are doormats ruled by dumb luck. Her gallery of spineless males includes ineffectual hoods (*Mikey and Nicky*), boobish songwriters (*Ishtar*), a larcenous gold digger (*A New Leaf*), and a shiksa-obsessed social climber (*The Heartbreak Kid*). In these oddball films, the battle of the sexes is a draw. In May's male-dominated universe, women are either prizes or obstacles, but men are fools for not being able to recognize who is which.—ROBERT PARDI

Mayron, Melanie

American actress and director

Born *Philadelphia, Pennsylvania, 20 October 1952.* ***Education*** *Studied at the American Academy of Dramatic Art.* ***Career*** *Early 1970s—toured in the musical* Godspell; *1980s-90s—made guest appearances on such television shows as* The New Twilight Zone, Lois and Clark, Tribeca, *and* Mad About You; *1987—began playing Melissa Steadman on the hit television series* thirtysomething, *on which she also directed series episodes; since 1993—directed episodes of such television series as* Tribeca, New York Undercover, *and* Nash Bridges; *1995—directed her first features,* The Baby-Sitters Club *and the television movie* Freaky Friday. ***Awards*** *1978—Bronze Leopard, for* Girlfriends; *1989, 1990, 1991—Emmy Award as Outstanding Supporting Actress in a Drama Series, for* thirtysomething.

Films as Actress: 1974: *Harry and Tonto* (Mazursky) (as Ginger). **1975:** *Hustling* (Sargent) (as Dee Dee) (for TV). **1976:** *The Great Smokey Roadblock* (*Last of the Cowboys*) (Leone) (as Lula); *Carwash* (Shultz) (as Marsha); *Gable and Lombard* (Furie) (as Dixie). **1977:** *You Light Up My Life* (Brooks) (as Annie Gerrard). **1978:** *Katie: Portrait of a Centerfold* (Greenwald) (as Madelaine) (for TV); *Girlfriends* (Weill) (as Susan Weinblatt). **1980:** *Playing for Time* (Mann) (as Marianne). **1981:** *Heartbeeps* (Arkush) (as Susan); *The Best Little Girl in the World* (O'Steen) (as Carol Link) (for TV). **1982:** *Will There Really Be a Morning?* (Cook) (as Sophie Rosenstein) (for TV); *Missing* (Costa-Gavras) (as Terry Simon). **1985:**

Melanie Mayron (left) in a scene from *Girlfriends*.

Wallenberg: A Hero's Story (Johnson) (for TV) (as Sonja Kahn). **1986:** *The Boss' Wife* (Steinberg) (as Janet Keefer). **1988:** *Sticky Fingers* (Adams) (as Lolly) (+ co-scr, co-pr). **1989:** *Checking Out* (Leland) (as Jenny Macklin). **1990:** *My Blue Heaven* (Ross) (as Crystal). **1993:** *Ordeal in the Arctic* (Sobel) (as Sue) (for TV); *Other Women's Children* (Wheeler) (as Dr. Amelia Stewart) (for TV). **1994:** *Drop Zone* (Badham) (as Mrs. Willins).

Films as Director: 1995: *The Baby-Sitters Club* (+ bit role); *Freaky Friday* (for TV). **1997:** *Toothless* (+ role) (for TV).

During the first section of her career, Melanie Mayron was a dependable actress who offered strong performances whenever landing a meaty role. After making her screen debut as a hitchhiker in *Harry and Tonto*, she established herself playing a tragic young prostitute in the television movie *Hustling*. Her signature screen role came in the independent feature *Girlfriends*. Here, she played Susan Weinblatt, a lonely and emotionally vulnerable young photographer attempting to establish her career. Her self-doubts are compounded when Susan's best friend and roommate announces her intention to marry. In describing the character, the *Variety* reviewer also characterized the actress: "Mayron as Susan Weinblatt is not beautiful: she's a bit chubby and suburban." It was just this sort of perception that helped pigeonhole Mayron as a character/supporting player.

To date, her highest profile role has been in the television series *thirtysomething*, in which Mayron won kudos for her knowing performance as insecure Baby Boomer photographer Melissa Steadman. Melissa is an older version of Mayron's character in *Girlfriends*. Both are sensitive souls who feel—and express—deep emotion as they relate to others and strive for achievement in a creative field. Yet Melissa is already a decade Susan's senior. Her career disappointments and long string of unsuccessful relationships have forced her to slowly reduce her personal and professional expectations.

More recently, Mayron has joined Ron Howard, Penny Marshall, Rob Reiner, and Betty Thomas as an actor-turned-director. Actually, her initial foray behind the motion picture camera was as co-producer and co-screenwriter (as well as star) of *Sticky Fingers*, a lackluster chick flick about a pair of best friends/struggling musicians who keep dipping into a bag filled with $900,000 that has been left in their apartment by a drug dealer. If guy movies are about blaring explosions, blasting guns and speeding cars, then the characters in chick flicks like *Sticky Fingers* spend an excessive amount of time obsessed with their shoes.

Mayron's sole theatrical feature as director to date has been *The Baby-Sitters Club*, based on a series of best-selling books by Ann M. Martin. Her made-for-television films are fantasies: *Freaky Friday*, a remake of the 1977 Disney feature about a mother and daughter who magically trade personalities; and *Toothless*, in which a female dentist dies in an accident, finds herself in Limbo Land (a place existing between Heaven and Hell), and is dispatched back to earth as the tooth fairy.

Mayron's films are populated by congenial characters who are meant to serve as role models for their target audience: middle school-age girls. The films feature implicit messages. Whether you are interested in baseball or boys, or whether you prefer wearing jeans and overalls or more feminine attire, it is okay to be whoever you want to be. Plus, girl-girl friendships are irreplaceable, as are the understandings between women and girls and mothers and daughters. With this in mind, Mayron chooses to work with scripts that portray adult females as paragons. The dentist in *Toothless*, for example, is a successful professional who operates her own business and owns her own house. The point is emphasized that a woman does not need a connection to a man in order to be a success. While her life is lacking because she has never allowed herself to love someone, it is also clear that this devotion need not be romantic. The character is humanized when she comes to feel love for children—and if she is fortunate enough to fall for a man along the way, so much the better. While her main connection is to a motherless boy, the first bit of advice she offers a girl is to read *Little Women* and never allow herself to be dominated by a male.

The intention of *The Baby-Sitter's Club*—to create solidarity among its audience members—is apparent from the film's beginning moments, as the song played over its opening (and, later, closing) credits is an ode to the "sisterhood" shared by its 12 and 13-year-old characters. The title association is comprised of seven girls—five Caucasian, one African-American, one Asian-American—who reside in an upscale community. Some of the youngsters are social butterflies, while others are bookworms. Some are tomboys, while others are ultra-feminine. Yet they are united in that they are nice kids who respect each other's differences. As Kristy, the club's founder and president, declares at the outset, "You know, we're more than just a club. We're friends. Best friends. Nothing could ever change that." Along the way, the girls act silly and giggle a lot, talk about (and, in some cases, begin dating) boys, interact with parents, and concoct zany schemes. Most important of all, they help each other, and are supportive of each other. Even though they are young, their sisterhood is indeed powerful.

Their world may not be obstacle-free. Kristy's parents are divorced, and her emotions and loyalties are scrambled when her irresponsible father pops up unexpectedly. Stacey, another club member, is a diabetic; she also falls for a cute 17-year-old boy, and fears he will be unresponsive because she is just 13. Nonetheless, in *The Baby-Sitters Club*, Mayron portrays an idealized world, one which is a 1990s updating of a 1950s sitcom. Unlike the adolescent girls in dozens of 1990s features, the best of which are independent productions, none of these kids know rootlessness, poverty or child abuse. Their first loves are just that: sweet, innocent, and non-sexual. All their problems have solutions, and most of their endings are happy. The lone threats among their peers are three snooty (but essentially harmless) "villainesses," the leader of whom receives a comical comeuppance. Despite its formulaic qualities, however, *The Baby-Sitters Club* does succeed as a message film for its targeted audience. As their lives progress, the club members will establish relationships with others. Invariably, they will grow and change. Yet their bond with each other will remain extra-special, and will serve as a rock-solid foundation upon which they will fashion the rest of their lives.

The manner in which Mayron depicts adults cannot be overemphasized. Unlike so many Hollywood features intended for youngsters, her films spotlight adult characters who are not cartoonish stereotypes. Those who are patronizing are admonished to listen to children, and not judge them. Furthermore, children and adults bond, and come to appreciate each other. The parents and neighbors in *The Baby-Sitters Club* are loving, caring, flawed, and human. An aging neighbor who is annoyed when the girls establish a next-door summer camp filled with sweetly mischievous children, and who threatens to close the camp down, ends up as the girls' ally. Upon viewing the world through different perceptions, the mother and daughter in *Freaky Friday* come to understand and sympathize with each other. The dentist in *Toothless* is a neat lady who, in her role as tooth fairy, becomes the mentor and pal to a group of youngsters.

One of the *Baby-Sitters Club* members is a short, bespectacled young girl who aspires to be a writer, and already is drafting a novel. This character might be a pint-sized Susan Weinblatt, Melissa Steadman—or Melanie Mayron.—ROB EDELMAN

The McDonagh Sisters

Australian actress (Isobel); producer, writer, and art director (Phyllis); director and writer (Paulette)

ISOBEL. Pseudonym *Marie Lorraine.* ***Born*** *Isobel Mercia McDonagh in Sydney, 1899.* ***Education*** *Attended Kincoppal, the Convent of the Sacred Heart, Elizabeth Bay.* ***Family*** *Married Charles Stewart, 1932, three children.* ***Career*** *Worked as a nurse; co-founded a photographic studio; modeled for the painter, Thea Proctor; 1924—billed as "Marie Lorraine," she made her film debut in* Joe; *1933—starred in her last film,* Two Minutes Silence; *1959—appeared with her three children in Tennessee Williams's play,* Orpheus Descending. ***Died*** *In London, 4 March 1982.*

PHYLLIS. Born *Phyllis Glory McDonagh in Sydney, 1900.* ***Education*** *Attended Kincoppal, the Convent of the Sacred Heart, Elizabeth Bay.* ***Family*** *Married Leo O'Brien, 1941.* ***Career*** *1933—retired from filmmaking; mid-to-late 1930s worked as editor of New Zealand newspaper* Truth; *after 1941—worked as a freelance journalist and short story writer; 1960-78—worked as social editor of* North Shore Times. ***Died*** *In Sydney, 17 October 1978.*

PAULETTE. Born *Paulette de Vere McDonagh in Sydney, 1901.* ***Education*** *Attended Kincoppal, the Convent of the Sacred Heart, Elizabeth Bay; studied acting at P. J. Ramster School.* ***Career*** *1924—worked as an extra in* The Mystery of a Hansom Cab; *1926—co-directed first feature film* Those Who Love; *1934—unsuccessfully tried to produce another film.* ***Died*** *In Australia, August 1978.*

1926—the sisters earned widespread attention in Australia for their first feature film collaboration, Those Who Love; *1933—the sisters produced their final film together,* Two Minutes Silence. ***Awards*** *The sisters received the Australian Film Institute's Raymond Longford Award for significant contributions to the Australian film industry, 1978.*

Films as Collaborators: 1926: *Those Who Love* (Paulette, co-d with Ramster). **1928:** *The Far Paradise.* **1930:** *The Cheaters.* **1933:** *Two Minutes Silence.*

Films as Actress (Isobel): 1924: *Joe* (B. Smith). **1925:** *Painted Daughters.*

Other Films (Paulette): 1924: *The Mystery of a Hansom Cab* (Shirley) (ro as extra). **Early 1930s:** *Australia in the Swim* (co-d with Macken—doc, short); *How I Play Cricket* (co-d with Macken—doc, short); *The Mighty Conqueror* (co-d with Macken—doc, short).

The McDonagh sisters were a trio of Australian filmmakers who funded and produced four feature films that reflected their admiration for Hollywood movies. In a truly unique partnership, the sisters worked together as a production team between 1926 and 1933: Paulette was the screenwriter and director; Phyllis was the production manager and collaborated on the stories and titles; and Isobel, billed as Marie Lorraine, starred in each of the films. They are noteworthy as the first women in Australia to produce feature films; it was not until Gillian Armstrong's 1979 film *My Brilliant Career* that their accomplishment would be repeated.

The McDonagh sisters' father worked as the honorary surgeon to J. C. Williamson's theatrical companies, so as children they became quite familiar with show business. Paulette worked as a movie extra in *The Mystery of a Hansom Cab,* after which she wrote two scenarios,

Those Who Love and *The Greater Love*. Then, she studied film acting briefly with P. J. Ramster. Yet Paulette learned about filmmaking by assiduously watching Hollywood films; she would go to a movie in the morning and if she liked it, she would return for the afternoon and evening screenings to study the techniques more closely. In addition, the cinematographer Jack Fletcher, who had worked briefly in Hollywood, helped teach her camera and editing techniques in order to craft the more delicate rhythms and moods that she favored. Paulette employed her acting teacher Ramster to direct their first film, *Those Who Love*. But, she soon took the director's reins herself in order to produce the effects she envisioned. The film proved to be commercially successful, and was commended by critics for its dramatic qualities and technical standards, especially compared to other Australian films. The press trumpeted the story that the Governor de Chair cried at its premiere. Their second film, *The Far Paradise,* was also critically applauded and is considered one of the best-directed of the pre-sound Australian films.

The sisters' aim was to counter the prevailing Australian genres. Paulette, in particular, objected to the vulgarities of the popular bush comedies and their macho sensibilities as well as the social issue films. She disliked Australian films in general for what she considered their technical limitations, their overly melodramatic qualities, and their overwrought acting styles. Instead, she chose to make cosmopolitan society dramas and she carefully studied Hollywood techniques for creating more delicate rhythms and moods.

The McDonagh sisters' films were low-budget affairs that featured the themes of family antagonism, the longing for vengeance, the power of beauty, and the joys and torments of love. In addition, Phyllis paid careful attention to the art direction and the sisters favored grand settings, including the family's colonial home, Drummoyne House, which was brimming with antiques and spectacular furnishings and came in handy for *Those Who Love* and *The Far Paradise*. In 1928, an Australian journalist suggested that the McDonaghs would be challenged and nurtured in Hollywood, especially Isobel whose career would benefit by the possibility of appearing in more films than was possible in Australia.

Critics and film historians generally praise the sisters' films for their authenticity and Paulette's skill in framing, lighting, and editing her films, as well as Isobel's "natural" and restrained performances. Their heroines are typically innocent victims of their fathers' efforts to keep them from their lovers, though they are usually reunited after considerable trials and tribulations. Both *The Far Paradise* and *The Cheaters* featured heroines who were torn by their loyalty to their criminal fathers versus the men they loved. *The Far Paradise* tells the story of Cherry who returns home from finishing school to discover that her father is a drunken swindler and the proclaimed nemesis of her lover's father. *Those Who Love* tells the story of a dancer Lola who willingly sacrifices her lover when she learns their relationship will mean the loss of his inheritance.

In *The Cheaters* the heroine is a safe-cracking thief who eventually realizes the wrongs of her cheating life and so confesses her reluctance to her father, a criminal patriarch. But *The Cheaters* was troubled by the coming of the "talkies"; originally produced as a silent film, before its release it was converted to a part-talkie by substituting a number of synchronized sound sequences and by embellishing other scenes with music. The effect was disappointing. One of the film's investors recalled that it "died a horrible death" at the premiere, in part because several recording mistakes produced howls of laughter from the audience. In 1931 it was converted to a full-talkie and some sequences were re-shot. The changes, however, failed to produce box-office profits. The story is occasionally overwrought and the style a bit slow, and the ending is too facile—as it is revealed that the cheating daughter is not really related to her criminal father, but rather to her adopted lover's father! Yet, her characterizations reveal more complexity and cynicism than was the case in Australia's earlier star-crossed romances.

The last film the McDonagh sisters made was *Two Minutes Silence,* a sound epic adapted from the antiwar play by Leslie Haylen that featured the painful memories of four people as they participate in the two-minutes silence customary on Armistice Day. It is noteworthy as the first Australian talkie that focused on a social issue and as the film of which Paulette was most proud. But the newspaper *Sunday Sun and Guardian* criticized the film for its deadly serious subject and for the failure to depict Australian characterizations, though outraged fans deluged the paper with letters supporting the film. Nevertheless, its failure at the box office meant the retirement of the team.

Before the sisters made *Two Minutes Silence* Paulette made a series of documentary shorts with Neville Macken that featured Australian sports heroes, including *Australia in the Swim* with the Olympic swim team, *How I Play Cricket,* and *The Mighty Conqueror* with the race horse Phar Lap. Only two of the four feature films produced by the McDonaghs are still extant, *The Far Paradise* and *The Cheaters.* In the 1970s, as feminist historians began to resurrect the work of noteworthy yet overlooked women, these two films were restored and the silent version of *The Cheaters* was widely screened as the work of a pioneering woman director.—CYNTHIA FELANDO

Meerapfel, Jeanine

Argentinean director and writer

***Born** Buenos Aires, Argentina, 14 June 1943. **Education** Received German Academic Exchange Service (DAAD) scholarship, Academy of Art and Design, Ulm, Germany, 1964. **Career** 1964—moved to Germany to pursue film studies; lecturer for Adult Education Center in Ulm and Goethe Institute in various countries. **Awards** Golden Ducat, Mannheim Film Festival, for* In the Country of My Parents, *1981; Prize for Young Filmmaker, San Sebastian Film Festival, FIPRESCI Award (International Film Critics), Cannes Film Festival, and First Prize, Chicago International Film Festival, for* Malou, *1981; Interfilm Award and Otto Dibielius Award, Berlin International Film Festival, for* Die Kümmeltürkin geht, *1985; Hessen-Film Award, for* Zwickel auf Bizykel, *1997.*

Films as Director: 1964-68: *Distanciamiento* (short); *Diario Regional* (doc, 16mm). **1966:** *Abstand.* **1967:** *Regionalzeitung.* **1968-97:** *Zwickel auf Bizykel* (co-d). **1969:** *Team Delphin*; *Am Ama am Amazons.* **1981:** *Im Land miener Eltern* (*In the Country of My Parents*) (doc) (+ sc); *Malou* (+ sc). **1983:** *Solange es Europa noch gibt—Fragen an den Freiden* (*As Long as There's Still a Europe—Questions on Peace*) (video) (co-d with Schäfer). **1985:** *Die Kümmeltürkin geht* (*Melek Leaves*) (doc) (+ sc). **1987:** *Die Verliebten* (*Days to Remember*) (+ sc). **1988:** *La Amiga* (+ sc). **1989:** *13 Minuten vor zwölf in Lima* (doc—for TV) (co-d with Chiesa); *Desembarcos* (*Es Gibt Kein Vergessen*; *When Memory Speaks*) (doc) (co-d with Chiesa, + co-sc). **1990:** *Im Glanze dieses Glückes* (doc) (co-d). **1993-95:** *Amigomío* (co-d with Chiesa, + co-sc).

Other Film: 1995: *Die Nacht der Regisseure* (*The Night of the Filmmakers*) (Reitz—doc) (appearance).

By the end of the 1930s Argentinean cinema had flourished, leading the film industry in Latin America and regaining its foothold in the international Spanish-language film market. The tango, that quintessential Argentinean musical form, had propelled this success. Tango's tragic legendary hero, Carlos Gardel, gave the tango its lasting sophistication and brought it to the big screen as its romantic hero. His contract with Paramount Pictures, resulting in seven feature-length films, gave Argentinean cinema international prominence, heightened by the star's untimely death in a 1935 airplane collision. The Argentinean cinema's meteoric rise, however, was curtailed by World War II—Argentina's neutrality, seen as veiled support of the Axis powers, brought the wrath of the United States, the only country then producing raw film stock. Cut off from necessary resources and poorly managed, the film industry collapsed.

In the 1940s, President Péron set up several initiatives to bolster the film industry. Most of these, however, did little to support its continuation and the industry saw further decline. In the early 1970s, when Péron returned from exile to lead his country once more, the film industry responded favorably to the new atmosphere and optimism of Argentina. Péron died in office and in 1976 the government that succeeded him was overthrown by a military junta. The military dictatorship imposed strict censorship on the mass media, seeing popular culture as related to politics and as a potential source of resistance. Once again, Argentinean cinema was stymied. This time, however, its filmmakers were blacklisted, "disappeared," or went into exile.

The return of democracy after the brutal military dictatorship brought with it the resurgence of Argentinean cinema. President Raúl Alfonsín (1983-89) could count among his successes the international acclaim and critical acceptance of Argentinean cinema. In the 1980s, Argentina's filmmakers, both the stars and the newcomers, explored the extent of their new expressive freedom in films that addressed national identity, conflicts raised by national history and by being part of the bourgeoisie. These films cannot easily be characterized in brief terms, but, as John King has noted, a great energy and inventiveness accompanied filmmakers' explorations of their new political freedom. Further, many of the films of this period directly address the traumas of recent history, perhaps most notably the Academy Award-winning film *The Official Story* (directed by Luis Puenzo, 1985).

Jeanine Meerapfel's work in many ways epitomizes the issues—economic, political, and emotional—with which Argentinean directors have grappled in the past two decades. Born in Buenos Aires, Meerapfel left Argentina in 1964 to study cinema in Ulm, Germany, and has resided in Germany ever since. Her films, however, frequently return to her Argentinean heritage. Meerapfel approaches exile, distance, and memory directly as in her documentary *When Memory Speaks* about how Argentina deals with its past. Similar themes crop up in her 1981 feature *Malou,* which shows the life of a woman (modeled on the experience of Meerapfel's mother), who follows her husband into a lonely exile in Argentina, an ocean away from her own native land. Again in 1993, Meerapfel approaches exile and the search for identity in *Amigomío,* a road movie in which a father and son flee Argentina after the disappearance of the boy's politically active mother.

We note in all of Meerapfel's work the continual struggle to reconcile exile, rootlessness, liminality, history, memory, and the continual quest for identity. These thematic touchstones connect Meerapfel's work to that of other contemporary Argentinean filmmakers (especially María Luisa Bemberg, Fernando Solanas, and Luis Puenzo). Meerapfel's artistic search also relates to that of Chilean filmmakers, both in exile and in the country, who struggle with similar issues and their own tortuous experience with a repressive dictatorship.

Like many Latin American filmmakers, Meerapfel has found co-production to be the only secure route to a finished film and, as the German titles indicate, many of her films have been

German-Argentinean co-productions. These factors, as well as her continued residence in Germany coupled with the Argentinean themes and setting of some of her films, create in Meerapfel a thoroughly Latin American filmmaker, one who cannot be pigeonholed as "feminist" or "Argentinean" and whose films resonate not only across Latin America, but throughout the contemporary world.

Meerapfel's most acclaimed and best-known film is *La Amiga*. Made in 1988, *La Amiga* concentrates on Argentina's painful recent history through its depiction of the formation and development of the political movement, Las madres de Plaza de Mayo (the Mothers of the Plaza de Mayo). As chronicled in the award-winning documentary *Las madres de la Plaza de Mayo* (directed by Susana Muñoz and Lourdes Portillo, 1986), Las madres began as a small group of women who in 1977 organized to protest the disappearance of their children and family members. Not able to cut through legal and bureaucratic red tape, Las madres began to demonstrate once a week in front of the government building, Casa Rosada, in Buenos Aires's main plaza. Growing in size and strength, the group defied political pressure to disband and gained worldwide media attention. By the 1980s, Las madres had evolved into a sophisticated human-rights organization. *La Amiga,* the first feature fiction film devoted to Las madres, centers on two friends, María and Raquel, who have grown apart due to Raquel's exile during the dictatorship. Their reunion is set against the backdrop of Las madres, for which María is the main spokeswoman, and the complexity of renegotiating identities and relationships in post-dictatorship Argentina.

Like María Luisa Bemberg's *Camila* (1984), *La Amiga* is a significant film not just because of its poignant story and strong filmmaking. In the late 1980s, Argentina's Radical government had declared an official end to the trials of military leaders accused of human-rights atrocities during the dictatorship. *La Amiga* is Meerapfel's contribution to the ongoing struggle, a loud refusal to let the human-rights debate end or to forget or forgive the crimes against Argentina by her own military. As Meerapfel herself said in an interview with John King, "Those who forget their story, repeat their story. Identity is formed by keeping memory alive."—ILENE S. GOLDMAN

Mehta, Deepa

Indian/Canadian director

Born *Amritsar, India, 1950.* ***Education*** *Earned a degree in philosophy from the University of New Delhi; learned the basics of filmmaking while working for a documentary film company in India.* ***Family*** *Married the Canadian filmmaker Paul Saltzman (divorced 1983), daughter: Devyani.* ***Career*** *Introduced to film as a child by her father, a film distributor in India; obtained a job with a documentary film company and wrote scripts for children's films; 1973—emigrated to Canada and co-founded Sunrise Films Ltd., with her husband, Paul Saltzman, and her brother, photojournalist Dilip Mehta; 1970s-80s—directed film and television documentaries; 1988—directed* The Twin, *a half-hour television drama, and acted in another episode of this (as well as other) series; 1988-89—directed four episodes of the television series* Danger Bay; *1992—directed an episode of the television series* Young Indiana Jones Chronicles; *1995—directed the final episode of* Young Indiana Jones Chronicles. ***Awards*** *Etrog Award, Best Documentary, for* At 99: A Portrait of Louise Tandy Murch, *1975; Best Feature Film, International Women's*

Film Festival, for Martha, Ruth & Edie, *1988; Special Prize of the Jury, International Filmfest Mannheim-Heidelberg; Most Popular Canadian Film, Vancouver International Film Festival, for* Fire, *1996.*

Films as Director: 1975: *At 99: A Portrait of Louise Tandy Murch* (doc, short); *What's the Weather Like Up There* (doc, short). **1985:** *K.Y.T.E.S.: How We Dream Ourselves* (doc). **1986:** *Travelling Light: The Photojournalism of Dilip Mehta* (doc). **1988:** *Martha, Ruth & Edie* (co-d with Bailey and Suissa, + pr). **1991:** *Sam & Me* (+ co-pr). **1994:** *Camilla.* **1996:** *Fire* (+ co-pr, sc). **1998:** *Earth* (+ co-pr, sc).

Other Films: 1974: *The Bakery* (Saltzman—doc) (sc, ed). **1994:** *Skin Deep* (Onodera) (exec pr).

In her films, Deepa Mehta has mostly been concerned with the lives of women, and the manner in which women communicate on the deepest and most intimate levels. A common theme has been the unlikely union developing between two disparate individuals who end up transcending age differences and cultural barriers as they strike up a friendship, and an understanding. Another of her recurring topics is the depiction of older women as vital and active. This is evident in her very first film, the documentary short *At 99: A Portrait of Louise Tandy Murch,* in which her subject is shown doing yoga and making music and otherwise relishing her life.

Working with two other women filmmakers, Norma Bailey and Daniele J. Suissa, Mehta directed *Martha, Ruth & Edie,* consisting of a trio of vignettes in which the title characters attend a self-help conference and end up examining their innermost emotions. *Sam & Me,* Mehta's first solo feature, is an exception to her other work in that its protagonists are male. And it is her best film to date: a compassionate slice-of-life about Nikhil, a young Indian who comes to Toronto under the sponsorship of a manipulative uncle. Nikhil ends up looking after Sam Cohen, a cantankerous, elderly Jew. Despite their dissimilarities, Nikhil and Sam are united in that they are outcasts. Eventually, they develop a bond. Tragically, however, peer and family pressures on both sides result in the termination of their friendship. *Sam & Me* works as an indictment of those within ethnic communities who are more concerned with custom and convention than human interaction.

Camilla, her follow-up feature, is a redo of *Sam & Me* as an exploration of intergenerational camaraderie. Only here, the characters are women—and the end result is well-intentioned but deeply flawed. The title character, Camilla Cara (played by Jessica Tandy in her cinematic swan song), is an aged concert violinist who is lorded over by her fat, pompous son. She becomes the friend of, and mentor to, a young musician who desires a career as a composer and is weighed down by a thoughtless, patronizing husband.

Camilla often is obvious and silly, as the two women set out on the road and share experiences. But it is never uninteresting whenever Tandy is on screen. She rises above the film's shortcomings, and is especially luminous in her brief scenes with her husband Hume Cronyn (playing Camilla's long-ago lover). These sequences transcend the film, becoming a celebration of Tandy and Cronyn, their talent and their lives together.

The focus of *Fire,* Mehta's next feature, also is on the evolving relationship between two women who are victimized by unfeeling males—but with a decidedly sexual twist. And with *Sam & Me,* it serves as a lambasting of the stifling constraints of tradition.

The film (along with Mira Nair's *Kama Sutra: A Tale of Love,* which made the film-festival rounds with *Fire*) deals with a subject rarely seen on Western movie screens: sexuality and

Indian women. It is the story of Sita, an innocent young bride in an arranged marriage. The future seems to hold little for Sita, as her husband disregards her and prefers the company of his Chinese mistress. At one point he patronizingly orders Sita to occupy herself with "needlework," or by taking "a beauty course or something."

The other woman in the story is Radha, Sita's new, long-married sister-in-law. Radha may be a devoted wife, but because she has been unable to conceive a child she has brought shame to her husband. Both women are bound by custom and ritual, and their lives of drudgery, frustration, and isolation seem preordained. But each has a restless spirit; each yearns for freedom and liberation. And they are certain to cause contention in their household when they are drawn together out of their shared loneliness and yearning for tenderness, and eventually find solace in each other's arms.

Fire is valuable as a mirror of social change in contemporary India. Dramatically speaking, however, it is like a virulent 1970s feminist tract. The characters are one-dimensional stereotypes: *All* the men in the story are boorish, perverted, or good old-fashioned male chauvinist pigs, while the women are downtrodden and victimized. And there is plenty of shallow symbolism. It just so happens that Biji, Sita and Radha's elderly mother-in-law, is mute—this is meant to symbolize the state of women throughout Indian history—and thus is unable to cry out as a sleazy household servant watches X-rated videos in her presence.

Mehta has stated that she means for *Fire* to be "about the intolerance in class, culture and identity. And how we can cope with [the] burdens of society and the tug of war between tradition and the voice of personal independence." Despite the worthiness of these goals, the result is a superficial drama that lacks fully fleshed-out characters and a multilayered scenario.

Nonetheless, *Fire* serves as an example of how a woman filmmaker may go about exploring a topic—sex—that stereotypically is the domain of men. In India, the film was considered highly controversial. When it was presented at an Indian film festival, Mehta reported that "a lot of the [older] men wanted to shoot me dead. . . .They feel it is threatening their masculinity." *Fire* is scheduled as the first of a trilogy, to be followed by *Earth* and *Water*.—ROB EDELMAN

Menken, Marie

American director

Born *New York, 1910, of Lithuanian immigrant parents.* ***Family*** *Married the poet and filmmaker Willard Maas, 1937.* ***Career*** *Early 1930s—began painting; mid-1930s—received a residence grant from the Yaddo art colony, where she met Willard Maas; 1943—first film experience, photographing* Geography of the Body, *a film directed by Maas; 1945—first film as director* Visual Variations on Noguchi; *mid-1950s—founded the Gryphon Film Group with Willard Maas, Stan Brakhage, and Ben Moore; also worked at Time-Life most of her married life.* ***Awards*** *Special Citation, Creative Film Foundation for* Dwightiana, *1959.* ***Died*** *New York, 29 December 1970.*

Films as Director: 1945: *Visual Variations on Noguchi.* **1957:** *Hurry! Hurry!*; *Glimpse of the Garden*; *Dwightiana.* **1960:** *Faucets* (unfinished). **1961:** *Eye Music in Red Major*; *Arabesque for Kenneth Anger*; *Bagatelle for Willard Maas.* **1962:** *Moonplay*; *Here and There with My Octoscope and Zenscapes* (unfinished). **1963:** *Go! Go! Go!*; *Mood Mondrian*; *Notebook*; *Drips and Strips.* **1964:** *Wrestling.* **1965:** *Andy Warhol.* **1966:** *Lights*; *Sidewalks.* **1967:** *Watts with Eggs.* **1968:** *Excursion.*

Other Films: 1943: *Geography of the Body* (Maas) (ph). **1966:** *The Chelsea Girls* (*The Trip*) (Warhol) (ro as Mother); *Life of Juanita Castro* (Warhol) (ro).

Along with key experimental filmmakers such as Maya Deren, Sidney Peterson, and Kenneth Anger, Marie Menken formed a part of that generation of American avant-garde filmmakers who emerged in the early to mid-1940s. Menken was a painter/collagist and filmmaker whose first film experience was photographing *Geography of the Body* (1943), a film made by her husband, Willard Maas, that featured poetic text by George Barker. It was made with a 16mm camera left with Menken by animator Frances Lee when she went into the army, and features distorted images of the human body produced by dime-store magnifying glasses taped to the camera lens. Although Menken's contribution to the film was substantial, it does not reflect the kind of films she would eventually make on her own.

Menken's true first film was the beautiful *Visual Variations on Noguchi* (1945), which was made in the artist's studio and features several techniques that we now associate with Menken's visual style, in particular exhilarating handheld camera work and rhythmical editing patterns. In later films such as *Hurry! Hurry!* (1957), *Notebook* (1963), *Moonplay* (1962), and *Arabesque for Kenneth Anger* (1961), Menken would add to her visual repertoire such techniques as "nightwriting" (night lights filmed with such speed that they seem to be dancing) and fast motion photography (achieved by under-cranking the camera), which in *Moonplay* make the moon appear to be dancing in the night sky. Menken's films are short, lyrical, and poetic. She also helped create a new form of experimental film: the poetic, diary film.

One of her most notorious films, *Hurry! Hurry!,* was made from footage of spermatozoa shot in microscopic close-up. This found-footage film incorporated scientific footage not shot by the filmmaker, but the film is made her own by the addition of a complex formal structure and editing patterns. The resulting film is one of Menken's most impressive. *Eye Music in Red Major* (1961) creates a symphony of color, shape, and movement through the rhythmical photographing and editing of Christmas-tree decorations. Equally appealing is *Arabesque for Kenneth Anger,* made while traveling with the filmmaker in Alhambra. The references to music and dance in these films are not casual. Menken's films have a musical quality, and they often involve a dance between the camera and its subject. At times camera movement is the guiding structural principle, as in *Moonplay,* and at others it is the movement of the object within the frame. *Notebook,* a film constructed from footage dating to the late 1940s though not given final shape until the early 1960s, is a fine example of Menken's editing strategies of cutting on shape, color, and length of shot. Though Menken's films represent serious investigations into the rhythmical possibilities of cinema, her work always remains exuberant and playful.

Menken's films also bear the imprint of the economy of means that went into their making. The simplicity of her shooting and editing techniques is one of their great charms and connects her to other women artists working in different media, as well as to many other experimental filmmakers. Stan Brakhage describes how Menken's editing process involved hanging strips of film and looking at the shapes within the frame to determine the length of each shot visually (Brakhage 1989). He relates her work to collage techniques in painting. Menken rarely used an editing machine, and it was only when the films were projected that she could judge if the film was in its final shape. The handcrafted aspect of her films emphasizes the filmic material and the physicality of making art.

It can be argued that her influence on other filmmakers such as Stan Brakhage and Jonas Mekas, and her encouragement of others such as Kenneth Anger and Andy Warhol, is as great a legacy as the body of work she left behind. P. Adams Sitney in *Visionary Film* credits Menken as being a key influence on the lyrical film of the 1950s and 1960s, which reached its apotheosis in the great lyric films of Brakhage and Bruce Baillie. Menken's attachment to Andy Warhol's Factory in the mid-1960s undoubtedly had some influence on the films produced by Warhol in this period as well. Additionally, Menken turns up in several of Warhol's key films, most notably in *Life of Juanita Castro* and *The Chelsea Girls*. Despite this certain influence on other filmmakers, the power and accomplishment of Menken's own work as a filmmaker should not be underestimated. Menken's films have been undervalued to some extent because of their seeming simplicity and naive faith in the power of cinema to produce a fresh perspective of the world. They are also not as readily available or as well known as they should be.

Menken's personal life was noteworthy in that her long marriage to poet and filmmaker Willard Maas was notoriously tempestuous in part due to Maas's homosexuality. Menken's Catholicism prevented her from seeking a divorce, although Brakhage argues that Menken could not bear to leave Maas because "she loved him, all the same" (Brakhage 1989). Menken's difficult personal life was also exacerbated by alcohol. Notwithstanding her turbulent personal history, Marie Menken's impact on experimental film is substantial. She is a key figure whose work deserves a wider audience and critical reevaluation.—MARIO FALSETTO

Meredyth, Bess

American writer and actress

Born *Helen MacGlashan in Buffalo, New York, 1890.* ***Family*** *Married the director Michael Curtiz, 1928 (died 1962).* ***Career*** *1911—extra for Griffith at Biograph: first role in* A Sailor's Heart, *1912; 1917—first feature film as writer,* The Midnight Man. ***Died*** *In Woodland Hills, California, 13 July 1969.*

Films as Writer: 1913: *At Midnight* (Lucas); *The Honor of the Regiment* (Lucas). **1914:** *The Forbidden Room* (Dwan); *The Love Victorious* (Lucas); *The Mystery of Wickham Hall*; *The Outlaw Reforms*; *The Smuggler's Daughter*; *The Trey O'Hearts* (Lucas—serial). **1915:** *The Blood of the Children* (McRae); *Their Hour*; *The Mystery Woman*; *Stronger than Death* (DeGrasse); *The Fascination of the Fleur de Lis* (DeGrasse). **1917:** *Three Women of France* (Baldwin); *The Midnight Man* (Clifton); *Scandal* (Giblyn); *Pay Me* (DeGrasse). **1918:** *The Romance of Tarzan* (+ co-d with Lucas); *Morgan's Raiders* (+ co-d with Lucas). **1919:** *The Man from Kangaroo* (+ co-d). **1921:** *The Fighting Breed* (Lucas); *The Grim Comedian* (Lloyd); *The Shadow of Lightning Ridge* (Lucas). **1922:** *The Dangerous Age* (Stahl); *Grand Larceny* (Worsley); *One Clear Call* (Stahl); *Rose o' the Sea* (Niblo); *The Song of Life* (Stahl); *The Woman He Married* (Niblo). **1923:** *Strangers of the Night* (Niblo). **1924:** *The Red Lily* (Niblo); *Thy Name Is Woman* (Niblo). **1925:** *The Love Hour* (Raymaker); *The Slave of Fashion* (Henley); *The Wife Who Wasn't Wanted* (Flood). **1926:** *Ben-Hur* (Niblo); *Don Juan* (Crosland); *The Sea Beast* (Webb). **1927:** *Irish Hearts* (Haskin); *The Magic Flame* (H. King); *Rose of the Golden West* (Fitzmaurice); *When a Man Loves* (Crosland). **1928:** *The Little Shepherd of Kingdom Come* (Santell); *The Mysterious Lady* (Niblo); *Sailors' Wives* (Henabery); *The Scarlet Lady* (Crosland); *A Woman of Affairs* (C. Brown); *The Yellow Lily* (A. Korda). **1929:** *Wonder of Women* (C. Brown). **1930:** *Chasing Rainbows* (*The Road Show*) (Reisner); *In Gay Madrid* (Leonard); *The Sea Bat* (Ruggles); *Our Blushing Brides* (Beaumont); *Romance* (C. Brown). **1931:** *Laughing Sinners* (Beaumont); *Phantom of Paris* (Robertson); *The Prodigal* (*The Southerner*) (Pollard); *Cuban Love Song* (Van Dyke). **1932:** *Strange Interlude* (*Strange Interval*) (Leonard); *West of Broadway* (Beaumont). **1933:** *Looking Forward* (C. Brown). **1934:** *The Affairs of Cellini* (La Cava); *The Mighty Barnum* (W. Lang). **1935:** *Folies Bergère* (Del Ruth); *Metropolitan*

(Boleslawsky); *Charlie Chan at the Opera* (Humberstone); *The Iron Duke* (Saville). **1936:** *Half Angel* (Lanfield); *Under Two Flags* (Lloyd). **1937:** *The Great Hospital Mystery* (Tinling). **1940:** *The Mark of Zorro* (Mamoulian). **1941:** *That Night in Rio* (Cummings). **1947:** *The Unsuspected* (Curtiz).

Films as Actress: 1912: *A Sailor's Heart* (Lucas). **1914:** *The Magnet*; *Bess the Detectress, or The Old Mill at Midnight*; *When Bess Got in Wrong*; *The Little Autogomobile*; *Father's Bride*; *Willie Walrus and the Awful Confession*; *Bess the Detectress, or The Dog Watch*; *Bess the Detectress in Tick, Tick, Tick*; *Her Twin Brother*; *The Desert's Sting*.

Bess Meredyth was one of the solid core of first-class screenwriters, the majority of whom were women, who began their careers in the silent era and continued to enjoy success on into the coming of sound. Like many of the other women writers, Meredyth had early work in short-story and newspaper writing, as well as in vaudeville and stage acting. She began her career in films as an actress, starting in 1911 as an extra for D. W. Griffith at Biograph in New York, and soon went to Hollywood. Her screen-acting work for Biograph, Universal, and other studios includes the Western *The Desert's Sting,* in which she played the woman with whom the white husband of an Indian—played by Jeanie Macpherson—falls in love; both Macpherson and Meredyth would go on to successful screenwriting careers.

Meredyth had success writing and selling scenarios as early as 1913. In 1915 she was selected to be assistant to Joseph Vance in the preparation of all scripts for Fiction Pictures Inc., following several months during which she worked with Vance in the preparation of the 30-reel serial picture *The Trey O'Hearts* (Vance writing the story, Meredyth the scenario). By this time, Meredyth had written some 140 scenarios. In 1918 she co-directed with Wilfred Lucas *The Romance of Tarzan* (sequel to *Tarzan of the Apes*) for the National Film Corporation.

Meredyth later wrote for MGM, Warner Bros., Columbia, and other major studios; her scripts included vehicles for stars such as John Barrymore, Greta Garbo, Joan Crawford, and Clark Gable. Notable screenwriting credits include the Roman epic *Ben-Hur,* starring Ramon Novarro, and directed by Fred Niblo (with whom Meredyth would work on other productions). Bess Meredyth and Carey Wilson were hired to replace scenarist June Mathis; the high budget (more than $4.5 million) spectacle, shot in Italy, and incorporating two-color Technicolor sequences, proved to be a big success for MGM. Meredyth was also the scenarist on another hit, *Don Juan,* a lavish costume drama starring John Barrymore and directed by Alan Crosland. Warners' first feature film using the revolutionary Vitaphone sound process, the film began with a synchronized speech, and featured an elaborate recorded orchestral score performed by the New York Philharmonic.

Other notable work among Meredyth's many screen credits includes *The Mysterious Lady* (starring Greta Garbo), *Strange Interlude* (with Norma Shearer and Clark Gable), *The Mighty Barnum* (co-written with Gene Fowler for Darryl F. Zanuck), *Folies Bergère* (starring Maurice Chevalier and Ann Sothern), *Under Two Flags* (Ronald Colman and Claudette Colbert), and *That Night in Rio* (with Alice Faye, Don Ameche, and Carmen Miranda).—VIRGINIA M. CLARK

Mészáros, Márta

Hungarian director

Born *Budapest, 19 September 1931.* ***Education*** *Attended VGIK (film school), Moscow, 1957.* ***Family*** *Married 1) 1957 (divorced 1959); 2) the director Miklós Jancsó, 1960*

Márta Mészáros

(divorced 1973), three children; 3) the actor Jan Nowicki. ***Career*** *1936—emigrated with family to U.S.S.R.; 1946—returned to Hungary; 1954—worked at Newsreel Studio, Budapest; 1957-59—worked for the Alexandru Sahia documentary studio, Bucharest, Romania; 1959-68—made science popularization shorts and documentary shorts, Budapest; mid-1960s—joined Mafilm Group 4; 1968—directed first feature.* ***Address*** *c/o MAFILM Studio, Lumumba utca 174, Budapest, 1149 Hungary.*

Films as Director: **1954:** *Ujra mosolyognak* (*Smiling Again*). **1955:** *Albertfalvai történet* (*A History of Albertfalva*); *Tul a Kálvin-téren* (*Beyond the Square*); *Mindennapi történetek* (*Everyday Stories*). **1956:** *Országutak vándora* (*Wandering on Highways*). **1959:** *Az élet megy tovább* (*Life Goes On*). **1960:** *Az eladás müvészete* (*Salesmanship*); *Riport egy TSZ-elnökröl* (*Report on the Chairman of a Farmers' Co-Operative*); *Rajtunk is mulik* (*It Depends on Us Too . . .*). **1961:** *Szivdobogás* (*Heartbeat*); *Vásárhelyi szinek* (*Colors of Vásárhely*); *Danulon gyártás* (*Danulon Production*); *A szár és a gyökér fejlödése* (*The Development of the Stalk and the Root*). **1962:** *Tornyai János* (*János Tornyai*); *Gyermekek, könyvek* (*Children, Books*); *Kamaszváros* (*A Town in the Awkward Age*); *Nagyüzemi tojástermelés* (*Mass*

Production of Eggs); *A labda varásza* (*The Spell of the Ball*). **1963:** *1963.julius 27.szombat* (*Saturday, July 27, 1963*); *Munka vagy hivatás?* (*Work or Profession?*); *Szeretet* (*Care and Affection*). **1964:** *Festök városa—Szentendre* (*Szentendre—Town of Painters*); *Bóbita* (*Blow-Ball*); *Kiáltó* (*Proclamation*). **1965:** *15 perc 15 évröl* (*Fifteen Minutes on Fifteen Years*). **1966:** *Borsós Miklós* (*Miklós Borsós*); *Harangok városa—Veszprém* (*Veszprém—Town of Bells*).

Films as director (short films in Romania): 1957: *Sa zimbeasca toti copiii.* **1958:** *Femeile zilelor noastre*; *Popas in tabara de vara.* **1959:** *Schimbul de miine.*

Films as director (feature films): 1968: *Eltávozott nap* (*The Girl*) (+ sc); *Mészáros László emlékére* (*In Memoriam László Mészáros*) (short); *A "holdudvar"* (*Binding Sentiments*) (+ sc). **1970:** *Szép lányok, ne sirjatok* (*Don't Cry, Pretty Girls*). **1971:** *A lörinci fonóban* (*Woman in the Spinnery*; *At the Lörinc Spinnery*) (short). **1973:** *Szabad lélegzet* (*Riddance*; *Free Breathing*) (+ sc). **1975:** *Örökbefogadás* (*Adoption*) (+ co-sc). **1976:** *Kilenc hónap* (*Nine Months*) (+ co-sc). **1977:** *Ök ketten* (*Two Women*; *The Two of Them*). **1978:** *Olyan, mint otthon* (*Just Like at Home*). **1979:** *Utközben* (*En cours de route*; *On the Move*). **1980:** *Örökseg* (*The Heiresses*; *The Inheritance*). **1981:** *Anya és leánya* (*Mother and Daughter*) (+ co-sc). **1982:** *Nema Kiáltás* (*Silent Cry*) (+ sc); *Napló gyermekeimnek* (*Diary for My Children*) (+ sc). **1983:** *Délibábok országa* (*The Land of Mirages*). **1987:** *Napló szerelmeimnek* (*Diary for My Loves*) (+ sc). **1988:** *Piroska és a farkas* (*Bye-Bye Red Riding Hood*) (+ co-sc). **1989:** *Utinapló* (doc). **1990:** *Napló apámnak, anyámnak* (*Diary for My Father and My Mother*). **1992:** *Edith és Marlene* (for TV). **1993:** *A Magzat* (*Fetus*). **1995:** *Sióدmy pokój* (+ co-sc).

Márta Mészáros is one of few contemporary woman filmmakers consistently making films both critically and commercially successful for an international audience. Her eight feature films made from 1968 to 1979 are concerned with the social oppression, economic constraints, and emotional challenges faced by Hungarian women. Mészáros explains, "I tell banal, commonplace stories, and then in them the leads are women—I portray things from a woman's angle."

Trained in filmmaking on a scholarship at Moscow's film school, she worked at Newsreel Studios in Budapest, made four short films at the Bucharest Documentary Studios, married a Romanian citizen in 1957, and was divorced in 1959. She returned to Budapest, where she made more than 30 documentaries before attempting a feature. Mészáros's documentaries deal with subjects as diverse as science (*Mass Production of Eggs*), a Hungarian hero (*Saturday, July 27, 1963*), orphans (*Care and Affection*), and artists (*Szentendre—Town of Painters,* which she considers her best documentary.)

In the mid-1960s Mészáros joined Mafilm Group 4, where she met Miklós Jancsó, whom she later married. She wrote and directed her first feature, *The Girl,* in 1968. A hopeless mood pervades this story of the quest by an orphan girl for her biological parents, who had abandoned her. The girl leaves her textile-factory job to comfort her mother, who introduces her as her niece to her husband and relatives. The girl meets a man whom she believes is her father. The man neither confirms nor denies this. The girl returns home and attends a factory dance where she meets a young man who is interested in her. As with most Mészáros features the film is open-ended, lacking a conventional plot. Dialogue is sparse. Derek Elley asserts that *The Girl* is a model to which Mészáros adheres in her subsequent features; her visual compositions are "carefully composed, rarely showy," and "characterisation never remains static."

In *Binding Sentiments* the conflicts between an aging mother and her son's fiancée are delineated with understated solemnity and subtle humor. A semi-musical, *Don't Cry, Pretty Girls,* lightheartedly captures the romance between a rural girl and a city musician in a hostel and youth-camp setting. Mészáros's short *Woman in the Spinnery* studies the working status and conditions of the factory worker, the same subjects that she explores in *Riddance*. In this generation gap tale, a pair of lovers must deceive the young man's parents, who object to his love for a girl who was raised in a children's home with no family. *Riddance* urges assertiveness and truth to oneself, and shows little sympathy for the older generation.

A fortyish woman wants a child from her unmarried lover in *Adoption*. She meets a teenager raised by the state who wants to marry her boyfriend. The relationship which develops between these two women and the men in their lives becomes the subject of Mészáros's most illuminating work.

A factory woman with one child has an affair with an engineer in *Nine Months*. The conflicts in their relationship are never resolved; they cannot agree on the terms and conditions of a life together; neither can surrender enough self to form a partnership. The woman leaves him to bear her second child alone. The actual birth of Lila Monari's child was photographed for the film.

The aptly titled *Two Women* depicts a friendship. Juli has a daughter and a husband attempting to find a cure for his alcoholism. Mari directs a hostel for working women, and tolerates a lackluster husband. Juli and Mari enjoy a greater rapport with each other than with the men in their lives. Situations depicting humiliation of and discrimination against women recur. The subject of Mészáros's next film, about a young man's attraction to a little girl, makes *Just Like at Home* a departure from her focus on women. In this film, Andras returns to Budapest after study in the United States and strikes up a friendship with a ten-year-old Zsuzsi, whose parents agree that she live with Andras in Budapest and be educated there. Their chaste friendship endures despite the intrusion of Andras's lady friend. Andras learns more from Zsuzsi than she learns from him, to the bewilderment of their parents.

In *The Heiresses* Mészáros used a period setting for the first time. A young, sterile woman marries a military officer during the World War II era. Because she needs an heir to inherit her father's money, she persuades a Jewish woman to bear a child sired by her husband. After the birth, the woman and her husband become deeply attached, and a second child is born. At that time the wife "turns in" the Jewish woman (Jews were deported from Hungary in 1944), the husband is arrested, and the wife is given custody of the second child.

Mészáros's films deal with realities usually ignored in Eastern European cinema: the subordination of women, conflicts of urban and rural cultures, antagonism between the bureaucracy and its employees, alcoholism, the generation gap, dissolution of traditional family structures, and the plight of state-reared children. In her unpretentious works, she creates a composite picture of life in Hungary today.

In Derek Elley's words, she "has created a body of feature work which, for sheer thematic and stylistic homogeneity, ranks among the best in current world cinema." Her features examine emotional struggles "in the search for human warmth and companionship in a present-day, industrialised society."—LOUISE HECK-RABI

Miró, Pilar

Spanish director and writer

Born *Pilar Miró Romero, in Madrid, 20 April 1940.* ***Education*** *Studied law and journalism, University of Madrid; attended Escuela Oficial de Cinematografí [Official*

school of cinematography], Madrid, graduating in screenwriting, 1968. ***Family*** *One son: Gonzalo.* ***Career*** *1960—began working as program assistant for Radiotelevisión Española, Spain's state television; 1964—wrote screenplay for first of two films directed by Manuel Summers,* The Girl in Mourning; *1966—directed made-for-TV movie* Lilí, *becoming the first woman to direct dramas for Spanish TV; subsequently made more than 300 programs for Spanish TV, primarily directing dramas based on noted literary works; 1976—directed first feature film,* The Engagement Party, *which was briefly banned; 1976—joined Socialist Party, member until 1989; 1979—directed* The Crime at Cuenca, *which after being banned for two years because of scenes depicting torture at the hands of the Civil Guard was released in 1981 and became a top box-office attraction; 1982—directed Bizet's opera* Carmen *in Madrid, one of her occasional forays into directing plays and operas; during general elections, served as media adviser to Felipe González in his successful campaign to become Spain's prime minister, an event ushering in almost 14 years of Socialist Party rule; 1982-85—served as director general of cinematography for the Culture Ministry; 1984—helped enact the "Miró Law," which provided generous subsidies to Spanish filmmakers; 1985—resigned from government post to return to directing, making the 1986-released* Werther; *1986-89—served as director general of Radiotelevisión Española, resigning in 1989 under controversy, cleared of wrongdoing in 1992 following lengthy court case; 1990—directed first of two video documentaries,* Velázquez *(also* Nacho Duato—la danza [Nacho Duato—The Dance], *1992); 1993—directed Christopher Hampton's play* Dangerous Liaisons *in Barcelona; 1995—directed Spanish state television coverage of the royal wedding in Seville of Princess Elena, eldest daughter of Spain's King Juan Carlos; her acclaimed* The Dog in the Manger *is released, a film that won seven prizes at the 1997 Goya Awards; 1996—her final film,* Your Name Poisons My Dreams, *is released; 1997—in October, two weeks prior to her death, directed Spanish state television coverage of the royal wedding in Barcelona of Princess Cristina, daughter of the king.* ***Awards*** *"Antena de oro" award for her overall work for Spanish state television, 1972; Sindicato Nacional de Espectáculo [National entertainment syndicate] award for best screenplay, and Círculo de Escritores Cinematográficos [The screenwriters' circle] award for best new director, for* The Engagement Party, *1976; Silver Bear, Berlin International Film Festival, for* Beltenebros, *1991; Best Film, Mar del Plata Film Festival, 1996, and Goya Film Award for Best Director, 1997, for* The Dog in the Manger. ***Died*** *In Madrid, of a heart attack, 19 October 1997.*

Films as Director: 1976: *La petición* (*The Engagement Party*; *The Request*; *The Betrothal*) (+ co-sc). **1981:** *El crimen de Cuenca* (*The Crime at Cuenca*; *The Cuenca Crime*) (produced 1979) (+ co-sc); *Gary Cooper que estás en los cielos* (*Gary Cooper Who Art in Heaven*) (+ co-sc, co-pr). **1982:** *Hablamos esta noche* (*Let's Talk Tonight*) (+ co-sc, co-pr). **1986:** *Werther* (+ co-sc, pr). **1991:** *Beltenebros* (*Prince of Shadows*) (+ co-sc). **1993:** *El pájaro de la felicidad* (*The Bird of Happiness*). **1995:** *El perro del hortelano* (*The Dog in the Manger*) (+ sc). **1996:** *Tu nombre envenena mis sueños* (*Your Name Poisons My Dreams*) (+ co-sc).

Other Films: 1964: *La niña de luto* (*The Girl in Mourning*) (Summers) (sc). **1965:** *El juego de la oca* (*Snakes and Ladders*) (Summers) (sc, st); *Luciano* (Claudio Guerín Hill) (dialogue writer).

Pilar Miró was undoubtedly one of the most important figures of the late-20th-century Spanish entertainment industry. In addition to winning acclaim—and enduring some controversy—for her direction of nine motion pictures from 1976 to 1996, Miró was also an award-winning and prolific director for Spanish television. Her more than 300 small-screen credits include made-for-television movies, dramatic series, plays, operas, and perhaps most famously the televising of the royal weddings of the two daughters of Spain's King Juan Carlos, whom she had befriended when they were both law students in Madrid in the late 1950s. In a more sporadic vein, Miró made occasional forays into the theater to direct plays and operas and made two video documentaries.

Miró, who had joined the Socialist Party as soon as it was legal to do so in 1976 and remained a member until 1989, also played a key role as media adviser to Felipe González in his victory in the 1982 general elections, after which the Socialists ruled for nearly 14 years. González then persuaded Miró to become director general of cinematography for the Culture Ministry starting in 1983, making her the first industry figure in what had been a post occupied only by political appointees. During her three years in the position, Miró achieved some success in improving the quality—if not the quantity—of Spanish films, mainly through what was known as the "Miró Law." In effect, from 1984 through 1989, the law provided generous subsidies to Spanish filmmakers, including such notables as Pedro Almodóvar and Fernando Trueba. Following her resignation from this post to direct *Werther* (based on a Goethe novel), Miró served as head of state radio and television from 1986 through 1989. She resigned under a cloud of controversial expenditures she had made for clothing and gifts, but was cleared of all charges in 1992 (during the last few years of her life, when she attended awards ceremonies, she wore tuxedo-like clothing as an effective form of silent protest over the obviously sexist accusations).

Beyond the overall quality of her creations, Miró the film director helped raise the technical bar for Spanish filmmaking through innovative use of Steadicams and other modern gadgets. She also played an important role in expanding the range of what could be depicted on the Spanish screen. Her very first film, *The Engagement Party*—adapted from an Émile Zola story called "For a Night of Love"—centered around a wealthy, sadistic, sexually voracious, and ultimately murderous woman ably and erotically played by Ana Belén. Although Spanish cinemas of the time were filled with the usual assortment of popular, low-budget sex comedies, Miró's decidedly feminist portrayal of a strong sexually aggressive woman—told from the woman's perspective—ran afoul of the censors of post-Franco Spain. A ban on the film was soon lifted after a press campaign emphasized the film's artistic merit.

Miró then encountered more serious difficulties with her follow-up to *The Engagement Party,* the 1979-produced *The Crime at Cuenca*. In depicting the true story of a rather obscure 1912 case of two anarchists falsely accused of murder, the film includes graphic scenes of the men being tortured into confession by the notorious Spanish Civil Guard. This politically explosive film was taken by the Civil Guard to be an attack on them, and Miró and the film's producer were indicted by a military court in early 1980 for "insults to the Civil Guard." *The Crime at Cuenca* was banned in Spain, although a print had already made its way to the February 1980 Berlin film festival, helping to make the film an international cause célèbre. Eventually the Guard was persuaded to let the case against Miró be shifted to a civil court, which soon dropped the charges. Upon its release in Spain in 1981, *The Crime at Cuenca* was an enormous hit, in part thanks to its notoriety, and it set a record in Spain for box-office gross receipts for a domestically made movie.

Of her films that followed *The Crime at Cuenca,* several of them were semiautobiographical in nature, with Mercedes Sampietro serving as Miró's cinematic alter ego. In the 1981 film *Gary*

Cooper Who Art in Heaven—which has been noted for its similarities to Agnès Varda's *Cleo from 5 to 7*—Sampietro portrays a television director who must undergo an abortion after learning she has ovarian cancer. The film covers a three-day period prior to and including the day of the operation (although it ends before the operation begins), during which time the character examines what she feels has been an unsuccessful life. The story draws upon and effectively—and realistically, even grimly—depicts the difficulties Miró faced in the male-dominated entertainment industry, as well as upon her own 1975 heart surgery (which would be followed by a second heart surgery in 1985). *Gary Cooper* is also noteworthy as the first film Miró produced herself, having been forced to do so when no one in the industry would work with her because of her then still-pending *Cuenca* trial.

In 1993, Miró, with Sampietro again as her stand-in, returned to depict another unfulfilled middle-aged woman taking stock of her life in *The Bird of Happiness*. Beginning with the character being robbed and nearly raped in Madrid, the film shows the character gradually escaping from various familial and communal ties to a remote rural village where at the end it appears that she will contentedly raise—alone—her grandson who has been abandoned to her. In addition to being a depiction of a woman finding an inner peace on her own, *The Bird of Happiness* also represents Miró's disillusionment with socialism in the 1990s.

Although *The Bird of Happiness* is perhaps her greatest achievement, Miró received much acclaim for her next-to-last film, *The Dog in the Manger*. It won seven Goya Awards, including best director, as well as the $650,000 first prize at the 1996 Mar del Plata Film Festival in Argentina. Based on a play by Lope de Vega, this period comedy is noteworthy for its depiction of a strong, complex woman (agilely played by Emma Suárez). Not as autobiographical as her earlier films, *The Dog in the Manger* nonetheless has at its center a woman who breaks with the female archetypes of her time, just as Miró during her most impressive and pioneering career broke through numerous barriers to create a new archetype for future women filmmakers the world over.—DAVID E. SALAMIE

Muratova, Kira

Russian/Ukrainian director and writer

Born *Kira Georgievna Korotkova, in Soroca, Romania (now Moldova), 5 November 1934.* ***Education*** *Attended Moscow State University for one year; attended All-Union State Institute of Cinematography (VGIK), studying with the director Sergei Gerasimov, graduating with a degree in directing, 1962.* ***Family*** *Married 1) the director Alexander Muratov (divorced); 2) Yevgeni Golunbenko.* ***Career*** *1963—made her directing debut with her diploma film,* By the Steep Ravine, *co-directed by her then-husband Muratov; 1967—her solo directing debut,* Brief Encounters, *receives only a limited release to film clubs and is otherwise banned; 1971—her film* Long Farewells *is banned and she is barred from directing for several years; 1979—allowed to return to directing with* Getting to Know the World; *1983—*Among the Grey Stones *is heavily reedited after she completes it, prompting her to have her name removed from the film, the directing of which is credited to "Ivan Sidorov"; 1987—comes to international attention following the general release of* Brief Encounters *and* Long Farewells, *which are shown widely at international film festivals, and with the release of her new film* A Change of Fate; *1989—her widely acclaimed* The

Asthenic Syndrome *is initially banned, then released in 1990.* ***Awards*** *Grand Prix, USSR Festival, and Fipressi Prize, Locarno International Film Festival, for* Long Farewells, *1987; Silver Bear, Special Jury Prize, Berlin Film Festival, and Nika Award, for* The Asthenic Syndrome, *1990; Best Director Nika Award, for* Passions, *1994.* ***Address*** *Proletarsky Boulevard 14B, Apartment 15, 270015 Odessa, Ukraine.*

Films as Director: 1963: *U krutogo yara* (*By the Steep Ravine*; *The She-Wolf*) (co-d with A. Muratov, + co-sc). **1964:** *Nash chestnyi khleb* (*Our Honest Bread*; *Honest Bread*) (co-d with A. Muratov). **1967:** *Korotkiye vstrechi* (*Brief Encounters*) (released 1987) (+ co-sc, ro as Valentina Ivanova); *Braslet-2.* **1971:** *Dolgie provody* (*Long Farewells*) (released 1987). **1972:** *Russia.* **1979:** *Poznavaya belyi svet* (*Getting to Know the World*) (released 1980). **1983:** *Sredi serykh kamnei* (*Among the Grey Stones*) (credited as Ivan Sidorov—released 1987) (+ sc). **1987:** *Peremena uchasti* (*A Change of Fate*) (+ sc). **1989:** *Astenicheskii Sindrom* (*The Asthenic Syndrome*; *The Weakness Syndrome*) (released 1990) (+ co-sc). **1992:** *Chuvstvitel'nyi militsioner* (*The Sentimental Policeman*) (+ co-sc). **1994:** *Uvletschenia* (*Passions*; *Avocations*; *Obsessions*) (+ sc). **1997:** *Tri istorii* (*Three Stories*).

Other Film: 1985: *Ya tebya pomnyu* (*I Remember You*) (Khamrayev) (ed).

Though Kira Muratova's career as a film director was seriously hindered by the censors of the Brezhnev-to-Gorbachev-era Soviet Union, she still managed to emerge as one of the leading figures in contemporary Russian cinema. She was born in 1934 in Soroca, Romania (which is now part of Moldova), with her family background being partly Western. Raised by a Russian grandmother while her parents were in prison for their Communist activities, Muratova moved to the Soviet Union in 1954, attended Moscow State University for one year, then studied under the director Sergei Gerasimov at the Soviet state film school (VGIK). She then joined the Odessa Film Studio (located in what is now the Ukraine), where she has made most of her films. Having co-directed two films with her then-husband Alexander Muratov, in 1967 she solo-directed *Brief Encounters,* a love-triangle tale with Muratova as one of the three in the only acting role of her career, and then in 1971 directed *Long Farewells,* which centers around a middle-class mother-son relationship. Both of these black-and-white films were effectively banned from general release, although *Brief Encounters* did receive a very limited release to some film clubs. On the surface, it seems puzzling why two intensely personal, relationship-oriented films would run afoul of the censor. But Muratova in all of her films has been intent upon depicting daily life in an honest manner, warts and all, and it was evidently the details that she included—water shortages in Odessa, stockings that run, contractors who cheat their clients—that made them threatening. *Long Farewells* was additionally condemned for its rather gloomy ending and its bourgeois sensibilities.

Long Farewells also led to Muratova being stripped of her VGIK degree and blacklisted from directing. She worked at a variety of jobs for the next several years, and tried without success to gain permission to film a couple of her scenarios. In 1978, Lenfilm invited Muratova to direct any of several scenarios they had on hand. She chose a story about another love triangle, this one taking place at the construction site of a huge new tractor factory. This was the 1979-produced, 1980-released (rather limitedly) *Getting to Know the World,* Muratova's first film in color. Though not banned outright, the authorities criticized the director for depicting negative types of characters, and she was barred from filming contemporary subjects.

Even when Muratova did then draw on a literary classic for her next film, 1983's *Among the Grey Stones,* she ran into trouble. An adaptation of an 1883 story by Russian writer Vladimir Korolenko, the film is a story of haves meeting have-nots, specifically a neglected son of a powerful judge befriending a strange community of hobos who live among the ruins of a castle.

Again criticized for making a pessimistic film, Muratova saw her film mutilated in the postproduction editing, leading her to request that her name be taken off the film.

The turning point in Muratova's career came with the advent of glasnost and the 1986-initiated review of banned films by the Filmmakers Union's Conflict Commission. This led to the 1987 release of all of her banned films, and *Brief Encounters* and *Long Farewells* in particular received long-overdue acclaim both at home and abroad. That same year, Muratova directed the aptly titled *A Change of Fate,* which she adapted from another literary classic, Somerset Maugham's short story "The Letter."

It was her next film, however, that has come to be considered her masterpiece. *The Asthenic Syndrome* is one of the key films of the glasnost period, and in its withering portrayal of a society in moral decay even managed to be briefly banned. In Muratova's vision, the syndrome of the title—which manifests itself in the face of extreme stress—implies not only a torpor as in the dictionary definition of "asthenic" but also extreme aggression. The film is extremely complex in its construction, including a film-within-a-film (which is in black and white), an innovative use of documentary style, and a long second sequence which is largely plotless and consists of a variety of vignettes that surreally and effectively depict a society largely out of control. Yet as much as it is of its late-glasnost time and place, *The Asthenic Syndrome* is actually much more universal; its critique can be seen as applying perfectly to contemporary Western society, whose stressed-out public face alternates between mean-spirited aggression and excessive apathy.

With this rather apocalyptic film behind her, Muratova next offered some hope in the amusing comedy *The Sentimental Policeman,* which was filmed as the Soviet Union was collapsing. The title character is a young policeman who finds an abandoned baby (in a cabbage patch!), takes her to the station house, and later returns with his wife after the couple decides they wish to adopt the child; complications then arise. Though set in the same indifferent society as her previous film, *The Sentimental Policeman* offers portraits of a few people persevering in a positive way through this chaotic world.

In the post-Soviet period, Muratova has continued to experiment with the cinematic form—though somewhat more obscurely, in an ironic twist. As she has throughout her career, Muratova continues to work with little-known actors, to rely on the spontaneity of these nonprofessionals, and to heavily utilize montage—her favorite cinematic device. *Passions* is a largely plotless, difficult to fathom film, centering around male jockeys and female circus trainers and their obsessions with horses. *Three Stories* consists of three episodes linked by the motif of violent death; the crimes in each episode, however, are not solved and the perpetrators are not brought to justice. Muratova has said that she wanted to simply lay out the events as they occurred and let the audience make their own judgments. This inherently noncommercial approach is typical of Muratova, who has also said that she is not a director who can please a large audience. Rather, she is one "who is able to please a small, indeed very small, number of viewers, but really please them."—DAVID E. SALAMIE

Murfin, Jane

American writer

Born *Quincy, Michigan, 1893.* ***Family*** *Married the actor and director Donald Crisp, 1932 (divorced 1944).* ***Career*** *Playwright from 1908, often with (and for) the actress Jane Cowl:* Lilac Time, Daybreak, Information Please, *and* Smilin' Through *(using the joint pseudonym Allan Langdon Martin); other plays include* The Right to Lie *and* Stripped; *1919—first film as writer,* The Right to Lie; *also produced some of her scripts in the early 1920s.* ***Died*** *In Brentwood, California, 10 August 1955.*

Films as Writer (selected list): 1919: *The Right to Lie* (Carewe); *Marie, Ltd.* (Webb). **1921:** *The Silent Call* (Trimble). **1922:** *Brawn of the North* (Trimble) (+ co-pr). **1924:** *The Love Master* (Trimble) (+ co-pr); *Flapper Wives* (+ co-pr, co-d). **1925:** *White Fang* (Trimble); *A Slave of Fashion* (Henley). **1926:** *The Savage* (Newmeyer); *Meet the Prince* (Henabery). **1927:** *The Notorious Lady* (Baggot); *The Prince of Headwaiters* (Dillon). **1929:** *Half Marriage* (Cowen); *Street Girl* (Ruggles); *Dance Hall* (M. Brown); *Seven Keys to Baldpate* (Barker). **1930:** *The Pay Off* (L. Sherman); *Leathernecking* (Cline); *Lawful Larceny* (Dwan); *The Runaway Bride* (Crisp); *Too Many Crooks* (G. King). **1931:** *Friends and Lovers* (Schertzinger); *White Shoulders* (M. Brown). **1932:** *What Price Hollywood?* (Cukor); *Young Bride* (Seiter); *Rockabye* (Cukor); *Way Back Home* (Seiter). **1933:** *After Tonight* (Archainbaud); *Ann Vickers* (Cromwell); *Double Harness* (Cromwell); *Our Betters* (Cukor); *The Silver Cord* (Cromwell); *Little Women* (Cukor). **1934:** *Crime Doctor* (Robertson); *The Fountain* (Cromwell); *The Life of Vergie Winters* (Santell); *The Little Minister* (Wallace); *Romance in Manhattan* (Roberts); *Spitfire* (Cromwell); *This Man Is Mine* (Cromwell). **1935:** *Alice Adams* (Stevens); *Roberta* (Seiter). **1936:** *Come and Get It* (Hawks and Wyler). **1937:** *I'll Take Romance* (Griffith). **1938:** *The Shining Hour* (Borzage). **1939:** *Stand Up and Fight* (Van Dyke); *The Women* (Cukor) (co). **1940:** *Pride and Prejudice* (Leonard) (co). **1941:** *Andy Hardy's Private Secretary* (Seitz). **1943:** *Flight for Freedom* (Mendes). **1944:** *Dragon Seed* (Conway and Bucquet).

Jane Murfin had a successful career as a playwright on Broadway before being lured to Hollywood in the late 1910s to become an equally successful screenwriter for many years. Murfin's first stage play, *The Right to Lie,* was produced in 1908; it was later turned into a motion picture, under the direction of Edwin Carewe. Other stage plays were written in collaboration with actress Jane Cowl: *Daybreak,* 1917 (filmed the same year); *Lilac Time* (filmed with Colleen Moore in 1928); *Smilin' Through* (filmed with Norma Talmadge in 1922, Norma Shearer in 1932, and Jeanette MacDonald in 1941).

Coming to Hollywood in the late 1910s, Murfin wrote numerous stories and screenplays, alone or in collaboration, mostly romantic comedies and dramas for RKO and MGM; she believed that human interest was the key to a successful story. Murfin had started writing scripts for Famous Players-Lasky while still in New York; in Hollywood, she wrote some 60-odd scripts, directing or producing a few of them. In one of her earliest projects, Murfin sponsored, and wrote a series of pictures for Strongheart—a German shepherd dog who had formerly served in a Red Cross unit in the army. Starting in 1922, five pictures were made for First National. Aided by the direction of dog trainer, writer, and producer Larry Trimble, Strongheart's success as a canine star in the 1920s was rivaled only by that of Rin-Tin-Tin.

Murfin wrote frequently for RKO, for directors such as George Cukor, and for stars such as Constance Bennett (*What Price Hollywood?* and *Rockabye*), Katharine Hepburn (*Little Women*), and Irene Dunne (*The Silver Cord*). In 1934 Pandro Berman appointed Murfin to be the first woman supervisor of motion pictures at RKO; some of her first writing projects included *The*

Little Minister (starring John Beal and Katharine Hepburn) and the sparkling Jerome Kern musical *Roberta* (featuring Irene Dunne, Randolph Scott, Fred Astaire, and Ginger Rogers).

In 1935 Murfin severed ties with RKO, and signed a long-term contract with Samuel Goldwyn. Some of the outstanding films that she wrote or co-wrote for MGM include *Come and Get It* (starring Edward Arnold and Frances Farmer and directed by William Wyler and Howard Hawks), *The Women* (co-written with Anita Loos; starring Norma Shearer, Joan Crawford, Rosalind Russell and Paulette Goddard and directed by George Cukor), and *Pride and Prejudice* (co-written with Aldous Huxley; starring Laurence Olivier and Greer Garson; directed by Robert Z. Leonard). Later work ranged from *Andy Hardy's Private Secretary* to *Dragon Seed*.—VIRGINIA M. CLARK

Murphy, Brianne

British/American cinematographer and director

Pseudonyms *Sometimes credited as Geraldine Brianne, Bri Murphy, G. B. Murphy, and Geraldine Brianne Murphy.* ***Born*** *London, 1 April 1937.* ***Education*** *Studied at Neighborhood Playhouse, 1952-54; Brown University, M.A., 1962.* ***Family*** *Married Ralph Brook, 1958 (deceased).* ***Career*** *1952-55—actress, various other jobs; from 1955—cinematographer; has served as cinematographer for TV series, including:* Breaking Away, Square Pegs, For Love and Honor, Highway to Heaven, In the Heat of the Night, Shades of L.A., *and* Love and War, *and episodes of* The Next Generation, Shortstories, *and* ABC Afterschool Special; *1973—admitted to cameraman's union; first woman member of the American Society of Cinematographers; 1995—ASC president, Columbia College, Hollywood.* ***Awards*** *Emmy Award, Best Cinematography, for* Five Finger Discount, *1978; Academy Award, Scientific or Technical Achievement, for design of the MISI camera insert safety car and trailer, 1982.* ***Address*** *c/o American Society of Cinematographers, 1782 North Orange Drive, Hollywood, CA 90028, U.S.A.*

Films as Cinematographer: **1955:** *Man Beast* (J. Warren) (+ script supervisor). **1960:** *The Barrier.* **1961:** *Chivato (Rebellion in Cuba)* (Gannaway). **1962:** *Panchito y El Gringo.* **1972:** *Pago.* **1973:** *Pocket Filled with Dreams.* **1976:** *Secrets of the Bermuda Triangle.* **1978:** *Like Mom, Like Me* (Pressman—for TV). **1979:** *Five Finger Discount* (for TV); *Before and After* (K. Friedman—for TV). **1980:** *Fatso* (Bancroft). **1983:** *Little House: Look Back to Yesterday* (French—for TV). **1985:** *There Were Times, Dear* (Malone—for TV). **1988:** *Destined to Live: 100 Roads to Recovery* (for TV). **1990:** *In the Best Interest of the Child* (David Greene—for TV). **1991:** *This Old Man.* **1992:** *Love & War* (for TV).

Films as Director: **1957:** *Virgins from Venus* (+ sc). **1958:** *Teenage Zombies* (sc, ro as Pam). **1962:** *Magic Tide.* **1968:** *Single Room Furnished* (uncredited). **1972:** *Blood Sabbath* (+ ph). **1992:** *To Die, to Sleep (Mortal Danger, Turn Your Pony Around)* (+ ph).

Other Films: **1960:** *The Incredible Petrified World* (J. Warren) (production supervisor, dialog d). **1961:** *Bloodlust!* (Brooke) (production manager). **1965:** *House of the Black Death (Blood of the Man Devil; Night of the Beast)* (H. Daniels) (script asst). **1981:** *Cheech and Chong's Nice Dreams* (Chong) (additional ph).

Perhaps the best understanding of Brianne Murphy's career as a cinematographer does not lie in a study of her camera work as such, because she does not seem to have had a full opportunity to explore her creative abilities. Even in 1996, Murphy—who has often used non-gender-specific aliases such as G. B. Murphy in order to increase her chances of getting jobs—was one of only four women belonging to the American Society of Cinematographers. With men dominating her profession more thoroughly than they have most other realms of film work, Murphy's talents have been relegated to television, or to light features such as *Cheech and Chong's Nice Dreams.*

Therefore the true essence of Murphy's career as a cinematographer lies in the story—which she tells with characteristic good humor—of how she broke into the "man's world" surrounding the operation of cameras. The first female member of the feature-film union, the International Alliance of Theatrical and Stage Employees (IATSE), Murphy fought a long battle, not for recognition, but simply for the right to work alongside men.

One of the principal themes of Murphy's story is her ability to turn a supposed disadvantage—that of being a woman—into an advantage. In her early Hollywood days, she would often quiz cameramen about what they did, and they would happily brag to her about their abilities, never dreaming that she was actually taking mental notes. Because she was a woman, she recalled: "I could take a cameraman out to lunch and ask him all kinds of questions. I think he felt flattered . . . whereas if a young man had taken him out and asked all these questions, he'd find some way to say 'Go find out for yourself.'"

Murphy has never considered herself above admitting it when she does not know something, and she has seldom disdained the advice of others. From the beginning of her film career, before she managed to find a place for herself behind the camera, she made it a point to get to know everyone on the set—to find out what they did, how they did it, and if she could help them. That same attitude helped her win an Oscar, when she used the assistance of race-car drivers to develop a newer, safer camera car. Up until that time, cameras had been mounted on conventional pick-up trucks, and they could become so top-heavy that they could overturn and kill someone—as one did her camera assistant Rodney Micchell in 1980. After this tragic event, while Murphy was in Georgia working on the television series *Breaking Away,* she talked to some race-car drivers on the NASCAR circuit about an idea that ultimately became the Micchell Camera Car, winner of a 1982 technical Academy Award.

Outgoing by nature and well-inclined to win friends and influence people, Murphy seemed in her early years to lead a charmed life. As a little girl in Bermuda, fleeing the Nazi bombing of her native Britain during World War II, she was "discovered" for a theater role as Emily in *Our Town*. Later producer Elia Kazan took an interest in her, and several times again in her later career, she seemed to have a talent for being at the right place at the right time. For instance, when she went to work on her first feature, the low-budget *Man Beast* in 1955, she came on the set as a props and wardrobe person, but ended up taking control of the camera because the cameraman was the only member of the crew who could fit into the monster suit needed for a particular scene. Even divine justice seemed to work in her favor, as in her oft-told story of the IATSE union boss who told her a woman would only get into the union over his dead body: he suddenly died.

Yet her story was not as smooth as it might have seemed. Her parents had divorced when she was young, and with no man around the house, she had grown up knowing how to take care of herself. "My sister asked me what I wanted for Christmas," Murphy commented. "I told her power tools. I never had a man around as a copout." And though she seemingly had people opening doors for her, those opportunities did not just happen: Murphy made them happen with her unbridled chutzpah. As a young woman, she got her first camera job working for the Ringling Brothers Circus, and she got it by dressing up as a clown and joining the circus parade when it came through town. Later, on the set of *Man Beast,* she told the film's backer that she could make two movies for the price of the one film, which she considered a staggering budget at $30,000. Suddenly she found herself in the driver's seat on *Virgins from Venus* and *Teenage Zombies.* Murphy delivered, and became one of a select-few female directors—even if the material was not exactly classic. (Though it was certainly classic schlock cinema.)

Again and again, Murphy managed to find herself at the right place, at the right time. In 1979 NBC needed a woman to shoot footage for a documentary on breast cancer in which the female patients refused to allow a male cameraman into the room. The choice was not difficult, since there was only one female cinematographer in Hollywood. Actress Anne Bancroft, when she was making *Fatso* in 1980, hired Murphy because, according to Murphy: "she couldn't give orders to men. . . . I was a woman and not fat [so] she chose me."

But for every time she got a job because she was a woman, she missed out on countless other ones for the same reason. "It's a sad thing," Murphy has said, "but it's true—as a woman, you just have to be better." She offers this advice to both women and men: "I think if you work cheap enough, come in early enough, and stay late enough, you can always get a job." Though she eschews any sort of role as a movement leader or spokeswoman, Murphy has been a pioneer for women, and because of her efforts, women will one day "man" the cameras of Oscar-winning blockbusters.—JUDSON KNIGHT

Musidora

French director, writer, and actress

Born *Jeanne Roques in Paris, 23 February 1889.* ***Education*** *Studied art at Académie Jullian, Atelier Schommer, and École des Beaux Arts.* ***Family*** *Married Clément Marot, 1927 (divorced 1944), one son.* ***Career*** *After deciding on stage career, took name "Musidora" from heroine of Théophile Gautier's novel* Fortunio; *1910—stage debut in vaudeville* La Nuit de noces, *Paris; 1910-12—member of troupe Théâtre Montparnasse; 1912—music-hall star, appearing at Ba-ta-clan and the Châtelet; 1913—film acting debut in production of syndicalist cooperative Le Cinéma du Peuple, a film protesting exploitation of domestic workers,* Les Misères de l'aiguille; *1914—hired by Feuillade for Gaumont company; 1915—began working on first of Feuillade serials,* Les Vampires; *created French version of much-imitated "vamp" character; 1916—first directing effort, adaptation of Colette's* Minne, *reportedly unreleased and no longer in existence; 1916-17—made several films for André Hugon; 1918—in first film adaptation of Colette novel,* La Vagabonde; *1919—first film as director released,* Vicenta, *produced by her own production company, La Société des Films Musidora; 1921-26—lived principally in Spain; 1926—last commercial film appearance in* Les Ombres du passé; *after 1926—active as writer of fiction, stage and radio plays, and popular songs; 1944—through Henri Langlois, actively involved with film preservation efforts of Cinémathèque Française; 1950—directed her last film* La Magique image. ***Died*** *11 December 1957.*

Films as Director and Actress: **1916:** *Minne* (incomplete or not distributed). **1917:** *Le Maillot noir* (*The Black Leotard*) (as herself, + co-sc). **1918:** *La Vagabonde* (*The Vagabond*) (Perego) (as Renée Néré, co-adapt only). **1919:** *Vicenta* (title role, + sc). **1920:** *La Flamme cachée* (*The Hidden Flame*) (co-d with Lion, ro as Anne Morin, + sc, ed—produced 1918). **1921:** *Pour Don Carlos* (*La Capitana Allegria*) (co-d with Lasseyre, ro as Allegria Detchard, + sc). **1922:** *Una aventura de Musidora en España* (*Musidora en Espagne*) (+ sc); *Soleil et ombre* (*Sol y sombra*; *Sun and Shadow*) (co-d with Lasseyre, ro as Juana/blond stranger, + sc). **1924:** *La Tierra de los toros* (*La Terre des Taureaux*; *Land of the Bulls*) (+ sc). **1926:** *Le Berceau de Dieu*. **1950:** *La Magique image* (+ sc—16mm compilation short).

Films as Actress: **1913:** *Les Misères de l'aiguille* (Clamour). **1914:** *La Ville de Madame Tango*; *Severo Torelli* (Feuillade) (as Portia); *Le Calvaire* (Feuillade) (as Bianca Flor); *Tu n'épouseras jamais un avocat* (Feuillade) (as Estelle); *Les Fiancés de 1914* (Feuillade). **1915:** *Sainte Odile* (Ravel); *Les Trois rats* (Ravel) (as young ballerina); *La Bouquetière des Catalans* (Ravel); *Les Leçons de la guerre* (Ravel); *La Petite refugiée* (Ravel); *L'Autre Victoire* (Ravel); *Bout de Zan et l'espion* (Feuillade); *Le Colonel Bontemps* (Feuillade); *L'Union sacrée* (Feuillade) (as the typist); *Celui qui reste* (Feuillade) (as Suzanne Gerson); *Le Coup du fakir* (Feuillade); *Deux Françaises* (Feuillade) (as Mme. Castel); *Fifi tambour* (Feuillade); *L'Escapade de Filoche* (Feuillade) (as Mme. Pichepin); *Les Noces d'argent* (Feuillade); *Le Roman de la midinette* (Ravel); *Le Sosie* (Feuillade); *Triple Entente* (Ravel); *La Barrière* (Feuillade); *Le Fer à cheval* (Feuillade); *Le Collier de perles* (Feuillade); *Le Trophée du zouave* (Ravel); *Le Grand Souffle* (Ravel); *Bout de Zan et le poilu* (Feuillade); *Une Page de gloire* (Perret). **1915-16:** *Les Vampires* (Feuillade—serial) (as Irma Vep). **1916:** *Le Troisième Larron*; *Jeunes Filles d'hier et d'aujourd'hui* (Feuillade); *Coeur fragile*; *Le Pied qui étreint* (Feyder—serial) (as Irma Vep); *Les Mariés d'un jour* (Feuillade); *Les Fourberies de Pingouin* (Feuillade); *Les Fiançailles d'Agenor* (Feuillade) (as Amélie); *Le Poète et sa folle amante* (Feuillade); *Fille d'Eve*; *Si vous ne m'aimez pas* (Feuillade) (as Simone); *La Peine de talion* (Feuillade) (as Rosa Larose); *Lagourdette, gentleman cambrioleur* (Feuillade); *Judex* (Feuillade—serial) (as Diana Monti/Marie Verdier). **1917:** *C'est pour les orphelins!* (Feuillade); *Mon Oncle* (Feuillade); *Débrouille-toi* (Feuillade) (as Mlle. Friquette); *Les Chacals* (Hugon) (as Dolorès Melrose). **1918:** *Johannès fils de Johannès* (Paglieri and Hugon) (as Gabrielle Baude). **1919:** *Mam'zelle Chiffon* (Hugon) (title role). **1921:** *La Geole* (Ravel—produced 1918) (as Marie-Ange Gaël). **1922:** *La Jeune fille la plus méritante de France*. **1926:** *Les Ombres du passé* (Leroy-Granville).

One of the greatest stars of the French silent cinema, Musidora gained extraordinary fame playing France's first screen vamp, Irma Vep (an anagram of "vampire") in Louis Feuillade's 1915-16 film series, *Les Vampires*. She played its femme fatale with great aplomb, appearing in each of its ten semi-independent episodes in a different disguise—both male and female. In addition, her sexy villainess wore a provocative black leotard and expressed an unashamed sexuality. Her characterizations earned Musidora an amazing fame, and she was embraced enthusiastically by popular audiences as well as by the surrealists who appreciated her subversive androgynous eroticism. But, Musidora was something of a "Renaissance woman": in addition to her work as a film actress, she was a novelist, poet, dancer, painter, songwriter, and playwright. Yet very little historical attention has been paid to Musidora's offscreen film roles, despite the fact that she became a film director in the mid-1910s when very few women had such opportunities. When she died, she left behind seven unpublished screenplays and several films that she directed or co-directed.

Musidora had rather auspicious roots: her mother was a feminist who started the journal *Le Vengeur* in 1897, which was devoted to feminism, sociology, and the arts. Clearly influenced by her mother, after she gained fame in *Les Vampires,* Musidora earned a reputation for her flamboyant lifestyle and avant-garde friends, including Colette, Germaine Dulac, Louis Delluc, André Breton, Marcel L'Herbier, and other surrealists.

Musidora's early forays into the arena of film directing involved collaborations with the legendary French writer Colette, with whom she worked on three films—*Minne, La Vagabonde,* and *La Flamme cachée*. Musidora's first directorial effort was an adaptation of Colette's *Minne,* based on *The Innocent Libertine,* in which she also starred. It was reportedly based on Colette's life, though it never was finished and its footage no longer exists. Next, she made *Le Maillot noir,* which she wrote in collaboration with Germaine Beaumont, and in which she revisited the vampire image she had created for Feuillade. 1918's *La Vagabonde* was a pivotal film for Musidora because it was both popular and well-received by critics. She also starred in and adapted it with Eugenio Perego (who also directed); the scenario was written by Colette. With *La Flamme cachée* she collaborated with Colette on the script and the production was the first from her own company, La Société des Films Musidora. The film was a "drama in four parts" that Musidora starred in, adapted, edited, and co-directed (with Roger Lion), from a scenario by Colette. Musidora's recollections of the film were published in *L'Ecran Français* in 1950; she described it as a story of a student (played by Musidora) who marries a fellow student who is a millionaire, despite the fact she loves another man who is poor. Hoping to change her life and be with her true love, she tries to compel her husband to commit suicide, but she dies in an explosion after offending her lover.

In 1919 Musidora made and starred in *Vicenta,* from her original script. Between 1920 and 1923, she collaborated with Jacques Lasseyre on the direction of *Pour Don Carlos* and *Soleil et Ombre*. In 1924 Musidora wrote a feminist screenplay for *La Tierra de los toros,* which she shot in Spain. While in that country, Musidora reportedly determined to prove that women were courageous enough to be given voting rights—by demonstrating her own bravery in the bull ring.

In 1926 Musidora was celebrated as the "queen of the cinema," but her film career came to an end with the arrival of sound, except for the 1951 compilation short film, *La Magique image,* which included clips from her early films. After she retired from filmmaking, she became a journalist, writing several articles about cinema, and she wrote fiction and poetry as well. In 1946 she began working at the Cinémathèque Française. In France, Musidora's legend as a woman with a charged sexual persona endures. In the 1970s feminists began to acknowledge and embrace her achievements as a brave filmmaker, and in 1973 the Musidora Association was founded. In 1974 the association organized the first Musidora International Festival of Women's Films, where Musidora's only surviving film, *Soleil et ombre,* was screened. According to the Musidora Association, the primary goal of the festival was to make the point that films made by women actually existed.—CYNTHIA FELANDO

Nair, Mira

Indian director

Born *Bhubaneshwar, Orissa, India, 1957.* ***Education*** *Studied sociology at Delhi University; studied sociology and cinema on scholarship at Harvard University, 1976.* ***Family*** *Married 1) the cinematographer Mitch Epstein; 2) Mahmood Mamdani, son: Zohran.* ***Career*** *1979—made first documentary,* Jama Masjid Street Journal; *1985—gained some notoriety for the controversial documentary,* India Cabaret; *1988—garnered critical acclaim and commercial success with first fiction feature,* Salaam Bombay!; *1996—created more controversy with the erotic* Kama Sutra. ***Awards*** *Best Documentary, Global Village Film Festival in New York, for* India Cabaret, *1985; Camera d'Or, Best First Feature, Cannes Film Festival, and Prix de Publique, Audience Favorite, Cannes Film Festival, for* Salaam Bombay!, *1988; Ciak Award for Most Popular Film at the Festival, and Best Screenplay, Venice Film Festival, for* Mississippi Masala, *1991; Muse Award for Outstanding Vision and Achievement, New York Women in Film and Television, 1997; Boston Film Video Association's Vision Award, 1997.* ***Agent*** *Bart Walker, International Creative Management, 40 West 57th Street, New York, NY 10019, U.S.A.* ***Address*** *Mirabai Films, 24 Belmont Avenue, Oranjezicht, Cape Town 8001, South Africa.*

Films as Director: 1979: *Jama Masjid Street Journal* (doc). **1983:** *So Far from India* (doc). **1984:** *Women and Development* (doc). **1985:** *India Cabaret* (doc). **1987:** *Children of Desired Sex* (doc). **1988:** *Salaam Bombay!* (+ pr, co-sc). **1991:** *Mississippi Masala* (+ pr, co-sc, ro as gossip). **1993:** *The Day the Mercedes Became a Hat* (short video) (+ pr, co-sc). **1995:** *The Perez Family* (+ ro as woman buying flowers). **1996:** *Kama Sutra* (*Kama Sutra: A Tale of Love*) (+ pr, co-sc). **1997:** *My Own Country* (+ ro as gossip).

After spending three years working as a theater actress in New Delhi, Mira Nair was inspired to pursue a career in filmmaking after taking a course in documentary production at Harvard University. Subsequently, she made four documentaries in India that focused on her country's changing culture. For example, the controversial *India Cabaret* is about Bombay strippers and their male audiences, and effectively illuminates the marginalized lives of the strippers as well as the double standards and patriarchal values whereby women in general are never moved to question or challenge their lot as oppressed citizens. Nair intended that this film would present an Indian woman's perspective that was unknown in Indian cinema, one that depicts men and women, as she put it, "as they are, the way they speak." *Jama Masjid Street Journal* is a documentary about India's culture that served as Nair's thesis film; it was screened at New York's Film Forum in 1986. Yet another documentary, *So Far from India* is about an Indian-American subway newsstand salesman living in New York, while his wife awaits his return to India. Like many women filmmakers, Nair made several documentaries before turning to fiction feature production.

Mira Nair. Photograph by Prabhuddo Dasgupta.

Nair's first fiction feature was *Salaam Bombay!* Her breakthrough film, it tells the compelling and heartrending story of the tremendous trials of a runaway boy from the country who survives in the mean streets and back alleys of Bombay with his wits, despite being surrounded by a proliferation of low-life hustlers, prostitutes, and junkies. A powerful successor to Héctor Babenco's film about street children, *Pixote,* Nair's film is filled with both pathos and humor. She developed the film, in addition to discovering and training her principal actors, by arranging a series of improvisational theater workshops with street children in Bombay. In 1989 it was nominated for an Oscar for Best Foreign Film and enjoyed considerable box-office success in India and the West. Putting her money where her heart is, Nair gave part of the film's profits to a foundation in order to help educate homeless children in the city.

Nair garnered additional critical and commercial success with the dramatic feature *Mississippi Masala,* about an Indian family living in exile in the southern United States where they must endure the region's racism. In addition, despite their determined attempts to retain their Indian culture, the daughter becomes attracted to and falls in love with a young, handsome African-American man. Thus, the family must cope with the couple's budding affair, a situation Nair uses to help underscore the equally pervasive racism that exists between minority groups. Nevertheless, her film celebrates the mélange of cultures and the possibilities created by migration. As Nair has said, she herself identifies with the notion of *masala*—a term that refers to those who dwell in two lands.

The Perez Family proved to be another critical success for Nair. A romantic fable set within the context of the 1980 Mariel boat-lift of Cuban refugees, it tells the story of a newly released Cuban prisoner who goes to Miami in order to search for his long-lost wife and daughter. But he hooks up with a lusty young woman while his wife, who mistakenly believes he missed the boat, finally permits herself to fall in love with another man.

Nair's recent film, *Kama Sutra,* which is set in 16th-century India, did not enjoy the critical praise of her earlier work. It features two girls, one a lowly servant and the other a noble princess, who grew up together. As children they are inseparable companions, though the princess enjoys the privileges of her class position, while the servant is acutely aware of her position of subordination. Yet the servant uses her striking beauty and her precocious skills of seduction in order to exact her revenge on the sexually repressed princess by seducing her husband, a king, on their wedding day. So begins a vengeful struggle for power that leads the servant to become an accomplished courtesan well-versed in the lessons of the *Kama Sutra,* the Indian book of love. But, ultimately the women's dissension produces tragic results. Nair's evocation of the look and tone of 16th-century India is impressive; as she explained, it is incredible to know that so much style surrounding pleasure could exist in one part of the world, while Puritanism dominated elsewhere. Some critics charged that the film played like a Harlequin Romance, as a result of its many beautiful bodies alluringly arrayed and photographed, as well as its dramatic, contrived, and breathless emotions. Such critics suggested that despite its nearly explicit depictions of sex, the film fails on the level of passion. On the other hand, some critics praised it as a lush, beautiful, voluptuous tale that was compellingly expressed with a quiet and impressive eroticism. Interestingly, Nair was reportedly unable to get the film screened in India, which she says prohibits scenes of kissing but has no problem with scenes of rape and violence toward women.

In *Salaam Bombay!, Mississippi Masala,* and *The Perez Family,* Nair provided compelling combinations of history with provocative tales of the marginalized. In addition, her films each focus in some way on class issues and other cultural differences. Further, since *Salaam Bombay!* her films have shared a focus on female sexuality and sensuality; indeed, she is refreshingly unafraid to depict beautiful, lusty women who openly express their attraction to men.—CYNTHIA FELANDO

Nelson, Gunvor

Swedish/American director

Born *Gunvor Grundel in Stockholm, 1931; naturalized American.* ***Education*** *Attended Humboldt State University, California, majoring in art, B.A. 1957; San Francisco Art Institute, studying painting and lithography with Nathan Olivera, 1957; Mills College, painting (with Richard Diebenkorn) and art history, M.F.A. 1958.* ***Family*** *Daughter, the artist Oona Nelson.* ***Career*** *Mid-1950s—came to United States to study art; pursued career in painting and filmmaking; made several films, especially in the mid-to-late 1960s and early 1970s, with Dorothy Wiley; late 1960s—began own 16mm films, several made in both the United States and Sweden, financed through grants from both countries; taught filmmaking for 24 years at the San Francisco Art Institute; since 1993—living and working in Sweden, based in Kristinehamn; now working with painting, collage, printmaking, photography, video, and computer animation.* ***Awards*** *Guggenheim Fellowship, 1973; American Association of University Women Fellowship, 1974; National Endowment for the Arts, 1975 and 1982; American Film Institute, 1977; Filmverkstan*

Fellowship, 1981 and 1987; Konstnarsnamden, 1982, 1990, and 1994; Swedish Short Film Fund, 1985; San Francisco Arts Commission Award, 1986; Western States Regional Media Arts Fellowship, 1987 and 1988; Marin Arts Council, 1988; Rockefeller Foundation, 1990. ***Address*** *Hovslagaregatan 2B, S 681 31, Kristinehamn, Sweden.*

Films as Director: 1965: *Schmeerguntz* (short) (co-d with Dorothy Wiley). **1967:** *Fog Pumas* (co-d with Wiley). **1969:** *Kirsa Nicholina* (short); *My Name Is Oona.* **1971:** *Five Artists: BillBobBillBillBob* (co-d with Wiley). **1972:** *One and the Same* (short) (co-d with Freude Solomon-Bartlett); *Take Off* (short) (co-d with Magda). **1973:** *Moons Pool* (short). **1973-76:** *Trollstenen.* **1979:** *Before Need* (co-d with Wiley). **1984:** *Frame Line* (short); *Red Shift.* **1987:** *Light Years* (short); *Light Years Expanding* (short). **1988:** *Field Study #2* (short). **1990:** *Natural Features* (short). **1991:** *Time Being* (short). **1993:** *Old Digs; Kristina's Harbor.* **1995:** *Before Need Redressed* (co-d with Wiley).

Trained as a painter and lithographer, currently working in a variety of media but not film, Gunvor Nelson describes herself as an artist rather than as a director. Her films have been widely screened in festivals and one-woman shows around the United States and Europe. Marked by engagements with surrealist and personal avant-garde film, they all, though differently, meld attention to color, light, shape, form, and texture with a keen sense of rhythm and time. Emotion and mood predominate: although careful choreography, always of images and frequently also of sound, underpins her individual and her collaborative works, such structurings are more often viscerally felt than directly perceived. For Nelson, an openness to associations and an appreciation of transformations are key.

Interested in animation from the start, Nelson's five "field studies" in particular (*Frame Line, Light Years, Light Years Expanding, Field Study #2,* and *Natural Features*) are created thanks to an amateur animation camera that she designed to accommodate the mixing of a variety of media, including cut-outs, photographs, fluids, toys, and live-action footage. *Frame Line* and *Natural Features* revolve around footage shot in Stockholm while *Light Years* and *Light Years Expanding* move into the Swedish countryside, but all represent reflections on cross- and trans-cultural commutations, evoking spaces and times recaptured, remembered, and reshaped within and through film frames and fields. Of the five, only *Frame Line* is in black and white.

Two of Nelson's most recent films, *Kristina's Harbor* and *Old Digs,* engage with similar themes, but are not made with her amateur animation camera. Both present lyrical excavations and poetic reassemblages of bits and pieces of Kristinehamn, Nelson's hometown, where she is again based after living for more than 30 years in the United States. *Old Digs* uses sounds from *Kristina's Harbor* (looped voices of old people, now indecipherably murmuring and mumbling; clock tones; a rainstorm; electronic music) as a subterranean backdrop for images of dead birds, insects, clouds, water, cut-outs, photographs, buildings, reflections. Shot with a different attitude, a lighter-weight camera, and no tripod, *Old Digs* varies appreciably in tone, seeming darker than *Kristina's Harbor* though equally, subtly, dramatic.

More overtly surrealist, *Schmeerguntz, Take Off, Fog Pumas, Before Need,* and *Before Need Redressed,* also explore the beauty in strange obsessions, and even decay, while mocking perfection as socially defined, limiting, and absurd, often through disjointed and absurd narratives and dialogue. In *Before Need* and *Before Need Redressed,* for example, close-ups and extreme close-ups of dental instruments and teeth are rendered with an eye to form and color, highlights and shadows, as are Faberge eggs, a block of ice melting under the impact of a hot iron, and more. Both films present viewers with a series of kaleidoscopic puzzles to be deciphered as, and if, they will. A recut and condensed version of *Before Need, Before Need*

Redressed stands as a quite different film, because even though many of the whispered voice-over reflections of an older woman "character" and snatches of string music remain, and even though, like the images, these sounds are presented in the same order, many of the original images and much of the synchronized dialogue of non sequiturs have been excised.

Nelson's early works often generated interest because she was one of a handful of women filmmakers working among the largely male West Coast avant-garde in the 1960s and 1970s. *Schmeerguntz,* a collage send-up that juxtaposes recycled images of magazine model femininity with select footage of more everyday female experiences, and *Take Off,* an animated *cum* live-action film about a stripper who ends up stripping her own body parts, then rocketing off into space, were and continue to be hailed by some critics as "feminist"; in fact they were quite diversely received among feminists at the time.

Other films, including *My Name Is Oona, Red Shift, Time Being, Kirsa Nicholina, Five Artists, One and the Same,* and *Trollstenen,* center on family, friends, and/or self, and emotion. Like Nelson's other work in film, all exceed gender-based or gender-limited labels. The haunting *My Name Is Oona,* a ten-minute black-and-white short, casts Nelson's young daughter as playful child and fairy-tale princess via multi-layered superimpositions of negative and positive images combined in varying speeds with choral and singular transformations of Oona's recorded voice, off, chanting, mantralike, "My name is Oona." The nearly feature-length *Red Shift* weaves exchanges among three generations of Grundel/Nelson women (Oona, Gunvor, and Gunvor's mother, Carin) together with the reflections of fictional characters and Calamity Jane's letters to her absent daughter, evoking some of the emotional connections experienced by mothers and daughters of differing ages, in differing epochs. *Time Being,* an eight-minute silent, moves from still photos of Nelson's vibrantly athletic middle-aged mother, smiling on skis, to three long takes, the first in close-up, the second in medium shot, the third in long shot, of Carin in old age, nearly motionless on a nursing home or hospital bed, struggling to breathe. Interspersed gestural camera work and manipulations of light exposure powerfully suggest the intensities of observation and feeling to be found in waiting, and being.—CHRIS HOLMLUND

Notari, Elvira

Italian director and writer

Born *Elvira Cody, in Salerno, Italy, 10 February 1875.* ***Family*** *Married Nicola Notari, 1902, three children.* ***Career*** *1906—founded Film Dora (later called Dora Film) and started producing films; 1906-11—produced film shorts intended to open or close a cinema show; 1909—started producing longer films; 1920—due to popular demand,* 'A Legge *screened for a full month rather than the usual two weeks; 1920s—Notari's films were censored and increasingly were shown in the United States; 1925-30—her company's film output declined drastically due to Italian censorship; 1930—made her last film,* Christian Triumph. ***Died*** *In Italy, 1946.*

Films as Director and Writer: 1906-11: *Arrivederci* and *Augurali* (at least 27 episodes of varying lengths). **1909:** *Capri Incantevole* (*Enchanting Capri*); *Posillipo da Napoli* (*Posillipo as Seen from Naples*); *L'Accalappiacani* (*The Dog Catcher*); *Il Processo Cuocolo* (*The Trial Cuocolo*). **1910:** *La Fuga del Gatto* (*Escape of the Cat*). **1911:** *La Corazzata San Giorgio* (*The Ship San Giorgio*); *Preparativi Guerreschi a Napoli* (*Preparing for the War in Naples*); *Bufera d'Anime* (*Blizzard of Passion*); *Carmela* *la Pazza* (*Carmela the Madwoman*); *Maria Rosa di Santa Flavia* (*Maria Rosa of Santa Flavia*). **1912:** *Capri Pittoresco* (*Picturesque Capri*); *Caratteristica Guerra Italo-Turca Tra i Nostri Scugnizzi Napoletani* (*Italo-Turkish War among Our Neapolitan Urchins*); *Cattura di un Pazzo a Bagnoli* (*Capture of a Madman in Bagnoli*); *Rivista Navale Dell' 11 Novembre 1912* (*Great Parade of the Fleet*); *L'Eroismo di un Aviatore a Tripoli* (*Heroism of an Aviator in Tripoli*); *La Figlia del Vesuvio* (*The Daughter of Vesuvius*); *I Nomadi* (*Nomadic People*); *Ritorna all'Onda* (*Return to the Wave*). **1913:** *Povera Tisa, Povera Madre* (*Poor Consumptive! Poor Mother!*); *Il Tricolore* (*The Italian Flag*); *A Marechiaro ce sta 'na Fenesta* (*At Marechiaro There Is a Window*). **1914:** *Fenesta che Lucive* (*Lighted Window*). **1915:** *Addio Mia Bella Addio, l'Armata se ne va* (*Farewell, My Dear, Farewell. . . the Army Is Going*); *Figlio del Reggimento* (*Son of the Regiment*); *Sempre Avanti Savoia* (*Forward, Savoia*). **1916:** *Carmela la Sartina di Montesanto* (*Carmela the Dressmaker of Montesanto*); *Ciccio il Pizzaiuolo del Carmine* (*Ciccio, the Pizzamaker of Carmine*); *Gloria ai Caduti* (*Glory to the Fallen Soldiers*). **1917:** *Mandolinata a Mare* (*Mandolin Music at Sea*); *La Maschera del Vizio* (*The Mask of Vice*); *Il Nano Rosso* (*The Red Dwarf*). **1918:** *Il Barcaiuolo d'Amalfi* (*The Boatman of Amalfi*); *Gnesella*; *Pusilleco Addiruso* (*Rimpianto*; *Urchins*; *Regret*). **1919:** *Chiarina la Modista* (*Chiarina the Milliner*); *Gabriele il Lampionaio di Porto* (*Gabriele the Lamplighter of the Harbor*); *La Medea di Porta Medina* (*The Medea of Porta Medina*). **1920:** *A Piedigrotta* (*At Piedigrotta*); *'A Legge* (*'O Festino e 'a Legge*; *The Law*; *The Feast and the Law*); *'A Mala Nova* (*The New Criminal Underworld*). **1921:** *Gennariello il Figlio del Galeotto* (*Gennariello the Son of the Convict*); *Gennariello Polizziotto* (*Gennariello the Policeman*); *Luciella* (*Luciella la Figlia Della Strada*; *Luciella*; *Luciella, the Daughter of the Street*); *'O Munaciello* (*The House of Spirit*). **1922:** *Cielo celeste*; *Cielo 'e Napule*; *E' Piccarella* (*The Little Girl's Wrong*); *Il Miracolo Della Madonna di Pompei* (*Mary the Crazy Woman*); *'A Santa notte* (*The Holy Night*). **1923:** *Core 'e Frata* (*Brother's Heart*); *'O Cuppe' d'a Morte* (*The Carriage of Death*); *Pupatella* (*Waltzer Dream*); *Reginella* (*Little Queen*); *Scugnizza* (*Orphan of Naples*); *Sotto il Carcere di San Francisco* (*Beneath the Prison*). **1924:** *A Marechiaro ce sta 'na Fenesta* (*At Marechiaro There Is a Window*) (2nd version); *La Fata di Borgo Loreto* (*The Fairy of Borgo Loreto*); *'Nfama* (*Voglio a Tte*; *Infamous Woman*; *I Fancy You*); *Otto e Novanta* (*8 and 90*); *Piange Pierrot* (*Cosi Piange Pierrot*; *Pierrot Cries*). **1925:** *Fenesta che Lucive* (*Lighted Window*) (2nd version); *Mettete l'Avvocato* (*Get a Lawyer*). **1927:** *Fantasia 'e Surdata* (*Soldier's Fantasy*); *L'Italia s'è Desta* (*Italy Has Risen*); *Mother and Country* (produced in 1925). **1928:** *Duie Paravise* (*Two Heavens*); *La Leggenda di Napoli* (*The Legend of Naples*); *La Madonnina del Pescatore* (*The Little Madonna of the Fisherman*); *Napoli Terra d'Amore* (*Naples, Land of Love*). **1929:** *Napoli Sirena Della Canzone* (*Naples, Singing Mermaid*). **1930:** *Passa a Bandiera* (*The Flag Passes By*); *Trionfo Cristiano* (*Christian Triumph*).

Though her name is now largely forgotten, Elvira Notari was Italy's first and most prolific woman filmmaker and her vast body of work is considered an important antecedent of Italian neorealism. Her films were distributed throughout Italy and other countries, especially to New York City (where Dora Film had an office). Unfortunately, the bulk of her work no longer exists, though the fragments that remain suggest that she brought a richly textured female perspective to her looks at love, violence, poverty, desire, and death.

After Notari finished school, unusual for a girl from the working class, she went to Naples to work as a milliner. After she married Nicola Notari, the couple supported themselves by hand-coloring photographs, and soon they started coloring motion pictures. In 1906 they started making their own films—shorts that were intended to open or close a cinema show, and which were called, *Augurali* and *Arrivederci* films. In addition, they made short documentaries that mostly consisted of brief scenes of street life and expansive city and natural vistas, as well as "actualities"—films of real events, including urban youth gang fights (*Italo-Turkish War among Our Neapolitan Urchins*) and the arrest of a madman (*Capture of a Madman in Bagnoli*). By 1909, under the name Film Dora, they were releasing feature films (they changed the studio's name in about 1915 to Dora Film). Their company was a family affair: Nicola was responsible for the cinematography and sets, and he developed, printed, and edited the films with Elvira. In addition, their son Edoardo appeared in nearly all of the films, playing the recurring character Gennariello.

During a career that spanned the years 1906-30, Elvira directed and co-produced all of Dora Film's output, including about 60 feature films, as well as more than a hundred documentaries and shorts. She selected the stories and wrote the original screenplays as well as the scripts that were adapted from popular novels and songs. Interestingly, at Dora Film she was known as "the general" for her serious and precise working style. Apparently, her films were extraordinarily popular: in the Naples's arcade theaters where they were regularly screened, each of her films generally ran for two weeks, from the morning until late at night, and each was likely seen by thousands of theater patrons. Further, her films were popular in the United States among Italian immigrants. Until her career was resurrected by Giuliana Bruno, however, film history had forgotten her. Historians routinely had propagated misinformation about Dora Film, in particular that Nicola had directed all of the films. Nevertheless, a local critic in 1916 praised her films and noted that what audiences appreciated in particular was that "the suggestive drama develops against the enchanting panorama of the city of Naples."

During Elvira's career, the Italian film industry was divided between the lively film production of the South, which included the popular Dora Film, and Northern film production, mostly near Rome and Turin. In particular, the Southern Neapolitan cinema was associated with depictions of "crude local scenes of poverty and violence." Elvira's films were of their region; indeed, her "cinema of the street" was far different from the slick Italian "super-spectacles" of her Northern contemporaries that were dominant in Italian cinema, and preferred by commercial American distributors. Her distinctive style arguably foreshadowed neorealism, in terms, for example, of mise-en-scène and subject matter. That is, Elvira shot her melodramas on location in the streets of Naples, and often with nonprofessional performers. Accordingly, her films revealed the conditions of urban living among the poor, as well as her interest in the experiences of women. But her work was usually not explicitly political—she made tearful melodramas with exciting crimes of passion and betrayal. Notably, the subjects of her melodramas were inspired by Neapolitan popular culture, 19th-century popular literature, and Italian women's romantic fiction. Often, the titles of her films were taken from contemporary popular songs, including *Fenesta che Lucive, A Marechiaro ce sta 'na Fenesta,* and *Pupatella*. They often featured women who reject prevailing social expectations, including women who are mad, violent, and highly sexual; and they were populated by temptresses and vamps and weak men all too eager to commit horrible crimes for them. *E' Piccarella,* for example, was a melodrama about a woman who is pursued by two men, and who favors the sinister over the good man, with tragic results. Indeed, one of Elvira Notari's recurrent female characters was the matriarchal *piccarella*; as her film suggested, the term refers to a strong-willed, outspoken, and somewhat bad girl. In addition, Notari's films often depicted a betrayed and abandoned mother who is instrumental in reestablishing the Law, as in *'A Legge. Core 'e Frata,* like many of her films, is a romance, but with a difference: it is about a woman who works as a lighthouse keeper and longs for a romance with a passionate assassin, instead of with her disinterested and drunken fiancé.

During the 1920s, with the rise of Italian Fascism, Dora Film increasingly experienced censorship problems because the films seemed to criticize the law, and because they depicted crime, neglect, and poverty, and employed authentic dialects, instead of adhering to the fascist regime's favored images of an ordered and honest Italy. Thus, for example, Notari's film *Mother and Country* was cut and reedited several times before the Italian censors finally approved it.

Nevertheless, when her films were refused censorship visas by Rome's authorities, they often were smuggled into the United States and distributed to Italian immigrant communities in New York's Little Italy and other urban areas where they were quite popular. Continuing censorship problems and the coming of sound, however, marked the end of Elvira Notari's film career.—CYNTHIA FELANDO

Novaro, María

Mexican director and writer

Born *Mexico City, Mexico, 11 September 1951.* ***Education*** *Studied sociology at the Universidad Autonoma de México (UNAM) and filmmaking at the Centro Universitario de Estudios Cinematográficos (CUEC).* ***Career*** *Feature film debut,* Lola, *1989.* ***Awards*** *Ariel, Best Short Fiction, Mexican Academy of Motion Picture Arts and Science, for* An Island Surrounded by Water, *1984; Ariel, Best Feature Debut and Best Film Script, Mexican Academy of Motion Picture Arts and Science, for* Lola, *1989.*

Films as Director: **1981:** *Sobre las olas* (*Over the Waves*) (short); *De encaje y azucar* (*Of Lace and Sugar*) (short); *Lavaderos* (*Laundry Shed*) (short); *Es primera vez* (*For the First Time*). **1982:** *Conmigo la pasas muy bien* (*With Me You Do Very Well*) (short). **1983:** *Querida Carmen* (*Dear Carmen*) (short); *7 AM* (short). **1984:** *Una Isla rodeada de agua* (*An Island Surrounded by Water*) (short). **1985:** *La Pervertida* (*Depraved*) (short). **1988:** "Azul celeste" ("Celestial Blue"; "Sky Blue") ep. of *Historias de ciudad* (co-d). **1989:** *Lola* (+ sc). **1990:** *Danzón* (+ co-sc, co-ed). **1992:** *Otoñal* (*Autumn*) (short). **1994:** *El jardín del Edén* (*The Garden of Eden*) (+ sc, ed). **1998:** "Cuando comenzamos a hablar" ep. of *Enredando sombras.*

Other Film: **1990:** *My Filmmaking, My Life: Matilde Landeta* (P. Diaz and J. Ryder—doc) (appearance).

The 1990s have been an exciting decade in Mexican cinema, especially for women filmmakers. Between 1989-92, five women debuted feature films—María Novaro, Busi Cortés, Dana Rotberg, Marysa Systach, and Guita Schyfter. Most of these women made their second features within two years of their first. María Novaro contributed to this renaissance of Mexican cinema with the production of *Danzón,* her second feature, which earned international acclaim. Even more impressive, films by these women have been among the nominees in several categories for the Ariel, Mexico's Academy Award, in the past ten years.

The decade did not begin auspiciously—rounding off the trouble in the industry in the 1980s, 992 theaters were closed between 1989-91. Feature-film production dropped from 100 films in 1989 to 52 in 1990 and only 34 in 1991. The difficulties affected not only state-supported cinema, but Mexico's independent production as well. As Mexican cinema rose from the ashes, complete state production (through IMCINE, the Mexican film institute) was discontinued, giving bureaucrats a lesser hold on films, and co-productions between IMCINE, independent producers, and foreign countries increased.

Despite the crisis in the Mexican film industry, exacerbated by the country's economic crisis in 1990-91, Mexican filmmakers persevered. In fact, 1990-91 was a great year for Mexican cinema—a number of internationally acclaimed films were released, many produced by new, young filmmakers. Even more notable, perhaps, was the fact that the Mexican film-going audience flocked to see Mexican films, keeping them in the theaters longer than expected and creating new excitement and demand for domestic cinema.

Novaro

María Novaro's films embody the spirit and the art of this new Mexican cinema. In the 1980s she produced a number of short films that were all well received. Novaro introduced in these shorts a number of aesthetic and political themes that resound throughout her oeuvre. She is unapologetically feminist, and continuously explores the role of women in Mexican society, gender inequity, the limits of fantasy and desire, and the political realities of being next-door neighbors with the mighty United States of America. In her combination of aesthetic and textual complexity, Novaro contributes to a strong movement of feminist filmmaking that began across Latin America in the late 1970s and continues today.

Her best-known short, *An Island Surrounded by Water,* lyrically narrates a young orphan girl's search for her mother. Its exquisite setting, Guerrero, on the coast of Costa Grande, enhances the girl's quest, which ultimately ends with two cameras—the filmmaker's and a portrait photographer's—presenting us with the girl's conflictual feelings about coming into womanhood. The search for her displaced mother becomes, in the end, a search for a guide into the next phase of life, or for the woman inside herself. The film received the Ariel for Best Fiction Short.

Novaro's other shorts examine distinct moments in the lives of Mexican women. *7 AM* (1983) allegorizes the contrast between the day of an average working woman and her fantasies of a life of leisure, informed by her experiences of mass media. This theme seemed to pulse throughout Latin America in the 1980s and, in fact, the Colombian feminist film and video collective Cine Mujer produced a very similar film in 1978 entitled *A primera vista* (*At First Glance*). Novaro's *Dear Carmen* (1983) also looks at the contradictions between reality and fantasy and the limits of desire, juxtaposing the life of a young professional woman with her fantasies about taming the Wild West as the legendary heroine Calamity Jane.

Novaro's feature-film debut, *Lola,* garnered several Ariel nominations including Best Feature Debut and Best Film Script. Like her subsequent films, *Lola* was written in collaboration with Novaro's sister, Beatriz. *Lola* is set in one of the shanty towns that surround Mexico City, just after the earthquake of 1985. Through its protagonists, a female street peddler and a "rockanrolero" (rock and roll fan), the film examines social and sexual politics.

In 1990, Novaro came to the attention of the international film community with *Danzón*. A beautiful and compelling film, *Danzón* tells the story of a telephone operator and single mother, Julia, whose ballroom dancing takes the place of any emotional life. She is devastated when her dancing partner disappears and she embarks on a dizzying quest to find him. As much inner voyage as odyssey, Julia's extraordinary journey is exuberant, difficult, and fulfilling. Novaro and actress María Rojo received Ariel nods, for Best Director and Best Actress respectively. The script, written with her sister Beatriz, was nominated for Best Original Screenplay. In a year seemingly jam-packed with exciting Latin American films, *Danzón* stands out as an uplifting tale about a woman's search for inner strength and happiness.

Novaro followed *Danzón* with a film about Mexicans in Tijuana struggling to cross the border into the United States. *El jardín de Edén* poignantly portrays the would-be emigrés as regular people, seeking a better life, and hoping to find it in "the Garden of Eden," the United States. Like the biblical garden, however, the mythical northern neighbor has hidden risks and dangers. Coinciding with the NAFTA agreement and the U.S. bailout of the Mexican economy, *El jardín de Edén* humanizes people who are generally portrayed by the U.S. press as dirty, backward, and subhuman, reminding us at the same time what it should mean to be a "neighbor."—ILENE S. GOLDMAN

Obomsawin, Alanis

Canadian director

Born *Lebanon, New Hampshire, 31 August 1932; moved to Canada in 1933 and was raised to age 9 on the Odonak Reserve in Quebec.* ***Family*** *One child, Kisos.* ***Career*** *Late 1950s—moved to Montreal, joining circle of writers, photographers, and artists; 1960—made professional singing debut at New York City's Town Hall; 1960s—traveled extensively throughout Canada, the United States, and Europe, earning a reputation as a singer, songwriter, storyteller, and activist; made several guest appearances on TV series* Sesame Street *(Canadian version); 1967—joined National Film Board of Canada as a consultant, beginning long-term relationship; 1971—directorial debut with the short,* Christmas at Moose Factory; *1973—directed first of two multimedia education packages,* Manowan (L'ilawat *followed in 1976); 1977—made first feature-length documentary,* Mother of Many Children; *1979—directed two shorts,* Old Crow *and* Gabriel Goes to the City, *for the educational TV series,* Sounds from Our People; *1982—as a guest of the music department, taught a course on oral tradition at Dartmouth College; 1988—released "Bush Lady," an album of traditional Abenaki and original songs, sung in Abenaki, English, or French; 1993—directed* Kanehsatake: 270 Years of Resistance, *winner of 18 awards and international acclaim.* ***Awards*** *"Outstanding Canadian of the Year,"* Maclean's *magazine, 1965; Grand Prix, International Festival of Arctic Film (Dieppe, France), and Best Documentary, American Indian Film Festival (San Francisco), for* Mother of Many Children, *1977; Order of Canada, 1983; Best Documentary, American Indian Film Festival (San Francisco), for* Richard Cardinal, *1986; Best Documentary, American Indian Film Festival (San Francisco), for* No Address, *1988; 125th Anniversary of the Confederation of Canada Medal, 1992; best Canadian feature award, Toronto Film Festival, for* Kanehsatake, *1993; Award for Outstanding Achievement in Direction, Toronto Women in Film and Television, Toronto, 1994; Outstanding Contribution*

Award, Canadian Sociology and Anthropology Association, 1994; Taos Mountain Award, Taos Talking Pictures, 1997. ***Address*** *c/o National Film Board, Box 6100, Station A, Montreal, PQ, Canada H3C 3H5.*

Films as Director: 1971: *Christmas at Moose Factory* (short) (+ sc). **1977:** *Mother of Many Children* (+ sc, co-pr, narrator); *Amisk* (+ co-pr). **1979:** *Old Crow* (short—for TV); *Gabriel Goes to the City* (short—for TV); *Canada Vignettes: Wild Rice Harvest Kenora* (short) (+ sc); *Canada Vignettes: June in Povungnituk—Quebec Arctic* (short) (+ sc, narrator). **1984:** *Incident at Restigouche* (+ sc, co-pr, narrator). **1986:** *Richard Cardinal: Cry from a Diary of a Métis Child* (short) (+ sc, co-pr). **1987:** *Poundmaker's Lodge: A Healing Place* (short) (+ sc, co-pr). **1988:** *No Address* (+ sc, co-pr); *A Way of Learning* (+ sc, co-pr). **1991:** *Le Patro Le Prévost 80 Years Later* (+ sc, co-pr). **1992:** *Walker* (short). **1993:** *Kanehsatake: 270 Years of Resistance* (+ sc, co-pr, narrator); *Voices of Experience, Voices for Change, Part 1* (compilation that includes *Richard Cardinal*). **1995:** *My Name Is Kahentiiosta* (short) (+ sc, co-pr, co-ph). **1996:** *Referendum—Take 2/Prise deux* (co-d). **1997:** *Spudwrench—Kahnawake Man* (+ pr).

Other Film: 1970: *Eliza's Horoscope* (appearance).

Documentarian Alanis Obomsawin has become one of Canada's leading native filmmakers—and has garnered international renown—in a career spanning more than a quarter of a century, a career that emerged out of a unique background. Soon after her birth in New Hampshire, her family moved to Canada, where they initially lived on the Odonak Reserve, northeast of Montreal. There, Obomsawin learned the songs and stories of her people, the Abenaki. When she was nine, her family moved again, this time settling in Trois-Rivières, a small town 75 miles northeast of Montreal, where Obomsawin was the only native child and had to endure cultural isolation and racial discrimination—experiences that had a profound effect on her later filmmaking. Following this typically difficult native childhood, Obomsawin moved to Montreal in the late 1950s, where she eventually emerged as a singer and storyteller out of the circle of writers, photographers, and artists she had joined. During the 1960s she traveled widely throughout Canada, the United States, and Europe performing in universities, prisons, art centers, and at folk festivals for humanitarian causes; she even made several guest appearances on the Canadian version of the television series *Sesame Street,* and was named "Outstanding Canadian of the Year" in 1965 by *Maclean's* magazine. In 1967, Canada's National Film Board (NFB) invited her to work as an adviser on several film projects, leading to her entrance into documentary filmmaking and a long-term relationship with the NFB. Making this move was a natural one for Obomsawin, the storyteller; she has said that "to make a film you have to be able to tell a story. Filmmaking for me is really storytelling."

All of Obomsawin's films deal with one or more aspects of native life, culture, and customs, conveyed through the sensitive and perceptive prism of an insider (it is worth noting that she also writes and co-produces, and often narrates, her films). Her 1971 debut, *Christmas at Moose Factory,* tells the story of life at the Cree settlement of Moose Factory through the artwork of its native children. After directing two multimedia educational packages in 1973 and 1976, she returned to film in 1977 with the award-winning *Mother of Many Children,* her first feature-length documentary. For this film, Obomsawin traveled throughout Canada to document the seminal role that women play—by using language and storytelling to pass on their culture—in what are largely matrilineal societies.

Also in 1977 came *Amisk,* in which Obomsawin showcased native music and dancing at a concert that was part of a week-long festival. Held in Montreal, the purpose of the festival was to raise funds in support of the Cree people of James Bay, who were battling to save their land from a massive hydroelectric project being built by the government of Quebec. This was the first of several films in which Obomsawin documents conflicts between native peoples and the government, which is somewhat ironic given that she was awarded the prestigious Order of Canada in 1983. In fact, the year following this honor, Obomsawin directed *Incident at Restigouche,* which portrays a showdown over salmon fishing rights between the Micmac people on the Restigouche Reserve and the Ontario Provincial Police. Snappily edited, the film draws on television coverage of two police raids of the reserve, montaged news photographs, maps, courtroom drawings, shots of Micmac fishermen, on-camera interviews, and footage of salmon migrating and spawning. Although it plays down the issue of overfishing and is thus not entirely even-handed in its approach, *Incident at Restigouche*—like many of Obomsawin's films—gives voice to native peoples whose rights are too often trampled upon.

In *Richard Cardinal,* Obomsawin drew upon a diary left behind by the Métis title character who had committed suicide in 1984 at age 17 after being shuttled—incredibly—between 28 foster homes, group homes, and shelters in Alberta. To tell this story of abuse and neglect inflicted by the child-welfare system, Obomsawin intersperses quotes from his diary with scenes from his life reconstructed by actors, interviews with some of his foster parents, and depictions of the squalid settings the agencies placed him in.

Obomsawin's next films continued to portray the difficulties of native life in Canada but also highlighted the importance of collective action and tradition in efforts to help native peoples overcome these difficulties. *Poundmaker's Lodge* focuses on a treatment center in St. Albert, Alberta, where native people attempt to rebuild their substance abuse-devastated lives through mutual support, the sweat lodge and other rituals, and the rediscovery of their traditions. In *No Address* Obomsawin depicts the plight of native people who become part of the homeless population of Montreal soon after arriving there in search of a better life; it also looks, however, at the work of various organizations, such as the Montreal Native Friendship Centre, which attempt to help these individuals. In yet another portrayal of a community organization, *Le Patro Le Prévost 80 Years Later* showcases the 1909-founded Patro Le Prévost, a downtown Montreal religious-oriented center that brings people in the community together through various programs and activities.

In the 1990s, Obomsawin has spent much of her time documenting the summer and early fall 1990 confrontation in the Mohawk village of Kanehsatake near Oka, Quebec, between the Mohawks, the provincial police, and Canadian army—and this historic event's aftermath. She has so far made three films centering on the Oka crisis, with the first, the 1993-released *Kanehsatake: 270 Years of Resistance,* becoming her most-celebrated film yet. During the entire 78-day standoff—which grew out of a scheme to have the government take over Mohawk pine-forest land to build a golf course—Obomsawin lived with the Mohawks, thus very much imparting an insider's perspective to the film. But this film, unlike *Incident at Restigouche,* is more even-handed in its politics, with, for example, an army major being portrayed rather sympathetically. More importantly, Obomsawin in this two-hour-long film takes the time to put the Oka crisis into a historical context, namely the nearly three centuries of land-grabbing in and around Montreal at the expense of the Mohawks. This powerful documentary—winner of 18 international awards—thus fulfilled her intention of presenting a community to itself, at the same time that it provided to outsiders a complex record of an important event and its impact on the people involved.

Obomsawin next provided intimate portraits of two of the Mohawks involved in the Oka crisis through 1995's *My Name Is Kahentiiosta* and 1997's *Spudwrench—Kahnawake Man*. The former focuses on a young woman named Kahentiiosta, who is arrested during the crisis and then detained for longer than the other women because the government will not accept her aboriginal name in court. *Spudwrench* tells the story of Randy Horne, a high-steel worker who adopted the code name "spudwrench" during the crisis, and of the generations of Mohawk high-steel workers who have traveled around North America to work on some of the tallest buildings in the world. In both films, Obomsawin is careful to detail the reasons why these and other Mohawks were willing to risk their lives to save their sacred land.

Throughout her increasingly impressive career, Obomsawin has lived up to her goal of making documentary films both for her own community and for the outside world. She concisely summed up her approach when she said, "I make films for the world, [but] first of all I think of the people who I am documenting."—DAVID E. SALAMIE

Ono, Yoko

Japanese director, composer, and actress

Born *Tokyo, 18 February 1933; permanent resident of the United States.* ***Education*** *Attended Gakushuin School; studied at Gakuishin University, Japan, and Sarah Lawrence College, without completing a degree.* ***Family*** *Married 1) Toshi Ichiyanagi, 1957 (divorced 1963); 2) Tony Cox, 1963 (divorced 1969), daughter: Kyoko Cox; 3) the musician John Lennon, 1969 (died 1980), son: Sean Ono Lennon.* ***Career*** *1960-61—held gatherings at her Lower Manhattan loft where experimental poets, composers, and performance artists, most later allied with the loose Fluxus group of "conceptual artists," plied their trades; 1961—had her first gallery show in Manhattan and performed "concerts" (her keening accompanying a woman shattering glass, for example) there; 1962—presented* Works of Yoko Ono *in Tokyo, a five and a half hour-long performance piece filmed for TV, to horrendous reviews, spent time in a mental hospital; 1963—recorded the soundtrack to Tasha Iimura's film* Love; *1964—published* Grapefruit, *a series of "instruction paintings" or written recipes for artworks to be constructed in the audience member's head; presented a series of conceptual pieces in* Yoko Ono's Final Performance *in Tokyo and then left Japan for New York City; 1966—contributed her first film shorts to the omnibus* Fluxfilm Program; *exhibited at the Indica Gallery in London, attained some British notoriety for her first long film,* Bottoms; *1966-71—shot a series of experimental films, often in collaboration with John Lennon; 1967—presented the exhibit* Half-a-Wind *at the Lisson Gallery in London, with partial underwriting by Lennon; 1968—recorded* Two Virgins *with Lennon, an experimental sound collage, the album's release brought horrendous reviews; from 1968 until the present, recorded and performed a unique and eventually fairly influential cross between avant-garde and rock music, with Lennon and on her own; late 1960s—Ono and Lennon also made antiwar, anti-hatred Happenings out of their world-famous love, such as the Acorn Event or the Bed-Ins for Peace; 1969—appeared in the cinema verité-styled* Honeymoon *short, about her seven days in (just postmarital) bed with Lennon surrounded by members of the press; 1970—presented*

Fluxfest, a festival of events and exhibits in Manhattan; 1971-72—showed a retrospective at Everson Art Museum, Syracuse, New York; 1980—released Double Fantasy *in collaboration with Lennon, their last record before he was shot dead in front of her; 1988—Rykodisc released* Onobox, *a 6-compact-disc retrospective of the past two decades of her music; 1989—the Whitney Museum of American Art in New York City presented a retrospective of her films and installations, including some old pieces redone in bronze to reflect the impact of the 1980's zeitgeist on a 1960's spirit; 1992—appeared on TV comedy series* Mad about You *as herself in the "Yoko Said" episode about documentary filmmaking; 1994—wrote score and book for an off-Broadway musical, "New York Rock," about love and violence in a modern cityscape; 1995—appeared in* The Beatles Anthology, *a TV history of the band, also released on video.* ***Address*** *c/o Starpeace, 1 West 72nd Street, New York, NY 10023, U.S.A.*

Films as Director: 1966: *Film No. 4 (Bottoms)*; *Match*; *Eyeblink* (shorts, all 3 part of *Fluxfilm Program* omnibus). **1967:** *Film No. 4 (Bottoms)* (80-minute version). **1968:** *Film No. 5 (Smile)* (co-d with Lennon); *Instant Karma* (music short); *Two Virgins* (co-d with Lennon). **1969:** *Honeymoon* (co-d); *Film No. 6 (Rape)*; *Self-Portrait* (co-d with Lennon); *Apotheosis* (co-d with Lennon); *Cold Turkey* (music short); *Apotheosis No. 2* (co-d); *Bed-In* (*Bedpeace*; *Give Peace a Chance*) (co-d with Lennon). **1970:** *Up Your Legs Forever* (co-d with Lennon); *Fly*; *Erection* (co-d with Lennon). **1971:** *Clock* (co-d with Lennon); *Imagine* (co-d with Lennon); *Freedom* (short); *The Museum of Modern Art Show*. **1981:** *Walking on Thin Ice* (music video); *Woman* (music video). **1982:** *Goodbye Sadness* (music video).

Films as Actress: 1967: *Satan's Bed* (*Judas City*) (Marshall Smith) (as Ito). **1969:** *The Magic Christian* (McGrath) (cameo). **1970:** *Let It Be* (Lindsay-Hogg—doc). **1971:** *Dynamite Chicken* (Pintoff). **1982:** *Scenes from the Life of Andy Warhol* (Mekas—doc) (as herself). **1988:** *Imagine: John Lennon* (Solt—doc) (as herself). **1993:** *The Misfits: 30 Years of Fluxus* (Movin—doc) (+ co-mus). **1994:** *Jonas in the Desert* (Sempel—doc). **1996:** *The Rolling Stones Rock-and-Roll Circus* (Lindsay-Hogg—doc for TV, produced in 1968).

Scholars have only barely begun to investigate Yoko Ono's filmmaking. She is of course best known as John Lennon's widow. Before the ex-Beatle was assassinated, she was cast as the "dragon lady" who broke up the band. Though mean-spirited biographers such as Albert Goldman continue to give a sleazy edge to her self-confidence and wide-ranging appetites for both art and life, Ono has candidly expressed her most intimate feelings—as visual artist, composer, lyricist, and performer as well as director—throughout her life, before and after her time with her third husband.

Ono's filmmaking career grew out of her work as part of the Fluxus group, an international collective of musicians, poets, visual artists, and proto-performance artists, united by their commitment to overturning ideas about what art is and what an audience does, primarily by blurring boundaries between art and nonart, and between art forms. In 1966 the impresario at the heart of the loose alliance of Dada-inspired artists, George Maciunas, acquired a fast-speed movie camera and asked several artists to contribute to the *Fluxfilm Program*. *Fluxfilm* was an omnibus of short film pieces, including Ono's *Match, Eyeblink,* and *No. 4 (Bottoms)*. Avant-garde film historian Scott MacDonald calls the latter two films the earliest-known examples of "single-shot films," whose slow-motion action consists of one take only: a blinking eye, a bare rear end walking away from the camera.

In 1967 Ono elaborated *Bottoms* into an 80-minute version: she placed a humorously notorious ad in a London paper asking for performers willing to bare their behinds. Ono writes in *Grapefruit* that her aim with the film was both political/historical (to reflect the funny side of the antiauthority, convention-busting 1960s) and formal. MacDonald calls the long *Bottoms* one of the first films with a "serial" structure. Ono tells him that her concept was to fill the screen completely with one moving object at a time, in a series of some 375 individual butts, each filling the frame for some 15 seconds. MacDonald notes the film's theme that human beings, precisely in their culturally proscribed, forbidden, or "ugly" aspects, are equal, united, and actually beautiful. This is an idea dear to Ono's heart across all her art.

In 1968 Ono made the 51-minute-long *Smile* with her new lover, Lennon. It consists of two shots, each of Lennon's face in slow motion. Lennon and Ono also collaborated that year on *Two Virgins.* This film's form parallels both the overlapping sound collage that Lennon's play with multitrack audio tape allows on the accompanying record project of the same title, and the multitracked form of rock-era music recording in general. The film superimposes, or visually "multitracks," images of Ono's and Lennon's faces, and images of nature, for its first part. (The second is a shot of the two lovers kissing.) *Two Virgins* reflects several themes also present in Ono's artwork and performance pieces: the idea that looking at nature with care makes it art, the idea that communication and blending between people is desirable if frightening, and the idea that techniques of looking, whether shaped by the form of a canvas or by a film's shot lengths and editing, can bring out beauty and eroticism in unexpectedly isolated and interconnected details of the everyday world, and everyday people. The effect of many of Ono's filmed ideas is much the same as her installations which ask the viewer to look at the sky or the room through a small eyehole in a canvas, or to reach out her or his hands through two holes in a canvas to greet new people. The art serves as the conduit toward an oddening, a freshening up, of the (only seemingly) mundane details of the natural, and the social.

In 1969 Ono and Lennon filmed *Bed-In,* a fairly conventional documentary of their second extended stay in bed, in touch with the media, for peace, in Montreal. Ono's film work as a whole—because it follows the Fluxus tradition of close focus upon one real-world object for extended periods, with an eye toward politics and toward the irritation/activation of the viewer—straddles the line between documentary and avant-garde, form-driven film. Also in 1969 Ono made the evil candid-camera film, *Rape,* wherein we watch a film crew chase a German-speaking girl around London for 77 minutes while she reacts to their unwanted intrusion. Again the themes of communication and its perils cross wires in Ono's work with the erotic politics of the gaze, here and in *Fly,* a 31-minute-long exploration of a female nude body—by the camera and also by, first, one and then several chloroformed-to-be-docile flies. At the end the camera "flies" out the window, the buried pun at once reinforcing and throwing up the parallel between the prying camera and the insects. Ono is similarly at once critiquing and reenergizing the typical cinematic form that takes the female form as its voyeuristic object. *Up Your Legs Forever* features such an unevenly unsettling pun only in its title. It is a serially structured film, this time about (some famous people's) thighs, up which the camera pans in what is edited to seem a continuum. Its levels of formal inventiveness and political shock value register lower than Ono's earlier efforts. *Apotheosis* is a seemingly single-shot film (actually edited once, unobtrusively) with a camera, mounted on a hot-air balloon, rising up past Ono's and Lennon's bodies, into the clouds, and finally above them into the sunlight.

Lennon and Ono's play with the sound/image relationship and with puns built on discrepancies between words and images, continued with their next films. *Erection* uses time-lapse photography to explore the raising of—not the Lennon penis that was the subject of *Self-Portrait,* but—a skyscraper. *Imagine* is silent except for an exchange of greetings at the start.

Ono's *The Museum of Modern Art Show* details her "show which didn't exist" at the New York museum; sidewalk sign-bearers induce passersby to inquire for an installation that existed only in Ono's mind and advertising. In this stunt, the Fluxus-inspired Ono, who once offered as an art object a list of her own artworks' prices, devises objects of pure exchange and no-use value—inviting passersby to try to pay to see art so purely conceptual that its "catalogue" is all of it that exists. The gall and freedom to redefine the world, of course, is the "real" use value of such art—whose price turns out to be the viewers' investment of time and perhaps willingness to be shocked or humiliated by the unexpected directions in which Ono will take them.

Ono made no new films or art projects between 1972-79 (though she and Lennon pulled off a form of concept art for billionaires in 1979 by running an obscurely motivated "love letter," preaching peace and brotherhood to their fans, in London, New York, and Tokyo newspapers). In the 1980s she directed several music videos for her own and the late Lennon's songs; they had collaborated on film shorts for several songs in their filmmaking period. MacDonald notes that the 1989 retrospective of her films and art at Manhattan's Whitney Museum was poised to lead to a redistribution of her films in the nineties. The prolific and yet evasive Ono is poised to receive the full measure of attention that it seems not only her unusual celebrity but her gender and race have prevented her filmmaking, and all her distinctive, affecting, and innovative art, from receiving thus far.—SUSAN KNOBLOCH

Ottinger, Ulrike

German director

Born *Konstanz, Germany, 6 June 1942.* ***Education*** *Attended Munich Academy of Arts, 1959-61.* ***Career*** *1962-68—worked independently as a painter, lived in Paris, learning engraving and photography; 1966—wrote first screenplay,* The Mongolian Double Drawer, *conceived as part animation and part live action; during this period also wrote the initial draft of* Laocoon and Sons; *1969—returned to Germany, where she founded and ran a gallery, "Galerie-Press," and opened a film club in Konstanz, "Visuell," which operated until 1972; 1985—directed a theater play in Stuttgart.* ***Awards*** *German Film Critics Award, for* China—The Arts—The People, *1985; HDF Short Film Prize, for* Usinimage, *1987; Federal German Film Gold Ribbon for Artistic Realization, for* Johanna d'Arc of Mongolia, *1988.* ***Address*** *Ulrike Ottinger Filmproduktion, Hasenheide 92, D-10967 Berlin, Germany.*

Films as Director: **1972-74:** *Laokoon und Söhne* (*Laocoon and Sons*) (co-d with Blumenschein). **1973:** *Vostell—Berlin-fieber* (*Berlin Fever—Wolf Vostell*). **1975:** *Die Betörung der blauen Matrosen* (*The Enchantment of the Blue Sailors*; *The Bewitchment of the Drunken Sailors*) (co-d with Blumenschein). **1977:** *Madame X—eine absolute Herrscherin* (*Madame X—An Absolute Ruler*). **1979:** *Bildnis Einer Trinkerin—Aller jamais retour* (*Ticket of No Return*) (+ sc, ph). **1981:** *Freak Orlando* (+ sc, ph, sets). **1984:** *Dorian Gray in spiegel der Boulevardprsse* (*The Image of Dorian Gray in the Yellow Press*) (+ sc, ph, sets). **1985:** *China—die Künste—der Alltag* (*China—The Arts—The People*) (doc) (+ ph). **1986:** *Sieben Frauen—Sieben Sünden* (*Seven Women—Seven Sins*) (+ sc, ph). **1986-87:** *Superbia—Der Stolz* (*Superbia—L'orgueil*; *Superbia—Pride*). **1987:** *Usinimage.* **1988:** *Johanna d'Arc of Mongolia* (+ pr, sc, ph, ed, sets). **1990:** *Countdown* (doc) (+ ph, sc). **1992:** *Taiga* (doc) (+ pr, sc, ph). **1997:** *Exil Shanghai* (doc) (+ pr, sc, ph).

Other Film: **1995:** *The Night of the Filmmakers* (Reitz—doc) (appearance).

Ulrike Ottinger emerged from a tradition of the avant-garde visual arts as a painter, lithographer, and photographer. This differentiates her from other West German women filmmakers who came to prominence in the mid-to-late 1970s, who were more traditional left-wing feminists. Ottinger is also, and has always been, openly lesbian. Both of these factors have made her somewhat marginal in the feminist community, though certainly no less interesting, and often, a great deal more fun than her contemporaries. She shares few of the thematic concerns of the New German Cinema, and has often been compared with Werner Schroeter, because of her proclivity for stylization and exaggeration, artifice, and parody. When once asked where she positioned herself in relation to the then-burgeoning New German Cinema, she exclaimed, "I wouldn't know what I have in common with [them]."

Her work has polarized critics. The feminist journal *Frauen und film* criticized her for her retrograde, degenerate aesthetic agenda, whereas others have called her films "a celebration of Lesbian punk anti-realism."

Unlike many of her more earnest contemporaries, Ottinger's films are playful, with a strong element of fantasy. The director explains: "The tragic thing is that reality and fantasy are always separated: fantasy here, reality there. This separation, like the separation of form and content of a work of art is the result of the invasion of certain areas by scientific thinking. Wishful dreaming and fantasy are the strongest forces in people's lives, the source of their actions. We have to stop rendering reality the way we see it, our surface perceptions of it. We have to learn how to deal with our wishes and our dreams as an integral part of ourselves."

Ottinger utilizes unusual juxtapositions of sound and image, highly saturated colors, nonnaturalistic performance styles, sometimes outrageous costume and set design, and disjunctive narrative, structures, to create a truly unique oeuvre. Those who claim her for feminism say she "radically subverts the terms in which patriarchal cinema has monopolized visual pleasure on behalf of the male gaze."

Ottinger's first feature film was *Madame X—An Absolute Ruler,* made in 1977. Seven women (including Yvonne Rainer) abandon their traditional roles to join the imperious, beautiful, lesbian pirate, the notorious Madame X, in a quest for love, adventure, and riches. The women have difficulty shedding their socialized roles, and under Madame X's ruthless domination, are eventually killed. Madame X searches for a new crew in her next port of call, and is rejoined by the same cast of characters—death has brought about renewal and change.

Highly stylized costume and set design (Madame X's severed hand is replaced by a decorative spike) and a series of bizarre performances are coupled with the imagery of sadism—chains and leather—making for a perverse, sexually charged, and ritualized atmosphere.

The director's next work was *Ticket of No Return,* once again starring Ottinger's sometime collaborator, and icon of the Berlin underground scene, Tabea Blumenschein (who also played Madame X). Blumenschein is introduced in the film as "a woman of antique grace and Raphaelic charm, a woman created like no other to be Medea, Madonna, Beatrice, Iphigenia, Aspasia"—in short, the classical, ideal Woman. Contrary to this euphoric introduction, "She" (known by no other name) buys a one-way ticket to Berlin with the specific project of drinking herself to death. The woman befriends a bag lady (Lutze—a well-known figure on the Berlin scene), and they begin a tour of Berlin that would be unlikely for any travel guide, visiting a variety of locations, from underground clubs (where punk diva Nina Hagen graces them with a song), to the Banhof Zoo, to a traditional Bavarian-style beer hall. Throughout, the woman—who becomes increasingly disoriented as she fulfills her alcoholic program, wears a series of bizarre, but visually enticing costumes that serve to mock haute couture, and raise the issue of woman as an object to be looked at. The woman remains silent throughout the film, miming gestures in a ritualized fashion, heightening the film's sense of dissociation with reality, as well as encouraging associations with the woman's lack of voice in the patriarchy. Ottinger says: "In my opinion film should not be based on dialogue. It makes the film lack a certain sensuality which I find very important. Think of the beginnings of film, the expressionist silents. They spoke almost exclusively in images. The relation of image to objects is quite different than that of words to objects. This is not to say that I consider words or sound to be superfluous. To the contrary, I am making very conscious use of sound. I am working with twelve tracks to achieve the kind of sound rhythm I want. But again, this sound rhythm does not rely on language alone but equally as much on music and noises, also on fragment of various things."

Ottinger has always claimed to be an ethnographer, and indeed, the tour of the underbelly of Berlin speaks to this sensibility. But it is combined at the same time with Ottinger's typical stylization, providing an interesting aesthetic tension.

The filmmaker next made *Freak Orlando,* starring art cinema icon Delphine Seyrig. The film is a conflation of Tod Browning's 1932 classic, *Freaks,* with Virginia Woolf's meditation on gender, *Orlando.* It charts the time-travels of a mythic, androgynous figure, who challenges the patriarchy in various historical epochs. Ottinger says the film is "a history of freaks from the Middle Ages until now and analyzes power structures like the Inquisition and psychiatric power." *The Image of Dorian Gray in the Yellow Press* was Ottinger's next venture into filmmaking, and is a retelling of Fritz Lang's *Dr. Mabuse* films with, of course, a female cast. The director questions the objectivity of the press and stages a trial that humorously challenges the veracity of the fifth estate.

Ottinger shifted into a more documentary mode with *China—The Arts—The People,* a 4½ hour exploration of city life in China, as well as an investigation of the minorities inhabiting the outer perimeters of the country. In the film, Ottinger examines various art forms, both ancient and modern.

The director's next significant work was *Johanna d'Arc of Mongolia,* which again starred Delphine Seyrig, and presents a juxtaposition of the ancient and modern world, of Mongolia tribal culture and European mores, and of older and younger women. The film again combines ethnographic elements—as the assembled cast of women wander through Mongolia—with female-based rituals. Two of Ottinger's most recent films have been documentaries. *Countdown* deals with the fall of the Berlin wall, while in *Taiga* (a 501-minute epic), the director returns to Mongolia, detailing the nomadic tribes and their shamanic rites.—CAROLE ZUCKER

Palcy, Euzhan

French West Indian director, writer, and producer

Born *In the French overseas department of Martinique, 1957.* ***Education*** *Studied French literature at the Sorbonne in Paris, cinema at the Rue Lumière School.* ***Career*** *1974—wrote, directed, and acted in first locally produced film for Martinique television station; moved to Paris to study literature and film; 1983—wrote and directed internationally recognized feature,* Sugar Cane Alley; *1989—co-wrote and directed* A Dry White Season, *the first Hollywood studio release directed by a black woman.* ***Awards*** *Silver Lion, Venice Film Festival, and César for Best First Film, for* Sugar Cane Alley, *1983; Orson Welles Prize for Special Cinematic Achievement, for* A Dry White Season, *1989; Golden Keops, Ouagadougou Film Festival, Golden Senghor for Best Director, Special Jury Prize, Brussels Film Festival, Prix de la Jeunesse, Milan Film Festival, and Ban Zil Kreol Award, Montreal Film Festival, for* Simeon, *1993.* ***Agent*** *Jeff Field, William Morris Agency, 151 El Camino Drive, Beverly Hills, CA 90212, U.S.A.* ***Address*** *Saligna and So On, 2435 21st Street, Santa Monica, CA 90405, U.S.A.*

Films as Director and Writer: 1974: *La messagère* (*The Messenger*) (doc—for TV). **1982:** *L'atelier du diable* (*The Devil's Workshop*) (doc—for TV). **1983:** *La Rue cases nègres* (*Sugar Cane Alley*; *Black Shack Alley*). **1989:** *A Dry White Season.* **1990:** *Hassane* (doc—for TV). **1992:** *Simeon* (+ pr). **1994:** *Aimé Césaire: A Voice for History* (doc—for TV). **1997:** *Ruby Bridges Story* (for TV) (+ pr). **1998:** *Wings against the Wind* (co-sc, + pr).

"For all the Black Shack Alleys of the world"—with these words, the opening dedication of her first feature, *La Rue cases nègres* (*Sugar Cane Alley*), Euzhan Palcy arrived on the scene of international filmmaking. The film not only garnered a César from the French Film Academy, and a Silver Lion from the Venice Film Festival, it also demonstrated that there was an audience for films with central black characters. The film proved to be remarkably successful in France; in Martinique, the setting of the story and Palcy's first home, *Sugar Cane Alley* outgrossed the Hollywood blockbuster of the year, *E.T.* The success of Palcy's initial feature led to her

Euzhan Palcy on the set of ***A Dry White Season.***

involvement in another landmark film, *A Dry White Season,* one of the few American films to depict the effects of South African apartheid, and, with Palcy at the helm, the first Hollywood production directed by a woman of color.

Growing up in Martinique, a French colony without local film or theater production—but swamped by an incessant flow of American media—Palcy became determined to be a filmmaker who created real images of her people. As a teenager, her success as a poet and songwriter led to her being asked to do a weekly poetry program on local television. While at the television station, Palcy—just 17 years old—wrote, directed, and performed in a 52-minute film entitled *The Messenger.* The drama, which centered on the relationship between a girl and her grandmother, and which explored the lives of workers on a banana plantation, was the first West Indian production mounted in Martinique.

Recognizing that to pursue a career as a filmmaker she would have to leave Martinique, Palcy moved to Paris in 1974. She went to film school, studied French literature at the highly competitive Sorbonne, worked as a film editor, and, for the first time, exchanged views with young African filmmakers. During this time she continued to revise her screenplay for *Sugar Cane Alley.* As she became acquainted with members of the French film community, Palcy received encouragement from New Wave filmmaker François Truffaut and his collaborator Suzanne Shiffman. Her work as an apprentice paid off. In 1982 the French government provided partial funding for the film. To secure funding from French television, one of the film's co-producers, Palcy wrote and directed a short entitled *The Devil's Workshop,* which traced an outline of the story that would be told in Palcy's first feature.

Palcy seized upon the subject for her first full-length film when as a girl she read *La Rue cases nègres,* a novel by Martinique author Josef Zobel. As she has explained, reading the novel was an "event," for it was the first time in her life she had encountered work by a black writer, moreover, a black writer from her own country. Palcy's own experience growing up in Martinique, and her years of living with the story resulted in a production that was clearly the work of a filmmaker who, in the words of Stanley Kauffmann, "understands absolutely everything about the lives she is touching." After watching this story of a poor black boy's coming of age, who survives the effects of the French colonial system because of his grandmother's courage and the wisdom of Mr. M, an aged storyteller who introduces him to African and Afro-Caribbean traditions, critics such as Stuart Klawans rightly argue that "few films have conveyed so vividly the thrill of intellectual awakening."

Following the international success of *Sugar Cane Alley,* and returning to a subject that had been at the heart of another novel central to her growing up, *Cry, the Beloved Country,* Palcy worked to secure financing for a film that would, as Nina Easton explains, reveal "the horrors of apartheid through the eyes of a young black girl." Eventually recognizing that it was almost impossible to secure funding for a film without a central white character, Palcy became part of a project that took as its source André Brink's novel, *A Dry White Season.* Originally a Warner Bros. property and a David Puttnam production, the film, with a screenplay by Colin Welland and Euzhan Palcy was, in the end, distributed by MGM/UA and produced by Paula Weinstein, who, like her mother, Hannah Weinstein, was an experienced Hollywood executive and a champion of progressive filmmaking.

A Dry White Season, which follows a white South African schoolteacher as he is drawn into the antiapartheid movement, shows the filmmaker's efforts to bring the experience of black

South Africans to the foreground—the film eliminates the novel's account of an affair between the schoolteacher (played by Donald Sutherland) and a proactive journalist (played by Susan Sarandon), and instead provides us with more detailed characterizations of the black South Africans involved. When the film was released, many reviewers argued that it was an emotionally potent film, and that it demonstrated—in contrast to other young directors whose second features represented a sellout—that Euzhan Palcy had remained true to her vision as a filmmaker. Other critics felt Palcy had not gone far enough to counter the commercial elements of the film.

Even Palcy's critics, however, recognize her remarkable ability to direct actors. For her performance in *Sugar Cane Alley,* veteran actress Darling Legitimus was named Best Actress at the Venice Film Festival, and in reviewing that film, Andrew Sarris argued that it was impossible to "overpraise the casting and acting which jumps out of the screen with an expressive vitality." Commenting on her direction of actors in *A Dry White Season,* Kauffmann underscores the fact that Palcy, who "deals empathetically with her cast . . . works with economy and flair—[a] sense of movement as gesture."

In one of her most recent productions, *Simeon,* Palcy returned to a Caribbean setting, working to make, as she has always intended, films with real images of her people. While her work has been critiqued for individualizing narratives that explore social conditions, taken together, Euzhan Palcy's films represent a thoughtful and often brilliant response to the conventions of First World Cinema.—CYNTHIA BARON

Parker, Claire

American director and animator

***Born** Boston, Massachusetts, 31 August 1906. **Family** Married the director and animator Alexander Alexeieff, 1941 (died 1982). **Career** 1931—with Alexander Alexeieff co-invented pinboard animation; 1933—co-creator of* Night on Bald Mountain, *a critical success, but commercially unmarketable; 1935-39—with Alexeieff and other collaborators (Georges Violet, Alexeieff's wife Alexandra Grinevsky, and others) collaborated on some 25 short advertising films that were shown in movie theaters, some with original musical scores by major composers such as Poulenc, Auric, and Milhaud; 1935-36—in Alexeieff's absence, directed documentary film on Rubens and one advertising film (*Étude sur l'harmonie des lignes*) on her own; 1940—emigrated to United States with Alexeieff and his family when Nazis invaded France; 1941—married Alexeieff soon after his divorce from Grinevsky, settled in White Plains, New York; 1943—created* En Passant, *second pinboard animation production, for the newly formed National Film Board of Canada; 1947—returned to Paris; 1952-64—created more advertising films with Alexeieff, using many different techniques, including "totalization" with compound pendulums; 1957—co-designed logo used on films of French distribution company Cocinor; 1962—co-produced pinboard prologue to Orson Welles's* The Trial; *1962-79—worked with Alexeieff on three more pinboard films,* The Nose, Pictures at an Exhibition, *and* Three Moods, *and assisted him with pinboard illustrations for several books (Dostoyevsky's* The

Gambler *and* Notes from Underground *and Pasternak's* Doctor Zhivago*).* ***Died 3 October 1981.***

Films as Director: 1935: *Étude sur l'harmonie des lignes* (advertising film). **1936:** *Rubens* (art film).

Pinboard Animation Films as Co-Director and Co-Animator with Alexander Alexeieff: 1933: *Une Nuit sur le Mont Chauve* (*Night on Bald Mountain*). **1943:** *En Passant.* **1962:** Prologue to *Le Procès* (*The Trial*) (Welles). **1963:** *Le Nez* (*The Nose*). **1972:** *Tableaux d'une exposition* (*Pictures at an Exhibition*). **1980:** *Trois Thèmes* (*Three Moods*).

Films as Co-Animator with Alexander Alexeieff and Others: 1935: *La Belle au bois dormant* (*Sleeping Beauty*) (puppet film). **1936-39:** *Parade des chapeaux*; *Le Trône de France*; *Grands Feux*; *La Crème Simon*; *Les Vêtements Sigrand*; *Huilor*; *L'eau d'Evian*; *Les Fonderies Martin*; *Balatrum*; *Les Oranges de Jaffa* (3 films); *Les Cigarettes Davros*; *Gulf Stream*; *Les Gaines Roussel*; *Cenpa*; *Le Gaz* (unfinished). **1951-66:** *Fumées* (first use of compound pendulum); *Masques*; *Nocturne*; *Pure beauté*; *Rîmes*; *Le Buisson ardent*; *La Sève de la terre*; *Quatre Temps*; *Bain d'X* (Bendix); *Constance*; *Anonyme*; *Osram* (for TV); *Cent pour cent*; Cocinor logo; *Automation*; *La Dauphine Java*; *Divertissement*; *L'eau.*

Claire Parker's unique and memorable place in the history of independent, non-cartoon animation is permanently and inextricably linked to that of her partner/husband Alexander Alexeieff. For some 50 years Alexeieff and Parker worked together, first on the invention of the world's first pinboard (1932); then on their celebrated *Night on Bald Mountain* (1933) and later pinboard films; between times, on a succession of innovative advertising films; and for many decades as promoters of animation as a fine art. Sometimes they introduced themselves as the artist and the animator, but even their close friends have found it impossible to know exactly who did what.

Parker always maintained that Alosha (his Russian nickname) was the genius, but without her many talents and steadfast dedication, his genius would certainly not have been expressed in motion-picture animation. Although her role was secondary and supportive, there is no indication that throughout their long relationship she aspired to anything more.

On only two occasions, early in her career, did she assume full filmmaking responsibilities: in 1936 when she shot a color art film on the Rubens exhibition at the Orangerie in Paris, and later during Alexeieff's absence when she directed a color advertising film of her own. For the remainder of her career in film, Parker remained Alexeieff's "constant collaborator."

When Parker and Alexeieff met in Paris in the late 1920s, she was a young American studying painting and drawing abroad, and he was a young Russian emigré already considered a master illustrator of fine books. She asked him for lessons in engraving copper, wood, and stone, but soon they were working together on a device he had begun working on—a device to make "animated engravings" (*gravures animées*), engravings that could move. The term was quickly abandoned for "pinboard" animation, later changed to "pinscreen" (a more accurate translation of the French *l'écran d'épingles*).

Their first "apparatus for producing images" was patented in Europe and the United States in Claire Parker's name alone, perhaps because she, with help from her wealthy Boston family, had financed the invention, along with the production of their first film. Both of them felt sure that marketable uses of the pinboard would more than repay Parker's investment and might also provide opportunities for work in the highly paid film industry.

Their first film, *Night on Bald Mountain,* won wide acclaim in European art circles, and is still considered one of the most important animation films ever made. Parker's mathematical and musical talents helped her synchronize Alexeieff's images to a phonograph recording of Moussorgsky's symphonic music "with the precision of a twenty-fourth of a second." It could not have been easy, with only the most primitive equipment at hand, just a few years after the introduction of sound-on-film.

Program notes of the London Film Society's 1935 showing incorrectly gave Parker first billing ("Engravings by C. Parker and Alexeieff"), but dozens of subsequent reviews and listings failed to even mention her name. To be accurate and fair, it should be made clear that the film's witches, goblins, and other creatures of the night, disappearing and reappearing, come straight from Russian folklore and from Alexeieff's boundless imagination. But the careful filming of these images, the sound analysis, and synchronization were Parker's self-taught achievements—along with her operation of the reverse side of the pinboard.

But no commercial use was found for a short film, however magical, that had taken 18 months to complete. To earn enough money to support himself and his wife and daughter, Alexeieff began making advertising films, the first in color to be shown publicly in France. Here Claire Parker felt she made her major contribution, since she (a painter) worked more comfortably in color than he (a graphic artist). In the United States during World War II, Parker became Mrs. Alexeieff following his divorce from his first wife. On their return to France in 1947, she took on new roles as housekeeper, hostess, stepmother to his daughter Svetlana (and later step-grandmother to her four children—one of whom—Alexandre Rockwell—later became a filmmaker himself).

Having no children of their own, which had been part of their marriage agreement, Claire and Alosha welcomed into their animation family a young Canadian animator, Jacques Drouin, who had mastered the pinscreen technique and made a magical film called *Mindscape*. This may have spurred them on to even more intricate techniques in their own pinscreen films, using multiple in-camera loops, or a small pinscreen revolving in front of a larger one, techniques requiring even more patience and precision on Parker's part. For her the reward seemed to be that her hard work allowed her to become what she called the "spellbound spectator" of a true artist's visions and visual memories.—CECILE STARR

Parmar, Pratibha

British director

Born *In 1955 to Indian parents in Kenya; family immigrated to England in 1967.* ***Education*** *Postgraduate studies at the Centre for Contemporary Cultural Studies at the University of Birmingham.* ***Awards*** *Audience award for Best Short Documentary, San Francisco Festival, for* Khush, *1991; Best Historical Documentary, National Black Programming Consortium, for* A Place of Rage, *1991; Frameline Award, 1993.* ***Address*** *c/o 78 Fonthill Road, Finsbury Park, London N4 3HT, England.*

Films as Director: **1986:** *Emergence* (short for TV). **1987:** *A Plague on You* (for TV). **1988:** *Sari Red* (short); *ReFraming AIDs* (doc). **1989:** *Memory Pictures* (doc). **1990:** *Flesh and Paper* (doc, short for TV). **1991:** *Khush* (doc, short for TV) (+ pr); *A Place of Rage* (doc for TV). **1992:** *Double the Trouble, Twice the Fun* (doc, short for TV). **1993:** *Warrior Marks* (doc for TV) (+ pr). **1994:** *The Colour of Britain* (doc). **1996:** *Jodie: An Icon* (short). **1997:** *Memsahib Rita* (short).

Pratibha Parmar's films reflect her experiences as a woman of the Asian and African diaspora, as a lesbian, and as a political and cultural activist. She attributes her desire to be a filmmaker to the anger and rage kindled by her first playground encounter with "Paki-bashing" schoolmates. Her resistance to being defined as a "marginal" person, as someone who can be pigeonholed according to race, gender, or sexual orientation, is a constant theme in her work.

Parmar was one of the founding members of the first black lesbian group in Britain in 1984 and discovered within that group a sense of community based on shared experiences and cultural backgrounds. She came to filmmaking from a background of activism rather than from film or art school. In her first experimental video, *Emergence,* Parmar uses interviews, poetry, and performance art, together with the juxtaposition of evocative images, to present issues of racial identity confronting women of the diaspora. The violence directed against these women is the subject of *Sari Red,* a short film commemorating Kalbinder Kaur Hayre who died when she and two other Asian women were run down by white racists. This film features the "look back," a confrontational technique used first on a poster created by the publishing house Black Women Talk, of which Parmar was also a founding member. The poster was one in a series called "In Our Own Image," and pictures a young South Asian woman practicing self-defense and confronting the viewer with the warning: "If anyone calls me a Paki, I'll bash their heads in." This "look-back" is a device used by Parmar in her films to redirect a gaze usually used as a means of domination back upon the viewer. In *Sari Red,* this gaze is found in the eyes of the mourners, of the three dolls symbolizing the victims of the racist attack, and in the eyes woven into the red sari featured in the film.

Parmar's choice of themes for her work has much to do with current issues, and reflects her own interest in activism. The British government's homophobic AIDS-awareness campaign of the 1980s inspired *A Plague on You,* produced by the Lesbian and Gay Media Group for British television, and *ReFraming AIDS.* The latter film brought Parmar criticism from fellow black lesbians because it included interviews with black and white gay men. *ReFraming AIDS* saw Parmar venture outside the black lesbian "community," and explore a broader territory.

This exploration continued in Parmar's next three works, *Memory Pictures, Flesh and Paper,* and *Khush,* which explore the attributes, histories, and eroticisms of individual lesbian and gay Asians. *Khush,* made for Channel 4's gay and lesbian series *Out on Tuesday,* won an award for Best Documentary Short at the San Francisco Festival in 1991, and has been shown at many lesbian and gay film festivals. In *Khush,* which is an Urdu word meaning "ecstatic pleasure," Parmar uses film clips, fantasy sequences, an erotic dance performance, and statements from western South Asian lesbians and gays to present the complexities of lesbian and gay identities. This interest in presenting the rich diversities that exist among gays and lesbians is further expressed in *Double the Trouble, Twice the Fun,* which features the gay Indian writer Firdaus Kanga, who also happens to be disabled.

A Place of Rage explores the role of women in the American civil rights movement, a study that Parmar undertook to further her understanding of racist violence and oppression. The documentary features interviews with Angela Davis, June Jordan, and writer Alice Walker, and is frequently screened at lesbian and gay film festivals. A collaboration with Walker on the documentary *Warrior Marks* followed in 1993. The film was inspired by Walker's book, *Possessing the Secret of Joy,* and treats the subject of female genital mutilation. Filming was done for *Warrior Marks* in Africa, Britain, and the United States and features interviews with women who have themselves endured this procedure, as well as those who perform it. In the book

Warrior Marks: Female Genital Mutilation and the Sexual Blinding of Women, written by Walker and Parmar, which chronicles the making of the film, Parmar discusses the problems in making a documentary on such a complex issue, one which involves race, culture, and the rights of women and young girls. In *Warrior Marks,* as in *Sari Red, Flesh and Paper, A Place of Rage,* and *Khush,* dance is used as an enhancement of the theme, in this case expressing joy of sexuality as well as the sorrow of its loss.

Parmar must have found the making of *The Colour of Britain* very satisfying, as it features the work of South Asian artists who are having an impact on British culture. The documentary includes interviews with sculptor Anish Kapoor, choreographer Shobana Jeyasingh, and theater director Jatinder Verma, as well as examples of their work. Parmar has ventured into a new area of exploration with the short drama *Memsahib Rita,* made for BBC Television, a thriller in which questions of mixed race play a part.—JEAN EDMUNDS

Pascal, Christine

French director, writer, and actress

Born *Lyons, France, 29 November 1953.* ***Family*** *Married producer-writer Robert Boner.* ***Career*** *1973—made her film debut as an actress in* Black Thursday; *1974—appeared in her first feature directed by Bertrand Tavernier,* The Clockmaker; *1979—directed her first feature,* Felicité. ***Awards*** *Best Script, Montreal Film Festival, and Louis Delluc Prize for Directing, for* The Little Prince Said, *1992.* ***Died*** *Suicide, outside Paris, 30 August 1996.*

Films as Director and Writer/Co-Writer: 1979: *Felicité* (+ ro). **1984:** *La Garce* (*The Bitch*). **1988:** *Zanzibar.* **1992:** *Le Petit prince à dit* (*The Little Prince Said*). **1995:** *Adultere (mode d'emploi)* (*Adultery [A User's Manual]*).

Other Films: 1973: *Les Guichets du Louvre* (*Black Thursday*) (Mitrani) (ro). **1974:** *L'Horloger de Saint-Paul* (*The Clockmaker*) (Tavernier) (ro as Liliane Terrini). **1975:** *Que la fête commence. . .* (*Let Joy Reign Supreme. . .*) (Tavernier) (ro as Emilie). **1976:** *Le Juge et l'assassin* (*The Judge and the Assassin*) (Tavernier) (ro); *La Meilleure façon de marcher* (*The Best Way*) (C. Miller) (ro as Chantal). **1977:** *Les Indiens sont encore loin* (*The Indians Are Still Far Away*) (Moraz) (ro); *Des enfants gâtés* (*Spoiled Children*) (Tavernier) (ro) (+ co-sc). **1979:** *Panny z Wilka* (*The Girls from Wilko*) (Wajda) (ro as Tunia). **1980:** *Pepi, Luci, Bom y otras chicas de montón* (Almodóvar) (ro); *Au bon beurre* (Molinaro) (ro). **1983:** *Coup de foudre* (*Entre nous; Between Us; At First Sight*) (Kurys) (ro as Sarah); *Entre tinieblas* (*Into the Dark; The Sisters of Darkness*) (Almodóvar) (ro). **1984:** *Train d'enfer* (Hanin) (ro as Isabelle). **1985:** *Elsa, Elsa* (Haudepin) (title role); *Private Show* (Kayko) (pr); *Signé Charlotte* (*Sincerely Charlotte; Signed Charlotte*) (Huppert) (ro as Christine). **1986:** *'Round Midnight* (*Autour de minuit*) (Tavernier) (ro as Sylvie). **1987:** *Le Grand chemin* (*The Grand Highway*) (Hubert) (ro as Claire). **1988:** *La Couleur du vent* (Granier-Deferre) (ro); *La Travestie* (Boisset) (ro as Christine). **1989:** *Promis. . .Jure!* (Monnet) (ro). **1990:** *The Island* (Leitao) (ro as Linda Walsh). **1991:** *Rien que des mensonges* (*Nothing but Lies*) (Muret) (ro as Lise); *La Femme de l'amant* (Frank) (ro as Ludmilla). **1994:** *Le Sourire* (*The Smile*) (C. Miller and Othenin-Girard) (ro); *Regarde les hommes tomber* (*See How They Fall*) (Audiard) (ro as Sandrine); *Les Patriotes* (*The Patriots*) (Rochant) (ro as Laurence).

From the mid-1970s through the early 1990s, Christine Pascal had starring or supporting roles as girlfriends and mothers, students and schoolteachers in more than two dozen European-made features. While never blossoming into a major international star, she lent charm and depth to films directed by Claude Miller, Pedro Almodóvar, Andrzej Wajda, Diane Kurys, and, most especially, Bertrand Tavernier. She appeared in a half-dozen Tavernier films and, most significantly, co-scripted (as well as starred in) one, *Spoiled Children*. This blatantly autobiographical film casts Michel Piccoli as a famous filmmaker/writer named Bernardi who rents an apartment in a high-rise in order to work on a new script. The real world intrudes as he becomes involved in a landlord-tenant dispute and commences an affair with a neighbor (played by Pascal), a sensitive young woman who is half his age.

The six features Pascal directed (all of which she either scripted or co-scripted) also are heavily autobiographical. Collectively, they are disturbing, revealing, achingly personal psychological portraits. In them, Pascal elicits a fascination with male and female sexuality and the jumble of feelings people experience over sexual issues. The films are punctuated by raw emotion, and jarring sequences illustrating erotic sexual encounters with strangers. All of her characters—and especially her psychologically unhinged heroines—experience deep emotional turmoil, attempt to exorcise childhood demons, are haunted by death, act out sexually, or become consumed by sexual fantasies.

Pascal directed her first feature, *Felicité,* when she was 25 years old. It is her lone directorial effort in which she stars, and she casts herself in the title role: a young woman who is spending an evening with her lover, who meets a female friend whom he invites to join them. Felicité then is overcome by jealousy. She returns home by herself, at which point she begins drinking nonstop. Via hallucinations, she recalls her childhood and her domineering mother, and she plays out sexual fantasies (including some anonymous copulation and a striptease in a cheap club).

In *The Bitch,* Pascal's heroine is a young woman who jumps between her gangster boyfriend and a policeman. In *Zanzibar,* she is a drug-addicted actress. In *The Little Prince Said,* she is an emotionally unstrung actress. In *Adultery (A User's Manual),* she is a married, career-driven architect who plays extramarital sexual games with a friend. Pascal may only have produced *Private Show,* a film directed by Sixto Kayko, but its heroine—a young woman who dances in a private sex club in order to alleviate the pain of her child's death—is linked to those in her own films.

Pascal's two most mature films are her last. *The Little Prince Said* is a sincere and stirring drama about a ten-year-old girl who is diagnosed with a lethal brain tumor. While the child can accept her impending demise, the same cannot be said for her divorced parents: the actress, and a doctor who is used to being in command of his life. *Adultery (A User's Manual)* is a pungent exploration of the professional aspirations and personal/sexual/romantic needs of contemporary men and women. It is the story of married architects who work as a team and are awaiting word if they have won a major competition. As they do so, both characters act out their trepidation via sexual promiscuity.

Meanwhile, *Zanzibar* is effective as an exploration of the frenzied world of independent filmmaking—a world Pascal knew all-too-well—in a scenario that focuses on three characters: a producer who is attempting to secure financing for a project even though there is no script; the actress; and a tyrannical director. *Zanzibar* works as a reality test for anyone who might romanticize the "artistic" process of filmmaking.

In the program guide of the 1995 Toronto Film Festival, Kay Armatage ended her description of *Adultery (A User's Manual)* by noting that, "If there is a new breed of French cinema that combines Godard's street-smarts, Beineix's sexiness, post-modern cultural knowledge and an independent's immediacy, Christine Pascal is one director to watch." Tragically, Pascal was unable to exorcise her demons artistically or otherwise—and *Adultery (A User's*

Manual) was to be her final film. A year after its release, she committed suicide, at age 42, as reported in *Variety,* by "throwing herself out the window of a clinic on the outskirts of Paris where she had apparently been battling depression."—ROB EDELMAN

Peng Xiaolian

Chinese director

Born *Shanghai, 26 June 1953.* ***Education*** *Attended Beijing Film Academy, 1978-82; visiting scholar at New York University, 1989-90.* ***Career*** *1969-78—sent to the countryside during the Cultural Revolution; 1976-78—actress in the Yi Chun County Opera Group; 1979—while in school directed her first television film,* Good-bye Yesterday, *then became assistant director for* Camel Xiang Zi; *1982—upon graduation was appointed director at the Shanghai Film Studio; 1982-85—co-director and assistant director on four features; 1986—assigned to direct her first feature, a children's film,* Me and My Classmates; *1989—her second feature,* Women's Story, *is temporarily banned in April by the Film Bureau; on 14 June her third feature,* Random Thoughts, *is canceled halfway through production.* ***Awards*** *Bronze Medal, Chinese Television Competition, for* Good-bye Yesterday, *1979; Best Film Script, Shanghai Young People's Cultural Competition, for* Come Back in the Summertime, *1985; Golden Rooster Award, Best Children's Film, and Best Film and Best Director, Chinese Children's Film Competition, for* Me and My Classmates, *1986; People's Choice Award, Hawaii International Film Festival, and Special Jury Prize, Créteil International Women's Film Festival, for* Women's Story, *1987.* ***Address*** *c/o International Film Circuit, Post Office Box 1151, Old Chelsea Station, New York, NY 10011, U.S.A.*

Films as Director: 1979: *Good-bye Yesterday* (for TV). **1982:** *The Assistant Lawyer* (co-d). **1986:** *Me and My Classmates* (+ co-sc). **1987:** *Nüren de gushi* (*Women's Story*) (+ co-sc).

Other Films: 1980: *Camel Xiang Zi* (asst d). **1983:** *Golden Autumn* (asst d); *The Unusual Tourney* (asst d). **1985:** *The Midnight Songs* (asst d); *Come Back in the Summertime* (sc). **1989:** *The Last Trial* (sc).

Along with Li Shaohong and Ning Ying, Peng Xiaolian is one of the few women who was graduated from the directing class of the Beijing Film Academy in 1982, and is therefore a member of the acclaimed "Fifth Generation" of Chinese directors. Born into a family of intellectuals (her father was a former Minister of Propaganda, her mother a translator) severely persecuted during the 1950s (her father was arrested when she was two and died in prison) and throughout the Cultural Revolution (during which her mother, then her brother were also arrested), Peng was sent to the countryside, like many "urban educated youths," and stayed there nine years. After the fall of the Gang of Four, schools and universities reopened, and, in order to escape the countryside, Peng applied to the Beijing Film Academy, where her schoolmates were other victims of the Cultural Revolution: Chen Kaige, Zhang Yimou, Tian Zhuangzhuang. Fifth Generation filmmakers shared the same experience of having had their childhood and teenage years cut short by the Cultural Revolution, and they all entered the Beijing Film Academy with hopes for a better, more creative life, and the possibility of pursuing artistic and formal experiments that were previously impossible.

Gender bias, however, still played a role and Peng found it was more difficult for a woman than for a man to be given a directing job. Her first assignment was a children's movie, whose original screenplay was "so bad" that she had to revise it six times. The film, however, was successful, which gave her credibility as a director, and allowed her to fight for her next production, a story she had co-written which was inspired by her intimate knowledge of peasant women. Criticized as a "bad movie" by most Chinese film critics, *Women's Story* was a huge success when screened at the Hawaii International Film Festival. Unfortunately, this attracted the attention of the Chinese Film Bureau, especially a newspaper article asserting that, since Peng was showing a peasant woman going into hiding to give birth to her second baby (in the hope of having a son), the film implicitly criticized China's one-child-per-family policy. The film was banned, but circulated in international circles in video form, and eventually the ban was lifted.

In *Women's Story,* only the point of view of the female protagonists is shown. Men are mostly kept off-screen. For the subject of the film is not how the three protagonists—Xiao Feng, "Lai's mother," and Jing Xiang—relate to the men in their lives, but how they find strength with or without them. Feng's one-night stand in the city is not an act of love, but a challenge to the life patriarchal society wants to impose on her as an "unmarriageable" girl. The older woman, defined only as "Lai's mother" (meaning she has borne a son), first reacts in a traditional way, upset at Feng's "shame." She eventually learns to respect the younger woman's decision, which implies a new understanding on her part. Xiang's revolt is clearer: arranged marriage is the stuff Chinese melodramas are made of. The socialist revolution eliminated the practice of selling girls as concubines or forcing them into marriage. But in the countryside, where kinship systems are economically determined and peasants are very poor, a young woman might have to accept her parents' decision in order to improve the family finances. Xiang's union to a man she abhors is a way to make her brother's marriage possible. A good Chinese daughter, she first tearfully submits. Later, she escapes to join Feng and "Lai's mother" when they leave the village to sell wool. Structurally, it is Xiang's story that brackets the often-humorous travels of the three women across China. What launches the narrative is her upcoming marriage; what closes it is the image of her husband arriving to retrieve his conjugal "property," while Feng and "Lai's mother" stand beside her. Will patriarchy win? Will Xiang be defeated? Significantly, the film stops here. *Women's Story* is situated within the space the three protagonists have created for themselves. When this space is threatened, the filmmaker remains silent.

After *Women's Story,* Peng spent two years researching a film about the writer Ba Jin, once a part of the May Fourth Movement of prerevolutionary intellectuals, who, in 1955, agreed to write an article attacking the poet Hu Feng (like Peng's father, Hu Feng was subsequently imprisoned for more than two decades). Later, Ba Jin courageously asserted, against the grain of political propaganda, that the Chinese people as a whole, and not only the reviled Gang of Four, bore responsibility for the excesses committed during the Cultural Revolution. Production for *Random Thoughts* started in the spring of 1989, and on 14 June, four days after the Tiananmen Square massacre, it was halted.

Peng received a fellowship to be a visiting scholar at New York University, and has lived mainly in the United States since. A prolific writer, she has continued publishing many stories in Chinese, and recently directed a television series in China.—BÉRÉNICE REYNAUD

Perry, Eleanor

American writer

***Born** Eleanor Rosenfeld in Cleveland, Ohio, 1915.* ***Education** Attended Western Reserve University, Cleveland, M.A. in social work.* ***Family** Married 1) Leo G. Bayer (divorced 1959), two children: Bill and Ann; 2) the director Frank Perry, 1960 (divorced 1971).* ***Career** 1943—first of several books written with Leo Bayer; 1959—play (co-written with Bayer) produced in New York,* Third Best Sport; *1962—first of several film scripts directed by Frank Perry,* David and Lisa; *also wrote for TV.* ***Died** Of cancer, in New York City, 14 March 1981.*

Films as Writer for Director Frank Perry: 1962: *David and Lisa.* **1963:** *Ladybug, Ladybug.* **1968:** *The Swimmer.* **1969:** *Last Summer, Trilogy* (co). **1970:** *Diary of a Mad Housewife.*

Other Films as Writer: 1970: *The Lady in a Car with Glasses and a Gun* (Litvak) (co). **1972:** *La Maison sous les arbres* (*The Deadly Trap*) (Clément) (co). **1973:** *The Man Who Loved Cat Dancing* (Sarafian) (co, + co-pr).

Eleanor Perry was a writer of carefully crafted screenplays, mainly adaptations realized in collaboration with her second husband, the director Frank Perry. Their first film was a low-budget, independently produced feature, *David and Lisa,* which Perry adapted from psychiatrist Theodore Rubin's book. Her script was a faithful, accomplished and—due to the subject matter—necessarily brooding account of the love between two troubled adolescent patients in a mental hospital. Here Perry developed a penetrating style that would characterize her screen writing: a penchant for unflinchingly probing character and situation to the bone. The controversy that surrounded many of the Perrys' films was due in large measure to Eleanor's commitment to the honest adaptation of source material without cutting dramatic corners or pandering to audience expectations or societal norms. Though *The Swimmer, Diary of a Mad Housewife,* and even *David and Lisa* and *Last Summer* may appear dated today, in their time these films marked significant departures from standard American movie fare.

The Swimmer, based on John Cheever's short story, is too solemnly "artistic" for its own good, but Perry's screenplay deftly manages to capture the stunning looniness of Cheever's vision. At the same time it is a shrewd sociological study of affluent suburban life in the northeast of America. Since Cheever's story is very short, Perry added numerous scenes and incidents that flesh out the story as well as economically convey the character of the swimmer (played by Burt Lancaster). For example, to reveal him as a man driven to do things the hard way, like the character in the short story who "never used the ladder" to get out of a pool, Perry shows him swimming a pool the long way, diagonally, and racing a thoroughbred horse barefooted. These actions effectively exhibit the exacting (and ultimately insane) nature of the swimmer's personal code of masculinity. Owing both to the brilliance of Cheever's cockeyed conceit and Perry's accomplished translation, *The Swimmer* is an unforgettable, if flawed, film.

Last Summer, based on Evan Hunter's novel, essays the same social milieu as *The Swimmer,* focusing on four teenagers on their summer vacation on Fire Island. Once again Perry held true to her source material right down to its disturbing climax: the sexual assault of one of the characters by the others. Along with other independently produced American films released at about the same time, such as *Easy Rider* and *Medium Cool, Last Summer* helped alter the face of the American cinema. What was distinctive about *Last Summer* can be traced back to Eleanor

Perry. Her script had the courage of its convictions, and she was willing to follow the narrative logic of the plot wherever it might lead without compromising the original material or softening the blow for the audience. The Perrys continued this new brand of realism in their next project, *Diary of a Mad Housewife,* based on the novel by Sue Kaufman. In retrospect, the film's feminism may seem dated (in later years Eleanor Perry thought so herself), but it exists as one of the first American films to seriously examine femininity in modern terms. As such, it is a groundbreaking film, more important today as a precedent than for any inherent quality. Three years after the film was released, Perry said she would have written the film differently, carrying "it one step further, to show Tina [the housewife] liberating herself, but not through a man."

In the late 1960s the Perrys, in collaboration with Truman Capote, also made short film adaptations for television of three of Capote's short stories. Two of them, *A Christmas Memory* and *A Thanksgiving Memory,* won Perry and her co-scenarist, Capote, best screenplay Emmy awards. The three films were later reedited and released as an anthology feature entitled *Trilogy.*

After her separation from her husband, Eleanor Perry co-produced and wrote a screenplay for *The Man Who Loved Cat Dancing*. She disowned the finished film, claiming that so many other writers—all male—had worked on the project (among them Robert Bolt, Bill Norton, Tracy Keenan Wynn, Steve Shagan, and Brian Hutton) that the resulting film bore little resemblance to her original intention, which was to tell a Western story from a woman's point of view.

Two years before she died, Perry published a thinly disguised roman à clef, *Blue Pages,* chronicling the exploitation of a woman screenwriter in the male-dominated American film industry. Among the myriad humiliations the female protagonist in the novel endures is being cajoled by her film-director husband to share a screenwriting credit with a "Great Writer" whose work she has been adapting, and whose contribution to the screenplay is nil, presumably to give the project credibility and stature.

In an introduction to the published screenplays of *Trilogy,* Perry wrote that she considered the two most important elements in developing literary material to film were "a deep empathy with the material, the author's theme, intention and view of life; and . . . an unblocked imagination which is able to flow freely from the original source, playing, embroidering, ornamenting, extending and, in the most successful adaptations, even enriching the original material." At its best, Eleanor Perry's work exhibits this kind of sympathetic and enriching sensibility.—CHARLES RAMÍREZ BERG

Pickford, Mary

American producer and actress

Born *Gladys Mary Smith in Toronto, Ontario, Canada, 8 April 1893.* ***Family*** *Married 1) the actor Owen Moore, 1911 (divorced 1920); 2) the actor Douglas Fairbanks, 1920 (divorced 1936); 3) the actor Charles "Buddy" Rogers, 1937, two adopted children.* ***Career*** *1898—debut as child actress in stage play* Bootle's Baby; *played other roles in Valentine Stock Company, and toured with other companies; 1907—Broadway debut in* The Warrens of Virginia; *1909—film debut as extra in* Her First Biscuits; *leading role in D. W. Griffith's* The Violin Maker of Cremona*: became known as "The Biograph Girl"; 1913-18—contract with Zukor; 1918—independent producer; 1919—co-founder, with Douglas Fairbanks, Charlie Chaplin, and D. W. Griffith, of United Artists; 1923-24—roles* *in* Rosita *and* Dorothy Vernon of Haddon Hall *attempted to break her "little girl" image; 1929—first sound film,* Coquette; *1936—formed Pickford-Lasky Productions with Jesse Lasky; 1937—formed Mary Pickford Cosmetic Company; 1946-49—produced several films for a variety of companies; 1956—sold the last of her United Artists stock.* ***Awards*** *Best Actress Academy Award, for* Coquette, *1929; Special Career Academy Award, for her "unique contributions to the film industry and the development of film as an artistic medium," 1975.* ***Died*** *Of cerebral hemorrhage, in Santa Monica, California, 29 May 1979.*

Films as Producer: **1919:** *Daddy Long-Legs* (Neilan) (+ ro); *The Hoodlum* (+ ro); *Heart o' the Hills* (S. Franklin) (+ ro). **1920:** *Pollyanna* (P. Powell) (+ title role); *Suds* (Dillon) (+ ro). **1921:** *The Love Light* (Marion) (+ ro as Angela); *Through the Back Door* (A. E. Green and J. Pickford) (+ ro as Jeanne Budamere); *Little Lord Fauntleroy* (A. E. Green and J. Pickford) (+ title role). **1922:** *Tess of the Storm Country* (Robertson) (+ title role). **1923:** *Rosita* (Lubitsch) (+ title role); *Garrison's Finish* (Rosson) (co-sc titles only). **1924:** *Dorothy Vernon of Haddon Hall* (Neilan) (+ title role). **1925:** *Little Annie Rooney* (Beaudine) (+ title role). **1926:** *Sparrows* (Beaudine) (+ ro as Mama Mollie). **1927:** *My Best Girl* (Sam Taylor) (+ ro as Maggie Johnson). **1929:** *Coquette* (Sam Taylor) (+ ro as Norma Besant); *The Taming of the Shrew* (Sam Taylor) (+ ro as Katherine). **1931:** *Kiki* (Sam Taylor) (+ title role). **1933:** *Secrets* (Borzage) (+ roles as Mary Marlow/Mary Carlton). **1936:** *One Rainy Afternoon* (R. V. Lee); *The Gay Desperado* (Mamoulian). **1946:** *Little Iodine* (Le Borg); *Susie Steps Out* (Le Borg). **1947:** *The Adventures of Don Coyote* (Le Borg); *Stork Bites Man* (Endfield). **1948:** *High Fury* (*White Cradle Inn*) (French); *Sleep, My Love* (Siodmak). **1949:** *Love Happy* (D. Miller).

Films as Actress: **1909:** *Her First Biscuits*; *The Violin Maker of Cremona*; *The Lonely Villa*; *The Son's Return*; *The Faded Lilies*; *The Peach Basket Hat*; *The Way of Man*; *The Necklace*; *The Mexican Sweethearts*; *The Country Doctor*; *The Cardinal's Conspiracy*; *The Renunciation*; *The Seventh Day*; *A Strange Meeting*; *Sweet and Twenty*; *The Slave*; *They Would Elope*; *The Indian Runner's Romance*; *His Wife's Visitor*; *Oh Uncle*; *The Sealed Room*; *1776, or The Hessian Renegades*; *The Little Darling*; *In Old Kentucky*; *Getting Even*; *The Broken Locket*; *What's Your Hurry*; *The Awakening*; *The Little Teacher*; *The Gibson Goddess*; *In the Watches of the Night*; *His Lost Love*; *The Restoration*; *The Light That Came*; *A Midnight Adventure*; *The Mountaineer's Honor*; *The Trick That Failed*; *The Test*; *To Save Her Soul*. **1910:** *All on Account of the Milk* (Powell); *The Woman from Mellon's*; *The Englishman and the Girl*; *The Newlyweds*; *The Thread of Destiny*; *The Twisted Trail*; *The Smoker*; *As It Is in Life*; *A Rich Revenge*; *A Romance of the Western Hills*; *May and December*; *Never Again!*; *The Unchanging Sea*; *Love among the Roses*; *The Two Brothers*; *Romona*; *In the Season of Buds*; *A Victim of Jealousy*; *A Child's Impulse*; *Muggsy's First Sweetheart*; *What the Daisy Said*; *The Call to Arms*; *An Arcadian Maid*; *Muggsy Becomes a Hero*; *The Sorrows of the Unfaithful*; *When We Were in Our Teens*; *Wilful Peggy*; *Examination Day at School*; *A Gold Necklace*; *A Lucky Toothache*; *Waiter No. 5*; *Simple Charity*; *The Masher*; *The Song of the Wildwood Flute*; *A Plain Song*. **1911:** *White Roses*; *When a Man Loves*; *The Italian Barber*; *Three Sisters*; *A Decree of Destiny*; *The First Misunderstanding* (Ince and Tucker); *The Dream* (Ince and Tucker) (+ sc); *Maid or Man* (Ince); *At the Duke's Command*; *The Mirror*; *While the Cat's Away*; *Her Darkest Hour* (Ince); *Artful Kate* (Ince); *A Manly Man* (Ince); *The Message in the Bottle* (Ince); *The Fisher-maid* (Ince); *In Old Madrid* (Ince); *Sweet Memories of Yesterday* (Ince); *The Stampede*; *Second Sight*; *The Fair Dentist*; *For Her Brother's Sake* (Ince and Tucker); *Back to the Soil*; *In the Sultan's Garden* (Ince); *The Master and the Man*; *The Lighthouse Keeper*; *For the Queen's Honor*; *A Gasoline Engagement*; *At a Quarter to Two*; *Science*; *The Skating Bug*; *The Call of the Song*; *A Toss of the Coin*; *The Sentinel Asleep*; *The Better Way*; *His Dress Shirt*; *'Tween Two Loves* (*The Stronger Love*); *The Rose's Story*; *From the Bottom of the Sea*; *The Courting of Mary* (Tucker); *Love Heeds Not the Showers* (Moore); *Little Red Riding Hood* (Moore); *The Caddy's Dream* (Moore). **1912:** *Honor Thy Father* (Moore); *The Mender of Nets*; *Iola's Promise*; *Fate's Inception*; *The Female of the Species*; *Just Like a Woman*; *Won by a Fish* (Sennett); *The Old Actor*; *A Lodging for the Night*; *A Beast at Bay*; *Home Folks*; *Lena and the Geese* (+ sc); *The School Teacher and the Waif*; *An Indian Summer*; *A Pueblo Legend*; *The Narrow Road*; *The Inner Circle*; *With the Enemy's Help*; *Friends*; *So Near, Yet So Far*; *A Feud in the Kentucky Hills*; *The One She Loved*; *My Baby*; *The Informer*; *The Unwelcome Guest*; *The New York Hat*. **1913:** *In the Bishop's Carriage* (Porter); *Caprice* (Dawley). **1914:** *A Good Little Devil* (Porter); *Hearts Adrift* (Porter); *Tess of the Storm Country* (Porter); *The Eagle's Mate* (Kirkwood); *Such a Little Queen* (Hugh Ford); *Behind the*

Scenes (Kirkwood); *Cinderella* (Kirkwood). **1915:** *Mistress Nell* (Kirkwood); *Fanchon, the Cricket* (Kirkwood); *The Dawn of Tomorrow* (Kirkwood); *Little Pal* (Kirkwood); *Rags* (Kirkwood); *Esmerelda* (Kirkwood); *A Girl of Yesterday* (Dwan); *Madame Butterfly* (Olcott). **1916:** *The Foundling* (O'Brien); *Poor Little Peppina* (Olcott); *The Eternal Grind* (O'Brien); *Hulda from Holland* (O'Brien); *Less Than Dust* (Emerson). **1917:** *The Pride of the Clan* (M. Tourneur); *The Poor Little Rich Girl* (M. Tourneur); *A Romance of the Redwoods* (C. B. DeMille); *Rebecca of Sunnybrook Farm* (Neilan) (title role); *A Little Princess* (Neilan). **1918:** *Stella Maris* (Neilan) (title role/Unity Blake); *Amarilly of Clothes-Line Alley* (Neilan); *M'Liss* (Neilan); *How Could You, Jean?* (W. Taylor); *Johanna Enlists* (W. Taylor); *One Hundred Percent American* (Rossen). **1919:** *Captain Kidd, Jr.* (W. Taylor). **1927:** *The Gaucho* (F. R. Jones).

Aptly dubbed "America's Sweetheart," Mary Pickford was the world's first motion-picture star. She was also an accomplished producer who successfully orchestrated a career that seemed, for a time, as though it would last forever. Very early in her movie career, Pickford demonstrated her business savvy by moving from one studio to another, negotiating each time for higher wages and greater creative control of her films. She was equally attentive to the importance of choosing roles that she thought would please her audience.

In 1918, when Pickford was renegotiating her contract with Adolph Zukor's Famous Players-Lasky company, she demanded more money, complete creative control of her movies, and that the studio act only as her distributor. But it was First National who agreed to meet her demands. Subsequently, she played only the roles she selected and she carefully controlled her star image in order to satisfy her audience's expectations. And she was very clear about the composition of her audience—mostly working-class women; she proudly declared, "I am a woman's woman. My success has been [because] women like the pictures in which I appear." Thus, her films were typically preoccupied with poverty and melodrama, and with plucky independent heroines who struggle relentlessly to survive in the harsh world. In addition, much of her success was due to her acute awareness of her star value, and her skill at picking directors and other crew members who would complement her talents and image.

In 1919 rumors made the rounds in Hollywood that Famous Players-Lasky and First National planned to merge. Seeking to avoid falling under the control of Zukor and losing control of her films, Pickford co-founded the United Artists Corporation (UA) with her fellow movie stars Charlie Chaplin and Douglas Fairbanks, and the star director D. W. Griffith. It was organized to distribute their high-end productions and to give them complete control of their films. Pickford's first film for UA was the sticky sweet *Pollyanna,* about the unfailingly optimistic little orphan girl who, despite a crippling accident, declares that because her grumpy aunt now loves her, she is happy she was hurt. Despite what critics called its uninspired direction, it was a huge hit. Her costume movie *Little Lord Fauntleroy* featured her in a dual role, and its box-office success confirmed Pickford's sense that her fans preferred her Victorian fables. She had moderate success with *Tess of the Storm Country,* a remake of an earlier Pickford hit; it featured one of her most exuberant performances in which she played a sweet, but bold girl who proves her mettle by tangling with swains and selflessly taking on the protection of orphaned babies.

Over time, Pickford produced films that were more and more elaborate, but they stuck with well-worn themes that were increasingly out of touch with the "Jazz Age." She tried to change her image by making *Rosita,* in which she played a gypsy heroine, but she and director Ernst Lubitsch continually clashed over their disparate conceptions of the film and the result was both mediocre and unpopular. She miscalculated again with *Dorothy Vernon of Haddon Hall,* an expensive costume romance set in the court of Elizabeth I in which Pickford played a grown-

Mary Pickford

up woman instead of a girl. After *Dorothy Vernon of Haddon Hall,* she returned to her girlish persona with *Little Annie Rooney,* an engaging, fluffy bit of fun, but weighty with ethnic stereotypes; it was a great hit. In the moderately successful Dickensian story *Sparrows,* Pickford played a guardian of ten children imprisoned on a baby farm who ultimately escorts the children to freedom. Her last silent film *My Best Girl* was a hit, in which she played a contemporary shop-girl who falls in love with the heir to the department store where she works. Her first sound film *Coquette* was a static, stagey film about the flighty daughter of a small-town doctor, but it was commercially successful and earned her the Academy Award for acting. Toward the end of her career, Pickford wanted to concentrate on classical roles, so she co-starred with her husband Douglas Fairbanks in an adaptation of *The Taming of the Shrew.* But it was overwrought with comedy gags, and although it returned a profit, it failed to meet her expectations and she claimed that she hated it. She had another "misadventure" with *Kiki,* in which she played a daring modern woman who ardently pursues the producer of her show; critics disparaged it and audiences were disinterested too.

More interested in commercial rather than artistic success, Pickford's career is characterized by her trepidation about alienating the audience. Consequently, she mostly hired directors who unquestioningly accepted her authority; in addition, she occasionally recut her movies according to her wishes. As the producer of her films, she freely exercised her extensive knowledge of and preferences for filmmaking. Charles Rosher recalled that she "knew everything there was to know about motion pictures," and often directed her own scenes while the official director did the crowd scenes. Pickford herself declared: "Nobody ever directed me, not even Mr. Griffith." According to Pickford, one of her most cherished filmmaking principles was that her function was not to educate her fans, but rather to entertain, and moreover, to "serve" them. In 1936, after she retired from acting, she formed Pickford-Lasky Productions, in order to produce "wholesome, healthy" movies that would counter Mae West's films, which Pickford thought were morally degrading to Hollywood. The partnership dissolved after only two films. During the late 1940s, however, she produced several films for different studios with her third husband, "Buddy" Rogers.—CYNTHIA FELANDO

Poirier, Anne-Claire

Canadian director and writer

Born *St. Hyacinthe, Quebec, Canada, 1932.* ***Education*** *Attended University of Montreal, law degree; studied theater at the Conservatoire d'art dramatique.* ***Career*** *1960—began*

working for the French section of the National Film Board of Canada; 1963—directed 30 Minutes, Mister Plummer, *her first film for the NFB; 1968—directed her first feature,* Mother-to-Be, *the initial Quebec feature directed by a woman; 1972—with Jeanne Morazain and Monique Larocque, established "En tant que femmes," a program for women at the NFB, which lasted three years; 1975-78—served as executive producer of the Challenge for Change Société nouvelle program and as studio head in the French production branch; mid-1970s—produced a series of documentaries for other filmmakers; formed a working partnership with screenwriter Marthe Blackburn.* ***Awards*** *Ordre national du Québec, 1985; Government of Quebec, Albert Tessier Award for lifetime achievement, 1988; Grand Prix Hydro-Quebec, Festival du Cinema International, for* Salut Victor!, *1988.* ***Address*** *c/o National Film Board of Canada, P.O. Box 6100, Station Centre-Ville Montreal, PQ H3C 3H5, Canada.*

Films as Director: 1963: *30 Minutes, Mister Plummer* (doc, short) (+ sc, ed, narration). **1964:** *La Fin des étés* (short) (+ co-sc, co-ed). **1965:** *Les Ludions* (short). **1968:** *De mère en fille* (*Mother-to-Be*) (+ sc). **1970:** *L'Impot, et tout et tout* (short, revision). **1971:** "1re partie" and "2e partie" of *Le savoir-faire s'impose* (shorts). **1974:** *Les Filles du Roi* (*They Called Us "Les Filles du Roy"*) (+ co-sc, co-pr). **1975:** *Le Temps de l'avant* (*Before the Time Comes*) (+ co-sc, pr). **1979:** *Mourir à tue-tête* (*A Scream of Silence*) (+ co-sc, co-pr). **1982:** *La Quarantaine* (*Over Forty*; *Beyond Forty*) (+ co-sc). **1988:** *Salut Victor!* (for TV) (+ co-sc, pr). **1989:** *Il y à longtemps que je t'aime.* **1997:** *Tu as Crie* (*Let Me Go*) (+ co-sc).

Other Films: 1962: *Jour apres jour* (*Day after Day*) (Perron—short) (ed). **1963:** *Voir Miami* (Groulx—short) (co-sc, co-narration). **1973:** *J'me marie, j'me marie pas* (Dansereau) (co-pr); *Souris, tu m'inquiétes* (Danis) (co-pr); *Á qui appartient ce gage?* (Blackburn, Gibbard, Morazin, Saia, and Warny) (co-pr). **1974:** *Les filles c'est pas pareil* (Girard) (pr). **1976:** *Shakti—"She Is Vital Energy"* (Crouillere) (pr); *Surtout l'hiver* (Gagne) (pr); *Tie-Dre* (De Bellefeuille) (pr). **1977:** *La P'tite Violence* (Girard) (pr); *Raison d'être* (Dion) (co-pr); *Quebec à vendre* (Garceau) (pr); *Le Mentour (1re partie)-L'Alcoholisme: la therapie* (Seguin) (pr); *Le Mentour (2e partie)-L'Alcoholisme: la maladie* (Seguin) (pr); *Famille et Variations* (Dansereau) (pr); *Les Heritiers de la violence* (Vamos) (pr).

Throughout her long career, Anne-Claire Poirier has consistently made films with feminist and humanist concerns. She explores serious issues facing young, contemporary women, from defining one's place in society and attaining personal satisfaction to dealing with the aftereffects of sexual violence. In the two outstanding fiction films she made in the 1980s, however, her characters are neither youthful nor fashionable. Rather, they respectively are aging, and aged.

Poirier's first film, *30 Minutes, Mister Plummer,* is a documentary portrait of actor Christopher Plummer as he prepares to play Cyrano de Bergerac; despite its title, the film actually runs 27-plus minutes. But she really hit her stride with her initial feature-length film, *Mother-to-Be,* a documentary about pregnancy and motherhood that provoked much debate about feminism in the Québécois cinema. In the film, Poirier explores the conflicting emotions of a young mother as she awaits the birth of her second child. *Mother-to-Be,* which was made in 1967, insightfully explores one of the key questions women were beginning to ask themselves as the modern feminist movement was taking shape: Can a woman attain self-fulfillment while devoting herself to a husband and children?

Through the 1970s, Poirier's films focused on feminist issues. *They Called Us "Les Filles du Roy"* examines the roles of women in the history of Quebec, from squaw and settler's wife to self-sufficient member of the workforce. In the film, Poirier differentiates between the historical role of women as wives and mothers and their contemporary, postfeminist identity, while spotlighting the challenges couples must face if they are to work together and thrive. *Before the Time Comes* deals with the abortion issue, as it charts the plight of a happily married woman who already has three children. She finds herself pregnant and, with her husband, must make the torturous decision of whether to abort or have the baby. *A Scream of Silence* chronicles the rape and subsequent suicide of a nurse, whose sense of self is destroyed as a result of the brutality she experiences. Here, Poirier examines the reasons why women may feel they somehow are to blame for their sexual victimization.

In the 1980s, Poirier expanded her thematic horizons and directed *Over Forty* and *Salut Victor!,* heartfelt, poetic dramas that sympathetically examine the lives of older characters. *Over Forty* is a *Return of the Secaucus Seven* and *The Big Chill* for those who grew up during the 1940s. It chronicles a reunion of The Gang, a clique of men and women who came of age together. After a three-decade-long separation, they meet one more time to sing, and recollect old times, and reveal the triumphs and disappointments of their lives. *Over Forty* is an enchanting jewel of a movie about the nature of camaraderie, the passing of time, and the ability to forget one's dissatisfaction and live in the moment.

Salut Victor! charts the evolving friendship between two elderly residents of an old-age home: Philippe, a new arrival who no longer can care for himself, and who has come there to pass his remaining time and die; and Victor, talkative and spirited, who cherishes life yet is pragmatic about his surroundings. Victor also is proudly gay, and has suffered for his lifestyle; he had left his wife and children for a man, an airline pilot who was killed in a plane crash, and remains estranged from his family. He quickly befriends, and positively impacts on, the less outgoing, more pessimistic Philippe. The pair share some eloquent repartee, with Philippe eventually admitting that he too is gay, and has spent his life deeply hidden in the closet. But the crux of the story is the relationship between these two elderly gentlemen, and the warmth and solace they find in their friendship.

If *Over Forty* is a poignant story of characters at midlife, *Salut Victor!* is an equally eloquent account of how the elderly may be patronized (or downright ignored) by society despite their feelings, fears, desires—and their humanity.

In Poirier's earliest films, she deals thoughtfully and compassionately with women's issues. In *Over Forty* and *Salut Victor!,* made as she herself matured, she explores the emotions and attitudes of those who are no longer young. Notwithstanding, all of her films are united in that they have a way of reverberating inside even the most seasoned moviegoer for days after they have been seen.—ROB EDELMAN

Pool, Léa

Swiss-Canadian director

Born *Geneva, Switzerland, 1950.* ***Education*** *In 1975 traveled to Canada to study film and video production; graduated from the University of Quebec with a degree in communications.* ***Career*** *Teacher in Switzerland; 1978-83—taught film and video at the University of Quebec; 1980—made first short film, the documentary* Un Strass café; *1980-81—directed nine episodes of the "Planete" series for Radio Québec; 1980-83—directed a series of programs about cultural minorities for Quebec television; 1984—made her critically acclaimed debut feature film,* A Woman in Transit. ***Awards*** *Critics Prize* *and International Critics Prize, Montreal World Film Festival, and Best Canadian Film, Toronto Festival of Festivals, for* A Woman in Transit, *1984; First Prize, Namur Film Festival, and First Prize, Atlantic Film Festival, for* Straight for the Heart, *1988.* ***Address*** *c/o: Groupe MultiMédia du Canada, 525 Berri, Bureau 200, Montreal PQ H2J 2S4, Canada.*

Films as Director: **1978:** *Laurent Lamerre, portier* (co-d). **1980:** *Un Strass café* (doc, short) (+ sc, pr, ed). **1984:** *La Femme de l'hôtel* (*A Woman in Transit*) (+ co-sc). **1986:** *Anne Trister* (+ co-sc). **1988:** *À corps perdu* (*Straight for the Heart*; *Straight to the Heart*) (+ co-sc). **1990:** *Hotel Chronicles.* **1991:** *La Demoiselle sauvage* (*The Savage Woman*) (+ co-sc); "Rispondetemi" ep. of *Montréal vu par* (*Montreal Sextet*). **1992:** *Blanche* (for TV). **1993:** *C'était le 12 du 12 et chili avait les blues.* **1994:** *Mouvements du désir* (*Desire in Motion*) (+ sc). **1996:** *Letter to My Daughter.* **1997:** *Marguerite Volant* (for TV). **1998:** *Emporte-moi.*

Other Film: **1993:** *Cap Tourmente* (Langlois) (adviser).

Léa Pool is a celebrated Canadian filmmaker who works in both film and video, fiction and documentary. Her work is highly intimate and introspective, refuses to follow familiar narrative conventions, and typically employs lengthy, subjective shots. Not surprisingly, she has expressed admiration for the films of her contemporary (and friend) Chantal Akerman. In addition, Pool has acknowledged that she is interested in images and perspectives of women, and she aligns herself with those filmmakers whose urges do not include the pursuit of commercial success by making Hollywood-style films. Indeed, she has lamented that, it is "very rare to see films that come from the heart" due to the commercial constraints of Hollywood.

After working as a teacher in her native Switzerland, Pool went to Montreal to study film production, where she garnered attention for a student film. Since 1975, she has lived in Quebec. After working on several student films, Pool made her first solo film, the low-budget experimental short documentary, *Strass café,* made at the National Film Board of Canada in 1980. It uses black-and-white cinematography and a poetic voice over to meditate upon the city, exile, solitude, identity, and a woman and man who desire but never meet each other.

Pool's debut feature was *A Woman in Transit,* an intense story of loneliness and creative frustration. Set in a downtown Montreal hotel, it features three female characters. Specifically, filmmaker Andrea returns to her native Montreal to make a musical drama; upon checking into her hotel, she briefly encounters a strange older woman who, distraught from a broken love affair, soon tries to commit suicide with drugs and alcohol. The film's third woman is an actress who has a part as a singer in Andrea's film. When Andrea and the older woman finally talk at length, it becomes clear that Andrea's film bears striking similarities to the older woman's life. Thus, the film treats the theme of life imitating art, and vice versa. In this film, Pool has explained that her intention was to address the three sides of a woman—the conscious, unconscious, and the combination of the two. To do so, she chose three different characters, and, as she put it, "each one is a side of me in a way." The film has a slow, contemplative pace, and critics generally praised it, calling it "introspective" and "arty." Significantly, its critical and popular success enabled Pool to raise the money for her next script very quickly.

Although *A Woman in Transit* alludes to lesbian desire, her second feature, *Anne Trister,* deals with the subject more explicitly. Funded by the National Film Board of Canada, it is the partly autobiographical tale of a Jewish woman who leaves her native Switzerland after the death of her father, in order to establish her own identity in Quebec, where she falls in love with an older woman. The film prompted considerable commentary for its subject matter at the Berlin Film Festival and it was lauded by Canadian critics. Moreover, although at the time gay and lesbian themes were considered commercially risky, it was an economic success. Some critics have disagreed, however, with Pool's portrayal of the lesbian relationship because it is decidedly unerotic. That is, the heterosexual love scene is more graphic than the lesbian love scene. The disparity was motivated by Pool's intention to express the desire that permeates a new love relationship, and to symbolically explore the primal mother-daughter love—a woman's "first love." Therefore, she chose to emphasize the women's emotions with their eyes and physical gestures rather than by using more sexually explicit means.

Pool's third feature, *Straight for the Heart,* is the story of Pierre, a photojournalist who returns to Montreal from an assignment in Nicaragua to discover that his ménage à trois of ten years has ended unexpectedly when his former lovers, David and Sarah, leave together. Pierre then nurtures his obsession to discover why they have deserted him, and undertakes a photographic study of Montreal's urban corrosion. Certainly, images of the city constitute a visual theme in Pool's work, as in *Un Strass café, A Woman in Transit,* and *Straight for the Heart.* In addition, her characters often exist in alienating transitional spaces; for example, the hotel in *A Woman in Transit,* and a train in *Desire in Motion.* Certainly, movement is an essential element of cinema—as is desire. Thus, in Pool's more recent film, *Desire in Motion,* she deploys the "strangers on a train" device, but with a difference—as the film's title suggests. The story concerns a woman who has recently ended a relationship and is traveling with her seven-year-old daughter on a train from Montreal to Vancouver. She meets a shy man traveling to meet his lover, but eventually the two strangers give full vent to their passion, to the chagrin of the little girl. The film's several surreal dream sequences and assortment of unusual characters are pure Pool. Critics called it "ultra steamy," and claimed it was her most "viewer friendly" film. Quebec critics, in particular, praised her juxtaposition of the tight, claustrophobic train interiors with the expansive Canadian landscapes.

Pool's films are better received in Europe than in English-speaking Canada or the United States. She is that rare Quebec filmmaker, however, whose films are screened in commercial theaters; and her success has prompted considerable attention from film critics and academics, particularly feminists. Notably, although mainstream film critics have characterized her films as feminist, many academic feminists have challenged them on the grounds that they are not clearly "feminist" because, for example, they tend to focus on individual, private tensions, rather than on the larger issue of the unequal distribution of power between men and women.—CYNTHIA FELANDO

Potter, Sally

British director

Born *London, 1947.* ***Education*** *Attended London School of Contemporary Dance; St. Martin's Art School.* ***Career*** *1968—began making 8-millimeter films; 1974—performed and choreographed for the Strider Dance Company; founded Limited Dance Company; toured Britain and United States in performance shows, both solo and in collaboration, including the Feminist Improvising Group (FIG); 1979—released short feminist comedy,* Thriller, *funded by the Arts Council of Great Britain; 1980—formed Marx Bros. group with Lindsay Cooper and Georgie Born; choreographed solo dances for Maedee Dupres; lectured on feminism and feminism and cinema; 1983—made first feature film,* The Gold

Diggers, *financed by the British Film Institute; 1980s—made films for television.* **Agent** *Alexandra Cann Representation, 337 Fulham Road, London SW10 9TW, England.* **Address** *Adventure Pictures, Blackbird Yard, London E2, England.*

Films as Director: 1968-73: *Hors d'oeuvres* (8mm short); *Play* (16mm short); *The Building* (expanded cinema event). **1979:** *Thriller* (short) (+ pr, sc); *The London Story* (short) (+ pr, sc). **1983:** *The Gold Diggers* (+ co-sc, co-ed, composer of lyrics, performer of song "Seeing Red," choreographer). **1986:** *Tears Laughter Fear and Rage* (for TV). **1988:** *I Am an Ox—Women in Soviet Cinema* (doc for TV). **1993:** *Orlando* (+ sc, co-mus). **1997:** *The Tango Lesson* (+ ro as Sally).

Sally Potter's career so far exemplifies the best and the worst features of British film culture: the best in its imaginativeness, inventiveness, and biting integrity; the worst in the extreme parsimony, both financial and critical, in which it existed. Potter's work in performance art, dance, and at the London Film Makers' Co-op was both culturally and financially "on the margins." Aware of these categories of "avant-garde" or "independent," "feminist" or "experimental," Potter has in quite serious ways never accepted them. Quite early on she spoke of herself as working within "avant-garde show business." Performance art and dance brought her into intimate contact with audiences, and she maintained this contact when she turned to film—regularly traveling with her films, watching and rewatching with different audiences, and involving herself in discussions afterwards. In various ways the idea of "the big screen" and the richness of the history of classical narrative cinema has been from the beginning part of her project. When making *Thriller,* a short but disconcerting deconstruction of *La Bohème,* she has said that she always asked herself, as she shot and then edited it, how it would look on the big screen in a Leicester Square cinema.

Changes in the structure of funding independent films in Britain during the 1980s enabled Potter to make her first feature film, *The Gold Diggers*. Using Colette Lafont, with whom she had worked in *Thriller,* and dramatic landscapes of "virginal purity" in Iceland, which she had visited with her performance group, she put together a film in which the circulation of finance and the circulation of images are both scrutinized. Lafont plays a computer programmer in a bank who becomes fascinated by gold—the touchstone of value, the basis of the calculations that appear daily on her screen. Julie Christie plays an actress on the run from her image. The film's radical quality extended to its mode of production. All participants took a salary of £30 per day and the film was shot with an all-women crew, including Babette Mangolte on camera, who had had previous experience with Chantal Akerman and Yvonne Rainer. The film was shot in black and white. Christie brought with her memories of her role within the traditional cinema epic, David Lean's *Doctor Zhivago,* but also a sense of the new, postwar woman from her work in British cinema of the sixties (*Billy Liar, Darling*). Lafont was deliberately cast against the stereotype of the black woman who is primarily a physical and sensual being. In the course of the action each woman attempts to locate a value system of her own, her own kind of gold. The film is full of affectionate references to cinema history and to the representations of women within it. Its very English quality lies in what has been called its narrative of "Alice in Wonderland-like inconsequentiality." In this lack of narrative seriousness, and in the sense in which its twin protagonists are experienced almost as a single entity, the film nicely prefigures *Orlando.*

With *Orlando* Potter seemed to be attempting to film the unfilmable, so much of the charm and persuasiveness of Virginia Woolf's thinly veiled love letter to Vita Sackville-West—and to history and to language—lies in its literary mode of address, the joy of words on paper. In the event Potter's intellectual adventurousness, allied to her equally strong awareness of the cinema's potential for magic, proved precisely right. Its rich, late-20th-century nouveau-rococo mise-en-scène (well within the English tradition of masque and display, explored also by Derek Jarman and Peter Greenaway), its quirky humor and laconic way with big themes, were purely cinematic. Central to the success of the film was the casting of Tilda Swinton as the protagonist who lives for 400 years, changing gender in the process—a role which Potter had envisaged for her from the beginning. The intelligent performance Swinton gives provides the film with an unshakable focus.

Financial necessity again nudged Potter towards radical production solutions. Funding was cobbled together from a handful of European sources, which included Russia. From Russia also came Elem Klimov's miraculous cinematographer Alexei Rodionov, the strange landscapes of Khiva, and St. Petersburg's snow. There is a sense in *Orlando* of everything—discourses on Englishness and the foreign, history and class, gender and identity—being thrown into the air to fall almost where they will. Gender, argues *Orlando,* is not central to the person but inconsequential. "Same person," says *Orlando,* "different sex."

Visual excitement comes not from narrative drive and the surrender to the merely sensational. "I edit," Potter has said, "not to narrative, but to an idea." Likewise her early work on performance and display inhibits her from an automatic recourse to the well-nigh ubiquitous language of the tight close-up with its concomitant fetishising of body parts at the expense of the person. Craft, a sense of timing, the awareness that an audience finds pleasure in a whole complex of feelings and ideas—"ethics too are pleasurable"—all play a part.

As the language of commercial cinema becomes more homogenous across the world, films that keep alive other ways of representation and response become increasingly valuable, and indeed necessary. Potter's work so far does so with considerable wit and aplomb.—VERINA GLAESSNER

Preobrazhenskaya, Olga

Russian director and actress

Born *Moscow, 1881.* ***Education*** *Studied drama at the Moscow Art Theatre; was student of Konstantin Stanislavsky.* ***Family*** *Married the film director Ivan Pravov.* ***Career*** *Worked extensively as actress in provincial Russian theaters; 1913—became overnight success via her screen acting debut in Yakov Protazanov and Vladimir Gardin's immensely popular* The Keys to Happiness; *altogether, starred in more than 20 silent films, many directed by Protazanov and/or Gardin; 1916—made directing debut as co-director with Gardin of* The Lady Peasant, *becoming Russia's first female director; early 1920s—taught in the first Soviet film school, the State Cinema Technicum (GTK); 1927—filmed her masterpiece,* Peasant Women of Ryazan; *1927-41—taught at the All-Union State Institute of Cinematography (VGIK); 1930s-early 1940s—worked primarily in a collaborative vein with Pravov; 1940s—career cut short by Stalin's purges.* ***Died*** *31 October 1971.*

Films as Director: 1916: *Baryshnia krestianka* (*The Lady Peasant*; *Miss Peasant*) (co-d with Gardin). **1917:** *Viktoriya* (*Victoria*). **1923:** *Slesar i kantzler* (*Locksmith and Chancellor*) (co-d with Gardin). **1925:** *Fedka's Truth* (short). **1926:** *Kashtanka.* **1927:** *Anya*; *Baby ryazanskie* (*Peasant Women of Ryazan*; *The Village of Sin*; *Women of Ryazan*). **1928:** *Svetlyi gorod* (*Bright City*; *Luminous City*). **1929:** *Poslednyi attraktzion* (*The Last Attraction*). **1930:** *Tikhiy Don* (*Cossacks of the Don*; *The Quiet Don*) (co-d with Pravov, + sc). **1935:** *Vrazhi tropi* (*Enemy Paths*). **1936:** *Grain* (co-d with Pravov). **1939:** *Stepan Razin* (co-d with Pravov). **1941:** *Prairie Station*; *Paren iz taigi* (*Boy from the Taiga*; *Children of the Taiga*) (co-d with Pravov).

Films as Actress (selected): 1913: *Klyuchi shchastya* (*The Keys to Happiness*) (Protazanov and Gardin). **1915:** *Petersburgskiye trushchobi* (*Petersburg Slums*) Protazanov and Gardin—serial); *Voina i mir* (*War and Peace*) (Protazanov and Gardin); *A Nest of Noblemen* (Gardin); *Plebei* (*Plebian*) (Protazanov).

Though little known in the West today, Olga Preobrazhenskaya was one of the pioneers of the Russian and early Soviet cinema. Beginning as a Moscow Art Theatre- and Stanislavsky-trained actress for the stage, Preobrazhenskaya made a smashing screen debut in 1913's *The Keys to Happiness*—an adaptation of a popular novel by Anastasiya Verbitskaya, which was directed by Yakov Protazanov and Vladimir Gardin. Preobrazhenskaya played a young Russian woman who has a liaison with an older, Jewish businessman (at the time, she was in her early thirties, considered "too old" for starring roles by many filmmakers). Propelled by the film's stature as the greatest box-office success in Russia to date, Preobrazhenskaya went on to star in more than 20 other features, establishing herself as a leading actress of the pre-Revolutionary cinema in such "big-budget" films as the elaborate *War and Peace* (also directed by Protazanov and Gardin) and *Plebian,* an adaptation of August Strindberg's *Miss Julie* directed by Protazanov alone.

Like many other early cinematic actresses the world over, Preobrazhenskaya was not content with just performing but quickly moved behind the camera. In 1916 she became the first female director in Russia with her co-direction with Gardin of *The Lady Peasant,* which already represented two of the primary themes of her directing career: the place of women in Russian society and the lives of the Russian peasantry. In 1917—the year of the Russian Revolution—Preobrazhenskaya solo-directed for the first time with *Victoria.* After teaching at the first Soviet film school in the early 1920s, she returned to direct several films for and about children: *Fedka's Truth*; the popular *Kashtanka,* which was based on a Chekhov story; and *Anya.*

In 1927—the same year that she directed *Anya*—Preobrazhenskaya also returned to films for adults with what is generally considered her greatest film, the classically melodramatic *Peasant Women of Ryazan.* The film centers around two village women, one representing tradition (Anna) and the other change (Vassilisa). In a story based on *snokharchestvo* (the persistent problem in Russian villages of sexual abuse of daughters-in-law), Anna is raped by her vicious father-in-law—a kulak—after her husband leaves to fight in World War I. She bears the rapist's child, and in the end drowns herself when her husband returns and rejects her. In contrast, the independent-minded Vassilisa, daughter of the kulak, shacks up with the lowly blacksmith whom she loves, after her father refuses to give his consent to their marriage. Vassilisa also sets up an orphanage for homeless children in the country, thus completely establishing her as a "new Soviet woman"—nearly a proto-feminist. She even takes charge of Anna's child after the mother's suicide.

Although criticized by Soviet authorities at the time for—among other things—being "unrealistic," in particular for its cursory coverage of the Revolution and civil war, Preobrazhenskaya is now credited with making a masterpiece; Denise J. Youngblood has called it "a Soviet melodrama of the highest order." Following the launch of the Cultural Revolution in the spring of 1928, films about the collectivization campaign were encouraged, leading to a spate of "peasant films" in the 1930s; in this way, Preobrazhenskaya's *Peasant Women of Ryazan* was a pioneering film—Youngblood calls it "the only major Soviet film about peasant life made prior to the

Cultural Revolution." *Peasant Women* also helped launch the career of Emma Tsesarskaya (in the role of Vassilisa), who became a star of the 1930s peasant films, including Preobrazhenskaya's own *Grain*—a 1936 film depicting Soviet collective farms battling on one hand with peasants clinging to the past and on the other with the standby-villain kulaks.

Grain was among several films that Preobrazhenskaya made from the late 1920s through 1941 in collaboration with her husband, Ivan Pravov. Among these, 1930's *Cossacks of the Don,* which was adapted from Mikhail Sholokhov's acclaimed novel *The Quiet Don,* is one of the best known. (Tsesarskaya has another starring role in this film.) Taking place during the civil war, it portrays the customs and morals of the Cossacks—and their role in the civil war—in a remarkably even-handed and realistic way, thus staying true to its novel source. A *New York Times* reviewer of the era raved: "The theme is one in which the tragic and the comic are well intermingled, and the ending—the dawn of a new era in Czarist-oppressed Russia—comes as a maturely conceived climax to a story of unusual merit." It is thus almost tragic that, following the completion of the historical epic *Stepan Razin* in 1939 and two more films in 1941, Preobrazhenskaya's career would come to an abrupt end via the Stalin-led purges of the 1940s, fading to black the vision of one of the most important women filmmakers of Russian and Soviet cinema.—DAVID E. SALAMIE

Rainer, Yvonne

American director

Born *San Francisco, 1934.* ***Career*** *From 1957—modern dancer, then choreographer, New York; 1962—co-founder of Judson Dance Theater; 1962-75—presented choreographic work in United States and Europe; 1968—began to integrate slides and short films into dance performances; 1972—completed first feature-length film,* Lives of Performers; *teacher at New School for Social Research, New York, California Institute of the Arts, Valencia, and elsewhere.* ***Awards*** *Maya Deren Award, American Film Institute, 1988; Guggenheim Fellowship, 1969, 1989; MacArthur Fellowship, 1990-95; Wexner Prize, 1995.* ***Address*** *72 Franklin Street, New York, NY 10013, U.S.A.*

Films as Director: 1967: *Volleyball* (*Foot Film*) (short). **1968:** *Hand Movie* (short); *Rhode Island Red* (short); *Trio Film* (short). **1969:** *Line.* **1972:** *Lives of Performers.* **1974:** *Film about a Woman Who. . . .* **1976:** *Kristina Talking Pictures.* **1980:** *Journeys from Berlin/1971.* **1985:** *The Man Who Envied Women.* **1990:** *Privilege.* **1996:** *Murder and Murder.*

Films as Actress Only: 1977: *Madame X—eine absolute Herrscherin* (*Madame X—An Absolute Ruler*) (Ottinger) (as Josephine de Collage).

Although Yvonne Rainer made her first feature-length film in 1972, she had already been prominent in the New York avant-garde art scene for nearly a decade. She moved to New York from San Francisco in 1957 to study acting, but started taking dance lessons and soon committed herself to dance. By the mid-1960s, she emerged as an influential dancer and choreographer, initially drawing the attention of critics and audiences through her work with the Judson Dance Theater.

Rainer saw a problem inherent in dance as an art form, namely its involvement with "narcissism, virtuosity, and display." Her alternative conception was of the performance as a kind of work or task, as opposed to an exhibition, carried out by "neutral 'doers'" rather than performers. Thus the minimalist dance that she pioneered, which depended on ordinary movements, departed radically from the dramatic, emotive forms of both its classical and modern dance precursors.

Rainer was not long content with merely stripping dance of its artifice and conventions. She became interested in psychology and sexuality, in the everyday emotions that people share, and grew dissatisfied with abstract dance, which she found too limited to express her new concerns. To communicate more personal and emotional content, Rainer began experimenting with combining movements with other media, such as recorded and spoken texts, slides, film stills, and music, creating a performance collage. Language and narrative became increasingly important components of her performance.

Rainer's first films, shorts made to be part of these performances in the late 1960s, were "filmed choreographic exercises," as she wrote in 1971, "that were meant to be viewed with one's peripheral vision . . . not to be taken seriously." Her interest in the narrative potential of film and the director's dominance of the medium drew Rainer further into filmmaking.

Her first two feature films, *Lives of Performers* and *Film about a Woman Who . . . ,* both with cinematographer Babette Mangolte, originated as performance pieces. In these and her two other films, *Kristina Talking Pictures* and *Journeys from Berlin/1971,* Rainer interweaves the real and the fictional, the personal and the political, the concrete and the abstract. She preserves the collagist methods of her performances, juxtaposing personal recollections, previous works, historical documents, and original dialogue and narration, her soundtracks often having the same richness, and the same disjunction, as the visual portions of her films.

Like Brecht, Rainer believes that an audience should contemplate what they see; they should participate in the creative process of the film rather than simply receive it passively. Thus, instead of systematically telling a story, she apposes and layers narrative elements to create meaning. The discontinuity, ambiguity, and even contradiction that often result keep Rainer's audience at a distance, so they can examine the feminist, psychological, political, or purely emotional issues she addresses. Consistent with her dance and performance, Rainer's films are theoretical, even intellectual, not dramatic, sentimental, or emotional, despite her subject matter, which is often controversial and emotion-laden.—JESSICA WOLFF

Reiniger, Lotte

British animator

Born *Berlin, 2 June 1899; became citizen of Great Britain.* ***Education*** *Attended Max Reinhardt theater school, Berlin, 1916-17.* ***Family*** *Married Carl Koch, 1921 (died 1963).* ***Career*** *1916—created silhouettes for intertitles of Paul Wegener's* Rübezahls Hochzeit; *1918—introduced by Wegener to film group associated with Dr. Hans Cürlis; 1919—Cürlis's newly founded Institut für Kulturforschung, Berlin, sponsored Reiniger's first film; mid-1930s—with Koch moved to Britain, worked with G.P.O. Film Unit with Len Lye and Norman McLaren; 1936—made* The King's Breakfast, *first film in England; 1946—worked with Märchentheater of city of Berlin at Theater am Schiffbauerdamm; beginning 1950—lived and worked mainly for TV, in England; 1950s and 1960s—created sets and figures for English puppet and shadow theater Hoghart's Puppets; 1953—Primrose Productions set up, sponsored productions for American TV; 1975—began collaboration*

Lotte Reiniger

*with National Film Board of Canada; 1979—*The Rose and the Ring *premiered at American Film Festival.* **Awards** *Silver Dolphin, Venice Biennale, for* Gallant Little Tailor, *1955; Filmband in Gold, West Germany, for service to German cinema, 1972; Verdienst Kreuz, West Germany, 1978.* **Died** *19 June 1981.*

Films as Animator: 1919: *Das Ornament des verliebten Herzens* (*The Ornament of the Loving Heart*). **1920:** *Amor und das standhafte Liebespaar* (*Love and the Steadfast Sweethearts*). **1921:** *Der fliegende Koffer* (*The Flying Coffer*); *Der Stern von Bethlehem* (*The Star of Bethlehem*). **1922:** *Aschenputtel*; *Dornröschen.* **1923-26:** *Die Geschichte des Prinzen Achmed* (*Die Abenteuer des Prinzen Achmed*; *Wak-Wak, ein Märchenzauber*, *The Adventures of Prince Achmed*). **1928:** *Der scheintote Chinese* (originally part of *Die Geschichte des Prinzen Achmed*); *Doktor Dolittle und seine Tiere* (*The Adventures of Dr. Dolittle*) (in 3 parts: *Abenteuer: Die Reise nach Afrika*; *Abenteuer: Die Affenbrücke*; *Abenteuer: Die Affenkrankheit*). **1930:** *Zehn Minuten Mozart.* **1931:** *Harlekin.* **1932:** *Sissi* (intended as interlude for premiere of operetta *Sissi* by Fritz Kreisler, Vienna 1932). **1933:** *Carmen.* **1934:** *Das rollende Rad*; *Der Graf von Carabas*; *Das gestohlene Herz* (*The Stolen Heart*). **1935:** *Der kleine Schornsteinfeger* (*The Little Chimney Sweep*); *Galathea*; *Papageno.* **1936:** *The King's Breakfast.* **1937:** *Tocher.* **1939:** *Dream Circus* (not completed); *L'elisir d'amore* (not released). **1944:** *Die goldene Gans* (not completed). **1951:** *Mary's Birthday.* **1953:** *Aladdin* (for U.S. TV); *The Magic Horse* (for U.S. TV); *Snow White and Rose Red* (for U.S. TV). **1954:** *The Three Wishes* (for U.S. TV); *The Grasshopper and the Ant* (for U.S. TV); *The Frog Prince* (for U.S. TV); *The Gallant Little Tailor* (for U.S. TV); *The Sleeping Beauty* (for U.S. TV); *Caliph Storch* (for U.S. TV). **1955:** *Hansel and Gretel* (for U.S. TV); *Thumbelina* (for U.S. TV); *Jack and the Beanstalk* (for U.S. TV). **1956:** *The Star of Bethlehem* (theatrical film). **1957:** *Helen la Belle* (theatrical film). **1958:** *The Seraglio* (theatrical film). **1960:** *The Pied Piper of Hamelin* (interlude for theatrical performance). **1961:** *The Frog Prince* (interlude for theatrical performance). **1962:** *Wee Sandy* (interlude for theatrical performance). **1963:** *Cinderella* (interlude for theatrical performance). **1974:** *The Lost Son* (interlude for theatrical performance). **1976:** *Aucassin et Nicolette* (Avoine) (interlude for theatrical performance) (short). **1979:** *The Rose and the Ring* (interlude for theatrical performance).

Other Films: 1916: *Rübezahls Hochzeit* (Wegener) (silhouettes for intertitles); *Die Schöne Prinzessin von China* (Gliese) (set decoration, props, and costumes). **1918:** *Apokalypse* (Gliese) (silhouettes for intertitles); *Der Rattenfänger von Hameln* (*The Pied Piper of Hamelin*) (Wegener) (silhouettes for intertitles). **1920:** *Der verlorene Schatten* (Gliese) (silhouette sequence). **1923:** *Die Nibelungen* (F. Lang) (silhouette sequence, not used). **1929-30:** *Die Jagd nach dem Glück* (*Running after Luck*) (Gliese) (co-story, co-sc, co-sound). **1933:** *Don Quichotte* (Pabst) (opening silhouette sequence). **1937:** *La Marseillaise* (Renoir) (created shadow theater seen in film). **1942:** *Una Signora dell'ovest* (Koch) (co-sc).

Lotte Reiniger's career as an independent filmmaker is among the longest and most singular in film history, spanning some 60 years (1919-79) of actively creating silhouette animation films. Her *The Adventures of Prince Achmed* is the world's first feature-length animation film, made when she was in her mid-twenties and winning considerable acclaim.

Silhouette animation existed before 1919, but Reiniger was its preeminent practitioner, transforming a technically and esthetically bland genre to a recognized art form. Since childhood she had excelled at freehand cut-outs and shadow theaters. As a teenager at Max Reinhardt's acting studio, she was invited by actor-director Paul Wegener to make silhouette decorations for the credits and intertitles of *The Pied Piper of Hamelin* (1918); she also helped animate the film's wooden rats, when live guinea pigs proved unmanageable. The rest of Reiniger's professional life was wholeheartedly devoted to silhouette animation, with an occasional retreat to shadow plays or book illustrations when money was not available for films.

Prominent among Reiniger's talents was her transcendence of the inherent flatness and awkwardness of silhouette animation through her dramatic mise en scène and her balletic movements. Her female characters are especially lively and original, displaying wit, sensuousness, and self-awareness rarely found in animated cartoons (from whose creative ranks women animators were virtually excluded until the 1970s). Few real-life actresses could match the expressiveness with which Reiniger inspirited the gestures of her lead-jointed figures as she moved and filmed them fraction by fraction, frame by frame.

For more than four decades, Lotte Reiniger shared her professional life with her husband, Carl Koch, who designed her animation studio and, until his death in 1963, served as her producer and camera operator. "There was nothing about what is called film-technique that he did not know," Jean Renoir wrote in his autobiography. (In the late 1930s, Koch collaborated on the scripts and production of Renoir's celebrated *Grand Illusion* and *Rules of the Game,* and on *La Marseillaise* for which Reiniger created a shadow-play sequence.)

Aside from *The Adventures of Prince Achmed,* Reiniger ventured into feature filmmaking only once, in *Running after Luck,* the story of a wandering showman, part animation and part live-action, which she co-directed with Rochus Gliese. It was a critical and financial failure, perhaps because of its imperfect sound system. The rest of her films were shorts, mainly one or two reels in length.

Reiniger worked outside commercial channels, with minimal support. She said she never felt discrimination because she was a woman, but she did admit resenting that great sums were spent on films of little or no imagination while so little was available for the films she wanted to make. In the 1970s she was coaxed from her retirement to make two films in Canada; she also toured much of Europe, Canada, and the United States under the auspices of the Goethe House cultural centers of the West German government, showing her films and demonstrating her cut-out animation technique.

Hans Richter, who knew Reiniger in the early Berlin years, later wrote that she "belonged to the avant-garde as far as independent production and courage were concerned," but that the spirit of her work seemed Victorian. Jean Renoir placed her even further back in time, as "a visual expression of Mozart's music." It is more likely that, like the fables and myths and fairy tales on which many of her films are based, her work transcends time and fashion.—CECILE STARR

Reville, Alma

British writer

Born *England, 14 August 1899.* ***Family*** *Married the director Alfred Hitchcock, 1926 (died 1980), daughter: Patricia.* ***Career*** *Early 1920s—editor's assistant, London Film, then Famous Players-Lasky, London; 1925—script girl on Hitchcock's* The Pleasure Garden, *then writer of many of his scripts, as well as scripts for other directors; 1939—emigrated to the United States with Hitchcock.* ***Died*** *In Los Angeles, 6 July 1982.*

Films as Co-writer for Director Alfred Hitchcock: **1927:** *The Ring.* **1929:** *Juno and the Paycock.* **1930:** *Murder.* **1931:** *The Skin Game*; *Rich and Strange* (*East of Shanghai*). **1932:** *Number Seventeen.* **1934:** *Waltzes from Vienna* (*Strauss's Great Waltz*). **1935:** *The 39 Steps.* **1936:** *The Secret Agent*; *Sabotage* (*A Woman Alone*). **1937:** *Young and Innocent* (*The Girl Was Young*). **1938:** *The Lady Vanishes.* **1939:** *Jamaica Inn.* **1941:** *Suspicion.* **1943:** *Shadow of a Doubt.* **1947:** *The Paradine Case.* **1950:** *Stage Fright.* **1953:** *I Confess* (uncredited).

Other Films as Co-writer: **1928:** *The Constant Nymph* (Brunel); *The First Born* (Mander). **1929:** *After the Verdict* (Galeen); *A Romance of Seville* (N. Walker). **1931:** *The Outsider* (Lachman); *Sally in Our Alley* (Elvey). **1932:** *The Water Gipsies* (Elvey); *Nine till Six* (Dean). **1934:** *Forbidden Country* (Rosen). **1935:** *The Passing of the Third Floor Back* (Viertel). **1945:** *It's in the Bag* (Wallace).

Films as Editor: **1915:** *The Prisoner of Zenda.* **1923:** *Woman to Woman* (Cutts).

Alma Reville with Alfred Hitchcock

Alma Reville's career is difficult to assess, since during most of it she worked exclusively on the films of her husband, director Alfred Hitchcock. Her contribution to his work fluctuated during the course of their 50-year marriage. It was sometimes that of a professional screenwriter or consultant, more often that of a supportive and knowledgeable wife.

Reville entered the British film industry even earlier than her husband, whose career spanned both the silent and sound eras. From the age of 16, Reville worked as a cutter (editor), first at the London Film Company, then at Famous Players-Lasky's English branch at Islington. Hitchcock's courtship of her began at the latter studio when he invited her to work as a cutter on *Woman to Woman,* an independent production that he was assistant directing under Graham Cutts at Islington; thus from the beginning, the couple's relationship was based on a combination of personal and professional interests. She shared her first screenwriting credit with Hitchcock as co-writer of his boxing melodrama *The Ring* in 1927, while continuing to work with other directors as scriptwriter, continuity girl, and assistant director.

Ambitious and talented, Reville sought to move into the director's chair herself. But the birth of a daughter, Patricia Alma, in 1928 and the family's subsequent move to America altered her ambitions. Joan Harrison, whom Hitchcock hired as a secretary in 1935, quickly took over many of the routine production duties which had previously been Reville's responsibility, while Reville focused exclusively on preparation of her husband's scripts. Harrison eventually became involved in this capacity too, often sharing screen credit with Reville. When the Hitchcocks moved to America in 1939 so that Hitchcock could work under personal contract to David O. Selznick, Harrison went along.

The scripts Reville worked on for Hitchcock in Hollywood were *Suspicion,* a troubled project which was nearly not released; *The Paradine Case,* on which producer Selznick was more exasperating in his interference with Hitchcock than usual; *Stage Fright*; and *I Confess,* which was made on Reville's initiative, but proved to be a box-office failure. Three of these films concern a man who betrays a woman. Reville was partly responsible for this pattern, which probably reflected her attitude toward her husband, whose interest in her waxed and waned; the couple's marriage was reportedly celibate after the birth of their daughter as Hitchcock's romantic fancy attached itself silently and unreciprocally to the various glamorous blonds in his films.

In the mid-1950s, at the peak of Hitchcock's confidence and power, Reville retreated firmly into the background and stayed there. He still sought and respected his wife's judgment on potential projects and relied on her keen eye for detail during the editing process. A famous story about *Psycho* has it that Reville saved its most famous sequence from being marred by a significant blemish that no one else had caught during months of editing. As the final cut was being prepared for release, Hitchcock showed it to her. She alone spotted a single blink of Janet Leigh's eye as the actress lay "dead" following the notorious shower murder scene. The gaffe was replaced with a cutaway shot, and *Psycho* went out to theaters, the sequence shocking audiences around the world and making film history.—PATRICIA FERRARA and JOHN McCARTY

Riefenstahl, Leni

German director

Born *Helene Berta Amalie Riefenstahl in Berlin, 22 August 1902.* ***Education*** *Studied Russian Ballet at the Mary Wigmann School for Dance, Dresden, and Jutta Klamt School for Dance, Berlin.* ***Family*** *Married Peter Jacob, 1944 (divorced 1946).* ***Career*** *From 1920—dancer; from 1936—appeared in "mountain films" directed by Arnold Fanck; 1931—established own production company, Riefenstahl Films; 1932—first film,* Das blaue Licht, *released; 1933—appointed "film expert to the National Socialist Party" by Hitler; 1945-48—detained in various prison camps by Allied Forces on charges of pro-Nazi activity; 1952—charges dismissed by Berlin court, allowed to work in film industry again; 1956—suffered serious auto accident while working in Africa; 1972—commissioned by* The Times *(London) to photograph the Munich Olympics; 1974—honored at Telluride Film Festival, Colorado (festival picketed by anti-Nazi groups); 1993—was the subject of the documentary* The Wonderful, Horrible Life of Leni Riefenstahl, *directed by Ray Müller.* ***Awards*** *Silver Medal, Venice Festival, for* Das blaue Licht, *1932; Exposition Internationale des Arts et des Techniques, Paris, Diplome de Grand Prix, for* Triumph des Willens, *1935; Polar Prize, Sweden, for* Olympia, *1938.* ***Address*** *20 Tengstrasse, 80798 Munich, Germany.*

Films as Director: 1932: *Das blaue Licht* (*The Blue Light*) (+ co-sc, co-pr, ro as Junta). **1933:** *Sieg des Glaubens* (*Victory of the Faith*). **1935:** *Triumph des Willens* (*Triumph of the Will*) (+ pr, ed); *Tag der Freiheit: unsere Wermacht* (+ ed). **1938:** *Olympia* (*Olympische Spiele 1936*) (+ sc, co-ph, ed). **1944:** *Tiefland* (*Lowland*) (co-d with Pabst, + sc, ed, ro as Marta) (released 1954).

Films as Actress: 1926: *Der heilige Berg* (Fanck) (as Diotima). **1927:** *Der grosse Sprung* (Fanck). **1929:** *Das Schiscksal derer von Hapsburg* (*The White Hell of Piz Palü* (Raffé); *Die weisses Hölle vom Piz Palü* (Fanck). **1930:** *Stürme über dem Montblanc* (Fanck). **1931:** *Der weiss Rausch* (Fanck). **1933:** *S.O.S. Eisberg* (Garnett and Fanck). **1995:** *Die Nacht der Regisseure* (*The Night of the Filmmakers*) (Reitz—doc) (appearance).

The years 1932-45 define the major filmmaking efforts of Leni Riefenstahl. Because she remained a German citizen making films in Hitler's Third Reich, two at the Fuhrer's request, she and her films were viewed as pro-Nazi. Riefenstahl claims she took no political position and committed no crimes. In 1948, a German court ruled that she was a follower of, not active in, the Nazi Party. Another court in 1952 reconfirmed her innocence of war crimes. But she is destined to remain a politically controversial filmmaker who made two films rated as masterpieces.

She began to learn filmmaking while acting in the mountain films of Arnold Fanck, her mentor. She made a mountain film of her own, *The Blue Light,* using smoke bombs to create "fog." She used a red and green filter on the camera lens, over her cameraman's objections, to obtain a novel magical effect. This film is Riefenstahl's own favorite. She says it is the story of her own life. Hitler admired *The Blue Light* and asked her to photograph the Nazi Party Congress in Nuremburg. She agreed to make *Victory of the Faith,* which was not publicly viewed. Hitler then asked her to film the 1934 Nazi Party rally.

Triumph of the Will, an extraordinary work, shows Hitler arriving by plane to attend the rally. He proceeds through the crowded streets of Nuremburg, addresses speeches to civilians and uniformed troops, and reviews a five-hour parade. The question is: Did Riefenstahl make

Leni Riefenstahl

Triumph as pro-Nazi propaganda or not? "Cinematically dazzling and ideologically vicious," is R. M. Barsam's judgment. According to Barsam, three basic critical views of *Triumph* exist: 1) those who cannot appreciate the film at all, 2) those who can appreciate and understand the film, and 3) those who appreciate it in spite of the politics in the film.

Triumph premiered 29 March 1935, was declared a masterpiece, and subsequently earned three awards. *Triumph* poses questions of staging. Was the rally staged so that it could be filmed? Did the filming process shape the rally, give it meaning? Riefenstahl's next film, *Olympia,* posed the question of financing. Did Nazi officialdom pay for the film to be made? Riefenstahl claims the film was made independently of any government support. Other opinions differ.

The improvisatory techniques Riefenstahl used to make *Triumph* were improved and elaborated to make *Olympia*. She and her crew worked 16-hour days, seven days a week. *Olympia* opens as *Triumph* does, with aerial scenes. Filmed in two parts, the peak of Olympia I is Jesse Owens's running feat. The peak of Olympia II is the diving scenes. In an interview with Gordon Hitchens in 1964, Riefenstahl revealed her guidelines for making *Olympia*. She decided to make two films instead of one because "the form must excite the content and give it shape. . . . The law of film is architecture, balance. If the image is weak, strengthen the sound, and vice-versa; the total impact on the viewer should be 100 percent." The secret of *Olympia*'s success, she affirmed, was its sound—all laboratory-made. Riefenstahl edited the film for a year and a half. It premiered 20 April 1938 and was declared a masterpiece, being awarded four prizes.

Riefenstahl's career after the beginning of World War II is comprised of a dozen unfinished film projects. She began *Penthesilea* in 1939, *Van Gogh* in 1943, and *Lowland* in 1944, releasing it in 1954. Riefenstahl acted the role of a Spanish girl in it while co-directing with G. W. Pabst this drama of peasant-landowner conflicts. Visiting Africa in 1956, she filmed *Black Cargo,* documenting the slave trade, but her film was ruined by incorrect laboratory procedures. In the 1960s, she lived with and photographed the Mesakin Nuba tribe in Africa.

Riefenstahl's *Triumph of the Will* and *Olympia* are two of the greatest documentaries ever made. That is indisputable. And it also is indisputable that they are among the most notorious and controversial. Each has been lauded for its sheer artistry, yet damned for its content and vision of Adolf Hitler and a German nation poised on the edge of totalitarian barbarism. After years as a name in the cinema history books, Riefenstahl was back in the news in 1992. *Memoirnen,* her autobiography, was first published in English as *The Sieve of Time: The Memoirs of Leni Riefenstahl,* and she was the subject of a documentary, Ray Müller's *The Wonderful, Horrible Life of Leni Riefenstahl.* Clearly, Riefenstahl had written the book and participated in the documentary in an attempt to have the final word regarding the debate over her involvement with Hitler and the Third Reich.

The documentary, which is three hours in length, traces Riefenstahl's undeniably remarkable life, from her success as a dancer and movie actress during the 1920s to her career as a director, her post-World War II censure, and her latter-day exploits as a still photographer. Still very much alive at age ninety-five, Riefenstahl is shown scuba diving, an activity she first took up in her seventies.

Riefenstahl is described at the outset as a "legend with many faces" and "the most influential filmmaker of the Third Reich." The film goes on to serve as an investigation of her life. Was she an opportunist, as she so vehemently denies, or a victim? Was she a "feminist pioneer, or a woman of evil?" Riefenstahl wishes history to view her as she views herself: not as a collaborator but as an artist first and foremost, whose sole fault was to have been alive in the wrong place at the wrong moment in history, and who was exploited by political forces of which she was unaware.

Upon meeting Hitler, she says, "He seemed a modest, private individual." She was "ignorant" of his ideas and politics, and "didn't see the danger of anti-Semitism." She claims to have acquiesced to making *Triumph of the Will* only after Hitler agreed that she would never have to make another film for him. To her, shooting *Triumph* was just a job. She wanted to make a film that was "interesting, one that was not with posed shots. . . . It had to be filmed the way an artist, not a politician, sees it." The same holds true for *Olympia,* which features images of perfectly proportioned, God-like German athletes. When queried regarding the issue of whether these visuals reflect a fascist aesthetic, Riefenstahl refuses to answer directly, replaying again that art and politics are separate entities.

"If an artist dedicates himself totally to his work, he cannot think politically," Riefenstahl says. Even in the late 1930s, she chose not to leave Germany because, as she observes, "I loved my homeland." She claims that she hoped that reports of anti-Semitism were "isolated events." And her image of Hitler was "shattered much too late. . . . My life fell apart because I believed in Hitler. People say of me, 'She doesn't want to know. She'll always be a Nazi.' [But] I was never a Nazi."

"What am I guilty of?" Riefenstahl asks. "I regret [that I was alive during that period]. But I was never anti-Semitic. I never dropped any bombs." Explained director Müller, after a New York Film Festival screening of the film, "She was an emancipated woman before there was even such a term. She has a super ego, which has been trod upon for half a century. . . . [She is] an artist and a perfectionist. I believe that she was purposefully blind not to look in the direction that would get her into trouble."

In this regard, *The Wonderful, Horrible Life of Leni Riefenstahl* ultimately works as a portrait of denial. As Müller so aptly observes, "Any artist has a great responsibility. Anyone who influences the public has this. She is possessed with her art. She says, 'I'm only doing my thing.' I think this is irresponsible. She may be obsessed and possessed, and a genius. But that does not exempt her from responsibility."

In 1995, Riefenstahl briefly resurfaced in Edgar Reitz's *The Night of the Filmmakers,* consisting of interviews with German filmmakers from Frank Beyer to Wim Wenders. Eric Hansen, writing in *Variety,* summed up the essence of her appearance by noting, "Names like the ninety-two-year-old Leni Riefenstahl and young director Detlev Buck are allowed only a few self-glorifying or sarcastic comments."

Perhaps the final word on Riefenstahl is found in Istvan Szabo's *Hanussen,* a 1988 German-Hungarian film. Much of *Hanussen* is set in Germany between the World Wars. One of the minor characters is a celebrated, egocentric woman artist, a member of the political inner circle, who surrounds herself with physical beauty while remaining callously unconcerned with all but her own vanity. Clearly, this character is based on Riefenstahl.—LOUISE HECK-RABI and ROB EDELMAN

Rose, Helen

American costume designer

Born *Chicago, c. 1904.* ***Education*** *Attended Chicago Academy of Fine Arts.* ***Family*** *Married Harry Rose, 1929, daughter: Jode.* ***Career*** *Worked for Lester Costume Company and Ernie Young's costume house, Chicago; designer for Fanchon and Marco's Ice Follies, 14 years; 1942—costume designer for MGM until her retirement, 1966.* ***Awards*** *Academy Awards, for* The Bad and the Beautiful, *1952, and* I'll Cry Tomorrow, *1955.* ***Died*** *In Palm Springs, California, 9 November 1985.*

Films as Costume Designer: 1943: *Coney Island* (W. Lang) (co); *Hello Frisco, Hello* (Humberstone) (co); *Stormy Weather* (A. L. Stone). **1946:** *The Harvey Girls* (Sidney) (co); *Two Sisters from Boston* (Koster) (co); *Ziegfeld Follies* (Minnelli) (co); *Till the Clouds Roll By* (Whorf) (co). **1947:** *Good News* (Walters) (co); *Merton of the Movies* (Alton) (co); *The Unfinished Dance* (Koster). **1948:** *A Date with Judy* (Thorpe); *Homecoming* (LeRoy); *Words and Music* (Taurog) (co); *Luxury Liner* (Whorf) (co); *The Bride Goes Wild* (Taurog); *Big City* (Taurog). **1949:** *Act of Violence* (Zinnemann); *On the Town* (Kelly and Donen); *The Red Danube* (Sidney); *The Stratton Story* (Wood); *Take Me Out to the Ball Game* (Berkeley) (co); *East Side, West Side* (LeRoy); *That Midnight Kiss* (Taurog). **1950:** *A Life of Her Own* (Cukor); *Nancy Goes to Rio* (Leonard); *Pagan Love Song* (Alton); *Summer Stock* (Walters) (co); *Three Little Words* (Thorpe); *To Please a Lady* (*Red Hot Wheels*) (C. Brown); *The Toast of New Orleans* (Taurog) (co); *The Reformer and the Redhead* (Panama and Frank); *Annie Get Your Gun* (Sidney) (co); *Father of the Bride* (Minnelli) (co); *The Duchess of Idaho* (Leonard); *The Big Hangover* (Minnelli); *Grounds for Marriage* (Leonard); *Two Weeks with Love* (Rowland) (co); *Right Cross* (J. Sturges); *Three Guys Named Mike* (Walters). **1951:** *Father's Little Dividend* (Minnelli); *The Great Caruso* (Thorpe) (co); *The Light Touch* (R. Brooks); *Texas Carnival* (Walters); *The Unknown Man* (Thorpe); *Excuse My Dust* (Rowland) (co); *No Questions Asked* (Kress); *Strictly Dishonorable* (Panama and Frank); *The Strip* (Kardos); *Too Young to Kiss* (Leonard); *Callaway Went Thataway* (Frank and Panama); *The People against O'Hara* (J. Sturges) (co); *Love Is Better Than Ever* (Donen); *Rich, Young and Pretty* (Taurog); *Bannerline* (Weis). **1952:** *The Girl in White* (J. Sturges) (co); *Because You're Mine* (Hall); *Above and Beyond* (Panama and Frank); *Glory Alley* (Walsh); *The Bad and the Beautiful* (Minnelli); *Invitation* (Bernhardt); *Holiday for Sinners* (Mayer); *The Merry Widow* (Bernhardt) (co); *Million Dollar Mermaid* (LeRoy) (co); *Skirts Ahoy!* (Lanfield); *The Belle of New York* (Walters) (co); *Washington Story* (Pirosh); *Everything I Have Is Yours* (Leonard). **1953:** *Dangerous When Wet* (Walters); *Dream Wife* (Sheldon) (co); *Jeopardy* (J. Sturges); *Latin Lovers* (LeRoy) (co); *Mogambo* (Ford); *Sombrero* (N. Foster); *The Story of Three Loves* (Reinhardt and Minnelli); *Torch Song* (Walters); *I Love Melvin* (Weis); *Small Town Girl* (Kardos); *Remains to Be Seen* (Weis); *Easy to Love* (Walters); *Give a Girl a Break* (Donen) (co); *The Girl Who Had Everything* (Thorpe); *Escape from Fort Bravo* (J. Sturges). **1954:** *Athena* (Thorpe) (co); *Executive Suite* (Wise); *Green Fire* (Marton); *Her Twelve Men* (Leonard); *The Last Time I Saw Paris* (R. Brooks); *Rhapsody* (C. Vidor); *The Long, Long Trailer* (Minnelli); *Rogue Cop* (Rowland); *Rose Marie* (LeRoy) (co); *The Student Prince* (Thorpe) (co); *The Glass Slipper* (Walters) (co); *The Flame and the Flesh* (R. Brooks). **1955:** *Bedevilled* (Leisen) (co); *Deep in My Heart* (Donen) (co); *Hit the Deck* (Rowland); *I'll Cry Tomorrow* (Daniel Mann); *Interrupted Melody* (Bernhardt); *It's Always Fair Weather* (Kelly and Donen); *Jupiter's Darling* (Sidney) (co); *Love Me or Leave Me* (C. Vidor); *The Rains of Ranchipur* (Negulesco) (co); *The Tender Trap* (Walters). **1956:** *Forbidden Planet* (Wilcox) (co); *Gaby* (Beaumont); *High Society* (Beaudine); *Meet Me in Las Vegas* (Rowland); *The Opposite Sex* (Miller); *The Power and the Prize* (Koster); *Ransom!* (Segal); *The Swan* (C. Vidor); *Tea and Sympathy* (Minnelli); *These Wilder Years* (Rowland). **1957:** *Designing Woman* (Minnelli); *Don't Go Near the Water* (Walters); *The Seventh Sin* (Neame); *Silk Stockings* (Mamoulian); *Something of Value* (R. Brooks); *Tip on a Dead Jockey* (Thorpe); *Ten Thousand Bedrooms* (Thorpe); *This Could Be the Night* (Wise). **1958:** *Cat on a Hot Tin Roof* (R. Brooks); *Party Girl* (N. Ray); *The High Cost of Loving* (J. Ferrer); *Saddle the Wind* (Parrish); *The Reluctant Debutante* (Minnelli) (co); *The Tunnel of Love* (Kelly); *Torpedo Run* (Pevney). **1959:** *Ask Any Girl* (Walters); *Count Your Blessings* (Negulesco); *It Started with a Kiss* (George Marshall); *The Mating Game* (George Marshall). **1960:** *All the Fine Young Cannibals* (M. Anderson);

Butterfield 8 (Daniel Mann); *The Gazebo* (George Marshall); *Never So Few* (J. Sturges). **1961:** *Ada* (Daniel Mann); *Bachelor in Paradise* (Arnold); *Go Naked in the World* (MacDougall); *The Honeymoon Machine* (Thorpe); *Two Loves* (Walters). **1963:** *The Courtship of Eddie's Father* (Minnelli). **1964:** *Goodbye Charlie* (Minnelli). **1966:** *Made in Paris* (Sagal); *Mister Buddwing* (*Woman without a Face*) (Delbert Mann); *The Singing Nun* (Koster). **1968:** *How Sweet It Is!* (Paris).

Helen Rose was born on Chicago's south side on a yet undetermined date (Rose came from an era when women felt compelled not to reveal their true age). Dates vary from 1904-18. Because of this, she often appears as precocious as Mozart with her list of early achievements. It is most likely, however, that Rose started her career in her late teens.

She began studies at the Chicago Academy of Fine Arts. While still in school she got a job at the Lester Costume Company creating "girlie" costumes for vaudeville and nightclub extravaganzas. She developed tremendous versatility turning chorus girls into, amongst other things, dancing cupcakes. She then worked at Ernie Young's costume house for three years gaining more experience and earning a highly regarded reputation as a theatrical designer. She expanded creatively and technically working for Young and at other companies, and learned the difficult art of chiffon design, a skill that she would later find useful in Hollywood. Continuing in the costume business, Rose moved to Los Angeles in 1929 to a company that supplied wardrobes for film studios. For several months she worked at 20th Century-Fox until a political upheaval in their costume department put an end to that assignment. She then became designer for the Ice Follies and stayed with them for 14 years. She was content with this work until MGM gave her a financial offer she could not refuse. The studio was still searching for a replacement for Adrian and did not feel confident that any of their current designers had taken his place. Irene was working at MGM at the time and Rose was assigned to design clothes only for the younger stars. Nevertheless, while the two designers were jointly doing a film for director Joe Pasternak, he so openly preferred Rose that Irene angrily left the studio.

Pasternak was not the only one who favored Rose. Even in their private lives, stars would ask for her. She created wedding gowns for Liz Taylor, Ann Blyth, Jane Powell, Pier Angeli, and Debbie Reynolds. It greatly upset Edith Head when Head's good friend Grace Kelly requested a Helen Rose gown for her marriage to the Prince of Monaco. Rose was also a favorite of Louis B. Mayer, who referred to her as "my sweetheart Rose." In general she was well-liked at the studio and dressed almost every major actress for MGM. Others who wore her costumes in addition to those mentioned above were Ava Gardner, Deborah Kerr, Cyd Charisse, Jane Powell, and Lena Horne.

Rose's designs were well structured with a strong emphasis on the silhouette. She kept her use of decoration simple and subdued. Her designs were elegant and understated, yet innovative, looking natural in spite of their theatrical nature. Like her rival at Paramount, Edith Head, Rose used designs that suited the new demands of the 1950s. They were more practical than fanciful; the sort of clothes a nice upper-middle-class suburbanite might wear. These clothes were also a goal to which less affluent members of the audience could aspire. Rose was not limited to the contemporary look, however, and could equally design excellent and accurate period costuming, as in *The Swan*.

Clothing manufacturers were not blind to the fact that Rose's designs were popular with the public. Her wedding dress for *Father of the Bride* was extensively copied by New York fashion designers. Her inventive bathing suits for the Esther Williams pictures, made of light new fabrics, influenced bathing-suit manufacturers such as Catalina, Jantzen, and Rose Marie Reid. In the 1958 film *Cat on a Hot Tin Roof,* Liz Taylor's white chiffon gown with the revealing décolletage caused a sensation. The star asked for a copy for her personal wardrobe and Rose received so many additional requests for copies that she decided to enter the wholesale garment business. Her expensive ready-to-wear was sold under franchise to exclusive department stores and speciality shops across the country. In making this move Rose may have reasoned that she could express herself more creatively and make a better living as a ready-to-wear designer. She might have also suspected, however, that the time of the great studio costume designers was coming to an end.

By the time she left the studio in 1966, Helen Rose had designed more than 200 pictures and had received two Academy Awards, for *The Bad and the Beautiful* and *I'll Cry Tomorrow.*—EDITH C. LEE

Russell, Shirley

British costume designer

Born *Shirley Ann Kingdon in London, 1935.* ***Education*** *Attended Royal College of Art, London.* ***Family*** *Married the director Ken Russell, 1957 (divorced 1979), sons: Alex, James, Xavier, and Toby, daughter: Victoria.* ***Career*** *Worked as costume designer on documentary, then on feature films directed by Ken Russell, and for other directors.*

Films as Costume Designer: 1963: *French Dressing* (K. Russell). **1967:** *Billion Dollar Brain* (K. Russell); *Dante's Inferno* (K. Russell—for TV). **1969:** *Women in Love* (K. Russell). **1970:** *The Music Lovers* (K. Russell); *The Boys in the Band* (Friedkin). **1971:** *The Devils* (K. Russell); *The Boy Friend* (K. Russell). **1972:** *Savage Messiah* (K. Russell). **1974:** *Mahler* (K. Russell); *Tommy* (K. Russell); *The Little Prince* (Donen). **1975:** *Lisztomania* (K. Russell); *Inserts* (Byrum). **1977:** *Valentino* (K. Russell). **1978:** *Clouds of Glory* (K. Russell—2 parts, for TV). **1979:** *Yanks* (Schlesinger); *Cuba* (Lester); *Agatha* (Apted). **1981:** *Reds* (Beatty); *Lady Chatterley's Lover* (Jaeckin). **1982:** *The Return of the Soldier* (Bridges). **1983:** *Wagner* (Palmer). **1984:** *The Razor's Edge* (Byrum); *Greystoke: The Legend of Tarzan, Lord of the Apes* (Hudson). **1985:** *The Bride* (Roddam). **1987:** *Hope and Glory* (Boorman). **1996:** *Gulliver's Travels* (Sturridge—for TV). **1997:** *Illumination* (Sturridge).

Shirley Russell rose to prominence as a costume designer during the 1960s and 1970s working with her then-husband, the director Ken Russell. Her work remained precisely detailed and delicately stylized even as that of her husband became more extreme and outrageous. In *Women in Love,* Shirley Russell's costumes are brilliantly accurate not only in rendering the Edwardian period in general, but in sketching crucial class distinctions and even in lampooning characters' social aspirations. The clearest indication of her talents is in the differences of garb between the Brangwens and the Criches, but even more persuasive are the small nuances of costume, in the film's early scenes, that demarcate the contrasting styles of Rupert's and Gerald's dandyism. In *The Music Lovers,* the character of Nina Tchaikovsky seems almost as much a product of Russell's costumes as of Glenda Jackson's exquisite performance. Nina's descent from fresh-faced maiden to besotted madwoman is aptly reflected in the explosions of color and texture of her early costumes that gradually give way, as she becomes more frustrated and unhappy, to monochromatic rags. *The Devils* was very much a turning point in its director's career, but it was also a turning point in his collaboration with Shirley Russell. While Ken Russell's vision becomes ever more Baroque, Shirley Russell remains concerned with minute

Shirley Russell

observations of specific social manners. In *The Devils,* Russell's costumes expertly match Derek Jarman's wildly stylized production design, from the stark, hauntingly jet-gray robes of Sister Jeanne to the imperious attire of Grandier. At the same time, however, the intricacy of Shirley Russell's costumes may begin to seem out of keeping with the much broader strokes—to put it mildly—of her husband's direction.

After the end of their collaboration, Ken Russell's directorial strokes—to continue putting it mildly—become even broader, and many of his period pieces lack the flavor that had been provided by the meticulously exact costumes of his ex-wife. Perhaps sensing this lack, Russell even went so far as to set his adaptation of Bram Stoker's *The Lair of the White Worm* in the present, with predictably disastrous results. Shirley Russell, meanwhile, seemed very much at home in such comparatively realistic projects as Schlesinger's *Yanks* or Warren Beatty's *Reds,* continuing to explore the social and personal ramifications of costume.—JAMES MORRISON

Sagan, Leontine

Austrian director

Born *Leontine Schlesinger in Vienna, Austria, 1899 (some sources say 1889); moved to Johannesburg with her family.* ***Education*** *Trained with Max Reinhardt in Berlin.* ***Family*** *Married Dr. Victor Fleischer.* ***Career*** *1910s-20s—won her initial fame as a stage actress and director in Germany and Austria; 1931—won international fame with her debut feature,* Mädchen in Uniform; *1932—went to England to direct her next feature,* Men of Tomorrow, *for Alexander Korda; mid-1930s—worked at Korda's studios; returned to working on the stage in England; from 1939—moved to South Africa, where she had spent her childhood, and became one of the key directors in South African theater, and co-founded the National Theatre in Johannesburg.* ***Died*** *In Pretoria, South Africa, 23 May 1974.*

Films as Director: 1931: *Mädchen in Uniform* (*Girls in Uniform; Maidens in Uniform*). **1932:** *Men of Tomorrow* (co-d with Z. Korda, + ed). **1946:** *Gaiety George* (*Showtime*) (co-d with G. King and F. Carpenter).

Throughout her long career, most of which was spent as a stage director, Leontine Sagan directed only three films. The latter two were made in England, and are all but forgotten: *Men of Tomorrow,* chronicling the travails of a rebellious young Oxford University student; and *Gaiety George,* a biography of Irish-born stage producer George Edwardes (who is inexplicably called "George Howard" on screen).

But Sagan's first, *Mädchen in Uniform,* is a classic of pre-Hitler German cinema, a profoundly antifascist political tract as well as a groundbreaking and liberating depiction of a crystal-clear eroticism between women.

Mädchen in Uniform is the story of Manuela, a pretty 14-year-old who arrives at a Potsdam boarding school run in a strict, militaristic manner by Prussian Frau Oberin, the headmistress. "I demand absolute discipline," declares Oberin. Many of her charges are the children of Prussian soldiers, she observes, and hopefully they will grow up to be the wives of Prussian soldiers. Her

Prussianism is ever-apparent upon her declaration, as the girls gripe about their lack of food, that "through discipline and hunger, hunger and discipline, we shall rise again."

Despite their preordained destiny as dutiful soldiers' wives, there are hints of romantic attachments (if not downright physical relations) between the girls. Upon her arrival, one of her fellow students tells Manuela, "Well, don't fall in love. . . ." Meanwhile, all the girls have developed crushes on Fräulein von Bernburg, their sole sympathetic, nonauthoritarian teacher/housemistress.

On one level, the students are like typical adolescents as they act girlishly silly, talk about movie stars, and comically imitate their teachers. Yet it seems as if every last one has formed a romantic or physical attachment within the boundaries of their school. They have made such connections not necessarily because they are lesbians; these girls are lonely and desperate for affection, and are turning to each other because they live in a world completely devoid of boys and men.

The female-to-female eroticism in *Mädchen in Uniform,* both implied and obvious, is unmistakable throughout. There is much talk (as well as footage) of the girls dressing and undressing. Girls constantly walk hand-in-hand, or arm-in-arm. There is an emphasis on the girls' developing bodies. At one point, a girl rehearses dialogue for a school play while another sits at her feet, stroking her naked leg.

Fräulein von Bernburg is depicted as a responsible and caring adult who is deeply concerned with the welfare of the students, and who tells Manuela to make up her mind to be happy at school. Yet her involvement with the girls is not restricted to disseminating kindly advice. Each night, as they are about to retire, von Bernburg presents each girl with a kiss on the forehead. It becomes clear that a special attachment is developing between von Bernburg and Manuela when, after bidding goodnight to the others, she kisses the youngster on the lips.

From that point on, Manuela is enraptured by the Fräulein. Manuela does well in every other class but von Bernburg's, because she is so distracted by the teacher. She announces that, at night, she would like to enter von Bernburg's room, talk with her, and hold her hand.

Mädchen in Uniform ends on an idealistically upbeat note. Upon Manuela's publicly declaring her feelings toward her cherished teacher, Oberin pronounces that she is to be isolated from the others and blames von Bernburg for the "revolutionary ideas" instilled inside the girls. After the girls ignore Oberin and collectively save Manuela from committing suicide, the headmistress is shown walking down a flight of stairs in defeat, which symbolizes her loss of power and influence.

Mädchen in Uniform is a film about physical and spiritual liberation, in which caring, warmth, and intimacy triumph over blind authority, militarism, and repression. Unfortunately, just as the film was playing in movie houses, it was the Frau Oberins who were seizing power in Germany. Two years after its release, Hitler became the nation's chancellor—and dictator. While *Mädchen in Uniform* initially was greeted enthusiastically by critics in Germany and abroad, it eventually was banned by Goebbels. But the film remains significant not just for its antiauthoritarianism/militarism theme and female-to-female imagery. By way of its union of dialogue and sound, gleaned from her formidable theatrical experience, Sagan displayed a mastery of the then-new sound film medium. Her use of visuals is equally impressive. By superimposing the images of Manuela and Fräulein von Bernburg, she communicates their intense psychological association.

Soon after directing *Mädchen in Uniform,* Sagan abandoned Germany for England, and eventually became a preeminent stage director in South Africa. But with this film, her place in the history of both German and gay cinema is assured.—ROB EDELMAN

Sander, Helke

German director and writer

Born *Berlin, 31 January 1937.* ***Education*** *Attended drama school, studying with Ida Ehre, Hamburg, 1957-58; studied German and psychology at the University of Helsinki, 1960-62; studied at the Deutsche Film-und Fernsehakademie, Berlin, 1966-69.* ***Family*** *Married the Finnish writer Markku Lahtela, 1959, one son: Silvio.* ***Career*** *1962—worked in Finnish theater; 1964—worked for Finnish television; 1965—returned to Germany; 1966—directed first short film* Subjectivity; *1974—founded* Frauen und Film; *since 1981—professor at the Hamburg University for Visual Arts; co-director for the Bremen Institute for Film and Television.* ***Awards*** *Women's Film Hyères, and Prix l'age d'or, Brussels, for* Redupers, *1977; Golden Bear and German Film Prize, Filmband in Gold, for* No. 1—From the Reports of Security Guards and Patrol Services, *1984.* ***Address*** *Hochschule für Bildende Künste, Hamburg, Germany.*

Films as Director and Writer: **1966:** *Subjektitüde* (*Subjectivity*). **1967:** *Silvio*; *Brecht die Macht der Manipulateure* (*Crush the Power of the Manipulators*). **1969:** *Kindergärtnerin, was nun?* (*What Now, Nursery Workers*); *Kinder sind nicht Rinder* (*Children Are Not Cattle*). **1971:** *Eine Prämie für Irene* (*A Bonus for Irene*) (co-d). **1972:** *Macht die Pille Frei?* (*Does the Pill Liberate?*) (co-d). **1973:** *Männerbunde* (*Male Bonding*) (co-d). **1977:** *Die allseitig reduzierte Persönlichkeit* (*Redupers*; *The All-Around Reduced Personality*) (+ ro as Edda Chiemnyjewski). **1981:** *Der subjektive Faktor* (*The Subjective Factor*). **1983:** *Der Beginn aller Schrecken ist Liebe* (*The Trouble with Love*) (+ ro as lover). **1984:** *Nr. 1—Aus Berichten der Wach—und Patrouillendienst* (*No. 1—From the Reports of Security Guards and Patrol Services*) (doc); *Nr. 8—Aus Berichten der Wach—und Patrouillendienst* (*No. 8—From the Reports of Security Guards and Patrol Services*) (doc). **1986:** "Füttern" ("Gluttony") ep. of *Sieben Frauen—Sieben Sünden* (*Seven Women—Seven Sins*). **1987:** *Felix* (co-d with Buschmann, Sanders-Brahms, and von Trotta). **1990:** *Die Deutschen und ihre Männer* (*The Germans and Their Men*). **1992:** *BeFreier und Befreite Krieg, Vergewaltigung, Kinder* (*Liberators Take Liberties: War, Rape, Children*) (doc). **1997:** *Dazlak.*

Other Films: **1983:** *Vater und Sohn* (*Father and Son*) (Mitscherlich) (ro). **1988:** *Das schwache Geschlecht muss stärker werden* (*The Weaker Sex Must Become Stronger*) (ro as herself). **1992:** *Des Lebens schönste Seiten* (*Life's Most Beautiful Sides*) (Heine—for TV) (ro as Neri). **1995:** *Die Nacht der Regisseure* (*The Night of the Filmmakers*) (Reitz—doc) (appearance).

Helke Sander's name has become synonymous with the advent of Germany's second wave women's movement and feminist filmmaking. Provocative in style and subject matter, her self-reflexive documentaries and later fictional explorations of women's experiences reveal the ambition to politicize the private sphere and to challenge habitual ways of seeing. Owing to her unconventional choice of topics, Sander received no funding for a period of about five years with the justification that her proposed themes addressed only women instead of appealing to a general public. It was not until 1977 that Sander was able to direct her break-through and best-known feature-length film, *Redupers* which focuses on the life of Edda, a freelance

Helke Sander

photographer, mother, and activist who faces the conflicting demands of her private and professional life and who confronts sexism in the media when a photoessay of women's views of Berlin, commissioned by a mainstream magazine, is rejected.

While still at the Film and Television Academy, Sander became active in the student movement. In her 1968 address at the Socialist Student's Association ("Speech by the Action Council for Women's Liberation"), Sander criticized the male Left for its disregard of women's issues and, more generally, for a political analysis that overlooked the private realm. Disaffected with the Left's blind spots, Sander co-founded the Council for Women's Liberation. This experience is reflected in *The Subjective Factor,* a work of memory that traces the beginnings of the women's movement in Germany and the break with the socialist student movement and the APO (extraparliamentary opposition). Interspersed with documentary footage, the subjective, autobiographical fiction challenges the claim of the objectivity of historical narration and the documentary genre. In *The Trouble with Love* the paradoxical politics of emotion are parodied when two liberated, though jealous, women vie for the same man and perform for his gaze. The film addresses the oppressive structures that shape interpersonal relations as well as collective histories commented on in a voice-over. *The Germans and Their Men* similarly explores the failure to link the deeply entrenched public and private divide in numerous interviews with men who neglect to contemplate their conduct toward women. In *Liberators Take Liberties,* an ambitious three-and-one-half-hour documentary film, Sander probes the stories of German women who were raped predominately by soldiers of the Red Army in the last days of World War II. A montage of present-day interviews breaks through the silence that has beleaguered personal and public memory. Sander's film *Duzlak,* a road movie/comedy, depicts chance meeting between Jenny and a skinhead whom she tries to help after he hits a tree with his car while driving under the influence.

Throughout her career, in her films, essays, and most recently in her short stories, Sander has remained provocative and unveering in her pursuit to expose the asymmetrical power structures that disadvantage women and the general resistance to an analysis of gendered relations. Besides her own filmmaking interests, her formidable accomplishments include founding the first, and only, feminist film journal in Europe, *Frauen und Film,* in 1974—recovering works of women directors, actors, and scriptwriters either forgotten or ignored by film history, addressing the conditions under which women make films and the policies and preferences of funding agencies, and supporting women filmmakers who found little backing or visibility. In 1974 she co-organized the International Women's Film Seminar to promote women's productions.—BARBARA KOSTA

Sanders-Brahms, Helma

German director and writer

Born *Helma Sanders in Emden, Germany, 20 November 1940; added her mother's maiden name to her own to differentiate herself from another New German Cinema filmmaker, Helke Sander.* ***Education*** *Studied acting in Hanover, Germany; studied drama and literature at Cologne University.* ***Family*** *Daughter, the actress Anna Sanders.* ***Career*** *1960s—worked as an announcer and interviewer for a Cologne television station; 1970-began directing shorts and documentaries for German television; 1971—directed first feature,* Gewelt; *1974—made* Erdbeben in Chile, *her first film for the Filmverlag der Autoren, set up by 13 New German Cinema directors as a production and distribution co-operative.*

Helma Sanders-Brahms: *Deutschland, Bleiche Mutter.*

Films as Director and Writer: **1970:** *Angelika Urban, Verkaüferin, Verlobt* (*Angelika Urban, Salesgirl, Engaged*) (short). **1971:** *Gewalt* (*Violence*) (for TV); *Die industrielle Reservarmee* (*The Industrial Reserve Army*) (doc—for TV). **1972:** *Der Angestellte* (*The Employee*) (for TV). **1973:** *Die maschine* (*The Machine*) (doc). **1974:** *Die letzten Tage von Gomorrah* (*The Last Days of Gomorrah*) (for TV); *Erdbeben in Chile* (*Earthquake in Chile*) (for TV). **1975:** *Unter dem Pflaster ist der Strand* (*The Sand under the Pavement*). **1976:** *Shirins Hochzeit* (*Shirin's Wedding*) (for TV). **1977:** *Heinrich.* **1980:** *Deutschland, bleiche Mutter* (*Germany, Pale Mother*) (+ pr); *Vringsveedeler Triptichon* (*The Vringsveedel Tryptych*) (doc). **1981:** *Die Berührte* (*No Mercy No Future, No Exit No Panic*) (+ pr, costumes, makeup). **1982:** *Die Erbtöchter* (*The Daughters' Inheritance*) (co-d). **1984:** *Flügel und Fesseln* (*L'Avenir d'Emilie, The Future of Emily*). **1985:** *Alte Liebe* (*Old Love*) (doc—for TV) (co-sc). **1986:** *Laputa.* **1987:** *Felix* (co-d with Buschmann, Sander, and von Trotta). **1988:** *Geteilte Liebe* (*Divided Love, Manoever*) (+ pr). **1992:** *Apfelbaume* (*Apple Trees*). **1995:** *Lumière et compagnie* (*Lumière and Company*) (doc) (co-d); *Jetzt leben—Juden in Berlin.* **1997:** *Mein Herz-Niemandem* (*My Heart Is Mine Alone*). **2000:** *Clara.*

Other Films: **1981:** *Der Subjektive Faktor* (ro). **1995:** *Die Nacht der Regisseure* (*The Night of the Filmmakers*) (Reitz—doc) (appearance).

The films of Helma Sanders-Brahms have been programmed with some amount of relish at film festivals and in art houses and cinematheques, but it is a safe bet that they never will be mainstream movie fare. They are not engrossing dramas in which the audience can become emotionally involved in the on-screen action. Instead, Sanders-Brahms presents, from a distance, observable archetypes of life, often with a deliberate pacing. Rather than directing actors to express emotion, she prefers "pent-up" performers who hide their real feelings. In fact, actor Heinrich Giskes found himself so emotionally "pent-up" while shooting a scene for *Heinrich* that he broke a glass over his director's head as soon as she yelled cut.

Sanders-Brahms is a rebel to Hollywood conventions. She avoids casting glamorous leading ladies or hunky actors in order to sell tickets, and her films are often very slowly paced. She does not make "road movies," because she does not revel in what she calls "the poetry of the road, the journey. The autobahn and the factory assembly line are the same thing, the same prison."

A producer and writer in addition to director, Sanders-Brahms is a member of the New German Cinema movement, and as such she builds her scripts around the concerns of the political left. Many of her films present themes pertaining to the plight of the worker in Germany: the inequities of modern working conditions; how workers have been pitted against one another in order to attain Germany's capitalist "economic miracle"; and how the Gastarbeiter ("guest worker," or foreign migrant worker in Germany) is exploited. *Shirin's Wedding* addresses the Gastarbeiter problem, focusing on the suffering of a Turkish woman. As a child, Shirin was betrothed to Mahmud, but he left for Germany to become a Gastarbeiter. To escape an arranged marriage, Shirin travels to Germany to find Mahmud. She obtains work in a factory in Cologne and later as a cleaner, a job that disappears after she is raped by her boss. She winds up a prostitute, with Mahmud paying to have sex with her. Eventually, she is killed by a pimp's bullet. In *No Mercy No Future,* the daughter of a bourgeois family seeks sexual partners in the streets, including black migrant workers, derelicts, and aged, crippled cast-offs of society. In these neglected people, she sees the essence of Christ. Finally, *Apple Trees* shows the destruction of a family whose members are adversely affected by the politics of reunification.

Other motifs in Sanders-Brahms's work are the independent woman under fire and the mother-daughter relationship. She herself was raised by her self-reliant mother while her father was away fighting in Hitler's armies. He did not return until she was five years old. Much of her perception of her parents' relationship and her own childhood is depicted in *Germany, Pale*

Mother, one of her best-known films. The mother is shown as a strong and independent woman who gives birth to her daughter (played by Sanders-Brahms's own baby girl) during an air raid. When the war ends, this woman is expected to file away her independence in order to be an obedient wife. She does so, but her frustrations take hold in the form of a disease which paralyzes her face and, in a gut-wrenching scene, calls for the removal of all her teeth. *The Future of Emily* tells of an actress who lives a single, unconventional lifestyle. She returns to her parents' home to retrieve her daughter, only to be told by her own mother that she is a bad influence on the child. In a powerful scene the actress and her little girl visit the beach, where they spin fantasy adventures with each other. The movie makes reference to the myth of an Amazon queen, a woman who has killed off the man she loves and is living quite nicely without the company of men. Sanders-Brahms's point is that, in modern society, there are women who also are living well without men, but they are brainwashed into thinking that they would be better off with male partners.

Sanders-Brahms's us-against-them brand of feminism mirrors the early 1970s, when the modern feminist movement was new and women who had grown up in a male-dominated society were feeling confrontational. Indeed, *Felix,* released in 1987, might have been made in the early 1970s. It is the politically loaded story of an egocentric, hypocritical modern male whose lack of self-awareness borders on the ridiculous. He has just been left by his lover, and he finds himself cast adrift in a world in which women no longer need men, or want men. *Felix* is filmed in four episodes, each shot by a different woman director—Christel Buschmann, Helke Sander, and Margarethe von Trotta, in addition to Sanders-Brahms. All are guilty of stereotyping men as jabbering idiots, and women as collectively sensitive, sensuous, and perceptive—practically perfect.

Sanders-Brahms's films are united in that they are reflective of the society in which she came of age. Along with her fellow members of the New German Cinema, she has a mission: to point out what is wrong with the world as she sees it.—AUDREY E. KUPFERBERG

Sarmiento, Valeria

Chilean director, writer, and editor

Born *Valparaiso, Chile, 1948.* ***Education*** *Studied film and philosophy at the Universidad de Chile, Viña del Mar.* ***Family*** *Married the director Raúl Ruiz.* ***Career*** *1973—fled General Pinochet's Chile for Paris; began working as editor; 1975—directed* The Housewife, *her first documentary made in exile.* ***Awards*** *San Sebastian International Film Festival award, for* Our Marriage, *1984.*

Films as Director: 1968-69: *Sueño como de colores* (*I Dream in Color*) (doc, short). **1972:** *Poesia popular: la teoría y la práctica* (*Popular Poetry: Theory and Practice*) (doc, short) (co-d with Ruiz, + co-pr, co-ed). **1973:** *Nueva canción (chilena)* (*New Song [Chilean]*) (unfinished short) (co-d, + ed). **1975:** *La Femme au foyer* (*La dueña de casa; The Housewife*) (doc, short). **1979:** *Le Mal du pays* (*The Bad Thing about This Country*) (doc). **1980:** *Gens de toutes partes, Gens de nulle parte* (*Gente de todas partes . . . Gente de ninguna parte; People from Everywhere, People from Nowhere*) (doc). **1982:** *El hombre cuando es hombre* (*A Man, When He Is a Man*) (doc). **1984:** *Notre mariage* (*Our Marriage*). **1991:** *Amelia Lópes O'Neill; Le planète des enfants* (*The Planet of Children*). **1992:** *Latin Women* (doc—for TV). **1995:** *Elle* (*She*) (+ sc). **1998:** *L'Inconnu de Strasbourg.*

Films as Editor: **1971:** *La Expropiación* (*The Expropriation*) (Ruiz). **1972:** *Los Minuteros* (*The Minute Hands*; *The Street Photographer*) (Ruiz—doc, short) (+ co-pr). **1974:** *Dialogue d'exilés* (*Diálogo de exiliados*; *Exiles' Dialogue*) (Ruiz) (+ ro). **1975:** *Mensche verstreut und Welt verkehrt* (*El cuerpo repartido y el mundo al revés*; *The Body Repaired and the World in Reverse*) (Ruiz). **1976:** *Sotelo* (Ruiz—doc, short). **1977:** *La Vocation suspendue* (*The Suspended Vocation*) (Ruiz); *Colloque de chiens* (*Dog's Language*) (Ruiz). **1979:** *Des Grandes événements et des gens ordinaires: les élections* (*Big Events and Ordinary People: Elections*) (Ruiz—doc); *Petit Manuel d'histoire de France, ch. 1 "Des ancêtres les Gaulois à la prise du pouvoir par Louis X1V"* (*Short History of France, ch. 1 "From the Gaulle Ancestors to the Taking of Power by Louis XIV"*) (Ruiz—doc, video). **1980:** *Le Borgne* (Ruiz—for TV, 4 eps.); *Guns* (Kramer) (co). **1981:** *Le Territoire* (*The Territory*) (Ruiz); *Le Toit de la Baleine* (*On Top of the Whale*; *The Whale's Roof*; *Het dak van de walvis*) (Ruiz—doc for TV). **1982:** *Les Trois Couronnes du matelot* (*The Three Crowns of a Sailor*; *Las Tres coronas del marinera*) (Ruiz) (co). **1983:** *La Ville des pirates* (*The City of Pirates*) (Ruiz). **1985:** *Voyage autour d'une main* (*Voyage around a Hand*) (Ruiz—short). **1988:** *Derrière le mur* (*Behind the Wall*) (Ruiz). **1994:** *Il Viaggio clandestino* (*The Secret Journey*) (Ruiz). **1997:** *Généalogies d'une crime* (*Geneologies of a Crime*) (Ruiz); *Le Film à venir* (*Film in the Future*) (Ruiz—doc, short).

Although Chile's vibrant film culture gave birth in 1962 to the important international film festival at Viña del Mar, it is difficult to speak of a Chilean national cinema until the late 1960s. In the brief moment of Salvador Allende's presidency (1970-73), Chilean national cinema blossomed. Most of Chile's filmmakers supported Allende's Popular Unity coalition government. Despite political, ideological, and economic difficulties, they managed to make an unprecedented number of films, both independently and with state aid given through national universities, the Ministries of Agriculture and Education, and three state-owned television channels. In 1973 President Allende's government was ousted by a military coup. General Pinochet's repressive dictatorship brutally squelched opposition voices and many Chileans who had supported Allende fled their native land. Among those who went into exile were Chile's artists and filmmakers, most notably poet Pablo Neruda, novelist Isabel Allende, and filmmakers Miguel Littin, Raul Ruiz, his wife Valeria Sarmiento, and Marilú Mallet.

Chilean cinema in exile, particularly in the immediate postcoup years (1973-79), has been referred to as a Cinema of Resistance. These films, while not a movement in the traditional aesthetic, theoretical, or political sense, shared common themes and goals: a celebration of Chilean culture as it grew under Allende; building a consensus against the military junta; and the liberation of Chilean and Latin American peoples governed by repressive regimes.

Valeria Sarmiento is among this generation of Chilean filmmakers who began their careers in the 1960s and supported the Popular Unity government of Salvador Allende with their films. Her husband, Raul Ruiz, an internationally acclaimed filmmaker, was also politically active in the 1960s and throughout the Allende years. Sarmiento and Ruiz sought political asylum in Paris in the wake of the 1973 military coup. Sarmiento found it difficult to finance new film projects because she was not as well known as her husband. Many potential funders felt that Sarmiento's work was derivative of Ruiz's and did not merit their investments. Although she was able to make a living as an editor, Sarmiento still speaks of this period as one of the most difficult and demoralizing of her career. Her first films made in exile dealt specifically with exile and the exile's identity struggle in an adopted land. Subsequent projects explored constructions of Latin American identity in a more general sense. Although many of her films examine women's and feminist issues, their constant concern with Latin American realities prohibits pigeonholing her work as "feminist."

Sarmiento's first directorial effort, *Sueño como de colores* was made in Chile during the Popular Unity years. A documentary about two striptease workers, the film was poorly received by critics who felt it did not deal with the important issues of the moment. Specifically, although its subjects are working-class women struggling to get ahead, reviewers commented that the film did not deal with class and economic stratification, problems that the Allende government was trying to resolve.

Sarmiento's first documentary made in exile, *The Housewife,* finally produced in 1975, explores how the opposition mobilized Chile's bourgeois women against Popular Unity. The film revisits the inequities of Chile's classist society, picking up the dialogue of the Popular Unity cinema. For the second time, however, critics found this film to be only tangential to the issues of Chilean exile cinema. Sarmiento's approach to political issues, looking at them through the position of marginalized social players, sets her work apart from other Chilean filmmakers. Further, her innovative formal and aesthetic play teases the politics out even as it searches for a personal film language. As a result, Sarmiento's films are both intimate and pan-Latin American, a difficult balance that she reaches expertly.

In *The Bad Thing about this Country* Sarmiento concerns herself with the exile of working-class Chilean children who fled Chile's slums for working-class French neighborhoods. It is a poignant portrait of children ages 5 to 8 who long for their homeland and yet recognize the vast improvement in their quality of life.

Sarmiento made an international name for herself with *A Man, When He Is a Man,* a feature-length documentary that explores the theme of "machismo" in Latin American culture. *A Man* analyzes how machismo is continued by the attitudes of both men and women. Filmed in Costa Rica and told largely from the perspective of men, the film also touches on romanticism in Latin American culture, demonstrating how romanticism and machismo overlap and feed each other. *A Man* uses the rites that mark different phases of a woman's life to examine how machismo is produced, maintained, and reproduced.

The critical success of *A Man* gave Sarmiento the opportunity to direct her first feature fiction film, *Our Marriage.* An adaptation of a novel by Corín Tellado, one of the most widely read romance novelists in Latin America, the film tells the story of a girl put into foster care because her father cannot afford to provide for her. Years later when her foster mother has died, her biological father gives the girl's foster father permission to marry her. In this and her subsequent feature films, Sarmiento matches her canny observations about Latin American and female identity with melodrama, perhaps the most beloved film and television genre in Latin America. Through melodrama she can throw into relief obsession, desire, sexuality, and morality—topics laid bare by Latin American melodrama, but paradoxically greatly repressed in Latin American polite society.—ILENE S. GOLDMAN

Savoca, Nancy

American director and writer

Born *New York, 1959.* ***Education*** *Attended Queen's College (CUNY), and New York University Film School.* ***Family*** *Married Richard Guay (her co-writer and producer on two films), 1980, three children.* ***Career*** *While in film school, made two noteworthy films,*

Nancy Savoca directing *Household Saints.*

Renata *and* Bad Timing; *1989—directed and co-scripted first feature film,* True Love. ***Awards*** *Haig P. Manoogian Award for overall excellence, NYU Student Film Festival, 1984; Grand Jury Prize, U.S. Film Festival, for* True Love, *1989.* ***Agent*** *United Talent Agency, 9560 Wilshire Boulevard, Suite 500, Beverly Hills, CA 90212, U.S.A.*

Films as Director: 1983: *Bad Timing* (short) (+ co-sc). **1989:** *True Love* (+ co-sc). **1991:** *Dogfight.* **1993:** *Household Saints* (+ co-sc). **1996:** "1952" and "1974" eps. of *If These Walls Could Talk* (for TV) (+ co-sc). **1998:** *The 24 Hour Woman* (+ co-sc). **1999:** *Janis.*

Other Film: 1996: "1996" ep. of *If These Walls Could Talk* (Cher—for TV) (co-sc).

Nancy Savoca began as an amused chronicler of the courtship and wedding rituals of the Italian-American culture of her upbringing. Like her senior male counterparts, Coppola in the *Godfather* saga and Scorsese in *Mean Streets,* Savoca was inspired by the emotional volatility of such ferociously tight-knit communities. She works, however, on a more intimate cinematic scale, avoiding Coppola's expansive narratives and Scorsese's jittery manner in dramatizing how tribal life shapes, even deforms individual identity.

This drama is obviously not confined to any one ethnic group or community, and in fact, the social consciousness of Savoca's films extends beyond the confines of Italian-American culture, as *Dogfight* and her recent television work demonstrate. "I like," she revealed in an interview, " to look at people who are looking to follow the rules, looking desperately to get in." She is unsentimental, yet tactful in focusing on characters, usually of unexceptional looks, circumstances, and talents, who stand out in some small, but definitive way. The Group not only offers her characters a security that eludes them elsewhere, but promises them personal fulfillment in a socially sanctioned destiny—marriage in *True Love*; military camaraderie in *Dogfight. Household Saints* works a poignant reversal on this formula by giving us a heroine who takes the strictures of her Catholic upbringing so seriously that she aspires to sainthood, thus baffling the loving mother and tenderhearted, but secular father who want a less eccentric, self-denying life for her. Savoca's films observe a discrepancy between an established social consensus on the "good life" and the actual experience of men and women hampered in their desire to realize such a life.

This discrepancy, as Savoca understands and presents it, is mostly a comic one. But Savoca's comedy, like her irony, is gentle, even fragile, and on rare occasions is supplanted by pathos—as in the suicide of Michael, the emotionally dislocated and disabled Italian-American son of *Household Saints,* hopelessly adrift in the Orientalist fantasies spawned by *Madame Butterfly.* Still Savoca excels in revealing her characters not so much through their solitary moments as in their search for company or a night's diversion. Her films take on an invigorating satiric energy in representing boys on the town or hanging out at their favorite bar, women at a male strip club, or such ritual gatherings as family dinners and, of course, weddings.

True Love has the most contemporary feel of all of Savoca's work, although it is set in a community whose traditionalism makes it less susceptible to the convulsive changes that periodically rock American culture. Her second film, *Dogfight,* set in November 1963, ambitiously, if not always convincingly presents its story of a soldier on leave before being shipped off to Vietnam as an allegory of an America about to change its ways in the decade ahead. This film initially concerns a group of young soldiers who dub themselves "the four Bs," brought together, we suspect, primarily by the proximity of their names on the military rolls. On their last night Stateside, they stage a "dogfight," a party to which each soldier brings the ugliest girl—or dog—he can find, the winner to be determined by a panel of "judges" who rate the dogs as they take to the dance floor. It is a cruel game, but finally, one that only boys, especially those uncertain about their future, would play with such stupid intensity. Savoca seems to understand this, so while not excusing the game, she shows that a woman can be appreciative as Fellini of unsightly females. The "dogs" she rounds up for the competition are not freaks, however, but plain young women unused to male attention, so that when it comes their way, they are too grateful or surprised to question its sincerity.

Spiritedly playing, then renouncing the game is Eddie Birdlace, played winningly by River Phoenix, who settles on Lili Taylor's Rose. The second half of the film sweetly pursues the emotional adventures of this odd couple as they enjoy a "second" night on the town, having dinner at a restaurant they cannot afford, wandering through the romantic San Francisco streets until returning to her home to make awkward but fervent love. The film has two endings, both ambiguous. In the first we see Birdlace tear up Rose's address as he, reunited with his buddies, decides that his fate, if not his heart, is cast with the buddies on whom his life may one day depend. The second shows us the war-scarred Vietnam vet, returning four years later to a transformed city and a transformed, but still recognizable Rose, who welcomes him back in a quiet embrace.

Household Saints, based on Francine Prose's novel of the same name, is Savoca's most comically serene work to date. It genially takes its tone from those entertaining family legends recounted with droll solemnity after a hearty meal—in this instance, the story of how "it happened by the grace of God, that Joseph Santangelo won his wife in a pinochle game." It took, we learn, a perfect hand to win her, the first of many surreal occurrences that Savoca presents as co-existing imperturbably with commonplace happenings of everyday life. Tracey Ullman and Vincent D'Onofrio play the magically matched couple. Lili Taylor brings her talent for conveying spiritual insensity to the role as their daughter, whose religious ardor, denied any worldly outlet, surfaces as anorexia and culminates in a vision of a blond Christ who looks like a rock star and talks the King's English. Savoca never settles the question of whether Rose has suffered a mental breakdown (the official diagnosis) or has in fact been elected into a community of saints.

If These Walls Could Talk displays a talent for unadorned, even harrowing realism only vaguely hinted at in her earlier work. Her direction of the 1952 segment, featuring Demi Moore as a widow desperately seeking an abortionist, is unrelenting in showing us how a trained nurse might go about aborting herself. Nor does Savoca spare us the details of how an abortionist, making a house call with his seedy wares in hand, plies his trade on the kitchen table. The camera only pulls away in the final shot of Moore hemorrhaging and calling for help. Savoca does not pretend we can identify with such horror as easily as all that. Whether the matter before her be comic or grave, Savoca never slips into condescension or sanctimonious irony. Her gift is for understatement, trusting as she does to the surfaces of life to indicate the depths in which her characters are in danger of losing their footing, perhaps even drowning.—MARIA DiBATTISTA

Schiller, Greta

American director

Born *Detroit, 21 December 1954.* ***Education*** *Earned a BFA from the Picker Film Institute, City College, City University of New York.* ***Family*** *Life partner of the filmmaker and film historian Andrea Weiss.* ***Career*** *1977—directed first film,* Greta's Girls, *while still a student at City College; 1984—with Andrea Weiss, founded Jezebel Productions; 1985—won international acclaim for the documentary,* Before Stonewall: The Making of a Gay and Lesbian Community. ***Awards*** *Best Cultural or Historical Program, and Best Research, Emmy Awards, First Place, National Educational Film Festival, Best Film, Houston International Film Festival, and Best Documentary Feature, Los Angeles FILMEX, for* Before Stonewall, *1985; Blue Ribbon, American Film and Video Festival, Audience Prize, Fest. International de Films de Femmes, Cretail, Prize of the International Jury, Oberhausen Short Film Festival, and Jury Prize, Leipzig International Documentary Festival, for* International Sweethearts of Rhythm, *1986; Silver Plaque Award, Chicago International Film Festival, for* Tiny & Ruby: Hell-Divin' Women, *1989; Fulbright Fellowship in Film, 1988-89; Film Fellowship, New York Foundation for the Arts, 1990; Best Documentary (Audience Prize), Fest. International de Films de Femmes, Cretail, and Best Documentary (Audience Prize), Berlin Film Festival, for* Paris Was a Woman, *1996.*

Films as Director: **1977:** *Greta's Girls* (co-d with Seid, + pr, ph); *Rape Prevention* (video short) (+ pr, ph). **1979:** *Well, We Are Alive* (video short) (+ pr, ed, ph). **1985:** *Before Stonewall: The Making of a Gay and Lesbian Community* (co-d with Rosenberg, + pr, co-sc, additional ph). **1986:** *International Sweethearts of Rhythm* (short) (co-d, + co-pr, ph, ed). **1989:** *Tiny & Ruby: Hell-Divin' Women* (short) (co-d with Weiss, + co-pr, ph); *Waking Up: A Lesson in Love* (video). **1991:** *Maxine Sullivan: Love to Be in Love* (short) (+ pr, sc). **1994:** *Woman of the Wolf* (short) (+ sc). **1996:** *Paris Was a Woman* (+ co-pr, co-sc, ed, co-ph). **1998:** *The Moffie Who Drove with Mandela* (+ pr).

Other Films: **1981:** *Greetings from Washington, D.C.* (short) (co-pr, camera). **1982:** *Wild Style* (Ahearn) (camera operator). **1988:** *Die Jungfrauen Maschine* (*The Virgin Machine*) (Treut) (asst d); *Charlotte Bunch: One Woman's Legacy* (promo tape) (pr, ed). **1994:** *Age of Dissent* (short) (pr). **1997:** *Seed of Sarah* (Weiss) (pr). **1999:** *Escape to Life* (Weiss) (pr).

In her most representative films, Greta Schiller documents the stories of spirited and single-minded individuals—many of whom have been lost in the pages of history—whose lives transcend social and sexual taboos. Her breakthrough documentary, co-directed with Robert Rosenberg, is *Before Stonewall: The Making of a Gay and Lesbian Community,* which outlines the beginnings of America's queer subculture. Using archival footage and interviews, Schiller and Rosenberg chart the history of the 1920s lesbian bar scene and gay GI experiences during World War II. In so doing, they portray queer lifestyles in the decades before the Stonewall rebellion of 1969, before gays and lesbians were celebrated on the covers of mainstream magazines, when oppression was the rule and gay-pride parades were unimaginable. As a full-bodied documentary exploration of its subject, *Before Stonewall* is a seminal work.

More often than not, Schiller's subjects have been connected to the arts or the entertainment industry. In collaboration with Andrea Weiss, she made *International Sweethearts of Rhythm,* which records the history of an interracial, all-woman jazz band that came to prominence during the 1940s: an era when female drummers, trombonists, and trumpet players were viewed as little more than novelties. One of the significant issues raised in *International Sweethearts of Rhythm* is that, had they not been women—let alone black women—a number of the band members might have enjoyed mainstream careers, and a more lasting fame. Another is that despite the prejudice of the time, these musicians experienced a freedom that then was rare for women, and that helped shape their lives.

An offshoot/companion piece to *International Sweethearts of Rhythm* is *Tiny & Ruby: Hell-Divin' Women,* which Schiller also directed with Weiss. The film's subjects are two larger-than-life personalities: jazz singer/trumpeter Ernestine "Tiny" Davis, a performer with the International Sweethearts (who, in the 1940s, was billed as "the female Louis Armstrong"), and her life partner, drummer Ruby Lucas. Another of Schiller's documentaries, *Maxine Sullivan: Love to Be in Love,* is a portrait of the black jazz singer whose prominence may have transcended that of the International Sweethearts of Rhythm but who nonetheless, because of her race and her sex, was denied the opportunity to cross over from radio to television during the 1950s.

One of Schiller's most recent films, *Paris Was a Woman,* records the lives of American expatriate women who, in the early 20th century, flocked to the Left Bank and created a community all their own. None fitted into mainstream society. None were defined by their relationships to men. All rejected the conventional social and sexual roles of women. In fact, many were lesbian and bisexual. All became writers and artists, publishers and editors, poets and photographers, journalists and salon hostesses. And all lived fiercely independent lives in an artistic community that flourished in the post-World War I years and ended upon the occupation of Paris by the German army in 1940.

Some of these women, such as Gertrude Stein, Alice B. Toklas, and Janet Flanner, are well-known today. Others, such as writer Djuna Barnes, have become cult figures. Still others, such as bookshop proprietresses Adrienne Monnier and Sylvia Beach and heiress/poet Natalie Barney, have been obscured by the course of time. It is the information on these women in particular that makes *Paris Was a Woman* so illuminating.

Schiller's documentaries, chock full of vintage clips and information, are meaningful as histories of times and places. Especially revealing are the found and filmed footage and recordings of many of her subjects. When the surviving members of the International Sweethearts of Rhythm recall their triumphs and difficulties, or when the effervescent personalities of

Tiny and Ruby take hold, or when Gertrude Stein's voice fills the soundtrack and Janet Flanner's impressive presence fills the screen, these films becomes living, breathing histories.

An essay on Schiller would be incomplete without mention of her partner and frequent collaborator, Andrea Weiss, with whom she founded the New York/London-based Jezebel Productions in 1984. Weiss is, in her own right, an award-winning filmmaker and film historian. She was the research director of *Before Stonewall*; she produced (as well as co-directed) *The International Sweethearts of Rhythm* and *Tiny & Ruby: Hell-Divin' Women*, and wrote and produced *Paris Was a Woman*. Schiller has also produced two films directed by Weiss: *Seed of Sarah* and *Escape to Life*.

To date, Schiller's nondocumentary works are footnotes to her career. They include *Greta's Girls*, co-directed with Thomas Seid and made while a student at New York's City College, which chronicles the daily life of a lesbian couple; and *Waking Up: A Lesson in Love*, a drama about a promiscuous lesbian named Susan. Both films are notable for offering candid views of lesbian characters, whether at the beginning of a relationship (in *Greta's Girls*) or in the process of exploring sex in the hope of finding love (in *Waking Up*).—ROB EDELMAN

Schneemann, Carolee

American director

Born *Fox Chase, Pennsylvania, 1939.* ***Education*** *Attended Bard College, B.A.; University of Illinois at Urbana, M.F.A.; attended Columbia University School of Painting and Sculpture, New York, and New School for Social Research, New York.* ***Career*** *Founded Kinetic Theatre, New York; has had numerous exhibitions in New York, Milan, Paris, California, and Vienna, including the Venice Biennale; the Museum of Modern Art, and the New Museum of Contemporary Art (retrospective, 1997), New York; San Francisco Museum of Modern Art; Centre Georges Pompidou, Paris; Frauen Museum, Bonn, Germany; the Museum of Contemporary Art, Los Angeles; and many other venues; has been an instructor of art at the Art Institute of Chicago, University of Colorado at Boulder, University of Ohio, Pratt Institute, New York, and University of California, Los Angeles.* ***Awards*** *Individual Artist Grant, Gottlieb Foundation, 1987; Guggenheim Fellowship, 1993; Pollock-Krasner Grant, 1996.* ***Address*** *114 West 29th Street, New York, NY 10001, U.S.A.*

Films as Director: 1963: *Carl Ruggles' Christmas Breakfast.* **1965:** *Viet-Flakes.* **1966:** *Red News.* **1967:** *Fuses.* **1971:** *Plumb Line* (+ sound). **1971-72:** *Reel Time* (co-d with McCall). **1973-78:** *Kitch's Last Meal.* **1982:** *Up to and Including Her Limits* (video) (+ ed). **1992:** *Vesper's Stampede to My Holy Mouth* (video) (co-d with Vesna). **1993:** *Imaging Her Erotics: Carolee Schneemann* (video) (co-d with M. Beatty, + co-ed). **1995:** *Interior Scroll—The Cave* (video) (co-d with M. Beatty).

Performance Documentation Films: 1964: *Meat Joy* (Gaisseau and Giorgio). **1965:** *Water Light/Water Needle* (3 films: Film 1 [J. Jones] [+ co-ed], Film 2 [Rocklin] [+ ed], Film 3 [Summers]). **1966:** *Snows* (Shilling). **1967:** *Body Collage* (Bachmann); *Falling Bodies* (*Body Rotations*) (Whitehead). **1968:** *Illinois Central* (Heinz); *Illinois Central Transposed* (Dacey). **1972:** *Ices Strip Train Skating*; *American I Ching Apple Pie.* **1973:** *Acts of Perception*; *Cooking with Apes.* **1975:** *Interior Scroll* (Beskind—video). **1976-77:** *ABC—We Print Anything—In the Cards* (Sharits and Morgan). **1977:** *Homerunmuse* (Slater—video).

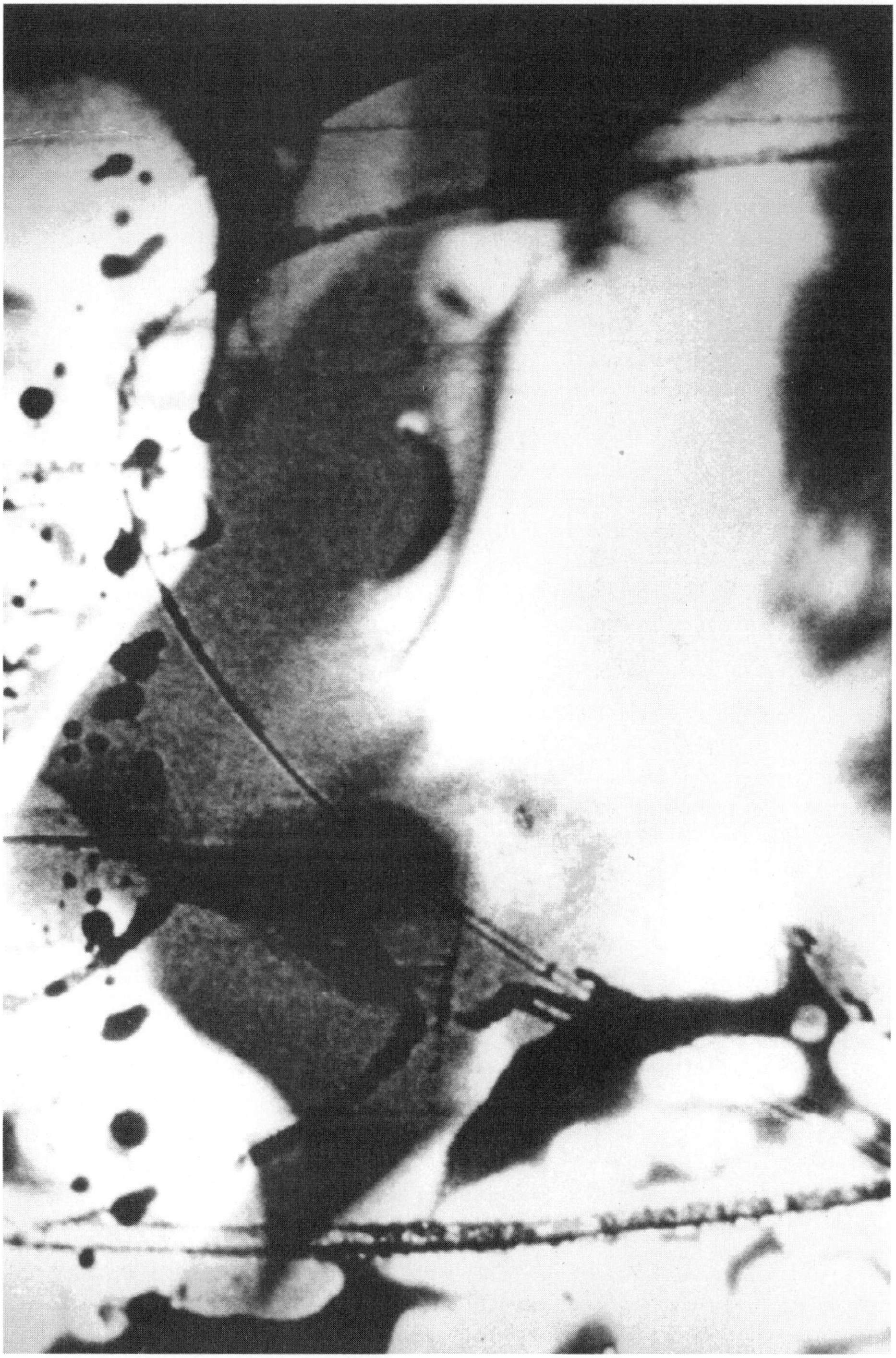

Carolee Schneemann: *Fuses.* Photograph by Carolee Schneemann.

Appearances in Other Films: 1957: *Daybreak* (Brakhage); *Whiteye* (Brakhage); *Loving* (Brakhage). **1959:** *Cat's Cradle* (Brakhage). **1961:** *Waves and Washes* (Vanderbeek—doc) (work by Oldenburg).

Carolee Schneemann is a performance artist, filmmaker, writer, and assemblage artist who has been creating art since the early 1960s. Her work as an artist has been influenced by the psychoanalytical theories of Wilhelm Reich and Antonin Artaud's theater of cruelty. Schneemann is known for using a wide variety of materials in her artwork and performances such as paint, sand, glue, glass, flour, lights, and perhaps most significantly, the human body. As Schneemann said in speaking of her early performance work, she set out "to eroticise my guilt-ridden culture and further to confound this culture's sexual rigidities—that the life of the body is more variously expressive than a sex-negative society can admit." (*More than Meat Joy*, 1979). Schneemann is also known for her fierce independence and shock tactics as an artist. Her work, including many of her films, privileges the human body, the materiality of whatever medium she is working in and the experiential. She is concerned with an examination of the ecstatic in her art, and this is never so clear as in her best film, the controversial *Fuses*.

Fuses offers a radical approach to representations of the human body. It is a graphic attempt to represent the ecstatic in heterosexual lovemaking, and powerfully represents the emotional state of two individuals involved in the act of making love. Schneemann's approach to her filmmaking is similar to her work as a visual artist. She is interested in breaking down barriers, both in terms of cultural taboos and in her process of making films. The film fragments and abstracts the human body to such an extent that all traces of the voyeuristic are eliminated from the viewing experience. It incorporates multiple superimpositions and extreme collage techniques that have a way of blurring the discreteness of the individual shot. Schneemann's process also involves working with the filmic material by means of scratching, painting, and baking the celluloid. This results in an anti-illusionistic, reflexive kind of filmmaking that constantly reminds the viewer of the actual work involved in the art-making process and the physicality of working with one's materials. This physicality gives her films a directness and authenticity that is all too rare in the cinema. She stated in an interview that "she worked on that film the way I work on a canvas. It was like an overall immediacy put into a prolonged time duration, a way of working with film as one extended frame in time" (MacDonald, 1988).

The film's diaristic approach to documenting the intense activities of two individuals making love is radical and shocking for its time, and the film can still register strong reactions with an audience. In the first decade of its release, however, it was notorious for almost always creating controversy each time it was publicly screened, especially if the filmmaker was in attendance. This was due in part to the graphicness of the sexual imagery, which did involve many shots of the vagina and penis, as well close-ups of bodily fluids, images which had hitherto been the province of pornography. It was also due to the seemingly haphazard approach and messiness of the imagery in the film. *Fuses* does not have the cool elegance of many of the structuralist films at the time made by filmmakers such as Michael Snow or Hollis Frampton. Neither does it have the lyrical, mythopoeic complexity of Brakhage's best work.

It is true Schneemann's accomplishment is not of that order. But neither did it deserve the critical neglect or public attacks it generally received at the time. Schneemann recounts the astonishing story of how 40 young men at a screening in France in the late 1960s were so incensed by the film that they slashed the seats with razors, shredding and throwing the padding throughout the screening room (MacDonald, 1988). Where the film celebrates the potential of human sexuality some viewers were so enraged and fearful that they could only respond with anger. It is the mark of a truly subversive work of art that it can provoke such a hostile reaction, so totally out of proportion to any possible provocation. *Fuses* was a truly fresh, innovative attempt to graphically represent and celebrate the human body. The film has grown in stature as years have passed, and today it remains a bold, innovative film.

Schneemann continued to explore the film medium by incorporating her own life as subject matter in her next few films. *Plumb Line* differs from *Fuses* in that it was made after a relationship had disintegrated. Although an interesting film it does not have the radical groundbreaking quality of her earlier, best-known film. *Plumb Line* was made primarily to take control and give some sense of emotional balance to her life after the devastation of her break-up. *Kitch's Last Meal* is a Super-8, double-projection film based on the filmmaker's observations of her cat and the impressions it might have observed in the last days of its life. The film explores the daily routines of the filmmaker and her partner such as gardening, chopping wood, cleaning, cooking, reading, etc. It exists in several versions ranging in length from one hour to five hours. Neither of these films has been extensively screened over the years, and Schneemann's reputation as a filmmaker essentially rests on the not inconsiderable accomplishment of *Fuses*.

Carolee Schneemann is perhaps better known today as a visual artist and painter but her contribution to the history of the American avant-garde cinema, though small, remains a significant one. She proved that it was possible to create a truly radical film out of the dailiness of one's life, and in one astonishing film she explored human sexuality with more originality and creativity than most other filmmakers, male or female, mainstream or avant-garde could ever hope to achieve. Schneemann made a lasting contribution to the art of cinema, and *Fuses* remains one of the key films of the 1960s. Any discussion of sexuality in the cinema, as well as films that radically attempt to create a new way of seeing the world, must surely include her work.—MARIO FALSETTO

Schoonmaker, Thelma

American editor

Born *Algiers, Algeria, 3 January 1940.* ***Education*** *Attended Cornell University, studying political science and Russian, B.A., 1961; Columbia University, studying primitive art; New York University Film School, six-week film course.* ***Family*** *Married the director Michael Powell, 1984 (died 1990).* ***Career*** *Met the director Martin Scorsese while both students at NYU; 1968—cut Scorsese's debut feature* Who's That Knocking at My Door?; *lack of union membership kept her from editing feature films until* Raging Bull, *1980.* ***Award*** *Academy Award, for* Raging Bull, *1980.* ***Address*** *c/o Cappa Productions, 445 Park Avenue, 7th Floor, New York, NY 10022, U.S.A.*

Films as Editor: 1965: *Finnegans Wake* (*Passages from James Joyce's Finnegans Wake*) (Bute) (co). **1968:** *The Virgin President* (Ferguson) (co); *Who's That Knocking at My Door?* (Scorsese). **1970:** *Street Scenes* (Scorsese—doc) (co); *Woodstock* (Wadleigh—doc) (chief ed, + asst d). **1979:** *The Kids Are Alright* (Stein) (special consultant). **1980:** *Raging Bull* (Scorsese); *Rockshow* (Cavalcanti—doc) (co). **1983:** *The King of Comedy* (Scorsese) (+ production supervisor). **1985:** *After Hours* (Scorsese). **1986:** *The Color of Money* (Scorsese). **1988:** *The Last Temptation of Christ* (Scorsese). **1989:** "Life Lessons" ep. of *New York Stories* (Scorsese). **1990:** *GoodFellas* (Scorsese); *Made in Milan* (Scorsese—doc, short). **1991:** *Cape Fear* (Scorsese). **1993:** *The Age of Innocence* (Scorsese). **1995:** *Casino* (Scorsese). **1996:** *Grace of My Heart* (Anders) (co). **1997:** *Kundun* (Scorsese). **1999:** *Bringing Out the Dead* (Scorsese).

Thelma Schoonmaker: *Raging Bull*

An axiom of Hollywood post-production holds that the best editing maintains a seamless invisibility; that the best editors do not draw attention to their work. Thelma Schoonmaker simultaneously embodies and shatters that axiom. On one hand, she is certainly one of Hollywood's most self-effacing editors, perhaps understandably so working as Martin Scorsese's editor. Editing all his films from *Raging Bull* on, she always claims the credit goes to Scorsese since he shoots for and edits with her. On the other hand, her editing is often far from self-effacing; although it functions within classical Hollywood parameters, it draws attention to itself as a fully realized art form and provides a compendium of what contemporary editing can accomplish. As Jeffrey Ressner says: *"Raging Bull, GoodFellas,* and *Casino* have pushed the editing craft into a postmodern, almost hallucinogenic art. They are what films can be."

Schoonmaker's "postmodern" editing synthesizes a number of different influences, approaches, and devices: Nouvelle Vague, music videos, classical continuity editing (particularly shot/reverse shot dialogue editing), long takes and intrasequence cutting, montage, freeze frames, dissolves, jump cuts, temporal ellipses, extreme close-ups, and irises. One might expect to see all these devices in a television commercial or a music video, yet Schoonmaker's films successfully employs them in narrative features. She established this "hallucinatory" battery of techniques in her first commercial narrative, *Raging Bull,* which according to Stephan Talty, "is one of the most obsessively crafted and exhaustively edited films in American cinema."

The techniques Schoonmaker initiated with *Raging Bull* won her an Oscar for best editing and she continued to use and expand them as her career progressed. Since 1980, her editing has become so innovative, complex, and continually evolving that addressing all aspects of it in a short essay is as unfair as it is impossible. Some of the above characteristics help describe her editorial signature.

Raging Bull appears documentary-like: shot in black and white, using subtitles to specify time and place, and telling the biography of Jake La Motta. Schoonmaker contributes to this appearance by utilizing long takes and intercutting "home movies" of La Motta and his friends and family. She also employs the naturalism associated with classical Hollywood editing by structuring much of the film around traditional shot/reverse shot dialogue sequences. But any sense of realism or naturalism these techniques may suggest shrinks behind the style she gives to the rest of the film. Most obviously, the eight fight sequences allow Schoonmaker to do anything she wants. She puts each sequence together in a different way with a different tempo, but all rely on montage and sound manipulation. Extreme close-ups are cut next to long shots; low angle shots are cut next to high angle shots; normal speed shots are cut next to slow and fast motion shots; long camera takes are cut next to split-second shots of camera flashes; the boxers and audience are cut next to objects (round cards, the bell, water buckets); freeze frames are cut next to Steadicam shots; sound intensifies, drops out, becomes subjective, becomes abstract. All of this makes each fight literally "explosive," especially when compared to the slower pacing of rest of the film. Schoonmaker explains that while working on "Round 13" of the third Sugar Ray Robinson fight, she first edited for narrative structure and then reworked the scene for movement, lighting, and effects—exactly the concerns that push her editing to the foreground.

Outside the fight sequences Schoonmaker employs subtler, but just as untraditional, editing techniques. Perhaps her most influential innovations occurred in this area: expanding the accepted boundary of the temporal ellipse and challenging the limitations of match-action editing. All editors eliminate unimportant information that a viewer can infer. For example, an editor will not bother showing a character getting into a car, driving to a new location, and then getting out of the car. Typically, we would see the character get into the car, drive out of the frame, and then exit the car at the new location. The viewer understands that the car was driven between two points without needing to see it. Schoonmaker pushes this in a number of ways, but most interestingly by using this technique when we do not expect to see it. For example, while standing at a poolside soda stand, La Motta first sees Vicki. Then a cut shows us Vicki in close-up (from La Motta's point of view). When another cut returns us to La Motta he is sitting down at a table. We do not see him move from the soda stand to the table, but we know he did. Later, during La Motta's courtship of Vicki, she accompanies him to his apartment. As he closes the refrigerator door, a cut shows him sitting down at a table across the room. Again, unorthodox but fully comprehendible.

Traditional match-action editing requires two things to make the cut "invisible": (1) cutting at the point of strongest action and (2) maintaining exact screen position and direction. Failure to follow these two conventions produces "bad editing" or "jump cuts." By traditional standards, Schoonmaker's editing borders on the "bad." But under contemporary editing aesthetics (heavily influenced by television and music videos) her editing delivers an excitement impossible under the strict parameters of match-action editing. Points of strongest action and exact screen position are replaced by jump cuts that produce a rhythmic pacing, an emphasis on character and dialogue (and actors' performances), and narrative intensification. In the many shot/reverse shot dialogue sequences, the street vernacular the characters speak, with its staccato tempo, perfectly complements and supports these editorial decisions and produces the edgy tension associated with Scorsese's films.

Schoonmaker also demonstrates a deft hand at intrasequence cutting. Brian Henderson defines intrasequence cutting as the linking of long takes to emphasize the rhythm and movement within a long duration shot. Each cut breaks that rhythm or movement but then replaces it with a different rhythm or movement of the next shot. Scorsese employs long takes usually with elaborate camera movements made possible by the Steadicam. In the Marcel Cerdan fight, the camera follows La Motta out of his dressing room, down a number of hallways, through the crowded arena, and into the ring as the camera (now on a crane) moves into a high angle shot. Schoonmaker uses such long takes in combination with her montage-inspired editing to break and establish different editing tempos.

Immediately before or after a montage sequence, cutting together long takes provides a needed respite from a taxing emotional or intensely physical scene. Combining long takes with shot/reverse shot editing allows characters to develop more naturally. The bookending sequences of La Motta in his dressing room set up the narrative and structure of the film with an efficiency no other editing technique could accomplish.

In *The King of Comedy,* she pushed the temporal ellipse to include a spatial aspect. Straight cutting on dialogue in a typical shot/reverse shot pattern we move freely between Rupert's basement and his (fantasized) luncheon at Sardi's with Jerry Langford. Rupert's first conversation with Rita at a bar does the same thing: on a line of continuous dialogue over a shot/reverse shot cut we relocate to a restaurant. Schoonmaker and Scorsese indulge in a bit of Nouvelle Vague reflexivity here. In the long takes and intrasequence cutting that structures this scene, a patron behind Rupert gazes at the camera and mocks Rupert's gestures and facial expressions. In a film that questions the thin line between reality and fantasy, this scene in particular demonstrates the impossibility of film to ever be real.

The opening title sequence of *The King of Comedy* superimposes credits over a freeze frame of Marsha's clawing hands. Schoonmaker develops the freeze frame until it becomes one of her signature devices. She uses the freeze frame extensively in *GoodFellas.* Whenever Henry Hill's voice-over makes an important point, Schoonmaker freezes the image. In *GoodFellas,* she also employs long takes (especially in the famous track-back/zoom-in-shot at the diner), intrasequence cutting (Karen and Henry and the Copacabana and the Saturday, 11 May sequence), spatial and temporal ellipses (all of the violence and the gifts of money at the wedding reception), and jump cuts (Karen at the beauty parlor and at Janet Rossi's apartment). Her work on *GoodFellas* earned her an Academy Award nomination.

In *The Color of Money,* she uses extreme close-ups of cue chalk, billiard balls, cigarettes, and money as a visual leitmotiv to stress the theme of the film. She balances long takes with montage sequences; Vincent's "Werewolves of London" pool-cue performance juxtaposed to the increased speed, overhead jump cuts, and extreme close-ups for a series of pool games. She plays much cutting on moving camera against a precise visual symmetry (the left/right balance of Vincent and Eddie's grudge match). In Vincent's game with Grady, Schoonmaker employs dissolves and superimpositions to convey the various deceits and facades of the two players.

Schoonmaker also develops the dissolve until it becomes another of her signature devices. She uses the dissolve extensively in *The Age of Innocence* and *Casino.* Whereas her earlier films used the dissolve traditionally (to indicate simultaneity or a passage of time), her later films use it to disorient. In *The Age of Innocence,* the opera sequence that opens the film immediately undercuts the period setting. Dissolves link shots that traditionally would be joined in one long take or through match action. Combining this unsettling technique with jump cuts (during the pan of the theater) and abandoned eye-line matches (an audience member looks up across the theater, yet the next shot is down to a performer on the stage) provides a commentary on the hidden meanings of exterior actions. Schoonmaker takes advantage of the period setting to employ irises. A silent-film device before editing used close-ups, an iris focused the viewer's attention on a specific part of the screen. Here Schoonmaker uses translucent irises as another visual metaphor for disguised appearances.

In *Casino,* Schoonmaker uses both devices but for different reasons. The dissolves work as point of view commentary (especially since the film is narrated in voice-over). For example, as Sam explains how he eliminated professional cheaters from the Tropicana we see him determine how two men have won $140,000 in blackjack. Schoonmaker presents this to us through dissolves that link Sam to the two tables involved in the scam. When Nicky and Jennifer first meet

Ginger, we see her through Nicky's eyes in a three-shot dissolve that augments her approach. In *Casino,* the iris functions to suggest blindness. Sam is so obsessed with Ginger he cannot see the destruction their relationship will cause; an iris leads us to his head and then an extreme close-up of a flashbulb exploding. Both films also make extensive use of intrasequence cutting, temporal ellipses, cutting on moving camera, and montage.

These techniques also work well in the context of a suspense film. In *Cape Fear,* Schoonmaker melded her editing techniques with the action cutting demanded of a genre film. The result was a film that frightened and exhibited an innovative twist on an old format. She used negative imagery to comment on the lack of clear difference between guilt and innocence. Her jump cutting and temporal ellipses added a new edge of terror and excitement to the final houseboat sequence (involving miniatures and special effects) as well as Saw Bowden's first sighting of Max Cady in town (three jump cuts from long shot to medium shot to close up on passing cars). Cady's seduction of Danielle on the school stage expertly demonstrates intrasequence cutting. Scorsese shot the improvised scene in one continuous, nine-minute take with two cameras. Schoonmaker seamlessly melded the two takes so it looks like a typical shot/reverse shot sequence even though she is linking long takes.

The approaches mentioned above outline the unique style of Schoonmaker's editing technique. Perhaps more than any other contemporary Hollywood editor, her distinct editorial signature positions her as an auteur. Working exclusively with Scorsese certainly supports this claim and demonstrates not only that editing must be viewed as an art but how film can function as a collaborative act of creativity.—GREG S. FALLER

Seidelman, Susan

American director

***Born** Near Philadelphia, Pennsylvania, 11 December 1952. **Education** Attended school in Philadelphia; studied design and film at Drexel University; New York University Graduate School of Film and TV, 1974-77. **Career** Directed first feature,* Smithereens, *1982. **Agent** William Morris Agency, 151 El Camino Drive, Beverly Hills, CA 90212, U.S.A. **Address** c/o Michael Shedler, 225 West 34th Street, Suite 1012, New York, NY 10122-0049, U.S.A.*

Films as Director: 1976/77: *And You Act Like One, Too* (short); *Deficit* (short); *Yours Truly, Andrea G. Stern* (short). **1982:** *Smithereens* (+ pr, st). **1985:** *Desperately Seeking Susan.* **1987:** *Making Mr. Right* (+ exec pr). **1989:** *Cookie* (+ sc); *She-Devil* (+ co-pr). **1992:** *Confessions of a Suburban Girl* (+ ro). **1995:** *The Dutch Master* (short, released as ep. in *Tales of Erotica* in 1996) (+ co-sc); *The Barefoot Executive* (for TV). **1998:** *Sex and the City* (for TV).

Other Films: 1982: *Chambre 666* (Wenders—doc, for TV) (appearance). **1993:** *The Night We Never Met* (Leight) (co-assoc pr).

Prior to directing *Smithereens,* her breakthrough independent feature, and *Desperately Seeking Susan,* the film that announced her as a major cinematic talent, Susan Seidelman made *Deficit,* a 40-minute drama about a young man who seeks revenge for a crime committed against his father. The film was funded in part by the American Film Institute Independent Filmmaker Program. Call it understatement or prophecy, but a comment on the film's evaluation form portended Seidelman's future, "The filmmaker shows a budding talent as a feature film director."

Susan Seidelman on the set of *Desperately Seeking Susan.*

That talent was realized in *Smithereens* and *Desperately Seeking Susan*. Both are likably funky and keenly observed films featuring spirited, independent-minded but refreshingly unromanticized heroines: refugees from stifling suburbia who come to New York City's East Village where they forge identities within a subculture. Both films are knowing depictions of New York punk/New Wave/No Wave culture, and are clearly defined observations of hipness and pseudo-hipness.

Smithereens, made for $80,000, is a minor landmark in the history of the then-burgeoning American independent film movement; for one thing, it was the first such film accepted as an official in-competition entry at the Cannes Film Festival. *Smithereens* benefits from its low budget, which allows it an authentic feel for time and place. Its heroine is Wren, a rootless 19-year-old whose motto might be "Desperately Seeking Celebrity." She lives in a shabby East Village apartment, from which she is evicted for nonpayment of rent; she may be energetic and determined, but her dreams of achieving fame, which are connected to the rock music industry and an idealized Southern California lifestyle, are hazy at best. Instead of educating herself and working to realize them, Wren pastes xeroxed photos of herself on subway car and station walls and attempts to link up with a rock singer whom she foolishly regards as a meal ticket. She will say and do anything and manipulate anyone, even if it results in her own debasement. Her rationale for her behavior is a line she repeats throughout the scenario, "I got a million and one places to go."

Seidelman entered the realm of mainstream filmmaking with her follow-up feature: *Desperately Seeking Susan,* a stylish screwball comedy that remained faithful to the feeling of its predecessor and became a surprise box-office smash. In retrospect, it is one of the more entertaining films of the mid-1980s. There are two heroines in *Desperately Seeking Susan.* The first is Roberta, a bored suburban housewife who sets out on a comic odyssey upon becoming intrigued by a series of "Desperately Seeking Susan" personal ads. Roberta's counterpart, the Susan of the title, is a variation of Wren. She is a homeless but nonetheless ultrahip East Village free spirit who has various boyfriends and sexual liaisons, and who will think nothing of pilfering jewelry or stiffing a taxi driver. Roberta and Susan become immersed in a frantic, funny scenario involving mistaken identity, amnesia, and other plot devices. *Desperately Seeking Susan* is especially successful in capturing the appeal of Madonna, who plays the title role and who then was blossoming as one of the era's elite pop stars. Prior to her playing *Evita* 12 years later, Susan was her preeminent screen role.

Unfortunately, *Desperately Seeking Susan* was to be a career apex for Seidelman; it and *Smithereens* are her foremost films to date. The clever female-oriented humor that worked so well in *Desperately Seeking Susan* is missing from *Making Mr. Right,* which attempts to squeeze laughs out of a supposedly successful career woman's inability to walk in high heels. The scenario (which is set in Miami Beach) has the heroine realizing she only can find true love with a robot. In *Smithereens* and *Desperately Seeking Susan,* the male characters run the gamut from boring and self-involved to sympathetic. In *Making Mr. Right,* the view of men is horribly clichéd and mean-spirited, and downright offensive in that a real man is insufficient as the heroine's romantic partner. Furthermore, the robot, which she has helped program, comes apart whenever it makes love.

In *She-Devil,* Seidelman directed one of the era's most distinguished film actresses (Meryl Streep) and popular television comediennes (Roseanne), and worked from an acclaimed feminist novel: Fay Weldon's *The Life and Loves of a She-Devil.* But the result, involving a frumpy housewife who seeks revenge after her husband leaves her, is slight and predictable. *Cookie,* which like *She-Devil* was scripted by Nora Ephron (working with Alice Arlen), is the story of a cheeky adolescent who forges a relationship with her mafioso father upon his release from jail. But the film was strictly formulaic, and paled beside Seidelman's earlier work. In these last three films, the feeling is that Seidelman abandoned her New York artistic roots, and in so doing lost her way as an idiosyncratic filmmaker.

In the 1990s Seidelman has been anything but prolific. But her films at least have been more than respectable, even if they have not established her as an A-list film maker. The luridly named *Confessions of a Suburban Girl,* whose title seems an attempted thematic throwback to *Smithereens* and *Desperately Seeking Susan,* actually is a revealing documentary account of the filmmaker and several of her friends as they parallel their youthful aspirations to the reality of their adult lives. *The Dutch Master,* a short film (which won Seidelman a Best Live Action Short

Oscar nomination), is the story of New York dental hygienist who becomes fascinated by, and begins fantasizing about, a 17th-century painting.

If you are, say, Martin Scorsese or Woody Allen and you choose to direct a short, that work will be considered an exercise in creativity. But if you are Susan Seidelman, and you have not had a critical or commercial hit in a decade, your short film, however fine, will be viewed as a comedown. Tellingly, *The Dutch Master* was released commercially, along with three other shorts, under the throwaway title *Tales of Erotica*. It was paired with films by Ken Russell, Melvin Van Peebles, and Bob Rafelson—who, like Seidelman, are once-innovative filmmakers whose foremost works most likely are in their past.—ROB EDELMAN

Serreau, Coline

French director, writer, and actress

Born *Paris, 1947; daughter of theater director Jean-Marie Serreau.* ***Education*** *Studied music, dance, and acrobatics.* ***Career*** *1970-76—actress for stage, film, and television; 1975—first documentary feature,* Mais qu'est-ce qu'elles veulent?; *1977—first feature film,* Pourquoi pas?; *1985—international success of* Trois hommes et un couffin. ***Awards*** *César, Best Film and Best Screenplay, for* Trois hommes et un couffin, *1985.*

Films as Director: 1976: *Le Rendez-vous* (short, for TV). **1977:** *Pourquoi pas?* (*Why Not?*) (+ sc). **1978:** *Mais qu'est-ce qu'elles veulent?* (*But What Do Women Want?*) (doc—produced 1975) (+ sc, sound). **1982:** *Qu'est-ce qu'on attend pour être heureux!* (*What Are You Waiting for to Be Happy!*) (+ sc). **1985:** *Trois hommes et un couffin* (*Three Men and a Cradle*) (+ sc). **1989:** *Romuald et Juliette* (*Mama, There's a Man in Your Bed*) (+ sc). **1991:** Ep. in *Contre l'oubli* (*Against Oblivion*; *Écrire contre*

Coline Serreau: ***Trois hommes et un couffin***

l'oubli; Lest We Forget). **1992:** *La Crise* (*The Crisis*) (+ sc). **1996:** *La Belle verte* (*The Green Planet*) (+ sc, mus, ro as Mila).

Other Films: 1970: *Un Peu beaucoup, passionnément* (Enrico) (ro). **1973:** *On s'est trompé d'histoire d'amour* (Bertucelli) (co-sc, ro as Anne). **1975:** *Sept morts sur ordonnance* (Rouffio) (ro as Mme. Mauvagne). **1977:** *Le Fou de Mai* (ro). **1987:** *Three Men and a Baby* (Nimoy) (st). **1990:** *Three Men and a Little Lady* (Ardolino) (technical adviser).

Ginette Vincendeau's insightful survey of Coline Serreau's career calls it a "high wire act," but one might shift the metaphor a little to "balancing act," for Serreau has managed to keep a steady balance between feminism and commercial success, outright farce, and drama of sentiment, while keeping a cool eye on her typically obtuse—but educable—male protagonists.

Serreau's first film, a documentary interviewing women as socially and economically diverse as a Swiss church minister and a sex-film star, was named after Freud's famous expression of bafflement, "What do women want?" Her second and third features, both fiction, explored the utopian possibilities of (respectively) a ménage à trois and a group of actors rebelling against the commercial film they are making. To be sure, Serreau's own next feature was commercial enough: *Trois hommes et un couffin* was the most widely attended French film in 20 years, and garnered César awards for both Best Picture and Best Screenplay. Projects to direct American remakes of this and her fifth film, *Romuald et Juliette,* came to naught, but she has continued in France to be a successful maker of satiric comedies.

Trois hommes explores the comic—and sentimental—possibilities of three Parisian bachelors having to curtail their usual amorous activities, and indeed even their professional careers, to raise an abandoned infant. Farce is the engine that drives the plot at first: the writer-director seems to have asked herself what *could,* after all, induce three perennial swingers to settle down even unwillingly to such a task. But the latter part of the film manages to be touching without becoming treacly or preachy (or indulging in chase scenes) as did the American version that eventually got made. The film has been accused of misogyny, in that the men eventually seem to claim exclusive rights over the realm of child care, while there are no sympathetic females in the picture other than the infant. But Serreau's droll observations of the bachelors—both their vanity (as when one of them, citing all the books he has read, tells off the equally haughty "Seconde Maman") and their deep affection for the child behind their masks of detached "professionalism" (as when they sing "Au clair de la lune" in three-part harmony to get her to sleep)—suggest a more complex perspective.

The farcical setup is considerably more ingenious in *Romuald et Juliette,* in which a yogurt tycoon on the eve of his greatest financial coup is the victim of three different and coincidental plots at the same time: his executive protégé is having an affair with his wife, another executive sabotages the yogurt plant to make Romuald and the protégé/lover look culpable, and a third executive is using Romuald's secretary/mistress to trap the boss in a phony insider-trading scheme. All this is the means of igniting the unlikely romance of the title, between the tycoon and his office cleaning woman, a black mother of five who lives in a cramped tenement. The *scène à faire,* in which Juliette tells her boss about one plot after the other that she has overheard, is truly hilarious, thanks not only to the explosive release of tension but to Daniel Auteuil's performance (and Serreau's direction), conveying genuine friendliness along with strained politeness and baffled incredulity. Equally brilliant is a later matching scene in which Juliette (the superb Firmine Richard) reacts to Romuald's marriage proposal with comparable astonishment but also indignation, even exasperation. Some have found the film's ending problematic, with Romuald's vast wealth seeming indeed to buy happiness, or at least serving to overcome Juliette's reservations, and with Juliette rather too neatly becoming an earth mother for the late 1980s. At least, in its delirious vision of family harmony despite racial and economic barriers it is consistent with Serreau's utopian/comic outlook.

La Crise follows to a considerable extent the pattern set by its predecessors. The opening crisis is actually a multiple one in which the protagonist loses his job, is deserted by his wife, and finds most of his friends and relatives having momentous quarrels with their spouses and lovers. In this case the outsider who leads the middle-class protagonist to reconciliation is not an infant girl or African woman but a lower-class sot who accompanies the "hero" on a sentimental journey. Most recently, *La Belle verte* carries Serreau's utopian proclivities a great deal further: in this comic fantasy the writer-director herself plays Mila, inhabitant of a "green planet," where everyone lives free of stress, pollution, and bureaucracy, while practicing vegetarianism and acrobatics. Mila's visit to Earth, armed with a device for "deprogramming" people so that they can be their "natural" selves (to the shock of other earthlings), allows Serreau herself to play the role of the beneficent outsider—to show up in her own cradle, as it were. Whether *La Belle verte* marks a new direction in her filmmaking or is a fanciful interlude amidst her more down-to-earth comedies remains to be seen.—JOSEPH MILICIA

Sharaff, Irene

American costume designer

Born *Boston, 1910.* ***Education*** *Attended the New York School of Fine and Applied Arts, Art Students League, New York, and La Grande Chaumiere, Paris.* ***Career*** *1928-30—assistant designer to Aline Bernstein, Civic Repertory Theatre Company; 1932—designer for Broadway plays, and for several ballet companies; 1943-45—costume designer, MGM, then freelance designer for films.* ***Awards*** *Academy Awards, for* An American in Paris, *1951;* The King and I, *1956;* West Side Story, *1961;* Cleopatra, *1963;* Who's Afraid of Virginia Woolf?, *1966.* ***Died*** *In New York City, 16 August 1993.*

Films as Costume Designer: 1943: *Girl Crazy* (Taurog); *I Dood It* (Minnelli) (co); *Madame Curie* (LeRoy) (co). **1944:** *Meet Me in St. Louis* (Minnelli). **1945:** *Yolanda and the Thief* (Minnelli) (co). **1946:** *The Best Years of Our Lives* (Wyler); *The Dark Mirror* (Siodmak). **1947:** *The Bishop's Wife* (Koster); *The Secret Life of Walter Mitty* (McLeod); *A Song Is Born* (Hawks). **1948:** *Every Girl Should Be Married* (Hartman). **1951:** *An American in Paris* (Minnelli). **1953:** *Call Me Madam* (W. Lang). **1954:** *A Star Is Born* (Cukor) (co); *Brigadoon* (Minnelli). **1955:** *Guys and Dolls* (J. L. Mankiewicz). **1956:** *The King and I* (W. Lang). **1959:** *Porgy and Bess* (Preminger). **1960:** *Can-Can* (W. Lang). **1961:** *Flower Drum Song* (Koster); *West Side Story* (Wise and Robbins). **1963:** *Cleopatra* (J. L. Mankiewicz) (co). **1965:** *The Sandpiper* (Minnelli). **1966:** *Who's Afraid of Virginia Woolf?* (M. Nichols). **1967:** *The Taming of the Shrew* (Zeffirelli) (co). **1968:** *Funny Girl* (Ross). **1969:** *Hello, Dolly!* (Kelly); *Justine* (Cukor). **1970:** *The Great White Hope* (Ritt). **1973:** *The Way We Were* (Pollack) (co). **1977:** *The Other Side of Midnight* (Jarrott). **1981:** *Mommie Dearest* (Perry).

Making motion pictures often demands more from an artist than the duties suggested by an official title. Had "costume designer" Irene Sharaff merely sketched pretty dresses for stunning starlets, prestigious MGM studios would have slammed shut the pages of her drawing pad. But Sharaff's talent included a strong intellect, a fine eye, intuitive insights, and ingenious ability for original adaptation, and an integrating mind that united all into workable designs.

Sharaff succeeded quickly as a New York stage designer. She showed a clever use of color in her costumes for Irving Berlin's *Easter Parade*. For this stage revue, various shades of browns, tans, and other neutrals mimicked the pages of the *New York Times* rotogravure. Sharaff's designs for *Alice in Wonderland* won acclaim as reconstructions of the original Tenniel illustrations. These successes caught the attention of MGM filmmakers who hoped to translate Sharaff's theatrical skills into bankable Hollywood ventures. Specifically, they sought a suitable designer to deal with the new Technicolor process. Sharaff did not disappoint them after she joined the staff in 1942.

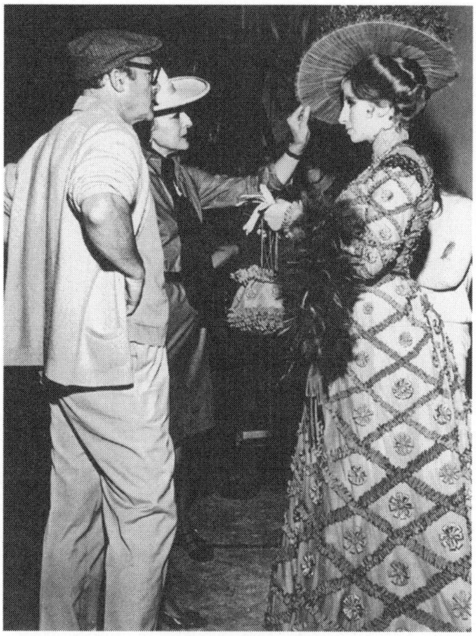

Irene Sharaff (center) with Gene Kelly and Barbra Streisand on the set of *Hello, Dolly!*

MGM designated Sharaff's skills to the Freed unit, which made some of the world's most memorable musicals. Almost immediately, her touch turned projects into screen gold. *Meet Me in St. Louis,* for instance, was a nostalgic valentine of lace, swiss dots, and ruffles. But the *An American in Paris* ballet sequence proved the costume designer's finest hour, as it utilized a multitude of her various talents. For this ballet, Sharaff based her visuals on a number of famous French painters. Paying homage to the Impressionists and several Post-Impressionists, she translated the colors and techniques of individual artists to set design and costume, even as she facilitated Gene Kelly's dances with garments constructed specifically for movement. Even the fabrics flowed with harmonizing rhythms.

Sharaff's career displayed considerable variety. *The King and I* sparkled with exotic ethnic dress. *Can-Can* offered an imaginative "Adam and Eve" ballet complete with guises from animal to insect. *West Side Story* glorified the uniforms of working-class New York toughs. A few years later, *The Sandpiper* peopled the beaches of Big Sur with contemporary bohemians. Sharaff often dressed Elizabeth Taylor, be it as Egyptian queen (*Cleopatra*), a brilliant but testy Renaissance jewel (*The Taming of the Shrew*), or an overweight, aging slob (*Who's Afraid of Virginia Woolf?*). Late in her career, Sharaff's designs for *Mommie Dearest* amplified the lurid luster of Hollywood glamour in the 1940s and 1950s.

Throughout her remarkable 50-year career, Irene Sharaff translated her visions from stage to screen, using all the artistries of the world as inspiration. Understanding the natures of film, the stage, and ballet, she recognized their similarities and differences. Starting with this knowledge, she splashed it with just the right colors and elevated each creation to optimum advantage. Sharaff will best be remembered for taking the superficial show out of show business and replacing it with the depth of fine art.—EDITH C. LEE and DENISE DELOREY

Shepitko, Larissa

Soviet Ukrainian director and writer

Born *Armtervosk, Eastern Ukraine, 1938 (some sources list 1939).* ***Education*** *Studied with Alexander Dovzhenko at the VGIK (State Film Institute), from which she was graduated.* ***Family*** *Married the director Elem Klimov.* ***Career*** *1958—assisted Yulia Solntseva, Alexander Dovzhenko's widow, in making* Poem of the Sea, *based on Dovzhenko's writings; early 1960s—directed the short films* The Blind Cook *and* Living Water *and the diploma feature* Heat *while at film school; 1978—a retrospective of her work presented at the Berlin Film Festival, where she was a member of the jury.* ***Awards*** *Second Prize, Venice Film Festival, for* You and I, *1971; Golden Bear and International Federation of Cinema Press, Berlin Film Festival, for* The Ascent, *1977.* ***Died*** *Near Moscow, July 1979.*

Films as Director: 1961: *The Blind Cook* (short). **1962:** *Living Water* (short). **1963:** *Znoy* (*Heat*) (+ co-sc). **1966:** *Krylya* (*Wings*). **1968:** *V trinadtsatom chasu* (*At One O'Clock*). **1971:** *Ti I Ya* (*You and I*) (co-sc). **1977:** *Voshojdenie* (*Kodiyettom*; *The Ascent*) (+ co-sc). **1987:** *The Homeland of Electricity* (*Rodina Electrichestva*) (short—filmed in 1967 and released with *Angel*, a short directed by Andrei Smirnov, as *The Beginning of an Unknown Century*).

Other Films: 1970: *Sport, Sport, Sport* (Klimov) (ro). **1981:** *Proschanie s Matyoroy* (*Farewell*; *Farewell to Matyora*) (Klimov) (script concept).

Barely two years after her greatest international triumph—winning the Golden Bear at the Berlin Film Festival for *The Ascent*—Ukrainian filmmaker Larissa Shepitko died in an automobile accident. The Soviet cinema thus prematurely lost one of the major talents of its postwar generation, and the international film community was robbed of one of its emerging—and potentially most significant—creative lights. Summarily, Shepitko and her work pretty much have remained unknown and ignored in North America, despite a small but fervent cult of admirers (including Martin Scorsese and Stan Brakhage).

Shepitko's films are visually stunning, and loaded with images that eloquently communicate her characters' deepest feelings, concerns, and conflicts. They also are linked in that their settings are such disparate physical extremes as snow-covered landscapes, arid deserts and rugged wastelands. Nature itself presents a threat to human life, with the basics of survival often the primary challenge for her characters.

Furthermore, relationships in Shepitko's films mostly are strained. Characters have their own personal visions and opposing views on key issues. While her first films explore clear-cut political questions within Soviet society, her work evolved to deal more with moral and ideological concerns. Ultimately, her films reflect on the use of cinema as a means of exploring such issues—and, accordingly, serve as expressions of the essence of the human spirit.

In her all-too-short life—she was 40 years old when she died—Shepitko directed just four features. Her first, *Heat,* was her diploma work for the VGIK state film school, and was completed when she was 24 years old. It is set during the 1950s, on a small collective farm in the U.S.S.R.'s arid central Asian territory of Kirghizia, where two males from different generations quarrel over the manner in which agricultural procedures may be used to modernize the farm. This crisply directed film is especially successful in connecting its characters to their parched surrounding.

Wings, which Shepitko made three years later, examines the friction between Russians who survived World War II and their offspring. Its main character is a fabled female fighter pilot who has difficulty reconciling her past with her present job as a school administrator. She is entering middle age, her lone true love died in the war, and her memories of the war at once fill her thoughts and adversely affect her present-day relationships with her students and adopted daughter. From a political perspective, *Wings* is a provocative depiction of a character who views collectivism and obligation as the backbone of the Soviet Union and is troubled by what she views as an increase in individualism among the younger generation. Adding resonance to the story is the fact that she is neither a Stalinist heavy nor a well-intentioned visionary, but rather an all-too-human being who is attempting to clarify her present-day identity and follow her convictions. *You and I* is a companion piece to *Wings* in that its main character, a brain surgeon, has come to question his role in society and the significance of his life and his work. For this reason, he leaves his job and family and sets out on an odyssey through Siberia in search of himself. Both *You and I* and *Wings* are noteworthy as probing looks at moral dilemmas facing then-contemporary Soviet society.

Finally, *The Ascent,* Shepitko's masterwork, is a chilling drama about honor and corruption, devotion and duplicity, and human endurance under the most trying conditions. It is set during a snowy, dreary World War II winter in Byelorussia, the provincial Soviet region then controlled by the occupying Germans. The three pivotal characters are individuals who each must achieve a personal reconciliation as they fathom the meaning of their accountability while struggling to endure the bloodshed in their midst. The first is a German-speaking Russian—whose profession, ironically, is that of a schoolteacher—who collaborates with the enemy and toils as a torturer of his fellow citizens. The other two are partisans. The first gutlessly attempts to save himself by sacrificing his comrade; the second heroically refuses to cave into his captors' pressure and comes to view his imminent demise on a religious-mystical level, as a sacrifice in the wake of society's horrors. Among the other characters are a trio of innocents sentenced to death for allegedly favoring the partisans.

In July 1979, while driving to Moscow after looking over locations for her next film, Shepitko and four of her crew members lost their lives in an automobile accident. The film, which ironically was to be titled *Farewell,* was completed by Shepitko's husband, director Elem Klimov—who also filmed a documentary homage to her, titled *Larissa.*

That Shepitko's star was ascending on the international film scene is unquestionable. For this reason alone, her premature death is especially heartbreaking.—ROB EDELMAN

Shipman, Nell

Canadian director and actress

Born *Helen Foster-Barham in Victoria, British Columbia, Canada, 15 October 1892.* ***Family*** *Married 1) the writer Ernest Shipman, 1911 (divorced 1920), son: the screenwriter Barry Shipman; 2) Charles Austin Ayers, 1925 (died 1964).* ***Career*** *1905—began appearing on stage in vaudeville and road shows; 1912—moved to Southern California and began writing for the screen, and serving as agent representing best-selling writers in their dealings with movie companies; 1916—had her first major on-screen success,* God's Country and the Woman; *1920—formed her own production company, Nell Shipman*

Productions, which produced The Girl from God's Country *and* The Grub Stake, *and moved to Priest Lake, Idaho; began co-directing films with Bert Van Tuyle; 1925—closed down her production company; 1985—National Archives of Canada premiered a restored print of* Back to God's Country; *1987—her autobiography is published; 1989—a program of Shipman films is presented in New York at the Museum of Modern Art.* ***Awards*** *A section of Priest Lake State Park at Priest Lake, Idaho, is named Nell Shipman Point, 1977.* ***Died*** *Cabazon, California, 12 January 1970.*

Films as Co-Director: 1920: *Something New* (co-d with Van Tuyle, + ro as Nell Shipman, pr, sc); *The Trail of the Arrow.* **1921:** *The Girl from God's Country* (co-d with Van Tuyle, + ro as Neeka Le Mort/ Marion Carslake, pr, sc, st); *A Bear, a Boy and a Dog* (*Saturday Off*) (co-d with Van Tuyle, + pr, sc).

Films as Actress: 1916: *God's Country and the Woman* (Sturgeon) (as Jo Barton); *Through the Wall* (Sturgeon) (as Alice Kittredge); *Fires of Conscience* (Apfel) (as Nell Blythe). **1917:** *The Black Wolf* (Reicher) (as Dona Isabel). **1918:** *Baree, Son of Kazan* (Smith) (as Nepeese); *Cavanaugh of the Forest Rangers* (Wolbert) (as Virginia Wetherford); *A Gentleman's Agreement* (Smith) (as Theresa Kane) (+ sc); *The Girl from Beyond* (Wolbert) (as Cynthia Stewart); *The Home Trail* (Wolbert) (as Clara); *The Wild Strain* (Wolbert) (as Winifred Hollywood). **1919:** *Back to God's Country* (Hartford) (as Dolores LeBeau, + pr, sc); *Tiger of the Sea* (+ sc). **1922:** *The Grub Stake* (Van Tuyle) (as Faith Diggs, + pr, sc, st). **1923:** *Little Dramas of the Big Places: Trail of the North Wind* (Van Tuyle) (+ pr, sc); *Little Dramas of the Big Places: The Light on Lookout* (Van Tuyle) (+ pr, sc); *Little Dramas of the Big Places: White Water* (Van Tuyle) (+ pr, sc). **1924:** *Little Dramas of the Big Places: The Love Tree* (Van Tuyle) (+ pr, sc) (not completed). **1927:** *The Golden Yukon* (shortened re-issue of *The Grub Stake*) (Van Tuyle) (as Faith Diggs, + pr, sc, st).

Other Films: 1913: *Outwitted by Billy* (sc); *One Hundred Years of Mormonism* (sc, st). **1914:** *Shepherd of the Southern Cross* (Butler) (sc). **1915:** *The Pine's Revenge* (DeGrasse—short) (sc, st); *Under the Crescent* (King—serial) (sc, st). **1916:** *The Melody of Love* (Kerrigan) (sc). **1917:** *My Fighting Gentleman* (Sloman) (st). **1935:** *Wings in the Dark* (Flood) (st). **1947:** *The Story of Mr. Hobbs* (*The Clam-Digger's Daughter*) (Varney-Serrao) (uncredited pr).

Between the mid-teens and early 1920s, Canadian-born and California-bred Nell Shipman had a fascinating but short-lived film career. During that period, which might be dubbed the brief but gilded age of women film pioneers, Shipman acted on-screen, directed, wrote screenplays and the stories upon which they were based, represented writers in their dealings with film companies, and even formed her own production company—thus becoming her own boss. She was a woman of incredible fortitude who insisted on shooting her films on location in the wilderness of Idaho and Canada, and was unafraid to take risks in order to realize her creative visions. As film historian William K. Everson has noted, however, "She was a maverick who . . . tried to lick the Hollywood system and failed."

Shipman's best-known films have a shared theme: The woman's experience in the harsh regions of the north country. In fact, upon her initial success, *God's Country and the Woman,* she won the nickname "The Girl from God's Country." Contemporary writers have categorized Shipman as a purveyor of feminist stories because the heroines she created and portrayed are capable of fighting back and surviving the harsh destinies that befall them. True as that may be, a closer look at the films of her peak years shows as much of an emphasis on the woman as victim rather than champion. The focus is less on the triumph of the heroine than on her melodramatic predicament as she struggles with the beastly powerful male arch villain—and the typical Shipman heroine winds up in the arms of the good and loving man she first encountered at the opening of the story.

While she was at Vitagraph in the mid-teens, Shipman starred in two feature films based on popular novels of north country adventures by James Oliver Curwood. In *God's Country and the Woman,* her mother is raped and subsequently made pregnant by a dastardly cad. Years later, he returns to "God's Country" to tyrannize Shipman by kidnapping her and threatening her fragile marriage of convenience. During a fight between the cad and the husband, the villain is eaten by a pack of ravenous sledge dogs. To call this a feminist theme is taking a skewed look at the scenario. Instead, the film explores the subject of a woman as the victim of an evil-minded man.

In *Baree, Son of Kazan,* another Curwood concoction about the Canadian northwest, Shipman plays the "half-breed" daughter of a trapper. Alone in her cabin, she is sexually attacked by a brutish trading-post owner. It is left to her dog Baree to trap the bad man so that Shipman eventually can marry the good man of the story.

As Shipman gained more control over her films, she remained true to the themes in these melodramas. In *Something New,* the setting may be Mexico but the story is similar as an infamous Mexican *bandito* absconds with the heroine to his hideaway. With the help of the good man and his dog and Maxwell car, she is saved.

The triangular tale of the victimized yet spunky heroine, the villain and the good man continues in her later features. These include *The Girl from God's Country,* another north country tale about a young woman who saves the life of a millionaire roué who actually is her father (who sexually ruined her mother years earlier!). And in *The Grub Stake,* Shipman again combines her tried-and-true melodramatic theme with an appreciation for the north country wilderness and animals as a blackguard entices an innocent named Faith into a fake marriage in order to betray her honor.

Evidence of the brief success Shipman had as a filmmaker lies in two career milestones. The first is an offer of a seven-year contract from Samuel Goldwyn, which she later regretted turning down. The second came in 1920 when she established her own independent production company in Priest Lake, Idaho. Along with her co-director-lover Bert Van Tuyle, 200 animals, and a small contingent of actors and crew, she created a string of films over the next few years. Unfortunately, her failure to link her productions with a major distribution outlet appears to be the cause of the demise of her studio in 1925, when she shut the books on her production company and retired her animals to the care of the San Diego Zoo. Much to Shipman's credit, she not only loved animals but recognized the necessity for their protection decades before this notion entered the mainstream consciousness.

Part of Shipman's problem surely lay in her choice of stories, which were becoming redundant to those who made up her audience and perhaps were becoming passé to an America that had entered the Jazz Age. Also, Shipman was far from a classic beauty. She did not retain her looks with the passing years; as she approached the age of 30, she was no longer able to adequately play the "young girl" starring roles she created. William K. Everson politely noted, "Nell Shipman was an attractive woman, though a difficult one to photograph." Anthony Slide is harsher in his judgment, claiming that Shipman was "a poor actress, coy and with bad teeth." He goes on to describe her films as "amateurish in extreme." Yet when these films are projected for today's audiences, there is enthusiasm for Shipman's predictable melodramas, in spite of the contrived put-upon heroines; the black-hat, white-hat male characters; and the loyal animal defenders. The irony appears to be that today's viewers do not take these photoplays seriously—but Shipman did.

Sources state that much of Shipman's work remains uncredited, so it is impossible to completely evaluate her career at this time. Lastly, her autobiography, *The Silent Screen and My Talking Heart,* published in 1987, is based on memoirs that were discovered after her death.—AUDREY E. KUPFERBERG

Shub, Esther

Soviet Ukrainian director

Born *Esfir Ilyianichna Shub in Chernigovsky district, Ukraine, 3 March 1894.* ***Education*** *Studied literature, Moscow; Institute for Women's Higher Education, Moscow.* ***Career*** *Administrator with Theatre Dept. of Narkompros (People's Commissariat of Education), collaborated on stage work with Meyerhold and Mayakovsky; 1922—joined film company Goskino, reediting imported films for Soviet distribution and producing compilation and documentary films; 1927—directed first "compilation film,"* The Fall of the Romanov Dynasty; *1933-35—taught montage for Eisenstein class at VGIK (film school); 1942—left Goskino to become chief editor of* Novosti Dnya *[The news of the day] for Central Studio for Documentary Film, Moscow.* ***Awards*** *Honored Artist of the Republic, 1935.* ***Died*** *In Moscow, 21 September 1959.*

Films as Director: 1927: *Padenye dinastii romanovykh* (*The Fall of the Romanov Dynasty*) (+ sc, ed); *Veliky put'* (*The Great Road*) (+ sc, ed). **1928:** *Rossiya Nikolaya II i Lev Tolstoi* (*The Russia of Nicholas II and Lev Tolstoy*) (+ sc, ed). **1930:** *Segodnya* (*Today*) (+ sc, ed). **1932:** *K-SH-E* (*Komsomol—Leader of Electrification*; *Komsomol—The Guide to Electrification*) (+ sc, ed). **1934:** *Moskva stroit metro* (*Moscow Builds the Subway*; *The Metro by Night*) (+ sc, ed). **1937:** *Strana Sovietov* (*Land of the Soviets*) (+ sc, ed); *Turtsiia na podeme* (*Turkey at the Turning Point*). **1939:** *Ispaniya* (*Spain*) (+ sc, ed). **1940:** *Kino za XX liet* (*20 let sovetskogo kino*; *Twenty Years of Soviet Cinema*) (co-d, co-ed, sc). **1941:** *Fashizm budet razbit* (*Fascism Will Be Destroyed*; *The Face of the Enemy*) (+ sc, ed). **1942:** *Strana rodnaya* (*The Native Country*) (+ sc, ed). **1946:** *Po tu storonu Araksa* (*Across the Araks*) (+ sc, ed); *Sud v Smolenske* (*The Trial in Smolensk*) (+ sc, ed).

Other Films: 1922-25: Edited 200 foreign fiction films and ten Soviet films, final one being *The Skotinins* (Roshal). **1926:** *Krylya kholopa* (*Wings of a Serf*) (Tarich) (ed); *Abrik Zaur* (Mikhin) (ed).

In Russia, as directors traditionally do their own editing, famous film editors are rare. A great exception to this rule was Esther Shub. After gaining her reputation and experience in the early 1920s on the strength of her reediting of foreign productions and a dozen Soviet features, she became, largely on her own initiative, a pioneer of the "compilation film," producing work that has seldom since been equaled. She brought to this genre far more than her speed, industry and flair; she brought a positive genius for using all sorts of ill-considered odd bits of old footage as a painter uses his palette, using them as if they had all been especially shot for her. In creating her first two brilliant compilations, *The Fall of the Romanov Dynasty* and *The Great Road,* about the first decade of the revolution (both released in 1927), she scavenged everywhere with indefatigable determination. Old newsreels, amateur footage shot by the imperial family and their friends, official footage from a pair of official imperial cinematographers, storage facilities (cellars, vaults, and closets) of wartime cameramen were all investigated by Shub. She even managed to purchase valuable material from the United States. All of this was against the original reluctance of her studios to go ahead with these projects, and they refused to recognize her rights as author when she had finished the films.

Shub originally planned a film biography of Tolstoy as her third work, but even she failed to dig out more than a few hundred feet of material. Undaunted, she wove the footage she did secure in with other early fragments with great effect, emerging with *The Russia of Nicholas II and Lev Tolstoy.*

With the advent of sound Shub made an abrupt change in her methods. For *K-SH-E* (*Komsomol—Leader of Electrification*) she created her own version of the Communist Hero—young, passionate and dedicated, complete with high-necked Russian blouse and leather jerkin. She forsook her cutting table to become a sort of investigative journalist, deliberately turning her back on archival material, sweeping generalizations, and bravura montage. Instead, she forged a new, original style of ultra-realism, predating by 30 years many of the practices and theories of cinema verité. Forty years later a Soviet film historian was to chide her for "indulging herself with a contemporary enthusiasm for the future of sound film and with the peculiar cult for film-apparatus." This was because she opened the film in a sound studio full of every kind of cinematic machinery with what she termed a "parade of film techniques," and occasionally cut back to this theme throughout the production. She purposely included shots in which people looked into the lens, screwed up their eyes at the arc-lamps, stumbled and stuttered in front of cameras and microphones visible in the scenes, and, in general, tried to augment reality by reminding the audience that the crew and camera were actually *there* instead of pretending that they were part of some all-seeing, omnipotent but unobtrusive eye.

Another important Shub film was *Spain,* a history of the Spanish Civil War. This work was seen once again as an "editor's film." Put together from newsreels and the frontline camera work of Roman Karmen and Boris Makaseyev, the film featured a commentary by Vsevolod Vishnevski, who also collaborated on the script. In the following year Pudovkin collaborated with Shub on her compilation *Twenty Years of Soviet Cinema,* a history of the Soviet industry. She continued her documentary work through the war years and into the late 1940s.

Although as a woman and an editor she perhaps suffered some bureaucratic indifference and obstruction ("they only join pieces of film together"), Shub was an influential filmmaker who deserves at least a niche in the Soviet film pantheon alongside such other originals (in both senses) as Pudovkin and Eisenstein, who certainly appreciated her work.—ROBERT DUNBAR

Silver, Joan Micklin

American director

Born *Omaha, Nebraska, 24 May 1935.* ***Education*** *Studied at Sarah Lawrence College, New York, B.A., 1956.* ***Family*** *Married Raphael D. Silver, three daughters: the directors Marisa Silver and Claudia Silver, and the producer Dina Silver.* ***Career*** *From 1967—freelance writer for an educational film company, New York; 1975—directed first feature,* Hester Street; *1979—directed* Chilly Scenes of Winter *for United Artists, studio changed the title and the ending, but released it in its original form in 1982; 1980s—director for stage and TV, as well as film.* ***Address*** *Silverfilm Productions, Inc., 510 Park Avenue, Suite 9B, New York, NY 10022-1105, U.S.A.*

Films as Director: 1972: *Immigrant Experience: The Long Long Journey* (short). **1975:** *Hester Street* (+ sc). **1976:** *Bernice Bobs Her Hair* (for TV). **1977:** *Between the Lines.* **1979:** *Chilly Scenes of Winter* (*Head over Heels*) (+ sc). **1985:** *Finnegan Begin Again* (for TV). **1988:** *Crossing Delancey.* **1990:** *Loverboy.* **1991:** "Parole Board" ep. of *Prison Stories: Women on the Inside* (for TV). **1992:** *Big Girls Don't Cry. . . They Get Even* (*Stepkids*); *A Private Matter* (for TV). **1997:** *In the Presence of Mine Enemies* (for TV). **1998:** *A Fish in the Bathtub.* **1999:** *Invisible Child* (for TV).

Other Films: 1972: *Limbo* (*Women in Limbo*; *Chained to Yesterday*) (Robson) (co-sc). **1979:** *On the Yard* (R. Silver) (pr).

Undoubtedly, the impact of the feminist movement during the 1960s and early 1970s was instrumental in making it possible for women to establish themselves as directors by the latter half of the 1970s. Joan Micklin Silver was one of the first to do so. Silver's films are not explicitly feminist in content, but she consistently displays an awareness of and sensitivity to women's identities and concerns.

As in her initial effort, *Hester Street,* Silver's films have tended to be intimate character studies centered on heterosexual relationships that are in a transitional process. In several of the films, Silver, while not minimizing her significance, decenters the film's female protagonist: in *Finnegan Begin Again,* for example, the Robert Preston character dominates the narrative. But the two most striking examples are the films featuring John Heard, *Between the Lines* and *Chilly Scenes of Winter.* In both films, Heard plays a character with similar characteristics: a tendency to be possessive about the woman he professes to love and a casting of the relationship in the terms of romantic love. In *Chilly Scenes of Winter,* Heard imbues the film with his consciousness. His fantasy regarding a meeting with the Mary Beth Hurt character is visualized and he frequently directly addresses the viewer, providing access to his mental and/or emotional responses to a specific situation. By the film's conclusion, Heard has relinquished his romantic passion, but not without undergoing a considerable psychic and emotional strain. While Hurt rejects Heard and his overwhelming demands, she appears, on the other hand, to have no clearly formed idea of what she either wants or needs from a love relationship. Interestingly, the film does not imply that Hurt's uncertainty is a negative condition—she is just beginning to discover that she can explore the range of sexual and/or romantic involvements available to a contemporary woman.

In *Chilly Scenes of Winter,* the most complex and disturbing of her films, Silver indicates that from Hurt's point of view romantic love is oppressive and destructive; in *Crossing Delancey,* Silver employs a woman, the Amy Irving character, to investigate what could be called a romantic "perception" about possible relationships. Irving rejects the Peter Riegert character before she gets to know him on the grounds that the conditions of their meeting and his profession preclude the possibility of a romance between them. To an extent, Irving's rejection is motivated by her desire to distance herself from her Jewish ghetto origins. In Silver's films, a character's attitude to his or her origins, profession, etc., is often shown to be a contributing factor in the shaping of the romantic fantasy. In the Heard films, the character is frustrated by (*Between the Lines*) or indifferent to (*Chilly Scenes of Winter*) his professional life. In *Crossing Delancey,* it is only after Irving distinguishes between her romantic notions of appropriate partners and the reality of the Riegert character that a romance between the two can develop.

With *Loverboy,* Silver addresses another aspect of the thematic: a young man, played by Patrick Dempsey, learns gradually through his experiences as the paid lover of a number of frustrated married women that sexual desire, pleasure, and fulfillment are enriched by having a romantic attitude towards intimate relationships (in courting women, Dempsey's musical tastes move from heavy metal to Fred Astaire). Silver's films feature a continual probing of what the romantic means—the various dimensions of the concept and its possible significance to both of the sexes. As a concept, the romantic ideal is not gender specific, and it is treated as something that can be either negative or positive in application.

Joan Micklin Silver. Photograph by Joyce Ravid.

In *Hollywood from Vietnam to Reagan,* Robin Wood argues that *Chilly Scenes of Winter,* to be fully appreciated, needs to be read in relation to the generic expectations it in part fulfills but also undermines. Wood's contention that the film belongs to the classical Hollywood tradition of the light comedy is well-taken; essentially, the same can be said of both *Crossing Delancey,* which is a reworking of the classical romantic comedy, and *Loverboy,* which has its antecedents in the 1930s screwball comedy. (Similarly, Silver's graceful but unobtrusive mise-en-scène is a reflection of the classical filmmaking tradition.) In making this claim, it is important to indicate that the films are not evoking these classical genres for nostalgic purposes; instead, the films, while utilizing the structural strengths and comic potentials of the generic formulas, are offering a contemporary vision of the tensions underpinning heterosexual relations, and Silver's films predominantly respond to these tensions in a progressive manner. From this perspective, Silver's films can be compared to Woody Allen's light romantic comedies (*Annie Hall, Manhattan, Broadway Danny Rose*), though of the two directors, Silver is much less sentimental and precious about her characters (particularly in her treatment of the films' male protagonists).

Silver mostly has been idle in the 1990s. Nevertheless, as more women directors emerge both outside and within the Hollywood establishment, she has come to be regarded as an elder statesman of women filmmakers. One of this new breed is her daughter, Marisa, whose films include *Old Enough, Permanent Record, Vital Signs,* and *He Said, She Said* (the latter codirected with Ken Kwapis).

Silver's feature after *Loverboy* is *Big Girls Don't Cry. . . They Get Even,* released in 1992 but screened the preceding year as *Stepkids.* It is a comedy which charts the plight of Laura (Hillary Wolf), a teen with a large family—and big problems. While a genial, generally likable film, it is far from Silver's best work, as it often plays like a television situation comedy, complete with overly adorable or precocious children and a too neatly wrapped-up finale.

In the last 20 years, Silver has produced a small but personal and distinguished body of work. She remains an underrated filmmaker; in part, this may be due to the fact that her films are not big-budget projects or star vehicles. (Consistently, her films are conceived as ensemble pieces and contain beautifully judged performances.) It may also be due to the fact that the tone of Silver's films tends to be decidedly offbeat: although the films are clearly "serious" examinations of the complexities of heterosexual relations, Silver infuses the films with a slightly absurdist humor. On the one hand, this may produce a distancing effect that alienates the viewer. But it also allows the viewer to take a more contemplative attitude towards her depiction of the often aching pleasures involved in love relationships.—RICHARD LIPPE and ROB EDELMAN

Šimková-Plívová, Věra

Czech director and writer

Pseudonym *Sometimes known as Věra Plívová-Šimková.* ***Born*** *Lomnice nad Popelkou, Czechoslovakia, 29 May 1934.* ***Education*** *Studied film direction at FAMU (Prague Film School), 1952-57, diploma film* Než se rozhrne opona. ***Family*** *Married Tomáš Šimek, one daughter, one son.* ***Career*** *1957-62—assistant to Jasný, Gajer, Kachyna, Vorlíček, Kašlík; 1964—first film as director,* Boys, Take Your Dancing Partners!

Films as Director: **1957:** *Než se rozhrne opona* (*Before the Curtain Goes Up*) (+ sc). **1958:** *Touha* (*Desire*) (Jasný) (asst d); *Sny na neděli* (*Dreams for Sunday*) (Gajer) (asst d). **1959:** *Král Šumavy* (*Smugglers of Death*) (Kachyňa) (asst d). **1960:** *Případ Lupínek* (*A Little Lupin's Investigation*) (Vorlíček) (asst d). **1962:** *Rusalka* (*Water Nymph*) (Kašlík) (asst d). **1964:** *Chlapci, zadejte se!* (*Boys, Take Your Dancing Partners!*) (short) (+ sc). **1965:** *Káta a krokodýl* (*Katia and the Crocodile*) (+ co-sc). **1968:** *Tony, tobě přeskočilo* (*Tony, You Have a Bee in Your Bonnet*) (co-d with Králová, + co-sc). **1970:** *Lišáci-myšáci a Šibeničák* (*Foxes, Mice and Gallows Hill*) (+ sc). **1972:** *O Sněhurce* (*Snow White*) (+ sc). **1973:** *Přijela k nám pout* (*The Funfair Has Arrived*) (+ sc). **1975:** *Páni kluci* (*Boys Will Be Boys*; *Gentlemen Boys*). **1977:** *Jak se točí Rozmarýny* (*Ring a Ring o' Roses*) (+ sc). **1979:** *Brontosaurus* (+sc). **1980:** *Krakonoš a lyžníci* (*The Mountain Giant and the Skiers*). **1982:** *Mrkáček Čiko* (*Cziko, the Blinking Boy*) (co-d with Králová, + co-sc). **1985:** *Hledám dům holubí* (*I Look for a House of Pigeons*) (+ sc). **1988:** *Nefňukej, veverko!* (*Dear Squirrel, Don't Snivel*; *Katy and the Twins*) (+ sc); *Veverka a kouzelná mušle* (*Squirrel's Magic Shell*) (+ sc). **1990:** *Houpačka* (*The Seesaw*) (+ sc).

There are not many directors in international film history who have specialized in productions for children and teenagers and have done so with artistic success. This is understandable because this type of genre does not immediately bring enormous profits. In the former Czechoslovakia the regular production of films for children was ensured by the existence of a nationalized film industry which put aside a certain sum for these types of films. As a result of state support, numerous films of various genres were made for children. Among filmmakers we can find prestigious producers who turned to the children's world once or twice during their career, but there are few of them who chose to depict children's life on the film screen as a lifetime mission. Věra Šimková-Plívová belongs to the latter group and kept faithful to this genre from her debut in 1965 through the 1990s.

During this period Šimková-Plívová cinematized many films that delved from different directions into mysteries of children's souls, thinking, joys, and troubles. She was never interested in fairy tales; the stories of her films are set in the present and are usually based on reality. Šimková-Plívová devoted her attention as much to preschool children as to the troubles of teenagers. Her films are entertaining and thrilling but they do not hide either the raw reality of life or the complicacy of the world.

One of her best films—*Tony, You Have a Bee in Your Bonnet*—begins with an extraordinary scene: people carry two coffins containing the adoptive parents of a little boy to the graveyard. The boy's fate is endangered by the loss of his home. The film heroes and heroines of

Šimková-Plívová must fight injustice, sorrow, and intolerance. For all that, she does not depict their world in dark or gray colors. Because she understands the children's world she also gives her heroes room for friendship, love, desires, and dreaming. She is able to advise children spontaneously of the values of good relationships with others, the variety of human characters, and the necessity to care for nature. Nevertheless, her films are not didactic.

Šimková-Plívová mastered her film profession. She wrote her scripts usually by herself and had a special ability to lead young "actors" to plausible performances. This ability also came from her life. Šimková-Plívová was born in a small town near the mountains. She rarely left this area, and far away from busy film studios, she shot most of her films there. Surrounded by forests, familiar houses, and familiar people, she explored—with her actors (many of whom came from this town)—the hidden problems of her heroes.

Her films were meant not only for children but for adults as well. She showed adults that children's fates can be complicated—more complicated than adults'—and that the suffering of children can be equal to the greatest of human tragedies. Šimková-Plívová chose a difficult branch of film voluntarily, "Because children haven't yet lost anything from their humanity."—BLAŽENA URGOŠÍKOVÁ

Solntseva, Yulia

Russian director and actress

Born *Iuliia Ippolitovna Solntseva, Moscow, 7 August 1901.* ***Family*** *Married the film director Alexander Dovzhenko, 1927 (died 1956).* ***Education*** *Studied philosophy at Moscow University; graduated from the State Institute of Music and Drama in Moscow.* ***Career*** *1924—began her career as an actress, first appearing on-screen in Protazanov's* Aelita; *1930—became the assistant and close collaborator of her husband, Alexander Dovzhenko; 1956—began directing the incomplete scripts of Dovzhenko at Mosfilm Studios after his death.* ***Awards*** *Named an Honored Artist of the Republic, 1935; Lenin Prize, for* Poem of the Sea, *1958; awarded the Dovzhenko Medal, 1972.* ***Died*** *October 1989.*

Films as Director: 1939: *Shchors* (co-d). **1940:** *Osvobozhdenie* (*Liberation*) (co-d); *Bukovyna-Zemlya* (*Bucovina-Ukrainian Land*; *Bucovina-Ukrainian Earth*). **1943:** *Bytva za nashu Radyansku Ukrayinu* (*The Battle for Our Soviet Ukraine*; *Ukraine in Flames*) (co-d). **1945:** *Pobeda na pravoberezhnoi Ukraine i izgnanie Nemetskikh zakhvatchikov za predeli Ukrainskikh Sovetskikh zemel* (*Victory in Right-Bank Ukraine and the Expulsion of the Germans from the Boundaries of the Ukrainian Soviet Earth*) (co-d). **1948:** *Michurin* (*Life in Bloom*) (co-d). **1953:** *Egor Bulychov i drugie* (*Egor Bulytchev and Others*; *Igor Bulichov*) (two parts). **1955:** *Revizory ponevole* (*Unwilling Inspectors*; *Reluctant Inspectors*) (short). **1958:** *Poema o more* (*Poem of the Sea*; *Poem of an Inland Sea*). **1961:** *Povest plamennykh let* (*Story of the Turbulent Years*; *The Flaming Years*; *Chronicle of Flaming Years*). **1965:** *Zacharovannaya Desna* (*The Enchanted Desna*). **1968:** *Nezabivaemoe* (*The Unforgettable*; *Ukraine in Flames*) (+ sc). **1969:** *Zolotye vorota* (*The Golden Gate*) (+ co-sc). **1974:** *Takie vysokie gory* (*Such High Mountains*). **1979:** *Mir v treh izmerenijah* (*The World in the Three Dimensions*).

Other Films: 1924: *Aelita* (*Aelita: Queen of Mars*) (Protazanov) (title role); *Papirosnitsa ot Mosselproma* (*Cigarette-Girl from Mosselprom*) (Zhelyabuzhsky) (ro). **1928:** *Glaza, kotorye videli* (*Eyes That Saw*; *Motele the Weaver*; *A Simple Tailor*) (Vilner) (ro as Rosas, asst). **1930:** *Zemlya* (*Earth*; *Soil*) (Dovzhenko) (ro as daughter, asst). **1932:** *Ivan* (Dovzhenko) (asst). **1935:** *Aerograd* (*Air City*; *Frontier*) (Dovzhenko) (asst).

One cannot consider the career of Soviet actress-filmmaker Yulia Solntseva without acknowledging the influence of her husband, Alexander Dovzhenko, who with Eisenstein and Pudovkin is one of the virtuosos of the Russian cinema. After establishing herself on screen in the 1920s, Solntseva married Dovzhenko and, from then on, was inexorably linked to her husband. In this regard, Solntseva's work behind the camera is not that of an independent creative artist.

Solntseva had more of a self-contained identity during her relatively brief time before the camera than she did upon becoming Dovzhenko's deputy and, later, the director of his unfinished scripts. Most notably, she starred as the scantily clad title character in Protazanov's science-fiction melodrama *Aelita,* and as the cigarette girl in Zhelyabuzhsky's *Cigarette-Girl from Mosselprom*. Her role in the latter, that of a beauty who becomes a film actress and falls in love with a cameraman, foreshadowed her own relationship with her husband-to-be. Her final acting role was a supporting part in Dovzhenko's *Earth*.

Just about all of Solntseva's creative output reflects on Dovzhenko. She may be listed with him as co-director of *Shchors, Liberation,* and *Life in Bloom,* but the content and artistic vision of these films were dictated by Dovzhenko. Her credit does not mean that she was a creative equal; rather, the "co-director" acknowledgment is a generous one, and should be viewed as gratitude bestowed by Dovzhenko on a valued subordinate.

Solntseva's most notable early works are documentaries/compilation films involving the plight of the Ukraine from the late 1930s through mid-1940s, as war clouds hovered over her homeland. Yet even here, the serene, poetic imagery found in all these films, which are contrasted to those of war's devastation, clearly are reflective of Dovzhenko's aesthetic. The first film for which she earned sole directorial credit was the documentary *Bucovina-Ukrainian Land,* made as the Red Army moved into the Western Ukraine and Byelorussia in the wake of Germany's assault on Poland. The compilation film *Victory in Right-Bank Ukraine and the Expulsion of the Germans from the Boundaries of the Ukrainian Soviet Earth,* however, was co-directed with Dovzhenko; Solntseva co-directed another compilation film, *The Battle for Our Soviet Ukraine,* with Yakov Avdeyenko, but it was produced under the close supervision of Dovzhenko.

Dovzhenko already had completed preproduction on *Poem of the Sea,* which was scheduled as the first of a trilogy involving the evolution of a Ukrainian village, when he died of a heart attack. Solntseva not only took over the direction of *Poem of the Sea* but also filmed the two additional scripts. Here, too, whatever lyrical quality contained in these films—not to mention their focus on Ukrainian folklore—may be attributed to the vision of Dovzhenko. Solntseva simply was following his orders as it were, adding life to his cinematic blueprint.

Upon Dovzhenko's death, Solntseva declared, "I must complete (*Poem of the Sea*) in accordance with Dovzhenko's artistic conception, putting aside every trace of my own individual vision." When that film won the Lenin Prize, she demanded that the award be bestowed upon Dovzhenko. In viewing *Poem of the Sea* and its sequels, the point is not so much the manner in which they were visualized by Solntseva but what they might have been had Dovzhenko lived to direct them.

Not all of Solntseva's films were completed in conjunction with Dovzhenko. For instance, in the early 1950s, when Dovzhenko was still alive, she was one of a number of directors who made two-part filmed plays culled from the repertoires of prominent Russian theater groups. Even after completing her husband's Ukrainian trilogy, however, she remained dedicated to fleshing out his ideas. Solntseva scripted as well as directed *The Unforgettable,* a chronicle of the Nazi occupation of the Ukraine, but the film was based on stories written by Dovzhenko. She directed and co-scripted *The Golden Gate,* a film in which she utilized her husband as subject matter. One exception to her Dovzhenko connection, in which she explored an independent theme, was *Such High Mountains,* which dealt with issues relating to contemporary education.

On one level, the fact that Solntseva directed films under her own name even before Dovzhenko's death may be viewed as a personal triumph, an act of individual liberation. Nevertheless, she closely aligned herself with Dovzhenko when he was alive, and after his death chose to work on projects based on his writing and ideas. The operative word here is "chose," and it is for this reason that Solntseva should not be viewed as a victim of sexism or creative repression. Her primary artistic motivation, after all, evolved from her respect for Dovzhenko as a cinema master.

Yulia Solntseva viewed herself as an interpreter of Dovzhenko's aesthetic vision. In the end, she made her creative choices, and apparently had no problem living with them.—ROB EDELMAN

Spencer, Dorothy

American editor

Nationality *American.* ***Born*** *Covington, Kentucky, 2 February, 1909.* ***Career*** *Hollywood film editor: first film,* Married in Hollywood, *1929; 1939—received first of four Academy Award nominations, for* Stagecoach; *1945-79—worked at 20th Century-Fox.*

Films as Editor: 1929: *Married in Hollywood* (Marcel Silver); *Nix on Dames* (Gallaher). **1934:** *As Husbands Go* (McFadden); *Coming Out Party*; *She Was a Lady* (McFadden). **1935:** *The Lottery Lover* (Thiele). **1936:** *The Case against Mrs. Ames* (Seiter); *The Luckiest Girl in the World* (Buzzell); *The Moon's Our Home* (Seiter). **1937:** *Stand-In* (Garnett); *Vogues* (*Vogues of 1938*) (Cummings). **1938:** *Blockade* (Dieterle); *Trade Winds* (Garnett). **1939:** *Eternally Yours* (Garnett); *Stagecoach* (Ford); *Winter Carnival* (Riesner). **1940:** *Foreign Correspondent* (Hitchcock); *The House across the Bay* (Mayo); *Slightly Honorable* (Garnett). **1941:** *Sundown* (Garnett). **1942:** *To Be or Not to Be* (Lubitsch). **1943:** *Happy Land* (Pichel); *Heaven Can Wait* (Lubitsch). **1944:** *Lifeboat* (Hitchcock); *Sweet and Low-Down* (Mayo). **1945:** *A Royal Scandal* (Lubitsch); *A Tree Grows in Brooklyn* (Kazan). **1946:** *Cluny Brown* (Lubitsch); *Dragonwyck* (J. L. Mankiewicz); *My Darling Clementine* (Ford). **1947:** *The Ghost and Mrs. Muir* (J. L. Mankiewicz). **1948:** *The Snake Pit* (Litvak); *That Lady in Ermine* (Lubitsch). **1949:** *Down to the Sea in Ships* (Hathaway). **1950:** *Three Came Home* (Hathaway); *Under My Skin* (Negulesco). **1951:** *Fourteen Hours* (Hathaway). **1952:** *Decision before Dawn* (Litvak); *Lydia Bailey* (Negulesco); *What Price Glory?* (Ford). **1953:** *Man on a Tightrope* (Kazan); *Tonight We Sing* (Leisen); *Vicki* (Horner). **1954:** *Black Widow* (N. Johnson); *Demetrius and the Gladiators* (Daves); *Night People* (N. Johnson); *Broken Lance* (Dmytryk). **1955:** *The Left Hand of God* (Dmytryk); *Prince of Players* (Dunne); *The Rains of Ranchipur* (Negulesco); *Soldier of Fortune* (Dmytryk). **1956:** *The Best Things in Life Are Free* (Curtiz); *The Man in the Gray Flannel Suit* (N. Johnson). **1957:** *A Hatful of Rain* (Zinnemann). **1958:** *The Young Lions* (Dmytryk). **1959:** *The Journey* (Litvak); *A Private's Affair* (Walsh). **1960:** *From the Terrace* (Robson); *North to Alaska* (Hathaway); *Seven Thieves* (Hathaway). **1961:** *Wild in the Country* (Dunne). **1963:** *Cleopatra* (J. L. Mankiewicz). **1964:** *Circus World* (Hathaway). **1965:** *Von Ryan's Express* (Robson). **1966:** *Lost Command* (Robson). **1967:** *A Guide for the Married Man* (Kelly); *Valley of the Dolls* (Robson). **1969:** *Daddy's Gone A-Hunting* (Robson). **1971:** *Happy Birthday, Wanda June* (Robson). **1972:** *Limbo* (*Women in Limbo*) (Robson). **1974:** *Earthquake* (Robson). **1979:** *The Concorde—Airport '79* (D. L. Rich).

Dorothy Spencer's career as film editor spanned five decades in the industry. Beginning at the dawn of talking pictures, her work continued through the glory days of the Hollywood studio system to the widescreen extravagance of the 1950s and 1960s, working under such directors as John Ford, Alfred Hitchcock, Ernst Lubitsch, Henry Hathaway, and Mark Robson. Though her early days are affiliated with independent producer Walter Wanger, she involved herself exclusively with 20th Century-Fox from the late 1940s until her retirement in 1979. Despite a distinguished and varied career, she was nominated for an Oscar only four times, losing out on each occasion.

Beginning her career at the age of 20, Spencer worked as cutter on many of Wanger's 1930s productions, including *The Case against Mrs. Ames* and *Winter Carnival.* She also found herself working with director Tay Garnett on *Stand-In, Trade Winds* and *Eternally Yours.* Her career with Wanger reached its peak with John Ford's seminal Western, *Stagecoach* and Hitchcock's *Foreign Correspondent.* In *Stagecoach* the editing principles of the Russian Formalists were deftly employed to convey suspense and pace. Most apparent is the chase sequence—in which the stagecoach is pursued by hostile Comanches—where the cutting is deliberately disorienting to convey the consternation of the passengers, while the crosscutting (alternating between the passengers' point of view and shots of the besetting Indians) increases the scene's tempo. The film was to earn Spencer her first Academy Award nomination.

In the early 1940s she began to work with Ernst Lubitsch, editing *To Be or Not to Be, Heaven Can Wait, A Royal Scandal,* and *Cluny Brown.* She also completed work on her second (and final) Hitchcock film, the propagandist wartime drama, *Lifeboat.* Notable for its expert use of limited space (the entire film is set on a lone lifeboat in the middle of the Atlantic), the film is by and large muted. Nevertheless, two scenes do stand out—the harrowing buildup to a necessary amputation and the lynching of a German U-boat commander—both of which build to their climax through a methodical use of montage.

A Tree Grows in Brooklyn, directed by Elia Kazan, marked her first film for 20th Century-Fox. Among her early projects for the corporation were *Dragonwyck, The Ghost and Mrs. Muir,* and John Ford's broodingly low-key Western, *My Darling Clementine.* Lacking significant mood music, *Clementine* achieved its suspense—most spectacularly in the famous O.K. Corral gunfight sequence—in its editing, a tight, pared-down construction in which only the barest (and most pertinent) of information is conveyed.

In 1948 Spencer began the first of her two assignments under producer/director Anatole Litvak; the acclaimed *The Snake Pit* was followed by *Decision before Dawn,* a suspenseful espionage thriller which afforded Spencer her second Oscar nomination. It was her success in the latter that gave rise to Spencer's long association with big-budget actioners, an association that would direct the rest of her career. In the same year as *Decision before Dawn,* she edited *Lydia Bailey* and *What Price Glory?,* and shortly thereafter embarked upon a long list of the Fox-patented CinemaScope pictures, beginning with *Black Widow* in 1954.

Though the widescreen format brought an initial rethinking of the medium's form—traditional framing was reformulated for the wider format and the duration of scenes increased to allow audiences time to register the spectacle—such modifications were limited. By and large the editor's task remained unaltered and Spencer's work, from the mid-1950s onward, shows no apparent change in technique. She worked on a variety of pictures, from large-scale Biblical epics (*Demetrius and the Gladiators*) to Cold War anticommunist pictures (*Night People*) to war movies (*The Young Lions*). Her career in editing widescreen blockbusters reached its peak with Joseph L. Mankiewicz's labored epic *Cleopatra*. Taking more than four years to produce, with countless writers and a $40 million budget, the film provided Spencer with more than 70,000 feet (120 miles) of film to reduce to the final print's 22,000 feet. A gargantuan task on every level, the film won four Academy Awards with Spencer receiving her third nomination.

Many of Spencer's later efforts were under the direction of Mark Robson. In total they worked together on seven pictures, including *Von Ryan's Express, Valley of the Dolls,* and *Earthquake*. Expressing many of the concerns of the industry at the time, being big, expensive, and destructive, *Earthquake* marked the crowning achievement of Spencer's work in the 1970s. A huge success, the film managed to enthrall audiences with the scale and magnitude of its destruction, much of which depended on Spencer's competent skills as editor. In between her collaborations with Robson, Spencer worked with directors Henry Hathaway on *Circus World* and Gene Kelly on *A Guide for the Married Man,* and with David Lowell Rich on her final picture, *The Concord—Airport '79.*

After 50 years in the industry Dorothy Spencer retired. A consummate studio craftsperson, her work traced the rise and fall of the Hollywood system. Rejecting the reactionist editing styles that emerged in the late 1960s, such as Dede Allen's work on *Bonnie and Clyde* and Sam O'Steen's on *The Graduate,* she continued to employ the classical style formulated in the mid-teens. As with all editors, however, her impact on the films she edited is difficult to gauge. Since the editor's role is secondary to that of the director's, and subservient to the nature and style of the film itself, a critical analysis of her own individual input is difficult to realize. Some of her best work was under such autocrats as John Ford, Alfred Hitchcock, and Ernst Lubitsch, all of whom would have assumed complete responsibility for the style of the cutting employed. Nevertheless, despite the lack of any auteurist evidence, her competence in the field, her success within the industry, and her devotion to her craft remain uncontested.—PETER FLYNN

Spheeris, Penelope

American director

Born *New Orleans, Louisiana, 2 December 1945.* ***Education*** *Attended School of Theater, Film, and Television, University of California at Los Angeles, M.F.A.* ***Family*** *Daughter, Anna.* ***Career*** *Voted Most Likely to Succeed by her high school classmates; early 1970s—made several short films while studying at UCLA; worked as an actress and film editor; 1974—founded Rock 'n' Reel, a company specializing in rock music promotion; mid-to-late 1970s—produced short films directed by Albert Brooks and presented on* Saturday Night Live; *1979—entered the motion picture industry as producer of Brooks's feature* Real Life; *1981—directed first theatrical feature, the documentary* The Decline of Western Civilization; *1984—directed first fictional feature,* Suburbia; *1993—co-created, co-wrote, and directed television series* Danger Theater. ***Agent*** *The Gersh Agency, 232 North Canon Drive, Beverly Hills, CA 90210, U.S.A.*

Films as Director: 1981: *The Decline of Western Civilization* (doc) (+ sc, pr). **1984:** *Suburbia* (*The Wild Side*) (+ sc). **1985:** *The Boys Next Door.* **1986:** *Hollywood Vice Squad.* **1987:** *Dudes.* **1988:** *The Decline of Western Civilization Part II: The Metal Years* (doc) (+ sc). **1991:** "New Chicks" ep. of *Prison Stories: Women on the Inside* (for TV). **1992:** *Wayne's World*; *Lifers Group: World Tour* (doc short).

1993: *The Beverly Hillbillies* (+ co-pr). **1994:** *The Little Rascals* (+ sc). **1996:** *Black Sheep.* **1998:** *The Decline of Western Civilization Part III* (doc); *Senseless*; *The Things in Bob's Garage.*

Other Films: 1979: *Real Life* (A. Brooks) (pr). **1987:** *Summer Camp Nightmare* (*The Butterfly Revolution*) (Dragin) (co-sc). **1990:** *Wedding Band* (Raskov) (ro).

Unlike many women directors, Penelope Spheeris does not make films that are sensitive at their core, that focus on women and their relationships and emotions. Rather, her films—at least the group she made in the first section of her career—are hard-edged and in-your-face brutal. In terms of subject matter, they often deal with male adolescent angst as it exists within a grim, realistic urban environment. If none are particularly distinguished, they certainly are linked thematically, and by their solemn and depressing outlook.

Suburbia, Spheeris's first nondocumentary feature, details the plight of a group of teen runaways residing on the edge of Los Angeles. It opens with a pack of wild dogs tearing a baby to shreds. *The Boys Next Door* is the saga of two teen boys who become serial killers. It included footage which had to be edited out in order to avoid an X rating. *Dudes* focuses on some young urban punk rockers who cross paths with murderous Southwestern rednecks. Not all of Spheeris's young protagonists are male, however. One of the characters in *Hollywood Vice Squad* is a runaway girl who has become a heroin-addicted prostitute.

Spheeris has admitted that her preoccupation with alienation and brutality is directly related to the incidents in her life. "I look at violence in a realistic way because I've experienced a lot of it in my own life," she once told an interviewer. While she grew up in a traveling side show called the Magic Empire Carnival, there was nothing enchanted about her childhood. When she was seven years old, her father was murdered. Her younger brother died at the hands of a drunken driver. Her mother, an alcoholic, was married nine times. And her lover, the father of her daughter Anna, overdosed on heroin in 1974. Perhaps the infant being torn apart at the beginning of *Suburbia* is a representation of innocent young Penelope Spheeris, whose childhood purity was ripped from her at a too-young age.

Penelope Spheeris

As a child, Spheeris became captivated by rock music as an expression of youthful rebellion. This interest led her into a career in the music industry (as she formed her own company, Rock 'n' Reel, which produced short promotional films for such groups as the Doobie Brothers) and to the subject matter of her initial feature, the one that established her as a director. It is the 1981 documentary *The Decline of Western Civilization,* which records the late 1970s punk rock scene in Los Angeles. Featured are groups with such names as Circle Jerks, Fear, X, and Catholic Discipline, which are made up of rockers who are alienated not only from the core of straight American society but from the established, old guard in the rock 'n' roll hierarchy; to these rockers, the Beatles, Rolling Stones, or Kinks are as much a part of the mainstream as Spiro Agnew. Six years later, Spheeris made *The Decline of Western Civilization Part II: The Metal Years,* which contrasted several veterans of the heavy metal scene (including Ozzy Osbourne, Gene Simmons, and members of Aerosmith) to younger punk wannabes. Indeed, Spheeris's attraction to individuals so far outside even the farthest degrees of the establishment may be traced to one of the films she made while a student at the UCLA Film School, *Hats Off to Hollywood,* about the romance between a drag queen and a lesbian.

Spheeris's first megahit came with *Wayne's World,* based on the nonsensical but nonetheless popular *Saturday Night Live* skit featuring Mike Myers and Dana Carvey as self-proclaimed "party dudes" who have their own cable TV show. Despite the film's box-office success, it is too often idiotic and dull. Her features since then, such as *The Beverly Hillbillies* and *The Little Rascals,* are even bigger disappointments, and far removed from the spirit of her earlier work: the first is a poorly done version of the silly but funny 1960s television sit-com, and the second a pale reworking of the beloved Hal Roach one- and two-reel comedies.—ROB EDELMAN

Steel, Dawn

American producer

Born *Bronx, New York, 19 August 1946.* ***Education*** *Marketing student, Boston University (1964-65), NYU (1966-67).* ***Family*** *Married producer Charles Roven: one daughter, Rebecca.* ***Career*** *1968-69—sportswriter,* Major League Baseball Digest *and* NFL/NY; *1969-75—editor of* Penthouse Magazine; *1975-78—president of Oh Dawn! merchandising; 1978-79—vice-president of merchandising, Paramount Pictures; 1979-80—senior vp of production, Paramount; 1980-85—president of production, Paramount; 1985-87—president, Columbia Pictures; 1990—Steel Pictures for Walt Disney.* ***Died*** *20 December 1998.*

Films as Producer: 1983: *Flashdance.* **1984:** *Footloose.* **1986:** *The Karate Kid, Part II; Top Gun; Star Trek IV: The Voyage Home.* **1987:** *Beverly Hills Cop II; Fatal Attraction; The Untouchables.* **1988:** *The Accused; Ghost; Good Morning, Vietnam.* **1989:** *Ghostbusters II; When Harry Met Sally; Lawrence of Arabia* (restoration). **1990:** *Casualties of War.* **1992:** *Honey, I Blew Up the Kid.* **1993:** *Cool Runnings; Sister Act 2.* **1995:** *Angus.* **1997:** *Fallen.* **1998:** *City of Angels.*

Dawn Steel was a pioneer in Hollywood, an audience-savvy producer, the first woman to head a major Hollywood studio (Columbia), and a seat-of-the-pants executive "movie-marketer" who readily admitted she was mostly learning as she went along. She broke through the industry's "glass ceiling" to produce hits like *Flashdance, Top Gun, The Accused,* and *When Harry Met Sally.* Rather than shoot from the hip like the men, pretending she had an answer when she didn't, "I learned my job by doing and watching," she wrote in her 1993 memoir *They Can Kill You but They Can't Eat You.* Such honesty, coupled with a reputation as the "Steely Queen of Mean" who fought hard for film projects she believed in, earned her both respect and admiration in an otherwise notoriously cutthroat field. "I'm not Mary Poppins," she was fond of saying.

Many in Hollywood agree that Steel was a threat because she mythologized herself, created herself from the same whole cloth that industrious men had used to create Hollywood in the first place. But while other studio-heads like Louis B. Mayer and Sam Goldwyn, and even

Dawn Steel and Charles Roven

Steel's male contemporaries, were lionized for their "terrorist" tactics, women like Steel were tagged with the B-word. "There's no equivalent word for men," Steel told *Playboy Magazine* (August 1995). "If I strap on my balls, he calls me a bitch. I loathe it. If you absolutely have to call a woman a name, you can call her a shithead."

Steel learned early on that even perceived power is an advantage in any business. "From my mother," she wrote in her book, "I got the notion (rare for the 1950s) that women are equal to men. From my father, I picked up a sense of humor and learned not to be afraid of men." Her grandparents were Russian Jews who came to the United States with very little. Her father, Nat, was a zipper salesman and an avid weightlifter who changed his name to Steel from Spielberg. (Dawn joked throughout her life that she might've had a better "leg-up" in the business with the original name). Her mother was an electronics executive. Dawn grew up as a self-described "poor girl in a rich neighborhood," a vantage point which bred an early interest in marketing as she watched her rich young friends plead with their parents for the latest fashions and toys. It was this fascination with how a product was sold to the public and then magically made indispensable that would fuel her success first in merchandising and then in film production.

At the age of sixteen, for example, while most of her friends were buying and wearing Pappagallos flats in all colors, she went to work for the famous shoe-designer. She studied marketing at Boston University for a time, but dropped-out for lack of funds, and likewise left New York University a few years later for lack of interest. Her first head-on battle, literally "with the boys," came when she took a job covering football games for *NFL Digest*. The management at Yankee Stadium refused her entry into the press box because she was a woman. "I was stunned," she wrote in her book, "then furious. But rather than slink away with my credentials between my legs, I raised an incredible stink." Management ended up building her a private auxiliary press box that hung out right over the fifty-yard line. Over time, her little turret became the hip place to be, attracting well-known sportscasters and luminaries.

By the early 1970s, Steel was both head of merchandising for *Penthouse Magazine* and moonlighting her own brand of novelty items like the Cock Sock and the Penis Plant (amaryllis actually). It wasn't until she was sued by the Gucci family for marketing Gucci toilet paper (named after her *Penthouse* boss Bob Guccione actually) that she fully realized the potential of the press, even BAD press, in promoting a product. She defended her stint at the magazine by claiming that Guccione was always respectful and willing to give a woman a chance in business, regardless of what some feminists thought of the magazine. By her own account, Steel did not consider herself a feminist at this point, even claims to have viewed other women as a threat. But in defending sometimes bad business decisions, Steel was already forging her trail to Hollywood. "If you can market smut and toilet paper," she told *Playboy,* "you can market movies."

In 1978, she joined Paramount Pictures as head of marketing, soon mastering the art of "high-concept Hollywood hardball" with the likes of Michael Eisner, Barry Diller, and Jeffrey Katzenberg. One of her most popular and clever merchandise tie-ins showed Klingons eating Big Macs at McDonald's to promote the first *Star Trek* feature. By 1980, she was appointed vice-president of production.

Her next big break came when she fought for the go-ahead on *Flashdance* (1983), largely because she simply believed in the integrity and timeliness of the script. It became a $90-million sleeper-sensation and sparked a nationwide merchandising rage for ripped T-shirts and rock-n-roll, MTV-style aerobics.

But success was not without its personal price. "The more successful and influential a woman becomes," she told *Cosmopolitan* (September 1996), the more possibilities diminish in terms of relationships with men. I think the opposite is true for men." When she first came to Paramount, she simply gave up on having a life. All her meals were business meetings, and all her free time was spent building and maintaining the crucial relationships—between agents, writers, directors, producers—so critical to getting a project on the screen. Friends began sending Steel material because they knew she would fight for it. But such fervent devotion to her work also brought about an emotional ending to a brief affair with Martin Scorsese, lost her a number of friends outside the business she no longer had time for, and nearly precipitated a nervous breakdown.

By 1985, Steel was again re-inventing herself. She met and married Charles Roven ("It's about fucking time," she claims to have said at their first introduction), and Paramount head Ned Tanen made Steel president of production. She was only the third woman in history to have a go at such a top spot, following Sherry Lansing at Fox and Paula Weinstein at United Artists. Here, Steel was responsible for blockbusters like *The Untouchables, Good Morning Vietnam,* and *Ghost,* and was rewarded by being replaced in 1987—a political studio move she found out about in the papers while she was in the hospital recuperating from the birth of her daughter Rebecca.

As it turned out, Paramount shut one door for her just as another was being opened. By mid-1987, she was being courted by Columbia Pictures, and in October she became the first woman ever to head a major motion-picture studio. Columbia was in dire need of an overhaul. In the previous five years, five separate administrative heads had come in, hired their own staffs and then left without taking anyone with them. Steel had a lot of "trimming" to do in order to make Columbia once again profitable; and, as in the past, it was not a task that would win her many new friends. David Puttnam (who had preceded her) had no experience in running a studio with a $400 million production and marketing budget and a release schedule of fifteen movies a year. But, as Steel herself was quick to point out, neither did she. "The good news was I had nowhere to go but up," she wrote in her book. "The bad news was I had nowhere to go but up."

Steel began by simply patching broken relationships and soothing bruised, stubborn egos. She brought *Ghostbusters II* and *Karate Kid II* to the screen after they had been languishing for months. She fought for the restoration of *Lawrence of Arabia,* once again proving to the public that commercialism and quality are not necessarily mutually exclusive concepts in the movie business.

In 1990, Steel was once again kicked downstairs when Sony bought Columbia and brought in Peter Guber and Jon Peters as chairmen of the board. But this time she was ready to leave, claiming she was happy to have been responsible for revitalizing the philosophical approach to making movies. She had certainly helped bring Columbia back from the economic brink, proving that the studio could once again make crowd-pleasing films both big and small. And she was ready to go independent, more hands-on both in her work and with her family.

With Disney and a handful of old colleagues from Paramount, she entered into a long-term producing arrangement that brought to the screen *Honey I Blew Up the Kid, Sister Act II,* and *Cool Runnings.* The latter was considered a laughable long-shot; it was the story of a Jamaican bobsled team, after all. But just as Steel had proved adamant (and usually right) when she fought for something early on in her career, whether she was marketing logo tchotchkes or pushing to make *Flashdance,* she championed the *Cool Runnings* script and it too became a surprising, quirky hit.

In March of 1996, Dawn Steel began what was to be the biggest battle of her life when she was diagnosed with brain cancer. She fought it valiantly for twenty months before she died on 20 December 1997. "She worked harder at getting well than anybody I've ever seen," said Amy Pascal (*People Weekly,* 12 January 1998), current president of Columbia Pictures and one of the many women who have since walked through the industry doors that Dawn Steel propped open. Certainly there are some who believe her acerbic style should not be the definitive model for women in the business, but given her meteoric rise to the top from such humble beginnings, there is little doubt that she continues to provide inspiration to girls with ambitious, filmic dreams. "The only way to combat sexism is through competence and being great at your job," she told *Playboy* in 1995. "It used to be about power. Now it's about passion for the work."—JEROME SZYMCZAK

Streisand, Barbra

American director, actress, producer, and writer

Born *Barbara Joan Streisand in Brooklyn, New York, 24 April 1942.* ***Education*** *Attended Erasmus Hall High School.* ***Family*** *Married actor Elliott Gould, 1963 (divorced 1971), son: Jason Emanuel; actor James Brolin, 1998.* ***Career*** *Singer in New York nightclub; 1961—professional stage debut in* Another Evening with Harry Stoones; *1963—Broadway debut in* I Can Get It for You Wholesale; *recording star; 1964—phenomenal success in stage play* Funny Girl, *and later in film version, 1968; 1969—co-founder, with Paul Newman and Sidney Poitier, First Artists Productions; 1976—executive producer,* A Star Is Born; *1983—producer and director, as well as actress,* Yentl; *1995—executive producer for the TV film,* Serving in Silence. ***Awards*** *Best Actress Academy Award, David Di Donatello award for Foreign Actress, and Golden Globe award for Best Actress, for* Funny Girl, *1968; David Di Donatello award for Foreign Actress, for* The Way We Were, *1973; Best Song Academy Award, and Golden Globe award for Best Song, for "Evergreen," in* A Star Is Born, *1976; Golden Globe award for Best Director, Silver Ribbon (Italy) as Best New Foreign Director, for* Yentl, *1983.* ***Agent*** *International Creative Management, 8942 Wilshire Boulevard, Beverly Hills, CA 90210, U.S.A.*

Films as Director: 1983: *Yentl* (+ co-pr, co-sc, title role). **1991:** *Prince of Tides* (+ co-pr, ro as Dr. Susan Lowenstein). **1996:** *The Mirror Has Two Faces* (+ pr, mus, ro as Rose Morgan).

Films as Producer: 1995: *Serving in Silence: The Margarethe Cammermeyer Story* (Bleckner—for TV) (co-exec pr). **1997:** *Rescuers: Stories of Courage—Two Women* (Bogdanovich—for TV) (co-exec pr). **1998:** *The Long Island Incident* (Sargent—for TV) (exec pr); *City at Peace* (Koch) (exec pr).

Films as Actress: 1968: *Funny Girl* (Wyler) (as Fanny Brice). **1969:** *Hello Dolly!* (Kelly) (as Dolly Levi). **1970:** *On a Clear Day You Can See Forever* (Minnelli) (as Daisy Gamble); *The Owl and the Pussycat* (Ross) (as Doris). **1972:** *What's Up, Doc?* (Bogdanovich) (as Judy Maxwell); *Up the Sandbox* (Kershner) (as Margaret Reynolds). **1973:** *The Way We Were* (Pollack) (as Katie Morosky). **1974:** *For Pete's Sake* (Yates) (as Henrietta). **1975:** *Funny Lady* (Ross) (as Fanny Brice). **1976:** *A Star Is Born* (Pierson) (as Esther Hoffman). **1979:** *The Main Event* (Zieff) (as Hillary Kramer). **1981:** *All Night Long*

Barbra Streisand directing *Yentl.*

(Tramont) (as Cheryl Gibbons). **1987:** *Nuts* (Ritt) (as Claudia Draper, + pr, mus). **1990:** *Listen Up!: The Lives of Quincy Jones* (Weissbrod—doc). **1995:** *Barbra Streisand: The Concert* (doc for TV) (+ co-pr).

Barbra Streisand's stardom as a singer and an actress underwrote the first movie she directed, literally. She told Dale Pollock that her previous success let her accept scale wages as director, no fee as co-writer, and a low salary as star of *Yentl. Yentl* was publicized by MGM/UA in 1983 as the first movie ever to feature one woman in all the above-listed capacities, as well as in the role of co-producer.

It is clear that Streisand's star image also underwrites *Yentl*'s aesthetics. Yentl is a young woman in turn of the century Eastern Europe whose love of the Talmud drives her to masquerade as a boy, the only way she can study the writings central to Judaism but prohibited to females at the time. The grounding in Jewish culture, the insistence upon women's rights, and the commitment to education all are part of Streisand's persona, as the many biographies of her and her philanthropic generosity detail. Formally, *Yentl* is a unique musical, predicated upon Streisand's grand, singular presence as a singer. At moments, Streisand sings Yentl's interior monologues, although (to the complaint of several critics) no one else in the film either sings or hears her.

At the yeshiva where s/he studies, Yentl meets Avigdor (Mandy Patinkin), and for love of him agrees to marry the girl he loves but cannot have, Hadass (Amy Irving). Allison Fernley and Paula Maloof make a strong case that Yentl's feelings of love and buried physical attraction for Hadass, in combination with Yentl's refusal at the end of the film to sacrifice her studies and retreat into a conventional marriage with Avigdor, mark *Yentl* as a uniquely feminist film. There was much speculation in the press that Streisand was refused an Oscar nomination for any of her work on the film, on sexist grounds.

Yentl shares a basic theme with Streisand's two subsequent directorial efforts: it is through each individual's ability to take on the roles and perspectives conventionally divided between genders that romantic love can best proceed between any two people, and that society can progress. Comparatively, however, the latter two films are less seditious in their promotion of this idea. *The Prince of Tides,* based upon Pat Conroy's novel, is a celebration of a strong woman's ability to reinvigorate a man by helping him admit past traumas, and by loving him for his vulnerability. Streisand cast herself as Lowenstein, psychotherapist to a suicidal (female) poet, and eventually lover to the poet's twin brother, Tom Wingo (Nick Nolte).

In *Yentl,* all three of the main characters serve as conduits between the other two. The crossed lines of desire, identification, and fear help all the characters grow, challenging norms of (especially female) gender and sexuality. But in *Prince,* while Lowenstein avails herself to Tom as the means whereby he can accept himself as he is and thus rekindle his love for his estranged wife, his daughters, and his teaching, Lowenstein remains a stranger to—unconnected and unconcerned with—these other females in his life. In the end, Tom and Lowenstein's play with conventional gender traits (she ordering a French dinner, he weeping in her arms) takes place only as temporary fantasy and dislocated experiment, much like their love itself, even though it is depicted as sexy and energizing.

Streisand's direction goes a long way toward contributing to that energy. She continues her preferred habit of using long takes wherever possible, allowing characters to overlap dialogue and react directly to one another. *Prince* bursts with characters—including, in a large sense, its South Carolina and New York City locations—and Streisand orchestrates a flow of full and active frames, in most of which Nolte is at the center.

Streisand's latest film integrates the personas and acting strengths of an impressively wide range of Hollywood, Broadway, and television stars, from Lauren Bacall, Brenda Vacarro, and Streisand's 1970 leading man George Segal, to Mimi Rogers and Pierce Brosnan. *The Mirror Has Two Faces* concerns Rose Morgan (Streisand), a Columbia English professor with a lackluster love life. Rose attracts the attention of a physically fit but priggish math professor (Jeff Bridges) so flustered by his desire, however well-met, that he now wants simply a companionate marriage. After he becomes her husband, he and Rose connect sexually as well as intellectually only after her mildly "unfeminine" style of dress—and love of learning, baseball, and her best pal—gives way, for a short period, to a "hyper-feminine" pursuit of physical beauty.

All three of Streisand's films are about an unconventionally gendered educator-student, at a crossroads in life, whose unexpected love for an intermediary enables her or him to (re)connect with a mate and find a future. The twist in *Mirror* is that the conduit figure for Rose is Rose herself, after a strenuous regimen of diet and exercise. Thought-provoking and involving as it is, *Mirror* seems the least certain of Streisand's trio of films, perhaps because the transitory function of the buff, blond Rose is not completely clear. The film does leave itself open to the charge that it celebrates variations from norms of feminine appearance, comportment, and appetites only ambivalently, after lingering upon its heroine's capability to adhere to them.—SUSAN KNOBLOCH

Tanaka, Kinuyo

Japanese director and actress

Born *Tokyo, 23 November 1910. (Other sources cite birthdate as 1907, or 29 December 1909, and birthplace as Shinomoseki City.)* ***Education*** *Attended Tennoji Elementary School, Osaka; studied the musical instrument the biwa (a lute-like instrument), gained license 1919.* ***Family*** *Married the director Hiroshi Shimizu, 1929 (divorced 1929); began relationship with the director Kenji Mizoguchi, 1947, which dissolved in the early 1950s.* ***Career*** *1920-23—member of the Biwa Shojo Kageki all-girl revue, Osaka; 1924—made film debut as actress in* Genroku onna; *1925—joined Shochiku Kamata Studio, Tokyo; by 1930—had become Japan's top female star; continued acting in prominent roles until 1976, altogether appeared in more than 240 films; 1953—directed her first film,* Koibumi. ***Awards*** *Japan Mainichi Eiga Concourse, 1947, 1948, 1957, 1960, 1974; Japan Kinema Jumpo Awards for Best Actress, for* Ballad of Narayama, *1958, and* Sandakan, House No. 8, *1974; Best Actress, Berlin Festival, for* Sandakan, House No. 8, *1975.* ***Died*** *Of a brain tumor, 21 March 1977.*

Films as Director: **1953:** *Koibumi* (*Love Letters*) (+ ro as landlady). **1955:** *Tsuki wa noborinu* (*The Moon Has Risen*) (+ ro as Yoneya); *Chibusa yo eien nare* (*The Eternal Breasts*) (+ ro as woman next door). **1958:** *Ruten no ohi* (*The Wandering Princess*) (+ ro). **1961:** *Onna bakari no yoru* (*Girls of the Night*). **1962:** *O-gin sama* (*Love under the Crucifix*).

Films as Actress (selected): **1924:** *Genroku onna* (Nomura) (as a maid). **1929:** *Daigaku wa detakeredo* (*I Graduated, But. . .*) (Ozu) (as Machiko). **1930:** *Ojosan* (*Young Miss*) (Ozu). **1931:** *Rakudai wa shitakeredo* (*I Flunked, But. . .*) (Ozu) (as Sayoko); *Madamu to nyobo* (*Madame and Wife*) (Gosho) (as the wife). **1932:** *Seishun no yume ima izuko* (*Where Now Are the Dreams of Youth?*) (Ozu) (as Oshige). **1933:** *Izu no odoriko* (*Dancing Girl of Izu*) (Gosho) (as Kaoru); *Tokyo no onna* (*A Woman of Tokyo*) (Ozu) (as Harue); *Hijosen no onna* (*Dragnet Girl*) (Ozu) (as Tokiko). **1935:** *Hakoiri musume* (*An Innocent Maid*) (Ozu); *Okoto to Sasuke* (*Okoto and Sasuke*) (Shimazu) (as Okoto). **1938:** *Aizen katsura* (*Yearning Laurel*) (Nomura) (as Katsue Takaishi). **1940:** *Naniwa ereji* (*Osaka Elegy*) (Mizoguchi) (as Ochika). **1941:** *Kanzashi* (*Ornamental Hairpin*) (Shimizu). **1944:** *Danjuro sandai* (*Three Generations of Danjuro*) (Mizoguchi) (as Okano); *Rikugun* (*The Army*) (Kinoshita) (as the mother); *Miyamoto musashi* (*Musashi Miyamoto*) (Mizoguchi) (as Shinobu). **1946:** *Josei no shori* (*The Victory of Women*) (Mizoguchi) (as Hiroko); *Utamaro o meburi go-nin no onna* (*Five Women around Utamaro*) (Mizoguchi) (as Okita). **1947:** *Joyu Sumako no koi* (*Love of Sumako*) (Mizoguchi) (as Sumako Matsui). **1948:** *Yoru no onna tachi* (*Women of the Night*) (Mizoguchi) (as Fusako); *Kaze no naka no mendori* (*A Hen in the Wind*) (Ozu) (as Tokiko Amamiya). **1949:** *Waga koi wa moenu* (*My Love Has Been Burning*) (Mizoguchi) (as Eiko Hirayama). **1950:** *Munekata shimai* (*The Munekata Sisters*) (Ozu) (as Setsuko). **1951:** *Ginza gesho* (*Ginza Cosmetics*) (Naruse); *Oyu-sama* (*Miss Oyu*) (Mizoguchi) (title role); *Musashino fujin* (*Lady Musashino*) (Mizoguchi) (as Michiko Akiyama). **1952:** *Nishijin no shimai* (*Sisters of Nishijin*) (Yoshimura); *Saikaku ichidai onna* (*Life of Oharu*) (Mizoguchi) (as Oharu); *Okasan* (*Mother*) (Naruse) (title role). **1953:** *Entotsu no mieru basho* (*Four Chimneys*) (Gosho) (as Hiroko Ogata); *Ugetsu monogotari* (*Ugetsu*) (Mizoguchi) (as Miyaki). **1954:** *Sansho dayu* (*Sansho the Bailiff*) (Mizoguchi) (as Tamaki); *Uwasa no onna* (*The Woman of Rumor*) (Mizoguchi) (as Hatsuko Mabuchi). **1956:** *Nagareru* (*Flowing*) (Naruse). **1957:** *Jotai wa kanashiku* (*Geisha in the Old City*) (Inagaki). **1958:** *Narayama bushi-ko* (*Ballad of Narayama*) (Kinoshita) (as Orin). **1959:** *Higanbana* (*Equinox Flower*) (Ozu) (as Kiyoko Hirayama). **1960:** *Ototo* (*Her Brother*) (Ichikawa) (as stepmother). **1962:** *Horoki* (*A Wandering Life*; *Lonely Lane*) (Naruse). **1963:** *Taiheyo hitoribochi* (*Alone in the Pacific*; *My Enemy the Sea*) (Ichikawa). **1965:** *Akahige* (*Red Beard*) (Kurosawa) (as Yasumoto's mother). **1974:** *Sandakan hachi-ban shokan: Bokyo* (*Sandakan, House No. 8*) (Kumai) (as Osaki).

Other Film: **1952:** *Ani imoto* (*Older Brother, Younger Sister*) (Naruse) (asst d).

For a woman to become accepted as a film director has rarely been easy, but in the Japan of the 1950s, a notoriously conventional society with rigidly traditional attitudes to the roles of the sexes, it was all but impossible. Only one woman achieved it, and then chiefly thanks to her status as Japan's most famous and respected cinema actress.

Kinuyo Tanaka's screen career began in the silent era, in 1924; still playing major roles, she made her last film in 1976, the year before she died. She starred in Japan's first talkie and first color film. Altogether she appeared in something more than 240 films and acted with almost every leading director of the period, starring in 10 films for Ozu and 14 for Mizoguchi. Yet despite her prestige she met with fierce opposition when she wanted to direct, and was able to make only six films as director. It says a lot for her talent and determination that not one of them is negligible, and that at their best they stand comparison with the finest films in which she acted.

Tanaka was inspired to take up direction on hearing that some of her female Hollywood contemporaries, such as Ida Lupino and Claudette Colbert, were contemplating directorial careers. In the winter of 1949-50 she visited Hollywood (in itself an audacious move for a Japanese actress) and came back resolved to work behind the camera. Her plan faced resistance from the directors' union, headed by Mizoguchi; though Tanaka's lover at the time, and director of some of the most sensitive films about women ever made (many of them starring Tanaka herself), he insisted that a woman should never direct. Other directors, including the supposed arch-traditionalist Ozu, were more supportive. Naruse took Tanaka on as assistant director to help her learn the ropes, Kinoshita scripted her first film, and Ozu co-scripted her second. (It was typical of Tanaka that even while battling on her own behalf she was ready to assist others. Her cousin, Masaki Kobayashi, always credited her with helping him launch his directorial career in 1952.)

As a director, Tanaka was not a formal innovator, and each of her six films fits into a prevailing genre such as *jidai-geki* (costume drama), *shomin-geki* (lower-middle-class melodrama), or *shin-geki* (realist drama). What distinguishes them is the female sensibility she brings to the established forms. Women, who take the key roles in all her films, are treated not just with sympathy, but with a humorous affection rare in Japanese cinema of the period. In *The Moon Has*

Risen family relationships, and specifically father-daughter relationships, display a relaxed spontaneous warmth that feels refreshingly natural; the same goes for *Love under the Crucifix*—even more unusual in a *jidai-geki* film, where stiff formality between generations is the norm.

Two of Tanaka's films, *The Eternal Breasts* and *Girls of the Night,* were scripted by a noted feminist writer, Sukie Tanaka (no relation to the director), but a compassionate feminism suffuses all Kinuyo Tanaka's work. Often the action focuses on a young woman who, like Tanaka herself, refuses to conform to the rigid codes of behavior expected of Japanese women. In *The Moon Has Risen* it is the youngest of three daughters who bucks convention, a situation handled as gentle comedy. Kuniko, the ex-prostitute in *Girls of the Night,* finds herself the victim of prejudice at every level as she tries to build a new life on her own terms. And in *Love under the Crucifix* the heroine, trapped by implacable forces and unable to live the life she wants, chooses the dignity of death as the best available option.

The historical drama *The Wandering Princess* also centers on a woman trapped by convention—although since the princess in question, sister-in-law of the puppet emperor of Manchuria (as in Bertolucci's *The Last Emperor*) stands little chance of rebelling, the film misses something of the vitality of Tanaka's other work. But perhaps her most remarkable film is the clumsily titled *The Eternal Breasts.* Based on the biography of a young woman poet who contracted breast cancer, it brings to its subject a clear-eyed, unflinching physicality. Chilling, clinical images convey Fumiko's vulnerability and fear at the invasion of her body, first by the disease and then by a double mastectomy; while Tanaka celebrates the surge of sexuality her heroine experiences after the operation as a brief, defiant assertion of life and erotic joy in the face of approaching death.

Unlike many actor-directors, Tanaka never used her films to give herself plum starring roles. In the first three she takes small roles, scarcely even cameos, and in the others she does not appear at all. But all her films as director share the qualities of her screen persona (which by all accounts reflected her personality in real life): intelligent, tenacious, versatile, emotionally responsive, and unconcerned with spurious glamour. For all her tenacity, though, Tanaka finally abandoned the struggle to build a directorial career in the face of professional hostility and public indifference. Her last film, *Love under the Crucifix,* was her most ambitious in production terms, with 'scope, color, and a substantial historical subject set in a vividly re-created 16th century. Originally planned to follow *The Eternal Breasts,* it took six years to bring to the screen and, like its predecessors, met with no great response at the box office. Following its heroine's example, Tanaka chose to make a dignified exit, and in any case had her acting career. It would be many years before any other Japanese woman director ventured to follow her lead.—PHILIP KEMP

Thomas, Betty

American actress and director

Born *Betty Thomas Nienhauser in St. Louis, Missouri, 27 July 1947 (some sources say 1948, 1949).* ***Education*** *Earned a fine arts degree from Ohio University; attended the Chicago Art Institute.* ***Career*** *Early 1970s—taught in the Chicago public school system; 1974—began appearing with Second City, the Chicago-based improvisational comedy troupe; 1976—became a regular on* The Fun Factory, *a daytime TV show, and began appearing in small roles on screen and television; 1981—began playing Lucy Bates on the* *television series* Hill Street Blues; *1988—appeared on the ABC-TV pilot,* Home Again; *late 1980s-90s—directed episodes of the TV series* Hooperman, Mancuso, FBI, Doogie Howser, M. D., *and* Arresting Behavior, *and directed over a dozen episodes of the HBO sitcom* Dream On; *1992—directed her first feature film,* Only You. ***Awards*** *1985—Emmy Award as Outstanding Supporting Actress in a Drama Series, for* Hill Street Blues; *1986—Viewers for Quality Television winner as Best Supporting Actress in a Quality Drama Series, for* Hill Street Blues; *1993—Emmy Award for Outstanding Individual Achievement in Directing in a Comedy Series, for* Dream On; *1996—Directors Guild of America Award, Outstanding Directorial Achievement in Dramatic Specials, for* The Late Shift; *1997—Audience Award, Karlovy Vary International Film Festival, for* Private Parts. ***Address*** *International Creative Management, 8942 Wilshire Blvd., Beverly Hills, CA 90211.*

Films as Director: 1992: *Only You.* **1994:** *My Breast* (for TV). **1995:** *The Brady Bunch Movie.* **1996:** *The Late Shift* (for TV). **1997:** *Private Parts* (*Howard Stern's Private Parts*). **1998:** *Dr. Dolittle.* **1999:** *Male Pattern Baldness.*

Films as Actress: 1976: *Tunnelvision* (Israel, Swirnoff) (as Bridgit Bert Richards); *Jackson County Jail* (Miller) (as Waitress); *Chesty Anderson, USN* (*Anderson's Angels, Chesty Anderson, US Navy*) (Forsyth) (bit). **1977:** *Dog and Cat* (Kelljan) (as Waitress) (for TV). **1978:** *Outside Chance* (*Jackson County Jail*) (Miller) (as Katherine) (for TV). **1980:** *Used Cars* (Zemeckis) (as Bunny); *Loose Shoes* (*Coming Attractions, Quackers*) (Miller) (as Biker Chick #1). **1981:** *Nashville Grab* (Conway) (as Maxine Pearce) (for TV). **1982:** *Homework* (*Growing Pains, Short People*) (Beshears) (bit). **1983:** *When Your Lover Leaves* (Bleckner) (as Maude) (for TV). **1987:** *Prison for Children* (Peerce) (as Angela Brannon) (for TV). **1989:** *Troop Beverly Hills* (Kanew) (as Velda Plendor).

Other Films: 1998: *Can't Hardly Wait* (Elfont, Kaplan) (co-pr).

If Emmy Awards are a measure of an individual's achievement in the television industry, then Betty Thomas has been equally successful in front of and behind the camera. As of 1998, she had accumulated ten Emmy nominations, and had taken home two statues—one for acting (on *Hill Street Blues*), and the other for directing (an episode of the HBO comedy series *Dream On*).

Betty Thomas

When Thomas won her initial fame, for playing no-nonsense police officer Lucy Bates on *Hill Street Blues*, she was just another semi-obscure actress with a stage background and scant television and film credits. She started out in the business as a member of Chicago's Second City improvisational comedy troupe, and her acting roles in theatrical and made-for-TV movies had been small and forgettable. Given her comedy background, it was surprising that she was cast in what was to become one of television's landmark police dramas. Yet Thomas not only played Lucy Bates with grit and heart, but fashioned the character into a role model for women. Lucy was just a human being trying her best to do her job and, as the character evolved on the series, she served to validate that a woman is capable of being a reliable and even noble cop.

Given her stature (she is 6'1", and lacking in movie star looks), her age (she was nearing forty when her series left the air) and her familiarity among audiences as Lucy Bates, it would have been nearly impossible for Thomas to maintain a high-profile acting career post-*Hill Street Blues*. So she almost completely abandoned acting—her last role to date came in 1989—and instead focused exclusively on establishing herself as a director. Even while appearing on *Hill Street Blues*, Thomas was intrigued by directing. While performers on other hit series are allowed to helm episodes of their shows, she did not do so on *Hill Street Blues* because Steven Bochco, its producer/co-creator, refuses to let his ensemble actors work behind the cameras. Instead, beginning in the late 1980s, Thomas gained valuable experience directing other television series.

As a director, Thomas is recognized for her ability to work with actors, which is not surprising given her industry roots. With the exception of *My Breast*, a television film that is several cuts above the average disease-of-the-week weeper—it is based on New York journalist Joyce Wadler's memoir, which charts her plight upon learning she has breast cancer—all of Thomas' features have been comedies or spoofs. To date, she has specialized in gross-out humor (key elements of *Private Parts* and *Dr. Dolittle*) and behind-the-scenes portraits of media personalities (*Private Parts* and *The Late Shift*). While Thomas has developed into a proficient director, and possesses a nice touch for comedy and satire, her films ultimately only are as good as the material with which she has to work.

Her directorial debut, *Only You*, is a lackluster romantic comedy that was released directly to home video. She fared far better with her initial theatrical feature, *The Brady Bunch Movie*: a hip, likable spoof that captures the spirit of the 1970s TV sitcom it lampoons, with Thomas milking laughs out of the irony of the Bradys living in the 1990s while being stuck in a 1970s time warp. Next came *The Late Shift*, an HBO produced television movie that never would have been produced by the networks. *The Late Shift* records the off-camera politics involved in the selection of Johnny Carson's successor as host of *The Tonight Show*, with Jay Leno and David Letterman vying for the job. The film is a sharply observed (albeit familiar) portrait of a vicious, ego-driven entertainment industry. Leno and Letterman are depicted as vain, insecure overgrown children, while the real industry powers are the scheming agents and executives who fashion clandestine deals and manipulate talent and the media.

In *Private Parts*, Thomas managed to humanize (and elicit a credible performance from) the film's subject and star, notorious radio shock-jock Howard Stern. To her credit, even those who despise Stern might find the film amusing. Yet while she should be lauded for this considerable achievement, *Private Parts*, at its core, is the equivalent of a Howard Stern press release, a bogus valentine to the allure of its subject. Thomas' most recent feature, *Dr. Dolittle*, parallels *Private Parts* in that it occasionally is entertaining but mostly misguided. The film is a contemporary reworking of the charmless 1967 musical—arguably the worst film ever to earn a Best Picture Academy Award nomination—which was based on Hugh Lofting's stories of a doctor who can communicate with animals. While ostensibly a kiddie film, this new, PG-13-rated *Dr. Dolittle* is endemic of too many contemporary Hollywood films fashioned for youngsters. The script is loaded with butt and poop jokes and other gross-out humor, with Eddie Murphy playing straightman to some smart-mouthed sheep, dogs, guinea pigs, and laboratory rats. Pre-teen boys will laugh themselves silly at the toilet humor, as their parents shudder at all the salty language. Computer animation is utilized to make the animals' moving mouths appear authentic. However, its predecessor in this capacity, the sweet-natured *Babe*, is a far better film.

As one critic noted, Thomas "has a pokey screwball style that doesn't really connect to the imaginative children's universe of the Dolittle material. And since the screwball script is more like a deadball, she has nothing to fall back on." Her Emmy honors aside, these are words which Betty Thomas would be well advised to heed as she selects future projects.—ROB EDELMAN

Toye, Wendy

British director

***Born** London, 1 May 1917. **Career** 1921—began working as a professional dancer, and performed at Albert Hall; 1927—staged a ballet,* Japanese Legend of the Rainbow, *at the London Palladium; 1930s—danced, choreographed, and acted on the London stage; late 1930s—performed on BBC television; 1946—began directing and producing plays and ballets for Sadler Wells, the Old Vic, and other British theater companies; 1947—formed her own ballet company, Ballet-Hoo de Wendy Toye; 1950—directed* Peter Pan *on stage in the United States; 1953—directed her first short film,* The Stranger Left No Card; *1954—directed her first feature,* The Teckman Mystery; *1950s-90s—directed and produced scores of stage plays, operas, operettas, and television productions. **Awards** Best Short Fiction Film, Cannes Film Festival, for* The Stranger Left No Card, *1953; awarded the Order of the British Empire, 1992. **Address** Flat 5, 95 Lower Sloane Street, London LW1W S3Z, England.*

Films as Director: 1953: *The Stranger Left No Card* (short). **1954:** *The Teckman Mystery.* **1955:** "In the Picture" ep. of *Three Cases of Murder, Raising a Riot, All for Mary.* **1956:** *On the Twelfth Day* (short). **1957:** *True as a Turtle.* **1962:** *We Are in the Navy Now* (*We Joined the Navy*). **1963:** *The King's Breakfast* (short). **1979:** *Tales of the Unexpected* (*Roald Dahl's Tales of the Unexpected*) (for TV). **1982:** *Trial by Jury.*

Other Films: 1931: *Dance Pretty Lady* (Asquith) (ro). **1935:** *Invitation to the Waltz* (Herzbach) (ro as Signora Picci, choreographer). **1945:** *I'll Be Your Sweetheart* (Guest) (ro). **1946:** *Piccadilly Incident* (Wilcox) (choreographer). **1986:** *Barnum!* (Coe and T. Hughes) (assoc pr).

Among the directors active in the British film industry during the 1950s were David Lean, Michael Powell, Emeric Pressburger, Carol Reed, Robert Hamer, Charles Crichton, Henry Cornelius, Alexander MacKendrick, John and Roy Boulting, Basil Dearden, Anthony Asquith, Ronald Neame, Guy Hamilton, Roy Ward Baker, Brian Desmond Hurst, Michael Anderson, Ralph Thomas . . . and Wendy Toye.

Toye was not the only woman to direct a British film during the decade. Muriel Box (who, in the mid-1940s, won an Academy Award for co-scripting *The Seventh Veil* with her then-husband, Sydney Box) made over a dozen shorts and features between 1952-64. Animator/producer Joy Batchelor and her husband, John Halas, created (among other films) an animated feature version of George Orwell's *Animal Farm* in 1954. Nevertheless, women directors back then practically were invisible, in England as well as elsewhere—and Toye only was to direct films for a decade, beginning in 1953.

Toye had no aspirations to make films. Her background was as a dancer/choreographer/dance and theater director, and she became involved with filmmaking due to the encouragement of producer Alexander Korda. Collectively, her feature films are unexceptional; none are among the very best British films produced during the decade. Her features include *The Teckman Mystery,* a drama about a writer investigating the supposedly accidental death of a pilot during a test flight, and a quartet of comedies: *Raising a Riot,* in which a wife/mother goes off to care for a sick parent, leaving her befuddled mate to cope with their hyperactive children; *All for Mary,* in which the title character is pursued by various men while on a Swiss vacation; *True as a Turtle,* about newlyweds who spend their honeymoon aboard a beat-up yacht; and her last feature, *We Are in the Navy Now,* in which a navy commander must reestablish his reputation after being relegated to training cadets.

Wendy Toye

It is tempting to decipher a subtle feminist agenda in *Raising a Riot,* in which a male character takes on a woman's role. After cooking, shopping, cleaning, and disciplining the children, this househusband declares, on his wife's return, "I wouldn't be a woman if the entire United Nations got down on their knees and begged me." In countless 1950s British comedies, however, male characters were feminized in order to evoke laughter. *Raising a Riot,* with its Brit-as-twit main character, is fashioned as a commercial entertainment. That it was directed by a woman is coincidental.

By far, Toye's best films were her short films. "In the Picture," her segment in *Three Cases of Murder,* is an eerie, surreal tale of terror in which a dead artist "resides" inside a house depicted in one of his paintings, which hangs in a museum. He emerges from the painting and lures a museum guide into it, and to his doom. *The Stranger Left No Card,* Toye's directorial debut—which she remade for television in 1981—is her finest overall work: a nifty yarn about a murderous outsider who arrives in a village and is taken in by the citizenry. Jean Cocteau dubbed *The Stranger Left No Card* a masterpiece, while British film critic Leslie Halliwell labeled it a "smart little trick film which as a novelty has not been surpassed." Toye employed her ballet expertise in *On the Twelfth Day,* a dance-oriented visualization of the song "The Twelve Days of Christmas," which Halliwell called "a refreshing and extravagant novelty."

Toye remained active as a stage director well into the 1990s—30-plus years after making her last film. In retrospect, even her best screen work seems a footnote to her long and prolific stage career.—ROB EDELMAN

Treut, Monika

German director

Born *Dusseldorf, Germany, 6 April 1954.* ***Education*** *Studied philosophy and literature in college, earning a Ph.D in literature, with a dissertation on the depiction of women in the Marquis de Sade's* Juliette *and Leopold von Sacher-Masoch's* Venus in Furs. ***Career*** *1970s-early 1980s—worked as an avant-garde performance artist, and made videos; 1985—co-directed* Verfuhrung: Die Grausame Frau, *her controversial feature debut, with Elfi Mikesch; co-founded the Women's Media Centre at Bildwechsel; 1996—visiting instructor at Vassar College.*

Films as Director: 1980: *Space Chaser* (short) (co-d). **1981:** *Ich Brauche unbedingt Kommunikation* (*I Really Need Communication*) (short); *Bitchband* (short). **1983:** *Bondage* (short). **1985:** *Verführung: Die grausame Frau* (*Seduction: The Cruel Woman*) (co-d with Mikesch, + co-sc, co-pr, video ph). **1988:** *Die Jungfrauen Maschine* (*The Virgin Machine*) (+ sc, pr). **1989:** *Annie* (short). **1991:** *My Father Is Coming* (+ co-sc, co-pr). **1992:** *Dr. Paglia* (short); *Max* (short); *Female Misbehavior* (+ pr). **1994:** "Taboo Parlor" ep. of *Erotique* (+ sc, co-pr). **1996:** *Danish Girls Show Everything.* **1997:** *Didn't Do It for Love.*

Film as Actress: 1993: *Domenica* (Kern) (as social worker).

To her supporters, the films of Monika Treut are daring and forceful, politically radical and groundbreaking in the manner in which they depict female sexuality. Her detractors, meanwhile, consider her most extreme works trashy and exploitive, even pornographic. These wildly divergent views crystallized during the world premiere, at the 1985 Berlin Film Festival, of this provocative filmmaker's very first feature: *Seduction: The Cruel Woman* (inspired by Sacher-Masoch's *Venus in Furs* and co-directed with her frequent collaborator, Elfi Mikesch), which was greeted with a combination of hearty applause and massive walkouts.

In her films, Treut suggests alternative—and highly radical—ideas and actions for fulfilling one's emotional needs. She portrays women as sexual aggressors. Men either are extraneous or undesirable sexually; they are completely missing from (and thus irrelevant to) sexual activity, or are victimized by the actions of women. Furthermore, a woman's sexual assertiveness is not depicted simply by having the female character on top of the male during the sexual act. In *Seduction: The Cruel Woman,* the main character is Wanda, an aloof, imperturbable dominatrix who operates a sex-performance gallery; she entices potential lovers of both sexes to her sanctuary of torture, where they become willing players in her sadistic erotic games. "It is my profession, being cruel," Wanda declares, simply and to-the-point.

The Virgin Machine and *My Father Is Coming* are stories of women who are struggling to find their identities, as well as someone to love. In the former, the main character, Dorothee, is addicted to romantic love, which only has brought her disappointment. She commences a sexual voyage that, geographically speaking, takes her from Hamburg to San Francisco. As she experiences various erotic encounters, she comes to grasp the lesbian aspect of her makeup.

My Father Is Coming is the story of Vicky, a German living in New York who waits tables while struggling to succeed as an actress. Like Dorothee, Vicky is desperate to find love. Her potential romantic partners are male—a female-to-male transsexual—and female. But more to the point, she has communicated to her father that she is happily married and a successful actress, and feels she must put up a front when he comes to New York for a visit. At its best, *My*

Father Is Coming is an astute observation of the significance of learning to accept who you are, along with the diversity in others.

Female Misbehavior consists of four of Treut's short films: *Bondage,* in which a lesbian expounds on the enjoyment and feelings of security she experiences in her sadomasochistic contacts; *Annie,* in which porn star/performance artist/sexual activist Annie Sprinkle (who also is featured in *My Father Is Coming*) takes the viewer on a tour of her cervix; *Dr. Paglia,* an interview with Camille Paglia, the controversial academic, author, and egocentric "feminist fatale"; and *Max,* featuring ex-lesbian Anita, whose sex-change operation transformed her into Max, a heterosexual male.

"Taboo Parlor," Treut's episode in *Erotique* (which includes three other short films, directed by Lizzie Borden, Ana Maria Magalhaes, and Clara Law), is an allegory about women's sexual power. It involves two lesbian lovers, Claire and Julia, who pick up Victor, a "100 per cent hetero" hunk, in a S&M bar. Victor's sexual presence is more brutal than amorous, and his sense of eroticism is thus sorely limited; he is none-too-pleased when Claire straps on a dildo and initiates anal intercourse with him. Treut depicts most of the other males on screen as bystanders, who clearly feel left out as they observe Claire and Julia kissing by a swimming pool or in the throes of foreplay with Victor on a public bus.

Monika Treut's films shatter conceptions of "normal" sexuality. Such taboos as lesbianism, sadomasochism, and transsexuality are depicted frankly, and sympathetically. An unlikely union of antipornography feminists and members of the religious right might join in condemning Treut because of her stance that pornography is emotionally healthy for women as long as it is female-controlled. In *The Virgin Machine,* Dorothee has an amusing encounter with Susie Sexpert, a pseudonym for author-editor-performer-activist-sex educator Susie Bright, who displays an array of sex toys and passes out flyers advertising for-women-only strip shows featuring female strippers. Afterwards, Dorothee declares, "The sex industry is lousy because women have no say. Feminists should go there instead of being uptight. It's the perfect place to live out their fantasies."

On a more emotional level, Treut examines what it means to fall in love, or be feminine, or feel desire; in her films, characters who search for romantic love are destined to find only frustration. This is articulated in the very first bit of dialogue in *The Virgin Machine*: "For many lambs, love is worse than going to slaughter." What Treut offers as an antithesis to romantic love is passion and eroticism, as exemplified by a line from *Seduction: The Cruel Woman*: "Happiness consists of feeling different passions, and living different passions."—ROB EDELMAN

Trinh T. Minh-Ha

American director

Born *Trinh Thi Minh-Ha, in Vietnam, 1953; came to the United States in 1970.* ***Education*** *Studied music composition, ethnomusicology, and French literature at the University of Illinois, Champaign-Urbana, received M.F.A. and Ph.D. degrees.* ***Career*** *Before becoming a filmmaker, she completed three years of ethnographic field research in West Africa and co-directed a research expedition there for the Research Expedition Program of the University of California, Berkeley; 1981—published first book* Un Art Sans

Oeuvre; *1982—completed first film* Reassemblage; *1985—with Jean-Paul Bourdier published a second book (*African Spaces: Designs for Living in Upper Volta*) and made a closely related film (*Naked Spaces: Living Is Round*); from 1994—Film and Women's Studies professor at the University of California, Berkeley; 1995—completed her first fiction and 35mm feature film,* A Tale of Love. ***Awards*** *Blue Ribbon Award for Best Experimental Feature, American International Film Festival, and Golden Athena Award for Best Feature Documentary, Athens International Film Festival, for* Naked Spaces, *1985; Merit Award, Bombay International Film Festival, Film as Art Award, Society for the Encouragement of Contemporary Art, San Francisco Museum of Modern Art, and the Blue Ribbon Award, American Film and Video Festival, for* Surname Viet, Given Name Nam; *Best Documentary Cinematography, Sundance Film Festival, and Best Feature Documentary Award, Athens International Film Festival, for* Shoot for the Contents, *1991; Maya Deren Award, American Film Institute, 1991.* ***Address*** *Women's Studies Department, 2241 College #4, University of California, Berkeley, CA 94720, U.S.A.*

Films as Director: 1982: *Reassemblage* (+ pr, sc, ed). **1985:** *Naked Spaces: Living Is Round* (+ pr, sc, ed). **1989:** *Surname Viet, Given Name Nam* (+ pr, sc, ed). **1991:** *Shoot for the Contents* (+ sc, ed). **1995:** *A Tale of Love* (co-d with Bourdier, + pr, sc, ed).

Originally trained as a musical composer, Trinh T. Minh-ha is a world-renowned feminist filmmaker, theorist, writer, and poet who is considered an expert on avant-garde and Third World, postcolonial film theory. Emigrating from Vietnam at the age of 17, she has developed a wide range of interests and talents that she consistently brings to her film work. Like the "theory films" of 1970's feminist filmmakers, Trinh's films offer theoretical musings into the subject of women, to which she adds the interrelated issue of ethnicity. She is known for such unique experimental documentaries as *Reassemblage,* about Senegalese village women and the aims of ethnography; *Surname Viet, Given Name Nam,* a film about identity and culture and the struggle of Vietnamese women; and *Shoot for the Contents,* a film about culture, art, and politics in China.

Trinh's films consistently prompt impassioned discussions, which have included denunciations of their "subjectivity," as well as praise for their refusals to adhere to ethnographic and documentary film conventions. That is, she generally blurs the line between fiction and documentary, thus questioning the meanings and expectations of audiences (and filmmakers) about both kinds of filmmaking practices. Moreover, she seeks not only to question the notion of "ethnic identity" but also of "female identity"—indeed, she has said she considers them as one issue that has been artificially separated. Trinh's affinity for music is also palpable in her films; she notes that her films' "non-expressive, non-melodic, non-narrative" aspects require a different kind of attention from its viewers, which hears "sound as sound, word as word, and sees images as image."

Her first film, *Reassemblage,* is a dynamic short film that refuses either to fit neatly into the categories of "documentary" or "fiction," or to provide easy answers to the questions it poses. Its style is highly experimental, using jump cuts, black leader, unfinished pans, fragmented compositions, multiple framings, and repetition. Accordingly, it challenges and comments on both the conventions of documentary film and ethnographic methodology. The soundtrack asks a suggestive question, "What can we expect from ethnology?" Later, it declares, "Filming in Africa means for many of us, colorful images, naked breast women, exotic dances and fearful rites, the unusual." Accordingly, Trinh dismisses the notion of "objectivity" among ethnographers who cannot help but express their personal values in their examinations of the "other," and she implies that ethnographers are unacknowledged voyeurs, not bias-free scientists.

Naked Spaces: Living Is Round is a feature-length film (Trinh calls it "exactingly long") that was shot in rural Senegal, Mauritania, Mali, Burkina Faso, Togo, and Benin. It explores the relationships between people and their living environments. But her best-known film is *Surname Viet, Given Name Nam,* which is a highly personal documentary that explores the status of women in contemporary Vietnam from a historical perspective. Interestingly, it consists largely of confessional interviews with five contemporary Vietnamese women whose words have been translated by Trinh and are delivered by amateur actresses. Despite somewhat disparate backgrounds, each of the women shares the "four virtues" and "three submissions" that constrain Vietnamese women's male-dominated lives. Trinh thereby suggests, but never asserts, that the Communist ascension to power had no effect on the subordinate status of women in Vietnamese society. Nevertheless, the women express an enduring love for their country—thus the film's title.

A Tale of Love is Trinh's most-recent film, and also her first fictional narrative, which provides a meditation about the tangled meanings of love. It traces the intellectual and emotional musings of a young Vietnamese-American journalist who moonlights as a photographer's model, and who shares the name of the heroine in Vietnam's national poem, "The Tale of Kieu"—considered by many Vietnamese to be an allegory of the "motherland's" history of strife and foreign domination. Written in the early 19th century, it relates the misfortunes of Kieu, a martyred woman who sacrificed her "purity" and prostituted herself for the good of her family. The modern Kieu sees parallels between the poem's Kieu and her own search for her self, since she finds herself struggling between two cultures and her own desires, and using her body as an economic resource. The film has a slow, contemplative pace and is peppered with painterly, often dreamy, images. Nevertheless, it is a challenging film that can be difficult to follow; that is, it has many scenes that have heavily didactic dialogue. In addition, the performances are stiff and amateurish, and Trinh contends that they are meant to be Brechtian. In large part, Trinh returns to feminist film theorist Laura Mulvey's important essay, "Visual Pleasure and Narrative Cinema," and its important thesis that Hollywood's movies are constructed for the pleasure of male viewers, largely, by fetishizing women's passive, glamorized bodies. Trinh extends Mulvey's thesis, however, by linking it to the subject of postcolonialism and the position of exile women.

In addition to her ongoing film career, since 1994 Trinh T. Minh-Ha has been a professor of women's studies and film at the University of California, Berkeley. As a professor, she aims to teach courses that, like her films, help to situate "women's work in the larger context of cultural politics, of post-coloniality, contemporary theory and the arts."—CYNTHIA FELANDO

Trintignant, Nadine

French director and writer

Pseudonym *Some of her earlier work was done under the name Nadine Marquand.* ***Born*** *Nadine Marquand in Nice, France, 11 November 1934; sister of the actors Serge and Christian Marquand.* ***Family*** *Married the actor Jean-Louis Trintignant, 1960 (divorced), daughter: the actress Marie Trintignant, and son: Vincent.* ***Career*** *1949—dropped out of high school and began working in the film industry as a lab assistant; 1950s-60s—worked*

Nadine Trintignant

as a "script girl," assistant editor, and film editor; 1960s—began directing television programs; 1965—directed a short film, Fragilité—ton nom est femme; *1967—directed her first feature,* My Love, My Love. ***Address*** *French Film Office, 745 Fifth Avenue, New York, NY 10151, U.S.A.*

Films as Director and Writer/Co-Writer: 1965: *Fragilité—ton nom est femme* (short). **1967:** *Mon amour, mon amour* (*My Love, My Love*). **1969:** *Le Voleur de crimes* (*The Crime Thief*). **1971:** *Ça n'arrive qu'aux autres* (*It Only Happens to Others*). **1973:** *Defense de savoir* (*Forbidden to Know*). **1976:** *Le Voyage de noces* (*The Honeymoon Trip*). **1980:** *Premier voyage* (*First Voyage*). **1985:** *L'Été prochain* (*Next Summer*). **1986:** *Tiroy senet.* **1987:** *Qui c'est ce garçon.* **1988:** *La Maison de jade* (*The House of Jade*) (co-sc). **1991:** Ep. in *Contre l'oubli* (*Against Oblivion*; *Écrire contre l'oubli*; *Lest We Forget*). **1992:** *Rè vense jeunesse.* **1993:** *Lucas.* **1995:** *Fugueuses* (*Runaways*; *Une Fille Galante*) (co-sc); *Lumière et Compagnie* (*Lumière and Company*) (co-d, one of 40). **1996:** *L'Insoumise* (for TV) (co-sc); *Balade en ville* (for TV).

Other Films: 1960: *L'Eau à la bouche* (*A Game for Six Lovers*) (Doniol-Valcroze) (co-ed). **1961:** *Leon Morin, pretre* (*Leon Morin, Priest*) (Melville) (co-ed). **1962:** *Le Coeur battant* (*The French Game*) (Doniol-Valcroze) (ed). **1963:** *Le Petit Soldat* (*The Little Soldier*) (Godard—produced 1960) (co-ed); *Les Grands chemins* (*Of Flesh and Blood*) (C. Marquand) (ed). **1996:** *Balade en ville* (Angelo) (sc).

From the very beginnings of the career of Nadine Trintignant, the filmmaking process has been a family affair. One of her early credits, *Of Flesh and Blood,* on which she is the editor, was directed and co-scripted by her brother, actor-director Christian Marquand, and features another brother, actor Serge Marquand, in a supporting role. Trintignant's husband, from whom she separated during the 1970s, was actor-director Jean-Louis Trintignant; he frequently appeared in her films, beginning with a starring role in her debut feature, *My Love, My Love*. Their daughter is actress Marie Trintignant, who also has been a regular in her mother's films, first appearing as a nine year old in *It Only Happens to Others*. Little brother Vincent and Marie play the two children who are the focus of *First Voyage,* while *L'Insoumise,* a television movie that is one of Nadine Trintignant's most recent credits, is scripted by mother and son.

Trintignant's films explore the issues of trust and devotion within families and relationships. They occasionally examine the fragility of new romances, and how they are doomed by a lack of communication. But in the majority of her work, her concerns are the quandaries existing within family structures, from the impact of infidelities on both sides of marital relationships to the manner in which couples deal with life-and-death crises to the way in which children respond to the actions or fates of their parents. At their worst, Trintignant's films are unoriginal, and by-the-numbers: scenarios whose basics have been more profoundly explored by other, more distinguished directors. But at their best, they are genuinely emotional, and visually stylish.

After serving her apprenticeship as an editor or co-editor on several films, and directing a short film, *Fragilité—ton nom est femme,* Trintignant made her debut feature in 1967: *My Love, My Love,* a romantic drama about a young pop-singer wannabe who is having an affair with an idealistic architect; she becomes pregnant, but does not inform her lover. The relationship ends, and it remains unclear if the woman has an abortion. Trintignant's follow-up, *The Crime Thief,* is the based-on-fact account of a drab henpecked husband who observes a woman commit suicide. In order to gain attention, he claims responsibility for her death; eventually, he does in fact kill a young model. Murder also is of consequence in *Forbidden to Know*; among its characters is a woman charged with slaying her lover.

Trintignant's first truly intimate family-oriented feature is *It Only Happens to Others,* which chronicles the death of an 18-month-old girl and its impact on her anguished parents. *The Honeymoon Trip* is the story of a married couple who go on a second honeymoon, at which point their various infidelities are revealed. *First Voyage* charts the plight of two siblings whose mother abruptly dies and who set out in search of their father, who had abandoned them years earlier. *Next Summer* is a generational portrait of a large, diverse family. At its center is a couple, with six children, who break up because of the husband's faithlessness but are reunited at the finale; during the course of the story, the various family members must evaluate their lives and face up to their inadequacies. *The House of Jade* follows the relationship between an older woman and younger man; the woman's earlier marriage ended because of her inability to become a mother and her commitment to her writing career, and this romance is doomed when her lover resolves to also have a family. *Runaways* is the story of two young women who both have had harsh relations with men, and who meet and become fast friends. One is on her way to see her estranged father as she escapes an unhappy home life with her mother. Upon her drowning, the other takes over her identity.

Even when her films fit into genres—*Forbidden to Know* is a suspense drama about an ambulance-chasing lawyer battling political chicanery; *Runaways* is part female buddy movie, part psychological drama—the manner in which Trintignant's characters respond to familial dilemmas plays a key role in her scenarios. And beyond the fact that she casts family members in her films, quite a few clearly are autobiographical. *It Only Happens to Others,* arguably Trintignant's most deeply personal film, is based on a real-life occurrence in the lives of the filmmaker and her husband. *The Honeymoon Trip,* meanwhile, is based on an incident in their marriage, while the characters in *Next Summer* are modeled after those in Trintignant's family.

As they explore deeply imbedded emotions, Nadine Trintignant's films observe the flow of everyday life. This is reflected in the choice she made for her participation in *Lumière and*

Company, an homage to the art of cinema, in which 40-odd filmmakers contribute 52-second-long "movies" shot with an original Lumière camera. Trintignant places her camera on a primitive dolly and glides it along an urban setting in which she captures an image of people sitting, standing, and walking in front of several buildings and water fountains. There may be strength in the image of the architecture, but the primary components to the shot are the people, and the panorama of life she records.—ROB EDELMAN

Ullmann, Liv

Norwegian director, writer, and actress

Born *In Tokyo, 16 December 1939.* ***Education*** *Studied acting in London; continued apprenticeship in repertory theater.* ***Family*** *Married 1) Gappe Stang, 1960 (divorced 1965); five-year relationship with the director Ingmar Bergman, one child, Linne Ullmann; 2) Donald Saunders, 1985.* ***Career*** *1957—film debut; 1960—acted with*

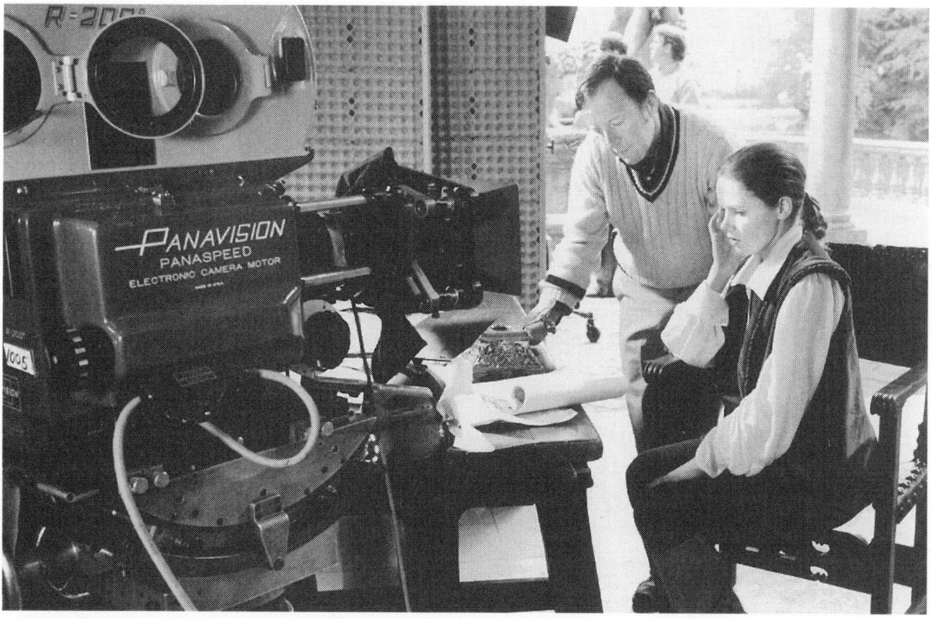

Liv Ullmann with Anthony Harvey on the set of *The Abdication.*

National Theatre and Norwegian Theatre; 1966—role in Persona, *the first of many performances in films by Ingmar Bergman; 1992—solo directorial debut; 1996—directed TV miniseries* Enskilda samtal (Private Confessions*). **Awards** Swedish Gold Bug for Best Actress, for* Skammen, *1968; Best Actress, New York Film Critics, for* Cries and Whispers *and* The Emigrants, *1972; Best Actress, Golden Globe, for* The Emigrants, *1972; Best Actress, New York Film Critics, for* Scenes from a Marriage, *1973; Best Actress, New York Film Critics, for* Face to Face, *1976; Seattle International Film Festival, New Directors Showcase, First Prize, for* Sofie, *1992. **Agent** Robert Lantz, 888 Seventh Avenue, New York, NY 10106, U.S.A.*

Films as Director: **1982:** *Love* (co-d with Zetterling, Cohen, and Dowd). **1992:** *Sofie* (*Sophie*) (+ co-sc). **1995:** *Kristin Lavransdatter* (*Kransen*; *Kristin Lavransdotter*) (+ sc); *Lumière et compagnie* (*Lumière and Company*) (co, one of 40 directors). **1996:** *Enskilda samtal* (*Private Confessions*) (for TV). **2000:** *Trolösa.*

Film as Actress: **1957:** *Fjols til Fjells* (*Fools in the Mountains*) (Carlmar). **1959:** *Ung flukt* (*Young Escape*) (Carlmar). **1962:** *Kort är sommaren* (*Short Is the Summer*) (B. Henning-Jensen) (as Eva). **1965:** *De kalte ham Skarven* (*They Call Him Skarven*) (Gustavson) (as Ragna). **1966:** *Persona* (I. Bergman) (as Elisabeth Vogler). **1968:** *Vargtimmen* (*Hour of the Wolf*) (I. Bergman) (as Alma); *An-Magritt* (Skouen) (title role); *Skammen* (*Shame*) (I. Bergman) (as Eva Rosenberg). **1969:** *En Passion* (*A Passion*; *The Passion of Anna*) (I. Bergman) (as Anna Fromm). **1971:** *The Night Visitor* (Benedek) (as Esther Jenks). **1972:** *Pope Joan* (*The Devil's Imposter*) (M. Anderson) (title role); *Viskningar och rop* (*Cries and Whispers*) (I. Bergman) (as a sister); *Utvandrarna* (*The Emigrants*) (Troell) (as Kristina). **1973:** *Nybyggarna* (*The New Land*) (Troell) (as Kristina); *Lost Horizon* (Jarrott) (as Catherine); *40 Carats* (Katselar) (as Ann Stanley); *Scener ur ett äktenskap* (*Scenes from a Marriage*) (I. Bergman—for TV) (as Marianne). **1974:** *Zandy's Bride* (Troell) (as Hannah Land); *The Abdication* (Harvey) (as Queen Christina); *L'uomo dalle due ombre* (*De la part des copains*; *Cold Sweat*) (T. Young) (as Fabienne); *Léonor* (Juan Buñuel) (title role). **1976:** *Ansikte mot ansikte* (*Face to Face*) (I. Bergman—for TV) (as Jenny). **1977:** *A Bridge Too Far* (Attenborough) (as Kate ter Horst); *The Serpent's Egg* (*Das Schlangenei*; *Örmens ägg*) (I. Bergman) (as Manuela Rosenberg). **1978:** *Herbstsonate* (*Autumn Sonata*) (I. Bergman) (as Eva); *Couleur chair* (Wyergans). **1980:** *The Gates of the Forest.* **1981:** *Richard's Things* (Harvey) (as Kate). **1983:** *Children in the Holocaust* (Eisner—doc) (as narrator); *Jacobo Timerman: Prisoner without a Name, Cell without a Number* (*Prisoner without a Name, Cell without a Number*) (Yellen—for TV). **1984:** *Jenny* (Bronken—for TV); *The Wild Duck* (Safran) (as Gina); *La Diagonale du fou* (*Dangerous Moves*) (Dembo) (as Marina Fromm). **1985:** *The Bay Boy* (Petrie) (as Jennie Campbell); *Ingrid* (Annakin, Crabtree, and French). **1986:** *Speriamo che sia femmina* (*Let's Hope It's a Girl*) (Monicelli) (as Elena). **1987:** *Gaby: A True Story* (Mandoki) (as Sari Brimmer); *Mosca Addio* (*Moscow Goodbye*) (Bolognini) (as Ida Nudel). **1988:** *La Amiga* (Meerapfel) (as Maria). **1989:** *The Rose Garden* (Rademakers) (as Gabriele Schlueter-Freund). **1991:** *Mindwalk* (B. Capra) (as Sonia Hoffman); *The Ox* (Nykvist) (as Maria). **1992:** *The Long Shadow* (Zsigmond) (as Katherine). **1994:** *Drømspel* (*Dreamplay*) (Straume) (as ticket seller); *Zorn* (G. Hallström) (as Emma Zorn).

Liv Ullmann created a place for herself in cinema history with her performances in films such as *Persona, Cries and Whispers, Scenes from a Marriage,* and *Autumn Sonata.* As an actress, Ullmann's singular beauty and ability to convey meaning through subtle but expressive gesture brought grace and emotional resonance to the work of Ingmar Bergman, and, for three decades, to scores of film and theatre productions in Europe and America. In 1992 Ullmann began her own directorial career. Because her films have been thoughtful character studies that draw on the creative resources of cast and crew members considered part of a company established by Ingmar Bergman, Ullmann's films are often compared to Bergman's—or perhaps more accurately, to critics' memories of films directed by Bergman. Close study of Ullmann's films reveals, however, that while her work explores relationships, settings, and philosophical terrain found in Bergman's work, Ullmann invites us to see things through a slightly different filter, one which, in particular, offers us a more self-affirming vision of women.

Born in the opening months of World War II, Ullmann lived in Toronto with her family during the war in a community known as Little Norway. When the war ended, Ullmann returned to Norway with her widowed mother and older sister. As a young girl, Ullmann, an avid reader and prolific writer of condensed classics, formed a drama club for which she presented her first stage performances. Out of school, her first success as an actress was as the lead in a local repertory production of *The Diary of Anne Frank.* In 1972 she received an Academy Award nomination for her performance in *The Emigrants,* and in 1976 another nomination for her work in *Face to Face.* During this period Ullmann returned to her interest in writing, and published the first of two autobiographical works. While continuing to work as an actress, Ullmann began broadening her range in another direction—in the seventies and eighties she became actively involved in humanitarian projects.

In the 1990s Ullmann's growth as an artist has allowed her to bring together a range of experience. *Sofie* represents not only Ullmann's debut as a director, but as a screenwriter as well. The script, co-written by Ullmann and Peter Poulsen, is an adaptation of the 1932 novel, *Mendel Philipsen og soen,* by Danish author Henri Nathansen. Set in Denmark at the turn of the century, the film's thoughtful account of a woman's passage from daughter to wife to mother, and its detailed depiction of the rituals that create a sense of order for a small Jewish community living at a distance from Danish life, combine to offer us a deft portrayal of the way in which contentment—in Sofie's case, the contentment of her parents—can, as Hal Hinson aptly puts it, "destroy a life as profoundly as misery can." Yet the film is not only a clear-eyed look into the complexities of even nurturing domestic life. It also stands as a compelling alternative to commercial cinema. In much the same way orthodox tradition provides the characters with a sense of meaning not found in modern, secular Denmark, on a formal level, the film's muted colors, long-take aesthetic, and casting of actors with "imperfect" features give audiences the opportunity to enter a richly detailed world of lifelike characters not found in productions driven by special-effects and star personas.

While *Sofie* has received the most critical attention and widest distribution of the films directed by Liv Ullmann, work following her directorial debut is also noteworthy. For her next project, an adaptation of the 1920s novel, *Kristin Lavransdatter,* by Nobel Laureate Sigrid Undset, Ullmann not only directed the film, but wrote the screenplay as well. While Ullmann's second film is set in the Christian world of medieval Norway, the narrative recalls dilemmas presented to *Sofie*'s central character, for again the direction of the woman's life is defined by the opposing demands of filial duty and passion. Here, however, the narrative explores the consequences of rejecting social convention.

Kristin Lavransdatter not only reveals thematic connections with Ullmann's earlier work—because the film's meaning is colored by the cinematography of Sven Nykvist—it also suggests a formal bridge to Ullmann's next piece, her contribution to the compilation film, *Lumière et compagnie,* for which Ullmann designed a self-reflective sequence in which Nykvist is seen filming the camera that films him. Produced in 1995 and shown at a collection of film festivals around the world, *Lumière et compagnie* celebrates the first 100 years of cinema with vignettes created by 40 filmmakers who produced work just as August and Louis Lumière had in 1895—using refurbished Lumière cameras, shooting films no longer than 52 seconds, and creating films using only natural light and nonsynchronous sound. Ullmann's contribution to the

Lumière film echoes the economy of gesture one finds in her work as an actress and her direction of actors, for without fanfare, it invites us to acknowledge that film has always depended on the performance of brilliant cinematographers.

Ullmann's most recent project is a film/television miniseries, *Enskilda samtal* (*Private Confessions*). The film, based on a largely autobiographical screenplay by Ingmar Bergman, examines the domestic life of its central character, Anna. The project brings together several members of "Bergman's company," for Nykvist is the film's cinematographer and the cast includes Max von Sydow and Pernilla August. First shown in Sweden and Norway, the film was screened at the Cannes Film Festival in 1997 to accompany the awarding of the Palm of Palms to Bergman.

Ullmann acknowledges that, like Bergman, she is interested in filmmaking that explores the geography of the human face. She points out, however, that she is concerned as well with figures in settings, and with what bodies as a whole can suggest about the inner lives of characters. Looking at Liv Ullmann's films as work that exists in its own right, what is perhaps most striking is that her aesthetic choices ask us to reckon with despair—and beyond that, they invite us to see the wonder and expressiveness of simple human gestures.—CYNTHIA BARON

Vachon, Christine

American producer

Born *New York, 1962.* **Education** *Attended Brown University; studied in Paris with Julia Kristeva and Christian Metz.* **Career** *1984—began working as a gofer on the sets of independent films; 1985—worked as an assistant and extra on Bill Sherwood's* Parting Glances; *1987—worked as third assistant director and production coordinator/second unit director on* Magic Sticks *and* My Demon Lover; *formed Apparatus, a production company, with Todd Haynes; 1989—co-produced (with Todd Haynes) her first feature,* He Once Was; *1990s—with Tom Kalin, established Kalin Vachon Productions, Inc. (KVPI); later established her own production company, Killer Films, in which she is partnered with Pamela Koffler.* **Awards** *1994—Frameline Award for Outstanding Achievement in Lesbian and Gay Media; 1996—New York Women in Film and Television's Muse Award for Outstanding Vision and Achievement.* **Address** *Killer Films, 380 Lafayette Street, New York, NY 10003-6933.*

Films as Producer/Co-Producer/Executive Producer: 1989: *He Was Once* (Hestand). **1991:** *Poison* (Haynes) (+ first asst dir). **1992:** *Swoon* (Kalin). **1993:** *Dottie Gets Spanked* (Haynes) (short, for TV). **1994:** *Postcards from America* (McLean); *Go Fish* (Troche). **1995:** *Stonewall* (Finch); *Safe* (Haynes); *Kids* (Clark). **1996:** *Plain Pleasures* (Kalin); *I Shot Andy Warhol* (Harron). **1997:** *Office Killer* (Sherman); *Kiss Me, Guido* (Vitale). **1998:** *Wild Flowers* (Painter); *Velvet Goldmine* (Haynes); *I'm Losing You* (Wagner); *Happiness* (Solondz). **1999:** *Take It Like a Man* (Pierce).

Other films: 1987: *Magic Sticks* (Keglevic) (third asst dir); *My Demon Lover* (Loventhal) (production coordinator, second unit dir).

Motion pictures are rarely controversial, since controversy often breeds contempt, and any sort of contempt for a film inevitably results in a dearth of box office dollars. Furthermore, in

Christine Vachon

the 1990s, the line between Hollywood and non-Hollywood product has become ever-so finer as once-"independent" film companies have been acquired by major studios. As a result, the term "independent film" has become increasingly ambiguous, if not altogether meaningless.

These facts of film business life have not deterred Christine Vachon, producer of some of the most cutting-edge and incendiary independent features released during the 1990s. From the very beginning of her career, Vachon has shown no interest in working on independents that are escapist fluff or low-budget derivations of Hollywood genre fare—or, for that matter, using her independent credits as a mainstream calling card. Vachon remains fiercely and proudly outside the mainstream. Her dedication to aligning herself with politically and socially committed filmmakers, and shooting politically and socially committed scripts, is reflected in the title of the combination memoir/independent film handbook she co-authored in 1998—*Shooting to Kill: How an Independent Producer Blasts Through the Barriers to Make Movies That Matter.*

Despite her book's ballsy title, in no way does Vachon romanticize the life of an independent producer. Filmmakers of all stripes may look hip and composed when they are photographed for magazine spreads. They may exude glamour as they attend film festivals, or appear to be all-knowing when they speak on panels in which they offer in-the-trenches advice to film biz neophytes. Yet Vachon is quick to admit that the everyday existence of the independent filmmaker is anything but alluring. On the first page of *Shooting to Kill. . .*, she observes: "Low-budget filmmaking is like childbirth. You have to repress the horror or you'll never do it again." In the decade in which she has been active as a producer, Vachon has continuously crushed whatever terror her experience has taught her to anticipate as she embarks on each new project.

As producer, Vachon's self-imposed role is to insure that the director's point-of-view has not been compromised by the time his or her film is ready to be screened for the public. In so doing, she plunges into the roll-up-your-sleeves, crisis-laden fact-of-life of low-budget filmmaking. During pre-production, she immerses herself in the script's evolution, the film's budgeting and financing, and the securing of appropriate talent to compliment the director and each other. Once the film is in production, her involvement remains hands-on. She strives to guarantee that the shoot does not go over budget or over schedule as she deals with the differing personalities working in front of and behind the camera. Then, when the film is completed, she labors to insure that it receives the best distribution deal, and highest-profile theatrical release. As Vachon has observed: "Basically, a low-budget movie is a crisis waiting to happen. You stretch every one of your resources to the limit, and then you constantly push that limit."

If the auteur theory has any relevance in the 1990s, then Vachon qualifies as an auteur producer. Most of her films feature characters who are deeply troubled, and disconnected from everyday society. Many are gay-themed—in fact, Vachon has been dubbed the queen of the New Queer Cinema—with her films exploring the insidiousness of homophobia by portraying the manner in which anti-gay attitudes affect the psyche. Not all of her gay characters are alienated, however; some live fulfilling lives while savoring friendships and searching for romance.

Collectively, the main characters in Vachon's films are reflective of the "outsider" aspect of society she is interested in exploring: a sensitive seven-year-old boy who disappears after shooting and killing his father, a disfigured scientist who becomes a sex killer, and an incarcerated gay male (*Poison*); an emotionally disconnected woman who comes to comprehend that she is being fatally poisoned by modern society (*Safe*); a downsized, ill-treated office worker who becomes a murderess (*Office Killer*); Valerie Solanas, the radical lesbian who attempted to assassinate Andy Warhol (*I Shot Andy Warhol*); David Wojnarowicz, the gay writer who died of AIDS (*Postcards from America*); an out-of-the-closet Leopold and Loeb (*Swoon*); drag queens who become involved in the Stonewall riots (*Stonewall*); lesbians who seek love (*Go Fish*); bisexual glam rockers and pop androgyny (*Velvet Goldmine*); aimless, hedonistic young teens (*Kids*); and gay male actors, and a straight Sylvester Stallone wannabe who thinks that GWM stands for "Guys With Money" (*Kiss Me, Guido*). Keeping in mind that the majority of independent features are artistic or commercial washouts—they will screen at the Independent Feature Film Market, where filmmakers bring their work to secure completion funds or find distribution, and then disappear without earning slots at film festivals or theatrical releases—the quality of Vachon's productions has been consistently and remarkably high.

Vachon most often has worked with Todd Haynes and Tom Kalin. Haynes is the director of *Poison, Safe,* and *Velvet Goldmine,* and he and Vachon co-produced *He Once Was.* Kalin is the director of *Swoon* and *Plain Pleasures*; together, they co-produced *Swoon* and *I Shot Andy Warhol*, and were the executive producers of *Go Fish*. To date, however, *Happiness*, directed by Todd Solondz, is Vachon's penultimate credit. *Happiness*, the filmmaker's follow-up to *Welcome to the Dollhouse*, is a savagely brilliant movie about middle-class alienation and desperation. It is the audacious, laced-in-acid story of a severely dysfunctional middle-class New Jersey family and their equally disconnected friends and neighbors. Each of the family members—a mother, father, and three grown daughters—has been unable to attain any sense of joy in life. While the parents have endured a loveless forty-year marriage, their problems are inconsequential when compared to those of their offspring. Trish, one of the daughters, professes to "have it all" in a picture-perfect marriage, yet little does she realize that her therapist husband is a deep-in-the-closet pedophile. Not only does he get a rise out of the sex discussions he has with his pubescent son, but he commences acting out his desires with the boy's schoolmates. *Happiness* is not the kind of film that features on-the-edge sex scenes that may be edited in order to avoid an NC-17 rating. Rather, it is the tone of the entire film that makes it so provocative.

Herein lies the controversy in *Happiness*. Some will find the film tasteless—just as some view the characterizations in *Poison* and *Kids* as especially offensive—while others will admire the brutal honesty with which the pretenses of the characters' lives are stripped away. Because of its content, the film—despite winning the International Critics' Prize at the Cannes Film Festival—was dropped by its distributor, October Films, the "independent" arm of Universal Pictures. *Happiness* eventually was released by Good Machine, which co-produced it with Killer Films, Vachon's production company.

It is fair to say that, had she not added her expertise to their productions, quite a few of Vachon's films might never have been made. Yet given the distribution plight of *Happiness*, along with its domestic box office—despite laudatory reviews and placement on many critics' ten-best lists, the film earned a paltry $2.5 million—it will not get any easier for Christine Vachon to maintain her goal of producing provocative films about characters who are the antithesis of Ozzie and Harriet and Andy Hardy.—ROB EDELMAN

van Dongen, Helen

Dutch editor and director

Born *Amsterdam, 5 January 1909.* ***Family*** *Married Kenneth Durant, 1950.* ***Career*** *1928—assisted Joris Ivens on* The Bridge, *and later works; 1930—studied soundtrack recording and editing, Tobis Klangfilm Studios, and also studied at UFA, Berlin; 1934—assistant and observer at Joinville Studios, Paris, studied at the Academy of Cinematography, Moscow, under Eisenstein, Pudovkin, and Vertov, 1934-36, and observer in Hollywood studios, 1936; late 1930s—worked as producer on education films; abortive job as editor on film project of Nelson Rockefeller, the co-ordinator of Inter-American Affairs, during World War II; another abortive project as deputy commissioner for the Netherlands East Indies (Ivens was to serve as Commissioner); 1950—retired from filmmaking when she married.*

Films as Editor: 1928: *De brug* (*The Bridge*) (Ivens) (asst). **1929:** *Regen* (*Rain*) (Ivens) (asst); *Wy brouwen* (*We Are Building*) (Ivens) (asst). **1931:** *Philips-Radio* (*Industrial Symphony*) (Ivens); *Zuiderzee Dike* (doc); *Nieuwe polders* (doc); *Creosoot* (*Creosote*) (Ivens) (asst). **1933:** *Zuyderzee*

(Ivens). **1934:** *Nieuwe Gronden (New Earth)* (Ivens); *Misère au Borinage (Borinage)* (Ivens). **1935:** *Borza (The Struggle)* (von Wagenheim). **1936:** *Spain in Flames* (+ pr). **1937:** *The Spanish Earth* (Ivens). **1938:** *You Can Draw* (+ d, ph). **1939:** *The 400 Million (China's 400 Million)* (Ivens); *Pete Roleum and His Cousins* (Losey). **1940:** *Power and the Land* (Ivens). **1942:** *The Land* (Flaherty); *Russians at War* (compilation) (+ pr). **1943:** *Netherlands America* (+ d); *Peoples of Indonesia* (+ d). **1945:** *News Review No. 2* (compilation). **1946:** *Gift of Green* (+ co-d—16 mm). **1948:** *Louisiana Story* (Flaherty) (+ assoc pr). **1950:** *Of Human Rights* (+ d).

There is a famous story recounted by *Time* magazine's Richard Corliss in a 1980 essay on Robert Flaherty. Helen van Dongen, working as the editor of the filmmaker's *The Land,* showed him a sequence she had cut together and he fervently disapproved. A few days later she screened the same sequence for him and he said "Now you've got it." Van Dongen proved ably up to the task of working with Flaherty, transmuting the director's seemingly random and chaotic footage into, as Corliss writes, "a brilliant 'as told to' autobiography. If [Flaherty's] spirit informed their project, then [van Dongen's] will gave its final form."

In the truest spirit of the title, van Dongen was an editor whose techniques, honed by early work with Joris Ivens, extended beyond mere physical assemblage and continuity supervision to thoughtful documentary theory and to complex and creative sound work. In Flaherty's *Louisiana Story,* in which she served as editor and as associate producer, she worked closely with composer Virgil Thompson in creating specific themes for characters and sequences, and manipulated the soundtrack by disassembling sounds and then reconfiguring them: a scene on a bridge at night may contain up to 20 separate sounds (some of which were not endemic to the location) or a human scream could be a fusing of a dozen voices. Her exhaustive analysis of the film can be found in *The Technique of Film Editing* and is a fascinating look not only at how sequences were structured and sound was used, but also the reasons why—both the pragmatic and the dramatic.

Though her two World War II compilation documentaries, *Russians at War* and *News Review No. 2* were well received, having been compared favorably with the *World at War* series by Frank Capra, her two films with Flaherty have proven her most enduring works. Her extensive diaries of the production histories of *The Land* and *Louisiana Story* provide a telling memoir of working on location and in the editing room with the often opaque and stubborn Flaherty (he referred to her as his "Dutch mule"), while also revealing a uniquely productive and successful collaboration. Though certainly a tempestuous relationship, it was never overtly adversarial; in fact when van Dongen had to trick Flaherty into providing the narration for *The Land* because no narrator could capture his intonations (she earlier had corralled Ernest Hemingway into reciting his own written words on Ivens's *The Spanish Earth*), he was by all accounts incensed, but later conceded van Dongen was right because it benefited the film. While their goals were the same, van Dongen admitted her greatest challenge was in having to continually interpret and reinterpret Flaherty's admittedly elusive vision (which often led to gross continuity gaps and over- and undershooting) and then shape it into a cohesive and viewable motion picture. When she first began to work with Flaherty, she said she was "completely baffled by his method" and wrote to Ivens for help in understanding. Ivens's reply was equally cryptic: "Observe, look and listen and you'll find what he wants." Only when she was able to view the footage through Flaherty's realm of understanding, she said, and then decipher Flaherty's reaction while watching footage could she gauge the direction—and ultimately, the success—of the film. She wrote, "Had I myself gone to direct Flaherty's story, it would have looked quite different. But working with already filmed material, filmed under the influence of Flaherty . . . essentially my editing would have resulted in approximately the same story and form. This would have been inevitable because, to use the random material to full value, the editor has to discover not only the inherent qualities of each shot but also must know the how's and why's, the director's reasoning behind each shot, or must know that no one else but Flaherty would have shot such a scene." Her ability to read the director in this way no doubt made her the best editor for Flaherty, but more importantly, made Flaherty's films better.

Though both *The Land* and *Louisiana Story* are prime examples of Flaherty's filmmaking sensibility, much of the beauty and emotional gravity of the films is owed to van Dongen's delicately focused sound and film editing. They move beyond what film history regards as documentary (and perhaps to a degree beyond what fiction can do as well), and into something ultimately more lyrical. In an interview with Ben Achtenberg, van Dongen herself resisted the label of documentary: "To me Flaherty is *not* a documentarian; he makes it all up. He does use the documentary style and background but, except for *The Land,* they are all, to a degree, stories. . . . They are part of our history of filmmaking, but I do hesitate to call them documentaries. They are Flaherty-films, and worthwhile enjoying."—JON LUPO

Van Runkle, Theadora

American costume designer

Born *c.1940.* ***Education*** *Attended Chouinard Art Institute, Los Angeles.* ***Career*** *Commercial artist; then sketch artist on* Hawaii; *1967—first film as costume designer,* Bonnie and Clyde, *for which she received her first of three Academy Award nominations; 1983—costume designer for TV series* Wizards and Warriors; *1997—costume designer for TV miniseries* The Last Don. ***Agent*** *Darrin Sugar.* ***Address*** *8805 Lookout Mountain Road, Los Angeles, CA 90046, U.S.A.*

Films as Costume Designer: 1966: *Hawaii* (G. R. Hill) (sketch artist). **1967:** *Bonnie and Clyde* (A. Penn). **1968:** *Bullitt* (Yates); *The Thomas Crown Affair* (Jewison) (co); *I Love You, Alice B. Toklas!* (Averback); *Amanti* (*A Place for Lovers*) (De Sica) (co). **1969:** *The Reivers* (Rydell); *The Arrangement* (Kazan). **1970:** *Myra Breckenridge* (Sarne). **1971:** *Johnny Got His Gun* (Trumbo). **1973:** *Kid Blue* (Frawley); *Ace Eli and Rodger of the Skies* (Erman). **1974:** *Mame* (Saks); *The Godfather, Part II* (F. F. Coppola). **1976:** *Nickelodeon* (Bogdanovich). **1977:** *New York, New York* (Scorsese). **1978:** *Heaven Can Wait* (Beatty and Henry) (co); *Same Time, Next Year* (Mulligan). **1979:** *The Jerk* (C. Reiner). **1981:** *S.O.B.* (Edwards); *Heartbeeps* (Arkush) (co). **1982:** *The Best Little Whorehouse in Texas* (Higgins). **1984:** *Rhinestone* (Clark). **1986:** *Peggy Sue Got Married* (F. F. Coppola). **1988:** *Everybody's All-American* (Hackford); *Wildfire* (Z. King). **1989:** *Troop Beverly Hills* (Kanew). **1990:** *Stella* (Erman). **1991:** *The Butcher's Wife* (T. Hughes). **1992:** *Leap of Faith* (Pearce). **1995:** *Kiss of Death* (Schroeder); *White Dwarf* (Markle—for TV). **1997:** *Good-bye, Lover* (R. Joffé); *The Last Don* (Clifford—for TV). **1998:** *I'm Losing You* (Wagner).

In 1967 miniskirts maintained their hold on the world of women's fashions. With the release of *Bonnie and Clyde,* however, hemlines began to fall as fashion magazines featured the midi-look Theadora Van Runkle revived for that film. And while women were wearing midi-skirts with silk blouses, men began sporting wide lapelled, double-breasted suits.

Prior to *Bonnie and Clyde,* Van Runkle had worked as an ad illustrator before making her film debut as a sketch artist for Dorothy Jeakins on *Hawaii.* When Jeakins had to turn down *Bonnie and Clyde* due to a prior commitment, she recommended Van Runkle: it was a golden opportunity for the young designer with an admitted passion for 1930s clothing design. With her debut as a designer, Van Runkle was thrust into the spotlight: an Oscar nomination (she lost to John Truscott for *Camelot*), a Golden Tiberius from the Italian design industry, and numerous offers for more film work.

Bonnie and Clyde catapulted not only Van Runkle to fame, but Faye Dunaway as well; over the next few years, the star used Van Runkle to design her clothes both offscreen and on, establishing her fashion image as one based on soft silks which both reveal and disguise. In discussing her approach to dressing Dunaway for *The Thomas Crown Affair,* Van Runkle noted her use of accessories to counterpoint the outfit: Dunaway's passion is signified by her clothing, her control by her jewelry.

While Van Runkle has done a wide variety of period pieces, from the sock-hop styles of the 1950s in *Peggy Sue Got Married* to the hippie atrocities of *I Love You, Alice B. Toklas!,* she claims her favorite period is that from the beginning of World War I to the end of World War II. With *Mame* Van Runkle re-created a fashion obsession with hats that prompted the Millinery Institute of America to award her their Golden Crown, while with *New York, New York,* she redefined Liza Minnelli's fashion image by dressing her in tailored outfits. With *The Godfather, Part II* Van Runkle was able to cover much of the period between the wars, outfitting the mob in an exquisite array of tailored suits.

That tailored look remains one of her two favorites, the other being what she calls her "romantic" style: sensual satins, furs, lace, and velvet. With *The Best Little Whorehouse in Texas,* Theadora Van Runkle was allowed to indulge that latter penchant to great effect, director Colin Higgins agreeing with her that costumes are an effective shorthand to character. In that film Dolly Parton was never more appropriately, nor more lavishly attired: one costume, dubbed "Miss Mona Aflame with Passion," cost $7,000.—DOUG TOMLINSON

Van Upp, Virginia

American writer and producer

Born *Chicago, 1902.* ***Family*** *Married (second) the former Paramount unit manager Ralph W. Nelson (divorced 1949); one daughter, Gay Harden, and one stepdaughter.* ***Career*** *Began professional career as child actor in silent films; acted as script assistant, casting director, agent, scenarist, screenwriter; 1930s—scripted scenarios for Paramount Pictures, before moving to Columbia Pictures where she took the role of scriptwriter, producer, and executive producer and second-in-command to studio boss Harry Cohn; 1950s—while in West Germany, made propaganda films for the U.S. government; retired.* ***Died*** *In Hollywood, of complications following an accident, 25 March 1970.*

Films as Writer: 1934: *The Pursuit of Happiness* (A. Hall) (co). **1936:** *Timothy's Quest* (Barton) (co); *Poppy* (A. E. Sutherland) (co); *Easy to Take* (Tryon); *My American Wife* (H. Young) (co); *Too Many Parents* (McGowan) (co). **1937:** *Swing High, Swing Low* (*The Dance of Life*) (Leisen) (co). **1938:** *You and Me* (F. Lang). **1939:** *Cafe Society* (E. H. Griffith); *St. Louis Blues* (*Best of the Blues*) (Walsh) (co); *Honeymoon in Bali* (*My Love for Yours*) (E. H. Griffith). **1941:** *One Night in Lisbon* (E. H. Griffith); *Virginia* (E. H. Griffith); *Bahama Passage* (E. H. Griffith). **1943:** *Young and Willing* (*Out of the Frying Pan*) (E. H. Griffith); *The Crystal Ball* (Nugent). **1944:** *Cover Girl* (C. Vidor) (co); *The Impatient Years*

(Cummings) (+ co-pr); *Together Again* (C. Vidor) (co-sc, + co-pr). **1945:** *She Wouldn't Say Yes* (A. Hall) (co-sc, + co-pr). **1951:** *Here Comes the Groom* (Capra) (co).

Film as Producer: 1946: *Gilda* (C. Vidor).

Other Films: 1941: *Come Live with Me* (C. Brown) (st). **1948:** *The Lady from Shanghai* (Welles) (contributed to script and assumed role of producer, uncredited). **1952:** *Affair in Trinidad* (V. Sherman) (co-st, assoc pr).

Not until more than a decade after her death was the long and illustrious career of actress-screenwriter-producer Virginia Van Upp properly documented as a significant chapter of the history of Hollywood film. Her life was unique, multifaceted and singular. She was a producer, a studio executive, and an accomplished screenwriter with a significant body of work to her credit (and in some cases noncredit); her remarkable career in the Hollywood film industry spanned nearly half a century.

To some, she is considered a "first," perhaps the first woman to crash Hollywood's proverbial glass ceiling during a period when patriarchal studio bosses controlled their empires with an iron hand. The recent work of film scholars, however, most notably Ally Acker, attest to the fact that there were many women before Van Upp who assumed important positions in various facets of the early film industry. But whether she was truly a first or not, Van Upp's career was at the very least, states Acker, "unusual for the era in which she was working."

Van Upp was born in Chicago, Illinois, in 1902. As a child of perhaps seven, she appeared in silent films, working with directors Thomas Ince and Lois Weber and alongside such actors as film star John Gilbert. Her father, Harry Van Upp appears to have also had some connection with the film industry; her mother, Helen Van Upp, had been an editor and title writer for the Ince Company. As a young woman, Virginia Van Upp's life in motion pictures included a host of different occupations. She acted in the position of casting director for the 1925 production of *Ben Hur,* as an agent, as secretary for RKO-Pathé writer Horace Jackson, as a film cutter, and as a script assistant. Perhaps influenced by her work with Jackson, she discovered her true calling as a scriptwriter.

At Paramount Pictures in the 1930s, her co-written scripts and adaptations of stage plays and stories often explored in humorous terms, marital, interpersonal relationships, and comedies of "romantic dilemma." Later, at Columbia, she was often paired with director-writer Edward H. Griffith on a number of wartime, "enjoyable trifles."

But more than simply being skilled in the art and craft of the motion-picture screenplay, Van Upp, by all accounts, possessed a certain measure of savvy that allowed her to move easily amongst the various operatives of film production. Van Upp "appreciated the myriad details involved in getting a movie made," writes Bernard Dick in his book on Harry Cohn; amongst these details was "the need to subject a script to a diversity of opinion."

In 1945 a writer for the *Los Angeles Times* wrote about Van Upp's success at Columbia Pictures, making a point of describing her as bespectacled and small in stature. Nevertheless, her small size had little relation to the enormous power she wielded in her position as executive producer and second-in-command to studio boss Harry Cohn. Working closely with Cohn, in

Virginia Van Upp

1945 she was directly responsible for the production of approximately 40 features and some $20 million of "stockholders coin."

Perhaps Van Upp's most remarkable achievement was Columbia's 1946 release of the film *Gilda,* starring World War II film-goddess Rita Hayworth. *Gilda* was a big picture with a big budget and Van Upp was in charge. In this picture, Van Upp solely is credited as the producer. The film, now considered an early archetype of the postwar film-noir style, was replete with a dark, sinister mood and overt sexual overtones. It went on to become one of the more commercially successful pictures of the year.

The post-World War II period was a turbulent one for the film industry as antitrust litigation, Communist witch-hunts, television, and the changing tastes of a society experiencing social upheaval, signaled the end of the so-called Golden Age of Hollywood. It is interesting to note Van Upp's involvement in the production of the 1948 classic, *Lady from Shanghai.* Considered filmmaker Orson Welles's masterpiece, the film may not have occurred at all had it not been for the intervention of Van Upp. Welles had gone well over budget. He erected elaborate sets and chose expensive on-location shooting in luxurious and expensive resorts in Acapulco. It was Van Upp who was assigned to save the day, patch the ragged script, and rein in Welles, the impetuous "Boy Wonder." One can only speculate how many other film "classics" occurred because of Virginia Van Upp's direct intervention.

In 1951 Van Upp co-wrote the screenplay for *Here Comes the Groom* and in 1952, for her last Hollywood film, she served as the associate producer for *Affair in Trinidad,* which was based on a story she co-wrote. A subsequent film for Republic Pictures was abandoned when Van Upp took ill.

Although one can only surmise what led to the end of Van Upp's professional career—the changing film industry and her poor health were most likely contributing factors—her career had already spanned almost 50 years. She had been a performer and had written or co-written more than a dozen respectable motion pictures. She had worked with internationally known directors from Fritz Lang to Frank Capra. She had saved *The Lady from Shanghai* from disaster and assumed one of the most powerful positions ever shouldered by a woman in modern film history. And notes Acker, it would be more than another 20 years before another woman would do the same.—PAMALA S. DEANE

Varda, Agnès

Belgian director

Born *Brussels, 30 May 1928.* ***Education*** *Studied literature and psychology at the Sorbonne, Paris; studied art history at the École du Louvre; studied photography at night school.* ***Family*** *Married the director Jacques Demy, 1962 (died 1990), son: Mathieu, daughter: Rosalie.* ***Career*** *Stage photographer for Théâtre Festival of Avignon, then for Théâtre National Populaire, Paris, Jean Vilar; 1954—directed first film,* La Pointe courte; *1955—accompanied Chris Marker to China as adviser for* Dimanche à Pekin; *1968—directed two shorts in United States; 1977—founded production company Ciné-Tamaris.* ***Awards*** *Prix Méliès, for* Cléo de cinq à sept, *1961; Bronze Lion, Venice Festival, for* Salut les Cubains, *1963; Prix Louis Delluc, David Selznick Award, and Silver Bear, Berlin Festival, for* Le Bonheur, *1965; First Prize, Oberhausen, for* Black Panthers, *1968; Grand Prix, Taormina, for* L'Une chante l'autre pas, *1977; César Award, for* Ulysse, *1983; Golden Lion, Venice Festival, Prix Méliès, and Best Foreign Film, Los Angeles Film Critics Association, for* Vagabond, *1985; Commander des Arts et des Lettres, Chevalier Legion d'honneur.* ***Address*** *c/o Ciné-Tamaris, 86 rue Daguerre, 75014 Paris, France.*

Films as Director: 1954: *La Pointe courte* (+ pr, sc). **1957:** *O saisons, o châteaux* (doc short). **1958:** *L'Opéra-Mouffe* (short); *Du côté de la Côte* (short). **1961:** *Cléo de cinq à sept* (*Cleo from 5 to 7*) (+ sc). **1963:** *Salut les Cubains* (*Salute to Cuba*) (+ text) (doc short). **1965:** *Le Bonheur* (*Happiness*) (+ sc). **1966:** *Les Créatures* (*Varelserna*; *The Creatures*) (+ sc); *Elsa*. **1967:** *Uncle Janco* (short); ep. of *Loin du Vietnam* (*Far from Vietnam*). **1968:** *Black Panthers* (*Huey*) (doc). **1969:** *Lions Love* (+ pr, sc). **1970:** *Nausicaa* (for TV). **1975:** *Daguerrotypes* (for TV) (+ pr); *Réponses de femmes* (8mm). **1977:** *L'Une chante l'autre pas* (*One Sings, the Other Doesn't*) (+ sc, lyrics). **1980:** *Mur Murs* (*Wall Walls*; *Mural Murals*) (+ pr). **1981:** *Documenteur: An Emotion Picture* (+ pr). **1983:** *Ulysse*. **1984:** *Les Dites cariatides*; *Sept P., Cuis., S. de B.,. . . a saisir.* **1985:** *Vagabonde* (*Sans Toit ni loi*; *Vagabond*). **1988:** *Le Petit Amour* (*Kung Fu Master*; *Don't Say It*) (+ pr, sc); *Jane B. par Agnès V.* (doc) (+ appearance). **1991:** *Jacquot de Nantes* (+ co-pr, sc). **1993:** *Des demoiselles ont en 25 ans* (*The Young Girls Turn 25*) (doc). **1995:** *Les cent et une nuits* (*A Hundred and One Nights*) (+ sc); *L'universe de Jacques Demy* (*The World of Jacques Demy*) (doc).

Other Films: 1967: *Les Demoiselles de Rochefort* (*The Young Girls of Rochefort*) (Demy) (ro as nun). **1971:** *Last Tango in Paris* (Bertolucci) (co-dialogue). **1978:** *Lady Oscar* (Demy) (pr). **1995:** *Kulonbozo helyek* (*Different Places*) (doc short).

Agnès Varda's startlingly individualistic films have earned her the title "grandmother of the New Wave" of French filmmaking. Her statement that a filmmaker must exercise as much freedom as a novelist became a mandate for New Wave directors, especially Chris Marker and Alain Resnais. Varda's first film, *La Pointe courte,* edited by Resnais, is regarded, as Georges Sadoul affirms, as "the first film of the French nouvelle vague. Its interplay between conscience, emotions, and the real world make it a direct antecedent of *Hiroshima mon amour.*"

The use of doubling, and twin story lines; the personification of objects; the artistic determination of cinematic composition, color, texture, form, and time; and the correlation of individual subjectivity to societal objectivity to depict sociopolitical issues are denominators of Varda's films, which she writes, produces, and directs.

After *La Pointe courte* Varda made three documentaries in 1957 and 1958. The best of these was *L'Opéra-Mouffe,* portraying the Mouffetard district of Paris. Segments of the film are prefaced by handwritten intertitles, a literary element Varda is fond of using. In 1961-62 Varda began but did not complete two film projects: *La Cocotte d'azur* and *Melangite*. Her next film, *Cléo de cinq à sept,* records the time a pop singer waits for results of her exam for cancer. Varda used physical time in *Cléo*: events happening at the same tempo as they would in actual life. The film is divided into chapters, using tarot cards which symbolize fate. Varda next photographed 4,000 still photos of Castro's revolution-in-progress, resulting in *Salute to Cuba*.

Happiness is considered Varda's most stunning and controversial achievement. Critics were puzzled and pleased. Of her first color film, Varda says it was "essentially a pursuit of the palette. . . . Psychology takes first place." A young carpenter lives with his wife and children. Then he takes a mistress; when his wife drowns, his mistress takes her place. The film was commended for its superb visual beauties, the use of narrative in *le nouveau roman* literary pattern, and its tonal contrasts and spatial configurations. Critics continue to debate the film's theme.

Elsa is an essay portraying authors Elsa Triolet and her husband Louis Aragon. *The Creatures* uses a black-and-white-with-red color scheme in a fantasy-thriller utilizing an inside-outside plot that mingles real and unreal events. As in *La Pointe courte,* a young couple retreat to a rural locale. The pregnant wife is mute, due to an accident. Her husband is writing a book. He meets a recluse who operates a machine forcing people to behave as their subconscious would dictate. The wife gives birth, regaining her speech.

Visiting the United States, Varda and her husband Jacques Demy each made a film. Varda honored her *Uncle Janco* in the film so named. *The Black Panthers* (or *Huey*) followed. Both documentaries were shown at the London Film Festival in 1968. She next directed a segment of the antiwar short *Far from Vietnam*.

Using an American setting and an English-speaking cast, including the co-authors of the musical *Hair,* Varda made *Lions Love* in Hollywood. This jigsaw-puzzle work includes a fake suicide and images of a television set reporting Robert Kennedy's assassination. G. Roy Levin declared that it was hard to distinguish between the actual and the invented film realities. *Nausicaa* deals with Greeks living in France. Made for television, it was not shown, Varda says, because it was against military-ruled Greece.

In 1971, Varda helped write the script for *Last Tango in Paris*. Varda's involvement in the women's movement began about 1972; a film dealing with feminist issues, *Réponses de femmes,* has yet to be shown. Made for German television, *Daguerreotypes* has no cast. Varda filmed the residents and shops of the Rue Daguerre, a tribute to L. J. M. Daguerre.

In 1977, Varda made *One Sings, the Other Doesn't* and established her own company, Ciné-Tamaris, to finance it. This "family" of workers created the film. Chronicling the friendship of two women over 15 years, it earned mixed reviews, some referring to it as feminist propaganda or as sentimental syrup. But Varda, narrating the film and writing the song lyrics, does not impose her views. In *One Sings,* she wanted to portray the happiness of being a woman, she says.

Easily Varda's most potent film of the 1980s, and one of the best of her career, is *Vagabond,* an evocative drama about the death and life of a young woman, Mona (Sandrine Bonnaire). She is an ex-secretary who has chosen to become a drifter, and her fate is apparent at the outset. As the film begins, Mona has died. Her frost-bitten corpse is seen in a ditch. Her body is claimed by no one, and she is laid to rest in a potter's field. As *Vagabond* unfolds, Varda explores Mona's identity as she wanders through the rural French countryside hitching rides and begging for the necessities that will sustain her. The scenario also spotlights the manner in which she impacts on those she meets: truck drivers; a gas station owner and his son; a vineyard worker; a professor-researcher; and other, fellow drifters. Varda constructs the film as a series of sequences, some comprised of a single shot lasting several seconds, in which Mona passes through the lives of these people. The result is an eloquent film about one average, ill-fated young woman and the choices she makes, as well as a meditation on chance meetings and missed opportunities. On a much broader level, the film serves as an allegory of the travails a woman must face if she desires to completely liberate herself from the shackles of society.

Varda's most notable recent films have been valentines to her late husband, filmmaker Jacques Demy. *The Young Girls Turn 25* is a nostalgia piece about the filming of Demy's *The Young Girls of Rochefort*; *The World of Jacques Demy* is an up-close-and-personal documentary-biography consisting of interviews and clips from Demy's films.

A third title, *Jacquot de Nantes,* was the most widely seen. It is an exquisite film: a penetrating, heartrending account of the measure of a man's life, with Varda moving between sequences of Demy in conversation, filmed in extreme close-up; clips from his films; and a re-creation of his childhood in Nantes and the manner in which he developed a passion for cinema. Varda illustrates how Demy's life and world view influenced his films; for example, his hatred of violence, which is ever so apparent in his films, was forged by his memories of Nantes being bombed during World War II. But *Jacquot de Nantes* (which was conceived prior to Demy's death) is most effective as a tender love letter from one life partner to another. Varda visually evokes her feeling towards her departed mate in one of the film's opening shots. She pans her camera across a watercolor, whose composition is that of a nude woman and man who are holding hands. With over three decades of filmmaking experience, Varda's reputation as a filmmaker dazzles and endures.—LOUISE HECK-RABI and ROB EDELMAN

von Brandenstein, Patrizia

American production designer

Born *Arizona.* ***Education*** *Attended boarding school in Germany; Comedie Française school.* ***Family*** *Married (second) the production designer Stuart Wurtzel, daughter: Kimberly.* ***Career*** *Late 1960s-early 1970s—worked on stage productions for the American Conservatory Theater in San Francisco; assistant to production designer Stuart Wurtzel; 1975-77—served as art director on* Hester Street; *painted scenery for PBS; worked as costume designer on* Saturday Night Fever; *1979—first major production-design work on* Breaking Away. ***Awards*** *Academy Award for Art Direction, for* Amadeus, *1984.* ***Agent*** *Lawrence Mirisch, The Mirisch Agency, 10100 Santa Monica Boulevard, Suite 700, Los Angeles, CA 90067-4011, U.S.A.*

Films as Costume Designer: 1977: *Between the Lines* (J. Silver); *Saturday Night Fever* (Badham) (co). **1982:** *A Little Sex* (Paltrow).

Films as Production Designer: 1977: *The Gardener's Son* (for TV). **1978:** *Girlfriends* (Weill); *Summer of My German Soldier* (Tuchner—for TV). **1979:** *My Old Man* (Erman—for TV); *Breaking Away* (Yates). **1980:** *Tell Me a Riddle* (L. Grant). **1981:** *Heartland* (Pearce). **1983:** *Silkwood* (M.

Nichols); *Touched* (Flynn). **1984:** *Amadeus* (Forman); *Beat Street* (Lathan). **1985:** *A Chorus Line* (Attenborough). **1986:** *The Money Pit* (Benjamin); *No Mercy* (Pearce). **1987:** *The Untouchables* (De Palma). **1988:** *Betrayed* (Costa-Gavras); *Working Girl* (M. Nichols). **1990:** *The Lemon Sisters* (Chopra); *Postcards from the Edge* (M. Nichols); *State of Grace* (Joanou). **1991:** *Billy Bathgate* (Benton). **1992:** *Leap of Faith* (Pearce); *Sneakers* (Robinson). **1993:** *Six Degrees of Separation* (Schepisi). **1995:** *Just Cause* (Glimcher); *The Quick and the Dead* (Raimi). **1996:** *The People vs. Larry Flint* (Forman). **1998:** *Mercury Rising* (Becker); *A Simple Plan* (Raimi).

Other Films: 1972: *The Candidate* (Ritchie) (set designer). **1978:** *The Last Tenant* (J. Taylor—for TV) (art d). **1980:** *Hardhat and Legs* (Philips—for TV) (art d). **1981:** *Ragtime* (Forman) (art d).

Patrizia von Brandenstein made history in 1985 by becoming the first woman ever to win an Oscar for production design, for Milos Forman's ornate, pictorial *Amadeus.* But even if she had never won an Oscar, or never worked on *Amadeus,* her versatility alone would rank her at the top of her profession. Her credits show an astonishing range of subjects, styles, and periods: what does the low-budget, break-dancing musical *Beat Street* have in common with the expensive plutonium-plant melodrama *Silkwood,* besides von Brandenstein? Believing that a production designer can become as typecast as actors and actresses, and despite receiving Academy recognition only for her big-budgeted period pieces (*Ragtime, Amadeus,* and *The Untouchables*), von Brandenstein makes a concerted effort to avoid repeating herself or latching onto familiar subjects. This openness to challenge and diversity complicates any analysis of von Brandenstein's designing "style," for she has worked in so many genres her achievements resist categorization. Although not every film she worked on was a success—critically or financially—the enthusiasm she brings to such disparate pictures as *A Chorus Line* and *The Quick and the Dead* is always visible: these films, however flawed, catch the eye.

Von Brandenstein won some instant notoriety in 1977 as costume designer on *Saturday Night Fever*: the white disco-dance outfit she created for John Travolta appeared on the cover of *Newsweek,* sparking a fad. But it was her association with Stuart Wurtzel, her production design mentor (and future husband) that established ties with director Milos Forman. As Wurtzel's assistant on *Hair,* von Brandenstein worked well with Forman, and later served as art director on *Ragtime,* supervising construction of a nickelodeon and a lush rooftop garden that captured the film's nostalgic tone: they are relics of a bygone era, still glowing and functional, as if dropped from a time capsule. Her ability to establish historical verisimilitude dominates *Ragtime* and later films such as *Amadeus, The Untouchables,* and *Billy Bathgate,* where the visual design is so vivid and evocative the story and characters seem less interesting. For example, von Brandenstein and Forman scouted castles and palaces in Czechoslovakia to select appropriate sets for *Amadeus,* and even gained access to Prague's Tyl Theatre, where Mozart conducted the premiere of *Don Giovanni* in 1787. With all this rich architecture as background scenery, the dynamics of Peter Shaffer's stage play are somewhat stifled; the viewer is too busy gawking at the sets to concentrate on the vicious envy of F. Murray Abraham's mediocre composer. Less problematic are *The Untouchables* and *The Quick and the Dead,* period films by flamboyant directors uninterested in the psychological dimensions of their characters: here, von Brandenstein's bold re-creation of 1920s Chicago, and her hilarious rendering of a rotting, ramshackle western town match the films' comic-book plots and directorial flourishes.

Some of her best work, however, is not pure re-creation. Films with contemporary settings can challenge von Brandenstein even more than period pieces. She believes that for every picture, a production designer's main goal is to orchestrate visual material to establish the director's idea of the story's characters and central ideas, whatever the setting. Two films directed by Mike Nichols show her labors: in *Silkwood,* she conveys Karen Silkwood's paranoia and feelings of entrapment by designing her home in the same featureless, pale-green hue as the plutonium plant where she works; only Drew, Karen's freewheeling lover, brings life to the place with his American flags and bright-red hot rod. And in *Postcards from the Edge,* von Brandenstein plays illusion/reality games meant to represent the Hollywood heroine's disorientation: a tree-lined background proves to be a set painting when a stagehand walks right through it; a building shifts behind Dennis Quaid as Meryl Streep drives away, but it is the building that is on wheels; and, most famously, Streep hangs off a ledge over moving traffic, an illusion broken when Streep lifts her hands and does not fall—both the ledge and the traffic are fake. The viewer reads these images subconsciously, hardly aware that von Brandenstein is building emotion with colors and giant props. The sets are an outgrowth of the characters' personalities and conflicts, as in *The Money Pit,* where a crumbling mansion is a comic metaphor for a crumbling marriage.

Von Brandenstein also enjoys tricking an audience with realistic sets that, in terms of the plot and the characters, become absurd and unsettling. The first half of Costa-Gavras's race-hate picture *Betrayed* depicts an underground network of paramilitary bigots as deceptively simple country boys fond of beer, horses, and barbecues, an extended conceit tailored to the subjective view of outsiders like ourselves. (As soon as the country boys are exposed as out-and-out racists, though, the picture loses tension and belabors the obvious Klan rallies and right-wing militia training exercises.) The eclectic *Six Degrees of Separation* extends the visual trickery to knock down social barriers: vastly different New York environments (penthouse, hovel, bookstore, police station) are inhabited by the same characters at various points, making everyone look slightly out of place. A dirt-poor young actress, for instance, barges into a high-priced apartment complex to meet a rich art dealer, who has to come downstairs to a grubby little boiler room—it is a double clash of cultures. The production design in *Six Degrees* achieves total authenticity, unlike the broad, expressionist *Silkwood*; but it is the authenticity of the locations that parodies the characters in their bizarre explorations. The art dealer would not be laughable if the boiler room did not look real.

A film designed by von Brandenstein is guaranteed to be visually interesting, and von Brandenstein herself continues to expand her territory. *The Quick and the Dead* is her first Western after 20 years of movie work, and her memorable, dilapidated designs for that film prove both her virtuosity and her readiness to take a risk.—KEN PROVENCHER

von Harbou, Thea

German writer

Born *Tauperlitz, 27 December 1888.* ***Family*** *Married 1) the actor Rudolf Klein-Rogge (divorced); 2) the director Fritz Lang, 1924 (divorced 1934).* ***Career*** *Actress in Dusseldorf, 1906, Weimar, 1908-10, Chemnitz, 1911-12, and Aachen, 1913-14; novelist; 1920—first film script,* Die heilige Simplizie; *also wrote several scripts with Lang; 1930s—joined Nazi party, and appointed official scriptwriter; directed two films.* ***Died*** *In Berlin, 1 July 1954.*

Films as Writer: 1920: *Die heilige Simplizie* (J. May); *Das wandernde Bild* (*Wandernder Held; Wandering Image*) (F. Lang). **1921:** *Die Frauen von Gnadenstein* (Dinesen); *Kämpfende Herzen* (*Die*

Vier um die Frau; Four around a Woman) (F. Lang); *Das indische Grabmal (The Indian Tomb)* (J. May); *Der müde Tod (Between Two Worlds; Beyond the Wall)* (F. Lang); *Der Leidensweg der Inge Krafft* (J. May). **1922:** *Der brennende Acker (Burning Soil)* (Murnau); *Dr. Mabuse, der Spieler (Dr. Mabuse, the Gambler)* (F. Lang); *Phantom* (Murnau). **1923:** *Die Austreibung (Driven from Home; The Expulsion)* (Murnau); *Die Prinzessin Suwarin* (Guter). **1924:** *Die Finanzen des Grossherzogs (The Grand Duke's Finances)* (Murnau); *Michael* (Dreyer); *Die Nibelungen* (F. Lang—2 parts). **1925:** *Zur Chronik von Grieshuus (At the Grey House)* (von Gerlach). **1927:** *Metropolis* (F. Lang). **1928:** *Spione (Spies)* (F. Lang). **1929:** *Die Frau im Mond (By Rocket to the Moon; The Woman in the Moon)* (F. Lang). **1931:** *M* (F. Lang). **1932:** *Das erste Recht des Kindes (Aus dem Tagebuch einer Frauenärzin)* (Wendhausen). **1933:** *Das Testament des Dr. Mabuse (The Testament of Dr. Mabuse)* (F. Lang); *Der Läufer von Marathon* (Dupont). **1934:** *Hanneles Himmelfahrt* (+ d); *Prinzessin Tourandot* (Lamprecht); *Was bin ich ohne Dich?* (Rabenalt). **1935:** *Der alte und der junge König* (Steinhoff); *Ein idealer Gatte* (Selpin); *Ich war Jack Mortimer* (Froelich); *Der Mann mit der Pranke* (van der Noss). **1936:** *Eine Frau ohne Bedetung (A Woman of No Importance)* (Steinhoff); *Eskapade (Seine offizielle Frau)* (Waschneck); *Die unmögliche Frau* (Meyer). **1937:** *Der Herrscher (The Ruler)* (Harlan); *Versprich mir nichts!* (Liebeneiner); *Mutterlied* (Gallone); *Der zerbrochene Krug (The Broken Jug)* (Ucicky); *Solo per te* (Gallone). **1938:** *Jugend (Youth)* (Harlan); *Verwehte Spuren* (Harlan); *Die Frau am Scheidewege* (von Báky); *Menschen im Variete* (von Báky). **1939:** *Hurra! Ich bin Papa!* (Hoffmann). **1940:** *Lauter Liebe* (Rühmann); *Wie konntest du, Veronika?* (Habich). **1941:** *Annelie (Die Geschichte eines Lebens)* (von Báky); *Am Abend auf der Heide* (von Alten). **1942:** *Mit den Augen einer Frau* (Külb). **1943:** *Die Gattin* (Jacoby); *Gefährten meines Sommers* (Buch). **1944:** *Eine Frau für drei Tage* (Kirchhoff). **1945:** *Kolberg (Burning Hearts)* (Harlan) (co). **1948:** *Fahrt ins Glück* (Engel—produced 1945); *Via Mala (Die Strasse des Bösen)* (von Báky—produced 1944). **1950:** *Es kommt ein Tag* (Jugert); *Erzieherin gesucht* (Erfurth—produced 1944). **1951:** *Angelika* (Hansen) (*Dr. Holl; Affairs of Dr. Holl*). **1953:** *Dein Herz ist meine Heimat* (Häussler).

Film as Director: **1933:** *Elisabeth und der Narr.* **1934:** *Hanneles Himmelfahrt.*

Thea von Harbou worked as Fritz Lang's principal scenarist from 1924-32, when she split with Lang on political matters, and enthusiastically joined the Nazi Party. If we are to believe Fritz Lang's later statements, made in the 1960s in America, it was von Harbou who turned Lang in to Joseph Goebbels, the head of the Reich Propaganda Ministry.

Von Harbou's work as a scenarist for Lang includes her scripts for *Metropolis, By Rocket to the Moon, Dr. Mabuse, the Gambler,* and *Spies*. She also worked with Murnau, Dreyer, and Joe May. After writing the screenplay of Lang's most anti-Nazi film, *The Testament of Dr. Mabuse* (in which Hitler's words are put in the mouth of Dr. Mabuse, a criminal madman), von Harbou made a fatal decision, deciding for the nihilistic vision of the Nazis over the humanistic if sometimes brooding realism of the best of Lang's works. She worked continually up to her death on screen fare of decreasing distinction, ending her career with the screenplay for the mediocre film *Dein Herz ist meine Heimat.*

In all of von Harbou's screenplays, one can easily detect the strident notes of propaganda. Her work with Lang is the most restrained and fleshed-out of her long career, but, Lang later claimed that von Harbou was, at her best, merely a journeyman screenwriter who lacked the ability to get inside the motivations of her characters. Because von Harbou supported a regime that took a dim view of individualism or artistry without state direction, it is to be expected that her work under the Hitler regime, such as the screenplay for *Youth,* a study of the Hitler Youth Movement, would fail as both propaganda and cinematic art.

Between 1945-51 von Harbou was prevented from working in the German cinema by order of the Nuremberg Tribunal, but clearly her major work, for better or worse, was long behind her. She also directed two films under the Nazis, *Elisabeth und der Narr* and *Hanneles*

Himmelfahrt. Neither was a commercial or critical success. The same must be said of her work as a screenwriter between 1933-45. That her resultant efforts were quickly forgotten by both the public and the critics seems an inescapable by-product of von Harbou's ardent espousal of the Nazi cause. For the researcher, prints of von Harbou's work during World War II are available for screening at the National Archive in Washington, D.C. Although von Harbou was undoubtedly one of the key figures in the Expressionist movement of the 1920s, her work from 1937-45, founded as it inevitably was on a doctrine of racial hatred, simply has no place in a thoughtful or caring society.—WHEELER WINSTON DIXON

von Trotta, Margarethe

German director, writer, and actress

Born *Berlin, 21 February 1942.* ***Education*** *Attended the Universities of Munich and Paris; studied acting in Munich.* ***Family*** *Married the director Volker Schlöndorff, 1969 (divorced).* ***Career*** *1960s—actress in theaters in Dinkelsbül, Stuttgart, and Frankfurt; from 1969—worked only in TV and film; 1975—directed first film,* The Lost Honor of Katharina Blum. ***Awards*** *Golden Lion, Venice Festival, for* The German Sisters, *1981.* ***Address*** *Bioskop-Film, Turkenstrasse 91, D-80799 Munich, Germany.*

Films as Director: 1975: *Die verlorene Ehre der Katharina Blum* (*The Lost Honor of Katharina Blum*) (co-d with Schlöndorff, co-sc). **1977:** *Das zweite Erwachen der Christa Klages* (*The Second Awakening of Christa Klages*) (+ sc). **1979:** *Schwestern oder Die Balance des Glücks* (*Sisters, or The Balance of Happiness*) (+ co-sc). **1981:** *Die Bleierne Zeit* (*The German Sisters*; *Marianne and Juliane*; *Leaden Times*) (+ sc). **1983:** *Heller Wahn* (*L'Amie*; *Sheer Madness*; *A Labor of Love*; *Friends and Husbands*) (+ sc). **1986:** *Rosa Luxemburg* (+ sc). **1987:** *Felix* (co-d with Buschmann, Sander, and Sanders-Brahms); *Eva*. **1988:** *Paura e amore* (*Love and Fear*; *Fuerchten und Liebe*) (+ co-sc). **1990:** *Die Rückkehr* (*The Return*; *L'Africana*). **1993:** *Il lungo silenzio* (*The Long Silence*); *Zeit des Zorns*. **1994:** *Das versprechen* (*The Promise*) (+ co-sc). **1997:** *Winterkind* (for TV).

Margarethe von Trotta

Other Films: **1968:** *Schräge Vögel* (Ehmck) (ro). **1969:** *Brandstifter* (Lemke) (ro); *Götter der Pest* (Fassbinder) (ro as Margarethe). **1970:** *Baal* (Schlöndorff) (ro as Sophie); *Der amerikanische Soldat* (*The American Soldier*) (Fassbinder) (ro as maid). **1971:** *Der plötzliche Reichtum der armen Leute von Kombach* (Schlöndorff) (co-sc, ro as Heinrich's woman); *Die Moral der Ruth Halbfass* (Schlöndorff) (ro as Doris Vogelsang). **1972:** *Strohfeuer* (*Summer Lightning*) (Schlöndorff) (ro as Elisabeth, co-sc). **1973:** *Desaster* (Hauff) (ro); *Übernachtung in Tirol* (Schlöndorff) (ro as Katja). **1974:** *Invitation à la chasse* (Chabrol—for TV) (ro as Paulette); *Georgina's Gründe* (Schlöndorff—for TV) (ro as Kate Theory). **1975:** *Das andechser Gefühl* (Achternbusch) (ro as film actress). **1976:** *Der Fangschuss* (*Coup de grâce*) (Schlöndorff) (co-sc, ro as Sophie von Reval). **1981:** *Die Fälschung* (*The Forgery*; *Circle of Deceit*; *False Witness*) (Schlöndorff) (co-sc). **1984:** *Blaubart* (*Bluebeard*) (Zanussi) (ro); *Unerreichbare Nahe* (Hirtz) (sc). **1995:** *Die Nacht der Regisseure* (*The Night of the Filmmakers*) (Reitz—doc) (appearance); *Die Neugier immer weiter treiben* (Buchka—doc) (appearance).

An important aspect of Margarethe von Trotta's filmmaking, which affects not only the content but also the representation of that content, is her emphasis on women and the relationships that can develop between them. For example, von Trotta chose as the central theme in two of her films (*Sisters, or The Balance of Happiness* and *The German Sisters*) one of the most intense and complex relationships that can exist between two women, that of sisters. Whether von Trotta is dealing with overtly political themes as in *The Second Awakening of Christa Klages* (based on the true story of a woman who robs a bank in order to subsidize a day-care center) and *The German Sisters* (based on the experiences of Christine Ensslin and her "terrorist" sister) or with the lives of ordinary women as in *Sisters, or The Balance of Happiness* or *Sheer Madness,* von Trotta shows the political nature of relationships between women. By paying close attention to these relationships, von Trotta brings into question the social and political systems that either sustain them or do not allow them to exist.

Although the essence of von Trotta's films is political and critical of the status quo, their structures are quite conventional. Her films are expensively made and highly subsidized by the film production company Bioskop, which was started by her husband Volker Schlöndorff and Reinhard Hauff, both filmmakers. Von Trotta joined the company when she started making her own films. She did not go through the complicated system of incentives and grants available to independent filmmakers in Germany. Rather, she began working for Schlöndorff as an actress and then as a scriptwriter, and finally on her own as a director and co-owner in the production company that subsidizes their films.

Von Trotta has been criticized by some feminists for working too closely within the system and for creating characters and structures that are too conventional to be of any political value. Other critics find that a feminist aesthetic can be found in her choice of themes. For although von Trotta uses conventional women characters, she does not represent them in traditional fashion. Nor does she describe them with stereotyped, sexist clichés; instead, she allows her characters to develop on screen through gestures, glances, and nuances. Great importance is given to the psychological and subconscious delineation of her characters, for von Trotta pays constant attention to dreams, visions, flashbacks, and personal obsessions. In this way, her work can be seen as inspired by the films of Bresson and Bergman, filmmakers who also use the film medium to portray psychological depth.

"The unconscious and subconscious behavior of the characters is more important to me than what they do," says von Trotta. For this reason, von Trotta spends a great deal of time with her actors and actresses to be sure that they really understand the emotions and motivations of the characters that they portray. This aspect of her filmmaking caused her to separate her work from that of her husband, Volker Schlöndorff. During their joint direction of *The Lost Honor of*

Katharina Blum, it became apparent that Schlöndorff's manner of directing, which focused on action shots, did not mix with his wife's predilections for exploring the internal motivation of the characters. Her films are often criticized for paying too much attention to the psychological, and thus becoming too personal and inaccessible.

Von Trotta has caused much controversy within the feminist movement and outside of it. Nevertheless, her films have won several awards not only in her native Germany but also internationally, drawing large, diverse audiences. Her importance cannot be minimized. Although she employs the commonly used and accepted structures of popular filmmakers, her message is quite different. Her main characters are women and her films treat them in a serious and innovative fashion. Such treatment of women within a traditional form has in the past been undervalued or ignored. Her presentation of women has opened up possibilities for the development of the image of women on screen and contributed to the development of film itself.

Von Trotta's films have continued to express other concerns that were central to her earlier work as well. These include examinations of German identity and the impact of recent German history on the present; the view of historical events through the perceptions of the individuals those events affect; the personal risks that individuals take when speaking the truth or exposing the hypocrisy of those in power; and, in particular, the strengths of women and the manner in which they relate to each other and evolve as their own individual selves.

Rosa Luxemburg is a highly intelligent, multifaceted biopic of the idealistic, politically committed, but ill-fated humanist and democratic socialist who had such a high profile on the German political scene near the beginning of the 20th century. *Love and Fear,* loosely based on Chekhov's *The Three Sisters,* is an absorbing (if sometimes overdone) allegory about how life is forever in transition. It focuses on a trio of sisters, each with a different personality. The senior sibling is a scholarly type who is too cognizant of how quickly time goes by; the middle one lives an aimless life, and is ruled by her feelings; the junior in the group is a fervent, optimistic pre-med student.

The Long Silence is the story of a judge whose life is in danger because of his prosecution of corrupt government officials. After his murder—an unavoidable occurrence, given the circumstances—his gynecologist wife perseveres in continuing his work. *The Promise,* which reflects on the downfall of communism and the demise of the Berlin Wall, tells of two lovers who are separated in 1961 during a failed attempt to escape from East to West. With the exception of a brief reunion in Prague in 1968, they are held apart until 1989 and the death of communism in East Germany.—GRETCHEN ELSNER-SOMMER and ROB EDELMAN

Weber, Lois

American director

Born *Allegheny City, Pennsylvania, 13 June 1882.* ***Family*** *Married the director and actor Phillips Smalley, 1906 (divorced 1922).* ***Career*** *1890s—touring concert pianist, then Church Home Missionary in Pittsburgh; 1905—actress in touring melodrama* Why Girls Leave Home *for company managed by future husband Smalley; from 1908—writer and director (then actor) for Gaumont Talking Pictures; teamed up with Smalley, moved to Reliance, then Rex, working for Edwin S. Porter; 1912—the Smalleys (as they were known) took over Rex, a member of the Universal conglomerate, following Porter's departure; 1914—joined Hobart Bosworth's company; 1915—Universal funded private studio for Weber at 4634 Sunset Boulevard; 1917—founded own studio; 1920—signed contract with Famous Players-Lasky for $50,000 per picture and a percentage of profits; 1921—dropped by company after three unprofitable films, subsequently lost company, divorced husband, and suffered nervous collapse; late 1920s briefly resumed directing; 1930s—script-doctor for Universal.* ***Died*** *In Hollywood, 13 November 1939.*

Films as Director: 1912: *The Troubadour's Triumph* (co-d); *The Japanese Idyll* (co-d). **1913:** *The Eyes of God* (co-d); *The Jew's Christmas* (co-d, + sc, ro); *The Female of the Species* (+ ro); *Suspense* (co-d); *His Brand.* **1914:** *The Merchant of Venice* (co-d with Smalley, + ro as Portia); *Traitor*; *Like Most Wives*; *Hypocrites!* (+ sc); *False Colors* (co-d, + co-sc, ro); *It's No Laughing Matter* (+ sc); *A Fool and His Money* (+ ro); *Behind the Veil* (co-d, + sc, ro); *The Leper's Coat*; *The Career of Waterloo Peterson.* **1915:** *Sunshine Molly* (co-d, ro, sc); *Scandal* (co-d, + sc, ro); *Jewel*; *A Cigarette, That's All* (co-d, + sc). **1916:** *Discontent* (short); *Hop, the Devil's Brew* (co-d, + sc, ro); *Where Are My Children?* (co-d, + sc); *The French Downstairs*; *Alone in the World* (short); *The People vs. John Doe* (+ ro); *The Rock of Riches* (short); *John Needham's Double*; *Saving the Family Name* (co-d, ro); *Shoes*; *The Dumb Girl of Portici* (co-d); *The Flirt* (co-d); *Idle Wives*; *Wanted—a Home.* **1917:** *The Hand that Rocks the Cradle* (co-d, + pr, ro); *Even as You and I*; *The Mysterious Mrs. M*; *The Price of a Good Time*; *The Man Who Dared God*; *There's No Place Like Home*; *For Husbands Only* (+ pr). **1918:** *The Doctor and the Woman*; *Borrowed Clothes.* **1919:** *When a Girl Loves*; *Mary Regan*; *Midnight Romance* (+ sc); *Scandal Mongers*; *Home*; *Forbidden.* **1921:** *Too Wise Wives* (+ pr, sc); *What's Worth While?* (+ pr); *To Please One Woman* (+ sc);

Lois Weber (left) with Billie Dove

The Blot (+ pr, sc); *What Do Men Want?* (+ pr, sc). **1923:** *A Chapter in Her Life* (+ co-sc). **1926:** *The Marriage Clause* (+ sc). **1927:** *Sensation Seekers* (+ sc); *The Angel of Broadway.* **1934:** *White Heat* (+ co-sc).

Lois Weber was a unique silent film director. Not only was she a woman who was certainly the most important female director the American film industry has known, but unlike many of her colleagues up to the present, her work was regarded in its day as equal to, if not a little better than that of most male directors. She was a committed filmmaker in an era when commitment was virtually unknown, a filmmaker who was not afraid to make features with subject matter in which she devoutly believed, subjects as varied as Christian Science (*Jewel* and *A Chapter in Her Life*) or birth control (*Where Are My Children?*). *Hypocrites!* was an indictment of hypocrisy and corruption in big business, politics, and religion, while *The People vs. John Doe* opposed capital punishment. At the same time, Lois Weber was quite capable of handling with ease a major spectacular feature such as the historical drama *The Dumb Girl of Portici,* which introduced Anna Pavlova to the screen.

During the 1910s, Lois Weber was under contract to Universal. While at Universal, she appears to have been given total freedom as to the subject matter of her films, all of which where among the studio's biggest moneymakers and highly regarded by the critics of the day. (The Weber films, however, did run into censorship problems, and the director was the subject of a vicious attack in a 1918 issue of *Theatre Magazine* over the "indecent and suggestive" nature of her titles.) Eventually the director felt the urge to move on to independent production, and during 1920 and 1921 she released a series of highly personal intimate dramas dealing with married life and the types of problems which beset ordinary people. None of these films was particularly well received by the critics, who unanimously declared them dull, while the public displayed an equal lack of enthusiasm. Nonetheless, features such as *Too Wise Wives* and *The Blot* demonstrate Weber at her directorial best. In the former she presents a study of two married couples. Not very much happens, but in her characterizations and attention to detail (something for which Weber was always noted), the director is as contemporary as a Robert Altman or an Ingmar Bergman. *The Blot* is concerned with "genteel poverty" and is marked by the underplaying of its principals—Claire Windsor and Louis Calhern—and an enigmatic ending which leaves the viewer uninformed as to the characters' future, an ending unlike any in the entire history of the American silent film. These films, as with virtually all of the director's work, were also written by Lois Weber.

Through the end of her independent productions in 1921, Lois Weber worked in association with her husband Phillips Smalley, who usually received credit as associate or advisory director. After the two were divorced, Lois Weber's career went to pieces. She directed one or two minor program features together with one talkie, but none equaled her work from the 1910s and early 1920s. She was a liberated filmmaker who seemed lost without the companionship, both at home and in the studio, of a husband. Her career and life were in many ways as enigmatic as the ending of *The Blot.*—ANTHONY SLIDE

Weill, Claudia

American director

Born *New York City, 1947; distant cousin of the composer Kurt Weill.* ***Education*** *Studied photography at Radcliffe College, degree in photography, 1969; studied painting with Oskar Kokoschka in Salzburg; studied still photography with Walker Evans at Yale.* ***Career*** *1972—co-directed landmark feminist short for PBS,* Joyce at 34; *1978—directed and co-wrote the critically well-received independent feature* Girlfriends; *1980—directed bigger-budget feature* It's My Turn *for Columbia; 1980s-1990s—worked as a director of television movies and series television, including episodes of the TV series* Once a Hero, thirtysomething, My So-Called Life, *and* Chicago Hope. ***Awards*** *Emmy Award, Best Afterschool Special, for* The Great Love Experiment, *1984.* ***Agent*** *Walter Teller, Esq., Hansen, Jacobsen, Teller, & Hoberman, 450 North Roxbury Drive, 8th Floor, Beverly Hills, CA 90210, U.S.A.*

Films as Director: 1968: *Metropole*; *Radcliffe Blues.* **1969:** *Putney School.* **1971:** *This Is the Home of Mrs. Levant Grahame* (doc, short); *IDCA—1970*; *Roaches' Serenade* (doc, short). **1972:** *Belly Dancing*

Claudia Weill (right) with Jill Clayburgh on the set of *It's My Turn.*

Class; Commuters; Joyce at 34 (co-d with Chopra—short); *Lost and Found; Marriage; Yoga.* **1974:** *Matine Horner—Portrait of a Person* (doc—short); *The Other Half of the Sky: A China Memoir* (doc—co-d with MacLaine, + ph, co-ed). **1978:** *Girlfriends* (+ co-sc, pr). **1980:** *It's My Turn.* **1984:** *The Great Love Experiment* (for TV). **1986:** *Johnny Bull* (for TV). **1988:** *Once a Hero.* **1991:** *Face of a Stranger* (for TV). **1992:** *A Child Lost Forever* (for TV). **1996:** *Critical Choices* (for TV). **1998:** *Giving Up the Ghost* (for TV).

Other Films: **1973:** *The Year of the Woman* (ph). **1978:** *The Scenic Route* (ro). **1988:** *Calling the Shots* (Cole and Dale—doc) (ro as herself).

Director Claudia Weill started making amateur films as a student at Radcliffe College, and thereafter worked for a decade as a cinematographer. In addition, she made a variety of experimental and documentary shorts, including *This Is the Home of Mrs. Levant Grahame* and *Roaches' Serenade,* and directed 20 segments for *Sesame Street* as well as several other PBS television programs. She gained visibility as a filmmaker with her best known short, *Joyce at 34,* which she co-directed with her friend and colleague Joyce Chopra for public television.

Joyce at 34, features filmmaker Joyce Chopra as she contemplates her social conditioning and repressed anger at having to balance the conflicting demands of her life as a mother and as a professional. Its feminist perspective is evident in its suggestion that women can find some relief and moral community in their shared experiences. Subsequently, the actress Shirley MacLaine recruited Weill for *The Other Half of the Sky: A China Memoir,* which Weill co-directed, photographed, and co-edited, and which earned an Academy Award nomination.

The attention that *The Other Half of the Sky* garnered was instrumental in enabling Weill to secure the grant money that helped her piece together a small $140,000 budget to make her first fiction feature, *Girlfriends.* Using a conventional narrative structure, the film was considered groundbreaking for its depiction of female friendship and the divergence that arises between two best friends when one chooses to pursue a career as a photographer and the other as a housewife. Its enthusiastic reception when it was screened at the Cannes Film Festival in 1978 prompted Warner Bros. to pick it up for distribution. But, although it was a critical success, it was not a great commercial success. Nevertheless, Weill subsequently was offered a number of big studio directorial assignments and she chose Columbia Studio's seven-million dollar project, *It's My Turn.* The film's heroine is a successful math professor, played by Jill Clayburgh, stuck in an unsatisfying long-term relationship with a self-absorbed, noncommittal man. When she attends her father's wedding, she becomes attracted to the son of her father's bride, a sensitive and handsome former baseball player. The film reflected Hollywood's efforts to produce films that featured women who expressed the challenges, choices, and pleasures of contemporary feminism. Written by Eleanor Bergstein, it echoed the earlier *Joyce at 34* and *Girlfriends* in terms of its focus on women who desire professional lives that satisfactorily complement their personal and family lives. As Weill put it, "It's hard to do everything, but I think it's important to try." The film's poor performance at the box office, however, inspired Weill to turn to directing several plays in New York.

Currently, Weill works in television where she has directed episodes for such critically acclaimed series as *thirtysomething, Chicago Hope,* and *My So-Called Life,* in addition to several made-for-television movies, and an after-school special. Earlier in her career, critics suggested that Weill had been hampered because she was unfairly stigmatized by being labeled a "feminist filmmaker." Perhaps not surprisingly then, after she made *Girlfriends* (prior to which she unhesitatingly acknowledged her feminist ideals), she denied altogether that she was a feminist. Although she has not achieved enormous success as a feature-film director, Weill has been involved in television film projects that have featured strong actresses playing women who are committed to women and women's issues. For example, *Face of a Stranger* stars Tyne Daly and Gena Rowlands as two apparently disparate women who find strength with each other in their time of need. After the death of her husband, Pat discovers that he squandered all of their savings and she is now nearly destitute. To the horror of her daughter who wants to marry a rich man, Pat helps the homeless woman who lives in a cardboard box near her building and they become friends. Subsequently, Weill directed the television movie about child abuse, *A Child Lost Forever,* in which a teenager who gives her baby up for adoption attempts, 19 years later, to contact her son only to learn that he died under questionable circumstances when he was three years old. More recently, Weill directed *Critical Choices* about a woman who operates the only abortion clinic in Madison, Wisconsin, and another woman who is an avid abortion-rights supporter; their views are countered by a woman who is a right-wing antiabortionist. Testimony to the film's evenhandedness is that although their views differ dramatically, their dedication and respect for each other remains strong.—CYNTHIA FELANDO

Wertmüller, Lina

Italian director and writer

Born *Arcangela Felice Assunta Wertmüller von Elgg Spanol von Braueich in Rome, 14 August 1928.* ***Education*** *Attended several Catholic schools; Academy of Theatre, Rome, 1947-51.* ***Family*** *Married the artist Enrico Job, 1968.* ***Career*** *1951-52—joined Maria Signorelli's puppet troupe; from 1952—actress, stage manager, set designer, publicist, and writer for theater, radio and TV; 1962—assistant to Fellini on 8½; 1963—directed first feature,* I basilischi; *1973—first film to be given U.S. release,* Film d'amore e d'anarchia; *hired by Warner Bros. to direct four films, contract terminated after financial failure of first film.* ***Address*** *Piazza Clotilde 5, 00196 Rome, Italy.*

Films as Director and Writer: **1963:** *I basilischi* (*The Lizards*). **1965:** *Questa volta parliamo di uomini* (*Now Let's Talk about Men*; *This Time Let's Talk about Men*). **1967:** *Non stuzzicate la zanzara* (*Don't Tease the Mosquito*). **1972:** *Mimi metallurgio ferito nell'onore* (*The Seduction of Mimi*; *Mimi the Metalworker, Wounded in Honour*). **1973:** *Film d'amore e d'anarchia, ovvero stamattina alle 10 in Via dei fiori nella nota casa di toleranza* (*Film of Love and Anarchy, or This Morning at Ten in the Via dei fiori at the Well-Known House of Tolerance*). **1974:** *Tutto a posto e niente in ordine* (*Everything's in Order but Nothing Works*; *All Screwed Up*); *Travolti da un insolito destino nell'azzurro mare d'agosto* (*Swept Away. . . by an Unusual Destiny in the Blue Sea of August*; *Swept Away. . .*). **1976:** *Pasqualino settebellezze* (*Pasqualino: Seven Beauties*; *Seven Beauties*). **1978:** *The End of the World in Our Usual Bed in a Night Full of Rain* (*La Fine del mondo in una notte piena di poggia*; *A Night Full of Rain*); *Shimmy lagarno tarantelle e vino*; *Fatto di sangue fra due uomini per causa di una vedova* (*Blood Feud*; *Revenge*). **1979:** *Belle Starr* (under name "Nathan Wich"—for TV). **1981:** *E una Domenica sera di novembre* (for TV). **1983:** *Scherzo del destinoin aqquato dietro l'angelo come un brigante di strada* (*A Joke of Destiny, Lying in Wait around the Corner Like a Street Bandit*) (co-sc). **1984:** *Sotto, Sotto* (co-sc). **1986:** *Camorra* (*Vicoli e delitti*; *Un complicato intrigo di donne, vicoli e delitti*; *The Naples Connection*) (co-sc); *Notte d'estate, con profilo Greco, occhi amandorla e odore di basilico* (*Summer Night with Greek Profile, Almond Eyes and Scent of Basil*). **1989:** *In una notte di chiaro luna* (*In a Full Moon Night*); *Il Decimo clandestino*. **1990:** *Saturday, Sunday, Monday*. **1994:** *Io speriamo che me la cavo* (*Ciao, Professore!*) (co-sc). **1996:** *Ninfa plebea*; *Metal meccanico e parrucchiera in un turbine di sesso e di politica*. **1999:** *An Interesting State*; *Ferdinando e Carolina*.

Other Films: **1963:** *Otto e mezzo* (*8½*) (Fellini) (asst d). **1966:** *Rita la zanzara* (*Rita the Mosquito*) (d musical numbers only, sc). **1970:** *Quando de donne avevano la coda* (*When Women Had Tails*) (Festa Campanile) (co-sc); *Città violenta* (*Violent City*; *The Family*) (Sollima) (co-sc). **1972:** *Fratelli sole, sorella luna* (*Brother Sun, Sister Moon*) (Zeffirelli) (co-sc).

By the mid-1970s, Lina Wertmüller had directed a series of sharply observed (though, in retrospect, markedly uneven) features that made her one of the shining lights of European cinema. At their best, her films were crammed with pointed humor, astute social commentary, and outrageous sexuality. In 1976 she even became the first woman to win a Best Director Academy Award nomination, for *Seven Beauties*.

In recent years, Wertmüller's critical reputation has been tarnished. For one thing, the quality of her work has sharply deteriorated. For another, her detractors have dubbed her a reactionary, labeling her films as grotesque and self-absorbed, with little love for humanity.

Lina Wertmüller

Meanwhile, her champions hail her as a defender of the downtrodden, an idealistic anarchist who realizes anarchy is impractical yet still cherishes the notion of total individual freedom. Upon examining her films, one might decide that most of her characters are caricatures, or might consider them sympathetic human beings. It all depends on the interpretation.

Wertmüller's films most characteristically focus on the eternal battle between the sexes, fought with noisy screaming matches and comical seductions in a class-warfare setting. Her most typical features—those that cemented her reputation—may be found in the midsection of her filmography, from *The Seduction of Mimi* through *Swept Away. . . .* All are imperfect: for every inspired sequence—most notably, in *The Seduction of Mimi,* Giancarlo Giannini's antics between the sheets with a ridiculously obese woman—there are long stretches of repetitious ax-grinding on sex, love, anarchy, fascism, and the class struggle. All but *All Screwed Up* star Giannini, Wertmüller's favorite actor. His characters think they are suave, but they really are stubborn and stupid, in constant trouble both politically and sexually. An example: in *Film of Love and Anarchy,* set in 1932, Giannini plays an anarchist, hiding in a brothel, who plans to assassinate Mussolini but instead falls for a prostitute. Wertmüller's women, on the other hand, are not politically aware, and are uninterested in struggling for self-sufficiency.

Seven Beauties, filled with stunning images, is Wertmüller's penultimate feature: a searing drama about survival in a surreal, insane world. It chronicles the odyssey of a Don Juan (Giannini) through the horrors of World War II, with the highlight a typically gruesome Wertmüllian seduction sequence in which the "hero" entices a piggish female concentration-camp commandant.

Over the decades, the reputation of *Seven Beauties* has suffered because most of the features Wertmüller has made in its wake have been misfires. *The End of the World in Our Usual Bed in a Night Full of Rain,* her first English-language effort, is a verbose marital boxing match pitting journalist/communist Giannini and photographer/feminist Candice Bergen. *Revenge,* also known as *Blood Feud,* is the overbaked tale of a radical lawyer (Marcello Mastroianni) and a gangster (Giannini) who love widow Sophia Loren during the early years of Fascist rule in Italy. Both were released in the late 1970s, and were followed by close to a dozen forgettable films made over the next two decades.

Easily Wertmüller's most accessible later-career films are *Sotto, Sotto* and *Ciao, Professore!* Thematically speaking, *Sotto, Sotto* is related to her earlier work in that it is a tale of sexual combat, but with a twist. It is the story of a married woman who becomes romantically attracted to her best (female) friend, which predictably piques her brutally sexist husband. *Ciao, Professore!* is a social comedy about a Northern Italian grade-school teacher, used to working with affluent children, who is mistakenly assigned to an impoverished village near Naples, with the scenario detailing how he influences his students and how they impact on him. While not as disappointing as her other post-*Seven Beauties* features, *Sotto, Sotto* and *Ciao, Professore!* are by-the-numbers stories whose best moments cannot compare to their counterparts in *Love and Anarchy, Swept Away. . . ,* and, most certainly, *Seven Beauties.*

Wertmüller's films have remained consistent in one regard: many have lengthy, flowery titles. The complete name of *Swept Away. . .* is *Swept Away. . . by an Unusual Destiny in the Blue Sea of August.* Joining it and *The End of the World. . .* are *A Joke of Destiny, Lying in Wait around the Corner Like a Street Bandit*; and *Summer Night with Greek Profile, Almond Eyes and Scent of Basil.*

Once upon a time, these titles might have seemed clever and unique. Given the declining quality of Wertmüller's work, they now are overindulgent and pretentious.—ROB EDELMAN

West, Mae

American writer and actress

Born *Brooklyn, New York, 17 August 1892.* ***Education*** *Attended Brooklyn public schools to age 13.* ***Family*** *Married the entertainer Frank Wallace, 1911 (divorced 1942).* ***Career*** *Child entertainer: joined Hal Clarendon's stock company, Brooklyn, at age eight; toured with Frank Wallace; 1911—Broadway debut in the revue* A la Broadway and Hello, Paris; *then returned to vaudeville tour with star billing; 1907-18—frequently rewrote her vaudeville acts; early 1920s—toured in nightclub act with Harry Richman; 1926—on Broadway in her own play* Sex *(later plays produced include* The Drag, *1926,* The Wicked Age, *1927,* Diamond Lil, *1928 and several revivals,* The Pleasure Man, *1928,* The Constant Sinner, *1931, and* Catherine Was Great, *1944); 1932—film debut in* Night After Night*: contract with Paramount; 1933—adapted her stage hit* Diamond Lil *for the movie, in which she also starred,* She Done Him Wrong; *1933-40—starred in a series of popular films in the 1930s for which she often wrote the screenplay; 1954-56—toured with nightclub act; 1955—first of several albums of her songs,* The Fabulous Mae West; *1970—returned to the screen in* Myra Breckenridge. ***Died*** *In Los Angeles, 22 November 1980.*

Films as Writer and Actress: 1933: *She Done Him Wrong* (L. Sherman) (as Lady Lou); *I'm No Angel* (Ruggles) (as Tira). **1934:** *Belle of the Nineties* (McCarey) (as Ruby Carter). **1935:** *Goin' to Town* (A. Hall) (as Cleo Borden). **1936:** *Klondike Annie* (Walsh) (co-sc, as the Frisco Doll/Rose Carlton); *Go West, Young Man* (Hathaway) (as Mavis Arden). **1938:** *Every Day's a Holiday* (A. E. Sutherland) (as Peaches O'Day/Mademoiselle Fifi). **1940:** *My Little Chickadee* (Cline) (co-sc, as Flower Belle Lee).

Films as Actress: 1932: *Night after Night* (Mayo) (as Maudie Triplett). **1943:** *The Heat's On* (*Tropicana*) (Ratoff) (as Fay Lawrence). **1970:** *Myra Breckenridge* (Sarne) (as Leticia Van Allen, + co-dialogue). **1978:** *Sextette* (K. Hughes) (as Marlo Manners).

Mae West was Hollywood's most flamboyant symbol of sexual satire in the 1930s, though she was known perhaps more for her swagger than for writing the witty screenplays for the films in which she starred. In 1933 Paramount invited West to adapt her enormously popular play *Diamond Lil* for the screen—despite the studio's reservations that its Gay Nineties setting would be hopelessly out-of-sync with the tastes of the all-important youth audience. But her bawdy humor struck a profitable chord with a vast audience. West had a shrewd sense of comic timing, and the determination to tap into and extend contemporary themes and rhythms, especially, of course, about sex. The ribald one-liners that peppered her scripts were endlessly repeated, and attest to their simple brilliance, including "I used to be Snow White, but I drifted."

By the time she arrived in Hollywood, West was already well known. From the age of five, she worked as a performer, and by her teens she was doing vaudeville routines that attracted attention for her scandalous dances, especially the "shimmy." By the mid-1920s, she was writing stage plays with sexual themes, such as *The Constant Sinner*. The play that assured her fame was 1926's sensation, *Sex,* which she wrote, produced, and directed on Broadway. Huffy critics lambasted it as "disgusting," but audiences adored it. After 385 performances, it was raided and

Mae West

West was charged and jailed briefly for obscenity. It was her Broadway hit *Diamond Lil'* that proved to be her ticket to Hollywood.

In 1932, at the age of 40, West made her movie debut in *Night after Night,* though it employed her acting rather than her writing skills. Yet, in her brief but much-noticed appearance, she uttered a now-famous line: to a coat-check girl's exclamation, "Goodness! What lovely diamonds!," West drawled, "Goodness had nothing to do with it." Her second film was her adaptation of *Diamond Lil,* retitled *She Done Him Wrong*. Her most noteworthy film, it features West as a saloon songstress in the Gay Nineties; Cary Grant plays the undercover cop who has been assigned to haul her in. But, West has other plans; she entices him to "Come up sometime and see me," thus ensuring a successful seduction. Although the film ends with the promise of West's marriage, there is no suggestion that she will be a docile wife. Her screenplay was a surprising combination of sexual satire and moral uplift that toyed mercilessly with conventional masculine and feminine sex roles. Thus, not a few critics have related her flamboyant sexuality to the excesses of camp. *She Done Him Wrong* was a smash hit, and West followed it with another, *I'm No Angel,* which also starred Cary Grant. The character she wrote for herself was a familiar provocateur; she plays a lion tamer with an uncanny ability to separate wealthy old men from their money. One of the film's highlights is a courtroom scene in which West acts as her own attorney and proves to be a disruptingly seductive presence, especially to the judge.

In addition to writing or collaborating on the scripts for her films, Paramount gave West enormous control over their production, including final cut, full creative control, and her choice of directors and leading men. West's films not only reiterated the cheeky "sex goddess" persona she had cultivated on Broadway, they also rescued Paramount from the threat of bankruptcy. Plot was less important in her scripts than her quips and characterizations. They capitalized on her image—curvaceous figure, big blond hair, tight corset, and suggestive saunter, and usually featured her in roles in which she played independent adventurers, often entertainers, who unashamedly express their desire for the hunks who catch her gaze. Her characters are never subservient to men, and it is the pleasure of sex rather than the security of romantic love that her characters seek. Further, they refuse to reform by film's end, in the manner of other "modern women" heroines; instead, her films flaunted her sexuality and its myriad rewards—men, money, freedom, and irreverence. Indeed, her scripts brim with her witticisms and innuendo, which temporarily confounded Hollywood's censors. But, Depression-era audiences were both titillated and charmed by the sexual suggestiveness of her films, along with their implication that anyone could succeed if he or she had enough stubborn determination.

Following the enormous success of *She Done Him Wrong,* conservatives and reformers who thought her work was morally despicable prompted the Production Code Administration to demand that she tame her scripts. *She Done Him Wrong,* in particular, is routinely cited as one of the key reasons that the Production Code—Hollywood's moral code—was restructured. Eventually, West's trademark sexual parody and double entendre were diluted and her films sold fewer tickets. Her script for *Belle of the Nineties,* for example, was rewritten extensively to conform to the new Code, and many local censors trimmed it even further. By the end of the 1930s, she was called "box-office" poison by a major exhibitor, but she bounced back with the minor classic, *My Little Chickadee,* in which she traded quips with W. C. Fields. In 1943, after her disappointing film *The Heat's On,* West retired from Hollywood and returned to the stage. In the 1970s she made two more films for which she wrote her own lines. The ill-conceived and realized *Myra*

Breckenridge was a failure at the box office, but succeeded in renewing West's popularity. At the age of 85, she made her last film, *Sextette*.

Film critics have long been preoccupied with the question of whether West's films have feminist intentions, or merely pander to male fantasies about sex-obsessed women. Such questions, however, are a tribute to the rich and wry complexity of her work, especially her clever parodies of her own sex-symbol persona.—CYNTHIA FELANDO

Wieland, Joyce

Canadian director

Born *Toronto, 30 June 1931.* ***Education*** *Attended Central Technical Vocational High School, Toronto.* ***Family*** *Married the artist Michael Snow, 1957.* ***Career*** *1950s—independent artist and commercial artist, Toronto; 1955-56—animator for Jim McKay and George Dunning's Graphic Films; 1963—with Snow moved to New York City; 1964—formed company Corrective film; 1971—moved back to Toronto; instructor at Nova Scotia College of Art; 1971-76—worked on funding, producing and directing* The Far Shore; *1979-82—taught at Arts Sake, Toronto; 1985-86—instructor at the San Francisco Art Institute; from 1987—continues working as visual artist; retrospective of art and films at Art Gallery of Ontario.* ***Awards*** *Three Canadian film awards, 1977.* ***Died*** *27 June 1998.*

Films as Director: 1958: *Tea in the Garden* (co-d). **1959:** *A Salt in the Park* (co-d). **1963:** *Larry's Recent Behaviour.* **1964:** *Peggy's Blue Skylight*; *Patriotism* (Parts 1 and 2). **1965:** *Watersark*; *Barbara's Blindness* (co-d with B. Ferguson). **1967:** *Bill's Hat*; *Sailboat*; *1933*; *Hand-tinting.* **1968:** *Catfood*; *Rat Life and Diet in North America.* **1969:** *La Raison avant la passion* (*Reason over Passion*); *Dripping Water* (co-d with Snow); *One Second in Montreal* (co-d with Snow). **1972:** *Pierre Vallières*; *Birds at Sunrise.* **1973:** *Solidarity.* **1976:** *The Far Shore* (+ co-pr). **1984:** *A & B in Ontario* (co-d with Frampton). **1985:** *Birds at Sunrise*; *Wendy and Joyce* (incomplete).

Other Films as Actress: 1967: *Sky Socialist* (Jacobs); *Wavelength* (Snow); *Standard Time* (Snow). **1972:** *Knocturne* (George and Mike Kuchar); *"Rameau's Nephew" by Diderot (Thanx to Dennis Young) by Wilma Schoen* (Snow).

Joyce Wieland achieved her reputation as one of a group of experimental filmmakers who contributed to the creation of an avant-garde film style in the middle and late 1960s. Wieland's films formally investigate the limitations and shared properties of several media while they developed increasingly pointed themes regarding Canadian nationalism and feminism.

When Toronto developed into a leading Canadian art center in the late 1950s and 1960s, Wieland became the only woman who achieved artistic prominence among the new group of Canadian painters influenced by Abstract Expressionism and Pop Art. Concerned about being even closer to the most recent developments among vanguard artists, Wieland and her husband Michael Snow moved to New York City in 1963. Although they remained expatriates until 1971, Wieland continued to exhibit her work throughout Canada and established a reputation during the next decade as the country's leading woman artist.

In New York City, Wieland became friendly with many members of the "underground" film community, a group whose bohemian behavior and outrageously styled home movies were gaining increased notoriety. Influenced by underground filmmakers Harry Smith, Ken Jacobs, and George Kuchar, Wieland began making short, personal films, and her movies were soon included in the group's regular Greenwich Village screenings.

The cinematic style that evolved out of several underground filmmakers' works became known by the late 1960s as "structural film." These films addressed the nature of the film viewing experience itself and created self-reflexive statements about such basic materials of filmmaking as projected light, celluloid, and the camera apparatus. Structural filmmaking paralleled painterly developments in minimal art and received international recognition as the new radical forefront of avant-garde film. Wieland's films—often grouped and discussed with those by such other structural filmmakers as Snow, Jacobs, Hollis Frampton, and Ernie Gehr—played at museums, film festivals, and colleges in Europe and North America.

In 1969 Wieland directed a feature-length movie that wedded the highly conceptual and experimental concerns of structural film with her own political feelings regarding Canada. The result, *Reason over Passion,* is an experimental documentary film about the country of Canada and Canadian culture and identity. Following the film's release, Wieland expressed and developed the same themes in an art show entitled "True Patriot Love" at the National Gallery of Canada in 1971. The show's Pop Art-styled quilts, embroideries, and knittings served as patriotic banners for nationalism and feminism.

Because of the direction her work was taking, and because of her increased involvement in Canadian artists' political groups and causes, Wieland returned in 1971 to Toronto. There she completed two additional short structural documentaries. *Pierre Vallières* is about a French-Canadian revolutionary and the problems between French and English Canada. *Solidarity* is about a labor strike at an Ontario factory whose workers were mostly women. At the same time, Wieland co-wrote, co-produced, and directed a theatrical feature-length film. *The Far Shore* is a romantic melodrama that tells the story of a French-Canadian woman whose failing marriage to a stuffy Toronto bourgeois results in her liberating affair with a Canadian painter. The film was not commercially successful but has subsequently been featured at film festivals, colleges, and museums in North America and Europe. After the completion of *The Far Shore,* Wieland returned primarily to drawing, painting, and printmaking and has since produced several series of new works. In 1987 the Art Gallery of Ontario hosted a retrospective of her art and films. It was the museum's first such honoring a living woman artist.—LAUREN RABINOVITZ

Winfrey, Oprah

American talk show host, actress, and producer

Born *Kosciusko, Mississippi, 29 January 1954.* ***Education*** *Earned a BA in Speech and Drama at Tennessee State University.* ***Career*** *1971-72—worked as a news reporter at WVOL radio, Nashville; 1973-76—worked as a reporter and news anchor at WTVF-TV, Nashville; 1976-77—worked as a news anchor and talk show host at WJZ-TV, Baltimore; 1977-83—hosted a morning TV talk show in Baltimore,* People Are Talking; *1984—hosted the TV talk show* A.M. Chicago; *1985—made her screen debut in Steven Spielberg's* The Color Purple; *began hosting the daytime talk show,* The Oprah Winfrey Show, *which was syndicated nationally a year later; 1986—became owner, producer, chairperson and CEO of Harpo Productions, her own production company; 1990—reprised her role as*

Oprah Winfrey in *Beloved.*

Mattie Michael in the television movie The Women of Brewster Place *on the TV series* Brewster Place; *1992—became the host and supervising producer of* Oprah: Behind the Scenes, *a celebrity interview series; 1997—signed a contract that will pay her $130-million for continuing* The Oprah Winfrey Show *through the 1999-2000 television season; 1998—appeared on the final episode of the television sitcom* Ellen. ***Awards*** *1986—NOW Woman of Achievement Award; 1987, 1991, 1992, 1993, 1994, 1995, 1998—Emmy Award as Outstanding Talk Show Host, for* The Oprah Winfrey Show; *1989, 1991, 1992, 1994, 1995, 1996, 1997—Emmy Award as Supervising Producer, Outstanding Talk Show, for* The Oprah Winfrey Show; *1989—NAACP Entertainer of the Year Award; 1989, 1990, 1991, 1992—NAACP Image Award; 1990—America's Hope Award; 1993—Emmy Award for Outstanding Children's Special, as Supervising Producer of* Shades of a Single Protein; *1995-96—George Foster Peabody Individual Achievement Award; 1998—Lifetime Achievement Award, National Academy of Television Arts and Sciences; named one of the 100 most influential people of the 20th-century by* Time *magazine; named Most Important Person in Books and Media by* Newsweek *magazine.* ***Address*** *Harpo Productions, 110 North Carpenter Street, Chicago, IL 60607-2145.*

Films as Actress: 1985: *The Color Purple* (Spielberg) (as Sofia). **1986:** *Native Son* (Freedman) (as Mrs. Thomas). **1987:** *Throw Momma from the Train* (De Vito) (as herself). **1989:** *The Women of Brewster Place* (Deitch) (as Mattie Michael) (for TV) (+exec prod). **1991:** *Listen Up: The Lives of Quincy Jones* (Weissbrod) (doc) (as herself). **1992:** *Lincoln* (Kunhardt) (doc) (as the voice of Elizabeth Keckley) (for TV). **1993:** *There Are No Children Here* (Addison) (as LaJoe Rivers) (for TV). **1997:** *Before Women Had Wings* (*Oprah Winfrey Presents: Before Women Had Wings*) (Kramer) (as Miss Zora) (for TV) (+ co-pr). **1998:** *Beloved* (Demme) (as Sethe) (+ co-pr).

Other Films: 1992: *Overexposed* (Markowitz) (for TV) (exec pr). **1998:** *The Wedding* (*Oprah Winfrey Presents The Wedding*) (Burnett) (for TV) (co-exec pr); *David and Lisa* (*Oprah Winfrey Presents David and Lisa*) (Kramer) (for TV) (co-exec pr).

Oprah Winfrey is one of the powerhouses of the entertainment industry. She was the first African-American woman to host her own daytime talkfest, the exceptionally successful *The Oprah Winfrey Show*, on which she also is supervising producer. The program, which originated in Chicago, premiered in 1985, was an immediate ratings winner, and was syndicated nationally a year later. At the core of her popularity is her mastery at empathizing with the predicaments of her guests and the everyday experiences of her viewers, to the point where she has publicly bared many of her own personal demons, from her being sexually abused as a child to the problems she has faced maintaining a desirable weight. A shrewd businesswoman, Winfrey opted to purchase her show outright, and acquired a production facility in which to produce it. She also founded Harpo ("Oprah" spelled backwards), her own production company. By 1989, she had become the wealthiest woman in television.

While Winfrey's fame rests on her visibility on TV, she has used that celebrity to propel deserving works of art to the forefront. A simple word from her and a book will earn reams of publicity, and be catapulted to the top of the best-seller list. She has also forged a career as an actress and producer of intelligent and serious-minded narratives. By the late 1990s, Winfrey had become increasingly active as a producer of made-for-television movies and mini-series. Three of her projects are: *The Wedding*, which charts the travails of an upper-class, light-skinned black woman; *Before Women Had Wings*, in which Winfrey appears as the wise, kindly Miss Zora, who becomes the mentor of a young white girl who is the product of a dysfunctional family; and *David and Lisa*, a remake of Frank Perry's acclaimed 1962 independent drama about two psychologically damaged adolescents, featuring Sidney Poitier as a empathetic psychologist. These films also are known as *Oprah Winfrey Presents The Wedding*, *Oprah Winfrey Presents Before Women Had Wings* and *Oprah Winfrey Presents David and Lisa*, all of which emphasizes the power her name and fame holds as a marketing ploy. Conversely, in her role as actress, Winfrey effectively immerses herself in her characters, rather than offering star turns that are constant reminders of her off-camera marquee value.

But for the drive of Steven Spielberg, *Schindler's List*, *Amistad* and *Saving Private Ryan* could not have been made within the climate of the present-day entertainment industry, where the bottom line is high profits derived from special effects-laden extravaganzas that sacrifice characterization and story. If not for the authority of Warren Beatty, an audacious and deeply personal political satire like *Bulworth* never would be a product of the Hollywood system. Without the backing of Tom Cruise, in his role as co-producer, Robert Towne's *Without Limits*, an exploration of the psychology of athletic competition, would not have been green-lighted. Similarly, in her role as motion picture executive, Winfrey has instigated projects which otherwise never would be filmed.

Such is the case with *Beloved*, an ambitious adaptation of Toni Morrison's Pulitzer Prize-winning novel. *Beloved*, set in the years immediately following the Civil War, is a depiction of the manner in which the degradation of slavery left piercing and painful wounds on the individual soul. Winfrey appears on camera in the role of Sethe, an escaped slave who resides with Denver, her reclusive daughter, in a house on the Cincinnati side of the Ohio River. Also present in the dwelling is an apparition, whose existence results from the tumult of Sethe's past. Sethe and Denver soon are joined by Paul D, another former slave who Sethe knew back in Kentucky, and

Beloved, a strange child-woman whose identity is a mystery. She may be a most unconventional interloper. Or, she may be the physical incarnation of the apparition haunting Sethe's house: the living ghost of the daughter Sethe slew years earlier, to prevent her from being taken back to the plantation as a slave.

Beloved, unfortunately, proved to be one of Winfrey's few missteps. She and director Jonathan Demme do deserve kudos for attempting to tackle Morrison's novel as it is written, and the film is loaded with flashes of undeniable power and poignancy. But these are fragments, which rarely constitute a whole. Because of its subtlety and complexity, what is needed is a reordering of the book's structure, a less literal and more basic and simple cinematic rendering. Because Winfrey and Demme chose to be true to their source material, *Beloved* is difficult to follow because of its sequences, which were so crucial to the book's success, are disconnected. Throughout, the characters ramble on and on; the almost-three hour running time might have been pared down without negatively impacting on the film's content. Additionally—and ironically—the special effects distract from the material. In the film's first, lengthy sequence, the ghost makes its presence known in Sethe's house. Here, the whoosh and fury of the special effects become a sideshow, taking away from the impact of the ghost on the individual characters. Later on, when Beloved first appears, there is too much emphasis on her grotesque physical state. This too initially distracts from her role in the story. Despite the power of Winfrey's public relations machine resulting in the film's being massively hyped in the media prior to its release, *Beloved* was a major box office disappointment.

Notwithstanding, the character of Sethe does fit the mold of Winfrey's most representative roles: Sofia in Spielberg's *The Color Purple*, released just as Winfrey was entering the national conscious; and Mattie Michael in *The Women of Brewster Place*, the television mini-series that was her first major work as actress-producer. Like Sethe, Sofia and Mattie are the creations of African-American women writers: Alice Walker (*The Color Purple*) and Gloria Naylor (*The Women of Brewster Place*). Their stories are further united in that they deal with the experiences and struggles of African-American women.

Sofia, as Sethe, is a victim of the time in which she lives: the American South, in the early years of the 20th-century. She at first is a large and powerful woman who is bent on marrying the man of her choice, and even does the unthinkable: she mouths off to her town's white mayor. This act results in her being beaten up and imprisoned, which depletes her spirit. On the other hand, Mattie is a strong, stubborn woman who remains resolute despite enduring incredible hardships. She is seduced and made pregnant by a local lothario, and beaten and booted out of her Tennessee home by her domineering father. She ends up living on the title street, located in a dead-end urban neighborhood. Years later, she is victimized by her now-grown son, a ne'er-do-well who runs out on her after she puts up all her assets to bail him out of jail. Yet Mattie survives. By the 1960s, when much of *The Women of Brewster Place* and *Brewster Place* (the brief TV series spawned from the film) are set, Mattie has become a matriarchal fixture in her community.

As it records the lives of Mattie and her African-American female neighbors, *The Women of Brewster Place* is a story of motherhood, responsibility and friendship, mother-child relationships and women's often incendiary connection to men. Like *Beloved* and *The Color Purple*, it is an homage to African-American womanhood. The essence of all three—and the essence of Oprah Winfrey—are summed up by a line from *The Women of Brewster Place*: "We learned that when we women come together, there was a power inside us. . . "—ROB EDELMAN

Yamasaki, Tizuka

Brazilian director

Born *Porto Alegre, Brazil, 12 May 1949.* ***Education*** *Studied architecture and then transferred to communications with a specialty in film at the Universities of Brasilia, 1970-72, and Federal Fluminense in Rio de Janeiro, 1972-75.* ***Career*** *1973 and 1977—assistant director to Nelson Pereira dos Santos; 1978—assistant director to Glauber Rocha; 1980—first feature film,* Gaijin: Road to Freedom; *1989—directed TV miniseries* Kananga du Japão. ***Awards:*** *Gran Premio Coral, Havana International Film Festival, for* Gaijin, *1980.*

Films as Director: 1973: *Bon Odoni* (short). **1978:** *Viva 24 de Maio* (short) (co-d, + co-pr). **1980:** *Gaijin: Caminhos da Liberdade* (*Gaijin: Road to Freedom*) (+ co-sc). **1981:** *Cinéma: Embaixada do Brasil* (*The Cinema's Embassy*) (doc) (+ ed); *Alcool, alternativa para o furturo* (doc). **1983:** *Parahyba Mulher-macho* (*Parahyba, a Macho Woman*) (+ co-sc). **1985:** *Patriamada* (*Beloved Motherland*) (+ sc). **1990:** *Luna de Cristal.* **1997:** *Fica Comigo*; *O noviço Rebelde.*

Other Films: 1973: *O Amuleto de Ogum* (Pereira dos Santos) (asst d). **1977:** *Tenda Dos Milagros* (Pereira dos Santos) (asst d). **1978:** *A Idade de Terra* (Rocha) (asst d).

A Brazilian-born daughter of Japanese immigrants, Tizuka Yamasaki embodies one of Brazil's most complicated identity matrices. Negotiating her own identity means juggling her gender, race, and nationality to arrive at a "Brazilian" balance. Not surprisingly, many of Yamasaki's films deal with gender and racial identity, immigration, the hybridity of Brazilian culture, and democracy. In questioning country, patria, and culture, Yamasaki asks repeatedly, "What is it to be Brazilian?"

Yamasaki was born in Porto Alegre and grew up São Paulo. Her parents lived from the land and tried to make a good life for their children. Both geographically and ideologically, a career in filmmaking seemed out of place in such a context. Yamasaki began, instead, to study architecture. She quickly found that she was drawn to filmmaking and changed academic tracks. There was for Yamasaki a tangible risk in choosing filmmaking in the early seventies in Brazil. As she told Luis Trelles Plazaola in a recent interview, the cinema guaranteed her nothing.

After university, Yamasaki began her career under the tutelage of two of Brazil's most important filmmakers and contributors to its politically oriented Cinema Novo movement of the 1960s. As assistant director to Nelson Pereira dos Santos on two films, Yamasaki was given enough responsibility and trust to be able to explore her own relationship to the camera and to the films' subject. From these experiences she learned to rediscover the familiar, taking note of everyday gestures and recognizing how to integrate them into a poetic film language. With new eyes, she began for the first time to really see her country and understand its complexities. Glauber Rocha taught her the formal nuances of the medium, such as camera position and composition. Under his wing Yamasaki learned the basic tenets of the Cinema Novo and learned to fictionalize reality, to "turn it into cinema."

Yamasaki's approach to filmmaking combines these lessons from Brazil's master filmmakers with her own poetic and feminine instincts. The result, she believes, is that she can think of film as a feeling. An audience can watch the film, absorb the expression and the emotion, and then carry it with them, to think about later.

Yamasaki's first feature film, *Gaijin: Road to Freedom,* won her international acclaim and a Gran Premio Coral at the Second Annual International Festival of New Latin American Cinema in Havana, Cuba. Set at the turn of the century, *Gaijin* presents an intimate portrait of Japanese emigration to Brazil through the story of one family who come to seek their fortune on Brazil's coffee plantations. While her protagonists are Japanese, their story resonates for many other ethnic and national groups who toiled in the plantations at the turn of the century.

Her next feature, *Parahyba, a Macho Woman,* is about Anayde Beiriz, a Brazilian "any-woman," who wishes to be able to express herself and to love freely, defying the patriarchal, prejudiced, and moralistic society in which she lives. Set in 1930, the film sets Anayde's personal revolution within the political friction between conservatives and liberals in the northeast state of Parahyba. Anayde's personal struggle, then, allegorizes the struggle of this state to achieve modernity and autonomy.

In *Beloved Motherland,* Yamasaki looks at contemporary Brazil, combining fiction and documentary in a stunning portrait of Brazil's return to democracy following 20 years of military dictatorship. The film's fictional characters are Goias, a filmmaker documenting the impressive Candelaria demonstration in favor of popular presidential elections, and Lina, a reporter whom Goias has asked to interview celebrities in the crowd. Reportedly, the actress playing Lina, Debora Bloch, got so involved in her role that she pushed real reporters out of the way in order to "get her story." *Beloved Motherland* was made without a written script—the actors and director collaborated on writing scenes responding to daily events. In the end, this process allowed *Beloved Motherland* to reflect both the exhilaration and the ambiguity Brazilians experienced in this crucial moment.

Despite the critical success of her films, Yamasaki has not had many production options for further feature films. This is due, in large part, to the difficulties the Brazilian film industry suffered in the 1980s. During this time Yamasaki turned to television soap operas and even directed a stage production of the opera *Madame Butterfly* in Bello Horizonte. She has directed several projects for Embrafilme and a miniseries, *Kananga du Japão.*—ILENE S. GOLDMAN

Zetterling, Mai (Elisabeth)

Swedish director and actress

Born *Västerås, 24 May 1925.* ***Education*** *Attended Ordtuery Theatre School, 1941; Royal Dramatic Theatre School, Stockholm, 1942-45.* ***Family*** *Married 1) the ballet dancer Tutte Lemkow (divorced), two sons: Etienne and Louis; 2) the writer David Hughes (divorced).* ***Career*** *1941—stage debut and film debut; 1942-44—in repertory with the Royal Dramatic Theatre, Stockholm; 1960—turned director with the BBC documentary* The Polite Invasion; *1960s—began collaborating on television documentaries with husband Hughes; 1990—directed episode of* Mistress of Suspense *for television.* ***Awards*** *Golden Lion, Venice Festival, for* The War Game, *1961.* ***Died*** *Of cancer, in London, 15 March 1994.*

Films as Director: 1960: *The Polite Invasion* (short, for TV). **1961:** *Lords of Little Egypt* (short, for TV); *The War Game* (short) (+ pr). **1962:** *The Prosperity Race* (short, for TV). **1963:** *The Do-It-Yourself Democracy* (short, for TV). **1964:** *Älskande par* (*Loving Couples*) (+ co-sc). **1966:** *Nattlek* (*Night Games*). **1967:** *Doktor Glas* (co-d with D. Hughes). **1968:** *Flickorna* (*The Girls*) (+ co-sc). **1971:** *Vincent the Dutchman* (co-d with D. Hughes, + pr—doc for TV). **1973:** "The Strongest" ep. of *Visions of Eight* (co-d with D. Hughes). **1976:** *We har manje namn* (*We Have Many Names*) (+ ro, sc, ed). **1977:** *Stockholm* (for TV) (+ ro). **1978:** *The Rain's Hat* (for TV) (+ ed). **1980:** *Of Seals and Men* (co-d). **1982:** *Love* (co-d, + co-sc—for TV). **1983:** *Scrubbers* (+ co-sc). **1986:** *Amorosa* (+ sc, co-ed). **1990:** *Sunday Pursuit*; *The Stuff of Madness* (for TV).

Other Films: 1941: *Lasse-Maja* (Olsson) (ro). **1943:** *Jag drapte* (Molander) (ro). **1944:** *Hets* (*Torment*; *Frenzy*) (Sjöberg) (ro as Bertha Olsson); *Prins Gustaf* (Bauman) (ro). **1946:** *Iris och Lojtnantshjarta* (*Iris and the Lieutenant*) (Sjöberg) (ro as Iris); *Driver dagg faller Regn* (*Sunshine Follows Rain*) (ro). **1947:** *Frieda* (Dearden) (title role). **1948:** *Musik i moerker* (*Music in Darkness*; *Night Is My Future*) (I. Bergman) (ro as Ingrid); *Nu borjar livet* (Molander) (ro); *The Bad Lord Byron* (Macdonald) (ro as Teresa Guiccioli); *Portrait from Life* (*The Girl in the Painting*) (Fisher) (ro as Hildegarde). **1949:** "The Facts of Life" ep. of *Quartet* (Smart and others) (ro as Jeanne); *The Romantic Age* (*Naughty Arlette*) (Gréville) (ro as Arlette). **1950:** *Blackmailed* (Marc Allégret) (ro as Carol Edwards); *The Lost People* (Knowles and Box) (ro as Lili). **1951:** *Hell Is Sold Out* (M. Anderson) (ro as Valerie Martin). **1952:** *The Tall Headlines* (*The Frightened Bride*) (T. Young) (ro as Doris Richardson); *The Ringer* (*The Gaunt Stranger*) (Hamilton) (ro as Lisa). **1953:** *Desperate Moment* (Bennett) (ro as Anna de Burgh). **1954:** *Dance Little Lady* (Guest) (ro as Nina Gordon); *Knock on Wood* (Frank and Panama) (ro as Ilse Nordstrom). **1955:** *A Prize of Gold* (Robson) (ro as Maria). **1956:** "Ett dockhem" ("A Doll's House") ep. of *Giftas* (Henriksson) (ro). **1957:** *Abandon Ship!* (*Seven Waves Away*) (Sale) (ro as Julie). **1958:** *The Truth about Women* (Box) (ro as Julie); *Lek pa regnbagen* (Kjellgren) (ro). **1959:** *Jet Storm* (Endfield) (ro as Carol Tilley). **1960:** *Faces in the Dark* (Eady) (ro as Christiane Hammond); *Piccadilly Third Stop* (Rilla) (ro as Christine Pready). **1961:** *Offbeat* (Owen) (ro as Ruth Lombard). **1962:** *The Man Who Finally Died* (Lawrence) (ro as Lisa); *Only Two Can Play* (Gilliat) (ro as Elizabeth Gruffydd Williams); *The Main Attraction* (Petrie) (ro as Gina). **1963:** *The Bay of St. Michel* (Ainsworth) (ro as Helene Bretton). **1965:** *The Vine Bridge* (Nykvist) (ro). **1988:** *Calling the Shots* (Cole—doc) (appearance). **1990:** *The Witches* (Roeg) (ro as Helga); *Hidden Agenda* (Loach) (ro as Moa). **1993:** *Morfars Resa* (*Grandfather's Journey*) (Staffan Lamm) (ro as Elin Fromm).

Mai Zetterling's career as a filmmaker stemmed from her disillusionment with acting. Trained at Stockholm's Royal Dramatic Theatre, Zetterling debuted on stage and screen in 1941. She considered the film *Torment* her best acting achievement. She worked in British theater, enacting roles in Chekhov, Anouilh, and Ibsen plays, and in British films. After one part in a

Hollywood film, *Knock on Wood* with Danny Kaye, she spurned contract offers and returned home.

With her husband, David Hughes, she made several documentaries in the 1960s dealing with political issues. Zetterling's feature films depict the social status and psyche of women, reflecting her feminist concerns. The uncompromising honesty of perception and technical virtuosity in her films correspond to the pervasive and dominant themes of loneliness and obsession. Zetterling says: "I want very strongly to do things I believe in. I can't do jobs for the money. I just can't do it."

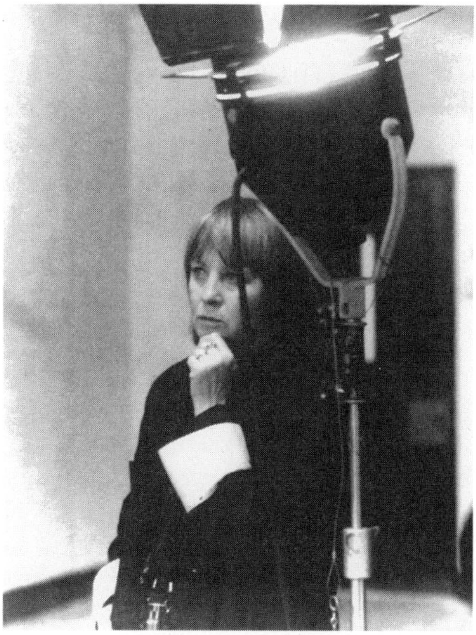

Mai Zetterling on the set of *Scrubbers*.

In 1960 Roger Moorfoot of the BBC financed her idea for a film on the immigration of Swedes to Lapland, *The Polite Invasion*. Three more followed: *Lords of Little Egypt* depicted the gypsies at Saintes-Maries-de-la-Mer; her view of Swedish affluence in *The Prosperity Race* was not appreciated in Stockholm; and *The Do-It-Yourself Democracy* commented on Icelandic society and government. Her first independent effort was the fifteen-minute antiwar film *The War Game,* in which two boys tussle for possession of a toy gun.

Zetterling's first feature film, *Loving Couples,* was based on the fifth volume of Swedish author Agnes von Krusenstjerna's seven-volume novel, *The Misses von Pahlen*. Zetterling wrote the script in one year, with sketches of each shot to indicate camera positions. In it, three expectant mothers in a Stockholm hospital recall their lives in the moment of, and then beyond, the births of their babies. Critic Derek Elley suggests that Zetterling developed her theories and themes of film in *Loving Couples* and rarely deviated from them in later works. She employed elaborate timelines as well as flashbacks, which she used often and well, intertwining them one within another. Her films peak emotionally in scenes of parties and social gatherings. Her films are cohesive compositions, with a literary base, filmed in the stark contrasts of black to white, with a range of grays intervening. Zetterling's scenes of sexual behavior are integral to her themes of loneliness and obsession. *Loving Couples* exemplifies these characteristics.

Night Games, derived from Zetterling's novel with the same title, was banned from the Venice Film Festival. The critics who saw it were angered by the Marxist and Freudian elements in it; shocked by scenes of vomiting, masturbation, and childbirth. Based on Hjalmar Soderberg's 1905 novel, her next film, *Doktor Glas,* records the haunted love of a young physician for a pastor's wife. Even though the wife does not respond to the physician's erotic overtures, he administers a lethal drug to the pastor. It is Zetterling's grimmest study of loneliness, as Derek Elley observes, and her most pessimistic film, told in one extended flashback, "a far cry from *Night Games*."

She returned to a strongly feminist story in *Flickorna* and, as in *Loving Couples,* it contains three female roles of equal weight. In *Flickorna* three actresses perform *Lysistrata* on tour, acting out the views of the play in their private lives. Some critics reacted negatively, finding it self-indulgent, a mix of Greek comedy and soap opera, with heavy symbolism and confusing time structures. Other critics liked the various forms of humor effectively employed, and the arresting imagery.

In 1971 Zetterling filmed a documentary in color about Vincent Van Gogh. Titled *Vincent the Dutchman,* it was shown on American and British television. David Wolper then asked her to film any phase of the 1972 Olympics she chose; she filmed the weight-lifting sequence, "The Strongest," for *Visions of Eight*.

In the 1970s Zetterling published three novels, pursuing creative directions other than filmmaking. She also continued making documentaries (one on tennis champion Stan Smith, one dealing with Stockholm, another on marriage customs), along with a seven-hour adaptation for French television of Simone de Beauvoir's *The Second Sex.* Zetterling asserted that whatever she filmed, it would be "something I believe in."—LOUISE HECK-RABI

Zhang Nuanxin

Chinese director and writer

Born *Hohhot, Inner Mongolia, October 1940; her father was a doctor who immersed himself in Chinese literature and art.* ***Education*** *Studied directing at the Beijing Film Academy, 1958-62.* ***Family*** *Married the Beijing writer/critic Li Tuo.* ***Career*** *After graduation, stayed on to teach in the directing department of the Beijing Film Academy, where she helped train members of China's "Fifth Generation" filmmakers; assigned to the Beijing Film Academy's Youth Film Studio as director; in her early career, she assisted prominent directors Sang Hu and Xie Jin, before progressing to directing her own films; 1985—invited to Paris for a year-long stay as a visiting researcher; upon her return, she served as primary consultant to the Sino-French production of* Tears of Huajiao. ***Awards*** *PRC Special Prize, for* Sha'ou's Seagull, *1981; PRC Best Picture, and Hong Kong Best Chinese Language Film, for* Good Morning, Beijing, *1991.* ***Died*** *In Beijing, of cancer, 28 May 1995.*

Films as Director and Co-Writer: 1981: *Sha Ou* (*Sha'ou's Seagull*; *The Seagull*; *The Drive to Win*). **1985:** *Qingchunji* (*Sacrificed Youth*).

Films as Director: 1991: *Beijing Nin Zao* (*Good Morning, Beijing*). **1994:** *Yunnan Qiu Shi* (*The Story of Yunnan*).

Other Films: 1979: *Li Siguang* (Ling Zingfeng) (co-sc). **c. 1986:** *Huajiao Lei* (*Tears of Huajiao*) (consultant).

Zhang Nuanxin declared that Chinese cinema at the end of the Great Proletariat Cultural Revolution (1966-76) was 20 years behind world filmmaking. Influenced first by the Italian neorealists and then by the French new wave, she and husband Li Tuo co-wrote the controversial essay "On the Modernization of the Language of Film" in 1979, in which she argued against the prevailing focus on content over form.

Zhang Nuanxin: *Qingchunji*

Although the ideas in the article were initially widely criticized, as she began to put them into practice in directing her films, critics began to concede that her approach was both fresh and palatable. It featured the director as auteur, utilizing cinematic realism as a tool to achieve a lyrical effect. The feature film, she urged, should retreat from its over reliance on theatricality and spectacle, and need not always revolve, as it usually does, around a core conflict and its resolution.

Zhang held that cinema could be better if it were closer to real life, but at the same time she sought to go beyond merely capturing an external reality on screen—her goal was to express her subjectivity by capturing dominant features of her own inner landscape in her work. The form of the film, she felt, could and should be used to express the filmmaker's deepest feelings and emotions.—CYNTHIA Y. NING

notes on contributors

Baron, Cynthia Visiting assistant professor, Washington University, St. Louis. Contributor to anthologies such as *Screen Acting*; and to journals such as *Film and Philosophy,* and *Spectator.* **Essays:** Hammer; Palcy; Ullmann.

Barr, Charles Lecturer in film, University of East Anglia, Norwich, England. Author of *Ealing Studios,* 1977. **Essay:** B. Box.

Bartoni, Doreen Artist-in-residence, Columbia College, Chicago, 1986-87. **Essay:** Loos.

Basinger, Jeanine Corwin-Fuller Professor of Film Studies, Wesleyan University, Middletown, Connecticut; also chair, film studies program, and curator/founder, Wesleyan Cinema Archives. Trustee, American Film Institute; steering committee, National Center for Film and Video Preservation; and formerly on the board of advisers of the AIVF. Author of *Anthony Mann,* 1979; *The World War II Combat Film: Anatomy of a Genre,* 1986; *The "It's a Wonderful Life" Book,* 1986; *A Woman's View: How Hollywood Spoke to Women, 1930-1960,* 1993; and *American Cinema: 100 Years of Filmmaking,* 1994, and numerous articles. **Essays:** Harrison; Levien.

Berg, Charles Ramírez Instructor in film, University of Texas, Austin. Author of *Cinema of Solitude: A Critical Study of Mexican Film, 1967-1983,* 1992. **Essay:** Perry.

Bowers, Ronald Financial editor, E. F. Hutton and Company. Editor, *Films in Review,* 1979-81. Author of *The Selznick Players,* 1976. Co-author (with James Robert Parrish) of *The MGM Stock Company,* 1973. **Essay:** Lennart.

Brophy, Stephen Film critic for *L. A. Times, Washington Post,* and others. Co-author (with Peter Harry Brown) of *Howard Hughes: The Untold Story,* 1996. **Essay:** Bute.

Clark, Virginia M. Assistant professor, English and film, Frostburg State College, Maryland. Film archivist, Library of Congress, 1985, and researcher/cataloger, American Film Institute Catalog of Feature Films, 1985-86. Author of *Aldous Huxley and Film,* 1987. Editor of *What Women Wrote: Scenarios 1912-1929,* 1987. **Essays:** Meredyth; Murfin.

Cook, Samantha Freelance editor, researcher, and writer, London. Editor of *1989 Women's Film List*; and contributor to *Neglected Audiences,* 1990. Compiler of *Women and Film Bibliography,* 1992. **Essay:** Bemberg.

Deane, Pamala S. Independent writer, Maryland; instructor of writing for media; producer-writer of educational television programming; screenwriter, author. **Essays:** Larkin; Van Upp.

Delorey, Denise Writer and educator. Instructor, history of narrative film, Massachusetts Institute of Technology, 1989 and 1991, and American literature, Emerson College, 1994-95. Author of "Parsing the Female Sentence: The Paradox of Containment in Virginia Woolf's Narratives," in *Ambiguous Discourse: Feminist Narratology and British Women Writers,* 1996. **Essay:** Sharaff.

Derry, Charles Head of Motion Picture Studies, Wright State University, Dayton, Ohio, since 1978. Author of *Dark Dreams: A Psychological History of the Horror Film,* 1977; and *The Suspense Thriller: Films in the Shadow of Alfred Hitchcock,* 1988; co-author (with Jack Ellis and Sharon Kern) of *The Film Book Bibliography: 1940-1975,* 1979. Writer/director of *Cerebral Accident,* 1986, and *Joan Crawford Died for Your Sins,* 1987; fiction published in *Reclaiming the Heartland: Gay & Lesbian Voices from the Midwest,* 1996. **Essay:** J. Allen.

DiBattista, Maria Professor of English and comparative literature, Princeton University. Author of *First Love: The Affectations of Modern Fiction,* 1991. Co-editor (with Lucy McDiarmid) *High and Low Moderns: Literature and Culture, 1889-1939,* 1996. **Essay:** Savoca.

Dixon, Wheeler Winston Professor, Film Studies Program, University of Nebraska at Lincoln. Filmmaker. Author of *The "B" Directors: A Biographical Directory,* 1985; *The Cinematic Vision of F. Scott Fitzgerald,* 1986; *The Charm of Evil: The Life and Films of Terence Fisher,* 1991; *The Films of Freddie Francis,* 1991; *The Early Film Criticism of François Truffaut,* 1992; *The Films of Reginald LeBorg,* 1992; *Reviewing British Cinema, 1900-1992,* 1994; *It Looks at You,* 1995; *The Films of Jean-Luc Godard,* 1997; *The Exploding Eye,* 1997; and *The Transparency of Spectacle,* 1998. Contributor to *Films in Review, Velvet Light Trap, Literature/Film Quarterly,* and *Post Script.* **Essay:** Von Harbou.

Dunbar, Robert Freelance film critic and historian; held various visiting professorships and lectureships, from 1975. Worked for Gainsborough and Gaumont-British Studios, 1933-38, 1948-49; director of public and cultural relations, British Embassy, Moscow, 1944-47; general manager, Imperadio Pictures, 1949-51; independent producer of feature films and documentaries, 1952-63; chairman, London School of Film Technique, 1963-74. Died 1988. **Essay:** Shub.

Edelman, Rob Author of *Great Baseball Films,* 1994; and *Baseball on the Web,* 1998; co-author of *Angela Lansbury: A Life on Stage and Screen,* 1996; *The John Travolta Scrapbook,* 1997; and *Meet the Mertzes,* forthcoming. Contributing editor of *Leonard Maltin's Movie and Video Guide* and *Leonard Maltin's Movie Encyclopedia.* Director of programming of Home Film Festival. Contributor to *International Dictionary of Films and Filmmakers, The Political Companion to American Film, Total Baseball, The Total Baseball Catalog, International Film Guide,* and *The Whole Film Sourcebook.* Film critic/columnist, *New Haven Register* and *Gazette Newspapers.* Film critic/commentator, WAMC (Northeast) Public Radio. Former adjunct instructor, The School of Visual Arts, Iona College, Sacred Heart University. **Essays:** Amaral; Anders; Armstrong; Audry; Beth B; Batchelor; Bauchens; Bemberg; Bird; Breien; Campion; Choy; Dörrie; Elek; Godmilow; Gordon; Hänsel; Harris; Holland; Hui; Huillet; Jhabvala; Keaton; Kidron; Livingston; Maclean; Marshall; Mayron; Mehta; Pascal; Poirier; Riefenstahl; Sagan; Schiller; Seidelman; Shepitko; Silver; Solntseva; Spheeris; Thomas; Toye; Treut; Trintignant; Vachon; Varda; Von Trotta; Wertmüller; Winfrey.

Edmunds, Jean Freelance writer. Contributor to encyclopedias. **Essay:** Parmar.

Elsner-Sommer, Gretchen Film critic and director of Foreign Images distribution company. Formerly associate editor of *Jump Cut.* **Essay:** von Trotta.

Faller, Greg S. Associate professor of film, Towson State University, Baltimore, since 1986. Taught at Northwestern University, 1984-86. Assistant/associate editor of *International Dictionary of Films and Filmmakers,* first edition, vols. 3, 4, and 5; and of *Journal of Film and Video,* 1985-87. Editor of *Film Reader 6,* 1985. **Essays:** D. Allen; Guillemot; Schoonmaker.

Falsetto, Mario Associate professor, Cinema Department, Concordia University, Montreal. Author of *Stanley Kubrick: A Narrative and Stylistic Analysis,* 1994. Editor of *Perspectives on Stanley Kubrick,* 1996. **Essays:** Child; Friedrich; Greenwald; Menken; Schneemann.

Felando, Cynthia Film and television instructor and freelance writer; coordinator for the Los Angeles International Women's Film Festival. **Essays:** Angelou; Apon; Borden; Cantrill; Cavani; Chopra; Citron; Cole and Dale; Coolidge; Dash; Deitch; Denis; Epstein; Export; Gish; Glyn; Gorris; Heckerling; Hein; Kaplan; Law; Lupino; Lyell; McDonagh sisters; Musidora; Nair; Notari; Pickford; Pool; Trinh; Weill; West.

Felperin, Leslie Contributor to *Sight and Sound*. **Essay:** Armstrong.

Ferrara, Patricia Member of the faculty, Georgia State University, Atlanta. Contributor to *New Orleans Review*. **Essay:** Reville.

Ferrari, Lilie Writer and researcher, London. **Essay:** Arzner.

Flynn, Peter Freelance writer. **Essay:** Spencer.

Foreman, Alexa L. Account executive, Video Duplications, Atlanta. Formerly theater manager, American Film Institute. Author of *Women in Motion*, 1983. **Essays:** Brackett; Macpherson.

Foster, Gwendolyn Audrey Assistant professor, University of Nebraska, Lincoln. Author of *Women Film Directors: An International Bio-Critical Dictionary*, 1995; and *Women Filmmakers of the African and Asian Diaspora*, 1997. Filmmaker, *The Women Who Made the Movies*, 1992. **Essay:** Foreword.

Gateward, Frances K. Film scholar and independent film and video maker. Has taught at Indiana University, University of Illinois, Urbana-Champaign, and Howard University. Contributor to *Angles, The Paper Channel*, and *The Television Encyclopedia*. **Essays:** Chenzira; Davis; Faye.

Glaessner, Verina Freelance critic and lecturer, London. Contributor to *Economist, Guardian, Monthly Film Bulletin, Sight and Sound*, and *Focus on Film*. **Essays:** Cecchi d'Amico; Chytilová; Potter.

Goldman, Ilene S. Film studies instructor, Chicago. Contributor to *Jump Cut, Independent*, and *Studies in Latin American Popular Culture*. **Essays:** Abreu; Carolina; Fernández Violante; Mallet; Meerapfel; Novaro; Sarmiento; Yamasaki.

Gomery, Douglas Professor, College of Journalism, University of Maryland. Author of nine books, including *The Hollywood Studio System*, 1986; and *Shared Pleasures*, 1992. Co-editor of *The Future of News*, 1992. Contributor of numerous articles to periodicals including *Village Voice, American Journalism Review*, and *Screen*. **Essays:** Booth; Fields.

Heck-Rabi, Louise Teacher and freelance writer. Author of *Women Filmmakers: A Critical Reception*, 1984. Died 1995. **Essays:** Akins; Deren; Guy; Mészáros; Riefenstahl; Varda; Zetterling.

Hoffman, Judy Acting director of Documentary Film Center, Columbia College. Co-founder of Kartemquin Films and contributor to most of their film productions, including as associate producer of *Golub*. Active in Alternative Media movement of the 1970s; became one of the first women to work professionally as a film technician in Chicago, apprenticing with IATSE Camera Local 666. Camera assistant on numerous independent documentary films, including *Family Business; Seeing Red; American Dream;* and *Daley: The Last Boss*. Researcher for PBS series *On the Waterways*. Associate producer of film *Box of Treasures*. Video instructor and media consultant for Kwakiut'l Indians for ten years. Director and editor of museum video on Kwakiut'l salmon fishing for Chicago's Shedd Aquarium. Teacher of video with Community Television Network. Producer and editor of student production *Time to Make That Change*. Recipient of VOICE Award from Chicago's Center for Community and Media, 1994. **Essay:** Kopple.

Holmlund, Chris Associate professor of French, film, and women's studies, University of Tennessee, Knoxville. Co-editor (with Cynthia Fuchs) of *Between the Sheets, in the Streets: Queer, Lesbian, and Gay Documentary*, 1997. Contributor to *Screening the Male, Retakes on Remakes, Discourse of the Other, Feminism and Documentary, Camera Obscura, Cinema Journal, Discourse, Jump Cut, New Formations, Screen*, and *Social Text*. **Essay:** Nelson.

Johnson, Mark Freelance writer. Author of *The Swedish Sexpot Stereotype Anita Ekberg and the American Fifties*, 1993. Associate editor of the *Velvet Light Trap*, 1989-91. **Essay:** J. Allen.

Kemp, Philip Freelance writer and film historian. Author of *Lethal Innocence: The Cinema of Alexander Mackendrick*, 1991. Reviewer for *Sight and Sound*. Contributor to periodicals, including *Variety, Film Comment, Metro* (Melbourne), *Liber* (Paris), and *Kino* (Seoul). **Essays:** Bigelow; Craigie; Tanaka.

Knight, Judson Freelance writer, Atlanta. Ghost writer or co-writer for a number of prominent clients; researcher; editorial consultant for the Knight Agency, a firm specializing in literary representation and marketing. **Essays:** Hubley; Murphy.

Knobloch, Susan Doctoral candidate in film and television critical studies, University of California, Los Angeles. Contributor to several anthologies, including *Feminism and Documentary,* edited by Diane Waldman and Janet Walker. **Essays:** Ephron; Ono; Streisand.

Kosta, Barbara Assistant professor, University of Arizona, since 1989. Author of *Recasting Autobiography: Women's Counterfictions in Contemporary German Literature and Film,* 1994. Contributor to *Gender and German Cinema, Signs,* and *German Studies Review.* **Essay:** Sander.

Kupferberg, Audrey E. Film historian, appraiser, and archivist. Co-author of *Angela Lansbury: A Life on Stage and Screen,* 1996; *The John Travolta Scrapbook,* 1997; and *Meet the Mertzes,* forthcoming. Contributor to *International Dictionary of Films and Filmmakers.* Film consultant to the Peary-MacMillan Arctic Museum at Bowdoin College. Former director, Yale University Film Study Center. Former assistant director, the National Center for Film and Video Preservation at the American Film Institute. Former instructor, University of Bridgeport. **Essays:** Bauchens; Comden; Madison; Sanders-Brahms; Shipman.

Lee, Edith C. Staff member, Synthesis Concepts, Chicago. Editor, *META Magazine.* Worked in video division, Columbia Pictures, 1981-82. **Essays:** Dillon; Rose; Sharaff.

Lippe, Richard Lecturer in film at Atkinson College, York University, Ontario. On the editorial board of *CineAction!* **Essay:** Silver.

López, Ana M. Associate professor, Department of Communications, Tulane University, New Orleans. Co-editor of *Mediating Two Worlds: Cinematic Encounters in the Americas* (with John King and Manuel Alvarado), 1993; and *The Ethnic Eye: Latino Media Arts* (with Chon A. Noriega), 1996. **Essay:** Landeta.

Lorenz, Janet Associate editor and film critic *Z Channel Magazine,* since 1984. Assistant supervisor, University of Southern California Cinema Research Library, Los Angeles, 1979-82, and film critic, *SelecTV Magazine,* 1980-84. **Essay:** Jhabvala.

Lupo, Jon Freelance writer. Film editor and critic, *Massachusetts Daily Collegian,* 1991-96. Editor and publisher, *Cinefile cinema journal,* since 1995. **Essay:** Van Dongen.

Manvell, Roger Formerly professor of film, Boston University. Director, British Film Academy, London, 1947-59, and governor and head of Department of Film History, London Film School, until 1974; Bingham Professor of the Humanities, University of Louisville, 1973. Editor, *Penguin Film Review,* 1946-49, and the *Pelican Annual Cinema,* 1950-52; associate editor, *New Humanist,* 1968-75, and director, Rationalist Press, London, from 1966; editor-in-chief, *International Encyclopaedia of Film,* 1972. Author of *Film,* 1944; *The Animated Film,* 1954; *The Film and the Public,* 1955; *On the Air,* 1955; *The Technique of Film Music,* 1957, 1976; *The Living Screen,* 1961; *What Is a Film?,* 1965; *New Cinema in the U.S.A.,* 1968; *New Cinema in Britain,* 1969; *Art in Movement,* 1970; *Shakespeare and the Film,* 1971; *Films and the Second World War,* 1975; *Love Goddesses of the Movies,* 1975; *Theatre and Film,* 1979; *Art and Animation: Halas and Batchelor, 1940-1980,* 1980; and *Ingmar Bergman,* 1980; co-author of *The Technique of Film Animation* (with John Halas), 1959; *Design in Motion* (with John Halas), 1962; *The German Cinema* (with Heinrich Fraenkel), 1971; and *Images of Madness: The Portrayal of Insanity in the Feature Film* (with Michael Fleming), 1985; also author of novels, biographies of theatrical personalities and of personalities of the Third Reich. Died 1987. **Essay:** Mathis.

McCaffrey, Donald W. Emeritus professor of English, University of North Dakota. Author of *Four Great Comedians: Chaplin, Lloyd, Keaton, and Langdon,* 1968; *The Golden Age of Sound Comedy: Comic Films and Comedians of the Thirties,* 1973; *Three Classic Silent Film Comedies Starring Harold Lloyd,* 1976; and *Assault on Society: Satirical Literature to Film,* 1992. Editor of *Focus on Chaplin,* 1971. **Essay:** Goodrich.

McCarty, John Author and freelance writer. Assistant editor of *Mystery Scene.* Author of *Splatter Movies,* 1984; *The Films of John Huston,* 1987; *The Modern Horror Film,* 1990; *Hollywood Gangland,* 1993; *Movie Psychos and Madmen,* 1993; *The Fearmakers,* 1994; *The Sleaze Merchants,* 1995; *The Films of Mel*

Gibson, 1997, and other books on film and television history. **Essay:** Reville.

Merz, Caroline Freelance journalist and television researcher, Norwich, England. **Essay:** M. Box.

Milicia, Joseph Professor of English, University of Wisconsin, Sheboygan Center. Contributor to *Multicultural Review, New York Review of Science Fiction, Contemporary Literature,* and others. Author of articles on science-fiction films for Gregg Press. **Essays:** Kurys; Serreau.

Mitchell, John E. Humor writer/comic book writer, and publisher. Author of *Very Vicky* comic books, 1993-95; *That Skinny Bastard: Frank Sinatra,* 1995; *Calling All Hillbillies* comic books, 1995; and *Very Vicky Junior Hepcat Funbook,* 1996. **Essay:** Irene.

Monty, Ib Director of Det Danske Filmmuseum, Copenhagen, since 1960. Literary and film critic for the newspaper *Morgenavisen Jyllands-Posten,* since 1958. Editor-in-chief of the film periodical *Kosmorama,* 1960-67. Author of *Leonardo da Vinci,* 1953. Co-editor (with Morten Piil) of *Se-det-er film I-iii* (anthology of articles on film), 1964-66; editor of *TV Broadcasts on Films and Filmmakers,* 1972. **Essay:** Henning-Jensen.

Morrison, James Assistant professor, English Department, North Carolina State University, Raleigh. Contributor to *New Orleans Review, Centennial Review,* and *Film Criticism.* **Essay:** Russell.

Mraz, John Researcher, Center for the Study of Contemporary History, University of Puebla, Mexico, since 1984. Distinguished visiting professor, Mexican-American studies, San Diego State University, 1991; visiting professor, art and Latin American studies, University of Connecticut, 1990, and history, University of California, Santa Cruz, 1988. Coordinator of Graphic History, Center for the Historical Study of the Mexican Labor Movement, 1981-83. Contributor to *Jump Cut.* **Essay:** Gómez.

Ning, Cynthia Associate director, Center for Chinese Studies, University of Hawaii. Instructor on Chinese cinema, literature, and language. Consultant to the Hawaii International Film Festival. Author of *Communicating in Chinese* (3 vols.), 1993, 1994. **Essay:** Zhang.

Palmer, R. Barton Chair and professor of English, Clemson University; formerly professor of English, Georgia State University. Author of *Hollywood's Dark Cinema: The American Film Noir,* 1994; and *Perspectives on Film Noir,* 1996. Editor of *Studies in the Literary Imagination.* **Essay:** Foster.

Pardi, Robert Staff writer for *The Motion Picture Guide.* Managing editor/chief reviewer of *Movies on TV* for six editions. Author of *Cable and TV*; co-author of *Movie Blockbusters*; and *The Complete Guide to Videocassette Movies.* Contributor to *International Dictionary of Films and Filmmakers.* Contributor to *Baseline, Delphi Internet, Billboard, Cinemax, Film Journal, Video Business,* and *Cineaste.* **Essay:** May.

Prichard, Susan Perez Freelance writer. Author of *Film Costume: An Annotated Bibliography,* 1981. **Essay:** Jeakins.

Provencher, Ken Arts and entertainment staff writer and editor, *Lowell Connector,* 1991-94. **Essay:** von Brandenstein.

Rabinovitz, Lauren Associate professor of American studies and communication studies, University of Iowa, since 1986. Author of *Points of Resistance: Women, Power and Politics in the New York Avant-Garde Cinema, 1943-71,* 1991; and *For the Love of Pleasure: Women, Movies, and Culture in Turn-of-the Century Chicago,* 1998; co-author (with Greg Easley) of *The Rebecca Project,* 1995. Co-editor (with Susan Jeffords) of *Seeing through the Media: The Persian Gulf War,* 1994. **Essays:** Clarke; Wieland.

Reynaud, Bérénice Member of staff of permanent faculty, California Institute of Arts. U.S. correspondent for *Cahiers du Cinéma.* Co-editor of *Vingt ans de theories feministes sur le cinéma,* 1993. Contributor to *Sight and Sound, Film Comment, Cinemaya,* and *Afterimage.* **Essays:** Bani-Etemad; Maldoror; Peng.

Richards, Allen Grant Freelance writer. **Essay:** Littleton.

Robson, Arthur G. Professor and chairman, Department of Classics, and professor of comparative literature, Beloit College, Wisconsin, since 1966. Author of *Euripides' Electra: An Interpretive Commentary.* Editor of *Latin: Our Living Heritage, Book III,* 1964. **Essay:** Leaf.

Salamie, David E. Contributing editor, *Women Filmmakers & Their Films.* Contributing editor and contributor, third edition of *Interna-*

tional Dictionary of Films and Filmmakers: Actors and Actresses. Freelance writer and editor. Co-owner of InfoWorks Development Group, a reference publication development and editorial services company. **Essays:** Chronology of Women Filmmakers; Ahrne; Miró; Muratova; Obomsawin; Preobrazhenskaya.

Schiff, Lillian Freelance film critic and consultant, New York. Author of *Getting Started in Filmmaking,* 1978. **Essay:** Akerman.

Skvorecký, Josef Professor of English and film, University of Toronto, Canada, since 1969. Author of *All the Bright Young Men and Women: A Personal History of the Czech Cinema,* 1972; and *Jiri Menzel and the History of Closely Watched Trains,* 1982. Works as novelist include *Miss Silver's Past,* 1975; *The Bass Saxophone,* 1977; *The Engineer of Human Souls,* 1984; and *The Miracle Game,* 1990. **Essay:** Chytilová.

Slide, Anthony Author and editor of more than 50 books on the history of popular entertainment, including *The Films of D. W. Griffith,* 1975; *The American Film Industry: A Historical Dictionary,* 1986; *Nitrate Won't Wait: A History of Film Preservation in the United States,* 1992; *The Encyclopedia of Vaudeville,* 1994; and *Paramount in Paris,* 1998. Also editor of the Scarecrow Press "Filmmakers Series," and a documentary filmmaker. **Essay:** Weber.

Starr, Cecile Freelance writer, lecturer, and filmmaker. Film reviewer (16mm) for *Saturday Review, New York,* 1949-59. Author of *Ideas on Film,* 1951; and *Discovering the Movies,* 1977; co-author (with Robert Russett) of *Experimental Animation,* 1976, 1988. Director of the Women's Independent Film Exchange, since 1977. **Essays:** De Hirsch; Dulac; Grayson; Marion; Parker; Reiniger.

Szymczak, Jerome Researcher and writer, Alameda, California. **Essays:** Alberti; Haines; Littman; Steel.

Tomlinson, Doug Associate professor of film studies, Montclair State College, New Jersey. Principal researcher for *Voices of Film Experience,* edited by Jay Leyda, 1977; editor of *Actors on Acting for the Screen,* 1994. Died 1992. **Essay:** Van Runkle.

Unterburger, Amy L. Editor, *Women Filmmakers & Their Films.* Editor, third edition of *International Dictionary of Films and Filmmakers: Actors and Actresses.* Co-owner of InfoWorks Development Group, a reference publication development and editorial services company.

Urgošíková, Blažena Film historian. Head of Department of Film History and Cataloguing, Národní filmovyarchiv Praha. Author of *A Famous Era of the Swedish Cinema,* 1969; *Rudolph Valentino,* 1970; *History of Science Fiction Films,* 1973, 1982; *Remakes,* 1977; and *Czech Fiction Films,* 1995. **Essays:** Jakubowska; Krumbachová; Simková-Plívová.

Valentine, Fiona Member of faculty, School of Speech, Northwestern University, Evanston, Illinois. **Essay:** Head.

White, M. B. Assistant professor, Department of Radio-TV-Film, Northwestern University, Evanston, Illinois, since 1982. Contributor to *Enclitic, Purdue Film Studies Annual,* and other periodicals. **Essay:** Duras.

Wolff, Jessica Freelance researcher, writer, and editor. **Essay:** Rainer.

Yeck, Joanne L. Lecturer on humanities and film, Art Center College of Design, Pasadena. Coauthor (with Tom McGreevey) of *Movie Westerns,* 1994; and *Our Movie Heritage,* 1997. **Essay:** Coffee.

Zants, Emily Professor of French, University of Hawaii. Author of *Creative Encounters with French Films,* 1993; and *Chaos Theory, Complexity, Cinema, and the Evolution of the French Novel,* 1996. **Essay:** Colette.

Zucker, Carole Associate professor, Department of Cinema, Concordia University, Montreal. Author of *The Idea of Image: Josef von Sternberg's Dietrich Films,* 1988; and *Figures of Light: Actors and Directors Illuminate the Art of Film Acting,* 1995. Editor of *Making Visible the Invisible: An Anthology of Original Essays on Film Acting,* 1990. **Essays:** Brückner; Ottinger.

nationality index

American
Zoë Akins
Dede Allen
Jay Presson Allen
Allison Anders
Maya Angelou
Dorothy Arzner
Beth B
Anne Bauchens
Kathryn Bigelow
Margaret Booth
Lizzie Borden
Leigh Brackett
Mary Ellen Bute
Ayoka Chenzira
Abigail Child
Joyce Chopra
Christine Choy
Michelle Citron
Shirley Clarke
Lenore J. Coffee
Betty Comden
Martha Coolidge
Julie Dash
Zeinabu irene Davis
Storm De Hirsch
Donna Deitch
Maya Deren
Nora Ephron
Verna Fields
Jodie Foster
Su Friedrich
Lillian Gish
Jill Godmilow
Frances Goodrich
Bette Gordon
Helen Grayson
Maggie Greenwald
Randa Haines
Barbara Hammer
Leslie Harris
Edith Head
Amy Heckerling
Faith Elliott Hubley
Irene
Dorothy Jeakins
Ruth Prawer Jhabvala
Diane Keaton
Barbara Kopple
Alile Sharon Larkin
Caroline Leaf
Isobel Lennart
Sonya Levien
Carol Littleton
Lynne Littman
Jennie Livingston
Anita Loos
Ida Lupino
Jeanie Macpherson
Cleo Madison
Frances Marion
Penny Marshall
June Mathis
Elaine May
Melanie Mayron
Marie Menken
Bess Meredyth
Jane Murfin
Brianne Murphy
Gunvor Nelson
Claire Parker
Eleanor Perry
Mary Pickford
Yvonne Rainer
Helen Rose
Nancy Savoca
Greta Schiller
Carolee Schneemann
Thelma Schoonmaker
Susan Seidelman
Irene Sharaff
Joan Micklin Silver
Dorothy Spencer
Penelope Spheeris
Dawn Steel
Barbra Streisand
Betty Thomas
Trinh T. Minh-Ha
Christine Vachon
Theadora Van Runkle
Virginia Van Upp
Patrizia von Brandenstein
Lois Weber
Claudia Weill
Mae West
Oprah Winfrey

Argentinean
María Luisa Bemberg
Nelly Kaplan
Jeanine Meerapfel

Australian
Gillian Armstrong
Corinne Cantrill
Lottie Lyell
Isobel McDonagh
Paulette McDonagh
Phyllis McDonagh

Austrian
Valie Export
Leontine Sagan

Belgian
Chantal Akerman
Marion Hänsel
Agnès Varda

Brazilian
Gilda de Abreu
Suzana Amaral
Ana Carolina
Tizuka Yamasaki

British
Joy Batchelor
Antonia Bird
Betty E. Box
Muriel Box
Jill Craigie
Carmen Dillon
Elinor Glyn
Joan Harrison
Beeban Kidron
Brianne Murphy
Pratibha Parmar
Sally Potter
Lotte Reiniger

Alma Reville
Shirley Russell
Wendy Toye

Canadian
Janis Cole
Holly Dale
Caroline Leaf
Alison Maclean
Deepa Mehta
Alanis Obomsawin
Anne-Claire Poirier
Léa Pool
Nell Shipman
Joyce Wieland

Chilean
Marilú Mallet
Valeria Sarmiento

Chinese
Clara Law
Peng Xiaolian
Zhang Nuanxin

Chinese/Hong Kong
Ann Hui

Cuban
Sara Gómez

Czech
Vera Chytilová
Ester Krumbachová
Vera imková-Plívová

Danish
Astrid Henning-Jensen

Dutch
Annette Apon
Marleen Gorris
Helen van Dongen

French
Maryse Alberti
Jacqueline Audry
Colette
Claire Denis
Germaine Dulac
Marguerite Duras
Marie Epstein
Agnès Guillemot
Alice Guy
Marion Hänsel
Danièle Huillet
Nelly Kaplan
Diane Kurys
Sarah Maldoror
Musidora
Euzhan Palcy
Christine Pascal
Coline Serreau
Nadine Trintignant

German
Jutta Brückner
Doris Dörrie
Birgit Hein
Ulrike Ottinger
Leni Riefenstahl
Helke Sander
Helma Sanders-Brahms
Monika Treut
Thea von Harbou
Margarethe von Trotta

Hungarian
Judit Elek
Márta Mészáros

Indian
Deepa Mehta
Mira Nair

Iranian
Rakhshan Bani-Etemad

Italian
Liliana Cavani
Suso Cecchi d'Amico
Elvira Notari
Lina Wertmüller

Japanese
Yoko Ono
Kinuyo Tanaka

Mexican
Marcela Fernández Violante
Matilde Soto Landeta
María Novaro

New Zealander
Jane Campion
Alison Maclean

Norwegian
Anja Breien
Liv Ullmann

Polish
Agnieszka Holland
Wanda Jakubowska

Russian
Kira Muratova
Olga Preobrazhenskaya
Yulia Solntseva

Senegalese
Safi Faye

Spanish
Pilar Miró

Soviet Ukrainian
Larissa Shepitko
Esther Shub

Swedish
Marianne Ahrne
Gunvor Nelson
Mai Zetterling

Swiss
Léa Pool

Ukrainian
Kira Muratova

West Indian
Euzhan Palcy

The *St. James Women Filmmakers Encyclopedia* Index includes page references for all filmmakers entries, as well as all film titles listed in the various Filmographies thoughout the book. Also included are cross-references for alternative or translation titles. The name(s) in parentheses after a title refers to the name of the entrant(s) in whose entry the reference appears.

10 Modern Commandments (Arzner): 25
$1,000 a Touchdown (Head): 184
10:30 P.M. Summer (Duras): 124
10th Avenue Angel (Irene): 205
13 Minuten vor zwölf in Lima (Meerapfel): 280
13 West Street (Brackett): 52
15 perc 15 évröl (Mészáros): 289
150 km per Hour
See *150 na godzinę*
150 na godzinę (Jakubowska): 207
15/8 (Akerman): 4
17, maj—en film om ritualer (Breien): 55
17 May, a Film about Rituals
See *17, maj—en film om ritualer*
1776, or The Hessian Renegades (Pickford): 334
1933 (Wieland): 455
1-94 (Gordon): 157
1941 (Marshall): 268
1963.julius 27.szombat (Mészáros): 289
1968 Persian Letters
See *Petit à petit ou Les Lettres persanes 1968*
2 Friends (Campion): 61
2, Rue de la Memoire (Mallet): 263
20 let sovetskogo kino
See *Kino za XX liet*
24 Hour Woman (Savoca): 368
29 Acacia Avenue (Box, M.): 51
3 ans 5 mois (Faye): 137
3 Men Missing
See *Ztracenci*
3 Years Five Months
See *3 ans 5 mois*
30 Minutes, Mister Plummer (Poirier): 337
333 (Export): 134
39 Steps (Box, B.): 48; (Reville): 349
40 Carats (Ullmann): 424
400 Million (van Dongen): 430
4000 Frames, an Eye-Opener Film (Cantrill): 65
625 (Hein): 192
6½ x 11
See *Six et demi-onze*
7 AM (Novaro): 309
8 and 90
See *Otto e Novanta*
8½
See *Otto e mezzo*

A

A & B in Ontario (Wieland): 455
À corps perdu (Pool): 339
A "holdudvar" (Mészáros): 289
À la folie (Kurys): 225
À la source, la femme aimée (Kaplan): 213
À la recherche d'un appartement (Guy): 168
A Labda varásza (Mészáros): 289
'A Legge (Notari): 307
A lörinci fonóban (Mészáros): 289

Magzat (Mészáros): 289
'A Mala Nova (Notari): 307
. . . a pátý jezdec je Strach (Krumbachová): 223
A Marechiaro ce sta 'na Fenesta (Notari): 307
A Piedigrotta (Notari): 307
À qui appartient ce gage? (Poirier): 337
'A Santa notte (Notari): 307
A szár és a gyökér fejlődése (Mészáros): 288
Aaron Slick from Punkin Crick (Head): 185
Abandon Ship! (Zetterling): 462
Abblenden
See *Aufblenden*
Abbott and Costello in Hollywood (Irene): 205
ABC—We Print Anything—In the Cards (Schneemann): 372
Abdication (Ullmann): 424
Abel Gance et son Napoléon (Kaplan): 213
Abel Gance, hier et demain (Kaplan): 213
Abenteuer des Prinzen Achmed
See *Geschichte des Prinzen Achmed*
Abenteuer: Die Affenbrücke
See *Doktor Dolittle und seine Tiere*
Abenteuer: Die Affenkrankheit
See *Doktor Dolittle und seine Tiere*
Abenteuer: Die Reise nach Afrika
See *Doktor Dolittle und seine Tiere*
Abortion Problems in France
See *Abortproblem i Frankrike*
Abortproblem i Frankrike (Ahrne): 2
About Mrs. Leslie (Head): 186
About Overtime and Voluntary Labor
See *Sobre horas extras y trabajo voluntario*
Above and Beyond (Rose): 355
Above Suspicion (Irene): 203
Abraham Lincoln (Marion): 265
Abreu, Gilda de: **1**
Abrik Zaur (Shub): 390
Abstand (Meerapfel): 280
Abstract Film No. 1 (Export): 134
Abstronic (Bute): 59
Abu series (Batchelor): 34
Accident (Dillon): 118
Accidental Tourist (Littleton): 239
Accused (Akins): 6; (Foster): 143; (Head): 185; (Steel): 401
Accusing Finger (Head): 183
Ace Eli and Rodger of the Skies (Van Runkle): 431
Across the Araks
See *Po tu storonu Araksa*
Across the Mexican Line (Guy): 168
Act of Violence (Rose): 355
Acts of Perception (Schneemann): 372
Ada (Rose): 356
Adam's Rib (Bauchens): 37; (Macpherson): 255
Addams Family (Allen, D.): 10
Addio Mia Bella Addio, l'Armata se ne va (Notari): 307
Adjoined Dislocations
See *Adjungierte Dislokationen*
Adjungierte Dislokationen (Export): 134
Adoption
See *Örökbefogadás*
Adultere (mode d'emploi) (Pascal): 328
Adultery [A User's Manual]
See *Adultere (mode d'emploi)*
Adventure (Irene): 205
Adventure for Two
See *Demi-Paradise*
Adventure in Diamonds (Head): 184
Adventure Playground (Cantrill): 65
Adventurer (Guy): 169
*Adventures of an ** (Hubley): 197
Adventures of Don Coyote (Pickford): 334
Adventures of Dr. Dolittle
See *Doktor Dolittle und seine Tiere*
Adventures of Huckleberry Finn (Gish): 148
Adventures of Prince Achmed
See *Geschichte des Prinzen Achmed*
Adventures of Sherlock Holmes (Lupino): 247
A.E.I. (Mallet): 263
Aelita (Solntseva): 395
Aerograd (Solntseva): 395
Aesop
See *Ezop*
Affair in Berlin
See *Interno Berlinese*
Affair in Trinidad (Van Upp): 433
Affair of Hearts (Macpherson): 256
Affair of the Skin (Fields): 141
Affairs of Anatol (Bauchens): 37; (Glyn): 150; (Macpherson): 255
Affairs of Cellini (Meredyth): 286
Affairs of Dr. Holl
See *Angelika*
Affairs of Martha (Lennart): 236
Affairs of Susan (Head): 185
Aftab Nechinha (Bani-Etemad): 32
After Hours (Campion): 61; (Schoonmaker): 375
After the Thin Man (Goodrich): 155
After the Verdict (Reville): 349
After Tomorrow (Levien): 237
After Tonight (Murfin): 296
Against Oblivion
See *Contre l'oubli*
Agatha (Russell): 357
Agatha et les lectures limitées (Duras): 124
Age of Desire (Coffee): 90
Age of Dissent (Schiller): 370
Age of Indiscretion (Coffee): 90

Age of Innocence (Schoonmaker): 375
Age of Stalin
See *L'eta' di Stalin*
Agent 8¾
See *Hot Enough for June*
Agnes Kempler's Sacrifice (Madison): 258
Agung Gives Ivor a Haircut (Cantrill): 65
Ah Kam (Hui): 199
Ah, Wilderness! (Goodrich): 155
Ahrne, Marianne: **2**
Ai zai biexiang de jijie (Law): 232
Aimé Césaire: A Voice for History (Palcy): 321
Aimé Césaire, le masque des mots (Maldoror): 261
Air City
See *Aerograd*
Airport (Head): 187
Airport 75 (Head): 187
Airport 77 (Head): 187
Aizen katsura (Tanaka): 409
Akahige (Tanaka): 410
Akerman, Chantal: **4**
Akins, Zoë: **5**
Aktorzy prowincjonalni (Holland): 195
Al di là del bene e del male (Cavani): 69
Aladdin (Reiniger): 347
Aladdin's Other Lamp (Mathis): 269
Alas and Alack (Madison): 258
Alaska Seas (Head): 186
Albertfalvai történet (Mészáros): 288
Alberti, Maryse: **7**
Alberto Carliski, Sculpteur (Maldoror): 261
Alcool, alternativa para o furturo (Yamasaki): 460
Alex (Kidron): 217
Alfred Hitchcock Presents (Haines): 171
Algiers (Irene): 203
Algorithm (Gordon): 157
Alias Jane Jones (Madison): 258
Alias Jesse James (Head): 186
Alias Ladyfingers
See *Ladyfingers*
Alibi Inn (Box, M.): 51
Alice Adams (Murfin): 296
Alice Doesn't Live Here Anymore (Foster): 143
Alice et Elsa
See *À la folie*
Alice's Restaurant (Allen, D.): 10
Alien Encounter
See *Starship Invasions*
All about Eve (Head): 185
All Fall Down (Jeakins): 208
All-Around Reduced Personality
See *allseitig reduzierte Persönlichkeit*
All for Mary (Toye): 414
All Good Countrymen . . .
See *Všichni dobří rodáci*
All in a Night's Work (Head): 186
All Lit Up (Batchelor): 34
All Man (Marion): 264
All Men Are Enemies (Coffee): 90
All Night Long
See *Toute une nuit*
All Night Long (Streisand): 405
All on Account of the Milk (Pickford): 334
All Screwed Up
See *Tutto a posto e niente in ordine*
All the Fine Young Cannibals (Rose): 355
All Women Have Secrets (Head): 184
Allen, Dede: **9**
Allen, Jay Presson: **12**
Allseitig reduzierte Persönlichkeit (Sander): 361
Alma's Rainbow (Chenzira): 75
Aloma of the South Seas (Head): 184
Alone in the Pacific
See *Taiheyo hitoribochi*
Alone in the World (Weber): 444
Along Came Jones (Fields): 141
Along Came Youth (Head): 183
Along the Malibu (Madison): 258
Alphaville (Guillemot): 165
Älskande par (Zetterling): 462
Alt werden in der Fremde (Dörrie): 121
Alte Liebe (Sanders-Brahms): 364
Altered Message (Guy): 168
Altes Material; Zoom—lange Fassung (Hein): 192
Altitude 3200 (Epstein): 132
Altri tempi (Cecchi d'Amico): 71
Am Abend auf der Heide (von Harbou): 440
Am Ama am Amazons (Meerapfel): 280
Amadeus (von Brandenstein): 438
Amanti (Van Runkle): 431
Amaral, Suzana: **13**
Amarilly of Clothes-Line Alley (Marion): 264; (Pickford): 335
Amazing Mrs. Holliday (Levien): 237
Amazonia (Hubley): 197
Amazons (Marion): 264
Ambassades Nourricières (Faye): 137
Ame d'artiste (Dulac): 123
Amelia Earhart: The Final Flight (Keaton): 215
Amelia Lópes O'Neill (Sarmiento): 365
America, America (Allen, D.): 10
American Aristocracy (Loos): 245
American Dream (Kopple): 221
American Graffiti (Fields): 141; (Hein): 192
American I Ching Apple Pie (Schneemann): 372
American in Paris (Sharaff): 384
American Romance (Irene): 203

American Soldier
See *Der amerikanische Soldat*
American Stories
See *Histoires d'Amérique: Food, Family and Philosophy*
American Writer's Congress (Choy): 81
Americano (Loos): 245
America's Dream (Angelou): 17
Âmes au soleil (Faye): 137
Ames de fous (Dulac): 122
Âmes d'enfants (Epstein): 132
Amiche (Cecchi d'Amico): 71
Amiga (Holland): 195; (Meerapfel): 280; (Ullmann): 424
Amigomío (Meerapfel): 280
Amisk (Obomsawin): 313
Amnesia (B): 30
Among Noisy Sheep
See *Unter Schafen*
Among the Grey Stones
See *Sredi serykh kamnei*
Among the Living (Head): 184
Amor und das standhafte Liebespaar (Reiniger): 347
Amore amaro (Cecchi d'Amico): 72
Amore e ginnastica (Cecchi d'Amico): 72
Amore e rabbia (Guillemot): 165
Amorosa (Zetterling): 462
Amuhuelai-Mi (Mallet): 263
An Interesting State (Wertmüller): 449
Anatolian Smile
See *America, America*
Anatomía do Espectador (Carolina): 67
Anatomy of Love
See *Tempi nostri*
Anchors Aweigh (Irene): 205; (Lennart): 236
And Now Tomorrow (Head): 185
And the Angels Sing (Head): 185
And the Dogs Kept Silent
See *Et les Chiens se taisaient*
. . . and the Fifth Rider Is Fear
See *. . . a pátý jezdec je Strach*
And the Wild, Wild Women
See *Nella città l'inferno*
And We've Got "Sabor"
See *Y tenemos sabor*
And You Act Like One, Too (Seidelman): 379
Andechser Gefühl (von Trotta): 442
Anders, Allison: **15**
Anderson's Angels
See *Chesty Anderson, USN*
Andy Hardy's Blonde Trouble (Irene): 203
Andy Hardy's Private Secretary (Murfin): 296
Andy Warhol (Menken): 285
Angel (Shepitko): 386
Angel at My Table (Campion): 61
Angel Falls (Chopra): 78
Angel of Broadway (Coffee): 90; (Weber): 445
Angel of Contention (Gish): 148
Angel on My Shoulder (Deitch): 112
Angelika (von Harbou): 440
Angelika Urban, Salesgirl, Engaged
See *Angelika Urban, Verkaüferin, Verlobt*
Angelika Urban, Verkaüferin, Verlobt (Sanders-Brahms): 364
Angelina
See *L'onorevole Angelina*
Angelou, Maya: **17**
Angie (Coolidge): 99
Angophora and Sandstone (Cantrill): 65
Angry Harvest
See *Bittere ernte*
Angus (Steel): 401
Ani imoto (Tanaka): 410
Animal Farm (Batchelor): 34
Animal Kingdom (Irene): 203
Animal Vegetable Mineral (Batchelor): 34
Anitra's Dance (Bute): 59
An-Magritt (Ullmann): 424
Ann Vickers (Murfin): 296
Anna (Holland): 195
Anna Christie (Marion): 266
Anna Karenina (Levien): 238
Anne of Green Gables (Marion): 265
Anne Trister (Pool): 339
Années 25 (Kaplan): 213
Années 80 (Akerman): 4
Annelie (von Harbou): 440
Annie (Booth): 45; (Treut): 416
Annie Get Your Gun (Rose): 355
Annie Hall (Keaton): 215
Annie Laurie (Gish): 148
Año uno (Gómez): 154
Anonyme (Parker): 325
Another Thin Man (Goodrich): 155
Another Time, Another Place (Coffee): 91
Another Way of Life
See *O něčem jiném*
Ansikte mot ansikte (Ullmann): 424
Anskiter (Breien): 55
Ansprache Aussprache (Export): 134
Antigone (Huillet): 201
Antoinette Sabrier (Dulac): 123
Antonia (Gorris): 159
Antonia & Jane (Kidron): 217
Antonia: A Portrait of the Woman (Godmilow): 152
Antonia's Line
See *Antonia*
Any Wednesday (Jeakins): 208
Anya (Preobrazhenskaya): 342
Anya és leánya (Mészáros): 289

Anybody's Woman (Akins): 6; (Arzner): 25
Anything Can Happen (Head): 185
Anything Goes (Head): 186; (Lupino): 247
Apaches pas veinards (Guy): 168
Apfelbaume (Sanders-Brahms): 364
Apokalypse (Reiniger): 348
Apon, Annette: **19**
Apotheosis (Ono): 316
Apotheosis No. 2 (Ono): 316
Apple Game
See *Hra o jablko*
Apple Trees
See *Apfelbaume*
Appointment with Venus (Box, B.): 48
Après l'amour (Kurys): 225
April 3, 1973 (Citron): 86
Arabesque for Kenneth Anger (Menken): 284
Arcadian Maid (Pickford): 334
Arch of Triumph (Head): 185
Archa bláznů aneb Vyprávění z konce života (Krumbachová): 223
Are Husbands Necessary? (Head): 184
Arequipa (Hammer): 173
Arise, My Love (Head): 184
Arise My Love (Irene): 203
Aristotle (De Hirsch): 110
Arizona Mahoney (Head): 183
Ark of Fools
See *Archa bláznů aneb Vyprávění z konce života*
Arkansas Traveler (Head): 183
Armed Eye
See *Bewaffnete Auge*
Armstrong, Gillian: **21**
Army
See *Rikugun*
Arnelo Affair (Irene): 205
Arrangement (Van Runkle): 431
Arrest Bulldog Drummond (Head): 184
Arrivederci (Notari): 306
Arrowhead (Head): 185
Ars Lucis (Export): 134
Arsène Lupin (Coffee): 90
Art for Art's Sake (Batchelor): 35
Art Lovers (Batchelor): 35
Artful Kate (Pickford): 334
Articulações (Carolina): 67
Artists and Models (Head): 183; (Head): 186; (Lupino): 247
Artists and Models Abroad (Head): 183
Arvácska (Elek): 127
Arven (Breien): 55
Arzner, Dorothy: **25**
As Fate Ordained
See *Enoch Arden*
As Fiandeiras (Carolina): 67
As Husbands Go (Levien): 237; (Spencer): 397
As It Is in Life (Pickford): 334
As Long as There's Still a Europe—Questions on Peace
See *Solange es Europa noch gibt—Fragen an den Freiden*
As Man Made Her (Marion): 264
As Old as the Hills (Batchelor): 34
As Young as You Are (Head): 186
Ascent
See *Voshojdenie*
Aschenputtel (Reiniger): 347
Asemie (Export): 134
Ash Wednesday (Head): 187
Ask Any Girl (Rose): 355
Ass and the Stick (Batchelor): 35
Assassin
See *Venetian Bird*
Assault on a Queen (Head): 187
Assignment in Britanny (Irene): 203
Assistant Lawyer (Peng): 330
Astenicheskii Sindrom (Muratova): 294
Asthenic Syndrome
See *Astenicheskii Sindrom*
Astonished Heart (Box, M.): 51
At 99: A Portrait of Louise Tandy Murch (Mehta): 283
At a Quarter to Two (Pickford): 334
At Black Range (Cantrill): 65
At Eltham (Cantrill): 65
At First Sight
See *Coup de foudre*
At Land (Deren): 116
At Marechiaro There Is a Window
See *A Marechiaro ce sta 'na Fenesta*
At Midnight (Meredyth): 286
At One O'Clock
See *V trinadtsatom chasu*
At Piedigrotta
See *A Piedigrotta*
At the Duke's Command (Pickford): 334
At the Grey House
See *Zur Chronik von Grieshuus*
At the Lörinc Spinnery
See *A lörinci fonóban*
At the Phone (Guy): 169
At žije republika (Krumbachová): 223
Atencion prenatal (Gómez): 154
Athena (Rose): 355
Atlantic Story
See *Opowieść Atlantycka*
Au Bal de Flore (Guy): 168
Au bon beurre (Pascal): 328
Au cabaret (Guy): 167
Au Poulailler! (Guy): 168
Au réfectoire (Guy): 167

Au Verre de l'amitié (Kaplan): 213
Aucassin et Nicolette (Reiniger): 347
Audience (Hammer): 173
Audre Lord Story (Choy): 81
Audrey Rose (Jeakins): 208
Audry, Jacqueline: **27**
Auf+Zu+Ab+An (Export): 134
Aufblenden (Hein): 192
Augen wollen sich nicht zu jeder Zeit schliessen oder Vielleicht eines Tages wird Rom sich erlauben, seinerseits zu wählen
See *Othon*
Augurali (Notari): 306
Auntie Mame (Comden): 96
Aurélia Steiner series (Duras): 124
Aus dem Tagebuch einer Frauenärzin
See *Erste Recht des Kindes*
Ausdatiertes Material (Hein): 192
Aussi longue absence (Duras): 124
Austerlitz/Napoleone ad Austerlitz (Kaplan): 213
Australia Calls (Lyell): 250
Australia in the Swim (McDonagh Sisters): 278
Australian by Marriage (Lyell): 250
Austreibung (von Harbou): 440
Auszüge aus einer Biographie (Hein): 192
Autobahn. 2 Teile (Hein): 192
Autobiography of a Princess (Jhabvala): 210
Automania 2000 (Batchelor): 35
Automation (Parker): 325
Automation Blues (Batchelor): 35
Autour de minuit
See *'Round Midnight*
Autumn
See *Otoñal*
Autumn Moon
See *Qiuyue*
Autumn Sonata
See *Herbstsonate*
Available Space (Hammer): 173
Aventura de Musidora en España (Musidora): 300
Aventures d'un voyageur trop pressé (Guy): 168
Avenue de l'Opéra (Guy): 168
Avocations
See *Uvletschenia*
Awakening
See *Ébredés*
Awakening (Marion): 266; (Pickford): 334
Awakenings (Marshall): 268
Az eladás müvészete (Mészáros): 288
Az élet megy tovább (Mészáros): 288
Azul (Fernández Violante): 139

B

B, Beth: **30**
Baal (von Trotta): 442
Baby Boom (Keaton): 215
Baby, I Will Make You Sweat (Hein): 192
Baby ryazanskie (Preobrazhenskaya): 342
Baby Snatcher (Chopra): 78
Baby-Sitters Club (Mayron): 276
Bachelor in Paradise (Rose): 356
Bachelor Mother (Irene): 203
Back Door to Heaven (Head): 184
Back Pay (Marion): 265
Back to God's Country (Shipman): 388
Back to the Soil (Pickford): 334
Backtrack (Foster): 143; (Lupino): 248
Bad and the Beautiful (Rose): 355
Bad Bascomb (Irene): 205
Bad Lord Byron (Zetterling): 462
Bad Thing about This Country
See *Mal du pays*
Bad Timing (Savoca): 368
Bag of Fleas
See *Pytel blech*
Bagatelle for Willard Maas (Menken): 284
Bagpipes (Batchelor): 35
Bahama Passage (Head): 184; (Van Upp): 432
Baignade dans le torrent (Guy): 167
Bain d'X (Parker): 325
Baises volés (Guillemot): 165
Bakery (Mehta): 283
Bakti (Hänsel): 176
Balade en ville (Trintignant): 420
Balatrum (Parker): 325
Balcony (Fields): 141
Bali Film (Cantrill): 65
Ball of Fire (Head): 184
Ballad of Little Jo (Greenwald): 163
Ballad of Narayama
See *Narayama bushi-ko*
Ballad of Therese
See *Balladen om Therese*
Balladen om Therese (Ahrne): 2
Ballet de Singe
See *vérité sur l'homme-singe*
Ballet Girl
See *Ballettens børn*
Ballet Japonais (Guy): 168
Ballet Libella (Guy): 167
Ballettens børn (Henning-Jensen): 194
Bamboo Xerox (Hammer): 173
Band of Outsiders
See *Bande à part*
Band Wagon (Comden): 96
Bande à part (Guillemot): 165
Bani-Etemad, Rakhshan: **32**
Bannerline (Rose): 355

Baptême (Hänsel): 176
Bar 20 Justice (Head): 183
Barbara Frietchie (Guy): 169
Barbara Ward Will Never Die (Hammer): 173
Barbara's Blindness (Wieland): 455
Barbarian (Loos): 245
Barbra Streisand: The Concert (Streisand): 407
Barcaiuolo d'Amalfi (Notari): 307
Bare Essentials (Coolidge): 99
Baree, Son of Kazan (Shipman): 388
Barefoot Executive (Seidelman): 379
Barefoot in the Park (Head): 187
Barkleys of Broadway (Comden): 96; (Irene): 205
Barnaby—Father Dear Father (Batchelor): 35
Barnaby—Overdue Dues Blues (Batchelor): 35
Barndommens gade (Henning-Jensen): 194
Barnum! (Toye): 414
Barretts of Wimpole Street (Booth): 45
Barrier (Head): 183; (Murphy): 297
Barrière (Musidora): 300
Baryshnia krestianka (Preobrazhenskaya): 342
Basic Fleetwork (Batchelor): 34
Basilique de Saint Denis (Maldoror): 261
Bataille de boules de neige (Guy): 168
Bataille d'oreillers (Guy): 168
Batchelor, Joy: **34**
Bathing Beauty (Irene): 205
Battle at Elderbush Gulch (Gish): 148
Battle for Our Soviet Ukraine
See *Bytva za nashu Radyansku Ukrayinu*
Battle of Austerlitz
See *Austerlitz/Napoleone ad Austerlitz*
Battle of the Sexes (Gish): 148
Battle of the Villa Fiorita (Dillon): 118
Bauchens, Anne: **36**
Baule-les-Pins (Kurys): 225
Baxter, Vera Baxter (Duras): 124
Bay Boy (Ullmann): 424
Bay of St. Michel (Zetterling): 462
Beach House
See *Casotto*
Beachcomber (Box, M.): 51; (Head): 184
Bear
See Medvěd
Bear, a Boy and a Dog (Shipman): 388
Beast at Bay (Pickford): 334
Beast of the City (Bauchens): 37
Beasts of the Jungle (Guy): 169
Beat Street (von Brandenstein): 438
Beau Geste (Head): 184
Beau James (Head): 186
Beautiful Swindlers
See *Plus Belles Escroqueries du monde*
Beauty
See *Mossane*
Beauty Treatment (Batchelor): 35
Bébé embarrassant (Guy): 168
Because of Eve
See *Story of Life*
Because You're Mine (Rose): 355
Bed
See *Lit*
Bed and Board
See *Domicile conjugal*
Bedevilled (Rose): 355
Bed-In (Ono): 316
Bedpeace
See *Bed-In*
Bedtime Stories (Hammer): 173
Bedtime Story (Irene): 203
Before and After (Murphy): 297
Before Need (Nelson): 305
Before Need Redressed (Nelson): 305
Before Stonewall: The Making of a Gay and Lesbian Community (Schiller): 370
Before the Curtain Goes Up
See *Než se rozhrne opona*
Before the Time Comes
See *Temps de l'avant*
Before Women Had Wings (Winfrey): 457
BeFreier und Befreite Krieg, Vergewaltigung, Kinder (Sander): 361
Begegnung im Zwielicht
See *Spotkania w mroku*
Beggar's Uproar (Batchelor): 35
Beginning of an Unknown Century (Shepitko): 386
Beginning of the End (Irene): 205
Behind that Curtain (Levien): 237
Behind the Makeup (Arzner): 25
Behind the Mask (Guy): 169
Behind the Scenes (Pickford): 334
Behind the Veil (Weber): 444
Behind the Wall
See *Derrière le mur*
Beijing Nin Zao (Zhang): 464
Bell Partout (Leaf): 235
Bella, My Bella (Henning-Jensen): 194
Belladonna (B): 30
Bellboy (Head): 186
Belle affaire (Hänsel): 176
Belle au bois dormant (Parker): 325
Belle dame sans merci (Dulac): 123
Belle of New York (Rose): 355
Belle of the Nineties (West): 452
Belle of the Yukon (Fields): 141
Belle Starr (Wertmüller): 449
Belle verte (Serreau): 383
Belles on Their Toes (Jeakins): 208
Bellissima (Cecchi d'Amico): 71
Bells Are Ringing (Comden): 96

Bells of St. Mary's (Head): 185
Belly Dancing Class (Weill): 446
Beloved (Littleton): 239; (Winfrey): 457
Beloved Adventuress (Marion): 264
Beloved Child
  See *L'Enfant aimé*
Beloved Motherland
  See *Patriamada*
Beltenebros (Miró): 291
Bemberg, María Luisa: **38**
Bemused Tourist (Cantrill): 65
Ben Bolt (Guy): 169
Beneath the Czar (Guy): 169
Beneath the Prison
  See *Sotto il Carcere di San Francisco*
Beneath the Twelve Mile Reef (Jeakins): 208
Benefactors
  See *Salvation!*
Ben-Hur (Mathis): 270; (Meredyth): 286
Benny & Joon (Littleton): 239
Bent Time (Hammer): 173
Bequest to the Nation (Dillon): 118
Berceau de Dieu (Musidora): 300
Berkeley 12 to 1 (Deitch): 112
Berkeley Square (Levien): 237
Berlin Affair
  See *Interno Berlinese*
Berlin Apartment (Cantrill): 65
Berlin Fever—Wolf Vostell
  See *Vostell—Berlin-fieber*
Bernice Bobs Her Hair (Silver): 392
Berthe (Hänsel): 176
Bertoldo, Bertoldino e Cacasenno (Cecchi d'Amico): 72
Berührte (Sanders-Brahms): 364
Bess the Detectress in Tick, Tick, Tick (Meredyth): 287
Bess the Detectress, or The Dog Watch (Meredyth): 287
Bess the Detectress, or The Old Mill at Midnight (Meredyth): 287
Best Foot Forward (Irene): 203
Best Hotel on Skid Row (Choy): 81
Best Little Girl in the World (Mayron): 275
Best Little Whorehouse in Texas (Van Runkle): 431
Best Man (Jeakins): 208
Best of Enemies
  See *I due nemici*
Best of the Blues
  See *St. Louis Blues*
Best Seller (Batchelor): 35
Best Things in Life Are Free (Spencer): 397
Best Way
  See *Meilleure façon de marcher*
Best Years of Our Lives (Sharaff): 384
Betörung der blauen Matrosen (Ottinger): 318
Betrayed (von Brandenstein): 438
Betrothal
  See *Petición*
Betsy (Jeakins): 208
Better Spirit (Batchelor): 34
Better Way (Pickford): 334
Better Wife (Coffee): 90
Betty in Search of a Thrill (Marion): 266
Between Heaven and Earth
  See *Sur la terre comme au ciel*
Between the Devil and the Deep Blue Sea (Hänsel): 176
Between the Lines (Silver): 392; (von Brandenstein): 437
Between Two Women (Irene): 203
Between Two Worlds
  See *Müde Tod*
Between Us
  See *Coup de foudre*
Between Us (Pascal): 328
Beverly Hillbillies (Spheeris): 400
Beverly Hills Cop II (Steel): 401
Beverly Hills Cop III (Coolidge): 99
Bewaffnete Auge (Export): 134
Beware, My Lovely (Lupino): 248
Beware of Children
  See *No Kidding*
Bewitchment of the Drunken Sailors
  See *Betörung der blauen Matrosen*
Beyond Forty
  See *Quarantaine*
Beyond Glory (Head): 185
Beyond Good and Evil
  See *Al di là del bene e del male*
Beyond JFK: The Question of Conspiracy (Kopple): 221
Beyond the Blue Horizon (Head): 184
Beyond the Door (Cavani): 69
Beyond the Forest (Coffee): 91; (Head): 185
Beyond the Rocks (Glyn): 150
Beyond the Shadow Place (Hubley): 197
Beyond the Square
  See *Tul a Kálvin-téren*
Beyond the Wall
  See *Müde Tod*
Bez znieczulenia (Holland): 195
B.F.'s Daughter (Irene): 205
Bhowani Junction (Levien): 237
Biały mazur (Jakubowska): 207
Bicycle Thief
  See *Ladri di biciclette*
Bienfaits du cinématographe (Guy): 168
Big (Marshall): 268
Big Bang and Other Creation Myths (Hubley): 197

Big Broadcast of 1932 (Head): 183
Big Broadcast of 1936 (Head): 183
Big Broadcast of 1937 (Head): 183
Big Broadcast of 1938 (Head): 183
Big Carnival (Head): 185
Big Chill (Littleton): 239
Big City (Rose): 355
Big-City Vampires
See *Storstadsvampyrer*
Big Clock (Head): 185
Big Deal on Madonna Street
See *I soliti ignoti*
Big Deal on Madonna Street. . . 20 Years Later
See *I soliti ignoti vent'anni dopo*
Big Events and Ordinary People: Elections
See *Des Grandes événements et des gens ordinaires: les élections*
Big Fix (Head): 187
Big Girls Don't Cry. . . They Get Even (Silver): 392
Big Hangover (Rose): 355
Big House (Marion): 266
Big Knife (Lupino): 248
Big Race (Batchelor): 35
Big Sky (Jeakins): 208
Big Sleep (Brackett): 52
Bigamist (Lupino): 247
Bigelow, Kathryn: **40**
Bildnis Einer Trinkerin—Aller jamais retour (Ottinger): 318
Billion Dollar Brain (Russell): 357
Bill's Hat (Wieland): 455
Billy Bathgate (von Brandenstein): 438
Billy's Rival (Loos): 244
Bimbo (Coolidge): 99
Binding Sentiments
See *A "holdudvar"*
Bingo, Bridesmaids and Braces (Armstrong): 21
Bink Runs Away
See *Bink's Vacation*
Bink's Vacation (Loos): 244
Biography of a Bachelor Girl (Loos): 245
Bird, Antonia: **42**
Bird of Happiness
See *El pájaro de la felicidad*
Birdcage (May): 271
Birds (Head): 186
Birds and the Bees (Head): 186
Birds at Sunrise (Wieland): 455
Birth of a Nation (Gish): 148
Birth of the Blues (Head): 184
Birthday Cake (Batchelor): 35
Birthday Treat (Batchelor): 35
Biscuit Eater (Head): 184
Bishop Murder Case (Coffee): 90
Bishop's Wife (Sharaff): 384
Bitch
See *Garce*
Bitchband (Treut): 416
Bitter Fruit
See *Fruits amers*
Bittere ernte (Holland): 195
Bittersweet Survival (Choy): 81
Black Angustias
See *Negra Angustias*
Black Bird (Booth): 45
Black Box (B): 30
Black Leotard
See *Maillot noir*
Black Orchid (Head): 186
Black Orchids (Madison): 258
Black Panthers (Varda): 435
Black Roots
See *Racines noires*
Black Shack Alley
See *Rue cases nègres*
Black Sheep (Spheeris): 400
Black Sins
See *Schwarze Sunde*
Black South: The Life and Lifework of Zora Neale Hurston (Dash): 105
Black Thursday
See *Guichets du Louvre*
Black Widow (Spencer): 397
Black Wolf (Shipman): 388
Blackmailed (Zetterling): 462
Blanche (Pool): 339
Blast (Cantrill): 65
Blaubart (von Trotta): 442
Blaue Licht (Riefenstahl): 351
Blaze of Noon (Head): 185
Blé en herbe (Colette): 95
Bleierne Zeit (von Trotta): 441
Blind Cook (Shepitko): 386
Blind Goddess (Box, B.): 48; (Box, M.): 51
Blind Princess and the Poet (Macpherson): 256
Blitz on Bugs (Batchelor): 34
Blizzard of Passion
See *Bufera d'Anime*
Blockade (Irene): 203; (Spencer): 397
Blonde Fever (Irene): 205
Blonde Gypsy
See *Caraque blonde*
Blonde Trouble (Head): 183
Blondie of the Follies (Loos): 245; (Marion): 266
Blood & Donuts (Cole and Dale): 93
Blood and Sand (Arzner): 25; (Mathis): 270
Blood and Water (Guy): 169
Blood Feud
See *Fatto di sangue fra due uomini per causa di una vedova*

Blood of Others
See *Sang des autres*
Blood of the Children (Meredyth): 286
Blood of the Man Devil
See *House of the Black Death*
Blood Sabbath (Murphy): 297
Bloodlust! (Murphy): 297
Bloodstain (Guy): 169
Blossoms in the Dust (Loos): 245
Blossoms on Broadway (Head): 183
Blot (Weber): 445
Blow-Ball
See *Bóbita*
Blow up My Town
See *Saute ma ville*
Blue
See *Azul*
Blue Country
See *Pays bleu*
Blue Dahlia (Head): 185
Blue Hawaii (Head): 186
Blue Jeans (Mathis): 269
Blue Light
See *Blaue Licht*
Blue Mountains Mystery (Lyell): 250
Blue or the Gray (Gish): 148
Blue Scar (Craigie): 101
Blue Skies (Head): 185
Blue Steel (Bigelow): 41
Bluebeard
See *Blaubart*
Blueberry Hill (Hänsel): 176
Bluebird (Head): 187
Blue-Veiled
See *Rusariye Abi*
Boa Morte (Chenzira): 75
Boarding House for Single Gentlemen
See *Pension pro svobodné pány*
Boat People
See *T'ou-Pen Nu-Hai*
Boatman of Amalfi
See *Barcaiuolo d'Amalfi*
Bóbita (Mészáros): 289
Boccaccio '70 (Cecchi d'Amico): 72
Body Collage (Schneemann): 372
Body Heat (Littleton): 239
Body Politics (Export): 134
Body Repaired and the World in Reverse
See *Mensche verstreut und Welt verkehrt*
Body Rotations
See *Falling Bodies*
Boeing, Boeing (Head): 186
Bohème (Gish): 148
Boiling Electric Jug Film (Cantrill): 65
Bolly (Batchelor): 35
Bombay Talkie (Jhabvala): 210
Bombshell (Booth): 45
Bon Odoni (Yamasaki): 460
Bondage (Treut): 416
Bonheur (Varda): 435
Bonheur des autres (Dulac): 122
Bonne Absinthe (Guy): 168
Bonnie and Clyde (Allen, D.): 10; (Van Runkle): 431
Bonus for Irene
See *Eine Prämie für Irene*
Booloo (Head): 183
Boom, Boom (Denis): 114
Booth, Margaret: **44**
Borden, Lizzie: **46**
Border Flight (Head): 183
Border Radio (Anders): 15
Border Vigilantes (Head): 184
Borderland (Head): 183
Borgne (Sarmiento): 366
Borinage
See *Misère au Borinage*
Born in Flames (Bigelow): 41; (Borden): 46
Born to the West (Head): 183
Borrowed Clothes (Weber): 444
Borrowers (Allen, J.): 12
Borsós Miklós (Mészáros): 289
Borza (van Dongen): 430
Boss' Wife (Mayron): 276
Bostonians (Jhabvala): 210
Both (Child): 76
Both Sides of the Law
See *Street Corner*
Bottoms
See *Film No. 4*
Bouddi (Cantrill): 65
Bought and Paid For (Marion): 264
Bouquetière des Catalans (Musidora): 300
Bout de Zan et le poilu (Musidora): 300
Bout de Zan et l'espion (Musidora): 300
Box, Betty E.: **48**
Box, Muriel: **50**
Boy and Tarzan Appear in a Clearing (Choy): 81
Boy Friend (Russell): 357
Boy from the Taiga
See *Paren iz taigi*
Boy Next Door (Gordon): 157
Boy of Two Worlds
See *Paw*
Boy Trouble (Head): 184
Boy Who Saw Through (Bute): 59
Boys from the West Coast
See *Vesterhavs drenge*
Boys in the Band (Russell): 357
Boys Next Door (Spheeris): 399
Boys' Ranch (Irene): 205

Boys, Take Your Dancing Partners!
See *Chlapci, zadejte se!*
Boys Will Be Boys
See *Páni kluci*
Brackett, Leigh: **52**
Braconniers (Guy): 168
Brady Bunch Movie (Thomas): 412
Brain Battle (Leaf): 235
Branded (Head): 185
Branded Woman (Loos): 246
Brandstifter (von Trotta): 442
Braslet-2 (Muratova): 294
Brat (Guy): 169; (Levien): 237; (Mathis): 269
Brave Blacksmith
See *O statečném kováři*
Brave Tin Soldier (Batchelor): 34
Brawn of the North (Murfin): 296
Bread (Coffee): 90
Bread of the Border (Arzner): 25
Breakdown
See *Loveless*
Breakfast at Tiffany's (Head): 186
Breakfast Club (Allen, D.): 10
Breaking Away (von Brandenstein): 437
Breaking the Silence (Dash): 105
Breath of Scandal (Head): 186
Breaths (Dash): 105
Brecht die Macht der Manipulateure (Sander): 361
Breien, Anja: **53**
Bribe (Irene): 205
Bride (Russell): 357
Bride Goes Wild (Rose): 355
Bride Wore Boots (Head): 185
Bride Wore Red (Arzner): 25
Bridegroom, the Comedienne and the Pimp
See *Der Bräutigam, die Komödiantin und der Zuhälter*
Bridge
See *De brug*
Bridge of San Luis Rey (Booth): 44
Bridge Too Far (Ullmann): 424
Bridges at Toko-ri (Head): 186
Bridges-Go-Round (Clarke): 88
Brief Encounters
See *Korotkiye vstrechi*
Brigadoon (Sharaff): 384
Bright City
See *Svetlyi gorod*
Brighton Beach Memoirs (Littleton): 239
Bring on the Girls (Head): 185
Bringing Out the Dead (Schoonmaker): 375
Bringing Up Father (Booth): 44; (Marion): 266
Britain Must Export (Batchelor): 34
British Army at Your Service (Batchelor): 34
Broadway Rhythm (Irene): 203
Broken Blossoms (Gish): 148
Broken Jug
See *Der zerbrochene Krug*
Broken Lance (Spencer): 397
Broken Locket (Pickford): 334
Broken Mirrors
See *Gebroken Spiegels*
Brontosaurus (Šimková-Plívová): 394
Brother Sun, Sister Moon
See *Fratelli sole, sorella luna*
Brothers (Box, M.): 51
Brother's Heart
See *Core 'e Frata*
Browning Version (Dillon): 118
Brückner, Jutta: **56**
Bruno aspetta in macchna (Cecchi d'Amico): 72
Brussels "Loops" (Clarke): 88
Brute (Guillemot): 165
Bryn Mawr College (Grayson): 161
B/Side (Child): 76
Buccaneer (Bauchens): 37; (Head): 183; (Head): 186; (Macpherson): 255
Buccaneers (Madison): 258
Buck Benny Rides Again (Head): 184
Bucovina-Ukrainian Earth
See *Bukovyna-Zemlya*
Budujemy (Jakubowska): 207
Budujemy nowe wsi (Jakubowska): 207
Bufera d'Anime (Notari): 306
Bugsy Malone (Foster): 143
Building (Potter): 341
Buisson ardent (Parker): 325
Bukovyna-Zemlya (Solntseva): 395
Bulldog Drummond series (Bauchens): 37; (Head): 183, 184
Bullfight (Clarke): 88
Bullitt (Van Runkle): 431
Bunch of Flowers (Loos): 244
Buon Giorno, elefante! (Cecchi d'Amico): 71
Burglar Catcher (Batchelor): 35
Burglar's Dilemma (Gish): 147
Burning Hearts
See *Kolberg*
Burning Soil
See *Der Brennende Acker*
Bus (Fields): 141
Bushwackers (Lyell): 250
Buster Keaton Story (Head): 186
But No One (Friedrich): 144
But Not for Me (Head): 186
But What Do Women Want?
See *Mais qu'est-ce qu'elles veulent?*
Butch Cassidy and the Sundance Kid (Head): 187
Butcher's Wife (Van Runkle): 431

Bute, Mary Ellen: **58**
Butley (Dillon): 118
Butterfield 8 (Rose): 356
Butterfly Revolution
See *Summer Camp Nightmare*
Buy Me That Town (Head): 184
By Rocket to the Moon
See *Frau im Mond*
By the Steep Ravine
See *U krutogo yara*
Bye-Bye Red Riding Hood
See *Piroska és a farkas*
Bytva za nashu Radyansku Ukrayinu (Solntseva): 395

C

Ça n'arrive qu'aux autres (Trintignant): 420
Cabaret (Allen, J.): 12
Cabbage Fairy
See *Fée aux choux*
Cabin in the Sky (Irene): 203
Cadavres en Vacances (Audry): 27
Caddies (Batchelor): 35
Caddy (Head): 185
Caddy's Dream (Pickford): 334
Café Society (Head): 184
Cafe Society (Van Upp): 432
Cage of Doom
See *Terror from the Year 5000*
Cake-Walk de la pendule (Guy): 168
Calamity
See *Kalamita*
Calcutta (Head): 185
Calendar Girl (Marshall): 268
Calico Vampire (Loos): 244
California (Head): 185
California Suite (Booth): 45; (May): 271
Caliph Storch (Reiniger): 347
Call (Macpherson): 256
Call Me Madam (Sharaff): 384
Call of the Rose (Guy): 169
Call of the Song (Pickford): 334
Call to Arms (Pickford): 334
Callahans and the Murphys (Marion): 266
Callaway Went Thataway (Rose): 355
Calling the Shots (Cole and Dale): 93; (Weill): 447; (Zetterling): 462
Calvaire (Musidora): 300
Calypso Heat Wave (Angelou): 17
Camargue, det forlorade landet (Ahrne): 2
Cambrioleur et agent (Guy): 168
Cambrioleurs (Guy): 167
Cambrioleurs de Paris (Guy): 168
Camel Xiang Zi (Peng): 330
Camila (Bemberg): 38
Camilla (Mehta): 283
Camille (Akins): 6; (Booth): 45; (Marion): 264; (Marion): 266; (Mathis): 270
Camille without Camellias
See *signora senza camelie*
Camion (Duras): 124
Camorra (Wertmüller): 449
Campbell's Kingdom (Box, B.): 48
Campion, Jane: **61**
Campus Confessions (Head): 183
Canada Vignettes: June in Povungnituk—Quebec Arctic (Obomsawin): 313
Canada Vignettes: Wild Rice Harvest Kenora (Obomsawin): 313
Cananea (Fernández Violante): 139
Canary Yellow
See *Zard-e Ghanari*
Can-Can (Sharaff): 384
Cançao de Amor (Abreu): 1
Candidate (von Brandenstein): 438
Candlemaker (Batchelor): 34
Candleshoe (Foster): 143
Canned Harmony (Guy): 169
Cannibals
See *I Cannibali*
Can't Hardly Wait (Thomas): 412
Canta for Our Sisters (Davis): 107
Cantrill, Corinne: **64**
Cap Tourmente (Pool): 339
Cape Fear (Schoonmaker): 375
Caper of the Golden Bulls (Head): 187
Capitana Allegria
See *Pour Don Carlos*
Capri Incantevole (Notari): 306
Capri Pittoresco (Notari): 307
Caprice (Pickford): 334
Caprices of Kitty (Marion): 266
Captain Courtesy (Marion): 266
Captain Kidd (Madison): 258
Captain Kidd, Jr. (Marion): 264; (Pickford): 335
Captain Macklin (Gish): 148
Captain Midnight, the Bush King (Lyell): 250
Captain Starlight (Lyell): 250
Captive (Macpherson): 255
Capture of a Madman in Bagnoli
See *Cattura di un Pazzo a Bagnoli*
Car 99 (Head): 183
Carabiniers (Guillemot): 165
Caraque blonde (Audry): 27
Caratteristica Guerra Italo-Turca Tra i Nostri Scugnizzi Napoletani (Notari): 307
Cardboard Cavalier (Dillon): 118
Cardinal's Conspiracy (Pickford): 334
Care and Affection
See *Szeretet*
Career (Head): 186

Career of Waterloo Peterson (Weber): 444
Cari fottutissimi amici (Cecchi d'Amico): 72
Caribbean (Head): 185
Carl Ruggles' Christmas Breakfast (Schneemann): 372
Carmela la Pazza (Notari): 306
Carmela la Sartina di Montesanto (Notari): 307
Carmela the Dressmaker of Montesanto
See *Carmela la Sartina di Montesanto*
Carmela the Madwoman
See *Carmela la Pazza*
Carmen (Guy): 168; (Reiniger): 347
Carnaby, M.D.
See *Doctor in Clover*
Carnaval dans le Sahel (Maldoror): 261
Carnaval en Guinée-Bissau (Maldoror): 261
Carnival (Dillon): 118
Carnival in Guinea-Bissau
See *Carnaval en Guinée-Bissau*
Carnival in Sahel
See *Carnaval dans le Sahel*
Carnival in the Clothes Cupboard (Batchelor): 34
Carny (Foster): 143
Caro Michele (Cecchi d'Amico): 72
Carolina, Ana: **67**
Carpetbaggers (Head): 186
Carriage Going to Vienna
See *Kočár do Vídně*
Carriage of Death
See *'O Cuppe' d'a Morte*
Carrie (Head): 185
Carrot Top
See *Poil de carotte*
Carry Greenham Home (Kidron): 217
Carry on Constable (Dillon): 118
Carry on Cruising (Dillon): 118
Carry on Milkmaids (Batchelor): 35
Carwash (Mayron): 275
Cas je neúprosný (Chytilová): 83
Casa in Italia (Cavani): 69
Casanova (Kurys): 225
Casanova '70 (Cecchi d'Amico): 72
Casanova Brown (Fields): 141
Case against Mrs. Ames (Spencer): 397
Cash McCall (Coffee): 91
Cash on Delivery
See *To Dorothy a Son*
Casino (Schoonmaker): 375
Casotto (Foster): 143
Cass Timberlane (Irene): 205; (Levien): 237
Cassidy of Bar 20 (Head): 183
Cast and Credits: A Film to Be Read
See *Vorspann: Ein Lesefilm*
Casualties of War (Steel): 401
Cat and the Canary (Head): 184
Cat on a Hot Tin Roof (Rose): 355
Catch Me a Spy (Dillon): 118
Catchfire
See *Backtrack*
Catfood (Wieland): 455
Cat's Cradle (Schneemann): 374
Cattura di un Pazzo a Bagnoli (Notari): 307
Caught in the Draft (Head): 184
Cavalcade (Levien): 237
Cavanaugh of the Forest Rangers (Shipman): 388
Cavani, Liliana: **69**
Cayuga Run (De Hirsch): 110
Ce fut un bel été (Kaplan): 213
Cecchi d'Amico, Suso: **71**
Ceiling
See *Strop*
Celluloid Closet (Allen, J.): 12
Celui qui reste (Musidora): 300
Cenpa (Parker): 325
Cent et une nuits (Varda): 435
Cent pour cent (Parker): 325
Center
See *Hothouse*
Cento anni d'amore (Cecchi d'Amico): 71
Centralization
See *Tamarkoze*
Century of Women (Kopple): 221
Certain Smile (Goodrich): 155
Cesarée (Duras): 124
C'est la faute d'Adam (Audry): 27
C'est la vie
See *Baule-les-Pins*
C'est pour les orphelins! (Musidora): 300
Cesta z Prahy do Českého Krumlova aneb Jak jsem sestavoval novou vládu
See *Co dělat?*
C'était le 12 du 12 et chili avait les blues (Pool): 339
Cézanne (Huillet): 201
Chacals (Musidora): 300
Chained to Yesterday
See *Limbo*
Chalice of Sorrow (Madison): 258
Chalk Garden (Dillon): 118
Challenge
See *sfida*
Challenge of a Lifetime (Marshall): 268
Chambre 1 (Akerman): 4
Chambre 2 (Akerman): 4
Chambre 666 (Seidelman): 379
Champ (Marion): 266
Change of Fate
See *Peremena uchasti*
Change of Heart (Levien): 237

Change of Place (Deitch): 112
Chapter in Her Life (Weber): 445
Chapter Two (Booth): 45
Charité du prestidigitateur (Guy): 168
Charles et Lucie (Kaplan): 213
Charley series (Batchelor): 34
Charlie Chan at the Opera (Meredyth): 287
Charlotte Bunch: One Woman's Legacy (Schiller): 370
Charlotte Moorman's Avant-Garde Festival #9 (De Hirsch): 110
Charmant FrouFrou (Guy): 168
Charming Sinners (Arzner): 25
Chasing Rainbows (Meredyth): 286
Chasse au cambrioleur (Guy): 168
Chaussette (Guy): 168
Cheap Detective (Booth): 45
Cheated Love (Levien): 237
Cheaters (McDonagh Sisters): 278
Check to Song (Batchelor): 35
Checking Out (Mayron): 276
Checkpoint (Box, B.): 48; (Dillon): 118
Cheech and Chong's Nice Dreams (Murphy): 297
Chelsea Girls (Menken): 285
Chenzira, Ayoka: **74**
Chère Amérique (Mallet): 263
Chéri (Colette): 95
Cherokee Strip (Head): 184
Chesty Anderson, US Navy
See *Chesty Anderson, USN*
Chesty Anderson, USN (Thomas): 412
Chevaux du Vercors (Audry): 27
Chez le magnétiseur (Guy): 167
Chez le Maréchal-Ferrant (Guy): 168
Chez le photographe (Guy): 168
Chiarina la Modista (Notari): 307
Chiarina the Milliner
See *Chiarina la Modista*
Chibusa yo eien nare (Tanaka): 409
Chicago (Bauchens): 37; (Coffee): 90
Chico Viola Didn't Die
See *Chico Viola Não Morreu*
Chico Viola Não Morreu (Abreu): 1
Chien fou (Guillemot): 165
Chien jouant á la balle (Guy): 168
Chiens savants (Guy): 168
Chiffonier (Guy): 168
Child, Abigail: **76**
Child Lost Forever (Weill): 447
Child of the Andes
See *Mémoires d'un enfant des Andes*
Children
See *Enfants*
Children and Cars (Batchelor): 35
Children Are Not Cattle
See *Kinder sind nicht Rinder*
Children, Books
See *Gyermekek, könyvek*
Children in the Holocaust (Ullmann): 424
Children Making Cartoons (Batchelor): 35
Children of a Lesser God (Haines): 171
Children of Desired Sex (Nair): 302
Children of Montmartre
See *Maternelle*
Children of the Ruins (Craigie): 101
Children of the Sun (Hubley): 197
Children of the Taiga
See *Paren iz taigi*
Children Pay (Gish): 148
Children's Hour (Jeakins): 208
Children's Souls
See *Âmes d'enfants*
Child's Impulse (Pickford): 334
Child's Sacrifice (Guy): 168
Chilly Scenes of Winter (Silver): 392
Chimmie Fadden Out West (Macpherson): 255
China (Head): 184
China—die Künste—der Alltag (Ottinger): 318
China Moon (Littleton): 239
China Today (Choy): 81
China's 400 Million
See *400 Million*
Chinoise (Guillemot): 165
Chirurgie fin de siècle (Guy): 168
Chivato (Murphy): 297
Chlapci, zadejte se! (Šimková-Plívová): 394
Chocolat (Denis): 114
Chopra, Joyce: **78**
Chorus Line (von Brandenstein): 438
Choy, Christine: **80**
Christian Triumph
See *Trionfo Cristiano*
Christine of the Big Top (Levien): 237
Christmas at Moose Factory (Obomsawin): 313
Christmas Feast (Batchelor): 35
Christmas in Connecticut (Head): 185
Christmas in July (Head): 184
Christmas Visitor (Batchelor): 35
Christmas Wishes (Batchelor): 34
Christopher Columbus (Box, M.): 51
Christopher Strong (Akins): 6; (Arzner): 25
Chronicle of a Woman
See *Cronica de una Señora*
Chronicle of Anna Magdalena Bach
See *Chronik der Anna Magdalena Bach*
Chronicle of Flaming Years
See *Povest plamennykh let*
Chronicle of Hope: Nicaragua (Choy): 81
Chronik der Anna Magdalena Bach (Huillet): 201

Chroniques de France (Denis): 114
Chuka (Head): 187
Church and the Woman (Lyell): 250
Chuvstvitel'nyi militsioner (Muratova): 294
Chytilová, Věra: **83**
Chytilová versus Forman (Chytilová): 83
Ciao, Professore!
See *Io speriamo che me la cavo*
Cible humaine (Guy): 168
Ciccio il Pizzaiuolo del Carmine (Notari): 307
Ciccio, the Pizzamaker of Carmine
See *Ciccio il Pizzaiuolo del Carmine*
Cielo celeste (Notari): 307
Cielo 'e Napule (Notari): 307
Cielo sulla palude (Cecchi d'Amico): 71
Cigarette (Dulac): 122
Cigarette, That's All (Weber): 444
Cigarette-Girl from Mosselprom
See *Papirosnitsa ot Mosselproma*
Cigarettes Davros (Parker): 325
Cimetière du Père Lachaise (Maldoror): 261
Cinderella (Pickford): 335; (Reiniger): 347
Cinderfella (Head): 186
Cinéma au service de l'histoire (Dulac): 123
Cinéma: Embaixada do Brasil (Yamasaki): 460
Cinema Murder (Marion): 265
Cinema-Child
See *L'enfant-cinéma*
Cinema's Embassy
See *Cinéma: Embaixada do Brasil*
"Cine-Sonnets" Series (De Hirsch): 110
Circle of Danger (Harrison): 180
Circle of Deceit
See *Fälschung*
Circus Star (Batchelor): 35
Circus World (Spencer): 397
Citron, Michelle: **86**
Città violenta (Wertmüller): 449
City (Cantrill): 65
City at Peace (Streisand): 405
City Girl (Coolidge): 99
City of Angels (Steel): 401
City of Bad Men (Jeakins): 208
City of Dim Faces (Marion): 264
City of Pirates
See *Ville des pirates*
City Sentinel
See *Beast of the City*
City Vamp (Marion): 266
Civil Rights: The Struggle Continues (Kopple): 221
Clam-Digger's Daughter
See *Story of Mr. Hobbs*
Clara (Sanders-Brahms): 364
Clarence (Head): 183
Clarke, Shirley: **87**
Class Relations
See *Klassenverhältnisse*
Classic Fairy Tales (Batchelor): 35
Classified (Mathis): 270
Claudine à l'école (Colette): 95
Cléo de cinq à sept (Varda): 435
Cleopatra (Bauchens): 37; (Sharaff): 384; (Spencer): 397
Clock (Irene): 205; (Ono): 316
Clockmaker
See *L'Horloger de Saint-Paul*
Clorae & Albie (Chopra): 78
Clouded Yellow (Box, B.): 48
Cloudland (Hubley): 197
Clouds of Glory (Russell): 357
Clown en sac (Guy): 168
Clowns (Guy): 168
Clubman and the Tramp (Macpherson): 256
Clueless (Heckerling): 189
Cluny Brown (Spencer): 397
Co dělat? (Krumbachová): 224
Coast at Pearl Beach (Cantrill): 65
Coastal Navigation and Pilotage (Batchelor): 34
Cobweb (Gish): 148
Cocher de fiacre endormi (Guy): 167
Cockaboody (Hubley): 197
Cockpit
See *Lost People*
Cocktail (Henning-Jensen): 194
Cocktail Molotov (Kurys): 225
Coconut Grove (Head): 183
Coeur battant (Trintignant): 420
Coeur de Paris (Epstein): 132
Coeur fidèle (Epstein): 132
Coeur fragile (Musidora): 300
Coffee, Lenore J.: **90**
Cold Comfort (Batchelor): 34
Cold Sweat
See *L'uomo dalle due ombre*
Cold Turkey (Ono): 316
Cole, Janis and Holly Dale: **92**
Coleçao de marfil (Amaral): 13
Colette: **94**
College Holiday (Head): 183
College Swing (Head): 183
Collegiate (Head): 183
Collier de perles (Musidora): 300
Colloque de chiens (Sarmiento): 366
Colombo Plan (Batchelor): 35
Colonel Bontemps (Musidora): 300
Color of Money (Schoonmaker): 375
Color Purple (Winfrey): 457
Color Rhapsodie (Bute): 59
Colors of Love
See *Kolory kochania*

Colors of Vásárhely
See *Vásárhelyi szinek*
Colossal Love
See *Kolossale Liebe*
Colossus: The Forbin Project (Head): 187
Colour of Britain (Parmar): 326
Comden, Betty: **96**
Come and Get It (Murfin): 296
Come and Work
See *Fad'jal*
Come Back in the Summertime (Peng): 330
Come Back, Little Sheba (Head): 185
Come Blow Your Horn (Head): 186
Come Live with Me (Van Upp): 433
Come-On (Head): 186
Come on In (Loos): 245
Come on, Marines! (Lupino): 247
Come Rain or Shine
See *Ob's stürmt oder schneit*
Come West with Me (Gorris): 159
Comedians (Gish): 148
Comedians in Africa (Gish): 148
Comin' round the Mountain (Head): 184
Coming Attractions
See *Loose Shoes*
Coming Out Party (Spencer): 397
Commandos Strike at Dawn (Bauchens): 37; (Gish): 148
Comme on fait son lit on se couche (Guy): 168
Comment monsieur prend son bain (Guy): 168
Comment on disperse les foules (Guy): 168
Comment on dort á Paris! (Guy): 168
Commonplace Story
See *EgyszerŰ történet*
Commonwealth (Batchelor): 35
Commuters (Weill): 447
Compagnons de voyage encombrants (Guy): 168
Compensation (Davis): 107
Complicato intrigo di donne, vicoli e delitti
See *Camorra*
Complot
See *To Kill a Priest*
Concealing a Burglar (Macpherson): 256
Concierge (Guy): 168
Concierge revient de suite (Guillemot): 165
Concorde—Airport '79 (Spencer): 397
Concours de bébés (Guy): 168
Coney Island (Rose): 355
Confessions
See *L.A. Johns*
Confessions of a Suburban Girl (Alberti): 7; (Seidelman): 379
Confidence (Macpherson): 256
Conmigo la pasas muy bien (Novaro): 309
Connection (Clarke): 88
Conquering Power (Mathis): 270
Conquest of Space (Head): 186
Conscience de prêtre (Guy): 168
Conscience of Hassan Bey (Gish): 148
Conspiracy of Hearts (Box, B.): 48
Constance (Parker): 325
Constant Nymph (Reville): 349
Consumer Culture
See *Farahang-e-Massraffi*
Contact (Batchelor): 34; (Foster): 143
Contempt
See *Mépris*
Contessa azzurra (Cecchi d'Amico): 71
Contre l'oubli (Akerman): 4; (Denis): 114; (Serreau): 382; (Trintignant): 420
Conversation Piece
See *Gruppo di famiglia in un interno*
Convictions (Chopra): 78
Convoy Leaving Paradise
See *Transport z ráje*
Cookie (Ephron): 130; (Seidelman): 379
Cooking with Apes (Schneemann): 372
Cool Hands, Warm Heart (Friedrich): 144
Cool Runnings (Steel): 401
Cool World (Clarke): 88
Coolidge, Martha: **99**
Copper Canyon (Head): 185
Copycat (Allen, J.): 12
Coquette (Pickford): 334
Coquille et le clergyman (Dulac): 123
Coração Materno (Abreu): 1
Corazzata San Giorgio (Notari): 306
Core 'e Frata (Notari): 307
Corn Is Green (Dillon): 118
Corner in Cotton (Loos): 244
Corner in Hats (Loos): 244
Corner in Wheat (Macpherson): 256
Corporeal (Cantrill): 65
Corpse Had a Familiar Face (Chopra): 78
Cós za cós (Holland): 195
Cosi Piange Pierrot
See *Piange Pierrot*
Cosmic Eye (Hubley): 197
Cossacks (Marion): 266
Cossacks of the Don
See *Tikhiy Don*
Couch in New York
See *Divan à New York*
Coucher d'une Parisienne (Guy): 168
Coucher d'Yvette (Guy): 167
Couleur chair (Ullmann): 424
Couleur du vent (Pascal): 328
Count Your Blessings (Rose): 355
Countdown (Ottinger): 318
Counterfeit Traitor (Head): 186
Country Boy (Fields): 141

Country Doctor (Levien): 237; (Pickford): 334
Country Girl (Head): 186
Coup de foudre (Kurys): 225; (Pascal): 328
Coup de grâce
See *Der fangschuss*
Coup du fakir (Musidora): 300
Couple Takes a Wife (Marshall): 268
Cour des miracles (Guy): 168
Courage of Lassie (Irene): 205
Course de taureaux à Nîmes (Guy): 168
Court Jester (Head): 186
Courte échelle (Guy): 168
Courtesans of Bombay (Jhabvala): 210
Courting of Mary (Pickford): 334
Courtship of Eddie's Father (Rose): 356
Cousin cousine (Guillemot): 165
Cover Girl (Van Upp): 432
Covered Wagon (Arzner): 25
Covert Action (Child): 76
Cowboy and the Lady (Levien): 238
Cradle Song (Bauchens): 37; (Head): 183
Craigie, Jill: **101**
Craig's Wife (Arzner): 25; (Bauchens): 37
Crazy in Love (Coolidge): 99
Cream Soda (Cole and Dale): 92
Créatures (Varda): 435
Crème Simon (Parker): 325
Creosoot (van Dongen): 429
Cricket on the Hearth (Guy): 169
Cries and Whispers
See *Viskningar och rop*
Crime at Cuenca
See *El crimen de Cuenca*
Crime de la rue du Temple
See *L'Assassinat de la rue du Temple*
Crime Doctor (Murfin): 296
Crime Doctor's Man Hunt (Brackett): 52
Crime Gives Orders
See *Hunted Men*
Crime Nobody Saw (Head): 183
Crime of the Century (Head): 183
Crime Thief
See *Voleur de crimes*
Crimes and Misdemeanors (Ephron): 130
Crimes of the Heart (Keaton): 215
Criminal Passion (Deitch): 112
Crimson Dove (Marion): 264
Crimson Yoke (Madison): 258
Crinoline (Guy): 168
Crise (Serreau): 383
Crisis
See *Crise*
Critical Choices (Weill): 447
Critic's Choice (Head): 186
Crocodile Conspiracy (Davis): 107
Crocodiles in Amsterdam
See *Krokodillen in Amsterdam*
Cronica de una Señora (Bemberg): 38
Crooked Hearts (Marshall): 268
Crooks in Clover
See *Penthouse*
Cross My Heart (Head): 185
Cross Purposes (Madison): 258
Crossing Delancey (Silver): 392
Crosswinds (Head): 185
Crucial Test (Marion): 264
Cruel Embrace
See *Noces barbares*
Crumb (Alberti): 7
Crusades (Bauchens): 37; (Head): 183; (Macpherson): 255
Crush (Maclean): 253
Crush the Power of the Manipulators
See *Brecht die Macht der Manipulateure*
Cry for Help (Gish): 147
Cry Havoc (Irene): 203
Cry of Battle (Fields): 141
Cry Wolf (Head): 185
Crystal Ball (Van Upp): 432
Crystal Bell (Head): 184
Cuba (Russell): 357
Cuban Love Song (Booth): 45; (Meredyth): 286
Cuenca Crime
See *El crimen de Cuenca*
Culinary Embassies
See *Ambassades Nourricières*
Culture intensive ou Le Vieux Mari (Guy): 168
Cummington Story (Grayson): 161
Cuore (Cecchi d'Amico): 72
Cure for Suffragettes (Loos): 244
Curtain Pole (Macpherson): 256
Cuts
See *Schnitte*
Cutting (Export): 134
Cycles (Davis): 107
Cynara (Marion): 266
Cynthia (Irene): 205
Cyrano et d'Artagnan (Kaplan): 213
Cytherea (Marion): 265
Cziko, the Blinking Boy
See *Mrkáček Čiko*
Człowiek z Żelaza (Holland): 195

D

Dada (Bute): 59
Daddy Long Legs (Levien): 237
Daddy Long-Legs (Pickford): 334
Daddy's Gone A-Hunting (Spencer): 397
Daguerrotypes (Varda): 435
Daigaku wa detakeredo (Tanaka): 409

Daily-Life Racism
See *Racisme au quotidien*
Daisies
See *Sedmikrásky*
Daisy Miller (Fields): 141
Dam the Delta (Batchelor): 34
Damned if You Don't (Friedrich): 144
Damon and Pythias (Madison): 258
Dance, Girl, Dance (Arzner): 25
Dance Hall (Murfin): 296
Dance in Chains
See *Biały mazur*
Dance in the Sun (Clarke): 88
Dance Little Lady (Zetterling): 462
Dance of Life
See *Swing High, Swing Low*
Dance Pretty Lady (Toye): 414
Dance with Me (Haines): 171
Dancer (Madison): 258
Dancing Girl of Izu
See *Izu no odoriko*
Dancing Lady (Booth): 45
Dancing on a Dime (Head): 184
Dandelion Child
See *Maskrosbarn*
Dandy in Aspic (Dillon): 118
Danger of Love (Chopra): 78
Dangerous Age (Coffee): 90; (Madison): 259; (Meredyth): 286
Dangerous Business (Loos): 246
Dangerous Minds (May): 271
Dangerous Moves
See *Diagonale du fou*
Dangerous Offender (Cole and Dale): 93
Dangerous Partners (Irene): 205
Dangerous to Know (Head): 183
Dangerous When Wet (Rose): 355
Dangers de l'acoolisme (Guy): 168
Danish Brigade in Sweden
See *Dansk politi i Sverige*
Danish Girls Show Everything (Treut): 416
Danjuro sandai (Tanaka): 409
Dans les coulisses (Guy): 168
Dans l'ouragan de la vie (Dulac): 122
Danse basque (Guy): 168
Danse de l'ivresse (Guy): 168
Danse des Saisons (Guy): 168
Danse du papillon (Guy): 168
Danse du pas des foulards par des almées (Guy): 168
Danse du ventre (Guy): 168
Danse fleur de lotus (Guy): 167
Danse mauresque (Guy): 168
Danse serpentine (Guy): 168
Danse serpentine par Mme Bob Walter (Guy): 168
Danses (Guy): 168
Dansk politi i Sverige (Henning-Jensen): 193
Danske piger viser alt (Henning-Jensen): 194
Dante's Inferno (Russell): 357
Danton (Holland): 195
Danulon gyártás (Mészáros): 288
Danulon Production
See *Danulon gyártás*
Danzón (Novaro): 309
Daphne and the Pirate (Gish): 148
Dark Angel (Marion): 265
Dark City (Head): 185
Dark Delusion (Irene): 205
Dark Eyes
See *Oci ciornie*
Dark Mirror (Sharaff): 384
Dark Star (Marion): 265
Dark Waters (Harrison): 180
Darkest Russia (Marion): 264
Darling, How Could You? (Head): 185
Dash, Julie: **105**
Date with Judy (Rose): 355
Daughter of Luxury
See *Five and Ten*
Daughter of Shanghai (Head): 183
Daughter of the Navajos (Guy): 168
Daughter of the Poor (Loos): 245
Daughter of Vesuvius
See *Figlia del Vesuvio*
Daughter Rite (Citron): 86
Daughters' Inheritance
See *Erbtöchter*
Daughters of the Dust (Dash): 105
Dauphine Java (Parker): 325
David and Lisa (Perry): 332; (Winfrey): 458
David Copperfield (Coffee): 90
David: Off and On (Coolidge): 99
David Wheeler: Theater Company of Boston (Chopra): 78
Davis, Zeinabu irene: **107**
Dawn of Tomorrow (Pickford): 335
Day after Day
See *Jour apres jour*
Day of Peace
See *Giorno Della Pace*
Day the Mercedes Became a Hat (Nair): 302
Day the Sun Turned Cold
See *Tianguo Niezi*
Day to Remember (Box, B.): 48
Daybreak (Box, M.): 51; (Schneemann): 374
Daylight Test Section (Child): 76
Days in the Trees
See *Des journées entières dans les arbres*
Days of Betrayal
See *Dny zrady*

Days to Remember
See *Verliebten*
Daytime Wives (Coffee): 90
Dazlak (Sander): 361
Dazwischen (Dörrie): 121
De blå undulater (Henning-Jensen): 194
De brug (van Dongen): 429
De cierta manera (Gómez): 154
De encaje y azucar (Novaro): 309
De eso no se habla (Bemberg): 38
De guerre lasse (Hänsel): 176
De Hirsch, Storm: **109**
De kalte ham Skarven (Ullmann): 424
De la part des copains
See *L'uomo dalle due ombre*
De l'amour (Guillemot): 165
De mère en fille (Poirier): 337
De pokkers unger (Henning-Jensen): 194
De Stilte Rond Christine M (Gorris): 159
De todos modos Juan te llamas (Fernández Violante): 139
Deacon's Whiskers (Loos): 244
Dead (Jeakins): 208
Dead Case (Holland): 195
Dead Earth (Choy): 81
Dead Man Talking (Deitch): 112
Dead Man Who Killed (Madison): 258
Dead Men Don't Wear Plaid (Head): 187
Deadfall (Alberti): 7
Deadhead Miles (Lupino): 248
Deadlier than the Male (Box, B.): 48
Deadline for Murder: From the Files of Edna Buchanan (Chopra): 78
Deadly Glass of Beer (Loos): 245
Deadly Trap
See *Maison sous les arbres*
Dear America
See *Chère Amérique*
Dear Brat (Head): 185
Dear Carmen
See *Querida Carmen*
Dear Diary (Alberti): 7
Dear Murderer (Box, B.): 48; (Box, M.): 51
Dear Ruth (Head): 185
Dear Squirrel, Don't Snivel
See *Nefňukej, veverko!*
Death Disc (Macpherson): 256
Death of a Champion (Head): 184
Death of Empedocles
See *Der Tod des Empedokles*
Deathtrap (Allen, J.): 12
Deathwatch (Fields): 141
Débrouille-toi (Musidora): 300
Deceiver (Loos): 244
Decimo clandestino (Wertmüller): 449
Decision before Dawn (Spencer): 397
Déclassée (Akins): 6
Decline of Western Civilization (Spheeris): 399
Decline of Western Civilization Part II: The Metal Years (Spheeris): 399
Decline of Western Civilization Part III (Spheeris): 400
Decree of Destiny (Pickford): 334
Dědictví aneb Kurvahošigutntag (Chytilová): 83
Deep in My Heart (Rose): 355
Deep in the Mirror Embedded (De Hirsch): 110
Deep Valley (Lupino): 247
Defense de savoir (Trintignant): 420
Deficit (Seidelman): 379
Dein Herz ist meine Heimat (von Harbou): 440
Deitch, Donna: **112**
Déjeuner des enfants (Guy): 167
Délibábok országa (Mészáros): 289
Delicate Delinquent (Head): 186
Delicious (Levien): 237
Delitto di Giovanni Episcopo (Cecchi d'Amico): 71
Della nube alla resistenza (Huillet): 201
Delta: Ein Stück (Export): 134
Démanty noci (Krumbachová): 223
Déménagement
See *Moving In*
Déménagement à la cloche de bois (Guy): 167; (Guy): 168
Demetrius and the Gladiators (Spencer): 397
Demi-Paradise (Dillon): 118
Demoiselle sauvage (Pool): 339
Demoiselles de Rochefort (Varda): 435
Den Allvarsamma leken (Breien): 55
Den sista riddarvampyren (Ahrne): 2
Denis, Claire: **114**
Denmark Grows Up (Henning-Jensen): 193
Dent récalcitrante (Guy): 168
Denture Adventure (Batchelor): 35
Denver and Rio Grande (Head): 185
Départ pour les vacances (Guy): 168
Depraved
See *Pervertida*
Der alte und der junge König (von Harbou): 440
Der amerikanische Soldat (von Trotta): 442
Der Angestellte (Sanders-Brahms): 364
Der Augenblick des Friedens (Duras): 124
Der Beginn aller Schrecken ist Liebe (Sander): 361
Der Bräutigam,die Komödiantin und der Zuhälter (Huillet): 201
Der brennende Acker (von Harbou): 440
Der Erste Walzer (Dörrie): 121
Der fangschuss (Brückner): 57; (von Trotta): 442

Der fliegende Koffer (Reiniger): 347
Der Graf von Carabas (Reiniger): 347
Der grosse Sprung (Riefenstahl): 351
Der Hauptdarsteller (Dörrie): 121
Der heilige Berg (Riefenstahl): 351
Der Herrscher (von Harbou): 440
Der Himmel über Berlin (Denis): 115
Der Kleine Schornsteinfeger (Reiniger): 347
Der Kuss (Export): 134
Der läufer von Marathon (von Harbou): 440
Der leidensweg der Inge Krafft (von Harbou): 440
Der letzte Sommer-Wenn Du nicht Willst (Cecchi d'Amico): 72
Der Mann mit der Pranke (von Harbou): 440
Der Müde Tod (von Harbou): 440
Der plötzliche Reichtum der armen Leute von Kombach (von Trotta): 442
Der Rattenfänger von Hameln (Reiniger): 348
Der Scheintote Chinese (Reiniger): 347
Der Stern von Bethlehem (Reiniger): 347
Der subjektive Faktor (Sander): 361; (Sanders-Brahms): 364
Der Tod des Empedokles (Huillet): 201
Der verlorene Schatten (Reiniger): 348
Der weiss Rausch (Riefenstahl): 351
Der zerbrochene Krug (von Harbou): 440
Deren, Maya: **116**
Derrière le mur (Sarmiento): 366
Des demoiselles ont en 25 ans (Varda): 435
Des enfants gâtés (Pascal): 328
Des Fusils pour Banta (Maldoror): 261
Des Grandes événements et des gens ordinaires: les élections (Sarmiento): 366
Des journées entières dans les arbres (Duras): 124
Des Lebens schönste Seiten (Sander): 361
Desaster (von Trotta): 442
Desembarcos (Meerapfel): 280
Desert Flower (Mathis): 270
Desert Fury (Head): 185
Desert Hearts (Deitch): 112
Desert Nights (Coffee): 90
Desert's Sting (Macpherson): 256; (Meredyth): 287
Designing Woman (Rose): 355
Desire
See *Touba*
Desire in Motion
See *Mouvements du désir*
Desire Me (Akins): 6; (Irene): 205
Desperate Hours (Head): 186
Desperate Moment (Zetterling): 462
Desperately Seeking Susan (Seidelman): 379
Dessert pour Constance (Maldoror): 261
Dessins et merveilles (Kaplan): 213
D'est (Akerman): 4
Destined to Live: 100 Roads to Recovery (Murphy): 297
Destroy, She Said
See *Détruire, dit-elle*
Detective Story (Head): 185
Detective's Dog (Guy): 169
Détruire, dit-elle (Duras): 124
Deutschen und ihre Männer (Sander): 361
Deutschland, bleiche Mutter (Sanders-Brahms): 364
Deux Françaises (Musidora): 300
Deux Rivaux (Guy): 168
Development of the Stalk and the Root
See *A szár és a gyökér fejlődése*
Devil (Macpherson): 256
Devil Stone (Macpherson): 255
Devils (Russell): 357
Devil's Brother
See *Fra Diavolo*
Devil's Hairpin (Head): 186
Devil's Imposter
See *Pope Joan*
Devil's Rain (Lupino): 248
Devil's Rainbow (Deitch): 112
Devil's Workshop
See *L'atelier du diable*
Devotion (Lupino): 247
Diable dans la ville (Dulac): 123
Diabolique (Littleton): 239
Diabolo menthe (Kurys): 225
Diagonale du fou (Guillemot): 165; (Ullmann): 424
Dialectique (Guillemot): 165
Diálogo de exiliados
See *Dialogue d'exilés*
Dialogo di Roma (Duras): 124
Dialogue d'exilés (Sarmiento): 366
Diamonds of the Night
See *Démanty noci*
Diane of the Follies (Gish): 148
Diario Regional (Meerapfel): 280
Diary for My Children
See *Napló gyermekeimnek*
Diary for My Father and My Mother
See *Napló apámnak, anyámnak*
Diary for My Loves
See *Napló szerelmeimnek*
Diary of a Mad Housewife (Perry): 332
Diary of an African Nun (Dash): 105
Diary of Anne Frank (Goodrich): 155
Diavolo nel cervello (Cecchi d'Amico): 72
Dick Whittington and His Cat (Guy): 169
Didn't Do It for Love (Treut): 416
Difendo il mio amore (Cecchi d'Amico): 71
Different Image (Larkin): 231

Different Places
See *Kulonbozo helyek*
Dig: A Journey into the Earth (Hubley): 197
Diga sul Pacifico (Duras): 124
Digging for Victory (Batchelor): 34
Dillon, Carmen: **118**
Dimmi che fai tutto per mei (Cecchi d'Amico): 72
Dinkum Bloke (Lyell): 250
Dinner at Eight (Marion): 266
Dinner Date (Batchelor): 35
Dirty Like an Angel
See *Sale comme un ange*
Dirty Mary
See *Fiancée du pirate*
Disappearance of Aimee (Head): 187
Disappearance of Nora (Chopra): 78
Disbarred (Head): 184
Discontent (Weber): 444
Discontented Husbands (Madison): 259
Dis-moi (Akerman): 4
Disorderly Orderly (Head): 186
Disputed Passage (Head): 184
Disque 927 (Dulac): 123
Dissociated States (Cavani): 69
Distanciamiento (Meerapfel): 280
Dites cariatides (Varda): 435
Ditte: Child of Man
See *Ditte Menneskebarn*
Ditte Menneskebarn (Henning-Jensen): 194
Divan à New York (Akerman): 4
Divertissement (Parker): 325
Divided Love
See *Geteilte Liebe*
Divinations (De Hirsch): 110
Divine (Colette): 95
Divine Horsemen (Deren): 116
Divorce Game (Marion): 264
Divorce His, Divorce Hers (Head): 187
Divorce Problems in Italy
See *Skilsmässoproblem i italien*
Divorcee (Guy): 169; (Mathis): 269
Dix heures et demie du soir en été
See *10:30 P.M. Summer*
Dny zrady (Krumbachová): 224
Do Right and Fear No-one
See *Tue recht und scheue niemand*
Doctor (Haines): 171
Doctor and the Woman (Weber): 444
Doctor at Large (Box, B.): 48
Doctor at Sea (Box, B.): 48; (Dillon): 118
Doctor Cyclops (Head): 184
Dr. Dolittle (Thomas): 412
Dr. Gillespie's Criminal Case (Irene): 203
Doctor in Clover (Box, B.): 48
Doctor in Distress (Box, B.): 48
Doctor in Love (Box, B.): 48
Doctor in the House (Box, B.): 48; (Dillon): 118
Doctor in Trouble (Box, B.): 48
Dr. Holl
See *Angelika*
Dr. Mabuse, der Spieler (von Harbou): 440
Dr. Mabuse, the Gambler
See *Dr. Mabuse, der Spieler*
Dr. Paglia (Treut): 416
Doctor Rhythm (Head): 183
Dr. Watson's X-Rays (Hammer): 173
Doctors at War (Goodrich): 155
Doctor's Diary (Head): 183
Documental a proposito del transito (Gómez): 154
Documentary about Mass Transit
See *documental a proposito del transito*
Documenteur: An Emotion Picture (Varda): 435
Does the Pill Liberate?
See *Macht die Pille Frei?*
Dog and Cat (Thomas): 412
Dog Catcher
See *L'Accalappiacani*
Dog Day Afternoon (Allen, D.): 10
Dog in the Manger
See *El perro del hortelano*
Dog Pound (Batchelor): 35
Dogfight (Savoca): 368
Dogs and People
See *Psi a lidé*
Dog's Language
See *Colloque de chiens*
Dogs of Sinai
See *Fortini/Cani*
Dog's Tale: A Mexican Parable (Leaf): 235
Do-It-Yourself Democracy (Zetterling): 462
Doktor Dolittle und seine Tiere (Reiniger): 347
Doktor Glas (Zetterling): 462
Dokumentation (Hein): 192
Dokumente zum Internationalen Aktionismus (Export): 134
Dolce cinema (Cecchi d'Amico): 72
Dolgie provody (Muratova): 294
Doll
See *Child's Sacrifice*
Doll House (Hammer): 173
Doll's House (Head): 187
Dolly Put the Kettle On (Batchelor): 34
Domenica (Treut): 416
Domicile conjugal (Guillemot): 165
Don Is Dead (Head): 187
Don Juan (Meredyth): 286
Don Quichotte (Reiniger): 348
Donde voy a encontrar otra Violeta (Mallet): 263

Donna Nella Resistenza (Cavani): 69
Donovan's Reef (Head): 186
Don't Change Your Husband (Bauchens): 37; (Macpherson): 255
Don't Cry, Pretty Girls
See *Szép lányok, ne sirjatok*
Don't Ever Leave Me (Box, B.): 48
Don't Forget You're Going to Die
See *N'oublie pas que tu vas mourir*
Don't Give Up the Ship (Head): 186
Don't Go Near the Water (Rose): 355
Don't Say It
See *Petit Amour*
Don't Tease the Mosquito
See *Non stuzzicate la zanzara*
Doomed Caravan (Head): 184
Doonesbury Special (Hubley): 197
Doppelprojektion I (Hein): 192
Doppelprojektion II-IV (Hein): 192
Dorian Gray in spiegel der Boulevardprsse (Ottinger): 318
Dornröschen (Reiniger): 347
Dorothy Dandridge (Coolidge): 99
Dorothy Vernon of Haddon Hall (Pickford): 334
Dörrie, Doris: **120**
Dottie Gets Spanked (Alberti): 7; (Vachon): 426
Douaniers et contrebandiers (Guy): 168
Double Harness (Murfin): 296
Double Indemnity (Head): 185
Double or Nothing (Head): 183
Double Strength (Hammer): 173
Double the Trouble, Twice the Fun (Parmar): 326
Double Trouble (Loos): 244
Dove siete? Io sono qui (Cavani): 69
Down a Long Way (Batchelor): 34
Down by Law (Denis): 115
Down in the Delta (Angelou): 17
Down to Earth (Loos): 245
Down to the Sea in Ships (Spencer): 397
Downhill Racer (Head): 187
Downstairs (Coffee): 90
Dragnet Girl
See *Hijosen no onna*
Dragon Seed (Irene): 205; (Murfin): 296
Dragons de Villars (Guy): 168
Dragons, Dreams—and a Girl from Reality
See *Drakar, drümmar och en flicka från verkligheten*
Dragonwyck (Spencer): 397
Drakar, drümmar och en flicka från verkligheten (Ahrne): 2
Dranem (Guy): 168
Dreadlocks and the Three Bears (Larkin): 231
Dream (Cantrill): 65; (Pickford): 334
Dream Age (Hammer): 173
Dream Circus (Reiniger): 347
Dream Girl (Head): 185; (Macpherson): 255
Dream Is What You Wake Up From (Choy): 81
Dream Wife (Rose): 355
Dream Woman (Guy): 169
Dreamplay
See *Drømspel*
Dreams for Sunday
See *Sny na neděli*
Dripping Water (Wieland): 455
Drips and Strips (Menken): 285
Drive to Win
See *Sha Ou*
Driven from Home
See *Austreibung*
Driver dagg faller Regn (Zetterling): 462
Drømspel (Ullmann): 424
Drop Zone (Mayron): 276
Druides (Guy): 168
Drums along the Mohawk (Levien): 237
Drunkard
See *O Ébrio*
Dry White Season (Palcy): 321
Du Barry Was a Lady (Irene): 203
Du côté de la Côte (Varda): 435
Duality of Nature
See *Zweiheit der Natur*
Dubliners
See *Dead*
Duchess of Idaho (Rose): 355
Duck Soup (Head): 183
Dudes (Spheeris): 399
Due mogli sono troppe (Cecchi d'Amico): 71
Duel in the Sun (Gish): 148
Duel tragique (Guy): 168
Dueña de casa
See *Femme au foyer*
Duffy's Tavern (Head): 185
Duie Paravise (Notari): 307
Dulac, Germaine: **122**
Dulcy (Loos): 246
Dumb Girl of Portici (Weber): 444
Duo (Colette): 95
Duras, Marguerite: **124**
During the Round Up (Gish): 148
Dust (Hänsel): 176
Dustbin Parade (Batchelor): 34
Dutch Master (Alberti): 7; (Seidelman): 379
Dwightiana (Menken): 284
Dying for a Smoke (Batchelor): 35
Dying Swan
See *Mort du cygne*
Dyketactics (Hammer): 173
Dynamite (Bauchens): 37; (Macpherson): 255
Dynamite Chicken (Ono): 316

E

E' Piccarella (Notari): 307
E più facile che un cammello (Cecchi d'Amico): 71
E primavera (Cecchi d'Amico): 71
E una Domenica sera di novembre (Wertmüller): 449
Eagle's Mate (Pickford): 334
Ear
See *Ucho*
Early Morning at Borobudur (Cantrill): 65
Early Spring
See *Barndommens gade*
Earth
See *Zemlya*
Earth (Mehta): 283
Earth Message (Cantrill): 65
Earthquake (Spencer): 397
Earthquake in Chile
See *Erdbeben in Chile*
East Is West (Marion): 265
East Lynne (Coffee): 90
East of Shanghai
See *Rich and Strange*
East Side, West Side (Lennart): 236; (Rose): 355
Easter Parade (Goodrich): 155; (Irene): 205
Easy Come, Easy Go (Head): 185; (Head): 187
Easy Living (Head): 183
Easy Money (Box, M.): 51
Easy to Love (Rose): 355
Easy to Take (Van Upp): 432
Easy to Wed (Irene): 205
Ebb Tide (Head): 183
Ébredés (Elek): 127
Echoes of a Summer (Foster): 143
Eclipse (Guy): 168
Economic Measures at the Time of War
See *Ta'dabir Eghtessadi-y-Jangbi*
Écrire contre l'oubli
See *Contre l'oubli*
Edison Street
See *Ulica Edisona*
Edith és Marlene (Mészáros): 289
Een blandt mange (Henning-Jensen): 194
Een Schijntje Vrijheid (Apon): 19
Een Winter in Zuiderwoude (Apon): 19
Eggs (Hammer): 173; (Hubley): 197
Egor Bulychov i drugie (Solntseva): 395
Egor Bulytchev and Others
See *Egor Bulychov i drugie*
Egyszerű történet (Elek): 127
Eigen Haard is Goud Waard (Apon): 19
Eighties
See *Années 80*
Eikon (Cantrill): 65
Ein Blick—und die Liebe bricht aus (Brückner): 57
Ein Familienfilm von Waltraut Lehner (Export): 134
Ein ganz und gar verwahrlostes Mädchen (Brückner): 56
Ein Idealer Gatte (von Harbou): 440
Ein Liebe en Deutschland (Holland): 195
Ein Perfektes Paar oder die Unzucht wechselt ihre Haut (Export): 134
Eine Frau für drei Tage (von Harbou): 440
Eine Frau mit Verantwortung (Brückner): 57
Eine Frau ohne Bedetung (von Harbou): 440
Eine Prämie für Irene (Sander): 361
Eine Reise ist eine Reise Wert (Export): 134
Einleitung zu Arnold Schoenberg Begleit Musik zu einer Lichtspielscene (Huillet): 201
El Cid (Fields): 141
El crimen de Cuenca (Miró): 291
El Cuerpo repartido y el mundo al revés
See *Mensche verstreut und Welt verkehrt*
El Dorado (Brackett): 52
El hombre cuando es hombre (Sarmiento): 365
El jardín del Edén (Novaro): 309
El juego de la oca (Miró): 291
El Mundo de la Mujer (Bemberg): 38
El Niño Raramuri
See *En el país de los pies ligeros*
El pájaro de la felicidad (Miró): 291
El perro del hortelano (Miró): 291
Eleanor's Catch (Madison): 258
Electrocutée (Guy): 168
Elek, Judit: **127**
Element of Crime
See *Forbrydelsens Element*
Elephant Walk (Head): 186
Elisabeth und der Narr (von Harbou): 440
Eliza's Horoscope (Obomsawin): 313
Elle (Sarmiento): 365
Elle à passe tant d'heures sous les sunlights (Akerman): 4
Elle court, elle court la banlieue (Kurys): 225
Elmer Gantry (Jeakins): 208
Elsa (Varda): 435
Elsa, Elsa (Pascal): 328
Elsie Haas (Faye): 137
Eltávozott nap (Mészáros): 289
Emergence (Parmar): 326
Emergency Squad (Head): 184
Emigrants
See *Utvandrarna*
Emma (Marion): 266
Emmanuel Ungaro, Couturier (Maldoror): 261
Emperor Waltz (Head): 185
Empire Strikes Back (Brackett): 52

Employee
See *Der Angestellte*
Employment of the Rural Migrants in Town
See *Mohojereen Roustai*
Emporte-moi (Pool): 339
Empress (Guy): 169
Empty Suitcases (Gordon): 157
En avoir (ou pas) (Denis): 115
En classe (Guy): 167
En cours de route
See *Utközben*
En el país de los pies ligeros (Fernández Violante): 139
En faction (Guy): 168
En la otra isla (Gómez): 154
En Passant (Parker): 325
En Passion (Ullmann): 424
En Rachachant (Huillet): 201
Enchanted Desna
See *Zacharovannaya Desna*
Enchanting Capri
See *Capri Incantevole*
Enchantment (Head): 185
Enchantment of the Blue Sailors
See *Betörung der blauen Matrosen*
Encounter
See *Találkozás*
Encounters in the Dark
See *Spotkania w mroku*
End of a Clairvoyant
See *Konec jasnovidce*
End of Our World
See *Koniec naszego świata*
End of the Affair (Coffee): 91
End of the World in Our Usual Bed in a Night Full of Rain (Wertmüller): 449
Endangered (Hammer): 173
Endowing Your Future (Allen, D.): 10
Ene, mene, mink (Dörrie): 121
Enemy (Booth): 44; (Gish): 148
Enemy Paths
See *Vrazhi tropi*
Energy Picture (Batchelor): 35
Enfants (Duras): 124
Enfants du miracle (Guy): 168
Enfants du siècle (Kurys): 225
Engagement Party
See *petición*
Englishman and the Girl (Pickford): 334
Enlèvement en automobile et mariage précipite (Guy): 168
Enlisted Man's Honor (Guy): 168
Enoch Arden (Gish): 148; (Macpherson): 256
Enredando Sombras (Fernández Violante): 139
Enredando sombras (Novaro): 309
Ensemble for Somnambulists (Deren): 116
Ensign Pulver (Jeakins): 208
Enskilda samtal (Ullmann): 424
Enter Laughing (May): 271
Enter Life (Hubley): 197
Entotsu no mieru basho (Tanaka): 410
Entre Deux Soeurs (Leaf): 235
Entre el cielo y la tierre
See *Sur la terre comme au ciel*
Entre nous
See *Coup de foudre*
Entre tinieblas (Pascal): 328
Ephron, Nora: **129**
Epstein, Marie: **132**
Equal Opportunity (Leaf): 235
Equilibres (Hänsel): 176
Equine Spy (Guy): 169
Equinox Flower
See *Higanbana*
Erbtöchter (Brückner): 57; (Sanders-Brahms): 364
Erdbeben in Chile (Sanders-Brahms): 364
Erection (Ono): 316
Eros/ion (Export): 134
Erotique (Borden): 46; (Law): 232; (Treut): 416
Errand Boy (Head): 186
Erreur de poivrot (Guy): 168
Erreur judiciaire (Guy): 168
Erste Recht des Kindes (von Harbou): 440
Erzieherin gesucht (von Harbou): 440
Es Gibt Kein Vergessen
See *Desembarcos*
Es hilft nicht, wo Gewalt herrscht
See *Nicht versöhnt oder Es hilft nur Gewalt, wo Gewalt herrscht*
Es kommt ein Tag (von Harbou): 440
Es primera vez (Novaro): 309
Escalier C (Guillemot): 165
Escape (Bute): 59; (Gish): 148
Escape from Fort Bravo (Rose): 355
Escape from Zahrain (Head): 186
Escape Me Never (Coffee): 90; (Lupino): 247
Escape of the Cat
See *Fuga del Gatto*
Escape to Glory (Irene): 203
Escape to Life (Schiller): 370
Eskapade (von Harbou): 440
Esmeralda (Guy): 168
Esmerelda (Pickford): 335
Estate violenta (Cecchi d'Amico): 71
Et les Chiens se taisaient (Maldoror): 261
Eternal Breasts
See *Chibusa yo eien nare*
Eternal Flame (Marion): 265
Eternal Grind (Pickford): 335
Eternally Yours (Irene): 203; (Spencer): 397
E.T.—The Extraterrestrial (Littleton): 239

Etude cinégraphique sur une arabesque (Dulac): 123
Étude sur l'harmonie des lignes (Parker): 325
Europa, Europa (Holland): 195
Europeans (Jhabvala): 210
Eva (von Trotta): 441
Evelyn Prentice (Coffee): 90
Even as You and I (Weber): 444
Evening at Abdon
See *Wieczór u Abdona*
Evening at Abdon's
See *Wieczór u Abdona*
Evening Star (Bute): 59
Every Day's a Holiday (West): 452
Every Girl Should Be Married (Sharaff): 384
Every Other Weekend
See *Week-End sur deux*
Every Revolution Is a Throw of the Dice
See *Toute révolution est un coup de dés*
Everybody Rides the Carousel (Hubley): 197
Everybody's All-American (Van Runkle): 431
Everybody's Cheering
See *Take Me Out to the Ball Game*
Everyday Stories
See *Mindennapi történetek*
Everything I Have Is Yours (Rose): 355
Everything's in Order but Nothing Works
See *Tutto a posto e niente in ordine*
Eve's Secret (Akins): 6
Evil Roy Slade (Marshall): 268
Examination Day at School (Pickford): 334
Ex-Bad Boy (Loos): 246
Except the People (Child): 76
Excess Baggage (Marion): 266
Exchanges (Gordon): 157
Exciters (Levien): 237
Exclusive (Head): 183
Excursion (Menken): 285
Excursion a Vueltabajo (Gómez): 154
Excuse My Dust (Rose): 355
Executive Suite (Rose): 355
Exil Shanghai (Ottinger): 318
Exiles' Dialogue
See *Dialogue d'exilés*
Experiment in Meditation (De Hirsch): 110
Experiments in Three-Colour Separation (Cantrill): 65
Export! Export! Export! (Batchelor): 34
Export or Die (Batchelor): 34
Export, Valie: **133**
Expropiación (Sarmiento): 366
Expulsion
See *Austreibung*
Extravagance (Madison): 258
Eye for an Eye
See *Dead Man Who Killed*
Eye for an Eye (Mathis): 269
Eye Music in Red Major (Menken): 284
Eye of the Cat (Head): 187
Eye Witness
See *Your Witness*
Eyeblink (Ono): 316
Eyes Do Not Want to Close at All Times or Perhaps One Day Rome Will Permit Herself to Choose in Her Turn, Othon
See *Othon*
Eyes of God (Weber): 444
Eyes that Could Not Close (Guy): 169
Eyes That Saw
See *Glaza, kotorye videli*
Eyewitness (Box, M.): 51
Ezop (Krumbachová): 223

F

Få mig att skratta (Ahrne): 2
Fabiola (Cecchi d'Amico): 71
Facciamo paradiso (Cecchi d'Amico): 72
Face (Bird): 42
Face at the Window (Guy): 169
Face Between (Coffee): 90
Face in the Rain (Fields): 141
Face of a Stranger (Weill): 447
Face of Hope (Chytilová): 83
Face of the Enemy
See *Fashizm budet razbit*
Face to Face
See *Ansikte mot ansikte*
Faces
See *Anskiter*
Faces in the Dark (Zetterling): 462
Facial Grimaces
See *Gesichtsgrimassen*
Facing a Family (Export): 134
Facts of Life (Head): 186
Facts of Love
See *29 Acacia Avenue*
Faded Lilies (Macpherson): 256; (Pickford): 334
Fad'jal (Faye): 137
Fahrt ins Glück (von Harbou): 440
Faim . . . L' occasion . . . L'herbe tendre (Guy): 168
Fair Dentist (Pickford): 334
Fairy of Borgo Loreto
See *Fata di Borgo Loreto*
Fait d'hiver (Kaplan): 213
Faith of Her Fathers (Madison): 258
Faithful in My Fashion (Irene): 205
Fall of Eve (Loos): 246
Fall of the Romanov Dynasty
See *Padenye dinastii romanovykh*
Fallen (Steel): 401

Fallen Champ: The Untold Story of Mike Tyson (Kopple): 221
Fallen Hero (Loos): 244
Falling Bodies (Schneemann): 372
Falling Leaves (Guy): 169
Fälschung (von Trotta): 442
False Colors (Marion): 266; (Weber): 444
False Witness
See *Fälschung*
Famille et Variations (Poirier): 337
Family
See *Città violenta*
Family Business (Akerman): 4
Family Film by Waltraud Lehner
See *Ein Familienfilm von Waltraut Lehner*
Family Jewels (Head): 186
Family Plot (Head): 187
Famous Mrs. Fair (Marion): 265
Fanchon, the Cricket (Marion): 264; (Pickford): 335
Fancy Pants (Head): 185
Fanny Hill (Ahrne): 3
Fantasia 'e Surdata (Notari): 307
Fantassin Guignard (Guy): 168
Far from Poland (Godmilow): 152
Far from Vietnam
See *Loin du Vietnam*
Far Horizon (Head): 186
Far Paradise (McDonagh Sisters): 278
Far Shore (Wieland): 455
Farahang-e-Massraffi (Bani-Etemad): 32
Farces de cuisinière (Guy): 168
Farces de Jocko (Guy): 167
Farewell
See *Proschanie s Matyoroy*
Farewell China
See *Ai zai biexiang de jijie*
Farewell, My Dear, Farewell. . . the Army Is Going
See *Addio Mia Bella Addio, l'Armata se ne va*
Farewell to Arms (Head): 183
Farewell to Matyora
See *Proschanie s Matyoroy*
Farewell to the Devil
See *Pożegnanie z diabłem*
Farmer Charley (Batchelor): 34
Farmer's Daughter (Head): 184
Fascination of the Fleur de Lis (Madison): 258; (Meredyth): 286
Fascism Will Be Destroyed
See *Fashizm budet razbit*
Fashions for Women (Arzner): 25
Fashizm budet razbit (Shub): 390
Fast Times at Ridgemont High (Heckerling): 189
Fat City (Booth): 45; (Jeakins): 208
Fata di Borgo Loreto (Notari): 307
Fatal Attraction (Steel): 401
Fatal Dress Suit (Loos): 244
Fatal Finger Prints (Loos): 244
Fatal Hour (Macpherson): 256
Fatal Wedding (Lyell): 250
Fate (Cecchi d'Amico): 72
Fate's Inception (Pickford): 334
Father and Son
See *Vater und Sohn*
Father Brown, Detective (Head): 183
Father Gets in the Game (Macpherson): 256
Father of the Bride (Goodrich): 155; (Keaton): 215; (Rose): 355
Father of the Bride, Part II (Keaton): 215
Father's Bride (Meredyth): 287
Father's Little Dividend (Goodrich): 155; (Rose): 355
Fatso (Murphy): 297
Fatto di sangue fra due uomini per causa di una vedova (Wertmüller): 449
Faucets (Menken): 284
Faunovo prilis pozdni odpoledne (Chytilová): 83; (Krumbachová): 224
Faust (Guy): 168
Faust et Méphistophélès (Guy): 168
Faut vivre dangereusement (Kaplan): 213
Faute des autres (Guillemot): 165
Faye, Safi: **137**
Fear Strikes Out (Head): 186
Feast and the Law
See *'A Legge*
Feast of Life (Marion): 264
Febbre di vivere (Cecchi d'Amico): 71
Fedka's Truth (Preobrazhenskaya): 342
Fée au printemps (Guy): 168
Fée aux choux (Guy): 167
Feet of Clay (Bauchens): 37
Fei Tien, Goddess in Flight (Choy): 81
Feira (Carolina): 67
Felicité (Pascal): 328
Felix (Sander): 361; (Sanders-Brahms): 364; (von Trotta): 441
Fem dagar i Falköping (Ahrne): 2
Female Artillery (Lupino): 248
Female Closet (Hammer): 173
Female Misbehavior (Treut): 416
Female of the Species (Pickford): 334; (Weber): 444
Femeile zilelor noastre (Mészáros): 289
Feminist and the Fuzz (Marshall): 268
Femme au foyer (Sarmiento): 365
Femme de l'amant (Pascal): 328
Femme de l'hôtel (Pool): 339
Femme du Ganges (Duras): 124

Femme est une femme (Guillemot): 165
Femme mariée (Guillemot): 165
Fenesta che Lucive (Notari): 307
Feng Jie (Hui): 199
Fer à cheval (Musidora): 300
Ferai (Ahrne): 2
Ferdinando e Carolina (Wertmüller): 449
Fernández Violante, Marcela: **139**
Festök városa—Szentendre (Mészáros): 289
Fête espagnole (Dulac): 122
Fetus
See *A Magzat*
Feu de paille (Epstein): 132
Feud (Madison): 258
Feud in the Kentucky Hills (Pickford): 334
Fever
See *Gorączka*
Fever: The Story of the Bomb
See *Gorączka*
Fiançailles d'Agenor (Musidora): 300
Fiancé ensorcelé (Guy): 168
Fiancée du pirate (Kaplan): 213
Fiancés de 1914 (Musidora): 300
Fica Comigo (Yamasaki): 460
Fidgety Little Bouton
See *O neposedném knoflíčku*
Field Study #2 (Nelson): 305
Fields, Verna: **140**
Fiery Introduction (Madison): 258
Fiesta (Irene): 205
Fifi tambour (Musidora): 300
Fifteen Minutes on Fifteen Years
See *15 perc 15 évröl*
Fifth Horseman Is Fear
See *. . . a pátý jezdec je Strach*
Fight for Your Lady (Lupino): 247
Fighting Breed (Meredyth): 286
Fighting Shepherdess (Coffee): 90
Figlia del Vesuvio (Notari): 307
Figlio del Reggimento (Notari): 307
Figure behind the Glass (Krumbachová): 224
Figurehead (Batchelor): 34
File on Thelma Jordan (Head): 185
Fille à la dérive (Guillemot): 165
Fille d'Eve (Musidora): 300
Fille Galante
See *Fugueuses*
Filles c'est pas pareil (Poirier): 337
Filles du Roi (Poirier): 337
Filling the Gap (Batchelor): 34
Film à venir (Sarmiento): 366
Film about a Woman Who. . . (Rainer): 345
Film d'amore e d'anarchia, ovvero stamattina alle 10 in Via dei fiori nella nota casa di toleranza (Wertmüller): 449
Film in the Future
See *Film à venir*
Film No. 4 (Ono): 316
Film No. 5 (Ono): 316
Film No. 6 (Ono): 316
Film of Love and Anarchy, or This Morning at Ten in the Via dei fiori at the Well-Known House of Tolerance
See *Film d'amore e d'anarchia, ovvero stamattina alle 10 in Via dei fiori nella nota casa di toleranza*
Filmraum: Reproduktionsimmanente Ästhetik (Hein): 192
Filmstatement (Davis): 107
Fils du garde-chasse (Guy): 168
Fin des étés (Poirier): 337
Finanzen des Grossherzogs (von Harbou): 440
Fine Clothes (Booth): 44
Fine del mondo in una notte piena di poggia
See *End of the World in Our Usual Bed in a Night Full of Rain*
Fine e nota (Cecchi d'Amico): 72
Finestra sul Luna Park (Cecchi d'Amico): 71
Finian's Rainbow (Jeakins): 208
Finnegan Begin Again (Silver): 392
Finnegans Wake (Bute): 59; (Schoonmaker): 375
Fiole enchantée (Guy): 168
Fire (Mehta): 283
Fire in the Straw
See *Feu de paille*
Firefly (Goodrich): 155
Fires of Conscience (Shipman): 388
Fires Within (Armstrong): 21
First Born (Reville): 349
First Cigarette
See *Première Cigarette*
First Comes Courage (Arzner): 25
First Comes Love (Friedrich): 144
First Line of Defence (Batchelor): 34
First Love (Levien): 237
First Misunderstanding (Pickford): 334
First Ninety-Nine (Batchelor): 35
First of the Few (Dillon): 118
First Voyage
See *Premier voyage*
First Waltz
See *Der Erste Walzer*
First Wives Club (Keaton): 215
First Year (Marion): 265
Fish in the Bathtub (Silver): 392
Fisher Folks (Macpherson): 256
Fisher-maid (Pickford): 334
Fisher's Ghost (Lyell): 250
Fitzwilly (Lennart): 236
Five (Batchelor): 35

Five and Ten (Booth): 45
Five Angles on Murder
See *Woman in Question*
Five Artists: BillBobBillBillBob (Nelson): 305
Five Corners (Foster): 143
Five Days in Falköping
See *Fem dagar i Falköping*
Five Finger Discount (Murphy): 297
Five Finger Exercise (Goodrich): 155
Five Graves to Cairo (Head): 184
Five Out of Five (Chenzira): 75
Five Pennies (Head): 186
Five Pound Man (Dillon): 118
Five Women around Utamaro
See *Utamaro o meburi go-nin no onna*
Fixer (Jeakins): 208
Fjols til Fjells (Ullmann): 424
Flag Passes By
See *Passa a Bandiera*
Flamboyant Ladies Speak Out (Chenzira): 75
Flame and the Flesh (Rose): 355
Flame of the West (Madison): 258
Flaming Forties (Marion): 265
Flaming Years
See *Povest plamennykh let*
Flamme cachée (Colette): 95; (Musidora): 300
Flapper (Marion): 265
Flapper Wives (Murfin): 296
Flash of Light (Macpherson): 256
Flashdance (Steel): 401
Fleay's Fauna Centre (Leaf): 235
Fleet's In (Head): 184
Flemish Farm (Craigie): 101
Flesh and Blood (Guy): 169
Flesh and Fantasy (Head): 184
Flesh and Paper (Parmar): 326
Flesh Will Surrender
See *Delitto di Giovanni Episcopo*
Flickor, kvinnor och en och annan drake (Ahrne): 2
Flickorna (Zetterling): 462
Flight for Freedom (Murfin): 296
Flight of a Nightbird (Madison): 258
Flim-Flam Man (Jeakins): 208
Flirt (Weber): 444
Flirting with Fate (Gish): 148
Floating Life (Law): 232
Floterian—Hand Printings from a Film History (Cantrill): 65
Flower Drum Song (Sharaff): 384
Flowing
See *Nagareru*
Flügel und Fesseln (Sanders-Brahms): 364
Flu-ing Squad (Batchelor): 34
Flurina (Batchelor): 35
Flurry in Art (Loos): 244
Fluxfilm Program (Ono): 316
Fly (Ono): 316
Fly about the House (Batchelor): 34
Flying Blind (Head): 184
Flying Coffer
See *Der fliegende Koffer*
Flying Down to Rio (Irene): 203
Flyktingar finner en hamn (Henning-Jensen): 194
Fog Pumas (Nelson): 305
Fogo, Ile de Feu (Maldoror): 261
Folie des vaillants (Dulac): 123
Folies Bergère (Meredyth): 286
Folies douces (Guillemot): 165
Folies Masquées (Guy): 168
Folketingsvalg 1945 (Henning-Jensen): 194
Follow Me, Boys! (Gish): 148
Follow that Car (Batchelor): 35
Follow the Leader (Head): 183
Folly of Anne (Gish): 148
Fonderies Martin (Parker): 325
Fong Sai-Yuk (Hui): 199
Food of the Gods (Lupino): 248
Foo-Foo's New Hat (Batchelor): 35
Foo-Foo's Sleepless Night (Batchelor): 35
Fool and His Money (Weber): 444
Fool Killer (Jeakins): 208
Fool's Highway (Coffee): 90
Fools in the Mountains
See *Fjols til Fjells*
Fool's Paradise (Bauchens): 37
Foot Film
See *Volleyball*
Footloose (Steel): 401
Footsteps in the Fog (Coffee): 91
For Alimony Only (Coffee): 90
For Better for Worse (Batchelor): 34
For Better, for Worse (Bauchens): 37; (Macpherson): 255
"For George, Love Donna" (Deitch): 112
For Her Brother's Sake (Pickford): 334
For Her Father's Sins (Loos): 244
For Husbands Only (Weber): 444
For Pete's Sake (Streisand): 405
For Sasha
See *Pour Sacha*
For the First Time
See *Es primera vez*
For the Queen's Honor (Pickford): 334
For the Soul of Rafael (Coffee): 90
For Whom the Bell Tolls (Head): 185
Forbidden (Weber): 444
Forbidden Country (Reville): 349
Forbidden Fruit (Bauchens): 37; (Macpherson): 255
Forbidden Planet (Rose): 355

Forbidden Room (Meredyth): 286
Forbidden to Know
See *Defense de savoir*
Forbidden Woman (Coffee): 90
Forbrydelsens Element (Henning-Jensen): 194
Forced Landing (Head): 184
Foreign Affair (Head): 185
Foreign Correspondent (Harrison): 180; (Spencer): 397
Foreign Currency
See *Poul-e Khareji*
Forever and a Day (Lupino): 247
Forever Female (Head): 185
Forfølgelsen (Breien): 55
Forgery
See *Fälschung*
Forget-Me-Not (Marion): 264
Forlorn River (Head): 183
Fortini/Cani (Huillet): 201
Fortuna di essere donna (Cecchi d'Amico): 71
Fortune Cookies: The Myth of the Model Minority (Choy): 81
Fortune Hunters (Guy): 169
Forward, Savoia
See *Sempre Avanti Savoia*
Foster, Jodie: **142**
Foto-Film (Hein): 192
Fou de Mai (Serreau): 383
Foundling (Marion): 264; (Pickford): 335
Fountain (Murfin): 296
Four around a Woman
See *Kämpfende Herzen*
Four Chimneys
See *Entotsu no mieru basho*
Four Daughters (Coffee): 90
Four Frightened People (Bauchens): 37; (Coffee): 90
Four Horsemen of the Apocalypse (Mathis): 270
Four Hours to Kill (Head): 183
Four Men and a Prayer (Levien): 237
Four Rooms (Anders): 15
Four Women (Dash): 105
Fourberies de Pingouin (Musidora): 300
Fourteen Hours (Spencer): 397
Fourteen's Good, Eighteen's Better (Armstrong): 21
Fowl Play (Batchelor): 34
Fox and the Tiger (Leaf): 235
Foxes (Foster): 143
Foxes, Mice and Gallows Hill
See *Lišáci-myšáci a Šibeničák*
Fra Diavolo (Guy): 169; (Macpherson): 255
Fragilité—ton nom est femme (Trintignant): 420
Fragments (Cantrill): 65
Frame Line (Nelson): 305
Francesco (Cavani): 69
Francesco d'Assisi (Cavani): 69
Frank Capra's American Dream (Heckerling): 189
Franz Schubert's Last Three Sonatas
See *Trois dernières sonatas de Franz Shubert*
Fratelli sole, sorella luna (Wertmüller): 449
Fratello sole, sorella luna (Cecchi d'Amico): 72
Frau am Scheidewege (von Harbou): 440
Frau im Mond (von Harbou): 440
Frauen von Gnadenstein (von Harbou): 439
Freak Orlando (Ottinger): 318
Freaky Friday (Foster): 143; (Mayron): 276
Fredaines de Pierrette (Guy): 168
Free Breathing
See *Szabad lélegzet*
Freedom (Ono): 316
Freedom Radio (Dillon): 118
French Doll (Marion): 265
French Downstairs (Weber): 444
French Dressing (Russell): 357
French Game
See *Coeur battant*
French Milliner (Loos): 244
French Postcards (Littleton): 239
French without Tears (Dillon): 118; (Head): 184
Frenzy
See *Hets*
Fresh Seeds in a Big Apple (Choy): 81
Freundin
See *Amiga*
Frida Kahlo (Fernández Violante): 139
Friday, the 13th (Marion): 264
Frieda (Zetterling): 462
Friedrich, Su: **144**
Friendly (Coolidge): 99
Friendly Persuasion (Jeakins): 208
Friends (Pickford): 334
Friends and Husbands
See *Heller Wahn*
Friends and Lovers (Murfin): 296
Frightened Bride
See *Tall Headlines*
Frightening Women
See *Unheimlichen Frauen*
Fribetens murar (Ahrne): 2
Frivolité (Guy): 168
Frog Prince (Reiniger): 347
From Here to Eternity
See *Verdammt in alle Ewigkeit*
From Rags to Stitches (Batchelor): 34
From Spikes to Spindles (Choy): 81
From the Bottom of the Sea (Pickford): 334

From the Cloud to the Resistance
See *Della nube alla resistenza*
From the Terrace (Spencer): 397
Frontier
See *Aerograd*
Frontiersman (Head): 183
Frozen Justice (Levien): 237
Fruit Bowl
See *Yes! Yi zu*
Fruit of Paradise
See *Ovoce stromů rajských jíme*
Fruit Punch (Law): 232
Fruits amers (Audry): 27
Fruits de saison (Guy): 168
Fud 69 (Cantrill): 65
Fuegos (Guillemot): 165
Fuerchten und Liebe
See *Paura e amore*
Fuga del Gatto (Notari): 306
Fugitive Lovers (Goodrich): 155
Fugitives Find Shelter
See *Flyktingar finner en hamn*
Fugueuses (Trintignant): 420
Full Moon, Saturday Night (Deitch): 112
Full Rich Life
See *Cynthia*
Fumées (Parker): 325
Fun in Acapulco (Head): 186
Fun with Music
See *Polka Graph*
Funfair Has Arrived
See *Přijela k nám pout*
Funny Face (Head): 186
Funny Girl (Lennart): 236; (Sharaff): 384; (Streisand): 405
Funny Lady (Allen, J.): 12; (Booth): 45; (Streisand): 405
Funny Valentine (Dash): 105
Furies (Head): 185
Fuses (Schneemann): 372
Fussball (Hein): 192
Fusswaschung (Hein): 192
Future of Emily
See *Flügel und Fesseln*
Future of Saint Denis
See *Saint-Denis sur Avenir*
Fuzz (Jeakins): 208

G

Gable and Lombard (Head): 187; (Mayron): 275
Gabriel Goes to the City (Obomsawin): 313
Gabriele il Lampionaio di Porto (Notari): 307
Gaby (Goodrich): 155; (Rose): 355
Gaby: A True Story (Ullmann): 424
Gage d'amour (Guy): 168
Gaiety George (Sagan): 359
Gaijin: Caminhos da Liberdade (Yamasaki): 460
Gaines Roussel (Parker): 325
Galathea (Reiniger): 347
Galaxy (Cantrill): 65
Galileo (Cavani): 69
Gallant Little Tailor (Reiniger): 347
Gambling Ship (Head): 183
Game (Child): 76
Game for Six Lovers
See *L'Eau à la bouche*
Game of Love
See *Blé en herbe*
Games of Love and Loneliness
See *Den Allvarsamma leken*
Gangsters of New York (Loos): 244
Garbo Talks (Comden): 96
Garce (Pascal): 328
Garçonne (Audry): 27
Garden of Eden
See *El jardín del Edén*
Gardener (Batchelor): 35
Gardener's Son (von Brandenstein): 437
Garrison's Finish (Pickford): 334
Gary Cooper que estás en los cielos (Miró): 291
Gas Food Lodging (Anders): 15
Gaslight (Irene): 205
Gasoline Engagement (Pickford): 334
Gates of the Forest (Ullmann): 424
Gathering of Eagles (Irene): 205
Gattin (von Harbou): 440
Gattopardo (Cecchi d'Amico): 72
Gaucho (Pickford): 335
Gauloises bleues (Guillemot): 165
Gaunt Stranger
See *Ringer*
Gavotte (Guy): 168
Gay Day (Hammer): 173
Gay Deceiver (Booth): 44
Gay Desperado (Lupino): 247; (Pickford): 334
Gay Mrs. Trexel
See *Susan and God*
Gay Sisters (Coffee): 90; (Head): 184
Gayosso de descuentos (Fernández Violante): 139
Gaz (Parker): 325
Gaz de Lacq (Guillemot): 165
Gazebo (Rose): 356
Gebroken Spiegels (Gorris): 159
Gefährten meines Sommers (von Harbou): 440
Geisha Boy (Head): 186
Geisha in the Old City
See *Jotai wa kanashiku*
Geld (Dörrie): 121

Gendarmes (Guy): 168
Généalogies d'une crime (Sarmiento): 366
General's Daughter
See *De todos modos Juan te llamas*
Generation of the Railroad Builder (Choy): 81
Genitalpanik (Export): 134
Gennariello il Figlio del Galeotto (Notari): 307
Gennariello Polizziotto (Notari): 307
Gennariello the Policeman
See *Gennariello Polizziotto*
Gennariello the Son of the Convict
See *Gennariello il Figlio del Galeotto*
Genroku onna (Tanaka): 409
Gens de toutes partes, Gens de nulle parte (Sarmiento): 365
Gente de todas partes . . . Gente de ninguna parte
See *Gens de toutes partes, Gens de nulle parte*
Gentle Arm
See *Street Corner*
Gentle Sex (Dillon): 118
Gentleman or Thief (Loos): 244
Gentleman's Agreement (Shipman): 388
Gentlemen Boys
See *Páni kluci*
Gentlemen Marry Brunettes (Loos): 246
Gentlemen Prefer Blondes (Loos): 246
Gently down the Stream (Friedrich): 144
Genus: The Life of Jitka and Květa Válovy
See *Genus: Život Jitky a Květy Válových*
Genus: The Live of Theater Maker Ota Ornest
See *Genus: Život divadelníka Oty Ornesta*
Genus: Život divadelníka Oty Ornesta (Krumbachová): 224
Genus: Život Jitky a Květy Válových (Krumbachová): 224
Géo le mystérieux (Dulac): 122
Geography of the Body (Menken): 285
Geole (Musidora): 300
Geometrics of the Kabballah (De Hirsch): 110
Georgia, Georgia (Angelou): 17
Georgina's Gründe (von Trotta): 442
German Sisters
See *Bleierne Zeit*
Germans and Their Men
See *Deutschen und ihre Männer*
Germany, Pale Mother
See *Deutschland, bleiche Mutter*
Germination d'un haricot (Dulac): 123
Geronimo (Head): 184
Geschichte des Prinzen Achmed (Reiniger): 347
Geschichte eines Lebens
See *Annelie*
Geschichtsunterricht (Huillet): 201
Gesichtsgrimassen (Export): 134
Gestohlene Herz (Reiniger): 347
Gesu' mio Fratello (Cavani): 69
Get a Lawyer
See *Mettete l'Avvocato*
Get Shorty (Marshall): 268
Get Your Man (Arzner): 25
Geteilte Liebe (Sanders-Brahms): 364
Getting Away with Murder (Marshall): 268
Getting Even (Pickford): 334
Getting It Over With (Heckerling): 189
Getting Mary Married (Loos): 245
Getting to Know the World
See *Poznavaya belyi svet*
Getúlio Vargas (Carolina): 67
Gewalt (Sanders-Brahms): 364
Ghost (Steel): 401
Ghost and Mrs. Muir (Spencer): 397
Ghost Breaker (Macpherson): 255; (Macpherson): 256
Ghost Breakers (Head): 184
Ghost Camera (Lupino): 247
Ghostbusters II (Steel): 401
G.I. Blues (Head): 186
Gibson Goddess (Pickford): 334
Gift of Green (van Dongen): 430
Giftas (Zetterling): 462
Gigi (Audry): 27; (Colette): 95
Gilda (Van Upp): 433
Gilded Cage (Marion): 264
Ginger Mick (Lyell): 250
Ginza Cosmetics
See *Ginza gesho*
Ginza gesho (Tanaka): 410
Giorno Della Pace (Cavani): 69
Giovanni (Apon): 19
Girl
See *Eltávozott nap*
Girl and the Bronco Buster (Guy): 168
Girl Crazy (Sharaff): 384
Girl from Beyond (Shipman): 388
Girl from God's Country (Shipman): 388
Girl from Missouri (Loos): 246
Girl from Nowhere (Madison): 258
Girl from Scotland Yard (Head): 183
Girl in a Million (Box, M.): 51
Girl in Lower 9 (Madison): 258
Girl in Mourning
See *niña de luto*
Girl in Overalls
See *Swing Shift Maisie*
Girl in the Armchair (Guy): 169
Girl in the Painting
See *Portrait from Life*
Girl in the Shack (Loos): 244
Girl in White (Rose): 355
Girl Named Tamiko (Head): 186

Girl Next Door (Lennart): 236
Girl of the Golden West (Macpherson): 256
Girl of Yesterday (Marion): 266; (Pickford): 335
Girl Rush (Head): 186
Girl Was Young
See *Young and Innocent*
Girl Who Had Everything (Rose): 355
Girl Who Lost (Madison): 258
Girl With the Crazy Brother (Keaton): 215
Girl with the Green Eyes (Guy): 169
Girlfriends
See *Amiche*
Girlfriends (Mayron): 275; (von Brandenstein): 437; (Weill): 447
Girls
See *Flickorna*
Girls about Town (Akins): 6
Girls at 12 (Chopra): 78
Girl's Folly (Marion): 264
Girls from Wilko
See *Panny z Wilka*
Girls! Girls! Girls! (Head): 186
Girls in Uniform
See *Mädchen in Uniform*
Girls of the Night
See *Onna bakari no yoru*
Girl's Own Story (Campion): 61
Girls, Women—and Once in a While a Dragon
See *Flickor, kvinnor och en och annan drake*
Gish, Lillian: **147**
Give a Girl a Break (Goodrich): 155; (Rose): 355
Give Me a Sailor (Head): 183
Give Peace a Chance
See *Bed-In*
Giving Up the Ghost (Weill): 447
Glamour Boy (Head): 184
Glass Key (Head): 183; (Head): 184
Glass Slipper (Rose): 355
Glaza, kotorye videli (Solntseva): 395
Gli indifferenti (Cecchi d'Amico): 72
Glimpse of the Garden (Menken): 284
Global Gamble (Kidron): 217
Gloria ai Caduti (Notari): 307
Glory Alley (Rose): 355
Glory to the Fallen Soldiers
See *Gloria ai Caduti*
Glyn, Elinor: **150**
G-Man (B): 30
Gnesella (Notari): 307
Go Between (Choy): 81
Go Fish (Vachon): 426
Go! Go! Go! (Menken): 285
Go Naked in the World (Rose): 356
Go West, Young Man (West): 452
Goat (Marion): 264
Go-Between (Dillon): 118
God Bless America (Hein): 192
Godfather (Keaton): 215
Godfather, Part II (Keaton): 215; (Van Runkle): 431
Godfather, Part III (Keaton): 215
Godfather Trilogy: 1901-1980 (Keaton): 215
Godless Girl (Bauchens): 37; (Macpherson): 255
Godmilow, Jill: **152**
God's Country and the Woman (Shipman): 388
Goin' to Town (West): 452
Going Hollywood (Marion): 266
Going My Way (Head): 185
Gold and Glitter (Gish): 147
Gold Diggers (Potter): 341
Gold Fugue (Cantrill): 65
Gold Madness (Madison): 259
Gold Necklace (Pickford): 334
Gold of the Seven Saints (Brackett): 52
Golden Autumn (Peng): 330
Golden Bed (Bauchens): 37; (Head): 183; (Macpherson): 255
Golden Boat (Alberti): 7
Golden Chance (Macpherson): 255
Golden Eighties
See *Window Shopping*
Golden Gate
See *Zolotye vorota*
Golden Gloves (Head): 184
Golden Yukon (Shipman): 388
Goldene Gans (Reiniger): 347
Goldie Gets Along (Irene): 203
Golhayeh Davoodi (Bani-Etemad): 32
Golpe de suerte (Fernández Violante): 139
Golven (Apon): 19
Gómez, Sara: **154**
Gongola (Hänsel): 176
Goob na nu (Faye): 137
Good Earth (Marion): 266
Good Fellows (Head): 185
Good Girls Go to Paris (Coffee): 90
Good King Wenceslas (Batchelor): 34
Good Little Devil (Pickford): 334
Good Morning, Beijing
See *Beijing Nin Zao*
Good Morning, Vietnam (Steel): 401
Good Mother (Keaton): 215
Good News (Comden): 96; (Marion): 266; (Rose): 355
Good Time Girl (Box, M.): 51
Good-bye-Bill (Loos): 245
Goodbye Charlie (Rose): 356
Goodbye Girl (Booth): 45
Goodbye in the Mirror (De Hirsch): 109

Good-bye, Lover (Van Runkle): 431
Goodbye Sadness (Ono): 316
Good-bye Yesterday (Peng): 330
GoodFellas (Schoonmaker): 375
Goodrich, Frances: **155**
Goodwill to All Dogs (Batchelor): 35
Gorąca linia (Jakubowska): 207
Gorączka (Holland): 195
Gordon, Bette: **157**
Gorris, Marleen: **159**
Gossette (Dulac): 123
Gott om pojkar—ont om män? (Ahrne): 2
Götter der Pest (von Trotta): 442
Grace of My Heart (Anders): 15; (Schoonmaker): 375
Gracie Allen Murder Case (Head): 184
Grain (Preobrazhenskaya): 343
Grain of the Voice Series: Rock Wallaby and Blackbird (Cantrill): 65
Grand amour de Balzac (Audry): 27
Grand Canyon (Littleton): 239
Grand chemin (Pascal): 328
Grand Concert (Batchelor): 35
Grand Duke's Finances
See *Finanzen des Grossherzogs*
Grand Highway
See *Grand chemin*
Grand Jury Secrets (Head): 184
Grand Larceny (Meredyth): 286
Grand Matin (Guillemot): 165
Grand Souffle (Musidora): 300
Grande espérance (Epstein): 132
Grandfather's Journey
See *Morfars Resa*
Grand-père raconte
See *Fad'jal*
Grands chemins (Trintignant): 420
Grands Feux (Parker): 325
Grasshopper (Marshall): 268
Grasshopper and the Ant (Reiniger): 347
Graustark (Coffee): 90; (Marion): 265
Grayson, Helen: **161**
Graziella (Cecchi d'Amico): 71
Great Adventure (Guy): 169
Great Big World and Little Children
See *Wielka Wielksza Najwielksza*
Great Caruso (Levien): 237; (Rose): 355
Great Chase (Gish): 148
Great Divide (Coffee): 90
Great Gambini (Head): 183
Great Gatsby (Head): 185
Great Goddess (Hammer): 173
Great Hospital Mystery (Meredyth): 287
Great Lie (Coffee): 90
Great Love (Gish): 148
Great Love Experiment (Weill): 447
Great Lover (Head): 185
Great Man's Lady (Head): 184
Great McGinty (Head): 184
Great Meadow (Bauchens): 37
Great Moment (Glyn): 150; (Head): 185
Great Moments in Aviation (Kidron): 217
Great Parade of the Fleet
See *Rivista Navale Dell' 11 Novembre 1912*
Great Race (Head): 186
Great Radium Mystery (Madison): 258
Great Road
See *Veliky put'*
Great Sinner (Irene): 205
Great Smokey Roadblock (Mayron): 275
Great Victor Herbert (Head): 184
Great Waldo Pepper (Head): 187
Great Wall of Los Angeles (Deitch): 112
Great White Hope (Sharaff): 384
Greater Glory (Mathis): 270
Greater Love Hath No Man (Guy): 169
Greatest Question (Gish): 148
Greatest Show on Earth (Bauchens): 37; (Head): 185; (Jeakins): 208
Greatest Thing in Life (Gish): 148
Greed (Mathis): 270
Greeks Had a Word for Them (Akins): 6
Green Dolphin Street (Irene): 205
Green Eyed Woman
See *Take a Letter, Darling*
Green Fire (Rose): 355
Green Hell (Marion): 266
Green Mansions (Jeakins): 208
Green Planet
See *Belle verte*
Green Years (Irene): 205; (Levien): 237
Green-Eyed Devil (Gish): 148
Greenwald, Maggie: **163**
Greenwich Village (Comden): 96
Greetings from Washington, D.C. (Schiller): 370
Greta's Girls (Schiller): 370
Gretel (Armstrong): 21
Greystoke: The Legend of Tarzan, Lord of the Apes (Russell): 357
Grim Comedian (Meredyth): 286
Grip Till It Hurts (Dash): 105
Grosse Tête (Guillemot): 165
Grounds for Marriage (Rose): 355
Growing Pains
See *Homework*
Grub Stake (Shipman): 388
Grün (Hein): 192
Gruppo di famiglia in un interno (Cecchi d'Amico): 72
Guaglio
See *Probibito rubare*

Guérité
See *Douaniers et contrebandiers*
Guerra do Paraguai (Carolina): 67
Guest
See *L'Ospite*
Guichets du Louvre (Pascal): 328
Guide for the Married Man (Spencer): 397
Guillemot, Agnès: **165**
Guilt of Janet Ames (Coffee): 90
Guilty Hands (Bauchens): 37
Guilty One (Madison): 258
Gulf Stream (Parker): 325
Gulliver's Travels (Russell): 357
Gunfight at the O.K. Corral (Head): 186
Guns (Sarmiento): 366
Guns for Banta
See *Des Fusils pour Banta*
Guru (Jhabvala): 210
Gustave Moreau (Kaplan): 213
Guy, Alice: **167**
Guy Named Joe (Irene): 203
Guys and Dolls (Sharaff): 384
Gyermekek, könyvek (Mészáros): 288
Gypsy Girl
See *Sky, West, and Crooked*

H

H2 Worker (Alberti): 7
Hablamos esta noche (Miró): 291
Haiku (Deren): 116
Hail the Conquering Hero (Head): 185
Haines, Randa: **171**
Hair Piece: A Film for Nappyheaded People (Chenzira): 75
Haircut (Hammer): 173
Haitian Corner (Choy): 81
Hakoiri musume (Tanaka): 409
Half Angel (Meredyth): 287
Half-Breed (Loos): 245
Half Marriage (Murfin): 296
Hallelujah Trail (Head): 186
Hambone and Hillie (Gish): 148
Hamilton in the Musical Festival (Batchelor): 35
Hamilton the Musical Elephant (Batchelor): 35
Hamlet (Dillon): 118
Hammer
See *Marteau*
Hammer, Barbara: **173**
Hammered: The Best of Sledge (Coolidge): 99
Hammersmith Is Out (Head): 187
Hand Movie (Rainer): 345
Hand that Rocks the Cradle (Weber): 444
Handling Ships (Batchelor): 34
Hand-tinting (Wieland): 455
Hanging out—Yonkers (Akerman): 4
Hanging Up (Ephron): 130; (Keaton): 215
Hangman (Head): 186
Hanneles Himmelfahrt (von Harbou): 440
Hansel and Gretel (Reiniger): 347
Hänsel, Marion: **175**
Happiness
See *Bonheur*
Happiness (Alberti): 7; (Vachon): 426
Happy Birthday Türke! (Dörrie): 121
Happy Birthday, Wanda June (Spencer): 397
Happy Family (Box, M.): 51
Happy Go Lucky (Head): 185
Happy Land (Spencer): 397
Happy Mother's Day (Chopra): 78
Harangok városa—Veszprém (Mészáros): 289
Hard, Fast, and Beautiful (Lupino): 247
Hard to Handle: Bob Dylan with Tom Petty and the Heartbreakers (Armstrong): 21
Hard Way (Lupino): 247; (Marshall): 268
Hardhat and Legs (von Brandenstein): 438
Harlan County, U.S.A. (Kopple): 221
Harlekin (Reiniger): 347
Harlem Wednesday (Hubley): 197
Harlow (Head): 186
Harp in Hock (Levien): 237
Harris, Leslie: **178**
Harrison, Joan: **180**
Harry & Son (Allen, D.): 10
Harry and Tonto (Mayron): 275
Harry and Walter Go to New York (Keaton): 215
Harry Hooton (Cantrill): 65
Harvest Is In
See *Goob na nu*
Harvey Girls (Irene): 205; (Rose): 355
Hassane (Palcy): 321
Hat (Hubley): 197
Hatari! (Brackett): 52; (Head): 186
Hate (Mathis): 270
Hatful of Rain (Spencer): 397
Hättest was Gescheites gelernt (Dörrie): 121
Hauchtext: Liebesgedicht (1970) (Export): 134
Haunted Hearts (Madison): 258
Having a Go (Armstrong): 21
Having Our Say: The Delany Sisters first 100 Years (Littman): 240
Hawaii (Jeakins): 208; (Van Runkle): 431
He Comes Up Smiling (Marion): 264
He Learned about Women (Head): 183
He Liu (Hui): 199
He Stayed for Breakfast (Irene): 203
He Was Once (Vachon): 426
Head, Edith: **181**
Head over Heels
See *Chilly Scenes of Winter*

Hear Me Good (Head): 186
Heart Beats of Long Ago (Macpherson): 256
Heart o' the Hills (Pickford): 334
Heart of a Cracksman (Madison): 258
Heart of a Hero (Marion): 264
Heart of a Painted Woman (Guy): 169
Heart of Arizona (Head): 183
Heart of Nora Flynn (Macpherson): 255
Heart Thief (Levien): 237
Heartbeat
See *Szivdobogás*
Heartbeeps (Mayron): 275; (Van Runkle): 431
Heartbreak Kid (May): 271
Heartburn (Ephron): 130
Heartland (von Brandenstein): 437
Hearts Adrift (Pickford): 334
Hearts and Guts
See *Tripas Coração*
Hearts Are Trumps (Mathis): 269
Heart's Crucible (Madison): 258
Hearts of the World (Gish): 148
Heat
See *Znoy*
Heat and Dust (Jhabvala): 210
Heat Shimmer (Cantrill): 65
Heat's On (West): 452
Heave Away My Johnny (Batchelor): 34
Heaven (Keaton): 215
Heaven Can Wait (May): 271; (Spencer): 397; (Van Runkle): 431
Heaven over the Marshes
See *Cielo sulla palude*
Heavenly Body (Irene): 203
Heckerling, Amy: **189**
Heilige Simplizie (von Harbou): 439
Hein, Birgit: **191**
Heinrich (Sanders-Brahms): 364
Heiress (Head): 185
Heiresses
See *Örökseg*
Helen la Belle (Reiniger): 347
Hélène (Epstein): 132
Hell Is Sold Out (Zetterling): 462
Heller in Pink Tights (Head): 186
Heller Wahn (von Trotta): 441
Hellfighters (Head): 187
Hello (Hubley): 197
Hello, Dolly! (Sharaff): 384; (Streisand): 405
Hello, Elephant!
See *Buon Giorno, elefante!*
Hello, Everybody (Head): 183
Hello Frisco, Hello (Rose): 355
Hell's Highroad (Coffee): 90
Hell's Island (Head): 186
Hen in the Wind
See *Kaze no naka no mendori*
Henning-Jensen, Astrid: **193**
Henri Gaudier-Brzeska (Cantrill): 65
Henri Langlois (Gish): 148
Henry Aldrich, Editor (Head): 184
Henry Aldrich for President (Head): 184
Henry Aldrich Gets Glamour (Head): 185
Henry Aldrich Haunts a House (Head): 185
Henry Aldrich's Little Secret (Head): 185
Henry and June (Allen, D.): 10
Henry V (Dillon): 118
Her Bitter Cup (Madison): 258
Her Brother
See *Ototo*
Her Darkest Hour (Pickford): 334
Her Defiance (Madison): 258
Her First Affaire (Lupino): 247
Her First Biscuits (Pickford): 334
Her Husband Lies (Head): 183
Her Jungle Love (Head): 183
Her Man o' War (Macpherson): 255
Her Private Life (Akins): 6
Her Twelve Men (Rose): 355
Her Twin Brother (Meredyth): 287
Herb Alpert and the Tijuana Brass Double Feature (Hubley): 197
Herbstsonate (Ullmann): 424
Here and There with My Octoscope and Zenscapes (Menken): 284
Here Come the Girls (Head): 185
Here Come the Huggetts (Box, B.): 48; (Box, M.): 51
Here Come the Waves (Head): 185
Here Comes Cookie (Head): 183
Here Comes Mr. Jordan (Head): 184
Here Comes the Groom (Head): 185; (Van Upp): 433
Here's to Romance (Levien): 237
Heritage of the Desert (Head): 184
Heritiers de la violence (Poirier): 337
Heroism of an Aviator in Tripoli
See *L'Eroismo di un Aviatore a Tripoli*
Hest på sommerferie (Henning-Jensen): 194
Hester Street (Silver): 392
Het Bosplan (Apon): 19
Het dak van de walvis
See *Toit de la Baleine*
Het is de Schraapzucht, Gentlemen (Apon): 19
Hets (Zetterling): 462
Hicksville Epicure (Loos): 244
Hickville's Finest (Loos): 244
Hidden Agenda (Zetterling): 462
Hidden Eye (Irene): 205
Hidden Flame
See *Flamme cachée*
Hidden Gold (Head): 184
Hidden Scar (Marion): 264

Hide and Seek (Friedrich): 144
Hideaway Girl (Head): 183
Hide-Out (Goodrich): 155
Higanbana (Tanaka): 410
High Barbaree (Irene): 205
High Bright Sun (Box, B.): 48
High Commissioner
See *Nobody Runs Forever*
High Cost of Loving (Rose): 355
High Finance (Lupino): 247
High Fury
See *White Cradle Inn*
High Fury (Pickford): 334
High Heel Nights (B): 30
High Road
See *Lady of Scandal*
High Sierra (Lupino): 247
High Society (Rose): 355
High Tide (Armstrong): 21
Highbrow Love (Loos): 244
Hijosen no onna (Tanaka): 409
Hills of Old Wyoming (Head): 183
Hillside at Chauritchi (Cantrill): 65
Hindenburg (Jeakins): 208
Hiroshima mon amour (Duras): 124
His Awful Vengeance (Loos): 244
His Better Self (Guy): 168
His Brand (Weber): 444
His Country
See *Ship Comes In*
His Double Life (Gish): 148
His Dress Shirt (Pickford): 334
His Hoodoo (Loos): 244
His Hour (Glyn): 150
His Last Twelve Hours
See *mondo le condanna*
His Lesson (Gish): 148
His Lordship's White Feather (Guy): 169
His Lost Love (Pickford): 334
His Pal's Request (Madison): 258
His Picture in the Papers (Loos): 245
His Return (Madison): 258
His Sister's Sweetheart (Guy): 168
His Supreme Moment (Marion): 265
His Wife's Visitor (Pickford): 334
Histoires d'Amérique: Food, Family and Philosophy (Akerman): 4
Historia współczesna (Jakubowska): 207
Historias de ciudad (Novaro): 309
History
See *Storia*
History Lessons
See *Geschichtsunterricht*
History of Albertfalva
See *Albertfalvai történet*
History of the Chinese Patriot Movement in the U.S. (Choy): 81
History of the Cinema (Batchelor): 35
History of the World According to a Lesbian (Hammer): 173
Hit the Deck (Levien): 237; (Rose): 355
Hit-the-Trail Holliday (Loos): 245
Hitch-Hiker (Lupino): 247
Hitler Gang (Goodrich): 155; (Head): 185
Hledám dům holubí (Šimková-Plívová): 394
Hobson's Choice (Gish): 148
Hocus Pocus (Marshall): 268
Hodja fra Pjort (Henning-Jensen): 194
Hold back the Dawn (Head): 184
Hold 'em, Navy (Head): 183
Hold 'em, Yale (Head): 183
Hold That Blonde (Head): 185
Hold-Up (Guy): 168
Hold Your Man (Loos): 245
Hole (Hubley): 197
Hole in the Head (Head): 186
Holiday Affair (Lennart): 236
Holiday Camp (Box, M.): 51
Holiday for Sinners (Rose): 355
Holiday in Mexico (Irene): 205; (Lennart): 236
Holiday Inn (Head): 184
Holland, Agnieszka: **195**
Hollywood (Macpherson): 256
Hollywood Boulevard (Head): 183
Hollywood Canteen (Lupino): 247
Hollywood or Bust (Head): 186
Hollywood Vice Squad (Spheeris): 399
Holy Night
See *'A Santa notte*
Holy Smoke (Campion): 61
Home (Deitch): 112; (Hammer): 173; (Weber): 444
Home Folks (Pickford): 334
Home for the Holidays (Foster): 143
Home Movie—A Day in the Bush (Cantrill): 65
Home Remedy (Greenwald): 163
Home, Sweet Home (Gish): 148
Home Trail (Shipman): 388
Homecoming (Rose): 355
Homeland of Electricity (Shepitko): 386
Homerunmuse (Schneemann): 372
Homes Apart: Korea (Choy): 81
Homework (Thomas): 412
Homme amoureux
See *Man in Love*
Homme, une Terre (Maldoror): 261
Hommes de la Wahgi (Guillemot): 165
Homometer II (Export): 134
Honest Bread
See *Nash chestnyi khleb*
Honey, I Blew Up the Kid (Steel): 401

Honeymoon (Ono): 316
Honeymoon Deferred
See *Due mogli sono troppe*
Honeymoon in Bali (Head): 184; (Van Upp): 432
Honeymoon Machine (Rose): 356
Honeymoon Trip
See *Voyage de noces*
Hong Kong (Head): 185
Honor among Lovers (Arzner): 25
Honor of the Family (Coffee): 90
Honor of the Regiment (Meredyth): 286
Honor Thy Father (Pickford): 334
Honorin et la Lorelei (Kaplan): 213
Honorin et l'Enfant prodigue (Kaplan): 213
Honza, Jakub Kosteczka and a Little Paper Window
See *O Honzovi, Jakubovi Kostečkovi a papírovém okénku*
Hoodlum (Pickford): 334
Hoodlum Saint (Irene): 205
Hook and Hand (Guy): 169
Hookers, Hustlers, Pimps and Their Johns (Kidron): 217
Hookers on Davie (Cole and Dale): 93
Hoop Skirt
See *Robe à Cerceaux*
Hop, the Devil's Brew (Weber): 444
Hopalong Rides Again (Head): 183
Hope and Glory (Russell): 357
Hora da Estrêla (Amaral): 13
Horoki (Tanaka): 410
Hors d'oeuvres (Potter): 341
Horse on Bill (Loos): 244
Horse on Holiday
See *Hest på sommerferie*
Hospital
See *L'Ospite*
Hostages (Head): 185
Hot Enough for June (Box, B.): 48
Hot Flash (Hammer): 173
Hot Line
See *Gorąca linia*
Hot Saturday (Head): 183
Hot Spell (Head): 186
Hot Water (Friedrich): 144
Hotel (Head): 187
Hotel Chronicles (Pool): 339
Hotel for Strangers
See *Hotel pro cizince*
Hotel Haywire (Head): 183
Hotel Honeymoon (Guy): 169
Hotel Imperial (Head): 184
Hotel Monterey (Akerman): 4
Hotel New Hampshire (Foster): 143
Hotel pro cizince (Krumbachová): 223
Hotheads (Livingston): 242
Hothouse (Allen, J.): 12
Houdini (Head): 185
Houpačka (Šimková-Plívová): 394
Hour before the Dawn (Head): 185
Hour of the Star
See *Hora da Estrêla*
Hour of the Wolf
See *Vargtimmen*
House Across the Bay (Irene): 203; (Spencer): 397
House Built upon Sand (Gish): 148
House Divided (Guy): 169
House in Italy
See *Casa in Italia*
House in Sea Cliff (Grayson): 161
House Is Not a Home (Head): 186
House of Cards (Guy): 169; (Head): 187
House of Darkness (Gish): 148
House of Jade
See *Maison de jade*
House of Spirit
See *'O Munaciello*
House of the Black Death (Murphy): 297
Houseboat (Head): 186
Household Saints (Savoca): 368
Householder (Jhabvala): 210
Housekeeper's Daughter (Irene): 203
Housewife
See *Femme au foyer*
How Beaver Stole Fire (Leaf): 235
How Come Nobody's on Our Side? (Marshall): 268
How Could You, Jean? (Marion): 264; (Pickford): 335
How I Play Cricket (McDonagh Sisters): 278
How Long Does Man Matter?
See *Meddig él az ember?*
How Sweet It Is! (Marshall): 268; (Rose): 356
How the Day Was Saved (Loos): 244
How the Motor Car Works: The Carburettor (Batchelor): 35
How to Be a Hostess (Batchelor): 35
How to Keep a Husband (Loos): 244
How to Make an American Quilt (Angelou): 17
How to Marry a Millionaire (Akins): 6
Howard Stern's Private Parts
See *Private Parts*
Howards End (Jhabvala): 210
Hra o jablko (Chytilová): 83
Hu Yueh Te Ku Shih (Hui): 199
Huajiao Lei (Zhang): 464
Hubley, Faith Elliott: **197**
Hucksters (Irene): 205
Hud (Head): 186
"Hudson River Diary" series (De Hirsch): 110

Huey
See *Black Panthers*
Huggetts Abroad (Box, B.): 48
Hui, Ann: **199**
Huillet, Danièle: **201**
Huilor (Parker): 325
Huis clos (Audry): 27
Hulda from Holland (Pickford): 335
Hullabaloo over Georgie and Bonnie's Pictures (Jhabvala): 210
Human Comedy (Irene): 203
Humoresque (Marion): 265
Hunchback (Gish): 148; (Loos): 244
Hunchback of Notre Dame (Levien): 237
Hundred and One Nights
See *Cent et une nuits*
Hungarian Village
See *Istenmezején 1972-73*
Hunger
See *Sult*
Hungerjahre (Brückner): 57
Hungry Dog (Batchelor): 35
Hungry Heart (Marion): 264
Hunted Men (Bauchens): 37; (Head): 183
Hunting We Will Go (Batchelor): 35
Hurra! Ich bin Papa! (von Harbou): 440
Hurricane Irene (Kopple): 221
Hurricane Smith (Head): 185
Hurry! Hurry! (Menken): 284
Husbands and Lovers (Booth): 44
Husbands and Wives (Ephron): 130
Hush (Coffee): 90
Hussards et grisettes (Guy): 168
Hustler (Allen, D.): 10
Hustling (Mayron): 275
Hustruer (Breien): 55
Hustruer—10 år etter (Breien): 55
Hustruer III (Breien): 55
Huyue de gushi
See *Hu Yueh Te Ku Shih*
Hydraulip (Hänsel): 176
Hyperbulie (Export): 134
Hypnotist (Batchelor): 35
Hypocrites (Marion): 266; (Weber): 444

I

I Am an Ox—Women in Soviet Cinema (Potter): 341
I basilischi (Wertmüller): 449
I [(Beat) It] (Export): 134
I Can Jump over Puddles Again
See *Už zase skáču přes kaluže*
I cani del Sinai
See *Fortini/Cani*
I Cannibali (Cavani): 69
I Can't Sleep
See *J'ai pas sommeil*
I Confess (Reville): 349
I Could Go On Singing (Head): 186
I Don't Want to Talk about It
See *De eso no se habla*
I Dood It (Sharaff): 384
I Dream in Color
See *Sueño como de colores*
I Due nemici (Cecchi d'Amico): 71
I Due vite di Mattia Pascal (Cecchi d'Amico): 72
I Fancy You
See *'Nfama*
I figli chiedono perche (Cecchi d'Amico): 72
I Flunked, But. . .
See *Rakudai wa shitakeredo*
I Graduated, But. . .
See *Daigaku wa detakeredo*
I Know Why the Caged Bird Sings (Angelou): 17
I Lived with You (Lupino): 247
I Look for a House of Pigeons
See *Hledám dům holubí*
I Love a Mystery (Lupino): 248
I Love a Soldier (Head): 185
I Love Melvin (Rose): 355
I Love You, Alice B. Toklas! (Van Runkle): 431
I Love You, I Love You Not (Alberti): 7
I Magliari (Cecchi d'Amico): 71
I Married a Monster from Outer Space (Head): 186
I Married a Witch (Head): 184
I Married an Angel (Loos): 245
I Met a Man (Leaf): 235
I Nomadi (Notari): 307
I nostri figli
See *I vinti*
I picari (Cecchi d'Amico): 72
I Really Need Communication
See *Ich Brauche unbedingt Kommunikation*
I Remember You
See *Ya tebya pomnyu*
I Shall Go to Santiago
See *Iré a Santiago*
I Shot Andy Warhol (Vachon): 426
I Soliti ignoti (Cecchi d'Amico): 71
I Soliti ignoti vent'anni dopo (Cecchi d'Amico): 72
I Suggest Mine (Friedrich): 144
I, the Worst of Them All
See *Yo, la peor de todas*
I vinti (Cecchi d'Amico): 71
I Walk Alone (Head): 185
I Want a Divorce (Head): 184

I Want You to Be Rich (Hein): 192
I Wanted Wings (Head): 184
I Was/I Am (Hammer): 173
I, Your Mother
See *Man Sa Yay*
Icarus XB 1
See *Ikarie XB 1*
Iceman Cometh (Jeakins): 208
Ices Strip Train Skating (Schneemann): 372
Ich Brauche unbedingt Kommunikation (Treut): 416
Ich und Er (Dörrie): 121
Ich war Jack Mortimer (von Harbou): 440
Iconoclast (Macpherson): 256
Idade de Terra (Yamasaki): 460
IDCA—1970 (Weill): 446
Idle Rich (Mathis): 270
Idle Wives (Weber): 444
Idylle (Guy): 167
Idylle interrompue (Guy): 167
If a Thousand Clarinets . . .
See *Kdyby tisíc klarinetu*
If These Walls Could Talk (Savoca): 368
If Winter Comes (Irene): 205
Igor Bulichov
See *Egor Bulychov i drugie*
Ikarie XB 1 (Krumbachová): 223
Il n'y à pas d'oubli (Mallet): 263
Il y a longtemps que je t'aime (Guillemot): 165
Il y à longtemps que je t'aime (Poirier): 337
I'll Be Seeing You (Head): 185
I'll Be Your Sweetheart (Toye): 414
I'll Cry Tomorrow (Rose): 355
I'll Take Romance (Murfin): 296
Illegal Traffic (Head): 183
Illinois Central (Schneemann): 372
Illinois Central Transposed (Schneemann): 372
Illumination (Russell): 357
Illusionernas Natt (Ahrne): 2
Illusioniste renversant (Guy): 168
Illusions (Dash): 105
I'm from Missouri (Head): 184
Im Glanze dieses Glückes (Meerapfel): 280
Im Innern des Wals (Dörrie): 121
Im Land miener Eltern (Meerapfel): 280
I'm Losing You (Vachon): 426; (Van Runkle): 431
I'm No Angel (Head): 183; (West): 452
Image of Dorian Gray in the Yellow Press
See *Dorian Gray in spiegel der Boulevardprsse*
Imaginations (Bute): 59
Imagine (Ono): 316
Imagine: John Lennon (Ono): 316
Imaging Her Erotics: Carolee Schneemann (Schneemann): 372
Immigrant Experience: The Long Long Journey (Silver): 392
Impalement (Macpherson): 256
Impatient Years (Van Upp): 432
Imperfect Lady (Head): 185
Importance of Being Earnest (Dillon): 118
Impressions of April
See *Stemning i April*
Imprints (Cantrill): 65
In a Full Moon Night
See *In una notte di chiaro luna*
In Again, Out Again (Loos): 245
In Any Case, Your Name Is Juan
See *De todos modos Juan te llamas*
In Between
See *Dazwischen*
In Enemy Country (Head): 187
In Gay Madrid (Meredyth): 286
In Heaven as on Earth
See *Sur la terre comme au ciel*
In Her Own Time (Littman): 240
In Hollywood with Potash and Perlmutter (Marion): 265
In Life's Cycle (Macpherson): 256
In Memoriam László Mészáros
See *Mészáros László emlékére*
In Name Only (Irene): 203
In Old Chicago (Levien): 237
In Old Colorado (Head): 184
In Old Kentucky (Booth): 44; (Pickford): 334
In Old Madrid (Pickford): 334
In Old Mexico (Head): 183
In Our Time (Lupino): 247
In Paris Parks (Clarke): 88
In Search of a Sinner (Loos): 246
In Spite Of (Henning-Jensen): 194
In the Aisles of the Wild (Gish): 147
In the Belly of the Whale
See *Im Innern des Wals*
In the Best Interest of the Child (Murphy): 297
In the Bishop's Carriage (Pickford): 334
In the Cellar (Batchelor): 35
In the Country of Fast Runners
See *En el país de los pies ligeros*
In the Country of My Parents
See *Im Land miener Eltern*
In the Event That Anyone Disappears (Choy): 81
In the Good Old Summertime (Goodrich): 155; (Irene): 205
In the Jungle (Batchelor): 35
In The Matter of Kenneth (Littman): 240
In the Name of the Emperor (Choy): 81
In the Palace of the King (Mathis): 270
In the Presence of Mine Enemies (Silver): 392
In the Rivers of Mercy Angst (Chenzira): 75

In the Season of Buds (Pickford): 334
In the Shadow of Gunung Batur (Cantrill): 65
In the Spirit (May): 271
In the Sultan's Garden (Pickford): 334
In the Watches of the Night (Pickford): 334
In the Year 2000 (Guy): 169
In This House of Brede (Dillon): 118
In This Life's Body (Cantrill): 65
In Time of Pestilence (Batchelor): 35
In una notte di chiaro luna (Wertmüller): 449
Incendiary Blonde (Head): 185
Incident at Oglala (Alberti): 7
Incident at Restigouche (Obomsawin): 313
Incised Image (Cantrill): 65
Incontro notturno (Cavani): 69
Incredible Petrified World (Murphy): 297
India Cabaret (Nair): 302
India Song (Duras): 124
Indian Runner's Romance (Pickford): 334
Indian Summer (Pickford): 334
Indian Tomb
See *Indische Grabmal*
Indians Are Still Far Away
See *Indiens sont encore loin*
Indian's Loyalty (Gish): 148
Indiens sont encore loin (Pascal): 328
Indische Grabmal (von Harbou): 440
Indústria (Carolina): 67
Industrial Reserve Army
See *Industrielle Reservarmee*
Industrial Symphony
See *Philips-Radio*
Industrielle Reservarmee (Sanders-Brahms): 364
Inexorable Time
See *Cas je neúprosný*
Inez from Hollywood (Arzner): 25
Infamous Woman
See *'Nfama*
Infanzia, vocazione, e prime esperienze di Giacomo Casanova, Veneziano (Cecchi d'Amico): 72
Inferno (Jeakins): 208
Informer (Pickford): 334
Ingrid (Ullmann): 424
Inhabitants of Castles
See *Kastélyok lakói*
Inheritance
See *Örökseg*
Inheritance or Fuckoffguysgoodbye
See *Dědictví aneb Kurvahošigutntag*
Initiation (Clarke): 88
Inn of the Sixth Happiness (Lennart): 236
Inner Circle (Pickford): 334
Innocent
See *L'innocente*
Innocent Magdalene (Gish): 148
Innocent Maid
See *Hakoiri musume*
Inserts (Russell): 357
Inside Daisy Clover (Head): 186
Inside Out (Borden): 46
Inside Women Inside (Choy): 81
Inspector Morse (Bird): 42
Inspirations (Alberti): 7
Instant de la paix
See *Der augenblick des Friedens*
Instant Film (Export): 134
Instant Karma (Ono): 316
Insured for Life (Batchelor): 35
Integration (Citron): 86
Intelligence Men (Dillon): 118
Interior Scroll (Schneemann): 372
Interior Scroll—The Cave (Schneemann): 372
Interior/Exterior (Cantrill): 65
Interiors (Keaton): 215
Intermezzo (Irene): 203
International Sweethearts of Rhythm (Schiller): 370
Interno Berlinese (Cavani): 69
Interns Can't Take Money (Head): 183
Interrogation
See *Przesluchanie*
Interrupted Line (Export): 134
Interrupted Melody (Levien): 237; (Rose): 355
Interview (Leaf): 235
Into the Dark
See *Entre tinieblas*
Into the Night (Heckerling): 189
Intolerance (Gish): 148; (Loos): 244
Introduction to Arnold Schoenberg's Accompaniment for a Cinematographic Scene
See *Einleitung zu Arnold Schoenberg Begleit Musik zu einer Lichtspielscene*
Invisible Adversaries
See *Unsichtbare Gegner*
Invisible Child (Silver): 392
Invisible Exchange (Batchelor): 35
Invitation (Rose): 355
Invitation
See *Zaproszenie*
Invitation à la chasse (von Trotta): 442
Invitation au voyage (Guillemot): 165
Invitation to Happiness (Head): 184
Invitation to the Waltz (Toye): 414
Io, io, io . . . e gli altri (Cecchi d'Amico): 72
Io speriamo che me la cavo (Wertmüller): 449
Iola's Promise (Pickford): 334
Iré a Santiago (Gómez): 154
Irene: **203**
Irene (Mathis): 270
Iris och Lojtnantshjarta (Zetterling): 462

Irish Hearts (Meredyth): 286
Iron Duke (Meredyth): 287
Iron Maiden (Dillon): 118
Iron Petticoat (Box, B.): 48; (Dillon): 118
Is This What You Were Born For? (Child): 76
Ishtar (May): 271
Isla del tesero (Gómez): 154
Isla rodeada de agua (Novaro): 309
Island (Pascal): 328
Island Fuse (Cantrill): 65
Island of Intrigue (Mathis): 269
Island of Lost Men (Head): 184
Island on the Continent
See *Sziget a szárazföldön*
Island Rescue
See *Appointment with Venus*
Island Surrounded by Water
See *Isla rodeada de agua*
Islas Revillagigedo (Landeta): 229
Isle of Conquest (Loos): 245
Isn't It Romantic? (Head): 185
Ispaniya (Shub): 390
Istenmezején 1972-73 (Elek): 127
It (Glyn): 150
It Depends on Us Too . . .
See *Rajtunk is mulik*
It Happened in Brooklyn (Lennart): 236
It Only Happens to Others
See *Ça n'arrive qu'aux autres*
It Started in Naples (Cecchi d'Amico): 71; (Head): 186
It Started with a Kiss (Rose): 355
It Was a Wonderful Life (Foster): 143
Italian Barber (Pickford): 334
Italian Flag
See *Tricolore*
Italo-Turkish War among Our Neapolitan Urchins
See *Caratteristica Guerra Italo-Turca Tra i Nostri Scugnizzi Napoletani*
Italy Has Risen
See *L'Italia s'è Desta*
Itch (Kidron): 217
It's a 2' 6" above the Ground World
See *Love Ban*
It's a Big Country (Lennart): 236
It's a Good Day (Fields): 141
It's a Wise Child (Booth): 45
It's a Wonderful Life (Goodrich): 155
It's All Right Now (Littman): 240
It's Always Fair Weather (Comden): 96; (Rose): 355
It's Always Now (Allen, D.): 10
It's Forever Springtime
See *E primavera*
It's in the Bag (Reville): 349
It's My Turn (Allen, J.): 12; (Weill): 447
It's No Laughing Matter (Marion): 266; (Weber): 444
It's Not Cricket (Box, B.): 48
It's Not the Size that Counts (Box, B.): 48
It's Now or Never (Law): 232
It's Only Money (Head): 186
Itto (Epstein): 132
Ivan (Solntseva): 395
Ives House: Woodstock (De Hirsch): 110
Ivor Paints (Cantrill): 65
Ivor's Exhibition (Cantrill): 65
Ivor's Tiger Xmas Card (Cantrill): 65
Ivory Collection
See *Coleçao de marfil*
Izu no odoriko (Tanaka): 409
Izzy and His Rival
See *Billy's Rival*

J

Jack and the Beanstalk (Reiniger): 347
Jack Smith (Hein): 192
Jackson County Jail
See *Outside Chance*
Jacobo Timerman: Prisoner without a Name, Cell without a Number (Ullmann): 424
Jacques Rivette, Le Veilleur (Denis): 114
Jacquot de Nantes (Varda): 435
Jag drapte (Zetterling): 462
Jag skall bli Sveriges Rembrandt eller dö! (Ahrne): 3
Jagd nach dem Glück (Reiniger): 348
J'ai pas sommeil (Denis): 114
J'ai un hanneton dans mon pantalon (Guy): 168
Jak se točí Rozmarýny (Šimková-Plívová): 394
Jakubowska, Wanda: **206**
Jalan Raya, Ubud (Cantrill): 65
Jama Masjid Street Journal (Nair): 302
Jamaica Inn (Harrison): 180; (Reville): 349
Jamaica Run (Head): 185
Jane Austen in Manhattan (Jhabvala): 210
Jane B. par Agnès V. (Varda): 435
Jane Brakhage (Hammer): 173
Janis (Savoca): 368
János Tornyai
See *Tornyai János*
Japanese Idyll (Weber): 444
Jaune le soleil (Duras): 124
Jaws (Fields): 141
Jayhawkers (Head): 186
Je, tu, il, elle (Akerman): 4
Je vous y prrrends! (Guy): 167
Jeakins, Dorothy: **208**
Jean de la lune (Guillemot): 165

Jeanne Dielman, 23 Quai du Commerce, 1080 Bruxelles (Akerman): 4
Jeanne Eagels (Levien): 237
Jefferson in Paris (Jhabvala): 210
Jennie
See *Portrait of Jennie*
Jennifer (Lupino): 248
Jenny (Ullmann): 424
Jenny Lind
See *Lady's Morals*
Jeopardy (Rose): 355
Jerk (Van Runkle): 431
Jérôme Bosch (Guillemot): 165
Jester and the Queen
See *Sasek a kralovna*
Jesus, My Brother
See *Gesu' mio Fratello*
Jet Storm (Zetterling): 462
Jetzt leben—Juden in Berlin (Sanders-Brahms): 364
Jeune fille la plus méritante de France (Musidora): 300
Jeunes Filles d'hier et d'aujourd'hui (Musidora): 300
Jewel (Weber): 444
Jew's Christmas (Weber): 444
Jhabvala, Ruth Prawer: **209**
Jidao Zhuizhong (Hui): 199
Jilting of Granny Weatherall (Haines): 171
Jimmy Bruiteur (Epstein): 132
Jin de gu shi
See *Ah Kam*
Jinye Xingguang Canlan (Hui): 199
Jivaro (Head): 186
J'me marie, j'me marie pas (Poirier): 337
Joan of Arc (Jeakins): 208
Joan the Woman (Macpherson): 255
Jocko musicien (Guy): 168
Jodie: An Icon (Parmar): 326
Joe (McDonagh Sisters): 278
Johanna d'Arc of Mongolia (Ottinger): 318
Johanna Enlists (Marion): 264; (Pickford): 335
Johannès fils de Johannès (Musidora): 300
John Gilpin (Batchelor): 35
John Goldfarb, Please Come Home (Head): 186
John Meade's Woman (Head): 183
John Needham's Double (Weber): 444
Johnny Bull (Weill): 447
Johnny Dangerously (Heckerling): 189
Johnny Got His Gun (Van Runkle): 431
Johnny in the Clouds
See *Way to the Stars*
Joke of Destiny, Lying in Wait around the Corner Like a Street Bandit
See *Scherzo del destinoin aqquato dietro l'angelo come un brigante di strada*
Joker Is Wild (Head): 186
Jonas in the Desert (Ono): 316
Jonque (Guillemot): 165
Josei no shori (Tanaka): 410
Jostedalsrypa (Breien): 55
Jotai wa kanashiku (Tanaka): 410
Jour apres jour (Poirier): 337
Jour du terme (Guy): 168
Jour Pina m'a demandé (Akerman): 4
Journal inachevé (Mallet): 263
Journey (Spencer): 397
Journey around a Zero (De Hirsch): 109
Journey Is Worth the Trip
See *Eine Reise ist eine Reise Wert*
Journey to the Pacific (Fields): 141
Journeys from Berlin/1971 (Rainer): 345
Joy of Sex (Coolidge): 99
Joyce at 34 (Chopra): 78; (Weill): 447
Joyu Sumako no koi (Tanaka): 410
Judas City
See *Satan's Bed*
Judex (Musidora): 300
Judge and the Assassin
See *Juge et l'assassin*
Judith of Bethulia (Gish): 148
Juge et l'assassin (Pascal): 328
Jugend (von Harbou): 440
Juguetes (Bemberg): 38
Julia (Dillon): 118
Julia Misbehaves (Irene): 205
Julie de Carneilhan (Colette): 95
Jumpin' Jack Flash (Marshall): 268
Jumping Jacks (Head): 185
June Bride (Head): 185
Jungfrauen Maschine (Schiller): 370; (Treut): 416
Jungle Princess (Head): 183
Jungle Warfare (Batchelor): 34
Junior Bonner (Lupino): 248
Juno and the Paycock (Reville): 349
Jupiter's Darling (Rose): 355
Just Another Girl on the I.R.T. (Harris): 178
Just around the Corner (Marion): 265
Just Cause (von Brandenstein): 438
Just for You (Head): 185
Just Gold (Gish): 148
Just Kids (Gish): 148
Just Like a Woman (Pickford): 334
Just Like at Home
See *Olyan, mint otthon*
Just Pals (Haines): 171
Just Tell Me What You Want (Allen, J.): 12
Justice for Sale
See *Night Court*
Justine (Sharaff): 384

K

K-SH-E (Shub): 390
K.Y.T.E.S.: How We Dream Ourselves (Mehta): 283
Kaddu Beykat (Faye): 137
Kaerlighed pa kredit (Henning-Jensen): 194
Kakafonische Notities (Apon): 19
Kalamita (Chytilová): 83
Kali-filme (Hein): 192
Kam Parenky (Chytilová): 83
Kama Sutra (Nair): 302
Kama Sutra: A Tale of Love
See *Kama Sutra*
Kamaszváros (Mészáros): 288
Kämpfende Herzen (von Harbou): 439
Kanehsatake: 270 Years of Resistance (Obomsawin): 313
Kansas City Bomber (Foster): 143
Kanzashi (Tanaka): 409
Kaplan, Nelly: **212**
Karate Kid, Part II (Steel): 401
Kashtanka (Preobrazhenskaya): 342
Kastélyok lakói (Elek): 127
Káta a krokodýl (Šimková-Plívová): 394
Kate and Anna McGarrigle (Leaf): 235
Katharina Eiselt (Dörrie): 121
Katia and the Crocodile
See *Káta a krokodýl*
Katie: Portrait of a Centerfold (Mayron): 275
Katy and the Twins
See *Nefňukej, veverko!*
Kaze no naka no mendori (Tanaka): 410
Kdyby tisíc klarinetu (Krumbachová): 223
Kean (Cecchi d'Amico): 71
Keaton, Diane: **214**
Keep It for Yourself (Denis): 114
Keep Your Powder Dry (Irene): 205
Keeping On (Kopple): 221
Keiner Liebt Mich (Dörrie): 121
Kelly from the Emerald Isle (Guy): 169
Kempy
See *Wise Girls*
Képi (Guy): 168
Ketu Qiuhen (Hui): 199
Key to the City (Irene): 205
Keys of Heaven (Batchelor): 34
Keys to Happiness
See *Klyuchi shchastya*
Kharejaz Mahdoudeh (Bani-Etemad): 32
Khush (Parmar): 326
Kiáltó (Mészáros): 289
Kid Blue (Van Runkle): 431
Kid from Left Field (Jeakins): 208
Kidnapped (Dillon): 118; (Levien): 237
Kidron, Beeban: **217**
Kids (Vachon): 426
Kids Are Alright (Schoonmaker): 375
Kiki (Pickford): 334
Kilenc hónap (Mészáros): 289
Kill-Off (Greenwald): 163
Kinder sind nicht Rinder (Sander): 361
Kindergärtnerin, was nun? (Sander): 361
Kinegraffiti (Cantrill): 65
King and I (Sharaff): 384
King Creole (Head): 186
King Kongs Faust (Dörrie): 121
King Matthew I
See *Król Maciuś I*
King Matthias I
See *Król Maciuś I*
King of Alcatraz (Head): 183
King of Chinatown (Head): 184
King of Comedy (Schoonmaker): 375
King of Gamblers (Head): 183
King of Kings (Bauchens): 37; (Macpherson): 255
King of Kings
See *Král Králu*
Kingdom for a Guitar
See *Království za kytaru*
King's Breakfast (Reiniger): 347; (Toye): 414
Kino za XX liet (Shub): 390
Kirsa Nicholina (Nelson): 305
Kismet (Irene): 203
Kiss
See *Der Kuss*
Kiss Me, Guido (Vachon): 426
Kiss of Death (Van Runkle): 431
Kiss the Boys Goodbye (Head): 184
Kisses (Mathis): 270
Kissing Bandit (Lennart): 236
Kitchen Sink (Maclean): 253
Kitch's Last Meal (Schneemann): 372
Kladivo na čarodějnice (Krumbachová): 224
Klassenverhältnisse (Huillet): 201
Klondike Annie (West): 452
Klyuchi shchastya (Preobrazhenskaya): 343
Kneegrays in Russia (Davis): 107
Knight without Armour (Marion): 266
Knights of the Range (Head): 184
Knock on Wood (Head): 186; (Zetterling): 462
Knocturne (Wieland): 455
Knowing Men (Glyn): 150
Kobieta samotna (Holland): 195
Kočár do Vídně (Krumbachová): 223
Kodiyettom
See *Voshojdenie*
Koibumi (Tanaka): 409
Kolberg (von Harbou): 440
Kolory kochania (Jakubowska): 207
Kolossale Liebe (Brückner): 57

Komsomol—Leader of Electrification
See *K-SH-E*
Komsomol—The Guide to Electrification
See *K-SH-E*
Konec jasnovidce (Chytilová): 83
Koniec naszego świata (Jakubowska): 207
Kopple, Barbara: **220**
Kopytem Sem, Kopytem Tam (Chytilová): 83
Korczak (Holland): 195
Korotkiye vstrechi (Muratova): 294
Kort år sommaren (Henning-Jensen): 194; (Ullmann): 424
Krakonoš a lyžníci (Šimková-Plívová): 394
Král Králu (Krumbachová): 223
Král Šumavy (Šimková-Plívová): 394
Království za kytaru (Krumbachová): 223
Krane's Bakery Shop
See *Kranes Konditori*
Kranes Konditori (Henning-Jensen): 193
Kransen
See *Kristin Lavransdatter*
Kristin Lavransdatter (Ullmann): 424
Kristina Talking Pictures (Rainer): 345
Kristina's Harbor (Nelson): 305
Kristinus Bergman (Henning-Jensen): 194
Krokodillen in Amsterdam (Apon): 19
Król Maciuś I (Jakubowska): 207
Krumbachová, Ester: **223**
Krylya (Shepitko): 386
Krylya kholopa (Shub): 390
Kulonbozo helyek (Varda): 435
Kümmeltürkin geht (Meerapfel): 280
Kundun (Schoonmaker): 375
Kung Fu Master
See *Petit Amour*
Künstlerfilme I (Hein): 192
Künstlerfilme II (Hein): 192
Kurt Kren. Porträt eines experimentellen Fulmmachers (Hein): 192
Kurys, Diane: **225**

L

L.A. Johns (Chopra): 78
Laagland (Apon): 19
Labor of Love
See *Heller Wahn*
Lac-aux-Dames (Colette): 95
L'Accalappiacani (Notari): 306
Lace of Summer (De Hirsch): 110
Ladies in Retirement (Lupino): 247
Ladies' Man (Head): 186
Ladies Must Live (Madison): 259
Ladies Should Listen (Head): 183
Ladri di biciclette (Cecchi d'Amico): 71
Lady (Marion): 265
Lady and the Mob (Lupino): 247
Lady and the Mouse (Gish): 148; (Loos): 244
Lady Be Careful (Head): 183
Lady Bodyguard (Head): 185
Lady Caroline Lamb (Dillon): 118
Lady Chatterley's Lover (Russell): 357
Lady Eve (Head): 184
Lady from Constantinople
See *Sziget a szárazföldön*
Lady from Shanghai (Van Upp): 433
Lady Has Plans (Head): 184
Lady Helen's Escapade (Macpherson): 256
Lady in a Cage (Head): 186
Lady in a Car with Glasses and a Gun (Perry): 332
Lady in Black (Loos): 244
Lady in Shining Armor
See *Sonho de Valsa*
Lady in the Dark (Goodrich): 155; (Head): 185
Lady in the Lake (Irene): 205
Lady Is Willing (Irene): 203
Lady Liberty
See *Mortadella*
Lady Musashino
See *Musashino fujin*
Lady of Burlesque (Head): 185
Lady of Chance (Booth): 44
Lady of Scandal (Booth): 45
Lady of Secrets (Akins): 6
Lady of the Boulevards
See *Nana*
Lady Oscar (Varda): 435
Lady Peasant
See *Baryshnia krestianka*
Lady Vanishes (Reville): 349
Lady without Camellias
See *Signora senza camelie*
Ladybug, Ladybug (Perry): 332
Ladyfingers (Coffee): 90
Lady's from Kentucky (Head): 184
Lady's Morals (Booth): 45
L'Affiche (Epstein): 132
L'Africana
See *Rückkehr*
L'Age tendre (Guillemot): 165
Lagourdette, gentleman cambrioleur (Musidora): 300
L'allegro squadrone (Cecchi d'Amico): 71
L'Amie
See *Heller Wahn*
La Naissance du jour (Colette): 95
Land (van Dongen): 430
Land of Liberty (Bauchens): 37; (Macpherson): 255
Land of Mirages
See *Délibábok országa*

Land of the Bulls
See *Tierra de los toros*
Land of the Soviets
See *Strana Sovietov*
Landeta, Matilde Soto: **229**
L'Angélus (Guy): 168
Långt borta och nära (Ahrne): 2
Laocoon and Sons
See *Laokoon und Söhne*
Laokoon und Söhne (Ottinger): 318
Laputa (Sanders-Brahms): 364
Largo Desolato (Holland): 195
Larkin, Alile Sharon: **231**
L'Arroseur arrosé (Guy): 167
Larry's Recent Behaviour (Wieland): 455
Las Tres coronas del marinera
See *Trois Couronnes du matelot*
Las Vegas Nights (Head): 184
L'Assassinat de la rue du Temple (Guy): 168
L'Assassinat du Courrier de Lyon (Guy): 168
Lasse-Maja (Zetterling): 462
Last Attraction
See *Poslednyi attraktzion*
Last Butterfly
See *Poslední motýl*
Last Castle
See *Echoes of a Summer*
Last Days of Chez Nous (Armstrong): 21
Last Days of Gomorrah
See *Letzten Tage von Gomorrah*
Last Don (Van Runkle): 431
Last Drink of Whiskey (Loos): 244
Last Drop of Water (Macpherson): 256
Last Island (Gorris): 159
Last Knight Vampire
See *Den sista riddarvampyren*
Last Married Couple in America (Head): 187
Last of Mrs. Cheyney (Arzner): 25
Last of the Cowboys
See *Great Smokey Roadblock*
Last of the Secret Agents (Head): 187
Last of Their Race (Madison): 258
Last Outpost (Head): 183, 185
Last Stage
See *Ostatni etap*
Last Stop
See *Ostatni etap*
Last Summer (Perry): 332
Last Tango in Paris (Varda): 435
Last Temptation of Christ (Schoonmaker): 375
Last Tenant (von Brandenstein): 438
Last Time I Saw Paris (Rose): 355
Last Train from Gun Hill (Head): 186
Last Train from Madrid (Head): 183
Last Trial (Peng): 330
Last Visit to Ms. Iran Daftari (Bani-Etemad): 32
Late Shift (Thomas): 412
L'atelier du diable (Palcy): 321
Latin Lovers (Lennart): 236; (Rose): 355
Latin Women (Sarmiento): 365
L'Attaque d'un diligence (Guy): 168
L'Auberge rouge (Epstein): 132
Laufen lernen (Brückner): 57
Laughing Sinners (Meredyth): 286
Laundry Liz (Loos): 244
Laundry Shed
See *Lavaderos*
Laurent Lamerre, portier (Pool): 339
Lauter Liebe (von Harbou): 440
L'Autre Victoire (Musidora): 300
Lavaderos (Novaro): 309
Lavatory moderne (Guy): 168
L'Avenir d'Emilie
See *Flügel und Fesseln*
L'Aveugle (Guy): 167, 168
Lavrador (Carolina): 67
Law
See *'A Legge*
Law, Clara: **232**
Law of the Pampas (Head): 184
Law of Their Kind (Madison): 258
Lawful Larceny (Murfin): 296
Lawrence of Arabia (Steel): 401
Lazy Bones (Marion): 265
Leaden Times
See *Bleierne Zeit*
Leaf, Caroline: **234**
League of Their Own (Marshall): 268
Leap of Faith (Van Runkle): 431; (von Brandenstein): 438
Learning to Love (Loos): 246
Learning to Run
See *Laufen lernen*
Leather Saint (Head): 186
Leathernecking (Murfin): 296
L'eau (Parker): 325
L'Eau à la bouche (Trintignant): 420
L'eau d'Evian (Parker): 325
L'École des cocottes (Audry): 27
Leçon de danse (Guy): 167, 168
Leçons de boxe (Guy): 167
Leçons de la guerre (Musidora): 300
Lecture quotidienne (Guy): 168
Left Hand of God (Spencer): 397
Left-Handed Man (Gish): 148
Legacy
See *Dědictví aneb Kurvahošigutntag*
Legacy (Littleton): 239
Legacy of the Hollywood Blacklist (Littman): 240
Legend of Fong Sai-Yuk
See *Fong Sai-Yuk*

Legend of Naples
See *Leggenda di Napoli*
Legend of the Boy and the Eagle (Fields): 141
Leggenda di Napoli (Notari): 307
Lek pa regnbagen (Zetterling): 462
L'elisir d'amore (Reiniger): 347
Lemon Drop Kid (Head): 185
Lemon Sisters (Chopra): 78; (Keaton): 215; (von Brandenstein): 438
Lena and the Geese (Pickford): 334
L'Enfant aimé (Akerman): 4
L'enfant-cinéma (Maldoror): 261
L'enfant de la barricade
See *Sur la barricade*
L'Enfant sauvage (Guillemot): 165
Leningrad Hospital
See *L'hôpital de Leningrad*
Lennart, Isobel: **236**
Lentement (Mallet): 263
Léon G. Damas (Maldoror): 261
Leon Morin, pretre (Trintignant): 420
Léonor (Ullmann): 424
Leopard
See *Gattopardo*
Leoš Janáček (Krumbachová): 224
Leper's Coat (Weber): 444
L'Equilibriste (Guy): 168
L'Eroismo di un Aviatore a Tripoli (Notari): 307
Lesbian Avengers Eat Fire Too (Friedrich): 144
Lesbos Film (Hammer): 173
L'Escapade de Filoche (Musidora): 300
Less Than Dust (Pickford): 335
Lesson in Mechanics (Loos): 244
Lest We Forget
See *Contre l'oubli*
Let It Be (Ono): 316
Let It Ride (Allen, D.): 10
Let Joy Reign Supreme. . .
See *Que la fête commence. . .*
Let Me Go
See *Tu as Crie*
Let Us Be Gay (Marion): 266
L'eta' di Stalin (Cavani): 69
L'Été prochain (Trintignant): 420
L'étrange aventure de Lemmy Caution
See *Alphaville*
Let's Dance (Head): 185
Let's Face It (Head): 185
Let's Get a Divorce (Loos): 245
Let's Get Married (Lupino): 247
Let's Hope It's a Girl
See *Speriamo che sia femmina*
Let's Make a Million (Head): 183
Let's Make Love (Jeakins): 208
Let's Switch (Marshall): 268
Let's Talk Tonight
See *Hablamos esta noche*
Letter from a Filmmaker
See *Lettre d'un cineaste*
Letter from the Village
See *Kaddu Beykat*
Letter to My Daughter (Pool): 339
Letters (Lupino): 248
Letters to Dad (B): 30
Lettre d'un cineaste (Akerman): 4
Lettre paysanne
See *Kaddu Beykat*
Letzten Tage von Gomorrah (Sanders-Brahms): 364
L'évangile à Solentiname (Mallet): 263
L'evento (Cavani): 69
Levien, Sonya: **237**
Lèvres closes (Guy): 168
L'Heritage
See *Arven*
L'Homme à la valise (Akerman): 4
L'Honneur du Corse (Guy): 168
L'hôpital de Leningrad (Maldoror): 261
L'Horloger de Saint-Paul (Pascal): 328
Li
See *Between the Devil and the Deep Blue Sea*
Li Siguang (Zhang): 464
Liberation
See *Osvobozhdenie*
Liberators Take Liberties: War, Rape, Children
See *BeFreier und Befreite Krieg, Vergewaltigung, Kinder*
Lie (Macpherson): 255
Liebesgrüsse (Hein): 192
Life and Times of Judge Roy Bean (Head): 187
Life Begins at 8:30 (Lupino): 247
Life Goes On
See *Az élet megy tovább*
Life in Bloom
See *Michurin*
Life of Her Own (Lennart): 236; (Rose): 355
Life of Juanita Castro (Menken): 285
Life of Oharu
See *Saikaku ichidai onna*
Life of Rufus Dawes (Lyell): 250
Life of Vergie Winters (Murfin): 296
Life on the Flipside (Heckerling): 189
Life with Henry (Head): 184
Life without a Guitar
See *Život bez kytary*
Lifeboat (Spencer): 397
Lifers Group: World Tour (Spheeris): 399
Life's Most Beautiful Sides
See *Des Lebens schönste Seiten*
Lighea (Cecchi d'Amico): 72

Light of Heart
See *Life Begins at 8:30*
Light of Western Stars (Head): 184
Light That Came (Pickford): 334
Light That Failed (Coffee): 90; (Head): 184; (Lupino): 247
Light Touch (Rose): 355
Light Years (Nelson): 305
Light Years Expanding (Nelson): 305
Lighted Window
See *Fenesta che Lucive*
Lighthouse Keeper (Pickford): 334
Lightnin' (Levien): 237; (Marion): 265
Lightning Strikes Twice (Coffee): 91
Lights (Menken): 285
Like Mom, Like Me (Murphy): 297
Like Most Wives (Marion): 266; (Weber): 444
Liliom (Levien): 237
Lily and the Rose (Gish): 148
Limbo (Silver): 392; (Spencer): 397
L'Impot, et tout et tout (Poirier): 337
L'inchiesta (Cecchi d'Amico): 72
Lincoln (Winfrey): 457
L'Inconnu de Strasbourg (Sarmiento): 365
Line (Rainer): 345
Linear Accelerator (Batchelor): 34
Lines of White on the Sullen Sea (Macpherson): 256
L'innocente (Cecchi d'Amico): 72
L'Insoumise (Trintignant): 420
L'Invitation au voyage (Dulac): 123
Lion savant (Guy): 168
Lions Love (Clarke): 88; (Varda): 435
Liqueur du couvent (Guy): 168
Liquid Dynamite (Madison): 258
Lis de mer (Audry): 27
Lišáci-myšáci a Šibeničák (Šimková-Plívová): 394
Listen Up!: The Lives of Quincy Jones (Streisand): 407; (Winfrey): 457
Lisztomania (Russell): 357
Lit (Hänsel): 176
L'Italia s'è Desta (Notari): 307
Litany for Survival: The Life and Work of Audre Lord (Choy): 81
Littérature tunisienne de la Bibliothèque Nationale (Maldoror): 261
Little American (Macpherson): 255
Little Annie Rooney (Pickford): 334
Little Autogomobile (Meredyth): 287
Little Big Man (Allen, D.): 10; (Jeakins): 208
Little Boy Lost (Head): 186
Little by Little
See *Petit à petit ou Les Lettres persanes 1968*
Little Chimney Sweep
See *Der kleine Schornsteinfeger*
Little Darling (Pickford): 334
Little Dramas of the Big Places: The Light on Lookout (Shipman): 388
Little Dramas of the Big Places: The Love Tree (Shipman): 388
Little Dramas of the Big Places: Trail of the North Wind (Shipman): 388
Little Dramas of the Big Places: White Water (Shipman): 388
Little Drummer Girl (Keaton): 215
Little Forethought (Batchelor): 34
Little Girl Who Lives down the Lane (Foster): 143
Little Girl's Wrong
See *E' Piccarella*
Little House: Look Back to Yesterday (Murphy): 297
Little Iodine (Pickford): 334
Little Liar (Loos): 244
Little Life-Opera
See *Yi Sheng Yitai Xi*
Little Lord Fauntleroy (Pickford): 334
Little Lupin's Investigation
See *Případ Lupínek*
Little Madonna of the Fisherman
See *Madonnina del Pescatore*
Little Man Tate (Foster): 143
Little Mermaid
See *Malá mořská víla*
Little Minister (Murfin): 296
Little Miss Marker (Head): 183
Little Mister Jim (Irene): 205
Little Orphan Annie (Head): 183
Little Pal (Pickford): 335
Little Prince (Russell): 357
Little Prince Said
See *Petit prince à dit*
Little Princess (Marion): 264; (Pickford): 335
Little Queen
See *Reginella*
Little Rascals (Spheeris): 400
Little Red Riding Hood (Pickford): 334
Little Sex (von Brandenstein): 437
Little Shepherd of Kingdom Come (Meredyth): 286
Little Soldier
See *Petit Soldat*
Little Teacher (Pickford): 334
Little Women (Murfin): 296; (Armstrong): 21
Littleton, Carol: **239**
Littman, Lynne: **240**
Live From Baghdad (Marshall): 268
Live Water
See *O živej vode*

Lives of a Bengal Lancer (Head): 183
Lives of Performers (Rainer): 345
Living in a Big Way (Irene): 205
Living It Up (Head): 186
Living Water (Shepitko): 386
Livingston, Jennie: **242**
Livingstone (Kaplan): 213
Lizards
See *I basilischi*
Llano Kid (Head): 184
Lo Straniero (Cecchi d'Amico): 72
Local Power, People's Power
See *Poder local, poder popular*
Locked Out: Ravenswood (Kopple): 221
Locksmith and Chancellor
See *Slesar i kantzler*
Lodging for the Night (Pickford): 334
L'Odyssée du Capitaine Steve
See *Walk into Paradise*
Loin du Vietnam (Varda): 435
Lola (Novaro): 309
Lola Casanova (Landeta): 229
London (Hein): 192
London Story (Potter): 341
Lone Wolf Spy Hunt (Lupino): 247
Lone World Sail (Batchelor): 35
Lonely Lane
See *Horoki*
Lonely Man (Head): 186
Lonely Villa (Pickford): 334
Lonely Woman
See *Kobieta samotna*
Lonesome Ladies (Coffee): 90
Long Absence
See *Aussi longue absence*
Long Farewells
See *Dolgie provody*
Long Goodbye (Brackett): 52
Long Island Incident (Streisand): 405
Long Live the Republic!
See *At žije republika*
Long, Long Trailer (Goodrich): 155; (Rose): 355
Long Shadow (Ullmann): 424
Long Silence
See *Lungo silenzio*
L'onorevole Angelina (Cecchi d'Amico): 71
Look Who's Talking (Heckerling): 189
Look Who's Talking Now (Keaton): 215
Look Who's Talking Too (Heckerling): 189
Looking for Mr. Goodbar (Keaton): 215
Looking Forward (Meredyth): 286
Loos, Anita: **244**
Loose Pages Bound (Choy): 81
Loose Shoes (Thomas): 412
L'Opéra-Mouffe (Varda): 435
Lord Byron of Broadway (Bauchens): 37
Lord Chumley (Gish): 148; (Loos): 244
Lord of the Flies (Allen, J.): 12
Lords of Little Egypt (Zetterling): 462
Lorgnon accusateur (Guy): 168
Los Borges (Mallet): 263
Los Caminos de la vida (Landeta): 229
Los Minuteros (Sarmiento): 366
L'Ospite (Cavani): 69
Lost and Found (Weill): 447
Lost Angel (Irene): 203; (Lennart): 236
Lost Command (Spencer): 397
Lost Honor of Katharina Blum
See *Verlorene Ehre der Katharina Blum*
Lost Horizon (Ullmann): 424
Lost House (Gish): 148; (Loos): 244
Lost in Yonkers (Coolidge): 99
Lost Man (Head): 187
Lost People (Box, M.): 51; (Zetterling): 462
Lost Revue
See *Ztracená revue*
Lost Son (Reiniger): 347
Lost Weekend (Head): 185
Lothringen! (Huillet): 201
Lottery Lover (Spencer): 397
Louis Aragon—Un Masque à Paris (Maldoror): 261
Louisiana Story (van Dongen): 430
Love (Marion): 266; (Ullmann): 424; (Zetterling): 462
Love & War (Murphy): 297
Love after Love
See *Après l'amour*
Love among the Roses (Pickford): 334
Love among the Ruins (Dillon): 118
Love and Bullets (Jeakins): 208
Love and Death (Keaton): 215
Love and Fear
See *Paura e amore*
Love and the Steadfast Sweethearts
See *Amor und das standhafte Liebespaar*
Love Ban (Box, B.): 48
Love Crimes (Borden): 46
Love Expert (Loos): 246
Love from a Stranger (Marion): 266
Love Happy (Pickford): 334
Love Has Many Faces (Head): 186
Love Heeds Not the Showers (Pickford): 334
Love Hour (Meredyth): 286
Love in a Fallen City
See *Qing Cheng Zhi Lian*
Love in a Goldfish Bowl (Head): 186
Love in Germany
See *Liebe en Deutschland*
Love in Germany (Dörrie): 121
Love Is a Dog from Hell (Hänsel): 176
Love Is Better Than Ever (Rose): 355

Love Laughs at Andy Hardy (Irene): 205
Love Letters
See *Koibumi*
Love Letters (Bauchens): 37; (Head): 185
Love Light (Marion): 265; (Pickford): 334
Love Mask (Macpherson): 255
Love Master (Murfin): 296
Love Me or Leave Me (Lennart): 236; (Rose): 355
Love Me Tonight (Head): 183
Love of Sumako
See *Joyu Sumako no koi*
Love of Sunya (Coffee): 90
Love on Credit
See *Kaerlighed pa kredit*
Love on Toast (Head): 183
Love Piker (Marion): 265
Love Poem
See *Hauchtext: Liebesgedicht (1970)*
Love Potion (Chenzira): 75
Love Stinks—Bilder des taeglichen Wahnsinns (Hein): 192
Love Thy Neighbor (Head): 184; (Marshall): 268
Love Toy (Levien): 237
Love under the Crucifix
See *O-gin sama*
Love Victorious (Madison): 258; (Meredyth): 286
Love with a Song
See *Ta naše písnička česká*
Love with the Proper Stranger (Head): 186
Loveless (Bigelow): 41
Lover (Duras): 124
Lover Come Back (Irene): 205
Loverboy (Silver): 392
Love's Blindness (Glyn): 150
Lovers? (Booth): 44
Lovers and Other Strangers (Keaton): 215
Lovers Courageous (Booth): 45
Loving (Schneemann): 374
Loving Couples
See *Älskande par*
Loving You (Head): 186
Low Finance (Batchelor): 35
Lowland
See *Tiefland*
Lucas (Trintignant): 420
Luciano (Miró): 291
Luciella (Notari): 307
Luciella la Figlia Della Strada
See *Luciella*
Luciella, the Daughter of the Street
See *Luciella*
Luckiest Girl in the World (Spencer): 397
Lucky Break
See *Golpe de suerte*
Lucky Jordan (Head): 184
Lucky Partners (Irene): 203
Lucky Star (Levien): 237
Lucky Street (Batchelor): 35
Lucky to Be a Woman
See *Fortuna di essere donna*
Lucky Toothache (Pickford): 334
Lucy Gallant (Head): 186
Ludions (Poirier): 337
Ludwig (Cecchi d'Amico): 72
Lullaby (Madison): 259
Lumière and Company
See *Lumière et compagnie*
Lumière du lac (Guillemot): 165
Lumière et compagnie (Sanders-Brahms): 364; (Trintignant): 420; (Ullmann): 424
Luminous City
See *Svetlyi gorod*
Luna de Cristal (Yamasaki): 460
Lunch (Guy): 168
L'Une chante l'autre pas (Hänsel): 176; (Varda): 435
Lungo silenzio (von Trotta): 441
L'Union sacrée (Musidora): 300
L'universe de Jacques Demy (Varda): 435
L'uomo dalle due ombre (Ullmann): 424
L'uomo, l'orgoglio, la vendetta (Cecchi d'Amico): 72
Lupino, Ida: **247**
Lure (Guy): 169
Lure and the Lore (Chenzira): 75
Lure of the Jungle
See *Paw*
Lure of the Wilderness (Jeakins): 208
Lure of Youth (Madison): 259
Lust for Gold (Lupino): 247
Lutteurs américains (Guy): 168
Luv (May): 271
Luxury Liner (Rose): 355
Lydia Bailey (Spencer): 397
Lyell, Lottie: **250**

M

M (von Harbou): 440
Ma Hoggan's New Boarder (Lyell): 250
Macbeth (Loos): 244
Machine
See *maschine*
Machine-Bodies/Body-Space/Body-Machines
See *Maschinenkörper-Körperraum-Körpermaschinen*
Machorka-Muff (Huillet): 201
Macht die Pille Frei? (Sander): 361
Machu Picchu (Hammer): 173
Maclean, Alison: **253**

Maçons (Guy): 168
Macpherson, Jeanie: **255**
Mad about Men (Box, B.): 48
Mad Doctor (Head): 184
Mad Love (Bird): 42
Madam Satan (Bauchens): 37; (Macpherson): 255
Madame and Wife
See *Madamu to nyobo*
Madame Butterfly (Pickford): 335
Madame Curie (Sharaff): 384
Madame Pompadour (Marion): 266
Madame Satan
See *Madam Satan*
Madame Sousatska (Jhabvala): 210
Madame X—An Absolute Ruler
See *Madame X—eine absolute Herrscherin*
Madame X—eine absolute Herrscherin (Ottinger): 318; (Rainer): 345
Madamu to nyobo (Tanaka): 409
Mädchen in Uniform (Sagan): 359
Made in Milan (Schoonmaker): 375
Made in Paris (Rose): 356
Made in U.S.A. (Guillemot): 165
Mademoiselle (Duras): 124
Mademoiselle France
See *Reunion in France*
Madigan (Head): 187
Madison, Cleo: **258**
Madison/Wis (Hein): 192
Madonna of the Storm (Gish): 148
Madonnina del Pescatore (Notari): 307
Maestro (Hänsel): 176
Maeva (Deren): 116
Mafu Cage (Littleton): 239
Magic Book (Batchelor): 35
Magic Canvas (Batchelor): 34
Magic Christian (Ono): 316
Magic Flame (Mathis): 270; (Meredyth): 286
Magic Horse (Reiniger): 347
Magic Sticks (Vachon): 426
Magic Tide (Murphy): 297
Magical Eye
See *Magische Auge*
Magician (Batchelor): 35
Magie noire (Guy): 168
Magique image (Musidora): 300
Magische Auge (Export): 134
Magnet (Meredyth): 287
Magnificent Fraud (Head): 184
Mahler (Russell): 357
Maid or Man (Pickford): 334
Maidens in Uniform
See *Mädchen in Uniform*
Maillot noir (Musidora): 300
Main Attraction (Zetterling): 462
Main du professeur Hamilton ou Le Roi des dollars (Guy): 168
Main Event (Streisand): 405
Mains négatives (Duras): 124
Mais où et donc Ornicar (Denis): 115
Mais qu'est-ce qu'elles veulent? (Serreau): 382
Maisie Goes to Reno (Irene): 203
Maison de jade (Trintignant): 420
Maison sous les arbres (Perry): 332
Majd holnap (Elek): 127
Major and the Minor (Head): 184
Make Me Laugh
See *Få mig att skratta*
Make Mine Mink (Dillon): 118
Make Way for Tomorrow (Head): 183
Make-Up (Craigie): 101
Making Mr. Right (Seidelman): 379
Making of Agnes of God
See *Quiet on the Set: Filming Agnes of God*
Making of an American Citizen (Guy): 169
Making of the Sun City (Choy): 81
Mal du pays (Sarmiento): 365
Malá mořská víla (Krumbachová): 224
Malaya (Head): 185; (Irene): 205
Maldoror, Sarah: **260**
Male and Female (Bauchens): 37; (Macpherson): 255
Male Bonding
See *Männerbunde*
Male oscuro (Cecchi d'Amico): 72
Male Pattern Baldness (Thomas): 412
Malencontre (Dulac): 123
Malevitch at the Guggenheim (De Hirsch): 110
Malheurs du Sophie (Audry): 27
Mallet, Marilú: **262**
Malou (Meerapfel): 280
Mama Steps Out (Loos): 245
Mama, There's a Man in Your Bed
See *Romuald et Juliette*
Mama's Affair (Loos): 246
Mame (Van Runkle): 431
Mam'zelle Chiffon (Musidora): 300
Man, a Country
See *Homme, une Terre*
Man about Town (Head): 184
Man and Maid (Glyn): 150
Man and the Woman (Guy): 169
Man Beast (Murphy): 297
Man Between (Madison): 258
Man from Down Under (Irene): 203
Man from Kangaroo (Meredyth): 286
Man from the First Century
See *Muž z prvního století*
Man I Love (Lupino): 247
Man in Half Moon Street (Head): 185
Man in Love (Kurys): 225

Man in Polar Regions (Clarke): 88
Man in the Gray Flannel Suit (Spencer): 397
Man No Run (Denis): 114
Man of Conquest (Head): 184
Man of Iron
See *Człowiek z Żelaza*
Man of the Family
See *Top Man*
Man on a Tightrope (Spencer): 397
Man on the Flying Trapeze (Head): 183
Man, Pride and Vengeance
See *L'uomo, l'orgoglio, la vendetta*
Man Sa Yay (Faye): 137
Man, When He Is a Man
See *El hombre cuando es hombre*
Man Who Dared God (Weber): 444
Man Who Envied Women (Rainer): 345
Man Who Finally Died (Zetterling): 462
Man Who Knew Too Much (Head): 186
Man Who Loved Cat Dancing (Perry): 332
Man Who Rose in Price
See *Muž, který stoupl v ceně*
Man Who Shot Liberty Valance (Head): 186
Man Who Stayed at Home (Mathis): 269
Man Who Would Be King (Head): 187
Man with a Million
See *Million Pound Note*
Man with the Suitcase
See *L'Homme à la valise*
Man Within (Box, M.): 51
Man, Woman and Animal
See *Mann & Frau & Animal*
Mandolin Music at Sea
See *Mandolinata a Mare*
Mandolinata a Mare (Notari): 307
Manhandled (Head): 185
Manhattan (Keaton): 215
Manhattan Cocktail (Arzner): 25
Manhattan Madness (Loos): 245
Manhattan Murder Mystery (Keaton): 215
Manly Man (Pickford): 334
Mann & Frau & Animal (Export): 134
Männer. . . (Dörrie): 121
Männerbunde (Sander): 361
Manoever
See *Geteilte Liebe*
Man's Enemy (Gish): 148
Manslaughter (Bauchens): 37; (Macpherson): 255
Mantrap (Head): 183, 186
Many Happy Returns (Head): 183
Maori Maid's Love (Lyell): 250
Mar de Rosas (Carolina): 67
Maracaibo (Head): 186
Marâtre (Guy): 168
March on Paris 1914—Of General Obrest Alexander von Kluck—and His Memory of Jessie Holladay (Clarke): 88
Marchand de ballons (Guy): 168
Marchand de coco (Guy): 168
Marché à la volaille (Guy): 168
Marguerite Volant (Pool): 339
Maria Rosa (Macpherson): 255
Maria Rosa di Santa Flavia (Notari): 307
Mária-nap (Elek): 127
Mariage du Hibou (Leaf): 235
Marian (Krumbachová): 223
Marianne and Juliane
See *Bleierne Zeit*
Maria's Day
See *Mária-nap*
Marie, Ltd. (Murfin): 296
Mariés d'un jour (Musidora): 300
Marion, Frances: **264**
Mariti in città (Cecchi d'Amico): 71
Mark of Zorro (Meredyth): 287
Marnie (Allen, J.): 12; (Head): 186
Marriage (Weill): 447
Marriage Clause (Weber): 445
Marriage Is a Private Affair (Coffee): 90; (Irene): 205
Married in Hollywood (Spencer): 397
Married Woman
See *Femme mariée*
Marry Me! (Box, B.): 48
Marseillaise (Reiniger): 348
Marshall, Penny: **267**
Marteau (Akerman): 4
Martha Clarke Light and Dark: A Dancer's Journal (Chopra): 78
Martha, Ruth & Edie (Mehta): 283
Martinovics (Elek): 127
Martyrs of Love
See *Mučedníci lásky*
Marvin's Room (Keaton): 215
Mary Regan (Weber): 444
Mary the Crazy Woman
See *Miracolo Della Madonna di Pompei*
Mary's Birthday (Reiniger): 347
Maschera del Vizio (Notari): 307
Maschine (Sanders-Brahms): 364
Maschinenkörper-Körperraum-Körpermaschinen (Export): 134
Mascot of Troop "C" (Guy): 168
Masculine Ending (Bird): 42
Masculin-féminin (Guillemot): 165
Masher (Pickford): 334
Mask of Vice
See *Maschera del Vizio*
Masked Woman (Mathis): 270
Maskrosbarn (Ahrne): 2

Masks of the Devil (Marion): 266
Masquerade in Mexico (Head): 185
Masques (Parker): 325
Mass Production of Eggs
See *Nagyüzemi tojástermelés*
Master and the Man (Pickford): 334
Master Key (Madison): 258
Match (Ono): 316
Matchmaker (Head): 186
Matelas alcoolique (Guy): 168
Materialfilme I (Hein): 192
Materialfilme II (Hein): 192
Maternelle (Epstein): 132
Maternité (Epstein): 132
Mathis, June: **269**
Matine Horner—Portrait of a Person (Weill): 447
Matinee Scandal
See *One Rainy Afternoon*
Mating Game (Rose): 355
Matrimaniac (Loos): 245
Matrimony's Speed Limit (Guy): 169
Matter of Life and Death
See *På liv och död*
Mauprat (Epstein): 132
Mauvais coeur puni (Guy): 168
Mauvaise Soupe (Guy): 167
Maverick (Foster): 143
Max (Treut): 416
Maxine Sullivan: Love to Be in Love (Schiller): 370
May and December (Pickford): 334
May, Elaine: **271**
May Lady (Bani-Etemad): 32
Maybe Tomorrow
See *Majd holnap*
Mayhem (Child): 76
Mayol series (Guy): 168
Mayron, Melanie: **275**
McDonagh Sisters: **278**
McGuire, Go Home!
See *High Bright Sun*
Me and Him
See *Ich und Er*
Me and My Classmates (Peng): 330
Me and the Colonel (Head): 186
Me and You
See *Mej och dej*
Meal Ticket (Loos): 244
Meat Joy (Schneemann): 372
Medal for Benny (Head): 185
Meddig él az ember? (Elek): 127
Medea di Porta Medina (Notari): 307
Medicine Bottle (Macpherson): 256
Medien und das Bild. Andy Warhol's Kunst (Hein): 192
Meditation on Violence (Deren): 116
Meditations (Cantrill): 65
Medium Cool (Fields): 141
Medusa (Deren): 116
Medvěd (Krumbachová): 223
Meerapfel, Jeanine: **280**
Meet Me in Las Vegas (Lennart): 236; (Rose): 355
Meet Me in St. Louis (Sharaff): 384
Meet Me Tonight (Dillon): 118
Meet the People (Irene): 205
Meet the Prince (Murfin): 296
Mehta, Deepa: **282**
Meilleure façon de marcher (Pascal): 328
Mein Herz-Niemandem (Sanders-Brahms): 364
Mej och dej (Henning-Jensen): 194
Melek Leaves
See *Kümmeltürkin geht*
Melody of Love (Shipman): 388
Mémoires d'un enfant des Andes (Mallet): 263
Memoires d'un jeune con (Guillemot): 165
Memoirs of a River
See *Tutajosok*
Memorabilia P P 1 (Deitch): 112
Memories of Us (Fields): 141
Memory Lane (Booth): 44
Memory Pictures (Parmar): 326
Memsahib Rita (Parmar): 326
Men. . .
See *Männer. . .*
Men in Crisis: The Harvey Wallinger Story (Keaton): 215
Men of Tomorrow (Sagan): 359
Men with Wings (Head): 183
Men without Names (Head): 183
Menace (Bauchens): 37
Menace on the Mountain (Foster): 143
Mender of Nets (Pickford): 334
Menken, Marie: **284**
Men's Favorite Sport? (Head): 186
Men's Room (Bird): 42
Mensche verstreut und Welt verkehrt (Sarmiento): 366
Menschen im Variete (von Harbou): 440
Menschenfrauen (Export): 134
Menses (Hammer): 173
Menstruation Film
See *Menstruationsfilm*
Menstruationsfilm (Export): 134
Mental Images, Oder der Zugang der Welt (Export): 134
Mental Images, or, the Gateway to the World
See *Mental Images, Oder der Zugang der Welt*
Mentour (1re partie)-L'Alcoholisme: la therapie (Poirier): 337

Mentour (2e partie)-L'Alcoholisme: la maladie (Poirier): 337
Mépris (Guillemot): 165
Merchant of Venice (Macpherson): 256; (Weber): 444
Mercury Rising (von Brandenstein): 438
Mercy (Child): 76
Meredyth, Bess: **286**
Merrily We Go to Hell (Arzner): 25
Merrily We Live (Irene): 203
Merry Andrew (Lennart): 236
Merry Widow (Levien): 237; (Loos): 245; (Rose): 355
Merton of the Movies (Irene): 205; (Rose): 355
Mésaventure d'un charbonnier (Guy): 168
Meshes of the Afternoon (Deren): 116
Mesmerized (Foster): 143
Message (Macpherson): 256
Message in the Bottle (Pickford): 334
Messagère (Palcy): 321
Messe de minuit (Guy): 168
Messenger
See *messagère*
Mestiça, a Escrava Indomavel (Abreu): 1
Mészáros László emlékére (Mészáros): 289
Mészáros, Márta: **287**
Metal meccanico e parrucchiera in un turbine di sesso e di politica (Wertmüller): 449
Meta-Morphose (Export): 134
Metamorphosis of Mr. Samsa (Leaf): 235
Metello (Cecchi d'Amico): 72
Meteor Crater, Gosse Bluff (Cantrill): 65
Metro by Night
See *Moskva stroit metro*
Metropole (Weill): 446
Metropolis (von Harbou): 440
Metropolitan (Meredyth): 286
Mettete l'Avvocato (Notari): 307
Mexican Sweethearts (Pickford): 334
Mexican's Last Raid (Madison): 258
Mi Prazane me Rozùmeji (Chytilová): 83
Mi Vida Loca (Anders): 15
Michael (Ephron): 130; (von Harbou): 440
Michael Strogoff or The Courier to the Czar (Guy): 169
Michigan Avenue (Gordon): 157
Michurin (Solntseva): 395
Mickey's Pal (Guy): 169
Microbe (Mathis): 269
Midnight (Head): 184; (Irene): 203
Midnight Adventure (Macpherson): 256; (Pickford): 334
Midnight Lace (Irene): 205
Midnight Madonna (Head): 183
Midnight Man (Meredyth): 286
Midnight Mary (Loos): 245
Midnight Romance (Weber): 444
Midnight Songs (Peng): 330
Midnight Wedding (Lyell): 250
Midsummer Nightmare (Batchelor): 35
Mig og dig
See *Mej och dej*
Mighty Barnum (Meredyth): 286
Mighty Conqueror (McDonagh Sisters): 278
Mighty McGurk (Irene): 205
Mignon (Guy): 168
Mignon or The Child of Fate (Guy): 168
Mikado (Dillon): 118
Mike's Murder (Allen, D.): 10
Mikey and Nicky (May): 271
Miklós Borsós
See *Borsós Miklós*
Milagro Beanfield War (Allen, D.): 10
Milarepa (Cavani): 69
Militaire et nourrice (Guy): 168
Milky Way (Head): 183
Milky Way Special (Cantrill): 65
Million Dollar Bride (Loos): 244
Million Dollar Legs (Head): 184
Million Dollar Mermaid (Rose): 355
Million Dollar Robbery (Guy): 169
Million Pound Note (Craigie): 101
Mimi metallurgio ferito nell'onore (Wertmüller): 449
Mimi the Metalworker
See *Mimi metallurgio ferito nell'onore*
Min and Bill (Marion): 266
Min bedstefar er en stok (Henning-Jensen): 194
Mind Your Own Business (Head): 183
Mindennapi történetek (Mészáros): 288
Mindwalk (Ullmann): 424
Ming-Wei to Singaraja (Cantrill): 65
Minimum Charge No Cover (Cole and Dale): 92
Ministry of Fear (Head): 185
Minne (Colette): 95; (Musidora): 300
Minne, l'Ingénue libertine (Audry): 27; (Colette): 95
Minne, the Innocent Libertine
See *Minne, l'Ingénue libertine*
Minnie (Marion): 265
Minute Hands
See *Los Minuteros*
Mio figlio professore (Cecchi d'Amico): 71
Mir v treh izmerenijah (Solntseva): 395
Miracle in Milan
See *Miracolo a Milano*
Miracle in Soho (Dillon): 118
Miracle of Morgan's Creek (Head): 185
Miracolo a Milano (Cecchi d'Amico): 71
Miracolo Della Madonna di Pompei (Notari): 307

Miranda (Box, B.): 48
Mireille (Guy): 168
Miró (Maldoror): 261
Miró, Pilar: **290**
Mirror (Pickford): 334
Mirror Has Two Faces (Streisand): 405
Misérables (Jeakins): 208
Misère au Borinage (van Dongen): 430
Misères de l'aiguille (Musidora): 300
Misfits: 30 Years of Fluxus (Ono): 316
Misguided Tour (Batchelor): 35
Mishaps of Seduction and Conquest (Campion): 61
Misleading Widow (Marion): 264
Miss Fluci Moses (Larkin): 231
Miss Lina Esbrard Danseuse Cosmopolite et Serpentine series (Guy): 168
Miss Mary (Bemberg): 38
Miss Oyu
See *Oyu-sama*
Miss Peasant
See *Baryshnia krestianka*
Miss Susie Slagle's (Gish): 148; (Head): 185
Miss Tatlock's Millions (Head): 185
Missing (Mayron): 275
Mississippi (Head): 183
Mississippi Mah Jong Blues
See *Mississippi Triangle*
Mississippi Masala (Nair): 302
Mississippi Mermaid
See *Sirène du Mississippi*
Mississippi Triangle (Choy): 81
Missouri Breaks (Allen, D.): 10
Mistake (Loos): 244
Mr. and Mrs. Bridge (Jhabvala): 210
Mr. and Mrs. Smith (Irene): 203
Mister Buddwing (Rose): 356
Mr. Casanova (Head): 186
Mr. Jones at the Ball (Macpherson): 256
Mr. Jones Has a Card Party (Macpherson): 256
Mr. Lord Says No!
See *Happy Family*
Mr. Music (Head): 185
Mr. Skitch (Levien): 237
Misterio (Fernández Violante): 139
Mrs. Dalloway (Gorris): 159
Mrs. Jones Entertains (Macpherson): 256
Mistress Nell (Pickford): 335
Mrs. Parkington (Irene): 203
Mrs. Sew and Sew (Batchelor): 34
Mrs. Soffel (Armstrong): 21; (Keaton): 215
Mrs. Wiggs of the Cabbage Patch (Bauchens): 37; (Head): 184
Misunderstood Boy (Gish): 147
Mit den Augen einer Frau (von Harbou): 440
Mitsou (Audry): 27; (Colette): 95
Mitten ins Herz (Dörrie): 121
Mixed Nuts (Ephron): 130
Mixed Values (Loos): 244
Miyamoto musashi (Tanaka): 410
M'Liss (Marion): 264; (Pickford): 335
Modelage express (Guy): 168
Moderato Cantabile (Duras): 124
Modern Guide to Health (Batchelor): 34
Modern Story
See *Historia współczesna*
Modest Hero (Gish): 148
Moffie Who Drove with Mandela (Schiller): 370
Mogambo (Rose): 355
Mohojereen Roustai (Bani-Etemad): 32
Moi, Fleur Bleue (Foster): 143
Moi, ta mère
See *Man Sa Yay*
Molly Maguires (Jeakins): 208
Molotov Cocktail
See *Cocktail Molotov*
Moment
See *Øjeblikket*
Moment in Love (Clarke): 88
Momentos (Bemberg): 38
Mommie Dearest (Sharaff): 384
Mom's on the Roof
See *With Friends Like These. . .*
Mon amour, mon amour (Trintignant): 420
Mon Oncle (Musidora): 300
Mon Paris (Dulac): 123
Monangambée (Maldoror): 261
Mondani a mondhatatlant: Elie Wiesel üzenete (Elek): 127
Mondo le condanna (Cecchi d'Amico): 71
Money
See *Geld*
Money for Speed (Lupino): 247
Money from Home (Head): 186
Money Pit (von Brandenstein): 438
Monkey King Looks West (Choy): 81
Monnaie de lapin (Guy): 168
Monolutteur (Guy): 168
Monsieur Badin (Guillemot): 165
Monsieur Beaucaire (Head): 185
Monster and the Girl (Guy): 169; (Head): 184
Monster of Highgate Pond (Batchelor): 35
Monsters (Borden): 46
Monteiro Lobato (Carolina): 67
Montreal Sextet
See *Montréal vu par*
Montréal vu par (Pool): 339
Mood Contrasts (Bute): 59
Mood Lyric (Bute): 59
Mood Mondrian (Menken): 285
Moon Goddess (Hammer): 173

Moon Has Risen
See *Tsuki wa noborinu*
Moon over Burma (Head): 184
Moonbird (Hubley): 197
Moonplay (Menken): 284
Moon's Our Home (Spencer): 397
Moons Pool (Nelson): 305
Moonstruck (Batchelor): 35
Moontide (Lupino): 247
Moral der Ruth Halbfass (von Trotta): 442
More Than a School (Coolidge): 99
More than Friends (Marshall): 268
Morfars Resa (Zetterling): 462
Morgan's Raiders (Meredyth): 286
Morning After (Allen, J.): 12
Morning Glory (Akins): 6
Mort de Robert Macaire et Bertrand (Guy): 168
Mort du cygne (Epstein): 132
Mort du soleil (Dulac): 123
Mortadella (Cecchi d'Amico): 72
Mortal Danger
See *To Die, to Sleep*
Morze (Jakubowska): 207
Mosca Addio (Ullmann): 424
Moscow Builds the Subway
See *Moskva stroit metro*
Moscow Goodbye
See *Mosca Addio*
Moses und Aron (Huillet): 201
Moskva stroit metro (Shub): 390
Mossane (Faye): 137
Motele the Weaver
See *Glaza, kotorye videli*
Mother
See *Okasan*
Mother (Loos): 244
Mother and Country (Notari): 307
Mother and Daughter
See *Anya és leánya*
Mother and Son (Krumbachová): 223
Mother of Many Children (Obomsawin): 313
Mother of the River (Davis): 107
Mother Right (Citron): 86
Mothering Heart (Gish): 148
Mother's Atonement (Madison): 258
Mother's Cry (Coffee): 90
Mother's Heart
See *Coração Materno*
Mother's Helper (Keaton): 215
Mother's Instinct (Madison): 258
Mother-to-Be
See *De mère en fille*
Mots pour le dire (Cecchi d'Amico): 72
MOTV (Chenzira): 75
Mouche (Guy): 168
Mouettes (Kaplan): 213
Mountain (Head): 186
Mountain Giant and the Skiers
See *Krakonoš a lyžníci*
Mountain Music (Head): 183
Mountaineer's Honor (Pickford): 334
Mourir à tue-tête (Poirier): 337
Mouvements du désir (Pool): 339
Movers & Shakers (Marshall): 268
Moving In (Akerman): 4
Moving Picture Postcards (Cantrill): 65
Moving Spirit (Batchelor): 34
Moving the Mountain (Alberti): 7
Moyen Montrage
See *Keep It for Yourself*
Mrkáček Čiko (Šimková-Plívová): 394
Mučedníci lásky (Krumbachová): 223
Mud (Cantrill): 65
Muggsy Becomes a Hero (Pickford): 334
Muggsy's First Sweetheart (Pickford): 334
Multiple Orgasm (Hammer): 173
Munekata shimai (Tanaka): 410
Munekata Sisters
See *Munekata shimai*
Munka vagy hivatás? (Mészáros): 289
Mur Murs (Varda): 435
Mura di Malapaga (Cecchi d'Amico): 71
Mural Murals
See *Mur Murs*
Muratova, Kira: **293**
Murder (Reville): 349
Murder and Murder (Rainer): 345
Murder by Death (Booth): 45
Murder Goes to College (Head): 183
Murder, He Says (Head): 185
Murder in a Small Town (Chopra): 78
Murder in New Hampshire: The Pamela Wojas Smart Story (Chopra): 78
Murder in Thornton Square
See *Gaslight*
Murder of Mr. Devil
See *Vražda ing. Čerta*
Murder One: Diary of a Serial Killer (Deitch): 112
Murder with Pictures (Head): 183
Murfin, Jane: **296**
Murphy, Brianne: **297**
Musashi Miyamoto
See *Miyamoto musashi*
Musashino fujin (Tanaka): 410
Museum of Modern Art Show (Ono): 316
Music for Millions (Irene): 205
Music in Darkness
See *Musik i moerker*
Music Lovers (Russell): 357
Music Man (Batchelor): 34; (Jeakins): 208
Musica (Duras): 124

Musical May
See *Maestro*
Musidora: **299**
Musidora en Espagne
See *Aventura de Musidora en España*
Musik i moerker (Zetterling): 462
Musique d'Amérique latine (Mallet): 263
Musketeers of Pig Alley (Gish): 147; (Loos): 244
Mutiny (Child): 76
Mutiny of the Bounty (Lyell): 250
Mutiny on the Bounty (Booth): 45
Mutterlied (von Harbou): 440
Muž, který stoupl v ceně (Krumbachová): 223
Muž z prvního století (Krumbachová): 223
My America . . . or Honk if You Love Buddha (Choy): 81
My American Grandson
See *Shanghai Jiaqi*
My American Wife (Van Upp): 432
My Baby (Gish): 147; (Loos): 244; (Pickford): 334
My Best Girl (Pickford): 334
My Blue Heaven (Ephron): 130; (Mayron): 276
My Boys Are Good Boys (Lupino): 248
My Breast (Thomas): 412
My Brilliant Career (Armstrong): 21
My Brother Talks to Horses (Irene): 205
My Cousin Rachel (Jeakins): 208
My Crazy Life
See *Mi Vida Loca*
My Darling Clementine (Spencer): 397
My Demon Lover (Vachon): 426
My Dream Is to Marry an African Prince (Larkin): 231
My Enemy the Sea
See *Taiheyo hitoribochi*
My Father Is Coming (Treut): 416
My Favorite Blonde (Head): 184
My Favorite Brunette (Head): 185
My Favorite Spy (Head): 185
My Fighting Gentleman (Shipman): 388
My Filmmaking, My Life: Matilde Landeta (Fernández Violante): 139; (Novaro): 309
My Foolish Heart (Head): 185
My Friend Irma (Head): 185
My Friend Irma Goes West (Head): 185
My Geisha (Head): 186
My Heart Belongs to Daddy (Head): 184
My Heart Is Mine Alone
See *Mein Herz-Niemandem*
My Life to Live
See *Vivre sa vie*
My Little Chickadee (West): 452
My Love for Yours
See *Honeymoon in Bali*
My Love Has Been Burning
See *Waga koi wa moenu*
My Love, My Love
See *Mon amour, mon amour*
My Madonna (Guy): 169
My Name Is Kahentiiosta (Obomsawin): 313
My Name Is Oona (Nelson): 305
My Old Man (von Brandenstein): 437
My Own Country (Nair): 302
My Own True Love (Head): 185
My Own TV
See *MOTV*
My Praguers Understand Me
See *Mi Prazane me Rozùmeji*
My Reputation (Head): 185
My Sister, My Love
See *Mafu Cage*
My Six Loves (Head): 186
My Son John (Head): 185
My Son, My Son! (Coffee): 90
My Universe Inside Out (Hubley): 197
My Wife's Best Friend (Lennart): 236
Myra Breckenridge (Head): 187; (Van Runkle): 431; (West): 452
Myself When Fourteen (Cantrill): 65
Mysterious Lady (Booth): 44; (Meredyth): 286
Mysterious Mrs. M (Weber): 444
Mysterious Rider (Head): 183
Mysterium (Clarke): 88
Mystery
See *Misterio*
Mystery of a Hansom Cab (McDonagh Sisters): 278
Mystery of Wickham Hall (Madison): 258; (Meredyth): 286
Mystery Sea Raider (Head): 184
Mystery Woman (Madison): 258; (Meredyth): 286

N

Naar man kun er ung (Henning-Jensen): 194
Naarden Vesting (Apon): 19
Nacht der Regisseure (Meerapfel): 280; (Riefenstahl): 351; (Sander): 361; (Sanders-Brahms): 364; (von Trotta): 442
Nad Niemnem (Jakubowska): 207
Nagareru (Tanaka): 410
Nagyüzemi tojástermelés (Mészáros): 288
Náhrdelník melancholie (Krumbachová): 224
Nails (Kopple): 221
Nair, Mira: **302**
Naked Edge (Dillon): 118
Naked Jungle (Head): 186
Naked Spaces: Living Is Round (Trinh): 418
Namibia, Independence Now (Choy): 81

Nana (Arzner): 25
Nancy Goes to Rio (Rose): 355
Naniwa ereji (Tanaka): 409
Nano Rosso (Notari): 307
Naples Connection
See *Camorra*
Naples, Land of Love
See *Napoli Terra d'Amore*
Naples, Singing Mermaid
See *Napoli Sirena Della Canzone*
Napló apámnak, anyámnak (Mészáros): 289
Napló gyermekeimnek (Henning-Jensen): 194; (Mészáros): 289
Napló szerelmeimnek (Mészáros): 289
Napoleon and Samantha (Foster): 143
Napoli Sirena Della Canzone (Notari): 307
Napoli Terra d'Amore (Notari): 307
Narayama bushi-ko (Tanaka): 410
Nargess (Bani-Etemad): 32
Narrow Escape (Loos): 244
Narrow Road (Pickford): 334
Nash chestnyi khleb (Muratova): 294
Nashville Grab (Thomas): 412
Nathalie Granger (Duras): 124
Nation Sets Its Course (Grayson): 161
National Barn Dance (Head): 185
National Lampoon's European Vacation (Heckerling): 189
National Velvet (Irene): 205
Native Country
See *Strana rodnaya*
Native Son (Winfrey): 457
Nattlek (Zetterling): 462
Natural Features (Nelson): 305
Nature morte (Guillemot): 165
Naughty Arlette
See *Romantic Age*
Naughty Marietta (Goodrich): 155
Nausicaa (Varda): 435
Navire Night (Duras): 124
Navy Wife (Levien): 237
Ne bougeons plus (Guy): 168
Néa (Kaplan): 213
Near and Far Away
See *Långt borta och nära*
Near Dark (Bigelow): 41
Near Wilmington (Cantrill): 65
Nearly a Burglar's Bride (Loos): 244
Nearly a Lady (Marion): 264
'Neath Austral Skies (Lyell): 250
Nebulae (Cantrill): 65
Necklace (Pickford): 334
Necklace of Melancholy
See *Náhrdelník melancholie*
Ned McCobb's Daughter (Bauchens): 37; (Coffee): 90
Nefňukej, veverko! (Šimková-Plívová): 394
Negative/Positive on Three Images by Baldwin Spencer, 1901 (Cantrill): 65
Negra Angustias (Landeta): 229
Nell (Foster): 143
Nella città l'inferno (Cecchi d'Amico): 71
Nell's Eugenic Wedding (Loos): 244
Nelson Affair
See *Bequest to the Nation*
Nelson, Gunvor: **304**
Nelson Pereira Dos Santos (Carolina): 67
Nema Kiáltás (Mészáros): 289
Nénette et Boni (Denis): 114
Neptune's Daughter (Irene): 205
Nest of Noblemen (Preobrazhenskaya): 343
Netherlands America (van Dongen): 430
Nevada Smith (Head): 187
Nevelson in Process (Godmilow): 152
Never Again! (Pickford): 334
Never Fear (Lupino): 247
Never Say Die (Head): 184
Never So Few (Rose): 356
New Criminal Underworld
See *'A Mala Nova*
New Earth
See *Nieuwe Gronden*
New Kind of Love (Head): 186
New Land
See *Nybyggarna*
New Leaf (May): 271
New Moon (Booth): 45
New Movements Generate New Thoughts (Cantrill): 65
New Song [Chilean]
See *Nueva canción (chilena)*
New World (Grayson): 161
New York Hat (Gish): 147; (Loos): 244; (Pickford): 334
New York Loft (Hammer): 173
New York, New York (Van Runkle): 431
New York, New York Bis (Akerman): 4
New York Stories (Schoonmaker): 375
New York Town (Head): 184
Newlyweds (Macpherson): 256; (Pickford): 334
News from Home (Akerman): 4
News Review No. 2 (van Dongen): 430
Newsreel: Jonas in The Brig (De Hirsch): 109
Next of Kin
See *Arven*
Next Summer
See *L'Été prochain*
Nez (Parker): 325
Než se rozhrne opona (Šimková-Plívová): 394
Nezabivaemoe (Solntseva): 395
'Nfama (Notari): 307
Ni Une, Ni Deux (Denis): 114

Niagara (Jeakins): 208
Nibelungen (Reiniger): 348; (von Harbou): 440
Nice, Very Nice (Denis): 114
Nicht versöhnt oder Es hilft nur Gewalt, wo Gewalt herrscht (Huillet): 201
Nickelodeon (Van Runkle): 431
Niedzielne Dzieci (Holland): 195
Nieuwe Gronden (van Dongen): 430
Nieuwe polders (van Dongen): 429
Nigeria, Nigeria One (Choy): 81
Night after Night (West): 452
Night and Day
See *Nuit et jour*
Night at Earl Carroll's (Head): 184
Night at the Roxbury (Heckerling): 189
Night Club Scandal (Head): 183
Night Court (Coffee): 90
Night Full of Rain
See *End of the World in Our Usual Bed in a Night Full of Rain*
Night Games
See *Nattlek*
Night Has a Thousand Eyes (Head): 185
Night Is My Future
See *Musik i moerker*
Night Moves (Allen, D.): 10
Night of January 16th (Head): 184
Night of Love (Coffee): 90
Night of Mystery (Head): 183
Night of Nights (Head): 184
Night of the Beast
See *House of the Black Death*
Night of the Filmmakers
See *Nacht der Regisseure*
Night of the Filmmakers (Ottinger): 318
Night of the Hunter (Gish): 148
Night of the Iguana (Jeakins): 208
Night of the Meek (Coolidge): 99
Night on Bald Mountain
See *Nuit sur le Mont Chauve*
Night People (Spencer): 397
Night Plane from Chungking (Head): 185
Night Porter
See *Portiere di notte*
Night Visitor (Ullmann): 424
Night We Never Met (Seidelman): 379
Night Work (Head): 184
Nikdo se nebude smát (Krumbachová): 223
Nille (Henning-Jensen): 194
Niña de luto (Miró): 291
Nine Image Film (Cantrill): 65
Nine Months
See *Kilenc hónap*
Nine till Six (Reville): 349
Ninfa plebea (Wertmüller): 449
Nishijin no shimai (Tanaka): 410
Nitrate Kisses (Hammer): 173
Nix on Dames (Spencer): 397
No Address (Obomsawin): 313
No Exit
See *Huis clos*
No Exit No Panic
See *Berührte*
No Fear, No Die
See *S'en fout la mort*
No-Gun Man (Arzner): 25
No Kidding (Dillon): 118
No Leave No Love (Irene): 205
No Love for Johnnie (Box, B.): 48
No Man of Her Own (Head): 185
No Mercy (von Brandenstein): 438
No Mercy No Future
See *Berührte*
No, My Darling Daughter (Box, B.): 48
No No Nooky TV (Hammer): 173
No Nukes (Kopple): 221
No Questions Asked (Rose): 355
No Time for Love (Head): 185; (Irene): 203
No Trace of Romanticism
See *Von Romantik keine Spur*
Nobody Gets the Laugh
See *Nikdo se nebude smát*
Nobody Loves Me
See *Keiner Liebt Mich*
Nobody Runs Forever (Box, B.): 48
Nobody's Woman
See *Señora de Nadie*
Noce au lac Saint-Fargeau (Guy): 168
Noces barbares (Hänsel): 176
Noces d'argent (Musidora): 300
Nocturnal Love That Leaves
See *Nocturno amor que te vas*
Nocturne (Harrison): 180; (Parker): 325
Nocturno a Rosario (Landeta): 229
Nocturno amor que te vas (Fernández Violante): 139
Noisy Neighbors (Bauchens): 37
Nomadic People
See *I Nomadi*
Non stuzzicate la zanzara (Wertmüller): 449
North Country Tour (Choy): 81
North Dalls Forty (Jeakins): 208
North of the Rio Grande (Head): 183
North to Alaska (Spencer): 397
Northern Lights (Keaton): 215
Northwest Mounted Police (Bauchens): 37; (Head): 184; (Macpherson): 255
Nos Bon Etudiants (Guy): 168
Nose
See *Nez*
Not a Pretty Picture (Coolidge): 99
Not a Simple Story (Choy): 81

Not Fourteen Again (Armstrong): 21
Not Just a Pretty Face (Armstrong): 21
Not Reconciled
See *Nicht versöhnt oder Es hilft nur Gewalt, wo Gewalt herrscht*
Not Wanted (Lupino): 247
Not with My Wife, You Don't! (Head): 187
Notari, Elvira: **306**
Notebook (Menken): 285
Notes on Berlin, the Divided City (Cantrill): 65
Notes on the Passage of Time (Cantrill): 65
Nothing but Lies
See *Rien que des mensonges*
Nothing But the Truth (Head): 184
Nothing but Trouble (Irene): 203
Notorious (Head): 185
Notorious Lady (Murfin): 296
Notorious Sophie Lang (Head): 183
Notre mariage (Sarmiento): 365
Notte d'estate, con profilo Greco, occhi amandorla e odore di basilico (Wertmüller): 449
Notti bianche (Cecchi d'Amico): 71
N'oublie pas que tu vas mourir (Guillemot): 165
Nouvelle orangerie (Kaplan): 213
Novaro, María: **309**
Novel Affair
See *Passionate Stranger*
Now Let's Talk about Men
See *Questa volta parliamo di uomini*
Nowhere to Run (Cole and Dale): 92
Noyes (Gordon): 157
Nr. 1—Aus Berichten der Wach—und Patrouillendienst (Sander): 361
Nr. 8—Aus Berichten der Wach—und Patrouillendienst (Sander): 361
Nth Commandment (Marion): 265
Nu borjar livet (Zetterling): 462
Nueva canción (chilena) (Sarmiento): 365
Nueva Vida (Godmilow): 152
Nuit agitée (Guy): 167
Nuit et jour (Akerman): 4
Nuit noire, Calcutta (Duras): 124
Nuit sur le Mont Chauve (Parker): 325
No. 1—From the Reports of Security Guards and Patrol Services
See *Nr. 1—Aus Berichten der Wach—und Patrouillendienst*
No. 8—From the Reports of Security Guards and Patrol Services
See *Nr. 8—Aus Berichten der Wach—und Patrouillendienst*
Number Our Days (Littman): 240
Number Seventeen (Reville): 349
Nüren de gushi (Peng): 330
Nuren sishi
See *Xiatian de Xue*
Nursery School
See *Maternelle*
Nuts (Streisand): 407
Nutty Professor (Head): 186
Nybyggarna (Ullmann): 424

O

O Amuleto de Ogum (Yamasaki): 460
'O Cuppe' d'a Morte (Notari): 307
O Ébrio (Abreu): 1
'O Festino e 'a Legge
See *'A Legge*
O-gin sama (Tanaka): 409
O Honzovi, Jakubovi Kostečkovi a papírovém okénku (Krumbachová): 224
'O Munaciello (Notari): 307
O něčem jiném (Chytilová): 83
O neposedném knoflíčku (Krumbachová): 224
O noviço Rebelde (Yamasaki): 460
O Regresso do Homem Que Não Gostava de Sair de Casa (Amaral): 13
O saisons, o châteaux (Varda): 435
O slavnosti a hostech (Krumbachová): 223
O Sněburce (Šimková-Plívová): 394
O Sonho Acabou (Carolina): 67
O statečném kováři (Krumbachová): 224
O živej vode (Krumbachová): 224
Obomsawin, Alanis: **312**
Ob's stürmt oder schneit (Dörrie): 121
Obsessions
See *Uvletschenia*
Occupants of Manor Houses
See *Kastélyok lakói*
Ocean (Cantrill): 65
Ocean Waif (Guy): 169
Oci ciornie (Cecchi d'Amico): 72
Odds against Tomorrow (Allen, D.): 10
Odyssey
See *Odyssey Tapes*
Odyssey Tapes (Godmilow): 152
Of Flesh and Blood
See *Grands chemins*
Of Human Rights (van Dongen): 430
Of Lace and Sugar
See *De encaje y azucar*
Of Men and Demons (Hubley): 197
Of Seals and Men (Zetterling): 462
Of Stars and Men (Hubley): 197
Off Beat (Allen, D.): 10
Off Limits (Head): 186
Off the Limits
See *Kharejaz Mahdoudeh*
Offbeat (Zetterling): 462

Offenders (B): 30
Office Killer (Vachon): 426
Oh Uncle (Pickford): 334
Oh, You Women! (Loos): 245
O'Hara's Wife (Foster): 143
Ohio (Bigelow): 41
Ohne Titel Nr. 2 (Export): 134
Ohne Titel xn (Export): 134
Oil and Water (Gish): 147
Øjeblikket (Henning-Jensen): 194
Ojosan (Tanaka): 409
Ök ketten (Mészáros): 289
Okasan (Tanaka): 410
Oklahoma! (Levien): 237
Okoto to Sasuke (Tanaka): 409
Old Acquaintance (Coffee): 90
Old Actor (Pickford): 334
Old Crow (Obomsawin): 313
Old Digs (Nelson): 305
Old-Fashioned Woman (Coolidge): 99
Old Ironsides (Arzner): 25
Old Lady 31 (Mathis): 269
Old Love
See *Alte Liebe*
Old Maid (Akins): 6
Old Man and Dog (Armstrong): 21
Old Wives for New (Macpherson): 255
Old Wives' Tales (Batchelor): 34
Older Brother, Younger Sister
See *Ani imoto*
Oldest Profession
See *Plus Vieux Métier du monde*
Ole (Hein): 192
Olivia (Audry): 27
Olivier, Olivier (Holland): 195
Olly Olly Oxen Free (Head): 187
Oltre il Bene e il Male
See *Al di là del bene e del male*
Oltre la Porta
See *Beyond the Door*
Olyan, mint otthon (Mészáros): 289
Olympia (Riefenstahl): 351
Olympische Spiele 1936
See *Olympia*
Ombres du passé (Musidora): 300
Omen (Dillon): 118
On a Clear Day You Can See Forever (Streisand): 405
On an Island with You (Irene): 205
On Becoming a Woman (Chenzira): 75
On Dangerous Ground (Lupino): 247; (Marion): 264
On est poivrot, mais on a du cœur (Guy): 168
On Golden Pond (Jeakins): 208
On s'est trompé d'histoire d'amour (Serreau): 383
On Such a Night (Head): 183
On the Double (Head): 186
On the Move
See *Utközben*
On the Neman River
See *Nad Niemnem*
On the Other Island
See *En la otra isla*
On the Town (Comden): 96; (Rose): 355
On the Twelfth Day (Toye): 414
On the Yard (Silver): 392
On Top of the Whale
See *Toit de la Baleine*
Once a Daughter (Littman): 240
Once a Hero (Weill): 447
Once a Lady (Akins): 6
Once More, My Darling (Harrison): 180
Once upon a Thursday
See *Affairs of Martha*
One among Many
See *Een blandt mange*
One and the Same (Nelson): 305
One Clear Call (Meredyth): 286
One Day Pina Asked Me
See *Jour Pina m'a demandé*
One Glance, and Love Breaks Out
See *Ein Blick—und die Liebe bricht aus*
One Good Turn (Dillon): 118
One Hour Late (Bauchens): 37
One Hundred a Day (Armstrong): 21
One Hundred Percent American (Pickford): 335
One Hundred Percent Pure
See *Girl from Missouri*
One Hundred Years of Mormonism (Shipman): 388
One Little Indian (Foster): 143
One Night in Lisbon (Head): 184; (Van Upp): 432
One Plus One (Guillemot): 165
One Rainy Afternoon (Lupino): 247; (Pickford): 334
One Romantic Night (Gish): 148
One Second in Montreal (Wieland): 455
One She Loved (Gish): 147; (Pickford): 334
One Sings, the Other Doesn't
See *L'Une chante l'autre pas*
One Two Three (Clarke): 88
One Way or Another
See *De cierta manera*
Only the Brave (Head): 183
Only Thing (Glyn): 150
Only Thrill (Keaton): 215
Only Two Can Play (Zetterling): 462
Only You (Thomas): 412
Onna bakari no yoru (Tanaka): 409

Ono, Yoko: **315**
Opened by Mistake (Head): 184
Opening in Moscow (Clarke): 88
Opowieść Atlantycka (Jakubowska): 207
Opposite Sex (Rose): 355
Optic Nerve (Hammer): 173
Oranges Are Not the Only Fruit (Kidron): 217
Oranges de Jaffa (Parker): 325
Ordeal in the Arctic (Mayron): 276
Orders to Kill (Gish): 148
Orfeo (Leaf): 235
Orlando (Potter): 341
Örmens ägg
See *Serpent's Egg*
Ornament des verliebten Herzens (Reiniger): 347
Ornament of the Loving Heart
See *Ornament des verliebten Herzens*
Ornamental Hairpin
See *Kanzashi*
Ornamentals (Child): 76
Ornette, Made in America (Clarke): 88
Ornithopter (Apon): 19
Örökbefogadás (Mészáros): 289
Örökseg (Mészáros): 289
Orphan of Naples
See *Scugnizza*
Orphans of the Storm (Gish): 148
Országutak vándora (Mészáros): 288
Osaka Elegy
See *Naniwa ereji*
Oscar (Head): 187
Oscar & Lucinda (Armstrong): 21
Osram (Parker): 325
Ostatni etap (Jakubowska): 207
Osvobozhdenie (Solntseva): 395
Other Half and the Other Half
See *Wo ai tai kung ten*
Other Half of the Sky: A China Memoir (Weill): 447
Other Love (Head): 185
Other Side of Midnight (Sharaff): 384
Other Sister (Keaton): 215
Other Women's Children (Mayron): 276
Othon (Huillet): 201
Otley (Dillon): 118
Otoñal (Novaro): 309
Ototo (Tanaka): 410
Ottinger, Ulrike: **318**
Otto e mezzo (Wertmüller): 449
Otto e Novanta (Notari): 307
Our Betters (Murfin): 296
Our Blushing Brides (Meredyth): 286
Our Hearts Were Growing Up (Head): 185
Our Hearts Were Young and Gay (Head): 185
Our Honest Bread
See *Nash chestnyi khleb*
Our Leading Citizen (Head): 184
Our Marriage
See *Notre mariage*
Our Neighbors, the Carters (Head): 184
Our São Paolo
See *São Paolo de todos nos*
Our Trip (Hammer): 173
Our Vines Have Tender Grapes (Irene): 205
Out from the Shadow (Macpherson): 256
Out in Silence (Choy): 81
Out in South Africa (Hammer): 173
Out of Chaos (Craigie): 101
Out of Darkness (Kopple): 221
Out of Sight/Out of Mind (B): 30
Out of the Fog (Lupino): 247; (Mathis): 269
Out of the Frying Pan
See *Young and Willing*
Out of this World (Head): 185
Out to Sea (Coolidge): 99
Outcast (Head): 183
Outcast Lady (Akins): 6
Outcasts of Poker Flat (Jeakins): 208
Outing to Vueltabajo
See *Excursion a Vueltabajo*
Outlaw Reforms (Meredyth): 286
Outrage (Lupino): 247
Outside Chance (Thomas): 412
Outsider (Reville): 349
Outwitted by Billy (Shipman): 388
Over Forty
See *Quarantaine*
Over the Waves
See *Sobre las olas*
Overexposed (Winfrey): 458
Overloop is Sloop (Apon): 19
Ovoce stromů rajských jíme (Chytilová): 83; (Krumbachová): 224
Owl and the Pussycat (Batchelor): 34; (Booth): 45; (Leaf): 235; (Streisand): 405
Owl Who Married a Goose
See *Mariage du Hibou*
Ox (Ullmann): 424
Oxo Parade (Batchelor): 34
Oyu-sama (Tanaka): 410

P

P4W (Cole and Dale): 92
På liv och död (Ahrne): 2
Pa Says (Loos): 244
Pacific Far East Line (Child): 76
Paddy O'Day (Levien): 237
Padenye dinastii romanovykh (Shub): 390
Pagan Love Song (Rose): 355

Page de gloire (Musidora): 300
Pago (Murphy): 297
Paid in Full (Head): 185
Painted Daughters (McDonagh Sisters): 278
Pair of Briefs (Box, B.): 48
Palace of Illusions
See *Illusionernas Natt*
Palcy, Euzhan: **321**
Palle alene i Verden (Henning-Jensen): 193
Palle Alone in the World
See *Palle alene i Verden*
Palm Beach Story (Head): 184; (Irene): 203
Pan jin lian zhi qian shii jin sheng (Law): 232
Panchito y El Gringo (Murphy): 297
Pan/Colour Separations (Cantrill): 65
Panelstory (Chytilová): 83
Páni kluci (Šimková-Plívová): 394
Panni sporchi (Cecchi d'Amico): 72
Panny z Wilka (Pascal): 328
Pantalon coupé (Guy): 168
Pantanal (Carolina): 67
Papa les petits bateaux (Kaplan): 213
Papageno (Reiniger): 347
Papa's Delicate Condition (Head): 186
Paper Bird
See *Papirfuglen*
Paper Moon (Fields): 141
Papirfuglen (Breien): 55
Papirosnitsa ot Mosselproma (Solntseva): 395
Pappersdraken
See *Papirfuglen*
Parabola (Bute): 59
Parade des chapeaux (Parker): 325
Paradies (Dörrie): 121
Paradine Case (Reville): 349
Paradise
See *Paradies*
Paradise Found (Leaf): 235
Paradise, Hawaiian Style (Head): 187
Parahyba, a Macho Woman
See *Parahyba Mulher-macho*
Parahyba Mulher-macho (Yamasaki): 460
Paralytic (Guy): 169
Paramount on Parade (Arzner): 25
Pardners (Head): 186
Pardon My Trunk
See *Buon Giorno, elefante!*
Paren iz taigi (Preobrazhenskaya): 343
Parenti serpenti (Cecchi d'Amico): 72
Paresse (Akerman): 4
Parfait amour (Guillemot): 165
Paris at Midnight (Marion): 265
Paris Honeymoon (Head): 184
Paris in Spring (Lupino): 247
Paris Is Burning (Alberti): 7; (Livingston): 242
Paris la nuit ou Exploits d' apaches à Montmartre (Guy): 168
Paris, Texas (Denis): 115
Paris vu par. . . 20 ans après (Akerman): 4
Paris Was a Woman (Schiller): 370
Parisian Blinds (Hammer): 173
Parker, Claire: **324**
Parlor, Bedroom and Bath (Mathis): 270
Parmar, Pratibha: **326**
Parnell (Coffee): 90
Parole Fixer (Head): 184
Parson of Panamint (Head): 184
Parthenogenesis (Citron): 86
Partners Again (Marion): 265
Partners in Crime (Head): 183
Partners of the Plains (Head): 183
Party and the Guests
See *O slavnosti a hostech*
Party Crashers (Head): 186
Party Girl (Rose): 355
Pascal, Christine: **328**
Pasqualino settebellezze (Wertmüller): 449
Pasqualino: Seven Beauties
See *Pasqualino settebellezze*
Passa a Bandiera (Notari): 307
Passage (Cantrill): 65
Passager du Tassili (Maldoror): 261
Passages from James Joyce's Finnegans Wake
See *Finnegans Wake*
Passante (Faye): 137
Passerby
See *Passante*
Passing of the Third Floor Back (Reville): 349
Passing Quietly Through (Coolidge): 99
Passion
See *En Passion*
Passion of Anna
See *En Passion*
Passionate Stranger (Box, M.): 51
Passionate Thief
See *Risate di gioia*
Passionless Moments (Campion): 61
Passions
See *Uvletschenia*
Pasti, Pasti, pasticky (Chytilová): 83
Pastorale (Bute): 59
Pathways of Life (Gish): 148
Pătissier et ramoneur (Guy): 168
Patriamada (Yamasaki): 460
Patriotes (Pascal): 328
Patriotism (Wieland): 455
Patriots
See *Patriotes*
Patro Le Prévost 80 Years Later (Obomsawin): 313
Patsy (Head): 186

Pattes de Velours (Kaplan): 213
Patto col diavolo (Cecchi d'Amico): 71
Paula aus Portugal (Dörrie): 121
Paura e amore (von Trotta): 441
Pause between Frames (Cantrill): 65
Pauvre pompier (Guy): 168
Pavé (Guy): 168
Paw (Henning-Jensen): 194
Pay Me (Meredyth): 286
Pay Off (Murfin): 296
Paying Bay (Batchelor): 35
Payment on Demand (Head): 185
Pays bleu (Guillemot): 165
Peach Basket Hat (Macpherson): 256; (Pickford): 334
Pearl Diver (Hammer): 173
Pearl Divers (Batchelor): 35
Pearls of the Deep
See *Perličky na dně*
Peasant Letter
See *Kaddu Beykat*
Peasant Women of Ryazan
See *Baby ryazanskie*
Peau de pêche (Epstein): 132
Peccato che sia una canaglia (Cecchi d'Amico): 71
Pêcheur dans le torrent (Guy): 167
Peel (Campion): 61
Peg o' My Heart (Booth): 45; (Marion): 266
Peggy Sue Got Married (Van Runkle): 431
Peggy's Blue Skylight (Wieland): 455
Pègre de Paris (Guy): 168
Peine de talion (Musidora): 300
Peintre et ivrogne (Guy): 168
Peking Express (Head): 185
Pelle (Cavani): 69
Penelope (Head): 187
Peng Xiaolian: **330**
Pennington's Choice (Loos): 244
Pension pro svobodné pány (Krumbachová): 223
Penthouse (Goodrich): 155
People against O'Hara (Rose): 355
People from Everywhere, People from Nowhere
See *Gens de toutes partes, Gens de nulle parte*
People of the Pit (Madison): 258
People People People (Hubley): 197
People vs. John Doe (Weber): 444
People vs. Larry Flint (von Brandenstein): 438
People Will Talk (Head): 183
People's Firehouse Number 1 (Choy): 81
Peoples of Indonesia (van Dongen): 430
Pepe (Head): 186; (Levien): 237
Pepi, Luci, Bom y otras chicas de montón (Pascal): 328
Peppermint Soda
See *Diabolo menthe*
Percussion, Impression & Reality (Choy): 81
Percy (Box, B.): 48
Percy's Progress
See *It's Not the Size that Counts*
Peremena uchasti (Muratova): 294
Perez Family (Nair): 302
Perfect Gentlemen (Ephron): 130
Perfect Marriage (Head): 185
Perfect Pair, or, Indecency Sheds Its Skin
See *Ein Perfektes Paar oder die Unzucht wechselt ihre Haut*
Perfect Woman (Loos): 246
Perils (Child): 76
Perils of Pauline (Head): 185
Period of Adjustment (Lennart): 236
Period Piece (Davis): 107
Peripeteia I (Child): 76
Peripeteia II (Child): 76
Perličky na dně (Chytilová): 83
Permanent Wave (Choy): 81
Perry, Eleanor: **332**
Persona (Ullmann): 424
Personal Memoir of Hong Kong: As Time Goes By (Hui): 199
Persons in Hiding (Head): 184
Pervertida (Novaro): 309
Pete 'n' Tillie (Head): 187
Pete Roleum and His Cousins (van Dongen): 430
Peter Ibbetson (Head): 183; (Lupino): 247
Peter Pan (Head): 183
Peter Vernon's Silence (Lyell): 250
Petersburg Slums
See *Petersburgskiye trushchobi*
Petersburgskiye trushchobi (Preobrazhenskaya): 343
Petición (Miró): 291
Petit à petit ou Les Lettres persanes 1968 (Faye): 137·
Petit Amour (Varda): 435
Petit Manuel d'histoire de France, ch. 1 "Des ancêtres les Gaulois à la prise du pouvoir par Louis X1V (Sarmiento): 366
Petit prince à dit (Pascal): 328
Petit Soldat (Guillemot): 165; (Trintignant): 420
Petite magicienne (Guy): 168
Petite refugiée (Musidora): 300
Petits Coupeurs de bois vert (Guy): 168
Petits matins (Audry): 27
Peu beaucoup, passionnément (Serreau): 383
Peyote Queen (De Hirsch): 110
Phantom (von Harbou): 440

Phantom Lady (Harrison): 180
Phantom of Paris (Meredyth): 286
Philippe Pétain: Processo a Vichy (Cavani): 69
Philippe Petain: Trial at Vichy
See *Philippe Pétain: Processo a Vichy*
Philips-Radio (van Dongen): 429
Phillis Wheatley (Dash): 105
Piange Pierrot (Notari): 307
Piano (Campion): 61
Picador (Dulac): 123
Piccadilly Incident (Toye): 414
Piccadilly Third Stop (Zetterling): 462
Pickford, Mary: **333**
Picture of Dorian Gray (Irene): 205
Pictures at an Exhibition
See *Tableaux d'une exposition*
Pictures for Barbara (Hammer): 173
Picturesque Capri
See *Capri Pittoresco*
Pied Piper of Hamelin
See *Der Rattenfänger von Hameln*
Pied Piper of Hamelin (Reiniger): 347
Pied qui étreint (Musidora): 300
Pierre Vallières (Wieland): 455
Pierrot assassin (Guy): 168
Pierrot Cries
See *Piange Pierrot*
Pies (Leaf): 235
Pigeon That Took Rome (Head): 186
Pillow to Post (Lupino): 247
Pine's Revenge (Madison): 258; (Shipman): 388
Ping Pong (Export): 134
Pinguinho de Gente (Abreu): 1
Pink Gods (Levien): 237
Pink Jungle (Head): 187
Pink Metronome (Cantrill): 65
Pinocchio (Cecchi d'Amico): 72
Pioneers (Lyell): 250
Piper's Tune (Box, M.): 51
Piping Hot (Batchelor): 34
Pirate (Goodrich): 155
Pirates on Horseback (Head): 184
Piroska és a farkas (Mészáros): 289
Pit and the Pendulum (Guy): 169
Pit of Loneliness
See *Olivia*
Place for Lovers
See *Amanti*
Place in the Sun (Head): 185
Place Mattes (Hammer): 173
Place of Rage (Parmar): 326
Places in the Heart (Littleton): 239
Plague on You (Parmar): 326
Plain Clothes (Coolidge): 99
Plain Pleasures (Vachon): 426
Plain Song (Pickford): 334
Plainsman (Bauchens): 37; (Macpherson): 255
Plaisir d'amour (Kaplan): 213
Planet of Children
See *Planète des enfants*
Planète des enfants (Sarmiento): 365
Planton du colonel (Guy): 167
Plateau (Guy): 168
Play (Potter): 341
Play It Again, Sam (Keaton): 215
Pleasantville (Godmilow): 152
Please Believe Me (Irene): 205
Please Don't Eat the Daisies (Lennart): 236
Please Turn Over (Dillon): 118
Pleasure Island (Head): 186
Pleasure of His Company (Head): 186
Plebei (Preobrazhenskaya): 343
Plebian
See *Plebei*
Plenty of Boys, Shortage of Men?
See *Gott om pojkar—ont om män?*
Plumb Line (Schneemann): 372
Plus Belles Escroqueries du monde (Guillemot): 165
Plus Vieux Métier du monde (Guillemot): 165
Po tu storonu Araksa (Shub): 390
Pobeda na pravoberezhnoi Ukraine i izgnanie Nemetskikh zakhvatchikov za predeli Ukrainskikh Sovetskikh zemel (Solntseva): 395
Pocket Cartoon (Batchelor): 34
Pocket Filled with Dreams (Murphy): 297
Pocketful of Miracles (Head): 186
Poder local, poder popular (Gómez): 154
Poem of an Inland Sea
See *Poema o more*
Poem of the Sea
See *Poema o more*
Poema o more (Solntseva): 395
Poesia popular: la teoría y la práctica (Sarmiento): 365
Poète et sa folle amante (Musidora): 300
Poetic Justice (Angelou): 17
Poil de carotte (Kurys): 225
Point Break (Bigelow): 41
Point of Terror (Fields): 141
Pointe courte (Varda): 435
Poirier, Anne-Claire: **336**
Poison (Alberti): 7; (Vachon): 426
Policewoman
See *Street Corner*
Polin (Guy): 168
Polite Invasion (Zetterling): 462
Politiewerk (Apon): 19
Polka Graph (Bute): 59
Polly of the Follies (Loos): 246
Polly West est de retour (Kaplan): 213

Polly with a Past (Mathis): 269
Pollyanna (Marion): 265; (Pickford): 334
Pommier (Guy): 168
Pommy Arrives in Australia (Lyell): 250
Pompon malencontreux 1 (Guy): 168
Pond and Waterfall (Hammer): 173
Pony Express (Head): 186
Pool, Léa: **338**
Pools (Hammer): 173
Poor Consumptive! Poor Mother!
See *Povera Tisa, Povera Madre*
Poor Little Peppina (Pickford): 335
Poor Little Rich Girl (Marion): 264; (Pickford): 335
Popas in tabara de vara (Mészáros): 289
Pope Joan (Ullmann): 424
Popovich Brothers of South Chicago (Godmilow): 152
Poppy (Head): 183; (Van Upp): 432
Popular Poetry: Theory and Practice
See *Poesia popular: la teoría y la práctica*
Porgy and Bess (Sharaff): 384
Portiere di notte (Cavani): 69
Portrait (Deitch): 112
Portrait d'une jeune fille de la fin des années 60 à Bruxelles (Akerman): 4
Portrait from Life (Box, M.): 51; (Zetterling): 462
Portrait of a Lady (Campion): 61
Portrait of a Young Girl at the End of the 1960s in Brussels
See *Portrait d'une jeune fille de la fin des années 60 à Bruxelles*
Portrait of Jason (Clarke): 88
Portrait of Jennie (Gish): 148
Porträts (Hein): 192
Porträts I (Hein): 192
Porträts II (Hein): 192
Porträts III (Hein): 192
Porträts. 4. Nina I-III (Hein): 192
Porträts. Kurt Schwitters I, II, III (Hein): 192
Posillipo as Seen from Naples
See *Posillipo da Napoli*
Posillipo da Napoli (Notari): 306
Positive (Maclean): 253
Poslední motýl (Krumbachová): 223
Poslednyi attraktzion (Preobrazhenskaya): 342
Possedes (Holland): 195
Possessed (Coffee): 90
Postcards from America (Vachon): 426
Postcards from the Edge (von Brandenstein): 438
Postman Always Rings Twice (Irene): 205; (Jeakins): 208
Potage indigeste (Guy): 168
Potash and Perlmutter (Marion): 265
Potter, Sally: **340**
Poule fantaisiste (Guy): 168
Poul-e Khareji (Bani-Etemad): 32
Poundmaker's Lodge: A Healing Place (Obomsawin): 313
Pour Don Carlos (Musidora): 300
Pour Sacha (Kurys): 225
Pour secourer la salade (Guy): 168
Pourquoi pas? (Serreau): 382
Povera Tisa, Povera Madre (Notari): 307
Povest plamennykh let (Solntseva): 395
Power and the Land (van Dongen): 430
Power and the Prize (Rose): 355
Power Dive (Head): 184
Power of Fascination (Madison): 258
Power of the Camera (Loos): 244
Power of the Press (Levien): 237
Power to Fly (Batchelor): 34
Powerful Thang (Davis): 107
Pożegnanie z diabłem (Jakubowska): 207
Poznavaya belyi svet (Muratova): 294
Practice of Love
See *Praxis der Liebe*
Prague, the Restless Heart of Europe
See *Praha, neklidne srace Europy*
Praha, neklidne srace Europy (Chytilová): 83
Prairie Station (Preobrazhenskaya): 343
Praise House (Dash): 105
Pravdivý příběh Josta Buergiho (Krumbachová): 224
Praxis der Liebe (Export): 134
Preacher's Wife (Marshall): 268
Prefab Story
See *Panelstory*
Prefaces (Child): 76
Premier voyage (Trintignant): 420
Première Cigarette (Guy): 168
Première Gamelle (Guy): 168
Prenatal Care in the First Year
See *Atencion prenatal*
Preobrazhenskaya, Olga: **342**
Preparativi Guerreschi a Napoli (Notari): 306
Preparing for the War in Naples
See *Preparativi Guerreschi a Napoli*
Prete, fai un miracolo (Cecchi d'Amico): 72
Preventing Cancer (Dash): 105
Price of a Good Time (Weber): 444
Price of Redemption (Madison): 258
Price of Things (Glyn): 150
Pride and Prejudice (Murfin): 296
Pride of the Clan (Marion): 264; (Pickford): 335
Pride of the West (Head): 183
Prière (Guy): 168
Priest (Bird): 42
Přijela k nám pout (Šimková-Plívová): 394
Prima donna (Kaplan): 213

Primary Colors (May): 271
Prime of Miss Jean Brodie (Allen, J.): 12
Primitive Lover (Marion): 265
Prince and the Showgirl (Dillon): 118
Prince for Cynthia (Box, M.): 51
Prince of Arcadia (Lupino): 247
Prince of Headwaiters (Murfin): 296
Prince of Players (Spencer): 397
Prince of Shadows
See *Beltenebros*
Prince of the City (Allen, J.): 12
Prince of Tides (Streisand): 405
Princess Fragrance
See *Xiang Xiang Gong Zhu*
Princess from Hoboken (Levien): 237
Princesse Mandane (Dulac): 123
Prins Gustaf (Zetterling): 462
Prinzessin Suwarin (von Harbou): 440
Prinzessin Tourandot (von Harbou): 440
Případ Lupínek (Šimková-Plívová): 394
Priscilla's Prisoner (Madison): 258
Prison Farm (Head): 183
Prison for Children (Thomas): 412
Prison for Women
See *P4W*
Prison Stories: Women on the Inside (Deitch): 112; (Silver): 392; (Spheeris): 399
Prisoner of the Harem (Guy): 169
Prisoner of Zenda (Reville): 349
Prisoner without a Name, Cell without a Number
See *Jacobo Timerman: Prisoner without a Name, Cell without a Number*
Prisoners of Hope (Kopple): 221
Private Confessions
See *Enskilda samtal*
Private Hell 36 (Lupino): 248
Private Life of a Cat (Deren): 116
Private Matter (Silver): 392
Private Parts (Thomas): 412
Private Show (Pascal): 328
Private's Affair (Spencer): 397
Privilege (Rainer): 345
Prize of Gold (Zetterling): 462
Prizefighter and the Lady (Marion): 266
Procès (Parker): 325
Processo alla città (Cecchi d'Amico): 71
Processo Cuocolo (Notari): 306
Proclamation
See *Kiáltó*
Prodigal
See *Southerner*
Prodigal (Meredyth): 286
Professor Beware (Head): 183
Professor My Son
See *Mio figlio professore*
Prohibito rubare (Cecchi d'Amico): 71
Proibito (Cecchi d'Amico): 71
Project for Thought and Speech
See *Projeto pensamiento e linguajen*
Projected Light (Cantrill): 65
Projekties (Apon): 19
Projeto pensamiento e linguajen (Amaral): 13
Promenad i de gamlas land (Ahrne): 2
Promenade in the Land of the Aged
See *Promenad i de gamlas land*
Promis. . . Jure! (Pascal): 328
Promise
See *Versprechen*
Proschanie s Matyoroy (Shepitko): 386
Proselyt (Export): 134
Proselyte
See *Proselyt*
Prosperity Race (Zetterling): 462
Proud and the Profane (Head): 186
Provincial Actors
See *Aktorzy prowincjonalni*
Przesluchanie (Holland): 195
Psi a lidé (Krumbachová): 223
Psychosynthesis (Hammer): 173
P'tite Violence (Poirier): 337
Publicity Madness (Loos): 245
Pueblo Legend (Pickford): 334
Pull Your Head to the Moon (Chenzira): 75
Pulmonary Function (Batchelor): 35
Pupatella (Notari): 307
Pure beauté (Parker): 325
Pursuit of Happiness (Head): 183; (Van Upp): 432
Pusilleco Addiruso (Notari): 307
Putney School (Weill): 446
Pytel blech (Chytilová): 83
Pythoness (Batchelor): 35

Q

Qing Cheng Zhi Lian (Hui): 199
Qingchunji (Zhang): 464
Qiuyue (Law): 232
Quackers
See *Loose Shoes*
Quadrille réaliste (Guy): 168
Quando de donne avevano la coda (Wertmüller): 449
Quarantaine (Poirier): 337
Quarry (Hänsel): 176
Quarterback (Head): 184
Quartet (Jhabvala): 210; (Zetterling): 462
Quatre Temps (Parker): 325
Quatre Vérités (Cecchi d'Amico): 72
Que la fête commence. . . (Pascal): 328
Quebec à vendre (Poirier): 337

Queen of Hearts (Batchelor): 35
Queen of the Mob (Head): 184
Queens
See *Fate*
Querida Carmen (Novaro): 309
Questa volta parliamo di uomini (Wertmüller): 449
Qu'est-ce qu'on attend pour être heureux! (Serreau): 382
Question of Silence
See *De Stilte Rond Christine M*
Qui c'est ce garçon (Trintignant): 420
Quick and the Dead (von Brandenstein): 438
Quicksands (Gish): 148
Quiet Don
See *Tikhiy Don*
Quiet on the Set: Filming Agnes of God (Cole and Dale): 93
Quiet Wedding (Dillon): 118
Quille (Guillemot): 165
Quo Vadis (Levien): 238

R

Rachel and the Stranger (Head): 185
Rachel, Rachel (Allen, D.): 10
Racines noires (Faye): 137
Racisme au quotidien (Maldoror): 261
Radcliffe Blues (Weill): 446
Radio Days (Keaton): 215
Radio Rock Detente (Leaf): 235
Rafle de chiens (Guy): 168
Raftsmen
See *Tutajosok*
Rage de dents (Guy): 168
Raging Bull (Schoonmaker): 375
Rags (Pickford): 335
Ragtime (von Brandenstein): 438
Rain
See *Regen*
Rainbow Island (Head): 185
Rainbows of Hawai'i (Hubley): 197
Rainer, Yvonne: **345**
Rainmaker (Head): 186
Rain's Hat (Zetterling): 462
Rains of Ranchipur (Rose): 355; (Spencer): 397
Raising a Riot (Toye): 414
Raising the Wind (Dillon): 118
Raison avant la passion (Wieland): 455
Raison d'être (Poirier): 337
Rajtunk is mulik (Mészáros): 288
Rakudai wa shitakeredo (Tanaka): 409
Ramayana/Legong (Cantrill): 65
Rambling Rose (Coolidge): 99
"Rameau's Nephew" by Diderot (Thanx to Dennis Young) by Wilma Schoen (Wieland): 455
Ramrod (Head): 185
Range War (Head): 184
Rangers of Fortune (Head): 184
Ransom! (Rose): 355
Rape
See *Film No. 6*
Rape Prevention (Schiller): 370
Rape—The Anders Case
See *Voldtekt-Tilfellet Anders*
Rapt d'enfant par les romanichels
See *Erreur de poivrot*
Raramuri Boy
See *En el país de los pies ligeros*
Rasputin and the Empress (Coffee): 90
Rat Life and Diet in North America (Wieland): 455
Rat Race (Head): 186
Rattle of a Simple Man (Box, M.): 51
Raumsehen und Raumhören (Export): 134
Razor's Edge (Russell): 357
RCA: New Sensations in Sound (Bute): 59
Rè venses jeunesse (Trintignant): 420
Reaching for the Moon (Loos): 245
Reaching for the Sun (Head): 184
Ready for Love (Lupino): 247
Real Genius (Coolidge): 99
Real Life (Spheeris): 400
Reap the Wild Wind (Bauchens): 37; (Macpherson): 255
Rear Window (Head): 186
Reason over Passion
See *Raison avant la passion*
Reassemblage (Trinh): 418
Rebecca (Harrison): 180
Rebecca of Sunnybrook Farm (Levien): 237; (Marion): 264; (Pickford): 335
Rebellion in Cuba
See *Chivato*
Rebellion of Kitty Belle (Gish): 148
Reckless (Booth): 45
Récolte est finie
See *Goob na nu*
Recreating Black Women's Media Image (Davis): 107
Recurring Dream (De Hirsch): 110
Red Beard
See *Akahige*
Red Danube (Rose): 355
Red Dice (Macpherson): 255
Red Dwarf
See *Nano Rosso*
Red Garters (Head): 186
Red Hair (Glyn): 150

Red-Headed Woman (Loos): 245
Red, Hot, and Blue (Head): 185
Red Hot Romance (Loos): 246
Red Hot Wheels
See *To Please a Lady*
Red Kimono (Arzner): 25
Red Lantern (Mathis): 269
Red Lily (Meredyth): 286
Red Line 7000 (Head): 186
Red Margaret, Moonshiner (Macpherson): 255
Red Mill (Marion): 265
Red Mountain (Head): 185
Red News (Schneemann): 372
Red Shift (Nelson): 305
Red Shoe Diaries (Borden): 46
Red Sky at Morning (Head): 187
Red Stone Dancer (Cantrill): 65
Red, White and Blue Blood (Mathis): 269
Redemption (Booth): 45
Reds (Allen, D.): 10; (Keaton): 215; (Russell): 357
Redupers
See *Allseitig reduzierte Persönlichkeit*
Reel Time (Schneemann): 372
Referendum—Take 2/Prise deux (Obomsawin): 313
Refinery at Work (Batchelor): 34
Reflections in a Golden Eye (Jeakins): 208
Reflections on Three Images by Baldwin Spencer, 1901 (Cantrill): 65
Reformer and the Redhead (Rose): 355
ReFraming AIDs (Parmar): 326
Regard dans le miroir (Kaplan): 213
Regard Picasso (Kaplan): 213
Regarde les hommes tomber (Pascal): 328
Regen (van Dongen): 429
Régiment moderne (Guy): 168
Reginella (Notari): 307
Regionalzeitung (Meerapfel): 280
Regret
See *Pusilleco Addiruso*
Regrouping (Borden): 46
Regular Girl (Marion): 265
Réhabilitation (Guy): 168
Rehearsal at the Arts Laboratory (Cantrill): 65
Reincarnation of Golden Lotus
See *Pan jin lian zhi qian shii jin sheng*
Reiniger, Lotte: **346**
Reis Zonder Einde (Apon): 19
Reivers (Van Runkle): 431
Relatives (Dash): 105
Relitto (Cecchi d'Amico): 71
Reluctant Debutante (Rose): 355
Reluctant Inspectors
See *Revizory ponevole*
Reluctant Widow (Dillon): 118
Remains of the Day (Jhabvala): 210
Remains to Be Seen (Rose): 355
Remarkable Andrew (Head): 184
Remember the Night (Head): 184
Remodeling Her Husband (Gish): 147
. . . Remote . . . Remote . . . (Export): 134
Renaissance Man (Marshall): 268
Rendez-vous (Serreau): 382
Rendez-vous d'Anna (Akerman): 4
Rendra's Place, Depok (Cantrill): 65
René Depestre, Poète (Maldoror): 261
Renegade Trail (Head): 184
Renunciation (Pickford): 334
Répétition dans un cirque (Guy): 168
Replay (Hein): 192
Réponses de femmes (Varda): 435
Report of 1993 (Bani-Etemad): 32
Report on the Chairman of a Farmers' Co-Operative
See *Riport egy TSZ-elnökröl*
Reportage no. 1
See *Reportaż nr 1*
Reportaż nr 1 (Jakubowska): 207
Reproductions (Hein): 192
Request
See *Petición*
Rescuers: Stories of Courage—Two Women (Streisand): 405
Ressac (Hänsel): 176
Restless Sex (Marion): 265
Restoration (Pickford): 334
Restricted Code
See *Restringierter Code*
Restringierter Code (Export): 134
Reticule of Love (De Hirsch): 110
Retour des champs (Guy): 168
Return
See *Rückkehr*
Return of Sophie Lang (Head): 183
Return of the Soldier (Russell): 357
Return to the Wave
See *Ritorna all'Onda*
Reunion (Levien): 237
Reunion in France (Irene): 203
Revanche (Faye): 137
Rêve du chasseur (Guy): 168
Réveil du jardinier (Guy): 168
Revenge
See *Fatto di sangue fra due uomini per causa di una vedova*
See also *Revanche*
Revillagigedo Islands
See *Islas Revillagigedo*
Reville, Alma: **349**
Revizory ponevole (Solntseva): 395
Revolt (Marion): 264

Revolutionary Romance (Guy): 168
Reward (Batchelor): 35
Rhapsody (Rose): 355
Rhapsody in Blue (Levien): 237
Rhinestone (Van Runkle): 431
Rhode Island Red (Rainer): 345
Rhubarb (Head): 185
Rhythm in Light (Bute): 59
Rhythm on the Range (Head): 183
Rhythm on the River (Head): 184
Rich and Strange (Reville): 349
Rich Revenge (Pickford): 334
Rich, Young and Pretty (Rose): 355
Richard Cardinal: Cry from a Diary of a Métis Child (Obomsawin): 313
Richard III (Dillon): 118; (Kopple): 221
Richard's Things (Ullmann): 424
Riddance
See *Szabad lélegzet*
Ride a Crooked Mile (Head): 183
Ride the Pink Horse (Harrison): 180
Riding High (Head): 185
Riefenstahl, Leni: **351**
Rien que des mensonges (Pascal): 328
Riffraff (Loos): 245; (Marion): 266
Right Cross (Rose): 355
Right of Way (Mathis): 270
Right to Lie (Murfin): 296
Right to Love (Akins): 6
Right to Refuse? (Leaf): 235
Rikugun (Tanaka): 409
Rîmes (Parker): 325
Rimpianto
See *Pusilleco Addiruso*
Ring (Reville): 349
Ring a Ring o' Roses
See *Jak se točí Rozmarýny*
Ring of Destiny (Madison): 258
Ringer (Zetterling): 462
Rio Bravo (Brackett): 52
Rio Lobo (Brackett): 52
Riport egy TSZ-elnökröl (Mészáros): 288
Riptide (Booth): 45
Risate di gioia (Cecchi d'Amico): 71
Rise and Rise of Michael Rimmer (Dillon): 118
Rise of Helga
See *Susan Lenox, Her Fall and Rise*
Rise of Susan (Marion): 264
Rita la zanzara (Wertmüller): 449
Rita the Mosquito
See *Rita la zanzara*
Ritorna all'Onda (Notari): 307
Ritual in Transfigured Time (Deren): 116
Ritzy (Glyn): 150
River
See *He Liu*
River-Ghost (De Hirsch): 110
Rivista Navale Dell' 11 Novembre 1912 (Notari): 307
Roaches' Serenade (Weill): 446
Road House (Lupino): 247
Road Safety (Batchelor): 34
Road Show
See *Chasing Rainbows*
Road to Bali (Head): 185
Road to Morocco (Head): 184
Road to Plaindale (Loos): 244
Road to Rio (Head): 185
Road to Singapore (Head): 184
Road to Utopia (Head): 185
Road to Yesterday (Bauchens): 37; (Macpherson): 255
Road to Zanzibar (Head): 184
Roadie (Littleton): 239
Roald Dahl's Tales of the Unexpected
See *Tales of the Unexpected*
Rob Roy, the Highland Rogue (Dillon): 118
Robe à Cerceaux (Denis): 114
Robert Doisneau, Photographe (Maldoror): 261
Robert Frost: A Lover's Quarrel with the World (Clarke): 88
Robert Klippel Drawings, 1947-1963 (Cantrill): 65
Robert Klippel Sculpture Studies (Cantrill): 65
Robert Lapoujade, Peintre (Maldoror): 261
Robert Macaire et Bertrand (Guy): 168
Roberta (Murfin): 296
Robinson Charley (Batchelor): 34
Rocco and His Brothers
See *Rocco e i suoi fratelli*
Rocco e i suoi fratelli (Cecchi d'Amico): 71
Rock of Riches (Weber): 444
Rockabye (Murfin): 296
Rock-a-Bye Baby (Head): 186
Rocking-Horse Winner (Dillon): 118
Rockshow (Schoonmaker): 375
Rodina Electrichestva
See *Homeland of Electricity*
Rodolphe Bresdin 1825-1885 (Kaplan): 213
Rogopag (Guillemot): 165
Rogue Cop (Rose): 355
Rogue Song (Booth): 44; (Marion): 266
Rogues of Paris (Guy): 169
Rohfilm (Hein): 192
Rollende Rad (Reiniger): 347
Rolling Stones Rock-and-Roll Circus (Ono): 316
Roma città libera (Cecchi d'Amico): 71
Roman de la midinette (Musidora): 300
Roman Holiday (Head): 186
Romance (Meredyth): 286
Romance for Cornet
See *Romance pro křídlovku*

Romance in Manhattan (Murfin): 296
Romance of a Queen
See Three Weeks
Romance of Book & Sword
See *Shu Jian En Chou Lu*
Romance of Happy Valley (Gish): 148
Romance of Rosy Ridge (Irene): 205
Romance of Seville (Reville): 349
Romance of Tarzan (Madison): 258; (Meredyth): 286
Romance of the Redwoods (Macpherson): 255; (Pickford): 335
Romance of the Western Hills (Pickford): 334
Romance pro křídlovku (Krumbachová): 223
Romantic Age (Zetterling): 462
Romantic Story of Margaret Catchpole (Lyell): 250
Romazo d'amore (Cecchi d'Amico): 71
Romeo and Juliet (Booth): 45
Roméo pris au piége (Guy): 168
Romola (Gish): 148
Romona (Pickford): 334
Romuald et Juliette (Serreau): 382
Roof Needs Mowing (Armstrong): 21
Rookie of the Year (Foster): 143
Room (Cantrill): 65
Room with a View (Jhabvala): 210
Roommates
See *Raising the Wind*
Rooster Cogburn (Head): 187
Roots of Grief
See *Fribetens murar*
Rope Dancing (Coolidge): 99
Rope of Sand (Head): 185
Rosa Luxemburg (von Trotta): 441
Rose and the Ring (Reiniger): 347
Rose Bowl (Head): 183
Rose Garden (Ullmann): 424
Rose, Helen: **355**
Rose Marie (Goodrich): 155; (Rose): 355
Rose o' the Sea (Meredyth): 286
Rose of Paris (Coffee): 90
Rose of the Circus (Guy): 168
Rose of the Golden West (Meredyth): 286
Rose of the Rancho (Macpherson): 256
Rose Tattoo (Head): 186
Roseland (Jhabvala): 210
Rosenholm (Ahrne): 2
Rose's Story (Pickford): 334
Rosita (Pickford): 334
Rossini, Rossini (Cecchi d'Amico): 72
Rossiya Nikolaya II i Lev Tolstoi (Shub): 390
Rough Treatment
See *Bez znieczulenia*
Roughhouse (Coolidge): 99
Roughneck (Madison): 259
'Round Midnight (Pascal): 328
Roundup (Head): 184
Roustabout (Head): 186
Roy Cohn/Jack Smith (Godmilow): 152
Royal Scandal (Spencer): 397
Rubens (Parker): 325
Rübezahls Hochzeit (Reiniger): 348
Ruby Bridges Story (Palcy): 321
Ruby Gentry (Head): 185
Rückkehr (von Trotta): 441
Ruddigore (Batchelor): 35
Rudd's New Selection (Lyell): 250
Rude Hostess (Macpherson): 256
Rud's Wife (Maclean): 253
Rue cases nègres (Palcy): 321
Rues de Hong Kong (Guillemot): 165
Ruggles of Red Gap (Head): 183
Ruler
See *Der Herrscher*
Rulers of the Sea (Head): 184
Rules of the Road (Friedrich): 144
Run for Cover (Head): 186
Runaway Bride (Murfin): 296
Runaways
See *Fugueuses*
Running after Luck
See *Jagd nach dem Glück*
Running Mates (Keaton): 215
Running My Way (Littman): 240
Rusalka (Šimková-Plívová): 394
Rusariye Abi (Bani-Etemad): 32
Russell, Shirley: **357**
Russia (Muratova): 294
Russia of Nicholas II and Lev Tolstoy
See *Rossiya Nikolaya II i Lev Tolstoi*
Russians at War (van Dongen): 430
Rustler's Valley (Head): 183
Ruten no ohi (Tanaka): 409

S

S&W (Hein): 192
SA-I-GU (Choy): 81
Sa zimbeasca toti copiii (Mészáros): 289
Sabotage (Reville): 349
Saboteur (Harrison): 180
Sabrina (Head): 186
Sacrificed Youth
See *Qingchunji*
Sad Sack (Head): 186
Saddle the Wind (Rose): 355
Safari (Head): 184
Safe (Bird): 42; (Vachon): 426
Sagan, Leontine: **359**
Sage-femme de première classe (Guy): 168
Saigon (Head): 185

Saikaku ichidai onna (Tanaka): 410
Sailboat (Wieland): 455
Sailor Beware (Head): 185
Sailor from Gibraltar (Duras): 124
Sailor Takes a Wife (Irene): 205
Sailor's Consolation (Batchelor): 35
Sailor's Heart (Meredyth): 287
Sailor's Return (Dillon): 118
Sailors' Wives (Meredyth): 286
Saint-Denis sur Avenir (Maldoror): 261
Sainte Odile (Musidora): 300
Sainted Sisters (Head): 185
Salaam Bombay! (Nair): 302
Sale comme un ange (Guillemot): 165
Salesman (Batchelor): 35
Salesmanship
See *Az eladás müvészete*
Sally (Mathis): 270
Sally in Our Alley (Reville): 349
Salome of the Tenements (Levien): 237
Salt in the Park (Wieland): 455
Salty O'Rourke (Head): 185
Salut les Cubains (Varda): 435
Salut Victor! (Poirier): 337
Salute for Three (Head): 185
Salute to Cuba
See *Salut les Cubains*
Salute to France (Grayson): 161
Salute to the Theatres (Gish): 148
Salvation! (B): 30
Salvation! Have You Said Your Prayers Today?
See *Salvation!*
Salvatore Giuiliano (Cecchi d'Amico): 71
Sam & Me (Mehta): 283
Sambizanga (Maldoror): 261
Same Time, Next Year (Van Runkle): 431
Samson (Madison): 258
Samson and Delilah (Bauchens): 37; (Head): 185; (Jeakins): 208
San Francisco (Loos): 245
Sanctus (Hammer): 173
Sand or Peter and the Wolf (Leaf): 235
Sand under the Pavement
See *Unter dem Pflaster ist der Strand*
Sandakan hachi-ban shokan: Bokyo (Tanaka): 410
Sandakan, House No. 8
See *Sandakan hachi-ban shokan: Bokyo*
Sander, Helke: **361**
Sanders-Brahms, Helma: **363**
Sandpiper (Sharaff): 384
Sandra
See *Vaghe stelle dell'orsa*
Sang des autres (Foster): 143
Sangaree (Head): 186
Sannu batture (Hänsel): 176
Sans Toit ni loi
See *Vagabonde*
Sansho dayu (Tanaka): 410
Sansho the Bailiff
See *Sansho dayu*
Santa Fe Marshal (Head): 184
Santa Fe Trail (Head): 183
São Paolo de todos nos (Amaral): 13
Saphead (Mathis): 270
Sapphire (Dillon): 118
Sappho (Hammer): 173
Sarah and Son (Akins): 6; (Arzner): 25
Saratoga (Loos): 245
Sari Red (Parmar): 326
Sarmiento, Valeria: **365**
Sasek a kralovna (Chytilová): 83
Satan Junior (Mathis): 269
Satan's Bed (Ono): 316
Satdee Night (Armstrong): 21
Saturday, July 27, 1963
See *1963.julius 27.szombat*
Saturday Night (Bauchens): 37; (Macpherson): 255
Saturday Night Fever (von Brandenstein): 437
Saturday Night Kid (Head): 183
Saturday Off
See *Bear, a Boy and a Dog*
Saturday, Sunday, Monday (Wertmüller): 449
Saut humidifié de M. Plick (Guy): 168
Saute ma ville (Akerman): 4
Savage (Head): 185; (Murfin): 296
Savage Eye (Fields): 141
Savage/Love (Clarke): 88
Savage Messiah (Russell): 357
Savage Seven (Marshall): 268
Savage Woman
See *Demoiselle sauvage*
Saving Grace (Loos): 244; (Marshall): 268
Saving Pound
See *Uspořená libra*
Saving Presence (Loos): 244
Saving the Family Name (Weber): 444
Savoca, Nancy: **367**
Savoir-faire s'impose (Poirier): 337
Say It in French (Head): 183
Scandal (Meredyth): 286; (Weber): 444
Scandal Mongers (Weber): 444
Scandal Sheet (Head): 183
Scapegoat (Batchelor): 35
Scar Tissue (Friedrich): 144
Scared Stiff (Head): 186
Scarlet Hour (Head): 186
Scarlet Lady (Meredyth): 286
Scarlet Letter (Gish): 148; (Marion): 265
Scary Time (Clarke): 88
Scène d'escamotage (Guy): 167

Scène en cabinet particulier vue à travers le trou de la serrure (Guy): 168
Scene of the Crime (Irene): 205
Scener ur ett äktenskap (Ullmann): 424
Scènes Directoire (Guy): 168
Scenes from a Marriage
See *Scener ur ett äktenskap*
Scenes from the Life of Andy Warhol (Ono): 316
Scenic Route (Weill): 447
Scherzo del destinoin aqquato dietro l'angelo come un brigante di strada (Wertmüller): 449
Schiller, Greta: **370**
Schimbul de miine (Mészáros): 289
Schiscksal derer von Hapsburg (Riefenstahl): 351
Schizy (Hammer): 173
Schlangenei
See *Serpent's Egg*
Schmeerguntz (Nelson): 305
Schneemann, Carolee: **372**
Schnitte (Export): 134
Schöne Prinzessin von China (Reiniger): 348
School for Coquettes
See *L'École des cocottes*
School for Secrets (Dillon): 118
School Teacher and the Waif (Pickford): 334
Schoonmaker, Thelma: **375**
Schräge Vögel (von Trotta): 442
Schwache Geschlecht muss stärker werden (Sander): 361
Schwarze Sunde (Huillet): 201
Schwestern oder Die Balance des Glücks (von Trotta): 441
Science (Pickford): 334
Scream of Silence
See *Mourir à tue-tête*
Screaming Woman (Head): 187
Screen Tests
See *Zdjecia probne*
Scrubbers (Zetterling): 462
Scugnizza (Notari): 307
Sea
See *Morze*
Sea Bat (Meredyth): 286
Sea Beast (Meredyth): 286
Sea Devils (Lupino): 247
Sea of Roses
See *Mar de Rosas*
Sea Urchin (Macpherson): 255
Sea Wall
See *Diga sul Pacifico*
Sea Wolf (Lupino): 247
Seagull
See *Sha Ou*
Sealed Lips
See *Lèvres closes*
Sealed Orders (Madison): 258
Sealed Room (Pickford): 334
Sealed Verdict (Head): 185
Search for Beauty (Lupino): 247
Search for Bridey Murphy (Head): 186
Search for Signs of Intelligent Life in the Universe (Littleton): 239
Search for the Evil One (Fields): 141
Seashell and the Clergyman
See *Coquille et le clergyman*
Second Awakening of Christa Klages
See *zweite Erwachen der Christa Klages*
Second Chance: Sea (Hubley): 197
Second Journey (To Uluru) (Cantrill): 65
Second Sight
See *Trollsyn*
Second Sight (Pickford): 334
Seconde (Colette): 95
Secours aux naufragés (Guy): 168
Secret
See *Feng Jie*
Secret Agent (Reville): 349
Secret du Chevalier d'Éon (Audry): 27
Secret Garden (Holland): 195
Secret Heart (Irene): 205
Secret Journey
See *Viaggio clandestino*
Secret Life of Walter Mitty (Sharaff): 384
Secret Mission (Dillon): 118
Secret of Madame Blanche (Goodrich): 155
Secret of the Great Story-Teller
See *Tajemství velikého vypravěče*
Secret of the Incas (Head): 186
Secret of the Wastelands (Head): 184
Secret Six (Marion): 266
Secret Sounds Screaming (Chenzira): 75
Secret War of Harry Frigg (Head): 187
Secrets (Marion): 265, 266; (Pickford): 334
Secrets de la prestidigitation dévoilés (Guy): 168
Secrets of the Bermuda Triangle (Murphy): 297
Sedmikrásky (Chytilová): 83; (Krumbachová): 223
Seduction of Mimi
See *Mimi metallurgio ferito nell'onore*
Seduction: The Cruel Woman
See *Verführung: Die grausame Frau*
See Here, Private Hargrove (Irene): 203
See How They Fall
See *Regarde les hommes tomber*
See What You Hear What You See (Hammer): 173
Seed of Sarah (Schiller): 370

Seeing Space and Hearing Space
See *Raumsehen und Raumhören*
Seems Like Old Times (Booth): 45
Seers & Clowns (Hubley): 197
Seesaw
See *Houpačka*
Segodnya (Shub): 390
Sehtext: Fingergedicht (Export): 134
Seidelman, Susan: **379**
Seine offizielle Frau
See *Eskapade*
Seishun no yume ima izuko (Tanaka): 409
Selbé et tant d'autres (Faye): 137
Selbé One among Others
See *Selbé et tant d'autres*
Self-Defense (Citron): 86
Self-Portrait (Ono): 316
Semaine en France (Guillemot): 165
Semana de 22 (Amaral): 13
Sempre Avanti Savoia (Notari): 307
S'en fout la mort (Denis): 114
Sénégalais en Normandie (Maldoror): 261
Senegalese in Normandy
See *Sénégalais en Normandie*
Señora de Nadie (Bemberg): 38
Sensation Seekers (Weber): 445
Senseless (Spheeris): 400
Senso (Cecchi d'Amico): 71
Sentimental Bloke (Lyell): 250
Sentimental Policeman
See *Chuvstvitel'nyi militsioner*
Sentinel Asleep (Pickford): 334
Sentry at the Gate: The Comedy of Jane Galvin-Lewis (Chenzira): 75
Senza sapere nulla di lei (Cecchi d'Amico): 72
Separate Tables (Head): 186
Sept morts sur ordonnance (Serreau): 383
Sept P., Cuis., S. de B.,. . . a saisir (Varda): 435
Sept péchés capitaux (Colette): 95
September Affair (Head): 185
September Express (De Hirsch): 110
Seraglio (Reiniger): 347
Serious Game
See *Den Allvarsamma leken*
Serpent's Egg (Ullmann): 424
Serpico (Allen, D.): 10
Serreau, Coline: **382**
Service De Luxe (Irene): 203
Service: Garage Handling (Batchelor): 34
Service précipité (Guy): 168
Serving in Silence: The Margarethe Cammermeyer Story (Streisand): 405
Set-Up (Bigelow): 41
Sève de la terre (Parker): 325
Seven Beauties
See *Pasqualino settebellezze*
Seven Brides for Seven Brothers (Goodrich): 155
Seven Deadly Sins
See *Sept péchés capitaux*
Seven Keys to Baldpate (Murfin): 296
Seven Little Foys (Head): 186
Seven Sinners (Irene): 203
Seven Sisters (Cantrill): 65
Seven Thieves (Spencer): 397
Seven Waves Away
See *Abandon Ship!*
Seven Women, Seven Sins (Akerman): 4; (Gordon): 157
Seven Women—Seven Sins
See *Sieben Frauen—Sieben Sünden*
Seventeen (Head): 184
Seventh Cross (Irene): 203
Seventh Day (Macpherson): 256; (Pickford): 334
Seventh Sin (Rose): 355
Seventh Veil (Box, B.): 48; (Box, M.): 51
Severed Hand (Madison): 258
Severo Torelli (Musidora): 300
Sewer (Guy): 169
Sex and the City (Seidelman): 379
Sex and the Married Woman (Head): 187
Sex and the Single Girl (Head): 186
Sextette (Head): 187; (West): 452
Sexual Advances (Deitch): 112
Sfida (Cecchi d'Amico): 71
Sha Ou (Zhang): 464
Shades of Fear
See *Great Moments in Aviation*
Shadow of a Doubt (Harrison): 180; (Reville): 349
Shadow of Lightning Ridge (Meredyth): 286
Shadow on the Wall (Irene): 205
Shadows and Fog (Foster): 143
Shadows of Life (Madison): 258
Shadows of the Moulin Rouge (Guy): 169
Shaggie (Cole and Dale): 93
Shakespeare Wallah (Jhabvala): 210
Shakti—"She Is Vital Energy" (Poirier): 337
Shall We Dance (Irene): 203
Shaman: A Tapestry for Sorcerers (De Hirsch): 110
Shame
See *Skammen*
Shane (Head): 186
Shanghai Jiaqi (Hui): 199
Shanghai Lil's (Choy): 81
Sha'ou's Seagull
See *Sha Ou*
Sharaff, Irene: **384**

Shchors (Solntseva): 395
She
See *Elle*
She Asked for It (Head): 183
She-Devil (Seidelman): 379
She Done Him Wrong (Head): 183; (West): 452
She Lives to Ride (Alberti): 7
She Wanted a Millionaire (Levien): 237
She Was a Lady (Spencer): 397
She Was a Visitor (Deitch): 112
She Went to the Races (Irene): 205
She-Wolf
See *U krutogo yara*
She Wouldn't Say Yes (Van Upp): 433
Sheer Madness
See *Heller Wahn*
Shelter Skelter (Coolidge): 99
Shepherd of the Hills (Head): 184
Shepherd of the Southern Cross (Shipman): 388
Shepitko, Larissa: **386**
Sherlock Brown (Coffee): 90
She's No Lady (Head): 183
Shimmy lagarno tarantelle e vino (Wertmüller): 449
Shining Hour (Murfin): 296
Ship Comes In (Levien): 237
Ship San Giorgio
See *Corazzata San Giorgio*
Shipman, Nell: **387**
Shirins Hochzeit (Sanders-Brahms): 364
Shirin's Wedding
See *Shirins Hochzeit*
Shocked
See *Mesmerized*
Shoe Show
See *Shoe show aneb Botky mají pré*
Shoe show aneb Botky mají pré (Krumbachová): 224
Shoemaker and the Hatter (Batchelor): 34
Shoes (Weber): 444
Shoot for the Contents (Trinh): 418
Shoot the Moon (Keaton): 215
Short Cut to Hell (Head): 186
Short History of France, ch. 1 "From the Gaulle Ancestors to the Taking of Power by Louis XIV"
See *Petit Manuel d'histoire de France, ch. 1 "Des ancêtres les Gaulois à la prise du pouvoir par Louis X1V*
Short Is the Summer
See *Kort år sommaren*
Short People (Thomas): 412
Short Tall Story (Batchelor): 35
Shot Heard 'Round the World (Choy): 81
Shout Loud, Louder . . . I Don't Understand
See *Spara forte, più forte . . . non capisco*
Showdown (Head): 184; (Head): 187
Showtime
See *Gaiety George*
Shu Jian En Chou Lu (Hui): 199
Shub, Esther: **390**
Shut Up and Suffer (B): 30
Si vous ne m'aimez pas (Musidora): 300
Siamo donne (Cecchi d'Amico): 71
Sichtbarmachung der Wirkungsweise optischer Gesetze am einfachen Beispiel (Hein): 192
Sidewalks (Menken): 285
Sidney's Joujoux (Guy): 168
Sie Suesse Nummer: Ein Konsumerlebnis (Export): 134
Sieben Frauen—Sieben Sünden (Ottinger): 318; (Sander): 361
Sieg des Glaubens (Riefenstahl): 351
Siempre estaré contigo (Landeta): 229
Siesta (Foster): 143
Sight Poem: Finger Poem
See *Sehtext: Fingergedicht*
Sign of the Cross (Bauchens): 37; (Head): 183
Signé Charlotte (Pascal): 328
Signed Charlotte
See *Signé Charlotte*
Signora dell'ovest (Reiniger): 348
Signora senza camelie (Cecchi d'Amico): 71
Silence of Dean Maitland (Lyell): 250
Silence of the Lambs (Foster): 143
Silent Call (Murfin): 296
Silent Cry
See *Nema Kiáltás*
Silent Language
See *Stille Sprache*
Silent Sandy (Gish): 148
Silent Signal (Guy): 168
Silently, Bearing Totem of a Bird (De Hirsch): 110
Silk Stockings (Rose): 355
Silkwood (Ephron): 130; (von Brandenstein): 437
Silver City (Head): 185
Silver Cord (Murfin): 296
Silver, Joan Micklin: **391**
Silver on the Sage (Head): 184
Silverado (Littleton): 239
Silvio (Sander): 361
Simeon (Palcy): 321
Šimková-Plívová, Věra: **394**
Simon and Laura (Box, M.): 51; (Dillon): 118
Simon the Jester (Marion): 265
Simple Charity (Pickford): 334
Simple Observations of a Solar Eclipse (Cantrill): 65
Simple Plan (von Brandenstein): 438

Simple Story
See *Egyszerű történet*
Simple Tailor
See *Glaza, kotorye videli*
Sincerely Charlotte
See *Signé Charlotte*
Sinful Davey (Dillon): 118
Sing Lotus (De Hirsch): 109
Sing, You Sinners (Head): 183
Singer and the Dancer (Armstrong): 21
Singin' in the Rain (Comden): 96
Singing Nun (Rose): 356
Single Room Furnished (Murphy): 297
Sink or Swim (Friedrich): 144
Siódmy pokój (Mészáros): 289
Sirène du Mississippi (Guillemot): 165
Sissi (Reiniger): 347
Sister Act 2 (Steel): 401
Sister, Sister (Angelou): 17
Sisters (Gish): 148; (Hammer): 173; (Loos): 244
Sisters of Darkness
See *Entre tinieblas*
Sisters of Nishijin
See *Nishijin no shimai*
Sisters, or The Balance of Happiness
See *Schwestern oder Die Balance des Glücks*
Sitting Pretty (Head): 183
Siu Ngo Gong Woo
See *Xiao Ao Jiang Hu*
Six Days, Six Nights
See *À la folie*
Six Degrees of Separation (von Brandenstein): 438
Six et demi-onze (Epstein): 132
Six Fifty (Coffee): 90
Six Hours (Glyn): 150
Six Little Jungle Boys (Batchelor): 34
Sixteen Springs (Hui): 199
Skammen (Ullmann): 424
Skating Bug (Pickford): 334
Ski Resort (Batchelor): 35
Skilsmässoproblem i italien (Ahrne): 2
Skin
See *Pelle*
Skin Deep (Mehta): 283
Skin Game (Reville): 349
Skin of Our Teeth (Bute): 59
Skin of Your Eye (Cantrill): 65
Skirts Ahoy! (Lennart): 236; (Rose): 355
Skotinins (Shub): 390
Skullduggery (Head): 187
Sky Dance (Hubley): 197
Sky Socialist (Wieland): 455
Sky, West, and Crooked (Dillon): 118
Skylark (Head): 184; (Irene): 203
Skyscraper (Clarke): 88
Slaměný klobouk (Krumbachová): 223
Slap Shot (Allen, D.): 10
Slaughterhouse-Five (Allen, D.): 10
Slave (Pickford): 334
Slave of Fashion (Meredyth): 286; (Murfin): 296
Slaves of New York (Comden): 96
Sleep, My Love (Pickford): 334
Sleeper (Keaton): 215
Sleeping Beauty
See *Belle au bois dormant*
Sleeping Beauty (Batchelor): 35; (Reiniger): 347
Sleepless in Seattle (Ephron): 130
Slender Thread (Head): 186
Slesar i kantzler (Preobrazhenskaya): 342
Slightly Dangerous (Irene): 203
Slightly Honorable (Spencer): 397
Sloth
See *Paresse*
Slowly
See *Lentement*
Slugger's Wife (Booth): 45
Slzy, které svět nevidí (Krumbachová): 223
Small Town Girl (Goodrich): 155; (Rose): 355
Smart Girl (Lupino): 247
Smile
See *Film No. 5*
See also *Sourire*
Smile Jenny, You're Dead (Foster): 143
Smilin' Through (Booth): 45
Smiling Again
See *Ujra mosolyognak*
Smiling Madame Beudet
See *Souriante Madame Beudet*
Smithereens (Seidelman): 379
Smoker (Pickford): 334
Smokes and Lollies (Armstrong): 21
Smooth Talk (Chopra): 78
Smugglers
See *Man Within*
Smuggler's Daughter (Meredyth): 286
Smugglers of Death
See *Král Šumavy*
Smykketyven (Breien): 55
Snake Pit (Spencer): 397
Snakes and Ladders
See *El juego de la oca*
Snakes and Ladders (Batchelor): 35
Snap and the Beanstalk (Batchelor): 35
Snap Goes East (Batchelor): 35
Sneakers (von Brandenstein): 438
Snow Bride (Levien): 237
Snow Job: The Media Hysteria of Aids (Hammer): 173
Snow White
See *O Sněhurce*

Snow White and Rose Red (Reiniger): 347
Snowfire (Chenzira): 75; (Fields): 141
Snows (Schneemann): 372
Sny na neděli (Šimková-Plívová): 394
So Evil My Love (Head): 185
So Far from India (Nair): 302
So Long at the Fair (Box, B.): 48; (Box, M.): 51
So Near, Yet So Far (Pickford): 334
So Runs the Way (Gish): 148
So This Is Hollywood
See *In Hollywood with Potash and Perlmutter*
So This Is London (Levien): 237
S.O.B. (Van Runkle): 431
Sobre horas extras y trabajo voluntario (Gómez): 154
Sobre las olas (Novaro): 309
Social Exile
See *Déclassée*
Social Highwayman (Marion): 264
Social Leper (Marion): 264
Social Quicksands (Mathis): 269
Social Register (Loos): 246
Social Secretary (Loos): 245
Society Lawyer (Goodrich): 155
Soeurs enemies (Dulac): 122
Sofie (Ullmann): 424
Soil
See *Zemlya*
Sol y sombra
See *Soleil et ombre*
Solange es Europa noch gibt—Fragen an den Freiden (Meerapfel): 280
Sold for Marriage (Gish): 148
Soldier of Fortune (Spencer): 397
Soldier of Victory
See *Żołnierz zwycięstwa*
Soldier's Daughter Never Cries (Jhabvala): 210
Soldier's Fantasy
See *Fantasia 'e Surdata*
Soledad
See *Fruits amers*
Soleil et ombre (Musidora): 300
Solidarity (Wieland): 455
Solntseva, Yulia: **395**
Solo per te (von Harbou): 440
Solstik (Henning-Jensen): 194
Sombre dimanche (Audry): 27
Sombrero (Rose): 355
Some Bull's Daughter (Loos): 244
Some Exterior Presence (Child): 76
Some Girls Do (Box, B.): 48
Some Like It Hot (Head): 184
Somebody Loves Me (Head): 185
Something About Amelia (Haines): 171
Something Different
See *O něčem jiném*
Something Else
See *O něčem jiném*
Something for Something
See *Cós za cós*
Something New (Shipman): 388
Something of Value (Rose): 355
Something to Live For (Head): 185
Something to Think About (Bauchens): 37; (Macpherson): 255
Sometimes a Great Notion (Head): 187
Sommersby (Foster): 143
Son nom de Venises dans Calcutta désert (Duras): 124
Son of Lassie (Irene): 205
Son of Paleface (Head): 185
Son of the Regiment
See *Figlio del Reggimento*
Son of the Sheik (Marion): 265
Son-Daughter (Booth): 45
Song Is Born (Sharaff): 384
Song o' My Heart (Levien): 237
Song of Life (Meredyth): 286
Song of Love
See *Cançao de Amor*
Song of Love (Irene): 205; (Marion): 265
Song of Russia (Irene): 203
Song of Surrender (Head): 185
Song of the Clinking Cup (Hammer): 173
Song of the Exile
See *Ketu Qiuhen*
Song of the Thin Man (Irene): 205
Song of the Wildwood Flute (Pickford): 334
Sonho de Valsa (Carolina): 67
Sonny (Marion): 265
Sons of Katie Elder (Head): 186
Sons of the Legion (Bauchens): 37; (Head): 183
Son's Return (Pickford): 334
Sophie
See *Sofie*
Sophie Lang Goes West (Head): 183
Sorceress (Madison): 258
Sorrows of the Unfaithful (Pickford): 334
Sorry, Wrong Number (Head): 185
S.O.S. Eisberg (Riefenstahl): 351
S.O.S. Kindtand (Henning-Jensen): 194
Sosie (Musidora): 300
Sotelo (Sarmiento): 366
Sotto il Carcere di San Francisco (Notari): 307
Sotto, Sotto (Wertmüller): 449
Soul Adrift (Guy): 169
Soul Enslaved (Madison): 258
Soul Kiss
See *Lady's Morals*
Souls at Sea (Head): 183

Souls for Sale (Mathis): 270
Souls in Bondage (Madison): 259
Souls in the Sun
See *Âmes au soleil*
Souls Triumphant (Gish): 148
Sound Film
See *Tonfilm*
Sound of Music (Jeakins): 208
Source (Guy): 168
Souriante Madame Beudet (Dulac): 123
Sourire (Pascal): 328
Souris, tu m'inquiétes (Poirier): 337
South Pacific (Jeakins): 208
South Sea Rose (Levien): 237
Southerner
See *Prodigal*
Southerner (Booth): 45
Space Chaser (Treut): 416
Spain
See *Ispaniya*
Spain in Flames (van Dongen): 430
Spanish Dancer (Mathis): 270
Spanish Earth (van Dongen): 430
Spanish Gypsy (Macpherson): 256
Spara forte, più forte . . . non capisco (Cecchi d'Amico): 72
Sparrows (Pickford): 334
Spawn of the North (Head): 183
Speak to, Speak Out
See *Ansprache Aussprache*
Speed the Plough (Batchelor): 35
Spell of the Ball
See *A labda varásza*
Spencer, Dorothy: **397**
Speriamo che sia femmina (Cecchi d'Amico): 72; (Ullmann): 424
Spheeris, Penelope: **399**
Spione (von Harbou): 440
Spitfire
See *First of the Few*
Spitfire (Murfin): 296
Split Reality (Export): 134
Splitscreen-Solipsismus (Export): 134
Spoiled Children
See *Des enfants gâtés*
Spook Sport (Bute): 59
Spooky Bunch
See *Zhuang Dao Zheng*
Sport, Sport, Sport (Shepitko): 386
Spotkania w mroku (Jakubowska): 207
Spring and Winter (Batchelor): 35
Spring Song (Batchelor): 35
Spring to Spring (Bani-Etemad): 32
Spudwrench—Kahnawake Man (Obomsawin): 313
Sputum (Batchelor): 35
Spy Train (Batchelor): 35
Spylarks
See *Intelligence Men*
Square Dance (Hein): 192
Square Deal (Marion): 264
Squaw Man (Bauchens): 37; (Coffee): 90
Squirrel's Magic Shell
See *Veverka a kouzelná mušle*
Sredi serykh kamnei (Muratova): 294
St. Francis of Assisi
See *Francesco*
St. Louis Blues (Head): 184, 186; (Van Upp): 432
Stag (Alberti): 7
Stage Fright (Reville): 349
Stage Struck (Akins): 6
Stagecoach (Spencer): 397
Stagecoach War (Head): 184
Stalag 17 (Head): 186
Stalking Moon (Jeakins): 208
Stampede (Guy): 168; (Pickford): 334
Stand Up and Fight (Murfin): 296
Standard Time (Wieland): 455
Stand-In (Spencer): 397
Standing Room Only (Head): 185
Stanza dello scirocco (Cecchi d'Amico): 72
Star Is Born (Sharaff): 384; (Streisand): 405
Star Maker (Head): 184
Star of Bethlehem
See *Der Stern von Bethlehem*
Star of Bethlehem (Reiniger): 347
Star of India (Guy): 169
Star Trek IV: The Voyage Home (Steel): 401
Starlore (Hubley): 197
Starry Is the Night
See *Jinye Xingguang Canlan*
Stars and Stripes Forever (Jeakins): 208
Stars Are Singing (Head): 186
Starship Invasions (Cole and Dale): 93
Star-Spangled Rhythm (Head): 184
Starstruck (Armstrong): 21
Start with What Is under Your Nose (Batchelor): 34
Starting Line (Grayson): 161
State Fair (Levien): 237
State of Grace (von Brandenstein): 438
State of the Union (Irene): 205
Statue (Guy): 168
Steak trop cuit (Guillemot): 165
Stealing Home (Foster): 143
Steel, Dawn: **401**
Stella (Van Runkle): 431
Stella Dallas (Marion): 265
Stella Maris (Marion): 264; (Pickford): 335
Stemning i April (Henning-Jensen): 194
Step by Step (Hubley): 197

Stepan Razin (Preobrazhenskaya): 343
Stepkids
See *Big Girls Don't Cry. . . They Get Even*
Sticky Fingers (Mayron): 276
Stigmata (B): 30
Still Life (Gordon): 157
Still Point (Hammer): 173
Stille Sprache (Export): 134
Stills (Hein): 192
Sting (Head): 187
Stockholm (Zetterling): 462
Stolen Bride (Gish): 147
Stolen Harmony (Head): 183
Stolen Heart
See *Gestohlene Herz*
Stolen Heaven (Head): 183
Stolen Kisses
See *Baises volés*
Stolen Masterpiece (Loos): 244
Stolen Paradise (Marion): 264
Stone Circles (Hammer): 173
Stonewall (Vachon): 426
Stooge (Head): 185
Stop Calling Me Baby!
See *Moi, Fleur Bleue*
Storia (Cecchi d'Amico): 72
Storia del terzo Reich (Cavani): 69
Storia di una donna (Allen, D.): 10
Stork Bites Man (Pickford): 334
Stork Club (Head): 185
Storm at Daybreak (Booth): 45
Stormy Weather (Rose): 355
Storstadsvampyrer (Ahrne): 2
Story of a Woman
See *Storia di una donna*
Story of a Woman (Head): 187
Story of Dr. Wassell (Bauchens): 37; (Macpherson): 255
Story of Life (Allen, D.): 10
Story of Mr. Hobbs (Shipman): 388
Story of Robin Hood and His Merrie Men (Dillon): 118
Story of the Third Reich
See *Storia del terzo Reich*
Story of the Turbulent Years
See *Povest plamennykh let*
Story of Three Loves (Rose): 355
Story of Woo Viet
See *Hu Yueh Te Ku Shih*
Story of Yunnan
See *Yunnan Qiu Shi*
Stowaway (Batchelor): 35
Stradivari (Cecchi d'Amico): 72
Straight for the Heart
See *À corps perdu*
Straight Is the Way (Marion): 265
Straight through the Heart
See *Mitten ins Herz*
Straight to the Heart
See *À corps perdu*
Strana rodnaya (Shub): 390
Strana Sovietov (Shub): 390
Stranded (Loos): 244; (Loos): 245
Strange Affair of Uncle Harry
See *Uncle Harry*
Strange Days (Bigelow): 41
Strange Interlude (Booth): 45; (Meredyth): 286
Strange Intruder (Lupino): 248
Strange Love of Martha Ivers (Head): 185
Strange Meeting (Pickford): 334
Stranger
See *Lo straniero*
Stranger in Town (Lennart): 236
Stranger Left No Card (Toye): 414
Strangers in 7A (Lupino): 248
Strangers of the Night (Coffee): 90; (Meredyth): 286
Strass café (Pool): 339
Strasse des Bösen
See *Via Mala*
Strategic Air Command (Head): 186
Stratton Story (Rose): 355
Strauss's Great Waltz
See *Waltzes from Vienna*
Straw Fire
See *Feu de paille*
Straw Hat
See *Slaměný klobouk*
Strawberries and Gold (Coolidge): 99
Street (Leaf): 235
Street Corner (Box, M.): 51
Street Girl (Murfin): 296
Street of Chance (Coffee): 90
Street of My Childhood
See *Barndommens gade*
Street Photographer
See *Los Minuteros*
Street Scenes (Schoonmaker): 375
Streetwalker
See *Trotacalles*
Streisand, Barbra: **405**
Strenuous Life (Madison): 258
Stress Scars and Pleasure Wrinkles (Hammer): 173
Strictly Dishonorable (Rose): 355
Strictly Personal (Head): 183
Strictly Unconventional (Booth): 45
Strip (Rose): 355
Strohfeuer (von Trotta): 442
Stroke of Luck
See *Golpe de suerte*

Stronger Love
See *'Tween Two Loves*
Stronger than Death (Guy): 169; (Meredyth): 286
Strop (Chytilová): 83
Struggle
See *Borza*
Struggle (Loos): 246
Strukturelle Studien (Hein): 192
Student Prince (Levien): 237; (Rose): 355
Studies in Image (De)Generation (Cantrill): 65
Studs Lonigan (Fields): 141
Study in Choreography for Camera (Deren): 116
Stuff of Madness, The (Zetterling): 462
Stunt Woman
See *Ah Kam*
Stuntwoman Ajin
See *Ah Kam*
Stürme über dem Montblanc (Riefenstahl): 351
Subjective Factor
See *Der Subjektive Faktor*
Subjectivity
See *Subjektitüde*
Subjektitüde (Sander): 361
Submarine Command (Head): 185
Submarine Control (Batchelor): 34
Submarine Zone
See *Escape to Glory*
Suburbia (Spheeris): 399
Subway in the Sky (Box, M.): 51
Subway Stories: Tales from the Underground (Dash): 105
Such a Little Queen (Pickford): 334
Such Good Friends (May): 271
Such High Mountains
See *Takie vysokie gory*
Such Women Are Dangerous (Coffee): 90
Sud v Smolenske (Shub): 390
Sudden Fear (Coffee): 91
Sudden Money (Head): 184
Suds (Pickford): 334
Sueño como de colores (Sarmiento): 365
Suffering of Susan (Loos): 244
Sugar
See *With or Without*
Sugar Cane Alley
See *Rue cases nègres*
Sugarland Express (Fields): 141
Suicide Pact (Loos): 244
Sullivan's Travels (Head): 184
Sult (Breien): 55
Summer and Smoke (Head): 186
Summer Camp Nightmare (Spheeris): 400
Summer Girl (Marion): 264
Summer Holiday (Goodrich): 155; (Irene): 205
Summer Lightning
See *Strohfeuer*
Summer Night with Greek Profile, Almond Eyes and Scent of Basil
See *Notte d'estate, con profilo Greco, occhi amandorla e odore di basilico*
Summer of My German Soldier (von Brandenstein): 437
Summer Snow
See *Xiatian de Xue*
Summer Stock (Rose): 355
Sun and Shadow
See *Soleil et ombre*
Sun Comes Up (Irene): 205
Sunday Children
See *Niedzielne Dzieci*
Sunday Pursuit (Zetterling): 462
Sundown (Irene): 203; (Marion): 265; (Spencer): 397
Sundowners (Lennart): 236
Sunset Boulevard (Head): 185
Sunset Trail (Head): 184
Sunshine Boys (Booth): 45
Sunshine Christmas (Head): 187
Sunshine Follows Rain
See *Driver dagg faller Regn*
Sunshine Molly (Marion): 266; (Weber): 444
Superbia—Der Stolz (Ottinger): 318
Superdyke (Hammer): 173
Superdyke Meets Madame X (Hammer): 173
Superman und Superwoman (Hein): 192
Sur la barricade (Guy): 168
Sur la terre comme au ciel (Hänsel): 176
Surname Viet, Given Name Nam (Trinh): 418
Surprises de l'affichage (Guy): 168
Surrender (Levien): 237
Surtout l'hiver (Poirier): 337
Surviving Picasso (Jhabvala): 210
Susan and God (Loos): 245
Susan Lenox, Her Fall and Rise (Booth): 45
Susie Steps Out (Pickford): 334
Suspended Vocation
See *Vocation suspendue*
Suspense (Weber): 444
Suspicion (Harrison): 180; (Reville): 349
Süsse Nummer: Ein Konsumerlebnis (Export): 134
Suzy (Coffee): 90
Svält
See *Sult*
Svengali (Foster): 143
Svenska färger (Ahrne): 2
Svetlyi gorod (Preobrazhenskaya): 342
Swagman's Story (Lyell): 250
Swan (Coffee): 90; (Rose): 355

Swedish Fanny Hill
See *Fanny Hill*
Sweet and Low-Down (Spencer): 397
Sweet and Twenty (Pickford): 334
Sweet Bird of Youth (Davis): 107
Sweet Charity (Head): 187
Sweet Liberty (Gish): 148
Sweet Memories of Yesterday (Pickford): 334
Sweet One: A Consumer Experience
See *Süsse Nummer: Ein Konsumerlebnis*
Sweetie (Campion): 61
Swept Away. . .
See *Travolti da un insolito destino nell'azzurro mare d'agosto*
Swept Away. . . by an Unusual Destiny in the Blue Sea of August
See *Travolti da un insolito destino nell'azzurro mare d'agosto*
Swept from the Sea (Kidron): 217
Swimmer (Perry): 332
Swimming to Cambodia (Littleton): 239
Swing High, Swing Low (Van Upp): 432
Swing Shift Maisie (Irene): 203
Swinger (Head): 187
Swingin' Maiden
See *Iron Maiden*
Swoon (Vachon): 426
Sword and the Dragon (Fields): 141
Sword and the Rose (Dillon): 118
Swordsman
See *Xiao Ao Jiang Hu*
Sylvia (Head): 186
Sympathy for the Devil
See *One Plus One*
Sympathy Sal (Loos): 244
Sync Touch (Hammer): 173
Synchromy No. 1 (Bute): 59
Synchromy No. 2 (Bute): 59
Synchromy No. 4
See *Escape*
Synchromy No. 9
See *Tarantella*
Synchronization
See *Synchromy No. 1*
Syntagma (Export): 134
Syvilla: They Dance to Her Drum (Chenzira): 75
Szabad lélegzet (Mészáros): 289
Szentendre—Town of Painters
See *Festök városa—Szentendre*
Szép lányok, ne sirjatok (Mészáros): 289
Szeretet (Mészáros): 289
Sziget a szárazföldön (Elek): 127
Szivdobogás (Mészáros): 288

T

T.G.M.—Osvoboditel (Chytilová): 83
T.V. Tart (Hammer): 173
Ta'dabir Eghtessadi-y-Janghi (Bani-Etemad): 32
Ta naše písnička česká (Krumbachová): 223
Table Quotes-November 1985
See *Tischbemerkungen-November 1985*
Tableaux d'une exposition (Parker): 325
Tag der Freiheit: unsere Wermacht (Riefenstahl): 351
Taiga (Ottinger): 318
Taiheyo hitoribochi (Tanaka): 410
Tailor Made Man (Irene): 205
Tainted Horseplay
See *Kopytem Sem, Kopytem Tam*
Tajemství velikého vypravěče (Krumbachová): 223
Take a Letter, Darling (Irene): 203
Take It Like a Man (Vachon): 426
Take Me Out to the Ball Game (Comden): 96; (Rose): 355
Take Off (Nelson): 305
Takie vysokie gory (Solntseva): 395
Taking His Chance (Lyell): 250
Találkozás (Elek): 127
Találkozunk 1972-ben (Elek): 127
Tale of Love (Trinh): 418
Tale of Two Cities (Box, B.): 48; (Dillon): 118
Tales (Godmilow): 152
Tales from a Street (Gorris): 159
Tales of Erotica
See *Dutch Master*
Tales of Manhattan (Irene): 203
Tales of the Unexpected (Toye): 414
Talk of the Town (Irene): 203
Talkback (Maclean): 253
Tall Headlines (Zetterling): 462
Tall Time Tales (Hubley): 197
Tamarkoze (Bani-Etemad): 32
Taming of the Shrew (Cecchi d'Amico): 72; (Pickford): 334; (Sharaff): 384
Tanaka, Kinuyo: **409**
Tangled Fates (Marion): 264
Tango Lesson (Potter): 341
Tanoureh Deev (Bani-Etemad): 32
Tapp und Tastkino (Export): 134
Tar People (Child): 76
Tarantella (Bute): 59
Tarantelle (Guy): 168
Tarantula (Macpherson): 255
Targets (Fields): 141
Tarnish (Marion): 265
Tarnished Reputations (Guy): 169
Tarzan versus I.B.M.
See *Alphaville*

Tassili Passenger
See *passager du Tassili*
Tattooed Man (De Hirsch): 110
Taunt (Maclean): 253
Taxi Driver (Foster): 143
Tea and Sympathy (Rose): 355
Tea in the Garden (Wieland): 455
Teach Our Children (Choy): 81
Teacher's Pet (Head): 186
Team Delphin (Meerapfel): 280
Tear on the Page (Loos): 244
Tear that Burned (Gish): 148
Tears Laughter Fear and Rage (Potter): 341
Tears of Huajiao
See *Huajiao Lei*
Tears That the World Doesn't See
See *Slzy, které svět nevidí*
Teckman Mystery (Toye): 414
Teenage Zombies (Murphy): 297
Tel est pris qui croyait prendre (Guy): 168
Telephone Girl and the Lady (Loos): 244
Television Spy (Bauchens): 37; (Head): 184
Tell Me
See *Dis-moi*
Tell Me a Riddle (von Brandenstein): 437
Tell Them Willie Boy Is Here (Head): 187
Telling the World (Booth): 44
Temperamental Wife (Loos): 245
Tempi nostri (Cecchi d'Amico): 71
Temple of Dusk (Marion): 264
Temps de l'avant (Poirier): 337
Temptation (Coffee): 90; (Macpherson): 255
Temptation of a Monk
See *You seng*
Ten-Cent Adventure (Loos): 244
Ten Commandments (Bauchens): 37; (Head): 186; (Jeakins): 208; (Macpherson): 255
Ten for Survival (Batchelor): 35
Ten Thousand Bedrooms (Rose): 355
Tenants of Castles
See *Kastélyok lakói*
Tenda Dos Milagros (Yamasaki): 460
Tender Comrade (Head): 185
Tender Fictions (Hammer): 173
Tender Game (Hubley): 197
Tender Trap (Rose): 355
Tentation d'Antoine (Kaplan): 213
Tentative d'assassinat en chemin de fer (Guy): 168
Terre des Taureaux
See *Tierra de los toros*
Terrible Lesson (Guy): 169
Terrible Night (Guy): 169
Territoire (Sarmiento): 366
Territory
See *Territoire*
Terror from the Year 5000 (Allen, D.): 10
Tesito (Faye): 137
Tess of the Storm Country (Levien): 237; (Pickford): 334
Test (Pickford): 334
Test of Friendship (Macpherson): 256
Testament (Littman): 240
Testament de Pierrot (Guy): 168
Testament des Dr. Mabuse (von Harbou): 440
Testament of Dr. Mabuse
See *Testament des Dr. Mabuse*
Texans (Head): 183
Texas Carnival (Rose): 355
Texas Rangers (Head): 183
Texas Rangers Ride Again (Head): 184
Texas Trail (Head): 183
TEXC (Bird): 42
Thanatopsis (B): 30
Thank You (Marion): 265
Thank Your Lucky Stars (Lupino): 247
Thanks for the Memory (Head): 183
That Certain Feeling (Head): 186
That Kind of Woman (Head): 186
That Lady in Ermine (Spencer): 397
That Midnight Kiss (Rose): 355
That Night in Rio (Meredyth): 287
That Our Children Will Not Die (Chopra): 78
That Uncertain Feeling (Irene): 203
That's Adequate (Coolidge): 99
That's My Boy (Head): 185
Thaumetopoea (Guillemot): 165
"The Color of Ritual, The Color of Thought" Series (De Hirsch): 110
Their Hour (Madison): 258; (Meredyth): 286
Their Own Desire (Marion): 266
Thèmes et variations (Dulac): 123
Then I'll Come Back to You (Marion): 264
Theodora Goes Wild (Arzner): 25
Theory of Ideas (Godmilow): 152
There Are No Children Here (Angelou): 17; (Winfrey): 457
There Goes My Heart (Irene): 203
There Is No Forgetting
See *Il n'y à pas d'oubli*
There Were Times, Dear (Murphy): 297
There's a Magic in the Music (Head): 184
There's No Place Like Home (Weber): 444
These Wilder Years (Rose): 355
They All Kissed the Bride (Irene): 203
They Call Him Skarven
See *De kalte ham Skarven*
They Called Us "Les Filles du Roy"
See *Filles du Roi*
They Drive by Night (Lupino): 247
They Got Me Covered (Head): 185
They Had to See Paris (Levien): 237

They Met in Bombay (Loos): 245
They Say the Moon Is Fuller Here (Law): 232
They Won't Believe Me (Harrison): 180
They Would Elope (Pickford): 334
Thief in Paradise (Marion): 265
Thin Air (Bird): 42
Thin Blue Line
See *Thin Line*
Thin Ice (Batchelor): 35; (Gish): 148
Thin Line (Cole and Dale): 92
Thin Man (Goodrich): 155
Thin Man Goes Home (Irene): 205
Things in Bob's Garage (Spheeris): 400
Think of the Future (Batchelor): 35
Third Eye Butterfly (De Hirsch): 110
Thirteen Hours by Air (Head): 183
Thirteenth Chamber
See *Třináctá komnata*
Thirty Seconds over Tokyo (Irene): 205
Thirty-Six Hours (Head): 186
This Angry Age
See *Diga sul Pacifico*
This Could Be the Night (Lennart): 236; (Rose): 355
This Day and Age (Bauchens): 37
This Gun for Hire (Head): 184
This Is Dynamite (Head): 185
This Is My Life (Ephron): 130
This Is the Air Force (Batchelor): 34
This Is the Home of Mrs. Levant Grahame (Weill): 446
This Love Thing (Batchelor): 35
This Mad World (Bauchens): 37
This Man Is Mine (Murfin): 296
This Man Is News (Head): 184
This Man's Navy (Irene): 205
This Old Man (Murphy): 297
This Other Eden (Box, M.): 51
This Property Is Condemned (Head): 187
This Thing Called Love (Irene): 203
This Time for Keeps (Irene): 205
This Time Let's Talk about Men
See *Questa volta parliamo di uomini*
This Way Please (Bauchens): 37; (Head): 183
Thomas, Betty: **411**
Thomas Crown Affair (Van Runkle): 431
Thoroughly Demoralized Girl: A Day in the Life of Rita Rischak
See *Ein ganz und gar verwahrlostes Mädchen*
Those Blasted Kids
See *De pokkers unger*
Those Redheads from Seattle (Head): 186
Those Were the Days (Head): 184
Those Who Love (McDonagh Sisters): 278
Thousands Cheer (Irene): 203
Thread of Destiny (Pickford): 334
Three Broadway Girls
See *Greeks Had a Word for Them*
Three Came Home (Spencer): 397
Three Cases of Murder (Toye): 414
Three Cheers for Love (Head): 183
Three Coins in the Fountain (Jeakins): 208
Three Colour Separation Studies—Landscapes (Cantrill): 65
Three Colour Separation Studies—Still Lifes (Cantrill): 65
Three Crowns of a Sailor
See *Trois Couronnes du matelot*
Three Daring Daughters (Irene): 205; (Levien): 237
Three Fables of Love
See *Quatre Vérités*
Three Generations of Danjuro
See *Danjuro sandai*
Three Guys Named Mike (Rose): 355
Three Hearts for Julia (Irene): 203
Three Little Words (Rose): 355
Three Men and a Baby (Serreau): 383
Three Men and a Cradle
See *Trois hommes et un couffin*
Three Men and a Little Lady (Serreau): 383
Three Men from Texas (Head): 184
Three Men in White (Irene): 205
Three Miles Out (Loos): 246
Three Moods
See *Trois Thèmes*
Three Mountaineers (Batchelor): 35
Three-Ring Circus (Head): 186
Three Sisters (Pickford): 334
Three Stanzas on the Name Sacher
See *Trois strophes sur le nom de Sacher*
Three Stories
See *Tri istorii*
Three Violent People (Head): 186
Three Weeks (Glyn): 150; (Mathis): 270
Three Wise Fools (Irene): 205; (Mathis): 270
Three Wishes (Coolidge): 99; (Reiniger): 347
Three Women of France (Meredyth): 286
Thrill of a Lifetime (Head): 183
Thrill of a Romance (Irene): 205
Thriller (Potter): 341
Through the Back Door (Pickford): 334
Through the Dark (Marion): 265
Through the Wall (Shipman): 388
Throw Momma from the Train (Winfrey): 457
Thumbelina (Reiniger): 347
Thunder in the East (Head): 186
Thunder Trail (Head): 183
Thundering Dawn (Coffee): 90
Thy Name Is Woman (Meredyth): 286
Ti I Ya (Shepitko): 386

Ti presento un'amica (Cecchi d'Amico): 72
Tianguo Niezi (Hui): 199
Ticket of No Return
See *Bildnis Einer Trinkerin—Aller jamais retour*
Tide of Death (Lyell): 250
Tie-Dre (Poirier): 337
Tiefland (Riefenstahl): 351
Tierra de los toros (Musidora): 300
Ties That Bind (Friedrich): 144
Tiger among Us
See *13 West Street*
Tiger of the Sea (Shipman): 388
Tigress (Guy): 169
Tikhiy Don (Preobrazhenskaya): 342
Till Death Do Us Part (Littman): 240
Till I Come Back to You (Bauchens): 37; (Macpherson): 255
Till the Clouds Roll By (Irene): 205; (Rose): 355
Till We Meet Again (Coffee): 90; (Head): 183; (Head): 185
Tillie, the Little Swede (Madison): 258
Tillie Wakes Up (Marion): 264
Time Being (Nelson): 305
Time/Colour Separations (Cantrill): 65
Time of Indifference
See *Gli indifferenti*
Time of the Angels (Hubley): 197
Time Tunnel: The Movie (Marshall): 268
Timely Interception (Gish): 148
Times Gone By
See *Altri tempi*
Timothy's Quest (Van Upp): 432
Tin Star (Head): 186
Tiny & Ruby: Hell-Divin' Women (Schiller): 370
Tiny Tot
See *Pinguinho de Gente*
Tip-Off Girls (Head): 184
Tip on a Dead Jockey (Rose): 355
Tiroy senet (Trintignant): 420
Tischbemerkungen-November 1985 (Export): 134
Tissues (Campion): 61
Titanic (Jeakins): 208
Tivoli Garden Games
See *Tivoligarden spiller*
Tivoligarden spiller (Henning-Jensen): 194
To Another Woman (Madison): 258
To Be a Woman (Craigie): 101
To Be or Not to Be (Irene): 203; (Spencer): 397
To Catch a Thief (Head): 186
To Die, to Sleep (Murphy): 297
To Dorothy a Son (Box, M.): 51
To Each His Own (Head): 185
To Freedom (Grayson): 161
To Have [or Not]
See *En avoir (ou pas)*
To Hell with the Kaiser (Mathis): 269
To Kill a Priest (Holland): 195
To Live in Peace
See *Vivere in pace*
To Love, Honor, and Obey (Choy): 81
To Please a Lady (Rose): 355
To Please One Woman (Weber): 444
To Save Her Soul (Pickford): 334
To Speak the Unspeakable: The Message of Elie Wiesel
See *Mondani a mondhatatlant: Elie Wiesel üzenete*
To the Limit
See *À la folie*
To Whom Are You Showing These Films? (Bani-Etemad): 32
To Wong Foo, Thanks for Everything! Julie Newmar (Kidron): 217
To Your Health (Batchelor): 34
Toast of New Orleans (Rose): 355
Toccata and Fugue (Bute): 59
Tocher (Reiniger): 347
Today
See *Segodnya*
Tog Dogs (Batchelor): 35
Together Again (Van Upp): 433
Together for Children: Principle 10
See *Ten for Survival*
Tohfehha (Bani-Etemad): 32
Toit de la Baleine (Sarmiento): 366
Tokyo no onna (Tanaka): 409
Tom Sawyer (Foster): 143
Tom Sawyer, Detective (Head): 184
Tomas G. Masaryk—The Liberator
See *T.G.M.—Osvoboditel*
Tommy (Russell): 357
Tommy's Double Trouble (Batchelor): 34
Tomorrow Is Forever (Coffee): 90
Tomorrow the World (Bauchens): 37
Tondeur de chiens (Guy): 167
Tonfilm (Export): 134
Tongues (Clarke): 88
Tonight Is Ours (Bauchens): 37
Tonight We Sing (Spencer): 397
Tonnelier (Guy): 168
Tony, tobě přeskočilo (Šimková-Plívová): 394
Too Bad She's Bad
See *Peccato che sia una canaglia*
Too Early, Too Late
See *Trop tot, trop tard*
Too Late Blues (Head): 186
Too Many Crooks (Murfin): 296
Too Many Husbands (Irene): 203
Too Many Parents (Head): 183; (Van Upp): 432

Too Wise Wives (Weber): 444
Too Young for Love (Head): 186
Too Young to Kiss (Goodrich): 155; (Rose): 355
Too Young to Love (Box, M.): 51
Toothless (Mayron): 276
Tootsie (May): 271
Top Gun (Steel): 401
Top Man (Gish): 148
Top of New York (Levien): 237
Topaz (Head): 187
Topper (Irene): 203
Topper Takes a Trip (Irene): 203
Tops Is the Limit
See *Anything Goes*
Torch Singer (Coffee): 90
Torch Song (Rose): 355
Torment
See *Hets*
Torn Curtain (Head): 187
Tornyai János (Mészáros): 288
Torpedo Run (Rose): 355
Toselli
See *Romazo d'amore*
Toss of the Coin (Pickford): 334
Total Eclipse (Holland): 195
Toto Bissainte, Chanteuse (Maldoror): 261
Tou Bun No Hoi
See *T'ou-Pen Nu-Hai*
Touch Cinema
See *Tapp und Tastkino*
Touch of Larceny (Head): 186
Touch Wood (Armstrong): 21
Touchdown Army (Head): 184
Touched (von Brandenstein): 438
Touching (1970) (Export): 134
Touching the Earth Series: Ocean at Point Lookout, near Coober Pedy, at Uluru, Katatjuta (Cantrill): 65
Touha (Šimková-Plívová): 394
T'ou-Pen Nu-Hai (Hui): 199
Tour de Nèsle (Kaplan): 213
Tourbiers (Guillemot): 165
Tourist (Hammer): 173
Tournage Mossane (Faye): 137
Toute révolution est un coup de dés (Huillet): 201
Toute une nuit (Akerman): 4
Town and Country (Keaton): 215
Town in the Awkward Age
See *Kamaszváros*
Town on Trial
See *Processo alla città*
Toy (Booth): 45
Toy Wife (Akins): 6
Toye, Wendy: **414**
Track of Thunder (Fields): 141
Trade Winds (Irene): 203; (Spencer): 397
Tragic Love (Macpherson): 256
Trail of the Arrow (Shipman): 388
Trail of the Lonesome Pine (Macpherson): 255
Train d'enfer (Pascal): 328
Train Trouble (Batchelor): 34
Traitor (Marion): 266; (Weber): 444
Trans (Clarke): 88
Transformations (Guy): 168
Transport z ráje (Krumbachová): 223
Trap (Head): 186; (Madison): 258
Trap Dance (De Hirsch): 110
Trap Door (B): 30
Trap, Trap, Little Trap
See *Pasti, Pasti, pasticky*
Traveling: Marie and Me (Hammer): 173
Travelling Light: The Photojournalism of Dilip Mehta (Mehta): 283
Travels with My Aunt (Allen, J.): 12
Travestie (Pascal): 328
Travolti da un insolito destino nell'azzurro mare d'agosto (Wertmüller): 449
Treasure Hunt (Batchelor): 35
Treasure Island
See *Isla del tesero*
Treasure of Ice Cake Island (Batchelor): 35
Treasure of the Golden Condor (Jeakins): 208
Tree Grows in Brooklyn (Spencer): 397
Trenchcoat in Paradise (Coolidge): 99
Tres Desenhos (Carolina): 67
Treut, Monika: **416**
Trêve (Guillemot): 165
Trey O' Hearts (Madison): 258; (Meredyth): 286
Tri istorii (Muratova): 294
Trial
See *Procès*
Trial by Jury (Toye): 414
Trial Cuocolo
See *Processo Cuocolo*
Trial in Smolensk
See *Sud v Smolenske*
Trial Marriage (Levien): 237
Triangulo de Cuatro (Bemberg): 38
Tribe of the "E" Wood
See *tribu du bois de l'é*
Tribu du bois de l'é (Maldoror): 261
Trick That Failed (Pickford): 334
Tricolore (Notari): 307
Trilogy (Perry): 332
Třináctá komnata (Krumbachová): 224
Trinh T. Minh-Ha: **417**
Trintignant, Nadine: **419**
Trio Film (Rainer): 345
Trionfo Cristiano (Notari): 307
Trip
See *Chelsea Girls*

Trip to Paradise (Mathis): 270
Tripas Coração (Carolina): 67
Triple Entente (Musidora): 300
Triste fin d'un vieux savant (Guy): 168
Triumph (Bauchens): 37; (Macpherson): 255
Triumph des Willens (Riefenstahl): 351
Triumph of Truth (Madison): 258
Trois Coleurs: Blanc (Holland): 195
Trois Coleurs: Bleu (Holland): 195
Trois Couronnes du matelot (Sarmiento): 366
Trois dernières sonatas de Franz Shubert (Akerman): 4
Trois hommes et un couffin (Serreau): 382
Trois rats (Musidora): 300
Trois strophes sur le nom de Sacher (Akerman): 4
Trois Thèmes (Parker): 325
Troisième Larron (Musidora): 300
Trollstenen (Nelson): 305
Trollsyn (Breien): 55
Trolösa (Ullmann): 424
Trompé mais content (Guy): 168
Trône de France (Parker): 325
Troop Beverly Hills (Thomas): 412; (Van Runkle): 431
Trooper Campbell (Lyell): 250
Trop tot, trop tard (Huillet): 201
Trophée du zouave (Musidora): 300
Tropic Holiday (Head): 184
Tropic Zone (Head): 186
Tropicana
See *Heat's On*
Trotacalles (Landeta): 229
Troubadour's Triumph (Weber): 444
Trouble with Angels (Lupino): 247
Trouble with Harry (Head): 186
Trouble with Love
See *Der Beginn aller Schrecken ist Liebe*
Trouble with Women (Head): 185
Troubleshooters (Coolidge): 99
Truck
See *Camion*
True as a Turtle (Toye): 414
True as Steel (Madison): 259
True Confession (Head): 183
True Grit (Jeakins): 208
True Heart Susie (Gish): 148
True Love (Savoca): 368
True Story of Jost Buergi
See *Pravdivý příběh Josta Buergiho*
True to Life (Head): 185
Trumpetistically, Clora Bryant (Davis): 107
Truth about Women (Box, M.): 51; (Zetterling): 462
Trying to Get Arrested (Macpherson): 256
Tsuki wa noborinu (Tanaka): 409
Tu as Crie (Poirier): 337
Tu n'épouseras jamais un avocat (Musidora): 300
Tu nombre envenena mis sueños (Miró): 291
Tue recht und scheue niemand (Brückner): 56
Tul a Kálvin-téren (Mészáros): 288
Tunisian Literature at the National Library
See *littérature tunisienne de la Bibliothèque Nationale*
Tunnel of Love (Rose): 355
Tunnelvision (Thomas): 412
Turkey at the Turning Point
See *Turtsiia na podeme*
Turn Off the Moon (Head): 183
Turn to the Right (Mathis): 270
Turn Your Pony Around
See *To Die, to Sleep*
Turning Point (Head): 185
Turtsiia na podeme (Shub): 390
Tutajosok (Elek): 127
Tutto a posto e niente in ordine (Wertmüller): 449
Två kvinnor (Ahrne): 2
Twa Corbies (Batchelor): 35
'Twas Ever Thus (Marion): 264
'Tween Two Loves (Pickford): 334
Twelve Angry Men (Hubley): 197
Twenty Years of Soviet Cinema
See *Kino za XX liet*
Twice Blessed (Irene): 205
Twice 'round the Daffodils (Dillon): 118
Twice upon a Time
See *Smykketyven*
Twilight (Littleton): 239
Twin Beds (Irene): 203
Twin Detectives (Gish): 148
Twisted Trail (Pickford): 334
Two Bad Daughters (Hammer): 173
Two Brothers (Pickford): 334
Two-Colour Separation Studies (Cantrill): 65
Two Daughters of Eve (Gish): 147
Two for the Seesaw (Lennart): 236
Two for Tonight (Head): 183
Two Girls and a Sailor (Irene): 203; (Irene): 205
Two Heavens
See *Duie Paravise*
Two Hours from London (Craigie): 101
Two Kinds of Women (Head): 183
Two Little Rangers (Guy): 169
Two Lives of Mattia Pascal
See *due vite di Mattia Pascal*
Two Loves (Rose): 356
Two Minutes Silence (McDonagh Sisters): 278
Two Mrs. Carrolls (Head): 185

Two of Them
See also *Ök ketten*
Two Sisters
See *Entre Deux Soeurs*
Two Sisters from Boston (Rose): 355
Two Small Bodies (B): 30
Two Smart People (Irene): 205
Two Virgins (Ono): 316
Two Weeks (Loos): 246
Two Weeks with Love (Rose): 355
Two Women
See *Två kvinnor*
See also *Ök ketten*
Two Women (Cantrill): 65
Type comme moi ne devrait jamais mourir (Guillemot): 165
Typhoon (Head): 184

U

U krutogo yara (Muratova): 294
U.S. Go Home (Denis): 114
Übernachtung in Tirol (von Trotta): 442
Ucho (Krumbachová): 224
Ugetsu
See *Ugetsu monogotari*
Ugetsu monogotari (Tanaka): 410
Ujra mosolyognak (Mészáros): 288
Ukjent mann (Henning-Jensen): 194
Ukraine in Flames
See *Bytva za nashu Radyansku Ukrayinu*
See also *Nezabivaemoe*
Ulica Edisona (Jakubowska): 207
Ullmann, Liv: **423**
Ulysse (Varda): 435
Unafraid (Macpherson): 255
Unchanging Sea (Pickford): 334
Uncle Harry (Harrison): 180
Uncle Janco (Varda): 435
Unconquered (Bauchens): 37
Und Sie? (Hein): 192
Under Lock and Key (B): 30
Under My Skin (Spencer): 397
Under the Black Flag (Madison): 258
Under the Clock
See *Clock*
Under the Crescent (Shipman): 388
Under the Skin of the City (Bani-Etemad): 32
Under the Top (Loos): 245
Under This Sky (Haines): 171
Under Two Flags (Meredyth): 287
Undercover Doctor (Head): 184
Undercover Maisie (Irene): 205
Undercover Man (Head): 183
Undercurrent (Irene): 205
Undertow (Bigelow): 41
Unerreichbare Nahe (von Trotta): 442
Unfaithful
See *Utro*
Unfinished Dance (Irene): 205; (Rose): 355
Unfinished Diary
See *Journal inachevé*
Unforgettable
See *Nezabivaemoe*
Unforgiven (Gish): 148; (Jeakins): 208
Ung flukt (Ullmann): 424
Unguarded Hour (Irene): 203
Unheimlichen Frauen (Hein): 192
Unica (Export): 134
Uninvited (Head): 185
Union City (Bigelow): 41
Union Pacific (Bauchens): 37; (Head): 184; (Macpherson): 255
United States of America (Gordon): 157
Universal Clip
See *Dada*
Unjustly Accused (Madison): 258
Unknown Man
See *Ukjent mann*
Unknown Man (Rose): 355
Unmarried (Head): 184
Unmögliche Frau (von Harbou): 440
Uno Scandale per bene (Cecchi d'Amico): 72
Unpublished Story (Dillon): 118
Unseen Enemy (Gish): 147
Unseen Hands (Madison): 259
Unsichtbare Gegner (Export): 134
Unstrung Heroes (Keaton): 215
Unsuspected (Meredyth): 287
Untamed (Head): 184
Unter dem Pflaster ist der Strand (Sanders-Brahms): 364
Unter Schafen (Dörrie): 121
Unthurqua (Cantrill): 65
Untouchables (Steel): 401; (von Brandenstein): 438
Unusual Tourney (Peng): 330
Unwelcome Guest (Gish): 147; (Pickford): 334
Unwilling Inspectors
See *Revizory ponevole*
Up+Down+On+Off
See *Auf+Zu+Ab+An*
Up Goes Maisie (Irene): 205
Up She Goes
See *Up Goes Maisie*
Up the Sandbox (Streisand): 405
Up to and Including Her Limits (Schneemann): 372
Up Your Legs Forever (Ono): 316
Upside Down (Hubley): 197
Upstairs and Downstairs (Box, B.): 48
Urbanissimo (Hubley): 197

Urchins
See *Pusilleco Addiruso*
Used Cars (Thomas): 412
Used People (Kidron): 217
Usinimage (Ottinger): 318
Uspořená libra (Krumbachová): 223
Utamaro o mehuri go-nin no onna (Tanaka): 410
Utinapló (Mészáros): 289
Utközben (Mészáros): 289
Utro (Henning-Jensen): 194
Utvandrarna (Ullmann): 424
Uvletschenia (Muratova): 294
Uwasa no onna (Tanaka): 410
Už zase skáču přes kaluže (Krumbachová): 224

V

V trinadtsatom chasu (Shepitko): 386
V.I.P.s (Booth): 45
Vachon, Christine: **426**
Vagabond
See *Vagabonde*
Vagabonde (Colette): 95; (Musidora): 300; (Varda): 435
Vaghe stelle dell'orsa (Cecchi d'Amico): 72
Vagues (Guy): 168
Valentino (Russell): 357
Valerie a týden divů (Krumbachová): 224
Valerie and a Week of Wonders
See *Valerie a týden divů*
Valie Export (Export): 134
Valise enchantée (Guy): 168
Valley Girl (Coolidge): 99
Valley of Decision (Irene): 205; (Levien): 237
Valley of the Dolls (Spencer): 397
Vampire (Guy): 169
Vampires (Musidora): 300
Vampire's Ghost (Brackett): 52
Van Brood Alleen Kan een Mens Niet Leven (Apon): 19
Van Dongen, Helen: **429**
Van Runkle, Theadora: **431**
Van Upp, Virginia: **432**
Vanessa: Her Love Story (Coffee): 90
Vangelo '70
See *Amore e rabbia*
Vanquished (Head): 186
Vaquero's Vow (Macpherson): 256
Varda, Agnès: **435**
Varelserna
See *Créatures*
Vargtimmen (Ullmann): 424
Variety (Gordon): 157
Variety Girl (Head): 185
Vásárhelyi szinek (Mészáros): 288
Vater und Sohn (Sander): 361
Velia (Cecchi d'Amico): 72
Veliky put' (Shub): 390
Velvet Goldmine (Alberti): 7; (Vachon): 426
Venetian Bird (Box, B.): 48
Vénus et Adonis (Guy): 168
Vénus Victrix (Dulac): 122
Verbotene Bilder (Hein): 192
Verdammt in alle Ewigkeit (Hein): 192
Verführung: Die grausame Frau (Treut): 416
Vérité sur l'homme-singe (Guy): 168
Verliebten (Meerapfel): 280
Verlorene Ehre der Katharina Blum (von Trotta): 441
Versprechen (von Trotta): 441
Versprich mir nichts! (von Harbou): 440
Vertigo (Head): 186
Verwehte Spuren (von Harbou): 440
Very Curious Girl
See *Fiancée du pirate*
Very Eye of Night (Deren): 116
Very Late Afternoon of a Faun
See *Faunovo prilis pozdni odpoledne*
Vesper's Stampede to My Holy Mouth (Schneemann): 372
Vesterhavs drenge (Henning-Jensen): 194
Veszprém—Town of Bells
See *Harangok városa—Veszprém*
Vêtements Sigrand (Parker): 325
Veverka a kouzelná mušle (Šimková-Plívová): 394
Via Mala (von Harbou): 440
Viaggio clandestino (Sarmiento): 366
Vibes (Littleton): 239
Vice Versa (Dillon): 118
Vicenta (Musidora): 300
Vicki (Spencer): 397
Vicoli e delitti
See *Camorra*
Victim of Jealousy (Macpherson): 256; (Pickford): 334
Victoria
See *Viktoriya*
Victory (Head): 184
Victory in Right-Bank Ukraine and the Expulsion of the Germans from the Boundaries of the Ukrainian Soviet Earth
See *Pobeda na pravoberezhnoi Ukraine i izgnanie Nemetskikh zakhvatchikov za predeli Ukrainskikh Sovetskikh zemel*
Victory of the Faith
See *Sieg des Glaubens*
Victory of Women
See *Josei no shori*
Video Self-Portrait (Cantrill): 65
Videotape I (Hein): 192

Vie de Bohème (Marion): 264
Vie du Christ (Guy): 168
Vie du marin (Guy): 168
Vieilles Estampes (Guy): 168
Vier um die Frau
See *Kämpfende Herzen*
Viet-Flakes (Schneemann): 372
View from the Balcony of the Marco Polo Hotel (Cantrill): 65
Vigil (Godmilow): 152
Viktoriya (Preobrazhenskaya): 342
Villa dévalisée (Guy): 168
Village of Sin
See *Baby ryazanskie*
Ville de Madame Tango (Musidora): 300
Ville des pirates (Sarmiento): 366
Vincent the Dutchman (Zetterling): 462
Vindication
See *Fighting Shepherdess*
Vine Bridge (Zetterling): 462
Vinterbørn (Henning-Jensen): 194
Violence
See *Gewalt*
Violence et Passion
See *Gruppo di famiglia in un interno*
Violent City
See *Città violenta*
Violent Journey
See *Fool Killer*
Violent Summer
See *Estate violenta*
Violin Maker of Cremona (Pickford): 334
Violin Maker of Nuremberg (Guy): 168
Violons parfois (Guillemot): 165
Virgin Machine
See *Jungfrauen Maschine*
Virgin President (Schoonmaker): 375
Virginia (Head): 184; (Madison): 258; (Van Upp): 432
Virginian (Goodrich): 155; (Head): 183; (Head): 185
Virgins from Venus (Murphy): 297
Virtuous Vamp (Loos): 245
Visions of Eight (Allen, D.): 10; (Zetterling): 462
Visit to a Small Planet (Head): 186
Visiting Desire (B): 30
Viskningar och rop (Ullmann): 424
Visual Variations on Noguchi (Menken): 284
Vital Signs (Hammer): 173
Viva 24 de Maio (Yamasaki): 460
Vivacious Lady (Irene): 203
Vivere in pace (Cecchi d'Amico): 71
Vivre sa vie (Guillemot): 165
Vlady, Peintre (Maldoror): 261
Vlci bouda (Chytilová): 83
Vocation suspendue (Sarmiento): 366
Voglio a Tte
See *'Nfama*
Vogues (Spencer): 397; (Irene): 203
Voice from the Minaret (Marion): 265
Voice in the Night
See *Freedom Radio*
Voices of Experience, Voices for Change, Part 1 (Obomsawin): 313
Voiles à Val (Guillemot): 165
Voina i mir (Preobrazhenskaya): 343
Voir Miami (Poirier): 337
Voiture cellulaire (Guy): 168
Voldtekt-Tilfellet Anders (Breien): 55
Voleur de crimes (Trintignant): 420
Voleur sacrilège (Guy): 168
Voleuse (Duras): 124
Volga Boatman (Bauchens): 37; (Coffee): 90
Volleyball (Rainer): 345
Von Brandenstein, Patrizia: **437**
Von Harbou, Thea: **439**
Von Romantik keine Spur (Dörrie): 121
Von Ryan's Express (Spencer): 397
Von Trotta, Margarethe: **441**
Vorspann: Ein Lesefilm (Export): 134
Vortex (B): 30
Voshojdenie (Shepitko): 386
Vostell—Berlin-fieber (Ottinger): 318
Vote for Huggett (Box, B.): 48
Vous n'avez rien contre la jeunesse (Guillemot): 165
Voyage around a Hand
See *Voyage autour d'une main*
Voyage autour d'une main (Sarmiento): 366
Voyage de noces (Trintignant): 420
Voyage en Boscavie (Guillemot): 165
Voyage en Espagne (Guy): 168
Voyage to Next (Hubley): 197
Vražda ing. Čerta (Krumbachová): 223
Vrazhi tropi (Preobrazhenskaya): 343
Vringsveedeler Triptichon (Sanders-Brahms): 364
Vroom (Kidron): 217
Všichni dobří rodáci (Krumbachová): 224

W

W. C. Fields and Me (Head): 187
W.O.W. (Hubley): 197
Waco (Head): 187
Waga koi wa moenu (Tanaka): 410
Wagner (Russell): 357
Wahine
See *Maeva*
Waikiki Wedding (Head): 183
Waiter No. 5 (Pickford): 334

Waiting for the Moon (Godmilow): 152
Wak-Wak, ein Märchenzauber
See *Geschichte des Prinzen Achmed*
Wake Island (Head): 184
Wakers and Dreamers
See *Wakers en Dromers*
Wakers en Dromers (Apon): 19
Waking Up: A Lesson in Love (Schiller): 370
Walk into Paradise (Guillemot): 165
Walker (Obomsawin): 313
Walking on Thin Ice (Ono): 316
Walking to Yeh Pelu (Cantrill): 65
Walking Track (Cantrill): 65
Wall Walls
See *Mur Murs*
Wallenberg: A Hero's Story (Mayron): 276
Walls of Freedom
See *Frihetens murar*
Walls of Malapaga
See *Mura di Malapaga*
Waltzer Dream
See *Pupatella*
Waltzes from Vienna (Reville): 349
Wanderer (Head): 183
Wandering Daughters (Coffee): 90
Wandering Image
See *Wandernde Bild*
Wandering Life
See *Horoki*
Wandering on Highways
See *Országutak vándora*
Wandering Princess
See *Ruten no ohi*
Wandernde Bild (von Harbou): 439
Wann ist der Mensch eine Frau? (Export): 134
Wann—Wenn Nicht Jetzt? (Dörrie): 121
Wanted: Operadadoras (Littman): 240
Wanted—a Home (Weber): 444
Wanton Contessa
See *Senso*
War and Peace
See *Voina i mir*
War Game (Zetterling): 462
War of Paraguay
See *Guerra do Paraguai*
War of the Worlds (Head): 186
War Series (Leaf): 235
Warning Shot (Gish): 148; (Head): 187
Warrah (Cantrill): 65
Warrior Marks (Parmar): 326
Warrior's Husband (Levien): 237
Was bin ich ohne Dich? (von Harbou): 440
Washington Square (Holland): 195
Washington Story (Rose): 355
Wastrel
See *relitto*
Watch Your Stern (Dillon): 118
Water for Firefighting (Batchelor): 34
Water Gipsies (Reville): 349
Water Light/Water Needle (Schneemann): 372
Water Nymph
See *Rusalka*
Waterfall (Cantrill): 65
Watersark (Wieland): 455
Watts with Eggs (Menken): 285
Wavelength (Wieland): 455
Waves
See *Golven*
Waves and Washes (Schneemann): 374
Way Back Home (Murfin): 296
Way Down East (Gish): 148
Way of All Flesh (Coffee): 90; (Head): 184
Way of Learning (Obomsawin): 313
Way of Man (Pickford): 334
Way of the World (Macpherson): 256
Way to the Stars (Dillon): 118
Way We Live (Craigie): 101
Way We Were (Booth): 45; (Jeakins): 208; (Sharaff): 384; (Streisand): 405
Wayne's World (Spheeris): 399
Ways of a Man (Madison): 258
Wayward (Head): 183
We Are Building
See *Budujemy*
See also *Wy brouwen*
We Are Building New Villages
See *Budujemy nowe wsi*
We Are in the Navy Now (Toye): 414
We Can't Have Everything (Bauchens): 37
We Eat the Fruit of the Trees of Paradise
See *Ovoce stromů rajských jíme*
We har manje namn (Zetterling): 462
We Have Many Names
See *We har manje namn*
We Joined the Navy
See *We Are in the Navy Now*
We Moderns (Mathis): 270
We the Women
See *Siamo donne*
We Were Dancing (Coffee): 90
Weaker Sex Must Become Stronger
See *schwache Geschlecht muss stärker werden*
Weakness Syndrome
See *Astenicheskii Sindrom*
Web (Madison): 258
Web of Desire (Marion): 264
Weber, Lois: **444**
Wedding (Gish): 148; (Winfrey): 458
Wedding Band (Spheeris): 400
Wedding Gown (Loos): 244
Wedding Present (Head): 183

Wee Sandy (Reiniger): 347
Week of 1922
See *Semana de 22*
Weekend (Guillemot): 165
Weekend at the Waldorf (Irene): 205
Week-End sur deux (Guillemot): 165
Weill, Claudia: **446**
Weisses Hölle vom Piz Palü (Riefenstahl): 351
Welcome, Foreigner
See *Sannu batture*
Welcome Stranger (Head): 185
Well-Groomed Bride (Head): 185
Well Kept Machine (Batchelor): 34
We'll Meet in 1972
See *Találkozunk 1972-ben*
We'll Take Her Children in Amongst Our Own (Lyell): 250
Well, We Are Alive (Schiller): 370
Wells Fargo (Head): 183
Wendy and Joyce (Wieland): 455
Werbefilm Nr. 1: Bamberg (Hein): 192
Werther (Dulac): 123; (Miró): 291
Wertmüller, Lina: **449**
West, Mae: **452**
West of Broadway (Meredyth): 286
West Point Widow (Head): 184
West Side Story (Sharaff): 384
Western Love (Guy): 169
Wet Parade (Bauchens): 37
We've Come a Long Way (Batchelor): 34
Whales of August (Gish): 148
Whale's Roof
See *Toit de la Baleine*
Wharf Rat (Loos): 245
What a Life (Head): 184
What a Way to Go! (Comden): 96; (Head): 186
What Are You Waiting for to Be Happy!
See *Qu'est-ce qu'on attend pour être heureux!*
What Can It Be (Dörrie): 121
What Color Is God? (Larkin): 231
What Do Men Want? (Weber): 445
What Does Dorrie Want (Keaton): 215
What Farocki Taught (Godmilow): 152
What Is It, Zach (Gordon): 157
What Next Corporal Hargrove? (Irene): 205
What Now, Nursery Workers
See *Kindergärtnerin, was nun?*
What Price Glory? (Spencer): 397
What Price Hollywood? (Murfin): 296
What the Daisy Said (Pickford): 334
What to Do?
See *Co dělat?*
What Will People Say? (Guy): 169
What You Take for Granted (Citron): 86
Whatever You Do, You Lose
See *De todos modos Juan te llamas*
What's Cooking? (Batchelor): 34
What's So Bad about Feeling Good? (Head): 187
What's the Weather Like Up There (Mehta): 283
What's Underground about Marshmallows (Godmilow): 152
What's Up, Doc? (Fields): 141; (Streisand): 405
What's Worth While? (Weber): 444
What's Your Hurry (Pickford): 334
When a Girl Loves (Weber): 444
When a Man Loves (Meredyth): 286; (Pickford): 334
When a Woman Guides (Loos): 244
When Bess Got in Wrong (Meredyth): 287
When Harry Met Sally . . . (Ephron): 130; (Steel): 401
When Husbands Flirt (Arzner): 25
When Is a Human Being a Woman?
See *Wann ist der Mensch eine Frau?*
When Ladies Meet (Loos): 245
When Memory Speaks
See *Desembarcos*
When the Bough Breaks (Box, B.): 48; (Box, M.): 51
When the Road Parts (Loos): 244
When the Wolf Howls (Madison): 258
When We Were in Our Teens (Pickford): 334
When We Were Kings (Alberti): 7
When Women Had Tails
See *Quando de donne avevano la coda*
When Worlds Collide (Head): 185
When You and I Were Young (Guy): 169
When Your Lover Leaves (Thomas): 412
Where Am I Going to Find Another Violeta
See *Donde voy a encontrar otra Violeta*
Where Are My Children? (Weber): 444
Where Are You? I'm Here
See *Dove siete? Io sono qui*
Where Have All the Mentally Ill Gone? (Godmilow): 152
Where Love Has Gone (Head): 186
Where Now Are the Dreams of Youth?
See *Seishun no yume ima izuko*
Where There's Life (Head): 185
While Still Young
See *Naar man kun er ung*
While the Cat's Away (Pickford): 334
While the City Sleeps (Fields): 141; (Lupino): 248
Whispering Chorus (Macpherson): 255
Whispering Smith (Head): 185
Whistling in Brooklyn (Irene): 203
White Banners (Coffee): 90
White Christmas (Head): 186

White Cliffs of Dover (Irene): 203
White Cradle Inn
See *High Fury*
White Cradle Inn (Dillon): 118
White Dwarf (Van Runkle): 431
White Fang (Murfin): 296
White Flower Passing (Choy): 81
White Heat (Weber): 445
White Hell of Piz Palü
See *Schiscksal derer von Hapsburg*
White Man
See *Squaw Man*
White Mazurka
See *Biały mazur*
White Nights
See *notti bianche*
White-Orange-Green (Cantrill): 65
White Palace (Littleton): 239
White Parade (Levien): 237
White Roses (Pickford): 334
White Shoulders (Murfin): 296
White Sister (Booth): 45; (Gish): 148
White Slave Catchers (Loos): 244
White Witch Doctor (Jeakins): 208
White Woman (Head): 183
Whiteye (Schneemann): 374
Whither Weather (Hubley): 197
Who Am I (Hubley): 197
Who Goes Next? (Dillon): 118
Who Has Seen the Wind? (Head): 186
Who Killed Vincent Chin? (Choy): 81
Who Will Marry Me? (Levien): 237
Whole Town's Talking (Loos): 246
Who's Afraid of Virginia Woolf? (Sharaff): 384
Who's Been Sleeping in My Bed? (Head): 186
Who's Got the Action? (Head): 186
Who's Minding the Store? (Head): 186
Who's That Knocking at My Door? (Schoonmaker): 375
Why Change Your Wife? (Bauchens): 37
Why Men Leave Home (Booth): 44
Why Not?
See *Pourquoi pas?*
Wide-Open Town (Head): 184
Widow's Kids (Loos): 244
Wie konntest du, Veronika? (von Harbou): 440
Wieczór u Abdona (Holland): 195
Wieland, Joyce: **455**
Wielka Wielksza Najwielksza (Jakubowska): 207
Wife (Gish): 148
Wife Takes a Flyer (Irene): 203
Wife Who Wasn't Wanted (Meredyth): 286
Wild and the Willing (Box, B.): 48
Wild and Woolly (Loos): 245
Wild Child
See *L'Enfant sauvage*
Wild Duck (Ullmann): 424
Wild Flowers (Vachon): 426
Wild Girl from the Hills (Marion): 266
Wild Girl of the Sierras (Loos): 244
Wild Harvest (Head): 185
Wild in the Country (Spencer): 397
Wild Irish Rose (Madison): 258
Wild Is the Wind (Head): 186
Wild Man Blues (Kopple): 221
Wild Money (Head): 183
Wild Party (Arzner): 25
Wild Racers (Fields): 141
Wild Side
See *Suburbia*
Wild Strain (Shipman): 388
Wild Style (Schiller): 370
Wildfire (Van Runkle): 431
Wildflower (Keaton): 215
Wilful Peggy (Pickford): 334
Will, I Will . . . For Now (Keaton): 215
Will There Really Be a Morning? (Mayron): 275
Williamswood (Chenzira): 75
Willie Walrus and the Awful Confession (Meredyth): 287
Wilpena (Cantrill): 65
Wind (Gish): 148; (Marion): 266
Wind Cannot Read (Box, B.): 48
Windom's Way (Craigie): 101
Window Shopping (Akerman): 4
Windy Day (Hubley): 197
Winfrey, Oprah: **456**
Wings
See *Krylya*
Wings (Head): 183
Wings against the Wind (Palcy): 321
Wings in the Dark (Head): 183; (Shipman): 388
Wings of a Serf
See *Krylya kholopa*
Wings of Desire
See *Der Himmel über Berlin*
Wings to Hawaii (Grayson): 161
Winning (Head): 187
Winning Back His Love (Macpherson): 256
Winning of Barbara Worth (Coffee): 90; (Marion): 265
Winsome but Wise (Guy): 169
Winter Carnival (Spencer): 397
Winter Children
See *Vinterbørn*
Winter Garden (Batchelor): 35
Winter in Zuiderwoude
See *Een Winter in Zuiderwoude*
Winter Soldier (Kopple): 221

Winterborn
See *Vinterbørn*
Wintergarden (De Hirsch): 110
Winterkind (von Trotta): 441
Wise Girls (Booth): 44
Witch Hunt
See *Forfølgelsen*
See also *Kladivo na čarodějnice*
Witches (Zetterling): 462
Witches' Cradle (Deren): 116
Witching Hour (Head): 183
With Friends Like These. . . (Marshall): 268
With Grotowski at Nienadowka (Godmilow): 152
With Her Card (Macpherson): 256
With Liberty and Justice for All (Kopple): 221
With Me You Do Very Well
See *Conmigo la pasas muy bien*
With or Without (Kidron): 217
With the Enemy's Help (Pickford): 334
Within the Law (Marion): 265
Without Anesthesia
See *Bez znieczulenia*
Without Apparent Motive (Bird): 42
Without Love (Irene): 205
Without Title No. 2
See *Ohne Titel Nr. 2*
Without Title xn
See *Ohne Titel xn*
Witness for the Prosecution (Head): 186
Wives
See *Hustruer*
Wives: 10 Years After
See *Hustruer—10 år etter*
Wives and Lovers (Head): 186
Wives III
See *Hustruer III*
Wives Never Know (Head): 183
Wiz (Allen, D.): 10
Wizard of Malta (Keaton): 215
Wo ai tai kung ten (Law): 232
Wolf Song (Head): 183
Wolf's Hole
See *Vlci bouda*
Woman (Ono): 316
Woman Alone
See *Kobieta samotna*
See also *Sabotage*
Woman Alone (Marion): 264
Woman from Mellon's (Pickford): 334
Woman God Forgot (Macpherson): 255
Woman Hater (Dillon): 118
Woman He Married (Meredyth): 286
Woman in Hiding (Lupino): 247
Woman in Question (Dillon): 118
Woman in the Moon
See *Frau im Mond*
Woman in the Spinnery
See *I lörinci fonóban*
Woman in the Ultimate (Gish): 148
Woman in the Window (Fields): 141
Woman in Transit
See *Femme de l'hôtel*
Woman Is a Woman
See *Femme est une femme*
Woman of Affairs (Meredyth): 286
Woman of Mystery (Guy): 169
Woman of No Importance
See *Eine Frau ohne Bedetung*
Woman of Rumor
See *Uwasa no onna*
Woman of the Ganges
See *Femme du Ganges*
Woman of the Wolf (Schiller): 370
Woman of Tokyo
See *Tokyo no onna*
Woman Suffers (Lyell): 250
Woman to Woman (Deitch): 112; (Reville): 349
Woman Trap (Head): 183
Woman Who Would Not Pay (Madison): 258
Woman with Responsibility
See *Eine Frau mit Verantwortung*
Woman without a Face
See *Mister Buddwing*
Woman's Debt (Madison): 258
Woman's Place (Loos): 246
Woman's Way (Marion): 264
Woman's Woman (Madison): 259
Women (Loos): 245; (Murfin): 296
Women and Development (Nair): 302
Women I Love (Hammer): 173
Women in Chains (Lupino): 248
Women in Limbo
See *Limbo*
Women in Love (Russell): 357
Women in Waiting (Littman): 240
Women Love Once (Akins): 6
Women of Brewster Place (Deitch): 112; (Winfrey): 457
Women of Ryazan
See *Baby ryazanskie*
Women of the Night
See *Yoru no onna tachi*
Women of the Resistance
See *Donna Nella Resistenza*
Women of the World
See *W.O.W.*
Women without Names (Bauchens): 37; (Head): 184
Women's Prison (Lupino): 248

Women's Rites or Truth Is the Daughter of Time (Hammer): 173
Women's Story
See *Nüren de gushi*
Won by a Fish (Pickford): 334
Wonder of Women (Meredyth): 286
Wonder of Wool (Batchelor): 35
Woodstock (Schoonmaker): 375
Woodstock '94 (Kopple): 221
Words and Music (Rose): 355
Work in Progress Teil A (Hein): 192
Work in Progress Teil B (Hein): 192
Work in Progress Teil C (Hein): 192
Work in Progress Teil D (Hein): 192
Work or Profession?
See *Munka vagy hivatás?*
Working Girl (von Brandenstein): 438
Working Girls (Akins): 6; (Arzner): 25; (Borden): 46
Working Models of Success (Dash): 105
World and His Wife (Marion): 265
Wor(l)d Cinema: Ein Sprachfest (Export): 134
World in Flames (Head): 184
World in the Three Dimensions
See *Mir v treh izmerenijah*
World of Jacques Demy
See *L'universe de Jacques Demy*
World of Little Ig (Batchelor): 34
World Premiere (Head): 184
World That Nature Forgot (Batchelor): 34
Wot Dot (Batchelor): 35
Would You Like to Meet Your Neighbor? (Hammer): 173
Wounded in Honour
See *Mimi metallurgio ferito nell'onore*
Wreath in Time (Macpherson): 256
Wreath of Orange Blossoms (Macpherson): 256
Wrestling (Menken): 285
Wrestling Ernest Hemingway (Haines): 171
Wu Li Chang (Marion): 266
Wy brouwen (van Dongen): 429
Wyatt Earp (Littleton): 239

X

X (Hammer): 173
Xiang Xiang Gong Zhu (Hui): 199
Xiao Ao Jiang Hu (Hui): 199
Xiaojie Zhuang Dao Gui
See *Zhuang Dao Zheng*
Xiatian de Xue (Hui): 199

Y

Y tenemos sabor (Gómez): 154
Ya tebya pomnyu (Muratova): 294
Yakuza (Jeakins): 208
Yamasaki, Tizuka: **460**
Yank at Oxford (Booth): 45
Yank in Dutch
See *Wife Takes a Flyer*
Yanks (Russell): 357
Year of the Gun (Allen, J.): 12
Year of the Horse (Hubley): 197
Year of the Woman (Weill): 447
Yearling (Irene): 205
Yearning Laurel
See *Aizen katsura*
Years Between (Box, B.): 48; (Box, M.): 51
Years of Hunger
See *Hungerjahre*
Yellow Lily (Meredyth): 286
Yellow Passport (Marion): 264
Yellow Rolls-Royce (Head): 186
Yellow Tale Blues: Two American Families (Choy): 81
Yellow Traffic (Guy): 169
Yentl (Streisand): 405
Yes to Europe (Hein): 192
Yes We Can (Hubley): 197
Yes! Yi zu (Law): 232
Yeux ne veulent pas en tout temps se fermer ou Peut-être qu'un jour Rome se permettra de choisir à son tour
See *Othon*
Yi Sheng Yitai Xi (Hui): 199
Yo, la peor de todas (Bemberg): 38
Yoga (Weill): 447
Yolanda and the Thief (Sharaff): 384
Yoru no onna tachi (Tanaka): 410
You and I
See *Ti I Ya*
You and Me (Head): 184; (Van Upp): 432
You Belong to Me (Head): 183; (Head): 184
You Came Along (Head): 185
You Can Draw (van Dongen): 430
You Can't Ration Love (Head): 185
You Can't Take It with You (Irene): 203
You Light Up My Life (Mayron): 275
You seng (Law): 232
You Were Never Lovelier (Irene): 203
Young and Innocent (Harrison): 180; (Reville): 349
Young and Willing
See *Wild and the Willing*
Young and Willing (Head): 184; (Van Upp): 432
Young April (Macpherson): 255
Young at Heart (Coffee): 91
Young Bride (Murfin): 296
Young Captives (Head): 186

Young Emmanuelle
See *Néa*
Young Escape
See *Ung flukt*
Young Frankenstein (Jeakins): 208
Young Girls of Rochefort
See *Demoiselles de Rochefort*
Young Girls Turn 25
See *Des demoiselles ont en 25 ans*
Young Lions (Spencer): 397
Young Lovers
See *Never Fear*
Young Miss
See *Ojosan*
Young Rajah (Mathis): 270
Younger Generation (Levien): 237
Youngest Profession (Irene): 203
Your Children Come Back to You (Larkin): 231
Your Name Poisons My Dreams
See *Tu nombre envenena mis sueños*
Your Witness (Harrison): 180
You're Never Too Young (Head): 186
You're the One (Head): 184
Yours for the Asking (Lupino): 247
Yours Truly, Andrea G. Stern (Seidelman): 379
Youth
See *Jugend*
Youth in Revolt
See *Altitude 3200*
You've Got Mail (Ephron): 130
Yukon Quest (Export): 134
Yunnan Qiu Shi (Zhang): 464

Z

Zacharovannaya Desna (Solntseva): 395
Zajota and the Boogie Spirit (Chenzira): 75
Zander the Great (Marion): 265
Zandy's Bride (Ullmann): 424
Zanzibar (Pascal): 328
Zap (Cantrill): 65
Zaproszenie (Jakubowska): 207
Zard-e Ghanari (Bani-Etemad): 32
Zaza (Akins): 6; (Head): 184
Zdjecia probne (Holland): 195
Zebrahead (Alberti): 7
Zehn Minuten Mozart (Reiniger): 347
Zeit des Zorns (von Trotta): 441
Zemlya (Solntseva): 395
Zetterling, Mai (Elisabeth): **462**
Zhang Nuanxin: **464**
Zhuang Dao Zheng (Hui): 199
Ziegfeld Follies (Irene): 205; (Levien): 237; (Rose): 355
Ziegfeld Girl (Levien): 237
Život bez kytary (Krumbachová): 223
Znoy (Shepitko): 386
Zodiac Killer
See *Jidao Zhuizhong*
Żołnierz zwycięstwa (Jakubowska): 207
Zolotye vorota (Solntseva): 395
Zoom—kurze Fassung (Hein): 192
Zorn (Ullmann): 424
Ztracená revue (Krumbachová): 223
Ztracenci (Chytilová): 83
Zu früh, zu spät
See *Trop tot, trop tard*
Zu Lucifer Rising von Kenneth Anger (Hein): 192
Zuiderzee Dike (van Dongen): 429
Zur Chronik von Grieshuus (von Harbou): 440
Zuyderzee (van Dongen): 429
Zweiheit der Natur (Export): 134
Zweite Erwachen der Christa Klages (von Trotta): 441
Zwickel auf Bizykel (Meerapfel): 280